Shattered Hope

Captain Jacobo Arbenz, October 1944. Arbenz was, the CIA later wrote, "brilliant . . . cultured."

Shattered Hope

THE GUATEMALAN REVOLUTION AND THE UNITED STATES, 1944–1954

Piero Gleijeses

PRINCETON UNIVERSITY PRESS

PRINCETON, NEW JERSEY

Library of Congress Cataloging-in-Publication Data

Gleijeses, Piero.
Shattered hope : the Guatemalan revolution and the United States, 1944–1954 / Piero Gleijeses.
Includes bibliographical references (p.   ) and index.
1. United States—Foreign relations—Guatemala. 2. Guatemala—Foreign relations—United
States. 3. United States—Foreign relations—1945–1953. 4. Guatemala—Politics and
government—1945–1985. I. Title.
E183.8.G9S48   1991   327.7307281'09044—dc20   90—8901

ISBN 0-691-07817-3
ISBN 0-691-02556-8 (pbk.)

The author gratefully acknowledges permission from the following publications in which
portions of chapters 1, 3, 5, and 8 previously appeared:
   Mesoamérica, "La aldea de Ubico: Guatemala, 1931–1944," June 1989 (chapter 1);
   Journal of Latin American Studies, "The Death of Arana," October 1990 (chapter 3);
   Journal of Latin American Studies, "Juan José Arévalo and the Caribbean Legion," February
1989 (chapter 5);
   Journal of Latin American Studies, "The Agrarian Reform of Jacobo Arbenz," October 1989
(chapter 8).
   The photographs appearing in this book were graciously provided from private collections.

To Setsuko Ono and Letterina Gleijeses

Contents

Illustrations

Figures

Acknowledgments

IT IS a pleasant task to thank those who have supported me during the writing of this volume. My wife, Setsuko Ono, stood by me at the inception; suffered through the first, most painful drafts; offered sensitive, intelligent, and frank criticism; and saved the manuscript at a decisive stage when I had worked myself into a dead end.

I received financial assistance from the Central American and Caribbean Center of Johns Hopkins University and from the Plumsock Foundation, whose director, Christopher Lutz, also shared his deep knowledge of Guatemalan history.

Doña María de Arbenz, Major Carlos Paz Tejada, and Robert Woodward, three of the protagonists of this story, graciously read the entire manuscript. Three U.S. officers who served in Guatemala in the early 1950s—Colonel Aloysius McCormick, Colonel Thomas Hanford, and Major Manuel Chavez— read those sections that dealt with the Guatemalan army. To them, and to all those Guatemalans, Americans, and others who agreed to be interviewed, my sincere thanks.

I talked late into many nights with my two closest Guatemalan friends. Their deep knowledge and love of their country inspired me. It is indicative of the culture of fear in Guatemala today that they have asked me not to mention them by name.

I was fortunate to benefit from the assistance and advice of friends and colleagues at the Johns Hopkins University, four above all—Bonnie Tenneriello, Thomas Thornton, Marta Velazquez, Bernard Wolfson. My task was made easier by two outstanding librarians, Linda Carlson and Barbara Prophet. After several barren years, I was finally able to count on the assistance of an excellent secretary, Paula Smith; when she left, I was taken under the wing of Florence Rotz, by general acclaim the best secretary to have graced these halls in a great many years.

My intellectual debt to Nancy Mitchell is truly deep. Her analytical skills, her great literary talent, her probing, irreverent questions, and her own deep knowledge of U.S. policy in the region gave new life to the manuscript. First as my research assistant, then as a colleague, we began an intellectual collaboration that I hope will last through many books—hers and mine.

Washington, D.C.
September 1990

A Note on Documentation

DOCUMENTS from the National Archives (NA) are always from Record Group (RG) 59.

Intelligence documents from the State Department (OSS, OIR) located in the NA do not have file numbers. They are in RG59, Research and Analysis File. They are identified only with NA.

The file number of the embassy's *Joint Weeka* (*JW*) is always 714.00(W). Prior to January 1954, the *JW* was divided into two sections, political (I) and economic (II). When citing *JW*, I and II refer to these sections, not to volume numbers.

The origin of all documents is either Washington, D.C., or Guatemala City, unless otherwise indicated.

Prior to June 1944, the NA gave each document in its Decimal Files a unique identifying number following its decimal number; after June 1944, only the date of the document is repeated after the decimal number. Whereas I cite the former, I do not cite the latter except in those rare instances when it differs from the actual date of the document.

Documents received through the Freedom of Information Act frequently have no file numbers and have not yet been filed. These documents are cited with no archival information.

Document numbers are given whenever they exist. Informal correspondence carries no document numbers, nor do memos of conversations; whenever the former has a title, it is included; for the latter, either the participants in the conversation or the title of the conversation, whichever is shorter, is included.

Whenever a document appears in its entirety in *Foreign Relations of the United States* (*FRUS*), I use the *FRUS* citation. When, however, the *FRUS* version is incomplete, I cite the original.

For articles from the press that are not cited in full in the notes, see the Bibliography. The place of publication is the United States or Guatemala, unless otherwise indicated.

Abbreviations

AGA	Asociación General de Agricultores
AGCA	Archivo General de Centroamérica
AHA	Archivo Histórico Arquidiocesano
AmEm	American embassy
AmEmG	American embassy, Guatemala
ARA	American Republics Area
AWD	Allen Welsh Dulles
CAD	departmental agrarian committee
CAL	local agrarian committee
CF	Confidential File
CGTG	Confederación General de Trabajadores de Guatemala
CM:G	Correspondencia Dirigida al Señor Ministro: Gobernación
CNCG	Confederación Nacional Campesina de Guatemala
CO:G	Copiador de Oficios: Gobernación
CPR	Correspondencia del Presidente de la República
CR	*Congressional Record*
CSC:DAT	Correspondencia Sindical Campesina: Departamento Administrativo del Trabajo
CSM	*Christian Science Monitor*
CT:DAT	Contratos de Trabajo: Departamento Administrativo del Trabajo
CTG	Confederación de Trabajadores de Guatemala
DCA	*Diario de Centro América*
DCM	Deputy Chief of Mission
DDE:DS	Dwight David Eisenhower Diary Series
DF	Decimal File
DP:SACS	Dulles Papers Special Assistant Chronological Series
DP:SS	Dulles Papers Subject Series
DP:TCS	Dulles Papers Telephone Conversation Series
DOS	Department of State
EL	Eisenhower Library
EL I	*El Imparcial*
FPL	Frente Popular Libertador
FRUS	*Foreign Relations of the United States*
GF	General File
GT	Guatemala Transcripts
HCFA	U.S. House Committee on Foreign Affairs

ID	Intelligence Document Files
IGT	Inspección General de Trabajo
IMJP:G	Informes Mensuales de Jefes´ Políticos: Gobernación
IRCA	International Railways of Central America
JFD:CS	John Foster Dulles Chronological Series
JP	Jefaturas Políticas
JW	*Joint Weeka*
MemoConv	Memorandum of conversation
MemoTel	Memorandum of telephone conversation
ML	Mudd Library, Princeton University
MP:G	Ministerio Público: Gobernación
NA	National Archives
NA-S	National Archives at Suitland
NYT	*New York Times*
OAS	Organization of American States
ODECA	Organización de Estados Centroamericanos
OF	Official File
OIR	Office of Intelligence and Research
OJR	Organismo Judicial de la República
PAR	Partido de Acción Revolucionaria
PGT	Partido Guatemalteco del Trabajo
PIN	Partido de Integridad Nacíonal
PRG	Partido de la Revolución Guatemalteca
RF	Regional Files
RG	Record Group
RN	Renovación Nacional
SCFR	U.S. Senate Committee on Foreign Relations
TL	Truman Library
UFCO	United Fruit Company
USIA	United States Information Agency
WF	Whitman File
WP	*Washington Post*
WSJ	*Wall Street Journal*

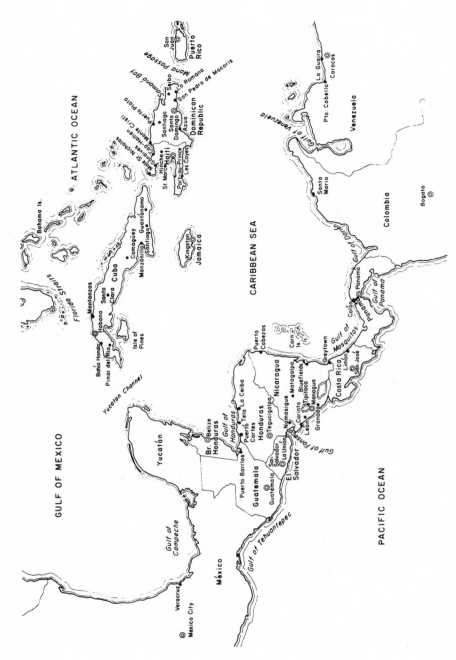

Map of Central America and the Caribbean. (From Dana Munro, *The United States and the Caribbean Republics, 1921–1933*)

Shattered Hope

Witnesses

"IT WASN'T a great conspiracy, and it wasn't a child's game. We were just a group of young men searching for our destiny." So said Alfredo Guerra Borges one evening in January eighteen years ago. He had been a leader of the Communist Party of Guatemala (PGT) in the early 1950s. Ours was not a formal interview. I was curious about the Guatemalan revolution; he was eager to relive a past of which he was still proud.

He spoke of Jacobo Arbenz—the Red Jacobo. He spoke of himself and of his friends, of what they accomplished, and of what they failed to achieve. He spoke of Moscow and of Alejandro, the Cuban communist who sat in on the councils of the PGT. He spoke of Washington and of Ambassador John Peurifoy, whom he had ridiculed in the columns of the PGT's *Tribuna Popular*. And he spoke, as in wonder, of the fall of Arbenz.

The CIA engineered the coup against Arbenz that ended the Guatemalan revolution—a revolution that had seen the PGT bask in the president's favor while communists were pariahs elsewhere in Latin America; a revolution that had seen the first true agrarian reform of Central America: half a million people (one-sixth of Guatemala's population) received the land they desperately needed.

Jacobo Arbenz and Juan José Arévalo presided over Guatemala during those ten "years of spring in the land of eternal tyranny."[1] Arévalo—eloquent and charismatic—was a prominent intellectual; Arbenz—introverted and, even by CIA accounts, brilliant[2]—was an unusual young colonel who cared passionately about social reform. The virus of communism had infected both of them, especially Arbenz, or so said American observers. A few months before the coup, the *New York Times* delivered its indictment: Arbenz was "a prisoner of the embrace he so long ago gave the Communists."[3]

Thirty-six years have passed. It is no longer fashionable to disparage Arévalo: he was, we are told, a Rooseveltian, a democrat whom Washington had misunderstood. But Arbenz is still controversial. Many believe that he too was misjudged and that the CIA plotted his overthrow because he had expropriated the land of the United Fruit Company. Others disagree. The former general

[1] Cardoza y Aragón, *La Revolución Guatemalteca*, p. 9.

[2] CIA, "Guatemala," SR-46, July 27, 1950, p. 39, Truman Papers, President's Secretary's File, Intelligence File, Box 261, TL.

[3] "Guatemala Reds Increase Powers," *NYT*, Nov. 6, 1953, p. 3.

secretary of the PGT, Arbenz's closest friend, observes dryly, "They would have overthrown us even if we had grown no bananas."[4]

Since I first spoke with Alfredo Guerra Borges in January 1973, several excellent studies have appeared that examine U.S. policy toward the Guatemalan revolution, but the contours of the revolution itself—the Guatemalan side of the story—remain hazy.[5] This is the story that I have sought to uncover.

My search led me to the Guatemalan and American press of the period; to the *Guatemalan Transcripts* (ninety-four boxes of documents seized by the CIA after the fall of Arbenz); to presidential libraries, the National Archives of the United States and of Guatemala, and to other public and private libraries.

But the mysteries of the revolution remained unsolved. Who killed Francisco Arana, the man who had hoped to be Arévalo's successor? Why did Arbenz import weapons from Czechoslovakia? How close was he to the Communist party? Why did the army turn against him? Why did he resign? The written record does not answer these questions. Much that transpired was not recorded at the time, and the protagonists have remained silent through the years. Even the loquacious Arévalo, who has written voluminous memoirs, has not written about his own presidency.

And so I pursued the survivors—in Guatemala, in Mexico, in the United States, in Cuba, in the Dominican Republic, in Nicaragua, in Costa Rica. I began in 1978, and my last interview was in 1990. Some people spoke for one hour, others for many hours, in interviews that spanned twelve years. This allowed me to check and cross-check their stories and to probe more deeply as I learned more.

Let me give, as an example, the case of Arbenz's widow, María. I first tried to interview her in August 1978, when I arrived at her house in San Salvador with a warm letter of introduction from a mutual friend, only to be told, "La señora is away. We don't know when she will be back." I persisted during the following years, as she moved to San José, Costa Rica. At last, in February 1982, I was invited to her sister-in-law's house for lunch. "Come," I was told. "Doña María will be here." I arrived—with two Guatemalan friends who knew her and who had helped arrange the encounter—like a prospective

---

[4] Interview with Fortuny.

[5] In the early 1980s several books were published that made good use of newly declassified documents to shed light on U.S. policy toward Guatemala: Immerman, *CIA in Guatemala*; Schlesinger and Kinzer, *Bitter Fruit*; Cook, *Declassified Eisenhower*, pp. 217–92. While these books overshadow everything that had been written previously on the subject, three earlier works deserve to be remembered: Jonas and Tobis, *Guatemala*, and Blasier, *Hovering Giant*, for their intelligent analyses; and Wise and Ross, *Invisible Government*, pp. 177–96, for its investigative skill. More recent works that rely on this new scholarship include Rabe, *Eisenhower and Latin America*, pp. 42–63, and Wood, *Dismantling*, pp. 152–90.

bridegroom, surrounded by matchmakers. Doña María did not appear. "She couldn't make it," her sister-in-law explained. "But, please, stay for lunch. Let's talk." I stayed. We talked through the afternoon and into the evening. As I was leaving, my hostess made a phone call. She then handed me a slip of paper. "Call this number tomorrow morning at nine."

At nine, I made my call, nervous, half-expecting to be told, "La señora is away." But Doña María came to the phone, and that same afternoon I went to her house. It was February 9, 1982. To my knowledge, I am the only person to whom she has granted an interview since the fall of Arbenz.

For three days she did not allow me to take notes, whereas she taped our conversations for her records. There was not a word about the Communist party; we were fencing. Gradually, she began to tell me her story. I interviewed her for three weeks in 1982, for ten days in 1984, and more briefly on later occasions when I was in San José. Most interviews lasted for three or four hours. But one, the one during which we discussed the fall of Arbenz, began, as always, at three-thirty in the afternoon and ended well past midnight.

By the time I met Doña María, I had been working on the book for several years. I could engage her in discussion rather than merely take notes. As the days and weeks passed, María's story unfolded. It corroborated what José Manuel Fortuny, the general secretary of the PGT, had already told me.

Of course, memory is treacherous and men lie. Are María de Arbenz and Fortuny entirely reliable? No, of course not. Do they have their own agendas? Yes, of course. But there are safeguards: (1) They were interviewed repeatedly, and always separately. Doña María did not see the notes of my interviews with Fortuny, and Fortuny did not see the notes of my interviews with Doña María. And yet their testimonies are strikingly similar. (2) Cui bono? María de Arbenz and Fortuny have no common agenda: María de Arbenz is no longer a communist and lives a quiet bourgeois life in Costa Rica; Fortuny is still a communist and lives in Mexico. They are not friends; they have not seen each other since the death of Jacobo Arbenz in 1971. While it might be in Fortuny's interest to stress Arbenz's communist past (although it could be used to justify the U.S. intervention),[6] it is certainly not in Doña María's interest. Yet their accounts concur both in broad outline and in most details. (3) There are very few points for which I rely exclusively on the testimonies of María de Arbenz and Fortuny. Even when addressing Arbenz's motivations for the agrarian reform program, an issue that is not discussed in the written record, the testimonies of Fortuny and María de Arbenz were weighed against those of Guerra Borges (who left the party in the mid-1960s and is no friend

[6] Indeed, the man who gave me the letter of introduction for Doña María in 1978 told me that he did not think it was wise to write about Arbenz's political sympathies. "It would play right into the CIA's hands."

of Fortuny), Alejandro (who has seen neither María nor Fortuny since the mid-1960s), Augusto Charnaud MacDonald (a noncommunist), and Guillermo Noriega Morales (the only surviving noncommunist who had helped to prepare the first draft of the agrarian reform program).

María de Arbenz is a key witness, but so are Guatemala's army officers, for the army held the balance of power in Arbenz's time. Most of the military officers of the period are still in Guatemala, and they are garrulous. Most had never been interviewed before. They arrived with a prepared script, but, to a man, they departed from it. Colonel Enrique Parinello, the army chief of staff under Arbenz, initially insisted that he had been loyal to the president, but as the interview progressed, he admitted that he had known that the army was going to betray Arbenz and that he had said nothing because the situation had seemed so hopeless—the United States had decided that Arbenz had to go. Colonel Rubén González Siguí began by regaling me with the standard army version of the fall of Arbenz. As he droned on, I put down my pen. I had delayed my flight from Guatemala in order to see him. It was September 1982, during Guatemala's dirty war, and I was uneasy, coming as I was from Mexico, where I had interviewed Guatemalan exiles. "Look," I told him. "What you're telling me makes no sense." I itemized the inconsistencies of this well rehearsed account. "I can leave now, if you want. Or we can talk. I won't quote you without your permission." We talked. With bitter pride, González Siguí recollected how Arbenz had stood up to the United States, and how the army had not.

There is a man in Guatemala City who has in his desk drawer a gun and a handkerchief stained with blood. When I first went to interview him, before bidding me welcome he opened the drawer and flourished the gun. I flinched. It was August 1978. Violence was increasing in the capital, and my host was a man of the far right, a fervent supporter of the Movimiento de Liberación Nacional, which had a long history of political assassinations. He wanted to impress upon me that in Guatemala one must live by the gun, that in Guatemala one must kill or be killed. The handkerchief, he explained, was stained with the blood of Carlos Castillo Armas, the man who had overthrown Arbenz and who was himself mysteriously assassinated three years later. And so I met Guayo Taracena de la Cerda, an enthusiastic supporter of Castillo Armas and a dedicated foe of Arbenz. Taracena is an idealist who has killed but not stolen, a man who fought for a cause, not for personal gain. I spent many hours with him through the summer of 1978 and again in 1982.

It is not only the Guatemalans who have a story to tell. So too do the Americans, from embassy officials who witnessed the unfolding of the revolution to CIA agents who plotted its demise. They were interviewed for this book, several on repeated occasions. They were, for the most part, professional and dispassionate. Richard Bissell, who participated in the CIA plot against Arbenz, spent six hours analyzing the weaknesses of the operation—weaknesses, he concluded, that were many and glaring. Ambassador Peurifoy's deputy, Bill Krieg, remarked that the communist leaders "were very honest, very committed. This was the tragedy: the only people who were committed to hard work were those who were, by definition, our worst enemies."[7]

Unlike the Guatemalan participants, most of the Americans had been interviewed by other researchers, but an understanding of the Guatemalan revolution casts new light on their accounts. My analysis of the Guatemalan side of the story has convinced me that the accuracy and subtlety of U.S. intelligence on Guatemala improved from Truman to Eisenhower and that in the course of the revolution, the influence of the communists in shaping Guatemalan policy increased, while the influence of the United Fruit Company in shaping American policy decreased. There is no convenient villain of the piece, but rather a complex interplay of imperial hubris, security concerns, and economic interests. It is against this constellation of forces that the story of the Guatemalan revolution was played out to its tragic end. The record—Guatemalan and American, oral and written—shows that Fortuny was right: "They would have overthrown us even if we had grown no bananas."

[7] Interview with Krieg.

CHAPTER 1

The Era of Ubico

ON JANUARY 22, 1932, a peasant revolt erupted in El Salvador. The uprising was quickly suppressed, as the government slaughtered from ten to thirty thousand peasants. The young Communist Party of El Salvador, which had participated in the revolt, was branded by the Salvadoran authorities as its sole organizer and the source of its every atrocity.[1]

Neighboring Guatemala shuddered. Fear spread through its upper class: a similar upheaval could take place at home. But President Jorge Ubico had already acted: on January 29, the Guatemalan government announced that a Bolshevik revolt had been narrowly averted "in one of the most efficient and beneficial operations executed in the Americas since the arrival of the conquistadores." The communists, it explained, had gained control of the trade unions and had been agitating in the countryside; their leader, the carpenter Antonio Obando Sánchez, had been appointed "High Commissar and Great Teacher of the Steppes in the Soviet of Guatemala" by the Kremlin.[2]

And so hundreds were arrested, as the upper class quaked. "There was a house," the police disclosed,

> in which the cook, the chauffeur, a maid and a gardener had joined the communists; they were ready to betray their masters—raping, murdering and robbing on the day of the uprising. In another household, a black servant was found carrying the tools needed to break into the bedroom of two of our most beautiful high society girls. In another house, the police confiscated ropes which were going to be used to hang a rich man and his family who lived in the heart of our capital city.[3]

The demonic nature of the communist leaders was exposed. Obando Sánchez, it was stated, "preaches slaughter first, and then the complete redistribution of private property, including—like pieces of furniture or slaves (and only to satisfy the biological needs of the species)—all the women of the defeated

---

[1] On the revolt, see Anderson, *Matanza*; Dalton, *Miguel Mármol*, pp. 229–367; "Los sucesos," *Abra*; Arias Gómez, *Farabundo Martí*; McClintock, *American Connection*, 1:99–121.

[2] *La Gaceta: Revista de policía y variedades*, Feb. 7, 1932, pp. 251–323, p. 306 (quoted). See also "Vasto plan del terrorismo comunista para Guatemala," *El I*, Jan. 29, 1932, p. 1; "Todos los cabecillas capturados," *El I*, Jan. 30, 1932, p. 1; "Sigue la limpia de agitadores del terrorismo," *El I*, Feb. 2, 1932, p. 1.

[3] *La Gaceta* (see n. 2 above), p. 306. This issue includes a long list of the detained "communist plotters."

bourgeoisie from age eight to thirty, sentencing those who are older to death by fire.'' Juan Pablo Wainwright, a young upper-class Honduran who had joined the party a few months earlier, was just as bloodthirsty: ''His only interest is burning, destroying, breaking, raping, cutting in two, in four, beating and redistributing private property.''[4]

There had been no plot: the Guatemalan Communist Party was far weaker than its Salvadoran counterpart. In 1932, the communists were thinking not of revolution but of survival.[5] Yet the Guatemalan upper class believed the government's propaganda. Then, as now, its acumen was warped by its fear of losing any of its privileges, by its proclivity to brand all suggestions of reform as communist subversion, and by its tendency to believe anything that might confirm its deformed view of reality.[6]

The upper class, the press, and the Church warmly praised the government's ''activism and vigor'' against international communism. They warned, however, that there must be no slackening of the vigilance and the repression needed to prevent further outbursts.[7]

They had no reason to fret. Ubico, himself a prominent landowner, crushed both the fledgling labor movement and the tiny Communist party. Most leading party members fell into the hands of the police and were tortured. Not one begged for mercy; not one repented. Among them was Wainwright, who is remembered for an act of courage unique in the thirteen years of Ubico's rule. ''Cruelly tortured,'' relates an inveterate anticommunist writer,

> Wainwright sent a note to General Ubico offering him sensational revelations. Ubico arrived at the penitentiary and entered the gloom of cell number 13.
>
> ''What do you have to tell me?'' asked the dictator.
>
> ''I sent for you,'' replied Wainwright, ''to tell you that you are a miserable murderer and an animal.'' He spat in Ubico's face. The dictator whipped him merci-

---

[4] Ibid., pp. 309, 279.

[5] Interview with a party leader, Vásquez, who notes that the party, which had been founded in 1922, never had more than one hundred members. The best source on the Communist Party of Guatemala in the twenties is Taracena Arriola: ''Les origines,'' pp. 282–390, 425–29 and ''El primer partido.'' Obando Sánchez, a leader of the party, includes valuable information in his *Memorias*, pp. 43–109. Useful studies by Guatemalan communists of the post–World War II period are: Alvarado Arellano, *Apuntes*, pp. 5–11 and *Esbozo histórico*, pp. 3–6; Gutiérrez, *Breve historia*, pp. 21–27 and *Apuntes*, pp. 14–20. The only worthwhile source in English is Alexander, *Communism*, pp. 350–53.

[6] See Gleijeses, *Politics and Culture*, pp. 24–26.

[7] Quoted from ''El comunismo,'' *El Apostol*, Jan. 31, 1932, p. 17. See also ''Manifestación social contra el comunismo,'' *El I*, Feb. 1, 1932, p. 1; ''Es una suerte para Guatemala represión oportuna al comunismo,'' *El I*, Feb. 5, 1932, p. 1; ''Orden de la gran parada anticomunista el domingo,'' *El I*, Feb. 11, 1932, p. 1.

lessly. He was almost dead when a bullet ended his suffering. Wainwright lived and died with honor.[8]

Several communists were executed a few days later. The party had been destroyed. It was the second year of the era of Ubico.

Lacking gold, sugar, and spices, Guatemala had been an impoverished and neglected colony throughout the three centuries of Spanish rule. Even after independence it remained an impoverished backwater. Coffee was to change this.

In the last decades of the nineteenth century, the rising demand for coffee wrenched Guatemala into the world economy. Great coffee estates were created, and, to bring the coffee to the sea, railroads were built. Agrarian "reforms" that dispossessed the Indians of their land and labor codes that legalized forced labor ensured that the Indian would supply the workforce.[9]

While the Indian tilled the land, the foreigner built the railroad. By 1912, the American-owned International Railways of Central America controlled Guatemala's railroads. Over the next two decades, the United Fruit Company acquired immense tracts of state land, offering in return paltry sums of money and perfunctory thanks. The State looked on, untroubled by the mergers and the acquisitions that tightened foreign control of the economy.

In 1920, Guatemala entered a period of limited political democracy. The Congress and the press were relatively free. Repression remained, but less than in the past, at least in the cities. The urban population demanded economic concessions and dared to stage strikes. Often the police intervened and arrested people, but wages did increase and several labor unions were legalized.[10] In 1922, thirteen Ladino artisans and a Salvadoran law student created the Communist Party of Guatemala. It was illegal, persecuted, and penniless. ("We were ignorant; we didn't know anything about Marxist theory; we didn't even own any Marxist books," recalls one of the party's founders.)[11] But due to the skill of its leaders, the party acquired influence in the labor movement out of proportion to its meager numbers. It had, however, no contacts in the

[8] Schlesinger, *Revolución comunista*, pp. 44–46, quoted from p. 46. On Wainwright, see also García, *Páginas de lucha*, pp. 73–75; Gaitán, "Los mártires"; Oqueli, "Un señor"; Rosenthal, *Guatemala*, pp. 192–93.

[9] The best works on the coffee era are by McCreery and Castellanos Cambranes. By McCreery, see esp. *Development and the State*, "Debt Servitude," and "An 'Odious Feudalism.' " By Castellanos Cambranes, see *Desarrollo* and *Café y campesinos*. A classic study is Rubio Sánchez, "Breve historia."

[10] On the democratic interlude of the 1920s, see Figueroa Ibarra, "Contenido de clase" and "La insurrección"; Arévalo Martínez, *Ecce Pericles!*, esp. vol. 2; Taracena Arriola, "Les origines," pp. 104–424; Quintana, *La generación de 1920*; Pitti, "Ubico."

[11] Interview with Vásquez.

rural areas. There, no unions were allowed, and democracy meant herding the Indians to the polls on election day.

With the crash of 1929, the coffee market collapsed, the Guatemalan economy went bankrupt, and unemployment spread through the land. "There is a great deal of unrest among the working classes," reported the U.S. embassy in April 1930.[12] Fearing "the gathering of red storm clouds,"[13] the Guatemalan elite knew that the times demanded a strong leader. That man was Jorge Ubico. As a governor, he had gained "a reputation for efficiency and cruelty." The U.S. embassy gave him its hearty endorsement.[14] In February 1931, he triumphed in a presidential election in which he was the sole candidate.

During his thirteen-year dictatorship, Ubico built a number of roads using largely unpaid Indian labor provided in lieu of a road tax; this age-old practice he enforced with particular vigor. He also erected several public buildings. Again, much of the labor was unpaid, supplied by convicts whose ranks were swelled by periodic police raids on Saturday evenings in poor sections of the capital and other towns to arrest drunken laborers and others who might have become drunk had they had the time. This, too, was an old practice, which had fallen into disuse during the more permissive twenties.[15]

By 1934, Ubico had balanced the national budget by slashing government expenditures. He had also reduced graft, which had been rampant in the twenties. For many members of the Guatemalan middle class, this austerity meant dismissal from the bureaucracy. For others, Ubico's rule meant a sharp reduction in salaries and pensions. Blue collar workers fared worse. When the workers of Novella & Company, the largest cement factory of Central America, went on strike in March 1931 to protest a wage cut, the newly inaugurated Ubico ordered the arrest of the ringleaders.[16] Then came the great wave of repression that accompanied the discovery of the 1932 "communist plot"; the

[12] Hawks to SecState, no. 19, Apr. 2, 1930, p. 4, NA 814.00/1011.

[13] David Vela, "Canción de alba porvenirista," *El I*, Nov. 27, 1930, p.3.

[14] Grieb, "American Involvement," p. 12. The best source on Ubico prior to his presidency is Pitti, "Ubico."

[15] See esp. Grieb, *Guatemalan Caudillo*, pp. 126–40, 163–76. This is superior to the only comparable study of the Ubico era: Arévalo Martínez, *Ubico*. It is less penetrating, however, than Pitti's magisterial "Ubico," which ends, unfortunately, with Ubico's accession to the presidency. The writings of former *Ubiquistas* convey the flavor of the times: Col. Ardón, *El señor general*, is a vivid apology by an unreconstructed *Ubiquista*; Col. Flores Avendaño, *Memorias*, 1:143–270, describes the Ubico era through one man's eyes; Samayoa Chinchilla, *El dictador*, is well written and at times incisive.

[16] See "Una protesta," *Nuestro Diario*, Mar. 20, 1931, p. 3; López Larrave, *Breve historia*, p. 23; Obando Sánchez, *Memorias*, pp. 77–78; Dosal, "Political Economy," pp. 341–43.

urban labor movement was destroyed. Thereafter, notes a labor lawyer, "began the long night of Guatemalan labor." The words "trade union, strike, labor rights, petitions" were proscribed, "and those who dared use them were automatically branded as 'communists.' "[17]

Ubico watched carefully that no naive soul spoiled the Guatemalan workers. He intervened in 1942, when the U.S. army (which was building military bases in the country) sought to pay its laborers more than the prevailing wage of twenty-five cents per day.[18] Wages failed to increase even when the Second World War brought sharp inflation to Guatemala.[19] His rule did, however, bring the workers one improvement: disgusted by the subversive connotation of the word, Ubico decreed that there would no longer be "obreros" in Guatemala; they all became "empleados."[20]

However important politically, cities and towns were only specks in the immense *finca* that was Guatemala. In 1940, about 90 percent of the approximately 2.25 million Guatemalans lived in communities of fewer than ten thousand inhabitants. Two-thirds of these Guatemalans were Indians, the descendants of the vanquished Maya.[21] Above the Indians were the Ladinos, an ambiguous category that encompassed all those who were not officially classed as Indians, blacks, or Chinese; it ranged from upper-class whites who boasted of their European lineage to landless Indians who had renounced the culture of their people.

Rare was the Ladino, whatever his status, who felt no contempt for the Indian. Contempt and fear. One day the Indians might rise in blind, destructive fury. No one could divine what lurked behind their subservient smiles, their tame demeanor, their silence. The aboriginal race was "cowardly, sad, fanatical, and cruel. . . . [It was] closer to beast than to man," lamented a young Guatemalan intellectual in 1927. "For the Indians there is only one law—the lash."[22]

---

[17] López Larrave, *Breve historia*, p. 24.

[18] FBI, "Guatemala Today," July 1944, p. 31, NA 814.00/8-944.

[19] For the inflation of the war years, see the Weekly Stability Reports of the U.S. military attaché in Guatemala, 1942–44, RG319 RF, Boxes 749 and 1564, NA-S. See also Bulmer-Thomas, *Political Economy*, pp. 95–100, and CT:DAT, 1944, AGCA.

[20] See Monteforte Toledo, *Guatemala*, p. 290, n. 1, and González Orellana, *Historia de la educación*, p. 374.

[21] Before they were published, these census figures were laundered by Ubico; he swelled the population by 1 million and cut the proportion of Indians from more than two-thirds of the total to one-half. See Naval Attaché June, "Intelligence Report" no. 464-42-R, Dec. 14, 1942, RG165 RF, Box 1574, NA-S; Early, *Demographic Structure*, pp. 20–21; "2.781.665 habitantes en Guatemala," *El I*, June 17, 1950, p. 1; Monteforte Toledo, *Guatemala*, pp. 61–70.

[22] Quotations from García Granados, *Evolución sociológica*, pp. 25–26, and a Guatemalan official quoted in Jones, *Guatemala*, p. 106.

On this beast rested the prosperity of Guatemala. "The Indian," the U.S. embassy noted, "illiterate, unshod, diseased, is the Guatemalan laborer."[23] Until 1934, he was bound to his master by debt peonage. After 1934, he was bound to the State by Ubico's vagrancy laws: all those Indians who owned no land or less than a prescribed amount were ordered to hire themselves out to landowners for at least one hundred days a year.[24] Theoretically, the Indians could choose their employers and negotiate their contracts according to the laws of supply and demand. But in a world ruled by the masters' violence, these laws hardly applied. When there was any trouble, the landowners banded together. Thus, in the department of Quezaltenango, they "joined forces to create a trust . . . which would maintain a wage level of 15 centavos per day. . . . Penalties were agreed upon for anyone who broke this rule."[25]

Only exceptionally were such steps necessary. The Indian laborers could not read the contracts to which they apposed their thumbs; they could not verify whether the written words matched the *patrón*'s oral promises. Moreover, all Indian men between eighteen and sixty years of age had to prove that they had hired themselves out for the prescribed number of days. To this end, they were required to carry cards on which their employers noted the days they had worked, and "it was the common occurrence that the *patrón* would keep a laborer on simply by refusing to sign the books."[26] If a dispute arose, the authorities sided with the landowners. But disputes were usually settled within the closed world of the fincas: whips and stocks were a standard part of the landowner's equipment.

Ubico, sympathetic to the landowners' concerns, legalized murder: Decree 1816 of April 1932 exempted landowners from the consequences of any action taken to protect their goods and lands.[27] From this to the cold-blooded murder of a stubborn Indian was a moot step. Yet, one wonders why this decree was necessary. Civilized Guatemalans had always understood the occasional need to kill an Indian.

By replacing debt peonage with the vagrancy laws, Ubico sought to improve Guatemala's image abroad. He also satisfied the requests of many land-

[23] Capt. Rose, "Military Attaché Report" no. 922, Oct. 25, 1943, p. 2, RG319 DF, Box 226, NA-S.

[24] See Skinner-Klée, *Legislación indigenista*, pp. 108–14 and 118–19 for Decree 1995 (May 7, 1934), Decree 1996 (May 10, 1934) and "Reglamento relativo a los jornaleros para trabajos agrícolas" (Sept. 24, 1935). In theory, the vagrancy laws applied to all Guatemalan citizens; in practice, they applied almost exclusively to Indians. Only those Indians who could convince the unsympathetic authorities that they did not earn their living through agriculture escaped the law. See also Jones, *Guatemala*, pp. 160–67, and Whetten, *Guatemala*, pp. 120–22.

[25] Jones, *Guatemala*, pp. 165–66.

[26] Adams, *Crucifixion*, p. 178.

[27] *DCA*, May 7, 1932, p. 14.

owners who had argued since the 1920s that debt peonage was ineffective and uneconomic.[28] The vagrancy laws increased the influence of the central government, which was given the responsibility of allocating Indians among competing landowners. This was part of Ubico's effort "to shift the locus of power that had generally rested locally and regionally in the hands of the local upper class," and as such it paralleled the 1935 Municipal Law, which replaced the country's elected mayors with *intendentes* appointed by the central government.[29] Just as the *intendente* system was not introduced to improve the lot of the lower classes, so the vagrancy laws were not concerned with the welfare of the Indians.

This is not to say that Ubico was unpopular with the Indians. The daily oppression they endured—an oppression that seemed as eternal as the land and the sky—came from their immediate masters: the landowners, the local authorities, and their Ladino neighbors. The president of the republic was a remote figure, nearly as remote as the concept of a country called Guatemala. Ubico, who traveled extensively through the country, may even have appeared as a benevolent figure who came from afar and spoke words that, though stern, lingered as an echo of hope after the great man had departed.[30] These are impressions; no one, save a few foreign anthropologists who eschewed political analysis, attempted to penetrate the world of the Indian.[31] For the Ladinos, the Indians were inferior beings, a featureless mass that understood only force.

The instruments of control were at hand. This was a militarized society. Every governor of Guatemala's twenty-two departments was a general. The

[28] See Pitti, "Ubico," pp. 230–32, 286, 369, 376, 404–5, 408, 487–88; McCreery, "Debt Servitude," esp. pp. 756–59; Castellanos Cambranes, "Los empresarios agrarios," pp. 276–79; Dawson, "Labor Legislation," esp. pp. 135–37.

[29] For an excellent analysis, see Adams, *Crucifixion*, pp. 174–79, quoted from p. 175.

[30] On these travels, see the apologetic but interesting Hernández de León, *Viajes*. For less partisan sketches published in later years by participants and other witnesses, see Samayoa Chinchilla, *El dictador*, pp. 93–94, 147–59; Torres Moss, "Justicia salomónica"; González, "Recuerdos."

[31] Outstanding among these anthropological studies is Tax, *Penny Capitalism*. More recent studies also offer insight. For example, in a superb book based on field research done in the 1960s, Carmack writes of the area of Momostenango: "The Indians seem to have believed that their problems were due to local ladino officials, but not to Ubico himself." (*Historia social*, p. 300.) For U.S. embassy accounts of unreported Indian riots and the attending executions and imprisonments, see Davis to Burnett, Aug. 13, 1936, RG165 RF, Box 1562, NA-S; R.McN, "Labor-General," July 8, 1942, RG165 RF, Box 1563, NA-S; F.G.M., "Roads and Highways," Sept. 7, 1942, RG165 RF, Box 1568, NA-S. For a poignant account written by Indians of the massacre at Tacaná in 1937 (that was officially described as the army's appropriate response to a riot), see Diego López P. et al. to Procurador General de la República, Tacaná, Dec. 2, 1945, MP:G, Leg. 32562, AGCA.

National Radio and the Department of Roads were staffed by military officers; officers led convicts and Indians to perform forced labor in the cities and the countryside. Secondary education was placed under military control: school principals were senior army officers; lieutenants and captains were in charge of discipline; students were required to undergo reserve training.[32] "With the militarization of these minor civil officials," the U.S. naval attaché explained, "President Ubico further extends his military control over the everyday life and every thought and action of the people of Guatemala."[33]

Not only did these measures enforce military discipline in the bureaucracy, they also employed some of the eighty generals who infested the Guatemalan army in the early 1940s. (Those who had no specific duties congregated every morning in the dictator's anteroom to await his pleasure.) Hated by their own officers, Ubico's generals were notorious for their ignorance, incompetence, and cruelty. Their sole qualification was their mindless obedience to Ubico's orders.

The Guatemalan army, noted a 1944 U.S. intelligence report, was a dismal affair, 798 officers and 5,528 enlisted men who were "poorly trained and poorly equipped." ("It is doubtful," the report pointed out, "whether many of the soldiers have ever fired their rifles.")[34] The officers were Ladinos; nearly all the soldiers were Indian conscripts drafted by force. Military service, Ubico explained, was enlightening for the Indians: "They arrive rude and brutish, but when they leave they are no longer like donkeys, they have good manners and are better equipped to face life."[35] Life in the barracks was similar, however, to life on the *patrones'* estates: despised and paid miserably, they slept on the floor, ate terrible food, donned ragged and dirty uniforms, and were whipped mercilessly at the least infraction. In the words of a Gua-

---

[32] González Orellana, *Historia de la educación*, pp. 360–62, 439–40; Valdes López, "Aspectos socioculturales," pp. 32–35; Carrillo Ramírez, *Evolución histórica*, 1: 242–57.

[33] Lamson-Scribner, "Attaché's Report" no. 670, July 14, 1938, RG165 RF, Box 1571, NA-S.

[34] FBI, "Guatemala Today" (see n. 18 above), pp. 77–81, quoted from p. 77. Counting the number of officers and men in the Guatemalan army was not an exact science: just as he did with the census (see above, n. 21), so Ubico inflated the size of the army, padding it with imaginary reserves. (See Military Intelligence Division, "Military Forces of the Central American Republics," no. 265-231, Oct. 15, 1940, RG165 RF, Box 1574, NA-S; Woodward to SecState, no. 538, Aug. 28, 1945, RG84 CF, Box 13, NA-S; HQs Panama Canal Department, "Weekly Intelligence Summary" no. 263, July 15, 1947, p. 5, RG319 ID 384002, NA-S.) There is no adequate study of the army in the Ubico era. Interviews with the following officers who were on active duty at the time were particularly useful: Lorenzana, Silva Girón, Paz Tejada, Cruz Salazar.

[35] Ubico, quoted in Hernández de León, *Viajes*, 2:17.

temalan officer who served under Ubico and who is not given to sentimentality, "Their treatment was atrocious"; they were, observes another officer, "inept, ill-prepared, illiterate and whipped into stupidity."[36]

Ubico's notorious parsimony was also evident in the treatment of his officers, at least until they reached the rank of colonel. Their salaries were mediocre, and they endured an oppressive discipline. Their role was to inspire fear on behalf of the dictator, but they, too, lived in a world of fear, where "the slightest hint of dissatisfaction could prove fatal."[37] To avoid contamination, officers were not sent to study abroad. They were jailers, forbidden to wander outside the prison walls. The "merciless system" worked. The officers were automata, ready to obey all orders, refraining from all initiative: "We were always scared; the military code was draconian, prescribing the death penalty for virtually every offense. Spies were everywhere."[38]

For added security, Ubico relied on an elite unit that served as his presidential guard. The Guardia de Honor received the bulk of the weapons given to Guatemala by the United States during the Second World War, including the only twelve tanks in the country. Its soldiers "slept on cots, not on the floor . . . and were somewhat better dressed and better fed."[39] The officers received higher pay; in return, they were expected to be particularly loyal to Ubico.

Special loyalty was also expected from the officers *de linea*. These were generally lower-middle-class Ladinos who rose through the ranks. For them, the life of an officer represented both an attractive station and one of the very few avenues of upward mobility in Guatemala. By contrast, the officers *de escuela*—those who had graduated from the military academy—were generally of middle-class extraction. Had it not been for the economic crisis of the 1930s, many would have attended the university; a military career offered them neither social nor economic advancement, particularly toward the end of the era, when the plethora of generals and colonels stifled the possibility of promotion.

However pitiful as a professional military force, the Guatemalan army was more than adequate to control the unarmed populace; indeed, it was impressive compared to the other ragtag armies of Central America. Moreover, it was supplemented by the police which, drawn almost exclusively from poor

[36] Quotations from interview with Lorenzana and from Silva Girón, *12 Horas*, p. 28.

[37] Lt. Col. Cruz Salazar, "El ejército," p. 77.

[38] Quotations from Lt. Col. Hardy, "Military Attaché Report" no. A/G 2028, Apr. 12, 1944, RG319 DF, Box 749, NA-S, and from interview with Col. Lorenzana. For a dramatic example, see the story of Roberto Barrios Peña recounted in Hunter, "Intelligence Report" no. 13-43-R, Jan. 15, 1943, RG165 RF, Box 1565, NA-S.

[39] Silva Girón, *12 Horas*, p. 32. Zamora Alvarez, *Las memorias de Andrés*, pp. 47-71, describes the life of a soldier in the Guardia de Honor in the last months of the dictatorship. For the early years of the Guardia de Honor, see Gen. Zamora Castellanos, *Nuestros cuarteles*, pp. 254–74.

Ladinos, had "the reputation of being one of the most efficient and secretive in Latin America."[40] Together, the army and the police formed a formidable barrier to domestic unrest, and they faced no difficult challenges. After the destruction of the 1932 "communist plot," Ubico crushed a true conspiracy in 1934. There were no other plots of any significance, and there were no disturbances, until 1944.[41]

Nor was there much crime, at least not in the usual sense: common criminals were swiftly and ruthlessly punished. Accounts abound of how safe Guatemala became under Ubico's rule. It was not safe, however, for the victims of the dictator's whims, for "subversive" Indians, or for poor Ladinos. "We had to endure not only the all-encompassing will of the dictator," recalls a former official, "but also the numerous 'Little Ubicos' who imitated him while doing his bidding: the chief of police, the governors of the departments, the local police chiefs and hundreds more. . . . In the early days of the dictatorship I became aware of murders perpetrated by the rural police. They had to set an example, their chiefs said, in order to escape the Man's wrath."[42]

Communists and criminals (insofar as he distinguished between them) were two of Ubico's phobias. The third was intellectuals, for whom he "felt an Olympian contempt."[43] His disdain was tinged with mistrust; people who read might fall prey to subversive ideas, that is, to communism. Thus he made sure that no subversive books entered Guatemala, and that no subversive ideas perturbed the Guatemalan youth. "We were political illiterates," recalls a student leader.[44]

Arrogant and suspicious, Ubico was loath to delegate authority. As a loyal minister stated, "His overestimation of himself led him to take care of everything without seeking advice." He had developed, noted the FBI, a clever system of "checking up on his ministers": he appointed their enemies as their deputies. "In this way they keep a check on each other and report to the President."[45] A U.S. official had seen this side of Ubico as early as 1923:

[40] FBI, "Guatemala Today" (see n. 18 above), pp. 66–77, quoted from p. 66. Ubico's jails were also famous for their efficiency; China requested permission to study them. (Tchou Che-Tsien, Consul General of China, to Ministro Gobernación, Jan. 7, 1944, CM:G, Leg. 32357, AGCA.)

[41] On the 1934 plot, see de los Rios, *Ombres*, 1:379–97 and 2:171–207; Sandoval Vásquez, *Leifugados*, pp. 74–78 and 217–57; Arévalo Martínez, *Ubico*, pp. 34–38; Aguilar P., *Vida*, pp. 25–52.

[42] Flores Avendaño, *Memorias*, 2:240–41.

[43] González Campo, "El general," p. 346.

[44] Interview with Galich, one of the leaders of the 1944 movement against Ubico in the university.

[45] Quotations from González Campo, "El general," pp. 347–48 and FBI, Hoover to Berle, Jan. 13, 1942, p. 2, NA 814.00/1371.

During the hour and a half that I spent with the General, I was impressed with . . . the almost Anglo-Saxon frankness of the man. He is what is known here as the white type, untainted by mixed blood. . . . The accession of General Ubico as President would be, however, the accession of a dictator. He has the suggestion complex, imagining that he is Napoleon, whom he does strongly resemble. This physicological [*sic*] state of mind is immediately apparent when one enters his drawing room. In conspicuous places are busts of Napoleon. . . . Above these statues is a large photograph of General Ubico.[46]

Ubico may have had delusions of grandeur, but his world was narrow; "he lacked the statesman's vision."[47] His was the Guatemala of the past, and he was suspicious of all change. "He opposed industrial development because factories spawned a proletariat from which the communists would emerge"; when Bata, a leading shoe manufacturer, sought to establish itself in Guatemala in the early 1940s, "Ubico categorically rejected the proposal."[48]

Ubico's bravery was legendary, as was his bravado: "I have no friends, but only domesticated enemies. . . . Be careful! I am a tiger, you are monkeys."[49] Considering Guatemala to be his personal domain, Ubico "ruled the country as if it were his hamlet. He controlled everything. It is true that there was less theft under Ubico. The only man with the freedom to steal was Ubico himself."[50] A 1944 U.S. intelligence report noted that after taking office, Ubico "became the greatest private landowner in Guatemala, despite his much-publicized campaign for honesty in government." He bought "many properties at a price fixed by himself." He also made sure that his salary and perquisites were generously increased while he slashed the bureaucrats' salaries, and he graciously accepted, in 1940, a gift of $200,000 from a servile Congress. This spontaneous token of gratitude aroused resentment, but the begrudgers were swiftly silenced: "The Legation has heard," the U.S. minister reported, "that some ninety persons in Guatemala have been put in jail for speaking out of turn regarding this gift."[51]

---

[46] G-2 Intelligence Report, "Interview with General Jorge Ubico," no. 839, Dec. 17, 1923, p. 3, RG165 RF, Box 1565, NA-S.

[47] González Campo, "El general," p. 346.

[48] Quotations from Alfonso Solorzano in Quan Rossell, *Guatemala*, 1:218, and González Campo, "El general," p. 354. The former was a foe of Ubico, the latter an apologist, but on this point they are in full agreement.

[49] Samayoa Chinchilla, *El dictador*, pp. 62, 107.

[50] José Luis Balcarcel in Quan Rossell, *Guatemala*, 2:497–98.

[51] Quotations from: Office of Strategic Services, Research and Analysis Branch, "The First Two Months of the New Guatemalan Government (November–December 1944)," no. 2791, Dec. 23, 1944, p. 6, NA; Cabot to SecState, no. 1599, Dec. 4, 1940, p. 3, NA 814.00/1340; DesPortes to SecState, no. 1250, May 8, 1940, p. 1, NA 814.001/101. For Ubico's salary and perquisites in July 1938 (totaling $11,790), see Samayoa Chinchilla, *El dictador*, p. 109.

Those who offended the dictator were harshly punished. The secret police "has earned for itself the odious title of the Guatemalan Gestapo," a U.S. official noted.[52] "The spy network was organized wisely and carefully. There were informers in all social classes. . . . The servant was a spy, and so was his master; the lady was a spy, and so was the whore; the priest was a spy, and so was the teacher."[53] As a result, recalls the son of a senior official, "In my friends' homes—and even in my home—in the streets, everyone spoke in hushed tones. . . . Suspicion was rife."[54] The immense majority of the elite submitted to the dictator's will, participated in his personality cult, and turned against those whom he branded as his enemies—even when they were friends or relatives. In return, they were allowed to live the lives of petty feudal lords.

Cold and contemptuous toward the Guatemalan upper class, Ubico was gentle with the United States. To be sure, the men he admired were not Roosevelt and Cordell Hull, but Franco and Mussolini. Admiration, however, did not stand in the way of common sense; the Caribbean belonged to the United States. Moreover, Ubico saw the Americans as a valuable shield against Mexico, a neighbor that in the nineteenth century had annexed vast regions claimed by Guatemala and had become—or so Ubico and his class believed—a breeding ground for communist infection.[55] The United States, by contrast, was relatively healthy, even though Ubico at times doubted Roosevelt's steadfastness. He was worried, he told a U.S. diplomat in 1941, "about communistic activities and so many strikes in the United States." The American Communist Party may have been small, but "the smallest rat left unmolested in a mansion would in time do considerable boring." Whether in Guatemala or the United States, he stressed, the communists should be given a "dose of lead," not freedom of speech.[56]

Only about communism did Ubico dare to offer advice to the United States. Otherwise, his attitude was that of the obsequious pupil. He "diligently courted American officials, diplomats, and businessmen, exhibited preference for Yankee investors, and showed considerable imagination in discovering ways to demonstrate his support."[57] For example, he appointed a U.S. officer as director of the Escuela Politécnica, an unprecedented gesture. Except for a few months in 1943, U.S. officers occupied that prestigious post throughout

[52] FBI, "Guatemala: Police and Penal System," no. 2710, Dec. 4, 1943, p. 4, RG165 RF, Box 1562, NA-S.

[53] Samayoa Chinchilla, *El dictador*, p. 68.

[54] Julio Gómez Padilla in Quan Rossell, *Guatemala*, 1:333.

[55] For Ubico and Mexico see Pitti, "Ubico," pp. 9–11, 63–64, 462–63; Grieb, *Guatemalan Caudillo*, pp. 206–18, 235–47; Zorrilla, *Relaciones*, pp. 691–734.

[56] MemoConv, Aug. 12, 1941, quoted from pp. 3–4, enclosed in DesPortes to SecState, no. 2057, Aug. 14, 1941, NA 814.00/1358.

[57] Grieb, *Guatemalan Caudillo*, p. 72.

Ubico's thirteen years; other U.S. officers were among the academy's professors.[58]

After hostilities broke out in Europe, Ubico asserted that Guatemala "was with the United States in any needed capacity 'all of the way.' "[59] He declared war on Japan on December 8, one day after Pearl Harbor; on Italy and Germany on December 11, the day they declared war on the United States. "General Ubico," the U.S. military attaché reported, "has always been quick to follow the lead of the United States in the war measures dictated by that country. He has given many unheard of concessions to the U.S. Army." American troops were stationed in Guatemala, and Ubico "cooperated in the maintenance of harmonious relations with United States military personnel."[60]

At Washington's behest, Ubico moved against the German community in Guatemala—five to six thousand individuals, mainly Guatemalans of German origin. This small but economically influential group had supported the dictator loyally, and there is no indication that he considered them a threat to his rule. The Americans wanted action, and he complied. Following Guatemala's declaration of war on Germany, Ubico allowed the FBI to deport several hundred German citizens and Guatemalans of German origin to the United States. Others faced discriminatory measures that culminated, in June 1944, in the expropriation of all the coffee estates belonging to the German community.[61]

[58] There is no good study of the Escuela Politécnica; still, the following are useful: Samayoa Coronado, *Escuela Politécnica*; Zamora Castellanos, *Nuestros cuarteles*, pp. 45–133; Escuela Politécnica, *La Escuela Politécnica* and *Centenario*. Carrillo Ramírez, *Evolución histórica*, 2:153–226, describes the curriculum at the academy. Francisco Morazán, who entered the Academy in 1933, has written a graphic account of his experiences, "Apuntes," pp. 104–570. For the U.S. view of the school in the Ubico era, see Harris, "The Military School," no. 1473, Dec. 1, 1931, and Lt. Col. Marsh, "National Military Academy," no. 414, May 18, 1942, both RG165 RF, Box 1572, NA-S.

[59] MemoConv, p. 1, included in DesPortes to SecState, no. 2057, Aug. 14, 1941, NA 814.00/1358.

[60] Quotations from Rose, "Military Attaché Report" no. 1105, Mar. 7, 1944, RG319 RF, Box 748, NA-S, and from FBI, "Guatemala Today" (see n. 18 above), p. 191.

[61] For the most comprehensive treatment, see FBI, "Guatemala Today" (see n. 18 above), pp. 82–193. See also June, "Intelligence Report" no. 582-41, Sept. 20, 1941, RG165 RF, Box 1566, NA-S; FBI, Hoover to Berle, Jan. 13, 1942, pp. 4–6, NA 814.00/1371; United States Tariff Commission, *Economic Controls*, pp. 18–19. Decree 3115 of June 22, 1944, stipulated that the former owners would be compensated after the war, according to the value they had declared for tax purposes. (See *DCA*, June 23, 1944, p. 805, and "Razones de la expropiación," *El I*, June 23, 1944, p. 1.) There is no definitive study of the German presence in Guatemala. The best sources

In the late 1930s, occasional articles in the U.S. press had castigated Ubico as sympathetic to the Axis powers. His behavior during the war allayed such fears. As a result, between 1940 and mid-1944, the American press displayed warm appreciation for Jorge Ubico, an exotic strongman who built roads, maintained stability and exhibited a touching admiration for the United States and Franklin Delano Roosevelt. Ubico, John Gunther told his many readers, "is the biggest man in Central America. Given local conditions, he has done a lot. . . . Relations between the United States and Guatemala are in every way excellent, better than they have ever been before."[62]

Ubico's treatment of American companies was exemplary. Not only did he respect their immense privileges, but he was forthcoming in the one case in which, for a less supple man, confrontation would have been inevitable. The matter involved a 1930 contract with the United Fruit Company (UFCO): in return for a grant of two hundred thousand hectares at Tiquisate on the Pacific coast, the company pledged to build a Pacific port within seven years.[63] For the landed elite, this had one significant benefit: cheaper transportation costs. The coffee grown on the Western Piedmont would no longer have to be carried by rail all the way to Puerto Barrios on the Atlantic, an economic absurdity from which the International Railways of Central America (IRCA) extracted a hefty profit.

Had UFCO honored the agreement, IRCA's losses would have been substantial. But the two American companies reached a friendly understanding, which was formalized in a September 1936 contract. UFCO, which already owned 17 percent of IRCA's stock, bought additional shares, bringing its total participation to 42.68 percent. It also pledged not to build a port on the Pacific. Thus the bananas from Tiquisate would have to be transported, like the coffee, all the way to Puerto Barrios—but IRCA would charge UFCO less than half its usual freight rate. It was a deal that promised to benefit both companies.[64]

Without Ubico's gentle forbearance, the agreement would not have been possible. In March 1936, Guatemala had freed UFCO of its obligation to build the port "because of the prevailing economic crisis" (which was less severe than in 1930, when the original contract had been signed). UFCO paid $50,000 and retained the land it had received for agreeing to build the port. The negotiations, UFCO's local manager told the American chargé, "had

---

are Castellanos Cambranes, *El imperialismo alemán*; Náñez Falcón, "Dieseldorff"; Wagner, "Actividades empresariales."

[62] Gunther, *Inside Latin America*, pp. 122, 126. See also Lawrence and Sylvia Martin, "Ubico—Boss of Guatemala," *CSM*, Oct. 18, 1941, p. 5; John Gunther, "Four Strong Men and a President," *Harper's*, Sept. 1942, pp. 418–27; Frank Taylor, "Guatemala's Hardheaded Ubico," *Reader's Digest*, Feb. 1944, pp. 25–27.

[63] See de León Aragón, *Los contratos*, pp. 261–73.

[64] For the 1936 agreement, see LaBarge, "A Study of United Fruit," pp. 19–20.

been carried on most amicably . . . [and the company] had not been subjected to any particular pressure."[65]

Once again, as so often in its empire-building in the Caribbean basin, UFCO reaped the benefits of dictatorial rule. Whereas the 1930 contract had been preceded by long and acrimonious debates in the Guatemalan Congress and the press, the 1936 agreement was approved swiftly and without debate.

There is no indication that U.S. officials intervened to help the company. Nor was such help requested by UFCO. Having just "reelected" himself in violation of the constitution, Ubico was particularly eager for American goodwill; he was also aware that in the early 1920s the State Department had applied massive pressure when the Guatemalan government had failed to satisfy the demands of American companies.[66] Moreover, UFCO and IRCA were powerful enough in their own right to elicit sympathetic treatment.

During his presidency, Ubico proved himself worthy of the Americans' favor, and the United States was not ungrateful. U.S. officials had welcomed Ubico's accession to the presidency in 1931, praising him in extravagant terms as the man who could best maintain pro-American stability in Guatemala during the world recession.[67] Their approval was steadfast until the last months of the dictator's rule.

Even useful dictators can become expendable. Throughout Latin America, the Depression had spawned strongmen; by the mid-1940s the economic crisis had waned, and the Allied victory over Hitler was spreading antidictatorial feelings among even the upper class. In the Caribbean arc, through the mid-1940s, dictators faltered and fell: Anastasio Somoza's control of Nicaragua was seriously threatened; Rafael Trujillo experienced difficulties in the Dominican Republic; in Cuba, Fulgencio Batista accepted defeat at the polls; while Isaias Medina Angarita was toppled in Venezuela.

At the University of San Carlos, Guatemala's only center of higher education, some students began to shake off the torpor that had becalmed the country. The creation of the Law Students' Association in October 1942 and of a Federation of University Students thirteen months later were tentative steps along a narrow path. The students appeared to eschew political issues and to seek only minimal academic freedom, but below the surface, tensions were rising.[68] U.S. officials reported that Ubico's decision to continue for a third

[65] O'Donaghue to SecState, no. 941, Apr. 8, 1936, p. 2, NA 814.6156/13. For the text of the contract and a critical analysis, see de León Aragón, *Los contratos*, pp. 95–105, 171–90, 274–84.

[66] For the State Department's efforts on behalf of Empresa Electrica and IRCA, see Pitti, "Ubico," pp. 68–72, 83, 88–104; see also below, p. 86.

[67] See Grieb, "American Involvement."

[68] The best source on the period of awakening within the university and on the weeks of unrest that preceded Ubico's resignation is Galich, *Del pánico al ataque*. Also useful

term (from March 1943 to March 1949) created "considerable public tension" and "latent opposition."[69] Ubico's police chief pointed to the Atlantic Charter as "the cause of political unrest. . . . He advised that the people [had] read Allied propaganda posters about the Four Freedoms and their ensuing thoughts on the matter led them to feel discontented under the present Guatemalan government."[70] In fact, the middle class hated Ubico, and even the upper class was turning against him. It no longer needed the arrogant strongman.

Ubico's departure was preceded by that of his Salvadoran colleague, General Maximiliano Hernández Martínez. After crushing a military revolt in April 1944, Martínez faced a mounting wave of urban strikes. Students and blue collar workers led the unrest, the army wavered, and the U.S. embassy, seeking an orderly transition, urged the beleaguered dictator to leave. On May 11, Martínez sought refuge in Guatemala.[71]

The fall of a neighboring dictator unnerved Ubico and inspired his restive subjects. Guatemala's university students were the first to react. Until late June their demands were confined to academic issues, but their assertiveness itself was a political challenge. The authorities responded with surprising irresolution, combining hesitant concessions with light punishments. A few students were detained briefly, and others lost their jobs as schoolteachers. The overall impression was one of weakness. The students were emboldened, and the grip of fear over the population began to loosen.

In mid-June the ferment spread to the capital's teachers. The preparations for Teachers' Day (June 30) provided the spark: "As in every year, the teachers' martyrdom had begun. Without regard for age or sex, they had to assem-

---

are Morales, *Derrocamiento*; Mejía, *El movimiento obrero*, pp. 41–76; Ruiz Franco, *Hambre*, pp. 17–51; Gómez Padilla in Quan Rossell, *Guatemala*, 1:333–46; Zea González, *El espejismo*, pp. 128–71; Arévalo Martínez, *Ubico*, pp. 64–137, 166–69. Of particular interest is a series of articles by university students in *Studium*, April 1945, no. 1. Samayoa Chinchilla, *El dictador*, pp. 178–81, describes Ubico's last days in power from the vantage point of an official in the presidential palace. Two accounts by loyal *Ubiquistas* are González Campo, "La caída," and Salazar, *Memoria*, pp. 316–23. The definitive study of the fall of Ubico has yet to be written.

[69] FBI, "Guatemala Today" (see n. 18 above), p. 48. See also June to Navy Department, no. 259-42, June 1, 1942 enclosed in DesPortes to SecState, no. 2949, June 10, 1942, NA 814.00/1390; June to Navy Department, 16-43-R, Jan. 19, 1943, NA 814.00/1429; Drew to SecState, no. 3593, Feb. 9, 1943, NA 814.00/1405; Drew to SecState, no. 3707, Mar. 19, 1943, NA 814.00/1419; FBI, Hoover to Berle, Oct. 25, 1943, NA 814.00/1449; FBI, Hoover to Berle, Mar. 6, 1944, NA 814.00/1401.

[70] FBI, Hoover to Berle, June 2, 1944, p. 8, NA 814.00/6-2444. See also June, "Intelligence Report" no. 16-43-R, Jan. 19, 1943, pp. 1–2, RG165 RF, Box 1565, NA-S.

[71] On the fall of Martínez, see Morán, *Las jornadas cívicas*, and Parkman, *Nonviolent Insurrection*.

ble every afternoon at the *Instituto Nacional Central de Varones*. There they practiced marching for two hours without a break. Led by army officers, they would have to parade on Teachers' Day in perfect order, carrying heavy flags under the blazing sun."[72] In growing numbers, the teachers boycotted the exercises. Soon other professionals, especially young lawyers, began to express their support for the students and to present demands of their own. But no one dared, as yet, to call for the dictator's resignation.

Ubico responded on June 22 by suspending constitutional guarantees. While no such guarantees had existed during his rule, their formal suspension indicated that a showdown was imminent. In the words of a student leader, "Everyone held their breath" that day and the next. "Beneath the anxiety, a new spirit was rising, nurtured by the bravery of the students and the whole-hearted support of the teachers."[73] On Saturday, June 24, two brave souls brought a petition signed by 311 prominent Guatemalans to the presidential palace. In a respectful but firm tone, the document called for the reestablishment of constitutional guarantees. It was an act of audacity that Ubico viewed as painful betrayal. That same day, for the first time in the Ubico era, crowds gathered in the capital to demonstrate against the government. Also for the first time, voices were heard—a few at first, then a swelling chorus—demanding the dictator's resignation. The poor joined the students, teachers, and other professionals in the streets. "The first organized demonstration" of the day, reported U.S. Ambassador Boaz Long, took place around noon "when students marched quietly through the streets, cheering the United States and President Roosevelt as they passed the American Consulate General and the office occupied by the Military and Naval Attachés."[74] Throughout the day there was little violence. During the night, the police sent thugs to loot and riot in some areas of the capital. Several people were killed. The authorities blamed the demonstrators.[75]

By the next morning, Sunday, June 25, "tension throughout the city had mounted with almost incredible rapidity," Long observed. Large crowds gathered. The police and the army intervened, wounding many. "To any person who has been familiar with the thirteen years of iron-bound discipline maintained by the Ubico administration," noted Long, "it was difficult to believe that an incident at first confined to a small group comprised of University students should so swiftly have spread as to involve the entire city in a serious

[72] Galich, *Del pánico al ataque*, pp. 256–57.

[73] Ibid., p. 332. For an eye-witness account of the students' reaction to the suspension of constitutional guarantees, see Catalán M., "Huelga."

[74] Long to SecState, no. 1256, June 27, 1944, p. 1, NA 814.00/6-2344.

[75] See "Actos de pillaje cometidos el sábado," *El Liberal Progresista*, June 26, 1944, p. 1, and "Fue una farsa vulgar de la policía el asalto al barrio de La Palmita y Colonia de Ubico," *El I*, July 3, 1944, p. 1.

situation marked by public disorder and general civic disobedience.''[76] In the afternoon, a thirty-one-year-old schoolteacher, María Chinchilla, was killed by a soldier. On Monday, June 26, "all stores and business houses, gasoline stations and newspaper offices closed.''[77] Guatemala City was challenging Ubico.

The confrontation would be brief and bloodless. For the next few days the police and the army were the unchallenged masters of the streets of the capital, but most offices and shops remained closed. Then, on June 30, the news spread: Ubico, it was said, had resigned.

And resign he did, on July 1. He abandoned a struggle he had not yet lost and might eventually have won. The capital was defiant, but the rest of the country was quiet, and the army had shown no sign of rebellion.[78] Nor had the Americans asked Ubico to step down. They did not, however, intervene to prop him up. Throughout June they were noncommittal. The State Department had told the embassy to limit its good offices, which had been requested by Ubico, "exclusively to the transmission of messages between the contending factions.''[79] U.S. officials were beginning to see the dictator as an anachronism, they considered his handling of the crisis ineffectual, and they were confident that should Ubico be replaced, his successors would be friendly to Washington.

American aloofness struck Ubico as a sharp rebuff, but it brought little comfort to his foes. A leader of the opposition contrasted the attitude of Ambassador Long to that of the Mexican ambassador after meeting them both in late June: "Long was tight-lipped; he neither said nor did anything that could give

[76] Long to SecState, no. 1256, June 27, 1944, p. 2, NA 814.00/6-2344.

[77] Long to SecState, no. 412, June 26, 1944, NA 814.00/1474. As the newspapers were either shut down or under government control, embassy memos and dispatches (NA 814.00 and RG84 GR, Box 106, NA-S) are the best source for the developments of the last week of June.

[78] For an overview, see the June reports of the Jefes Políticos (IMJP:G, Leg. 32376, AGCA). For the army, interviews with the officers listed in n. 34 above were instructive. For a corroborating sketch of the situation in the Guardia de Honor, see Zamora Alvarez, *Las memorias de Andrés*, pp. 73–76. Accounts by opposition leaders do not refer to any contact with active duty officers or to any wavering within the armed forces. The same telling silence is found in two army publications that deal at length with the events of 1944: *Revista de la Revolución*, Jan. 1945, and *Revista Militar*, Jan./Feb. 1945. In his Weekly Stability Reports for May and June 1944, the U.S. military attaché continued to assert that the army was loyal to Ubico (RG319 RF, Box 1564, NA-S). The only glimmer of a plot against Ubico was in the Escuela Politécnica among a mere handful of officers led by Jacobo Arbenz. They failed to gain adherents. (See below p. 139.)

[79] Quoted from Hull to AmEmG, no. 367, June 25, 1944, NA 814.00/1470. See also Long to SecState, no. 400, June 25, 1944, NA 814.00/1461; and Long to SecState, no. 402, June 25, 1944, NA 814.00/1470.

us the least comfort. But the Mexican Ambassador emphatically expressed his sympathy—and that of his government—for the Guatemalan people and the triumph of democracy in our country."[80] Mexican sympathy was welcome, but it was the attitude of the United States that could be decisive. Washington had not turned against the dictator. The army was still loyal. Ubico had a good chance to ride out the storm.

Why then did he step down? Was he convinced that his position had become hopeless? Was he moved by bitter disappointment, having swallowed his sycophants' assurances that the people loved him? Ubico, reported Long on the morning of June 30, was "deeply disillusioned and hurt with the realization that the majority of the country was against him." He was particularly embittered, Long added, by the petitions for his resignation submitted over the preceding days by a long list of prominent Guatemalans, including many whom he had considered absolutely loyal.[81]

Perhaps Ubico's decision was also influenced by his poor health, or even by the hope that soon he would be begged to return by a repentant people. No definitive answer has been offered by friend, foe, or even by Ubico himself; he left the presidential palace on the morning of July 1 with neither words nor overt emotion. He did not seek the safety of an embassy but went to his private residence in the capital—hardly the behavior of a cowed tyrant.

What is certain, however, is that he selected his successor in a most bizarre fashion. After signing his resignation decree on the morning of July 1, he ordered an aide, General Roderico Anzueto, "to choose three generals to take over the presidency." Anzueto decided to select men he thought he would be able to control. Stepping out of the president's office, he performed his task: to their great surprise, three undistinguished generals—Federico Ponce Vaides, Eduardo Villagran Ariza, and Buenaventura Pineda—learned that henceforth they would constitute a three-man military *junta* and take the place of Ubico. When another general started to ask Ubico to stay, the dictator "cut him short: 'Shut up!' he exclaimed. And he left." The first act of the new rulers, recalls the war minister, "was to get drunk."[82]

---

[80] Ernesto Viteri Bertrand, quoted by Morales, *Derrocamiento*, p. 108; see also pp. 95–97, 107–9, and Galich, *Del pánico al ataque*, p. 243. The role of the Mexican ambassador and his government's sympathy for the opposition to Ubico were widely noted. See Long to SecState, no. 1251, June 24, 1944; Long to SecState, no. 1261, June 27, 1944; FBI, Hoover to Berle, Aug. 23, 1944, p. 15; AmEm Mexico, Messersmith to SecState, no. 941, July 1, 1944; AmEm Mexico, Messersmith to SecState, no. 18733, July 12, 1944; Long to SecState, no. 1380, Aug. 1, 1944. All NA 814.00. See also: "Triunfo del civismo," *El I*, July 3, 1944, p. 1; Muñoz Meany, *El hombre*, pp. 141–44; Roberto Quintana, "Gesto heróico," *Studium*, Apr. 1945, no. 1, pp. 75–81; *Revista de la Revolución*, Jan. 1945, p. 28.

[81] Long to SecState, no. 1269, June 30, 1944, p. 2, NA 814.00.

[82] Quotations from: Rivas, "Versión inédita"; Villegas Rodas, "Como se produjo,"

On July 4, the most ambitious member of the *junta*, General Ponce, easily convinced a timorous Congress to elect him provisional president. "A Thompson sub-machine gun is a very good persuader," the U.S. military attaché observed dryly. Ponce was effusive. "I never dreamt, I never imagined, that one day I would be entrusted with the weighty responsibility which you now offer to me," he told the congressmen in his inaugural speech a few hours later.[83] In the weeks that followed, Ponce permitted the formation of political parties and trade unions and promised to hold free elections. Once again, students and teachers led the struggle. "The students," wrote Ambassador Long in August, "have injected themselves into all sorts of situations—labor, political, personal, congressional—ever since they succeeded in starting a movement which culminated in the resignation of President Ubico."[84] The country's two strongest opposition parties were the Frente Popular Libertador, whose leaders were university students, and Renovación Nacional, led by schoolteachers. Their candidate, university professor Juan José Arévalo, emerged as the leading contender for the presidency.

It became evident, however, that should elections indeed take place, they would be free only for those who were willing to choose General Ponce as Guatemala's next president.

Emboldened by their victory over the formidable Ubico, the inhabitants of the capital responded with mounting unrest. Ferment spread to many provincial towns, but the countryside remained quiet. Hoping to quell the opposition, Ponce exploited the Ladinos' fear of an Indian revolt. Beginning in late August, truckloads of Indians were carted to the capital to march in support of him; they were then shipped back to their villages, pawns in a struggle among

---

p. 3; Corado, "Yo no firmé." (These three senior government officials were eyewitnesses.) On Anzueto, interview with Rolz Bennett was useful. The U.S. embassy was told that the *junta* had been selected by the army's general staff, but this was certainly not the case. (See Salazar to Long, July 1, 1944, enclosed in Long to SecState, no. 1275, July 3, 1944; Long to SecState, no. 461, July 2, 1944; FBI, Hoover to Berle, July 15, 1944. All NA 814.00.) The manner in which Ubico chose his successors, coupled with the fact that there is no evidence that he tried to influence them after his resignation, disproves the theory that he stepped down in order to maintain power behind the throne.

[83] Quotations from Rose, "Weekly Conditions Report" no. 3020, July 6, 1944, p. 3, RG84 GR, Box 106, NA-S, and from "Discurso del General Ponce ante la Cámara," *El I*, July 5, 1944, p. 1. The best sources for the Ponce presidency are Arévalo Martínez, *Ubico*, pp. 166–343; Arévalo, *El candidato*, pp. 113–314; Ruiz Franco, *Hambre*, pp. 51–168; Flores Avendaño, *Memorias*, 2:271–317; Zea González, *El espejismo*, pp. 172–99. As with the fall of Ubico, much remains to be written; however in this case the Guatemalan press, which had become quite outspoken, is far more useful. For both periods, U.S. documents are a very important source.

[84] Long to SecState, no. 1428, Aug. 15, 1944, p. 2, NA 814.00.

Ladinos. The tactic culminated on Independence Day, September 15, with a parade of two thousand "imported" Indians marching through Guatemala City swinging clubs and machetes and shouting slogans in honor of "My President Ponce."[85] The government press praised "the magnificent parade . . . [and] the sincerity of the peasantry," and castigated those "power-hungry politicians who have contempt for the Indian."[86] The opposition offered a different assessment: "Sadness. . . . This is the only possible response to the pathetic parade of September 15. . . . What a sad spectacle! Illiterates, ignorants, marching through the streets of the capital without knowing why, shouting slurred slogans that they do not understand, repeating them by rote under the shadow of the whip." In tones of horror, of indignation, another paper described the marchers as "an unthinking mob . . . a host of illiterate Indians . . . armed with machetes, sticks, and clubs . . . with pictures of the provisional president hanging from their rags."[87]

Tensions grew. On October 1, the editor of the country's major opposition daily, El Imparcial, was assassinated by order of the government. Opposition leaders began to seek refuge in foreign embassies and in neighboring countries; others were deported. "Arévalo is in the Mexican Embassy," reported a U.S. official on October 18, "and his seeking refuge there is thought by many to mark the end of his serious candidacy."[88] It seemed increasingly likely that Ponce would triumph.

A conspiracy was hatching, however, among young army officers. It was spearheaded by Jacobo Arbenz Guzmán, a captain who had resigned from the army in early July, and by Major Carlos Aldana Sandoval, who belonged to the powerful Guardia de Honor. A few civilian leaders, particularly students, joined the officers. On the night of October 19, the plotters, minus Aldana Sandoval, struck. Frightened by his own audacity, Aldana Sandoval had fled to the safety of the Salvadoran border a few hours before the appointed time. His defection might have spelled disaster had it not been for an officer who had joined the plot in its later stages: Major Francisco Arana, the commander of the twelve tanks of the Guardia de Honor. Led by Arana, the Guardia de Honor rose in revolt. Throughout the night weapons were distributed to civil-

[85] The term "imported" is from Long to SecState, no. 1555, Sept. 22, 1944, p. 3, NA 814.00.

[86] "El día de la patria, los hijos del pueblo y el Ejército Nacional," El Independiente, Sept. 21, 1944, p. 2. See also "El indígena y su participación en la política" (edit.), La Nación, Sept. 18, 1944, p. 1.

[87] Quotations from "Magno desfile del día 15," Circuito Estudiantil, Sept. 22, 1944, p. 1, and from "Desvirtuación del 15 de Septiembre," El Libertador, Sept. 19, 1944, p. 1. See also Frente Unido de Partidos y Agrupaciones Cívicas to Diplomatic Corps, Sept. 21, 1944, enclosed in Long to SecState, no. 1554, Sept. 22, 1944, and Long to SecState, no. 1560, Sept. 25, 1944. All NA 814.00.

[88] Affeld to SecState, no. 687, Oct. 18, 1944, p. 1, NA 814.00.

ian volunteers; overall, between two and three thousand were armed. At first, the outcome was uncertain, as the other army units in the capital remained loyal to Ponce. But their resistance weakened as the hours went by. In the early afternoon of October 20, Ponce surrendered and was allowed to leave the country with his closest associates.[89]

On October 24, a car stopped for Ubico at the British embassy, where he had sought refuge when Ponce fell. It was bound for the airport. Upon leaving the country that he had ruled for thirteen years, Ubico lamented: "What they are doing to me is scandalous: to get rid of me as if I were a dog! They had better watch out: they have seized power; now they better muster the ability and the nerve to retain it. Beware of zealots and communists!"[90] Ubico flew to New Orleans, where he began pestering the U.S. government about his property, which had been confiscated in Guatemala.[91]

He died in New Orleans on June 14, 1946. In 1963, his remains were returned to Guatemala, where they were placed in a mausoleum and accorded full military honors.[92] The men who had ruled Guatemala since the overthrow of Arbenz admired Ubico's firm hand. They welcomed the old dictator home.

[89] On the plot and the fighting, see *Revista de la Revolución*, Jan. 1945; *Revista Militar*, Jan./Feb. 1945, pp. 3–7; *Studium*, Apr. 1945, pp. 36–39; U.S. embassy dispatches and internal memos Oct. 20–24, 1944 (esp. Affeld to SecState, no. 1658, Oct. 23, 1944, NA 814.00; Rose, "Revolution of October 20, 1944," enclosed in Affeld to SecState, no. 1662, Oct. 24, NA 814.00; all of Box 107, RG84 GR, NA-S). See also Arévalo, *El candidato*, pp. 297–327; Zea González, *El espejismo*, pp. 200–227; Arévalo Martínez, *Ubico*, pp. 299–343; Silva Girón, *12 horas*; Zamora Alvarez, *Las memorias de Andrés*, pp. 73–121. The best press coverage of the fighting was provided by *El I* in its issues of Oct. 21–24, 1944. Retrospective press accounts of the plot and the fighting include "Génesis de la revolución," *Nuestro Diario*, Oct. 27, 1944, p. 8; *El I*, Oct. 20, 1945, special supplement, section 3; Lt. Enrique de León Aragón, "Situaciones sobre el origen de la Revolución del Veinte de Octubre," *El Libertador*, Oct. 23, 1945, pp. 8, 10; Oscar de León Aragón, "Participación de los estudiantes universitarios en los sucesos del 20," ibid., pp. 9, 12–15; "Tengo pruebas de que Córdova fue todo un patriota, declara Silverio Ortiz," *El I*, June 8, 1946, p. 1; Toriello, "Revelaciones"; "¿Que pasó el 20 de Octubre?" *El Gráfico*; Pinto Recinos, "Lo que yo sé." Interviews with the following officers who participated in the revolt were particularly useful: Aldana Sandoval, Barrios Peña, Paz Tejada, Lorenzana, Mendoza. Also useful was an interview with Rolz Bennett, a civilian plotter against Ponce.

[90] "Sale el exdictador," *El I*, Oct. 25, 1944, p. 1 (quoted from p. 2).

[91] See Marta de Ubico to Eleanor Roosevelt, Dec. 15, 1944, enclosed in McLaughlin to Rockefeller, Jan. 20, 1945, NA 814.001/12-1544; MemoConv ("Conditions in Guatemala: President Ubico"), Jan. 5, 1945, p. 3, NA 814.00; MemoConv (Mrs. Ubico, Daniels, Newbegin), May 19, 1948, RG84 GR, Box 193, NA-S.

[92] "Ceremonial del ejército para inhumar los restos de Ubico," *El I*, Aug. 13, 1963, p. 1; "Inhumados los restos de Ubico hoy," *El I*, Aug. 14, 1963, p. 1. See also Zea Carrascosa, *Semblanzas*, pp. 223–25.

CHAPTER 2

The Presidency of Juan José Arévalo

THE FALL of Ponce marked the beginning of the Guatemalan revolution. It was a peculiar revolution, which saw urban workers, the middle class, the landed elite, and the officer corps celebrating together. "The quest for democracy had united them,"[1] but the definition of democracy would divide them.

The victorious rebels replaced Ponce with a three-man *junta*: Major Arana and Captain Arbenz, the two military heroes of the revolt, flanked the civilian Jorge Toriello, an upper-class youth who had played a prominent role in the struggle against Ponce. Toriello, the U.S. embassy later noted, "had an arbitrary, ruthless, impetuous character," but he also represented "an energetic conservative element in the Guatemalan government."[2]

Those were weeks of heady enthusiasm in the capital and the towns of the republic. A new Guatemala, it was said, was being born, a democratic Guatemala in which people would no longer live in fear. The *junta* promised free elections for a Constituent Assembly, a Congress, and a president. Political parties grew more vigorous, and trade unions stepped up their activities in the cities and on the plantations of the United Fruit Company.

Adorned by a new revolutionary veneer—had they not welcomed the fall of Ubico and Ponce?—Guatemala's latifundistas did not feel threatened. By eliminating the constraints imposed by the whims of a strongman, "democracy" might enhance their power and privilege. Furthermore, between 1940 and 1944 the international price of coffee had nearly doubled, promising Guatemala an economic boom, as in the 1920s.[3] Prosperity would enable the landed elite to buy off the middle class and the urban workers.

[1] Guerra Borges, *Pensamiento económico social*, p. 9.

[2] Quotations from Wells to DOS, no. 318, Mar. 10, 1950, p. 2, NA 714.00, and Woodward to SecState, no. 317, July 13, 1945, p. 2, NA 814.00. After the *junta*'s term had ended, Toriello's political role became marginal. Ambitious, shrill, violent, he was unable to retain a following even among conservative groups. For perceptive U.S. reports on Toriello and his political demise, see Cochran, "Guatemala-Political," June 29, 1945, p. 2, NA 814.00/6-1945; Woodward to SecState, no. 493, Aug. 17, 1945, pp. 2–4, NA 814.00; Donovan to SecState, no. 1025, Jan. 21, 1946, RG84 CF, Box 14, NA-S; Donovan to SecState, no. 1482, June 25, 1946, RG84 CF, Box 14, NA-S; DOS, Office of Research and Analysis, "Current US Policy toward Guatemala," no. 3569, Feb. 20, 1946, pp. 3–5, NA.

[3] See United Nations, FAO, *The World Coffee Economy*, pp. 55–56, 73, and Hennessey, "National Economy," p. 48.

To keep a democracy healthy, the upper class believed, the government had to promote the enlightened development of rural Guatemala. It must provide the *patrones* with easy credit and good prices for their products; it must let them look after the welfare of their workers without interference; it must clamp down on "all subversive propaganda."[4]

The countryside had remained quiet while urban Guatemala had turned against Ponce. But on October 22, 1944, two days after Ponce's demise, violence erupted at Patzicía, a small, predominantly Indian community about fifty miles west of the capital. "Armed with axes, machetes, clubs, stones and knives," approximately 1,000 Indians rose in a spontaneous outburst, killing more than twenty Ladinos. They chanted slogans in honor of "our General Ponce," but above all they cried: "We want land!"[5] The *junta* reacted swiftly. Soldiers were dispatched at once, and the rebellious Indians were punished in the traditional manner: with a bloodbath. "The troops summarily shot the rebels. They killed women, children and men indiscriminately," relates one of the few accounts of the episode; the exact death toll will never be known, but at least nine hundred Indians were killed. "This . . . would act as a warning throughout the Republic for any other disorders of this nature," the chief of staff of the Guatemalan army explained. In urban Guatemala no voices questioned the ferocity of the repression. This silence was considered auspicious by the landed elite, as was the fact that the revolt had encountered "the most drastic response of which the white and Ladino population is capable," in the words of the U.S. ambassador. After the slaughter of Patzicía, peace and tranquillity returned to the countryside.[6]

Middle-class youth had led the struggle against Ubico and Ponce, but the army emerged unscathed from the turmoil. Ponce had been overthrown neither

[4] For representative statements see Guatemala, *El triángulo de Escuintla*, esp. pp. 1, 123 (quoted), 135–37; Marroquín Rojas, *Crónicas*, pp. 98, 106; "Finqueros de Escuintla denuncian propaganda roja," *El I*, June 2, 1945, p. 1.

[5] "Al grito: Queremos las tierras que nos ofrecieron," *El I*, Oct. 24, 1944, p. 1. The passivity of the countryside during the struggle against Ponce is described in the monthly reports of the Jefes Políticos. (See IMJP:G, July–Oct. 1944, Leg. 32379, AGCA.)

[6] Quotations from: Hernández Sifontes, *Realidad jurídica*, p. 264; Rose, "Immediate Conditions in the Interior," no. 1348-44, Oct. 27, 1944, RG84 CF, Box 15, NA-S; Long to SecState, no. 1774, Nov. 24, 1944, NA 814.00. See also Long to SecState, no. 1682, Oct. 31, 1944, RG 84, Box 107, and Everardo Jiménez de León to Secretario de Estado de Gobernación y Justicia, Chimaltenango, Nov. 18, 1944, IMJP:G, Leg. 32379, AGCA. The Patzicía revolt is taboo in Guatemalan writing. Two brief accounts are Zamora Alvarez, *Las Memorias de Andrés*, pp. 147–53, and Santa Cruz Morales, "Hace 42 años." The figure of nine huundred killed is from Hernández Sifontes, *Realidad jurídica*, p. 264, and confirmed by interview with María de Rivera, a Guatemalan anthropologist who has interviewed survivors of the massacre.

by a general strike nor by an armed populace. The Guardia de Honor had spearheaded the insurrection, and army officers had led the rebel forces throughout the fighting. The purge within the military that followed Ponce's surrender was conducted without civilian interference, and it was limited to the crowd of generals, all of whom were dismissed, and several colonels.

The rebel officers had given arms to civilian volunteers during the fighting. But upon Ponce's defeat the *junta* moved to restore the military's monopoly of weapons. Its first bulletin demanded that all arms be returned within twenty-four hours: "all those who fail to comply . . . will be punished with the full weight of the law." Furthermore, those who returned the weapons would receive a small monetary compensation. Most of the weapons were returned.[7]

Thus the military remained the arbiter of the country's political life. For the landed elite, this was welcome. The Guatemalan army had never betrayed the country's latifundistas in favor of the lower classes. Should young hotheads try to turn democracy into license, the officers would restore order.

Nor was the upper class alarmed by the prospect that Juan José Arévalo, the charismatic presidential candidate, might win the December 1944 elections. Arévalo had the physique, voice and eloquence of a *caudillo*, but in Guatemala only the man on horseback could be a *caudillo*. Arévalo was a forty-year-old university professor who had written several books, not one of them about politics. Literature and the philosophy of education seemed to be his passions.

Arévalo, who was of middle class extraction, had become a primary school-teacher in 1922. Five years later, at age twenty-three, he went to Argentina, having won a scholarship to university. He left behind the memory of a brilliant and dynamic teacher and a gifted writer.[8]

Arévalo spent six years in Argentina, where he earned a doctorate in the philosophy of education; he was one of a handful of Guatemalans who had completed postgraduate studies in any field. From Argentina he sent 150 copies of his first book, *Viajar es vivir*, to Guatemala. "The Guatemalan press reviewed the book enthusiastically," he later wrote, but "after a few months

---

[7] Quoted from "Dan término perentorio de 24 horas," *El I*, Oct. 22, 1944, p. 1. See also "Severa medida," *El I*, Oct. 26, 1944, p. 1. Interviews with Galich, Paz Tejada, Charnaud, Fortuny, and other participants confirmed that almost all of the weapons were returned.

[8] There is no definitive biography of Arévalo. With more or less grace, his biographers lapse into uncritical praise. The list includes Dion, *Las ideas sociales*; Delli Sante-Arrocha, *Arévalo*; Mejía, *Juan José Arévalo*; Ordóñez Argüello, *Arévalo visto por América*; Alvarez Elizondo, *El Presidente Arévalo*; Barrios Archila, *Biografía mínima*. Arévalo has written his memoirs: *Memorias de aldea* and *La inquietud normalista* describe his life before he left for Argentina in 1927; *La Argentina* covers the 1927–1944 period; *El candidato* spans the months from June 1944 to March 1945; *Escritos complementarios* deals with 1951 to 1963.

no one read it. There was no one left who could appreciate its melding of philosophy and literature."[9]

In 1934 Arévalo returned to his homeland, confident of both his excellence and his brilliant future. He dutifully went to pay his respects to Ubico, sure that the dictator would appoint him undersecretary of education, a post which was vacant. He presented Ubico with a copy of his doctoral dissertation; his alma mater, he explained, intended to publish the manuscript. "Therefore I urged Ubico to have the government rush the book to print so that Guatemala would have the honor of the first edition."[10]

Arévalo received a rude shock: Ubico was not interested in his dissertation. Worse, two days later he appointed Arévalo to a mid-level post in the Ministry of Education.

"Stunned . . . I offered my thanks," relates Arévalo in his memoirs. "I would have only a typewriter and two chairs—no subordinates, not even a secretary. . . . I felt humiliated. Ubico had dealt me a blow that was as unexpected as it was undeserved. . . . I was a Doctor of Philosophy of Education, I had studied abroad for six years, and I had been deemed unworthy to be the undersecretary of education."[11]

Two years later, in 1936, Arévalo returned to Argentina—to escape dictatorship, his admirers have claimed;[12] to seek a better job, retort his critics, noting that while in Argentina he never once spoke out against the dictator.[13] Probably both the desire for a better job and aversion to Ubico's rule motivated Arévalo. Back in Guatemala after the fall of Ubico, he was categorical: "I left because I refused to submit to dictatorship."[14]

On July 2, 1944, in Guatemala City, eight friends—five of whom were teachers—assembled at the house of Mario Efraín Nájera Farfán. Ubico had stepped down the previous day; it was time, they argued, to create a political party, a

[9] Arévalo, *La Argentina*, pp. 258–59.

[10] Ibid., p. 281.

[11] Ibid., p. 282.

[12] See for instance "Rasgos biográficos del Dr. Juan José Arévalo," *El Libertador*, Dec. 9, 1944, p. 3; Mejía, *Juan José Arévalo*, p. 40; Alvarez Elizondo, *El Presidente Arévalo*, pp. 42–43.

[13] The one possible exception is a 1937 letter that Arévalo sent to a professor in Costa Rica. (See Arévalo, *Escritos políticos*, pp. 55–56, and Arévalo, *La Argentina*, pp. 405–6.)

[14] "Declaraciones del Dr. Juan José Arévalo," *Circuito Estudiantil*, Sept. 12, 1944, p. 2. But in fact Arévalo did submit: after the aborted 1934 plot against Ubico, he signed, as did many other government employees, a public statement that combined abject professions of loyalty to the dictator with furious invective against the defeated plotters. (See Arévalo, *La Argentina*, pp. 298–99. For the text of the statement, see "Una página del Partido Liberal," *La Hora*, Jan. 15, 1945, p. 1.)

party that should immediately select a presidential candidate in a bid to capture the people's attention.[15]

"We all agreed that our candidate had to be a new man," recalls Nájera Farfán. Such a man was his friend Arévalo, who was a distinguished professor at the University of Tucuman, Juan José Orozco asserted. Most of those present knew Arévalo personally, and some had been his colleagues when he had been a schoolteacher. A few were familiar with his books—"well-written, elegant and instructive."[16]

By the time the meeting adjourned, the eight had formed Renovación Nacional, the teachers' party, and they had a candidate, Juan José Arévalo. On July 3, they sent Arévalo a telegram announcing their momentous decision and urging him to return at once. Arévalo accepted.[17]

In a matter of days, in a phenomenon unprecedented in Guatemala, the suggestion of one man became the cry of many. Arévalo's candidacy was endorsed by the Frente Popular Libertador (FPL, the students' party) in early August. By September 3, when he returned to Guatemala, Arévalo's name had become a household word in the capital, spread through the front pages of the opposition press and invoked at political rallies. He, who had fought neither in word nor in deed against Ubico, was suddenly the leader of a movement in search of a soul; he was the symbol of the new Guatemala.

In 1944, recalls a witness, "there were many who remembered Arévalo as an honorable man who had not been tainted by Ubiquismo."[18] Those who had forgotten Arévalo and those who had never heard of him suddenly felt that they had long known and admired the man. Arévalo, the FPL's newspaper, *El Libertador*, announced on August 4, was "a man without blemish, with the experience, the talent, the strength of character, and the idealism that our people need. . . . While we Guatemalans were unaware of the virtues of Doctor Juan José Arévalo, several sophisticated nations, including Argentina, have benefitted from the intellectual achievements of our compatriot and have honored him."[19]

Little if anything was known of his political views; indeed, notes a judicious observer, Arévalo "had been away long enough to have become personally

[15] The best accounts of the meeting are by Nájera Farfán: *Los estafadores*, pp. 69–71, and "El Arevalismo y el momento actual," *El Libertador*, Jan. 25, 1945, p. 3. See also Alvarez Elizondo, *El Presidente Arévalo*, p. 93, n. 6; "Proyecciones de la Revolución del 44," *El Gráfico*.

[16] Quotations from Nájera Farfán, "El Arevalismo" (see n. 15 above), and Nájera Farfán, *Los estafadores*, p. 71.

[17] Nájera Farfán, "El Arevalismo," (see n. 15 above); Arévalo, *La Argentina*, pp. 514–18; Arévalo, *El candidato*, pp. 6–18.

[18] Interview with Lorenzana.

[19] "Por qué apoyamos la candidatura de Juan José Arévalo," *El Libertador*, Aug. 4, 1944, p. 1.

anonymous, an immeasurable help in his candidacy," since he could be all things to all people.[20] The fact that he was a professor fired the enthusiasm of students and teachers, the two groups that had led the struggle against Ubico and were now in the forefront of the opposition to Ponce. "In Argentina Arévalo is thought of as the new Sarmiento of the Americas," proclaimed an enthusiastic teacher. "Being a philosopher, Doctor Arévalo understands the deepest yearnings of the human soul," explained *El Libertador* with similar hyperbole a month before the philosopher had returned to Guatemala.[21]

Arévalo's relative youth was also to his advantage. "At that time the word youth was a political catchword which held out the promise of something new and bypassed the discussion of social and economic problems."[22] The fact that Arévalo was white and that his place of self-imposed exile had been Argentina, a white country ruled by conservatives (and not Mexico, mestizo and revolutionary), was reassuring to the Guatemalan landed elite. His books, which very few Guatemalans had read, had esoteric titles that bespoke of spiritual concerns, not socioeconomic issues, and this too comforted the upper class.[23]

The crowds that welcomed Arévalo when he arrived in Guatemala were not disappointed. "Arévalo won the elections the moment he stepped off the plane," recalls an eyewitness.[24] Even his critics acknowledge his charisma. One noted "his powerful physique, his eloquence, his exuberance, and his acute intelligence." Another remarked, "If nothing else, Arévalo looked every inch the president. Six feet tall, and weighing nearly 200 pounds, Arévalo furnished the young revolutionaries with a leader they could look up to, both literally and figuratively."[25]

The candidate "stumped the country," a U.S. embassy official recalled, "spellbinding the common people with his impressive physical appearance and excellent oratory."[26] His oratory, however, was as elusive as it was stir-

---

[20] Silvert, *Study in Government*, p. 8.

[21] Quotations from "Juan José Arévalo, candidato del F.P.L.," *El Libertador*, Aug. 4, 1944, p. 3, and "Juan José Arévalo y su candidatura," *El Libertador*, Aug. 7, 1944, p. 1.

[22] Alfonso Solorzano in Quan Rossell, *Guatemala*, 1:235.

[23] *Viajar es vivir, La pedagogía de la personalidad, La filosofía de los valores en la pedagogía, La adolescencia como evasión y retorno.*

[24] Interview with María de Rivera, Washington, D.C., Dec. 23, 1984. For press accounts, see "Desborde cívico," *El I*, p. 1; "Apoteósica recepción," *El Libertador*, p. 3; "Apoteósico recibimiento," *El Americano*, p. 1. All Sept. 4, 1944.

[25] Quotations from Samayoa Chinchilla, *El Quetzal no es rojo*, p. 91, and Schneider, *Communism*, p. 16.

[26] Siracusa, "Summary of Statements Made by Mr. Siracusa in Presentation of Guatemalan Situation," enclosed in Siracusa to Patterson, Aug. 22, 1949, p. 3, RG84 GR, Box 216, NA-S. Siracusa's remarks provide a revealing and comprehensive window

ring. He mentioned the economy, but stressed "the primacy of spiritual matters."[27] He suggested the need for social reforms but emphasized his opposition to "the naive redistribution of property. . . . The old class hatreds have been overcome," he asserted, and "spouting about materialism has been unmasked as the new propaganda tool of totalitarianism."[28] Sibylline statements reinforced the spiritual side of his message. "In Guatemala there are no longer conservatives, even though there is an aristocracy. Aristocracy is not a political category. It is an aesthetic category," he proclaimed on one occasion, stating on another, "The primary problems of Guatemala are spiritual problems. This is my theory, which is a little revolutionary and clashes with the materialist theories."[29]

As the December presidential elections drew near, several candidates withdrew in favor of Arévalo. The strongest of the remaining contenders was Adrian Recinos. A scholarly man who had long been Ubico's ambassador to the United States, Recinos was intelligent but uncharismatic. He enjoyed the support of a group of upper class friends, but not of the upper class as a whole. And he was tainted by his long collaboration with Ubico. He was, in short, no match for Arévalo, who won the presidency with 85 percent of the votes cast by literate men (the only enfranchised people). Arévalo's triumph represented the victory of the "revolution"—that is, no one's victory in particular. Time alone would reveal who Arévalo truly was and what the Guatemalan revolution would mean.[30]

On March 15, 1945, Arévalo assumed the presidency of Guatemala. The country presented a desolate spectacle. Despite Ubico's roads, internal transportation was woefully inadequate. Illiteracy was over 70 percent. Although the republic's agricultural potential was impressive—"In soils and climate," noted the World Bank, "few countries are better equipped for agricultural development"—agriculture was stifled by the pattern of landownership: 2 percent of landowners owned 72 percent of agricultural land; less than 1 percent of the land was cultivated, while half of those who owned land were crowded

---

on the embassy's attitude toward the Arévalo government. They were well received by the department.

[27] "Declaraciones del Dr. Juan José Arévalo," *Circuito Estudiantil*, Sept. 12, 1944, p. 4.

[28] "Pensamiento de J. José Arévalo," *La República*, Nov. 13, 1944, pp. 3–4.

[29] Quotations from "Socialismo espiritual preconiza el candidato Arévalo para Guatemala," *El I*, Oct. 30, 1944, p. 1 (quoted from p. 2) and "Declaraciones del Dr. Juan José Arévalo," *Circuito Estudiantil*, Sept. 12, 1944, p. 4.

[30] For two inside accounts of the electoral campaign, see Arévalo, *El candidato*, pp. 36–484, and Flores Avendaño, *Memorias*, 2:275–327. (Flores Avendaño was one of the defeated candidates.)

onto parcels too small to sustain a family.[31] Those who owned large estates directed them lackadaisically from afar, with the "prevailing viewpoint . . . that as long as the farm produces enough to provide a good financial return for the owner nothing more need be done."[32] Those who labored on these estates were trapped in the same cruel logic that had been noted in a U.S. report of 1925: "While everyone desires to increase the productive power of Indian labor, no one will make this possible by the obvious method of bettering the Indian's social and physical condition. And this is due to a curious mental deduction. If the Indian's physical condition is improved, he will produce more but he will demand more for his services, and then the essential element to national life—cheapness of labor—will be lost."[33] The impact of this "archaic culture"[34] on Guatemala's agricultural output is obvious: low productivity.

While agriculture engaged at least 75 percent of the labor force, industry was virtually nonexistent. According to the country's first industrial census of December 1946, there were 776 "industrial" establishments with five or more persons, for a total labor force of 23,914.[35] The leading products were beverages, foodstuffs, and textiles. Poor management and inadequate technology characterized Guatemalan industry. Labor was cheap, plentiful, and inefficient. "The Guatemalan worker is greatly handicapped," the World Bank pointed out in 1951. "His general level of health is poor. Malaria and intestinal disorders reduce his capacity and ambition. His nutrition often is not such as to permit him to do intensive work for long hours. Although inherently able to learn special skills, the local worker frequently lacks even a good elementary education. Without this background his vocational training is made more difficult."[36]

As the World Bank stated, in Guatemala sound economic development required a marked improvement in the standard of living of the populace. This was the challenge Arévalo faced. In this daunting task, he enjoyed two eco-

[31] International Bank for Reconstruction and Development (IBRD), *Economic Development*, pp. 5 (quoted), 22–89. For the statistics on land tenure, see Guatemala, *Censo Agropecuario 1950*, 1:17–39. For an insightful discussion, see Higbee, "The Agricultural Regions of Guatemala" and "Guatemala's Agrarian Problem." On the illiteracy rate, see González Orellana, *Historia de la educación*, pp. 401–2.

[32] AmEmG to DOS, no. 718, Jan. 22, 1951, p. 2, NA 814.2333. This report is an excellent and comprehensive analysis of the coffee culture in Guatemala.

[33] Military attaché to DOS, no. 1563, Dec. 4, 1925, p. 2, RG165 RF, Box 1562, NA-S.

[34] AmEmG to DOS, no. 718, Jan. 22, 1951, p. 46, NA 814.2333.

[35] *Boletín de la Dirección General de Estadística* (Guatemala), no. 11, Jan. 1948. See also Ovalle, *Industrial Report*; United States Tariff Commission, *Mining*; United Nations, ECLA, *Economic Development*, pp. 51–52.

[36] IBRD, *Economic Development*, p. 95.

nomic advantages: Ubico had paid the country's external debt,[37] and the international price of coffee would continue to rise through his presidency.

—Arévalo's six-year term was marked by the unprecedented existence of a multiparty system, the development of urban trade unions, and the enfranchisement of a large sector of the population. Yet democratization had severe limits: illiterate women could not vote, and the vote of illiterate men had to be public; the Communist party was still proscribed, and several communists and labor activists were deported; trade unionism in the countryside was drastically restricted—first legally, later de facto.

In the cities, unionization was accompanied by labor laws that brought significant benefits to the lower and middle classes. But these laws, or their implementation, did not extend to the countryside, home to 80 percent of the Guatemalan people. There, the government's failure to launch, or even to plan, an agrarian reform program overshadowed its timid efforts to improve the peasants' plight.

The failures and the achievements of the Arévalo presidency were embellished by an extraordinary flowering of rhetoric. From the very day he returned to Guatemala as a presidential candidate, Arévalo boasted that he had a unique message for his countrymen: Spiritual Socialism or, more prosaically, Arevalismo.

"Arevalismo," he explained, "is . . . the only political movement which has its own philosophy. We do not have simply a government program for the next three or four presidential terms; we have our own social and political theory; we have called it Spiritual Socialism, and it represents a true innovation for our America, which until now has been grappling with only conservatism, liberalism and Marxism."[38]

Perhaps Arévalo believed that he had forged a new political doctrine. Modesty was not one of his virtues. "He had the physique of a very big man," a former diplomat recalled, "and his opinion of himself was also very big."[39]

With the passing of time, the president's ill-starred theories became the butt of jokes of varying acrimony. "As he blanketed the country with his flowery dissertations, I was constantly trying to find out what the substance of spiritual socialism was, but I never succeeded," remarked a diplomat. More charitably, a sympathetic scholar concluded that "the weakness of the doctrine of Arevalismo may well lie in its having been overly spiritual and too little eco-

---

[37] The outstanding balance of a few hundred thousand dollars was paid by the Arévalo and Arbenz administrations. (See "Guatemala's Debt to Britain Paid," *NYT*, Mar. 25, 1947, p. 11; AmEmG, "Monthly Economic Report—June 1951," no. 1388, June 29, 1951, p. 3; Cardona, "Cooperativismo," p. 71.)

[38] Arévalo, *Escritos políticos*, p. 162.

[39] Interview with Steins.

nomic.''[40] This may have been true of the government's efforts in the country-side, but the reforms in favor of the urban middle and lower classes showed a clear grasp of the importance of economics.

The striking contradiction between Arévalo's urban and rural policies did not arise from the confused nature of Spiritual Socialism; its causes were concrete. In comparison to his predecessors, the president was exceptionally sympathetic to the rural masses. Yet, except geographically, the largely Indian world of the peasantry was far removed from that of Arévalo and the other middle class leaders who formed the new political elite. This distance muted the echo of the peasants' suffering. Among the government forces, only the trade unions showed an active desire for real change in the countryside, but their influence was limited, and their immediate interest was in the cities. The only powerful pressure group with direct interests in the countryside was the upper class, and it opposed all change.

Rather than a political theorist, Arévalo was a populist leader, personally honest, and without a comprehensive socioeconomic program for his country. He was a master, however, of politics—that is, he possessed an uncanny ability to manipulate men, including his own key supporters, the leaders of the revolutionary parties.[41]

These parties, which enjoyed a massive majority in Congress throughout Arévalo's term, were the Frente Popular Libertador (FPL), Renovación Nacional (RN), and the Partido Acción Revolucionaria (PAR). Created in November 1945 by the merger of the FPL and RN, the PAR survived the split of the FPL and RN eighteen months later. In terms of age and social extraction, the leadership of the three parties was similar: middle-class urban youth, particularly those university students and teachers who had distinguished themselves in 1944. The splintering of the PAR was due to personal ambitions, political differences, and the "influence of President Arévalo." Arévalo, noted a prominent administration figure, preferred to manipulate competing parties rather than to confront only one.[42]

[40] Quotations from interview with Woodward, and from Silvert, *Study in Government*, p. 11. Dion, *Las ideas sociales*, and Delli Sante-Arrocha, *Arévalo*, make sustained but vain attempts to penetrate the mysteries of Spiritual Socialism.

[41] The term *revolutionary parties* refers to all noncommunist parties that supported the Arévalo and Arbenz administrations.

[42] Monteforte Toledo, *Guatemala*, p. 311. See also Donovan to SecState, no. 2490, June 3, 1947, NA 814.00; Donovan to SecState, no. 2499, June 6, 1947, NA 814.00. There is no comprehensive study of the revolutionary parties. Important primary sources can be found in the *GT*, esp. boxes 9, 12, 66, 67, 68, 69. Despite a marked bias, reports from the U.S. embassy are valuable, as are some U.S. government studies, notably a 117-page analysis by the State Department's Office of Intelligence and Research ("Guatemala: Communist Influence," no. 5123, Oct. 23, 1950, NA). For the Arbenz years, see, in particular, the embassy's weekly *Joint Weeka* (*JW*). Among

Until 1949, when it was crippled by internal strife, the FPL was the largest of the revolutionary parties. Increasingly resistant to social reform, it competed with the more centrist RN for Arévalo's affection. To the left of both stood the PAR, which was more sympathetic to organized labor, locked in a bitter feud with the FPL, and ever more distant from Arévalo.

Within each party, rival factions clashed over the scope and speed of social reforms and over the division of the spoils of political power. Corruption was rampant, and graft became "the order of the day at high levels. While most, if not all, officials of the present government came into power as poor men," a U.S. official wrote in 1949, "few of them remain so today."[43] The story of Mario Méndez Montenegro is a case in point. As a student leader in 1944, he had displayed bravery and charisma. He became, under Arévalo, one of the leaders of the FPL, but when he served as mayor of Guatemala City (1946–1948), he demanded bribes from those who sought to do business with the city government.[44]

Among and above the squabbling factions, Arévalo adroitly mediated, using his well-honed political skills, his great personal charm, and "his largesse" with political leaders.[45] True, as time went on, he lost some of his prestige. But from the pack of revolutionary politicians, no civilian emerged who could challenge the president. Like Arévalo, most of these politicians lacked a comprehensive program for the country. They had grown up in Ubico's Guatemala—that is, in an intellectual desert. After 1944 much of their energy went to personal aggrandizement. There were exceptions, but they were few.

Arévalo and the revolutionary parties were urged forward by a combative labor movement regrouped in two rival confederations, the Federación Sindical de Guatemala (FSG) and the Confederación de Trabajadores de Guatemala (CTG). By early 1950 the FSG and the CTG claimed approximately ninety thousand members. While many of their unions existed on paper only, the number of effectively organized workers still ran into several tens of thousands; most were blue and white collar urban workers.[46]

---

published works, the most useful are Bishop, "Guatemalan Labor," pp. 109–58 (focusing on the relationship of the revolutionary parties to the labor movement); Schneider, *Communism*, esp. pp. 218–49; LeBaron, "Impaired Democracy," pp. 141–61. Particularly helpful were interviews with Galich, Charnaud, Fortuny, Bauer Paiz, Capuano, Monteforte Toledo.

[43] Siracusa (see n. 26 above), p. 4.

[44] On Méndez Montenegro, see Siracusa to SecState, no. 249, May 20, 1948, p. 2 ("Case 1") and p. 3 ("Case 4"), NA 814.00. For a devastating indictment of the corruption that permeated the 1950 Central American and Caribbean Games, see "Danza olímpica de los millones que se tornó despilfarro," *El I*, Apr. 2–12, 1951.

[45] Monteforte Toledo, *Guatemala*, p. 312.

[46] There was another labor confederation, the Federación Regional Central de Trabajadores, but in size and influence it was insignificant. In May 1950 still another labor

Important differences separated the leaders of the FSG and the CTG. As U.S. scholars have observed, the leaders of the CTG were more honest and more committed to the workers' interests, but also more open to communist influences. The following comparison is representative: Arturo Morales Cubas, the FSG's secretary general from its inception until January 1948, "was considered moderate in his views. . . . He might in time have furnished wider leadership to the labor movement had not his reputation and position been undercut by opportunism and corruption. He was unfortunately . . . a union leader who used his position to pilfer union funds." By contrast, Víctor Manuel Gutiérrez, who became secretary general of the CTG in October 1946, was "known as the Franciscan . . . because of his strict personal habits and devotion to work; he had a sense of the times and an urgent message for the laboring class." Gutiérrez and the leaders of the CTG "were the only ones who had a sure path to follow, a firm sense of direction." The FSG leaders, on the other hand, "never appeared to exercise a firm and well formulated approach either to their internal affairs or to the national problems. They were always the reluctant followers unable to seize the initiative."[47]

Their differences notwithstanding, the FSG and the CTG repeatedly joined together to press their demands on an often reluctant government. Using their leverage as the only group that could provide active support as well as votes to the various revolutionary parties, they achieved significant victories.

The most important was the Labor Code promulgated on May 1, 1947. In a more advanced country, the code would have been a moderate document; in Guatemala, it was radical. It affirmed the right to unionize (but set crippling limitations on agricultural unions). It afforded protection from unfair dismissals and guaranteed the right to strike within a conciliation mechanism. ("While helpful to labor," this mechanism "also served to set a limit on labor's right to strike," noted a U.S. government report.[48]) The code also stipulated a forty-eight-hour week, regulated the employment of women and adolescents, and established basic standards of health and safety in the workplace.[49]

---

confederation was created, the Confederación Nacional Campesina de Guatemala (CNCG), which is discussed below, pp. 172–73.

The best sources on organized labor in the Arévalo years are Bishop, "Guatemalan Labor," pp. 9–129, and Bush, "Organized Labor." Ramos Guzmán de Schmoock, "El movimiento sindical," pp. 21–119, taps some sources not used by Bishop and Bush. Ruiz Franco, *Hambre*, which covers the early stages of the labor movement, is a classic. Pearson, *"Confederación,"* pp. 1–40, focuses on the countryside.

[47] Bishop, "Guatemalan Labor," pp. 23, 25, 91, 130. Bishop's views are supported by those of the other authorities listed in n. 46 above.

[48] DOS, Office of Intelligence and Research, "Guatemala: Communist Influence," Oct. 23, 1950, p. 56, NA.

[49] The full text of the law, approved by Congress on Feb. 1, 1947, as Decree 330, is printed in *DCA*, Feb. 25, 1947, pp. 1113–30, and Feb. 26, 1947, pp. 1143–60.

The Labor Code was followed, in January 1948, by the inauguration of the Guatemalan Institute of Social Security (IGSS). Financed by the state, the employers, and the workers, the IGSS was designed and directed by two young bureaucrats from Costa Rica.[50] It soon earned the praise of even harsh critics of the Arévalo administration. The U.S. embassy reported that it was "undoubtedly the best administered and most effective of the social reforms of the Arévalo administration," and the conservative *El Imparcial* noted its "very constructive role."[51] Competently staffed by a well-paid bureaucracy, and shielded from outside interference, the IGSS was a signal exception to the morass of corruption, nepotism, and incompetence that engulfed the Arévalo administration.

By March 1951, when Arévalo's term ended, several tens of thousands of blue and white collar urban workers were insured by the IGSS, but rural workers remained unprotected. As time went by, the IGSS's financial straits worsened. The employers, particularly those in rural areas, did not pay their quotas; nor did many workers. In the summer of 1950, the IGSS asked the government for a special grant of $1 million; the alternative, it stressed, was "closing down or cutting sharply into its services."[52] The government did not help; worse, it too was behind in the payment of its quotas.

Likewise, many of the provisions of the Labor Code were implemented minimally or not at all. This was even true in the case of the urban workers, who were the main beneficiaries of the new legislation. Nonetheless, despite the inflation that plagued the Arévalo years, real wages for urban workers increased, at times significantly. The extent of the improvement often depended on the political muscle of individual unions; hence teachers and railwaymen were among those who fared best.[53]

Moreover, through occasional strikes, and more often through the conciliation mechanism established by the code, unionized workers were generally

---

[50] An excellent study of the IGSS is Suslow, "Social Security."

[51] Quotations from Fisher, "Memo: Oscar Barahona Streber," Aug. 17, 1950, RG84 CF, Box 15, NA-S, and from "Labor de seis años" (edit.), *El I*, Mar. 15, 1951, p. 2.

[52] Suslow, "Social Security," p. 118.

[53] On inflation and wages under Arévalo see Hendon, "Some Recent Economic Reforms," pp. 132–58; Bush, "Organized Labor," part 3, pp. 74, 77; Bishop, "Guatemalan Labor," pp. 54–56. Also valuable are economic and labor reports of the U.S. embassy. See, for instance: Donovan to SecState, A-539, Dec. 6, 1946, p. 3, NA 814.50; Wells to SecState, A-240, Oct. 14, 1948, pp. 6–7, NA 814.50; Larsen to SecState, no. 101, Jan. 26, 1950, p. 11, NA 814.10; "Quarterly Labor Review. Third Quarter—1950," no. 470, Nov. 3, 1950, p. 22, NA 814.06; "Annual Economic Report—1950," no. 980, Apr. 10, 1951, pp. 11–12, NA 814.00; "Annual Labor Report—1950," no. 989, Apr. 10, 1951, p. 26, NA 814.06.

able to secure protection from arbitrary dismissals—and this, in Guatemala, was a dramatic improvement.

The Arévalo years also brought political freedoms to the urban population: freedom to vote, freedom to express one's opinions, freedom to read a broader range of books and newspapers. Many members of the upper class soon branded these freedoms as intolerable excesses and began to reminisce about the times of Ubico, when "social peace" had reigned supreme. But to the lower and middle classes, Ubico had brought only hardship, and the political freedoms instituted by the 1944 revolution were very welcome.

There was also change in the countryside. Forced labor and the vagrancy laws were not enforced after the fall of Ponce. The 1945 constitution replaced Ubico's *intendentes* with elected mayors. In 1947 the Labor Code established the right of agricultural workers to unionize as long as the union had at least fifty members, two-thirds of whom were literate (a virtual impossibility that was removed the following year). Finally, Arévalo sought to bring education to the countryside and asserted that the Indians were Guatemalans and citizens, as the law stated.

But the cancer that rotted the countryside and the entire republic was the distribution of land. Prodded by organized labor, Congress established a committee to study the problem of agrarian reform. The members read books, made speeches, wrote reports. "We proceeded very slowly," the chairman of the committee recalls.[54] Nothing happened. "Except for the passage of compulsory land rental legislation in 1950, no positive action was taken by the Arévalo Administration" in the field of agrarian reform, concluded the Office of Intelligence and Research of the U.S. State Department in 1953. The land rental legislation, a mild measure designed to assist sharecroppers, was "honored far more in breach than in observance."[55]

When Arévalo assumed office, the Guatemalan state administered about 130 large estates—the Fincas Nacionales: the coffee estates of the German community that had been expropriated by Ubico in June 1944 and the estates of Ubico and some of his generals, which were confiscated a few days after the overthrow of Ponce. Together, these estates produced about 25 percent of the country's coffee crop. Had they been well administered, the Fincas Nacionales would have been a model of economic development and source of revenue; they could have improved the lot of tens of thousands of agricultural

[54] Interview with Monteforte Toledo.

[55] Quotations from DOS, Office of Intelligence and Research, no. 6001, Mar. 5, 1953, p. 1, NA, and from interview with Steins. On the lack of implementation of the land rental law enacted on Dec. 21, 1949, as Decree 712, see Comité Interamericano de Desarrollo Agrícola, *Tenencia de la tierra*, p. 37; García Añoveros, *La reforma agraria*, pp. 162–63. For the text of the law, see Méndez Montenegro, *444 años*, pp. 707–10.

laborers and demonstrated that not only the landed elite could manage Guatemala's most important export crop.

This opportunity was squandered. The administrators of the Fincas Nacionales were—almost to a man—as ignorant of agriculture as they were eager to enrich themselves. Following a tour of the Finca Santa Fe, a foreign scholar noted: "The administrator appeared to know nothing and care less. The house and garden of the Germans was in an abandoned state. . . . The majority of the machines were broken." After visiting several other Fincas Nacionales, the same scholar concluded: "The Directors of the various farms all hedged when questioned about production. Most of them seemed to lack knowledge of the functioning of their farms. . . . Only one of the Directors that I met . . . appeared capable." This grim assessment was shared by most outside observers, including the World Bank.[56]

Corruption and incompetence also characterized the bureaucracy that oversaw the Fincas from Guatemala City. Its director was inept and surrounded by corrupt aides. His one qualification was his birthright: he was the president's brother.[57]

It is hardly surprising that the output of the Fincas Nacionales decreased steadily. By 1950 their share of Guatemala's coffee production had fallen to 20 percent. Thus the state lost precious revenue and confirmed the landed barons in their conviction that they alone could manage Guatemala's agriculture.

In lieu of agrarian reform, Arévalo attempted colonization, spending several million dollars to establish an agricultural colony on untilled state land at Poptún, in faraway El Petén. The project began, with much fanfare, on November 14, 1945. "Road-building is a major expense," an observer noted three years later. "Most of the labor and equipment is devoted to this activity. The major problem is getting equipment. All equipment has to be flown to the colony. . . . Actual colonization has not yet begun."[58] Expenses soared because of the prohibitive transportation costs, inefficiency, and corruption.

[56] Quoted from Suslow, "Aspects of Social Reforms," pp. 67–68. See also IBRD, *Economic Development*, pp. 36–37; Biechler, "Coffee Industry," pp. 49–50; Hendon, "Some Recent Economic Reforms," pp. 177–81; Whetten, *Guatemala*, p. 128. A folder in the *GT*, Box 20, provides a glimpse of life on the Fincas Nacionales.

[57] In addition to many of the sources listed in n. 56 above, a 1953 series of front-page articles in *La Hora* is particularly instructive: "Vacías las cajas de Fincas Nacionales," Jan. 3; "Getellá ordena acción judicial pronta," Jan. 7; "Investigan maquinaria y ganado en Fincas," Jan. 9; "Aclara y la vez confirma una noticia de 'La Hora,' " Jan. 10; "Liquidador Getellá cuenta que es lo que sabe de los asuntos que él asumió," Jan. 12; "El ex-gerente Arévalo llamado a dar aclaraciones importantes," Jan. 13; "Grave denuncia recibe Getellá," Jan. 14; "Mariano Arévalo da declaraciones," Jan. 15.

[58] Suslow, "Aspects of Social Reforms," p. 75.

Arévalo was undaunted. Poptún was "the country's greatest political and economic undertaking," yet another proof of "the creative power of Arevalismo."[59] More soberly, the World Bank concluded, "The $3,000 spent on each of the present Poptún houses would probably have been enough to set a farmer up in business."[60] Guatemala was fortunate that this was Arévalo's only foray into colonization. As the president's term ended, Poptún accommodated only a few hundred colonists. "All kinds of supplies had to be brought by plane and there were no great hopes of future market outlets. Consequently, the colony was successful only so long as it received a heavy subsidy and it has been gradually dying as public funds assigned to it have been diminished," reported a Guatemalan economist a few years later.[61]

Of course, Arévalo was not an agronomist; he was an educator. And it was education, he asserted, that would transform the Indian into a citizen. The needs were immense, and his hopes were generous. But Arévalo's ambitious plans clashed with his country's strained budget and lack of human resources. Overwhelmingly Ladinos, rural teachers could overcome neither the cultural barriers to the Indian world nor their own prejudice. Most of these teachers, moreover, were among Guatemala's least qualified; they were the *empiricos*, who lacked even a secondary school degree and worked in the countryside because they could not find employment elsewhere.[62]

"All educational reform will ultimately fail," Arévalo had written in 1939, ". . . unless laws and governments help to eliminate . . . all types of economic exploitation."[63] As president, he chose to overlook these wise words. And in the absence of significant social reforms, minimal literacy in Spanish (which would soon be forgotten for lack of use) would not help the Indians to improve their lot. Their world would remain that of the agricultural laborer and minifundista eking out a substandard living. Books and newspapers would still belong to an alien world.

Most Indian parents believed that schools would offer their children little beyond the teacher's scorn. And an Indian child, as Ruben Reina noted in a classic study, "is needed for general assistance in the household and cannot

[59] Guatemala, *Primera colonia agrícola de Poptún*, pp. 3, 95.

[60] IBRD, *Economic Development*, p. 85.

[61] Fuentes-Mohr, "Land Settlement," p. 31.

[62] On rural education under Arévalo, see esp. González Orellana, *Historia de la educación*, pp. 394–423. Suslow, "Aspects of Social Reforms," pp. 18–27, 33–43, is informative and incisive; Noval, *Tres problemas*, makes valuable comments of a general nature that apply to the Arévalo period; Jimenez, *La educación rural*, pp. 66–307, is analytically poor but rich in detail; Casey, "Indigenismo," pp. 299–356, is a sympathetic study.

[63] "Marco social de la educación en nuestra América," *Revista de pedagogía*, Nov. 1939, reprinted in Arévalo, *Escritos pedagógicos y filosóficos*, pp. 33–45, quoted from p. 40.

easily be spared without causing sacrifice to his family.'' It was from the family, moreover, that children acquired the skills necessary for adult life.[64] In 1950 90 percent of the Indian children did not attend school.[65] All too often, there were no schools; when they existed, attendance was very low.

While Arévalo's interest in rural education was genuine, his commitment to rural labor unions was less certain. Labor organizers in the countryside faced formidable obstacles. Legal restrictions were compounded by the remoteness of the rural world in a country sorely deficient in transportation. The labor confederations did not have the resources for a sustained campaign in the countryside; indeed, noted a November 1948 report, the CTG ''had no vehicles of any kind, not even a horse, and . . . the CTG delegates operating in the rural areas could only depend upon their legs''; the FSG ''faced the same financial difficulties as the CTG.''[66] And the Arévalo Administration refused to lend vehicles to the labor organizations.[67]

Most landowners resisted unionization ''by every means at their disposal, including floggings'' and ''even killings.'' They enjoyed the support of the Church and the local authorities, who were unimpressed by the feeble admonitions emanating from the central government. There is no record of landowners or local officials who were successfully prosecuted or otherwise punished for acts of violence against their workers.[68]

As a result, organized labor made only scant inroads in the countryside. The major exceptions were the labor unions that developed on the plantations of United Fruit. (UFCO's workers had been militant in the 1920s and had begun organizing in the summer of 1944, shortly after the fall of Ubico.)[69] Elsewhere, noted a careful scholar, ''only on the coffee fincas owned by the national government did unionism make some headway, and even here the policies of the government were often contradictory and restrictive of unionism.''[70]

By the late 1940s, the vagrancy laws were no longer enforced, but population growth and soil erosion had made them unnecessary. Lacking sufficient land to support themselves and their families, many Indians—and some Ladinos—had no choice but to sell their labor in a market characterized by excess supply; the absence of labor unions sealed the landowners' advantage. Nomi-

[64] Reina, ''Chinautla,'' p. 91.

[65] See González Orellana, *Historia de la educación*, pp. 401–2.

[66] Bishop, ''Guatemalan Labor,'' pp. 82, 95.

[67] Pearson, *''Confederación*,'' p. 31.

[68] Quotations from Bishop, ''Guatemalan Labor,'' p. 76, and Bush ''Organized Labor,'' part 3, p. 38. See also the IMJP:G, the JP, and the CPR; all AGCA.

[69] On UFCO's unions see Bush, ''Organized Labor,'' part 2, pp. 13–39.

[70] Bishop, ''Guatemalan Labor,'' p. 74. For scattered reports on peasant unions, see CSC:DAT, AGCA.

nal wages for agricultural workers did increase in the Arévalo years, but inflation took its toll on the rural population. "The Indian who does not own enough land to be self-sufficient in staple products must pay the higher price for the corn," noted a perceptive study. The dearth of adequate statistics prevents a definitive judgement, but the existing data support the conclusion of a scholar who was quite sympathetic to Arévalo. Corn, he wrote, "sold on the market for between 1¢ and 2¢ per pound prior to the war. It now [mid-1949] costs between 5¢ and 6¢ per pound . . . while cash wages have generally risen in most areas, many [agricultural] workers have experienced an overall decline in real wages." The payment in kind that many of these workers received generally failed to increase through the 1940s.[71]

Arévalo's failure to bring real change to the countryside was not due solely to the opposition of the powerful in Guatemalan society. "Arévalo came from a family of middle-class landowners," recalls the president of the Guatemalan Congress. "He had no interest in agrarian reform."[72] Arévalo had indicated as much in an unusually candid speech in April 1945. "In Guatemala there is no agrarian problem," he averred. "The problem is that the peasants have lost their desire to till the soil because of the attitudes and politics of the past. My government will motivate them, but without resorting to any measures that hurt other classes."[73]

The urban-based labor movement—above all the CTG—was virtually alone in pressing for agrarian reform and rural unionization. These measures, the

[71] Quotations from Suslow, "Aspects of Social Reforms," p. 95, and Bush, "Organized Labor," part 2, p. 42. Reports by local authorities indicate that the vagrancy laws were enforced in the countryside at least through mid-1947. See, for instance, Gobernador Departamental de Izabal to Alcalde Municipal Morales, Feb. 11, 1946, JP (Puerto Barrios), AGCA; Gobernador Departamental de Izabal to Alcalde Municipal Morales, Mar. 23, 1946, p. 2, ibid.; Gobernador Departamental de Izabal to Alcalde Municipal Morales, Apr. 30, 1946, ibid.; Gobernador Departamental de Huehuetenango, no. 2372, Sept. 12, 1946, p. 1, IMJP:G, Leg. 32721, AGCA; Gobernador Departamental de Mazatenango, no. 2383/1, Oct. 14, 1946, p. 1, ibid.; Gobernador Departamental de Mazatenango, Dec. 15, 1946, p. 1, ibid.; José Angel Ico Delgado et al. to Ministro de Agricultura, May 8, 1947, IGT, Leg. 48750, AGCA; Manuel Mayo Cuc et al. to Inspector General del Trabajo, May 28, 1947, ibid. On agricultural wages and inflation under Arévalo see AmEmG to DOS, no. 162, Aug. 11, 1950, Table 1, p. 6, NA 814.231; AmEmG to DOS, no. 718, Jan. 22, 1951, pp. 23-25, NA 814.2333; Bush, "Organized Labor," part 2, pp. 40–55; Suslow, "Social Security," pp. 100–3, 110–14. (Suslow uses documents from the IGSS.) For the effects of population growth and erosion in a particular area, see Colby and van den Berghe, *Ixil Country*, pp. 74, 108–10. For an interesting editorial on the problem of erosion, see "Erosión: Enemigo público número uno de la vitalidad de la tierra," *DCA*, Aug. 11, 1948, p. 3.

[72] Interview with Monteforte Toledo.

[73] "Ideal de una Centroamerica como una sola nación culta, democrática, grande," *El I*, Apr. 4, 1945, p. 1.

CTG leaders argued, were also in the interest of the urban workers, for the labor movement would remain small, and hence weak, without the participation of the rural masses. Moreover, they stressed, agrarian reform would increase agricultural productivity and result in more abundant and cheaper foodstuffs for the cities. A less poor peasantry, they also noted, would be able to buy some of the products of the Guatemalan industries; production would increase and so would employment and wages in the cities. Finally, agrarian reform and rural unions would sap the power of the landed elite, organized labor's most bitter foe.[74]

Only a few PAR leaders truly supported these demands. In the final analysis, the Arévalo administration sought to cure some of the symptoms of the sickness that consumed Guatemala's rural world, not the sickness itself. For little could be done to improve the Indians' lot without first dealing with the country's land tenure system. Eloquent laws stating that the Indian was a citizen could not temper the contempt that most Ladinos felt for the Indians, that is, the age-old racism that justified extreme exploitation. Only a lessening of this exploitation could eventually transform the Indian into a full-fledged citizen.

If Arévalo's measures were sadly inadequate in terms of the peasants' needs, they seemed revolutionary to the Guatemalan latifundistas. To them any concession was excessive and dangerous. "The conservative elements," the U.S. military attaché reported, "attribute labor unrest to communism, look with horror on social reforms and reflect that it was easier to do business, easier to make money, and easier and safer to live during the dictator era."[75]

And so the upper class's honeymoon with Arévalo gave way, in 1946, to rising hostility. *El Imparcial*, the republic's major newspaper, reflected the mounting disappointment of its owners and their conservative friends. As Congress debated about the labor code, *El Imparcial* fustigated against the "impatience of the workers, both in city and country."[76] On February 1, 1947, the code was approved by the Congress, and the labor confederations

[74] For a representative statement of the CTG's position, see "La CTG frente a la política nacional e internacional," *El Libertador*, Oct. 31, Nov. 5, and Nov. 12, 1946. For a revealing document, see Gutiérrez to Arévalo, July 17, 1947, CPR, 1947, AGCA. For a comprehensive discussion, see Ramos Guzmán de Schmoock, "El movimiento sindical," pp. 37, 41–42, 49, 51–52, 63–70, 99–100, 107–9, 111–13, 116–17.

[75] Col. Devine, "Alleged Communist Penetrations," no. 104–46, Mar. 29, 1946, p. 2, RG84 CF, Box 14, NA-S.

[76] "A donde va Guatemala?" (edit.), *El I*, Oct. 24, 1946, p. 1. For an instructive comparison, see the still friendly editorial of *El I* on the first anniversary of the fall of Ponce ("Un año de revolución," Oct. 20, 1945, p. 1).

intensified their demands for social and economic change in the countryside. "How far have the seeds of subversion been cast?" asked *El Imparcial*.

The impact has been worst in the countryside. Day after day we read of discord, strikes and riots occurring in many areas where the Indians are a majority. . . . Not that the Indian is to blame: intellectually and socially he is a child. He believes what he is told by those who seek to excite his base desires and passions. . . . No one can foresee the consequences of a struggle that would engulf the entire republic. Until now we Guatemalans have looked to our army as the source of stability in the hour of danger. Who can be sure that the will of the army has not been sapped by the subversives? Will Indian soldiers participate in a war of extermination against their own race?[77]

Seeking the support of the Church, the upper class rose in defense of the values of "Christian" Guatemala, which were endangered by the government's "threats and attacks" against "the Catholic sensibilities of our people."[78] Led by Archbishop Mariano Rossell y Arellano, this was a deeply conservative church, whose model of political democracy and social justice was Franco's Spain. Deprived of its property in the 1870s, the Church had achieved a comfortable modus vivendi with Ubico, who had eased some of the restrictions to which it had been subjected. The 1945 constitution had further improved the Church's position, but it had not gone far enough in the eyes of Rossell y Arellano and his clergy. Therefore, the Church began its feud with the revolution.[79]

For too long the Guatemalan elite had lived under the shadow of dictators. Under Arévalo, right-wing parties remained ephemeral, unable to unite and reminiscent of social clubs. The scions of the upper class were not willing to invest energy or money in electoral politics, a distasteful and bothersome distraction from social and economic pursuits. They countered the *Arevalista* threat with invectives in the media and overtures to the Church. Above all, they resorted to their traditional ploy: they sought a military *caudillo* who would seize power and protect them. To this end they plotted, while raising their monotonous and shrill refrain. The government, they claimed, had fallen into the hands of communists.

[77] "Agitación campesina" (edit.), *El I*, Feb. 27, 1947, p. 1.

[78] "Cuatro puntos de la oposición," *El I*, Oct. 7, 1946, p. 1 (quoted from p. 7).

[79] For the Church under Ubico and Arévalo, see Holleran, *Church and State*, pp. 210–54; Frankel, "Political Development," pp. 169–265; Bendaña Perdomo, "Historia general," pp. 41–50; Miller, "Catholic Leaders"; Estrada Monroy, *Datos para la historia*, 3:495–640.

CHAPTER 3

The Death of Francisco Arana

"FROM THIS day forward the Guatemalan army will be an institution of impeccable professionalism," Arévalo promised in his inaugural address. "Led by men who have proven their patriotism and their love of the Guatemalan people, it will be the guardian of our domestic peace, and it will join in the great cultural awakening of our country."[1] Heady words, but as Arévalo knew, more tangible inducements were necessary to assure the army's loyalty. And so the officer corps became the pampered child of the revolution through large salary increases, generous scholarships to study abroad, well-paid positions in the government bureaucracy, and other alluring benefits. Aware of the limits of his power, the civilian president carefully refrained from interfering in military matters. It was, for the officer corps, a welcome change.

Major Francisco Arana and Captain Jacobo Arbenz were the two most influential officers when Arévalo's presidency began. Within the officer corps they were perhaps equal in prestige, but not in power. Arana was not only Arbenz's senior in age and rank, but luck had allowed him to play the decisive role in the overthrow of Ponce.

"Arana's emergence as one of the three leaders of the revolution . . . was," as the U.S. embassy reported, "something of an accident." He joined the plot only in its late stages, at the insistence of Major Aldana Sandoval. He was, however, the commander of the tank unit at the Guardia de Honor—that is, of the country's only tanks. The sudden defection of Aldana Sandoval on the eve of the revolt propelled Arana into the role of a leader, "a leader found at the last minute."[2] In the hours that followed, he fought with bravery and imagination.

Since 1937, Jacobo Arbenz had been a professor at the Escuela Politécnica, a post that gave him prestige but no troops. In the summer of 1944, he and Aldana Sandoval began to organize the uprising. He plotted as a civilian, having resigned from the army in early July to protest Ponce's takeover. Dressed as a civilian, leading a group of students, he had appeared on the night of October 19 at the Guardia de Honor, where Arana was already in charge. His brilliant career at the military academy and his role against Ponce earned Ar-

---

[1] Arévalo, *Discursos en la presidencia*, pp. 7–21. Quoted from pp. 13–14.

[2] Quotations from Affeld, "Confidential Biographic Data: Francisco Javier Arana," Apr. 4, 1945, p. 1, RG84 GR, Box 217, NA-S, and from interview with Mendoza.

benz the respect of many officers, particularly those *de escuela*, who, like him, had graduated from the academy.

During the uprising Arbenz and Arana fought with equal distinction. But Arana led the Guardia de Honor. As a result he became the senior member of the three-man *junta*.[3]

Arévalo first met Arbenz and Arana in the presidential palace a few days after the fall of Ponce. "The first to appear was a blond and blue-eyed young man, wearing a blue suit and a narrow red tie," Arévalo later wrote.

> He greeted me respectfully. . . . I had come, I told him, to meet and congratulate the two officers, Arbenz and Arana. The young man smiled and said: "I am Arbenz, Doctor Arévalo. . . ." Then Arana appeared. He was a man of average height and wide girth; a leather belt below his navel cinched his paunch. . . . His round face was expressionless, his eyes were evasive, and his smile fleeting. His handshake was limp. . . . When we were introduced he looked at me carefully and formally expressed his pleasure to meet me. He accepted my congratulations. But his reaction was not like that of Arbenz.[4]

The son of lower-middle-class parents, the thirty-nine-year-old Arana was "of mixed Spanish and Indian blood," an embassy official observed, "with the latter strain somewhat in predominance."[5] He had ascended from the ranks. He was "not a 'crusader' in any sense of the word."[6] The U.S. military attaché succinctly captured his personality:

EDUCATION: Little culture or polish . . .

MENTAL CHARACTERISTICS: Above average in general intelligence. Has initiative and a good intuitive grasp of the whole picture.

EMOTIONAL NATURE: Courageous and steady. Stolid Indian type.

PERSONALITY TRAITS: High ambition and tenacity of purpose. High sense of responsibility . . .

INTERPERSONAL RELATIONS: A good mixer, liked by superiors, equals and juniors. Has high qualities of leadership . . .

LOYALTY: Loyal under normal conditions.

POLITICAL VIEWS: Strongly nationalistic. Slightly pro-American.[7]

---

[3] "Had Major Aldana not been removed effectively from the fighting, no doubt he would have emerged in the place subsequently occupied by Major Arana." (Affeld [see n. 2 above], p. 2.)

[4] Arévalo, *El candidato*, pp. 327–29.

[5] Affeld (see n. 2 above), p. 1.

[6] Woodward to SecState, no. 2426, Apr. 24, 1945, p. 2, RG84 GR, Box 134, NA-S.

[7] Lt. Col. Morgan, "Lt. Col. Francisco Javier Arana," no. 313-46, Sept. 13, 1946, p. 1, RG84 GR, Box 217, NA-S.

Arana's Guatemalan contemporaries concurred.[8] "He was intelligent, canny like a peasant, and he could be charming," a political foe remembers. A poor speaker in public, he was "persuasive in small groups."[9] He might have lacked formal education, but he was intellectually curious and well-read by the pitiful standards of the Guatemalan officers, particularly those *de linea*. Generous with his friends, convivial—he excelled at telling jokes—he projected the image of a "good fellow" who had some charisma.[10]

This good fellow was now the most powerful man in the Guatemalan army. "Time alone will tell," an embassy official mused in March 1945, "whether Arana possesses the capacity to fill his role as intended, rather than using it . . . to handpick the next candidate for the Presidency." There was an undercurrent of uncertainty in embassy dispatches about Arana. "Arana has sufficient of the phlegmatic Indian strain to give him the laconic dignity, fearlessness and astuteness which seem frequently to be qualities that gravitate into positions of dictatorial control in the Latin American melting pot."[11]

Had Arana had his way, Arévalo would not have become president. After the fall of Ponce, Arana urged Arbenz and Toriello first to postpone the elections, then to disavow the results. "Don't forget," he wrote Toriello in a personal letter dated April 26, 1947, "what a hard time you had—the discussions, the arguments—convincing me to accept this situation [the election of Arévalo], which I never wanted because I knew that it meant handing the revolution over to civilians who would reap the benefits of what we, the military, had accomplished."[12]

---

[8] The portrait of Arana is based on (1) interviews with Guatemalans of different political sympathies, notably Cols. Lorenzana and Mendoza, Lt. Col. Cruz Salazar, Maj. Paz Tejada, Lt. Montenegro, and Charnaud, Galich, and Barrios Peña; (2) U.S. documents, esp. embassy reports; (3) works by Guatemalans, particularly a series by a well-informed if partisan friend of Arana, Avila Ayala, "La muerte del coronel Arana." A brazen apology of Arana that includes some useful information is Alvarado Rubio, *El asesinato*. For biographical data, see Zea Carrascosa, *Semblanzas*, pp. 279–80.

[9] Quoted from interview with Galich.

[10] Interview with Paz Tejada.

[11] Quotations from Affeld (see n. 2 above), p. 2, and Woodward to SecState, no. 215, June 19, 1945, p. 4, RG84 GR, Box 134, NA-S. For early expressions of this uncertainty, see also Col. Devine, "Intelligence Report" no. R75-46, Mar. 5, 1946, RG319 DF, Box 1621, NA-S; Lt. Col. Morgan, "Intelligence Report" no. R135-46, Apr. 29, 1946, RG319 ID 26044, NA-S; Col. Devine, "Intelligence Report" no. R254-46, July 11, 1946, RG319 DF, Box 1893, NA-S; Donovan to SecState, no. 1553, July 16, 1946, RG84 CF, Box 14, NA-S; enclosure no. 1 in Donovon to SecState, no. 2075, Jan. 2, 1947, NA 814.00; HQs Panama Canal Department, "Weekly Intelligence Summary" no. 255, May 21, 1947, RG319 ID 371556, NA-S.

[12] Arana to Jorge Toriello, Apr. 26, 1947, *El I*, Apr. 29, 1947, p. 9. See also "Carta abierta del Sr. Jorge Toriello al Jefe de las Fuerzas Armadas," Apr. 25, 1947, *El I*,

After Toriello indiscreetly published this letter, Arana issued a terse statement to the effect that, since the armed forces were apolitical, he would remain silent.[13] The damage had been done: Arana's letter to Toriello, noted the U.S. embassy, "quite frankly indicates . . . his belief that the government should not have been turned over to the civilian elements."[14]

Toriello and Arbenz demanded that the duly elected Arévalo be allowed to assume the presidency, and Arana finally agreed, but he exacted a price: the new constitution must guarantee his dominant position in the military. "After two private meetings" with Arana, President-elect Arévalo had little choice but to agree.[15] The 1945 constitution, prepared by an assembly dominated by Arévalo's supporters, established a new military position, patently absurd in an army of a few thousand men. Henceforth, there would be a chief of the armed forces, largely free of civilian control and more powerful than the minister of defense: "Military appointments," the constitution stipulated, "shall be made by the chief of the armed forces, through the minister of defense." His term would be six years. Unlike any other appointed official, he could be removed only by Congress, and then only if he had broken the law.[16] Upon Arévalo's inauguration, Arbenz became the minister of defense; Arana, the chief of the armed forces.

Arana's ambitions continued to grow. Soon an opportunity presented itself. On December 16, 1945, while cavorting in the countryside with a young American journalist, Arévalo drove his car into a deep ravine. It seemed at first that the president would be incapacitated for a long time.[17] Fearing that

---

Apr. 29, 1947, p. 1; Toriello, "Comentarios a la carta que recibí," Apr. 26, 1947, *El I*, Apr. 29, 1947, p. 9. On Arana's reluctance to hand the presidency to Arévalo, see also Affeld, "Memorandum for the Record," Jan. 26, 1945, RG84 GR, Box 134, NA-S.

[13] "Comunicado del Jefe de las Fuerzas Armadas coronel Francisco J. Arana," *El I*, Apr. 30, 1947, p. 1.

[14] Donovan to SecState, no. 2440, May 12, 1947, p. 2, NA 814.00.

[15] Cruz Salazar, "El ejército," p. 84.

[16] See arts. 149–61 of the 1945 constitution; quoted from art. 157. According to Cruz Salazar, the creation of this post was the result of Arana's pressure on Arévalo. Cruz Salazar served as intermediary in two secret meetings between Arana and Arévalo. (Interview with Cruz Salazar.) Arévalo refused to comment, beyond saying that Cruz Salazar's account was "largely correct" and that the decision to create the post of Chief of the Armed Forces was taken without him; "in fact, I wasn't even consulted." (Interview with Arévalo; see also Arévalo, *El candidato*, pp. 384–86, 610–14.) Cols. Lorenzana and Aldana Sandoval confirmed Cruz Salazar's account. (Interviews with Lorenzana and Aldana Sandoval.)

[17] For press accounts of the accident, see esp. *La Hora*, Dec. 17, 18, 1945, p. 1, and *El I*, Dec. 18, 19, 1945, p. 1. The press demurely overlooked the presence of the young lady. This was during the political honeymoon, and Arévalo was a married man. U.S. embassy reports were less discreet: "The young woman is understood to have

Arana might exploit the situation to seize power, a group of leaders of the PAR approached him. A secret deal was struck: the *Pacto del Barranco* (Pact of the ravine). In exchange for Arana's promise to refrain from a military coup, these leaders pledged in writing that their party would support his candidacy in the November 1950 presidential elections. Arévalo, who in fact recovered swiftly, reluctantly endorsed the arrangement.[18]

The U.S. State Department did not learn of the *Pacto del Barranco* until January 15, 1947:

> Lt. Col. Morgan, former Assistant Military Attaché in Guatemala, called on Mr. Newbegin [at the Central American desk of the State Department] . . . and told him that there was one bit of highly secret political information on Guatemala which had never been reported but was of great importance in analyzing current political trends in that country. This was the existence of an agreement between Col. Arana . . . and PAR, the dominant political party. Under this agreement Arana would be the candidate of PAR in the presidential election of 1951 [sic].
>
> This agreement, according to Colonel Morgan, explains Arana's unwillingness to join any movement to overthrow Arévalo. Arana does not want to incur unpopularity with his strongest supporters, the political party and liberal elements in the country, nor does he wish to endanger the institution of a six-year presidential term.
>
> This agreement, Colonel Morgan stated, is written and is known only to a very few people in Guatemala and is not known to anyone at the American Embassy.[19]

Left alone, Arana might indeed have remained content in his role as the heir apparent. But Guatemala's landed elite sought a champion to defend their privileges, and they turned to Arana "to use him as an instrument of disruption." With an ardor that blossomed as their hostility toward Arévalo deepened, the proud scions of the coffee elite began their humiliating courtship. They flocked around Arana, whom, in happier circumstances, they would have shunned as a parvenu. They invited him to their parties and their country

---

been Miss Lynn Cady Schnider, an American citizen who is rumored to have been very closely acquainted with President Arévalo. It is understood that Miss Schnider was not seriously injured and that she departed from Guatemala for Mexico or the United States on December 21, 1945.'' (Woodward to SecState, no. 965, Dec. 29, 1945; see also Woodward to SecState, no. 927, Dec. 18, 1945 and Woodward to SecState, no. 945, Dec. 22, 1945. All NA 814.001.)

[18] The existence of the pact is mentioned only by a few writers, notably Nájera Farfán, *Los estafadores*, pp. 105–6, Galich, *¿Por qué lucha Guatemala?*, p. 201, and Villagrán Kramer, "Los pactos," no. 1, July 12, 1987, p. 11. My sources include interviews with Galich, Charnaud, Fortuny, Monteforte Toledo, Barrios Peña, and Paz Tejada who, upon succeeding Arana as chief of the armed forces in August 1949, found the pact itself in a drawer of Arana's desk. (Among the signatures was that of Galich.)

[19] Williams, "Guatemalan Politics—Agreement between Arana and PAR," Jan. 16, 1947, NA 814.00.

estates. They showered him with praise, urging him to save Guatemala and overthrow the communist, Arévalo.[20]

Arana's drama had begun. He had no desire to sully his hands with a military coup. He wanted to retain his cachet as the democratic hero of the uprising against Ponce. He was not a violent man, as long as he could get what he wanted by other means, and the *Pacto del Barranco*, Arévalo's repeated assurances, and his own military power seemed to guarantee that he would be president in 1951—a president elected by an admiring populace, not a usurper ruling through force.

Yet Arana was not immune to the charm and the flattery of the elite. Lacking strong views on political and social affairs, he would not have complained about the government's reforms had it not been for the shrill protests of his new friends. He wanted their approval, but had no desire to antagonize the administration parties and the labor unions, the foot soldiers who would deliver the vote in the 1950 presidential elections. Caught between these contradictory desires, his behavior was inconsistent. He grumbled to his friends about the government's radicalism and labor's excesses ("What they are doing is unconscionable; I disapprove"), and occasionally he was outspoken to members of the government and to U.S. officials ("The present situation . . . [is] intolerable").[21] But these complaints rarely—very rarely—translated into action. Arana was openly defiant on only a few occasions. In September 1947, for instance, he hid a right-wing plotter in his house and demanded that several labor leaders be deported. As a rule, he did not actively oppose the government's policies, and, whatever he may have said behind Arévalo's back, "he visited the president in his house, in a respectful manner."[22]

Arana's grumblings, his occasional defiance, and his ties to some of the government's most bitter foes bred suspicion among administration politicians and labor leaders. In 1948, a few began to criticize him openly. "We believe it to be a mistake," admonished the prominent PAR leader Augusto Charnaud MacDonald, "to govern by force. Colonel Arana tried to deport two members of the FPL and the PAR whom he considered hostile to him. . . . A violent

[20] Quoted from Rivera to Ambassador and Donovan, May 9, 1946, RG84 CF, Box 14, NA-S. This is confirmed by the sources listed in n. 8 above, including Arana's adviser Barrios Peña, a prominent member of the upper class. See also FBI, Hoover to Neal, July 19, 1946, NA 814.00; FBI, Hoover to Neal, July 30, 1946, NA 814.00; Lt. Col. Morgan, "Lt. Col. Francisco Javier Arana," no. 313-46, Sept. 13, 1946, RG84 GR, Box 217, NA-S.

[21] Quotations from interviews with Barrios Peña and from Donovan to SecState, no. 1529, July 8, 1946, p. 2, NA 814.00.

[22] Quoted from interview with Galich. On the September 1947 incident, see HQs Panama Canal Department, "Weekly Intelligence Summary" no. 273, Sept. 25, 1947, pp. 7–8, RG319 ID 0400768, NA-S.

act such as forcing two citizens to leave their country . . . stabs democracy in the back.''[23]

For his part, Arana began to doubt the revolutionary parties' commitment to his presidential aspirations. In the November 1948 congressional elections, he ran his own slate of supporters. It was an inept effort, directed by men, like Ricardo Barrios Peña, who were more adept at plotting than at running a campaign. The outcome has been described by Clemente Marroquín Rojas, the most brilliant of Guatemala's right-wing journalists: ''In 1948 half of the Congress was up for reelection. . . . Colonel Arana lent his support to several candidates, but he chose undistinguished individuals who were virtually unknown; worse, he gave his money away indiscriminately, both to his friends and to his enemies—more than $30,000 from the Defense Ministry went to his enemies. Not one of Arana's candidates . . . was elected to Congress.''[24]

This futile attempt further strained Arana's relations with the revolutionary parties. A few days before the elections, the Guatemalan Congress overwhelmingly approved an unprecedented resolution that was clearly intended as a rebuke to Arana: ''The Legislature,'' it stated, ''has learned that some members of the army have been interfering in the Congressional campaign.'' Arana responded promptly with a curt statement that ''can only be interpreted,'' explained the U.S. embassy, ''as a sharp rebuff.''[25] A few days later, the embassy added:

Concurrent with increasing political activity in connection with the forthcoming Congressional elections are persistent reports of a possible early revolutionary attempt to be headed by Colonel . . . Arana. . . . While much of this talk is believed to be within the realm of speculation, it seems clear that recent political developments have distinctly cooled the relations between President Arévalo and Colonel Arana on one hand, and Congress and Colonel Arana on the other. The President is said to be annoyed by the ''Arana-for-President'' movement which has been launched by several independent groups in Guatemala City recently, probably with the encouragement of Arana. One informant of reliability reports that Arana approached a leading citizen . . . urging the latter to organize a political party to espouse Arana's candidacy in 1950. . . . Many observers believe that he much prefers to gain his ends through democratic elections, but that he is determined by any means to succeed Arévalo.

[23] Charnaud MacDonald, ''Arana y la unidad de las fuerzas revolucionarias,'' *El Libertador*, Aug. 21, 1948, p. 21.

[24] ''Ya no pierdan su tiempo, señores finqueros,'' *La Hora Dominical*, June 1, 1952, p. 1. An interview with Barrios Peña was particularly useful.

[25] Quotations from ''40 diputados firman punto resolutivo,'' *El I*, Nov. 4, 1948, p. 1, and Wells to SecState, no. 561, Nov. 10, 1948, NA 814.00/11-1248, p. 1. For Arana's response, see ''Proceder del Congreso causa extrañeza a Arana,'' *El I*, Nov. 8, 1948, p. 1.

Some months ago, there was considerable talk of an understanding between Colonel Arana and the *Frente Popular Libertador*. However recent developments cast doubts upon this possibility. . . . Arana's relations with the more leftist *Partido Acción Revolucionaria* and *Renovación Nacional* also obviously have cooled during recent weeks. . . .

The action of Congress in protesting the alleged intervention of the Armed Forces in politics . . . unquestionably has worsened Arana's relations with the Arevalista political parties. It is common knowledge that Congress gave serious consideration to adopting a curt resolution reaffirming its previous charge, in response to Arana's official communication of denial. . . . However, wiser counsel prevailed (one dissenter Deputy is reported to have observed that Congress could censure Arana if it wished, but to do so would invite dissolution the following day) and for the moment, at least, the incident is officially closed.

With the foregoing as background, it is difficult not to attach greater significance to current rumors that Colonel Arana has reached the end of his patience with the present "revolutionary" government, and is seeking the right opportunity and a reasonable excuse for a military coup d'etat. Although the Embassy believes that Arana sincerely desires to preserve constitutional government, and hopes to become President by means of the ballot, it must be admitted that all indications point to his having personal ambitions, as well as personal antipathy toward the extremism which all too frequently is identified with the Arévalo regime. For this reason, one may not rule out the possibility that the force of political developments may turn his ambitions in revolutionary channels.[26]

After his electoral fiasco, Arana still sought, through a combination of veiled threats and suasion, to secure the support of the leaders of the revolutionary parties, and they too wanted to avoid an open break. In early 1949, for instance, Arana twice approached José Manuel Fortuny, the leader of the radical wing of the PAR. In Fortuny's words, Arana asked, " 'Why don't you and your friends like me? I'm not a man of the right.' Arana was very direct: 'I am going to be a candidate,' " and he asked for the PAR's support. " 'The truth,' he complained, 'is that you people are ingrates.' " Fortuny responded: " 'We are not against you. We appreciate the role that you played in the revolt against Ponce. It's just that you have no sympathy for labor.' " He avoided stating categorically that the PAR would not support Arana. The party, he claimed, had not yet made a decision.[27]

The faltering minuet that had begun with the *Pacto del Barranco* was draw-

[26] Wells to SecState, no. 564, Nov. 12, 1948, NA 814.00. See also "Crisis between Col. Arana and President Arévalo May Result in a Coup d'état by the former," enclosed in Wells to de Zengotita, Nov. 5, 1948 (1); Wells to de Zengotita, Nov. 5, 1948 (2); Wells to de Zengotita, Nov. 15, 1948; Wells to de Zengotita, Nov. 19, 1948; Patterson to SecState, no. 462, Nov. 26, 1948. All RG84 GR, Box 192, NA-S.

[27] Interview with Fortuny.

ing to a close. The hostility of the PAR and RN toward Arana was obvious. Within the FPL, the most conservative of the revolutionary parties, only the faction led by Mario Méndez Montenegro still supported Arana. Some of them were motivated by loyalty; others, by opportunism. Their reasoning was, chided a critic, "The man with the weapons will win; it's best to back the winner; we're for Arana."[28] But in April 1949, the FPL held its first national convention and the *Aranistas* were soundly defeated.[29] They bolted from the party and created the FPL Ortodoxo. In the following weeks, recalls an observer sympathetic to Arana, "in almost all the departments of the republic the dissidents began to organize Arana's supporters. This premature campaign caused a lot of tension."[30] He was not a candidate, Arana explained to inquiring journalists, but he would run should the people of Guatemala so demand.[31] Meanwhile, writes another friendly witness, "many complained that his behavior was dishonorable because he was, in fact, running a presidential campaign while he was still chief of the armed forces, and he was funding it with government money. . . . Throughout the country one saw army jeeps carrying *Aranista* propaganda . . . and Arana himself would appear in uniform . . . in order to open branches of the FPL Ortodoxo."[32]

Yet Arana's chances appeared increasingly slim. The FPL Ortodoxo lacked popular appeal; the revolutionary parties were hostile, as was the labor movement. When some members of the powerful railway union (SAMF) declared their support of Arana's candidacy in January 1949, they were promptly rebuked by the SAMF leadership and by the country's two labor confederations.[33] Meanwhile, interest was growing in the government camp about the possible candidacy of Lieutenant Colonel Arbenz, the enigmatic minister of defense, who seemed to be sympathetic to labor and respectful of the constitution.

The first overtures toward Arbenz had taken place in September 1947, after the discovery of both a right-wing conspiracy to overthrow the government and an attempt by a few individuals to create a communist party. Directing his anger only at the "subversives" of the left, Arana had demanded that the

[28] "FPL define su postura," *Nuestro Diario*, June 11, 1949, p. 9.

[29] For the convention, see the issues of *Nuestro Diario* and *El I* of Mar. 31, Apr. 1, 2, 4, 1949. See also Wells to SecState, no. 179, Apr. 5, 1949, NA 814.00, and "Realizada la convención del Frente Popular Libertador," *El Libertador*, Apr. 16, 1949, p. 1.

[30] Nájera Farfán, *Los estafadores*, pp. 107–8.

[31] See, for instance, "Arana no gusta de camarillas," *El I*, Apr. 1, 1949, p. 1. and "Opinión que tiene Arana," *Nuestro Diario*, June 11, 1949, p. 1.

[32] Avila Ayala, "La muerte del coronel Arana," Aug. 2, 1954, p. 4.

[33] "Una rama del SAMF proclama la candidatura del coronel Arana," *Nuestro Diario*, Jan. 12, 1949, p. 9; "SAMF ajeno a los grupos políticos," *Nuestro Diario*, Jan. 13, 1949, p. 7.

government deport several labor leaders whom he considered particularly dangerous. Arbenz, who was usually reserved when nonmilitary matters were — discussed in the cabinet, clashed violently with Arana. His intervention limited the purge. A few days later, several PAR leaders (notably Charnaud, Morgan, and Fortuny) sought a meeting with Arbenz to become better acquainted with the colonel who had sprung to the defense of the labor movement.[34]

By mid-1949, many PAR, RN, and labor leaders had privately decided to back Arbenz. In a country in which the military was the most powerful institution, only a military man would have any chance to beat Arana, and in their opinion Arbenz was "the most progressive officer."[35]

It never came to a vote. On July 18, 1949, Arana was killed at the Puente de la Gloria, not far from the capital. His murderers were never apprehended.

Ignoring the published accounts of Arbenz and other government officials, some authors imply that the assassins were from the upper class: "Many of Arana's 'friends' felt that they would profit from his death in that he had obstructed several *coups* against Arévalo, thus casting a shadow on his 'loyalty.' His murder would at one stroke remove him and cast blame and subsequent public revulsion on Arbenz."[36] This reasoning defies logic. Arana was the elite's only hope to seize power. Arévalo had faced a plethora of plots, perhaps as many as thirty. As the former president himself remarked, "Some were family affairs, concocted behind closed doors; the police would arrive and cart them away. Others were military affairs. Tangay, for example, entered from Mexico and seized several villages in the department of San Marcos; the local police hauled him in before the army arrived."[37] Not one of these plots threatened Arévalo because not one had the support of either of the army's major factions, led by Arana and Arbenz. Arbenz would not plot against Arévalo. Therefore, the elite's only hope was Arana—a live Arana; not a martyr, but a *caudillo* who could lead a revolt. And while it is true that Arana had withstood many pleas to overthrow Arévalo, his scruples had weakened as his electoral chances had waned.

[34] Interviews with Charnaud, Morgan, and Fortuny. For the government's reaction and the debate in the congress, see esp. *DCA* and *El I*, issues of Sept. 16 to Oct. 2, 1947. For Arbenz's demeanor in the cabinet, see MemoConv (Hill, Silva Peña), Dec. 28, 1953, enclosed in Krieg to Fisher, Dec. 29, 1953, NA 714.00; also helpful were interviews with two cabinet members, Charnaud and Osegueda. For Arbenz's role in limiting the purge, see also Dalton, *Miguel Mármol*, pp. 518–20.

[35] Interviews with Charnaud (quoted), Morgan, Fortuny, Guerra Borges. See also Pellecer, "Crónica," pp. 91–92, and Bishop, "Guatemalan Labor," pp. 126–27.

[36] Melville, *Guatemala—Another Vietnam?* p. 59. See also Jonas, "Guatemala," p. 156, n. 8, and Immerman, *CIA in Guatemala*, pp. 59–60. For published accounts by Arbenz and others, see below nn. 78–81.

[37] Arévalo, "La revolución le enseñó al pueblo."

One evening in September or October 1948, Captain Carlos Paz Tejada, a respected young officer, was invited to dine with Arana. They spent the evening at a country estate, the Quinta Samayoa. Also present were leading *Aranista* officers and Ricardo Barrios Peña, the scion of one of Guatemala's most illustrious families and a close adviser to Arana. After listening to bitter denunciations of the government by Arana and his friends, Paz Tejada made an impassioned plea to the colonel not to become another Ubico. "You took the wind from our sails," Barrios Peña told Paz Tejada a few years later. "We were about to launch the coup."[38] Indeed, Barrios Peña stresses, "We already had Paco [Arana] convinced."[39]

In the late spring of 1949, senior *Aranista* officers, on Arana's instructions, assembled one night at the Guardia de Honor: Arana would come, he had promised, to lead them against the government. They waited until dawn, but Arana did not appear. He had spent the night, they later learned, drinking with Arévalo in the presidential palace.[40]

Arana knew that if he were to launch a coup, he would succeed. True, Arbenz had many supporters within the officer corps; there were also minor cliques that retained their independence, and many officers who remained indifferent. But Arana had used his authority as chief of the armed forces to place his supporters in key positions. They controlled the Guardia de Honor and the Base Militar, the two important military units in the capital. *Aranistas* were the commanders of each of the country's seven Zonas Militares. The sole *Arbencista* officer in command of troops was Colonel Francisco Cosenza, the head of the minuscule air force. The police force, under Arévalo's brother-in-law Colonel Víctor Sandoval, was not *Aranista*, but, poorly armed and poorly trained, its power was negligible. And Arévalo's Presidential Guard consisted of only a few men under a loyal officer.

What held Arana back was not fear of defeat, but his "inner conflict."[41] As long as he hoped that he could reach the presidency by more respectable means, Arana could not bring himself to launch a coup. This explains why at the Quinta Samayoa he was moved by the plea of Paz Tejada, an officer with much prestige but little power.

By July 1949, however, Arana could dally no longer. Facing the opposition of the revolutionary parties and labor unions, and unable to create a strong

[38] Interview with Paz Tejada.

[39] Interview with Barrios Peña, who confirmed Paz Tejada's account and added a wealth of detail.

[40] Interviews with Lt. Montenegro, who was at the Guardia de Honor, and with Col. Mendoza, whose brother, Col. Miguel Mendoza, was one of the senior officers who spent the night at the Guardia de Honor waiting for Arana.

[41] Interview with Col. Mendoza.

Aranista party, he would need the army to deliver the peasant vote. Yet his control of the military was threatened.

The constitution stipulated that a military officer could be elected president only if he quit active duty at least six months before election day; Arana would have to step down as armed forces chief by May 1950. His successor would be selected by the Guatemalan Congress from a list of three names submitted by the Consejo Superior de la Defensa (CSD), an advisory body composed of twenty-three officers. (Ten were members ex-officio, the others were elected every three years by all active duty officers.)[42] The 1946 elections for the CSD had attracted little attention, but by the spring of 1949 the CSD had acquired unforeseen importance. For it was obvious that the Guatemalan Congress, if offered the opportunity, would appoint a *non-Aranista* as chief of the armed forces. From Arana's perspective, therefore, it was imperative that the CSD submit the names of three *Aranista* officers. Arana lacked a clear majority within the CSD, but some of its members were up for reelection in early July 1949.

Through May and June 1949, "a quiet tug of war was waged" within the CSD. Ostensibly at issue were the rules for the forthcoming elections. The *Aranistas* wanted to ensure that the commanders of the Zonas Militares and the unit commanders had as much influence as possible over the ballot. Their opponents wanted to ensure that the vote be secret and free. The outcome of an unfettered ballot among the more than seven hundred active duty officers was unpredictable. As a witness recalls, "the situation within the officer corps was confused." The discussions in the CSD grew increasingly acrimonious. Arana and Arbenz, both members ex-officio, rarely attended; they were kept informed by their supporters.[43]

As election day approached, Arana convoked an extraordinary session of the CSD. This time both he and Arbenz participated. "It was an extremely tense session," recalls the president of the CSD, Paz Tejada.[44] Arbenz remained cold, impassive, arguing points of law. No agreement was reached beyond the decision to postpone the elections until late July.[45]

[42] See arts. 131/6, 152, 156, and 161 of the 1945 Constitution, and Congressional Decree no. 116, May 22, 1945. (*Recopilación de leyes*, vol. 64, p. 486.)

[43] Quotations from Clemente Marroquín Rojas, "Los lobos se han ido," *La Hora*, July 14, 1954, p. 4, and Avila Ayala, "La muerte del coronel Arana," Aug. 5, 1954, p. 4. My sources for this struggle include interviews with two members of the CSD: Maj. Paz Tejada (president) and Lt. Col. Paiz Novales; with Arana's adviser, Barrios Peña; and with María de Arbenz, Galich and Charnaud. Avila Ayala, "La muerte del coronel Arana," Aug. 5, 1954, p. 4 and Aug. 6, 1954, p. 4, is particularly useful. See also Galich, *Por qué lucha Guatemala?*, p. 203.

[44] Interview with Paz Tejada.

[45] See "Prórroga en las elecciones del Consejo Superior de la Defensa," *DCA*, July 13, 1949, p. 1, and "Elecciones del Consejo de Defensa prorrogan," *Nuestro Diario*,

On Friday, July 15, came the anticlimactic denouement: in a session of the CSD, the *Aranistas* suddenly accepted their opponents' demands. The elections would not be supervised by the local commanders; instead, teams of officers would be sent from the capital to oversee the vote in the different Zonas Militares; they would bring back the ballot boxes; each commission would include both *Aranistas* and *non-Aranistas*. The elections would begin in three days.

That same Friday Arana suddenly replaced Colonel Cosenza, the *Arbencista* commander of the air force, with one of his men, Colonel Arturo Altolaguirre Ubico. His order was promptly executed even though it had not been issued through the Defense Ministry, as required by the constitution.[46]

The following morning, Paz Tejada expressed his surprise at the unexpected turn of events within the CSD to Arbenz: "They gave in without a struggle." Arbenz replied: "They don't care any more. They've made up their minds to go for a coup."[47]

Arbenz was right. "Arana had tired of waiting, of arguing, pleading and threatening," his adviser Barrios Peña explains. He had been, or so he believed, exceedingly patient, listening to his own scruples rather than to his friends' advice. He had accepted rebuffs from upstart politicians who had conveniently forgotten that it was he who had overthrown Ponce in 1944, thereby enabling them to embark on their profitable careers. Their impudence was now imitated within the CSD by a clique of officers without troops. To be sure, Arévalo continued to reassure him of his presidential prospects, but the facts belied the president's promises. It was time to act. On the afternoon of Saturday, July 16, Arana went to the presidential palace and confronted Arévalo in his office.[48]

Had he launched a straightforward coup, Arana would have succeeded. But overconfidence and the lingering remnants of his "inner conflict" led him along a more tortuous path. He still longed to be a properly elected president.

July 13, 1949, p. 7. The rumor later spread that the elections for the CSD had taken place in the week before July 18 and had been won by the *Aranistas*. (See Wells to SecState, no. 311, July 18, 1949, NA 814.00 and Alvarado Rubio, *El asesinato*, pp. 29–30.)

[46] Monteforte Toledo, *Una democracia*, p. 23; Wells to SecState, no. 311, July 18, 1949, NA 814.00; Altolaguirre, "Entrevistamos." Arana also demanded that the police hand over some of their weapons to him. (See Víctor Sandoval, Director General de la Guardia Civil, to César Solís, Ministro de Gobernación, July 15, 1949, CO:G, June–July 1949, p. 919, AGCA, and Solís to Jefe de las Fuerzas Armadas, July 16, 1949, ibid., pp. 919–20.) Arana's motivation must have been to flaunt his power; the weapons of the poorly armed police would not have altered the balance of power in the country.

[47] Interview with Paz Tejada.

[48] An interview with Barrios Peña was particularly useful for this paragraph and the next.

Instead of toppling Arévalo, he delivered an ultimatum: Arévalo must dismiss his cabinet and replace his ministers with those of Arana's choice. Arbenz and his followers would be retired from the army. If Arévalo complied, he would be allowed to complete his presidential term. If he refused, he would be deposed.[49]

Arévalo listened with apparent resignation and asked only for a few days' time so that he could implement the changes in an orderly manner. Arana consented. The ultimatum would expire at 10 p.m. on Monday, July 18 (the day the elections for the CSD were to begin). Arana left triumphant. "Arévalo," remarks Barrios Peña, "willfully deceived Arana."[50]

In vain had Arana's advisers pleaded with him, before he went to the presidential palace, to forego complicated games and simply seize power. In vain did they argue, after he returned from the palace, that he could not rely on Arévalo's promises. In vain did they stress "that in a coup d'état there's no time for talk—you act or you fail."[51]

Arrogance and wishful thinking blinded Arana. He believed that Arévalo, lacking the means to resist, would capitulate. He believed that Arbenz, who could count only on officers without troops, would acquiesce in his own dismissal, just as he had acquiesced to the removal of Colonel Cosenza. The departure of Arbenz and senior *Arbencistas*, Arana concluded, would cinch his control of the military; congress would be cowed, and Arévalo would be in his pocket. Who, then, would dare resist his presidential ambitions? He would be a constitutional president, not a *golpista*. This Arana predicted on Sunday afternoon, July 17, to his skeptical friend Barrios Peña in the latter's estate in the department of Escuintla, a few hours from the capital. "It was the last time I saw Paco; he was sure that he had won."[52]

Arévalo had no intention of giving up so easily. While the details vary according to the informants, the main lines of what took place within the government are clear. After Arana left, Arévalo summoned Arbenz and other key aides and informed them of the ultimatum. They readily agreed that Arana must be sent into exile. The next day, while Arana dallied at Barrios Peña's estate, the Permanent Committee of the Guatemalan Congress met in secret session and voted unanimously that Arana be dismissed. At the request of his friend Arévalo, Cuban President Carlos Prío Socarrás agreed to give Arana asylum in his country. Colonel Cosenza would fly the disgraced plotter to Havana.[53]

[49] No one witnessed this conversation between Arana and Arévalo. My major sources are interviews with Barrios Peña, Galich, Charnaud, María de Arbenz, Lorenzana, and Mendoza. See also Arbenz, "Habla Arbenz," p. 120.

[50] Quoted from interview with Barrios Peña.

[51] Interviews with Col. Mendoza (quoted) and Barrios Peña.

[52] Interview with Barrios Peña.

[53] The main sources for this paragraph and the two that follow are interviews with Galich, Charnaud, María de Arbenz, Paz Tejada, Monteforte Toledo, Lorenzana, and

A formidable problem remained: how would these bold decisions be enforced? The government's hope was to seize Arana without warning, and even then, the likely response of the *Aranista* commanders would be a military uprising. No clear plan of action emerged, only the decision that somehow, somewhere, Arbenz would capture Arana the next day, Monday, July 18.

It was Arana himself, on Monday morning, who gave the government the help it needed. Appearing unexpectedly at the presidential palace, he told Arévalo that he was on his way to El Morlón, the presidential chalet on the shores of nearby Lake Amatitlán, to seize a cache of weapons that was hidden there.

The previous spring, with Arana's grudging consent, Arévalo had provided weapons and other assistance to Dominican exiles seeking to free their country from the Trujillo dictatorship.[54] Some of these weapons had been seized by the Mexican authorities while the exiles were in Cozumel, Quintana Roo. In early July, the weapons were returned to the Guatemalan government, and they were placed at the small air base of San José. "On Arbenz's orders, and with the complicity of Colonel Cosenza, the weapons were spirited away to El Morlón," the chief of army intelligence told Arana on July 14.[55] But Arana's attention was focused on his ultimatum to Arévalo, not on a paltry cache of arms.[56] He took no steps to seize the weapons for three days. Then, on the morning of the eighteenth, he went to see Arévalo.

Arévalo says now that "on the 18th Arana and I did not quarrel, much less exchange insults."[57] But at the time he told his aides that Arana had spoken to him "in an abusive and very threatening manner," that the armed forces chief had upbraided him as though he had been a disrespectful student, alternating threats with sarcastic remarks about his propensity to hide weapons. Whatever the true tone of the conversation (and Arévalo's private account at the time is more credible than the public disclaimer of a much changed Arévalo three decades later), Arana announced that he was on his way to El Morlón to recover the weapons.[58]

Mendoza. See also Arbenz, "Habla Arbenz," p. 120; Marroquín Rojas, *La "Carta política,"* p. 33; Pellecer, "Dos yanquis," Sept. 2, 1982, p. 2; Pérez, "Los oscuros acontecimientos." The account by Pellecer given in this chapter is indirectly confirmed by Arévalo in his "De Juan José Arévalo."

[54] See below, p. 114.

[55] Interview with Col. Lorenzana, chief of army intelligence.

[56] Interview with Barrios Peña. The sources listed in n. 49 above believe that Arana did not mention the arms in El Morlón when he saw Arévalo on July 16.

[57] Arévalo, "De Juan José Arévalo." Arévalo was responding to Pellecer's statement, "The conversation between the two was heated. The colonel . . . raised his voice and insulted and threatened the president." (Pellecer, "Dos yanquis," Sept. 2, 1982, p. 2.)

[58] Quoted from interview with Galich. The other sources are those listed in nn. 49 and 53 above (excepting Barrios Peña and Pérez).

The real reasons for Arana's visit to Arévalo can only be surmised. Arana knew that the arms stored at El Morlón—two hundred rifles without ammunition—in no way altered the balance of power; nor did he anticipate any resistance to his July 16 ultimatum. Furthermore, he had no need to go in person to El Morlón or, for that matter, to inform Arévalo of his whereabouts. Arana, an "impulsive" man whose patience was exhausted, went to the palace to flaunt his power and hurry the humbled president into the swift execution of his ultimatum.[59]

Once again, Arévalo deceived Arana. He raised no objection to Arana's decision to go to El Morlón and even suggested that the commander of his Presidential Guard, Colonel Felipe Antonio Girón, go with him.[60] Arana left the presidential palace savoring another Pyrrhic victory. He drove to El Morlón accompanied only by his driver Francisco Palacios, his aide Major Absalón Peralta, and the hapless Girón. "Arana," recalls a colonel who knew him well, "was very sure of himself. He knew that the officers in command of the troops were loyal to him. He never imagined that Arbenz and Arévalo would stand up to him, and his confidence was reinforced by the fact that he was accompanied on his trip to El Morlón by Arévalo's chief of staff."[61]

Upon Arana's departure, Arévalo contacted Arbenz. Now was the time. On Arbenz's orders, several armed men sped from the capital in two cars to intercept Arana as he returned from El Morlón. They were led by the deputy chief of police, Lt. Colonel Enrique Blanco, and by the chairman of the congressional Armed Forces committee, Alfonso Martínez, who was a retired army officer and a close friend of Arbenz.[62] Near a small bridge, the Puente de la Gloria, they waited. Their wait was not long.

Arana's business at El Morlón was swiftly concluded. According to his driver, they had found the chalet locked. "After blowing the horn several times, a man appeared from the garden, and they went to one of the boathouses where a red truck loaded with rifles was found." Soon thereafter Colonel Juan José de León "appeared with an army truck and two or three soldiers . . . and Colonel Arana said to him 'You already know what I ordered you.' " Leaving de León at the boathouse to load the weapons, Arana and his party began the return trip to Guatemala City. As they reached the Puente de la Gloria, "there was, on the other side, a grey Dodge, because of which, seeing that it was impossible to cross the bridge, Col. Arana stopped his car."[63]

---

[59] This is also the interpretation of Barrios Peña (quoted), and Cols. Lorenzana and Mendoza.

[60] My sources disagree as to who initiated this suggestion.

[61] Interview with Col. Mendoza. See also Alvarado Rubio, *El asesinato*, p. 49.

[62] Interview with Lt. García, who was Arbenz's aide and with him at the time; interviews with María de Arbenz, Guerra Borges, Charnaud, Galich, Paz Tejada. See also Pellecer, "Crónica," pp. 99–101, and Arbenz, "Habla Arbenz," p. 121.

[63] "Statement of Lt. Colonel Alberto Bone Summarizing Statement Made by Mr.

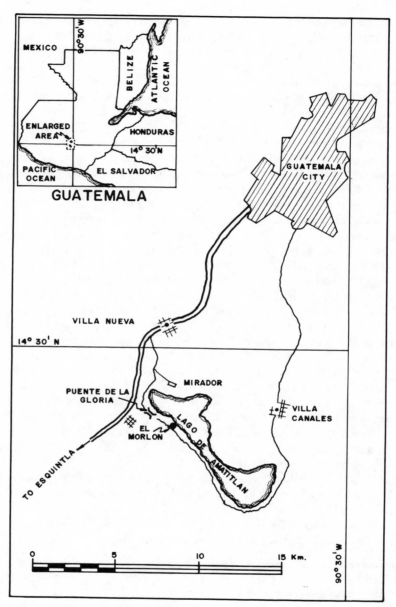

Map of Puente de la Gloria, where Arana was killed.

A brief shootout ensued and three men lay dead: Arana, his aide Peralta, and Lt. Colonel Blanco; others were wounded, including Arbenz's friend Alfonso Martínez. Did the ambushers open fire, without warning, as Arana's driver has claimed? Or did Peralta fire first, after Blanco had told Arana that he was under arrest and an argument had broken out? There is no definitive proof, but even some of Arana's friends believe that "the order was to capture Arana, not to kill him," that "his death was accidental."[64] Absalón Peralta and Blanco "first traded insults, then shots."[65]

News of Arana's death spread through the capital in a matter of hours. The Guardia de Honor rose in revolt.[66] For more than twenty-four hours the battle raged in the city. The rest of the country waited in tense expectation. More than once on the eighteenth, Arana's supporters seemed close to victory, but several factors were against them. Their intended victims had struck first, killing their *caudillo* and forcing them into a hasty reaction. While Arbenz led the loyalist forces with sang-froid and skill, no one rose to lead the rebels. Lt. Colonel Carlos Castillo Armas, possibly the most able of Arana's officers, was in Mazatenango, overseeing the elections for the CSD; he lacked the nerve to return to the capital.[67] The commander of the Guardia de Honor, Colonel Juan

---

Palacios J., Chauffeur of Colonel Arana, Concerning Events Associated With Arana's Death," pp. 1–2, enclosed in "Intelligence Report" no. IR-77-49, July 28, 1949. See also "Francisco Palacios hace sensacionales declaraciones," *Diario Latino*, San Salvador, Aug. 27, 1949, p. 1.

[64] Interview with Col. Lorenzana.

[65] Interview with Col. Mendoza. Also useful were interviews with Barrios Peña, Paz Tejada, Galich, García, María de Arbenz, Guerra Borges, Pellecer, Charnaud, and Aldana Sandoval (who pointed out that cold-blooded murderers would not have spared the life of Arana's driver). See also Pellecer, "Crónica," pp. 101–2, which gives a slightly different version of the scene.

[66] There is no definitive account of the fight. Following Arana's death, the government suspended publication of all newspapers, except the official *DCA*, which provided only sparse coverage. Upon resuming publication on August 1, the other newspapers wrote little on the subject. Coverage by the foreign press and by the U.S. embassy was superficial.

The government's version of the fighting was first outlined in "Mensaje del gobierno de la república a la ciudadanía," *DCA*, July 22, 1949, p. 1, and then in *Una democracia*, a 47-page pamphlet written by the president of the Guatemalan Congress, Monteforte Toledo. Useful information is included in Bush, "Organized Labor," part 4, pp. 11–14, in Sierra Roldán, *Diálogos*, pp. 44–46 and in Pellecer, "Dos yanquis," Sept. 3, 1982, p. 2. For an excellent series of articles by an *Aranista* officer, see Col. Pinto Recinos, "La rebelión." Particularly helpful were interviews with the following officers: García, Aldana Sandoval, Lorenzana, Mendoza, Montenegro, Paz Tejada; and with civilians Barrios Peña, Galich, and Charnaud.

[67] Castillo Armas was one of the few officers *de escuela* who was *Aranista*. An outstanding cadet (1933–1936), he attended classes at Fort Leavenworth, Kansas, from

Francisco Oliva, had been summoned by Arbenz to the Defense Ministry less than an hour after Arana's death; unaware of what had happened, he went and was arrested. Another *Aranista*, Colonel Gabino Santizo, the commander of the Base Militar, sided with the government. A few days later, with his customary eloquence, Arévalo told the people of Guatemala about the dialogue that, he said, had taken place between Arbenz and Santizo at the outset of the revolt: "Colonel Arbenz got in touch with . . . Colonel Gabino Santizo, a loyal soldier who immediately swore, 'My duty is to defend the government and the Constitution, and I guarantee you that all my commanders and officers will do their duty.' " The truth was more tawdry: Santizo had been bought for $75,000. That afternoon, while the *Aranista* officers at the base watched in sullen passivity, a group of loyalist officers arrived from the Defense Ministry "to place themselves under Santizo's orders," as the official story gently stated—or, more truthfully, to take control of his troops.[68]

Still, it was hours before the Base Militar stood solidly on the government's side, and in the meantime Arbenz had only the police, the tiny Presidential Guard, and loyal officers without troops. There were only a few weapons to arm the growing number of civilian volunteers.

The rebel officers squandered their advantage in ill-planned and poorly led attacks. Such were the incompetence and the disarray that effective command of the Guardia de Honor was assumed by a civilian, Mario Méndez Montenegro, the leader of the *Aranista* FPL Ortodoxo. Méndez Montenegro was brave, but untrained in military matters. Meanwhile, "some of the rebel colonels . . . were busy drinking."[69]

By dawn on July 19, the government was winning. The presidential palace and the police headquarters, the main targets of the rebels' attacks the previous

---

Oct. 1945 to Apr. 1946, and served as director of the Escuela Politécnica from Mar. 1947 to Mar. 1949. In Apr. 1949 he was appointed commander of the Fourth Military Zone (Mazatenango). His reaction to the news of Arana's death was provided by Paz Tejada, who was with him at the time. (Interview with Paz Tejada; see also Cáceres, *Aproximación*, pp. 46–47.)

[68] Quotations from "Mensaje del Gobierno" (see n. 66 above), p. 1 and from Monteforte Toledo, *Una democracia*, p. 19. A Guatemalan officer has written tactfully that on July 18, 1949, "the freedom of action of the Commander of the Base Militar was neutralized," without explaining how this was accomplished (Cruz Salazar, "El ejército," p. 86). Particularly informative were interviews with María de Arbenz, Paz Tejada, Guerra Borges, and Aldana Sandoval, the leader of the officers who took control of the Base Militar. See also Marroquín Rojas, "Los lobos se han ido," *La Hora*, July 17, 1954, p. 4. Santizo had a long pedigree as an *Aranista* plotter; he was one of the officers who were at the Quinta Samayoa in late 1948 (interview with Paz Tejada), and who later spent the night at the Guardia de Honor waiting for Arana (interview with Mendoza).

[69] Quoted from Pinto Recinos, "La rebelión," June 21, 1985, p. 2.

day, were in government hands. Government officers were now firmly in control of the Base Militar. The air force was also loyal: on Arbenz's orders, Colonel Cosenza arrested the officer whom Arana had appointed as his successor and resumed command. Civilian volunteers, mainly labor union members, had swelled the government ranks; they were armed with weapons from the Base Militar and the arms depot at Fort Matamoros, a small army barracks that Arbenz had seized during the night. Loyal officers and the cadets from the military academy hurriedly trained the volunteers.

By late morning soldiers from the Base Militar and armed civilians began to attack the Guardia de Honor. The air force's venerable planes strafed the rebel barracks and dropped a few bombs that rarely exploded. Even though the planes caused little physical damage, they deepened the rebels' demoralization. Through the Nuncio, at 1 p.m., the rebels sought negotiations. Desultory conversations ensued between representatives of both sides at the Salvadoran embassy; the government demanded unconditional surrender; the fighting resumed. At 5 p.m. the white flag was raised at the Guardia de Honor. The rebellion of the *Aranistas* had collapsed with approximately 150 dead and over two hundred wounded. In the words of a foe of Arbenz, the rebels' ineptitude "and the skill of the minister of defense determined the outcome of the battle."[70]

It remained for Arévalo to explain to the people of Guatemala the circumstances of Arana's death. On July 21, he declared five days of "national mourning."[71] Then, in a lengthy communiqué, he spun his tale.

Arana, Arévalo stated, was not blameless. Waylaid by the lure of the presidency and by self-seeking sycophants, "each day that passed he linked himself more and more closely with the political circles hostile to the president." But he resolutely resisted their entreaties that he overthrow the government. This refusal had cost him his life.

Arévalo did not name Arana's assassins, but he impugned the conservative opposition: the murderers were "reactionaries" who had finally realized that the colonel would never lead a coup d'état. Arana's death, the communiqué concluded, was a grave loss "for the nation, for the army, for the government and above all for his friend, President Arévalo."[72]

Before its publication, notes a PAR leader, "the official communiqué . . . was discussed in the cabinet; it was opposed by Arbenz, Foreign Minister Enrique Muñoz Meany and Carlos Aldana Sandoval, Minister of Public Works." These three asserted that Arévalo should tell the true story of Arana's death. ("There was no reason to lie," Aldana Sandoval exclaimed with a rare

---

[70] Cruz Salazar, "El ejército," p. 86.

[71] "Duelo nacional por la muerte del coronel Arana," *DCA*, July 21, 1949, p. 1.

[72] "Mensaje del Gobierno" (see n. 66 above), p. 3. "The official communiqué on Arana's death was written entirely by Arévalo" (Arévalo, "De Juan José Arévalo").

flash of emotion, more than forty years later.) Arévalo insisted on his version that, he explained, would avoid further inflaming passions; the other ministers agreed with the president.[73]

The next day, the official *Diario de Centro América* praised Arévalo's communiqué and drew a moral lesson: "Its eloquence has calmed us and given us the gift of truth, which comforts us. . . . Honesty seems defenseless, but it possesses a hidden weapon: truth, which always triumphs."[74]

Few Guatemalans agreed; few were so naive as to believe that Arana had been killed by his conservative friends. This contradicted both common sense and widely known facts. It was no secret, for instance, that Alfonso Martínez had been wounded at the Puente de la Gloria and that Martínez was close to Arbenz, not to the conservative opposition. Thus, the rumors and speculation surrounding the death of Arana took root.

At a massive rally in support of the administration, a prominent PAR leader, Carlos Manuel Pellecer, flatly contradicted the official story and alluded to Arana's disloyalty and to the true circumstances of his death. The government "rejects and officially condemns" Pellecer's declarations, a senior official announced the following day, on Arévalo's instructions. Pellecer was fired from his post in the Ministry of Education. "You were right to tell the truth," Arbenz later told him.[75]

In July 1950, on the first anniversary of the shootout at the Puente de la Gloria, opposition groups organized demonstrations accusing the government of the murder of Arana. Arévalo stuck to the official version. Arbenz remained silent, seeking to avoid an open break with the president. In the years that followed, first as president and then in lonely exile, Arbenz persisted in his silence even though he, far more than Arévalo, was branded as Arana's murderer. Shy, introverted, with a strict personal code of honor, he kept his promise not to speak out unless Arévalo agreed; the longer his silence, moreover, the more awkward a sudden reversal.[76] On one occasion, recalls his wife, he tried to convince Arévalo "to give a full and public account of the circumstances of Arana's death." It was in Montevideo, in the late 1950s, in one of the two ex-presidents' rare encounters during the years of exile. "But Arévalo said that it was better not to discuss it and changed the subject."[77]

[73] Pellecer, "Dos yanquis," Sept. 4, 1982, p. 2, and interview with Aldana Sandoval. As already noted, Arévalo indirectly endorsed Pellecer's account in "De Juan José Arévalo."

[74] "El gobierno dice al pueblo la verdad" (edit.), *DCA*, July 23, 1949, p. 3.

[75] Quotations from "El gobierno desaprueba el discurso del profesor Carlos Manuel Pellecer," *DCA*, July 25, 1949, p. 1 (quoted from p. 7), and Pellecer, "Dos yanquis," Sept. 4, 1982, p. 2.

[76] Interviews with María de Arbenz, Fortuny, and Guerra Borges.

[77] Interview with María de Arbenz.

Only in 1968, three years before his own death, did Arbenz finally state what had happened to Francisco Arana in those distant days of July 1949.[78]

Others did not wait so long. In July 1950, the communist weekly *Octubre* wrote that "prior to July 18 . . . Arana was ready to seize power," but it provided no details.[79] That same year, the communist leader Víctor Manuel Gutiérrez told a labor congress that Arana had died in an armed confrontation with "Police Coronel Enrique Blanco, who had a warrant for his arrest because he was plotting to overthrow Arévalo. . . . Therefore, comrade delegates, Arana was not assassinated: he died resisting arrest."[80] Information on the true circumstances of Arana's death was also provided in a 1956 book by Manuel Galich who, as secretary general of the FPL, had played a key role in July 1949.[81]

But Arévalo has remained evasive. At times he claims, as in a 1979 interview, that Arana's death is still an enigma, and probably "will remain a mystery forever."[82] On other occasions, as in a 1982 public letter, he has stated that he will reveal the truth in his memoirs, which will be published after his death.[83]

Why did Arévalo choose to cover up the facts? Perhaps in 1949 he honestly believed that his tale was the best way to restore domestic peace. Or perhaps he was keeping his options open: perhaps he believed that the *Aranistas* would one day regain power and that it was therefore not in his interest to malign their fallen hero. Or perhaps, as Arbenz speculated years later, "Arévalo played a very dirty trick on me."[84] For the residue of the official communiqué tarred Arbenz: in the absence of a plausible alternative and in the presence of the president's avowal of Arana's loyalty, speculation centered on the theory that Arana had been killed by *Arbencistas* in a showdown between military factions. As a key adviser to Arana muses, "Arévalo was very wily. He shifted all suspicion onto Arbenz."[85]

[78] Arbenz, "Habla Arbenz," pp. 119–22.

[79] "El 19 de Julio de 1949: Un gran golpe al imperialismo," *Octubre*, July 19, 1950, p. 1 (quoted from p. 3).

[80] Gutiérrez, "Informe rendido por el secretario general ante la novena asamblea confederal de la CTG," nd, p. 2, *GT*, Box 15.

[81] Galich, *¿Por qué lucha Guatemala?*, pp. 201–4.

[82] Interview with Arévalo.

[83] "De Juan José Arévalo." See also Alvarado Rubio, *El asesinato*, pp. 33–36, 41–48, 65–127.

[84] Interview with Fortuny quoting Arbenz.

[85] Interview with Barrios Peña. Since the late 1960s, Arévalo has spent most of his time in Guatemala, where the friends of Arana are again powerful. He has received honors and lives well. His lack of candor in July 1949 has served him well. See below, p. 394.

CHAPTER 4

The Election of Jacobo Arbenz

IT WAS THE HOUR of Jacobo Arbenz, the surviving military hero of 1944, the man who had led the government's defense against the *Aranistas*. After the rebels' defeat senior officers loyal to Arana were deported; others were retired, like Castillo Armas, or were shifted to positions of little importance.[1] Men loyal to Jacobo Arbenz now held the key military posts. On July 25, 1949, at Arbenz's request, Congress chose thirty-one-year old Paz Tejada as chief of the armed forces. Major Paz Tejada, noted the U.S. embassy, "was likeable . . . well-educated . . . well prepared for his job," and enjoyed "an unusual reputation for incorruptibility." He was also known for his independence of mind. Paz Tejada had joined the *Arbencista* group in order to counter the dictatorial propensities of Francisco Arana, but he remained very much his own man, and although he respected Arbenz, they were not close friends. He might become a powerful military leader, the embassy speculated, particularly if Arbenz's hold over the army were to weaken.[2] This appeared, for the moment, an unlikely prospect.

While the balance of power in the military had changed dramatically, the army's position in the country was unaffected. The military was, if anything, more powerful than before, because it was more united. And it retained its monopoly of the country's weapons.

During the revolt, as many as two thousand civilians, mainly students and union members, had been armed in the capital. At times, particularly on July 19, the volunteers had been asked their names and their addresses; on other occasions, the distribution had been indiscriminate.[3] But after the rebels' defeat, the government, prodded by the army, cajoled and threatened the civilians to return their weapons. As in October 1944, the labor leaders assisted the government; they feared a confrontation with the military that they were

[1] For a good summary, see Pinto Recinos, "La rebelión," July 3, 1985, p. 2.

[2] Patterson to SecState, no. 349, July 28, 1949, NA 814.00; quoted from Steins to SecState, no. 416, Aug. 3, 1949, p. 2, NA 814.20; Patterson to SecState, no. 421, Aug. 4, 1949, NA 814.20. Also useful were interviews with Paz Tejada, María de Arbenz, Guillén, Mendoza, Galich, García, Charnaud. For Paz Tejada's brilliant performance as a cadet and a young officer, see Samayoa Coronado, *La Escuela Politécnica*, 2:124, 370.

[3] In addition to the sources listed in p. 67, n. 66, see Patterson to SecState, no. 327, July 21, 1949, NA 814.00, and Tomás Yancos, "Una jornada gloriosa," *DCA*, July 28, 1949, p. 6.

bound to lose. While troops searched entire blocks of the city, the labor unions organized searches of their own and threatened to denounce all those found to be hiding weapons. In a matter of days, most of the arms had been returned. "We are surrendering the weapons that were given to us to defend our government," wrote the country's two foremost labor leaders to Arbenz. "We trust that they will be returned to us," should seditious officers again threaten "our freedom."[4]

Arbenz's behavior during the July uprising—firm in his support of the government, decisive in his military leadership—had reinforced his prestige, and the fact that there was no civilian who could unify the quarrelsome components of the government coalition and restrain the competing ambitions of a host of politicians further enhanced his status. Leaders such as Charnaud and Fortuny from the PAR and Gutiérrez from organized labor had first approached Arbenz out of expediency but had become his friends. They believed that they knew the true Jacobo, and that this man, so silent in public, would be not only an able leader but also a progressive one. By late 1949, the powerful PAR, the RN, and the country's two largest labor confederations were ready to declare their support of Jacobo Arbenz.[5]

Still another group was ready to raise Arbenz's standard: a handful of rich landowners and industrialists, most of whom, like Arbenz, hailed from Quezaltenango, Guatemala's second largest city. Having known the defense minister for many years, they too believed that they knew the private Jacobo. Arbenz, they argued, was courting the PAR and the labor movement because he needed their votes. As president, he would tolerate only modest social change. These men, unlike the immense majority of their peers, believed that limited concessions to the lower classes not only were politically necessary, but also would be economically beneficial. What Arbenz needed, they concluded, was the advice of well-bred and pragmatic friends. They were ready to educate the prince. In late 1949 these men—including Nicolás Brol, Joaquín Rivera Kunze, and Héctor Mazariegos—created the Partido de Integridad Nacional (PIN) to back Arbenz. Reflecting the geographical base of its leaders, the PIN was a regional party, with headquarters in Quezaltenango.[6]

Who would launch Arbenz's candidacy? The PAR, RN, and PIN bickered for the honor, until Arbenz, heeding the advice of a few friends—the leaders of Guatemala's clandestine Communist party—chose the PIN because it

[4] Gutiérrez and Pinto Usaga to Arbenz, Aug. 16, 1949, *GT*, Box 1. See also "La CTG denunciará a las personas que no han devuelto armas," *DCA*, July 26, 1949, p. 1; Paz Tejada to Gutiérrez and Pinto Usaga, Aug. 18, 1949, *GT*, Box 2. Interviews with Paz Tejada, Galich, Charnaud, and Guerra Borges were helpful.

[5] Particularly useful were interviews with Fortuny, Charnaud, Guerra Borges, Morgan, Galich, and María de Arbenz.

[6] On the PIN (which is virtually ignored in the literature), see *GT*, Boxes 9 and 69.

would lend an image of moderation to his candidacy.[7] On February 5, 1950, the PIN proudly nominated Jacobo Arbenz. This was followed, in short order, by the endorsements of the PAR, RN, and organized labor.[8]

Only the most conservative revolutionary party, the decaying FPL, held back. After protracted infighting, it nominated Health Minister Víctor Manuel Giordani. But some party members had already defected in order to support another moderate civilian, Jorge García Granados, and still others endorsed Arbenz. Meanwhile the FPL's frustrated secretary general, the able and ambitious Manuel Galich, expelled Giordani and was proclaimed presidential candidate by his own supporters. (As the polls opened on November 10, Galich abandoned his hopeless quest and rallied to Arbenz.)[9]

On February 20, Arbenz resigned as defense minister and announced his decision to run for the presidency. Arévalo responded with an effusive letter addressed to "My Great and Dear Friend."[10] While it was obvious that Arbenz was the administration's candidate, it was equally obvious that he was not Arévalo's choice. The relationship between the exuberant, self-centered president and his laconic minister, while always correct, lacked warmth. "Arévalo didn't trust Arbenz," the president of Congress remembers, "because he considered him too leftist." Nor did Arévalo, by 1950, have much in common with the PAR, whose leaders he also judged too radical and too independent. His sympathies went instead to the moribund FPL. Left to his own devices, he would have endorsed his close friend Giordani.[11] But the army and the civilian groups that formed the backbone of the administration supported Arbenz. Giordani stood no chance. Under Arbenz, Arévalo would

[7] Interviews with two of these friends, Fortuny and Guerra Borges. Confirmed by interview with María de Arbenz.

[8] "Arbenz nominado candidato del PIN," *El I*, Feb. 6, 1950, p. 1; "Postulación comunicarán a Arbenz" and "Nominación simultánea en el RN," *El I*, Feb. 20, 1950, p. 1; "Arbenz recibe la postulación suya de manos de laborantes," *El I*, Feb. 27, 1950, p. 1.

[9] For the García Granados split, see esp. *El I*: "Candidatura no apoyarán los partidos Arevalistas," Nov. 14, 1949, p.1; "Aceptará su candidatura a presidente" and "Hacia el candidato único va la trinca," Nov. 15, 1949, p. 1. For Giordani's nomination, the best coverage is again by *El I*: "Giordani gana la partida a Galich," Apr. 21, 1950, p. 1, and "Candidato de un partido y no partido de un candidato," May 2, 1950, p. 1. For Galich's antics, see "Galichistas violaron el estatuto del partido al expulsarlo, declara Giordani," *El I*, Sept. 30, 1950, p. 1; "Galich nominado candidato," *DCA*, Oct. 2, 1950, p. 1; "Las UPAS del FPL llegaron cuando ya el Arbencismo amarraba la victoria," *La Hora*, Nov. 13, 1950, p. 1; "Indignación y desbandada populista," *La Hora*, Nov. 14, 1950, p. 1.

[10] "Entrevista hoy con el presidente," *El I*, Feb. 21, 1950, p. 1, and "Aceptada la renuncia al candidato por el presidente," *El I*, Feb. 27, 1950, p. 1 (quoted from p. 9).

[11] Interviews with Monteforte Toledo (quoted), María de Arbenz, Galich, Charnaud, Fortuny, Guerra Borges, Arévalo, and Osegueda.

play no major political role; he could expect, however, honors and material rewards, provided he behaved graciously while Arbenz was still a candidate. He behaved graciously, and he was rewarded.[12]

While a few members of the upper class supported Arbenz, many more believed that he too was a communist like Arévalo. Others were unsure, and some were even hopeful. Though of merely middle-class extraction, Arbenz was white and had married an upper-class Salvadoran. Above all, he was a military officer. As president, he might behave as army officers had always behaved in Guatemala—and control the rabble. But rather than bank on an uncertain prospect, most members of the elite sought a candidate they could trust unconditionally.

They found him in fifty-five-year old Miguel Ydígoras Fuentes. Of Ubico's many generals, Ydígoras alone had discovered the virtues of democracy—at dawn on October 20, 1944, a few hours after the first rebel troops had left the Guardia de Honor to overthrow Ponce. "The [State] Department will recall," a U.S. official later wrote, that "Ydígoras Fuentes put in an appearance at our Embassy divested of all insignia . . . to offer his services as 'mediator,' to be useful, as he put it, in any negotiations that might be undertaken." He made the same offer to the rebels. Indeed, he was very active throughout the day, but he did not fight. (It would have been the first battle of his long military career.)[13] In short, noted the same U.S. official, Ydígoras' role had been "ambiguous and odd."[14] Yet his last moment betrayal of Ponce and his eagerness to serve the new rulers proved fruitful. The *junta* eventually appointed him Guatemala's minister to London, and he continued in the same post under Arévalo. In addition to his diplomatic duties, he cultivated Trujillo. He told the Dominican that Arévalo was a communist, that his immediate ouster was imperative, and that he, Ydígoras, was the man for the job. He would need, he added, $50,000.[15]

In the spring of 1950, the frustrated rebel returned from London to make his bid for the presidency, supported "by conservatives and ex-partisans of the dictator Ubico," as a State Department official put it.[16] He was not, by

[12] For Arévalo after 1950, see below, pp. 392–94.

[13] AmEm Tegucigalpa, Erwin to DOS, no. 181, Nov. 5, 1953, pp. 2–3, NA 714.00. See also Affeld to SecState, no. 1672, Oct. 25, 1944, NA 814.00; Mannion, "Memorandum for the Charge d'Affaires," enclosed in Affeld to SecState, no. 1672, Oct. 25, 1944, NA 814.00; *Revista de la revolución*, Jan. 1945, pp. 20, 21 and 27. For Ydígoras's military career, see the hagiography by de Zirión, *Datos biográficos*.

[14] Erwin to DOS (see n. 13 above), p. 3. See also CIA, SR-46, "Guatemala," July 27, 1950, p. 10, Truman Papers, President's Secretary's File, Intelligence File, Box 261, TL.

[15] Andrés Pastoriza, memo, enclosed in Pastoriza to Rafael Trujillo, London, Aug. 21, 1947, Vega File.

[16] Burr to Holland, June 1, 1954. For relevant newspaper articles, see "Carta abierta

Ubiquista standards, a bloody man; he was merely corrupt. Bewailing the stupidity of his conservative friends, Marroquín Rojas later wrote, "When they should have chosen a well-known, experienced and resolute candidate, they chose the shadow of dictatorship. When many people told me that they were supporting Ydígoras because he would resort to arms if he lost the elections, I assured them that Ydígoras . . . was not the man to lead a heroic rebellion."[17] Marroquín Rojas was right, on all counts.

The presidential campaign had just begun when an open letter was handed to the secretary general of the PAR. It was signed by ten prominent PAR members. Among them were the men who would later constitute the Secretariat of the Communist Party of Guatemala: José Manuel Fortuny, Alfredo Guerra Borges, Bernardo Alvarado Monzón, Mario Silva Jonama, and José Luis Ramos. In their letter, they announced their "irrevocable resignation" from the PAR and intimated their intention to create "a vanguard party, a party of the proletariat based on Marxism-Leninism."[18] One month later, on June 21, 1950, *Octubre* was launched. Edited by Fortuny, it carried on its masthead: "For a Great Communist Party, Vanguard of the Workers, the Peasants and the People." Would a communist party soon emerge, in open defiance of Arévalo?

The party already existed. The first attempt to reconstitute a communist party after its destruction by Ubico had been foiled by the police in September 1947, but no informer alerted the authorities two years later when a clandestine congress was held. To avoid suspicion, recalls Guerra Borges, "We only met on weekends and, occasionally, on weekday evenings."[19] No wonder, then, that the congress lasted from September 28 to December 18, 1949.

In numbers, the congress was not an impressive affair. The participants were less than fifty; most likely they were forty-three. No foreign party was represented, and none played a role in the creation of the Communist Party of Guatemala (PCG). "We met without any formalities," recalls Carlos Manuel Pellecer, "and we didn't give any thought to foreign delegates."[20] At age thirty-three, Fortuny, who was elected secretary general, seemed almost avun-

---

de Miguel Ydígoras Fuentes," *El I*, Feb. 2, 1950, p. 12; "Texto de la renuncia del general Ydígoras," *El I*, Mar. 29, 1950, p. 1; "El gran partido unificación anticomunista 'PUA': salvación con Ydígoras," *La Hora*, Nov. 3, 1950, p. 7.

[17] "Los ricos con el agua al cuello," *Impacto*, May 31, 1952, p. 1.

[18] For the full text of the six-page letter, dated May 20, see *GT*, Box 7, quoted pp. 1, 6. See also, "Diez izquierdistas renuncian del PAR," *El I*, May 27, 1950, p. 1.

[19] Interview with Guerra Borges.

[20] My major sources for the PCG in the Arévalo years are (1) interviews with Pellecer (quoted), Fortuny, and Guerra Borges; (2) Alvarado Arellano, *Apuntes*, pp. 11–28 and *Esbozo histórico*, pp. 6–18; Gutiérrez, *Apuntes*, pp. 20–27 and *Breve historia*, pp. 27–46. See also Fortuny's testimony in Cáceres, *Aproximación*, pp. 140–56, and Schneider, *Communism*, pp. 55–73.

cular. The other leaders were in their mid-twenties. They all shared urban lower-middle-class or middle-class backgrounds. Most were teachers or university students, who until 1944 had never lived outside Guatemala.[21]

Some, like twenty-four-year old Guerra Borges, had been totally apolitical when Ubico fell. Others, like Fortuny, had belonged to that restless youth that began the struggle against the dictator in late 1942. Not one had been a Marxist, let alone a Marxist-Leninist—not even Carlos Manuel Pellecer, who had lived in Mexico from 1940 to 1944 after a stint in Ubico's jails. (He had criticized army discipline while a cadet at the Escuela Politécnica.) In Mexico Pellecer had been preoccupied with earning a living, not with Marxism. "My love affair with communism," he later wrote, "began in Paris in 1947, when I read *Report from the Gallows* by [Czech communist writer Julius] Fucik."[22]

The "old communists" who emerged from the dictator's jails in 1944 played only a marginal role in the creation of the PCG. After twelve years of harsh imprisonment, "they had forgotten what little they had known of Marxism."[23] More influential were several exiles who had returned to Guatemala in 1944. But their effectiveness was hampered by the fact that they were Marxists, not Marxist-Leninists like the new leaders, and by their arrogance—their wisdom, they believed, gave them the right to lead. This was particularly true of the writer Luis Cardoza y Aragón.

Foreigners, particularly a handful of Salvadoran communists, were the major formative influence on the future leaders of the PCG. These men and women had not been sent by their party or by the Kremlin to spread the credo

[21] The hierarchy of the party was formalized at the second congress (Dec. 1952) as follows: (1) a 5-member Secretariat, led by the secretary general, which met daily; (2) a Political Commission of eleven members (including the Secretariat), which met once a week; (3) a 25-member Central Committee (including the Political Commission), which met every three months. The Secretariat was officially created at the second congress, but its members had constituted the inner core of the party from the outset. The next most important leaders were Víctor Manuel Gutiérrez, Carlos Manuel Pellecer, and José Alberto Cardoza. All were Guatemalans. See Partido Guatemalteco del Trabajo, *Estatutos*, pp. 18–25. For the composition of the Central Committee elected at the 1st Congress, see Alvarado Arellano, *Apuntes*, p. 18. Particularly useful were interviews with Fortuny, Guerra Borges, Pellecer, and Alejandro, the Cuban communist who served as adviser to the Guatemalan Communist Party in 1951–1954. For biographical sketches of the senior party leaders see Schneider, *Communism*, pp. 89–97.

[22] Pellecer, *Renuncia al comunismo*, p. 85. For Pellecer's version of his tribulations from his arrest in Guatemala to his return from Mexico, see his *Memoria en dos geografías*, pp. 111–499. On Fortuny as a student leader in 1942–1944, see Galich, *Del pánico al ataque*, pp. 84, 85, 134–35, 164, 185.

[23] Quoted from interview with Fortuny. Obando Sánchez, the only "old communist" who played more than a marginal role, refers to the 1944–1954 period in his *Memorias*, pp. 114–36. For insights on the "old communists" after 1944, see also Alfonso Solorzano in Quan Rossell, *Guatemala*, 1:245–46.

to Guatemala. They were exiles fleeing persecution; at home their party was in full disarray. In a cruel twist, just one day after Ponce surrendered in Guatemala, a military coup closed the democratic parenthesis in El Salvador that had been ushered in by the fall of Martínez: just as El Salvador had been a haven for Guatemalans between May and October 1944, so Guatemala became a refuge for Salvadorans. Among those who arrived in late 1944 were Miguel Mármol, Graciela García, Matilde Elena López, and Virgilio Guerra—communist party members of many years' standing, well-versed in clandestine work and familiar with Marxist-Leninist theory. They went into action at once, helping to mold the labor movement, working tirelessly, often unable to buy themselves a square meal: "The trade unions didn't have the money to pay their activists, let alone feed them. So I just ate whatever I could, whenever I could, and wherever I could," recalls Mármol.[24]

These Salvadorans were instrumental in the creation, in July 1945, of the labor school Escuela Claridad, which taught both labor organization and Marxism-Leninism. (The school, which had more than sixty students, was closed by Arévalo in January 1946.)[25] In the course of their work (public as union organizers, more discreet as Marxist proselytizers), they were harassed, and some were jailed for brief periods or deported. Yet their efforts bore fruit in the quality if not the quantity of their disciples. The Guatemalans who assembled at the founding congress in September 1949 could boast of impressive credentials: prominent journalists, congressmen, labor leaders, senior members of the PAR. They brought to the party a combination of dynamism, intellect, and integrity that was and would remain unequaled in Guatemalan politics. Two men, in particular, stood out: a twenty-six-year old teacher, Víctor Manuel Gutiérrez, who was a congressman and the secretary general of the CTG;[26] and Fortuny, also a member of Congress, a brilliant journalist and, until March 1949, the secretary general of the PAR.

[24] Dalton, *Miguel Mármol*, pp. 502–3. Two of these Salvadorans have written about their experiences in Guatemala: ibid., pp. 495–521, and García, *Páginas*, pp. 155–212, and *Las luchas revolucionarias*, pp. 57–131.

[25] In addition to the sources listed in nn. 20 and 24 above, see Bishop, "Guatemalan Labor," pp. 16–20, 26, and FBI, Hoover to Lyon, Nov. 23, 1945, NA 814.00.

[26] Gutiérrez resigned from the PCG in November 1949, even before the congress had ended, because of sincerely felt tactical differences. He created, in June 1950, the small Partido Revolucionario Obrero de Guatemala (PROG), which included both communists like Gutiérrez and others, mainly trade unionists, who were drawn by his personality or by the prospect of exploiting his prestige, but did not share his political views.

By 1951 the differences between Gutiérrez and the PCG had decreased markedly, and he was increasingly at odds with many leaders of his own party. Finally, in Feb. 1952, he was able to bring about the dissolution of the PROG. (He had tried in the previous months, but a majority of the leadership had refused to cooperate.) He im-

These may seem bold judgments—yet they parallel the conclusions that were reached by the U.S. embassy in the early 1950s, and they echo the conclusions of U.S. journalists and others whose anti-communist credentials are above suspicion, including those few, particularly Ronald Schneider, who have probed the vast documentary evidence in the *Guatemalan Transcripts*.[27] Schneider presents Gutiérrez as "the honest, humble and soft-spoken Gutiérrez, the revered leader of Guatemalan workers. . . . nicknamed the 'Franciscan' for his ascetic manner of living." Gutiérrez used his scarce free time to study and gave the bulk of his salary as a congressman to the party and the labor confederation, keeping only the bare minimum for himself. He neither sought nor accepted personal favors or privileges.[28] Of course, not all the communist leaders were pillars of virtue like Gutiérrez. Schneider points to Fortuny. "In spite of his obvious talents as a writer, speaker and theoretician," he states, "Fortuny's effectiveness was hampered by an unpleasant personality and the lack of morality in his private life. While Fortuny's contributions to the Guatemalan communist movement cannot be underestimated, he, less than any other leader, fits the image of the selfless, dedicated champion of the people."[29] Fortuny could indeed be abrasive; sure of his moral and intellectual superiority, he lacked Gutiérrez's modesty. His occasional extramarital flings contrast with Gutiérrez's impeccable private life. But not even the U.S. embassy, which devoted many hours to Fortuny, so much as hinted at an instance of corruption on his part. (Nor, for that matter, does Schneider.) One year after the fall of Arbenz, the *New York Times* noted that the communist leaders, unlike the other politicians, had not grown rich on their careers. Fortuny, in particular, "owned only a $200 share in the Communist daily *Tribuna Popular*"[30]—a remarkable feat for a man who had been one of Guatemala's

---

mediately rejoined the PCG and urged the members of the defunct PROG to follow his example. (Many did not.) He was elected forthwith to the Political Commission of the PCG.

For the PROG, and Gutiérrez's early differences with the PCG, see esp. Gutiérrez, *Apuntes*, pp. 25–26, and Alvarado Arellano, *Apuntes*, pp. 17–20, 24–26. The *GT*, Box 9, includes a folder of documents of the PROG. Schneider, *Communism*, pp. 61–68, is useful, but his conclusion, "the influence of the international Communist movement was used to induce Gutiérrez to submit to Communist Party discipline" (p. 68), overlooks the looseness of the Guatemalans' ties to other communist parties. (See below, pp. 183–89.) For a biographical sketch of Gutiérrez, see Thelma de Gutiérrez's testimony in Cáceres, *Aproximación*, pp. 59–76.

[27] See esp. Schneider, *Communism*, chs. 6–8.

[28] Ibid., pp. 94–95. For similar comments by other anticommunist writers, see Bishop, "Guatemalan Labor," p. 25; Suslow, "Social Security," p. 47; James, *Red Design*, p. 112.

[29] Schneider, *Communism*, p. 90.

[30] "Guatemala Reds Lose Properties," *NYT*, May 1, 1955, p. 17. Pellecer, who is

most influential politicians and the president's closest friend. And if Fortuny was scrupulously honest, he was equally gifted, hard-working, and devoted to the party that he has continued to serve, often under the most dangerous circumstances.[31] Marroquín Rojas first crossed swords with him during the 1945 Constituent Assembly. Fortuny is, he wrote, "rebellious, invincible . . . a courageous Congressman, indefatigable, astute and audacious. . . . Fortuny . . . is passionate and vigorous. He is an extremist."[32]

Some PCG leaders were temperamentally similar to Fortuny; others were more like Gutiérrez. They shared, however, honesty and dedication, setting their world far apart from that of Guatemala's other political groups. This was to be a great asset to the party and one of the sources of the ever growing attraction it held for Jacobo Arbenz.

Fortuny began considering himself a Marxist-Leninist in 1948, after joining Guerra Borges, Silva Jonama, Alvarado Monzón, and other PAR members in the Marxist circle Vanguardia Democrática. Together, they tried to lead the PAR toward Marxist positions. Their growing radicalism placed them in a minority within the party's councils; increasingly, they clashed with the anticommunist factions led by Charnaud MacDonald and Humberto González Juárez. At the PAR's convention of March 1949, they were decisively defeated—"We were massacred"—by a 382-to-120 vote.[33] In the name of party unity, they were given posts within the leadership, but they could no longer hope to sway the PAR's course. Aware that a communist party would be able to operate freely once Arbenz had assumed the presidency, they created the PCG in late 1949. A few months later, writes a PCG leader, "We decided that it was time for some of us to go public, while the others stayed underground to protect the party in case Arévalo struck."[34]

On May 20, 1950, Fortuny and his nine friends resigned from the PAR and intimated in their open letter their intention to create a communist party. Then on June 21 the first issue of *Octubre* appeared, and on September 8 the Jacobo

---

now a fervent anticommunist (see below p. 389) and no friend of Fortuny, asserts: "Fortuny was an honest man—an extremely honest man. He hated anything with even a whiff of corruption. This was typical of the leaders of the Communist party. It impressed and attracted me." (Interview with Pellecer.)

[31] See below, p. 389.

[32] Marroquín Rojas, *Crónicas*, pp. 61, 73, and 150.

[33] Interviews with Guerra Borges (quoted), Fortuny, Pellecer, and Charnaud. On the convention, see "Puñetazos y pistolas relucen en la sesión," *El I*, Mar. 16, 1949, p. 1; "Cambio de directiva," *DCA*, Mar. 16, 1949, p. 1; "Principios del Partido Acción Revolucionaria," *DCA*, Mar. 19, 1949, p. 1; Wells to SecState, no. 152, Mar. 22, 1949, NA 814.00; "Segunda convención nacional del PAR," *El Libertador*, Mar. 26, 1949, p. 1; "Nuevos principios de nuestro partido," *El Libertador*, Apr. 2, 1949, p. 1.

[34] Alvarado Arellano, *Apuntes*, p. 19.

Sánchez labor school was inaugurated. The school, explained *Octubre*, would offer "a short and basic course on Marxism."[35]

It was more than the government could tolerate. On September 13, the police closed *Octubre*—the communists had the right to express their views privately, but not to proselytize, explained Arévalo.[36] Two weeks later, the police closed the Jacobo Sánchez school, "and arrested those who were found on the premises—forty in all. . . . They also confiscated all written material, and even the paintings on the walls." Through Arbenz's personal intervention with the chief of police, those who had been detained were set free within a few hours.[37]

Octubre reappeared in November. The Jacobo Sánchez school was closed for two years,[38] at first to assuage anticommunist sensitivities during the electoral campaign, later because the communists had reassessed their priorities. They had too few qualified persons for too many tasks, a problem that would persist throughout the Arbenz years. As labor leaders, members of Congress, journalists, and members of Arbenz's inner circle, they were very busy with the electoral campaign, in addition to their tasks within the PCG. Fortuny, in particular, had a delicate assignment: at Arbenz's request, he wrote his campaign speeches, seeking to put a moderate spin on the issues that Arbenz wanted to address.[39] Unwitting praise for Fortuny's skill came from an exacting source: the Office of Intelligence and Research of the U.S. State Department noted, in late October, that Arbenz's speeches "have been essentially moderate in tone, containing few statements which could be construed as communist-inspired."[40]

While Arbenz was campaigning, Lt. Colonel Castillo Armas, the former *Aranista* commander, was plotting. His escapades would hardly deserve a foot-

[35] "Una escuela para la clase obrera," *Octubre*, Sept. 6, 1950, p. 3. See also "Un éxito la inauguración de la escuela 'Jacobo Sánchez,' " *Octubre*, Sept. 13, 1950, p. 2.

[36] "Cierre de Octubre ante el Congreso," *El I*, Sept. 14, 1950, p. 1; Arévalo to Fortuny, Sept. 20, 1950, *GT*, Box 8. See also Sierra Roldán, *Diálogos*, pp. 30–31. For *Octubre*'s absence in late July and August, see "Octubre de nuevo en la trinchera de lucha" (edit.), *Octubre*, Sept. 6, 1950, p. 1, and "Como vemos la situación actual," ibid., p. 3.

[37] "Escuela comunista 'Jacobo Sánchez' cierra Gobernación," *DCA*, Sept. 29, 1950, p. 1; "40 alumnos de la escuela comunista Jacobo Sánchez estuvieron detenidos," *El I*, Sept. 30, 1950, p. 1 (quoted); Fisher to DOS, no. 368, Oct. 5, 1950, NA 714.001. On Arbenz's role, interviews with Guerra Borges and Fortuny were useful.

[38] See "Segunda reaparición de Octubre," *Octubre*, Nov. 10, 1950, p. 1; "Actividad del partido," *Octubre*, Feb. 19, 1953, p. 7; *JW* 9, Feb. 27, 1953, I:3.

[39] Interviews with Fortuny, Guerra Borges, and María de Arbenz.

[40] "Guatemala: Communist Influence," report no. 5123, Oct. 23, 1950, p. 24, NA.

note were it not that in 1953 he was selected by the CIA to lead the "liberation" of Guatemala.

Castillo Armas and his plotters were united by their opposition to Arbenz and by their lack of realism. Some were former *Aranista* officers; like Castillo Armas, they had been dismissed from the army after the failure of the July uprising and were now bent on avenging their dead leader and their own disgrace. Others belonged to the landed elite. One was the former chief of Ubico's secret police, the notorious José Bernabé Linares, fresh out of jail.[41]

With the landowner Juan Córdova Cerna acting as intermediary, Castillo Armas approached General Ydígoras Fuentes. This was the first in a series of attempts at collaboration between these two intensely ambitious men. Ydígoras did indeed welcome the prospect of a military coup, but only if he lost the elections, that is (as he put it), if the government refused to honor his victory. A coup, he stressed, should be undertaken only to secure his claim to the presidency.[42]

This was not an attitude Castillo Armas could appreciate. His contacts with Ydígoras dragged on in growing acrimony as he continued to hatch his own plot. He struck on November 5, five days before the polls opened. With seventy men he attacked the Base Militar in the capital, confident that the element of surprise and the complicity of a few junior officers within the barracks would guarantee his success. (Castillo Armas, Marroquín Rojas later wrote, was "sure that the Base Militar would be his, as if it were a seat he had reserved at the theater."[43]) His initial victory, he believed, would spark a revolt in the army—a most bizarre proposition, since loyalist officers were in command of the troops.

[41] My main sources on the plot are: (1) CIA reports: "Col. Carlos Castillo Armas in Initial Stage of Organizing Armed Coup Against Guatemalan Government," no. deleted, Jan. 19, 1950; "Growing Opposition to Arbenz in Guatemalan Army Groups," no. S036757, Mar. 9, 1950; "Plans of Colonel Carlos Castillo Armas for Armed Revolt Against the Government," no. deleted, Aug. 24, 1950; "Plans of Colonel Carlos Castillo Armas to Overthrow Guatemalan Government," no. deleted, Nov. 3, 1950—while speaking highly of Castillo Armas, the reports were skeptical of his chances of success; (2) Clemente Marroquín Rojas, "Lo que fué el asalto a la Base Militar," *La Hora*, Sept. 18, 1953, p. 1, and "Temor a la verdad, virtud guatemalteca," *La Hora*, Sept. 21, 1953, p. 1; Pinto Recinos, "La rebelión," July 3, 1985, p. 2 and July 4, 1985, p. 2; Castillo Armas, "Organización del ataque"; (3) Interviews with Castillo Armas' supporters Taracena and Montenegro.

After Castillo Armas seized power in 1954, Linares resumed his old job. (See "J. Bernabé Linares tomó posesión de la Guardia Judicial," *El I*, Aug. 12, 1954, p. 1.)

[42] Interview with Taracena, who was involved in the plot.

[43] Marroquín Rojas, "Lo que fué el asalto a la Base Militar," *La Hora*, Sept. 18, 1953, p. 1.

As late as November 4, Lieutenant Montenegro, one of Castillo Armas' followers, had tried "to reason with him." The revolt, he argued, was hopeless even if they could seize the Base Militar.[44] But Castillo Armas didn't even seize the base. One of his accomplices betrayed him; the attackers were met with heavy fire and swiftly routed. Castillo Armas was wounded and captured; after spending some weeks in the military hospital, he was sent to the penitentiary to await trial.

"Nine Escape Like the Count of Montecristo," blared *El Imparcial* on June 12, 1951.[45] Castillo Armas, helped by other prisoners, had dug a long tunnel under the outer wall—or so he and his admirers have claimed, despite the fact that this would have required the guards to have been blind as well as deaf.[46] A less stirring but more plausible explanation is that some prison officials had been bribed, and the tunnel had been dug with their connivance in order to mask the true circumstances of the escape.[47]

Whatever the truth, Castillo Armas went straight from the penitentiary to the embassy of Colombia, where he sought asylum. On July 3, he left for Bogotá. He was the last of the *Aranistas*, a brave man who had failed to join the revolt of his friends on July 18, 1949, and who had now vindicated himself through his hopeless rebellion.

Castillo Armas was still in jail when on March 15, 1951, Arbenz was inaugurated president of Guatemala. Arbenz's victory at the polls, on November 10–12, 1950, had been massive: 258,987 out of 404,739 ballots cast. Ydígoras had come second, with 72,796 votes, while García Granados trailed as a distant third, followed by Giordani, in a field of ten candidates.[48]

Arbenz's victory had been assured. Ydígoras was the landowners' choice, but he lacked personal appeal and military support. García Granados and Giordani, two distinguished civilians who tempered their support for the revolution with pleas for moderation, had neither charisma nor political base. Arbenz, on the other hand, had the fervent backing of the country's two major political parties and of organized labor, which worked tirelessly on his behalf.[49] He

[44] Interview with Montenegro.

[45] "Nueve evadidos a lo Edmundo Dantés," *El I*, June 12, 1951, p. 1.

[46] For Castillo Armas' highly romanticized version of the escape, see L.A.H.A., *Así se gestó la Liberación*, pp. 10–17 and 51–54, and "Fuga de la Penitenciaria," *El Espectador*, July 3, 1955, p. 4.

[47] Some believe that Castillo Armas owed his freedom to Arbenz, who respected his courage and engineered his escape to avoid creating an unnecessary martyr. (See Cehelsky, "Guatemala's Frustrated Revolution," p. 43.) Arbenz's widow and two of his closest friends firmly reject this theory. (Interviews with María de Arbenz, Fortuny, and Guerra Borges.)

[48] For a breakdown of the vote, see Silvert, *Study in Government*, pp. 59–60.

[49] For two graphic examples, see Comité Político Nacional de los Trabajadores, "In-

would have won even had the elections been completely free, but in the Guatemala of 1950 elections could not be genuinely free. The 1945 constitution gave illiterate males only a public vote and disenfranchised illiterate women. It is naive to imagine that many Indians would have dared vote against the authorities' candidate—be it Ubico, Arana, Arbenz, or Ydígoras. Centuries of oppression had taught them the proper behavior. In the past, the army and the landowners had usually proceeded hand-in-hand; now they were divided. The military's influence reached farther than that of the landowners, and Arbenz was the military's candidate. But Arbenz also won a majority of the secret vote, conceded Marroquín Rojas, himself a defeated candidate. Despite a few incidents, he added, "the campaign was fair," and the elections were free, "as free as they could be in Guatemala."[50]

---

strucciones urgentes para las votaciones," Oct. 1950, *GT*, Box 15, and Comité Político Nacional de los Trabajadores, "Resolución adoptada por la Asamblea de Comités Políticos del departamento de Guatemala en su sesión de el 1o. de noviembre de 1950," ibid. See also Bishop, "Guatemalan Labor," pp. 121–29.

[50] Marroquín Rojas, "Comienzan las alegres elecciones," *La Hora*, Nov. 10, 1950 (quoted from pp. 1, 4); David Goliat (i.e., Marroquín Rojas), "Ya lo ves Chuchín Silva," *La Hora*, Dec. 8, 1950, p. 1; Marroquín Rojas, "Los analfabetos y las elecciones del Coronel Arbenz," *La Hora*, July 13, 1954, p. 4. Only the most partisan critics will find too mild the conclusion of Schneider: the government left "nothing . . . to chance," but "Arbenz was probably the choice of more voters than any of the opposition candidates." (*Communism*, p. 33.) See also Handy, "The Guatemalan Revolution and Civil Rights," esp. pp. 7–11.

CHAPTER 5

The United States and Arévalo: Arévalo's Sins

IN 1944, the United States had believed that Guatemala, with or without Ubico, would remain the docile little neighbor it had been for decades. Washington's confidence was soon shaken. Arévalo refused to show the customary deference to the State Department's "friendly representations."[1] This disquieting departure could be explained, many Americans believed, only by immaturity and the thrall of communism. During the previous half century, only one regime in all of Central America had offended Washington's sensibilities more: that of President José Santos Zelaya in Nicaragua, forced out by the United States in 1909. Washington's reaction to the Arévalo administration must be analyzed against this background of the past servility of Guatemala and the present servility of the other banana republics. While minor problems heightened tensions, the Guatemalans' major sins were two: their "persecution"[2] of American companies and their irresponsible attitude toward communism.

In the eyes of most Americans, it was self-evident that the country of Jefferson was not, and had never been, an imperialist power. The threat to the well-being and the sovereignty of the banana republics came from across the Atlantic. Monroe had been the first to challenge the ambitions of the European powers. Wilson had turned them back, nearly a century later, with his "Protective Imperialism" (strong medicine, perhaps, but administered for generous motives).[3] If at times the United States had been overbearing toward its Latin neighbors, the Good Neighbor Policy of Franklin Delano Roosevelt had removed all reasonable grounds for complaint.[4] Now, in the late 1940s, a new

[1] MemoTel, Aug. 2, 1949, *FRUS*, 1949, 2:659.

[2] The State Department used this term repeatedly, beginning in mid-1947.

[3] In 1940, Samuel Bemis wrote in his influential *The Latin American Policy of the United States*: "Wilson and Bryan . . . strove to strengthen [U.S.] influence and control in these regions in order to remove further than ever justification for any European intervention. All this they covered with a sincere Wilsonian zeal for saving the people from bad government, tyranny, and economic exploitation in order that they might be made fit and stable for self-government, liberty and the pursuit of happiness under protection of the United States. . . . All this the missionaries of Democracy desired in order that 'benighted' peoples might be saved from themselves by themselves" (p. 185).

[4] "Anti-American feeling has seldom been unknown in most countries south of us. A generation ago there was often good reason for it. That it should still exist in spite

enemy threatened the banana republics: Soviet imperialism, as barbarous as German nazism, but even more dangerous. Once again, America called her little sisters to a crusade against a common foe.

But Guatemala's new leaders failed to respond with proper enthusiasm, despite the fact that most of them were anticommunists. They acknowledged that the Soviet Union was an imperialist power, and they proclaimed their solidarity with the United States. But they lacked the zeal of a Somoza or a Trujillo. While Soviet armies threatened European countries, Europe was far away, and it was difficult to blame Russia for the trampled dignity of a banana republic. And the distinguishing mark of the middle-class leaders who came to sudden prominence after the fall of Ubico was their sense of national dignity. Many would discard their idealism as the rewards of power drew them from their roots, but few would discard their nationalism. The United States may have been the champion of the free world, but it was the United States that interfered in Guatemala's internal affairs, and it was American companies that held a stranglehold over the country's economy.

AMERICAN COMPANIES IN GUATEMALA

Total U.S. investment in Guatemala in 1944 was about $93 million,[5] concentrated in three companies: the Empresa Eléctrica de Guatemala, a subsidiary of Electric Bond and Share; the International Railways of Central America; and the United Fruit Company.

Empresa Eléctrica, originally a German company, had been seized by the Guatemalan government during World War I. The Wilson administration was as eager to pry this thriving concern from its new owners as the Guatemalans were reluctant to relinquish it. President Manuel Estrada Cabrera refused to sell the company to the Americans. He was overthrown in April 1920. His successor, Carlos Herrera, proved equally obtuse. In December 1921, he too was toppled. Herrera's successor eagerly agreed to the sale.[6] Nationalistic Guatemalans did not forget this story. Nor did they forget the paltry price that

---

of our Good Neighbor policy is baffling.'' ("The Guatemalan Incident," edit., *NYT*, Apr. 8, 1950, p. 12.)

[5] United States Treasury Department, *Census*, p. 70, table 2; CIA, "Guatemala," SR-46, July 27, 1950, p. 32, Truman Papers, President's Secretary's File, Intelligence File, Box 261, TL.

[6] As Munro argues, the Wilson administration had not plotted against Estrada Cabrera; yet "the erroneous belief that the United States had turned against the President seems to have been an important factor in the rapid growth of the opposition movement." The same belief contributed to the fall of Herrera. (*Intervention and Dollar Diplomacy*, p. 460.) See also Pitti, "Ubico," pp. 20–38, 48–61, 68–72, 83, 88–104; Baker, "Woodrow Wilson Administration"; Dinwoodie, "Expedient Diplomacy," pp. 146–78.

the Americans had paid. Nor were they blind to the privileges the U.S. company had received. Resentment was fueled by the high rates charged by Empresa Eléctrica, which exploited its position of virtual monopoly (it supplied about 80 percent of the country's electricity) and by the poor service it provided. In 1944 the company was using the same equipment it had used in the 1920s.[7]

Unlike Empresa Eléctrica, the International Railways of Central America (IRCA) did not owe its status to direct U.S. pressure. President Estrada Cabrera was responsible for its monopoly and its privileges. Except for the state-owned 29.5 mile Verapaz Railway (seized from German owners during World War II) and the 207.1 miles of rail owned by United Fruit on its plantations, Guatemala's railways belonged to IRCA: 580.7 miles of single-track rail.[8] The absence of an adequate road system reinforced IRCA's monopoly. In particular, no road connected the capital with the Caribbean harbor of Puerto Barrios—an "inexplicable failure," the World Bank noted in 1951, since Puerto Barrios was Guatemala's only deep water port and accounted for over 60 percent of the country's foreign trade.[9] Not only did IRCA control the rail link between Puerto Barrios and the capital, it also owned Puerto Barrios' only pier.

Two ports on Guatemala's Pacific coast (San José and Champerico) played a minor role in the country's foreign trade; IRCA owned the pier at San José, and that of Champerico belonged to a subsidiary of the Grace Line. In other words, the three ports of any significance in Guatemala's foreign trade belonged to U.S. companies. Guatemala was not alone. As the United Nations observed in 1953, only three of the major ports of Central America were controlled by nationals; the others were in the hands of American companies. "Thus, there is a virtual monopoly of the foreign trade of the Central American countries, and it is impossible for them to control the port fees which are frequently excessive and discriminatory." This was the case, the report stated, at Puerto Barrios.[10]

As long as Ubico ruled, no criticism of IRCA had been permitted in Guatemala. After his ouster, Guatemalans complained loudly that IRCA's rates

[7] For a detailed analysis of Empresa Eléctrica see IBRD, *Economic Development*, pp. 218–43. The report focused on 1950, but its comments are also valid for 1945, since there were no significant changes in the intervening years. Bush, "Organized Labor," part 2, pp. 97–102, discusses the company's labor relations under Arévalo.

[8] IBRD, *Economic Development*, pp. 132–210, is the best analysis of transportation in Guatemala in the late 1940s. Also important is United Nations, *El transporte*. For background on IRCA, see Solis, *Los ferrocarriles*.

[9] Quoted from IBRD, *Economic Development*, p. 184. For the percentages see LaBarge, "Impact of the United Fruit," pp. 16–17, table 4.

[10] United Nations, *El transporte*, p. 218. For San José and Champerico, see de León Aragón, *Los contratos*, pp. 195–231.

were exorbitant; with equal fervor, the company proclaimed its innocence. In 1951, the World Bank concluded that while IRCA's rates for passenger traffic were reasonable, its average freight rates "exceed[ed] those of many other countries." They were higher, for instance, than comparable rates in the United States although, the report pointed out, the reverse should have been true. "It is quite possible," the bank observed with customary caution, "that they are higher than they should be," and it went on to stress "the absence of effective competition" and "the lack of any governmental control over IRCA's rates."[11]

To one customer, however, IRCA charged a bargain basement price: United Fruit, which owned 42.68 percent of IRCA's shares, paid about half the normal rate. (The rate was, a New York court later found, "unfair and unconscionable.")[12] Special treatment extended beyond price setting. In 1953, the United Nations observed:

> The community of interest between the railroad company . . . and the banana company has created a situation that does not always benefit the economy of the country. . . . The trains that carry bananas are given absolute priority; when they are running, all other trains must wait in a siding. Furthermore, they receive special treatment in the ports and have priority in loading and unloading. Therefore the trains and ships that do not carry bananas are forced to wait. In fact, the loading and unloading of other goods is interrupted in order to attend to the bananas.[13]

The World Bank flatly concluded: "to all intents and purposes, [Puerto Barrios] . . . is under the complete control of the United Fruit Company and the International Railways Company. That control extends over the movement of practically all import and export cargo through the Atlantic area."[14]

If IRCA was powerful, United Fruit was a colossus. It had been created in 1899, the result of a merger between the personal empire of Minor Keith, who

---

[11] IBRD, *Economic Development*, p. 172.

[12] Quoted from "United Fruit Loses $4,500,000 Rail Suit," *NYT*, June 29, 1959, p. 17. In 1949, minority stockholders of IRCA sued United Fruit, claiming that the freight rates paid by the latter were excessively low. In a series of judgments between 1957 and 1960, the court ordered United Fruit to pay IRCA $4.5 million plus interest, to pay higher freight rates for future shipments, and to divest itself of all shares of IRCA. See the coverage in the *NYT*: "Damage Suit Lost by United Fruit Co.," July 2, 1957, p. 44; "Award Put At $5,519,000," July 16, 1957, p. 37; "United Fruit Debt to Railroad Set," Dec. 19, 1957, p. 49; "Appeal is Argued in United Fruit Suit," Feb. 11, 1959, p. 77; "United Fruit Loses $4,500,000 Rail Suit," June 24, 1959, p. 17; "65 Million Claim Is Filed in Court," Mar. 25, 1960, p. 37; "State Appeals Court Upholds the Award," Dec. 2, 1960, p. 41. See also "Resumen seleccionado," *Economía*, pp. 31–32, 37–42, and 51–52.

[13] United Nations, *El transporte*, p. 13.

[14] IBRD, *Economic Development*, p. 185.

built railroads in Central America, and the Boston Fruit Company, which imported bananas from the Caribbean islands. Managed with ruthlessness, skill, and ambition, UFCO earned its sobriquet: the Octopus. As Arévalo ascended to the presidency, it was the world's greatest grower and exporter of bananas.

The heart of its empire was in Guatemala, Honduras, and Costa Rica, where it owned well over 1 million acres of banana plantations; but it also had plantations in Panama, Colombia, Ecuador, Jamaica, Cuba, and the Dominican Republic.[15] The Great White Fleet—eighty-five ships—carried UFCO's bananas to North America and Europe, making the company the largest carrier of the fruit.[16] The ships also carried a significant percentage of the foreign trade of many of the smaller republics in which UFCO operated, as well as some passenger traffic. The fleet was "more than a source of income: it was a symbol of the company's dominions—at home, in the tropics, and on the seven seas."[17] Still another tentacle had been added to UFCO in 1913, when the Tropical Radio Telegraph Company was incorporated to assure communications between the field and UFCO's Boston headquarters. By 1945, it controlled an important part of the international radio and cable traffic of Central America. The last major component of this well-integrated empire was the railroad. UFCO itself owned 1,400 miles of rail, mostly within its plantations. It also owned 42.6 percent of IRCA, whose 794 miles of railroad constituted "the most extensive rail network between Mexico and Panama."[18]

UFCO's annual budget was larger than those of the Central American countries in which it operated. Although by U.S. standards the largest company in Central America was not a giant, it was a well respected and well connected company, particularly in Massachusetts. This was evident in the Massachu-

---

[15] See UFCO's Annual Reports for 1944 and 1945, and Pollan, *United Fruit Company.* There is a large and highly partisan literature on United Fruit. The most sophisticated apologists are LaBarge, "A Study of United Fruit"; May and Plaza, *United Fruit.* Two classic studies, critical and well-documented, are Kepner, *Social Aspects of the Banana Industry* and Kepner and Soothill, *Banana Empire.* On Minor Keith, see Stewart, *Keith and Costa Rica.* For studies focusing specifically on UFCO and Guatemala, see LaBarge, "Impact of the United Fruit," and Bauer Paiz, *Como opera el capital yanqui*; both studies are highly partisan, but interesting.

[16] There were eighty-five ships in UFCO's fleet in 1940, before the losses caused by World War II. As soon as the conflict ended, "replacements were rushed down the ways. . . . The new recruits are better and faster." ("Banana Split—a la Zemurray," *Business Week*, May 4, 1946, p. 42.) For the modernization of the fleet in the immediate postwar period, see also "Great White Fleet," *Unifruitco*, Aug.–Sept. 1948, pp. 14–21.

[17] McCann, *American Company*, p. 24.

[18] United Nations, *El transporte*, p. 9. "From a practical standpoint," a U.S. official explained, "the United Fruit Company probably may be said to control IRCA. However, to our knowledge, this has never been admitted." (Ballentine to Wells, enclosed in Wells to Clark, Apr. 10, 1951, NA 714.00.)

setts delegation to the U.S. Congress. UFCO's shareholders included the venerable Cabots—Thomas was briefly the company's president in 1948, and his brother, John Moors, was assistant secretary of state for inter-American affairs in 1953.

Several high-powered lobbyists were on call to remind the State Department and influential Americans that United Fruit deserved their affection and their support. These included the former senator, Robert La Follette, who could boast impressive liberal credentials, and the prominent Washington lawyer, Thomas Corcoran. In the early 1940s, UFCO had hired yet another liberal, Edward Bernays, "the father of public relations" and "the biggest name in his field."[19] A battery of lawyers from America's most prominent law firms complemented the lobbyists' efforts. Indeed, as many authors have stressed, when the prestigious law firm of Sullivan and Cromwell negotiated UFCO's contract with Ubico in 1936, one of the firm's senior associates was John Foster Dulles.[20]

UFCO had expanded swiftly and efficiently in Guatemala. In a 1924 agreement with President Orellana, it consolidated and enlarged its holdings on the Caribbean coast, creating the immense division of Bananera; in 1930 it moved onto Guatemala's Pacific shore, receiving an expansive tract at Tiquisate. By 1945, it was the country's largest private landowner and biggest employer, dwarfing all others with its 566,000 acres of land and more than 15,000 workers. (The second largest private employer was IRCA, which employed approximately five thousand.)

For years, apologists and critics of United Fruit have engaged in fierce debate. After diplomatically conceding that the record is not untarnished, the apologists point out that UFCO was not forced on Guatemala by gunboat diplomacy; they add that it played a very positive role in the development of the country's resources and paid millions of dollars in taxes. It centered its activities in undeveloped areas "that otherwise might have remained closed to settlement and productive use for many decades,"[21] and it introduced medical and sanitation services. The company's workers, they stress, were better paid, better fed, and better housed than those who toiled for other landowners.

There is some truth to these claims. Until the presidency of Arévalo, the State Department never intervened formally on behalf of UFCO: the company had never required such assistance. Yet there are more subtle forms of pressure. During the negotiations that led to the 1930 contract with President Chacón (the only time the company did not blithely get its way) the dispatches of the U.S. embassy to Washington expressed warm sympathy for UFCO's de-

[19] McCann, *American Company*, p. 45.
[20] On Dulles in the interwar period, see Pruessen, *Dulles*, chs. 4–7.
[21] May and Plaza, *United Fruit*, p. 230.

mands,[22] and it is inconceivable that the embassy hid this sympathy from the Guatemalan authorities.

Although UFCO developed previously neglected regions, it did so in return for immense privileges. Indeed, after the fall of Ubico, an internal State Department document acknowledged, "Foreign companies, through arrangements favorable to the dictator in power at the moment, have been able to obtain large concessions and large privileges." Among these privileges were the tax breaks granted to UFCO, IRCA, and Empresa Eléctrica—which were in no way modified under Arévalo. In a detailed 1950 study, three U.S. financial experts concluded, "A careful estimate indicates that in all three cases the tax liability is in the neighborhood of one-half of what it would be in the absence of the contracts."[23]

But Empresa Eléctrica and UFCO (evidence is lacking in the case of IRCA) evaded even their paltry fiscal obligations. As the Guatemalan government discovered when it audited the company in 1953, Empresa Eléctrica had consistently resorted to creative accounting.[24] And UFCO—like all large landowners in Guatemala—regularly undervalued its land in its tax declarations. Going beyond such elementary cheating, it also used methods that local landowners could not imitate. When UFCO shipped bananas to subsidiaries in North America and Europe, it recorded the sales at below market prices.[25] The fraud was exposed by the Canadian Trade Commissioner in a 1949 article:

> In total trade with Canada, Guatemala achieved [in 1948] a balance in her favor of $499,969, according to Guatemalan statistics. Canadian statistics show this balance to be much larger. This is due to the fact that the United Fruit Company, in its intercompany trading between Guatemala and the United States, only places a small nominal value on banana exports. On entry into Canada, they are recorded at their proper value which is some 700 percent higher than recorded in the Guatemalan export returns.[26]

Had UFCO declared the true value of the bananas, stated a 1950 CIA report, "bananas will be seen to contribute at least 39 percent of the total exports (by value) and coffee 47 percent or less," rather than the official averages of 20 percent and 60 percent respectively.[27] Reminiscing in 1976, a former United Fruit vice president cited other ways the company evaded its taxes. These gimmicks, he said, had become more sophisticated since the 1950s, but no

[22] See Pitti, "Ubico," p. 388.

[23] Quotations from "Current Relations with Guatemala," May 1950, *FRUS*, 1950, 2:898, and Adler, Schlesinger, and Olson, *Public Finance*, p. 124.

[24] See the well-documented analysis in Bauer Paiz, "La Electric Bond and Share Company," esp. pp. 31–34.

[25] Adler, Schlesinger, and Olson, *Public Finance*, p. 34.

[26] Birkett, "Confidence in Guatemala," p. 1010.

[27] CIA (see n. 5 above), p. 24.

one ever resorted to the "shell game" with "one shred more enthusiasm . . . than United Fruit demonstrated in those simpler days, starting with its very beginning."[28]

Until the fall of Ubico, the Guatemalan state allowed UFCO to operate as a private fiefdom, never interfering on behalf of the workers. While Guatemalan employers were similarly protected, UFCO had a special advantage: because of its power and the power of the American flag, it was spared the dictators' whims. Neither Estrada Cabrera (1898–1920) nor Ubico tolerated any show of disrespect toward United Fruit. Only in the 1920s, between dictators, did UFCO experience minor annoyances. Some criticism was voiced in the Guatemalan Congress and press, and there were uncharacteristic delays when the company requested more concessions.[29] Worse, in 1923 UFCO faced an assault from an unlikely quarter; its laborers went on strike. "The work is so well paid that . . . certain hidden motives" must be behind the strike, company officials told the U.S. embassy; agitators were "intimidating peaceful employees, and . . . spreading all kinds of Bolsheviki propaganda." The Guatemalan government promptly sent in the troops, but the company was not satisfied. The Minister of Development had urged UFCO to recognize the labor union, an attitude that was "nothing short of Bolshevism."[30]

Once Ubico assumed power, there were no more wayward ministers or ungrateful laborers, and UFCO remained undisturbed until 1944, an aloof feudal lord entrenched in its outlying domains and respected by the weak sovereign of the land. Dictatorship had served UFCO well in Guatemala—so well, in fact, that the company had become complacent and was unruffled at Ubico's fall.

UFCO's record on labor relations was indeed superior to that of the coffee elite. UFCO's workers were treated harshly by their white overlords,[31] but the coffee barons paid wages that were even more miserable and their brutality was seldom tempered by their much vaunted paternalism. Second to none in the virulence of their racism, they considered their Indian workers savages.[32]

[28] McCann, *American Company*, p. 41.

[29] See Pitti, "Ubico," pp. 286, 360–61, 386–90, 489.

[30] Quotations from R. K. Thomas, "Memorandum," Feb. 24, 1923, p. 3, and Thomas, "Memorandum re: Strike United Fruit Company Laborers," Mar. 4, 1923, pp. 4, 7, both enclosed in Thomas to Geissler, Mar. 7, 1923, RG165 RF, Box 1562, NA-S.

[31] See Williams, "Rise of the Banana Industry," pp. 111–22. Williams's account of UFCO's racism is particularly telling because he is generally sympathetic to UFCO.

[32] The extent to which UFCO's real wages were higher than those paid by the coffee elite has been the subject of fierce debate. The best study is Kepner, *Social Aspects of the Banana Industry*, pp. 109–59. Kepner concludes that UFCO's real wages were higher than those paid by other landowners, but that the difference was relatively small.

Judged by these standards, UFCO was a fair employer. For the company, its squalid record was a source of pride.

UNITED FRUIT AND THE ARÉVALO ADMINISTRATION

UFCO entered the Arévalo period confident of its power, its legal rights, and its position as Guatemala's model employer. It extended the hand of friendship to the new authorities, ready to entertain with them the same warm relations it had enjoyed with Ubico. It would not be long, however, before the company felt betrayed and persecuted. These feelings were shared by Empresa Eléctrica and IRCA, but UFCO would lead the struggle against the new government and, later, against Arbenz.

One of UFCO's grievances had some validity. The Arévalo administration was more vigorous in its protection of UFCO's workers than of other rural laborers. It may seem peculiar that a government so timid toward the native elite dared to disturb the American giant. In part, the paradox is explained by the nationalism of the revolutionary leaders. More disturbing than the plight of the peasants was the presence in their midst of an imperial enclave.[33] Another consideration was equally significant: unlike those who tilled the land of the coffee elite, UFCO's 15,000 workers had begun to organize in the summer of 1944, they had actively supported the candidacy of Arévalo, and they were closely connected with the urban labor movement.[34]

How grave were the sins of the Guatemalan government against United Fruit? Beyond offering some legal protection to the company's workers, Arévalo did not disturb UFCO's privileges. The day would come when, reeling under Arbenz's blows, United Fruit would remember Arévalo's "extremism" with something akin to nostalgia. At the time, however, the company was outraged by the Guatemalans' "aggressions."

While minor disputes between U.S. companies and the government had surfaced soon after Ponce's overthrow,[35] organized labor posed no serious

[33] For a vivid expression of this frustrated nationalism, see Bauer Paiz, *Como opera el capital yanqui*, and de León Aragón, *Los contratos*.

[34] For an eloquent statement to this effect by the Guatemalan ambassador in Washington, see MemoConv (García Granados, Braden), May 29, 1947, p. 1, NA 814.504. For the most comprehensive discussion of United Fruit's labor unions, see Bush, "Organized Labor," part 2, pp. 13–39.

[35] The first such dispute (the Denby affair) had pitted the Guatemalan government against Pan American Airways and Alfred Denby, an American citizen who had been a close associate of Ubico. The dispute, which provoked the intervention of the State Department, was settled in 1947 on terms that were satisfactory to the U.S. (For a good summary, see Immerman, *CIA in Guatemala*, pp. 86–87, and the *NYT*: "Guatemalan Line Set Up," Mar. 18, 1945, III-7; "Airline Seizure Approved," Nov. 25, 1945, p.

challenge to UFCO until 1947. The strike that broke out at Bananera in early October 1946 was only an annoyance. The strikers demanded higher wages and "an improvement in living conditions and treatment." It was the first strike in two decades, and it spread rapidly through the plantation. Even "the maids working for Americans have quit," noted the conservative *El Imparcial*. For the first time in the history of Bananera, white American women "are doing all their own housework—running errands and even cleaning their houses."[36] UFCO refused to negotiate. *El Imparcial* itself contrasted the intransigence of the company with the good behavior of the strikers and the moderate nature of their demands. Intransigence triumphed: when work resumed at the end of October, the company's only concession was to promise that it would take no reprisals. The settlement galled many Guatemalans.[37]

In May 1947, the Labor Code was enacted. For the remainder of the Arévalo presidency, this Labor Code was, to UFCO, the symbol of its persecution. While the list of the offending articles was long, one principle particularly riled UFCO. This principle established different degrees of protection and benefits for workers in industrial, commercial, or agricultural enterprises. Agricultural laborers employed in estates of five hundred or more permanent workers were granted many of the rights of industrial workers. While several Fincas Nacionales and at least four Guatemalan landowners fell into this category, so too did UFCO. The principle was blatantly discriminatory, UFCO charged; the offending articles had to be modified or removed.[38] The company turned to the State Department for support.

22; "Guatemala to Pay for Airline," May 22, 1947, p. 8; "Guatemala Paying Airline Claim," Dec. 22, 1947, p. 17.)

[36] "Toda Bananera está en huelga," *El I*, Oct. 16, 1946, p. 1 (quoted from p. 11). Writing in the late 1950s, LaBarge observed that in UFCO's plantations "the grievances that cause the most bitter conflicts are those which reflect upon the workers' status as human beings. . . . The attitude that 'these people' are an insensitive, inferior and stupid species for whom the most common courtesies are not required probably costs the Company more in strikes, in slowdowns, and in general bad relations and publicity than the entire battle against the banana diseases." ("A Study of United Fruit," p. 276.)

[37] *El I* provided the best coverage of this 1946 strike; see "A 60 fincas y 1,600 muelleros abarca el tremendo paro," Oct. 17, p. 1; "Junta en el Ministerio de Economía," Oct. 24, p. 1; "No acepta condiciones la Frutera," Oct. 25, p. 1; "El gobierno da fin a la huelga," Oct. 26, p. 1; "Terminada en firme la huelga," Oct. 30, p. 1; "Reanudada hoy la labor en el Atlantico," Oct. 31, p. 1. See also the reports for Oct. and Nov. 1946 by the Governor of Izabal, nos. 5568 and 5948, IMJP:G, Leg. 32721, AGCA.

[38] For representative statements by the company, listing the "discriminatory" articles, see La Follette to Braden, June 23, 1947, enclosed in La Follette to Newbegin, July 15, 1947; DOS, "Guatemalan Labor Code—Possible Discrimination against United Fruit Company," July 17, 1947; Corcoran to Newbegin, Aug. 1, 1947 (enclos-

The details of UFCO's interaction with the U.S. government during the presidencies of Arévalo and Arbenz will be known only when the company's archives are opened, and this, one of its lobbyists has delicately noted, "may take a very long time, since they [UFCO's successors at United Brands] may consider the record damning."[39] The available evidence indicates that the American Republics Area (ARA) of the State Department showed an "immediate grasp of the problem presented to the United Fruit Company by the . . . labor code," as an appreciative lobbyist wrote to Assistant Secretary Spruille Braden.[40] Braden's grasp was indeed so acute that he began to upbraid the Guatemalan ambassador without bothering to wait for the Legal Office of the State Department to determine whether the Labor Code was in fact discriminatory.[41] In mid-July, the legal adviser submitted his report. After conceding that two minor articles *might* be discriminatory, he categorically rejected the crux of UFCO's case: the State Department, he warned, "could hardly maintain" that the code's distinction between larger and smaller agricultural enterprises was discriminatory, since this same principle was recognized "in labor laws in the United States as well as in foreign countries."[42]

ARA was not perturbed. In late July, a senior ARA official left Washington for Guatemala. UFCO had requested that the State Department send "a good strong man" to press the company's case on the Guatemalan authorities.[43] Ever obliging, UFCO had even selected the ideal envoy, Raymond Geist, a Foreign Service officer stationed in Mexico. Braden, however, believed that it would be better if the special envoy spoke Spanish—not one of Geist's talents. He suggested the chief of ARA's Division of Central America and Panama Affairs, Robert Newbegin, "a person of backbone and initiative," who, he assured lobbyist La Follette, could be relied on "to present our case forcefully."[44]

---

ing copy of the memo of same date by William Taillon, UFCO manager in Guatemala, to Arévalo); La Follette to Newbegin, Aug. 12, 1947. All NA 814.504. For a list of employers with a permanent work force of more than five hundred, see Taillon to UFCO's Vice President S. G. Baggett, Nov. 29, 1948, NA 814.00.

[39] Interview with Robert Corrigan, a representative for United Brands, Washington, D.C., Sept. 15, 1981.

[40] La Follette to Braden, May 23, 1947, NA 814.504.

[41] MemoConv (García Granados, Braden), May 24, 1947, NA 814.504.

[42] MemoConv ("Guatemalan Labor Code and Possible Discrimination against United Fruit Company"), July 22, 1947, p. 1, NA 814.504. See also MemoConv (La Follette, Newbegin), July 18, 1947, NA 814.504.

[43] La Follette to Braden, May 23, 1947, NA 814.504.

[44] MemoConv ("Guatemalan Labor Code"), June 2, 1947 (quoted from p. 2); see also La Follette to Braden, June 23, 1947, enclosed in La Follette to Newbegin, July 15, 1947; MemoConv ("Effect of Guatemalan Labor Law on United Fruit Company"), July 10, 1947; Corcoran to Newbegin, July 21, 1947. All NA 814.504.

And so, Newbegin descended on Guatemala, as did several UFCO lobbyists and officials offering moral support and guidance. Newbegin was, indeed, a man of backbone and initiative. He began by informing the Guatemalan foreign minister that the purpose of his trip was "solely" to discuss the Labor Code and to urge the government to rewrite the offending articles "so that the Company could operate with sufficient guarantees and assurances."[45] While he resisted UFCO's suggestion that he file "an immediate protest," he sternly warned the Guatemalans that their treatment of UFCO "might well have a serious effect upon relations between the two countries."[46] It was a performance, concluded La Follette, that "impressed the Guatemalan authorities."[47]

Nevertheless, the Guatemalan government did not remove the offending articles, and UFCO's labor unions began to demand that the company comply with the code. While pressure mounted, UFCO officials and lobbyists flooded the State Department and the embassy with complaints and prognostications. At times they contended that the economic burden of compliance would be intolerable.[48] More often, they argued from a loftier height. It was not the cost that troubled them, but the injustice: UFCO was being penalized because it was owned by Americans. "The history of the Labor Code," explained lobbyist Corcoran, "indicated clearly that it had been adopted in order to discriminate against the United Fruit Company."[49] Where would appeasement lead? More than the survival of American investment in Guatemala was at stake; surrender in Guatemala would encourage "legal and pseudo-legal assaults on foreign enterprises in many places of Latin America."[50]

The discriminatory nature of the Labor Code was the result, UFCO asserted, of more than the greed of the labor leaders and the chauvinism of the Guatemalan authorities. Far more dangerous forces were at work: the Arévalo administration "was subjected to communistic influences emanating from outside Guatemala."[51] Addressing this accusation squarely, in June 1947 a junior official at the embassy in Guatemala introduced a note of caution:

[45] MemoConv, July 30, 1947, *FRUS*, 1947, 8:708–10, quoted from pp. 708, 709.

[46] Quotations from MemoConv ("United Fruit Company and Guatemalan Labor Code"), Aug. 4, 1947, p. 1, NA 814.504/7–2447, and MemoConv, July 30, 1947, *FRUS*, 1947, 8:709.

[47] MemoConv (La Follette, Newbegin), Aug. 7, 1947, NA 814.504.

[48] MemoConv ("Effect of Guatemalan Labor Law on United Fruit Company"), July 10, 1947, NA 814.504. ("Mr. Corcoran declared that the company might find it necessary to reduce its personnel now from 17,000 to less than 500 in order to avoid the penalties of the present law," p. 1.)

[49] MemoConv ("Guatemalan Labor Code and Possible Discrimination against United Fruit Company"), July 22, 1947, p. 2, NA 814.504.

[50] "Labor Pact Likely in Guatemala Now," *NYT*, Feb. 26, 1949, p. 5.

[51] MemoConv ("Effect of Guatemalan Labor Law on United Fruit Company"), July 10, 1947, p. 1, NA 814.504.

In its opening paragraph the United Fruit Company memorandum states that "foreign influence has evidently been very effective" in the preparation of the Code. This is of course true, since one of the principal drafters of the Code was Licenciado Oscar Barahona Streber, a Costa Rican. Most of the Code is modeled on the similar Costa Rican document. . . . The Labor Commission of the Guatemalan Legislature appears to have made every effort to take into consideration the observations of all sectors affected by the Code, and apparently took the advice of the United Fruit Company and the International Railways of Central America in many cases. The final document cannot be considered radical or revolutionary in any sense, except that no coordinated labor legislation existed in this country previously.[52]

No one else in the embassy expressed such iconoclastic views, not even the amiable Edwin Kyle, who served as U.S. ambassador from May 1945 to August 1948. Kyle was not unsympathetic to the Guatemalan government, and he believed that the suspicions of communist influence "were without foundation, at least in so far as President Arévalo is concerned." (He had misgivings, however, about Foreign Minister Enrique Muñoz Meany, "especially on the communist charge," and did not consider Arbenz as "dependable" as Arana.) Judiciously, Kyle pointed out that "a great deal" of the criticism directed at the Arévalo administration "came from the country's wealthy property owners and that it reminded him of opinions expressed by some of his wealthy fellow Texans relative to President Roosevelt."[53] It apparently never occurred to him that UFCO might also be a biased critic. On the contrary, he had only praise for the company. In June 1947, the same month that one of his subordinates challenged UFCO's assessment of the Labor Code, Kyle wrote, "I have every possible confidence in the United Fruit Company. As I told the [Guatemalan] Foreign Minister, I am convinced that next to what the Standard Oil Company is doing for the people and Government of Venezuela, that the United Fruit Company comes next in all of the Central and South American countries as doing the most for the territory in which it operates." His views did not change in the following year when the conflict between the company and the host government deepened. UFCO, he told the State Department as he returned to private life in the summer of 1948, "was doing a really constructive job in its Latin American relations."[54]

No one should accuse the unflappable Kyle of opportunism. He was an elderly dean of agriculture from Texas who had not sought to be an ambassa-

[52] Stines to Ives, June 6, 1947, quoted from p. 1, enclosed in Donovan to SecState, June 10, 1947, NA 814.504.

[53] MemoConv ("Final Remarks of Ambassador Edwin J. Kyle Relative to Guatemala"), Aug. 30 and Sept. 1, 1948, pp. 1, 2, NA 814.00. Muñoz Meany was foreign minister between June 1948 and August 1949.

[54] Quotations from Kyle to Newbegin, June 26, 1947, pp. 1–2, NA 814.504 and "Final Remarks" (see n. 53 above), p. 2.

dor and who looked forward to retirement.[55] Like a great many Americans, he believed in the virtues of big business and in the positive role it played in backward countries. He saw no contradiction between his exuberant praise of UFCO and his goodwill toward the Arévalo administration. He failed to realize that this praise lent credibility to UFCO's claim that sinister forces were at work in the Guatemalan government.

THE COMMUNIST THREAT

In July 1948, the legal adviser to the State Department intervened a second time, urging that "until we can establish that the United Fruit Company is, in practice, being discriminated against, we should take some steps to have the Embassy diminish its vigorous pressure on the Guatemalan Government."[56]

Such qualms did not trouble the officials at ARA. What concerned them was the communist threat. Nor was the new ambassador, Richard Patterson, who replaced Kyle in the summer of 1948, given to legalistic caution. Patterson was as arrogant as Kyle had been courteous; he was devoid of sympathy for the Guatemalan government and highly receptive to allegations of communist influence. He was, in short, in tune with United Fruit, as well as with the senior embassy staff and ARA officials in Washington.[57]

Initially the U.S. had viewed neither the revolution nor Arévalo with suspicion. There was some uneasiness, however, about the region as a whole. An August 1945 intelligence analysis had remarked that in Latin America "mass discontent is more acute than at any time in the past century," and it had listed Guatemala as one of the countries "where the old forms of society and government have completely broken down and new forms are in process of emergence." The assessment of the Arévalo administration was favorable; the only reservation was whether it would have the ability to direct the difficult transition.[58] Such concerns about the future of Latin America were amorphous and fleeting. A December 1946 intelligence report on Soviet objectives in the Western Hemisphere, for example, expressed no anxiety about communism in Central America, except in Costa Rica. In the other four republics, the report

[55] Interview with Woodward. For background on Kyle, see the Kyle Papers, Cornell University.

[56] MemoConv ("Section 130 of the Guatemalan Labor Code"), July 21, 1948, p. 2, NA 814.504.

[57] The Truman Library has two boxes of Patterson's personal papers that complement his dispatches from Guatemala and illuminate his personality.

[58] Office of Strategic Services, Research and Analysis Branch, "Estimate of the Situation in Central and South America," R&A no. 3356, Aug. 28, 1945, quoted from pp. 1 and 2, NA.

noted, the Communist party was banned, and "there is no indication that if any real communists exist, they have an appreciable influence."[59]

It was United Fruit that first raised the specter of serious communist infiltration in Guatemala, and it was the introduction of the Labor Code that provoked it to do so. In the months that followed, the company's accusations fell on fertile ground. It was evident that several labor leaders and politicians had veered sharply to the left. (The FBI had been collecting information on rogues such as Fortuny and Gutiérrez for over two years.)[60] Moreover, the Labor Code encouraged the fledgling labor movement and exasperated the upper class, which began to brandish charges of communist infiltration with even greater gusto than did UFCO.

Meanwhile the Cold War deepened. In 1945 and 1946 the Truman administration had shown antipathy toward dictatorial rule and sympathy for democratic regimes in its Latin American policy. By 1948, this stance had changed into appreciation for dictators as the strongest defense against communism. (Dictators, moreover, tended to be more friendly to American companies than were popularly elected presidents.)

Many U.S. officials accepted that social reforms were long overdue in Latin America, and some even intimated that such reforms could be the best antidote to communism. But reforms were acceptable only if they did not enhance the prestige of men whom Washington distrusted, such as Guatemala's labor leaders. Furthermore, these reforms must respect established American economic interests, and they must not antagonize the elites, those stalwart friends of the United States who benefited from the injustice of the status quo.

Although U.S. officials conceded that American firms abroad were at times persecuted simply because of the host governments naïveté, greed, and chauvinism, they were also on guard to the ever present danger of communism; very close scrutiny of the reformers was in order. The standards against which the Arévalo administration was judged were Ubico's Guatemala and the undemocratic regimes of El Salvador, Honduras, and Nicaragua.

U.S. officials were ill-equipped to assess the men who led Guatemala. They also lacked accurate information. They had been accustomed to a country where even in the moments of political opening (as in the 1920s) the relevant actors were few, well-known, and predictable: the upper class and aspiring military *caudillos*. Information was gathered in the beautiful houses of the

[59] DOS, Intelligence Research Report, "Soviet Policy and Objectives in the Other American Republics," OCL-4185, Dec. 31, 1946, quoted from p. 10, NA.

[60] See Hoover to Lyon, Jan. 14, 1946; Hoover to Lyon, Mar. 13, 1946; Lyon to Hoover, Apr. 5, 1946; Hoover to Lyon, Apr. 19, 1946; Hoover to Lyon, May 16, 1946; "José Manuel Fortuny," May 28, 1946; Hoover to Lyon et al., July 9, 1946; Hoover to Lyon et al., July 15, 1946; "Víctor Manuel Gutiérrez," Sept. 30, 1946; Hoover to Neal et al., Dec. 17, 1946. All NA 814.00B. In 1947, responsibility for intelligence gathering in Latin America passed from the FBI to the CIA.

upper class or by summoning the protagonists to the embassy. At other times, the relevant actors were even fewer: in Ubico's thirteen years, only one man mattered.

With the fall of Ponce, the United States faced a whirlwind of new groups, such as organized labor and the political parties of the middle class; groups that talked of changing Guatemalan society, although their rhetoric tended to be far more ardent than their actions; groups that were led by men with whom embassy officials were usually ill at ease; groups that were motivated by a nationalism that stood in sharp contrast to the accommodating greed of the leaders of happier days. "No one of the former governing class of old 'good families' was or has since been a member of this government," a U.S. diplomat lamented in 1949.[61]

To penetrate this strange new world of young revolutionary leaders, the embassy turned to those Guatemalans who appeared unswervingly pro-American; those who would be honest enough to acknowledge that the Labor Code was discriminatory, and that UFCO and its sister companies were being victimized; those who were sensitive to the communist threat. Not surprisingly, these worthies were found among Arévalo's enemies and particularly among the genteel upper class. These were the men who were eager to convince the Americans of the burgeoning communist threat. To be sure, Washington was not unaware that these men had their own agenda. But their warnings, U.S. officials believed, contained elements of truth; the more dangerous seemed the Arévalo regime, the less shrill seemed its critics. Governments hostile to Guatemala added damning information. Again, Washington did not uncritically accept these reports, but the accusations reinforced the mood of distrust.[62]

The Truman administration, and in particular the embassy in Guatemala, had another source of information, the one they valued most highly: those Americans who had long lived in the country. These men were the representatives of U.S. companies in Guatemala; foremost among them were two in-

---

[61] Siracusa, "Summary of Statements Made by Mr. Siracusa in Presentation of Guatemalan Situation," p. 3, enclosed in Siracusa to Patterson, Aug. 22, 1949, RG84 GR, Box 216, NA-S.

[62] For information from other governments, see AmEm Madrid, Moffitt to SecState, no. 141, Mar. 5, 1948, NA 814.00B, enclosing a five-page report "given the Embassy informally and voluntarily, by the Chief of the American Section of the Spanish Foreign Office"; HQs Panama Canal Department, "Weekly Intelligence Summary" no. 257, June 4, 1947, RG319 ID 373808, NA-S; Marshall to SecState, no. 1074, Oct. 23, 1947, NA 814.00B; Wells to DOS, no. 248, Sept. 6, 1950, NA 714.00. Alarmed by the Arévalo administration's insistent claims on British Honduras, British officials embarked on a campaign to impugn the Guatemalan government as communist. (Meers, "Pebble on the Beach," pp. 22–29.) For a revealing selection of British reports, see "Extract from Annual Review" and "Extract from Guatemala Report," RG84 CF, Box 15, NA-S.

telligent, persuasive and outspoken individuals, William Taillon, general manager of UFCO, and Thomas Bradshaw, president of IRCA. Milton Wells, the Foreign Service officer who essentially ran the embassy under both Kyle and Patterson, "entertained close ties with Taillon and Bradshaw," recalls an embassy official.[63]

Thus by the late 1940s, the Truman administration saw Guatemala as a nightmarish world infested not only by communists, but also by ill-defined yet dangerous species such as procommunists, fellow travelers, extreme leftists, and radical leftists. There was some truth to these fears; that Gutiérrez, for example, had become a communist was a fact that he himself hardly sought to hide. The same was true of a handful of labor leaders close to him.

But U.S. officials also branded as communists or communist sympathizers men who were at most mild leftists or even right of center. The prominent PAR leader Charnaud was not considered "a *proven* communist in the card-carrying sense," yet his strong procommunist orientation was flagrant, "since 1944 at least."[64] In fact Charnaud, who hardly knew who Marx was in 1944, was, by the end of Arévalo's term, an eloquent populist with slight leftist proclivities. The same virulent Red virus allegedly contaminated Foreign Minister Muñoz Meany, another moderate leftist whose major sins were strong hostility to dictatorship and sincere nationalism.[65] Other cases were still more farfetched. U.S. officials were not sure whether Jorge García Granados, a moderate candidate in the 1950 presidential elections, was a card-carrying communist—but he was certainly a communist sympathizer and a dangerous man.[66] The Honduran exile Medardo Mejía, who held mid-level positions in the Guatemalan bureaucracy and wrote in the progovernment press, was correctly identified as a "close friend of Arévalo." It was the Honduran Minister in Guatemala who had revealed Mejía's secret to the American embassy: he

[63] Interview with Steins.

[64] OIR, "Guatemala: Communist Influence," Oct. 23, 1950, p. 95, NA. An earlier in-depth report had noted that "there is good circumstantial evidence of party affiliation." (AmEmG, "Communism in Guatemala," p. 17, enclosed in Wells to SecState, no. 217, May 6, 1948, NA 814.00B.)

[65] For the U.S. view of Muñoz Meany, see HQs Panama Canal Department, "Weekly Intelligence Summary" no. 270, Sept. 3, 1947, p. 13, RG319 ID 397212, NA-S; "Communism in Guatemala" (see n. 64 above), p. 17; Wells to DOS, no. 794, June 27, 1950, NA 714.13; "Guatemala: Communist Influence" (see n. 64 above), pp. 43, 64.

[66] See Col. Devine, "Possible Russian and Communist Influence in Guatemala," Report 142-6, May 3, 1946, RG84 CF, Box 14, NA-S; HQs Panama Canal Department, "Weekly Intelligence Summary" no. 262, July 9, 1947, p. 11, RG319 ID 382208, NA-S; "Communism in Guatemala" (see n. 64 above), p. 10. By the end of the Arévalo administration, the U.S. perception of García Granados began to soften: see "Guatemala: Communist Influence" (see n. 64 above), p. 71, n. 1.

was "one of the principal agents" of communist penetration in Guatemala;[67] this information was accepted by U.S. officials even though it came from an obviously partisan source. Mejía, who shared the confused populist views of Arévalo, became, for the Americans, a dangerous character and was placed in the same gallery of scoundrels as Graciela García, a Salvadoran communist of many years' standing whom Arévalo had deported in 1947.[68]

Even Clemente Marroquín Rojas, a prominent right-wing intellectual, aroused the suspicions of U.S. officials. His nationalism, which was tinged with criticism of the United States, confused them, for they were accustomed to Guatemalan conservatives who loudly sang the praises of all things American. His daily *La Hora*, which had attacked Arévalo and his policies as extremist since late 1947, was branded as leftist.[69]

Given this hypersensitivity, it is hardly surprising that U.S. officials saw the revolutionary parties as ravaged by the Red virus. Once again, a distorted assessment grew around a grain of truth: the PAR had harbored communists—Fortuny and his friends. But even after their resignation, U.S. officials believed that communist influence in the PAR was significant,[70] not an unreasonable conclusion, given that they considered the party's major leader, the anticommunist Charnaud, to be at least a fellow traveler. U.S. officials also concluded that the infection had spread to RN, albeit to a "less pronounced" degree, and suspicions were even raised about the docile FPL.[71]

With hindsight, the embassy concluded that "demagogic incitement of the masses against the status quo [had] marked the first three years of the Arévalo Administration"[72]—a bold assessment that was not consonant with the embassy's own reporting in 1945 and 1946. The same hindsight colored the embassy's interpretation of the Labor Code. In 1947, U.S. officials had condemned merely its discriminatory nature, while UFCO had warned that it bore the signs of communist influence; by 1948, the embassy had discovered that the code was a "drastic document which, if enforced literally, would greatly facilitate the communist objective of state or worker control of industry." It warned that the social policies of the Arévalo administration were "motivated in part by a calculated effort to further class warfare, rather than being limited in scope to a sincere effort to bring about much needed social and economic adjustments."[73]

[67] "Guatemala: Communist Influence" (see n. 64 above), p. 41.

[68] Ibid., pp. 41–42. See also Comité Salvadoreño de Liberación Nacional, "Memorial dirigido por la emigración centroamericana al Presidente de la República de Guatemala," July 21, 1947, CPR, AGCA.

[69] "Guatemala: Communist Influence" (see n. 64 above), p. 74.

[70] Ibid., p. 22.

[71] See ibid., pp. 3, 22 (quoted), 80, and "Communism in Guatemala" (see n. 64 above), p. 5.

[72] "Communism in Guatemala" (see n. 64 above), p. 17.

[73] Ibid., pp. 18, 14.

THE STATE DEPARTMENT AND UFCO

While Washington's preoccupation with communism in Guatemala grew, American companies locked into an increasingly bitter conflict with the host government and organized labor. Once again, United Fruit led the way, resisting the demands of its labor unions that the Labor Code be implemented and that wages be increased.

The company remained firm: the code was discriminatory, and UFCO's wages were already the highest paid to agricultural workers in Guatemala. In a still-recent past, UFCO would have fired the insubordinate workers, and the government would have readily enforced the company's will. But now the Labor Code stipulated that workers could not be summarily dismissed and provided for inspectors to verify the unions' complaints. Furthermore, United Fruit was expected to use the mechanisms of conciliation and arbitration established by the new legislation.

The government's "persecution" of UFCO, however, should not be exaggerated. Between the summer of 1947 and early 1949, when the smoldering conflict erupted into a dangerous crisis, labor inspectors repeatedly found UFCO guilty of violations of the Labor Code, yet the total amount of the fines levied against the company was $690.[74] What exasperated UFCO, sure of its moral superiority and jealous of its autonomy, was the idea of any outside interference, even if this interference came from the sovereign government of the land.

Egged on by UFCO, the State Department exerted unrelenting pressure on the Arévalo administration to modify the Labor Code and to halt its "persecution" of American companies. In late July 1948, the legal adviser of the State Department had criticized ARA's stance, arguing that the discriminatory nature of the code had not yet been proven. ARA eventually conceded the point, and on November 2 it instructed the embassy to ascertain, "in as discreet a manner as possible," whether UFCO was indeed a victim of discrimination.[75] The nature of the debate, and its swift conclusion, were well summarized in a December 1948 memorandum to Robert Lovett, the undersecretary of state:

> In February 1947 there was enacted in Guatemala a labor code of more than 400 articles. In four of these . . . special benefits are conferred on employees of agricultural enterprises with more than 500 workers. In the specific Guatemalan setting it appeared clear that these articles were intended to place a special burden on the United Fruit Company. Consequently, the American Embassy, with the Depart-

[74] Bauer Paiz, *La Frutera*, p. 16. Bauer Paiz was the finance minister. For a vivid description of the travails of a labor inspector, see "Expediente relacionado con los conflictos tratados por el inspector de trabajo urbano Salvador Ruano Pimentel en la zona de Tiquisate," June 16, 1947, IGT, Leg. 48750, AGCA.

[75] Lovett to AmEmG, no. A-210, Nov. 2, 1948, NA 814.504/9-348.

ment's backing, in due course protested the seemingly discriminatory articles. . . . Later . . . doubts arose within the Department as to whether our government could, in view of much of its own legislation and the jurisprudence built up around it, properly represent that the four disputed articles were *prima facie* discriminatory in a legal sense. The views first expressed by our ambassador to the Guatemalan government were never retracted, but these doubts . . . were discussed by the Department with counsel and officers of the United Fruit Company. It was agreed between the Department and the Company that the Company would gather and present evidence to the Department as to whether there were enterprises besides the United Fruit Company covered by the articles in question, and, if so, whether such enterprises were complying with the law. These enterprises would possibly include a number of large farms operated by the Guatemalan government itself.

The Department could not and did not require of the United Fruit Company that it present clear and incontrovertible evidence on these points before proceeding further. In the nature of things Guatemalan it would be practically impossible for the Company and our Embassy to develop such evidence. It was only on December 9, 1948, that the company was able to present to the Department sufficient information to enable it to take a further step. On December 10, by telegram, the Department transmitted this information to the new Ambassador in Guatemala, Richard C. Patterson, Jr., and instructed him to verify it and then to renew representations in protection of the United Fruit Company's interests.

Representations were in the first instance begun by our Embassy as soon as the position in which the Guatemalan Labor Code placed the United Fruit Company had become clear and these representations were vigorously pushed by Ambassador Kyle. Our Government's stand has never been altered and with the new information at hand the case of the United Fruit Company will be vigorously pressed.[76]

Thus ended the ineffectual debate, in which United Fruit had been its own prosecutor, and the jury had been a most sympathetic embassy. A more serious investigation would have shown, as the Guatemalan government contended, that there were several agricultural enterprises with more than five hundred permanent workers, and that in some of these (Herrera y Cía and a few Fincas Nacionales), some provisions of the Labor Code were enforced.[77] The analysis would also have shown that the impetus to implement the code came from UFCO's labor unions, not from the Arévalo administration; as the Guatemalan

[76] Humelsine to Connelly, Dec. 15, 1948, pp. 1–2, enclosed in Connelly to Lovett, Dec 4 [sic], 1948. On the debate, see also Barber to Metzger, Sept. 3, 1948; MemoConv ("Article 130 of Guatemala Labor Code"), Sept. 27, 1948; Daniels to Barber and de Zengotita, Dec. 3, 1948, and enclosed Tate to Daniels of same date; Daniels to Acting Sec., Dec. 6, 1948; Brown to Daniels, Dec. 6, 1948. All NA 814.504.

[77] For the Fincas Nacionales and Herrera y Cía, see Taillon to Baggett, Nov. 29, 1948, NA 814.00.

ambassador had pointed out, agricultural workers elsewhere were far less combative.

The conclusion of the debate within the State Department came at a most opportune moment: less than a month later, United Fruit declared war on the Guatemalan government. Ordered by the government to submit its dispute with the labor unions to arbitration in the labor courts, UFCO responded by firing a large number of workers and stopping all shipping at Puerto Barrios. The impasse continued throughout February, while Arévalo threatened to sequester the company's properties and Ambassador Patterson, implementing Washington's orders with gusto, made it clear to Arévalo that the United States held his administration responsible for the conflict. "Recent developments [are] of deepest concern [to] U.S. Government and business circles," he warned, "and [are] being watched as testability and even willingness . . . [of the Guatemalan] Government to give American enterprises [in] this country the fair deal which certainly has been denied them during [the] past three years."[78]

It was an unequal contest. In March, a compromise was reached that reestablished normal relations between the company and the host government—that is, relations of extreme distrust. United Fruit had made good its refusal to submit to arbitration, and the unions had obtained only modest concessions, principally a wage increase of less than 10 percent. "It is clear," concluded *El Imparcial*, "that our country is too weak to challenge powerful American business interests."[79]

For the remainder of the Arévalo presidency, embassy reports and State Department communications referred repeatedly to Guatemala's "victimization" of American companies; "persecution" was the monotonous refrain. With rising irritation, Patterson lectured Arévalo about Guatemala's sins, and State Department officials administered the same medicine to the hapless Guatemalan ambassador in Washington.

And yet, in 1950, reviewing the record of many years of "persecution," the State Department concluded that American companies in Guatemala

---

[78] Patterson to SecState, no. 44, Feb. 1, 1949, p. 2, NA 814.504. For the origins of the conflict, see Juzgado de Trabajo y Previsión Social, Zona Sexta, Unión Sindical de Trabajadores de Puerto Barrios vs United Fruit Company, Leg. 2B, Pieza 84, Juzgado 1° de Trabajo de Izabal, OJR, AGCA.

[79] "Arreglo frutero," *El I*, Mar. 9, 1949, p. 1. For the terms of the agreement, see "Resuelto el conflicto frutero," *El I*, Mar. 5, 1949, p. 1, and "Suscrito el convenio entre la UFCO y los laborantes," *El I*, Mar. 7, 1949, p. 1. The 1949 contract was renegotiated the next year, in what was "actually a one-year extension of the old contract with a few modifications." (Steins to DOS, no. 474, Apr. 20, 1950, p. 2, NA 814.062.) For the continuing struggle between UFCO and its workers, see the "Inventarios del Juzgado de Trabajo y Previsión Social de la Sexta Zona Económica de los Juicios Laborales," Juzgado de Trabajo de Puerto Barrios, 1947–1958, OJR, AGCA.

"have suffered no serious harm."[80] This relatively happy situation, U.S. of-ficials believed, had been possible only because of their spirited defense of the companies, and they had a point. In spite of UFCO's economic power, it is unlikely that Arévalo would have been as forgiving had it not been for the heckling of the State Department.

After December 1948, the record indicates only one instance when a U.S. official dared to suggest that the Guatemalan government was anything less than the villain of the piece. In a comprehensive memorandum, the labor of-ficer of the Office of Regional American Affairs, John Fishburn, boldly stated that the State Department's embrace of UFCO was wrong. With only one exception, Fishburn argued, the "discriminatory" articles of the Labor Code were in fact "legitimate in terms of modern thinking." Noting UFCO's claim that it treated its Guatemalan workers generously, Fishburn responded: "The company will have to learn that labor often does not appreciate paternalism, but wishes to share in determining its fate. This trend to extend democracy in industrial relations is very powerful." Presciently, he warned: if UFCO "should attempt, with or without Embassy assistance, to fight this inevitable trend, . . . it will probably lead to the same conclusion experienced by the American and British oil companies in Mexico." That is, expropriation. He concluded:

> With respect to this Government's relations to the case, it would appear most unwise for us to be tied to the company's position, without regard for Guatemala's aspira-tions or sovereign feelings. It is my judgment that our unfortunate and necessarily ineffectual attempts to help the company have permitted the communists to pose as champions of labor and of national sovereignty, and have thereby aided them in achieving control over organized labor in Guatemala.[81]

The embassy in Guatemala shot off a sharply worded six-page rebuttal.[82] Edward W. Clark, of the Office of Middle American Affairs (MID), wrote to Milton Wells, the U.S. chargé in Guatemala: "All of us here in MID think Fishburn is way off the beam in his thinking on this matter and have told him so." A few days earlier, continued Clark, at the weekly meeting of assistant secretaries "the situation relating to our relations with Guatemala was dis-cussed thoroughly and full approval was given . . . to the policy which we are presently following."[83]

U.S. officials did not dispute Fishburn's assertion that the communists were

---

[80] "Current Relations with Guatemala," May 1950, *FRUS*, 1950, 2:900.

[81] Fishburn to Miller, Apr. 10, 1950, ibid., pp. 880–84.

[82] See Wells to DOS, May 17, 1950, ibid., pp. 889–91, and the enclosed "Memo-randum," ibid., pp. 891–96.

[83] Clark to Wells, June 6, 1950, ibid., p. 903. For the meeting of assistant secretaries mentioned by Clark, see ibid., pp. 901–2.

profiting from the labor conflicts and discrediting both UFCO and the U.S. government. But they believed that Fishburn's analysis was naive: any concessions on UFCO's part would have encouraged the communist bosses to raise new demands and enhanced their prestige among the workers. At fault was not the State Department's support of UFCO, but the Guatemalan government's tolerance, and even encouragement, of these communists. This connivance added an ominous dimension to the labor conflict and heightened U.S. suspicions about Arévalo.

THE CARIBBEAN LEGION

Not only did Arévalo persecute American companies and show a disquieting tenderness toward communist agitators, his foreign policy was equally reckless. Guatemala, the State Department asserted in 1950, was "one of the principal causes of unrest and instability in the Caribbean."[84] The accusation was not baseless; no government helped the semimythical Caribbean Legion more than that of Arévalo. Arévalo's involvement with the Caribbean Legion illuminates both his personality and the struggles that stirred the Caribbean in the late 1940s. Further, it highlights the paranoia that had seized the Truman administration. In a less distorted world, Arévalo's support for the Caribbean Legion would have been proof that the president was an anticommunist or at least that he was not a communist; instead it was added to the indictment as evidence of his communist proclivities.

Indeed, it was partly this worldview that made the Caribbean Legion seem more powerful to Washington than it ever was. As a structured, formal organization, the Caribbean Legion never existed. (The name was coined by U.S. journalists in 1948.) What did exist were nuclei of exiled leaders from various countries who were, at times, able to coordinate their activities and mobilize "foot-soldiers"—exiles living throughout the region.[85]

[84] "Current Relations with Guatemala," ibid., p. 899.

[85] There is no definitive study of the Caribbean Legion. The best treatment is Ameringer, *Democratic Left*, pp. 59–110. Useful material is included in Corominas, *In the Caribbean Political Areas*; Vega, *Los Estados Unidos*; Unión Panamericana, *Tratado interamericano*, 1:33–149. The most important accounts by participants are Arvelo, *Cayo Confite*; Ornes, *Desembarco*; Henríquez Vásquez, "Cayo Confites"; Bosch, "Cayo Confites"; Wangüemert y Máiquez, "El diario de Cayo Confites"; Argüello, *Quiénes*; Bayo, *Tempestad*; Silfa, *Guerra*, 1:175–299; Figueres, *El espíritu del 48*; Morazán, "Los siete primeros." U.S. documents shed light not only on U.S. perceptions and policies but occasionally on the activities of the exiles and the governments concerned. Particularly helpful were interviews with the Dominican participants Ramírez Alcantara, Arvelo, Martínez Bonilla (a "foot soldier"); with the Guatemalans Fortuny, Arévalo, María de Arbenz, Barrios Peña, Charnaud; with the Costa Rican Figueres; and with the Nicaraguan Torres Espinoza.

In the twilight of the Second World War, the sudden emergence of democracy in Cuba, Guatemala, and Venezuela had swelled the hopes of exiles from the less fortunate republics in the region. No longer lonely outcasts, they could now count on the assistance of friendly governments. Freedom was contagious, they believed, and resistance to dictatorship was growing in their own countries. Among the dictators, Trujillo and Somoza were the pillars of tyranny. Should they be toppled, the wind of democracy in the Caribbean would prove irresistible.

While others plotted, the Dominican exiles acted. In the summer of 1947, with the complicity of President Ramón Grau San Martin and other high Cuban officials, they assembled the largest exile force that had ever congregated in the Caribbean. A potpourri of approximately 1,200 armed men, mainly Cuban volunteers and Dominicans with a sprinkling of Hondurans and other exiles, gathered in Cuba at Cayo Confites. The leaders of the expedition were confident of their own strength and that of the underground that awaited their arrival in the Dominican Republic. The underground did indeed exist, although they exaggerated its power. Had the exiles invaded, Trujillo would have been the likely victor. Had they invaded. Secrecy was a virtue that the exiles and their Cuban protectors had spurned; the preparations for the invasion were public knowledge, and Cuban complicity was flagrant. While Trujillo's complaints grew, the United States pressed Grau to desist, as did Cuban opposition politicians and even government officials (including the chief of staff of the army). Grau capitulated; in late September the Cuban military detained the entire expeditionary force.

In a matter of days the exiles were set free, but their hopes had been shattered. The chastened Cuban government was no longer willing to offer its country as a base for future expeditions. Worse, it confiscated the weapons that the exiles had accumulated so laboriously.[86]

It was at this juncture that Arévalo assumed center stage. The previous summer, while the Dominicans had been organizing in Cuba under Grau's protection, Arévalo had acted as their intermediary to buy weapons in Argentina, using his good contacts with the Buenos Aires government and claiming that the arms were for Guatemala.[87] He had also broken diplomatic relations with Trujillo in July 1947. It had been a useful, though secondary, role. But now that Grau had abandoned the exiles, Arévalo stepped forward as the champion of the Caribbean Legion; he was to retain this role for two years, and he acted with far more discretion than had Grau. In Guatemala, Arévalo's policy,

[86] For two vivid accounts of the Dominicans' efforts to recover the weapons from the Cuban government, see Arvelo, *Cayo Confite*, pp. 120–22, and Henríquez Vásquez, "Cayo Confites," Jan. 17, 1984, p. 10.

[87] See especially Silfa, *Guerra*, 1:180–82, and Bosch, "Cayo Confites," pp. 3, 8, 13.

which was never discussed publicly, was endorsed by leaders of the revolutionary parties. Within the military, Arbenz was sympathetic, and Arana grumbled. ("It's just adolescent bravado," he confided to friends.) Yet he went along, as was his wont.[88]

Sincere hostility to dictators only partially explains Arévalo's daring role between 1947 and 1949.[89] A dream that had deep roots in Central American history moved him to risk a confrontation with Trujillo and Somoza and to incur Washington's anger. It was a passionate longing that Arévalo had expressed in two essays written in his youth and that he reiterated in his inaugural address:

> There is no Guatemalan who does not dream of the Greater Motherland of Central America. . . . We feel impotent whenever we pause to consider the fact that we are still five small republics, exposed to the machinations of any adventurer and the exploitation of the powerful. Terrible enemies keep us apart. These enemies are our very own governments. The Federation of Central America would exist now if our governments had renounced their selfish interests. . . . The Federation is not an illusion: it could become a reality in the near future. We need only to unite . . . in order to resurrect this Central American nation as a great democracy, with a powerful economy and a modern army.[90]

Upon becoming President, Arévalo sought to achieve his goal by diplomatic means, expounding the idea of a gradual but steady federative process for the five Central American republics. His efforts led, in 1945 and again in 1946, to two highly publicized meetings with General Salvador Castañeda Castro, the strongman who ruled El Salvador. Florid treaties for the progressive unification of the two countries were signed. Meanwhile, the other three Central

[88] Quoted from interview with Arana's close associate, Barrios Peña. Some exiles have written accounts, published after Arana's death, that distort Arana's position into one of active opposition and even slander him as an accomplice of Trujillo. (See Ornes, *Desembarco*, pp. 90, 119, and Silfa, *Guerra*, 1:280–89.) Interviews with Fortuny, Charnaud, María de Arbenz, Cruz Salazar, Lorenzana, and Torres Espinoza were instructive.

[89] This hostility was not limited to the dictatorships of the Caribbean. At both the Rio Conference (1947) and at Bogotá (1948), Guatemala advocated a policy of nonrecognition of regimes in the hemisphere that had come to power through force, particularly those that had overthrown democracies. The proposal was rejected, but Arévalo adopted it unilaterally. Guatemala was also a vocal critic of Franco. See Frankel, "Political Development," pp. 50–68, 87–91.

[90] "Al asumir la presidencia," Mar. 15, 1945, in Arévalo, *Discursos en la presidencia*, pp. 7–21, quoted from pp. 12–13. The two essays are "Istmania (tierras del Istmo)," written in 1935, and "Cultura y posibilidades de cultura en la América Central," written in 1939; both were first published in Arévalo's *Escritos políticos*, pp. 12–28, 57–69.

American governments remained aloof. By 1947 it was clear that the treaties were worthless. In the words of a sympathetic scholar, Arévalo had become "completely disillusioned as far as the possibility of a successful unification effort was concerned."[91]

Yet his zeal was unquenched. The failure of his diplomatic efforts merely led him to conclude that the dictators themselves were the obstacle to Central American unification and that with their overthrow Central America would be one and democratic. It was this conviction that moved him, in the wake of the Cuban fiasco, to respond to the Dominicans' appeal for help. On their behalf, he urged his friend, President Grau, to release the weapons of Cayo Confites. Grau surrendered some of the weapons; he gave them, however, not to the exiles but to the Guatemalan government.[92]

Thus Guatemala became Mecca, and Arévalo the prophet. Dominicans, Hondurans, and leaders of rival Nicaraguan exile factions flocked to him. Also present was an eloquent Costa Rican, José Figueres. To be sure, Figueres could hardly qualify as an exile. Deported from Costa Rica in 1942, he had returned in 1944. Since then he had indulged unmolested in one of his fondest occupations: inveighing in scathing and scurrilous public denunciations of the administrations of Presidents Rafael Angel Calderón Guardia (1940–1944) and Teodoro Picado (1944–1948). More discreetly, Figueres was busy plotting against the government.[93]

Within that cacophony, Arévalo arbitrated with the assurance of the man who holds all the cards. Under his firm guidance the exiles were forced to patch up their differences and to sign, on December 17, 1947, a most extraordinary document, the *Pacto del Caribe*. The pact established an alliance "of the groups representing the Dominican Republic, Nicaragua, and Costa Rica. . . . As we overthrow each of these dictators, the resources of the liberated countries will be used to reinforce our common endeavor."

While explicitly targeting only Costa Rica, the Dominican Republic, and Nicaragua, the *Pacto del Caribe* had a more ambitious scope: "All groups representing the oppressed peoples of the Caribbean are invited to join this pact, so that they too—with our help—can liberate their own countries." The ultimate aim, so dear to Arévalo, was powerfully stated:

[91] Bishop, "Arévalo and Central American Unification," p. 108.

[92] See esp. Henríquez Vásquez, "Cayo Confites," Jan. 17, 1984, p. 10. U.S. intelligence was anxious to follow the movement of the weapons: see Kyle to SecState, no. 32, Jan. 21, 1948; Feinberg, Paraphrase no. P-10, Jan. 22, 1948; Neruob to SecState, no. 55, Jan. 22, 1948; Siracusa to Wells, Feb. 4, 1948; Kyle to SecState, no. 62, Feb. 5, 1948. All RG84 GR, Box 193, NA-S.

[93] Two superb, well documented and dispassionate books that deal with the regimes of Calderón and Picado, as well as with Figueres's role, are Aguilar Bulgarelli, *Costa Rica*, and Bell, *Crisis*.

We, the undersigned, declare that the immediate reestablishment of the Republic of Central America is necessary for this continent; this principle will be affirmed in the new constitutions of the liberated countries, and each new government will immediately work to implement it with all the resources at its disposal.

The liberated countries pledge to establish a Democratic Alliance of the Caribbean, which will be open to all the democracies of the Caribbean, as well as to El Salvador and Ecuador. . . .

The Democratic Alliance of the Caribbean will constitute an indivisible bloc in all international crises. Its fundamental aims will be: to strengthen democracy in the region; to demand the respect of the international community for each of its members; to liberate the European colonies that still exist in the Caribbean; to promote the creation of the Republic of the Lesser Antilles; to act as one in defense of our common economic, military and political interests.

Discreetly, Arévalo refrained from signing the document, yet his hand was evident in the flowery language that was his trademark. "All differences in the interpretation and implementation of this pact," the document concluded, "will be submitted to the irrevocable decision of President Juan José Arévalo, in whose ability, honesty and impartiality we place full trust. We are confident that he will not withhold the invaluable gift of his wisdom."[94]

Of course, to brand the governments of Calderón and Picado as dictatorships—as the *Pacto del Caribe* did—was hyperbole and to lump Costa Rica with Trujillo's Dominican Republic and Somoza's Nicaragua was sheer nonsense. Costa Rica had a hybrid system where electoral fraud (as in 1944) alternated with clean elections (as those for Congress, in 1946). Under President Calderón, and "above all" under Picado, the foremost authority on the period points out, the opposition "could act almost freely"; it was rarely cowed and responded in kind to the government's excesses."[95] By Costa Rica's previous standards, democracy did not fare badly under Calderón and Picado. It was comparable to that of Cuba under Grau. Furthermore, the administrations of Calderón and Picado contrasted with those of their predecessors in their advocacy of social reforms and in their alliance with the Communist party, which had polled 10 percent of the votes in the 1940 elections. It was this strong reformist bent, and the alliance with the communists, that exasperated the Costa Rican upper class, which had blithely overlooked the brazen electoral fraud and high-handed practices of Calderón's predecessor, León Cortés (1936–1940). Figueres shared the upper class's hostility toward Calderón and Picado, not because he opposed social reform, but because he wanted power.

Costa Rica's domestic politics were of little concern to the Caribbean exiles, even though many disapproved of Calderón's and Picado's association with

---

[94] For the text of the *Pacto del Caribe*, see Aguilar Bulgarelli, *Costa Rica*, pp. 307–12.

[95] Ibid., p. 300.

the communists. However, in the eyes of many exiles, Calderón and Picado were guilty of a particularly heinous crime: intent on domestic reforms and aware of the military weakness of their country, they remained aloof from the struggle against dictatorship in the Caribbean, and they strove to maintain proper relations with the powerful Somoza.[96] This policy led a faction of Nicaraguan exiles to strike an alliance with Figueres in 1943. With their help, Figueres eventually won over Edelberto Torres Espinoza and Roberto Brenes Mesen, Nicaraguan and Costa Rican intellectuals who were friends of Arévalo. With them, and then with Arévalo in late 1947, Figueres argued a case that was as simple as it was straightforward: given its border with Nicaragua, Costa Rica was the ideal base from which to launch an attack against Somoza; should he, Figueres, seize power, he would offer his country and its resources to assist in the liberation of Nicaragua. With its risible army of three hundred men, the Costa Rican regime would be easily toppled.[97]

Figueres was eloquent, and Torres and Brenes were venerable figures. Although the *Pacto del Caribe* had established no sequence among the three regimes that were explicitly targeted for destruction, Arévalo had made his choice: Costa Rica would be first, followed by Nicaragua. Then, in ever stronger waves, other targets would be hit, until no dictator remained in the Caribbean. The Dominican exiles, the rightful owners of the weapons they no longer controlled, had no alternative but to accept this decision, which delayed their hour, but at least held out a promise of liberation for their country.

On March 1, 1948, the Costa Rican government annulled the February presidential elections, which had been won by the opposition, and thereby handed a welcome pretext to those who had already decreed its destruction. When, on March 12, the uprising that Figueres had been preparing for six years finally broke out, Arévalo promptly sent the weapons of Cayo Confites to the rebels.[98] Without this aid, a successful revolt could hardly have been staged, for Figueres had no arms. A handful of well-trained Caribbean exiles accompanied the weapons from Guatemala; they supplied "critical military skills that the traditionally pacific Costa Ricans lacked," and provided the insurgents

[96] See Schifter, *Las alianzas*, pp. 229–49.

[97] In a 1972 interview, Arévalo stated: "It's strange. I knew almost nothing about Figueres. I was first visited in my presidential office by Roberto Brenes Mesen, that great philosopher and writer who inspired the youth of our country. This was in 1947. He asked for help in his struggle against the government of Costa Rica that was infiltrated by communists." ("No sé si la ayuda que dimos a Figueres en 1948 fué para bien.")

[98] U.S. Intelligence had considerable difficulty in ascertaining Guatemala's role in this episode. See Kyle to SecState, no. 159, Mar. 23, 1948; Kyle to SecState, no. 162, Mar. 24, 1948; Wells to SecState, no. 177, Apr. 13, 1948; Wells to SecState, no. 206, Apr. 29, 1948 (all RG84 GR, Box 191, NA-S); Wells to Daniels, Sept. 1, 1948, RG84 GR, Box 190, NA-S.

with a "technical military advantage over the regular forces of the Costa Rican army"—an army whose officers demonstrated neither the ability nor the will to resist.[99]

Arévalo had honored his pledge to Figueres. Now it was Figueres' turn. Yet once in power, the Costa Rican was unable, and probably unwilling, to fulfill his promises. Granted, the Nicaraguan exiles who flocked to the country after Figueres's victory did not help their own cause. They were more interested in San José's bars than in military training. Their indiscreet, boisterous behavior alienated not only the Costa Rican public but also Figueres's supporters, who had not been privy to the commitments undertaken by their leader in the *Pacto del Caribe* and who had little desire to court unnecessary danger by challenging the mighty Somoza. In vain did Arévalo try to stiffen the resolve of the elusive Figueres; in vain did he beseech his erstwhile protegé to honor the *Pacto del Caribe*, "a pact," he pleaded, "signed in good conscience and that even included an oath to be loyal and disciplined until the fall of the last dictator."[100]

Months of inactivity were followed, in December 1948, by a small invasion of Costa Rica launched from Nicaragua by supporters of former President Calderón. At Figueres's urgent request, the Organization of American States intervened and swiftly rendered its predictable verdict: both Nicaragua and Costa Rica were guilty—Nicaragua of actual aggression, Costa Rica of potential aggression; they should desist at once and adhere strictly to the policy of nonintervention. Both governments happily complied: Somoza, who had intended merely to frighten Figueres, urged the invaders to withdraw to Nicaragua; Figueres, to the great joy of his supporters, told the Nicaraguan exiles to leave Costa Rica. Once again, it was to Guatemala that the leaders of Nicaraguan, Dominican, and other exile groups flocked, and it was to Guatemala that Figueres returned the bulk of the weapons that he had received from Arévalo.

Arévalo was prepared to make a final effort. This time, rather than to the

[99] Bell, *Crisis*, p. 138. The CIA also concluded, "The Caribbean Legion . . . was decisive" in Figueres's victory. (CIA, "The Caribbean Legion," ORE 11–49, Mar. 17, 1949, p. 2, Truman Papers, President's Secretary's File, Intelligence File, Box 256, TL.) In addition to Bell's *Crisis*, pp. 131–54, the best accounts of the uprising are Aguilar Bulgarelli, *Costa Rica*, pp. 317–98 and Acuña, *El 48*. Schifter's *Las alianzas* is a well-researched study of U.S. policy toward Costa Rica from 1940 to Figueres' victory. The "Diary (San José) 1948–1949" of U.S. Ambassador Nathaniel Davis is informative, insightful and entertaining. (Davis Papers, Box 1, TL.)

[100] Letter from Arévalo to Figueres, May 27, 1948, in Aguilar Bulgarelli, *Costa Rica*, pp. 414–15. For a scathing denunciation of Figueres' conduct, see Argüello, *Quiénes*—a biased but informative account. For a more balanced version by another participant, see Bayo, *Tempestad*, pp. 83–158. Among secondary sources, see esp. Aguilar Bulgarelli, *Costa Rica*, pp. 398–432.

discredited and faction-ridden Nicaraguans, his support went to the more co-hesive Dominicans. "Basically," one of these Dominicans has written, "our plan was the following: several groups of rebels with weapons for 500 or 600 men would be flown to the Dominican Republic. Unlike Cayo Confites, this would not be a full-fledged invasion, and we would not immediately confront Trujillo's army. . . . We had decided to land in three different places, and we would arrive by air, not by sea like in Cayo Confites."[101] About sixty men would participate in the invasion.

At Arévalo's behest, the Dominican exiles were trained at Guatemalan mil-itary facilities and were given the well-traveled weapons of Cayo Confites. Since President Prío, who replaced Grau in 1948, would not allow the rebels' planes to refuel in Cuba while en route to the Dominican Republic, Arévalo helped to persuade senior Mexican officials to permit refueling at the military airport of Cozumel in Quintana Roo.[102] Thus, while Figueres apparently con-tributed a small amount of money, and Prío a lame expression of sympathy, Arévalo was the only president to give active assistance to those fighting against the dictators. (The democratic government of Venezuela had been overthrown in November 1948.)

The Dominicans' plan was as foolhardy as it was brave. Due to bad weather and poor coordination at Cozumel, only one of the six planes of the invading squadron reached the Dominican Republic, landing near the town of Luperón on June 19, 1949, with fifteen men aboard, including the pilots. Had ten times their number arrived, disaster would have been inevitable. The underground no longer existed; some of its members had been killed, others were in jail, and those who had escaped detection were trying to forget that they had ever dared to plot against Trujillo.

The rebels who landed near Luperón were desperately alone. Within a few hours, ten had been killed. The others became Trujillo's prisoners; their public trial would expose the machinations of "international communism" (and of Moscow's puppet, Arévalo) against the peace-loving democracy of *Generali-simo* Trujillo.[103] The tragedy of Luperón closed the parenthesis of hope that had opened in 1944. The Caribbean Legion had fought its last battle.

Washington welcomed its demise. By the late 1940s the Truman adminis-tration considered Trujillo and Somoza to be stalwart members of the inter-American family. Their anticommunism and their loyalty to the United States were above reproach, something that could be said neither of Arévalo nor,

[101] Arvelo, *Cayo Confite*, pp. 122–23; see also Ornes, *Desembarco*, pp. 30–31.

[102] See Arvelo, *Cayo Confite*, pp. 130, 133, and Ornes, *Desembarco*, pp. 152–55. Confirmed by interviews with Fortuny, Charnaud and María de Arbenz.

[103] In addition to many of the sources listed above in n. 85, see Crassweller, *Trujillo*, pp. 241–42; Dominican Republic, *White Book*, pp. 105–49; Rodríguez Loeche, "Por qué fracasó."

Washington believed, of the exiles of the Caribbean Legion. These "political malcontents"[104] threatened the *Pax Americana* with their plots and counterplots. They had sown division among the countries of the area, distracting them from the all-consuming East-West confrontation. The turmoil provoked by the Caribbean exiles, lamented Secretary of State Dean Acheson in a September 1949 address, had created a "situation . . . repugnant to the entire fabric of the inter-American system." The sacred principle of nonintervention had been violated, and the "United States could not be faithful to its international obligations if it did not condemn it in the strongest terms."[105]

Repeatedly in 1948 and 1949, the U.S. embassy had urged Arévalo to renounce his support of the Caribbean Legion; repeatedly, he had denied all involvement. Washington knew these denials to be untrue. In calmer times, U.S. officials would have explained Guatemala's behavior in the same way that they had explained Cuba's involvement in the Cayo Confites expedition: a mixture of adventurism, naïveté, and hostility to the tropical dictators. But this was not 1947, and Arévalo was not Grau. Moreover, Washington harbored new doubts about the Caribbean Legion: it was in the communists' interest, the argument ran, to create turmoil and dissension in the region. Might not, then, communist agents be at work in the Caribbean Legion?

This was, noted a major intelligence report, another ambiguous situation in which Guatemalan foreign policy could be explained either by antidictatorial inclinations or by communist proclivities.[106] (This was also the case, for instance, with Guatemala's opposition to Franco.) And the latter possibility was particularly credible because Foreign Minister Muñoz Meany, whose communist sympathies were beyond doubt, was, reported Ambassador Patterson, " 'up to his neck' in Caribbean Legion affairs." [107] It was, recalls a CIA analyst, "one of those areas where there was disagreement within the intelligence community."[108] At times, however, the tension between the different interpretations gave way to a less complicated conclusion: the communists "have influenced the [Guatemalan] Government to support the so-called 'Caribbean Legion,' " asserted the undersecretary of state in a September 1950 memorandum to Truman.[109] (The Communist Party of Guatemala begged to differ: it considered Arévalo's "support for the reactionary Figueres in Costa Rica" to be one of his major sins.)[110]

[104] "Current Relations with Guatemala," May 1950, *FRUS*, 1950, 2:899.

[105] "Waging Peace in the Americas," Sept. 10, 1949, *State Department Bulletin*, 21:462–66, quoted from p. 463. For a stinging rejoinder, see Bosch, "Errores."

[106] "Guatemala: Communist Influence," (see n. 64 above), pp. 63–65.

[107] Patterson to SecState, May 12, 1949, *FRUS*, 1949, 2:445.

[108] Interview with Dillon.

[109] Webb to Truman, Sept. 9. 1950, *FRUS*, 1950, 2:912.

[110] "Arévalo, presidente demócrata," *Octubre*, Mar. 7, 1951, p. 1. See also Alvarado Arellano, *Apuntes*, p. 15.

In its indignation with those who dared violate the principle of nonintervention without U.S. permission, and blinded by its bias, Washington failed to see that Arévalo had helped the anticommunist and pro-American Figueres to overthrow the only government in the hemisphere that still accepted the Communist party as an ally; it also failed to see that the leaders of the Caribbean Legion opposed communism and would side with the United States against Soviet imperialism. Indeed, the secret *Pacto del Caribe* had stated, with Arévalo's approval, that the members of the future Democratic Alliance of the Caribbean would "ally themselves in perpetuity with the United States and Mexico for the common defense."[111]

[111] Art. 9 of the *Pacto del Caribe*.

CHAPTER 6

The United States and Arévalo: The U.S. Response

BEING a sincere nationalist, Arévalo could never have been the malleable friend that the United States expected the president of a banana republic to be. Yet he had hoped to maintain cordial relations with Washington. The rhetoric of Spiritual Socialism notwithstanding, ideology did not separate Arévalo from the Americans, for he believed in capitalism and sharply condemned communism. His opposition to Soviet imperialism made him all the more ready to accept the geopolitical reality that Guatemala was in the U.S. sphere of influence. Arévalo asked only that his country begin to develop from satellite to ally, and he sought to restrain the American companies that dominated Guatemala's economy.

But imperial attitudes are long in dying. Perhaps the most striking aspect of U.S. behavior toward the Arévalo regime was its self-righteousness. U.S. officials were convinced that legitimate American interests were being victimized. While they readily conceded that Ubico had been "one of the most ruthless of all Guatemalan dictators,"[1] they held up their relations with Ubico as exemplary. Given this model, Assistant Secretary of State Edward Miller was correct in emphasizing the "growing lack of concern of the Guatemalan Government for the traditional good relations between the two countries"; nor was Undersecretary James Webb wrong when he stated that "Guatemala currently was not following its traditional policy of cooperation with the U.S."[2] Washington's conviction that it had observed a "policy of patience and forbearance" vis-à-vis Guatemala[3] was sincere, as was its indignation when, in March 1950, Arévalo requested the recall of Ambassador Patterson because of his persistent meddling in Guatemala's internal affairs. This unprecedented demand was seen as one more example of Guatemala's hostility, patently inspired by the communists. Patterson was clearly innocent. He had merely executed his superiors' policy to "support the legitimate aspirations of the Guatemalan people"[4] and to respect that country's sovereignty. The *New York Times* joined the chorus of critics:

> The present Guatemalan Government arose out of a revolt against a particularly unsavory dictator. This revolt had at first some promising features. Now it seems fairly

[1] "Current Relations with Guatemala," May 1950, *FRUS*, 1950, 2:898.

[2] Quotations from MemoTel, Aug. 2, 1949, *FRUS*, 1949, 2:659, and MemoConv, Sept. 16, 1949, ibid., p. 665.

[3] Wells to DOS, no. 89, July 22, 1950, p. 3, NA 714.00.

[4] SecState to President, Oct. 19, 1950, *FRUS*, 1950, 2:918.

obvious that the present leaders of the Guatemalan Government are permitting themselves to be manipulated by Communist revolutionaries. They fail to realize—or for
political purposes refuse to admit—that the United States is not trying to block social
and economic progress, but is interested rather in seeing that Guatemala becomes a
liberal democracy and not a totalitarian slave state. We want to be friends with the
Guatemalan people, but we do not believe the road to friendship lies through the
uncomplaining acceptance of insults and discriminations. We applaud the State Department for its categorical rejection of such a policy.[5]

Unable to discern the blessings of traditional U.S.-Guatemalan relations,
Arévalo saw in the behavior of the Truman administration neither generosity
nor forbearance, but intolerance and contempt. If Arévalo had never been the
Americans' friend by Washington's standards, by the time he left the presidency he was not their friend by any standard.[6] The same evolution marked
the leaders of the revolutionary parties. Their bitter frustration, fueled by their
impotence vis à vis their generous neighbor to the north, explains their occasional acts of defiance. At the Central American and Caribbean games in Guatemala City in February 1950, the Puerto Rican athletes were honored with a
white flag bearing the Puerto Rican shield rather than the Stars and Stripes,
and a military band played "La Borinqueña" instead of the "Star Spangled
Banner."[7] The cooperative education program established in 1945 with the
U.S. Institute of Inter-American Affairs was not renewed in 1950,[8] and the
Guatemalan Congress postponed the ratification of the 1947 Rio Treaty until
September 1950, a delay that was harshly criticized by Truman and was explained by ARA as "a pertinent example of the influence on government
thinking by communist-minded individuals."[9] (In a recent study, Richard Im-

[5] "The Guatemalan Incident" (edit.), Apr. 8, 1950, p. 12. A rare exception to the
condemnation of Guatemala in the American press was the *Nation*. ("The Shape of
Things," edit., Apr. 22, 1950, pp. 358–59.)

[6] See Arévalo's speech on the day of Arbenz's inauguration, *DCA*, Mar. 15, 1951,
pp. 3, 6.

[7] See "No se espera ninguna protesta de Patterson," *El I*, Feb. 27, 1950, p. 1;
"Especulación sobre la ejecución de 'El Borinqueño,'" *DCA*, Feb. 27, 1950, p. 8;
"Guatemala Snubs U.S. with Music," *NYT*, Feb. 27, 1950, p. 1; "Guatemalan Band
Sounds Note of Harmony for U.S.," *NYT*, Feb. 28, 1950, p. 19; "Pulling Uncle's
Whiskers," *Newsweek*, Mar. 13, 1950, p. 46; "Musical Disharmony," *Senior Scho-
lastic*, Mar. 18, 1950, p. 8. La Borinqueña is a popular Puerto Rican song.

[8] For the Guatemalan decision, see Inman, *A New Day*, pp. 53–54, and González
Orellana, *Historia de la educación*, p. 420. For the U.S. reaction, see Bennett, "Some
Aspects of Communist Penetration in Guatemala," Mar. 23, 1950, pp. 17–19. On the
program itself, see Griffith, "A Recent Attempt"; Casey, "Indigenismo," pp. 323–
38; González Orellana, *Historia de la educación*, pp. 414–22.

[9] "Some Aspects of Communist Penetration" (see n. 8 above), p. 13. See also

merman argues that "Guatemala's opposition to the Rio Pact stemmed from its longstanding controversy over control of Belize," then a British colony. As he correctly notes, when Guatemala finally ratified the pact, it reserved its right to liberate the territory by any means. This amendment was rejected, and therefore the ratification was withheld.[10] But the delay had had nothing to do with Belize. In fact, Mario Fuentes Peruccini, chairman of the Foreign Relations Committee of the Guatemalan Congress, did not even mention Belize when explaining the delay; he stated merely that the committee had been preoccupied with more urgent matters. The Belize issue was raised only on the day before the final vote on the ratification.)[11]

To wary U.S. officials, these actions were further proof of communist influence. But to what extent was the Guatemalan government dominated by the communists? To those who sought to unravel the mysteries of Guatemalan politics, "the biggest enigma" was Arévalo.[12] "On occasion," U.S. officials conceded, he had adopted repressive measures against "overt manifestations of communist tendencies,"[13] but as U.S. suspicions waxed, the significance given to these measures waned. Arévalo deported very few communists relative to the number Washington had branded as Reds. (And on one occasion— "significantly"—he gave $100 "out of his private funds" to two Salvadoran communists prior to their deportation, which he had ordered.)[14]

Arévalo did condemn communism in his speeches and writings, but "these protestations of devotion to purely democratic principles," noted Chargé Wells, were "more and more . . . difficult to reconcile" with his friendship with "international communists" such as the Chilean Pablo Neruda. Neruda had not only been allowed to visit Guatemala, but he had been treated "virtually as a state guest."[15]

Two different views of democracy were clashing. In the United States the anticommunist witch-hunt was well under way. Not only was the party per-

---

FRUS, 1950, 2:866, 909, 920, 925–27. For Truman's remarks, see DOS, *Press Releases*, no. 29, Jan. 11, 1950.

[10] Immerman, *CIA in Guatemala*, p. 94.

[11] For Fuentes Peruccini's declaration, see "Pacto de Rio será suscrito próximamente," *El I*, Feb. 20, 1950, p. 1. The best coverage of the congressional debate on the ratification is by *El I*: "En brillante jornada ratifícase el tratado de Rio de Janeiro," Sept. 20, 1950, p. 1; "Reserva sobre Belice y Tratado de Rio debaten hoy finalmente en el Congreso," Sept. 21, 1950, p. 1; "Tratado de Rio sobre ruedas," Sept. 22, 1950, p. 1.

[12] Wells to SecState, no. 170, Mar. 31, 1949, p. 2, NA 814.00B.

[13] OIR, "Guatemala: Communist Influence," Oct. 23, 1950, p. 51, NA.

[14] Ibid., p. 39.

[15] Wells to DOS, Nov. 15, 1950, *FRUS*, 1950, 2:922. See also MemoConv, May 12, 1950, ibid., p. 886, and "Guatemala: Communist Influence" (see n. 13 above), p. 37.

secuted, but so too were individual communists and fellow travelers of every shade; no true American could have any ties, personal or professional, with them. McCarthyism antedated the notoriety of the man and continued well after him. But Arévalo, the obscure president of a banana republic, refused to humor Washington's paranoia. Anticommunism did not blind him, nor did it blind most of the revolutionary leaders. They believed a communist could be an honest and honorable person; he could even be a friend, as the Chilean communist César Godoy was Arévalo's friend. In Neruda they saw genius, not depravity.[16]

It was difficult for Arévalo and the revolutionary leaders to take the Red threat seriously when there were so few communists in Guatemala. Had the communists conspired against the country's first democratic government, Arévalo would have moved against them. "Their identities are known," he told Wells. "Come a crisis, they would be rounded up in twenty-four hours."[17] The communists, however, were not the plotters; the plotters were the pillars of the upper class.

American officials could not imagine that the president of a banana republic might hold a broader view of political democracy than did they; they also believed that communist influence in Guatemala was more pervasive than Arévalo claimed. His lofty anticommunist rhetoric rang hollow to them and did not mask the truth: "Arévalo and company . . . are responsible for inviting, yielding to, and instigating the move toward communism."[18]

While the indictment appeared devastating, the verdict was not yet in. "There was a lot of debate at all levels in the U.S. embassy as to whether

[16] Even *El I*, ever sensitive to the communist threat, was not critical of Neruda's visits to Guatemala in 1949 and 1950. See "Neruda viene al país," July 12, 1949, p. 1; "Pablo Neruda se reunió con la gente de prensa," Apr. 16, 1950, p. 1; "Homenaje de normalistas para Neruda," Apr. 21, 1950, p. 1.

Godoy had been a close friend of Arévalo since 1928. He was then a fervent anticommunist, something that he continued to be for many years. In 1944, Arévalo writes, Godoy told him that he was about to join the Communist party—"It is your business, César: these are personal matters." Godoy first visited Guatemala in 1945 to attend Arévalo's inauguration. He returned on two or three occasions in the late 1940s as Arévalo's guest. (He came from Mexico where he was living in exile following the anticommunist persecution unleashed by President Gabriel González Videla in Chile.) (Arévalo, *La Argentina*, quoted from p. 506. See also ibid., pp. 73, 76–77, 80, 82, and Arévalo, *El candidato*, pp. 60, 65, 638.) For U.S. indignation at Arévalo's friendship with Godoy, see Wells, "Cesar Godoy Urrutia, Chilean Communist," July 5, 1949, RG84 GR, Box 217, NA-S; Wells to Wise, Oct. 7, 1949, p. 2, NA 814.00B; Wells to DOS, Nov. 15, 1950, *FRUS*, 1950, 2:922.

[17] Wells to DOS, July 7, 1950, *FRUS*, 1950, 2:906.

[18] Siracusa, "Summary of Statements Made by Mr. Siracusa in Presentation of Guatemalan Situation," p. 17, enclosed in Siracusa to Patterson, Aug. 22, 1949, RG84 GR, Box 216, NA-S.

Arévalo and his government were communist, crypto-communist, under communist influence or not communist at all," recalls an embassy official.[19] The embassy's views were not always consistent. An extreme mood was reflected in a November 3, 1949, report by the Guatemala desk officer of the State Department:

> Many sources allege that the present Government of Guatemala is Communist (Moscow)-directed. When I visited there recently our Embassy did not go so far as that but did characterize the Guatemalan government as "almost" in that category and certainly as a menace to Inter-American unity and defense. Furthermore, some Embassy officers maintained that the present Guatemalan government is so far involved with international Communism that there is no possibility of its disentanglement.[20]

At other times more sober counsel prevailed. The embassy's most influential official, Milton Wells, pointed out in May 1948 that "the saying 'one is known by the company he keeps' definitively adds to the case against Arévalo" and compiled a long list of Arévalo's sins. And yet, his conclusion was equivocal: "On balance, the writer is convinced that, despite these disturbing circumstances, the record does not make a closed case against Arévalo for alleged Communism. It is felt that he is more of a political opportunist of the extreme left."[21]

With abrupt swings toward greater pessimism, this "centrist" view prevailed, both in the embassy and in Washington, for the remaining two years of the Arévalo presidency. Despite their fears and their irritation, U.S. officials conceded occasionally in 1949 and 1950 that Arévalo and his government could act in a constructive manner. In 1949, Guatemala renewed the agreement allowing two U.S. military missions (air force and army) to operate in the country. And in September 1950, the Guatemalan Congress finally ratified the Rio Treaty by an overwhelming majority "over stubborn communist opposition." Furthermore after the Korean War broke out in June 1950, a July 14 memo stated, "while equivocal at first, Guatemala has since given evidence of support for the United Nations and for the United States."[22] In the following weeks, at the UN General Assembly, the Guatemalan Foreign Minister condemned "the aggression perpetrated upon the Republic of Korea" and reiterated that Guatemala "fully supports the Security Council's timely and vigorous action" (the dispatch of troops to Korea), while on Arévalo's behalf the Guatemalan ambassador informed the State Department that his

[19] Interview with Steins.

[20] Oakley to Miller, Nov. 3, 1949, p. 1, NA 814.00B.

[21] AmEmG, "Communism in Guatemala," pp. 15–16, enclosed in Wells to SecState, no. 217, May 6, 1948, NA 814.00B.

[22] Quotations from Wells to DOS, Oct. 19, 1950, *FRUS*, 1950, 2:920, and Mann to Barber, July 14, 1950, ibid., pp. 908–9.

country, "was one hundred percent behind the United States and the United Nations, that if the United States needed bases in Guatemala it could have them and that Guatemala was prepared to make available to the United Nations men for the armed forces if needed. . . . He had been authorized to put the President's offer in the form of a note if the Department so desired."[23]

These developments should have reassured U.S. officials; instead they confused them and strengthened their belief that, whatever his precise ideology, Arévalo was "a master at intrigue despite his protestations of being 'just a simple school teacher.' "[24] This, at least, was an accurate perception.

Amid their confusion and their suspicions, U.S. officials acknowledged that the communists faced formidable obstacles in Guatemala. While "influential both within the Government and without, especially in the labor unions," the communists were fewer than five hundred, and their influence rested on "the personal patronage of Arévalo or members of his immediate official family."[25] They faced countervailing forces, including the Church, the upper class, and, above all, the Guatemalan armed forces—"the key to the situation," stressed the embassy.[26]

U.S. reporting on the Guatemalan military was bizarre—yet consistent with the Americans' confused analysis of the country. This is illustrated by the two major U.S. reports on communism in Guatemala in the Arévalo years: a 28-page study written by a senior embassy official in 1948, and a 120-page analysis prepared by the State Department's Office of Intelligence and Research in 1950. In both reports, the reader frequently has the feeling that the communists are in control of Guatemala, or at least that the threat is severe and accelerating. Pages are devoted to minor aspects of communist infiltration, such as the possible emigration to Guatemala of Spanish exiles who, U.S. officials suspect, would include a goodly number of Reds.[27] There follows a

---

[23] Quotations from speech by Foreign Minister Ismael González Arévalo to the UN General Assembly, Sept. 21, 1950, p. 2 (Truman Papers, OF, Box 1287/439, TL), and MemoConv (Goubaud, Mann, Clark), Aug. 14, 1950, p. 2, NA 714.00. See also "Guatemalan Chief Ties Nation to U.S.," *NYT*, July 18, 1950, p. 6, and "Declaraciones de nuestro canciller en Washington," *El I*, Sept. 22, 1950.

[24] "Some Aspects of Communist Penetration" (see n. 8 above), p. 8.

[25] Quotations from "Current Relations With Guatemala," May 1950, *FRUS*, 1950, 2:900, and Wells to DOS, Nov. 15, 1950, ibid., p. 922. For the figure of less than five hundred communists, see "Guatemala: Communist Influence" (see n. 13 above), p. 81.

[26] Kyle to SecState, no. 189, Apr. 21, 1948, p. 3, NA 814.00.

[27] "Communism in Guatemala" (see n. 21 above), pp. 11–12; "Guatemala: Communist Influence" (see n. 13 above), pp. 42–45. Concerning the suspect Spaniards, the Guatemalan official in Paris who dealt with them has written: "Our Finance Minister, Charnaud MacDonald, wanted to develop Guatemala's fishing industry, so we

brief treatment of the Guatemalan armed forces: less than half a page in the 1948 study, less than three in the lengthier 1950 report.[28] Suddenly, we enter the realm of objectivity.

While the Guatemalan upper class claimed that the army was deeply infiltrated by the communists, U.S. officials disagreed: "There is better reason to believe that Communist infiltration is nonconsequential," argued the May 1948 report, not a mean concession from an embassy so prone to see communists everywhere. Infiltration was "virtually non-existent at present," concluded the 1950 study.[29]

Throughout the Arévalo presidency, no U.S. report even raised the possibility that the communists had infiltrated the military; rather, the army was "a keystone of stability." The military, the embassy noted, occupies "a relatively privileged position: officers are well-paid, and many have handsomely profited since the 1944 Revolution."[30] Unlike labor unions and middle class politicians, the army was, for U.S. officials, a familiar institution, and one they had dealt with for decades. Their reports indicate a dearth of information about the internal politics of the military, but the Americans believed they understood the Guatemalan officer. He might be opportunistic and corrupt, but he was fundamentally anticommunist. And he would never risk his privileged status in suicidal adventures in the heart of the American sphere of influence. It was, as events would demonstrate, a sound assessment.

It was Arana, U.S. officials believed, who controlled the military, and he was the soul of moderation. "If anyone within the present Government is well disposed towards the United States, it is Arana." His anticommunism was "above question." Embassy reports consistently stressed "that his concern regarding communist infiltration in this country is genuine," praised his sympathetic stance in favor of American companies, and noted how "on more than one occasion . . . [he had] demonstrated undisguised antipathy toward certain Government policies and toward certain individuals (described as ex-

---

were told to get fishermen from among the Spanish refugees in France. After several meetings with officials of the Spanish government-in-exile, Spaniards began to arrive at our embassy. . . . Every single one claimed to be a fisherman. Frequently, they were accompanied by children and very beautiful women. They knew nothing about fish except how to eat them." (Pellecer, "Crónica," p. 84.) "All in all, about fifty Spaniards emigrated to Guatemala. Not one was a communist, or even a fisherman—except for the López family, who now own a fishmarket in Guatemala City called La Catalana." (Interview with Pellecer.)

[28] "Communism in Guatemala" (see n. 21 above), p. 20; "Guatemala: Communist Influence" (see n. 13 above), pp. 55, 71–72.

[29] Quotations from "Communism in Guatemala" (see n. 21 above), p. 20, and "Guatemala: Communist Influence" (see n. 13 above), p. 55.

[30] Quotations from Wells to SecState, no. 175, Apr. 1, 1949, p. 1, NA 814.00, and Kyle to SecState, no. 189, Apr. 21, 1948, p. 3, NA 814.00.

tremists or communist suspects) closely identified with Arévalo and his Government."[31] Arana had actively cultivated the embassy's goodwill, informing U.S. officials of his devotion to American ideals and his sympathy for American companies, yet he did not mention his schemes and plots. The evidence persuasively indicates that the United States was unaware of his bid for power in the weeks that preceded his death; indeed, in early June 1949 an embassy dispatch had indicated that Arana and Arbenz had "composed their differences."[32]

Arana's death and the defeat of his followers alarmed U.S. officials. Arana "has always represented [the] only positive conservative element in [the] Arévalo Administration and was determined [to] run for the Presidency," a senior ARA official lamented on July 19. "Regardless responsibility [for] assassination," cabled Patterson on July 20, "end result eliminates important moderate elements Government and strengthens Leftist materially"; the following day he warned: "Consensus . . . [is] that developments forecast sharp leftist trend within [the] government."[33]

Arbenz was now the strongest man in the military. U.S. officials did not know him well, but their initial sympathy for this "highly idealistic" officer had given way, as Arbenz had moved to the left, to wariness and distrust.[34] No one suggested that he was a communist or a communist sympathizer but, cabled Patterson on July 22, 1949, "Arbenz is associated politically with Par-

[31] Quotations from: Wells to de Zengotita, Nov. 15, 1948, RG84 GR, Box 192, NA-S; "Communism in Guatemala" (see n. 21 above), p. 20; Wells to SecState, no. 2757, Dec. 12, 1947, NA 814.00B; Wells to SecState, no. 175, Apr. 1, 1949, p. 1, NA 814.00. See also Col. Devine, "Intelligence Report" no. 52–46, Feb. 6, 1946, RG319 GF, Box 1582, NA-S; Donovan to SecState, no. 1538, July 10, 1946, RG84 CF, Box 14, NA-S; HQs Panama Canal Department, "Weekly Intelligence Summary" no. 262, July 9, 1947, RG319 ID 382208, NA-S; HQs Panama Canal Department, "Weekly Intelligence Summary" no. 265, July 30, 1947, RG319 ID 388826, NA-S; Donovan to SecState, no. 2601, Aug. 12, 1947, RG84 GR, Box 177, NA-S; Wells to de Zengotita, Nov. 19, 1948, RG84 GR, Box 192, NA-S.

[32] Wells to SecState, no. 267, June 3, 1949, p. 2, NA 814.00.

[33] Quotations from: Siracusa, "Guatemala Situation," July 19, 1949; Patterson to SecState, no. 324, July 20, 1949; Patterson to SecState, no. 327, July 21, 1949. All NA 814.00.

[34] Quoted from Affeld, "Confidential Biographic Data: Francisco Javier Arana," Apr. 4, 1945, p. 2, RG84 GR, Box 217, NA-S. See also: Woodward to SecState, no. 2426, Apr. 24, 1945, RG84 GR, Box 134, NA-S; Col. Devine, "Alleged Communist Penetrations," no. 104–46, Mar. 29, 1946, RG84 CF, Box 14, NA-S; Donovan to Newbegin, Aug. 1, 1946, NA 814.00; Enclosure no. 1 in Donovan to SecState, no. 2075, Jan. 2, 1947, NA 814.00; AmEmG, "Re: Guatemala Political," Feb. 26, 1947, p. 6, RG84 GR, Box 176, NA-S; HQs Panama Canal Department, "Weekly Intelligence Summary" no. 262, July 9, 1947, RG319 ID 382208, NA-S.

tido Acción Revolucionaria and is identified with the more radical fringe of the Arévalo regime.''[35] These were not good references.

U.S. fears quickly subsided. As early as July 29, 1949, an ARA official, Ernest Siracusa, who had a ''close association with the situation in Guatemala,''[36] struck a far more positive note. While not excluding the possibility that ''Arbenz may decide to string along with Arévalo, thereby making the possibility of further leftism very real,'' Siracusa outlined a more comforting scenario, based on his conclusion that Arbenz was dishonest and shallow:

> Arbenz is not, in my opinion, a person with any deep seated intellectual alliance to the leftist cause, and, as such, no real sympathy for the lower classes or for the many outside communists who have infiltrated Guatemala.
>
> Arbenz is, in my opinion, essentially an opportunist who has strung along with the Arévalo bandwagon principally as a means of accumulating personal wealth and of giving ascendancy to his own political star. He has no admixtures of Indian blood, and is basically of an autocratic character.
>
> . . . Arbenz seems strongly to want to be president and he has a wife, with strong ideas, who wants to be first lady.
>
> The conclusion is this: Arbenz . . . might effect a coup d'état, using as his excuse the necessity of saving Guatemala from Communism.
>
> Not being an intellectual nor an honest leftist, Arbenz would make of himself a strong dictator, a necessary thing if he is to rid Guatemala of its leftist penetration. He will also have to be a strong dictator in order to remove from Guatemala some of the truly liberal gains of the revolution.
>
> My estimation of Arbenz is that he is the type of man who could and might do just this, and who could be truly ruthless if necessary.
>
> My judgment of him is that I don't and never have liked him, as a man. He has appeared to me to be shifty and not trustworthy.
>
> Such an eventuality would probably mean the end of the coercion of U.S. capital, a return of Guatemala to cooperation with the United States, and the end of any personal freedom in Guatemala.[37]

The thrust of the argument was clear: Arbenz was an unsavory character with whom the United States could work well. Siracusa's assessment was echoed within the State Department, where another ''Guatemala watcher'' argued two weeks later: ''If Arbenz continues to ally himself with the leftists, this will probably be only a temporary move in the interests of expediency. . . .

---

[35] Patterson to SecState, no. 385, July 22, 1949, p. 1, NA 711.14.

[36] Wise to Miller, July 29, 1949. Siracusa had been second secretary of the U.S. embassy in Guatemala until Mar. 14, 1949. In July 1949, he was the Guatemala desk officer.

[37] Siracusa to Wise, July 29, 1949, NA 814.00. See also Siracusa to Patterson, Aug. 3, 1949, RG84 GR, Box 216, NA-S.

(My long run guess is that Arbenz no longer has anything to gain by alliance with leftists, that a clash will occur from his pressure to contain them, and that he will, sooner or later, use this as a pretext for overt action in his own interests.)"[38]

Abandoning his earlier pessimism, Patterson heartily concurred. After the defeat of the *Aranistas*, he wrote to UFCO's president:

> The first inclination of most people here was that it forecast a sharper leftward move in the Government. All along I have felt that this is not necessarily the case because of the kind of man I believe Arbenz to be. He is an opportunist with no deep seated leftist convictions. . . . Since he wants to be President and is clever, his best bet is an alliance with the United States. Therefore, if he remains in the saddle it means better results for American interests and the possible eradication of the foreign Communist element. In any event, I believe that United Fruit and other interests will not suffer because of the Revolution.[39]

Over the ensuing months, through the presidential elections of November 1950 and into the first weeks of the Arbenz presidency, this became the dominant view of U.S. officials, although a slight feeling of uneasiness persisted. From Guatemala, the State Department received comforting reports of conversations that senior embassy officials held with Arbenz between August 1949 and March 1951.[40] It is difficult to determine what most deluded U.S. officials in these conversations. Was it what Arbenz said, though judging from the embassy's reports he seldom ventured beyond banalities? Or was it, as his wife suggests, the polite silence with which he listened to the Americans' diatribes about developments in Guatemala?[41] In any case, U.S. officials were certainly led astray by their own bias. They had already decided that Arbenz was a man devoid of strong political beliefs. Moreover, he was a military officer: a left-wing colonel was an unknown species in Central America.

In August 1949, Milton Wells provided a rare glimpse of a different Arbenz:

> With obvious sincerity and clarity of language Colonel Arbenz spoke at length on the basic aims of the 1944 Revolution and the Arévalo regime—which, in simple

[38] Bennett to Barber and Miller, Aug. 9, 1949, p. 1, NA 711.14.

[39] Patterson to Zemurray (president of United Fruit), Aug. 11, 1949, Patterson Papers, Box 5, TL. See also Patterson to Miller and Patterson to Siracusa, both Aug. 12, 1949, RG84 GR, Box 216, NA-S.

[40] See esp. Patterson to SecState, no. 385, July 22, 1949, NA 711.14; Patterson to SecState, no. 417, Aug. 3, 1949, NA 711.14; Wells to SecState, no 433, Aug. 11, 1949, NA 814.00; Wells to SecState, no. 435, Aug. 12, 1949, NA 711.14; Wells to DOS, no. 395, Mar. 31, 1950, NA 611.14; CIA, "Guatemala," SR-46, July 27, 1950, pp. 45–46, Truman Papers, President's Secretary's File, Intelligence File, Box 261, TL; Wells to DOS, Nov. 15, 1950, *FRUS*, 1950, 2:922–25; Wells to Clark, Jan. 22, 1951, NA 714.00.

[41] Interview with María de Arbenz; also interviews with Fortuny and Guerra Borges.

terms, are to bring social and economic betterment to the people, and to establish a decent, democratic way of life, which will make impossible the old-style military coups d'etat and personal dictatorships under which the people have suffered for generations. It must be understood, he argued . . . that the laws of the land are general, affecting Guatemalan and United States firms and persons alike.[42]

This image of a compassionate man was utterly overlooked. Questions were raised neither by Wells who wrote the report, nor by those who read it. Arbenz's opportunism had become an article of faith for U.S. officials. This opportunist would have few qualms, they argued, at betraying his friends from the PAR and organized labor (including the communists) after he had used them to win the elections. He would sacrifice them in order to curry the favor of the dominant player—the United States. The military would welcome the reversal of Arévalo's radical policies: "The Army is going to back Arbenz in a determined anti-Communist policy," reported Wells. Thus, the embassy welcomed Arbenz's presidential victory with "restrained optimism."[43] On February 16, 1951, the embassy informed the State Department that the communists "are probably seeking to strengthen themselves against the possibility of finding themselves in disfavor with the future [Arbenz] administration."[44]

Thus, the Truman administration reassured itself that under Arbenz the Guatemalan army would remain a formidable bulwark against communism. Arbenz was a dishonest and unsavory character, but self-interest would drive him into the familiar embrace of Washington. Arana's death, which had initially unnerved the Americans, was not as disruptive as they had feared. The military, Guatemala's most powerful institution, was still healthy—that is, anticommunist.

It is this conviction, held before Arana's death and reestablished soon after it, that explains why, their indignation and their concern notwithstanding, U.S. officials did not plot to overthrow Arévalo. But short of that, they exerted whatever diplomatic, economic, and psychological pressure they could on the Guatemalan regime. They were hampered by two constraints. They wanted to avoid causing undue damage to the inter-American system and the most obvious sanction—the denial of economic aid—was hardly an option, given the minimal amount of aid offered to Latin America at the time. "Fortunately or

[42] MemoConv (Arbenz, Kielhauer, Patterson, Wells), Aug. 9, 1949, quoted from pp. 1–2, enclosed in Wells to SecState, no. 435, Aug. 12, 1949, NA 711.14.

[43] Wells to DOS, Nov. 15, 1950, *FRUS*, 1950, 2:923, 925. It was "the firm belief of the American Embassy . . . that he [Arbenz] would move to the Right," the British Legation reported. ("Extract from Guatemala Report dated 4th May, 1951," RG84 CF, Box 15, NA-S.)

[44] Wardlaw to DOS, no. 839, Feb. 16, 1951, p. 2, NA 714.00.

unfortunately," an embassy official moaned, "our most obvious weapons are useless."[45]

ARA officials briefly considered arraigning Guatemala before the Organization of American States, but they dismissed the idea because even they realized that none but the most servile of banana republics would have endorsed the proposition that Arévalo was the aggressor against the United States and a threat to inter-American security. In State Department parlance, this was translated into the bizarre observation that "even though Latin American states might feel a deep concern with developments in Guatemala, there would doubtless be many which would censor any United States act or policy which was or appeared to be interventionist."[46] Obviously, it had not occurred to U.S. officials that their relentless diplomatic pressure on the Arévalo regime might already be considered interventionist. Until 1950, the Truman administration provided only insignificant amounts of aid to Latin America; a termination of the tiny U.S. program of technical assistance to Guatemala, the State Department concluded, would have little practical effect on that country, while supplying potent fodder for leftist propaganda. Hence, a policy of "selective withholding of cooperation" was adopted by default.[47] This policy was extended to military affairs. Beginning in 1949, the United States imposed a systematic embargo on arms sales to Guatemala.[48]

Greater opportunities to punish the Arévalo administration arose in 1950, after Congress had approved Truman's Point Four foreign aid program. "Until such time as the overall situation in Guatemala changes," Secretary Acheson decreed, no Point Four money would be given to it.[49] In 1950 the World Bank,

[45] Siracusa (see n. 18 above), p. 20.

[46] MemoConv, Dec. 29, 1950, *FRUS*, 1950, 2:930 (quoted), and "Current Relations with Guatemala," May 1950, ibid., p. 900.

[47] Clark to Wise, Oct. 6, 1949, NA 711.14. See also de Zengotita to Barber, Woodward and Daniels, June 7, 1949, NA 711.14; MemoConv (Patterson, Daniels, Barber, de Zengotita), June 8, 1949, NA 814.00; Wise to Barber and Miller, Aug. 1, 1949, NA 814.00; "Current Relations with Guatemala," May 1950, *FRUS*, 1950, 2:901. For a detailed example of the thinking behind this policy, see Siracusa (see n. 18 above), pp. 20–23.

[48] For the arms' embargo, which was not made public at the time, see Clark to Bennett, Feb. 6, 1950, NA 714.5; Clark to Mann, Sept. 13, 1950, NA 714.56; MemoConv (Mara, Clark), Oct. 25, 1950, NA Lot 57D95, Box 2. For a telling exchange, see Col. Deerwester to Ambassador, July 10, 1951, RG84 CF, Box 15, NA-S, and DOS, "Guatemalan Request for Defence Order Priority for Five Hundred 38 Calibre Revolvers," July 23, 1951, NA 714.5614. In the former, the U.S. air attaché "recommends, from the standpoint of necessity for law enforcement, that favorable consideration be given this request [for 500 pistols for the police force]"; in the latter, the powers that be in Washington and Ambassador Schoenfeld in Guatemala deny the request.

[49] SecState to AmEmG, Oct. 11, 1950, *FRUS*, 1950, 2:918.

in which U.S. influence was decisive, refused "a much-needed loan to Guatemala." As Assistant Secretary Miller later explained to Congress, the World Bank "sent a mission down there . . . to make some recommendations for loans. We asked [them] . . . not to do that, that we . . . would exercise the veto power against such loans."[50]

There was only one significant deviation from this pattern of niggardly aid. Between 1945 and 1951, Washington contributed $6 million to the construction of the Guatemalan portion of the Inter-American Highway, which would link Texas to Panama. The project was beneficial to Guatemala—but also to the United States, as Miller stressed in his forceful May 1950 congressional testimony.[51]

While there is no evidence that U.S. officials urged Arana to overthrow Arévalo, the tenor of U.S. reports in 1948 and 1949 (including those reports dealing with the possibility that Arana might seize power) indicates that such a move would not have been unwelcome; this was in stark contrast to U.S. reports in 1945 and 1946, which had expressed frank opposition to any military coup. It is evident that, at least after 1947, Arana was restrained by his own scruples and hopes, not by Washington. And when he finally acted in July 1949, he did so without informing the United States.

In May 1950, several months after Arana's death, UFCO's lobbyist Corcoran paid a visit to Thomas Mann, director of the State Department's Office of Middle American Affairs. "He had been turning over in his mind the possibility that the American companies might agree between themselves on some method to bring moderate elements into power in Guatemala," and he wanted to know whether the State Department "had any program for bringing about the election of a middle-of-the-road candidate" in the November presidential contest. His overture was rebuffed by Mann, who argued that any attempt to interfere in the elections would become known, causing a backlash in Guatemala and throughout Latin America, and that it would, in any case, prove ineffectual. U.S. policy, Corcoran was told, was to wait and see. "Although," Mann went on, "I would not like to try to guess what the policy in the future might be if it were definitively determined that the Guatemalan Government and people had fallen under the totalitarian control of communist elements."[52]

By the time this exchange took place, some U.S. officials had been advo-

---

[50] Quotations from "Red Shadow in Elections," *Newsweek*, Nov. 13, 1950, p. 52, and U.S. Congress, *HCFA*, p. 399. See also MemoConv (Consolo, Waterson, Miller, Cady, Wise), Dec. 14, 1949, RG84 GR, Box 217, NA-S.

[51] See Miller's testimony before the Senate Committee on Public Works, May 25, 1950, Miller Papers, Box 2, TL, and Patterson's testimony before the same committee, May 25, 1950, Patterson Papers, Box 5, TL. See also United Nations, *El transporte*, pp. 17–18.

[52] MemoConv, May 15, 1950, *FRUS*, 1950, 2:888–89.

cating another form of punishment for the wayward Guatemalans: "We should encourage outstanding newspapers and magazines to take an interest in happenings in Guatemala, to study them on the spot, and to report them forthrightly." In an August 1949 cable to the State Department, Ambassador Patterson welcomed the appearance of a highly critical article in the *Wall Street Journal*. (A few months later, in a letter to UFCO President Samuel Zemurray, Patterson also urged that there be "an all-out barrage in the United States Senate on the bad treatment of American capital in Guatemala.")[53] In the same vein, in the fall of 1950, UFCO's consultant Edward Bernays proposed that the company engage in a public relations offensive on the communist threat in Guatemala. UFCO executives, Bernays complains in his memoirs, were slow to appreciate the wisdom of his suggestions; and the offensive began in earnest only two years later; this delay, he concludes philosophically, "was not unusual in corporate life, where do-nothing is rather safer than taking a chance."[54] Apparently UFCO, though having lost none of its arrogance, was no longer the risk-taking company it once had been; it preferred to rely on the exertions of the State Department and on its own economic muscle in its dealings with Arévalo. "Companies, like people," an UFCO executive has remarked, "have most of their energy when they are young, and as they age they lose their potency. . . . When I joined United Fruit in 1952 . . . the company was already well into middle age and its arteries had started to harden."[55]

Still, whether on their own initiative or prodded by the State Department, the conservative *New York Herald Tribune* and the liberal *New York Times* decided to probe developments in Guatemala. The results were strikingly similar. In February 1950, the *Herald Tribune* published a five-part series by Fitzburgh Turner entitled "Communism in the Caribbean," which was followed in June by Will Lissner's *New York Times* series on the same subject, both front page news.[56] The two series closely echoed the views of the State Department, with shrill cries about the communist threat and unabashed praise of UFCO. Turner and Lissner were instant experts who hid their ignorance behind glibness. Reading their articles, one had the impression that Guatemala's communist agents (both foreign and native) had trooped into the journalists' hotel rooms to confess their dastardly schemes. More likely, however, the revelations came from more respectable sources: embassy officials, represen-

[53] Quotations from Siracusa (see n. 18 above), p. 22 and Patterson to Zemurray, Jan. 11, 1950, Patterson Papers, Box 5, TL. See also Wise to Barber and Miller, Aug. 1, 1949, RG84 GR, Box 216, NA-S; "Things in Guatemala," *WSJ*, Aug. 10, 1949, p. 1; Patterson to SecState, no. 445, Aug. 18, 1949, NA 711.14.

[54] Bernays, *Biography of an Idea*, p. 760.

[55] McCann, *American Company*, p. 14.

[56] Turner, "Communism in the Caribbean," *New York Herald Tribune*, Feb. 8–13, 1950, and Lissner, "Soviet Agents Plotting to Ruin Unity, Defenses of Americas," *NYT*, June 22–27, 1950.

tatives of the American companies, and upper-class Guatemalans. Lurid details laced the stories: "communist goons resembling New York mobsters bullied students, workers, intellectuals. . . . democrats lived in terror for their lives," and so on. And the moral: as a result of the persecution of American companies, the Guatemalan people suffered while, thanks to Truman's Point Four, business was booming elsewhere in Central America; while Arévalo connived with the communists, rulers like Somoza were looking after the welfare of their people. It was yellow journalism in the style of the 1890s, and it was also typical of American journalists dealing with banana republics in the late 1940s. Cold war paranoia and sheer ignorance were more powerful than all the manipulations of Edward Bernays and other skillful minions in the pay of United Fruit.

A systematic press campaign against Guatemala was not under way. To be sure, by 1949 and 1950 friendly references to the Arévalo regime were extremely rare; the most conspicuous example was an article in *The Nation* in January 1950.[57] Communist penetration of Guatemala and Guatemala's persecution of American companies were generally treated in tandem; even the liberal *Hispanic American Report*—the voice of Stanford University on Latin American affairs—heaped scorn on the "Red-stained" Arévalo, the "unmistakable party-line nature of many of his policies," and the "communist tendencies" of his government.[58] Guatemala, however, did not loom large in the American press. Between Lissner's diatribe and the end of Arévalo's term, only four major stories appeared. In *The Reporter*, Theodore Draper presented the Guatemalan government as naughty and inept, but not communist; compared to the other stories, this was restraint. The *Reader's Digest* exposed Guatemala's role in the communists' "global master-plan against the United States." The *Saturday Evening Post* revealed that *Arevalismo* was a "systematic effort to make the Guatemalan revolution follow the course of the October Revolution in Russia." And *Life* ran a five-page spread, replete with photographs, on "Sam the Banana Man," the generous, misunderstood Samuel Zemurray, president of UFCO.[59]

---

[57] Ovidio Gondi, "Chaos on Our Doorstep," Jan. 28, 1950, pp. 81–83. Gondi's article evoked a stern response from UFCO's President Zemurray. (See "La Frutera's Record," *The Nation*, Mar. 25, 1950, pp. 287–89.) On March 18, *The Nation* had published an article that combined a contemptuous critique of the Arévalo administration with an even harsher assessment of Turner's series in the *New York Herald Tribune*. (Ellis Ogle, "Communism in the Caribbean?" pp. 246–47.)

[58] Quotations from *Hispanic American Report*: Dec. 1950, p. 13; Mar. 1950, p. 12; Aug. 1950, p. 12.

[59] Draper, "The Minutemen of Guatemala," *The Reporter*, Oct. 24, 1950, pp. 32–35 and "How Red is Guatemala?" *The Reporter*, Nov. 7, 1950, pp. 23–27; J. P. McEvoy, "Trouble in Our Own Back Yard," *Reader's Digest*, Aug. 11, 1950, pp. 7–11 (quoted p. 10); Leigh White, "Red Threat on Our Tropic Frontier," *Saturday Eve-*

The Congress of the United States occasionally turned its attention to Arévalo's Guatemala. The august body first noticed the tiny country in February 1949. Two issues sparked the congressmen's interest: UFCO's travails and Truman's Point Four. Not surprisingly, the Massachusetts delegation led the attack. Senator Henry Cabot Lodge delivered the first broadside on February 14: UFCO was being persecuted in Guatemala "through actions which, I am informed, can be directly traced to Communist influences"; aid was a two-way street, conditioned on the principle of just and equal treatment—Guatemala had disqualified itself from the benefits of Point Four.[60] Within the month two other senators and three representatives shared their wisdom on Guatemalan affairs with Congress: UFCO was being persecuted, the company's record deserved strong praise, and the communists were scheming.[61]

After the congressional outburst of February 1949 and the settlement between UFCO and the unions in March, Congress was silent on Guatemala for the rest of the year. There was a lone exception: Senator Francis Myers, noting the *Diario de Centro América*'s (Guatemala's government daily) tribute to George Washington on the Fourth of July, placed a tribute to Guatemalan and Central American independence in the *Congressional Record*.[62] In 1950, only two congressmen spoke out in Congress about Guatemala. Spurred by the Patterson incident, Alexander Wiley, a prominent member of the Senate Foreign Relations Committee, warned that while "redder pastures appear in the distance in Europe and in China . . . right on this continent we have a red pasture." The same warning had been given in the House a few days earlier by Representative John McCormack, who combined his scathing attacks on the Arévalo administration with unabashed praise of United Fruit.[63]

For a Congress that was busy unmasking traitors at home and debating the "loss" of China, entanglement in Europe, and war in Korea, Guatemala was a minor and unglamorous issue, an issue, moreover, that could not be exploited for partisan purposes. The Republicans had no quarrel with the administration's handling of Guatemalan matters: even crusty Senator Wiley—at first suspicious that the State Department might not be 100 percent behind Patterson after the ambassador had been "booted out" of Guatemala "by a

---

ning Post, Oct. 28, 1950, pp. 24–25, 146, 148–49 (quoted from p. 148); John Kobler, "Sam The Banana Man," *Life*, Feb. 19, 1951, pp. 83–84, 87–88, 91–92, 94.

[60] Lodge (R-Mass), Feb. 14, 1949, *CR*-Senate, p. 1172.

[61] Claude Pepper (D-Fla), Feb. 17, 1949, ibid., pp. 1353–54; Lister Hill (D-Ala), Feb. 14, 1949, ibid., p. 1353; John McCormack (D-Mass), Feb. 21, 1949, *CR*-House, pp. 1463–64; Christian Herter (R-Mass), Feb. 24, 1949, ibid., p. 1496; Mike Mansfield (D-Mont), Feb. 21, 1949, ibid., p. 1498.

[62] Myers (D-Pa), Sept. 15, 1949, *CR*-Senate, p. 12936. For the article in *DCA*, see "Nuestro saludo a la patria de Washington y Roosevelt," July 2, 1949, p. 1.

[63] Wiley (R-Wisc), Apr. 27, 1950, *CR*-Senate, pp. 5879–81 (quoted from p. 5879); McCormack, Apr. 3, 1950, *CR*-House, pp. A2538–41.

Red controlled government''—was mollified by the visit of a State Department delegation to the office of his legislative assistant.[64]

Guatemala was not yet perceived as the Soviet beachhead in the Western Hemisphere. It remained *terra incognita* for the immense majority of Americans. To President Truman and the senior members of his administration, Guatemala was but an eddy in a sea of worries. Washington was willing to give the unsavory Arbenz a chance. But American patience was not infinite: ''If the Arbenz Administration fails to take a positive stand, public opinion in the United States and elsewhere in the Hemisphere would probably support a more direct approach to the problem,'' the State Department concluded.[65] The words were not vehement, but the implications were ominous.

[64] Wiley to Miller, Aug. 26, 1950, Truman Papers, OF, Box 1352/558, TL.
[65] MemoConv, Dec. 29, 1950, *FRUS*, 1950, 2:930.

CHAPTER 7

The World of Jacobo Arbenz

JACOBO ARBENZ betrayed the hopes of the Truman administration. Had he been the opportunist the Americans anticipated, had he been the cynic they expected, he would have used the power of the presidency to court the Americans. Had he chosen this path, it is difficult to see who could have stopped him. The officer corps was loyal and had no desire for more reforms; urban labor was weak and unarmed; the countryside was quiet. Arbenz could easily have imposed a pause in the revolution. Instead he advanced along an unprecedented and increasingly dangerous road. His presidency would be marked by three departures: agrarian reform, close ties with the Communist party, stubborn defiance of the United States. As he pressed forward, he lost touch with his original power base, the military. He became a lonely man who had to act on two levels: the private Arbenz who confided only in his wife and the leaders of the Communist party, and the public Arbenz who hid his true beliefs. This secretive and increasingly harried man accomplished a unique feat: the first true agrarian reform of Central America. As in a Greek tragedy, the more he accomplished, the closer he came to his destruction and the destruction of his dream. When he fell, in June 1954, he was mentally and physically exhausted.

Many explanations have been offered for the fate of this enigmatic man. Conservative critics have seen in him a man driven by ambition and greed. Liberal analysts have seen in him a well-intentioned reformer who became to some degree a prisoner of the communists' embrace. Radical authors have spurned him as a petty bourgeois who was either unwilling or unable to deepen the revolution.[1]

A major influence on Jacobo Arbenz, friends and foes agree, was his Salvadoran wife, María Vilanova. Indeed, some have described her husband as putty in her hands. Jacobo and María were, in fact, partners in a process of radicalization that began slowly and became increasingly rapid. They shared the same evolution, the same beliefs, and the same friends.

They met in 1938, while María was spending a few weeks in Guatemala, her mother's country. She was immediately attracted to the good-looking and se-

---

[1] See for instance Martz, *Communist Infiltration*; James, *Red Design*; Immerman, *CIA in Guatemala*; Schlesinger and Kinzer, *Bitter Fruit*; Cardoza y Aragón, *La Revolución Guatemalteca*; Jonas and Tobis, *Guatemala*.

rious young officer, who spoke and laughed little, but had, at times, "a smile that made me fall in love."[2]

And yet they seemed very different. From a rich Salvadoran family, María had studied in the United States, was relatively well read, liked classical music and painting, and combined a deep intellectual curiosity with a gregarious personality. Jacobo had never left Guatemala, showed little interest in the arts, and found it difficult to express his feelings. María recalls of their courtship:

> At times, I would ask him, "Do you like Beethoven?" There would be a silence. Then, very seriously, he would answer, "I have never heard Beethoven." I would ask him, "Do you like this book?" Again, silence, and then, always very serious, he would answer, "I have never read this book," and I would despair, and wonder, "Why am I falling in love with this man, so different from me, with whom I share so few interests?" But then, once, I asked him, "What would you like to be?" And very seriously he answered, "I would like to be a reformer," and then I thought, "Yes. We do have something very important in common."[3]

Neither could have explained what it meant to be a reformer or how and what one should reform. They simply shared a feeling that something was wrong, deeply wrong, in the society that surrounded them. They were married a few months later, in early 1939, without the permission of María's parents, who bitterly disapproved of their daughter's match with a penniless lieutenant. ("My family was furious and refused to have anything to do with us," recalls María.)[4] Jacobo was twenty-six and his bride twenty-four years old.

Two people who would deeply influence one another had joined together. María had enjoyed a comfortable youth, untroubled by family dramas. Her father, a rich landowner, sent her to the College of Notre Dame in Belmont, California, but at the onset of the Great Depression she had returned to El Salvador. The family was rich, but not rich enough to afford the luxury of maintaining a daughter in the United States during an economic crisis. In a few years she would marry, and a woman of her class would have no need to work. It was, on the face of it, a most banal story.[5]

Less banal was that María, who spent her summers on her father's estates, became uneasy about the desperate plight of the peasants. Her father's participation in the peasants' massacre of 1932 troubled her. ("He spoke of it in

---

[2] Interview with María de Arbenz.

[3] Interview with María de Arbenz.

[4] Interview with María de Arbenz. "Jacobo was slow to propose. At last, when I was just about to return to El Salvador, he asked me, 'Will you come back to Guatemala? I would like to marry you. But I can't right now because I don't earn enough.' I left for El Salvador. But once back home, I thought: 'Why wait? What do I care about money? Let's get married right away!' I went back to Guatemala and we got married without my family's approval."

[5] Interview with María de Arbenz.

such a matter of fact way . . . 'We killed so many.' ") And her grandmother's piety failed to reassure her. ("She went in her beautiful car to hand out old clothes and food to destitute peasants.") Something was terribly wrong, even though she hardly knew what and why.[6] These were just doubts, shadows of questions that a conventional marriage might well have stifled. Instead she met Arbenz.

Arbenz's youth had been far less comfortable and was scarred by personal tragedy. His father, a Swiss German, had come to Guatemala in 1901 and had settled in Quetzaltenango, the country's second city. There he had opened a pharmacy and married a middle-class Ladino woman. Born in 1913, Jacobo grew up in comfortable circumstances, with the cachet of a European father whose Nordic complexion he inherited. (He was, a 1950 CIA study noted, "of upper-class European ancestry.")[7] Then disaster struck: Jacobo's father became addicted to morphine. He neglected his business. The pharmacy went bankrupt and the family was forced to retire to a small estate in the vicinity of Quetzaltenango that a German friend put at their disposal "out of charity." This was a trauma the young Jacobo never forgot.[8]

The family's financial disaster meant that Jacobo could no longer hope to go to the university. "He would have liked to have been an economist or an engineer." He had no desire to enter the military, but if he won a scholarship he could get a free education at the Escuela Politécnica.[9] He applied, passed the entrance examinations, and in 1932 entered the academy as a cadet. Two years later, his father committed suicide.

In the Escuela Politécnica, Jacobo Arbenz was occasionally rebellious and always reserved. He was also "an exceptional student," in the words of a 1971 history published by the Guatemalan armed forces.[10] Excelling both in athletics and in academics, he became first sergeant, the highest honor to which a cadet could aspire and a distinction that only six other cadets achieved between 1924 and 1944.[11] Indeed, notes a fellow officer, "his abilities were such that the officers treated him with a respect which was rarely granted to a

[6] Interview with María de Arbenz.

[7] CIA, "Guatemala," SR-46, July 27, 1950, p. 39, Truman Papers, President's Secretary's File, Intelligence File, Box 261, TL.

[8] Interviews with María de Arbenz (quoted), Fortuny, and Rolz Bennett, a childhood friend of Arbenz. For a biographical sketch of Arbenz, see Zea Carrascosa, *Semblanzas*, pp. 283–86. García Añoveros, *Jacobo Arbenz*, is the only biography of Arbenz, but it is disappointing and perfunctory.

[9] Interviews with María de Arbenz (quoted), Fortuny, Rolz Bennett, and Guerra Borges.

[10] Zea Carrascosa, *Semblanzas*, p. 284.

[11] On Arbenz as a cadet, see ibid., pp. 283–84; Samayoa Coronado, *La Escuela Politécnica*, 2:96, 98; Morazán, "Apuntes," pp. 248–57, 466–73, 522–33. For a list of the first sergeants between 1924 and 1944, see Escuela Politécnica, *Centenario*.

cadet." This respect was shared by Major John Considine, the American director of the Escuela Politécnica, and the other U.S. officers who served in the academy.[12]

Arbenz graduated in December 1935, having so impressed his superiors that they had him transferred back to the academy in early 1937, when a position became vacant. In the interval Arbenz experienced the squalid life of a junior officer in Ubico's army, serving first at Fort San José in the capital and then in the tiny army garrison in the small town of San Juan Sacatepéquez "under an illiterate colonel."[13] While at San José, he, like the other officers, had to lead squads of soldiers who escorted chain gangs of convicts (including political prisoners) to perform forced labor. For Arbenz, "it was yet another trauma; he felt like a *capataz*." It was then that he first met Arana, who was stationed at Fort Matamoros, also in the capital. They met while watching their convicts, jailers performing a degrading task.[14]

From March 1937 until the fall of Ubico, Arbenz was stationed at the Escuela Politécnica, an oasis in the grim world of the Guatemalan armed forces. "In a dismal lethargic Army," the U.S. military attaché reported, "it is the only alert unit."[15] Instead of supervising convicts and serving under illiterate colonels, he was in daily contact with competent military officers—the Americans on loan to the academy. In addition to his other duties, he became a professor, teaching cadets a wide range of courses (from military subjects to history and physics) and, in the process, broadening his own limited education. In 1943 he was promoted to captain and placed in command of the entire corps of cadets. It was the third highest position in the academy and "one of the most prestigious posts to which a young officer could aspire."[16]

The brilliant cadet had grown into a superb officer. Even colleagues who later turned against him remember his "magnetism," and readily acknowledge that he was "a born leader"[17]—characteristics that helped him, in later

[12] Interviews with Maj. Paz Tejada (quoted), Lt. Col. Mendizabal, and Cols. Guillén, Lorenzana, Mendoza, and González Siguí.

[13] Quoted from interview with Fortuny. See also Zea Carrascosa, *Semblanzas*, p. 283, and Samayoa Coronado, *La Escuela Politécnica*, 2:99.

[14] Interviews with Fortuny (quoted) and María de Arbenz. See also Lt. Enrique de León Aragón, "Situaciones sobre el origen de la Revolución del Veinte de Octubre," *El Libertador*, Oct. 23, 1945, p. 10.

[15] Marsh, "National Military Academy," no. 414, May 18, 1942, p. 3, RG165 RF, Box 1572, NA-S.

[16] Quoted from interview with Paz Tejada. Zea Carrascosa, *Semblanzas*, p. 284, lists the courses taught by Arbenz: military history of Central America, world history, military reporting, communications and fortifications, physics, mechanics, the art of war, geometry, and tactics.

[17] Quotations from interviews with Lt. Montenegro and Col. Lorenzana. All the Guatemalan officers interviewed by the author concurred with this assessment.

years, to retain the respect, if not the loyalty, of the Guatemalan officer corps. His keen intelligence was nourished by a growing interest in books that his wife helped to stimulate.

Arbenz could be affable, but he remained inscrutable. "It was difficult to know what he thought";[18] he had many acquaintances but few friends. "He lived in his own world, thinking his own thoughts," recalls a cadet who served under him; "he was a reformer who encouraged some of us to read books that other officers considered subversive."[19] A professor at the academy remembers Arbenz as an officer whose "grasp of civilian and military matters was unusually broad for a man of his age and surroundings, and whose concern for the future of his country was intense."[20]

One night when Arbenz was on duty, "he saw me arrive among those who were to be punished," writes Carlos Manuel Pellecer, who was then a cadet.

> He called me to his office and poured me a strong coffee. He gave me a copy of the *Essays* of Emerson. . . . Yes, the *Essays* of the North American philosopher Ralph Waldo Emerson, and he told me: "This will be more useful than punishment. Read it." Two hours later, he came and asked: "What have you learned?" I responded by quoting from the book: "As a plant upon the earth, so a man rests upon the bosom of God; he is nourished by unfailing fountains, and draws, at his need, inexhaustible power. Who can set bounds to the possibilities of man? Once inhale the upper air, being admitted to behold the absolute natures of justice and truth, and we learn that man has access to the entire mind of the Creator, is himself the creator in the finite."
> . . . Arbenz smiled and gave me permission to leave.[21]

Pellecer was an unusual cadet, highly intelligent, rebellious and full of intellectual curiosity; he was eventually expelled from the Escuela Politécnica and later became a leader of the Communist party. But in 1964, when he wrote of this encounter with Arbenz, he had renounced his past and was courting Arbenz's foes.[22] He had nothing to gain, and something to lose, from portraying Arbenz in a favorable light.

The world of Jacobo Arbenz and his wife, in those last years of Ubico's rule, was not that of the Guatemalan upper class. "But what did we care?" María muses. "They were parasites—like in El Salvador. I wanted to broaden my horizons. I hadn't come to Guatemala to be a socialite and play bridge or golf."[23] But if Arbenz did not belong to the upper class, neither was he the pauper that some have portrayed. His position at the Escuela Politécnica gave

[18] Interview with Col. Lorenzana.
[19] Interview with Lt. Col. Mendizabal.
[20] Interview with Arriola.
[21] Pellecer, *Memoria en dos geografías*, p. 140.
[22] For Pellecer after 1954, see below, p. 389.
[23] Interview with María de Arbenz.

him a degree of social prestige and a salary that, while modest, was three times that of an officer of similar rank who did not serve at the academy.[24] Nor were he and his wife outcasts. They had a number of upper-class acquaintances (particularly from Quetzaltenango, Arbenz's hometown), and one of Arbenz's sisters had married into one of Guatemala's most prominent families, the Aparicios. Upon the birth of their first child, nine months after the marriage, María's parents forgave the couple. (Yet the initial rejection had deeply hurt Arbenz.)[25] It was hardly a period of frustrations. "We were young; we were in love. Together we were learning and growing."[26] María indulged in one of her great passions, painting, as she still does today. One of their closest friends was Enrique Muñoz Meany, a civilian who taught at the Escuela Politécnica, an intellectual with progressive leanings who helped Jacobo Arbenz to imagine a world beyond Guatemala's narrow confines.[27]

They were, then, an attractive couple, both good-looking, both white (socially an important factor), he withdrawn but with "an imposing personality that inspired respect,"[28] she full of verve and *joie de vivre*. An interesting couple, of some social status, and an intellectual couple, especially by the abysmal standards of their milieu. But in no way were they, or did they appear to be, revolutionaries.

The first hint of revolt came in early 1944 when Arbenz and a small group of officers and civilian professors from the Escuela Politécnica began to plot against Ubico. Their plans, however, never got off the drawing board.[29]

The first act of revolt came in July 1944, in the wake of Ubico's resignation. On July 3, with several friends, Arbenz went in civilian clothes to the special session of Congress called to elect the provisional president of the republic. He was present, therefore, when troops occupied the building to remind the legislators that the man they wanted was General Ponce. "Jacobo," María wrote a few days later to her parents, "left the Congress seething. . . . He came home choking with rage." That same week he resigned from the army

[24] "The salary of a lieutenant was $30 per month. In the Escuela Politécnica, Arbenz earned $90." (Interview with Paz Tejada.)

[25] Interviews with María de Arbenz, Fortuny, and Rolz Bennett. The child, Arabella, was María's parents' first grandchild.

[26] Interview with María de Arbenz. See also María Vilanova de Arbenz, "Aclaración."

[27] Interview with María de Arbenz. On Muñoz Meany, see Saker-Ti, *Enrique Muñoz Meany*; "Enrique Muñoz Meany muere en Paris," *El I*, Dec. 22, 1951, p. 1; "Homenaje a Muñoz Meany," *DCA*, Dec. 9, 1953, p. 1.

[28] Interview with Col. Mendoza.

[29] Interview with Arriola, a civilian professor at the academy who joined the plot (as did Arbenz's friend Muñoz Meany). Confirmed by interview with María de Arbenz. See also de León Aragón, "Situaciones" (see n. 14 above), p. 8.

to protest the imposition of Ponce. He was the only Guatemalan officer to do so.[30]

Arbenz began plotting. He and Major Aldana Sandoval were the military leaders of the conspiracy that eventually overthrew Ponce. "It was Arbenz," muses Aldana Sandoval, "who insisted that civilians be included. At the Guardia de Honor, our position was: 'No civilians, military men only.' So all contact with the civilians was through Arbenz—only Arbenz."[31]

On October 4, Arbenz wrote to his wife, who was with her parents in El Salvador:

> All the players will soon be in place. The civilians have confidence in me; they support us. I think that you are going to enjoy what is in store. . . . We are almost ready and we will strike decisively. I have been authorized to form a *de facto* government. . . . We will call elections for a Constituent Assembly and then presidential elections, both of which will be completely free. Therefore, Arévalo will win. If we succeed, we will have written a brilliant and patriotic page in our history.[32]

Ponce fell, and Arbenz kept his promise. Overcoming Arana's resistance, he and Jorge Toriello made sure that president-elect Arévalo was inaugurated on schedule. Unlike Arana and Toriello, he never plotted against Arévalo.

Jacobo Arbenz and his wife knew nothing of Marxism when the Arévalo presidency began. They shared, however, "a love of books" and "restlessness and sensitivity to social problems."[33] In a Guatemala suddenly exposed to new ideas, their questions were becoming more urgent, as they searched for explanations of Guatemala's underdevelopment and of the plight of the lower classes. ("How can the country progress when its people don't have enough to eat? . . . I often thought of this and felt ashamed.") Their nationalism, too, was assuming more definite contours, and Arbenz, who had been so appreciated by his American superiors at the Escuela Politécnica, began to question the U.S. role in Guatemala. Muñoz Meany, a staunch nationalist and a *bête noire* of the U.S. embassy, remained a close friend, and relationships that were based on respect rather than warmth developed between Arbenz and some young leftist leaders, notably Charnaud MacDonald.[34]

[30] Quoted from María de Arbenz, letter to her parents, July 7, 1944; Arévalo Martínez, *Ubico*, pp. 299–300; de León Aragón, "Situaciones" (see n. 14 above), pp. 8, 10; Krehm, *Democracies and Tyrannies*, p. 52; Wardlaw to DOS, no. 617, Dec. 21, 1950, NA 714.11.

[31] Interview with Aldana Sandoval. Confirmed by interview with Rolz Bennett, a civilian plotter.

[32] Jacobo Arbenz, letter to his wife, Oct. 4, 1944. María had been sent by Arbenz to her parents' house in San Salvador to shield her from danger. Arbenz's letters to his wife are warm and affectionate. (María de Arbenz asked the author not to quote any personal passages.)

[33] Interview with Charnaud, who knew Arbenz well at the time.

[34] Interview with Charnaud, quoting Arbenz. Also helpful were interviews with

The first Marxist work came by chance into Jacobo's and María's hands. It was the *Communist Manifesto*, which María received at a women's congress, read, and placed on Jacobo's bedside table before leaving for a brief vacation. "When I returned," she recalls, "he asked me: 'What is this that you left for me?' He too had been moved. Together we talked about the *Manifesto*. It seemed to us that it explained what we had been feeling."[35] Increasingly, Arbenz read about history and economics; he also began to develop a taste for philosophy. Increasingly, his reading included Marxist writings, among them works by Marx, Lenin, and Stalin. "Marxist theory," María observes, "offered Jacobo explanations that weren't available in other theories. What other theory can one use to analyze our country's past? Marx is not perfect, but he comes closest to explaining the history of Guatemala."[36]

As U.S. relations with Arévalo soured and the conflict with American companies grew ever more bitter, Arbenz's frustrated nationalism stimulated first his curiosity, then his sympathy, for the Soviet Union. In the words of Charnaud MacDonald, for Arbenz the Soviet Union represented "something new in the world—rising in opposition to the old world. Three basic facts attracted Arbenz: it was governed by a class which had been ruthlessly exploited; it had defeated illiteracy and raised the standard of living in a very short time; it had never harmed Guatemala." As an officer, Arbenz was also deeply impressed by the Soviet triumph over Hitler; increasingly he attributed this triumph not only to the Russian people, but to their social system.[37]

This political radicalization went hand in hand with Arbenz's growing disenchantment with the revolutionary parties, which seemed to lack both the ability to conceptualize the radical changes that he believed Guatemala needed and the will to implement them.

Friends also played a role in his radicalization. By the late 1940s, Arbenz was growing closer to a group of young Guatemalan communists—the future leaders of the PGT[38]—men like Alfredo Guerra Borges, Víctor Manuel Gutiérrez, Mario Silva Jonama, Bernardo Alvarado Monzón. These were warm relationships, grounded both in politics and in friendship. But of all his friends, none would be as close as José Manuel Fortuny, who in 1948 became

María de Arbenz, Fortuny, Guerra Borges, Paz Tejada. Initially, Arbenz had discussed broadening the role of the U.S. military missions in Guatemala with embassy officials. See Woodward to SecState, no. 2426, Apr. 24, 1945, p. 2, RG84 GR, Box 134, NA-S.

[35] Interview with María de Arbenz.

[36] Interview with María de Arbenz. For a revealing report of a conversation between María de Arbenz and an embassy official, see MemoConv (Mrs. Arbenz, Wardlaw), Aug. 3, 1951, RG84 CF, Box 15, NA-S.

[37] Interviews with Charnaud (quoted), María de Arbenz, Fortuny, Guerra Borges.

[38] *Partido Guatemalteco del Trabajo*, the new name adopted by the Guatemalan Communist party in Dec. 1952.

the secretary general of Vanguardia Democrática, the clandestine forerunner of the Guatemalan Communist party.[39]

Arbenz and Fortuny had starkly different personalities. Fortuny, like María, was extroverted. He was full of wit, vivacious, interested in everything from movies to politics; he could talk for hours, without ever becoming boring (a quality he has retained).[40] Like Arbenz, he was moved by fierce nationalism and an ardent desire to improve the lot of the Guatemalan people; like Arbenz, he searched for answers in Marxist theory.

In Fortuny, Arbenz found the brother he had never had, the complement of himself, a man with whom he felt totally at ease, "without having to wear a mask, relaxed," sharing the most intimate thoughts, both personal and political. It was a relationship he would never have with anyone else, except María.[41]

Their friendship began in the fall of 1947, after Arbenz stood up in the cabinet and forcefully opposed the move to deport several labor leaders accused of being communists. Fortuny, who had seen no difference between Arbenz and Arana until then, paid a visit to the defense minister, intrigued by his unexpected behavior.[42]

He discovered a man unlike the stereotype of the military, a man who, with his wife, had "a burning desire" to learn more and to grapple with every issue that he considered vital to the future of Guatemala. "There was almost a competition between them to see who would learn more. . . . Soon Jacobo began to overtake María."[43] In 1950, the CIA paid Arbenz a handsome compliment: he was, a lengthy study noted, "brilliant . . . cultured."[44]

A first, rather formal encounter between Arbenz and Fortuny was followed by others that became increasingly frank. Arbenz began inviting Fortuny to his house; "the conversations would last until late in the night."[45] Jacobo and his wife had begun exploring Marxism (and the Soviet Union) before their relations with Fortuny grew close. In Fortuny, they found someone who had embarked along the same road, although he frankly acknowledged that he was still a novice. (Thus, recalls Fortuny, he was reading books by Soviet generals about the Russian front in the Second World War, notably one that focused on the battle of Kursk. Arbenz asked him: " 'What do you think is the cause of

---

[39] Interviews with María de Arbenz, Guerra Borges, and Fortuny. There is no evidence to support the oft-repeated assertion that Salvadoran and other foreign communists played a key role in the radicalization of Doña María. She herself denies it.

[40] Based on extended conversations with Fortuny between 1978 and 1988.

[41] Interviews with María de Arbenz (quoted), Fortuny, Pellecer, and Guerra Borges.

[42] Interview with Fortuny. See also above, pp. 58–59.

[43] Interview with Fortuny.

[44] CIA (see n. 7 above), p. 39.

[45] Interviews with Fortuny (quoted) and María de Arbenz.

the Soviet victory over the Germans?' I answered: 'I am not quite sure, but the laws of dialectic. . . . look, I don't really get it yet, but I think . . .' '')[46]

There were other friends too. Some belonged to the middle and the upper classes, people whom Arbenz and his wife had known for years. They danced together, they drank together, but they did not talk about politics. María enjoyed the company of artists. Arbenz, for his part, was genuinely fond of several young officers who had been his colleagues or students at the Escuela Politécnica, men such as Alfonso Martínez, Terencio Guillén, Amadeo García, Carlos Bracamonte, Carlos Enrique Díaz. With them, too, he remained reticent about what most preoccupied him. And he shared fewer and fewer of his political thoughts with earlier confidants like Muñoz Meany and Charnaud MacDonald. By the late 1940s, recalls his wife, "Of all the political leaders, the only ones with whom we had informal, relaxed conversations were those from the PGT, Fortuny above all."[47]

In 1950, when the presidential contest began, Arbenz asked Fortuny to write his campaign speeches. With Fortuny, and to a lesser degree with the other leaders of the fledgling Communist party, he explored the future of Guatemala; increasingly his thoughts turned to the necessity of agrarian reform, the battle cry of the Communist party. In Fortuny's words, "1950 was a decisive year in the ideological evolution of Jacobo Arbenz."[48]

After Arbenz became president, the leaders of the revolutionary parties besieged him in their incessant quest for personal gain, quarreling among themselves for his favor. More and more Arbenz appreciated the honesty and discipline of his communist friends, who sought advantage not for themselves, but for their cause; alone among the government's supporters, they had a program that was specific, at least by Guatemalan standards. Arbenz was increasingly attracted to this as the best hope for the Guatemalan people and nation. Ronald Schneider, whose *Communism in Guatemala* is not known for its sympathy for Arbenz, suggests how the president grew closer to the communists in the first eighteen months of his term:

> The Communists . . . impressed Arbenz as the most honest and trustworthy, as well as the hardest working of his supporters.
>
> . . . As the politicians of the other revolutionary parties lapsed into opportunism and concentrated upon getting the lion's share of the spoils of office, the Communists' stock rose in the President's eyes.
>
> The Communists worked hardest in support of the President's pet project, agrarian reform, and were able to provide the background studies, technical advice, mass

[46] Interview with Fortuny.

[47] Interview with María de Arbenz. Interviews with Rolz Bennett, Lt. García, and Col. Guillén were useful in developing this portrait of Arbenz.

[48] Interview with Fortuny.

support and enthusiasm which the project required. The struggle for the enactment of agrarian reform became a dividing line in the eyes of Arbenz; those who opposed it were his enemies and those whose support was only lukewarm dropped in his esteem. . . . In contrast to the other politicians, the Communists brought him answers and plans rather than problems and constant demands for the spoils of office.[49]

Agrarian reform was, indeed, Arbenz's "pet project." This passionate interest was "an aberration"[50] for a middle-class Ladino, an aberration that only a deep urge for social justice can explain. The revolutionary leaders showed little enthusiasm for comprehensive agrarian reform. Radical change, they feared, might trigger economic chaos and, worse, unleash forces that they might be unable to control. The awakening of the rural masses—largely Indians—alarmed revolutionary leaders content with the rewards of political life. These leaders were also preoccupied, one of their number concedes, with more immediate tasks: "When Arbenz became president," notes Charnaud MacDonald, "the revolutionary parties were fighting among themselves over who got what posts. What help could Arbenz expect from them in his struggle for agrarian reform? Their program was opportunistic; that of the PGT was honest."[51]

Nor was there strong pressure for reform from the countryside. Apart from UFCO's plantations, rural Guatemala had been largely untouched by the Arévalo years. The labor confederations had been calling for land reform, but they were impotent without the active support of the state. Under Arévalo the central government had provided no such support, and its representatives in the countryside, including the army and the police, had sided with the landowners.

While most of Guatemala's politicians considered that the revolution had peaked, Arbenz became ever more committed to the revolution which, in his view, had only begun. Agrarian reform would forge the political basis for the eventual radicalization of the Guatemalan revolution.[52]

Before becoming president Arbenz had been reading about agriculture, Guatemala's in particular. He profited from lengthy conversations with María's brother, Tonio, who was an agricultural expert, and in 1950 with a Mexican economist, Manuel Germán Parra. He also learned from his own finca, El Cajón, which he had bought in the late 1940s with money borrowed from his in-laws and turned into an experimental farm run by modern methods.[53] No higher compliment could be paid to Arbenz's grasp of agricultural affairs

[49] Schneider, *Communism*, pp. 195, 196 and 197.

[50] Silvert, *Study in Government*, p. 12.

[51] Interview with Charnaud.

[52] Interviews with María de Arbenz, Alejandro, Fortuny, and Guerra Borges.

[53] Interviews with Fortuny, María de Arbenz, Guerra Borges, Guillén (who became El Cajón's resident administrator), and Zachrisson (wife of Tonio Vilanova).

than that proffered by an eminent Guatemalan intellectual, Mario Monteforte Toledo, whose sympathy for Arbenz was, at best, tenuous. Monteforte writes, "In the meetings that President Arbenz had with the representatives of AGA to discuss agrarian reform [in May 1952], he knew more about the country's agrarian problems than they did."[54]

In late 1951, while public discussion about agrarian reform proceeded in dilatory fashion, Arbenz prepared to act. He secretly summoned three communist leaders: Fortuny, Gutiérrez, and Silva Jonama. In the following weeks they met informally to discuss "the basic structure of the agrarian reform."[55] After several meetings, Arbenz asked Fortuny to prepare the first draft of the law. As Fortuny proceeded article by article, each was reviewed by the PGT's Political Commission. (Some articles relating to the mode of compensation of expropriated landowners were first drafted by a noncommunist, the economist Guillermo Noriega Morales.) The complete draft was then presented to Arbenz. After introducing several modifications, Arbenz called a second working group, which included three PGT leaders—Fortuny, Gutiérrez, and Pellecer—and one noncommunist, the CNCG's secretary general, Leonardo Castillo Flores. After several more meetings, the draft acquired its final form, the brainchild of the PGT "with the extremely active participation of Jacobo Arbenz."[56]

In March 1952 Arbenz announced, "The first draft of an agrarian reform law will be sent this year to the Congress." These words, he noted a year later, "received little attention, except among the workers. . . . Perhaps so many promises had been made to the Guatemalan people in the past that this promise, too, seemed to be empty rhetoric."[57]

But in late April 1952 Arbenz presented an unsuspecting cabinet with a fait accompli: a fully developed program of agrarian reform. ("I can't tell you who prepared the document," remarks a minister. "It was handed to us, and we were asked for our reactions.") On May 10, after a few days of cursory discussion in the cabinet, the draft was formally introduced in Congress.[58]

Throughout the country passions rose, fear spread, and hope surged. The

[54] Monteforte Toledo, *Guatemala*, p. 435, n. 2.

[55] Interviews with Fortuny (quoted), María de Arbenz, and Guerra Borges.

[56] Interviews with Guerra Borges (quoted), María de Arbenz, Alejandro, Fortuny, and Pellecer. (Pellecer claims that he was included in the deliberations from the beginning and that he drafted several articles.) Interview with Noriega Morales confirmed the others' accounts of his participation.

[57] Arbenz, *Informe del ciudadano presidente*, pp. viii–ix.

[58] See "Proyecto entrega el Ejecutivo al Congreso," *El I*, May 10, 1952, p. 1, and "Proyecto de reforma agraria al Congreso," *DCA*, May 10, 1952, p. 1. For the full text of the draft see "Ley de reforma agraria," *DCA*, May 12, 14, 15, 16, 1952 (all p. 4). For the discussions in the cabinet, interviews with ministers Arriola (quoted), Charnaud, and Galich were helpful.

landed elite, represented by the Asociación General de Agricultores (AGA), responded with cries of pain and anger, pressing Arbenz to withdraw his bill and to accept instead its own hastily prepared project of agrarian reform, which emphasized generous government credits for its own members.[59] AGA inveighed against "a totalitarian law" that constituted "the most monstrous act of robbery ever perpetrated by any ruler in our history," and claimed that "the immense majority of the Guatemalan people . . . rejects categorically the communist origins of this law and its nefarious consequences for our motherland." Guatemala, AGA warned, was entering "the most dramatic and decisive days of its history."[60] The Church and most of the press supported AGA.[61] It was all to no avail. Jacobo Arbenz would not budge.

The leaders of the revolutionary parties were uneasy about a document they considered premature and radical, and they were taken aback by Arbenz's methods; they had been neither informed nor consulted about the preparation of the draft. They had, however, little choice but to support the president. Arbenz was more than the leader of the government coalition: he was a military caudillo and a formidable personality. By his actions, and through private and public remarks, he had made it clear that agrarian reform had become "the heart of his program, almost an obsession."[62] He had never been, the U.S. embassy reported, "so obstinate about any particular thing."[63] Open defiance would have created a dangerous crisis. Under intense presidential pressure and amid public demonstrations of support organized in the capital by the labor confederations, the bill was approved in Congress in the early hours of June 17, 1952. That same day, Arbenz signed it into law as Decree 900.[64] After

[59] See Asociación General de Agricultores, *Proyecto de ley agraria*. For the government's response see Guatemala, *Crítica al proyecto de ley agraria*.

[60] Quotations from "La AGA al pueblo de Guatemala," *La Hora*, June 18, 1952, p. 10, and from "La AGA ante la conciencia honrada del pueblo de Guatemala rechaza temerosas imputaciones," *La Hora*, June 19, 1952, p. 10. These are only two of an avalanche of communiqués published by the association. Some titles are particularly evocative, for instance: "The Wolves Cast Off Their Sheep's Clothing" (*La Hora*, May 30, 1952, p. 10), and "Selling the Leather Before Killing the Cow" (*La Hora*, June 3, 1952, p. 10).

[61] See below, pp. 210–15.

[62] Particularly useful were interviews with the following politicians: Galich (quoted), Charnaud, Morgan, and Capuano.

[63] Miller to Krieg and Larsen, May 27, 1952, p. 1, RG84 CF, Box 15, NA-S.

[64] For the debates in Congress, see Actas del Congreso, *Primer periodo ordinario de sesiones, 28 de febrero al 30 de mayo 1952* (Libro no. 15, 1952), and *Sesiones extraordinarias, 12 de junio a 3 de julio, 1952* (Libro no. 16, 1952). For the changes introduced in Congress to the government's bill, see Paredes Moreira, *Reforma agraria*, pp. 50–51. Of the press, *DCA* and the opposition dailies *El I* and *La Hora* are particularly useful.

years of sterile discussions, the country had a comprehensive agrarian reform law, thanks to Jacobo Arbenz and the PGT. If a revolution began in Guatemala, the date was not October 20, 1944, but June 17, 1952.

It was the preparation and the enactment of the agrarian reform bill that finally brought Arbenz over to the communists' side. By late 1952, President Arbenz had chosen the stand from which he would not deviate. His closest political friend was the PGT, and his closest personal friends were its leaders. Arbenz continued to read. "He read books on the Russian revolution, the history of the USSR, the military strategy of the Soviet generals in WWII. All this molded his way of looking at the world," observes Fortuny.[65] By 1952, "through all this reading," adds his wife, "Jacobo was convinced that the triumph of communism in the world was inevitable and desirable. The march of history was toward communism. Capitalism was doomed."[66]

Arbenz did not become a member of the PGT until 1957, three years after he had been overthrown; had he joined while president, he would have had to submit to party discipline. This could have created unnecessary conflicts and disturbed the close cooperation between him and the party. But in the last two years of his administration he considered himself a communist, and with his few confidants, he spoke like one. The PGT leaders formed his "kitchen cabinet," and with them he took his most important decisions; the only major disagreement between the president and the party occurred in the last two days of his presidency and concerned his eventual resignation. Perhaps Arbenz should not formally be called a communist, yet fellow traveler fails to convey the intensity of his commitment.[67]

Arbenz and the PGT did not think that a communist state, however desirable, could be established in Guatemala in the near future.[68] Guatemala, they believed, was a semifeudal country; therefore, it must first pass through a capitalist stage in which the material conditions for socialism would be developed by means of an agrarian reform program that would eventually lead to industrialization and the growth of a proletariat. This was the view of the international Communist movement toward semifeudal countries (as all Latin American Communist parties, at the time, saw their respective countries), and this is what Lenin had argued in his *Development of Capitalism in Russia*, a treatise that became a textbook for the Political Commission of the PGT. Only a

[65] Interview with Fortuny.

[66] Interview with María de Arbenz. (I had asked for her response to Fortuny's statement quoted immediately above.)

[67] Interviews with Fortuny, María de Arbenz, Guerra Borges, Alejandro, and Charnaud, who became a close friend of Arbenz after his overthrow.

[68] The remainder of this chapter is based primarily on interviews with María de Arbenz, Fortuny, Alejandro, and Guerra Borges.

country favored by geography could afford to skip the capitalist stage and move directly toward socialism: Mongolia, which had the good fortune "to border the Soviet Union," and the "tiny great nation of Albania."[69] Pragmatic considerations reinforced the theory. Guatemala was in the heart of the American empire. While Arbenz and the PGT underestimated the American threat, they were, nevertheless, convinced that in the foreseeable future Washington would not tolerate the emergence of a communist Guatemala. Thus, theory provided the welcome reassurance that the impossible need not be attempted. As a result, recalls Guerra Borges, the PGT "enthusiastically endorsed the thesis that Guatemala must first go through a capitalist stage. When we stated this we were not trying to hoodwink anyone. We were convinced of it."[70] This capitalist phase, the president and the party believed, had to be planned and executed carefully. Capitalist development under a government as corrupt and conservative as that of President Miguel Alemán in Mexico would be very different from that which would occur in Guatemala under a government led by Jacobo Arbenz. Moreover, while progressing into this capitalist stage, "the idea was to do nothing that would make the introduction of socialism more difficult, but rather to take steps that would make it easier."[71]

Arbenz, his wife, and the leaders of the PGT were convinced that the entire world would eventually become a socialist community. "Communism was inevitable, we thought,"[72] and it might come to Guatemala before it came to the United States. For this to happen, however, there had to be a change in the correlation of forces, both at the international level and within Guatemala itself. How long this would require they did not know. On those few occasions when they touched on the subject, the length of the delay (many years, a few decades) varied according to their optimism at the moment. Someday, they concluded, Guatemala would be Marxist-Leninist. But for the time being it was far more important to devote their energy to the tasks at hand than to indulge in idle speculation. Of the tasks at hand, none was more compelling than agrarian reform.

[69] Quotations from interview with Guerra Borges, and from Fortuny, *Informe sobre la actividad del Comité Central*, p. 35.

[70] Quoted from interview with Guerra Borges.

[71] Quoted from interview with María de Arbenz.

[72] María de Arbenz, letter to the author, Dec. 11, 1987, p. 10.

Jacobo Arbenz and his wife María, shortly after their marriage in 1939.

Jacobo and María, September 1945. Arbenz was the minister ot defense. María Vilanova was an upper-class Salvadoran. Together they could have led a charmed, upper-class life.

The civilian, Jorge Toriello, flanked by Francisco Arana on his right and Jacobo Arbenz on his left. This triumvirate assumed power after the fall of the dictator Ponce. (On the left is Aldana Sandoval, who helped plan the revolt, but lacked the courage to participate in it.) After the uprising, the civilians handed back their weapons, and effective power resided in the army.

Guatemalan soldiers being greeted by Jorge Toriello, October 22, 1944.

Juan José Arévalo returned to Guatemala from Argentina to become the first president of the Guatemalan revolution. A charismatic, honest, and self-confident man, he declared that his doctrine of Spiritual Socialism was "a true innovation for Latin America . . . which until now has been grappling with only conservatives, liberals and Marxists."

Francisco Arana, chief of the armed forces under Arévalo, was arguably the most powerful man in Guatemala. In 1949, he was poised to become the next president, but he was killed in a shootout near Guatemala City. His killers were never apprehended.

Arévalo "had the physique of a very big man," a U.S. diplomat recalls. "And his opinion of himself was also very big."

Arana courted U.S. officials. They considered him "the only positive, conservative element in the Arévalo administration" and were alarmed by his death.

Arana and Arévalo. It was not the army that prevented Arévalo from enacting an agrarian reform program: Arévalo was a middle-class Ladino; the world of the Indian was distant and fearsome.

Carlos Paz Tejada and Arévalo. Paz Tejada became chief of the armed forces after the death of Arana. As the U.S. air attaché reported, he was ''intelligent . . . gracious . . . a good organizer and administrator.''

President Arbenz on his inauguration day. Arbenz, U.S. officials believed, was
"an opportunist"; his presidency would mean "a return of Guatemala to
cooperation with the United States, and the end of any personal freedom in
Guatemala." In fact, his presidency was to be marked by agrarian reform, close
ties with the Communist party, and stubborn defiance of the United States.

María de Arbenz on inauguration day. Some have described her husband as
putty in her hands, but she was actually his partner in a process of radicalization
that became increasingly rapid. They shared the same evolution, the same
beliefs, and the same friends.

Arbenz in exile, painted by his wife in 1965.

Arbenz in Havana, 1962. ''The Cubans were very condescending,''
recalls María. ''They made Jacobo feel useless.''

CHAPTER 8

The Agrarian Reform

IN HIS INAUGURAL address, Arbenz set forth the goals of his economic program: "to transform Guatemala from a dependent nation with a semi-colonial economy into a country that is economically independent; to transform Guatemala from a backward country with a semifeudal economy into a modern capitalist country; to proceed in a way that will ensure the greatest possible improvement in the standard of living of the great masses of our people."[1]

Agrarian reform was the heart of Arbenz's program, but he also emphasized the need to modernize the country's physical infrastructure. Both were essential to the economic development of Guatemala and to the transformation of its rural population from serfs into citizens. In tackling these two fronts—agrarian reform and public works—Arbenz faced an added challenge: he would not rely on foreign capital. He had little choice. In view of the reputation of his administration, it was most unlikely that Americans would lend money to Guatemala, and the United States was, at the time, virtually the only source of foreign private capital available to a Central American country. Nor could the World Bank be relied upon. It had refused a "much needed loan" to Arévalo in 1950 at Washington's behest, and there was no reason to expect it to be more forthcoming. (In 1951, the World Bank asked the State Department's permission before showing its report on Guatemala to the Guatemalan authorities.)[2]

In the absence of foreign loans, Guatemala could undertake a program of public works only if the agrarian reform did not deplete the country's resources and decrease agricultural output. Good luck would also be necessary; the high international price of coffee that had blessed the Arévalo presidency would have to be maintained.

This, then, defined Arbenz's economic program: self-sustained economic development based on agrarian reform and public works. Together, they would provide the foundation for a more distant aim, the light industrialization of Guatemala. Industrialization, Arbenz stated, could not begin in earnest in the short span of his presidency, but he would support existing industries and look favorably on new ones.

[1] Arévalo, *Discursos del doctor Juan José Arévalo y del teniente coronel Jacobo Arbenz*, p. 26.

[2] For the 1950 incident, see above, pp. 128–29. For that of 1951, see MemoConv ("Mr. Lopéz-Herrarte's impressions of the situation in Guatemala"), Jan. 18, 1951, NA 714.00.

Arbenz was about to embark on the first comprehensive development plan in the history of Guatemala, whereas his predecessor had not even outlined such a plan. In his first speeches as president, Arbenz frankly acknowledged that he could only offer a blueprint and that much planning remained. He pledged, however, that he would transform his words into deeds. And he stressed, with a passion that many dismissed as empty rhetoric, the centrality of social justice:

> I grant great importance to economic policy, but only as a means to achieve our social goals. All the riches of Guatemala are not as important as the life, the freedom, the dignity, the health and the happiness of the most humble of its people. How wrong we would be if—mistaking the means for the end—we were to set financial stability and economic growth as the supreme goals of our policy, sacrificing to them the well being of our masses. . . . Our task is to work together in order to produce more wealth. . . . But we must distribute these riches so that those who have less—and they are the immense majority—benefit more, while those who have more—and they are so few—also benefit, but to a lesser extent. How could it be otherwise, given the poverty, the poor health, and the lack of education of our people?[3]

Arbenz spoke these words in April 1951. For the next twelve months the land tenure system remained unchanged, and no major public works were begun. Then the tempo accelerated, as Arbenz presented his draft of the agrarian reform law to a stunned Congress. Five weeks later, on June 17, 1952, Decree 900 was approved.

DECREE 900

The law, a senior FAO official reported, "was constructive and democratic in its aims. . . . It would bring about a land structure and a system of land tenure largely centering around the needs and aspirations of the individual peasant families."[4] It stipulated that all uncultivated land in private estates of more than 672 acres would be expropriated; idle land in estates of between 224 and 672 acres would be expropriated only if less than two thirds of the estate was under cultivation; estates of less than 224 acres would not be affected. By contrast, the government-owned Fincas Nacionales would be entirely parcelled out.[5]

[3] Arbenz, *Exposición*, pp. 8–9.

[4] AmEm Rome, Hayes, "Report of Director, Agriculture Division, FAO [Food and Agriculture Organization], on Land Reform Situation in Guatemala," Oct. 22, 1952, p. 2, RG84 CF, Box 15, NA-S.

[5] Arts. 9–12. For the text of Decree 900, see *El Guatemalteco*, June 17, 1952, 135:86, pp. 957–62.

Land expropriated from private estates would be given in private ownership or in lifetime tenure according to the recipient's wishes; in the latter case, upon the death of the beneficiary, his family would receive preferential consideration to rent the same land.[6] The Fincas Nacionales would be distributed in lifetime tenure only. For twenty-five years, every beneficiary would pay the government 3 percent of the annual value of the crop if he had received the land in lifetime tenure and 5 percent if he had received the land in outright ownership.

The former owners would be compensated with 3 percent agrarian bonds maturing in twenty-five years; the value of the expropriated land would be that declared by the owners on their tax returns prior to May 10, 1952, the day the agrarian reform bill had been presented to Congress.[7]

The introduction of the lifetime tenure system, the government claimed, would prevent large landowners from quickly recovering the parcels given to the peasants.[8] For Arbenz and the PGT, there was another, unstated rationale: "to introduce a progressive element into a capitalist reform." In Fortuny's words, "It was the PGT that proposed that land be given in lifetime tenure. Arbenz agreed."[9]

Decree 900 established a hierarchical system to implement the reform. At the bottom were the local agrarian committees (*comités agrarios locales* or CALs). Each CAL had five members, one appointed by the governor of the department in which the CAL was located, one by the municipality, and three by the local labor union. Where there was no labor organization or where there was more than one, the peasants and the agricultural workers would elect their representatives in popular assemblies.[10] Any people who thought they were entitled could petition the CAL for land that they considered eligible for expropriation. The CAL would assess the validity of the request and forward its recommendation to the departmental agrarian committee (*comité agrario departamental* or CAD).

The CADs, too, had five members: one chosen by the landowners' association (AGA), one each by the country's two labor confederations, one by the department's governor, and one by the newly created National Agrarian Department (*Departamento Agrario Nacional* or DAN). The CADs would supervise the work of the CALs and report to the DAN in the capital; the DAN

---

[6] Art. 39.

[7] Art. 6.

[8] See "Contestación a la AGA," *DCA*, June 3, 1952, p. 1, and "No hay contradicciones en el proyecto de ley de reforma agraria del Ejecutivo ni la AGA quiere hacer más 'propietarios,' " *DCA*, June 6, 1952, p. 8.

[9] Quotations from interviews with María de Arbenz and Fortuny. By June 1954, only 27.5 percent of the land had been given in freehold. (Paredes Moreira, "Aspectos y resultados," p. 59.)

[10] Art. 57.

would review the CADs' decisions. At the apex stood the president of the republic who "would serve as the final arbiter of all disputes raised by the implementation of the law." Thus, while the principle of administrative review was established throughout the expropriation process, the courts were expressly excluded.[11]

Many analysts portray Decree 900 as a moderate law cast in a capitalist mold. In particular, they note, only uncultivated land could be expropriated, and that only from large estates.[12] However, not only did Decree 900 introduce the lifetime tenure system, but it stipulated that the expropriation process would have to be completed in six weeks—a dramatic change in a country "accustomed to red tape and bureaucracy, where 'wait and see' is a way of life, where social legislation in the past had always been circumvented."[13] Moreover, through the CADs and the CALs, Decree 900 sought to stimulate the participation of the peasants and the labor organizations, rather than to impose the reform from the top alone. In Fortuny's words,

> We [the PGT] proposed the creation of peasant committees [CALs] in order to lay the groundwork for the eventual radicalization of the peasantry. We talked to Arbenz about this, and he agreed with us. What we wanted was to foster the control of the reform from below. This would give the peasants a strong sense of their common needs. And if, from the system of lifetime tenure, cooperatives developed, the seeds of a more collective society would have been sown.[14]

The Office of Intelligence Research (OIR) of the State Department had little criticism of the technical aspects of Decree 900. "If the Agrarian Law is fully implemented," it noted, "the impact upon private landholders would be borne chiefly by a minority. . . . Of 341,191 private agricultural holdings only 1,710 would be affected. These 1,710 holdings, however, comprise more than half of the total private acreage." The OIR went on to voice its deep concern: successful implementation of Decree 900 would strengthen the government's influence in the countryside and would provide the communists with "an excellent opportunity to extend their influence over the rural population."[15]

The months that followed the enactment of Decree 900 were, on all sides, a time of preparation. While the government began to establish the machinery

[11] Arts. 52, 54–56, 59 (quoted), and 60.

[12] Even the U.S. embassy concluded that the law was "relatively moderate in form." ("Economic and Financial Review—1953," no. 953, May 19, 1954, p. 21, NA 814.00.)

[13] Melville and Melville, *Guatemala: The Politics of Land Ownership*, p. 54. For the expropriation process, see arts. 63–83 of Decree 900.

[14] Interviews with Fortuny (quoted), María de Arbenz, and Guerra Borges.

[15] OIR, "Agrarian Reform in Guatemala," no. 6001, Mar. 5, 1953, pp. 7, 4, 5, NA.

for the administration of the agrarian reform, "representatives of labor and farm workers' unions toured the countryside instructing workers in the operation of the law and distributing forms for petitioning land."[16] Seeking to shield their workers from this plague, landowners closed the roads running through their plantations. "When one farm covered several thousand acres of land and straddled main highways," an authority has observed, "they could prevent people from travelling." In response, the government announced that all private roads would become public property on August 1, 1952; failure to open a road would result in fines of up to $2,000 per day.[17] The threat proved effective.

Strongly supported by the government, the labor confederations organized rural unions and helped to establish networks of CALs. They also began an intensive campaign to overcome the peasants' fears, spawned by landowners and priests, that the agrarian reform would lead to the collectivization of their wives and children, economic ruin, and eternal damnation. "It wasn't easy for the peasants to withstand the manipulations of the feudal landlords," noted the secretary general of the national peasant confederation (CNCG), Castillo Flores, in his report to its February 1954 Congress. "The propaganda unleashed by the landowners was hard-hitting. . . . And it met with some success. . . . The landowners also coopted some workers with good wages and bribes. . . . They offered many of the peasant leaders special privileges, and more than a few surrendered to temptation."[18] In the same vein, the PGT's secretary general, Fortuny, noted in August 1953 that "months of patient labor" had been necessary to convince the laborers of Concepción, one of the largest Fincas Nacionales, of the benefits of the agrarian reform.[19]

The distribution of land from the Fincas Nacionales began in August 1952. On January 5, 1953, Arbenz signed the first four decrees expropriating private land.[20] For the next eighteen months, the agrarian reform proceeded at a swift pace.

There is no question that mistakes and excesses marred the implementation of Decree 900. Arbitrary seizures took place at the hands of CALs that were

[16] AmEmG, "Monthly Economic Report—August 1952," no. 212, Aug. 28, 1952, p. 1, NA 814.00.

[17] Pearson, "*Confederación*," p. 174 (quoted); "Guatemala Opens Roads," *NYT*, July 24, 1952, p. 2.

[18] Castillo Flores, "Informe del Secretario General a el III Congreso Nacional Campesino," Feb. 19, 1954, pp. 1–2, *GT*, Box 11.

[19] Fortuny, "Sobre la parcelación de 'Concepción,' " *Tribuna Popular*, Aug. 26, 1953, p. 1 (quoted) and Aug. 27, 1953, p. 3.

[20] See "Positiva realidad el Decreto 900," *DCA*, Aug. 7, 1952, p. 1; *JW* 42, Oct. 16, 1952, I:4; *JW* 47, Nov. 20, 1952, I:2; "Acuerdase expropiación de las primeras fincas particulares," *DCA*, Jan. 6, 1953, p. 1; "Expropiadas las primeras fincas de particulares" (edit.), *DCA*, Jan. 7, 1953, p. 3.

strongly biased against landowners. At times, acts of violence were perpetrated against owners of large and middle-sized estates; on other occasions, landless peasants seized the holdings of their marginally better-off neighbors. Disputes erupted among peasants coveting the same land and between members of unions associated with different government parties. With the rapid pace of the agrarian reform, ancient tensions between neighboring peasant communities surfaced. On occasion, conflicts divided a single community.[21]

In his March 1954 message to Congress, Arbenz acknowledged, "There have been excesses [in the implementation of the law], such as the illegal occupation of estates and the seizure of land by some peasants to the detriment of others."[22] Castillo Flores struck the same note in his report to the third congress of the CNCG.[23] Letters written to Castillo Flores include poignant appeals. From Tecpán, in the department of Chimaltenango, a group of peasants complained: "Peasant Union of Chuatzunuj is full of greedy men. It has stolen our land"; from Senahú, in the department of Alta Verapaz, the peasants wrote: "Our neighbors have taken over our fields. . . . Please send a telegram on our behalf to the governor."[24] Other letters, telegrams, and reports addressed to the president of the republic, the DAN, members of Congress, and governors of departments tell of similar incidents.[25] Clashes between groups of peasants left several dead and wounded at San Pedro Ayampuc, at San Vicente Pacaya, at San Pedro Yepocapa, and at San Juan La Ermita.[26]

[21] The major primary sources on the implementation of the agrarian reform are (1) the reports of the U.S. embassy, particularly the *JW*, the Labor Reports (NA 814.06), and the Economic Reports (NA 814.00); (2) the Guatemalan press, esp. the official *DCA*, the PGT's *Octubre* and *Tribuna Popular*, and the opposition dailies *La Hora* and *El I*; (3) the *GT*.

The most important secondary sources on the implementation of the reform are by Paredes Moreira, *Reforma agraria*, *Aplicación*, and "Aspectos y resultados." On agricultural credit, see esp. Comité Interamericano de Desarrollo Agrícola, *Tenencia de la tierra*, pp. 31–54. On other aspects of the agrarian reform, see Pearson, "*Confederación*" and "Guatemala"; Aybar de Soto, *Dependency*; García Añoveros, "El 'caso Guatemala' "; Wasserstrom, "Revolution in Guatemala"; Handy, *Class and Community* and " 'The Most Precious Fruit' "; Whetten, *Guatemala* and "Land Reform."

[22] Arbenz, "Informe del ciudadano presidente," p. 3.

[23] Castillo Flores (see n. 18 above).

[24] Quotations from Diego Lares Bocal to Castillo Flores, Tecpán, Mar. 31, 1954, *GT*, Box 43, and Marcelino Tux, Secretario General Unión Campesina San Juan, to Castillo Flores, Senahú, May 23, 1954, *GT* Box 44.

[25] See *GT*, Boxes 11, 12, 42, and 43, and CO:G, AGCA for the relevant period.

[26] The incidents at San Pedro Ayampuc and San Vicente Pacaya occurred on Feb. 12 and 14, 1953; at San Pedro Yepocapa on Aug. 26, 1953; at San Juan La Ermita on Apr. 30, 1954. See esp. *DCA*, *El I*, *La Hora*, and *Tribuna Popular*.

The opposition press claimed that a wave of violence was engulfing the countryside, and many in Guatemala and the United States wept for the poor dispossessed landowners. Not only were they to be compensated in bonds rather than cash, but the amount of the compensation would be nugatory: it was common knowledge that the landowners had consistently and grossly understated the value of their estates on their tax returns.

In February 1953, yet another blow provoked howls of indignation from the opposition in Guatemala and struck many in the United States as definitive proof of the regime's totalitarian character. In two split decisions, the Supreme Court declared that Decree 900's exclusion of judicial review was unconstitutional, and it ordered the agrarian reform suspended until the lower courts could investigate charges that private lands were being expropriated illegally. This meant, as the *New York Times* pointed out, that "Guatemala's Land Law [was] halted."[27] Arbenz's response was swift: he summoned an extraordinary session of Congress. "You must decide," he told the deputies, "whether the Supreme Court can hear appeals on cases related to the agrarian reform, or whether, to the contrary, it must abide by . . . Decree 900 and refuse to hear them."[28] The message was couched in terms that were, conceded an opposition daily, "temperate,"[29] yet Arbenz's position was unmistakable.

Congress acted immediately. After a few hours of tumultuous debate, it impeached the errant judges by a 41 to 9 vote on grounds of "ignorance of the law which shows unfitness and manifest incapacity to administer justice," and replaced them with more sympathetic individuals. The new judges reversed their predecessors' rulings, and the agrarian reform continued free from judicial restraint.[30]

The difficulties associated with the implementation of the agrarian reform must be weighed against its results. Although the analysis is hampered by two constraints—the reform ran only until June 1954, when Arbenz was ousted, and many relevant documents were destroyed in the wake of his fall—enough data exist to assess its impact.

By June 1954, over 1.4 million acres had been expropriated (that is, one quarter of the total arable land of Guatemala). This represented "about half the acreage that the government contemplated would be affected by the law," the U.S. embassy noted. "Those persons who lost land owned extremely large quantities of it," an expert later wrote. "In many, if not most of these cases,

[27] "Guatemala's Land Law Halted," *NYT*, Feb. 6, 1953, p. 20.

[28] Arbenz's Feb. 5 message to Congress quoted in "Destituida hoy la corte," *El I*, Feb. 6, 1953, p. 9.

[29] "Destitución de la corte" (edit.), *El I*, Feb. 6, 1953, p. 1.

[30] The episode can be followed in *DCA*, *El I*, and *Prensa Libre*. For the Feb. 5 session of Congress, see "Actas de la séptima sesión extraordinaria," in *Sesiones extraordinarias, enero–febrero 1953*, (Libro no. 12, 1953), unpaginated.

the finqueros were absentee land-owners.''[31] There is no agreement as to the exact number of beneficiaries. Some scholars believe that as many as 138,000 families received land; others accept the figures of eighty to ninety thousand given by the government of Castillo Armas, who overthrew Arbenz. But on one occasion Castillo Armas's director of agrarian affairs, who was certainly in a position to know, assessed the total number at ''100,000 heads of families.'' This assessment is endorsed by some of the leading authorities on Arbenz's agrarian reform.[32] A simple calculation based on the 1950 census translates this figure to five hundred thousand Guatemalans.

From the moment of his inauguration, Arbenz had stressed that access to credit was crucial to any agrarian reform. For peasants in Guatemala, loans were a rare and costly privilege. ''Agricultural credit for the Indian is practically nonexistent,'' concluded the World Bank in 1951.[33] Enlarging on the same point, former State Department official Nathan Whetten wrote:

> Scarcity of rural credit facilities has made loans difficult to get and resulted in exorbitant rates of interest. A study of rural credit facilities in 37 *municipios* made in 1950–51 . . . estimated that 10 per cent of the Indian farmers of these *municipios* had obtained loans of some kind during the previous year. Usually these loans were small, ranging from 5 to 100 dollars per recipient and extended over short periods of time, ordinarily not more than a few months. The rates of interest, however, were generally extremely high and computed on a monthly basis. In the 37 *municipios* studied the average rate of interest varied from 3.2 per cent per month to 12.6 per cent per month. The average for the 37 *municipios* combined was 7.9 per cent per month. This is equivalent to a yearly rate of interest amounting to 94.8 per cent.[34]

Decree 900 stipulated that the provision of credit would be an integral part of the agrarian reform. In February 1953, the government presented a bill to Congress that established the National Agrarian Bank (*Banco Nacional Agrario* or BNA), whose sole purpose would be to provide credit to the beneficiaries of the agrarian reform and to other small farmers. The bill was accompanied by Arbenz's request that it be approved before the Congress adjourned on March 1.[35] In the meantime, credit would be granted through an established government agency, the Crédito Hypotecario Nacional (CHN).

[31] Quotations from Krieg to DOS, no. 818, Mar. 29, 1954, p. 3, NA 814.20, and Pearson, ''*Confederación*,'' p. 171. For statistical data see Paredes Moreira, *Reforma agraria* and *Aplicación*.

[32] Montenegro, ''El capitán Montenegro defiende''; see also Paredes Moreira, *Aplicación*, pp. 76–77, and Comité Interamericano de Desarrollo Agrícola, *Tenencia de la tierra*, p. 42.

[33] IBRD, *Economic Development*, p. 26.

[34] Whetten, *Guatemala*, p. 156.

[35] See *DCA*: ''Aprobado el anteproyecto del Banco Agrario,'' Feb. 3, 1953, p. 1; ''El Banco Agrario Nacional'' (edit.), Feb. 4, 1953, p. 3; ''Ultimos toques a la ley del

After months of delay, Congress bowed to strong executive pressure and approved the creation of the BNA on July 7, 1953. With the creation of this "new type of financial institution for Guatemala," reported the U.S. embassy, "the basic agrarian reform legislation was completed."[36] Between March 1953 and June 1954, the CHN and the BNA approved $11,881,432 in loans, of which $9 million was disbursed before the overthrow of Arbenz. An average of $225 was given to each of the 53,829 applicants—a sum that was almost twice Guatemala's annual per capita income in 1950 ($137) and well over twice per capita income in the countryside ($89).[37] In a dramatic break with the past, interest rates were fixed at 4 percent annually for loans of up to twelve months, and 6 percent for longer term loans (three to six years). To facilitate the procedure, the country was divided into six regions, and the BNA opened offices in each. Competently staffed, the bank earned its reputation as the most efficient government bureaucracy. (Even the U.S. embassy, which was deeply concerned by leftist influence within the BNA, offered no criticism of its structure or performance.)[38] The bank's director, Alfonso Bauer Paiz, was unusual among revolutionary politicians for his expertise and his honesty.

Of course, there were problems. As a senior BNA official recalls, "some borrowers used their loans to buy things like bikes, radios, etc. . . . You can't change everything at once. It takes time to educate the people. But these were isolated cases: most borrowers used their loans responsibly." In fact, of the $3,371,185 in loans granted by the CHN between March and November 1953, $3,049,092 had been repaid by June 1954, as had some of the loans given by the BNA, which began operations only in November 1953. This was crucial: "the BNA had limited resources, loans had to be turned over rapidly."[39] It was also proof that the beneficiaries were making good use of the opportunities created by the land reform.

Banco Agrario," Feb. 11, 1953, p. 1; "Proyecto del Banco Agrario fue enviado al Congreso," Feb. 12, 1953, p. 1; "Proyecto del Banco Agrario fué enviado ya al Congreso," Feb. 13, 1953, p. 1. For the draft, see "Texto del proyecto de creación del Banco Nacional Agrario," *DCA*, Feb. 16, 17, and 18, 1953 (all p. 8).

[36] *JW* 28, July 9, 1953, II:3. See also "Ley orgánica del Banco Agrario, aprobada," *DCA*, July 8, 1953, p. 1; " 'Publíquese y cúmplase' a la ley del Banco Nac. Agrario," *DCA*, July 9, 1953, p. 1; "El Banco Nacional Agrario" (edit.), *DCA*, July 11, 1953, p. 3.

[37] Comité Interamericano de Desarrollo Agrícola, *Tenencia de la tierra*, p. 43. (Paredes Moreira, *Reforma agraria*, p. 139, gives slightly different figures: $11,772,400 in loans and 53,950 successful applicants.) For per capita income in 1950, see Palacios, "Formas de redistribución," p. 430.

[38] Based on a reading of the embassy's reports. For the bank's organization, see *Informe mensual del Banco Nacional Agrario*, no. 1, May 1954, pp. 1–4.

[39] Quoted from interview with Noriega Morales, who was a senior official of the BNA. For the figures, see Comité Interamericano de Desarrollo Agrícola, *Tenencia de la tierra*, p. 42.

Some exacting critics point out that the government's efforts "to provide capital at low interest to *campesinos* needing farm equipment fell short of meeting the needs of the new landowners, with the result that many *campesinos* found themselves with land but with little or no capital to cultivate it profitably."[40] Arbenz was president, however, of poor and backward Guatemala, not of Sweden. The significance of the $12 million in loans approved by the government can be appreciated if one considers that in 1954 the total amount of loans processed by Guatemalan banks, excluding the BNA, was $45,292,000.[41] Similarly, it might be noted that the loans granted represented one sixth of the government's total expenditure for the 1953–1954 fiscal year.

In view of Guatemala's history, and of the severe economic and technical constraints faced by the government, the amount of credit provided by the CHN and the BNA is remarkable. A 1965 report sponsored by the Organization of American States—not a radical group—concluded, "The success of the agrarian credit policy was no less impressive than that of the land redistribution policy."[42] Indeed, Guatemala's experience was unprecedented in Latin America, where significant land redistribution was extremely rare and provision of credit to poor peasants even rarer.

Contrary to the hopes of the government's detractors, Decree 900 did not result in the collapse of agricultural output. Rather, notes an American scholar, the existing data, "seem to indicate that agrarian reform . . . unleashed new productive energies from both the peasants and those *finqueros* whose previously idle land was put into use."[43] Nor did the U.S. embassy, which closely monitored the country's economy, claim that agricultural production was declining. On the contrary, in August 1953 the embassy reported a 15 percent increase in the production of corn. Corn, it added, "is the chief crop of small landholders in Guatemala and is cultivated by the majority of persons who have received land under the Agrarian Reform Law."[44] Almost a year later, the embassy concluded that "production of food crops in 1953 was satisfactory." The corn harvest was "about 10 percent higher than 1952," rice and wheat production had increased by 74 percent and 21 percent respectively over 1952, and bean production had remained the same. In 1952–1953 coffee production did decrease slightly, but this was "due principally to weather conditions."[45] Furthermore, recovery was swift. The 1953–1954 coffee crop was

[40] LaCharite, *Case Study in Insurgency*, p. 60.

[41] See Aybar de Soto, *Dependency*, p. 195, n. 98.

[42] Comité Interamericano de Desarrollo Agrícola, *Tenencia de la tierra*, p. 42.

[43] Pearson, "*Confederación*," pp. 187–88.

[44] *JW* 34, Aug. 21, 1953, II:1.

[45] Quoted from "Economic and Financial Review—1953" (see n. 12 above), p. 6. See also McKnight to DOS, no. 238, Oct. 15, 1953, NA 814.231, and Paredes Moreira, *Reforma agraria*, p. 61, table 15.

the second highest in Guatemala's history.[46] In late 1954, in its postmortem of Decree 900, the embassy conceded, "The impact of agrarian reform during the Arbenz regime was principally political and did not greatly affect agricultural production."[47]

These results are particularly significant in light of the fact that agricultural production tends to decrease, often steeply, in the first years of a swift land reform. Such was the case in Bolivia in the 1950s, Cuba in the 1960s, Peru in the early 1970s, and Nicaragua in the early 1980s.

It would seem, moreover, that the reform led to an increase of the area under cultivation. Almost all of the private land expropriated (or otherwise seized) had not been cultivated. The landed elite, though cursing Decree 900 and the "communist" government, did not retaliate by reducing agricultural production. Some authorities even suggest that, fearing expropriation, many landowners hastened to cultivate land they had not previously tilled. In any case, production of rice and cotton, two crops grown mainly by large landowners, rose markedly during the life of Decree 900. Purchase of farm equipment by large landowners, which had dropped sharply after the enactment of the Agrarian Reform Law, was increasing by early 1954.[48] And not even U.S. officials, despite their dire prognostications, argued that Decree 900 was affecting the coffee crop of the landed elite.

About a quarter of Guatemala's coffee crop had been grown on the Fincas Nacionales. Their dismemberment, a chorus of Cassandras had warned, would prove disastrous. "The workers," they claimed, "knew nothing about coffee culture except performance of routine tasks. . . . coffee production would decline and . . . there would be a reversion to the mere subsistence crops of corn and beans."[49] In fact, Decree 900 had stipulated that in the Fincas Nacionales the beneficiaries could not change the existing crops without the permission of the agrarian authorities, and there is no indication that the acreage devoted to coffee in the Fincas Nacionales, or its productivity, decreased. The former workers, now acting as independent producers, proved at least as efficient as the administrators who had overseen the Fincas Nacionales under Arévalo.[50]

---

[46] United Nations, FAO, *World Coffee Economy*, Table 1A.

[47] McKnight to DOS, no. 309, Oct. 14, 1954, p. 5, NA 814.231.

[48] AmEmG: "Economic Summary—March 1954," no. 851, Apr. 12, 1954, p. 1; "Economic Summary—April 1954," no. 919, May 7, 1954, p. 1; "Economic Summary—May 1954," no. 995, June 9, 1954, p. 1. All NA 814.00.

[49] Whetten, *Guatemala*, p. 154 (quoting landowners).

[50] The U.S. agricultural attaché kept an eagle eye out for any loss of productivity in the cultivation of coffee due to the agrarian reform, but he was forced repeatedly to admit that he had no bad news to report. See McKnight to DOS: no. 748, Feb. 27, 1953; no. 902, Apr. 14, 1953; no. 304, Oct. 8, 1953; no. 854, Apr. 9, 1954; no. 308, Oct. 13, 1954. All NA 814.2333.

The Arbenz government sought to provide technical assistance to the beneficiaries of the agrarian reform through the newly created Oficina de Programas de Producción Agrícola and through special publications such as *El Campesino*, which explained in straightforward language how to increase productivity and fight blight; these educational efforts were made more effective by the development of the network of local agrarian committees and rural unions.[51]

Furthermore, contrary to what Fidel Castro later did in Cuba, Arbenz and his communist advisers did not attempt to impose a land tenancy system that went against the wishes of the rural population. Collectivization, they had concluded, was politically impossible in Guatemala and would remain so for a long time.[52]

Finally, the government did not turn the internal terms of trade against the rural producers in order to court the urban populace. As the U.S. embassy noted, it adopted a "policy of setting support prices for certain basic crops as a means of stimulating agricultural production."[53]

It is hardly surprising, then, that "many thousands of peasant families lived much better than ever before."[54] Decree 900 even benefited many of those who had not received land. By decreasing the labor pool, it pushed up real wages for agricultural workers, as did the growing unionization of rural labor and the government's sustained efforts on its behalf.[55]

Nor were the benefits simply material. What an anthropologist wrote of Guatemala in the early 1930s still held true in the fifties: "The land is for the Indian the symbol of his right to live, the connecting link between the material life with the divine existence."[56] For the first time since the Spanish conquest, the government returned land to the Indians. In the words of an unsympathetic U.S. official, "The Indians are not only to receive land, but they are in the process educated to regard it as a right."[57] For the first time, also, the rural workers and small peasants participated in trade union activities, even though their role was confined to the local level. The status of many landless agricultural workers was also enhanced by articles 13 and 14 of Decree 900, which stipulated that, on private estates, all settlements of agricultural workers con-

[51] One issue of *El Campesino* (Jan.–Mar. 1954) is in the *GT*, Box 7.

[52] Interviews with María de Arbenz, Fortuny, Guerra Borges, and Alejandro.

[53] *JW* 42, Oct. 16, 1953, II:2.

[54] Pearson, "Guatemala," p. 326. A glimpse of life in the countryside is provided by the voluminous documentation in CSC:DAT, AGCA for 1952 (which includes items for 1951 and 1953), 1953, and 1954.

[55] An examination of the labor contracts for the relevant period indicates an average of 35¢–50¢ per day in 1950 and 80¢ per day in 1953. (See CT:DAT, 1950–1953, AGCA.)

[56] Moisés Saenz, quoted in Reina, "Chinautla," p. 98.

[57] Hill to Ambassador, Oct. 2, 1952, p. 2, RG84 CF, Box 15, NA-S.

sisting of more than fifteen families would be designated urban centers, and private roads connecting these settlements with the outside world would be nationalized. This facilitated "state control" over the agricultural workers, lamented a State Department report.[58] Perhaps so, but only insofar as it weakened the landowner's grip over his workers' lives.

In early 1954, as a companion measure to Decree 900, the government began a literacy campaign in the rural areas. Although Arbenz, like Arévalo before him, was hampered by scarce resources, his campaign promised to be far more effective than the efforts of his predecessor. A network of support now existed in the countryside: the CNCG and the CGTG with their labor unions. These two labor confederations prodded their rural affiliates "to seize this magnificent opportunity." Literacy, land, and credit were, they stressed, intimately connected: the peasants needed to read and write in order to "present their demands [for land], transact their business with the agrarian authorities, and deal with other problems such as writing to the Agrarian Committees, asking for credit from the Agrarian Bank, buying and selling their crops, etc."[59]

This pragmatic approach was evident at the third congress of the CNCG in February 1954. As president of Guatemala, Arévalo had extolled the virtues of literacy for the rural masses, but he had offered them neither land nor credit and had thus robbed literacy of practical value. Now, at the congress of the CNCG, the impassioned appeal of a semiliterate peasant leader from the Indian department of Huehuetenango explained the importance of literacy with a clarity the eminent professor had lacked: "We must be able to read and write so that we can take advantage of the agrarian reform and take charge of our lives."[60]

Change was stirring in the countryside. In a study conducted in the summer of 1954 among peasants jailed after the overthrow of Arbenz, Richard Adams noted:

An awakening of profound import did take place for many . . . but it was not what usually has come under the rubric of "ideological." It could better be called a "sociological awakening," for it amounted to a realization that certain of the previously accepted roles and statuses within the social system were no longer bounded by the same rules, and that new channels were suddenly opened for the expression of and satisfaction of needs. The heretofore established series of relationships between political leader and countryman, between employer and laborer, between Indian and

[58] OIR, "Agrarian Reform in Guatemala," no. 6001, Mar. 5, 1953, p. 5, NA.

[59] Quotations from Castillo Flores to the Secretarios de Uniones Campesinas del Departamento de Izabal, June 2, 1954, *GT*, Box 12, and from CNCG, Circular, Feb. 15, 1954, p. 1, *GT*, Box 11. For other relevant documents, see ibid., Boxes 10–12.

[60] "Exposición de la federación campesina de Huehuetenango ante el Tercero Congreso Nacional Campesino," *GT*, Box 12.

Ladino, were not suddenly changed, but it abruptly became possible to introduce some change into them.[61]

The injustices of some arbitrary land seizures must be weighed against the massive injustices corrected by the implementation of Decree 900. The acts of violence among peasants struggling for the same land and those committed by peasants against landowners are regrettable, but such incidents were few, both in actual numbers and relative to the magnitude of the transformation taking place.

The reports of the Guatemalan opposition press were sensational, but they cited very few concrete cases of illegal land occupations or acts of violence against property or persons.[62] Equally instructive are the reports of the U.S. embassy. In February 1953, the embassy stated that "incidents" associated with the agrarian reform had been "local in scale and sporadic"; there were reports of "several minor clashes in rural areas," but "in general, the Administration moved forward without serious incident in its accelerated Agrarian Reform program."[63] On March 27, the embassy noted that "instances of violence in rural areas continued to be reported," but added that "in some cases" the local authorities had taken steps to restore order. "The pace of these lawless acts [has] diminished," it concluded at the end of April. And indeed a reader of U.S. reports will find little on the subject for the rest of the year.[64] In March 1954, reporting on land seizures in the department of Escuintla, the embassy stated: "Last year when the planting season got underway in March there was a marked decrease in such agrarian disturbances."[65]

It was only in the last weeks of the Arbenz regime that violence in the countryside increased—a time, that is, when fear of an attack abetted by the United States was mounting. Even so, the conclusion of Neale Pearson, the foremost American authority on Decree 900, is unimpeachable. There were cases, he wrote, "in which the peasants illegally occupied lands and a few in which they burned pastures or crops in order to have land declared uncultivated and subject to expropriation. But these cases were isolated and limited in numbers."[66] Moreover, the peasants' attacks against landowners were often acts of self-defense: "in a number of instances the plantation owner burned the shacks of the workers and drove them off the plantation," writes Whetten, a former State Department official.[67]

[61] Adams, "Receptivity," p. 361.

[62] Based on a thorough reading of El I and La Hora and a selective reading of El Espectador and Prensa Libre.

[63] Quotations from JW 8, Feb. 20, 1953, I:2 and JW 9, Feb. 27, 1953, I:2.

[64] Quotations from JW 13, Mar. 27, 1953, I:1 and JW 17, Apr. 24, 1953, I:3.

[65] JW 10, Mar. 12, 1954, p. 3.

[66] Pearson, "Confederación," p. 180.

[67] Whetten, Guatemala, p. 158. Reports of such incidents can be found in the GT,

On several occasions, particularly in the early months of Decree 900, the landowners' violence was condoned by the local authorities. Police officers, other officials and even some governors of departments found it difficult to curb their sympathy for the "genteel" elite that knew how to reward favors.[68] This was the time-honored response of a world that Arévalo had hardly disturbed. But now, under Arbenz, unprecedented orders emanated from the capital. A lengthy February 1953 circular from the national chief of the police is revealing. Noting that "lately peasants have voiced complaints against the police," he admonished the police chiefs of all the departments of the republic:

> Put an end to such abuses immediately. It is of utmost importance to avoid friction between the policemen and the peasants; otherwise the latter will think of the police . . . with the same revulsion they felt for them during the dictatorships of Ubico and Ponce. There have already been occasions when the peasants have asserted that today's policemen are the same as the bloodthirsty individuals from that nefarious past. Therefore I urge you, if you want to retain my trust, do not stuff these orders in a drawer without first being sure that your subordinates understand that they must absolutely avoid insulting or abusing the peasants.[69]

Abuses against the peasants by the local authorities continued, but they were sharply reduced because of pressure from the capital and the removal of some particularly obnoxious local policemen. Abandoned, therefore, to their own devices, and fearing the government's retribution, the landowners moderated their behavior.[70] As a result, violence in the countryside decreased, at least until the last weeks of the regime. In comparison with the land reform that occurred at roughly the same time in Bolivia, the Guatemalan reform was a model of order. Had the level of violence been significant, agricultural output would have suffered, as it did in Bolivia.

Indeed, some of the excesses were indispensible to the success of the agrarian reform. The impeachment of the four Supreme Court justices in February 1953 was the only illegal act committed by the Guatemalan Congress during the

---

esp. Boxes 10 and 12, in the government press and even, at times, in *La Hora*, whose owner, Marroquín Rojas, was the maverick of the Guatemalan right. (See, for instance: "CNC denuncia varios asesinatos," Jan. 3, 1953, p. 1; "Se incendiaron terrenos que habían entregado a los agraristas," Mar. 4, 1953, p. 1; "Cinco asesinatos cometidos en la laguna de Retana motivan protesta renovada de dirigentes campesinos," June 10, 1953, p. 1.)

[68] See *GT*, Boxes 1, 5, 12, and 20.

[69] "Rogelio Cruz Wer a señor jefe de la guardia civil departamental," Feb. 25, 1953, *GT*, Box 14. The circular was leaked to *El I*. (See "Curiosa circular," *El I*, Aug. 7, 1953, p. 1; "Circular de la Guardia Civil," *El I*, Aug. 8, 1953, p. 1.)

[70] See *GT*, Boxes 10 and 12.

entire Arbenz period, and it was done solely so that the agrarian reform would not be paralyzed. It is striking that those Americans who showed the most indulgence for the "pecadillos" of men like Somoza and Trujillo were the most outraged by this transgression by Arbenz and the Guatemalan Congress.

And was the system of compensation for expropriated lands as unjust as many claimed? Guatemala was, after all, following America's example: the U.S.-directed agrarian reform in Formosa and Japan had also stipulated payment in bonds over a twenty-to-twenty-five-year period with annual interest rates of 3 percent. Moreover, if the amount of compensation offered by Decree 900 was nugatory, who could be faulted but the "victimized" landowners? No one had forced them to cheat on their tax returns. Among these landowners was United Fruit. From May 1951 to March 1952, the company had been locked in an increasingly bitter conflict with its workers over the renewal of labor contracts. Throughout those months, the company proved that it had lost none of its arrogance and intransigence, as it laid off 3,746 workers without pay and resisted the government's attempts to mediate. In the final settlement, the workers largely accepted UFCO's conditions.[71] But the company had little time to celebrate. In June 1952, the Agrarian Reform Law was enacted. The following March President Arbenz upheld the DAN's decision to expropriate 234,000 acres of uncultivated land at UFCO's 295,000 acre plantation at Tiquisate. In February 1954 UFCO lost 173,000 acres of uncultivated land at Bananera, a plantation of 253,000 acres. The Guatemalan government assessed the value of the expropriated land at $1,185,000—that is, the amount declared by UFCO for tax purposes prior to May 10, 1952. UFCO immediately protested that the land was really worth $19,355,000, a claim that was steadfastly endorsed by the State Department.[72]

Champions of United Fruit have argued that the Arbenz administration acted in a discriminatory manner by expropriating such a high percentage of the company's land. UFCO, they contend, needed to keep most of its land fallow as a precaution in case of Panama disease (a blight that attacks banana plantations), as well as other natural disasters. The highly technical debate as to the exact amount of land UFCO needed to hold in reserve has never been resolved satisfactorily, but it is likely that the claims of both sides were exaggerated.[73]

[71] The crisis can best be followed in *DCA* and *El I*, and in embassy despatches filed in NA 814.062 (esp. despatches nos. 348, 454, 500, 697). See also the fifty-second and the fifty-third annual reports of United Fruit.

[72] On UFCO's claim and the State Department's response, see NA, Lot 57D618, Boxes 2 and 3; *Department of State Bulletin*, no. 29 (July–Dec. 1953), pp. 357–60, and no. 30 (Jan.–June 1954), pp. 678–79; *JW* 9 (Feb. 27, 1953), 10 (Mar. 6, 1953), 12 (Mar. 19, 1953), 33 (Aug. 14, 1953), 8 (Mar. 1, 1954).

[73] See the excellent discussion in Aybar de Soto, *Dependency*, pp. 200–204.

THE PUBLIC WORKS PROGRAM

Arbenz was seeking more than land. He intended to break the power of a foreign enclave that threatened the country's sovereignty. In this pursuit, he faced more than UFCO and would have to initiate more than agrarian reform. Vital sectors of the country's infrastructure were controlled by American companies that enjoyed immense privileges. Determined to loosen their grip on his country's economy, Arbenz moved forward with his public works program. This program would displace the Americans through competition rather than expropriation and call on foreign expertise, but not foreign capital. Largely following the blueprint suggested by a 1951 World Bank report on Guatemala, it had three major components.[74]

The first was the contruction of a large road network. "The inadequacy of present facilities for transportation," the World Bank had stated, "probably constitutes the greatest single barrier to the economic development and the cultural integration of the Republic." Particularly critical was a road linking the capital with the Caribbean coast; such a road would supplement the railway to Puerto Barrios, which was inadequate, expensive, and American. "Without this road—or at least positive proof that it will be constructed in the immediate future—there is no real indication that the Government is vitally interested in expediting or cheapening the movement of international freight," the World Bank had concluded.[75]

The second component was the construction of a port in the bay of Santo Tomás on the Caribbean coast, a few miles from Puerto Barrios—"a dream that had persisted for three and a half centuries."[76] Here, too, economic and political considerations went hand in hand. The inadequate facilities at Puerto Barrios created costly bottlenecks in the handling of foreign trade and were controlled by an American company. The third component of the program was the construction of a hydroelectric plant. The country's production of electricity was insufficient, uneconomical, and controlled by a U.S. company.

In April 1953 the government unveiled its road building plan. It proposed the construction of 750 miles of paved roads in the remaining four years of Arbenz's term. Except for its ambitious deadlines, the plan basically followed the 1951 World Bank report.[77]

Had the Guatemalan authorities attempted to accomplish so much in only

---

[74] For Arbenz's public works program, interviews with María de Arbenz, Fortuny, Guerra Borges, Paz Tejada, Charnaud, Bauer Paiz, and Capuano were particularly helpful. For the World Bank report, see IBRD, *Economic Development*.

[75] IBRD, *Economic Development*, pp. 132–210. Quoted from pp. 132 and 201.

[76] Griffith, "Santo Tomás," p. 40.

[77] From Apr. 10 to Apr. 28, 1953, *DCA* ran a series of articles on the plan, which presented the government's views. For comments by the U.S. embassy, see *JW* 16–18, Apr. 17–May 1, 1953.

four years, they would have courted disaster, for the country's technical and financial resources were inadequate. Fortunately, they followed a more pragmatic approach: they concentrated their efforts on the all-important 193-mile Atlantic Highway, which would connect the capital with the port of Santo Tomás. The necessary heavy equipment had been imported from the United States in 1952, and actual work began in earnest in the last months of that year. The U.S. embassy reported in mid-1953: "The Highway has continued to receive top priority among Guatemalan public works projects and has gained widening public support as results have been demonstrated."[78] The steady progress seemed to justify the government's promise that the highway would be completed by mid- or late-1955. (Arbenz's overthrow delayed the work, and the highway was not opened until mid-1957. As Arbenz and the World Bank had predicted, its existence forced the railway to lower its rates.)[79]

On July 2, 1953, Guatemala signed a contract with a subsidiary of the Morrison-Knudsen Company of San Francisco for the construction of the port of Santo Tomás, the future terminus of the Atlantic Highway. The contract stipulated that the port be completed within twenty-four months at a cost of $4.8 million. The government deposited this sum in foreign exchange in the United States as guarantee of payment, and the company posted a performance bond.[80] While the Guatemalan Congress, at Arbenz's request, declared the project to be one of public necessity (which insured certain priorities and immunities),[81] company representatives told the U.S. embassy that "they were satisfied with the contract." It was, the embassy concluded with little enthusiasm, "a major step in the Government's four-year economic development program."[82]

A few months earlier, in April 1953, Guatemala had contracted another U.S. firm, Westinghouse, to study the feasibility of a 28,000-kilowatt hydroelectric plant at Jurún in the department of Escuintla. This study would serve as the basis for the opening of competitive bidding for the construction of the plant, which would take approximately four years and cost $6 million.[83]

---

[78] *JW* 21, May 22, 1953, II:2.

[79] See Piedra-Santa, "La construcción de ferrocarriles," pp. 26–28.

[80] See "Firmado contrato con la Morrison," *DCA*, July 3, 1953, p. 1. The text of the contract was published in *DCA*, July 3, 6, 8, 9, 10, and 11, 1953.

[81] "Declaración de utilidad y necesidad públicas construcción del muelle de Santo Tomás," *DCA*, June 15, 1953, p. 1, and "Declarada de utilidad pública la expropiación de terrenos en donde se construirá puerto Santo Tomás," *DCA*, July 8, 1953, p. 1.

[82] *JW* 28, July 9, 1953, II:1–2. The port began operations in September 1955. (See "Decreto inaugural del puerto de Santo Tomás," *El I*, Sept. 13, 1955, p. 1.)

[83] See "Estudios técnicos para la construcción de la planta hidroeléctrica de Marinalá," *DCA*, June 1, 1953, p. 1; Government Information Bureau, *Guatemala*, no. 7,

A "Basically Prosperous" Economy

"The present Government . . . promises to leave a record of real accomplishments in the field of public works," conceded the U.S. embassy in May 1954.[84] In fact, both aspects of the government's economic program were proceeding successfully. The embassy had originally assumed that the agrarian reform would fail. Now it reserved its judgment. After listing Arbenz's claims of success in his March 1954 message to Congress, it concluded: "A preliminary analysis of the President's report left little doubt, as long as coffee prices are at their present high level, that the Guatemalan economy was basically prosperous."[85]

Despite UFCO's furious complaints that the government was strangling it and would force it to leave the country, 1953 saw the highest level of banana exports since 1948, thanks mainly to favorable weather conditions and to a diminution of labor conflicts.[86] Decree 900 had precipitated capital flight, but this loss was amply offset by the high coffee prices—in this regard, luck truly blessed Arbenz. As a result, the government's foreign currency reserves were sound: $39.4 million on December 31, 1950; $44 million two years later; $42.4 at the end of 1953.[87] Indeed, the U.S. embassy, after noting the $1.6 million drop in reserves between December 1952 and December 1953, explained,

Aug. 1, 1953, pp. 1–2; MemoConv (Schoenfeld, Whitbeck), Sept. 3, 1952, RG84 CF, Box 15, NA-S; MemoConv (Ford, Dyktor, Leddy), May 15, 1953, NA 814.2614; MemoConv (Schoenfeld, Dyktor), May 25, 1953, enclosed in Schoenfeld to Leddy, June 12, 1953, NA 814.2614; MemoConv (Partridge, Attwood, Leddy), Apr. 5, 1954, NA 814.2614.

[84] "Economic and Financial Review—1953" (see n. 12 above), p. 22.

[85] *JW* 9, Mar. 5, 1954, pp. 4–5. See also John Peurifoy, U.S. Congress, *HCFA*, Jan. 26, 1954, p. 463.

[86] See McKnight to DOS, no. 349, Oct. 23, 1953, NA 814.2376; McKnight to DOS, no. 875, Apr. 26, 1954, NA 814.2376; "Economic and Financial Review—1953" (see n. 12 above), pp. 6–7, 9–10.

[87] See "Economic and Financial Review—1953" (see n. 12 above), p. 10, and AmEmG, "Balance of Payments, Guatemala, 1953," no. 918, May 7, 1954, NA 814.10. Because of higher prices, the value of Guatemala's coffee exports soared from $33,670,000 in 1949 to $68,229,000 in 1953 and $71,380,000 in 1954. The effect was dramatic: Guatemala's balance of trade showed a small surplus in 1946 ($475,000); a deficit from 1947 to 1951 (1947, −$5,286,000; 1948, −$18,184,000; 1949, −$15,757,000; 1950, −$3,616,000; 1951, −$4,761,000). It showed a surplus in 1952 ($11,741,000) and in 1953 ($9,384,000). This surplus was achieved despite considerable increases in the cost of the imports. See Guatemala's *Anuario de comercio exterior* and the annual economic reports of the U.S. embassy (NA 814.00) for the relevant years.

not only were these [December 1953] totals much more than adequate for the requirements of the Guatemalan monetary laws, but they were higher than they had stood at the end of 1949, 1950 or 1951. Furthermore, the abnormally late coffee season in 1953 delayed the inflow of foreign exchange from the sale of the new coffee crop so that the drop below the mark of the year end of 1952 was of no significance, and in fact, with the heavy movements of the crop in January, February and March 1954, the Monetary Stabilization Fund and official international monetary reserves reached all-time highs.[88]

The funds needed for the agricultural credits provided by the government and for the public works program came mainly through indirect taxation. The rising value of Guatemala's foreign trade brought higher receipts from existing import and export duties. The authorities also sought to tighten collection and began, in late 1952, to raise taxes and duties. These measures hit the well-off hardest, but the urban poor were not unaffected.[89]

The emphasis on agrarian reform and public works meant, moreover, that Arbenz had been unable to focus on the needs of the urban population. Real income in urban areas did not rise during his presidency, as wage increases were offset by higher indirect taxes and inflation.[90] Nor did the government alleviate the housing crisis in the cities. In November 1953, Congress passed a rent control law, but, as *Diario de Centro América* noted, it did "not solve the housing problem. . . . The solution is to build more low cost housing, but this would take time and money that we do not have."[91] While the law brought some respite to the urban lower class, it also aggravated the slump in private sector housing construction.

Furthermore, the government was hampered by the graft and incompetence of many of its officials. (On both counts, the most striking example was the October 1953 Fair, a notorious fiasco that cost the state close to $1 million.)[92]

[88] "Economic and Financial Review—1953" (see n. 12 above), p. 16; see also the embassy's economic summaries for Feb.–June 1954 (NA 814.00).

[89] For the beginnings of the policy, see AmEmG, "Monthly Financial Statement—June 1951," no. 78, July 20, 1951, NA 814.10; for a useful summary see "Economic and Financial Review—1953" (see n. 12 above), pp. 14–15.

[90] While there is no study on this subject, there is a wealth of material in the Guatemalan press and in the economic and labor reports of the U.S. embassy. A series of articles in *DCA* about Guatemala's first Conference on the High Cost of Living is particularly instructive; see esp. "Llamamiento a la Conferencia Contra el Alto Costo de la Vida," July 30, 1953, p. 1; " El alto costo de la vida" (edit.), Aug. 7 and 21, 1953, both p. 3; "Ministro Fanjul inauguró la conferencia," Aug. 28, 1953, p. 1; "Clausurada la Conferencia del Alto Costo de la Vida," Aug. 29, 1953, p. 1; "Importantes resoluciones aprobadas," Aug. 31, 1953, p. 1; "Resoluciones de la Conferencia Contra el Alto Costo de la Vida," Sept. 4, 8, 10, 11, 12, and 17, 1953 (all p. 4).

[91] "La Ley de Inquilinato," *DCA*, Nov. 18, 1953, p. 3.

[92] See "La Feria de Octubre" (edit.), *DCA*, Aug. 3, 1953, p. 3; "Propaganda y

But Arbenz wisely concentrated his small pool of efficient bureaucrats in the most critical programs. He also sought technical assistance from international agencies. "Government cooperation in technical assistance programs has generally been fairly good," noted the U.S. embassy.[93] He did not hesitate to seek the services of U.S. companies for the construction of the port of Santo Tomás and the hydroelectric plant at Jurún.

Yet the government was unable to balance the 1953–1954 budget, the largest in the country's history. This failure led to a more realistic budget for the following year and to the determination to enact the first income tax in Guatemala's history. The tax would increase the government's receipts and democratize what U.S. experts justly considered a most regressive fiscal system.[94] Noted *Diario de Centro América*:

> Our poor millionaires yell bloody murder whenever the government touches their pocketbooks. . . . But whether they like it or not, the Revolution cannot go forward given the present tax system. It has become increasingly difficult for the State to develop its progressive programs under our feudal fiscal system that has barely changed since 1944. The time has come to correct this situation. Our unfortunate millionaires will have to pay taxes appropriate to our new circumstances, that is, to the capitalist development of our country. . . . The meaning of income tax is simple: the rich man pays as a rich man, and the poor man pays as a poor man. If there are differences in wealth and income, then there must also be in taxes.[95]

In December 1953, the government presented an income tax bill to Congress. During the next months the draft was revised first by a congressional committee and then by the executive. On May 28, the bill was approved by Congress in the first of three required readings;[96] the second reading was postponed to allow Congress to consider the government's budget for 1954-1955,

---

contrapropaganda a la Feria de Octubre en Estados Unidos" (edit.), *DCA*, Sept. 22, 1953, p. 3; "La Feria de Octubre culminará en éxito" (edit.), *DCA*, Oct. 14, 1953, p. 3; "La mala organización del coso originó el desorden de la Feria," *Tribuna Popular*, Oct. 22, 1953, p. 8; "La Feria que quisimos conocer" and "Una tarde en la Feria," *DCA*, Nov. 12, 1953, pp. 2 and 4; "Lo recaudado en la Feria no es ni la 10a. parte de lo invertido," *La Hora*, Nov. 18, 1953, p. 1. See also *JW* 43, Oct. 23, 1953, II.

[93] "Economic Development in Guatemala," no. 793, Mar. 13, 1953, p. 6, NA 814.00. The State Department had toyed with the idea of pressuring the UN to cut off its technical assistance to Guatemala but decided against it "since it was impossible to keep anything confidential in the United Nations." (MemoConv, "U.N. Technical Assistance to Guatemala," May 3, 1951, NA Lot 58D18 & 58D78, Box 3.)

[94] See Adler, Schlesinger, and Olson, *Public Finance*, pp. 41–66. See also United Nations, ECLA, *La política tributaria*, p. 123.

[95] "Desfeudalización de los impuestos," *DCA*, Jan. 4, 1954, p. 1.

[96] "Ley de impuesto sobre la renta conocida en primera lectura," *DCA*, May 29, 1954, p. 1; "Las leyes a toda maquina," *El I*, May 29, 1954, p. 1.

which was approved on June 7.[97] In a few more days, Guatemala would have had its first income tax law.

On the surface, the healthy state of the economy was matched by equally satisfactory developments in the political realm: the administration was popular, Arbenz's control of the government coalition appeared firm, and the opposition was in disarray. In the shadows, disaster loomed.

[97] "Aprobado ayer el presupuesto," *DCA*, June 8, 1954, p. 1. At $70,094,000, the FY 1954–1955 budget was $4,496,000 lower than that of the previous year. As the U.S. embassy noted, it made "no provision for some of the grandiose highway plans previously publicized by the government" and was realistic in its estimate of government income. (*JW* 14, Apr. 9, 1954, p. 4 [quoted], and Wardlaw to DOS, no. 1027, June 29, 1954, NA 814.10.)

CHAPTER 9

The Revolutionary Forces

ON DECEMBER 18, 1953, a squad of gun-toting braves stormed the headquarters of Renovación Nacional (RN), the party created by a group of teachers in July 1944. In the ensuing fistfight, the leader of the attackers, Jaime Díaz Rozzotto, pistol-whipped one of the defenders, an RN congressman. Before things got worse, the police intervened.

The affray at RN was not the prelude to an attack on the government. Díaz Rozzotto was not a right-wing plotter; he was, or rather had been, RN's secretary general. He was merely out to wrest the party headquarters—and his post—from his rivals, who had expelled him the previous day.

The Guatemalan Congress immediately censured Díaz Rozzotto. Undeterred, he proceeded to expel his adversaries from RN, and he was in turn expelled again. And so it continued, to the delight of the opposition press. The developments in RN, remarked the U.S. embassy, were "of the type which adds to the disciplined Guatemalan Communist Party's carefully cultivated reputation as the 'most honest' of the leftist parties supporting the Arbenz administration."[1]

Eventually, the warring factions convened a "Unity Congress"; it opened at noon, March 20, 1954, and closed a few hours later, amid gunshots, leaving one policeman dead and two delegates wounded. By the time Arbenz fell, there were four tiny "RNs" locked in fierce competition for the official party name and the government's patronage.[2]

[1] Krieg to DOS, no. 533, Dec. 21, 1953, p. 1, NA 714.00. For the battle and its immediate aftermath, see "Sucesos de ayer en Renovación Nacional," *DCA*, Dec. 19, 1953, p. 1; "Gangsterismo político sancionado" and "El escandalo de Renovación," *El I*, Dec. 19, 1953, p. 1; "Dos fracciones pugnan por la legitimidad en Renovación," *El I*, Dec. 21, 1953, p. 1. See also the series of interviews with the protagonists in *Tribuna Popular*: "Divergencias conmueven al Partido Renovación Nacional," Dec. 19, 1953, p. 1; "De las divergencias en Renovación Nacional," Dec. 20, 1953, p. 1; "Divergencias en Renovación Nacional," Dec. 22, 1953, p. 1; "De las divergencias en Renovación Nacional," Dec. 23, 1953, p. 1.

[2] The best press coverage of the congress is by *El I*: "Alas renovacionistas citan a consejo general," Mar. 17, 1954, p. 1; "Díaz Rozzotto o Fión Garma; convención RN empieza," Mar. 20, 1954, p. 1; "Alas RN rotas en sangre" and "Sucesos trágicos del Gimnasio Olímpico," Mar. 22, 1954, p. 1. For later developments in RN, see "Ultimatum a Renovación vence viernes," *El I*, Apr. 27, 1954, p. 1; "El partido RN en estertores de agonía," *La Hora*, Apr. 30, 1954, p. 1; "Directiva unitaria en el PRN,"

THE REVOLUTIONARY PARTIES

The schisms of RN notwithstanding, the coalition that supported Arbenz continued practically unchanged from the 1950 campaign to his fall. It included the revolutionary parties, the Communist party and the country's two labor confederations, the CGTG and the CNCG. Together, they formed the Frente Democrático Nacional (FDN), an advisory body chaired by Arbenz.[3]

To be sure, the names and the number of the revolutionary parties changed in the Arbenz years. They had been four as Arbenz became president—the PAR, RN, the FPL, and the PIN. They became five in July 1951, as a split in the PAR gave birth to the Partido Socialista (PS). (The PS, a judicious observer remarked, had "neither ideology nor platform.")[4] Eleven months later, the five suddenly merged and became one, the Partido de la Revolución Guatemalteca (PRG).[5] Within six weeks, most PAR and RN leaders had withdrawn to re-create their old parties amid a flurry of recriminations. Yet the PRG survived; it included the PS, the moribund FPL, the minuscule PIN, and former members of the PAR and RN.

Despite this tendency to split, reunite, and rename, the revolutionary parties scored massive victories in the congressional and municipal elections, and it was their leaders whom Arbenz chose as his ministers and senior officials. They had a powerful ally in the country's largest labor confederation, the peasant-based CNCG, whose leaders had little sympathy for communism and the PGT. By February 1954, the CNCG had 1,500 local unions and 150,000 to 190,000 members.[6] Its impressive growth—it had claimed only twenty-five local unions in May 1950—was due to Arbenz's unwavering support and to the dynamism unleashed in the countryside by the agrarian reform.

Tribuna Popular, May 7, 1954, p. 8; "No existe todavía unidad en Renovación Nacional," *DCA*, May 10, 1954, p. 1; "Cuatro alas renovacionistas," *El I*, May 17, 1954, p. 1; "Al morir Renovación, dejó huérfanos a siete diputados," *La Hora*, May 18, 1954, p. 1; "No inscriben planilla de Renovación," *DCA*, June 1, 1954, p. 1. See also *JW* 12, Mar. 26, 1954, p. 3, and *JW* 19, May 14, 1954, p. 2.

[3] The FDN was not Arbenz's "kitchen cabinet." It met irregularly, was not privy to the president's secret decisions, and dealt mainly with minor issues. Its significance is comparable to that of the cabinet: not an irrelevant body, but not one of great importance either. (Interviews with Charnaud, Guerra Borges, Capuano, Bauer Paiz, María de Arbenz; see also Gutiérrez, *Breve historia*, p. 70, and Unión Patriótica Gualtemalteca, *Guatemala*, p. 21.)

[4] Pearson, "*Confederación*," p. 102.

[5] See: "Fusión del PAR y PS, de gran importancia para la revolución," *DCA*, June 11, 1952, p. 1; "A toda la nación: Hacia un partido único de la Revolución de Octubre," *DCA*, June 12, 1952, p. 6; "Manifiesto del FPL," ibid., p. 1; "Manifiesto del Partido de la Revolución Guatemalteca," *DCA*, July 1, 1952, p. 6; *Boletín informativo del PRG*, no. 1, Aug. 9, 1952, *GT*, Box 9.

[6] See Pearson, "*Confederación*," pp. 40–43.

While careful to maintain its independence, the CNCG was solidly encamped within the fold of the revolutionary parties. Secretary General Castillo Flores was a PAR deputy when he had helped found the CNCG in May 1950. After joining the PS in July 1951 and the PRG one month later, he returned to the PAR in August 1952.[7] Throughout his wanderings, he retained firm— though not absolute—control of the CNCG, purging rivals when necessary. Most CNCG leaders followed him back to the PAR; others stayed with the PRG. The official line of the CNCG was that it was not a political organization; therefore its members could "belong to whatever party treats the peasants best."[8] In practice each leader told the peasants, more or less discreetly, which party to join. This resulted in a massive turnout for the PAR and, to a lesser degree, for the PRG.

While the CNCG was quite united under Castillo Flores, the revolutionary parties were plagued by infighting that acquired at times the character of a B western. Díaz Rozzotto's December exploit was not unprecedented. Two months earlier, on October 13, 1953, the recently ousted secretary general of the PAR, Francisco Fernández Foncea, had stormed the headquarters of his party with a band of armed associates. His motivation was as selfless as that of Díaz Rozzotto: to save the PAR from the grip of the newly installed Executive Committee, which had just expelled him. Mutual excommunications succeeded one another at a rapid clip, while telegrams from each faction poured into the offices of bemused party officials admonishing them, in peremptory terms, to reject the rival leadership. "These episodes in the PAR," reported U.S. Ambassador Schoenfeld, "once again illustrate the lack of ideological firmness and the opportunism which prevail in the leftist administration parties and the consequent improbability of the crystallization of a vigorous anticommunist left at the present juncture in Guatemalan politics."[9] Unlike RN, however, the PAR was able to regain some cohesion as one faction gained control and reestablished discipline.[10]

---

[7] Castillo Flores's peregrinations are well described by Pearson, ibid., pp. 101–10, and Schneider, *Communism*, pp. 158–63.

[8] Castillo Flores to López Fernández, Sept. 10, 1951, *GT*, Box 12.

[9] Schoenfeld to DOS, no. 333, Oct. 16, 1953, p. 2, NA 714.00.

[10] For the October affray and its aftermath, see "Consejo Nacional del PAR en sesión," *DCA*, Oct. 10, 1953, p. 1; "Nueva directiva del PAR," *Tribuna Popular*, Oct. 11, 1953, p. 1; "Fernández Foncea asumió hoy la dirección general del PAR," *DCA*, Oct. 13, 1953, p. 1; "Inscrita la planilla del PAR que encabeza Julio Estrada de la Hoz," *DCA*, Oct. 14, 1953, p. 1; "Decisión del Registro esperan hoy en el PAR," *Tribuna Popular*, Oct. 14, 1953, p. 1; "Al frente de cien marcha a las oficinas," *El I*, Oct. 15, 1953, p. 1; "Acuérdase no otorgar el amparo pedido por Fernández Foncea," *DCA*, Oct. 24, 1953, p. 1; "Manifiesto del grupo de diputados del PAR," *Tribuna Popular*, Nov. 11, 1953, p. 5; "Recurso de Fernández Foncea fué denegado," *DCA*, Nov. 20, 1953, p. 1; "Paristas del ala de Fernández Foncea retornaron al partido,"

Only the PRG escaped the indignity of having former secretaries general invade party headquarters. In its first year, its co–secretaries general, Roberto Alvarado Fuentes and Augusto Charnaud MacDonald, coexisted uneasily while each maneuvered to oust the other. Then, after a purge in August 1953, Alvarado Fuentes was dispatched into genteel exile as Guatemala's Ambassador to Mexico. Charnaud was in command; he was a highly intelligent and competent man, but he was distracted by ambition. In the months that followed his victory, he maintained unity in the PRG by purges and by the postponement of the party's first congress, which was not held until January 1954. Carefully orchestrated, the congress proceeded uneventfully, ratifying the existing leadership despite muted grumblings.[11]

The infighting that bedeviled the revolutionary parties owed little to ideological considerations; in fact, no faction had a coherent ideology or strategy. It was the ambitions of too many leaders that caused the dissension. Their squabbles and lack of direction reinforced the authority of Arbenz, a president with a program. One such squabble, and Arbenz's reaction to it, are described in the diary of a revolutionary politician. It was the fall of 1952, in a meeting in the presidential palace between Arbenz and the leaders of the administration parties.

"At our last meeting," Arbenz began, "we spent seven hours determining the slate of candidates for the upcoming [congressional] elections. I had assumed that we had been proceeding on the basis of revolutionary unity and loyalty, but I have just now learned that one of the parties here has been scheming against another. . . .

"Gentlemen, I am shocked and deeply worried." While saying this, his face was suffused with anger. "What kind of revolutionary unity is this? What do you think

---

DCA, Dec. 9, 1953, p. 1. For telegrams by the rival factions to local party officials, see *GT*, Boxes 1 and 6.

[11] For the PRG's congress and the infighting that preceded it, see "A todos los hombres y mujeres del Partido de la Revolución Guatemalteca," June 1953, *GT*, Box 8; "Comunicado de prensa," Aug. 8, 1953, *GT*, Box 9; "Fracción parlamentaria del PRG retiran del Frente Democrático," *DCA*, Sept. 25, 1953, p. 1; "Divergencias entre los diputados y la Comisión Política del PRG," *Tribuna Popular*, Sept. 26, 1953, p. 1; "Se reunirá bloque de diputados del PRG," *Tribuna Popular*, Sept. 27, 1953, p. 1; "Bloque de diputados del PRG por la unidad del partido," *DCA*, Sept. 29, 1953, p. 1; "Reafirman unidad en el PRG," *DCA*, Oct. 1, 1953, p. 1; "Fracción parlamentaria del PRG debe actuar conforme estatutos," *DCA*, Oct. 2, 1953, p. 1; "Texto de renuncias de 6 PRG," *El I*, Oct. 15, 1953, p. 1; "Sesiones de la Comisión Política y del Comité Ejecutivo Nacional," Dec. 23, 1953 (internal PRG document), *GT*, Box 9; "Instalada la Convención del PRG," *DCA*, Jan. 16, 1954, p. 1; "Directivo del PRG electo ayer," *DCA*, Jan. 18, 1954, p. 1; *Diario del Pueblo*, issues of Jan. 15, 16, 18, and 19, 1954. For the full text of Charnaud's speech at the congress, see "Informe a la Primera Convención Nacional del Partido de la Revolución Guatemalteca," Jan. 15, 1954, *GT*, Box 9. See also Krieg to DOS, no. 613, Jan. 19, 1954, NA 714.00.

we will achieve if we proceed like this? We are acting like spoiled brats without any sense of our responsibility toward the people. We quarrel among ourselves, and we betray each other without a backward glance. . . .

"God damm it!" He slammed his fist on the table. "There is only one president of the republic, one president of the Congress, one president of the judiciary, but everyone wants to be a president. Every jerk wants a seat in the Congress! Gentlemen, leave this farce behind. . . .

"Do you think that we will be able to sustain the revolution if we act like this? The political parties cannot be groups of village gossips. They must be strongly organized on the basis of a clear revolutionary ideology. Otherwise, what will happen?

"There are times, gentlemen, when I deeply regret that I am an officer. At times, I think that you believe that because I am an officer the army will always be behind us and we are sitting on foundations of granite. But you are completely wrong: the army may tire when we least expect it. And the only way to make sure that this does not happen is to remain united, honorable, and consistent in everything we do. Our task is to consolidate the revolution that began in 1944. We have to take momentous strides forward. We must leave behind our petty ambitions, our rancor, our greed.

"I am sorry that I have had to talk to you like this in the presidential office, but imagine that Jacobo Arbenz was talking to you in your party's offices. I am used to speaking the truth bluntly, and I want you to answer me in the same manner: honestly, without evasion."[12]

The revolutionary politicians endorsed Arbenz's vision of an industrialized Guatemala, but their support for his agrarian reform was lukewarm. They concentrated on garnering peasant support for their own parties and factions, rather than on implementing the reform. As a result, party rivalries deepened. As RN was paralyzed by its internal struggle, the rivalry between the PAR and the PRG intensified.[13]

The model of the revolutionary leaders, insofar as they had one, was Mexico's ruling Partido Revolucionario Institucional (PRI). Their desire to have a similar party in Guatemala led to the creation of the PRG in June 1952. A

[12] Zea González, *El espejismo*, pp. 333–35. I would like to thank José Antonio Montes, who sent me a copy of this privately published book.

[13] For a particularly sharp exchange, see "Manifiesto del Partido de la Revolución Guatemalteca (PRG) a toda la nación," *DCA*, Jan. 14, 1954, p. 4, and "El Partido Acción Revolucionaria—PAR," *DCA*, Jan. 25, 1954, p. 8. A series of documents in the *GT*—Box 13 in particular—illuminates the squabbling among revolutionary parties seeking to steal campesinos from each other and indicates that this concern was more important than the implementation of the agrarian reform. The documents also reveal that several leaders of the revolutionary parties in rural areas flirted with latifundistas— while in other instances latifundistas joined the local branch of a revolutionary party in order to protect their interests and subvert the agrarian reform.

united party would be in a stronger position vis-à-vis the president and his communist friends.[14] Arbenz's antipathy for the project contributed to its swift demise, but it would have failed in any case.[15] Too many self-proclaimed *caudillos* bloated the PRG; unity was impossible.

Many revolutionary leaders were not corrupt. Integrity and selfless commitment to his work characterized Alfonso Bauer Paiz, a senior member of the PRG. Under Arbenz he occupied several key positions with great distinction, notably as the director of the Banco Nacional Agrario. But there were many who took liberties with the country's monies. At times, scandals became public: some exposed or fabricated by the opposition press, others by revolutionary politicians bent on slandering their rivals. Thus the opposition *El Espectador* accused PAR Congressman José Felipe Dardón of attempting to extort $5,000 from auto-parts dealers by threatening to introduce a bill that would have limited their profits to 10 percent. In the course of a tumultuous congressional debate on Dardon's business practices, PAR and PRG deputies swapped insults and charges of corruption, while PGT deputy Pellecer vainly warned that it was a mistake "to stage such a demeaning spectacle for the benefit of the reactionaries." The PGT, Pellecer added drily, was the only party free of such scandals. ("A Mr. Galeano was recently expelled from our party for stealing 40 cents from the receipts of our paper, *Tribuna Popular*," he pointed out.)[16] The U.S. embassy concluded: "The scene in Congress fur-

[14] See de Wiche, "El comunismo en Guatemala," and Guerra Borges, "Apuntes," p. 117. Interviews with Charnaud, Galich, Capuano, and Bauer Paiz were helpful.

[15] Arbenz's opposition, voiced behind the scene, was adamant. (Interviews with María de Arbenz, Fortuny, Guerra Borges.) The PGT expressed its hostility in a four-part series in *Octubre*, which argued that the aim of the "petty bourgeois leaders" of the new party was to isolate the communists in order to stall "the growth of the labor movement and of the Communist party." (Fortuny, "Elementos para analizar la unificación de los partidos democráticos del Gobierno Arbenz," *Octubre*, July 3 [quoted], 10, 17 and 24, 1952.) See also Fortuny, "La ruptura del PRG," *Octubre*, July 31, 1952, p. 6, and letters from Pinto Usaga to Fortuny (Mexico, July 30, 1952, *GT*, Box 8) and from Cuenca, a senior PRG leader, to Fortuny (Aug. 1952, *GT.*, Box 9). Significantly, after delivering a bitter attack on Fortuny's *Octubre* articles (an attack in which Arbenz's name was not even mentioned), Cuenca felt the need to add, "N.B.: Even though it is clear from the text, I want to put in writing that this letter is not an attack on the president of the republic, Colonel Jacobo Arbenz Guzmán." Cuenca understood that Fortuny had expressed Arbenz's sentiments.

[16] Guatemala, *Diario de las sesiones del Congreso*, Nov. 27, 1953, vol. 16, no. 26, pp. 6–21, quoted from p. 16. For the most extensive press coverage of the session, see "Comisión especial investigará las denuncias," *DCA*, Nov. 28, 1953, p. 1, and "Se fijan en un pan y no en los ladrones de la revolución, dijo Fernández Foncea," *El I*, Nov. 28, 1953, p. 1. For the original accusation against Dardón, see "Chantaje usando el nombre del Congreso?" *El Espectador*, Nov. 17, 1953, p. 1.

Schneider provides ample support for Pellecer's statement about Galeano, and adds

ther lowered the prestige of the Administration politicians and gave the Communists an opportunity to claim superior dedication and honesty.''[17]

If venality characterized many revolutionary politicians, self-indulgence was even more widespread. Their penchant for soft desk jobs and perks stood in sharp contrast to the integrity of the PGT, which, the U.S. embassy lamented in late 1953, ''is now the only administration party that has not been shaken by a major scandal in many months.'' (The embassy had never reported any scandal, major or minor, involving the PGT.)[18]

Thus, the revolutionary leaders were not pure and hardy revolutionaries. On the contrary, they combined an increasingly hollow social conscience with a growing empathy for the ''sweet sorrows'' of the bourgeoisie. And their concern about their enigmatic president, whose communist proclivities (and communist friends) were ever more in evidence, deepened. They supported Arbenz with misgivings and looked forward to the 1956 presidential elections.

They compensated for their lack of revolutionary fervor with a fierce nationalism that had blossomed during the Arévalo years and was fanned by the arrogance of the U.S. government and the intransigence of the American companies. This nationalism was coddled, until late 1953, by a false sense of security. The revolutionary leaders believed that the United States might holler, threaten, and even impose limited sanctions on Guatemala. They did not believe, however, that the United States would overthrow the government. Arbenz and the PGT shared this illusion.

---

another example: ''Abel Mazariegos was expelled from the party for drinking, sleeping on the job of selling the Communist newspaper *Tribuna Popular*, as well as for following the usual bureaucratic practice of putting the 'bite' on those who fell under his jurisdiction as an Inspector of the Public Sanitation. . . . Jesús Galeano, a rising young Communist militant . . . was expelled as 'unworthy to be a Communist' for embezzling in excess of 63¢ from *Tribuna Popular*. Expelled by his cell, Galeano appealed to higher organs, but they upheld his expulsion. Galeano attempted to prove himself worthy of readmittance by working long and faithfully for the Third Congress of the CNCG, the peasant labor confederation under Communist influence, the Second Congress of the CGTG, and the Organizing Committee of the Festival of Friendship. He spread Communist propaganda . . . and used his job as Labor Inspector to the advantage of the party. Finally he humbly sought to be readmitted to the party, but the leadership ruled that his request was 'very premature' and that he would have to continue proving that he was worthy of the honor of being Communist.'' (Schneider, *Communism*, p. 112.) On Galeano, see also *GT*, Box 8.

[17] *JW* 49, Dec. 4, 1953, I:2. See also Krieg to DOS, no. 460, Nov. 30, 1953, NA 714.00. When the Guatemalan Congress legislated a pay raise of $200 a month for its members, the communist deputies handed the full amount to the PGT. (Schoenfeld to DOS, no. 1334, June 28, 1952, NA 714.2.)

[18] For the embassy's statement, see Krieg to DOS, no. 533, Dec. 21, 1953, p. 2, NA 714.00. Neither embassy's dispatches for the relevant period nor Schneider in his authoritative *Communism* implicate the PGT in any scandal.

The combination of frustrated nationalism and a heady sense of impunity helps to explain the strident rhetoric of most revolutionary leaders. Hostility to Washington easily translated into verbal support for the Soviet Union, according to the formula enunciated by a Mexican general in the early 1920s: "We are all Bolsheviks! . . . I don't know what Socialism is; but I am a Bolshevik, like all patriotic Mexicans. . . . The Yankees do not like the Bolsheviks; the Yankees are our enemies; therefore, the Bolsheviks must be our friends, and we must be their friends. We are all Bolsheviks!"[19] Radical rhetoric also polished the tarnished revolutionary credentials of its authors; above all, it might please Arbenz, whose patronage they all courted.

For Arbenz's sympathies were unmistakable. While the Guatemalan Foreign Ministry maintained a neutral line in international affairs, the government daily, *Diario de Centro América* (*DCA*), did not always disguise its preference for the Soviet bloc. A faithful reader of *DCA* was bound to develop respect for communist Czechoslovakia. In 1953 alone, fifty-three articles described life there, always in sympathetic terms; no other country received such attention. Some titles speak for themselves: "Czechoslovakia and Peace"; "Workers Visit Czechoslovakia: Impressed by Culture of Fellow Workers"; "The Victorious Path of the Slovak People"; "The High Standard of Living of the Czech Workers"; "Job Security in Czechoslovakia"; "All Czech Workers Enjoy Annual Vacations."[20] The following description of a visitor's encounter with Czechoslovakia epitomizes the general tone:

[19] Quoted by Roy, *Memoirs*, p. 154.

[20] DCA: Jan. 8, 1953, p. 6; Aug. 11, 1953, p. 8; Sept. 24, 1953, p. 8; Nov. 19, 1953, p. 4; ibid., p. 1; Dec. 30, 1953, p. 4. The other articles on Czechoslovakia that appeared in *DCA* in 1953 are "La historia del teatro checoslovaco de marionetas," Jan. 5, p. 2; "Interesante exposición en Praga," Jan. 10, p. 6; "Estudios superiores para los trabajadores checos," Jan. 12, p. 2; "Una nueva población surge en Karvina," Feb. 11, p. 8; "El prof. Zdenek Mejedly cumple sus 75 años," ibid.; "Dos mil representaciones de 'La Novia Vendida,' " Feb. 12, p. 6; "El pueblo checoslovaco recuerda al héroe nacional Julio Fucik," Mar. 4, p. 6; "Las fundiciones 'Klement Gottwald' la mayor obra que se realiza en Checoslovaquia," ibid.; "Condecoración del académico Zdenek Nejedly," ibid.; "Dos grandes películas checas," Mar. 13, p. 2; "La primera película para ciegos," Apr. 9, p. 2; "Estreno del drama 'Los de Stalingrado,' " Apr. 14, p. 6; "Mikolas Ales, el gran pintor del pueblo checo," Apr. 16, p. 2; "Una película sobre la vida de Julio Fucik," Apr. 21, p. 4; "Exito de las artes gráficas en Checoslovaquia," Apr. 22, p. 3; "Jaroslav Hasek, maestro del humor satírico," Apr. 24, p. 2; "Aumenta la producción en Checoslovaquia," May 15, p. 4; "Iniciase la televisión checa," May 19, p. 4; "Manifestación de paz en Terezin," May 29, p. 8; "Decreto de amnistía en Checoslovaquia," ibid.; "El deporte en Checoslovaquia," ibid., p. 5; "Nueva ley escolar en Checoslovaquia," June 11, p. 4; "Monumento a la literatura nacional en Praga," ibid., p. 8; "Sesión plenaria del Comité Checoeslovaco de Mujeres," ibid., p. 8; "Sesión plenaria del Comité Checoeslovaco de Defensores de la Paz," ibid.; "Reformarán la ley monetaria en Checoslovaquia," June 13, p. 8;

The sky of Czechoslovakia extends its blue hands to welcome all the youths who gather in the train stations along the border. We meet a youth of steel and hope, we meet a youth of fire and joy; workers step forward with music and bread, with accordions and apples, and join this celebration that even the dead applaud from the depths of the earth. It is a foretaste of the great victory, the victory that will return to man what is rightfully his. . . . Already Prague shimmers in the new light, it is the embodiment of our dreams. It is a flower that cannot be crushed. In the streets of Prague there are soldiers, there are girls, there are flowers, there are apples, there are prams with babies that the mothers push toward home and toward the future. Throughout the city one breathes an atmosphere of civic struggle. . . . Here in Czechoslovakia the new world has established one more pillar, whose granite foundations have deep roots in the heart of man. Here man begins to be man; he begins to rise from the swamp into which he has been thrown by the false prophets of fatalism and resignation, by the existentialists of all times, the bitter painters, the failed poets, the kings, the bankers, the businessmen.[21]

DCA did not consistently adopt a procommunist line in international affairs; its articles tended to be neutralist and only occasionally veered to a warm procommunist stance. Still, one can imagine the reaction of U.S. embassy officials when they saw in the cultural section of *DCA* a poem in honor of the ''Canal Volga-Don''[22] or when they read fulsome praise of Communist China in ''We embrace the women of China.''[23]

While the coverage of the Korean War generally avoided editorial comment

---

''Ludvik Kuba, el gran pintor del pueblo checoeslovaco,'' June 16, p. 3; ''Noticias de Checoeslovaquia,'' July 1, p. 8; ''La 'Primavera de Praga—1953,' '' July 23, p. 8; ''Nuevo éxito de la televisión checoeslovaca,'' ibid.; ''Intercambio de mercancias entre Checoeslovaquia y Austria,'' ibid.; ''Campos de entrenamiento para deportistas en Checoeslovaquia,'' Sept. 1, p. 5; ''Hace diez años fué ejecutado por el nazismo el gran Julio Fucik,'' Sept. 8, p. 8; ''En el noveno aniversario de la insurrección nacional eslovaca,'' Sept. 24, p. 3; ''Comienzo del año escolar en Checoeslovaquia,'' Sept. 28, p. 8; ''Homenaje a Julio Fucik rindió el pueblo de Checoeslovaquia,'' Oct. 26, p. 4; ''Desarrollo de la aviación en la república checoeslovaca,'' Nov. 7, p. 8; ''Films checoeslovacos en el extranjero,'' Nov. 13, p. 2; ''Primera exposición en México de productos industriales checoeslovacos,'' ibid., p. 8; ''Vida cultural de los extranjeros que residen en Checoeslovaquia,'' Nov. 14, p. 8; ''Inauguración de la exposición de productos industriales checoeslovacos,'' Nov. 19, p. 4; ''Leos Janacek en el 25 aniversario de su muerte,'' Nov. 20, p. 2; ''Los mercados campesinos en la república checoeslovaca,'' Nov. 21, p. 4; ''Varios artistas ingleses opinan sobre la situación checoslovaca,'' Dec. 15, p. 1; ''Escuelas cooperativistas del trabajo están funcionando en Checoeslovaquia,'' Dec. 28, p. 2; ''Exposición de Nicolas Copernico exhibiéndose en Checoeslovaquia,'' ibid., p. 8.

[21] Carlos Castro Saavedra, ''El mundo nuevo,'' *DCA*, May 21, 1953, p. 2.

[22] *DCA*, Jan. 8, 1953, p. 2.

[23] Atala Valenzuela, *DCA*, Mar. 7, 1953, p. 8.

on the nature of the conflict, there were significant exceptions, as if the editors had suddenly tired of restraint. When a January 2, 1953, editorial pointedly referred to "the unjustifiable origins" of the war,[24] the meaning could have escaped only the most obtuse readers; nor could there have been much confusion when another editorial argued that the United Nations Charter had been "abused in the Korean case by an interested party."[25] Perhaps the editorial which greeted the armistice at Panmunjom best conveys the *DCA*'s stance: "Mankind is tired of war. We have learned that for Big Business war is profit, but we have also learned that the World Peace Movement is not a futile and weak movement. It is strong and heroic."[26] The Departamento Agrario Nacional, a government agency, felt less compelled to be diplomatic; it firmly praised "the iron will of the people [of North Korea] . . . who proved the greatness of their ideals in their struggle to create a truly democratic government" and lambasted "the cynicism of the arms merchants."[27]

The government broadcasting network (whose director, Carlos Alvarado Jérez, was an alternate member of the PGT's Central Committee) followed a line on international affairs similar to that of *DCA*. And Arbenz himself, while generally cautious in his public statements, often sent messages of support to front organizations and at times provided government assistance to their meetings. When the Second Continental Congress of Democratic Lawyers was held in Guatemala in October 1953, it met in the Salón de Vistas of the Supreme Court, and the Guatemalan government provided $10,000. Arbenz sent Interior Minister Charnaud to convey his greetings, and the entire Supreme Court attended.[28]

It is hardly surprising that the revolutionary politicians declaimed speeches with a marked pro-Soviet bent—speeches that were usually couched in rudimentary Marxist jargon. The reaction to the armistice in Korea is a case in point. *Nuestro Diario*, which was controlled by the PAR, celebrated the ar-

---

[24] "Las posibilidades de este año," *DCA*, Jan. 2, 1953, p. 2.

[25] "Guatemala y la paz," *DCA*, July 28, 1953, p. 3.

[26] "La paz en Corea," *DCA*, July 27, 1953, p. 3.

[27] *Boletín Agrario*, no. 1, Aug. 1953, p. 2.

[28] For the 1953 coverage by *DCA* see esp. "Delegado al congreso jurídico de esta capital," Sept. 5, p. 1; "Adesiones a la Conferencia Continental de Juristas," Sept. 29, p. 1; "Convocada II Conferencia Continental de Juristas," Oct. 7, p. 1; "Repercusión americana del II Congreso de Juristas," Oct. 9, p. 1; "Brillante inauguración," Oct. 17, p. 1; "Clausurada la Conferencia de Juristas, ayer," Oct. 22, p. 1; "Resonancias del II Congreso Continental de Juristas," ibid., p. 3; "Resoluciones aprobadas en la Segunda Conferencia Continental de Juristas," in five parts, Nov. 2–6 (always p. 8). For two enthusiastic articles in the PGT's daily *Tribuna Popular*, see "II Conferencia Continental de Juristas iniciada anoche entre ovaciones," Oct. 17, p. 1, and "Soberanía, paz y democracia," Oct. 22, p. 8. Less warm was the coverage by the U.S. embassy: see *JW* 42, Oct. 16, I:3–4, and *JW* 43, Oct. 23, I:1, 3.

mistice as a triumph of the world peace movement over the ''warlike appetite of a great power'' and praised ''the Korean people who have endured horrible crimes at the hands of the western aggressor.''[29] In Congress, the revolutionary majority applauded enthusiastically when a PGT deputy extolled the victory of the peace-loving forces led by the Soviet Union over U.S. imperialism in Korea.[30] The president of the Congress, PAR Deputy Guillermo Ovando Arriola, gave free rein to his oratory. ''The warmongers,'' he asserted, had provoked the war in order to foster their own economic interests and had sent the youth of their countries to die for a sordid cause, ''turning them into butchers of a people whose only crime was their unquenchable yearning to be free.''[31] A few days later, at a massive rally to honor the armistice, the leaders of the PAR, the PRG, and RN pilloried the United States. Charnaud, who was both Arbenz's minister of the interior and the leader of the PRG, paid homage ''to the brave people of Korea who fought against the foreign aggressor''; PAR's Secretary General Fernández Foncea ''condemned the 'insane warmongers' who had caused the Korean conflict''; Díaz Rozzotto, the unsavory secretary general of RN, pointed out that the Korean people ''taught the imperialists an eloquent lesson.''[32] It was, Ambassador Schoenfeld observed, ''a public demonstration of the Arbenz administration's cooperation with the local communist group. President Arbenz,'' he added, ''did not attend the meeting or publicly endorse it. But since the rally was attended by ranking administration officials, political leaders and army officers subject to his discipline and dependent on his goodwill, it was evident that there was more than official tolerance for it.''[33] The logic was unimpeachable.

Nationalism and a longing to see the world impelled many revolutionary politicians to attend youth festivals, peace congresses and similar pro-Soviet gatherings in Western and Eastern Europe. (Their propensity to travel was invigorated by their hosts' willingness to defray their expenses.) To wary U.S. officials, these junkets appeared sinister.[34]

On March 12, 1953, thirty deputies of the Guatemalan Congress introduced a resolution asking for a minute of silence ''to honor the memory of the great statesman and leader of the Soviet Union, Joseph Vissarionovish Stalin, whose passing is mourned by all progressive men.'' Following a violent three-

---

[29] Quoted from ''Firmase la paz en Corea,'' *Nuestro Diario*, July 27, 1953, p. 1, and ''Jubilo por el armisticio,'' *Nuestro Diario*, July 31, 1953, p. 3.

[30] ''Gutiérrez aplaudido en el Congreso,'' *Nuestro Diario*, July 28, 1953, p. 1; Guatemala, *Diario de las sesiones del Congreso*, July 27, 1953, vol. 27, no. 18, p. 4.

[31] ''Duramente condenada la guerra,'' *DCA*, July 27, 1953, p. 1, quoted from p. 6.

[32] ''Triunfo de las fuerzas pacifistas celebrado anoche en un gran mitin,'' *DCA*, Aug. 1, 1953, p. 1 (quoted from p. 6) and ''Grandioso mitin de la paz,'' *Nuestro Diario*, Aug. 1, 1953, p. 1 (quoted from p. 6).

[33] *JW* 32, Aug. 8, 1953, I:1.

[34] See *JW* 12, Mar. 26, 1954, pp. 2–3.

hour debate with the handful of opposition deputies, all but two members of the majority voted in favor of the resolution and the Guatemalan Congress rose in silent homage to the late leader. It was, as a U.S. official pointed out, "the only government body in the Western Hemisphere to do so."[35]

The desire "to give a slap to the Yankees"[36] explains the overwhelming vote. (Few deputies failed to realize, moreover, that a negative vote would have offended Arbenz.) The roots of this desire were vividly expressed during the debate by PAR Deputy Julio Estrada de la Hoz in his reply to a deputy who had claimed that the Soviet Union was imperialistic. "I want to ask the opposition: is United Fruit a Soviet company? Who killed Sandino? Who stole the piers in our harbors?"[37] The debate occurred several months before fear of Yankee retribution would moderate the rhetoric of many revolutionary leaders. "Had Stalin died a year later, very few in Congress would have voted for the minute of silence," remarked the secretary general of the PGT three decades later.[38]

THE PARTIDO GUATEMALTECO DEL TRABAJO (PGT)

In the January 1953 congressional elections, the revolutionary parties increased their majority. In a Congress of fifty-six members, the PAR now held twenty-two seats, the PRG sixteen and RN seven. By contrast, the PGT had only four deputies, the opposition had five, and there were two progovernment independents. No one sympathetic to the PGT sat in Arbenz's cabinet, and very few senior government officials were close to the party; the two highest posts held by the PGT in the administration were those of director of national broadcasting (Carlos Alvarado Jérez) and deputy director of the Departamento Agrario Nacional (Waldemar Barrios Klée).

But Guatemala had a presidential system, and Arbenz was a strong president. With his backing, the communists gained influence far beyond their numbers. The PGT leaders—Fortuny foremost—were Arbenz's closest advisers and constituted his kitchen cabinet, which discussed all major decisions. This was true of the agrarian reform as well as of the purchase of weapons from Czechoslovakia; when Arbenz decided to resign, on June 26, 1954, he consulted only the PGT. By contrast, the official cabinet and the revolutionary leaders learned that weapons from Europe had reached Guatemala's shores only after the State Department loudly denounced their arrival; and when Ar-

---

[35] Leddy to Cabot, May 21, 1953, *FRUS*, 1952–1954, 4:1072. For the session of Congress, see "*1er periodo ordinario de sesiones, 22 febrero–29 mayo 1953* (Libro no. 13, 1953).

[36] Interview with a former member of Congress who asked to remain anonymous.

[37] "Minuto de silencio de Stalin al rojo," *El I*, Mar. 13, 1953, p. 1, quoted from p. 2.

[38] Interview with Fortuny.

benz told his assembled ministers of his decision to step down, Fortuny was already at work writing his resignation speech.

The first public documents signed by the Communist Party of Guatemala appeared in April 1951, one month after Arbenz's inauguration. On June 21, the first anniversary of the party's weekly *Octubre* was openly celebrated. "It is most interesting," the U.S. embassy reported, "that the Minister of Education . . . made an official request . . . that the theater be made available for this 'cultural activity.' "[39] The PGT had fewer than one hundred members, and it was still illegal, although it was obvious that its legalization was just a matter of time. That time came in December 1952, when the party held its second congress. It was a public affair, well advertised in the press and attended by high-ranking guests from the revolutionary parties, the labor confederations and the government. The congress changed the party's name to Partido Guatemalteco del Trabajo (PGT), since "the name Communist Party, however dear to us, makes it harder for us to reach the masses. . . . We must place the task of developing the party before any sentimental attachment to a name."[40] A few days later, the PGT was registered as a legal party despite the outcry of the opposition.[41] As a member of the recently created Frente Democrático Electoral, it was allied with the PAR, PRG, and RN in the January 1953 congressional elections.

The second congress had affirmed the PGT's status within the country, but the communist parties of only Cuba, Mexico, and Costa Rica had sent dele-

[39] *JW* 25, June 22, 1951, I:2. See also "Movimiento comunista sale sin mascara a la luz," *El I*, June 22, 1951, p. 1; "Mitin de aniversario de 'Octubre,' " *Octubre*, June 29, 1951, p. 1; "Communists in Guatemala" (edit.), *NYT*, July 14, 1951, p. 12.

[40] Partido Guatemalteco del Trabajo, *Estatutos*, p. 4. See also "Desarrollo del histórico II Congreso del PGT," *Octubre*, Dec. 18, 1952, p. 1, and Guerra Borges, "No sé por qué se hacen bolas," ibid., p. 3. This issue of *Octubre* is devoted to the congress; several relevant articles are also included in the issues of Dec. 26, 1952, and Jan. 9, 1953.

[41] "El PC cambia de montera," *La Hora*, Dec. 15, 1952, p. 1; "Partido Guatemalteco del Trabajo surge," *El I*, Dec. 15, 1952, p. 1; "Maniobras comunistas," *El I*, Dec. 16, 1952, p. 1; "Partido Guatemalteco del Trabajo queda inscrito," *El I*, Dec. 20, 1952, p. 1; "Doquiera que estéis, como quiera que os presentéis, siempre os reconoceremos," *La Hora* (edit.), Dec. 22, 1952, p. 1; "La flagrante violación incurrida por las autoridades electorales," *La Hora* (edit.), Dec. 24, 1952, p. 1; "CEUA pide la copia del acta de inscripción del PGT," *El I*, Dec. 24, 1952, p. 12; "Una gran victoria popular," *Octubre*, Dec. 26, 1952, p. 4; "Que la inscripción del PGT se cancele por ser completamente ilegal pide el PUA," *El I*, Dec. 29, 1952, p. 1; "La Junta Nacional Electoral busca salida," *La Hora* (edit.), Jan. 3, 1953, p. 1; "Cuando el pez por su boca muere," *La Hora* (edit.), Jan. 5, 1953, p. 1; "Puede la Junta Electoral apegarse con exclusividad a un procedimiento legalista?" *La Hora* (edit.), Jan. 13, 1953, p. 1.

gates.[42] This meager attendance from fraternal parties was not a ploy to disguise the fact that the PGT was part of the international communist movement; on the contrary, the PGT proclaimed this connection proudly. It merely reflected the party's low status and limited contacts.

The PGT had developed practically in isolation. In the late 1940s, no foreign party had made any effort to assist in the creation of a Guatemalan Communist party. Guatemala was too backward a country and its communists were too few to attract the attention of a Latin American communist movement that was reeling under the blows of the Cold War. Some Latin American communists who visited Guatemala were asked for advice and provided it, but these were sporadic and superficial contacts.[43]

It has been argued that the Chilean communist Deputy César Godoy was "of particular help to the Guatemalan Communists from 1947 to 1950."[44] Godoy visited Guatemala on two or three occasions in the late 1940s as Arévalo's guest.[45] The extent of his participation in the creation of the PGT is highlighted by one of the party's founders, Alfredo Guerra Borges:

> Godoy happened to be in Guatemala when we held the founding congress of the party. We invited him to the session in which we discussed the report on international affairs. He said that we were not paying enough attention to the Chinese revolution, which he considered as important as the Russian revolution. (We had only referred to it in passing, because of our lack of information.) This was Godoy's entire contribution to the creation of the party.[46]

Even later, in the Arbenz years, the PGT remained isolated in Latin America. Weakened by the Cold War and the attendant repression, the South American communist parties had little time for a fledgling organization in faraway Guatemala. Closer to home, Costa Rica's once powerful Vanguardia Popular was in disarray after its defeat in the 1948 civil war. The communist parties of Nicaragua and El Salvador were weak and persecuted. In the Dominican Republic, the communist Partido Socialista Popular had been destroyed by Trujillo in the late 1940s; no communist parties existed in Honduras and Haiti. The PGT and Arbenz could offer a safe haven to persecuted communists from the region, but they lacked the wherewithall to provide any active support to communist groups in neighboring countries.

The PGT maintained regular contacts with only two communist parties, those of Mexico and Cuba. The Partido Comunista Mexicano (PCM), minuscule and torn by internal strife, showed little interest in the PGT. The latter, in

[42] Interviews with Fortuny, Pellecer, and Guerra Borges.
[43] Interviews with Fortuny, Pellecer, and Guerra Borges.
[44] Schneider, *Communism*, p. 281.
[45] On Godoy and Arévalo, see above, p. 120, n. 16.
[46] Interview with Guerra Borges; confirmed by Fortuny.

turn, felt little respect for the PCM and its leaders; it never sought and never received any guidance.[47] This was not the case with the Cuban Communist Party (Partido Socialista Popular or PSP). In the words of Guerra Borges, "The PSP was our window on the world, and from time to time we gazed through it." The Guatemalan communists looked up to the PSP as an older, wiser brother. "We were very small in comparison to them," recalls Fortuny. "For us, the PSP was a mature party, fully developed; we considered ourselves a minor party, not only because of our small numbers, but also because of our lack of experience and our limited knowledge of Marxist theory."[48] In 1950, the Guatemalan communists approached the PSP for assistance, and the PSP, which had helped other fledgling parties from the region, responded positively. "The Cuban communists were the only party to truly help us. Not with money, but they sent us a member of their Central Committee (Alejandro) who stayed with us to help us strengthen our party. The PSP was the only Communist party that had the vision to see that a strong Communist party could be created in Guatemala."[49]

Alejandro arrived in Guatemala in mid-1951. PGT leaders remember him as "a wise comrade; he had a good grasp of theory and a lot of practical experience." He was "very good at dealing with people; he wasn't arrogant or dominating, and he was very discreet."[50] Yet his influence and that of his party should not be exaggerated. Batista's coup in Cuba in March 1952 made contacts between the two parties precarious, and Alejandro, who remained in Guatemala until the fall of Arbenz, failed to save the PGT from its mistakes and did not guide it to its successes. Until early 1954, the PGT's leadership was united behind the strong personality of Fortuny. Alejandro was in a country of which he had no previous knowledge, and during his stay he met few of its political leaders; few Guatemalans knew of his presence, and even fewer of his role. His strength may have been his understanding of the limits of this role.

On occasion PGT leaders did travel to the Soviet bloc. To wary U.S. officials, these trips were further proof of the growing international communist

---

[47] Interviews with Fortuny, Pellecer, and Guerra Borges. Tenuous contacts with the American Communist Party (CP) were maintained through infrequent correspondence with CP member A. B. Magil. (Interviews with Fortuny and Guerra Borges.) In the spring of 1954, Magil wrote a short book about Guatemala: Travis and Magil, *The Truth About Guatemala*.

[48] Quotations from interviews with Guerra Borges and Fortuny.

[49] Interviews with Guerra Borges (quoted), Fortuny and Alejandro.

[50] Quotation from interviews with Fortuny and Guerra Borges. This paragraph is based on interviews with Guerra Borges, Fortuny, Pellecer, and Alejandro. (Alejandro, who secretly returned to Cuba after the overthrow of Arbenz, has occupied several important official posts since 1959, notably as Cuba's ambassador to the Soviet Union.)

conspiracy against Guatemala. At times they recorded trips that had never taken place—thus they believed that Fortuny had been in Moscow in 1949 and 1953, when in fact he had not gone beyond Czechoslovakia, the only communist country he had visited before Arbenz fell. (Fortuny first went to the Soviet Union in 1957.) Actually, only one member of the PGT's Secretariat traveled to the Soviet Union before Arbenz's overthrow; en route to the Asian and Pacific Peace Conference in mid-1952, Mario Silva Jonama stopped briefly in Moscow, saw some low level Soviet officials ("they didn't pay much attention to him"), and resumed his journey.[51]

The evidence in the *Guatemalan Transcripts* (*GT*) supports the testimony of PGT leaders that their contacts with West European and Soviet bloc communist parties were very limited. The PGT was invited to attend meetings organized by front organizations such as the World Federation of Trade Unions and the World Peace Council, frequently at their own expense. Relations with the Soviet Union meant occasional visits to the Soviet embassy in Mexico by PGT leaders who happened to be there. "We only saw minor officials. They would ask us a few questions about the party, etc. They never offered us any advice. They never invited us to Moscow." The PGT was not even invited to the nineteenth congress of the Communist Party of the Soviet Union (PCUS), held in October 1952, and the first PGT leader to visit the Soviet Union on party business was Guerra Borges, who represented the PGT at the twentieth congress of the PCUS in October 1956. "We were knocking on the Soviets' door," explains Pellecer, "but they didn't answer."[52]

On two or three occasions, the PGT leaders told Soviet officials in Mexico that they, and Arbenz, would like the Soviet Union to open at least a consulate in their country. "We were told that they would pass on our request and that was always the end of it."[53] Fortunately so, one might add, for such a step would have had only one tangible byproduct, to supply ammunition to those

[51] Interviews with Fortuny (quoted), Alejandro, Pellecer, and Guerra Borges. For Fortuny's 1953 trip to Czechoslovakia, see below, pp. 279–81. For a brief account by Fortuny of his 1949 trip to Czechoslovakia, see Cáceres, *Aproximación*, pp. 145–48. For Silva Jonama's trip, see Krieg to DOS, no. 341, Oct. 14, 1952, NA 714.001.

[52] Interviews with Fortuny (quoted), Pellecer (quoted), Guerra Borges, and Alejandro. Some leading PGT members, including Gutiérrez, visited the Soviet Union in the Arévalo and Arbenz years, but only as guests of front organizations.

[53] Interviews with Guerra Borges (quoted), Fortuny, Pellecer, and Alejandro. Guatemala had established diplomatic relations with the USSR in April 1945, and the prominent writer Luis Cardoza y Aragón had been sent as minister to Moscow. But the Soviets failed to open a legation in Guatemala, and Arévalo took advantage of this lack of reciprocity to close the legation in May 1946. The two countries did not formally break diplomatic relations. In *Retorno al futuro*, Cardoza y Aragón describes his stay in the Soviet Union.

who charged that Guatemala was the Soviet bridgehead in the Western Hemisphere.

There is evidence of financial transactions between the Soviet Union and the PGT: the notorious "Moscow Gold" to which some Americans referred at the time. The PGT ordered a few books and magazines from the Soviet Union, and the *GT* include two letters from Moscow's *Mezhdunarodnaja Kniga*; these letters express impatience at the PGT's failure to settle its outstanding accounts of $12.35 and $10.60 and firmly demand that the debt be paid "as soon as possible."[54] Chastened, the PGT complied. With only slight exaggeration, Guerra Borges later protested, "We paid them religiously. We were the only ones in Latin America who paid them. People from the Mexican Communist Party told me: 'You people are crazy; we haven't paid them a cent for at least 10 years.' As for the 'Moscow Gold,' Moscow got money from us, not the other way around."[55] The PGT never received any financial assistance other than occasional travel expenses from foreign communist parties or front organizations.

Only on one occasion did the Soviet Union indicate an interest in developing ties with Guatemala. In late October 1953, Mikhail Samoilov, the Soviet commercial attaché in Mexico, visited Guatemala for three days. (Never before had a Soviet official come to the country.) He spoke with Arbenz and Fortuny and expressed his government's desire to establish commercial ties with Guatemala, something that both Arbenz and the PGT desired.[56] The Soviet Union, Samoilov stated, was willing to buy a very large quantity of Guatemalan bananas (more than the country actually produced); it offered agricultural equipment in exchange; since the Soviet Union did not have refrigerator ships, Guatemala would have to supply the transport. Arbenz and Fortuny explained that Guatemala had no ships; its bananas were exported in the bottoms of United Fruit, and it was unlikely that UFCO would hand over its ships to foster Soviet-Guatemalan friendship. However, they noted, Guatemala could sell coffee to the Soviet Union.

Samoilov was not impressed. The Soviet Union already had many long-term agreements to buy coffee abroad and could not purchase Guatemalan coffee in the near future. On this note, the conversation closed, "and that was

[54] Mezhdunarodnaja Kniga to Alfredo Mendoza, Apr. 17 and July 24, 1953, *GT*, Box 8. The expression is used in both letters.

[55] Interviews with Guerra Borges (quoted), Alejandro, Fortuny, and Pellecer.

[56] The account of Samoilov's conversation with Arbenz is based on interviews with Fortuny (who was present), María de Arbenz (who was told by Arbenz), and Guerra Borges and Alejandro (who were told by Fortuny). On Samoilov's visit to Guatemala see also: *JW* 44, Oct. 29, 1953, I:1, 3–4, and II:1–2; "Delegado del Soviet está en Guatemala," *El I*, Oct. 24, 1953, p. 1; "Competencia soviética tenemos en propia casa," *La Hora*, Oct. 24, 1953, p. 1; Col. McCormick, "Intelligence Report" no. R-8-54, Jan. 8, 1954, RG84 G&C, Box 4, NA-S.

that.''[57] It had been an exploratory mission that had revealed, above all, Moscow's ignorance of Guatemala, for it was no secret that Guatemala had no fleet, much less its own refrigerator ships.

One may speculate about the reasons for Moscow's lack of interest in the PGT and Guatemala. In Stalin's last years, mistrust characterized the Soviets' attitude toward Third World countries. Their attention was riveted on relations with the United States and on developments in Europe and Asia. Latin America was far from their preoccupations.[58] Within that inhospitable continent, Guatemala was a tiny and backward land thrust into the heart of the American empire. Arbenz was a military man, and the Soviet leaders dismissed Third World officers as imperialism's stooges. The PGT was a small group that lacked the traditions and international contacts of older Latin American communist parties.

Following Stalin's death, indications of greater flexibility began to appear in Moscow's attitude to the Third World. Samoilov's visit reflects the limits of this incipient change. Another reflection of the change was the Soviet decision, in December 1953, to allow Guatemala to buy weapons from Czechoslovakia. ''If Stalin had been alive,'' remarks Fortuny, ''they wouldn't have sold them to us.''[59]

In the spring of 1954, Soviet journals expressed a growing optimism that Latin American countries might be willing and able to lessen their dependence on the United States.[60] Eventually, this new appraisal might have led the Soviet Union to show greater interest in Guatemala, had Arbenz not been overthrown. But in the first six months of 1954 only one tangible change occurred: the PGT began receiving (gratis!) some issues of *Pravda*. In Guatemala, however, not even the most devout communist could read Russian.[61]

Yet the PGT was perturbed neither by Moscow's indifference nor by the paucity of its international contacts. ''We were a provincial party; we didn't look beyond our village; we didn't even have an international committee.'' The party's leaders were very busy: ''We were overwhelmed with work. We were preoccupied with the development of the PGT and with Guatemalan domestic politics.''[62] They sent delegates to the international congresses to which the PGT was invited, but usually the leaders stayed home;[63] they were content

[57] Interview with Fortuny.

[58] See Clissold, *Soviet Relations with Latin America*; Hough, *The Struggle for the Third World*; Kanet, *The Soviet Union and the Developing World*, ch. 1; Donaldson, *Soviet Policy toward India*, ch. 3.

[59] Interview with Fortuny.

[60] See Dinerstein, *The Making of a Missile Crisis*, pp. 10–14.

[61] Interviews with Fortuny and Guerra Borges.

[62] Quotations from interviews with Guerra Borges and Fortuny.

[63] The only senior party member to travel with relative frequency was Gutiérrez in his capacity as secretary general of the CGTG.

to applaud the Soviet Union and its policies from afar, with genuine enthusiasm. Other communist parties, small sects unable to influence events in their own countries, sought in endless congresses abroad and the occasional nods of minor Soviet officials the legitimacy they lacked at home. The PGT, however, unlike every other Communist party in the hemisphere, was gaining strength. If its leaders needed expert advice, they had Alejandro. He was well versed in Marxism and more familiar with Guatemala than party officials from distant lands. Success reinforced the provincial spirit of the PGT and might have led, over time, to a more sober assessment of the Soviet bloc.

Without Arbenz, the PGT would have been utterly isolated. Most revolutionary leaders felt little sympathy for the party. Left to their own devices, they would have spurned cooperation with the PGT and have barely tolerated its legalization. Instead, Arbenz's control of the government's purse and patronage, and his forceful personality, stirred politicians and bureaucrats to court the party that basked in the president's favor.

Arbenz was influential in the October 1951 merger of the two main labor confederations of the Arévalo period—the FSG and the CTG—into the communist-led CGTG.[64] In the spring of 1954, he helped the communists take control of the railway union (SAMF), the only important urban labor union that still opposed them.[65]

Even more critical was the president's impact on the peasant-based CNCG, created in May 1950 by a group of noncommunist and anticommunist labor leaders. Throughout the Arbenz years, these leaders resented the PGT's and the CGTG's efforts to gain influence in the countryside. But the CNCG was always penniless, and it needed the government's financial assistance.[66] Thus, its leaders spouted pro-Soviet rhetoric and even joined, after much hesitation, the Soviet-dominated World Federation of Trade Unions.[67] Above all, they sought a modus vivendi with the PGT and the CGTG. Verbal skirmishes in

[64] For the CGTG, see GT, Boxes 24, 27, 30–38. Among secondary sources, see esp. Bishop, "Guatemalan Labor," pp. 130–50; Schneider, Communism, pp. 141–55; Ramos Guzmán de Schmoock, "El movimiento sindical," pp. 118–69.

[65] The episode is well described by Schneider, Communism, pp. 176–84. Of the many boxes in the GT that deal with the SAMF (20, 21, 45–52, 80, 86, 87), particularly relevant are boxes 50–52.

[66] For the financial straits of the CNCG, see Pearson, "Confederación," pp. 47–54. For the government's assistance, see the following note signed by Castillo Flores on May 28, 1953: "I received $25,000 from the government to cover expenses related to the CNCG." (GT, Box 23.)

[67] For an excellent discussion of the CNCG's pro-Soviet rhetoric, see Pearson, "Confederación," pp. 81–83 and 88–95. For a thoughtful discussion of Castillo Flores's and of the CNCG's dilemma by a visiting American scholar, see MemoConv (Krieg, Alexander), Apr. 1, 1954, RG84 G&C, Box 4, NA-S.

1950 and 1951 gave way to tentative cooperation. Behind this friendly facade, tensions simmered. Years later, Gutiérrez lamented about "the lack of a true alliance between workers and peasants" under Arbenz and "the failure of the Coordinating Committee of the two labor confederations to foster closer ties between them."[68] Had the CNCG not needed Arbenz's support, its distrust of the communists would have turned into open hostility.

And yet, the men who led the PGT did not owe everything to Arbenz. They had acquired a leading role in the CTG in the Arévalo years. Their success was their own and not, as U.S. officials had believed, due to the patronage of Arévalo (who mistrusted the CTG and preferred the more moderate FSG). And if in 1951 Arbenz was instrumental in the unification of the FSG and the CTG under communist leadership, of equal or greater importance was the growing personal prestige of the CTG leaders among the rank and file of both labor confederations. As a U.S. scholar, Edwin Bishop, has pointed out, on one side stood the "opportunistic, corruptible anticommunist leaders"; on the other, "the dedicated, incorruptible Communist leaders like Gutiérrez." (Therefore, concludes the anticommunist Bishop, "it was the misfortune of the rank and file that they had but small choice.")[69]

This was at least as important as the role of Arbenz in determining the outcome of the conflict that rent the railway union, SAMF, in the spring of 1953. The anticommunist group that was decisively defeated in the June union elections was led by the prominent PRG labor leader Arturo Morales Cubas. Even the U.S. embassy, so sympathetic to any effort to weaken PGT influence, conceded that Morales Cubas was "unscrupulous," and that his management of the SAMF's Consumer Cooperative had been marred by serious financial irregularities.[70] Those SAMF leaders who supported Morales Cubas tended to

[68] Gutiérrez, *Breve historia*, pp. 71, 55.

[69] Bishop, "Guatemalan Labor," p. 148.

[70] *JW* 21, May 22, 1953, I:1. Morales Cubas, the embassy had earlier reported, "had been 'lending' himself and his friends large sums of Cooperative funds on no more than nominal security (e.g., $16,615 against an $85 deposit)." (*JW* 39, Sept. 25, 1952, I:3–4; see also: "Morales Cubas en la balanza," *El I*, Oct. 3, 1952, p. 1; Krieg to DOS, no. 379, Oct. 24, 1952, NA 814.062; "La cooperativa: Sección de préstamos en eso se ha convertido," *El I*, Dec. 23, 1952, p. 1; "En entredicho el estado financiero de la cooperativa de consumo del SAMF," *La Hora*, Feb. 2, 1953, p. 1.)

The embassy followed the denouement of the struggle within SAMF closely. See *JW* 21–24, 26 of 1953, and Schoenfeld to DOS: no. 1055, May 30, 1953; no. 1097, June 12, 1953; no. 1143, June 24, 1953; all NA 814.062. Press coverage was extensive. See esp. "El SAMF se sacudirá de los comunistas," *La Hora*, May 11, 1953, p. 1; "Mañana habrá tormenta en el SAMF," *La Hora*, May 14, 1953, p. 1; "Llamamiento de la CGTG," *DCA*, May 15, 1953, p. 1; "Golpe Cubista en el SAMF," *La Hora*, May 16, 1953, p. 1; "Triunfo rotundo," *DCA*, May 16, 1953, p. 1; "El PRG no puede enjuiciar a un lider," *La Hora*, May 23, 1953, p. 1; "Llamamiento de la

share his shortcomings. As Schneider has pointed out in his analysis of the SAMF elections:

> The moderate leaders themselves must bear partial responsibility for their failure and hence for the success of the Communists. The tragedy is that Morales Cubas and his followers discredited themselves, by taking advantage of their positions for personal gain at the workers' expense. Even when there were no sins of commission on the records of the opponents of Communism, they partially defaulted to the Communists and their allies. Many of the moderate leaders were too interested in their own economic well-being and job advancement to devote as much time to union affairs as did the extremists. Some moderate leaders stagnated once they tasted the better things of life and others gave up the fight and resigned to care for their personal or family interests. These actions and attitudes lost them the support of such dedicated leaders as José Luis Caceres R., who began to see in the Communist labor leaders a model more worthy of emulation.[71]

The PGT, however, never controlled the labor confederation. Its influence depended on Arbenz's support and on the personal prestige of a handful of CGTG leaders who belonged to the party, such as the CGTG's secretary general, Gutiérrez, and his deputy, José Alberto Cardoza. Within the CGTG, individual unions retained a large degree of autonomy, and only a few were led by PGT members. With the exception of union elections, the great majority of the hundred thousand CGTG members voted for the revolutionary parties and not for the PGT.[72]

A few revolutionary leaders were sincerely attracted to the PGT. Unable to forget their youthful dreams, they were distressed by the evolution of their own parties. To these men, the PGT appeared more and more as a model; weakness or ideology might keep them from joining this austere party but did

---

CGTG al SAMF hacia la unidad," *DCA*, May 23, 1953, p. 1; "Sosistas y Cubistas se disputarán en firme la directiva del SAMF," *La Hora*, May 25, 1953, p. 1; "El DAT manda al SAMF a convocar a elecciones," *DCA*, May 28, 1953, p. 1; "Comunicado sobre la situación actual del movimiento obrero," *DCA*, June 2, 1953, p. 1; "PRG ante el conflicto en el SAMF," *DCA*, June 18, 1953, p. 1; "Violenta pugna samfista," *El I*, June 19, 1953, p. 1; "Los votos samfistas en la capital," *La Hora*, June 22, 1953, p. 1; "Empezó escrutinio," *Nuestro Diario*, June 22, 1953, p. 13; "Planilla que encabeza Jaime Zabala triunfó en el SAMF," *DCA*, June 23, 1953, p. 1; "Rotundo triunfo," *Nuestro Diario*, June 23, 1953, p. 11; "Gran jubilo entre ferroviarios," *Nuestro Diario*, June 25, 1953, p. 8; "Posesionó la nueva directiva del SAMF," *DCA*, July 7, 1953, p. 1. See also above, n. 65.

[71] Schneider, *Communism*, p. 184.

[72] According to Gutiérrez, the CGTG had 104,000 members in late January 1954. (Gutiérrez, *Breve historia*, pp. 51–52.) "Convocatoria al Segundo Congreso Nacional Sindical de la C.G.T.G.," *DCA*, Dec. 12, 1953, p. 4, refers to 109,829 members.

not dampen their admiration. Their number, however, must not be over-stated—they were just a handful. Only a careless observer would include among them PAR Secretary General Fernández Foncea, who burst out in an October 5, 1953, session in Congress, "I endorse most of all the Communist party, the party of Pellecer, Cardoza and Gutiérrez, which is the most patri-otic, decent, honest and consistent in the country. The PAR is only a tempo-rary party, like the other parties of the revolution that are destined to disappear and be absorbed in the World Communist Party." This bold statement sur-prised the PGT, which had no inkling that Fernández Foncea might harbor such thoughts; predictably, it provoked an uproar in the PAR, which swiftly expelled him. The declaration, however, was not the public confession of a closet communist. On the contrary, Fernández Foncea fought tooth and nail to remain the PAR's secretary general. The explanation was more mundane: the man had been drinking.[73]

Had the PGT sought to impose its exacting standards on the revolutionary parties, it would have aroused fear and resentment. As it was, those within the government who resented the PGT's mounting influence and access to Arbenz were gratified that the party was indulgent of their peccadillos. The PGT also demonstrated welcome restraint in the division of bureaucratic spoils: its members let their noncommunist allies grow rich in soft jobs while they were content with less prestigious positions in which they soon became indispens-able. In short, concluded a *New York Times* correspondent, they did very little that was "sensational or extraordinary. They merely organized closely where others organized loosely. They worked devotedly for their group's interests where others worked for their own personal interest. They did the dreary, menial jobs while others sought the glamorous jobs. . . . They were a highly disciplined group."[74]

These dangerous qualities were acknowledged by the U.S. embassy and by some Guatemalans who loathed the PGT. "Licenciado Silva Peña," the em-bassy reported in December 1953, "said that the Communists made their in-fluence felt a great deal through hard work. For instance, once last year he was on a committee which had been unable to settle a question in a certain meeting. Everyone except the Communists had gone off that evening to see the 'Ice Festival' which was in town. The Communists had worked all night and came

[73] "Fernández Foncea preconiza el triunfo total de los comunistas en Guatemala," *Prensa Libre*, Oct. 6, 1953, p. 3. For Fernández Foncea's speech, see also "Fernández F. vociferó en favor del comunismo," *El I*, Oct. 6, 1953, p. 1; "Francisco Fernández Foncea ratifica sus conceptos," *DCA*, Oct. 8, 1953, p. 1; Guatemala, *Diario de las sesiones del Congreso*, Oct. 5, 1953, vol. 16, no. 10, pp. 29–30. For the PGT's reac-tion: interviews with Fortuny and Guerra Borges; and Fortuny, *Por un frente único*, pp. 32–34. For Fernández Foncea's attempts to hold onto power, see above, p. 173.

[74] Flora Lewis, "Communism in Guatemala: A Case History," *NYT*, Feb. 21, 1954, D11.

in the next day with a completely new set of proposals which carried the day.''[75] In a similar vein, an embassy dispatch reported a few weeks later:

> In a graphic illustration of the local Communists' ability quickly to exploit situations to their advantage, Carlos Manuel Pellecer . . . began to organize a relief committee for local market women within a few hours after a major fire in Guatemala City's No. 2 market burned down over 500 wooden shops and stalls. The Alianza Femenina Guatemalteca . . . , the Communist-front women's organization, also stepped in quickly with offers of aid, but the anti-Communist organizations apparently did nothing, although the market women have been among their strongest supporters.[76]

Thirty years later Bill Krieg, the embassy's deputy chief (DCM) in the Arbenz years, highlighted the contrast between the PGT and the other administration parties:

> The revolutionary parties were groups of bums of first order; lazy, ambitious, they wanted money, were palace hangers-on. Those who could work, had a sense of direction, ideas, knew where they wanted to go, were Fortuny and his PGT friends; they were very honest, very committed. This was the tragedy: the only people who were committed to hard work were those who were, by definition, our worst enemies.[77]

The communists' abilities, rather than merely Arbenz's favor, explain why the four PGT deputies acquired such influence in the National Congress. The PGT was represented in all fourteen committees elected by Congress in March 1954. PGT deputies chaired two committees of particular importance: Agrarian Reform (Gutiérrez), and Reform of the Labor Code (Cardoza).[78]

The PGT was moderate in its public statements. Although it acknowledged that its ultimate objective was the creation of a Marxist-Leninist Guatemala it stressed that this was a distant prospect. For the present, and for a long time to come, the party's task would be to assist in the creation of a modern, capitalist and fully independent Guatemala. No revolutionary politician could object. Lingering fears were assuaged by the comforting thought that in March 1957 Arbenz's presidency would end and the communists would lose their champion.

In the meantime, the PGT was growing. Profiting from the new climate of

[75] MemoConv (Hill, Silva Peña), Dec. 28, 1953, p. 2 enclosed in Krieg to Fisher, Dec. 29, 1953, NA 714.00.

[76] *JW* 4, Feb. 1, 1954, p. 4. For the fire, see " 'La Placita' reducida a cenizas," *DCA*, Jan. 25, 1954, p. 1, and several articles in *El I* of the same date.

[77] Interview with Krieg.

[78] For a list of the committees and their members, see "Comisiones del Congreso para el ciclo 1954–55," *GT*, Box 1. See also "Dirigente comunista por primera vez en directiva del Congreso," *El I*, Feb. 18, 1954, p. 1, and "Monopolizadas comisiones en el Congreso," *El I*, May 7, 1954, p. 1.

freedom, it sought to become a full-fledged party, able to compete in national elections. This led it to change its name and, shortly thereafter, to loosen the requirements for party membership. Secretariat member Bernardo Alvarado Monzón described the new approach:

> Our workers, our peasants and our middle class are very backward because of the semifeudal conditions in our country and because of the tyrants who oppressed us for so long. But these are our people, in whose midst we must forge our party. . . . This is why we are critical of those comrades who look down on our new members and welcome only those who are already "well-prepared." They forget that communists are molded within the party. . . . The belief that the party should be small, that it should be primarily a school of Marxist theory, and that its prospective members should arrive well-qualified . . . has isolated us from the masses and restricted the party's growth.
>
> There are comrades who cross themselves devoutly before entering a meeting, but they enter and listen to the party's teachings. These are the people whom the party must attract in order to enlist the best and transform them into good communists. . . .
>
> "Won't this weaken the party?" the most sectarian of our comrades will ask in fear. But . . . what weakens the party is to be cut off from the masses. . . . It would be worse if these honest peasants, after making the sign of the cross, went off to hear a venomous anticommunist diatribe.[79]

This approach differed sharply from the classic Leninist conception of a Bolshevik party, but the results seemed to vindicate the leaders' tactics. In particular, through the agrarian reform, the PGT began penetrating the countryside.

The communists and their sympathizers filled only a minority of the posts in the bureaucracies established by Decree 900, but to assess the PGT's role by a head count is misleading.[80] Schneider's assertion that the communists "sought and received virtual control of the machinery" implementing the agrarian reform is not without foundation.[81] Leaving abundant opportunities

[79] "Informe presentado por el camarada Bernardo Alvarado M. a nombre de la comisión de organización del comité central en la conferencia nacional de organización del Partido Guatemalteco del Trabajo—8 y 9 de agosto de 1953," *Organización*, no. 7, Sept. 1953, pp. 7–8.

[80] The most important positions held by PGT members in the Departamento Agrario Nacional were Waldemar Barrios Klée, deputy director, and Mario Sosa, chief inspector. Many agrarian inspectors belonged to the PGT. "There are communists in the DAN, but they are the best workers and the most honest," Arbenz told a group of officers in early June 1954. (*GT*, Box 11. See below, p. 307.) See also Pearson, "*Confederación*," pp. 170–71.

[81] Quoted from Schneider, *Communism*, p. 205. For a careful assessment of the

for graft to the revolutionary politicians, the PGT concentrated on garnering support in those areas of the countryside where the land redistribution process was gathering momentum, with the rich department of Escuintla as its first priority.

Of course, the party faced formidable obstacles: the relentless hostility of the Church; the deep suspicion of the Indians of anything that was Ladino and of the peasantry as a whole of all that was urban. The PGT was, after all, an urban-based Ladino party led by middle-class intellectuals, and the very word communist evoked fears inculcated by decades of state and Church propaganda.

Yet, the party's progress was real and afforded a reasonable hope that in a few years the PGT could develop a solid base of support in the countryside. By June 1954 the PGT had over five thousand members—a not insignificant number in a country of 3 million inhabitants and for a party that three years earlier had claimed less than a hundred. Many of the new members were agricultural workers, including Indians. "The PGT," notes Guerra Borges, "grew in the countryside because of the agrarian reform, even among the Indians, but our true strength was among the agricultural workers."[82]

Lenin would have been appalled: the inevitable result of a rapidly expanding membership in a backward society was that "the immense majority" of the PGT members "knew nothing of Marxism-Leninism." The number of *cuadros*—skilled activists who possessed a basic knowledge of Marxism-Leninism—was extremely small. "The good *cuadros*, well-prepared, who could think and organize, probably were no more than forty," recalls Fortuny. "And when I say forty, perhaps I am exaggerating." This was part of the legacy of underdevelopment and tyranny. And the frenetic activity of the party leaders had left them little time for anything but the most immediate tasks. "Had we been in the opposition [in the Arbenz period] we would have had more time

---

number of PGT members involved in the administration of the agrarian reform program, see Krieg to DOS, no. 818, Mar. 29, 1954, pp. 6–8, NA 814.20.

[82] Interviews with Fortuny and Guerra Borges (quoted). The PGT had close to five thousand members according to Fortuny, close to six thousand according to Guerra Borges. (Schneider's figure of four thousand is overly conservative [*Communism*, p. 101].)

According to the official party figures (which have been broadly confirmed in interviews with Fortuny and Guerra Borges), the membership of the PGT in Aug. 1953 included: 50 percent agricultural and industrial workers; 29 percent peasants; 21 percent members of the middle class. ("Informe presentado por el camarada Bernardo Alvarado M." [see n. 79 above], pp. 1–9; see also Fortuny, *Informe*, Dec. 11, 1952, p. 53.) The agricultural workers who joined the PGT were mainly from the departments of Escuintla, San Marcos, and Rhetaluleu. They usually belonged to peasant unions affiliated to the CGTG rather than to the CNCG. (See also Pearson, "*Confederación*," p. 134.)

to prepare *cuadros*," notes Fortuny. "But when you are in the government, there isn't enough time."[83]

The growth in membership was paralleled by success at the polls. In the January 1953 congressional elections, the PGT was the weakest of the four government parties. But the elections had been held only one month after the PGT's legalization, before it had launched its drive to transform itself into a broad-based organization, and before the agrarian reform had gained momentum. Less than a year later, in the November 1953 municipal elections, the PGT's progress was unmistakable. "It was the first time," remarked the U.S. embassy, "that the PGT had run as an independent party and it made an impressive showing."[84] Of the four provincial towns in which it fielded candidates, three elected communist mayors. Among them was Escuintla, capital of the important department of the same name, where the PGT's candidate won 40 percent of the vote in a four-way race.[85] By the following spring, knowledgeable observers predicted that in the November 1954 congressional elections, the PGT would gain an additional two or three seats.[86]

Given the president's support, the agrarian reform, the dissension of the other government parties—and its own cohesion and dedication—the PGT stood an excellent chance of increasing its strength in the November 1956 congressional elections, perhaps having close to a fifth of the seats in Congress by the time Arbenz's successor was inaugurated in March 1957. Was this a prospect that justified fears of a communist takeover, or at least of a controlling communist influence in Guatemala?

THE GUATEMALAN ARMED FORCES

It is striking that those who emphasize the "Red Threat" in Arbenz's Guatemala say so little about communist subversion in the armed forces. Those few American observers who did not mince words offered no corroboration.

[83] Interviews with Fortuny (quoted) and Guerra Borges.

[84] *JW* 48, Nov. 27, 1953, I:1–2.

[85] The administration parties won an overwhelming number of the 310 municipalities at stake, with the PAR, once again, the strongest, followed at a distance by the PRG. For press coverage, see esp. "Elecciones municipales," *El I*, Nov. 20, 1953, p. 1; "A vencer votando," *Tribuna Popular*, Nov. 21, 1953, p. 1; "Los candidatos del PGT y de unidad van a la cabeza," *Tribuna Popular*, Nov. 22, 1953, p. 1; "En la mayoría de los municipios triunfaron las fuerzas revolucionarias," *DCA*, Nov. 23, 1953, p. 1; "Rotunda victoria en las municipales," *Tribuna Popular*, Nov. 24, 1953, p. 1; "Confirman más triunfos de las fuerzas revolucionarias," *DCA*, Nov. 24, 1953, p. 1; "En los diversos departamentos mayoría para los revolucionarios," *El I*, Nov. 25, 1953, p. 1.

[86] See "Frente Democrático Nacional somete a consideración el reparto de curules," *El I*, May 24, 1954, p. 1; "Los comunistas van a tener más curules en el congreso," *La Hora*, May 24, 1954, p. 1; Schneider, *Communism*, p. 235.

"Russian sympathizers have top posts in the army," revealed *U.S. News and World Report* in early June 1954, but it said no more.[87] Daniel James, a respected journalist who was considered an authority on Guatemalan affairs, was equally blunt. "Even the army was infiltrated by the Red Virus," he stated boldly in his well-received *Red Design for the Americas*, the first retrospective of the Arbenz regime by a U.S. author. Colonel Arbenz was a traitor, and so was the chief of the armed forces, Colonel Carlos Enrique Díaz, who, after Arbenz's fall, "tried to save Guatemala for Communism." Many other members of the officer corps and of the ranks were "either communists or staunch sympathizers."[88] But in vain does the anxious reader wait for more details, the names of at least a few of the "many" communists and fellow travelers within the military, or a more precise estimate of the degree of infiltration of the Red virus. James's imagination failed him. After this one paragraph, he abandoned the topic. In a book of over three hundred pages about the communist threat in Guatemala, he never again mentioned the crucial subject of communist subversion in the armed forces.

James's assessment was not shared by U.S. officials. In May 1954, a lengthy State Department study noted that the PGT had "established its dominion over the key institutions in Guatemalan political life, with the exception of the armed forces, which, however, have not opposed Communism." In a fifteen-page description of the party's "Levers of Power," the document never once referred to the military. The armed forces were only briefly mentioned in a later section on the "Weaknesses of the PGT Position": "The PGT has yet made no palpable inroads on the Guatemalan army"[89]—a conclusion that was consistent with the reams of reports on Guatemala written by U.S. officials in the Arbenz years.

Ronald Schneider, who had access to an impressive array of Guatemalan primary sources, discusses communist infiltration in the different sectors of Guatemalan society at great length. To the military he devotes only two pages, roughly the same space allotted to the relatively marginal Alianza Femenina Guatemalteca, and much less than that reserved for the Comité Nacional de la Paz, a communist front organization of secondary significance.[90] His conclusions are undramatic:

[87] "Red Plan for War in the Americas," *U.S. News and World Report*, June 4, 1954, p. 30.

[88] James, *Red Design*, p. 19. On James' book, see Gillin and Silvert, "Ambiguities in Guatemala," p. 471, n. 1. Even these authorities on Guatemala described the book as "carefully written."

[89] "The Partido Guatemalteco del Trabajo: A Basic Study," in DOS, *Penetration of the Political Institutions*, quoted from pp. iii, 32. On the bizarre transformation of this document, see Wood, "Self-Plagiarism."

[90] See Schneider, *Communism*, pp. 214–16 for the army; pp. 110–11, 263–65 for the Alianza Femenina Guatemalteca; pp. 253–58 for the Comité Nacional de la Paz.

Communist infiltration of the army was perhaps less successful than in any other area of the government; that the army tolerated the Communists as long as it did was largely out of loyalty to the President. This is not to say that the Communists did not try, nor that they did not have success with some of the younger politically ambitious officers. (The greatest success of the Communists was of course with Arbenz himself.) The Communists did not have time to infiltrate the army from below; and with the exception of Arbenz and perhaps Paz Tejada and Aldana Sandoval, their wooing of the top officers proved to be far less effective than they had hoped.[91]

It is a sober assessment—and yet it still overstates reality.

An army of approximately 6,200 men, poorly-trained and badly equipped; an insignificant navy of 150 men; an air force of a few decrepit planes and 350 men: these were the Guatemalan armed forces under Arbenz. Hardly an impressive war machine, even though stronger than the other rag-tag armies of Central America. While the 1944 revolution had abolished the rank of general, colonels abounded: there were more than two hundred in the army alone. The officer corps numbered nine hundred: one officer for every six enlisted men. The officers were Ladinos. The enlisted men were mostly illiterate Indians, drafted for two years; they were treated less harshly than in the Ubico era, yet a chasm separated their world from that of the officers.[92]

Arbenz's military credentials were impressive: an outstanding cadet, a highly regarded professor at the Escuela Politécnica, and a hero of the 1944 revolution. As defense minister under Arévalo, he had led the anti-Arana faction; during the *Aranista* uprising he had displayed, even his foes acknowledge, outstanding bravery and skill. Many officers were drawn to him by a sense of loyalty or friendship. He elicited respect from his friends and fear from his enemies. When he succeeded Arévalo, in March 1951, many officers saw Arbenz as *their* president; others were indifferent but not hostile; only a minority secretly opposed him.

"I do not recall any doubts about Arbenz's political orientation prior to his winning the election," a U.S. military attaché has written. The Guatemalan officers "stated that he [Arbenz] had courted the labor groups to assure his election but in no way did they think that these leftist and labor groups would be permitted to influence him."[93] But in 1951, Arbenz knew what only a few officers had begun to suspect: the soldier was undergoing a process of political radicalization. This set him apart from the army whose leader he had become.

[91] Ibid., p. 214.

[92] The literature on the Guatemalan military in the revolutionary period is spare. The most useful studies are Adams, *Crucifixion*, pp. 238–77; Monteforte Toledo, *Guatemala*, pp. 359–74; Frankel, "Political Development," pp. 122–68; LaCharite, *Case Study in Insurgency*, pp. 81–97. All the Guatemalan officers interviewed for this book were asked about the issues examined in this section.

[93] Lt. Col. Manuel Chavez, letter to the author, June 11, 1989, p. 2.

Arbenz knew that this was potentially dangerous and that it could imperil his ability to lead. This knowledge shaped his policies toward the army.

The story of Major Carlos Paz Tejada is a case in point. Paz Tejada had distinguished himself in the October 1944 uprising against Ponce and again in July 1949 when the *Aranistas* rose in revolt. He was able, honest, efficient. His performance as chief of the armed forces after Arana's death had been, by all accounts, outstanding. As the U.S. air attaché reported, he was "intelligent . . . gracious . . . a good organizer and administrator." He was a superb candidate for a top military position in the Arbenz administration, such as chief of the armed forces or minister of defense.[94] Arbenz, who deeply respected Paz Tejada, carefully considered him for such a post.[95]

But Paz Tejada was flawed: not only was he anticommunist, he had a strong personality, and he could be neither bought nor seduced. He could become very dangerous, Arbenz concluded: he could lead the army in a revolt against a president who was too close to the Communist party. The key positions in the armed forces had to be held by officers who would be loyal and pliant. Military competence and personal integrity could not be the primary considerations.[96]

Arbenz appointed Paz Tejada minister of public works, removing him from active duty. As chief of the armed forces, he chose instead a gregarious, hard-drinking colonel, thirty-seven-year-old Carlos Enrique Díaz. Díaz was an unexceptional officer, but Arbenz believed he was loyal. As defense minister, he chose Colonel José Angel Sánchez, a man whom the U.S. embassy described as "ineffectual; heavy drinker . . . Loyal to Arbenz."[97] Arbenz had found the

[94] Maj. Chavez, "Intelligence Report" no. 11–53, Jan. 18, 1953, p. 2, RG84 G&C, Box 4, NA-S. See also Col. Lewis, "Intelligence Report" no. IR-80-49, Aug. 6, 1949, RG319 ID 591102, NA-S, and Wardlaw to DOS, no. 941, Mar. 27, 1951, NA 714.13.

Even three decades later, in conversations with the author, both former officers and civilians (including political adversaries) proved unstinting in their praise of Paz Tejada. For Paz Tejada during the uprising against Ponce, see Zamora Alvarez, *Las memorias de Andrés*, p. 116.

[95] Interviews with María de Arbenz and Col. Guillén, who was present once when Arbenz considered this matter. "I never heard Arbenz speak ill of Paz Tejada; on the contrary, he respected him." (Interview with Fortuny.)

[96] Interviews with María de Arbenz and Fortuny. Carlos Paz Tejada never curried the favor of Arbenz's enemies, and he opposed the overthrow of Arbenz. In 1960, it was Paz Tejada who first denounced—and from Guatemala—the training of Cuban exiles in his country for the Bay of Pigs. (Paz Tejada, "Aclaración y denuncia," *Prensa Libre*, Oct. 5, 1960, p. 19.) In 1962, he led one of the first guerrilla groups in an abortive attack against the undemocratic government of President Ydígoras. Thereafter, Paz Tejada has lived in exile, with quiet and impressive dignity.

[97] Confidential report (no name or date), p. 2, enclosed in Pearson to Attwood and Burrows, May 21, 1954, NA Lot 58D18 & 58D78, Box 2. See also Maj. Chavez, "Intelligence Report" no. 11–53, Jan. 18, 1953, RG84 G&C, Box 4, NA-S. For Ar-

malleable men he had sought, but he overestimated their loyalty, their nationalism and their competence.

Arbenz could have been an unchallenged military *caudillo*, but by being true to his political beliefs he weakened his support among the military. His charisma, the fear and the respect he inspired—and the sincere attachment some officers felt to him—would delay this process of erosion. But he was embarking on a most daring endeavor: he would govern the country with a kitchen cabinet of communists while the army was firmly anticommunist; he would impose unprecedented social reforms while the great majority of his officers were unsympathetic to social change and feared the power of organized labor. He knew, moreover, that even among dedicated *Arbencista* officers, revolutionary fervor had severe limits, and their loyalty, which was never unconditional, was to Arbenz the colonel, not to Arbenz the communists' friend.

Arbenz had intended, when he became president, to address the officers on a regular basis. He had hoped to educate them politically and to cultivate their loyalty.[98] He gave one such talk, and then a second—"and he did not return."[99] An indifferent public speaker, Arbenz was uncomfortable addressing large groups. There was, however, a more compelling reason to discontinue the talks. The gulf between him and the officer corps was too wide. He had wanted to educate them, but he had to hide his true political beliefs, and this rendered communication particularly awkward. Arbenz has been criticized for giving up the attempt, yet it is highly unlikely that mere words would have achieved much. Thus, in mid-1953, when he spoke at length about the benefits of the agrarian reform, the officers listened respectfully, but afterward they commented among themselves: "Look, the president thinks that he can fool us. These are all lies. The truth is that he's in bed with the communists."[100]

Arbenz tried to find other ways to retain the loyalty of his officers. He treated them "with kid gloves," and his wife was enlisted to help: "I had pages and pages of names of the officers, their children and their wives and all their birth dates so that I could send them presents (watches, etc.). I had a secretary who spent all her time doing this."[101]

It was a genteel touch, but more tangible signs of appreciation were required. Indeed, the claim that "the army never had it as good as under

---

benz's view of Díaz, particularly helpful were interviews with María de Arbenz and Fortuny. Sánchez, like Arbenz, was from Quetzaltenango. "The three of us had been friends since childhood," Rolz Bennett remembers. (Interview with Rolz Bennett.)

[98] Interviews with María de Arbenz and Fortuny.

[99] Interview with Col. González Siguí.

[100] Interview with Col. Guillén, who attended the meeting.

[101] Interview with María de Arbenz.

Arbenz''[102] is not exaggerated—if the comparison refers to previous regimes, rather than to those that followed. As had been true since the fall of Ponce, the officers' salaries increased far more rapidly than those of civil servants and blue collar workers. Arbenz expanded the commissaries established by Arévalo, where officers could buy imported goods at reduced prices.[103] Predictably, many officers purchased more than they needed and sold the surplus at a profit. Generous travel allowances and lucrative positions in the bureaucracy—all the governors of the country's twenty-two departments were colonels—helped to boost the morale of the officer corps. Attentive to the officers' needs, the Arbenz administration also began to build houses for them in preferred districts of the capital. The program was financed "with loans obtained from the Production Development Institute (INFOP)—a government agency. . . . Although the terms of these loans were easy, in most cases payments were in arrears. It was reported that INFOP employees were told not to press for payment.''[104] This, then, was the first prong of Arbenz's military policy: "coddling of the army to retain its loyalty," as the U.S. embassy put it.[105] It was a policy that had begun under Arévalo, the effects of which an officer aptly characterized years later: "Under Arévalo and Arbenz the officer corps was mollified with high salaries, elegant uniforms, expensive cars, beautiful country clubs, long vacations and readily available scholarships to study abroad.''[106]

These emoluments help to explain the military's acceptance of Decree 900. "The Army has swung completely behind President Arbenz and his Agrarian reform law," the U.S. air attaché reported in late May 1952.[107] Most officers disliked a measure that they thought would strengthen the labor unions in the countryside. The instinctive distrust and the contempt most officers felt for the "Indios" and the fear that agrarian reform would foster communist influence among them reinforced the army's uneasiness.[108]

Yet the officers failed even to express their misgivings to the strong-willed president who showered them with benefits and whose anger they feared. In

[102] "When Communists Take Over," *U.S. News and World Report*, Feb. 20, 1953, p. 15.

[103] See esp. "Dos decretos aprobados ayer por el h. Congreso," *DCA*, p. 1; "Las concesiones al ejército" (edit.), *La Hora*, p. 1; *JW* 37, I:4. All Sept. 11, 1953.

[104] LaCharite, *Case Study in Insurgency*, p. 96.

[105] *JW* 34, Aug. 21, 1953, I:1.

[106] Col. Silva Girón, *La batalla de Gualán*, p. 27.

[107] Col. Deerwester, "Intelligence Report" no. 106-52, May 29, 1952, p. 2, RG84 CF, Box 15, NA-S.

[108] On the officers' view of the Indians, see Monteforte Toledo, *Guatemala*, pp. 364–71. On land ownership among officers (and their reaction to Decree 900), see ibid., as well as Frankel, "Political Development," p. 139, and Sierra Roldán, *Diálogos*, pp. 72–73.

July 1952, the U.S. embassy predicted that the Guatemalan army would not take a strong stand against the agrarian reform. "During his term in office," it pointed out, "President Arbenz has made every effort to retain the goodwill and support of the armed forces. Army and Air officers have enjoyed preferred positions in the Guatemalan government and opportunities to engage in lucrative enterprises have been better than ever before. In general, Army and Air Force officers appear to be satisfied with their conditions. The majority take little interest in government policies which do not affect them directly."[109]

The agrarian reform did not affect the officers' economic interests. They were mainly of middle-class extraction. While many owned fincas, these were generally of small or middle size; in any case, they were carefully spared the pain of expropriation. A few officers even profited from the reform. Through a little-used article of Decree 900, a handful of them received parcels of land in lifetime tenure;[110] the transaction was legal, yet clearly contrary to the intent of the law. On other occasions, some profited through outright graft. Decree 900 stipulated that cultivated land could not be expropriated but failed to provide precise guidelines to determine whether land was, in fact, under cultivation. This enlarged the role of the local agrarian authorities, over whom the governors (all colonels) exerted a modicum of influence. In some instances, governors were swayed by the pleas of latifundistas who were eager to reward goodwill with tangible tokens of gratitude.

The opportunities for graft were deliberately limited, as were the perquisites that Arbenz bestowed on his officers. He saw material rewards as necessary to secure the officers' loyalty to a regime that sought radical change, but these rewards must not jeopardize his larger aims.

Economic rewards alone could not assure the army's loyalty. There were two further conditions, never openly stated but understood by all: the army had to retain the monopoly of weapons and it could not be the target of subversive infiltration—let the communists proselytize among the civilians, if such was the president's will; the military must remain inviolate. (As Doña María put it, "Don't corrupt our little soldiers.")[111]

Even officers who opposed the regime have emphatically stressed that under Arbenz "there was absolutely no communist influence in the armed forces." Indeed, "there was not even any sympathy."[112] The two senior officers men-

[109] *JW* 30, July 25, 1952, I:3.

[110] See: "Jefes y oficiales del ejército reciben tierra," *DCA*, May 9, 1953, p. 1; McKnight to DOS, no. 1009, May 15, 1953, NA 814.20; "Tierras para seis miembros del Ejército Nac. de la Revolución," *DCA*, Jan. 8, 1954, p. 1. (The relevant article of Decree 900 was 106.)

[111] Interview with María de Arbenz.

[112] Quotations from interviews with Col. Lorenzana and Lt. Col. Cruz Salazar. All the officers and other participants interviewed for this book have supported this conclusion.

tioned by Schneider as possible communist sympathizers (Paz Tejada and Aldana Sandoval) were no exception. Major Paz Tejada was distrusted by Arbenz because of his unusual combination of integrity, professional ability, and anticommunism. Colonel Aldana Sandoval, who possessed only the last of these attributes, was, until January 1952, ambassador to Washington, where he voiced his concern about his government's leftist tendencies to U.S. officials.[113] He then replaced Paz Tejada as minister of public works, and he later won the dubious distinction of being the first cabinet member to seek asylum—on June 26, 1954, the day before Arbenz resigned.[114]

"Communists have devoted little effort to military," Ambassador Schoenfeld cabled Secretary Dulles. "Communist influence within . . . armed forces is extremely slight. . . . No (rpt no) Guatemalan officer on active service is known to be a Communist. . . . There is thus no (rpt no) evidence of Communist indoctrination among military."[115] The PGT had indeed made no attempt to infiltrate the military. Both Arbenz and the party recognized the risks of such an undertaking ("it would have been like waving a red flag in front of a bull") and its difficulties ("the army was arcane and hostile territory; it would have been as hard to infiltrate as the Church").[116] Lacking both knowledge and resources, its few *cuadros* overextended and ignorant of military politics, the PGT concentrated on more promising domains. Arbenz, his wife recalls, "saw the army more or less as his preserve and did not discuss it much with the PGT. He had great confidence in Fortuny, and great respect for his political skill, but he thought that he knew much more than Fortuny and the PGT about military matters, and so he didn't consult the party about these things."[117] Arbenz, however, was steadily losing touch with military politics, and he relied increasingly on Armed Forces Chief Díaz and Defense Minister Sánchez, fair-weather friends of limited abilities.

This, then, was the ransom: perks, the monopoly of weapons, and the absence of communists in the ranks. In return, the officer corps remained loyal, or at least quiescent, while regretting that "Jacobo had changed so much."[118] A few malcontents banded together in loosely organized cliques—first the "Grupo de los Brujos" and then the "Club del Libro." Under the pretext of social gatherings, they met every one or two weeks, usually on a Saturday, "elaborating plans from late in the evening until five in the morning."[119] Their

[113] See MemoConv (Aldana Sandoval, López Herrarte, Nufer), June 12, 1951, and Nufer to Miller, July 31, 1951, both NA 714.00.

[114] See below, p. 346.

[115] Schoenfeld to SecState, no. 342, Feb. 28, 1953, p.1, NA 714.001.

[116] Quotations from interviews with María de Arbenz and Fortuny.

[117] Interview with María de Arbenz. Confirmed by Fortuny and Guerra Borges.

[118] These words were repeated by many of the military officers interviewed.

[119] Interview with Lt. Col. Cruz Salazar. Nothing has been written about these two

plotting never progressed beyond the venting of frustrations among friends fortified by strong drink. "We knew that we had to do something, but we didn't know what," recalls one of them.[120] Few of the would-be plotters occupied positions of any importance, and self-interest was sobering medicine. After all, life under Arbenz was not unpleasant even for disgruntled officers, and very few were willing to risk dismissal. They also lacked a leader. In the words of a lieutenant who eventually found the courage to rebel: "The opposition to Arbenz within the army never crystallized. Arana's death put an end to what could have been a serious, strong opposition to Arbenz in the officer corps." The Guatemalan army, the U.S. embassy noted as early as June 1951, "continues almost devoid of strong leaders and spokesmen."[121] Paz Tejada could have been such a leader, but Paz Tejada was no longer on active duty.

In March 1953, the U.S. army attaché had written, "It can be expected that the military leaders will hold fast to their present position of supporting President Arbenz . . . providing Arbenz continues to pursue his present policy of keeping the military contented."[122] By early 1954, however, a new situation had developed. Danger from the United States was undermining the army's toleration of Arbenz. Guatemalan officers, especially the younger ones, were not immune to nationalism.[123] Many did not resent, and some even welcomed, the president's firmness vis-à-vis the United States, but only as long as Washington's anger did not threaten them. For the Guatemalan military was above all prudent, and this led Arbenz to a contradictory policy. On the one hand, relations with the United States grew increasingly hostile. On the other hand, a U.S. army mission of four officers and an air force mission of three officers were stationed in Guatemala; when the 1945 agreement sanctioning their presence expired in early 1953, they continued their work "on the basis of the lapsed contracts with no difficulties."[124] This Arbenz conceded to assuage the sensitivities of his officers.

---

groups, whose importance was truly modest. My major sources are interviews with Cruz Salazar, Lt. Montenegro, and Col. Mendoza.

[120] Interview with Lt. Col. Cruz Salazar. Cruz Salazar was "hostile to Arbenz but unwilling to take any risks," a U.S. military attaché observed. (Interview with Col. McCormick.)

[121] Quotations from interview with Lt. Montenegro and from *JW* 26, June 28, 1951, I:3. Montenegro is one of the few officers who plotted with Castillo Armas.

[122] Col. McCormick, "Intelligence Report" no. R-18-53, Mar. 2, 1953, p.2, RG84 G&C, Box 4, NA-S.

[123] U.S. reports during the Arbenz years consistently noted the existence of this budding nationalism. See also Monteforte Toledo, *Guatemala*, p. 369, and Frankel, "Political Development," p. 143.

[124] *JW* 48, Nov. 27, 1953, I:3. See also MemoConv ("The Guatemalan Situation"), Feb. 5, 1953, NA 714.00, and "Second Progress Report on NSC 144/1," Nov. 20, 1953, *FRUS*, 1952–1954, 4:40–41.

These same sensitivities explain the cordial "social as well as business relations" that existed between "leading Guatemalan army officers and the American service attachés," as the *New York Times* noted in mid-1953.[125] Indeed, the chief of staff of the Guatemalan army, Colonel Enrique Parinello de León, proudly recalled, some twenty-five years later, "The American officers really liked me a lot. . . . On my birthday, the members of the military mission always gave me a party."[126] Like Parinello, a great many Guatemalan officers were eager to display their goodwill toward the United States. After a forty-eight-hour visit to Guatemala, U.S. General R. G. Partridge expressed his surprise at his conversation with Colonel Sánchez, Arbenz's defense minister. Sánchez, Partridge noted, spoke "almost exclusively . . . of his three children being educated in the United States and brought out pictures of them and his wife and talked at some length about his visits to the U.S. and his children's lives there. I considered this a rather striking attempt to impress me with his closeness to and friendly feelings for the United States."[127]

By demonstrating their pro-American feelings, the Guatemalan officers were trying to mitigate the danger of their government's bitter conflict with Washington. By early 1954, the exercise had become precarious, and cold fear haunted the officer corps. The threat of U.S. military aggression made the old rules obsolete. The time had come for Arbenz to distance himself from the communists; this was the only way to appease Washington. Arbenz stubbornly refused, yet he realized, albeit imperfectly, that the price could be the forfeiture of the army's loyalty.

COMMUNIST INFLUENCE AND THE 1956 ELECTIONS

The absence of communist sympathizers in the armed forces is of cardinal importance in examining the prospects for communist influence in Guatemala. Had Arbenz not been overthrown, the PGT's influence would have continued to increase through the remaining years of his presidency. Influence would not have become control because of the anticommunism of the military.

Arbenz's presidency was scheduled to end on March 15, 1957; the 1945 constitution forbade a second consecutive term; indeed, the constitution obliged the armed forces to overthrow a president who sought to succeed himself.

One might argue that Arbenz, urged on by his communist friends, would have tried to prolong his tenure. The president would have had few moral qualms about setting the bourgeois constitution aside, but this action, tanta-

---

[125] "Guatemalan Army Apathetic to Reds," *NYT*, Aug. 5, 1953, p. 5.
[126] Interview with Parinello.
[127] Partridge to Cabot, "Notes on Visit to Four Central American Countries," May 20, 1953, p. 2, NA 714.00/3-2053.

mount to a coup d'état, would have been possible only with the army's support. And why should the military cooperate? Loyalty to Arbenz was not unconditional even among *Arbencista* officers, and it was progressively weakened by the mounting evidence of the president's ties to the PGT. Nor would opportunism lead the officer corps to close ranks behind Jacobo Arbenz, the communists' friend. The military did not need Arbenz's protection; if anything, its privileges would have increased under a less forceful president. Arbenz's coup d'état would bring only danger: it would strengthen the PGT and provoke the wrath of the United States; it would undermine the regime's legitimacy in Latin America. Growing radicalization at home and decreasing support from Latin American governments would heighten the danger of U.S. aggression. And if the United States decided to remove Arbenz, what would be the fate of those officers who had been his accomplices? Dare they hope for indulgence, or would they face professional and economic ruin—even prison and death?

Another, more mundane concern would have led a number of senior officers and administration politicians to uphold the constitution: many of them nurtured presidential ambitions. By the spring of 1954 there were already a dozen presidential hopefuls, including Interior Minister Charnaud, Armed Forces Chief Díaz, and Defense Minister Sánchez. As Doña María would later remark, "Presidentitis is a very common illness in Latin America. Every man with a B.A. thinks he should be president." In 1954, Guatemala could ill afford these pretensions; they distracted the attention of administration politicians at the very moment that they should have been focusing on the international threat to Guatemala.[128]

The leaders of the PGT looked uneasily at the crowded field of presidential candidates. The most they could hope, they concluded, was that Arbenz's successor would not be actively hostile to the party. Arbenz had reached the same conclusion. He told his PGT friends that, under the circumstances, the best candidate would be Colonel Díaz. He had no illusions about Díaz's political leanings—the colonel was not a man of the left, much less a man sympathetic to the PGT, even though "to please Arbenz he smiled broadly on the party." But Arbenz believed that Díaz was loyal to him, that he had the support of the officer corps, and that he harbored no particular hostility to the communists.[129]

---

[128] Quoted from interview with Maria de Arbenz. For a list of prospective candidates, see "Los grupos revolucionarios temen nuevas divisiones," *La Hora*, Jan. 2, 1954, p. 1. See also Ramón Blanco, "Galera," *El I*, Jan. 6, 1954, p. 2, and "Primera lucha con vista a las elecciones de presidente," *El I*, Apr. 19, 1954, p. 1.

[129] Quoted from interview with Fortuny. Other sources for the paragraph include interviews with María de Arbenz, Alejandro, and Guerra Borges; Fortuny, *Por un frente único*, p. 31; entry of Nov. 5, 1953, in the diary of Secretariat member Silva Jonama; "Análisis de la situación," *Tribuna Popular*, Feb. 9, 1954, p. 1. For com-

The PGT leaders had made no formal decision—there was still time—but "deep down we thought of Díaz as the candidate." They knew that under Díaz they would no longer be the president's favorites; but neither, they hoped, would they become pariahs. In the meantime, what was crucial was to strengthen the party.[130]

---

ments by the U.S. embassy on Díaz's presidential ambitions, see *JW* 11, Mar. 19, 1954, pp. 2–3.

[130] Interviews with Guerra Borges (quoted), Alejandro, and Fortuny. Díaz was confident of his chances. Thus he told a fellow colonel: "Look, it's really possible—in fact I think it's going to happen—that I'll be the next president. You will be my right hand man." (Interview with Col. Guillén.)

CHAPTER 10

The "Christian" Opposition

AT 1 A.M. SUNDAY, March 29, 1953, one hundred rebels stormed the town of Salamá and the nearby village of San Jeronimo. At 6 p.m., a hundred government soldiers from the military base at Cobán regained possession of both towns "with little fighting." Only a few rebels escaped. There were fewer than twenty casualties.[1]

This was no valiant attempt of freedom-loving Guatemalans to overthrow a communist dictatorship. "The political opposition has been left to the lunatic fringe," a respected American scholar wrote, "which . . . is really against not only Communism and the Administration, but against the Revolution and all it implies: social security, trade unionism, agrarian reform, political democracy."[2] Sidney Gruson of the *New York Times* offered an equally unflattering assessment: "During his recent visit to Guatemala this correspondent could find out easily enough what these [opposition] groups were against. But they never showed they stood in favor of something."[3] A similar judgment was reached by Theodore Geiger in his influential *Communism Versus Progress in Guatemala*. Decrying the mounting communist conspiracy "against the people of Guatemala," Geiger asserted: "By far the most important reason for the failure of the opposition is its lack of a positive and constructive program for the country."[4] The State Department concurred: "The opposition groups . . . have no positive program of their own."[5]

By the time of the Salamá revolt, the Guatemalan upper class was in despair. In 1950 many members of the elite had hoped that as president, Arbenz would

[1] Quoted from CIA, "Revolt in Salamá," cs-6591, Apr. 6, 1953. For press coverage of the Salamá incident, see esp. *El I* and *DCA*, Mar. 30–Apr. 21, 1953. See also "Breve reseña de los acontecimientos surgidos a raíz del movimiento subversivo del 29 de marzo de 1953," Salamá, Apr. 15, 1953, *GT*, Box 22. See also below nn. 52–54.

[2] Alexander, "Revolution in Guatemala," p. 8.

[3] "Foes' Disunity Aids Guatemalan Reds," *NYT*, Feb. 24, 1953, p. 9.

[4] Geiger, *Communism versus Progress*, p. 28. Geiger's study was well received. (See "Red Grip Detailed within Guatemala," *NYT*, p. 27; "Reds in Guatemala Reported Extending," *WP*, p. 4; "Guatemala Faces Likely Conquest by Reds, Analysts Find," *Washington Star*, p. 13; "Guatemalan Communists Held Hemisphere Peril," *CSM*, p. 4. All Dec. 14, 1953.)

[5] DOS, *Intervention of International Communism*, pp. 85–86.

reverse Arévalo's "communistic" policies. A year later this hope had faded as Arbenz encouraged organized labor and the Communist party. Then came Decree 900, and doubt settled into hatred.

While the Asociación General de Agricultores (AGA) was intransigent in its opposition to the regime, the country's few industrialists were less cohesive. Some belonged to the small Cámara de Comercio e Industria de Guatemala (CCIG); others to the even smaller Asociación General de Industriales de Guatemala (AGIG). The former tended to be members of the landed elite, the latter were the nouveaux riches. Both opposed Decree 900, assailed the government's communist proclivities, and worried about the growing assertiveness of labor. But AGIG appreciated Arbenz's effort to assist Guatemala's fledgling industries through tariff adjustments; hence it was torn between limited collaboration with the regime and intransigent opposition to it.[6] For the CCIG, by contrast, collaboration was anathema. In December 1952, the two associations clashed openly. They had been invited by the government to participate in talks on the development of a national industrial policy. Only dupes or knaves would negotiate with a communist-dominated government, proclaimed the CCIG. To refuse to attend was unpatriotic, countered the AGIG, adding that it was ready to talk to anyone, "even the communists."[7] And so the bickering continued, until Arbenz was overthrown.

Those few members of the upper class who supported the government were almost all from Quetzaltenango, Arbenz's hometown. In 1949 they had founded the Partido Integridad Nacional (PIN) to back the candidacy of their friend Jacobo. This party of the "progressive bourgeoisie" was a small and dwindling group. It was led by Nicolás Brol and Roberto Fanjul, the former a rich landowner, the latter a successful businessman. In March 1951, Brol's appointment as minister of agriculture had been welcomed by the upper class. Then, after a year of heightening frustration, the elite was relieved when Fanjul joined Brol in the cabinet as minister of economy. "Señor Fanjul," noted the U.S. embassy, was "a successful and reputedly anti-communist businessman"; his appointment "raised hopes that relations between government and private capital might be improved."[8] But Fanjul and Brol remained in the

---

[6] AGIG's attitude was well summarized by the U.S. embassy: "The [Arbenz] administration has always been willing to aid domestic industry as long as the assistance does not adversely affect organized labor, small farmers, or the Government itself. Although the Association of Guatemalan Industrialists (AGIG) officially is pleased with such concessions, individual members privately doubt that there will be substantial private industrial expansion without a more responsible labor force, more realistic labor and financial legislation, and an improvement in the political atmosphere." (*JW* 52, Dec. 23, 1953, II:3; see also *JW* 47, Nov. 21, 1952, II:1-2.)

[7] *JW* 50, Dec. 12, 1952, II:3. The clash can be followed in the Guatemalan press of that month, esp. *El I.*

[8] Quotations from *JW* 13, Mar. 28, 1952, I:3 and *JW* 14, Apr. 4, 1952, II:1. See

cabinet even after the enactment of Decree 900. Indeed, at Arbenz's request, it was Fanjul who introduced the bill in Congress; he thus found himself, the *New York Times* observed, "in the odd situation of being attacked by the very people who hailed his recent appointment as an indication that President Arbenz was shaking off an asserted influence of Communists."[9]

Brol and Fanjul remained loyal to Arbenz. They believed that his policies favored the emergence of capitalism in Guatemala, but they were branded imbeciles or traitors by their former friends from the upper class. "The position of Minister Brol defies understanding," wrote Marroquín Rojas. "And Fanjul? Poor Fanjul! He will be a casualty of communism because a landowner . . . a captain of industry . . . can never be a socialist. When he received his ministerial portfolio he took leave of his senses: he imagines he is a 'comrade' of Víctor Manuel Gutiérrez! Tomorrow, when they no longer need him, they will throw him to the dogs."[10] Marroquín Rojas accepted the need for some social reforms, and he was a nationalist who resented Guatemala's status as a banana republic. Hence U.S. officials had labeled him leftist in the late 1940s. But he abhorred communism. If the choice was between social reforms with the slightest whiff of communism and the status quo, he opted for the latter. There were also idealists within the opposition, men like the student leader Eduardo Taracena de la Cerda, men who fought for what they believed to be the country's true interests,[11] but they were the exceptions. The overriding motivation of the men who led the opposition, as Marroquín Rojas at times intimated and U.S. reports freely conceded, was the implacable defense of privilege.

Waving the banner of anticommunism, these men engaged in a relentless campaign of opposition. Assisted by the country's major newspapers and radio stations, they sought to raise the specter of Armageddon among a people largely lacking political sophistication. Posing as champions of a Catholic faith threatened by Red hordes, they strove to inflame religious passions, and they received the full backing of the Church.

In 1950 Archbishop Rossell y Arellano had believed that Arbenz would purge the communists. How could it be otherwise, he had reasoned, when Arbenz "was married to a woman from a very rich family, was a military officer, lived in a house in Zone 10 of the capital (where the rich lived), and had the look of an aristocrat: white, distinguished."[12] Decree 900 persuaded

---

also Wells to SecState, no. 333, Mar. 15, 1951, NA 714.11; Wardlaw to DOS, no. 941, Mar. 27, 1951, NA 714.13; Krieg to DOS, no. 971, Mar. 26, 1952, NA 714.13.

[9] Gruson, "Guatemalan Foes Talk of Civil War," *NYT*, May 18, 1952, p. 10.

[10] "Los ricos con el agua al cuello," *Impacto*, May 31, 1952, p. 1.

[11] My view of Taracena is based on my conversations with him as well as with people who knew him well, both friends and enemies.

[12] Interview with Fr. Bendaña Perdomo.

Rossell y Arellano that he had been betrayed: the government was communist. Immediately, the archbishop lent his support, and the dignity of his office, to Arbenz's most bitter foes.[13]

Verbum, the mouthpiece of the Church, and the Catholic weekly *Acción Social Cristiana* assailed the government as fiercely as did AGA. There might be an agrarian problem in Guatemala, *Verbum* conceded, but it had been "provoked almost artificially by all the governments, especially by those called revolutionary, in order to gain the vote of the illiterates on behalf of their partisan interests. . . . If there really is a problem, it is not as flagrant or as grave as they have tried to make us believe."[14] Meanwhile, in the countryside, the clergy urged peasants and agricultural workers to resist a communist law that would bring them material and spiritual ruin.

In January 1953, Rossell y Arellano was the prime mover behind the creation of the Partido Anticomunista Demócrata Cristiano, which, he hoped, would become the political arm of the Church; but the party failed to thrive.[15] That same month he embarked on yet another undertaking, sending a reproduction of the statue of the "Black Christ" of Esquipulas on an extended perambulation through the country. It was, argued the official *Diario de Centro América*, a "bizarre pilgrimage," one that caused a near riot in the village of Esquipulas.[16] Rossell y Arellano, however, believed that he was countering

[13] On the Church in the Arbenz years, see Bendaña Perdomo, "Historia general," and Frankel, "Political Development." For Rossell y Arellano's collaboration with the plotters, interviews with Bendaña Perdomo and Taracena were helpful.

[14] "El ante-proyecto de ley agraria formulado por el Ejecutivo" (edit.), *Verbum*, May 25, 1952, p. 1. Decree 900 transformed Arbenz into an "agrarian dictator" and crudely violated "our sacred constitution," admonished *Acción Social Cristiana*, adding: "No reform is called for." ("La dictadura agraria," May 15, 1952, pp. 1–2.) *Acción Social Cristiana* was at least consistent. In 1947, it had warned, "Nothing would disrupt productivity more than agrarian reform." ("El comunismo y la reforma agraria," May 29, 1947, p. 1.) See also Frankel's excellent discussion, "Political Development," pp. 224–30.

[15] For the creation of the party see "Un Partido Demócrata Cristiano," *El I*, Jan. 24, 1953, p. 1; "Partido anticomunista cristiano," *La Hora*, Jan. 24, 1953, p. 1; *JW* 5, Jan. 30, 1953, I:3–4.

[16] "Miles de personas a Esquipulas," Jan. 3, 1953, p. 1. The population of Esquipulas loudly protested the archbishop's decision to send the statue through the country. It would have been the first time in three centuries that the statue had left the village. The uproar forced Rossell y Arellano to compromise: he sent a copy instead. For articles in the opposition press about the pilgrimage, see "Cristo de Esquipulas saldrá en peregrinación," *El I*, Dec. 22, 1952, p. 1; "El Cristo de Esquipulas recorrerá el país," *La Hora*, Dec. 22, 1952, p. 1; "Cristo de Esquipulas ingresará en la capital," *El I*, Dec. 29, 1952, p. 1; "No será movida de su sitial la imagen del Cristo de Esquipulas," *El I*, Dec. 31, 1952, p. 1; "Amenazado el parroco de Esquipulas," *La Hora*, Jan. 3, 1953, p. 1; "El Cristo de Esquipulas sale a peregrinación," *La Hora*, Jan. 16, 1953,

a challenge: the devil "was stalking the countryside" disguised as an agrarian reformer and "Christ would sally forth from Esquipulas to give him battle."[17]

Within the Church, one man opposed Rossell y Arellano's extremism. The papal nuncio, Genaro Verolino, did not believe that Decree 900 threatened Catholic Guatemala; there was an agrarian problem, he argued, and the decree had positive aspects. Communists did influence the government, and the communists' main champion was Arbenz, but Arbenz was not attacking the Church, and the military opposed communism. Therefore, Verolino concluded, the communists were not in control, and they would be greatly weakened when Arbenz left the presidency in 1957. In the meantime, he urged, the Church should bear with the government.[18]

A relationship marked by respect and some cordiality developed between Arbenz and the nuncio. This led to concessions on several issues important to the Church. In 1953, the government allowed a religious program ("The Voice of the Sacred Heart of Jesus") to be broadcast on the state radio; never before had such permission been granted in Guatemala. Acceding to the nuncio's request, the authorities also permitted an unprecedented number of foreign priests to work in Guatemala.[19]

They did, however, deport one priest, the American Sebastian Buccellato. Buccellato denied that he had ever advocated the overthrow of the government, as the authorities had intimated, but had merely done his duty as a Christian and as a priest. "The . . . agrarian reform Law . . . [was] a ruthless political tool that accomplished a bloodless Red revolution," he explained.

> I viewed the whole diabolical scheme with horror. . . . Those parish members who were offered land . . . asked my opinion. Naturally I told them that Communism and Christianity are irreconcilable. A few peasants, of course, accepted [the offer of land] . . . and left the parish. But with the help of 35 lay catechists, who toured the countryside, most of the members remained true and turned down the Communist

---

p. 1; "Abierta la inscripción para llevar en hombros al Cristo de Esquipulas," *La Hora*, Jan. 21, 1953, p. 1; "Imponente recibimiento al Cristo de Esquipulas," *La Hora*, Jan. 26, 1953, p. 1; "Multitudes desbordantes de fé," *El I*, Jan. 26, 1953, p. 1; "Una semana estará el Cristo de Esquipulas en Catedral," *La Hora*, Jan. 27, 1953, p. 1; "El Cristo de Esquipulas saldrá el próximo domingo para la Antigua," *La Hora*, Jan. 29, 1953, p. 1; "Desbordan de fé en Cristo la capital y Antigua," *El I*, Feb. 2, 1953, p. 1. See also "Memorial de los católicos de Esquipulas," no. 28, Feb. 27, 1953, Correspondencia, AHA.

[17] Interview with Bendaña Perdomo.

[18] Interview with Bendaña Perdomo; see also Bendaña Perdomo, "Historia general," p. 51, and Richard and Meléndez, *La iglesia*, p. 199.

[19] Interviews with Bendaña Perdomo and María de Arbenz. See also Bendaña Perdomo, "Historia general," p. 59; Calder, *Crecimiento*, p. 52; Alonso and Garrido, *La iglesia*, p. 191.

offer. . . . I left the country by plane on February 3 [1954], but not until I had broadcast the truth to the people over the anti-Communist radio in Guatemala City.[20]

Had the government been willing to risk a confrontation with the Church, many foreign priests would have shared Buccellato's fate, for many spoke the same inflammatory language and brazenly interfered in Guatemala's internal affairs. But the government did not openly attack the Church. It remonstrated, instead, that Decree 900 was in accordance with Catholic teachings.[21]

Arbenz's concessions and Verolino's arguments were to no avail. The clergy, from bishop to village priest, rallied behind Rossell y Arellano. Some were moved by chauvinism; the nuncio was a foreigner. But not even the foreign clergy supported Verolino, not even those priests who had come to Guatemala courtesy of his intercession. Deaf to the nuncio's subtle reasoning, they embraced the archbishop's simple and effective message: the government was communist and Christian virtue demanded opposition. "There is no indication," a Guatemalan Jesuit later remarked, "that a single priest opposed either the stance or the methods of Rossell y Arellano against Arbenz; nor do I know of any priest who had any sympathy for the government. In his conciliatory policy the nuncio was completely alone."[22]

The Church lent a veneer of legitimacy to the invectives of the upper class. It sparked the opposition's most combative battalion: "the outspoken market women of Guatemala City."[23] These women, wrote the *New York Times*, "were the only militants the opposition could put forward. Highly religious, and with a tough independence of spirit, [they were] willing not only to leave their sidewalk stalls and march to Government buildings in protests but also to use their scanty financial resources in their campaigns whether their wealthy

[20] Sebastian Buccellato, "I Saw the Reds Taking Over!" *This Week Magazine*, June 27, 1954, quoted from pp. 7, 18, 19. The government expelled Buccellato on a technicality; he had failed to renew his residence permit: see "Caso del Padre Buccellato," *El I*, Feb. 3, 1954, p. 1; "Buccellato estaba ilegalmente en el país," *DCA*, Feb. 4, 1954, p. 1; "Guatemalan Assures Press," *NYT*, Feb. 4, 1954, p. 2; "Foreign Minister of Guatemala Explains Ouster of Cleric," *NYT*, Feb. 5, 1954, p. 6. For background on Buccellato, see Federico Juarez Rodas to Ministro de Gobernación, May 26, 1954, CO:G, May 1954, p. 472, AGCA.

[21] See Frankel's authoritative discussion, "Political Development," pp. 233–35. Benites, *Meditaciones*, attempts to refute the Church's charges against Decree 900 point by point.

[22] Interview with Bendaña Perdomo. A possible exception is Fr. Augusto Herrera, parish priest of San Juan Sacátepequez. (See Augusto Herrera to Mgr. Gilberto Solorzano B., Feb. 1, 1952, no. 36, Correspondencia, AHA and Herrera to Carlos Alvarado Jérez, ibid.

[23] "Anti-Red Rifts Held Guatemala Threat," *CSM*, Jan. 24, 1953, p. 13.

compatriots support[ed] them or not."[24] Few among the lower classes shared the market women's selfless devotion to the political teachings of the Guatemalan Catholic Church. Three quarters of a century of anticlerical regimes, the U.S. embassy pointed out with regret, had weakened the clergy's hold over the people.[25] With its sparse ranks, the Church was unable to proselytize effectively, particularly in the rural areas. Even though the total number of priests rose from 114 in 1944 to 195 in 1954, Guatemala remained the country with the lowest priest-per-inhabitant ratio of Latin America.[26] Moreover, the message of the Guatemalan Church was not rousing: "To exorcise the communist demon, he [Rossell y Arellano] preached more charity from the rich and more humility from the poor." But the rich had little taste for charity, and the poor were weary of humility. The CIA's analysis was concise: "The Church has been handicapped by the small number of priests and by a lack of a constructive social program."[27]

The Church's attacks on Arbenz's agrarian reform in 1952 heightened many peasants' suspicions about the decree. As its implementation brought benefits rather than misery, the impact of the clergy's diatribes diminished. "In general, land reform has been popular with the masses," a December 1953 CIA report conceded,[28] while the following April a State Department study pointed out, "The large Guatemalan landowners and United Fruit Company have been the major targets of the reform. Neither has elicited any sympathy in Guatemalan public opinion. . . . The net internal political result of the implementation of [Decree 900] . . . has been to strengthen the Arbenz Administration."[29] The clergy had failed to generate widespread opposition to the regime, and the upper class was unable to garner enough popular support to warrant any hope of winning power through elections.

The opposition parties claimed that it was the government's repression that had rendered them impotent. Their shrill complaints were echoed by an op-

---

[24] "Foes' Disunity Aids Guatemalan Reds," *NYT*, Feb. 24, 1953, p. 9.

[25] *JW* 46, Nov. 13, 1953, I:4.

[26] Alonso and Garrido, *La iglesia*, p. 271, and Turner, *Catholicism*, pp. 135–36, 184, table 4. In 1954 Guatemala had one priest for every 14,611 inhabitants; ranked next was Honduras with one for every 12,103 inhabitants.

[27] Quotations from Frankel, "Political Development," p. 212 and CIA, "Present Political Situation In Guatemala and Possible Developments during 1952," NIE-62, Mar. 11, 1952, p. 3, Truman Papers, President's Secretary's File, Intelligence File, Box 254, TL. Frankel provides the best overall treatment of Rossell y Arellano. More sympathetic but less persuasive is Turner, *Catholicism*, pp. 131–40. Pike, "Catholic Church," is an apology; see esp. pp. 92, 102, 111–12.

[28] CIA, "Evaluation of Recent Political and Economic Developments," number deleted, Dec. 3, 1953, p. 2.

[29] "Political Developments in Guatemala since May 1953," IR-6579, quoted from pp. 1, 2, enclosed in Burgin to Leddy, Apr. 22, 1954, NA 714.00.

position press that was remarkably outspoken. The following titles of editorials from *La Hora* are illustrative: "Guerra Borges incites a massacre" (Guerra Borges was a member of the PGT's Secretariat); "The duplicity of Poncho Bauer" (Bauer Paiz was the director of the Banco Nacional Agrario); "The stupidity of our leaders"; "Blood is still flowing, Colonel Arbenz."[30] *El Imparcial* and *Prensa Libre*, the other major opposition dailies, were equally intemperate; some publications virtually advocated the overthrow of the regime.[31] The government did not intervene. Freedom of the press in Arbenz's Guatemala greatly surpassed that of neighboring Mexico; in Latin America, it was equaled only by Uruguay and, perhaps, by Chile and Costa Rica.

Even unsympathetic American journalists were struck by the degree of freedom that existed in Guatemala. In an essay that applauded the overthrow of Arbenz, one such journalist, Keith Monroe, wrote that in a 1953 visit to Guatemala he had found that "anti-communist and pro-American newspapers were still in business. They attacked the government as hotly as Hearst used to attack the New Deal, yet their editors walked the streets unharmed. Fences and adobe walls were daubed with damn-the-Communists slogans. Shops and homes displayed cards in their windows: 'THERE IS NO COMMUNISM IN THIS HOUSE.' "[32] By West European standards, political democracy in Guatemala was limited, in part because the Indians traditionally voted as the local authorities wished. But the reports of the U.S. embassy highlighted the lack of violence in the elections that were held under Arbenz; these reports include no allegations of government pressure on the people or of restrictions on the opposition's freedom to campaign in the rural areas.[33] The January 1953 congressional elections were praised by Marroquín Rojas: "Now that this most recent election is behind us, we can state with confidence that democracy has taken root."[34]

When several dozen people were detained in the wake of Salamá, the opposition press lambasted the regime. Several months later, however, the U.S.

[30] *La Hora*: Jan. 18, 1954, p. 3; Feb. 26, 1954, p. 3; Mar. 3, 1954, p. 3; Mar. 18, 1954, p. 3.

[31] See, for example, the daily *El Espectador* and the many leaflets and bulletins of the often ephemeral anticommunist committees. For a compilation of articles from *El I*, see Blanco, *25 galeras*, a collection of twenty-five of this prominent journalist's columns written between Sept. 30, 1953, and June 1, 1954. *25 galeras* conveys the intensity of his hostility for the Arbenz regime and provides graphic proof of the freedom of the press in that time.

[32] Monroe, "Guatemala: What the Reds Left Behind," p. 61.

[33] On the Jan. 1953 elections, see *JW* 1–5 (Jan. 1–30, 1953). See also Schoenfeld to DOS, no. 490, Jan. 8, 1953; Schoenfeld to DOS, no. 621, Jan. 21, 1953; Schoenfeld to DOS, no. 660, Jan. 30, 1953. All NA 714.2. On the Nov. 1953 elections, see *JW* 48, Nov. 27, 1953.

[34] "Lo que puede salir de la experiencia electoral que acaba de sucederse," *La Hora*, Jan. 20, 1953, p. 1.

embassy observed: "Most of the people arrested subsequent to the [Salamá] uprising were actually involved in the group seeking to overthrow the Government."[35] The following January, in a second wave of arrests, two dozen were detained; again the opposition press vented its indignation, and again the embassy reported that the "victims" had been plotting the overthrow of the regime. Repression in Arbenz's Guatemala began only in late May 1954, in dramatic circumstances brought about by the United States.

It was neither political repression nor electoral fraud that robbed Arbenz's foes of victory at the polls. Bitter, petty divisions sapped their strength. In October 1952, the U.S. embassy noted "the ineffectiveness of the Guatemalan anti-communist movement"; complained about the "multiplicity of anti-communist organizations, their frictions and jealousies"; and lamented the resulting "wave of disillusionments . . . in the anti-administration sector."[36] That same month, a prominent opposition journalist pushed the analysis further:

> Anticommunist activities have achieved to date the most complete failure. . . . The explanation is very simple: in the first place, they lack a leader. . . . In the second place, they lack what Clemente [Marroquín Rojas] calls "guts." . . . In the third place, they lack the will to sacrifice. . . . The communists are prominent because of their intellectual abilities. . . . The anticommunists move without organization, discipline, or cooperation. Many "anticommunists at heart" don't even reach into their pockets to give a small donation when a committee or group asks for a few cents to aid at least in the propaganda campaign. . . . The so-called "leaders" incite the fray from their homes and vanish from even the telephone directory at the first sign of a clash.[37]

They lacked guts, and they lacked popular support. Both a Guatemalan protagonist and an American scholar, neither swayed by sympathy for the regime, came to similar conclusions. In a February 1954 editorial, the Guatemalan, Marroquín Rojas, frankly acknowledged that the rural masses backed the government:

> The peasants do not support the opposition. They support the government, for they have been seduced by the agrarian reform and other promises. True, there are smart peasants who have understood how hollow are the government's words. But there are just a few. . . . In the present circumstances, it is the rich—the landowners and the landlords—who would have to fight in the streets, and they will never do it. The members of AGA are good marksmen, but they only know how to shoot ducks and other defenseless birds; they couldn't shoot a man holding a gun. . . . Somoza has

---

[35] Wardlaw to Peurifoy ("Conversation Regarding Possibility of Attempt against Guatemalan Government"), Dec. 29, 1953, p. 1, NA 714.00/1-454.

[36] Krieg to DOS, no. 334, Oct. 10, 1952, quoted from pp. 1, 3, NA 714.00.

[37] Alvaro Contreras Velez, "Cacto," *Prensa Libre*, Oct. 2, 1952, p. 3.

told them: "I'll give you the weapons, the ammunition and the money; you find the men." But neither Ydígoras, nor Castillo Armas, nor Córdova Cerna, nor Coronado Lira has been able to find ten men willing to fight.[38]

The scholar, Ronald Schneider, concluded in 1958:

> Most Guatemalans . . . were greatly concerned about the preservation of the fruits of the Revolution of 1944, and there was little in the attitudes or actions of the opposition to indicate sincere support for that goal. . . . The working class had particular reason to feel loyal to the revolutionary regime. . . . The lower classes enjoyed the novelty of living in a new atmosphere, officially fostered, in which they were treated with a measure of respect and dignity.[39]

Lacking popular support, the scions of the upper class had little alternative but to seek a foreign patron. The pilgrimages to U.S. embassies of would-be liberators eager to oust Arbenz began even before his inauguration. General Ydígoras Fuentes, the unsavory presidential candidate of November 1950, appeared at the U.S. embassy in San Salvador on January 10, 1951. He presented Chargé d'Affaires William Wieland with a dramatic revelation and a bold offer. "He asked," Wieland wrote, "if I would have time to listen to his story concerning Arévalo. Without waiting for an answer," Ydígoras proceeded to reveal how, at a gathering in London in 1946, he had met a Chilean professor whose name he couldn't quite recall. Mistaking Ydígoras for a communist, the professor had immediately confided that both he and Arévalo were Soviet agents and that Arévalo had been sent to Guatemala "to take over the country" on the Kremlin's behalf. Arévalo, the garrulous professor had continued, "had done a masterful job in applying his Communist orders in Guatemala."

Ydígoras explained that he was ready and eager to defend his homeland. He would need, however, assistance. Wieland politely "thanked the general for his very pleasant and informative visit." Not for the last time, Ydígoras had made a dismal impression on an American whose support he had courted.[40]

A few weeks later, two of Ydígoras's men visited Somoza. "They claimed," the U.S. embassy reported, "that they had all the military assistance they needed, that their plans were laid and the coup would take place February 28, but that they needed money." Somoza assured them of his high regard for Ydígoras and sent them packing; he did not believe that the Guatemalan army would support a coup.[41]

Throughout Arbenz's first year, Ydígoras and other exiles pursued their

[38] "El caso del diputado José Luis Arenas R.," *La Hora*, Feb. 27, 1954, p. 3.

[39] Schneider, *Communism*, pp. 302–3.

[40] AmEm San Salvador, Wieland to DOS, no. 518, Jan. 11, 1951, quoted from pp. 1–4, NA 714.00.

[41] AmEm Managua, Waynick to DOS, no. 759, Feb. 25, 1951, NA 714.00.

quest for a foreign patron. In Guatemala a few hotheads engaged in sporadic acts of violence,[42] but most opposition leaders, acutely aware of their own weakness and still hopeful that Arbenz would move to the right, were content with rhetorical outbursts, upbraiding the government for its dalliance with the communists and urging the populace to give no quarter to the Reds. "The communist in the department of Quetzaltenango is outlawed," warned the Partido Independiente Anti-Comunista Occidental. "He will not be allowed to buy or sell anything, he will not be given work, and he will be despised as though he were a rabid dog."[43]

The opposition occasionally organized demonstrations to demand that the authorities wipe out communism. After a series of particularly noisy rallies in the capital and other towns, the U.S. embassy reported that the demonstrators, who were "mostly fairly well-dressed," had been neither attacked nor harassed; the government's willingness to allow the opposition forces "to express their feelings," noted the *New York Times*, suggested to many Guatemalans and Americans that Arbenz's commitment to the Reds might be superficial.[44]

Decree 900 plunged the upper class into despair. Marroquín Rojas, in a May 31, 1952 editorial, castigated his conservative friends:

> Many of the rich were *Arbencistas* [in the 1950 election]. Asturias Beltranena and many others were sure that Colonel Arbenz was a man of the right; that he couldn't be a Marxist because he was a military man, because he was associated with capitalists, and "because he liked the good life." I, on the other hand, had become acquainted with the true Arbenz in the Council of Ministers, and notwithstanding my personal regard for him, I understood . . . that he would never be parted from his extremist inclinations. . . . For this reason, I always said that he would turn either to the right or to the left. The proposed agrarian reform has shown it to be the

---

[42] Taracena recalls: "In 1951, I participated in some terrorist acts—against property, not people. I was found out, and I had to go into exile." (Interview with Taracena.) In January 1952, there were two bomb attacks against the PGT. (See "Bomba misteriosa estalla," *El I*, Jan. 19, 1952, p. 1; "Deben ser castigados," *Octubre*, Jan. 24, 1952, p. 1; "Atentado terrorista con bomba nylon," *El I*, Jan. 28, 1952, p. 1; "Desesperados ante auge de la lucha popular los anticomunistas arrojaron otra bomba," *Octubre*, Jan. 31, 1952, p. 1.) For additional examples, see L.A.H.A., *Así se gestó la Liberación*, pp. 57–58; MemoConv (Schoenfeld, Whitbeck), June 9, 1952, RG84 CF, Box 15, NA-S; Schoenfeld to DOS, no. 1288, June 17, 1952, NA 714.52.

[43] "ALERTA PUEBLO!!" Partido Independiente Anti-Comunista Occidental, Quetzaltenango, Aug. 1951.

[44] Quotations from *JW* 13, Mar. 28, 1952, I:1 and "Guatemalans Firm in Anti-Red Effort," *NYT*, Mar. 24, 1952, p. 5. See also "Guatemalan Ban on Reds Is Sought," *NYT*, Mar. 22, 1952, p. 4; "Anti-Red Meeting Stirs Guatemala," *NYT*, Mar. 23, 1952, p. 26; "Rallies Are Peaceful in Rural Guatemala," *NYT*, Mar. 25, 1952, p. 10; "Anti-Reds' Views Asked," *NYT*, Mar. 30, 1952, p. 27.

latter. There now can be neither hope nor doubt. . . . Arbenz will be true to his beliefs until he is brought down. . . . But . . . the rich still hope for compromise. . . . That is their mistake.[45]

This was a call to war, because—as Marroquín Rojas well knew—the opposition would not gain power through elections. Spurred on by the agrarian reform, the number of plotters increased. So did the frequency of the plotters' visits to U.S. embassies in Guatemala and other Central American republics. (Some went directly to the State Department in Washington.) As always, they wanted U.S. support, particularly dollars. As always, each poured scorn on the other plotters—the competition for favor was ruthless. Overestimating American credulity, some inflated their own importance to the point of absurdity. Colonel (ret.) Roberto Barrios Peña, who appeared in May 1952 at the State Department unbidden and "extremely agitated about the agrarian reform law," claimed that he was "the leader of the anti-communist movement in Guatemala which . . . had some 300,000 followers."[46] The figure must have been charmed: a year later, Guillermo Putzeys, who belonged to a rival and equally insignificant group, announced to U.S. officials that "his movement had 300,000 members."[47] This out of a total population of 3 million.

U.S. officials gave a courteous hearing to all and, until the summer of 1953, gave them all the same answer: the United States was concerned about communist influence in Guatemala, but it was not prepared to back a coup. From Guatemala, Ambassador Schoenfeld, who was aware of the weakness of the would-be rebels, warned the State Department of "the constant danger that confronts the anti-communist movement in this country from intemperate elements who undertake premature subversive action."[48]

Though the plotters' words were bold, their actions were cautious. The saga of Lt. Colonel Castillo Armas is representative. After his failed November 1950 uprising, he escaped from jail in July 1951 and left within a few days for exile in Colombia. Upon arriving in Bogotá, he predicted with bland assurance "that before the end of the year, the armed forces and the anti-communist civilian forces will have overthrown the government."[49] In late 1951, he

---

[45] "Los ricos con el agua al cuello," *Impacto*, May 31, 1952, p. 1.

[46] MemoConv (Barrios Peña, Siracusa, Clark), May 27, 1952, p. 1, NA 714.00. See also MemoConv (Barrios Peña, Mann, Clark), May 28, 1952, NA 714.00.

[47] MemoConv (Putzeys, Padilla, Fisher), May 14, 1953, p. 1, NA 714.00.

[48] Schoenfeld to DOS, no. 1075, Apr. 25, 1952, p. 2, NA 714.00. He was referring to the activities of a Comité Ejecutivo de la Liberación Nacional, which had initiated a series of chain letters "calling in thinly veiled terms for a rising" against Arbenz (p. 1).

[49] CIA, "Colonel Castillo Armas, Guatemalan Exile," number deleted, Aug. 2, 1951, quote p. 2. See also above, pp. 81–83.

moved to Tegucigalpa. He intended to enter Guatemala from El Salvador on January 25, 1952, a CIA report noted. He would be met at the border by one of his most loyal followers, the student leader Mario Sandoval Alarcón. The revolt would begin that night.[50]

Castillo Armas did not cross the border, and the uprising was postponed until late February—when, once again, nothing happened. In June, rebel sources informed the CIA that the bellicose colonel would invade Guatemala within a few days, this time from Honduras; as soon as he crossed the border, most of the Guatemalan army would rise in revolt, and in the capital a "civilian large scale uprising" would begin. (The CIA report ended with a note of caution: "Time and possible success highly unpredictable. Will primarily depend on degree of army support, principally in Guatemala City, of which we have no reliable information.")[51] Again, nothing happened. Castillo Armas lacked organization, popular support, and influence in the military. Prudently, he, like the rest of the plotters, refrained from launching an uprising.

The one exception to this pattern of caution was the ill-fated attack on Salamá. This "premature and poorly planned attempt by a small group," as a CIA report called it, took the agency by surprise. Swamped by warnings of uprisings that never materialized, it had ignored rumors that a revolt "will be attempted in Guatemala during Holy Week."[52]

The leaders of the revolt were César Izaguirre, an inveterate plotter, and Carlos Simmons. Simmons, the U.S. embassy reported, "was until recently employed by the Tropical Radio Company, a subsidiary of the United Fruit Company." Izaguirre and Simmons had received a large sum of money and,

---

[50] CIA, number and day deleted, Jan. 1952. Forty years later, upon hearing this report, a close aide of Castillo Armas exclaimed, "Ah! The inexperience of youth! Yes, we thought there were six or seven officers on our side in the military zone of Jutiapa. And we imagined that with them, we'd be able to take control of the zone, and that then Castillo Armas could arrive from El Salvador." (Interview with Taracena.)

[51] CIA, IN 75738, June 23, 1952, quoted from pp. 1, 2. See also CIA, "Possible Revolution in Guatemala," SO 90855, June 25, 1952; CIA, "Plot to Overthrow Arbenz Government," 00-B-53060, July 1, 1952; Smith to Undersec. of State, Dec. 12, 1952, *FRUS*, 1952-54, 4:1055–56.

[52] Quotations from CIA, "Revolutionary Activity in Guatemala," CS-9229, May 1, 1953 and AmEm Managua, Whelan to SecState, no. 152, Mar. 4, 1953, NA 714.00. See also CIA, "Revolt in Salamá," CS-6591, Apr. 6, 1953; CIA, CS-9934, May 14, 1953; CIA, "Attitude of the Guatemalan Army toward Current Political Developments," CS-10050, May 14, 1953.

Following the fashion to see the CIA behind every tree, some authors assert that the agency sponsored Salamá, despite the fact that all the evidence indicates that it was surprised by it. One of the most inventive is Higgins (*Perfect Failure*, p. 19), who flashes two sources (one of which is *FRUS*) to support his claim. One source does indeed mention Salamá, but not the CIA; the other mentions neither.

apparently, weapons from Trujillo and United Fruit. Emboldened, these "hot-headed anti-Communists" had acted without seeking the support of other groups of plotters, hoping to preempt the competition and savor the rewards of success alone.[53]

After the inevitable debacle, Izaguirre and Simmons escaped to foreign embassies and soon left the country. Their motley band of followers, who had been assured that they were but the vanguard, was left to reflect on their credulity in jail. Meanwhile, rival plotters hastened to express their disapproval of the untimely undertaking to U.S. officials. Throughout, the Guatemalan army had shown no disloyalty to the government, and the garrison of Cobán had acted "promptly and efficiently to put down the revolt," the U.S. embassy reported. This confirmed Arbenz in his belief that he could rely on his officers. "Jacobo," his wife recalls, "was not unduly disturbed. He felt that the army was loyal. The outcome of Salamá gave him a sense of security."[54]

This was the Guatemala that the Eisenhower administration faced in the summer of 1953 when it decided to engineer the overthrow of Arbenz. Within the country the opposition was weak and ineffectual. Small groups of bickering exiles hovered on Guatemala's borders, particularly in Honduras and El Salvador. They included "democrats" who had left the country rather than submit to a "communist" regime, and "democrats" who, having engaged in subversive activities, had fled to escape arrest or had been deported. By mid-1953, a majority of those who had congregated in Honduras acknowledged Castillo Armas as their leader; he enjoyed Somoza's protection and was the favorite of Archbishop Rossell y Arellano. Most of those who lived in El Sal-

[53] Quotations from *JW* 16, Apr. 17, 1953, I:3, and Krieg to Ambassador, Apr. 20, 1953, p. 1, RG84 G&C, Box 3, NA-S. On Izaguirre, see Krieg to SecState, no. 392, Mar. 30, 1953, NA 714.00. On UFCO's role, the following memo is suggestive: "Mr. Orray Taft, Jr., Office of Munitions Control, called me at 5 p.m., to tell me that he had just received a call from Mr. Emerick, Deputy Commissioner of Customs in Charge of Investigations, who told him that his agents in New York were investigating acquisitions of arms by [UFCO President] Zemurray for the overthrow of the Guatemalan government, and that he would supply Mr. Taft with a copy of the report on the investigation." (Fisher to Mann, May 19, 1953, NA 714.00.)

[54] Quotations from Krieg to SecState, no. 393, Mar. 31, 1953, NA 714.00, and from interview with María de Arbenz. In addition to those cited in nn. 1, 52, and 53 above, useful U.S. documents on Salamá are: *JW* 14, Apr. 3, 1953, I; *JW* 15, Apr. 10, 1953, I; *JW* 18, May 1, 1953, I; *JW* 23, June 5, 1953, I; Krieg to SecState, no. 390, Mar. 30, 1953, NA 714.00; Maj. Chavez, "Intelligence Report" no. IR-49-53, Apr. 9, 1953, RG84 G&C, Box 3, NA-S; Schoenfeld to DOS, no. 905, Apr. 15, 1953, NA 714.00; Schoenfeld to DOS, no. 1002, May 13, 1953, NA 714.00; MemoConv (Barrios Peña, Leddy, Fisher), Apr. 28, 1953, NA 714.00.

vador followed Ydígoras Fuentes, who competed for Trujillo's favor with Colonel Roberto Barrios Peña.[55]

Castillo Armas and Ydígoras did try to unite. On March 31, 1952, they signed the *Pacto de los Caballeros* in San Salvador, but the pact was stillborn. It was "ratified" in August 1953, again to no avail.[56] Intense rivalry drove these two champions apart. Each wanted to be the "supreme savior" of Guatemala, and each wanted to replace Arbenz. Relations between the two remained "acrimonious."[57] Without U.S. support, Ydígoras and Castillo Armas would have been insignificant even had they united; divided, they were pathetic.

[55] According to the well-informed Cehelsky, Barrios Peña was Trujillo's chosen man, and Ydígoras was his second choice. ("Guatemala's Frustrated Revolution," pp. 53–54.) Confirmed by interview with Taracena.

[56] For the text of the pact, see Guatemala, *La democracia amenazada*, pp. 8–31.

[57] Quoted from interview with Taracena. Both Taracena and Barrios Peña, another Castillo Armas supporter, waxed eloquent on Ydígoras' perfidy. Ydígoras, for his part, pilloried Castillo Armas. (Interviews with Taracena, Barrios Peña and Ydígoras.)

CHAPTER 11

The International Conspiracy against Guatemala

WHEN ARÉVALO became president in March 1945, democracy was on the rise in the Caribbean; the dictators were on the defensive. Somoza and Trujillo were kept at arm's length by the Truman administration, and the fledgling democracies of Cuba, Venezuela, and Guatemala symbolized the new era.

When Arévalo stepped down six years later, Trujillo and Somoza were more powerful than ever. The Truman administration now praised the tropical dictators as steadfast allies in the war against communism. Venezuela's young democracy had ended in November 1948, as a military coup ushered in the dictatorship of Marcos Pérez Jiménez. Then, in March 1952, Fulgencio Batista seized power in Cuba. Only two democracies remained in the Caribbean: Guatemala and Costa Rica.

Three countries bordered on Guatemala: Mexico, El Salvador and Honduras. The Mexican authorities accepted that Central America was Washington's backyard. Their relations with Guatemala—strained under Ubico, cordial under Arévalo—grew distant as Arbenz moved to the left and Mexican President Adolfo Ruiz Cortines (1952–1958) moved to the right.

In El Salvador a young officer, Major Oscar Osorio, had won carefully staged elections in 1950. Osorio spouted populism, occasionally comparing his "revolution" to that of Guatemala. He granted some political freedom, as long as it did not threaten his rule, and enacted highly circumscribed social reforms in the cities, where a minority of Salvadorans lived. In the countryside, where the land tenure structure was as unjust as in pre-1952 Guatemala, agrarian reform remained taboo, and unionization was strictly forbidden. In foreign policy, while willing to follow Washington's lead, he tried to retain a degree of independence. The limited amount of U.S. investment in the country minimized the possible flashpoints.

Whereas El Salvador grew no bananas, Honduras was the country in which UFCO's plantations were the most extensive; it was the quintessential banana republic. After fifteen years of iron rule, General Tiburcio Carías had stepped down in 1948 in favor of his protegé, Secretary of War Juan Manuel Gálvez, a civilian who had long been United Fruit's lawyer. Gálvez carefully cultivated his ties with the United States and UFCO. Like Osorio, he allowed some freedom in the cities and firmly opposed change in the countryside. As elsewhere in the region the Communist party was illegal.

When Arbenz became president, Guatemala was isolated. Arévalo's support for the Caribbean Legion had aroused the wrath of Trujillo and Somoza and the suspicion of the ruling elites of El Salvador and Honduras. In 1947, Guatemala had broken diplomatic relations with Nicaragua and the Dominican Republic; in 1948, it had severed ties with Venezuela.

But by 1950, for all practical purposes, the Caribbean Legion had ceased to exist, and, keenly aware of his country's isolation, Arbenz sought to reassure his Central American neighbors. In September 1951, he reestablished diplomatic relations with Nicaragua, and, setting aside Arévalo's practice, he did not break relations with Cuba despite Batista's coup. At the prompting of Foreign Minister Manuel Galich, Guatemala became a moving force behind the creation, in October 1951, of the Organización de Estados Centroamericanos (ODECA), which included the five republics of Central America. Arévalo had believed that unification would be possible only when all the Central American countries were democracies. The theory underlying ODECA was that steps toward unification should be undertaken immediately despite the diversity of regimes. This position was unrealistic, but useful to Guatemala: through ODECA, Arbenz tried to calm his suspicious neighbors. In this, he was reminiscent of Calderón Guardia (1940–1944) and Picado (1944–1948) of Costa Rica, both of whom had implemented significant social reforms and collaborated with the Communist party, but had avoided all interference in Nicaragua's affairs; in return, Somoza had left them alone.[1]

But in Guatemala the pace of social change was frighteningly rapid, and the communists wielded far more influence than they had in Costa Rica. The Guatemalan example was too dangerous to ignore, as even Osorio of El Salvador made clear. Osorio had been the Central American president most sympathetic to Arbenz. Both were military officers, Osorio liked to consider himself a revolutionary, and the fact that Arbenz's wife was an upper-class Salvadoran

[1] On the reestablishment of diplomatic relations with Nicaragua and the creation of ODECA, see AmEm San Salvador, Shaw to DOS, May 29, 1951, RG84 CF, Box 15, NA-S; AmEm Managua, Ellis to DOS, no. 172, Aug. 31, 1951, NA 713.00; AmEm San José, Cohen to DOS, no. 274, Sept. 5, 1951, NA 713.00; AmEm Managua, Ellis to DOS, no. 202, Sept. 10, 1951, NA 713.00; AmEm Managua, Ellis to DOS, Sept. 15, 1951, RG84 CF, Box 15, NA-S; AmEm San Salvador, Silberstein to DOS, no. 359, Oct. 16, 1951, NA 713.00; MemoConv (Schoenfeld, Galich), Oct. 30, 1951, RG84 CF, Box 15, NA-S; DOS, "Monthly Political Summary—Central America and Panama," Oct. 31, 1951, pp. 2–3, NA 713.00. An interesting, though not always reliable account of Guatemala and ODECA is Galich, *Por qué lucha Guatemala?*, pp. 240–57. Interviews with Galich, Fortuny, María de Arbenz, and Sol were helpful.

Arbenz was also less provocative vis-à-vis British Honduras than his predecessor had been. Arévalo had pursued Guatemala's claims on the territory with robust energy, earning in the process the hostility of the British government. (See above, p. 100, n. 62.) Under Arbenz, Guatemala's demands on British Honduras softened—as did the British allegations of communist influence in Guatemala. (Meers, "Pebble on the Beach," pp. 23, 33–35, 72.)

added a gentle touch to the relationship. Nevertheless, in August 1952—two months after the enactment of Decree 900—El Salvador introduced a resolution urging that ODECA adopt a policy against the "subversive actions of International Communism in Central America."[2] The resolution was not formally directed against Guatemala. As a member of ODECA, Guatemala was actually asked to join in the anticommunist crusade. Agreement was, of course, impossible for Arbenz. An impasse ensued, paralyzing the organization. Then, in late September, Osorio unearthed a nonexistent communist plot in his country and unleashed a wave of repression against the Salvadoran labor movement. This, noted the U.S. embassy in Guatemala, was Osorio's response to Decree 900. While the Arbenz administration maintained an uneasy silence, the Guatemalan opposition loudly praised Osorio. Stressing that the communists also threatened Guatemala, they pointed out "how right the Salvadoran foreign minister had been in proposing that the five Central American states unite against the communist advance in the region." Returning the compliment, Osorio praised his Guatemalan admirers as good patriots—"an action," the U.S. embassy remarked, "which is little likely to endear him to the Guatemalan authorities."[3]

Bitterness and distrust had replaced the tentative cordiality that had marked relations between the two countries in Arbenz's first year. Relations with Honduras and Costa Rica were equally strained, and Nicaragua was openly hostile. ODECA was doomed. In April 1953 Guatemala withdrew from the organization.[4]

[2] "Ponencia contra infiltración comunista," *El I*, Aug. 12, 1952, p. 1.

[3] Quotations from "Sucesos de El Salvador," *El I*, Sept. 29, 1952, p. 2 and from *JW* 41, Oct. 9, 1952, I:2. See also: "Redada de rojos bajo el estado de sitio," *El I*, Sept. 27, 1952, p. 1; "Salvador Charges a Communist Plot," *NYT*, Sept. 27, 1952, p. 6; "Celulas se adiestraban para acción subversiva," *El I*, Sept. 29, 1952, p. 1; "Cinco comités solidarios con Osorio" and "Sucesos de El Salvador," *El I*, Oct. 3, 1952, p. 1; "El Salvador Protests," *NYT*, Oct. 5, 1952, p. 27; DOS, "Monthly Political Summary—Central America and Panama," Oct. 28, 1952, pp. 1, 3, NA 713.00; "Sigue la tragicomedia en El Salvador," *Octubre*, Feb. 19, 1953, p. 3. For a haunting account by one of Osorio's victims, see Carpio, *Secuestro y capucha*. Particularly useful on the relations between Osorio and Arbenz were interviews with María de Arbenz, Sol, Fortuny, and Galich.

[4] On the protracted demise of ODECA, see AmEm San Salvador, Duke to DOS, no. 45, July 23, 1952, NA 713.00; Clark to Duke, Aug. 4, 1952, NA 713.00; MemoConv (Krieg, Tattenbach), Oct. 8, 1952, RG84 CF, Box 15, NA-S; AmEm San José, MemoConv (Cohen, Canessa), Feb. 4, 1953, enclosed in Fleming to DOS, no. 743, Feb. 5, 1953, NA 713.00; AmEm San Salvador, Donovan to DOS, no. 642, Apr. 9, 1953, NA 713.00. For the government's communiqué announcing the withdrawal, see "Guatemala denuncia la Carta de San Salvador," *DCA*, Apr. 7, 1953, p. 1. See also the editorial of the same title in *DCA*, Apr. 8, 1953, p. 3; "Repercusiones de nuestra salida de la ODECA" (edit.), *DCA*, Apr. 9, 1953, p. 3; "Razones de Guatemala para

By that time Trujillo and United Fruit were busy plotting against Arbenz, and so was Somoza. Indeed in the summer of 1952, Somoza had enlisted Truman's help.

Washington's hopes that Arbenz would reverse Arévalo's extremist policies had soured before the introduction of the Agrarian Reform Bill. In March 1951, Assistant Secretary Miller had stated that "Arbenz is a much less woolly-headed man than the previous president. . . . The situation is going to improve in our favor." By July, the State Department's Office of Intelligence and Research (OIR) observed dryly, "The reverse seems to have happened." The following April the same agency, whose reports were among the most professional of the U.S. government, remarked, "other Latin American governments . . . have in the past worked with Communists, generally because of their influence in labor unions. In no other Latin American country, however, has the ruling group in power accepted the Communists with such cordiality into a political partnership including the frequent support of the Communist line by administration media."[5]

Similar concerns were being heard in Congress. "Vociferous anti-American people [are] in the saddle [in Guatemala]," Secretary of State Acheson testified. "The Guatemalan situation is a very troublesome one. . . . The Communists . . . have gotten into the Government and they are causing a great deal of trouble and concern to us."[6] The same shift from hope to hostility was seen in the American press. As early as June 1951, the *New York Times* had warned: "Despite the hope that President Arbenz would curb their activities and purge the Government and labor unions of their influence, the power of the Communists has grown at an alarming rate. Regardless of good intentions, President Arbenz has been able to accomplish little and his dismissal of the question by saying that there is no Communist Party in Guatemala and his pointing to the register of political parties to prove it, does not represent reality." Three days later, a *New York Times* editorial concluded: "It is time to register a sense of deep disappointment and disillusionment over the trend of Guatemalan politics in the two months since Colonel Arbenz became President. . . . the Communist trend, far from being reversed, has been strengthened."[7]

---

retirarse de la ODECA," ibid., p. 1; "Centroamericanismo de Guatemala en evidencia," *DCA*, Apr. 10, 1953, p. 3; "Hacia la dignificación," *DCA*, Apr. 14, 1953, p. 2.

[5] Quotations from: Miller, Mar. 16, 1951, U.S. Congress, HCFA, p. 393; OIR, "Communism in the other American Republics: Quarterly Survey, April–June 1951," No. 5180.6, July 19, 1951, p. 10, NA; OIR, "Communism in the other American Republics: Quarterly Survey, January–March 1952," No. 5180.9, Apr. 18, 1952, p. 6, NA.

[6] U.S. Congress, SCFR, vol. 4, 1952, p. 28. (Acheson testified on Jan. 14, 1952.)

[7] Quotations from "Guatemalan Reds Trade on Old Ills," June 5, 1951, p. 6, and "The Guatemalan Cancer" (edit.), June 8, 1951, p. 26.

Yet throughout Arbenz's first year, the concern of U.S. officials and journalists lacked urgency. Congressional speeches about Guatemala, while critical, were few and brief; press coverage was infrequent. The hope lingered that Arbenz was "essentially an opportunist" who would ultimately betray his leftist friends. In the words of Bill Krieg, the DCM at the U.S. embassy in Guatemala, "incident after incident accumulated and we became increasingly concerned and pessimistic, but no irrevocable line had been crossed."[8] Arbenz had not yet enacted any legislation that would have caused an irreparable break with the upper class. Relations with the American companies were strained, but no worse than they had been under Arévalo. And the Communist party, although enjoying the president's favor, was not yet legal. This indicated, many hoped, that Arbenz could still turn to the right.

Until the spring of 1952, Truman's policy toward Arbenz was similar to that adopted toward Arévalo in the late 1940s. Diplomatic pressure was accompanied by the denial of economic aid. Washington continued to refuse to sell weapons to Guatemala and began a successful effort to prevent Arbenz from acquiring arms in other Western countries. In June 1951, the United States halted financial assistance for the construction of the Guatemalan segment of the Inter-American Highway.[9]

[8] Quotations from CIA, "Present Political Situation in Guatemala and Possible Developments During 1952," NIE-62, Mar. 11, 1952, p. 2, Truman Papers, President's Secretary's File, Intelligence File, Box 254, TL, and from interview with Krieg. Between Mar. 1951 and Apr. 11, 1952, Guatemala was attacked ten times in the House of Representatives and once in the Senate. See CR-House, 1951, pp. 3803–5, 9808–9; CR-House, 1952, pp. 1336, 1338, 2975–78, A1316, A1426, A1449, A1714; CR-Senate, 1952, pp. 2278–81. For a representative sample of the press during the same period, see: "A Round for the Reds," Time, May 7, 1951, p. 42; "The Reds and the President," Newsweek, July 16, 1951, p. 40; "Anti-Red Outburst," Newsweek, July 23, 1951, p. 46; "Under Western Eyes," Time, July 23, 1951, p. 24; "There's More Than Meets the Eye," Business Week, Oct. 13, 1951, p. 168; "Harassed United Fruit," The Commonweal, Nov. 9, 1951, p. 108; "Showdown in Guatemala," Business Week, Dec. 8, 1951, pp. 177–78; "Fruit Trade Rift Widens in Guatemala," CSM, Dec. 18, 1951, p. 9; "Bananas and Politics," New Republic, Jan. 28, 1952, p. 7; "Economic Suicide in Guatemala," Washington Daily News, Feb. 14, 1952, p. 8; "Red Front Tightens Grip on Guatemala," WP, Feb. 17, 1952, p. 2; "Red Cell in Guatemala," WP, Mar. 4, 1952, p. 12; "Red Footprints Get Bigger in Guatemala," CSM, Mar. 4, 1952, p. 10; "Communists Are Making Inroads in U.S. 'Back Yard,' " U.S. News and World Report, Mar. 7, 1952, pp. 38–41; "Operations in Guatemala Resumed by United Fruit," CSM, Mar. 15, 1952, p. 1; "The Reds Lose a Round," Time, Mar. 17, 1952, p. 36; "Banana Bonanza," Newsweek, Mar. 24, 1952, p. 62; "Guatemala's Distrust of U.S. Feeds Communist Cauldron," NYT, Mar. 27, 1952, p. 15; "United Fruit Becomes Victim of Guatemala's Awakening," NYT, Mar. 28, 1952, p. 5; "Guatemalan Reds Are Strong but They Don't Run Country," NYT, Mar. 29, 1952, p. 4.

[9] On the arms embargo by third parties, see Col. McCormick, "Intelligence Report"

Then, in May 1952, the Agrarian Reform Bill burst upon the scene. In the weeks that followed, embassy officials witnessed the prominent role played by the communist deputies in the congressional debates that led to the enactment of Decree 900, and they understood that the bill's champions were the president and the PGT. The canard that Arbenz was an opportunist who would betray his friends was finally discarded. Some U.S. officials condemned Decree 900 because they were clearly sympathetic to the landed elite and United Fruit. Others were less biased. But on one point they all agreed: "the law opened the way for a further extension of Communist influence."[10]

It was at this juncture that Somoza approached the United States with a proposal to overthrow Arbenz. Only the outlines of the plan are known. The major protagonists have long since died, and the main source is *New York Times* correspondent Herbert Matthews, who has related what Assistant Secretary Miller told him a year after the scheme was hatched.[11] Additional information is provided by the written report of a March 1953 conversation between Rolland Welch, first secretary of the U.S. embassy in Managua, and Somoza's son Tachito. Tachito, noted Welch, claimed that "the 'Guatemalan matter' was first proposed in a conversation between his father and an attorney for the United Fruit Company."[12]

---

no. R-22-52, Nov. 13, 1952, RG84 CF, Box 15, NA-S; Schoenfeld to DOS, no. 68, July 24, 1953, NA 714.56; *JW* 45, Nov. 6, 1953, I:4–5; Krieg to DOS, no. 443, Nov. 23, 1953, p. 3, NA 714.00; AmEm Stockholm, Abbott to SecState, no. 776, Mar. 19, 1954, NA 714.56; AmEm Stockholm, Abbott to SecState, no. 788, Mar. 24, 1954, NA 714.56; Fisher to Holland, May 18, 1954, NA Lot 58D18 & 58D78, Box 2; Holland to SecState, May 25, 1954, ibid.; AmEm Stockholm, Cabot to SecState, no. 1040, June 2, 1954, NA 714.5614; Hanford, "Communist Beachhead," pp. 20, 35–36; Meers, "Pebble on the Beach," pp. 37–38, 40–41.

For Guatemala's repeated requests for aid for the Inter-American Highway and for the repeated U.S. refusals, see Ballentine to DOS, no. 223, Aug. 29, 1951, NA 814.2612; Siracusa to Schoenfeld, Sept. 13, 1951, NA 814.2612; U.S. Congress, HCFA, Feb. 29, 1952, pp. 399–400; *JW* 24, June 13, 1952, II:2; MemoConv (Schoenfeld, Arbenz), Sept. 25, 1952, *FRUS*, 1952–1954, 4:1039–40; "Truman no ha dicho la verdad," *La Hora*, Jan. 14, 1953, p. 1; "Guatemala ha iniciado gestiones para que se reanude colaboración norteamericana," *DCA*, Apr. 20, 1953, p. 1; Minutes of Cabinet Meeting, Mar. 5, 1954, p. 2, WF, Cabinet Series, Box 3, EL.

[10] Quoted from *JW* 25, June 20, 1952, I:2. See also Siracusa to Nufer et al., May 22, 1952, NA 714.34; *JW* 23, June 6, 1952; *JW* 24, June 13, 1952; Schoenfeld to DOS, no. 1261, June 10, 1952, NA 714.00. Interviews with DCM Krieg, Second Secretary Wardlaw, and OIR analyst Hyman were particularly helpful.

[11] Matthews, *World in Revolution*, pp. 262–64.

[12] AmEm Managua, Welch to Ohmans, Mar. 11, 1953, NA 714.00 (quoted) and enclosed MemoConv (Somoza, Welch), Mar. 9, 1953. Also useful are papers of Truman's assistant military aide, Col. Cornelius Mara, Truman Papers, OF, esp. Boxes

Somoza had arrived in the United States on April 28, 1952, on a private trip. His visit was marked by great cordiality on both sides. The Nicaraguan dictator was duly effusive in his praise of the United States as the champion of democracy—democracy that he had crushed at home. He was honored with New York City's Medal of Honor and responded appropriately: the Nicaraguan people, he pledged, were and would always be the best friends of the United States in Latin America. "We appreciate the kindness, protection and help you have given us"; the United States was a "big brother, always willing to help small countries."[13]

Somoza stressed his personal ties to America. Not only had he, his wife, and his three children been educated in the United States, but his daughter's six children had been born there, and one of his sons was graduating from the University of Maryland, and the other from West Point. "I have always considered the United States my second country," he said time and again.[14]

Beyond these pleasantries, Somoza had a serious message. "Just give me the arms, and I'll clean up Guatemala for you in no time," he promised Truman, Acheson, and other U.S. officials. The offer was laughed off as a good joke. There the matter rested until early July when Somoza left for Managua aboard a U.S. military plane.[15]

With him flew Colonel Cornelius Mara, assistant military aide to Truman and a close associate of General Harry Vaughan, Truman's trusted friend. Mara had met Somoza previously on trips that he and Vaughan had taken to Central America. His presence on the plane was intended as mere protocol— a mark of respect for a loyal dictator—but it turned out to be much more. By the time they landed in Managua, Somoza had persuaded Mara that if the United States provided the arms, he could engineer Arbenz's overthrow; together, they had decided what weapons would be needed.[16] Back in Washington, Mara became Somoza's champion. His report to Truman must have been truly eloquent; so eloquent, in fact, that Truman immediately "initialed the report" and instructed General Walter Bedell Smith, the CIA Director, "to

---

1286/432 and 1287/439, TL. Schlesinger and Kinzer, *Bitter Fruit*, pp. 92, 102, contribute additional data based on their interviews with lobbyist Tom Corcoran and on an unpublished manuscript by Richard Harris Smith about Allen Dulles.

[13] "Head of Nicaragua Gets City's Medal," *NYT*, June 21, 1952, p. 6 (quoted) and "General Somoza Honored," *NYT*, June 19, 1952, p. 10.

[14] "Somoza in Washington," *NYT*, May 2, 1952, p. 2 (quoted), and "Head of Nicaragua Gets City's Medal," p. 6.

[15] Quoted from Matthews, *World in Revolution*, p. 262.

[16] Ibid., p. 263. See also "Cornelius J. Mara," Truman Papers, OF, Box 1663/1420, TL; Waynick to Truman, Jan. 20, 1951, ibid., Box 1286/432; Somoza to Vaughan, June 23, 1952, ibid.; Vaughan to Somoza, June 25, 1952, ibid.; Cross Reference Sheet ("Somoza"), Apr. 28 [sic.], 1952, ibid., Box 1287/439.

put it into effect.'' Truman did not inform Acheson or any other State Department official.[17]

And so Smith unleashed his cowboys from the CIA's Directorate of Plans. The plot, code named OPERATION FORTUNE, took shape over the next few weeks. State Department officials ''were at all times ignorant of what was brewing''; the CIA, United Fruit, and Somoza were the schemers. Trujillo and Venezuela's Pérez Jiménez were contacted; they responded enthusiastically and apparently contributed money. OPERATION FORTUNE did not contemplate direct intervention by a foreign power: the job would be done by Somoza's protegé, Castillo Armas. The plan depended on one crucial assumption—that ''important officers of the Guatemalan army'' would rise in revolt, as Castillo Armas had promised, as soon as he had crossed the border with his band of exiles.[18]

It was not the first time that Castillo Armas had proffered such bold assurances, and as late as June 1952, the CIA had responded with a healthy dose of skepticism. Now, under Somoza's spell, skepticism turned into credulity.

As summer faded into autumn, the plotters pressed forward with their preparations. ''The arms were gathered. A representative of the United Fruit in Nicaragua was assigned to receive them. The United Fruit turned over one of its freighters which it had specially refitted for this purpose. Two leaders of the stevedores in New Orleans had to be told about it. The arms were loaded into the ship as 'agricultural machinery' in cases, and the ship sailed for Nicaragua.'' The ship was still en route when Acheson learned of the plot: ''A CIA representative went to Miller and asked him to initial a paper on behalf of the Munitions Department of the State Department. . . . Miller refused and showed the document to [Deputy Undersecretary] Doc Freeman Matthews and David Bruce, Undersecretary of State, both of whom hit the ceiling, went to Acheson, who went to Truman and a message was sent redirecting the ship to Panama, where the arms were unloaded.''[19]

Thus ended the first U.S. conspiracy against Arbenz. Castillo Armas was utterly deflated. ''Always at the last minute difficulties arose,'' he grumbled. Whereas a few weeks earlier he had been ''full of the almost certain success in the future,'' an informant reported in late October, ''his attitude has distinctly changed. He had certainly managed to get hold of some money . . .

[17] Matthews, *World in Revolution*, p. 263. See also Mara, memo for the President, July 11, 1952, Truman Papers, OF, Box 1286/432, TL.

[18] Quotations from Matthews, *World in Revolution*, p. 263, and from AmEm Managua, MemoConv (Somoza, Welch), (see n. 12 above), p. 1. (Matthews misidentifies Castillo Armas as a ''Castillo Moreno'' and calls Mara ''Marrow.'') See also Schlesinger and Kinzer, *Bitter Fruit*, p. 92. It was probably on this occasion that Trujillo provided $60,000 for Castillo Armas. (See Crassweller, *Trujillo*, p. 335, and Paniagua to Trujillo, Tegucigalpa, May 14, 1953, Vega File.)

[19] Matthews, *World in Revolution*, p. 264.

[but] he was losing hope.''[20] It was just as well. The plan was madness. The Guatemalan military had not yet been subjected to months of psychological warfare by the United States, and its support for Arbenz was still firm. Had Castillo Armas invaded, he would have been defeated as easily as were the Salamá rebels a few months later.

The most likely explanation for the abrupt termination of OPERATION FORTUNE is that Acheson had convinced Truman that it would fail. Perhaps he had also argued that Guatemala's sins were not yet so grevious as to justify an attempt to overthrow Arbenz. But Acheson's thinking, and the entire operation, remain mysterious. Years later, in the wake of the Bay of Pigs, he wrote to Truman: ''Why we ever engaged in this asinine Cuban adventure, I cannot imagine. Before I left [for Europe] it was mentioned to me and I told my informants how you and I had turned down similar suggestions for Iran and Guatemala and why.'' Unfortunately, he did not elaborate.[21]

In the weeks that followed the demise of OPERATION FORTUNE, events that were bound to heighten U.S. anxieties occurred in Guatemala.

On December 11, 1952, the Communist party opened its second congress; senior government officials and administration politicians were present. Eight days later, the party was legalized. That same month, noted the State Department's Office of Intelligence and Research (OIR), the PGT scored ''the outstanding political victory of the quarter'' when it was formally included in the administration's electoral coalition for the January 1953 congressional elections.[22] These were striking developments. Since 1948, no other Latin American government had collaborated with the Communist party; communists were persecuted in most Latin American countries.

In January 1953, the implementation of Decree 900 began in earnest. The PGT, reported OIR, ''continued in the forefront of agrarian reform agitation and Communist propagandists were especially active in rural areas.''[23] In the weeks that followed, UFCO land at Tiquisate was expropriated, and the four Supreme Court justices were dismissed by the Guatemalan Congress.

By April 1953, when OIR's next quarterly report appeared, Arbenz's Guatemala had committed even more damnable crimes:

> In Guatemala, now the only country in the world outside the Soviet orbit (except San Marino) where the Communist Party has formal membership in a government

[20] Letter to Col. Sawyer, U.S. army attaché, Tegucigalpa, Oct. 27, 1952, RG84 CF, Box 15, NA-S.

[21] Acheson to Truman, May 3, 1961, in McLellan and Acheson, *Among Friends*, pp. 206–7.

[22] OIR, ''Communism in the other American Republics: Quarterly Survey, October–December 1952,'' no. 5180.12, Jan. 28, 1953, p. ii, NA.

[23] Ibid., p.11.

coalition, official and pro-administration channels continued to be freely available for Communist propaganda. The administration press featured reports of the Guatemalans who had recently made the grand tour of "the popular republics of the Soviet Union and New China," serialized Jean Paul Sartre on the subject of the December 1952 Vienna peace front congress, and played up Communist youth front preparations for a Vienna meeting in March 1953. The Guatemalan Congress paid a "minute of silence" tribute to Stalin. Communist *Octubre*, in an impressive 12-page special edition commemorating Stalin, carried eulogies by leaders of the administration parties as well as by Communist leaders.[24]

The American press followed developments in Guatemala with growing concern. In mid-1952, the Agrarian Reform Law had provoked a spate of articles, some very sympathetic to UFCO and the Guatemalan landed elite, others stressing the need for land reform and highlighting the plight of the Indians. There was a common thread running through all these articles: fear of the spread of communist influence in the countryside. Some journalists expressed this fear in lurid terms. Others were more restrained. All sensed that the established order was crumbling in rural Guatemala, and all feared for the future.

The legalization of the PGT, its participation in the electoral alliance, and the January 1953 expropriations of private land triggered a fresh flurry of articles. In mid-January, *U.S. News and World Report* pointed out that Arbenz was a weak executive who, while not a communist himself, "usually does what the Communists want him to do." The following month, it warned: "What Guatemala is getting in the way of Government, and land reform, is a startling example of Russian-type action in the Western Hemisphere"; the country was moving into a period of "widespread strife, maybe revolution"; its airfields were but two hours from the Panama Canal, and less than three from vital oil and chemical industries in Texas.[25]

Newsweek announced that the PGT had "armed shock troopers in every town, village, and hamlet," and that "hordes of armed Indians" had been invading plantations "all over the republic"[26]—gross distortion that echoed tales spun in the fashionable cafés of Guatemala City. With even richer imagination, *American Mercury* stated that in Guatemala "a great espionage, sabotage, and propaganda organization works day and night for the Soviet Union"; there was "documentary proof" that the country's labor and agrarian

[24] "OIR, Communism in the other American Republics: Quarterly Survey, January–March 1953," no. 5180.13, Apr. 23, 1953, p. 1, NA.
[25] "Communists Get New Toe Holds," *U.S. News and World Report*, Jan. 16, 1953, pp. 31–32, and "When Communists Take Over," *U.S. News and World Report*, Feb. 20, 1953, pp. 14–16.
[26] "Reds at the Polls," *Newsweek*, Jan. 26, 1953, p. 59, and "The Fog Lifts," *Newsweek*, Feb. 9, 1953, p. 46.

legislation had been "consciously planned [by the communists] to bring about slow strangulation of the economy . . . [and] to create economic chaos."[27]

Agrarian reform was necessary, but Decree 900 had given the communists "their greatest opportunity to supplement their tough city cadres with peasant battalions," Sidney Gruson, the *New York Times'* Guatemala expert, warned on February 23. A few days later, the *Times* ran another article by Gruson, entitled "How Communists Won Control of Guatemala." Accompanying the article was "Moscow Samba" a cartoon of a Guatemalan dancing to Stalin's tune. Unlike many of his colleagues, Gruson told no lurid tales of Indian hordes running amok or Soviet agents manipulating Guatemala from smoke-filled rooms; he merely stressed the "superior organization" of the Guatemalan communists, their "missionary zeal and devotion to party causes rather than self-enrichment." Their influence was growing, he asserted, but they

Moscow Samba. (From *The San Diego Union*, February 18, 1953. Reprinted with permission from *The San Diego Union*.)

[27] Ralph de Toledano, "The Soft UNDERBELLY of the U.S.A.," *American Mercury*, Feb. 1953, pp. 114–28, quoted from pp. 114, 115.

were not yet in control. A similar conclusion had been reached by Robert Hallett, another outstanding journalist, in a long article in the *Christian Science Monitor*: because the communists were more honest, hardworking, and devoted than any other political group in Guatemala, they were gaining ground.[28]

A series by Daniel James in the *New York Herald Tribune* contributed the alarming information that Guatemala was but five hours from New Orleans. James agreed that the communists did not control Guatemala, but he was disturbed by their growing influence. After comparing the tactics of the PGT with those of Mao Zedong and the Yenan Way (communist wolves in agrarian reformers' clothing), he ended by stating ominously that Guatemala had recently quit ODECA because it objected to El Salvador's proposed united front against communism.[29]

When James' series appeared, the Eisenhower Administration had been in power for two months. The Republicans had triumphed in the November 1952 elections after a campaign waged under the shadow of McCarthyism. Relentlessly, they had charged that the Democrats had embarked on a road to surrender that had led to Yalta, the loss of China, and disaster in Korea—"twenty years of treason," in the words of Eisenhower's running mate. Containment, the Republicans charged, was negative, futile, immoral. To the American people, they now offered a credo of victory: rollback. Under Eisenhower, they pledged, the United States would seize the initiative and liberate the captive nations of Europe. More important still, they promised that the hero of World War II would end the war in Korea. Furthermore, they would reduce Truman's military budget, and hence taxes. It mattered little that the new crusaders failed to explain how this would be achieved; their vagueness was rewarded at the polls.[30] The Democrats were chased from the White House and lost (if barely) the control of the Congress. Eisenhower became president, and John Foster Dulles secretary of state.

The conventional wisdom that Eisenhower gave "an unparallelled gift of authority"[31] to Dulles, amiably following his secretary's lead in foreign pol-

[28] Gruson, "Guatemalan Reds Seek Full Power," *NYT*, Feb. 23, 1953, p. 4; Gruson, "How Communists Won Control of Guatemala," *NYT*, Mar. 1, 1953, D6; Hallett, "Communists Move Cautiously to Safeguard Gains Chalked Up in Guatemala," *CSM*, Jan. 15, 1953, p. 7.

[29] "The Truth About Guatemala," *New York Herald Tribune*, Apr. 7–9, 1953, always p. 22.

[30] On the 1952 campaign, see Bernstein, "Election of 1952"; Divine, *Foreign Policy*, pp. 3–85; Parmet, *Eisenhower*, pp. 83–149; Ambrose, *Eisenhower*, 1:529–72.

[31] Quoted in Reichard, "Eisenhower as President," p. 273.

icy, has been debunked as documents have been declassified.[32] As Stephen Rabe writes, "Few still doubt that Eisenhower was a strong, decisive, and intelligent leader."[33] He was in charge of his administration's foreign policy, and this foreign policy was in many respects a continuation of Truman's. Like his predecessor, he followed a policy of containment vis-à-vis the Soviet Union. Like his predecessor, the linchpin of his policy was Europe, where he continued and developed Truman's work. Like Truman, he knew very little of the Third World; he was aware that emerging nationalism and rising expectations confronted the United States with challenges that required innovative responses, but he, too, was distracted by other problems and crippled by bias and by narrow anticommunism. He tended to gloss over Latin America—until the late 1950s, when Castro forced a wrenching reassessment. Until then, Eisenhower believed, he had faced only one significant challenge in the hemisphere, the Guatemalan revolution. And in his memoirs, while by no means revealing the full extent of his administration's role in the overthrow of Arbenz, he listed it as one of his proudest accomplishments.[34]

But if Eisenhower presided over the overthrow of Arbenz, other men executed his orders. Within the high councils of the new administration, three men, other than the president, were to be instrumental in the fall of Arbenz: John Foster Dulles, his brother Allen, and General Bedell Smith.

Eisenhower actually liked John Foster Dulles. In this he was virtually unique, notes Stephen Ambrose, the president's foremost biographer. "Nearly everyone else found Dulles impossibly pompous, a prig, and unbearably dull."[35] Behind an unpleasant exterior lay, however, a mind of "considerable breadth . . . notable depth as well."[36] By 1952, at age sixty-four, Dulles had proven his abilities as a very successful corporate lawyer, as a diplomat, and to a lesser extent as a writer. But as he attained his lifelong ambition to be secretary of state, "much of the subtlety and sophistication of vision that Dulles had possessed was lost." He had grappled intellectually with the problems of war and decolonization, "but when it came to working for, or adjusting to, some new global order, he . . . fell back on a very traditional pursuit of national interest. . . . He increasingly camouflaged this pur-

[32] For the conventional view, see Childs, *Eisenhower*, and Hughes, *Ordeal of Power*. For the revisionist view, see Immerman, "Eisenhower and Dulles"; Divine, *Eisenhower and the Cold War*; Cook, *Declassified Eisenhower*; Greenstein, *Hidden-Hand Presidency*; Ambrose, *Eisenhower*, vol. 2. For review essays, see De Santis, "Eisenhower Revisionism"; Reichard, "Eisenhower as President"; McAuliffe, "Eisenhower, the President"; Schlesinger, "Ike Age Revisited"; Joes, "Eisenhower Revisionism"; McMahon, "Eisenhower and Third World Nationalism."

[33] Rabe, *Eisenhower and Latin America*, p. 5.

[34] Eisenhower, *Mandate*, pp. 421–27 and 573–75.

[35] Ambrose, *Eisenhower*, 2:21

[36] Pruessen, *Dulles*, p. 500.

suit with a series of facile assumptions about the profundity of his proposals, the benefits that would prevail for mankind, and the divine approval which seemed manifest.''[37]

Dulles hailed from the international wing of the Republican party and had supported Truman's policy of containment until the Republican defeat in the 1948 presidential elections and the ''loss'' of China made it politically expedient to abandon bipartisanship in foreign policy. In the 1952 presidential campaign, few had waved the flag of liberation with more enthusiasm than had John Foster Dulles. This had been Dulles the campaigner. As secretary of state, however, ''he understood that the Eisenhower administration could not *act* much more forcefully than its predecessor; the facts of nuclear life dictated caution. But the administration could, and through Dulles it would, *speak* more forcefully.''[38]

Like his predecessor, Dean Acheson, Dulles knew very little of Latin America; his meager exposure had been gained in the interwar years as a corporate lawyer. (He had, for instance, represented Electric Bond and Share in Guatemala in the early 1920s.)[39] He, like Acheson, had no interest in inter-American questions, ''except peripherally as a side issue in his anticommunist crusade.''[40] He knew, however, who his country's best friends in the region were. ''His instructions are flat,'' remarked an aide. ''Do nothing to offend the dictators; they are the only people we can depend on.''[41] The Truman administration had also embraced the dictators, but never as warmly as did Dulles.

Unlike his elder brother, CIA Director Allen Dulles had an engaging personality. He deferred to Foster, who in turn trusted him implicitly. He too had been a highly successful lawyer—until the United States entered World War II and his great adventure began. As head of the Bern office of the Office of Strategic Services, he had directed American espionage in Europe. He had found his true calling. He had returned from Europe after the war's end with an impressive reputation and a consuming passion for the secret world of covert operations. Under Truman, he became deputy director of the CIA. Eisenhower promoted him to director.

In government, as before, the two brothers were in constant, easy commu-

---

[37] Ibid., p. 508.

[38] Brands, *Cold Warriors*, p. 14.

[39] See Pruessen, *Dulles*, chs. 4–7 (esp. p. 64), and Pitti, ''Ubico,'' p. 100. Contrary to a persistent allegation (see, for instance, Treverton, *Covert Action*, p. 53), Dulles never represented United Fruit.

[40] Cabot, *First Line*, p. 90. In 1953, Cabot was assistant secretary for inter-American affairs.

[41] Robert Woodward (who was deputy assistant secretary for inter-American affairs in 1953), quoted in the diary of Adolph Berle, Feb. 8, 1955, Berle Papers. Berle and Jacobs, *Navigating the Rapids*, is an abridged version of the original diaries. It omits much that is important.

nication. Often, after a day's work, Allen would drop by Foster's house to go over unfinished business.[42] Never have a secretary of state and a CIA director enjoyed so close a relationship—so close, in fact, that it bothered some. "It is a relationship that it would be better not have to exist," remarked the chairman of a committee appointed by Eisenhower to investigate the agency. Eisenhower disagreed: "Part of CIA's work is extension of work of State Department."[43]

As Eisenhower's chief of staff during World War II, General Walter Bedell Smith had earned the trust and the respect of the future president. He was, according to Eisenhower, "a godsend—a master of detail with clear comprehension of the main issues."[44] He was also a "formidable personality"[45] who was quick to anger. His years as ambassador in Moscow after the war may not have mellowed his temper, but they sharpened his anticommunist sensitivities. "He had come away with a deep suspicion of Marxist philosophy, a hatred of Soviet cruelty, deception, and hostility, and a contempt for any 'parlor pinks,' as he called them, in the United States. . . . He was a rabid enemy of the Soviet system abroad and *any* form of socialism at home. . . . He was once, for instance, reputed to have called Nelson D. Rockfeller a 'red' for a lukewarm statement in favor of the unions."[46] In the wake of the outbreak of the Korean War and the CIA's failure to predict North Korea's attack, Truman made him DCI, director of the CIA. And a dynamic director he was. "He was the boss," Kim Philby wrote later, "and a boss of outstanding intellect and character."[47] As DCI, General Smith had been the frustrated patron of OPERATION FORTUNE. A champion of covert operations, he had chafed under the Truman-Acheson refusal to move against Mohammed Mossadegh. Kim Roosevelt, who eventually directed the CIA plot in Iran, relates a conversation with the general in early 1953. Eisenhower had not yet been inaugurated, but Smith was raring to go: " 'When is our goddam operation going to get underway?' [Smith asked] in his usual aggressive fashion."[48]

Smith was not to oversee the fall of Mossadegh from the CIA: Eisenhower shifted him to the State Department's number two slot, the undersecretary. Within a few weeks, the proud Smith had developed a hearty dislike for Foster

[42] See DP, *passim*, e.g. TelConv (JFD, AWD), Mar. 18, 1954, 2:11 p.m., JFD:CS, Box 7, EL; TelConv (JFD, AWD), Mar. 23, 1954, 5:45 p.m., ibid.; TelConv (JFD, AWD), Apr. 5, 1954, 6:10 p.m., ibid.; MemoTel (JFD, AWD), June 5, 1954, 12:50 p.m., ibid., Box 8.

[43] Gen. Doolittle and DDE, Oct. 19, 1954, WF, Adm. Series, Box 13, EL.

[44] Ambrose, *Eisenhower*, 1:187.

[45] Kirkpatrick, *The Real CIA*, p. 91. Kirkpatrick was Smith's executive assistant.

[46] Mosley, *Dulles*, pp. 269–70; see also Ambrose, *Eisenhower*, 2:56.

[47] Philby, quoted in Mosley, *Dulles*, p. 270.

[48] Roosevelt, *Countercoup*, p. 115.

Dulles.[49] Concerning Guatemala, however, he had no differences with the secretary.

By appointing the Dulles brothers and Smith to these key posts, Eisenhower assured that the State Department and the CIA would act in concert. Under his leadership, the CIA was given increased latitude, and its covert operations were emphasized.

As soon as Eisenhower became president, the CIA began plotting the overthrow of Mossadegh; OPERATION AJAX was formally approved on June 25 in a session chaired by Foster Dulles.[50] Eisenhower stayed in the wings, but he was very much in control.

> Before going into operation, AJAX had to have the approval of the President. Eisenhower participated in none of the meetings that set up AJAX; he received only oral reports on the plan; and he did not discuss it with his Cabinet or the NSC. Establishing a pattern he would hold to throughout his Presidency, he kept his distance and left no documents behind that could implicate the President in any projected coup. But in the privacy of the Oval Office, over cocktails, he was kept informed by Foster Dulles, and he maintained a tight control over the activities of the CIA.[51]

While preparing to overthrow Mossadegh, the administration was also under pressure to move against Arbenz. The prestigious Council on Foreign Relations urged Eisenhower to be bold. "The Guatemalan situation," its confidential report stressed, "is quite simply the penetration of Central America by a frankly Russian-dominated Communist group. . . . There should be no hesitation . . . in quite overtly working with the forces opposed to Communism, and eventually backing a political tide which will force the Guatemalan government either to exclude its Communists or to change."[52] Among the council's members was Adolph Berle, a distinguished former diplomat, an intellectual activist well-connected with both parties. Berle considered himself a liberal; he had been a member of Roosevelt's brain trust, and he would later be, under Kennedy, one of the fathers of the Alliance for Progress. He was also something of an expert on Latin America, a rarity among prominent Americans. However, as his diary attests, he knew very little about Central America, but this did not stop him from sharing his wisdom about it.

Guatemala worried him. On October 17, 1952, he jotted down what a high Salvadoran official, Miguel Magaña, had just told him. Magaña's tale, which Berle soon relayed to senior CIA officials, ran as follows:

[49] See Jackson Papers, Aug. 18, 1953, Box 56, EL, and Hanes, memo, Aug. 17, 1953, DP, Subject Series, Box 6, EL.

[50] Roosevelt, *Countercoup*, pp. 1–19.

[51] Ambrose, *Eisenhower*, 2:111.

[52] Quoted by Immerman, *CIA in Guatemala*, p. 128. See also Shoup and Minter, *Imperial Brain Trust*, pp. 195–99.

He said that the government of El Salvador is thoroughly worried and unhappy about the situation in Guatemala. This is a Communist government, net: hardly even disguised. They captured on the border the documents shipped in from Moscow and headed for El Salvador via Guatemala, setting up organization to eventually seize El Salvador's government. They have likewise been intercepting steady shipment of arms into Guatemala; these arms were all Czechoslovak.[53]

In March 1953, Berle spent five days in Nicaragua; from there, on an impulse, he went to Costa Rica for a day. He wanted to assess José Figueres, who was branded a communist by U.S. officials in Managua; he also wanted to discuss Arbenz with Figueres.[54] Two liberals—the prominent American and the leading Costa Rican politician—were about to meet.

It had been in Costa Rica, in early 1948, that Arévalo had scored the one success of his Caribbean policy: he had helped Figueres to overthrow the communist-supported government of Picado. After Picado's fall, Figueres ruled the country with semidictatorial powers and a harsh hand toward his defeated foes. In late 1949, he was succeeded by a conservative president, Otilio Ulate. By the time Berle arrived in Costa Rica, Ulate's term was coming to an end; elections were scheduled for July 1953, and it was common knowledge that Figueres would win.

Figueres combined an obvious lust for power with a frank hostility for the dictators of the region—above all, Somoza. He favored moderate social change; timely reforms, he argued, would strengthen the capitalist system. To the Central American upper class, this was heresy. To Somoza, the issue was clear: Figueres was a communist. Others were more open-minded: Figueres was probably not a party member, but he was a fellow traveler. "President Figueres," *El Diario de Hoy* warned from San Salvador in 1954, "is still playing the same wily trick he played in 1948—he talks tough to the communists, but in fact he supports them and their program."[55] He baffled U.S. officials. Assistant Secretary Miller told Congress in 1952, "I am a little worried

[53] Berle Diary, Oct. 17, 1952, Berle Papers; see also entries of June 18, Dec. 2, and Dec. 8, 1952.

[54] See ibid., Apr. 1, 1953. This entry includes Berle's account of his Mar. 19–26 Central American trip.

[55] "Conjeturas sobre la abstención de Costa Rica," *El Diario de Hoy*, San Salvador, Mar. 1, 1954, p. 7. While the Guatemalan upper class generally shared Somoza's view, *La Hora* was less consistent. At times it castigated Figueres "as an underhanded communist . . . who embraced subversives from everywhere"; on other occasions, it merely branded him an unsavory rogue with dangerous Red proclivities. See "Incógnita electoral en Costa Rica," July 25, 1953, p. 1; "Contradicciones de quien viaja en hombros soviéticos," Sept. 12, 1953, p. 1; "La reunión de Caracas puede fracasar," Nov. 17, 1953, p. 1; "Parece que le llega el turno a Figueres," July 12, 1954, p. 1 (quoted).

about Figueres because you can be a demagogue without being a Communist.'' Miller's successor was no less confused: ''It is one of those never never situations that could only happen in a Latin American country. . . . The Communists are ostensibly supporting . . . Figueres' opponent, [but] Figueres is receiving considerable wads of dough from official sources in Guatemala. It does not make any sense but that is the way it is.'' Eisenhower's ambassador to Costa Rica described Figueres as ''an extreme socialist . . . a very strange personality . . . who is supposed to be anti-communist, but is probably as dangerous a man as there is in all of the Latin American countries.''[56]

Of one thing U.S. officials were certain: Figueres' gestures of independence betrayed his leftist leanings. The March 1954 Inter-American Conference was a case in point. Withstanding U.S. pressure, Costa Rica, alone among its sister republics, refused to attend because the conference was held in Caracas, the seat of one of the most ferocious dictatorships of the hemisphere. Although Figueres immediately endorsed the anticommunist resolution sponsored by the United States, Dulles was not mollified.[57]

Only men blinded by anticommunist paranoia and imperial hubris could have failed to realize that Figueres was a fervent anticommunist who readily embraced the principle of U.S. hegemony in the Caribbean. ''I was one of the first to recognize the menace of communism in our hemisphere,'' he countered his critics, ''and I defeated communism in my country in 1948 at a time when many still failed to recognize the threat.'' Had he not overthrown a communist-supported regime? Had he not outlawed the Communist party, which had been legal since the early 1930s?[58] From Guatemala, the PGT vigorously confirmed Figueres' anticommunist credentials. Figueres, wrote *Octubre*, ''established a regime of terror. He is a fawning servant of U.S. imperialism.''[59] These accusations, however exaggerated, underlined a basic truth: there could be no friendship between José Figueres and Jacobo Arbenz. As Berle was to discover in Costa Rica, Figueres was very much Arbenz's foe.

Figueres, Berle recorded in his diary, ''said that he and all his friends fully recognized that a Kremlin-Communist government in this hemisphere was impossible.'' Years later, recalling this encounter with Berle, Figueres was

[56] Miller, Feb. 29, 1952, U.S. Congress, *HCFA*, p. 406; Cabot, May 22, 1953, ibid., pp. 418–19; Hill, Jan. 26, 1954, ibid., p. 477.

[57] See Ameringer, *Don Pepe*, pp. 117–19. For Washington's reaction, see also Figueres, ''Oral History Interview,'' pp. 33–35; Davis to Figueres, Feb. 22, 1954, Davis Papers, Box 1, TL; Hill to Davis, Mar. 1, 1954, ibid.; TelConv (JFD, Pearson), Mar. 24, 1954, 10:25 a.m., DP, JFD:CS, Box 7, EL; Berle Diary, Feb. 8, 1955, Berle Papers.

[58] ''En la emergencia de Guatemala estamos cooperando con otros miembros del sistema americano,'' *La Prensa Libre*, San José, June 1, 1954, p. 1 (quoted from p. 14).

[59] ''La elección de Figueres,'' *Octubre*, Aug. 6, 1953, p. 3.

straightforward: "Berle asked me whether I was ready to cooperate in a plan to overthrow Arbenz, and I answered that I had no moral qualms. In fact, I was all for overthrowing Arbenz, who was a communist, but on one condition: that Somoza not be involved."[60]

Spurred by his conversations with Figueres, Berle went to work as soon as he had returned to the United States. On March 31, he presented the fruit of his labor—a sixteen-page memorandum—to C. D. Jackson, a senior White House official. "The United States cannot tolerate a Kremlin-controlled Communist government in this hemisphere," the memorandum began. U.S. military intervention should be ruled out, however, "except as an extremely bad last resort, because of the immense complications which it would raise all over the hemisphere." An alternative was to organize a "counter-movement, capable of using force if necessary," and led by Nicaragua. But Somoza was an unsavory and discredited dictator. He should not be allowed to lead the movement against Arbenz, yet he could not be completely excluded, since "it is difficult to expect that anything effective could be done from the Central American side without Nicaragua in the picture." Berle saw a way out of this dilemma:

> The course of action I should recommend is . . . to work out a Central American "Political Defense" action, using . . . Salvador, Nicaragua and Costa Rica as chief elements, with what help can be obtained from Honduras. . . . The key to such action . . . seems to be Costa Rica. There . . . the summer's elections will result in putting in as President José Figueres. . . . Of the men who have . . . popular support in Central America, Figueres is easily the most dynamic, and I should think the fairest-minded. As between betting on him and betting on a senescent dictatorship in Nicaragua, I should immensely prefer the one democracy which has made its way. . . . A theatre commander for a job like the Guatemalan operation does not, apparently, exist in Central America. So, the *first* job is to get a theatre commander for the operation. . . . Guatemala is an unfriendly country and our own people—or Costa Ricans or Salvadorians friendly to us—ought to go in and organize in the country. This would have to be sub-rosa. In other countries whose governments will be brought to cooperate, the organization can be in the open and it should be done by nationals of those countries.
>
> . . . A quiet understanding should be reached between the governments of Costa Rica, Salvador, Honduras and at least some powerful elements in Nicaragua. This last, I think, can be done.
>
> . . . Some powerful Central American figure—I suggest Figueres—should be encouraged to take leadership and deal with the problem, all-out.
>
> The result ought to be an organization of a party of Democratic Defense in the five

[60] Quotations from Berle Diary, Apr. 1, 1953, Berle Papers, and from interview with Figueres.

Central American republics, taking as its first job the clearing out of the Communists in Guatemala.[61]

A few days later Berle met with C. D. Jackson.[62] He was thanked—and heard no more.

Even if his plan had been sound, it would have found little favor in an administration which, in Foster Dulles' words, saw Figueres as a "pretty rotten fellow"[63] and praised Somoza as a pillar of virtue. But Berle's plan was naive. How could one expect the governments of Honduras and El Salvador to participate in an enterprise led by Figueres, a man they loathed? Similarly, it was preposterous to imagine that Somoza would assist such an undertaking, or to believe that "some powerful elements in Nicaragua" would dare participate without the dictator's permission. Berle also overlooked the fact that the leaders of the Guatemalan opposition fought not for political democracy, but against social reform; they were, in other words, Somoza's natural allies and Figueres's foes. There was no liberal way to overthrow Arbenz—the road to Guatemala City passed through Managua, not through San José.

In May 1953, a senior Pentagon official, General Richard Partridge, spent forty-eight hours in Guatemala while on an official trip to Central America. Upon his return he wrote a memorandum on the Guatemalan question that was more brief and more cogent than that penned by Berle:

> It appears to me that right now we are holding a middle position between two definite policies, one of which we should choose and start implementing. One policy would be to support Arbenz in making his reforms and insist that in return for our support he use some moderation and eliminate the known Communists from power in his regime. The other policy is to oppose Arbenz seriously with the intention of knocking him and his regime out of power. . . . Acting as we are in between these policies without coming out strongly either one way or another, we are providing Arbenz good propaganda to justify his extreme acts. We are not moving either in the direction of controlling him or of getting rid of him but are simply accepting his activity on his own terms. There is no question but what these drastic reforms which he is implementing do affect the neighboring countries which are only slightly less overdue for reforms of a similar nature. That explains the great concern of the neighboring countries over his activities.[64]

[61] Memo to the Jackson Committee, Mar. 31, 1953, Berle Diary, Apr. 1, 1953, Berle Papers.

[62] Berle Diary, Apr. 1, 1953, ibid.

[63] TelConv (DDE, JFD), Oct. 7, 1953, WF, DDE:DS, Box 5, EL.

[64] Partridge, "Notes On Visit to Four Central American Countries," p. 3, enclosed in Partridge to Cabot, May 20, 1953, NA 714.00/3-2053.

The first policy outlined by General Partridge was out of the question. Even the Truman administration had contemplated a modus vivendi with Arbenz only if he first adopted an anticommunist and pro-American course. The only choice, then, was whether to continue Truman's policy of cold hostility and limited sanctions, or to seek to overthrow Arbenz. In the spring of 1953, Eisenhower's "passivity" vis-à-vis Guatemala was due to very prosaic and transient considerations: the new administration was just settling in after two decades of Democratic presidents, it was preoccupied with ending the Korean War and defining a policy toward the Soviet Union, and it had already embarked on a major covert operation in Iran.

But if the judges were temporarily busy elsewhere, they had already decided that the accused was guilty, and the hour for sentencing was fast approaching. In September 1953, writes John Moors Cabot, Miller's successor as assistant secretary for inter-American affairs, "I went to Bedell Smith and said that I thought that a CIA-organized coup was the only solution [in Guatemala]. He nodded and smiled, and I got the impression that the plan was already underway."[65] Cabot was right: Operation Success—PBSUCCESS—had begun.[66]

The precise date and the exact circumstances of the birth of PBSUCCESS are unknown. It was in the late summer of 1953—most likely in August, when AJAX was either on the verge of fruition, or in the immediate aftermath of its success.[67] The decision was taken with little internal debate and a heartening unanimity among the few policymakers involved. Eisenhower reserved the right to grant or deny final approval before H-hour, but this was a standard procedure for operations of this nature.

The planning of PBSUCCESS "took place with the utmost stealth. Only Eisenhower, the Dulles brothers, and a few other top-level members of the White House, State Department, and Central Intelligence Agency knew that an operation was even being considered, let alone were privy to its details."[68] The Pentagon, which later played a limited but not insignificant role in the Bay of Pigs, was involved neither at the policy nor the operational level; its contribution consisted at most of "some military personnel who were on loan to the CIA—but this was a constant practice."[69]

[65] Cabot, *First Line*, p. 90.

[66] "PB doesn't mean anything. The names of most covert operations have a two letter prefix that is arbitrary." (Interview with Bissell.)

[67] See Immerman, *CIA in Guatemala*, pp. 134–36, and Schlesinger and Kinzer, *Bitter Fruit*, p. 108.

[68] Immerman, *CIA in Guatemala*, p. 133.

[69] Interviews with Bissell (quoted) and Kirkpatrick. In 1963, Thruston Morton, who had been assistant secretary for congressional relations in 1954, was the first Eisenhower administration official to make a public statement confirming U.S. involvement in the overthrow of Arbenz. In his brief account, he exaggerated the role of the Pentagon. ("History: Damn Good and Sure," *Newsweek*.)

The conduct of PBSUCCESS was placed in the hands of the CIA's Directorate of Plans (DDP), which was in charge of covert operations. Within the DDP, "typically, the operation was closely held." A special unit was set up, with "its own communication facilities, financial officers, support people, covert agents, and special authority to requisition confidential funds."[70] The DDP's Western Hemisphere chief, Colonel J. C. King, was "shunted aside," because the Deputy Director of Plans, Frank Wisner, "wanted to run the show. King was very upset."[71] Wisner assumed the direction of PBSUCCESS under the overall control of Allen Dulles. Throughout the life of the operation, approximately ten months, Wisner focused on it with such intensity that he left his deputy, Richard Helms, "more or less in charge of all other things. PBSUCCESS became Wisner's project."[72]

The other side of the CIA, the Directorate of Intelligence, was not involved in PBSUCCESS, "absolutely not." Robert Amory, who as deputy director of intelligence was Wisner's counterpart, was never briefed. He sensed something was afoot, but he knew no details, no timetables. "If I had been captured by Arbenz and tortured to death," he has observed, "I would not have been able to tell them anything that could have done me any good." During PBSUCCESS, the CIA station in Guatemala did report to the Directorate of Intelligence about developments in the country—"but to the exclusion of anything dealing with or referring to the plot to overthrow Arbenz."[73] This was a crippling limitation, as Richard Bissell, who participated in PBSUCCESS and later rose to be deputy director of plans, admits. "With hindsight, one of the major mistakes of my career was my failure to include people from the analytical side in covert operations."[74]

If the analysts of the CIA lacked the "union cards"[75] to work for PBSUCCESS, so did State Department officials, with two major exceptions: Secretary Dulles and Undersecretary Smith. Foster Dulles was, with his brother Allen, a prime mover and enthusiastic supporter of PBSUCCESS, just as he had been of AJAX. As in the case of AJAX, he paid relatively little attention to the operation once the decision to act had been taken.[76] Distracted by his many duties and confident that the undertaking was in good hands (Allen's), he saw his role as briefing Eisenhower and ensuring that the CIA avoided doing anything that might embarrass the government. More intimately involved in PBSUCCESS was

[70] Quotations from Powers, *The Man Who Kept the Secrets*, p. 108, and Immerman, *CIA in Guatemala*, pp. 138–39.

[71] Interviews with Roettinger (quoted), Bissell, and Helms.

[72] Interviews with Bissell (quoted) and Helms.

[73] Interview with Amory.

[74] Interview with Bissell.

[75] "The intelligence people of the CIA are not operators; they don't have the union cards, so to speak." (Interview with Amory.)

[76] Interviews with Bissell and Amory.

Undersecretary Smith. "He was, at high level, the immediate contact of the CIA with the State Department; Wisner dealt with him on many issues without the need to go up all the way to Foster Dulles."[77]

The rest of the State Department was kept in the dark. The department's senior official for Latin America, John Moors Cabot, knew of the plot but played no active role. "An officer in ARA," he writes, "was designated liaison with other agencies involved in developing the plans. For the rest of my tour as Assistant Secretary I was in constant touch with this officer, but I never knew the details of the planned operation, nor did I want to know them; my principal concern was to keep secret any United States involvement in the projected coup."[78] The official in question, Raymond Leddy, "could clam up very well," remembers a colleague. Leddy, who was the officer in charge of Central American and Panamanian affairs, acted as the CIA's day-to-day contact in the State Department; "they dealt with him on those issues that did not require the immediate attention of Beedle Smith or Foster Dulles."[79]

In March 1954 Cabot was replaced by Henry Holland, a well-connected Texas lawyer. "Cabot," notes Deputy Assistant Secretary Robert Woodward, "left his job without ever telling me anything about PBSUCCESS, though he was fully aware of it since August or September 1953. All I was told by Cabot was that Leddy was working on something confidential (something pertaining to Central America and Guatemala), and that I should not bother with it."

In the first week of April, Holland went to Woodward. " 'Bob,' Holland said to me, 'I've just been told about a plan to overthrow Arbenz. I'm tempted to resign. Take two or three hours to think it over, and come back and tell me what you think I should do.' A few hours later, I urged Holland: 'Don't resign. Try to buck it. This CIA plot will destroy our nonintervention policy and throw us back to 1931–32, before Roosevelt's Good Neighbor Policy.' I doubted that the plan would succeed, and that, if successful, the U.S. role could be hidden; I also questioned whether the extent of the communist threat in Guatemala justified taking the risk. The next day Holland told me: 'I spoke with [Foster] Dulles; he's given me until the end of the year to come up with other ways to take care of the communist problem in Guatemala.' "[80]

Woodward had been tested, found wanting and fed a lie. Years later, when told of the incident, Bissell remarked: "This is common practice when an officer is opposed to this kind of plan, in order to avoid leaks. Although in Woodward's case, he was an honorable man and would have kept silent."[81]

On one point Holland had spoken the truth: he was opposed to the CIA plot

---

[77] Interview with Bissell.
[78] Cabot, *First Line*, pp. 90–91.
[79] Quotations from interviews with Jamison and Bissell.
[80] Interview with Woodward.
[81] Interview with Bissell.

against Arbenz. PBSUCCESS, notes Bissell, "was Holland's first encounter with a major covert operation, and he thought it was not the way to proceed. As a result, he was regarded by Wisner and others in the Directorate of Plans as one of our opponents within the State Department." After Arbenz fell, "Holland changed completely and became a very strong supporter of the CIA and of covert operations. This has happened to quite a lot of men in the State Department."[82] Holland's initial opposition meant, however, that he was excluded from the closeknit group who oversaw PBSUCCESS.

The planners of PBSUCCESS had no delusions about the Guatemalan opposition. Their attention was riveted on the army. "The Army is the key to the stability of the Arbenz regime," an intelligence report had underlined in June 1953,

> and could effect a rapid and decisive change in the Guatemalan political situation if it were to take concerted action. Although a quick change of attitude is always possible, there is no present reason to doubt the continued loyalty of the Army high command and of most of the Army officer corps to Arbenz. The Army would be unlikely to take revolutionary action [against Arbenz] unless the high command or a substantial body of unit commanders became convinced that their personal security and well-being were threatened. . . . The Communists have little power of their own.[83]

From its inception, PBSUCCESS was based on one premise: only the Guatemalan army could overthrow Arbenz. Psychological warfare would be the CIA's main weapon to convince the Guatemalan officers that their security and well-being were at stake, and thus prod them toward treason. As part of this effort, the United States would attempt to isolate Guatemala and wave the specter of multilateral sanctions. In the process, the civilian forces loyal to the regime would be demoralized and the civilian opposition would gather strength.

The Guatemalan exiles were to serve as the spark[84] if the army failed to rise against Arbenz on its own. At no moment did PBSUCCESS assume that the exiles would be able to defeat the Guatemalan army. The purpose of the invasion—coming after months of psychological destabilization and supported, it was hoped, by an active fifth column organized by the CIA—was to confront the Guatemalan officers with the stark choice: they could defeat the rebels and face the wrath of the United States, or they could turn against Arbenz and save themselves. The threat would be credible only if Washington had persuaded

[82] Interview with Bissell.

[83] Division of Research for Latin America, "Effect upon Guatemala of Arms Procurement by El Salvador, Honduras, and Nicaragua," Special Paper no. 21, June 12, 1953, pp. 2 and 4, enclosed in Armstrong to Cabot, June 16, 1953, NA 714.00.

[84] The term *spark* was used in separate interviews by DCM Krieg and by Taracena.

the officers that the exiles were U.S. proxies whose defeat would trigger a U.S. invasion.

President Eisenhower and Secretary Dulles wanted to protect the image of the United States abroad, particularly in Latin America. Just a few weeks before Eisenhower assumed the presidency, a CIA National Intelligence Estimate had stressed that Latin America was threatened by "the pressure of exaggerated nationalism," and that this trend might eventually "affect Hemispheric solidarity and U.S. security interests"; the same warning was repeated by Allen Dulles at a February 18, 1953, meeting of the National Security Council (NSC), and in mid-March, NSC 144/1 stated that the United States must "avoid the appearance of unilateral action" in the internal affairs of the Latin American republics.[85]

Thus, there was "a paradox at the heart of PBSUCCESS," a paradox that was resolved by a figleaf. "The figleaf was designed to deny U.S. involvement," muses Bissell, "yet the success of the operation hinged on convincing the Guatemalans that the U.S. was indeed involved."[86] This concern for appearances is evident in the handling of the president's press conference that was held the day before the exiles were set to invade Guatemala. Prior to the conference, Allen Dulles sent the press secretary, James Hagerty, a "Draft of Possible Press Conference Statement on Guatemala" that was couched in very harsh language. In response, Holland fired off an angry memo: "I most vigorously oppose the use of this statement." Holland feared that the use of such language by the president just before D-Day would strip away the figleaf. "I have reiterated . . . again and again to every Latin American Ambassador," he noted, "that the United States is undertaking to solve the problem [of communism in Guatemala] without unilateral intervention, whether political or economic, in Guatemalan affairs." Secretary Dulles decided in Holland's favor. Eisenhower, he reminded Allen, must not give the impression that he was issuing "an open call for revolution." Allen agreed and the secretary told Hagerty the following day "to avoid the implication we were seeking a revolution there."[87]

[85] Quotations from: "Conditions and Trends in Latin America Affecting U.S. Security," NIE-70, Dec. 12, 1952, p. 9, Truman Papers, President's Secretary's File, Intelligence File, Box 254, TL; "Discussion at the 132 Meeting of the National Security Council on Wednesday, February 18, 1953," Feb. 19, 1953, WF, NSC Series, Box 4, EL; "United States Objectives and Courses of Action with Respect to Latin America," NSC 144/1, Mar. 18, 1953, *FRUS*, 1952–1954, 4:7.

[86] Interview with Bissell. In 1952, a U.S. official had posed the dilemma starkly: "We must be careful in our own minds to distinguish between intervention and being caught at it." (Hill to Ambassador, Oct. 2, 1952, p. 3, RG84 CF, Box 15, NA-S.)

[87] Quotations from: Holland to JFD, June 15, 1954, *FRUS*, 1952–1954, 4:1168; TelConv (JFD, AWD), June 15, 1954, 6:24 p.m., DP: TCS, Box 2, EL; TelConv (JFD, Hagerty), June 16, 1954, 9:37 a.m., DP, JFD:CS, Box 8, EL. AWD, "Draft of

As would become clear as PBSUCCESS gathered momentum, it was not difficult to maintain the fiction. The governments of Western Europe and Latin America were willing to overlook U.S. violations of international law, as long as a pretense of compliance was maintained. In the United States, ignorance, anticommunism, and self-righteousness blended seamlessly to generate the comforting conviction in the political and intellectual elites, in the press, in the Congress, and in the public at large that Guatemala was the aggressor and the United States, the long-suffering victim.

PBSUCCESS was hatched at a time when the Guatemalan opposition was particularly weak. The arrests that followed the Salamá uprising had dealt a heavy blow to the various cliques of plotters; the agrarian reform was strengthening the government in the countryside; the military showed no signs of disloyalty. *New York Times* correspondent Sidney Gruson wrote in late July:

> To an observer revisiting Guatemala after six months, the overriding factor in the political situation is the disintegration that has occurred among the organized opposition. . . . What remains of it has lost what little confidence it once may have had. The accepted thing seems to be . . . to hope that somehow from somewhere something will happen to salvage the cause. This wishful thinking that someone else will eventually do the job of opposing the Communists is an old fault of the Guatemalan opposition.[88]

The exiles were still plotting, and United Fruit still gave them encouragement and, apparently, some material assistance.[89] But the region's strongmen were tiring of the exiles' incompetence, their perennial squabbles, and the gulf between their wild promises and pitiful performances. Trujillo now rebuffed his protegé, Colonel Roberto Barrios, complaining that "every time something started there were twenty people who wanted to be president after the uprising, and none who would cooperate with the other nineteen." Trujillo had concluded that "the only way the [Guatemalan] government would be overthrown was if the United States did it." This was also Somoza's view.[90] "When the United States decided to help us, in the fall of 1953, we were isolated," recalls a close aide of Castillo Armas. "Somoza was helping us very little. He would never have dared to act on his own. He needed the OK

Possible Press Conference Statement on Guatemala" is enclosed in Holland to JFD, June 15, 1954, *FRUS*, 1952–1954, 4:1168. See also Hagerty Diary, June 14–16, 1954, EL.

[88] "Anti-Reds Give Up Guatemalan Role," *NYT*, Aug. 1, 1953, p. 3.

[89] See Fisher to Mann, "Alleged Implication of Mr. Samuel Zemurray in Illicit Arms Traffic," May 22, 1953, NA 714.00, and Keay to Belmont, "Possible Anti-Communist Revolution in Guatemala," June 2, 1953.

[90] Hill, Memo, Nov. 3, 1953 (quoted) and MemoConv (Montenegro, Peurifoy, Krieg), Nov. 6, 1953. Both enclosed in Krieg to Leddy, Nov. 10, 1953, NA 714.00.

and the participation of the United States. And Honduras had done nothing for us."[91]

Washington's decision to move against Arbenz raised Somoza's spirits. PBSUCCESS called for a small Liberation army to be organized and trained in Nicaragua. It would eventually move into Honduras, which would serve as the springboard for the invasion. A fifth column of saboteurs, also trained in Nicaragua, would be infiltrated into Guatemala before D-Day. The invasion would begin no later than June 1954, that is, before the onset of the rainy season. Trujillo was left on the sidelines. Lacking a border with Guatemala, the Dominican Republic had little to contribute to PBSUCCESS. It is doubtful that the Dominican dictator was even informed of the plot.

In August 1953, Washington asked the embassy in Guatemala to suggest someone to lead a movement against Arbenz. (The question was framed in hypothetical terms.) "We decided," recalls DCM Krieg, "that among poor starters Castillo Armas was probably the best."[92]

Years later, in his autobiography, Castillo Armas's main rival, General Ydígoras Fuentes, sought to explain why the Eisenhower administration had spurned a man of his ability:

> A former executive of the United Fruit Company, now retired, Mr. Walter Turnbull, came to see me with two gentlemen whom he introduced as agents of the CIA. They said that I was a popular figure in Guatemala and that they wanted to lend their assistance to overthrow Arbenz. When I asked their conditions for the assistance I found them unacceptable. Among other things, I was to promise to favor the United Fruit Company and the International Railways of Central America; to destroy the railroad workers labor union; to suspend claims against Great Britain for the Belize territory; to establish a strong-arm government, on the style of Ubico. Further, I was to pay back every cent that was invested in the undertaking on the basis of accounts that would be presented to me afterwards. I told them that I would have to be given time to prepare my conditions, as theirs seemed to me to be unfavorable to Guatemala. They withdrew, promising to return; I never saw them again.[93]

Ydígoras' explanation is straightforward: he was passed over because of his unbending nationalism; Castillo Armas must have been more pliant.

Many writers have accepted Ydígoras's words at face value. Yet as president of Guatemala (1958–1963), Ydígoras was subservient to American companies, undemocratic, and corrupt.[94] Why then believe a self-serving state-

---

[91] Interview with Taracena.

[92] Interview with Krieg.

[93] Ydígoras Fuentes, *My War with Communism*, pp. 49–50.

[94] Jonas calls Ydígoras "a corrupt *ubiquista* with close ties to Dominican dictator Trujillo" yet accepts his claim that he refused the CIA/UFCO offer. ("Guatemala," p. 195. See also Jonas and Tobis, *Guatemala*, p. 68, and Schlesinger and Kinzer, *Bitter Fruit*, pp. 120–21.)

ment so out of character with the man? His autobiography—a rambling apologia remarkable only for its distortions and lies—is hardly a reliable source. His entire record indicates that, had he been offered the leadership of the crusade, Ydígoras would have accepted any conditions.

Castillo Armas was a more attractive candidate. He had been an excellent cadet and a highly competent officer, whereas Ydígoras was notorious as one of Ubico's subservient generals. In Arbenz's words, Castillo Armas "performed with great bravery" in the 1944 uprising against Ponce; Ydígoras's role, noted a U.S. official, had been "ambiguous and odd."[95] On July 18, 1949, a demoralized Castillo Armas failed to join the revolt of his *Aranista* friends, but his lonely uprising of November 1950 and his dramatic escape from prison restored his reputation for bravery.

Ydígoras had never risked his life, for any cause. He was a *bon vivant* and, in the words of a U.S. official who knew him well, "as crooked as they come."[96] Castillo Armas, on the other hand, was a fanatic. He sought to avenge Arana's death and to atone for his failure to fight in July 1949. Ambition, anticommunism, and the frustrations of exile propelled him forward. He was ready to side with anyone who wanted to overthrow Arbenz: the landed elite, the "tropical dictators," the United States—anyone, as long as they would anoint him Arbenz's successor. He was not distracted by a social conscience. As president he would tolerate corruption and champion the status quo. And yet he was courageous, not unintelligent, honest, and able to command the devotion of a small band of followers.

Furthermore, Castillo Armas was the favorite of Archbishop Rossell y Arellano and of Somoza. Ydígoras was merely one of Trujillo's protegés, and PBSUCCESS had cast the Dominican dictator in a supporting role, giving Somoza the lead. Thus, between the two aspiring and pliant *caudillos*, Washington's choice was eminently sensible.[97]

[95] Quotations from Arbenz, "Habla Arbenz," p. 122, and AmEm Tegucigalpa, Erwin to DOS, no. 181, Nov. 5, 1953, p. 3, NA 714.00.

[96] Interview with Jamison.

[97] According to Immerman, many CIA officials preferred the lawyer Juan Córdova Cerna, a prominent member of the landed elite, to Castillo Armas, but a routine medical examination revealed that Córdova Cerna had cancer. (*CIA in Guatemala*, p. 142; see also Phillips, *Night Watch*, p. 53.) This is highly questionable on several grounds: (1) Immerman's only source is the entertaining but unreliable Howard Hunt; (2) Córdova Cerna was active and in good health when the CIA chose Castillo Armas and remained active throughout the following year; U.S. reports attest to his vitality and ambition, and say nothing of his health (see for instance *FRUS*, 1952–1954, 4:1219, 1223–24); (3) Córdova Cerna was a civilian while the focus of PBSUCCESS was the military; (4) Córdova Cerna had been an attorney for United Fruit, and the U.S. government had no desire to hand ammunition to those who claimed that its quarrel with

On September 20, 1953, Castillo Armas wrote to Somoza from Tegucigalpa: "I have been informed by our friends here that the government of the North . . . has decided to let us develop our plans. Because of the importance of this decision, I immediately sent confidential messages so that it could be confirmed to me directly. Nevertheless up to now I have not received any reply which apparently can be interpreted as confirming the foregoing."[98]

A few days later, recalls his aide, Taracena de la Cerda, the CIA told Castillo Armas that he was the chosen one.[99] On October 15, in a letter to Somoza's son Tachito, Castillo Armas exulted: "Our work with our friends from the North has ended in our complete triumph. . . . We will soon enter into a very active phase which will lead inevitably to the victory that we all desire." The letter ended with warm thanks for the "generous support that we have received from those men who understand the nature of our struggle, especially from your Dad and you, who have been our true protectors in this difficult crusade."[100]

The selection of Castillo Armas to be the future liberator of Guatemala did not stop his rivals from importuning U.S. officials. Some were unaware of PBSUCCESS; others knew that something was afoot and that Castillo Armas was the anointed, but found it difficult to bow to the inevitable. Reports by U.S. officials make for amusing reading. José Luis Arenas, a member of the Guatemalan Congress, told DCM Krieg that he had a scheme to overthrow Arbenz that was "sure to work." Wasting no time on details, Arenas "inquired without ambiguity" if the embassy would provide him with $200,000 "to do the job." Upon being politely turned down, he asked whether he could not receive at least a "down payment."[101]

Even Ponce, Ubico's unlucky successor, surfaced from obscurity to press his claims. In January 1954, he appeared twice at the U.S. embassy in Managua. He was, he explained, "still the legal president of Guatemala," the only one, he insisted, with "legal and moral rights to the Presidency." The Guatemalan people and the Guatemalan army "would follow no one but him." His plans were ready, though he preferred not to discuss them in detail "at this time." If the United States would provide money to buy weapons, he would return to Guatemala "among the cheers of the multitude" and oust Arbenz.[102]

Guatemala was rooted in bananas. On Córdova Cerna, see also Villagrán Kramer, "Los pactos," July 12, 1987, p. 11.

[98] Guatemala, *La democracia amenazada*, pp. 92–93.

[99] Interview with Taracena.

[100] Guatemala, *La democracia amenazada*, p. 46.

[101] Quotations from Krieg to Fisher, Nov. 24, 1953, p. 1, NA 714.00, and from the enclosed MemoConv (Arenas, Ocaña, Krieg), Nov. 18, 1953, p. 2. See also Leddy to Fisher, Jan. 5, 1954.

[102] AmEm Managua, Welch to DOS, no. 272, Jan. 12, 1954, p. 1, NA 714.00.

None of the supplicants was as persistent as Ydígoras. To the very end, he harassed U.S. officials, waxing eloquent about Castillo Armas's sins and his own virtues; his followers did the same. Ydígoras's "henchmen," a June 1, 1954, State Department memo noted, "frequently call at the Department pleading for U.S. support, the latest being one Cesar Lanuza . . . on May 17. The *Ydigoristas* claim to have a large underground organization in Guatemala with good army connections, but they have thus far shown themselves totally ineffective in opposition to the present government and with the passage of time their prestige has steadily declined."[103] Ydígoras was indefatigable in his efforts to unseat Castillo Armas, but the other aspiring *caudillos* gradually fell in line, with more or less grace, behind Washington's man.

While searching for a Liberator, in the summer of 1953 the planners of PBSUC-CESS also sought a new U.S. ambassador for Guatemala—a team player. They found him in John Peurifoy. Peurifoy's predecessor, Rudolph Schoenfeld, was a career official who had become a harsh critic of the Arbenz administration. ("The Communist power-drive in Guatemala has reached an advanced state of infiltration," he asserted in his debriefing.) Schoenfeld, however, lacked the inclination and the training to participate effectively in a major covert operation. He was, Eleanor Lansing Dulles told her brother Foster, "first class . . . intelligent, intellectual . . . but . . . a bit cautious."[104]

In October 1953, as Peurifoy arrived in Guatemala, the local CIA station began to expand rapidly.[105] The rest of the embassy staff was not informed about a covert operation against Arbenz. It was only in February or March 1954 that Peurifoy told DCM Krieg and a few other embassy officials (including the military attachés and members of the military missions) that a plot was underway.[106]

Peurifoy told them that he knew only the broadest outlines of PBSUCCESS. In fact, he was "very involved."[107] Before he left for Guatemala, the CIA

---

[103] Burr to Holland, June 1, 1954. For Lanuza's May 17 visit, see MemoConv (Lanuza, Woodward, Fisher), May 17, 1954, NA 714.00. After claiming that Castillo Armas was revealing the names of army officers who favored Ydígoras to Arbenz, Lanuza ended with a parting shot: "It was obvious" that in his 1951 escape from jail, Castillo Armas "had bought his way out and not dug a tunnel as alleged"—an irrelevant detail to his American audience.

[104] Quotations from "Debriefing of Ambassador Rudolph E. Schoenfeld, October 28, 1953," *FRUS*, 1952–1954, 4:1087, and TelConv (JFD, Eleanor L. Dulles), Aug. 1, 1953, 4:35 p.m., DP, JFD:CS, Box 4, EL. Schoenfeld had presented his credentials to Arbenz on Apr. 24, 1951. Since the Patterson incident, the United States had been represented by a chargé.

[105] Interview with Bissell.

[106] Interview with Krieg; confirmed by interview with Bissell.

[107] Interview with Bissell.

"made certain that it would have a direct line to him at all times"; to avoid leaks, the agency communicated with Peurifoy through " 'back channels.' Once received by the CIA Guatemala station, the messages would be hand-carried or conveyed verbally to the Ambassador by Birch O'Neil, the CIA station chief."[108]

He was no suave diplomat, the "pistol packing" Peurifoy.[109] Indeed, wrote an admiring journalist, Flora Lewis, it was "jarringly wrong" to call him a diplomat at all. His loud checkered shirts, and his preference for a "jaunty, bright-green Borsalino . . . in place of the diplomat's black homburg," matched his ideas of diplomatic intercourse. "He is much more the politician than the diplomat," Lewis remarked, "but he is striking at it because he goes politicking around foreign countries instead of at home among the voters. "[110]

Peurifoy came to Guatemala from Greece, where at age forty-three he had landed his first ambassadorial appointment. His colorful career had included stints as a Capitol Hill elevator operator and as a salesperson at Woodward and Lothrop. Once in the State Department, he demonstrated that he was an effective organizer and administrator.[111] In 1950 he was sent to Greece, where the civil war had just ended with the communists' defeat, to shore up the corrupt conservative government and to prevent even a hint of communist resurgence. He began in characteristic fashion: "He told dignified old Sophocles Venizelos, then foreign minister and deputy premier, 'Look Soph, you call me Jack. Let's talk frankly about all this.' "[112] He intervened so brazenly in the country's internal affairs that even the meek Greek government felt compelled, on one occasion, to complain publicly that decisions in purely domestic matters should be left "to the Greek people and government."[113] Throughout his tenure in Greece, Peurifoy worked closely with the embassy's CIA station, "proving himself a most willing and able ally."[114]

This was the ambassador whom the planners of PBSUCCESS had chosen for

[108] Schlesinger and Kinzer, *Bitter Fruit*, p. 135.

[109] The expression is from a poem that Peurifoy's wife, Betty Jane, composed to celebrate the overthrow of Arbenz. See *Time*, July 26, 1954, p. 34.

[110] Flora Lewis, "Ambassador Extraordinary: John Peurifoy," *NYT Magazine*, July 18, 1954, p. 9. Lewis's piece is a model of good taste when compared with other feature articles on Peurifoy that appeared in the U.S. press after Arbenz's overthrow. See, for instance, Donald Grant, "Ambassador John E. Peurifoy," *St. Louis Post-Dispatch*, July 11, 1954, C1, and Ralph de Toledano, "Unconventional Ambassador," *American Mercury*, Oct. 1954, pp. 28–32.

[111] For Peurifoy's background, in addition to the sources cited in n. 110 above, see Schlesinger and Kinzer, *Bitter Fruit*, pp. 132–35; Immerman, *CIA in Guatemala*, pp. 137–38; Eisenhower Records Central File, OF, Box 163, EL.

[112] Lewis, "Ambassador Extraordinary" (see n. 110 above), p. 26.

[113] Couloumbis, *Greek Political Reaction*, pp. 53–68, quoted from p. 55.

[114] Immerman, *CIA in Guatemala*, p. 137.

Guatemala: a man used to upbraiding the officials of a client government, a doer rather than a thinker, a militant anticommunist, an ambitious career officer. His loud, aggressive personality, so different from the aloof politeness of Schoenfeld, was an asset. He was sent to frighten. In the words of a Guatemalan colonel who turned against Arbenz, Peurifoy was "an abusive, arrogant ambassador—but this was very effective: he scared a lot of officers."[115]

Peurifoy was preceded by his reputation as the high-handed proconsul who had presided over the anticommunist witch hunt in Greece. Sidney Gruson, the well-informed *New York Times* correspondent, reported: "It is generally expected in Guatemala that his advent means a change in the asserted passivity with which the United States has watched the growth of the Communists' influence to the point where, at least to the outsider, they seem to be masters of the country in all but name."[116] Peurifoy immediately vindicated these expectations. On the very day of his arrival, he had a long interview with Foreign Minister Raúl Osegueda. He did not suggest, as he had done with old Venizelos in Greece, that they be on a first-name basis. Rather, he immediately raised the issue of communist influence and all but called Osegueda a liar to his face. For his performance he was warmly praised from Washington by Leddy, the PBSUCCESS man at the State Department.[117] In a different vein, the PGT's daily *Tribuna Popular* wrote:

> The new U.S. ambassador, Señor Peurifoy, has arrived; like the ancient gods, he has been preceded by flashes of lightning and the rumbling of thunder. It is easy to divine why a man who has been in Greece—more as the mastermind of its struggle against the communists and Greek patriots than as an ambassador—has been sent to our country. The State Department does not need men like Peurifoy in Honduras, El Salvador or Nicaragua. These countries are led by men who are the lap dogs of Yankee monopolies.[118]

The embassy closely monitored the impact of Peurifoy's arrival. He presented his credentials on November 4 "amid a flurry of press and official speculation concerning United States intentions toward Guatemala." Two weeks later, Peurifoy himself observed: "I have psychological advantage of being new and government feels I have come to Guatemala to use the big stick. We have been letting them stew." The mere arrival of Peurifoy, stressed DCM Krieg, had

> provided a milepost for the smaller politically-conscious element of Guatemala to reassess the internal situation and set off the greatest wave of press and public spec-

[115] Interview with González Siguí.

[116] "U.S. To Re-Examine Guatemalan Role," *NYT*, Nov. 8, 1953, p. 9.

[117] See Peurifoy to Leddy, Oct. 30, 1953; Krieg to DOS, no. 378, Nov. 2, 1953, NA 611.14, and enclosed MemoConv (Osegueda, Peurifoy, Krieg), Oct. 29, 1953; Leddy to Peurifoy, Nov. 6, 1953, NA 611.14.

[118] "El nuevo embajador yanqui" (edit.), *Tribuna Popular*, Nov. 11, 1953, p. 5.

ulation in recent times as to what the U.S. would do about Communist influences in Guatemala. . . . The more conservative elements naturally seized upon the change of Chief of Mission as a portent that forceful action by the United States was imminent, as they had previously done when President Eisenhower succeeded President Truman. But on this occasion persons formerly sympathetic to the [Arbenz] Administration joined in by privately complaining that unbridled Communism was imperiling the country. In the past two weeks . . . this embassy has heard from . . . informed sources . . . that many Administration politicians are dissatisfied with the situation. . . . the non Communist politicians feel . . . that they are on a roller coaster over which they have no control but from which it would be dangerous to jump.[119]

Peurifoy had one serious conversation with Arbenz, a six-hour dinner on December 16, 1953. Only the ambassador, the president and their wives were present. Since Peurifoy knew only two Spanish words ("muchos [sic] gracias"), Doña María served as interpreter. (Arbenz, she notes, "understood English pretty well, but it gave him more time if I translated.")[120] Peurifoy played the role of the inquisitor, besieging his host with precise questions about communist influence in Guatemala; Arbenz, on the defensive, offered lame responses.

Two days later, Peurifoy sent Secretary Dulles a five-page report about the dinner. "I am definitely convinced that if the President is not a Communist, he will certainly do until one comes along," he concluded.[121] Thereafter, Peurifoy's contacts with Arbenz were purely formal, as were his contacts with the foreign ministry. Relations between the embassy and Guatemalan officials, already cold under Schoenfeld, were now icy.[122]

There was, however, one exception. U.S. officials intensified their contacts with the Guatemalan army. The State Department had decided in early 1953 to maintain the military missions in Guatemala unless Arbenz asked for their removal. Peurifoy endorsed this decision. The "army is anti-Communist . . . day may not be too far off when we will need friends where it will count," he wrote in a November 19 dispatch to the State Department. Despite occasional complaints by naive congressmen, who could not understand why such a favor should be bestowed on a procommunist regime, the military missions re-

[119] Quotations from: *JW* 45, Nov. 6, 1953, I:1–2; Peurifoy to SecState, no. 124, Nov. 19, 1953, NA 611.14; Krieg to DOS, no. 427, Nov. 18, 1953, pp. 1–2, NA 714.00.

[120] Interview with María de Arbenz. (Peurifoy's ignorance of Spanish was confirmed by interviews with the following embassy officials: Krieg, Wardlaw, and Wright.) For a discussion of the meeting between Arbenz and Peurifoy, see below, pp. 363–64.

[121] MemoConv (Pres. Arbenz, Mrs. Arbenz, Amb. Peurifoy, Mrs. Peurifoy), Dec. 17, 1953, p. 5, enclosed in Peurifoy to DOS, no. 522, Dec. 18, 1953, NA 611.14. An edited version of this document appears in *FRUS*, 1952–1954, 4:1091–93.

[122] Interviews with María de Arbenz, Krieg, Wardlaw, Osegueda, and Toriello.

mained in the country; they were "in constant touch with the Guatemalan officers," whom they urged to betray Arbenz.[123]

In the same month that Peurifoy arrived in Guatemala, two major developments added to the foreboding atmosphere. On October 6, the State Department suddenly asked the Council of the Organization of American States to include a new item, "Intervention of International Communism in the American Republics," in the agenda of the Tenth Inter-American Conference, to be held in March 1954.[124] Guatemala, the only country to vote against this request, was the target, as everyone understood.[125]

Also in October, U.S. officials began a sustained campaign of public denunciations of the Arbenz administraton. Assistant Secretary Cabot launched the first broadside. He assailed the Guatemalan authorities for "openly playing the Communist game," and asked ominously whether the "activities of the international Communist conspiracy to destroy free governments are prejudicing the independence" of Guatemala and its neighbors. Senator Wiley, chairman of the Senate Foreign Affairs Committee, added his own fulminations to the growing chorus.[126] There had been earlier attacks by the U.S. press, the Congress, and the State Department, but they had not been as systematic and virulent as they were from October 1953 until Arbenz fell.

It was all part of PBSUCCESS. The United States Information Agency (USIA) and the CIA helped to write and disseminate articles attacking the Arbenz regime.[127] Many of these articles were reprinted in the Guatemalan opposition press as proof that U.S. patience was fast coming to an end. "These . . . outstanding, courageous newspapers . . . will reprint anything against the Government," Peurifoy explained to the House Committee on Foreign Affairs

---

[123] Quotations from Peurifoy to SecState, no. 124, Nov. 19, 1953, NA 611.14, and from interview with Col. González Siguí. Peurifoy vacillated on this issue: see Peurifoy to SecState, Dec. 23, 1953, *FRUS, 1952–1954,* 4:1094; and Peurifoy to Fisher, May 24, 1954, NA 714.58.

[124] OAS, *Annals,* pp. 293–302.

[125] The vote came on Nov. 10. For the position of the Guatemalan government, see "Defensa de la soberanía," *DCA,* Nov. 12, 1953, p. 1; "Democracia e intervención" (edit.), *DCA,* Nov. 13, 1953, p. 3; "Pueblo y gobierno solidamente únidos en defensa de la soberanía," *DCA,* Nov. 30, 1953, p. 4; Guerra Borges, "El voto de Guatemala en la OEA," *Tribuna Popular,* Nov. 14, Nov. 17, and Nov. 18, 1953, p. 5.

[126] See Cabot, *Toward Our Common American Destiny,* pp. 41–60, 82–121 (quoted from p. 88), and "Wiley Scores Guatemala," *NYT,* Oct. 17, 1953, p. 13. For a more detailed account of Wiley's speech, see "Reds Gaining in Guatemala," *Milwaukee Journal,* Oct. 16, 1953, p. 4.

[127] On USIA, see "Report on Actions Taken by the United States Information Agency in the Guatemalan Situation," July 27, 1954, *FRUS, 1952–1954,* 4:1212–17.

in January 1954 as he urged the congressmen to make more speeches lambasting the Arbenz administration.[128]

In the same month, Peurifoy intensified the scare campaign. "Public opinion in the U.S.," he told *Time*, "might force us to take some measures to prevent Guatemala from falling into the lap of international Communism. We cannot permit a Soviet republic to be established between Texas and the Panama Canal."[129] In Guatemala, Peurifoy's statement was understood by all as a threat of military intervention. ("If the situation in Guatemala continues to deteriorate, the ultimate possibility of unilateral U.S. action cannot be ruled out," *Time* had added.)[130] The fears were hardly assuaged, or the hopes dimmed, by Peurifoy's half-hearted claim that he had been misquoted. "The statements attributed by *Time* to Ambassador Peurifoy," an embassy note stated, "were taken out of context and without authorization. They are not a fair representation of the ambassador's point of view. . . . The ambassador did not mean to imply that the Pan-American concern about communism in Guatemala need necessarily precipitate unilateral action by the United States."[131]

As Gruson later reported, the incident "only confirmed the worst fears of Guatemalan officials that Mr. Peurifoy's appointment was the forerunner of energetic United States action against them."[132] Marroquín Rojas patiently drove the point home:

Our foreign minister has officially accepted Ambassador Peurifoy's explanation of his interview in *Time*. But Dr. Osegueda knows that a magazine like *Time*, published in a country where lies are severely punished, would not falsify the words that it put so emphatically in Peurifoy's mouth. There is no doubt that Peurifoy said what *Time* printed, and there is no doubt that he was expressing the opinion of the White House, the Congress, and the Pentagon. How could the leaders of Guatemala imagine that the United States would tolerate a nest of enemies on its very doorstep? It would be absurd; indeed another country . . . would already have sent in the troops. To argue otherwise, and to spout about our "sovereignty" is childish. It is naive. Germany, powerful even though defeated, is still occupied, and so is Japan—and we will be too, we poor fools who don't even produce fireworks, much less the ammunition for a token resistance.[133]

[128] U.S. Congress, *HCFA*, pp. 481 (quoted), 468, 477.
[129] "The Problem of Guatemala," *Time*, Jan. 11, 1954, p. 27.
[130] Ibid.
[131] "Nota del Embajador Peurifoy," *La Hora*, Jan. 13, 1954, p. 1.
[132] "Guatemala Story of Plot Scouted," *NYT*, Jan. 31, 1954, p. 13. See also Osegueda, *Operación Guatemala*, pp. 202–12.
[133] Marroquín Rojas, "Y usted: ¿Qué deduce, señor ministro?" *La Hora*, Jan. 14, 1954, pp. 1, 10.

In the following weeks, Marroquín Rojas hammered away at the same theme. The principle of nonintervention would not inhibit the United States; the Americans did not hesitate to intervene militarily when they deemed it necessary; legal niceties would not restrain them.[134] As if in confirmation, two weeks after Peurifoy's *Time* interview, the Arbenz administration exposed a plot against it abetted by the United States.

In late September 1953, a man by the name of Isaac Delgado had approached Francisco Morazán, an aide of Arbenz. Delgado, who was Panama's commercial attaché in Managua, moonlighted as a secret courier for Castillo Armas. Was the Guatemalan government interested, he inquired, in his services?

Indeed, the government was very interested. Over the next few months, Delgado performed well as a double agent; among the many documents he sold were Castillo Armas's September 20 and October 15 letters to the Somozas, with their damning references to the government and friends from the North.[135]

But in January 1954, Delgado's lucrative career abruptly ended, as the Guatemalan government decided to publish the documents he had stolen. It was time, Arbenz and his advisers had concluded, to seize the initiative. "This decision," recalls PGT leader Guerra Borges, "was connected to our strategy for the Caracas conference." The publication of Delgado's incriminating material would unmask the aggressor and provoke indignation throughout Latin America. At Caracas, Washington's attempt to impose sanctions on Guatemala would be blocked.[136]

On January 21, the Guatemalan police arrested a former army major, Enrique Trinidad Oliva. This was a "severe blow," opposition sources told the U.S. embassy, since Oliva was a "key figure" of the Castillo Armas group in the country.[137] Over the next five days, two dozen plotters were detained. On

[134] See esp. *La Hora* articles: "El perrito del señor embajador," Jan. 16, 1954, p. 3; "Pues ni la realidad los convence," Jan. 19, 1954, p. 3; "Un comunista que invoca a Dios," Mar. 15, 1954, p. 1.

[135] Interviews with Fortuny, Guerra Borges, and Toriello. Delgado's role was first described in "125 hombres iniciaron la invasión a Guatemala," *La Nación*, San José, July 7, 1954, p. 1, and "Vivo o muerto se busca al nica Isaac Delgado," *La Hora*, July 22, 1954, p. 1. See also: Krieg to SecState, no. 250, Jan. 26, 1954, NA 714.00; Krieg to DOS, no. 643, Jan. 27, 1954, NA 714.00; L.A.H.A., *Así se gestó la Liberación*, p. 166; Selser, *El Guatemalazo*, pp. 101–3.

[136] Interviews with Guerra Borges (quoted), Fortuny, and Toriello. Toriello, who became foreign minister in January 1954, was involved in the decision to publish the documents.

[137] Krieg to SecState, no. 234, NA 714.00 (quoted); "Jeep que transportaba granadas de mano capturado," *DCA*, p. 1; "Exhibición personal del mayor Enrique Oliva," *El I*, p. 1. All Jan. 22, 1954.

January 28, the government announced that a press conference would be held the following day, at 10 a.m.; telegrams had already been sent to invite foreign journalists.[138]

"COUNTERREVOLUTIONARY PLOT," was the title splashed across the front page of the government daily on January 29. Below were several of Delgado's documents, including Castillo Armas's September 20 and October 15 letters to the Somozas.[139] The authorities did not identify the "Government of the North" that had pledged to assist Castillo Armas, but among Mexico, Canada, and the United States it was not difficult to choose.

The leaders of the opposition responded to the January arrests with impotent rage. Those who had been detained, they claimed, were the innocent victims of a repressive state. Loudly supported by the opposition press, they sought to arouse public indignation—"without much success," lamented the U.S. embassy. Aware that the innocent victims were in fact inveterate plotters, the embassy urged USIA "promptest press, radio coverage. . . . Imply arrests made arbitrarily and form part of campaign to intimidate anti-Communist opposition to Communist-influenced Arbenz administration."[140]

From Washington, Undersecretary Smith joined the fray. He urged that Serafino Romualdi, the representative for Latin America of the American Federation of Labor (AFL), persuade the AFL-sponsored Inter-American Organization of Labor (ORIT) to denounce Arbenz's persecution of labor. (Four of the arrested plotters were members of a very small antigovernment trade union.) But ORIT's Secretary General Luis Monge (a future president of Costa Rica and a close associate of Figueres) refused to comply. Monge's hostility

[138] "Mañana se emitirá comunicado," *DCA*, Jan. 28, 1954, p. 1. The best source on the arrests (Jan. 21–26) is the U.S. embassy. See: Krieg to SecState, nos. 233 and 234, Jan. 22, 1954; Krieg to SecState, no. 246, Jan. 25, 1954; Krieg to SecState, nos. 247, 250, and 252, Jan. 26, 1954; Krieg to DOS, no. 643, Jan. 27, 1954; Krieg to SecState, no. 264, Jan. 28, 1954; Krieg to DOS, no. 663, Feb. 3, 1954; Wardlaw to DOS, no. 664, Feb. 3, 1954. All NA 714.00. For an official Guatemalan perspective on the arrests, see Charnaud to Jefe de la Guardia Judicial, and Charnaud to Director General de la Guardia Civil, both Jan. 25, 1954, CO:G, Jan. 1954, unpag., AGCA. For press reports, see esp. "Enrique Oliva nada sabe de complot," *El I*, Jan. 23, 1954, p. 1; "La policía no está obligada a informar, dice Charnaud M.," *La Hora*, Jan. 26, 1954, p. 1; "El tráfico de la alarma" (edit.), *DCA*, Jan. 27, 1954, p. 3; "Guatemala Aide Explains Arrests," *NYT*, Jan. 27, 1954, p. 10; "Situación de zozobra," *El I*, Jan. 27, 1954, p. 1.

[139] The official communiqué, the press conference of the secretario de propaganda y divulgación, and several incriminating letters can be found in the major Guatemalan newspapers of Jan. 29 and 30, 1954. More documents were later published by the government in *La democracia amenazada*.

[140] Quotations from Krieg to SecState, no. 263, Jan. 28, 1954, and Krieg to USIA, TOUSI 26, Jan. 26, 1954. Both NA 714.00. For the embassy's cognizance that those arrested had been plotting, see the documents cited in n. 138 above.

to the Arbenz regime was not in question, but in South America, he argued, "the public and labor are quite ignorant of the true conditions [in Guatemala]." Any statement from him condemning Arbenz would "redound to the benefit of Guatemala rather than the free world." And so ORIT remained silent, and the AFL was left to write an open letter expressing great anxiety over "the growing influence of the Communist elements in Guatemala."[141]

In the United States, the revelations and the January arrests provoked contempt and anger. The State Department set the tone. An official press release began ritualistically, "it is the policy of the United States not to intervene in the internal affairs of other nations." It then dissected Guatemala's behavior: the detention of innocent opposition leaders and the slanderous charges against the United States, "coming as the climax of an increasingly mendacious propaganda campaign," were typical communist techniques. The timing of the accusations—"immediately prior" to the Caracas Conference—betrayed their purpose. They were "a Communist effort to disrupt the work of this conference and the Inter-American solidarity which is so vital to all the nations of the Hemisphere."[142]

The U.S. media were not likely to credit the wild charges of a procommunist banana republic over the lofty denials of the State Department. Their mistrust of the Guatemalans was heightened by two untimely actions. On February 3, the Arbenz administration deported Father Buccellato, that relentless foe of Decree 900; Buccellato was a priest and an American. The previous day, in an unprecedented move, Guatemala had expelled two journalists: Marshall Bannell of the National Broadcasting Company and Sydney Gruson of the *New York Times*.[143]

Gruson was, with Robert Hallett of the *Christian Science Monitor*, the most insightful of the American journalists covering Guatemala. Unlike most of his colleagues, he rarely resorted to sensationalism. In a sober style, he repeatedly acknowledged that the Arbenz government enjoyed popular support, that its

[141] Smith to AmEm San José, no. 69, Jan. 27, 1954, NA 714.00; AmEm San José, Stewart to SecState, no. 72, Jan. 28, 1954, NA 714.00; Krieg to SecState, no. 268, Jan. 29, 1954, NA 714.00; AmEm San José, Cohen to DOS, no. 613, Feb. 9, 1954, NA 714.00 (quoted); "Guatemalans Get Plea from A.F.L.," *NYT*, Feb. 7, 1954, p. 1 (quoted); Schlesinger and Kinzer, *Bitter Fruit*, pp. 141–42; Immerman, *CIA in Guatemala*, p. 105, p. 232, n. 14.

[142] Press release, Jan. 30, 1954, *Department of State Bulletin*, Jan. 25–31, 1954, pp. 251–52.

[143] See "Sydney Gruson expulsado del país," *DCA*, Feb. 2, 1954, p. 1 (includes the official communiqué); "Bannell se dedicó a actividades que no le estaban permitidas en el país," *El I*, Feb. 3, 1954, p. 1; "Rechazo a protesta de la SIP" and "El periodista no es un difamador público," *DCA*, Feb. 4, 1954, p. 1; "Guatemala Ousts Two U.S. Newsmen," *NYT*, Feb. 3, 1954, p. 7.

The government rescinded the orders against Gruson and Bannell a few weeks later.

social reforms were necessary, and that the opposition lacked a constructive program. But in a widely quoted November 1953 article he announced that Arbenz had become "a prisoner of the embrace he so long ago gave the Communists."[144] And he heaped scorn on the January plot revelations in an article that he wrote in Mexico City, where he was based.[145] As the article appeared in the *New York Times*, he landed in Guatemala—only to be expelled. Sydney Gruson, charged the official communiqué, "has systematically defamed and slandered this republic." The Guatemalan government may have hoped that irrefutable evidence of a plot abetted by Washington would dampen the American reaction to the deportation of three particularly nettlesome individuals. Or perhaps it merely acted impulsively, in a spasm of exasperation. To American eyes, however, the arrests and the plot revelations fit into the same pattern as the deportations of Buccellato, Bannell, and Gruson. "It all seemed to add up," concluded *Newsweek* in a mid-February article that closely paralleled the State Department's line. "The immediate object" of these fresh outrages was to provoke "some kind of drastic action by the United States. This could be built up into the standard charge of 'yanqui imperialism' with a consequent strain on hemispheric solidarity—all to the greater glory of World Communism."[146] *Time* also endorsed the State Department's "coolly reasoned explanation." The Guatemalan plot revelations were "a sort of Reichstag fire in reverse, masterminded in Moscow" on behalf of the "Red-wired" Arbenz government; their aim was to disrupt the upcoming Caracas Conference.[147]

In April 1953, Daniel James, an influential editor of the *New Leader*, had argued that the communists, though gaining ground, were far from controlling Guatemala.[148] In February 1954, he no longer entertained such hopes. The plot revelations, he charged, were only "the most disturbing of a series of unfortunate events." Until the late spring of 1953, "there was a possibility that the Guatemalan Communists would slow down their drive toward power. . . . There was also a possibility that Arbenz might decide to jettison the Communists or that the Army might do so. . . . Those possibilities apparently no longer exist." Within the last year, "rumors of Communist infiltration of the Army have increased, and its chief, Colonel Diaz, is now reported to be a fellow-traveler."[149]

The *Saturday Evening Post*, *The Atlantic*, and even the *Christian Science Monitor* (which had provided some of the best reporting on Guatemala) pub-

[144] "Guatemala Reds Increase Powers," *NYT*, Nov. 6, 1953, p. 3.

[145] "Guatemala Story of Plot Scouted," *NYT*, Jan. 31, 1954, p. 13.

[146] "Guatemala: Made in Moscow," *Newsweek*, Feb. 15, 1954; p. 54.

[147] "Plot Within A Plot," *Time*, Feb. 8, 1954, p. 36.

[148] "Is Guatemala Communist?" *New Leader*, Apr. 13, 1953, pp. 3–5; "The Truth about Guatemala," *New York Herald Tribune*, Apr. 7–9, 1953, always p. 22.

[149] "Showdown in Guatemala?" *New Leader*, Feb. 15, 1954, pp. 6–8 (quoted from pp. 6, 7).

lished articles along similar lines, while the scholarly *Hispanic American Report* derided the Guatemalan charges as "fantastic." More conservative publications, such as *American Mercury* and *Reader's Digest*, had long been preaching that Guatemala was a Soviet colony: Soviet agents crowded Guatemala City and were busy establishing military bases from which to threaten not only Guatemala's unfortunate neighbors but also the United States.[150]

Every American publication within the liberal-conservative arc blithely dismissed the charge that the United States was plotting against Arbenz. *The Nation*, which generally offered the most balanced coverage of Guatemalan matters, remained silent.[151] True, the *New York Times*, after harshly condemning the expulsion of Gruson and Bannell,[152] introduced a sober note: "The swiftness with which events appear to be moving in Guatemala is probably deceptive," a February 9 editorial told the Cassandras. "As in almost all Latin-American countries the ultimate power rests with the military, who are not Communists in Guatemala." But the *Times* was not naive. The plot charges were, of course, sheer fabrication, and the editorial lectured the mendacious Guatemalans: "The Guatemalan Government could help itself and the whole hemisphere by being less sensitive and less prone to carrying a chip on its shoulder. In railing against 'Yankee Imperialism' it is fighting a ghost of the dead past, resurrected only in the imagination of extreme nationalists and Communists. Guatemalans have no right to accuse North Americans of misunderstanding them when their own misunderstandings are so colossal."[153]

The Congress of the United States was not as restrained as the *New York Times*. On January 14, Senator Wiley had offered twenty-two proofs that Guatemala had become "a serious beachhead for international communism in this hemisphere." Following the plot revelations, a more intelligent man, Senator William Fulbright, rose to fulminate against the "vicious propaganda attack" of the "Communist-dominated Government of Guatemala." Meanwhile, Wiley added to his catalogue proof number twenty-three. The plot charges and the expulsion of two American correspondents, he explained, were just "the latest sickening demonstration of the Communist octopus at work"; the "ten-

---

[150] "The Reds Must Get No American Beachhead," *Saturday Evening Post* (edit.), Mar. 20, 1954, p. 10; "Guatemala," *Atlantic*, Apr. 1954, pp. 4, 6; Hallett, "Guatemalan Turmoil Linked to Communism," *CSM*, Feb. 3, 1954, p. 4; *Hispanic American Report*, Feb. 1954, p. 1 (quoted); Ralph de Toledano, "The Soft UNDERBELLY of the U.S.A.," *American Mercury*, Feb. 1953, pp. 114–28; Michael Scully, "Red Ruin for Guatemala?" *Reader's Digest*, Dec. 1953, pp. 25–30.

[151] Flora Lewis, "The Peril Is Not Red," merely noted that Guatemala "recently charged that the United States was involved in an 'invasion plot' against it." (*The Nation*, Feb. 13, 1954, pp. 127–29, quoted from p. 127.)

[152] "Censors in Guatemala" (edit.), *NYT*, Feb. 3, 1954, p. 22, and "Guatemala's Explanation" (edit.), *NYT*, Feb. 4, 1954, p. 24.

[153] "Guatemalan Reforms" (edit.), *NYT*, Feb. 9, 1954, p. 26.

tacles [of the] dangerous Communist octopus,'' he repeated, ''are tightening around every segment'' of Guatemala. This was blatant communist aggression against the people of Guatemala and against the Western Hemisphere.[154]

Representative Frances Bolton had never before addressed Congress on matters Guatemalan; her specialty was the Middle East. But it required no great expertise, she asserted, to understand what was occurring in Guatemala. Though her language was less colorful than Wiley's, the gentlewoman from Ohio was every bit as inflamed. The expulsion of Gruson and Bannell was ''one more fact in evidence that the Government of Guatemala is Communist.'' Guatemala, she reminded her fellow representatives, ''is about four hours' flight from New Orleans and considerably less than that from the Panama Canal. We can only interpret the recent actions by the Guatemalan Government as an open threat to the way of life we in this country—and most of our neighbors—hold dear.''[155]

Representative Donald Jackson, chairman of the House Subcommittee on Inter-American Affairs, considered himself an expert on Latin America. He now rose to denounce a grave error: two U.S. military missions were still operating in Guatemala. Unaware that his protest would make the planners of PBSUCCESS shudder, he demanded that the missions be withdrawn at once:

> The obvious purpose of such training missions in any country is to strengthen the ability of a nation to withstand aggression from without and generally to contribute to the overall defenses of the free world. Obviously, in the instance of Guatemala, there is no further purpose to be served in the training of the armed services to withstand outside aggression in light of the fact that the principal forces of world slavery and confusion are already at work within the country and in the rear of the military establishment. . . . The military leaders of the nation approve and support the actions of the Red-dominated government.[156]

Other members of Congress advocated economic sanctions. On February 8, Senator Margaret Chase Smith introduced Senate Resolution 211. The resolution stated the apparently twin points that the price of Guatemalan coffee was exorbitant and that the communists dominated the economic and political affairs of Guatemala. Eisenhower should ''take such action as may be required to exclude from importation into the United States all coffee originating in the Republic of Guatemala until such time as he is satisfied that (1) the economic and political affairs of that country no longer are dominated and controlled by

---

[154] Wiley, Jan. 14, 1954, *CR*-Senate, pp. 248–50 (quoted from p. 248); Fulbright (D-Ark), Feb. 1, 1954, ibid., p. 1073; Wiley, Feb. 4, 1954, ibid., pp. 1321–23 (quoted from p. 1322).

[155] Bolton (R-Ohio), Feb. 3, 1954, *CR*-House, p. 1258.

[156] Jackson (R-Cal), Feb. 25, 1954, ibid., pp. 2305–7 (quoted from p. 2306).

the Communist movement, and (2) the unjustified prices of coffee imposed by producers in that country have been undercut to reasonable levels."[157]

In Guatemala, the resolution was attacked bitterly in both the administration and the opposition press, while the landed elite vehemently rejected any insinuation that the high price of coffee might be due to communist manipulations.[158] Throughout Latin America, the response was indignation. The prospect of U.S. economic sanctions rekindled deep fears. The Coffee Committee of the OAS's Inter-American Economic and Social Council immediately adopted a resolution condemning a coffee boycott. On February 11, the council voted to give this resolution the "widest dissemination"; foes as bitter as Trujillo's Dominican Republic and Arbenz's Guatemala voted as one, while the lone dissenting vote was cast by the United States.[159]

Nor was Smith's resolution welcomed by the Eisenhower administration. The State Department had earlier considered and rejected a coffee embargo. It would be difficult to enforce, they reckoned, and in a seller's market (as was coffee at the time), Guatemala would find alternative buyers—whereas the political costs for the United States would be high. It might hurt the present regime in Guatemala a little economically, but it would give that regime a good weapon to attack our economic imperialism throughout the hemisphere," Assistant Secretary Cabot had noted.[160]

The planners of PBSUCCESS were equally unenthusiastic: Senator Smith was not the first, nor would she be the last, to suggest that the administration adopt economic sanctions against Guatemala, and these suggestions they consistently rejected. In a Janus-faced approach, they sought to frighten the Guatemalans with the specter of sanctions and yet to assure the Latin Americans that the United States would not impose unilateral sanctions.[161] Furthermore, "the

[157] Smith (R-Maine), Feb. 8, 1954, *CR*-Senate, p. 1475.

[158] "Boycot al café de Guatemala sería 'inoperante,' " *El I*, Feb. 9, 1954, p. 1; "El boycot al café perjudica no solo América, sino a los EU," *DCA*, Feb. 10, 1954, p. 8; "La propuesta de la senadora Smith," *Prensa Libre*, Feb. 10, 1954, p. 2; "La senadora Smith desconoce las realidades económicas," *La Hora*, Feb. 9, 1954, p. 1; *JW* 6, Feb. 12, 1954, pp. 1, 3–4; Wardlaw to DOS, no. 706, Feb. 15, 1954, NA 814.2333. The editor of the opposition paper *Prensa Libre* became "excited and irrational over the . . . proposed boycott," a U.S. official reported. "He was absolutely furious." (MemoConv [Urist, Pedro Julio García], Feb. 26, 1954, RG84 G&C, Box 4, NA-S.)

[159] "Americas Issue Coffee Warning," *NYT*, Feb. 12, 1954, p. 1.

[160] Cabot to McDermott, Sept. 12, 1953, *FRUS*, 1952–1954, 4:1009; see also MemoConv ("Guatemalan Coffee"), Nov. 25, 1953, ibid., pp. 1088–91. For a thorough exposition of the arguments against coffee sanctions, see Department of Commerce to Wiley, [Mar. 1954], filed in NA 714.001, and Department of Agriculture to Wiley, enclosed in Hyde to Brown, Apr. 7, 1954, NA Lot 58D18 & 58D78, Box 1.

[161] When Peurifoy urged the abrogation of the trade treaty with Guatemala, Dulles cabled: "Department desires avoid action suggestive of unilateral economic sanc-

intelligence community was very skeptical of the efficacy of economic sanctions."[162]

Senator Smith's proposal was particularly untimely, a confidential State Department memorandum noted. "On the eve of the Caracas conference, the Communist-influenced Government of Guatemala is thus served the most perfectly tailor-made issue it could seek in order to disrupt the conference."[163] On behalf of the State Department, Thruston Morton, assistant secretary for congressional affairs, hastened to explain to Congress that the high price of Guatemalan coffee was due not to communist machinations, but to the worldwide coffee shortage; the exclusion of Guatemalan coffee would be likely to further inflate coffee prices in the United States. "I do not feel," he concluded, "that the proposed measure would be advisable at the present time."[164] The Smith resolution did not resurface.

Congressman Jackson, perhaps enlightened by the CIA, dropped the subject of U.S. military missions in Guatemala. He seized instead on another idea. It was true, he conceded in a February 25 speech, that a coffee embargo would violate the 1936 Reciprocal Trade Agreement with Guatemala. But no one could rob the American people of their right to express their opposition to the Red plague. American companies should refuse to sell oil and gasoline to Soviet Guatemala; America's housewives should refuse to buy Guatemalan coffee; and the nations of the OAS, too, should demonstrate their love of freedom. Within a few days they would assemble at Caracas. There, they must adopt strong measures against the Arbenz regime, lest Caracas become "the Munich of our hemisphere." Let no one deny the truth: "The Soviet threat in Guatemala is aggression and as surely so as if it were backed by the bayonets of the Red army."[165]

While in the United States, the victim was branded as the aggressor, in Managua, Somoza responded to the publication of Delgado's incriminating documents with furious denials and *macho* defiance. For many years, he claimed, he had been the target of plots abetted by Guatemala, "but I don't complain because I have prepared a welcoming committee for those who

---

tions." (Dulles to AmEmG, no. 1194, June 8, 1954, NA 714.00. See also Peurifoy to SecState, June 2, 1954, *FRUS*, 1952–1954, 4:1156.)

[162] Interview with Hyman of the OIR who adds: "In 1953, the question was put to us as to what economic sanctions against Guatemala would be available and feasible (coffee, etc.). We decided in the negative." The attitude of the intelligence community toward economic sanctions, and particularly toward their usefulness in Guatemala, was confirmed in interviews with Kirkpatrick and Bissell. For the special case of oil, see below, p. 376.

[163] "The Coffee Problem as It Affects Communist Plans in Guatemala," p. 2, NA Lot 57D95, Box 5.

[164] Morton to Sen. Potter, Feb. 12, 1954, *CR*-Senate, Feb. 17, 1954, pp. 1896–97.

[165] Feb. 25, 1954, *CR*-House, pp. 2305–7 (quoted from p. 2307).

threaten the peace and security of Nicaragua. I am ready for them.''[166] Undersecretary Smith hastened to soothe the ruffled dictator: ''Inform President,'' he cabled the U.S. embassy in Managua, ''this Government . . . applauds Somoza's . . . strong rejection of false Guatemalan accusations.'' In Costa Rica, the prestigious *La Nación* ridiculed the alleged plot: ''Anyone who has followed developments in Guatemala over the last month will appreciate the true meaning of these accusations.''[167]

Few in Guatemala had *La Nación*'s insight. The evidence presented by the Arbenz administration seemed highly persuasive, and the State Department's denials sounded even more hollow than had those of Peurifoy a few weeks earlier. The Guatemalan government scored a moral victory—for Washington's lies were transparent—but it had also suffered a severe defeat. By exposing U.S. plotting, it had exacerbated the fears of many military officers and administration politicians. Worse, the threats and the abuse of the United States press and Congress in response to the plot revelations dashed the hope that American public opinion might restrain Eisenhower's hand.

Arbenz reacted with defiance, pledging that his administration would not retreat one step.[168] Meanwhile, *Diario de Centro América* assailed the State Department's hypocrisy and lambasted the ignorance and the arrogance of American journalists and congressmen alike. ''The Success of Our Revolution Has Aroused the Imperialists' Anger,'' ''The Imperialists Distrust Any Manifestation of Patriotism,'' ''The U.S. Spouts a Language That Befits a Master'': these are the titles of the articles that filled the pages of *DCA* in those tense days.[169]

It was a dignified response. But should the weak challenge the mighty, particularly when the latter is stalking? For many of his supporters, Arbenz's defiance inspired not pride but anxiety.[170] This anxiety was heightened by the fear of what might happen at Caracas, where the Tenth Inter-American Conference was about to begin.

[166] ''Embajador nica lleva la respuesta,'' *La Prensa*, Managua, Jan. 31, 1954, p. 1 (quoted from p. 2). See also AmEm Managua, Welch to SecState, no. 80, Feb. 2, 1954, NA 714.00; and AmEm Managua, Welch to DOS, no. 306, Feb. 9, 1954.

[167] Smith to AmEm Managua, no. 72, Feb. 1, 1954, NA 714.00; ''Los complots internacionales contra Guatemala'' (edit.), *La Nación*, San José, Feb. 2, 1954, p. 6.

[168] ''Arbenz afirma su fé en la victoria contra traidores,'' *DCA*, Feb. 2, 1954, p. 1; ''Guatemala Chief Hits Critics in U.S.,'' *NYT*, Feb. 5, 1954, p. 6; Krieg to DOS, no. 677, Feb. 8, 1954, NA 714.00.

[169] *DCA*: Feb. 5, 8, and 9, 1954, always p. 1.

[170] Confirmed by the testimonies of virtually all the Guatemalans interviewed by the author.

CHAPTER 12

The Caracas Conference

Two VIEWS clashed at Caracas. The Latin American governments sought U.S. aid in the form of development loans, higher prices for their raw materials, and easier access to the U.S. market. These had been their demands since the end of the Second World War. They had been repeatedly rebuffed by the Truman administration, which gave less aid to the twenty Latin American countries combined than to Belgium and Luxembourg. Privately, U.S. officials derided the Latin Americans' "deplorable tendency to extend their empty palms collectively in our direction";[1] publicly, they stated that what these countries needed was private investment, not U.S. loans. The Latin Americans were told to create a suitable climate for foreign investment. Economic nationalism was counterproductive, and any laws that violated free trade and investment principles must be expunged.

Predictably, the niggardliness and the haughtiness of the Truman administration stirred resentment in Latin America. In the 1952 presidential campaign, Eisenhower chided the Truman administration for its failed Latin American policy. He promised change.[2]

In the first year of the Eisenhower administration, a new development added to the Latin Americans' plight. The region's postwar economic growth "had ended abruptly."[3] Overall GNP had declined in real terms in 1952 and barely returned to the 1951 level in 1953. Meanwhile, the population continued to increase by 2.5 percent each year. Caracas was the Latin Americans' hope; from the unsavory dictators of the Caribbean to the democratic government of Uruguay, all agreed that, this time, the United States had to address their grievances.

Hope was edged with fear. The Latin Americans were convinced that Washington was preparing to violate the principle of nonintervention. To American journalists, these fears were patently anachronistic: couldn't the Latins see that since FDR, the United States had forsworn interference in the affairs of its sisters? But the Latin Americans saw instead the rising fury of the United States toward Guatemala and the documents released by Arbenz that pointed

---

[1] Assistant Secretary Miller to his father, Mar. 30, 1951, Miller Papers, Box 5, TL.

[2] For an excellent analysis of the economic relations between the Truman administration and Latin America, see Rabe, "Elusive Conference." For Eisenhower's criticism of Truman, see Rabe, *Eisenhower and Latin America*, p. 6.

[3] NSC 5407, Feb. 17, 1954, *FRUS*, 1952–1954, 4:209.

to a U.S. conspiracy. At Caracas, they expected Foster Dulles to try to loosen the legal knots that had been woven in the inter-American fabric in order to restrain the United States. To some Latin American governments, this would have been an acceptable price for Arbenz's fall, but a majority sharply disagreed, more in dread of a dangerous precedent than in sympathy with the Guatemalans.

At its outset, the Eisenhower administration sensed that all was not well in Latin America. In March 1953, the National Security Council warned that there was a "drift in the area toward radical and nationalistic regimes" (NSC 144/1). Its recommendations, however, differed little from those of the past. The United States should encourage "Latin American governments to recognize that the bulk of the capital required for their economic development can best be supplied by private enterprise and that their own self-interest requires the creation of a climate which will attract private investment." The United States should refrain "from overt unilateral intervention in the internal political affairs of the other American states." This prescription, however, was not unconditional. NSC 144/1 included a sentence that is still routinely deleted from the public record: should the inter-American system "fail to protect vital United States national interests in this hemisphere, it is recognized that unilateral action by the United States may be necessary."[4] Eisenhower was "extremely pleased" with the document. "Let us all look for a new approach" to Latin America, he exhorted his cabinet.[5]

To this end, the president sent his brother and highly trusted adviser, Milton, on a well-publicized visit to ten South American republics in the summer of 1953. But Milton Eisenhower, despite his genuine sympathy for Latin America, failed to come up with any bold or imaginative ideas in the report he submitted to the president on his return. "Economic cooperation," he stressed, "is without question the key to better relations between the United States and the nations to the South." Economic aid should be granted in par-

[4] "United States Objectives and Courses of Action with Respect to Latin America," NSC 144/1, Mar. 18, 1953, ibid., pp. 6–10, quotations from pp. 6, 8, and 7. The sentence on unilateral intervention has been deleted from the copy of NSC 144/1 deposited at the Eisenhower Library and from *FRUS* (see ibid., p. 7) but can be found in "Discussion at the 137th Meeting of the National Security Council on Wednesday, Mar. 18, 1953," Mar. 19, 1953, p. 12, WF, NSC Series, Box 4, EL. This document states unequivocally that NSC 144 was adopted by the NSC "subject to the following changes," which include the sentence on unilateral action. The document concludes with the statement: "NSC 144 as amended subsequently circulated as NSC 144/1" (ibid.). See also "Minutes of the 137th Meeting of the National Security Council," p. 4, White House Office, Special Assistant for National Security Affairs: Records 1952–61, NSC Series, Administration Subseries, Box 1, EL.

[5] See "Discussion at the 137th Meeting," *FRUS*, 1952–1954, 4:3, and Eisenhower, Handwritten Minutes of the July 3, 1953 Cabinet Meeting, unpaginated, White House Office, Staff Secretary: Records, 1952–1961, Cabinet Series, Box 1, EL.

ticular circumstances, and U.S. trade policy must respect the legitimate interests of the Latin Americans. The emphasis, however, was on private capital. U.S. companies, Milton Eisenhower noted, were already playing "an important role in promoting better understanding and friendship among the peoples of the American republics." Unfortunately, most Latin American governments were not yet reciprocating with fair treatment of American capital.[6]

Dr. Eisenhower's analysis was not such as to stir U.S. policymakers into action. The true difficulty in U.S. relations with Latin America, he argued, lay not in the policies of the United States, but in the Latin Americans' "misunderstanding and lack of information" about U.S. economic policy. "Fortunately," he stated, "the misunderstandings we found with respect to economic affairs are not matched in other areas. We were delighted to find a growing understanding of the United States as a nation and as a people . . . [and a] genuine pride in the Inter-American system." With one exception, the Latin American republics "share our desire for peace, freedom, and independence, and continue to cooperate effectively in the political councils of the world." The exception was Guatemala, which "has succumbed to Communist infiltration."[7]

More instrumental than Dr. Eisenhower in shaping the administration's economic policy toward Latin America was Secretary of the Treasury George Humphrey. "One of Eisenhower's closest and most trusted advisers," Humphrey was a rock of conservative orthodoxy and a champion of economic retrenchment. "On fiscal matters he was even more conservative than the president."[8] His formula for assisting the region was straightforward: "If we could find a few first-rate business men and send them as our ambassadors to the key Latin American nations, it would do far more good than any amount of money we could dole out."[9] Both President Eisenhower and Secretary Dulles tended to share Humphrey's views. "I want you to devise an imaginative policy for Latin America—but don't spend any money," Dulles warned Assistant Secretary Cabot in early 1953.[10] Foreign aid, the president explained to his brother, was appropriate only for those countries directly threatened by "the Communist menace."[11] Other than in Guatemala, however, the communist

[6] "Report to the President: United States–Latin American Relations," Nov. 18, 1953, pp. 17 and 29, DP:SS, Box 4, EL.

[7] Ibid., pp. 15, 14, 16, and 6.

[8] Kaufman, *Trade and Aid*, p. 30. This is the best study of Eisenhower's foreign aid policy. See also Rostow, *Eisenhower, Kennedy, and Foreign Aid*, pp. 75–151. On aid to Latin America during the Eisenhower administration, see Rabe, *Eisenhower and Latin America*, and Zoumaras, "Eisenhower's Foreign Economic Policy."

[9] "Discussion at the 137th Meeting," *FRUS*, 1952–1954, 4:4.

[10] Cabot, *First Line*, p. 87.

[11] DDE to Milton, Dec. 1, 1954, quoted in Rabe, *Eisenhower and Latin America*, p. 65.

threat in the hemisphere seemed too remote to require medicine, and in Guatemala, by contrast, the threat had progressed too far for anything but surgery.

It is not surprising, then, that Foster Dulles traveled to Caracas bereft of economic concessions or proposals. His one concern was his anticommunist resolution, the attack on Guatemala. In February 1954, a State Department memorandum had posited: "The minimum United States objective at Caracas with respect to the Communist item is to achieve adoption of a resolution which will lay ground work for subsequent positive action against Guatemala by the Organization of American States. Our maximum objective would be the adoption, should conditions permit, of effective multilateral measures against Guatemala."[12] By the time the conference convened, U.S. policymakers, aware of the Latin Americans' suspicions, had decided to focus on the minimum objective outlined in the February memo: the "adoption of a resolution which, without mentioning Guatemala by name, . . . would in effect express the serious concern of the OAS over the penetration of Communism in Guatemala and would lay the necessary ground work for subsequent positive multilateral action."[13] The mere prospect of collective sanctions, they reasoned, would demoralize Arbenz's supporters in Guatemala. It was only fitting that Secretary Dulles, in preparing his keynote speech for Caracas, sought the assistance of his brother Allen, the director of the CIA.[14]

As the seat of one of the most repressive dictatorships of the hemisphere, Caracas was not the most appropriate venue for a meeting of the OAS, an organization that boasted about its devotion to democracy. In Latin America several legislative assemblies, labor and political organizations, and major newspapers had demanded that if Pérez Jiménez wanted to host the conference, he must first free his political prisoners and restore basic political freedoms. President Figueres was blunt: Costa Rica would not send a delegation to Caracas.[15]

Few in the United States had shared these scruples. The U.S. Congress, vociferous on behalf of Guatemalan democracy, was apparently unaware that Pérez Jiménez was a dictator. The State Department firmly supported meeting in the Venezuelan capital and denounced any contrary view as interference in the internal affairs of a sister republic.

To many Latin Americans, this lofty stance was a poor disguise: Washing-

[12] "Guatemala and the Discussion of Communism at the Tenth Inter-American Conference," Feb. 10, 1954, *FRUS*, 1952–1954, 4:290.

[13] Ibid., p. 292.

[14] TelConv (JFD, AWD), Feb. 25, 1954, 11:10 a.m., John Foster Dulles Files, ML.

[15] See Figueres et al. to the Secretary of the OAS, enclosed in AmEm San José, Cohen to DOS, no. 639, Feb. 19, 1954, RG84 G&C, Box 2, NA-S; Betancourt, "La opinión continental"; Inman, *Inter-American Conferences*, pp. 257, 259; Kolb, *Democracy and Dictatorship*, pp. 127–28 and 135–39.

ton's best friends in the hemisphere were the dictators, men like Pérez Jiménez. Their cynicism was well founded. "I was glad we were meeting in Venezuela," Secretary Dulles told a House committee. "Venezuela is a country
which has adopted the kind of policies which we think that the other countries
of South America should adopt. Namely, they have adopted policies which
provide in Venezuela a climate which is attractive to foreign capital to come
in." If all Latin America followed suit, the danger of communism and social
disorder would disappear.[16] President Eisenhower had honored the dictator
with the Legion of Merit for his "spirit of collaboration and friendship toward
the United States," his encouragement of the "expansion of foreign invest-
ments . . . his constant concern toward the problem of Communist infiltration," and his recognition of the "similarity of interests of the United States
and Venezuela."[17]

The jails of Venezuela were still packed with political prisoners, and the
ruthless repression continued as the delegations of the United States and nineteen Latin American republics assembled in the magnificent Aula Magna of
the University of Caracas. At 4 p.m. on March 1, 1954, as Pérez Jiménez
welcomed his illustrious guests, the Tenth Inter-American Conference
opened. The battle would now begin.

The Guatemalan delegation had left for Caracas optimistic. "We were confident," recalls Foreign Minister Guillermo Toriello, "that the countries of
Latin America would rally around us and reject Dulles' proposal because that
was the only way to preserve the inter-American system." Mexico, Argentina, Chile, Uruguay, and probably Bolivia would vote with Guatemala; several other countries would abstain, and Dulles' resolution would fall short of
the required two-thirds majority.[18] This was also the thinking of Arbenz and
most leaders of his administration, including those of the PGT. This confidence had sustained them through the first two months of 1954, as the press,
the Congress, and the administration of the United States intensified their verbal onslaught, and the pressure became "brutal." Caracas would demonstrate
to the Americans, and to those Guatemalans whose loyalty was increasingly
frayed, that Latin America stood behind Guatemala, firm in defense of the
principle of nonintervention.[19] For weeks now, *Diario de Centro América* had
been delivering this message of hope to a population that heard only dire warnings from the opposition press. "Today it is Guatemala," wrote *DCA*. "Who

[16] Quotations from U.S. Congress, *HCFA*, p. 516, and Smith, *The United States
and Cuba*, p. 184.

[17] Kolb, *Democracy and Dictatorship*, pp. 142–43.

[18] Interviews with Toriello (quoted) and Noriega Morales, another member of the
delegation.

[19] Interviews with María de Arbenz, Guerra Borges (quoted), Fortuny, and Charnaud.

knows what country will be next? This is the burning question on the minds of all Latin American officials, while their people are demanding that they resist anything that smacks of aggression against Guatemala.'' At Caracas, Dulles would be defeated.[20]

On March 4, Foster Dulles addressed the conference. He quoted Bolívar, stressed Eisenhower's deep concern for the economic well-being of Latin America and assailed the international communist conspiracy that threatened the hemisphere. ''The danger mounts,'' he warned, and he proffered his anti-communist resolution.[21] Its key passage read: ''The domination or control of the political institutions of any American state by the international Communist movement . . . would constitute a threat to the sovereignty and political independence of the American states, endangering the peace of America, and would call for appropriate action in accordance with existing treaties.''[22] Among these existing treaties was that of Rio, which stipulated that diplomatic and economic sanctions were mandatory when supported by a two-thirds majority.

Toriello rose to respond. Never before had a banana republic dared to challenge the United States in an international forum. Dulles had spoken of the menace of communism—but Toriello spoke of the menace of the United States. Dulles had sought to enrobe his country in the PanAmerican mantle, but Toriello assailed the arrogant meddling of the United States in the internal affairs of the Latin American republics. Dulles's resolution, he argued, was not aimed at a threat from across the seas: it was aimed at Guatemala. It sought to legitimize aggression. Guatemala's only sin, Toriello concluded, was its attempt to assert its sovereignty.[23]

[20] ''La intervención: Amenaza para todos los gobiernos,'' *DCA*, Feb. 11, 1954, p. 1. The following is a representative sample of articles from *DCA*: ''México está con Guatemala,'' Dec. 17, 1953, p. 4; ''Pueblo haitiano concede a Arbenz la más alta prueba de amistad,'' Dec. 28, 1953, p. 8; ''Chile solidario con Guatemala,'' Jan. 8, 1954, p. 1; ''Defensa de nuestra revolución,'' Jan. 18, 1954, p. 1; ''Trabajadores bolivianos con Guatemala,'' Feb. 1, 1954, p. 1; ''Buena impresión dejó en Haití nuestra delegación especial,'' ibid., p. 8; ''Solidaridad continental con la democracia guatemalteca,'' Feb. 5, 1954, p. 1; ''Sociedad de amigos de Guatemala en Bolivia,'' ibid.; ''Personalidades chilenas repudian la intervención,'' ibid.; ''Responden los parlamentarios de Ecuador y de Costa Rica,'' ibid.; ''Solidaridad del continente con Guatemala,'' ibid., p. 3; ''Senadores chilenos pronuncianse en favor de Guatemala,'' Feb. 10, 1954, p. 1; ''Cárdenas está con Guatemala,'' Feb. 11, 1954, p. 1; ''Costa Rica contra la intervención,'' Feb. 13, 1954, p. 1; ''Bolivia solidaria con Guatemala,'' Feb. 16, 1954, p. 1; ''Caluroso recibimiento tributado al Dr Arévalo,'' ibid.; ''Rechazo a moción contra Guatemala,'' Feb. 17, 1954, p. 4.

[21] ''Address by the Secretary of State at the Second Plenary Session,'' Mar. 4, 1954, in DOS, *Tenth Inter-American Conference*, pp. 43–51, quoted from p. 45.

[22] Ibid., p. 157.

[23] See ''Address by His Excellency Guillermo Toriello Garrido, Minister of Foreign

The applause that greeted Toriello's speech, wrote the *New York Times*, was almost twice as long as that received by Dulles.[24] "He said many of the things some of the rest of us would like to say if we dared," observed a South American delegate.[25]

At Caracas, Toriello became a hero—but he had been dragged to glory. For he spoke words that he had not intended to speak. At Arbenz's request, a few weeks before the conference convened, the Foreign Ministry and the PGT had each presented a draft of the address that Toriello would deliver at Caracas. One was prepared by José Luis Mendoza, a senior Foreign Ministry official; the other was written for the PGT by Guerra Borges, a man of evident literary talents.[26] Mendoza sought to avoid a direct challenge to the United States and wrote in sober, legalistic terms. Over Toriello's objections, Arbenz chose Guerra Borges's draft, more passionate, more direct, openly crying out the bitterness of Guatemala's wounded nationalism and its abhorrence of U.S. arrogance.

As the Guatemalan delegation left for Caracas, Arbenz was uneasy. Would Toriello, who did not belong to his inner circle, spurn his instructions and deliver Mendoza's speech?[27] When Julio Estrada de la Hoz, secretary general of the PAR, left Guatemala to join the delegation at Caracas, he received an urgent message from Arbenz: he must make sure that Toriello obeyed his orders.

In Caracas, Estrada de la Hoz found the delegation in turmoil. Two of its members, Carlos González Orellana and Julio Gómez Padilla, were preparing to return to Guatemala in protest; Toriello had decided to use Mendoza's draft. But on March 5, when Toriello addressed the conference, his speech was that of Guerra Borges. Estrada de la Hoz's intervention had succeeded.

In 1944, Toriello had been one of the most impassioned speakers of the youth that had challenged Ubico. As ambassador to Washington from 1952 to January 1954, however, he had sought to assuage the Americans' growing anger. Now at Caracas, listening to the thunderous applause that greeted his speech, he reverted to the young man of 1944. Eagerly assuming, then and forever, full credit for a speech he had been loath to deliver, he spoke, throughout the conference, with passion and daring. "The brilliant Toriello,"

Affairs of Guatemala, in the Third Plenary Session, March 5, 1954," in OAS, *Tenth Inter-American Conference*, Document 95.

[24] "Guatemala Lays Plotting to U.S.," *NYT*, Mar. 6, 1954, p. 1, quoted from p. 6.

[25] "Keeping Communists Out," *Time*, Mar. 15, 1954, p. 30.

[26] For the genesis of Toriello's speech: interviews with Fortuny, Guerra Borges, María de Arbenz, and Noriega Morales; another member of the delegation, Julio Gómez Padilla, refers to the episode in Quan Rossell, *Guatemala*, 1:375–77. Toriello's own account of the Caracas conference does not mention the origins of his speech. (*La batalla de Guatemala*, pp. 59–94.) For Guerra Borges's literary talents, see his articles in *Tribuna Popular*.

[27] Interviews with María de Arbenz, Fortuny, and Guerra Borges.

praised a Mexican magazine, "played the music we love and attacked the things we hate."[28]

The duel between Toriello and the American secretary of state dominated the first half of the conference. Foster Dulles, Eisenhower had noted in his diary, "is not particularly persuasive in presentation and, at times, seems to have a curious lack of understanding as to how his words and manner may affect another personality."[29] To most Latin Americans and to a handful of sensitive U.S. observers, these traits were very much in evidence at Caracas.

After days of debate, it was clear that the democratic and semidemocratic governments of Latin America—notably Uruguay, Chile, Mexico, and Argentina—were unimpressed with Dulles's arguments. Among Washington's staunchest supporters were Trujillo, Somoza, Pérez Jiménez, and Batista. "It was embarrassing to see all the minor dictatorships of Latin America rush to support the United States," complained *Hispanic American Report*.[30] From Montevideo, *Marcha* expressed the same truth more sardonically: "It is in Caracas, once the proud city of Bolívar, now the domain of Pérez Jiménez, that a conference to promote peace and assail dictatorship is being held. The representatives of Trujillo, Batista and Odría are leading the democratic wave."[31] Even Dulles conceded to a closed congressional hearing that "the support of the so-called dictator countries . . . was sometimes a bit embarrassing."[32]

After rejecting wide-ranging amendments submitted by Mexico, Argentina, and Uruguay, Dulles consented to an insignificant change proposed by Colombia. Henceforth, the last sentence of his key paragraph (". . . and would call for appropriate action in accordance with existing treaties") would read ". . . and would call for *a meeting of consultation* [of OAS foreign ministers] *to consider the adoption of* appropriate action in accordance with existing treaties." He also tacked a final paragraph onto the resolution: "This declaration of foreign policy made by the American Republics in relation to dangers originating outside this Hemisphere is designed to protect and not to impair the inalienable right of each American State freely to choose its own form of government and economic system and to live its own social and cultural life."[33]

On March 13, the resolution was approved. Seventeen countries voted in

---

[28] "Guatemala en Caracas," *Humanismo*, Mexico City, Mar.–May 1954, pp. 11–16, quoted from pp. 13, 15.

[29] Ferrell, *Eisenhower Diaries*, p. 237, entry of May 14, 1953.

[30] *Hispanic American Report*, Apr. 1954, p. 1.

[31] "La farsa continúa," *Marcha*, Montevideo, Mar. 12, 1954, p. 1.

[32] U.S. Congress, *HCFA*, p. 502. Dulles's testimony to the House committee upon his return from Caracas is on pp. 499–505. (See also pp. 521–36 for the testimony of Assistant Secretary Holland.)

[33] DOS, *Tenth Inter-American Conference*, pp. 156–58.

favor. Argentina and Mexico abstained. Costa Rica was absent, but Figueres immediately endorsed the resolution. Guatemala cast the lone negative vote.

The additional paragraph, remarks an American scholar, made the resolution "either inconsistent or meaningless."[34] This was not the view of the U.S. press, however, which hailed the vote as "a triumph for Secretary Dulles, for the United States and for common sense in the Western Hemisphere."[35] Nor was it the view of Dulles and his delegation: "We didn't see it [the additional paragraph] as a major qualifier; it was primarily Latin American window dressing—somehow they have to stress their independence."[36] And it was certainly not the view of the Latin Americans themselves: "We contributed our approval without enthusiasm, without optimism, and without feeling that we were contributing to the adoption of a constructive measure," averred a Uruguayan delegate.[37]

Caracas, lamented the prominent Mexican jurist Isidro Fabela, "marks a deplorable assault on the principle of nonintervention which is the keystone of PanAmericanism." How could the qualifier be significant when everyone knew that the people and the government of the United States believed that no communist regime could ever be established with the consent of the governed, and the mere possibility of such a regime, to paraphrase Congressman Jackson, was considered evidence of aggression as flagrant as if it had been perpetrated by Soviet bayonets? The Caracas resolution did not specify how to determine if a country was dominated by international communism. Today against Guatemala, later against another wayward country, the United States could invoke the resolution to summon a meeting of OAS foreign ministers and demand the imposition of multilateral sanctions. And if the Latin Ameri-

[34] Slater, *The OAS*, p. 120.

[35] "Victory at Caracas" (edit.), *NYT*, Mar. 14, 1954, p. E10. It was a "striking victory for freedom and self-government in this part of the world." ("Declaration of Caracas," edit., *WP*, Mar. 15, 1954, p. 10.)

[36] Interview with Jamison. See also Dulles' testimony in U.S. Congress, *HCFA*, p. 503, and in "Memorandum of Discussion at the 189th Meeting of the National Security Council on Thursday, Mar. 18, 1954," *FRUS*, 1952–1954, 4:306. See also "Third Progress Report on NSC 144/1," May 25, 1954, ibid., p.45: "The United States achieved its primary objective of obtaining a clear-cut policy statement against Communism." For a rare expression of dissent by a U.S. official, see a May 28, 1954, memorandum by Louis Halle, of the State Department's Policy Planning Staff: "The 17 votes for our anti-Communist resolution at Caracas were granted only after the resolution had been watered down to the point of saying virtually nothing, and then grudgingly" (ibid., p. 1148). Halle's point was accurate, but narrow; this was not the way the Guatemalans saw it (see below, pp. 277–78)—and perception was paramount.

[37] "Guatemala reafirma su actitud frente al voto anticomunista," *El I*, Mar. 16, 1954, p. 1 (quoted from p. 2).

cans had failed to restrain the United States at Caracas, asked Fabela, what guarantee was there that they could mount a more effective resistance at a later date? "It would not be impossible for the United States to get the necessary two thirds majority: there are dictators in our Latin America who are beholden to Washington."[38]

The imposing majority that voted for the Caracas resolution had not been swayed by, as *Time* patriotically averred, the "intellectual force of Dulles' arguments."[39] They had surrendered, instead, to "very severe arm twisting." Foster Dulles, recalls a senior U.S. official, "spared no effort and spared no blandishment to get this Caracas Resolution through."[40] Decades of submission and "sordid calculations . . . [based on] the hope of receiving a *quid pro quo* on economic issues"[41] ensured the pitiful capitulation.

Those Latin Americans who had sold Guatemala for the lure of U.S. dollars were robbed of the payment. One hour after his resolution had been approved, Dulles boarded the plane back to Washington. His abrupt departure, comments a member of his delegation, was seen by the Latin Americans as "one more example of callous U.S. indifference to their economic problems."[42] Manners aside, the secretary's continued presence would have served no purpose; the U.S. delegation had nothing to offer on economic matters. It made only one concession: a special meeting of the Economic and Social Council of the OAS would be held to address the Latin Americans' concerns in Rio de Janeiro in late 1954. (The Rio meeting, notes a Dulles aide, proved to be "one of the worst failures of any conference that we've ever had. It was just a completely negative thing from the beginning.")[43]

It was with deep frustration that the Latin American delegates left Caracas at the end of March. "Caracas was a fiasco," blurted the foreign minister of El Salvador with uncharacteristic boldness. "Nothing was achieved in economic matters. . . . The resolution should have been accompanied by con-

[38] Fabela, "La conferencia de Caracas," pp. 32, 12.

[39] "Keeping Communists Out," *Time*, Mar. 15, 1954, p. 30.

[40] Rubottom, "Oral History Interview," p. 9.

[41] *Hispanic American Report*, Apr. 1954, p. 1.

[42] Interview with Jamison.

[43] Rubottom "Oral History Interview," p. 29. See also Rabe, *Eisenhower and Latin America*, pp. 70–77. For Milton Eisenhower's critique of the U.S. position for the Rio Conference and the president's response, see Milton to DDE, Sept. 7, 1954, WF, Name Series, Box 12; Milton to DDE, Oct. 22, 1954, ibid.; DDE to Milton, Oct. 25, 1954, WF, DDE:DS, Box 8; MemoTel, Oct. 30, 1954, ibid., Box 7; MemoTel, Nov. 9, 1954, ibid.; MemoTel, Nov. 20, 1954, ibid.; Milton to DDE, Monday [n.d.], WF, Name Series, Box 12; DDE to Milton, Nov. 23, 1954, WF, DDE:DS, Box 8; Milton to DDE, Nov. 30, 1954, WF, Name Series, Box 12. See also TelConv (JFD, Milton), Oct. 27, 1954, 1:11 p.m., DP:TCS, Box 3; TelConv (Holland, JFD), Oct. 29, 12:40 p.m., ibid. All EL.

structive agreements on economic matters. What we need is better prices for our raw materials. . . . Only with better prices will we be able to give a better life to our people."[44]

In Guatemala, tens of thousands greeted Toriello as he marched from the airport to the presidential palace, a flag in his hand. "Our delegates bring us a great moral victory," stated Arbenz in his welcoming speech. Even "many anti-Government Guatemalans," reported DCM Krieg, "got a feeling of perverse national pride from the spectacle of Willy Toriello standing up to Mr. Dulles."[45]

As with the January plot revelations, moral victory was overshadowed by a psychological defeat. At Caracas, the delegates of Mexico and Argentina had spoken with passion against Dulles's resolution, but they had abstained from voting against it. Other delegations, like that of Uruguay, had openly expressed their displeasure, yet they had voted with Dulles. Seventeen votes in favor, one against—it was a crushing defeat. While Arbenz stressed that "at Caracas not only did we not surrender our independence, but we voiced the hopes of all the peoples of Latin America,"[46] many of his supporters, civilians as well as military, somberly reflected that moral victories and the applause of spectators are of little help against a powerful aggressor. "At Caracas, our delegates were courageous, and we applauded them," recalls a Guatemalan officer, "but the net effect of the conference on most Guatemalans was fear. It was all part of the psychological warfare against Guatemala. Our moral victory was pyrrhic."[47]

For all his brave words, for all his efforts to inspire confidence, Arbenz himself was deeply shaken by the vote. The whoops of triumph in the United States, and the expressions of regret and fear in Latin America provided the Greek chorus: Guatemala, standing alone, was being led inexorably to her fate. "Our ship had been crippled; we were slipping with dignity beneath the waves," María de Arbenz remembers. "Yes, this is the way the bell tolls."[48]

The fact that Dulles succeeded despite his rude behavior made the situation

[44] "Conferencia de Caracas fué un fracaso," *La Prensa Libre*, San José, Mar. 30, 1954, pp. 1, 14.

[45] Quotations from "Recepción triunfal se ofreció a Toriello," *El I*, Mar. 30, 1954, p. 1 (quoted from p. 6) and from Krieg to Peurifoy, "Considerations Regarding U.S. Policy towards Guatemala," Apr. 27, 1954, p. 2, RG84 G&C, Box 3, NA-S.

[46] "Texto del discurso pronunciado por el ciudadano Presidente de la República," *DCA*, May 3, 1954, p. 1 (quoted from p. 8). On the government's efforts to present Caracas as a success, see also *JW* 11, Mar. 19, 1954, pp. 1–2; *JW* 12, Mar. 26, 1954, p. 1; *JW* 13, Apr. 2, 1954, pp. 1–2.

[47] Interview with Paz Tejada. His analysis and conclusions have been confirmed by the overwhelming majority of the Guatemalans I have interviewed, both civilian and military, friends and foes of the regime.

[48] Interview with María de Arbenz.

seem even more hopeless to Arbenz's supporters. American brazenness had not rallied the Latin American delegates. If an emboldened Eisenhower should strike Guatemala, what would the sister republics do? They would lament the aggression, certainly, but their lamentations would be of little comfort. The Guatemalans would pay the price of their loyalty to President Arbenz.

Some revolutionary politicians responded to the rising American threat with spasms of nationalism. Many more rued Arbenz's defiant stance. The president's ties with the PGT, always distasteful, were now dangerous. Inchoate ideas floated among many administration politicians: the revolution must take a step backward in order to pacify Washington; Arbenz should loosen his ties with the communists; some PGT leaders should leave the country for an extended "period of study"; others should renounce their positions in the bureaucracy; the agrarian reform should be slowed, if not altogether halted.

Few dared broach these ideas with Arbenz; when they did, the reaction was so negative as to paralyze any further attempt.[49] Deep malaise descended over the revolutionary camp. Without openly breaking with the regime, many politicians began to distance themselves from it. Meanwhile, unbeknownst to them and to most of his government, Arbenz had a daring plan.

[49] Interviews with María de Arbenz, Fortuny, Charnaud, Galich, and Guerra Borges.

CHAPTER 13

The Agony of the Regime

THE UNITED STATES had refused to sell weapons from Guatemala since 1949. In 1951 it began to frustrate the attempts of the Arbenz administration to buy weapons from other countries, to the dismay of the Guatemalan officer corps. This dismay, however, was not shared by Jacobo Arbenz, his public protestations notwithstanding. "Jacobo was not eager to buy weapons for the army," recalls his wife. "He was afraid that the officers would become overconfident and use them against him or the people."[1]

Nevertheless, in October 1953, when Arbenz learned from the documents delivered by Delgado that the United States was plotting his overthrow, he and the Secretariat of the PGT responded with a desperate gamble. Secretly, they would import weapons from Czechoslovakia, and secretly, some of these weapons would be given to the PGT to arm workers' militias should the need arise. It would be the first time that Arbenz had breached the army's monopoly of weapons and the first time that a Soviet bloc country had sent arms to the Western Hemisphere. The project was dangerous, for its discovery could trigger a military coup. But Arbenz felt he had little choice. Fear of the United States threatened to undermine the army's loyalty.[2]

Strict secrecy would be maintained. The military would learn that the weapons had reached Guatemala only after the arms earmarked for the PGT had been spirited away; it would not be told the true origin of the shipment. No cabinet member would be informed.[3] The PGT alone knew of the operation.

On November 16, an opposition paper reported that Fortuny had been spotted a week earlier in Mexico City boarding a plane for Vienna. He had been

[1] Interview with María de Arbenz; confirmed by Fortuny.

[2] Interviews with Fortuny, María de Arbenz, Guerra Borges, and Alejandro. Arbenz stated in a 1968 interview: "Because the threat was growing, I decided to get weapons from Czechoslovakia, so that I could arm the workers if necessary. . . . I did not inform the army." (Arbenz, "Habla Arbenz," p. 122.) As Fortuny notes, the PGT "had a great deal of influence among the dockers of Puerto Barrios." (Interview with Fortuny.) There is no agreement among my sources as to the exact percentage of weapons to be set aside for the civilians; their recollections vary from 25 percent to 50 percent of the total. In any case, these weapons were to be rifles and a few machine guns; the army would also receive heavier equipment such as mortars. The weapons set aside would be hidden in Arbenz's finca and in PGT safe houses.

[3] Confirmed by interviews with Interior Minister Charnaud and Army Chief of Staff Parinello.

on his way to Moscow to participate in the November 7 celebrations of the thirty-sixth anniversary of the Bolshevik revolution, responded the PGT daily, *Tribuna Popular*.[4] The U.S. embassy in Guatemala conscientiously relayed the information to Washington; it became an article of faith for U.S. officials that in November 1953 Fortuny had gone to the Soviet Union. And yet, as Ronald Schneider has pointed out, *Tribuna Popular* "did not explain how he [Fortuny] could be in Mexico on the 9th and get to Moscow by the 7th," that is, in time for the celebrations.[5] In fact, Fortuny was headed for Prague.

Soon after his arrival, Fortuny was received by Antonín Novotný, first secretary of the Communist Party of Czechoslovakia. "I told Novotný," he recalls, "about the dangers that Guatemala was facing, and I asked him if Czechoslovakia would sell weapons to us." Fortuny also explained that the weapons were not destined for the army alone, "but that we would keep some of them in case it became necessary to arm the people." If Novotný agreed, a Guatemalan military expert would arrange the details of the transaction later.[6]

Novotný was profuse in his expressions of sympathy for the struggle of the Guatemalan people; his government would study Fortuny's request. "He told me that he could not make any promises, but that I should trust him, and he assured me, 'You will not leave empty-handed.' " Fortuny waited: "I thought that they would reply in a week or two at most, but after more than fifteen days had gone by, I decided that the Czechs must be consulting the Soviets, and I asked them to arrange a trip to Moscow for me. I didn't tell them, but I had decided that it would be better if I talked directly to the Russians." The Czechs were noncommittal; they would transmit his request, they said. A few days later, a curt answer arrived: "They told me that it was not necessary to go to Moscow."

Ten more days passed before Fortuny was finally informed that Czechoslovakia would sell weapons to Guatemala. On January 8, 1954, he was back home after an absence of more than two months.[7] The unexpected length of

---

[4] "Rodeandose de completo misterio José Manuel Fortuny salió el 5 hacia Viena," *Prensa Libre*, Nov. 16, 1953, p. 2; "El viaje de José Manuel Fortuny," *Tribuna Popular*, Nov. 17, 1953, p. 5.

[5] Schneider, *Communism*, p. 100, n. 6.

[6] The account of Fortuny's stay in Prague and the quotations in this and the subsequent paragraphs are from interviews with Fortuny. Guerra Borges, Alejandro, and María de Arbenz confirmed Fortuny's account.

[7] "Fortuny regresó ayer," *Tribuna Popular*, Jan. 9, 1954, p. 1. In reporting Fortuny's return, the U.S. embassy concluded, "His trip to Moscow was thus of over two months duration." (Krieg to DOS, no. 583, Jan. 11, 1954, NA 714.001. See also *JW* 2, Jan. 15, 1954, p. 2.) The embassy was more successful in keeping tabs on Fortuny after his return. On January 21, an embassy official reported to Peurifoy: "A source told me today that Arbenz and Fortuny spent the weekend of January 8–10 alone at Arbenz's 'El Cajón' finca. The source said this information was absolutely reliable as

his stay in Prague, Fortuny believes, was due to the fact that his hosts consulted Moscow, that both they and the Russians knew little of Guatemala, had only loose ties with the PGT, and had more pressing concerns than the plight of Jacobo Arbenz.

On January 19, 1954, a few days after Fortuny's return, an incident surprised Guatemalan and foreign observers alike: the "mysterious departure" (to quote the U.S. embassy) of retired army major Alfonso Martínez, the head of the National Agrarian Department.[8] Martínez had boarded a plane for Mexico, explaining that his final destination was Switzerland. "No family members or government officials accompanied him to the airport," noted La Hora; his departure, stressed El Imparcial, "took government officials by surprise."[9]

Rumors spread. In view of Martínez's prominence and of the well-known fact that he was a close friend and protegé of Arbenz, the incident attracted attention in Guatemala and abroad. Some believed that Martínez, who had never fully recovered from a serious wound received at the Puente de la Gloria on July 18, 1949, had left for medical reasons. (He had gone to Switzerland for a check-up, a government communiqué stated flatly on January 23.) Many more, including the U.S. embassy and the New York Times, were suspicious.[10] It was no secret that Martínez resented the growing influence of the communists in "his" department of agrarian reform. It was also common knowledge that on January 18, the day before he left, Martínez had had lunch with Arbenz in a fashionable restaurant on the outskirts of the capital. No one had overheard their conversation, but they had appeared tense, agitated; they seemed to be quarreling. The explanation was obvious: they had been arguing, La Hora stated, about "matters related to the agrarian reform" and, in particular, the role of the PGT. Arbenz had sided with the communists. The next day, Martínez had left Guatemala.[11] "Lively rumors," reported the U.S. embassy on February 1, ". . . continued to circulate in the press and among the public throughout the week and those gaining the widest credence held that Martínez

---

he had obtained it from a personal employee of Arbenz." (Hill to Ambassador, Jan. 21, 1954, NA Lot 58D18 & 58D78, Box 1.) This information was correct. (Interviews with Fortuny and María de Arbenz.)

[8] JW 4, Feb. 1, 1954, p. 1.

[9] "No dan importancia política al viaje del jefe del DAN a Suiza," La Hora, Jan. 20, 1954, p. 4; "Alfonso Martínez a México y de allí a Europa y a Suiza," El I, Jan. 19, 1954, p. 1.

[10] See esp. JW 3, Jan. 22, 1954, pp. 1, 2; JW 4, Feb. 1, 1954, pp. 1, 3–4; Krieg, "Political Situation in Guatemala," Mar. 17, 1954, RG84 G&C, Box 3, NA-S; "Top Arbenz Aide Quits Guatemala," NYT, Feb. 8, 1954, p. 7.

[11] "No dan importancia política al viaje del jefe del DAN a Suiza," La Hora, Jan. 20, 1954, p. 4.

had clashed with President Arbenz's pro-Communist views and had decided or been told to get out of the country."[12]

No one told the story with more flair than the influential *Diario de Hoy* in neighboring El Salvador. Like so many other politicians in Guatemala, Alfonso Martínez had "flirted with the communists: he cynically encouraged them, naively believing that it would always be possible to control them. He, like many others, ignored the fact that the Reds are Frankensteins who destroy those who help them." A disgraced Martínez had now fled Guatemala, "to seek refuge in democratic Switzerland." *Diario de Hoy* saw it as a cautionary tale: "Martínez was able to escape from the communists' clutches, but few have been so lucky. All those Central American 'leaders' who flirt with the Reds should be forewarned."[13]

On February 20, however, Martínez returned to Guatemala. "Smiling and relaxed" at a press conference, he explained that he had been in a Swiss sanatorium attending to a heart problem; "I didn't even visit Rome or Paris."[14] In fact, he was returning from Prague, the one and only destination of his trip.

Arbenz had asked Martínez to handle the technical aspects of the arms sale. The selection of Martínez, who had pressing and important duties as head of the agrarian reform, illustrates the extent of Arbenz's alienation from the officer corps. The thirty-one-year old Martínez was his friend. He was not a man of the left, but he owed his high position to Arbenz alone. The bond between them had been sealed by the death of Arana; it had been Martínez whom Arbenz had sent to arrest the rebel colonel on July 18, 1949. His loyalty and discretion were proven. Keenly intelligent, he would conduct the sensitive mission with skill. Arbenz believed that no other officer had comparable credentials.[15]

The secret of the mission would be best guarded, Arbenz concluded, if it were thought that Martínez had left Guatemala because of a rift with him. Hence the circumstances of Martínez's departure. He left without informing his closest aides; no government official went to the airport to see him off; once he had gone, the authorities remained silent for several days as rumors spread—only belatedly did they issue a brief communiqué. Extraneous events

[12] *JW* 4, Feb. 1, 1954, p. 3.

[13] "El caso del coronel Martínez y las maniobras rojas en Centro América," *Diario de Hoy*, San Salvador, Jan. 30, 1954, p. 7.

[14] Quotations from "Guatemala Aide Back, Denies Rift," *NYT*, Feb. 24, 1954, p. 12, and "Alfonso Martínez asumió nuevamente la jefatura del DAN," *El I*, Feb. 23, 1954, p. 1 (quoted from p. 2).

[15] Interviews with María de Arbenz and Fortuny were particularly helpful for the story of Arbenz and Martínez. On Martínez, see Rose, Military Attaché Report no. 1224, June 9, 1944, RG165 RF, Box 1574, NA-S; Schoenfeld to Miller, Aug. 13, 1951, NA Lot 53D26, Box 7; Hill, "Alfonso Martínez Estevez," Aug. 12, 1952, RG84 CF, Box 15, NA-S.

facilitated the deception. Martínez's relations with the PGT were indeed strained. Moreover, Guatemala City was tense. On January 11, Peurifoy's *Time* interview had appeared; in late January (just a few days after Martínez's departure) several plotters were arrested, and then the conspiracy abetted by the "Government of the North" was revealed. Even implausible rumors became credible.

Arbenz added a personal touch to the ploy. He and Martínez were not quarreling when they lunched together on January 18. They were acting, and Arbenz had purposefully chosen one of the most fashionable restaurants as the stage. The following day, after Martínez had boarded his plane, the luncheon quarrel and the departure would be linked.

What was not faked, however, was Martínez's satisfaction when he returned to Guatemala. Not only had the secret been maintained, but he brought back the news that Prague would soon send two thousand tons of light weapons seized from the Germans in the Second World War. Captured German equipment was common in Europe and would mask the identity of the supplier.[16] The Czechs would arrange the transportation. "Payment," Martínez later explained, "was made directly from the Banco de Guatemala to a secret account at the Union des Banques Suisses in Zurich." The first dispatch of weapons from the Soviet Bloc to Latin America was neither a gift nor a loan. It was a sale, to be paid, at once, in cash.[17]

Meanwhile, a debate was unfolding within the Secretariat of the PGT. It had begun in early 1954, and it reached its climax in the weeks following Caracas. Guatemala was besieged; how should the party respond?[18]

For Alfredo Guerra Borges, for Bernardo Alvarado Monzón, for Mario Silva Jonama, for José Luis Ramos—and for Alejandro, the Secretariat's nonvoting Cuban adviser—only one answer was possible: the revolution must accelerate. Too much effort had been spent; too many successes had been achieved; time and again the forces of reaction had been defeated; Guatemala could not capitulate to U.S. imperialism; the revolutionaries could not retreat. They drew comfort from the weakness of the domestic opposition and from their faith in the population's growing revolutionary fervor.

[16] The weapons were in satisfactory condition. (Interviews with Col. Parinello, Lt. Cols. Hernández and Mendizabal, and Maj. Paz Tejada.) For a list of the weapons, see Hanford, "Communist Beachhead," appendix 6.

[17] Alfonso Martínez, "En México se pelea duro el Arevalismo y Martínez Estévez," *La Hora*, Mar. 4, 1963, p. 7. The payment was made with funds from the budget of the Atlantic Highway. There is disagreement as to the exact amount paid. The most likely figure is $1 million. See also Hill to DOS, no. 269, Oct. 4, 1954, NA 714.00; Wardlaw to DOS, no. 328, Oct. 19, 1954, NA 714.00.

[18] My main sources for this debate are interviews with Fortuny, Guerra Borges, and Alejandro, as well as Fortuny, "Autocrítica."

And so the revolutionary process surged forward. The pace of the agrarian reform was accelerated in January 1954, particularly in the important department of Escuintla, where the PGT had considerable influence. While their eyes scanned the horizon for the ship with its secret cargo, these leaders of the PGT intended, with Arbenz's support, to create as many *faits accomplis* as possible and to stiffen the will of the people.

Fortuny found himself isolated within the Secretariat that he had once dominated. He had fully supported the decision to buy weapons from Czechoslovakia. Yet, as the weeks passed, he felt that his friends were failing to grasp the gravity of the threat facing Guatemala. He agreed with them that the regime could handily repel the forthcoming invasion led by Castillo Armas, but this, he believed, was only the overture. Washington would respond to Castillo Armas's defeat by intensifying its aggression—even, if necessary, by sending in the troops.

There was no way that Guatemala alone could defeat a U.S. invasion, and Guatemala was alone. Caracas had exposed her isolation, and the messages of support that had poured in from politicians, intellectuals, and trade unionists of several Latin American countries were of little solace.[19] Searching for a viable policy, Fortuny decided that the party should "exercise self-restraint": the pace of the agrarian reform should not be accelerated; those communists in highly visible government positions should resign for "reasons of health"; and the government and the PGT should moderate their rhetoric. He hoped that such steps would give pause to the United States so that after the defeat of Castillo Armas, Eisenhower would hesitate before ordering more extreme measures.

The lines of the debate were confused. Fortuny was hesitant. He was afraid that he might appear defeatist, and he was afraid that his policy had very little chance of success—that it was too little, too late. In the past, his self-assurance had been a powerful weapon; now it was shaken, and the other members of the Secretariat argued with the fervor of desperation. In his "Autocrítica," written a year after Arbenz fell, Fortuny bares the doubts that enfeebled his warnings: "I was aware that my influence in the Secretariat was waning. . . . I was also worried that my views might be considered cowardly and that they would split the Political Commission at a time when unity was essential. But also, I was not sure of myself; I was not sure that I was right. These were my inner thoughts, and I made the mistake of not voicing them."[20]

Sickness also sapped Fortuny's strength,[21] but more debilitating was his growing sense of impotence. His calls for "self-restraint" were spurned. On

---

[19] Many of these messages were published in *DCA*; still others can be found in the *GT*, esp. Box 5.

[20] Fortuny, "Autocrítica," pp. 2–3.

[21] Ibid., p. 1.

May 1, there was the traditional workers' parade, purportedly organized by the labor confederations, but directed in fact by the PGT. A gigantic portrait of Ho Chi Minh opened the march and set the tone.[22] This was a flagrant rejection of Fortuny's advice that the government should moderate its tone, a rejection made more painful by the fact that he had not even been consulted.

For some time, Fortuny recalls, he had been considering stepping down, at least temporarily, from the leadership of a Secretariat he no longer led. The only alternative was to bring the disagreements within the Secretariat to the attention of the Political Commission and the Central Committee (CC) of the PGT. This, he believed, would have been divisive precisely when unity was imperative; the move would have been particularly unjustified, he may have felt, since he was not confident that he had a viable policy to offer. He was also aware that most members of the CC and the Political Commission supported the stance of the majority of the Secretariat.

Fortuny, Alejandro counters, "did not resign of his own accord. He was asked to resign."[23] The other members of the Secretariat considered him "burnt out."[24] His poor health provided a convenient pretext. In two sessions of the Secretariat—one in late April, the other in early May—Fortuny repeated his reservations: "I was worried that the party might go beyond what was realistically possible, and no longer take into account the objective conditions of the struggle, the political level of the people, or the constraints on the government." Then he and the other Secretariat members agreed on the immediate solution: "I would be temporarily relieved of my post as secretary general for medical reasons."[25] He would remain, however, as the link between the party and Arbenz. The decision was relayed to the Political Commission and the CC of the PGT. The explanation focused on Fortuny's poor health and only alluded to political differences.[26] On May 27, the PGT publicly announced Fortuny's temporary withdrawal; Bernardo Alvarado Monzón would be secretary general *ad interim*.[27]

[22] See "Gigantesco desfile," *DCA*, May 3, p. 1; "El 1° de mayo: Una respuesta," ibid., p. 4; "Guatemalan Fete Is Anti-U.S. Affair," *NYT*, May 2, p. 32; "60 mil desfilaron," *Tribuna Popular*, May 4, p. 1; "Orden, júbilo marcan ritmo con carrozas en profusión," *El I*, May 3, p. 1. All 1954.

[23] Interview with Alejandro.

[24] Interview with Guerra Borges.

[25] Fortuny, "Autocrítica," pp. 2, 3.

[26] Ibid., pp. 3–4.

[27] "Reunión del Comité Central del PGT," *Tribuna Popular*, May 27, 1954, p. 1. For the views of the U.S. embassy, which was confounded by Fortuny's resignation, see Wardlaw to DOS, no. 994, June 9, 1954, NA 714.001. For the views of the opposition, which was equally confused, see "Resoluciones que, según los afiliados, pueden aliviar la posición del gobierno," *La Hora*, May 28, 1954, p. 1, and "Profunda escisión dentro del Partido Comunista trasciende," *El Espectador*, June 7, 1954, p. 1.

Arbenz was not aware of the debate within the Secretariat. "It is true," Fortuny stressed in his "Autocrítica," that "President Arbenz and I were very close friends . . . that we talked of very personal matters, but I did not discuss internal party business with him."[28] Fortuny's resignation was a blow to Arbenz. "Jacobo knew Fortuny wasn't telling him the whole truth," recalls Doña María, "but he respected Fortuny's discretion, and he didn't pursue the matter. But it did bother him."[29]

One may wonder whether Fortuny's silence was due solely to discretion. Had Fortuny been more sure that he had an alternative to offer, he might have been less reticent. As it was, until mid-June—roughly until Castillo Armas attacked—the two friends maintained a mutual silence about their worst fears, each perhaps wary of demoralizing the other, each perhaps afraid that had he voiced his deepest fears they would have become more real.[30]

Arbenz, like the PGT, believed that the army would remain loyal if faced with Castillo Armas. Like Fortuny, he looked beyond the exiles' attack. What would the United States do after Castillo's Armas's defeat? Caracas had shaken him. "Now we are truly in danger," he confided in a rare moment of openness to an old friend, Colonel Terencio Guillén, governor of the department of Escuintla. "We must press on with the agrarian reform. We have to get tangible benefits for the people, benefits that it will be very hard to take away. Please help me. We must do as much as we can."[31]

One suspects that had Arbenz sat on the Secretariat of the PGT, he would have sided against Fortuny, not because he did not share his fears, but because he saw no salvation in retreat. "We cannot relent," he told Guillén. "It is better to remain at our posts until we are overwhelmed than to retreat; if we must, let us die fighting. If we waver, we will be routed."[32]

In public and in private, Arbenz sought to strengthen the morale of the population and to rally administration politicians who fervently hoped for a step backward. In his March 1 annual message to Congress, in his address welcoming the return of the Caracas delegation, in his May 1 speech, he spoke as a man who was self-assured and in control. The revolution faced external difficulties, he conceded, but these could be overcome—through firmness, not retreat. He stood by his policies, he warned, and there would be no "step backward." (Privately, to the leaders of the PGT he pledged: "I will be by

---

[28] Fortuny, "Autocrítica," p. 6.

[29] Interview with María de Arbenz; interview with Fortuny confirmed Arbenz's reticence in asking questions about the internal affairs of the PGT.

[30] Interviews with María de Arbenz and Fortuny.

[31] Interview with Guillén. Interviews with María de Arbenz and Fortuny were very useful.

[32] Interview with Guillén.

your side until the end.'')[33] The U.S. embassy found him "defiant," but neither shrill nor petulant.[34]

Yet Arbenz was anxious. He alternated between waves of deep pessimism and surges of optimism. His optimism, notes his wife, who was his closest confidante through those harrowing weeks, "was a means of self-defense: it was better to grasp at straws than to be defeated psychologically before the final battle."[35] In fact, Arbenz lived in a private world fraught with ghosts and contradictions, and nowhere were these contradictions more apparent than in the decision to import arms from Czechoslovakia. The weapons would build the morale of an army that had long been frustrated in its desire for new materiel. They would also increase its capacity to defeat a U.S. sponsored invasion of Guatemala. Yet the decision to set aside some of the weapons derived from mistrust of the very institution that would be strengthened by the remainder. In one stroke, Arbenz and the PGT were providing for a workers' militia they knew the army would never countenance, and they were giving the army weapons to crush it should it appear.

Arbenz, Fortuny, and the other members of the PGT's Secretariat were groping tensely and awkwardly for a way to save the revolution, but their political instincts had been dulled by the relentless pressure from Washington. And their enemies were circling.

Among them was Archbishop Rossell y Arellano, the highest Catholic authority in the land. On April 9, he issued a pastoral letter. Read in every church and echoed in the opposition press and radio stations, the pastoral was, in effect, a call to rebellion:

We again raise our voice to alert Catholics that anti-Christian communism—the worst atheist doctrine of all time—is stalking our country under the cloak of social justice. We warn you that those whom the communists help today, they will condemn to forced labor and terrible suffering tomorrow. Everyone who loves his country must fight against those who—loyal to no country, the scum of the earth—have repaid Guatemala's generous hospitality by fomenting class hatred, in preparation for the day of destruction and slaughter which they anticipate with such enthusiasm. . . . Guatemala must rise as one against this enemy of God and country.[36]

[33] Interviews with María de Arbenz (quoted), Fortuny, and Guerra Borges.
[34] See for instance *JW* 9, Mar. 5, 1954, pp. 1–2; *JW* 10, Mar. 12, 1954, p. 1 (quoted); *JW* 18, May 7, 1954, pp. 1–2.
[35] Interview with María de Arbenz.
[36] Carta Pastoral "Sobre los avances del comunismo," *El I*, Apr. 9, 1954, pp. 1, 6 (quoted). The archbishop's words, the U.S. embassy remarked, gave "sanction to activities outside of the confining limits of 'legal and constitutional' opposition." They constituted, "his strongest anti-communist pronouncement to date." (Quotations from

In vain did the nuncio, who had not been consulted about the pastoral, urge Rossell y Arellano to soften his rhetoric. Months of tension between the two clergymen culminated in "a very violent clash."[37] Rossell y Arellano pressed forward with the attack: "Any relationship between the Church and the government of Guatemala has ceased to exist," he told the *New York Times*.[38] He failed to mention that his attack was part of a larger effort; the timing and the venom of the pastoral were weapons in the rising war of nerves orchestrated by the planners of PBSUCCESS.[39]

While Rossell y Arellano's pastoral resonated through the churches of the republic, other Guatemalans were training in CIA camps in Nicaragua and Honduras, and still others were the guests of the CIA at Opa Locka, a semi-abandoned air force base near Miami.

In command at Opa Locka was Al Haney, a "handsome, rugged six-footer," with a pugnacious personality.[40] In October 1953, Allen Dulles had summoned Haney from Seoul, where he was CIA station chief, to take charge of the day-to-day conduct of PBSUCCESS. Under his vigorous leadership, Opa Locka became the nerve center of the operation. "He got all the funds," recalls an agent who was on the scene. Closely supervising and directing the work of the CIA stations in Central America, Haney steadily increased his autonomy, to the rising irritation of Frank Wisner, who was in charge of PBSUCCESS in Washington. "It was," explains Richard Bissell, "a system of double headquarters that led to a lot of squabbling. It was a mistake that we

---

Krieg to DOS, no. 852, Apr. 12, 1954, p. 2, NA 814.413, and *JW* 15, Apr. 14, 1954, p. 1.)

[37] Interview with Fr. Bendaña Perdomo. See also: Bendaña Perdomo, "Historia general," p. 52; "Si non e Vero-Lino e ven trovatino," *La Hora*, July 14, 1954, p. l; "Si non Vero-lino e ven trovato," *La Hora*, July 21, 1954, p. 1; "Varios católicos protestan por una alusión al Excelentísimo Nuncio Apostólico," *La Hora*, July 27, 1954, p. 1; "El Nuncio Verolino negó que haya diferencia alguna con el Arzobispo," *El I*, Feb. 4, 1956, p. 1.

[38] "Guatemala Cleric Vows War on Reds," *NYT*, Apr. 18, 1954, p. 12.

[39] Interviews with Bendaña Perdomo and Taracena. For the role played by the Catholic press (*Acción Social Cristiana* and *Verbum*) in the spring of 1954, see L.A.H.A., *Así se gestó la Liberación*, pp. 139, 148, 151, 153, 155–57, 160, 165. Following the publication of the pastoral, and as part of PBSUCCESS's psychological offensive, the rumor was spread that "the government is considering the expulsion of the Archbishop and of all foreign priests." (Ibid., p. 158.)

According to some sources, Cardinal Francis Spellman of New York helped the CIA to establish contact with Rossell y Arellano. (See Schlesinger and Kinzer, *Bitter Fruit*, p. 155, and Frankel, "Political Development," p. 235.) It should be noted, however, that the archbishop was plotting with Castillo Armas before PBSUCCESS began.

[40] Schlesinger and Kinzer, *Bitter Fruit*, p. 109. "I didn't know anyone who liked Haney." (Interview with Roettinger who was based at Opa Loca from February to April 1954.)

avoided in the Bay of Pigs operation; Opa Locka was used again, but there was only one headquarters—Washington, period!''[41]

Among the CIA officials who worked under Haney was Howard Hunt. Hunt, who enjoyed modest fame as a writer of spy thrillers, later gained notoriety when he was arrested in the Democratic Party Headquarters in the Watergate.[42] During PBSUCCESS, he served as political action officer. He was flamboyant, intelligent, and articulate. He also had, notes a colleague, ''a penchant for the devious [that] was apparent in almost every conversation. For example, most propaganda undertaken covertly is handled in this fashion only because it cannot be handled overtly, but Howard was inclined to consider the option of using the Department of State only if the effort was not possible by CIA stealth.''[43]

The propaganda put out by the CIA during PBSUCCESS had more than a touch of the melodrama that characterized Hunt's thrillers. And it is to the misfortune of historians that Hunt, certainly the most loquacious of the CIA agents who participated in the operation, demonstrated the same penchant for the devious and love of the melodramatic in his accounts of the plot.[44]

The planners of PBSUCCESS had counted on the collaboration of Honduras and Nicaragua. Honduras was key, as it would serve as the launching pad of the invasion, but President Gálvez and his associates lacked the requisite zeal and backbone. They required constant prodding. Not to worry: Whiting Willauer was there.

In February 1954, just as a handful of CIA instructors began training a few dozen exiles in a finca near Tegucigalpa, Willauer arrived at his post.[45] He had learned about communism at first hand. As General Claire Chennault's right-hand man in the Civil Air Transport Company, he had worked with the CIA and the Chinese Nationalists in the late 1940s; in the process he had witnessed the communist triumph in China.[46]

Entries in the log of C. D. Jackson, a senior White House aide who worked very closely with the CIA, suggest that in the spring of 1953 Willauer was a leading contender for the post of ambassador to Guatemala; they also indicate that Frank Wisner was deeply involved in the selection process. As late as July

---

[41] Quotations from interviews with Roettinger and Bissell; see also Schlesinger and Kinzer, *Bitter Fruit*, pp. 109–10 and Immerman, *CIA in Guatemala*, pp. 139–40. Until the late spring of 1954, ''It was really Opa Locka that was giving directions and making policy. Then Washington stepped in and took control. By that time, headquarters at Opa Locka had grown to about 100 people.'' (Interview with Bissell.)

[42] For a biography of Hunt, see Szulc, *Compulsive Spy*.

[43] Phillips, *Night Watch*, p. 36.

[44] See esp. Hunt, *Undercover*, pp. 83–101.

[45] Interview with Roettinger who joined the group in April.

[46] See Leary, *Perilous Missions*. See also Eisenhower Records Central File, OF, Box 165 OF8-F, Willauer, EL, and U.S. Congress, *Communist Threat*, pp. 861–88.

18, the log noted: "Lunch—Willauer-Wisner—on Guatemalan ambassador-ship. . . . Looks good right now, but you never know."[47]

In the end, Willauer lost out to Peurifoy and landed as ambassador in Honduras.[48] He had gone to his new job, he later told a congressional committee, as part of a "team"—activist ambassadors who worked closely with the CIA to implement PBSUCCESS. This team, he added, also included Ambassador Tom Whelan in Nicaragua and, of course, Jack Peurifoy.[49]

[47] Entries of Apr. 15, May 2, and July 18 (quoted), 1953, Jackson Papers, Box 56, EL.

[48] See entry of Sept. 22, 1953, ibid.; Hanes to Undersecretary of State, Nov. 20, 1953, DP:SACS, Box 4; MemoTel (JFD, Saltonstall), Jan. 19, 1954, DP, JFD:CS, Box 6. All EL.

Some authors suggest that Willauer, who was a Republican, lost to Peurifoy, a Democrat, because the administration preferred to have a member of the opposition party on the front line should PBSUCCESS fail. (See Immerman, *CIA in Guatemala*, pp. 136–37, and Schlesinger and Kinzer, *Bitter Fruit*, p. 132.) While Willauer was being considered as ambassador to Guatemala, Peurifoy was the leading candidate to be ambassador to Honduras. (See SecState, "Memorandum for the President," n.d., DP:SS, Box 6, EL.) Given the importance of the operation, it is more likely that the Administration chose Peurifoy because he was considered the better man.

[49] See U.S. Congress, *Communist Threat*, p. 866. Whelan, who had developed close personal ties to Somoza, was one of the handful of Truman's political appointees who survived Dulles's 1953 purge of the State Department.

In his testimony, Willauer included Robert Hill, the ambassador to Costa Rica from late 1953 to late 1954, in the "team." Hill himself declined the honor. (Immerman, *CIA in Guatemala*, p. 141.) Immerman, the only scholar to have examined this issue, notes that "documents refer to him [Hill] in connection with the Guatemalan project." He cites an Apr. 11, 1958 letter by C. D. Jackson, who was well informed about PBSUCCESS: "Dear Ambassador Hill was the character," wrote Jackson, "who made so much trouble for us in his previous post." Immerman's other major item of evidence is an Apr. 21, 1958 memo, again by Jackson, that mentions "all the trouble we had with Hill when he was in Guatemala." (Ibid.)

The following points must, however, be borne in mind:

1. PBSUCCESS assigned no active role to Costa Rica.
2. Hill's appointment was not engineered by the CIA. It was due, rather, to Styles Bridges, the powerful Republican senator from his home state of New Hampshire, who was friendly with Hill's family and respected Hill as a successful young businessman. (See: TelConv [JFD, Bridges], Oct. 19, 1953, 12:10 p.m., DP, JFD:CS, Box 5, EL; Hill, "Oral History Interview," 1964, pp. 1, 2, 18–19; and Hill, "Oral History Interview," 1973, pp. 7–13.)
3. Hill never served in Guatemala. While C. D. Jackson's Apr. 21, 1958, memo mentions "all the trouble we had with Hill when he was in Guatemala," the enclosures that Jackson attached to the memo indicate that he meant El Salvador. The "trouble" did not have to do with PBSUCCESS, but with an intemperate attack that Hill made in the Salvadoran press against *Time*'s critical reporting on Salvadoran affairs: " 'The unfortunate inaccuracy and often fraudulent articles written

"I suppose most of you have looked up Honduras on your maps before coming here," Willauer told a meeting of the World Affairs Council in 1960. "I must confess that I had to do so when it was first suggested that I should become ambassador."[50] Like Peurifoy, he had not set foot in Central America before he arrived as ambassador. But if his knowledge was faulty, his instincts were sure. By stealth and deception, the communists were preparing to reenact their Asian triumphs in the heart of the American Mediterranean. Should they consolidate their control of Guatemala, the infection would spread. Honduras would fall next, and then the other Central American republics.[51]

Willauer was proud to help reverse the tide. To be sure, he has acknowledged modestly that Peurifoy was "the principal man" in the ambassadorial team unleashed against Arbenz, but he, too, "was called upon to perform very important duties, particularly to keep the Honduran government . . . in line,

---

about the Latin American Republics make the work of our embassy much more difficult than it would be otherwise,' says the Ambassador." (*Prensa Gráfica*, Aug. 19, 1955, Jackson Papers, Box 49, EL. See also Dubois to Alexander, ibid.) After leaving the Eisenhower administration in 1954, Jackson had been a senior *Time* executive—hence his remarks on the trouble "we" had with Hill. In the same vein, when he mentioned Hill's "previous post" (where the trouble had occurred) in his Apr. 11, 1958, letter, he was not referring to Costa Rica. In 1958 Hill was ambassador to Mexico; his previous post, therefore, had been in El Salvador.

4. The only documents connecting Hill to Guatemala deal with diplomatic matters such as Hill's efforts to convince Figueres to participate in the Caracas conference and to endorse the U.S. preparations, in May–June 1954, for another OAS conference directed against Guatemala. With the one exception of Willauer's brief reference in his 1961 testimony, no document implicates Hill in PBSUCCESS.

Also not involved was Michael McDermott, who was appointed ambassador to El Salvador on May 21, 1953, that is, before PBSUCCESS was born. McDermott had been the State Department's press secretary since 1927. He was liked by State Department officials, including Secretary Dulles. Since he was nearing retirement, he was rewarded with an ambassadorship, the first and last of his life. No evidence links him to PBSUCCESS. (On McDermott's appointment, an interview with Deputy Assistant Secretary Woodward was particularly helpful. See also Purse to Willis, May 18, 1953, Eisenhower Records Central File, OF, Box 162, EL; Willis to Adams, July 28, 1954, ibid., Box 165; McDermott to Eisenhower, Aug. 13, 1954, ibid., Box 162. For a biographical sketch of McDermott see "Michael J. McDermott," ibid.)

To conclude, the CIA's "ambassadorial team" to Central America included only Peurifoy, Willauer, and Whelan, who served in the three countries that participated directly in the plot. Costa Rica and El Salvador were expected to provide only diplomatic support.

[50] Willauer, "Draft no. 1. Speech for World Affairs Council," Nov. 12, 1960, p. 1, Willauer Papers, ML.

[51] See ibid., esp. pp. 7–21. See also Willauer to Harrington, June 15, 1954, ibid., and Willauer to Sherry, June 9, 1954, ibid.

so they would allow this revolutionary activity [by Castillo Armas] to continue, based in Honduras.'' President Gálvez and his government were eager to see Arbenz overthrown, but they were afraid of what would happen if Castillo Armas failed. They feared the Guatemalans, and they feared their own people. In fact, explained Willauer, they were ''scared to death about the possibilities of themselves being overthrown.''[52] And so Willauer, flaunting the power of the United States and his own aggressive personality, did his best to cajole and bully his hosts and keep them in line. And in line they stood.[53]

There was no need to bully Somoza; the dictator was eager and enthusiastic. In February 1954, the CIA opened two training camps in Nicaragua: at Momotombito, an island in Lake Managua, and at El Tamarindo, a Somoza estate. Meanwhile, at an abandoned air strip near Puerto Cabezas, a handful of Guatemalan pilots was training for Castillo Armas's air force, while the CIA gathered the planes through dummy companies. Since the planners of PBSUCCESS were eager ''to give the impression that the rebels had bought the planes on the international market,'' the rebel airforce finally consisted of a motley assortment of a dozen or so World War II P-47s and C-47s.[54] Most of the pilots were Americans hired by the CIA—men like Jerry Fred DeLarm, ''a slim, short, hawk-featured man who liked to lay a 45 down on the table in front of him when talking to a stranger.''[55] Theatrics apart, these Americans were congenial fellows, gregarious and happy-going, just a mite too boisterous and indiscreet. ''Your pal will be in the middle of the blood and thunder . . . on June 18, 19 or 20,'' one of them wrote to a friend a week before D-Day.[56]

While the pilots were trained at Puerto Cabezas, a force of another kind was being organized at El Tamarindo and at Momotombito. PBSUCCESS called for

[52] Willauer testimony, in U.S. Congress, *Communist Threat*, p. 866. On U.S. concerns about domestic instability in Honduras, see Erwin to SecState, no. 50, Jan. 24, 1954; Erwin to DOS, no. 331, Feb. 2, 1954; Erwin to DOS, no. 339, Feb. 9, 1954; Erwin to SecState, no. 84, Feb. 21, 1954; Willauer to SecState, no. 154, Apr. 1, 1954; Willauer to DOS, no. 408, Apr. 2, 1954. All AmEm Tegucigalpa; all NA 715.00.

[53] ''The Gálvez regime in Honduras became generally frightened about the Castillo Armas movement, to the point where in February 1954 they forced him to bring his activities to a near standstill. Very fortunately, however, this loss of courage was short-lived and finally by April 1954 Castillo Armas was again permitted to continue with the preparations in Honduras.'' (Willauer, [see n. 50 above], p. 23.)

[54] Interview with Bissell (quoted). There is some disagreement as to the exact size and composition of Castillo Armas's air force. See Cline, *Secrets, Spies and Scholars*, p. 132; Phillips, *Night Watch*, p. 36; Willauer to Chennault, June 30, 1954, *FRUS*, 1952–1954, 4:1308. On the dummy companies, see Schlesinger and Kinzer, *Bitter Fruit*, pp. 115–16.

[55] Wise and Ross, *Invisible Government*, p. 186. For a creative and melodramatic account of Delarm's exploits, see Larsen, ''Sulfato.''

[56] ''U.S. Citizen Joins Anti-Red Rebels,'' *NYT*, June 22, 1954, p. 3 (quoted); FBI, report no. 1 from Havana, Cuba, June 8, 1954; FBI, Belmont to Boardman, June 10, 1954; FBI, Hoover to Olney, 2-14Oc-4, June 11, 1954.

two to three hundred men to invade Guatemala on D-Day. In the preceding weeks, 150 "hornets" would infiltrate the country.[57] With recruits from the "home front," they would organize a fifth column that would strike as soon as the invasion had begun. The would-be saboteurs learned their trade at El Tamarindo, whereas a couple hundred invaders were whipped into shape at Momotombito. "We trained for about six weeks," recalls Eduardo Taracena, a close aide of Castillo Armas who reached Momotombito in March. "Our instructors were taciturn, friendly Americans whom we knew only by first name. (They were all called Pepe or José.) They told us when we arrived that the invasion would begin in May."[58]

As the training progressed, the host, President Somoza, was very much in the news. Prominently featured with him was his nemesis, Figueres of Costa Rica. On April 5, the Nicaraguan government announced the discovery of an armed band of approximately twenty-five men who had been preparing an attack on Somoza; pursued by the National Guard, some had been killed, some had been captured, and others had escaped.[59] The plot was no CIA concoction to implicate Arbenz in an attack on his peaceful neighbor. The agency, in this case, was innocent, as was Somoza. Arbenz was equally innocent, and so were his communist friends, but it soon became evident that the plotters, who had entered Nicaragua from Costa Rica, had benefited from the complicity of high Costa Rican officials—even, perhaps, Figueres himself.[60]

Somoza was delighted to blame Arbenz for the plot, but he also wanted revenge against Figueres. His approach was straightforward: damn them both. Arbenz, he pointed out, was a communist, but then, so was Figueres, "who has been secretly conniving for many years with Soviet agents based in Guatemala and other Caribbean countries"; both belonged to the international communist conspiracy that had targeted him because he was the "foremost anticommunist leader of Central America."[61] Therefore, argued Somoza, a meeting of OAS foreign ministers should be convened to consider sanctions

[57] Tracy Barnes, a senior aide to Wisner, coined the term. (Interview with Roettinger.)

[58] Interviews with Taracena (quoted) and Bissell. See also L.A.H.A., *Así se gestó la Liberación*, pp. 181, 184; Wise and Ross, *Invisible Government*, pp. 185–86; Schlesinger and Kinzer, *Bitter Fruit*, p. 114.

[59] "Comunican el cierre de frontera sur," *La Prensa*, Managua, Apr. 6, 1954, p. 1; "Nicaragua Foils Assassins' Plot," *NYT*, Apr. 6, 1954, p. 7; "Frontier Is Closed," *NYT*, Apr. 7, 1954, p. 26; "6 Slain in Nicaragua," *NYT*, Apr. 8, 1954, p. 8; "3 Slain in Nicaragua," *NYT*, Apr. 9, 1954, p. 3; "Nicaraguan Rebel Chief Slain," *NYT*, Apr. 10, 1954, p. 6.

[60] For the plot, see Martz, *Central America*, pp. 186–93 and Ameringer, *Democratic Left*, pp. 205–12.

[61] "Memorandum confidencial sobre la infiltración comunista en Centro América," Managua, [May 1954], p. 2, Archives of the Nicaraguan embassy, Washington, D.C.

against both Costa Rica and Guatemala.[62] Without first consulting the United States, he approached Honduras and El Salvador to inquire whether they "would be willing to back the Nicaraguan request."[63]

Busy as they were cinching the noose around Arbenz, the planners of PBSUCCESS now had to placate the infuriated dictator. Gently, but firmly, Washington reminded Somoza that Arbenz was the target and that an OAS conference condemning both Guatemala and Costa Rica would deflect attention from this primary concern.[64] Reluctantly, Somoza relented.

On May 6 the Nicaraguan delivered another bombshell: a large cache of weapons had just been discovered on the country's Pacific coast; a few days earlier, he added, a mysterious submarine had been sighted in the area. For anyone who couldn't divine the source of the weapons and the nationality of the submarine, a clue was obligingly provided: the arms "were stamped with a hammer and sickle."[65] The weapons had, in fact, been planted by the CIA, with Somoza's enthusiastic complicity.[66] The ploy, however, was too crude to have much value as propaganda and received only limited attention at the time.

While Somoza spluttered, a small group of Guatemalans and their American adviser were setting up camp on a hillside near Managua.[67] The American, David Atlee Phillips, had been living in Chile, where he edited an English-language newspaper and moonlighted for the CIA.[68] In early March 1954, Phillips writes, he had been urgently summoned to the United States and offered a special assignment. A clandestine radio station, "which would pretend to be broadcasting from Guatemala," would be set up in Nicaragua. "A team of radio technicians, writers and announcers, including two women, was being recruited in Guatemala City. They would come to Florida for planning sessions before going off to the third country [Nicaragua] where the transmitter was now being erected. I was to act as an adviser to the team."[69] He was

---

[62] See Ministerio de relaciones exteriores, Managua, "Memorandum confidencial," May 24, 1954, Archives of the Nicaraguan Embassy, Washington, D.C.

[63] Foreign Minister Oscar Sevilla Sacasa to Amb. Guillermo Sevilla Sacasa, Managua, no. 232, May 24, 1954, Archives of the Nicaraguan Embassy, Washington, D.C.; see also Ministerio de Relaciones Exteriores, "Memorandum confidencial" (see n. 62 above), and AmEm Tegucigalpa, Willauer to SecState, no. 353, May 21, 1954, NA 714.00.

[64] See MemoConv (Dulles, Sevilla Sacasa), May 20, 1954, and MemoConv (Sevilla Sacasa, Holland), May 21, 1954. Both NA 714.00.

[65] "Armas en sacos impermeables hallan en costa del Pacifico," *La Prensa*, Managua, May 7, 1954, p. 1.

[66] See Schlesinger and Kinzer, *Bitter Fruit*, p. 150.

[67] Interview with Roettinger, who was there in late June.

[68] Phillips describes his Chilean days in *Night Watch*, pp. 4–29.

[69] Ibid., p. 36. For Phillips' account of his participation in PBSUCCESS, see pp. 30–54.

selected for the job, Phillips believes, because he possessed two skills unusual among CIA agents: he spoke flawless Spanish and had acting and broadcasting experience.[70] For the next few weeks he and his Guatemalan charges were guests of the CIA at Opa Locka. In late April they left for Managua.

The facilities were spartan: "the jungle transmitter was being set up in an old cow barn, and living quarters would be in a dilapidated shack."[71] Phillips knew that they had little time. Before leaving, he had been told that the radio had to start broadcasting on May 1 and that Castillo Armas's invasion would begin in mid-June;[72] his Guatemalans, writes Phillips, had "just six weeks to build toward the climax of their propaganda campaign."[73]

On May 1, *La Voz de la Liberación* broadcast its first message, announcing amid popular American songs that the hours of the "traitor Jacobo" were numbered.[74] The radio reception was excellent, and the country "was swept by speculation as to where the station was located and who was its sponsor."[75] The station, claimed its announcers and the Guatemalan opposition press, was operating from inside Guatemala, outwitting Arbenz's police.[76] The broadcasts were useful fodder in the war of nerves but by mid-May they had "lessened in effectiveness," noted the embassy, because of government jamming.[77]

The embassy's report was dated May 14. Three days later, tension in Guatemala reached a new high as the State Department announced that a Swedish ship, the *Alfhem*, had just landed at Puerto Barrios, loaded with arms from behind the Iron Curtain.[78]

It was true. The weapons promised by Novotný were aboard the ship in

[70] Interview with Phillips.

[71] Phillips, *Night Watch*, p. 38.

[72] Interview with Phillips.

[73] Phillips, *Night Watch*, p. 42.

[74] See, for example, the testimony of López Villatoro, one of the Guatemalan radio broadcasters, in U.S. Congress, *Communist Aggression*, pp. 97–111.

[75] *JW* 18, May 7, 1954, p. 3; see also Krieg to McCormick, et al., "Clandestine Radio Station in Guatemala," May 6, 1954, RG84 G&C, Box 3, NA-S, and Krieg to DOS, no. 915, May 6, 1954, NA 714.00.

[76] See, for instance: "Sigue la radioemisora clandestina" (edit.), *La Hora*, May 6, 1954, p. 4; "Vuela avión para localizar la radioemisora clandestina," *La Hora*, May 8, 1954, p. 1; "Radio Clandestina sigue siendo un fantasma," *El I*, May 8, 1954, p. 1; "Dónde se halla emplazada la radioemisora clandestina?" *La Hora*, May 14, 1954, p. 1.

[77] *JW* 19, May 14, 1954, p. 4. See also Marroquín Rojas, "Los cuatros entusiasmos de los últimos meses," *La Hora*, May 31, 1954, p. 4.

[78] "Communist Arms Unloaded in Guatemala by Vessel from Polish Port, U.S. Learns," *NYT*, May 18, 1954, p. 1. For the text of the State Department's press release see *Department of State Bulletin*, May 31, 1954, p. 835.

crates labeled optical equipment. In April, the CIA had learned from an agent in the Polish port of Stettin (where the weapons had been loaded) that military equipment was on its way to a country "in the Western Hemisphere"[79]— obviously Guatemala. But the CIA lost track of the *Alfhem* as it proceeded along a circuitous route to Puerto Barrios. ("The deception . . . was excellent," Wisner later told Secretary Dulles.)[80] The ship was rediscovered only as it reached Guatemalan waters.[81] On May 16, a few hours after the *Alfhem*'s arrival, the State Department instructed its embassy in Stockholm to persuade the Swedish government "to order *Alfhem* sail from Puerto Barrios at once without unloading," while Peurifoy was told "to encourage IRCA to cause maximum delay" while investigating the cargo.[82]

U.S. officials were alarmed by the *Alfhem*. They feared that it would strengthen support for Arbenz among the officer corps that longed for new weapons.[83] Its arrival, some analysts have argued, triggered the decision to launch PBSUCCESS: "When the *Alfhem* docked in Puerto Barrios," writes Immerman, "Eisenhower and his advisers decided thay they could no longer delay the authorization to effect PBSUCCESS. Castillo Armas's invasion had to begin before Arbenz distributed the new supplies, either to the peasants or to his cohorts elsewhere in Central America."[84]

The evidence does not support this assertion. Taracena recalls that before the arrival of the *Alfhem*, "Castillo Armas had been told that the invasion would begin in May. The date was postponed because we were not ready."[85] David Phillips, the CIA operative in charge of the clandestine radio, writes in his memoirs that he was told in late April that there were "just six weeks" before the invasion was launched.[86] Assistant Secretary Holland wrote on

[79] Tully, *CIA*, p. 64.

[80] TelConv (JFD, Wisner), May 17, 1954, 4:32 p.m., DP:TCS, Box 2, EL.

[81] The most exhaustive account of the CIA and the *Alfhem* is Tully, *CIA*, pp. 62–65. See also Richard and Gladys Harkness, "America's Secret Agents: The Mysterious Doings of CIA," *Saturday Evening Post*, Oct. 30, 1954, pp. 19–20. (This article was submitted to Allen Dulles for approval and revised according to his suggestions. See Fuoss to Grogan, Aug. 9, 1954, and Harkness to AWD, rec'd Aug. 13, 1954, AWD Papers, Box 62, ML.)

[82] DOS, "Chronology of Events (Secret)," entry of May 16, 1954 (quoted), RG84 G&C, Box 3, NA-S, and Holland to SecState, "Action to Prevent Delivery of Czech Arms to Guatemala," May 18, 1954, NA Lot 58D18 & 58D78, Box 2.

[83] Both Peurifoy and the CIA soon concluded, however, that there was no evidence that the shipment had in fact improved Arbenz's position. See Peurifoy to SecState, no. 854, June 1, 1954, NA 714.00, and CIA, *Current Intelligence Digest*, June 3, 1954, p.16.

[84] Immerman, *CIA in Guatemala*, p. 160 (quoted); Higgins, *Perfect Failure*, p. 26; Ranelagh, *Agency*, p. 266.

[85] Interview with Taracena.

[86] Phillips, *Night Watch*, p. 42.

April 20, "There are possibilities of new developments in the Guatemalan situation between now and the end of June."[87] Holland was one of the few who knew about PBSUCCESS; "new developments" was, clearly, a guarded reference to the invasion. The evidence suggests that well before the *Alfhem* appeared on the scene, the invasion was planned for May or June. There is no indication that the arrival of the *Alfhem* accelerated its tempo.[88]

It did, however, present the planners of PBSUCCESS with an opportunity they were determined to exploit: violent condemnations of this flagrant act of aggression by the Soviet Union and its Guatemalan puppet were accompanied by ostentatious measures purportedly designed to protect Nicaragua and Honduras. The United States had signed a Mutual Security Treaty on April 23 with Nicaragua; it now hastened to conclude a similar pact with Honduras.[89] On May 24, the Pentagon airlifted fifty tons of weapons to Nicaragua and Honduras. The United States, wrote the *New York Times*, would be sending additional arms to these two countries that were threatened by "Guatemalan aggression or . . . Communist subversion."[90] Other highly publicized military measures were taken rapidly: on May 23, the U.S. navy dispatched two submarines from Key West, "saying only that they were going 'south.' "[91] Four days later, the air force sent three intercontinental bombers, B-36s, to partici-

[87] Holland to Acting Secretary, Apr. 20, 1954, *FRUS*, 1952–1954, 4:1101.

[88] Exactly when Eisenhower gave the final go-ahead for the operation is not known. Ambrose and Immerman offer no source for their claim that in the wake of the *Alfhem*, "at a secret, emergency session of the National Security Council . . . Eisenhower approved the program [Allen] Dulles outlined. The CIA-sponsored invasion of Guatemala was on." (*Ike's Spies*, pp. 216–17.) It is likely that, as he had done with AJAX, Eisenhower gave the final okay very shortly before the invasion was launched. (This was also Kennedy's procedure in the Bay of Pigs.) Therefore, while the final authorization was probably given after the arrival of the *Alfhem*, this does not prove any causal relationship between the two events.

[89] "U.S. and Honduras Sign Arms Accord," *NYT*, May 22, 1954, p. 4. In fact, the United States, Nicaragua, and Honduras had agreed on the military assistance pacts several months earlier; they had been waiting for an opportune moment to announce them. Peurifoy had urged that "unless other considerations are overriding, announcement be deferred until after Caracas meeting since prior announcement would doubtless be used there by Guatemalans to claim United States was preparing for armed intervention in Guatemala." (Peurifoy to SecState, no. 321, Feb. 12, 1954, NA 714.00. For background, see *FRUS*, 1952–1954, 4:144–46, 150–53, 168–69; MemoConv [McDermott, Canessa], Feb. 9, 1954, NA Lot 58D18 & 58D78, Box 3; Leddy to Peurifoy, Mar. 8, 1954, NA 611.14, and Peurifoy to Leddy, Mar. 2, 1954, [enclosed].)

[90] "U.S. Flying Arms to 2 Latin Lands near Guatemala," *NYT*, May 25, 1954, p. 1. See also "U.S. Tanks for Honduras," *NYT*, June 2, 1954, p. 12, and "U.S. Aid to Grow," *NYT*, June 3, 1954, p. 10.

[91] Schlesinger and Kinzer, *Bitter Fruit*, p. 160.

pate in the celebrations for Nicaragua's Army Day—which coincided with Mrs. Somoza's birthday. The B-36, the *New York Times* stated dryly, "is capable of delivering the atomic bomb." As the planes flew overhead, the Nicaraguan crowds cried: "Long live the United States! Long live Somoza!"[92] For Nicaragua, it was a singular distinction: "this is the first time," the *Times* pointed out, "that any of the big strategic bombers have taken part in a foreign holiday."[93] Those who sent the planes were not thinking, however, of Mrs. Somoza's birthday. The "goodwill mission," explained a prominent columnist, "is merely a maneuver reminiscent of the 1910 muscular diplomacy celebrated by Richard Harding Davis."[94] The bombers flew over Nicaragua; their shadow fell on Guatemala.

The State Department, meanwhile, warned that the arrival of Soviet-bloc weapons in Guatemala might be in contravention of the Rio Treaty and justify the adoption of sanctions.[95] Foster Dulles was eloquent: the "extension of Soviet Colonialism to this hemisphere would, in the words of the Caracas Resolution, endanger the peace of America." He elaborated, "No member of the Rio Pact gives up what the Charter of the United Nations calls the inherent right of individual or collective self-defense: that right is reserved. Nevertheless, it is contemplated that, if the circumstances permit, there should be an effort, a sincere effort, at collective action, and we would expect to comply with both the letter and the spirit of our country's obligations."[96]

Hysteria seized the U.S. Congress and the American press. "The threat of Communist imperialism is no longer academic; it has arrived," proclaimed the *Washington Post* in an editorial, which asserted that "the shipment of arms from . . . Stettin ought to remove any lingering doubts that Guatemala is the beachhead for active Communist designs in the Western Hemisphere."[97] The *Wall Street Journal* saw the arms as a means of spreading the germ of communism like "Typhoid Mary,"[98] while the *New York Times* speculated about

[92] Quotations from "U.S. Detains Ship for Arms Search," *NYT*, May 27, 1954, p. 6, and "Vuelan los aviones atómicos sobre la ciudad de Managua," *El I*, May 28, 1954, p. 1. See also "Aviones atómicos a Managua," *El I*, May 27, 1954, p. 1; "U.S. Bombers Visit Nicaragua," *NYT*, May 28, 1954, p. 7; "Día del Ejército," *La Prensa*, Managua, May 28, 1954, p. 1.

[93] "U.S. Detains Ship for Arms Search," *NYT*, May 27, 1954, p. 6.

[94] Arthur Krock, "A Communist Arms Depot in Central America?" *NYT*, May 27, 1954, p. 26.

[95] "U.S. Wants Rio Pact Inquiry on Arms Sent to Guatemala," *NYT*, May 19, 1954, p. 1; "Latin Arms Cargo Upsets President," *NYT*, May 20, 1954, p. 1.

[96] Quotations from "Communist Influence in Guatemala," May 25, 1954, *Department of State Bulletin*, June 7, 1954, p. 874, and "Dulles Cites Danger of Reds Near Canal," *NYT*, May 26, 1954, p. 12.

[97] "Communist Beachhead" (edit.), *WP*, May 21, 1954, p. 22.

[98] "Repeating History," *WSJ*, June 1, 1954, p. 12.

the "secret jungle paths" along which the *Alfhem*'s machine guns would travel on their way to communist groups in other Central American countries.[99] Only *The Nation* observed that it was Guatemala, rather than its neighbors, that was threatened.[100]

In newspaper articles and in congressional speeches, the Monroe Doctrine was unearthed and batted around. "We find that one of our most cherished basic doctrines, which we have long considered to be a protection for North and South American countries, is now under direct attack by the Communists," warned Senator George Smathers. "We must decide whether we are to stand on the principle of the Monroe Doctrine or are we to retreat from it and let it become a meaningless memory."[101]

Guatemala endangered the hemisphere. "This cargo of arms is like an atom bomb planted in the rear of our backyard," argued Congressman McCormack. "It is as if a Soviet ship brought an atom bomb in her hold and berthed at a slip in the New York harbor calmly confident that at any time it could blow up the City of New York." The bones of American history were rattled in the chambers: "If Paul Revere were living today," said Representative William Lantaff, "he would view the landing of Red arms in Guatemala as a signal to ride and warn the Americas of the present acute danger of Communist infiltration in Latin America." Representative Robert Sikes compared the arrival of the *Alfhem* to Italy's invasion of Ethiopia in 1935 and noted how the failure of the democracies to respond had led to World War II.[102] The storm raged on, as congressman after congressman rose to denounce the Guatemalan regime.

The arrival of the *Alfhem* reignited the issue of the U.S. military missions in Guatemala. On May 18, at 11:38 a.m., Senator William Knowland, one of the most powerful Republicans in Congress, phoned Foster Dulles. He was "confused," Knowland said. He had just realized that "we have a military

[99] Krock, "A Communist Arms Depot in Central America?" *NYT*, May 27, 1954, p. 26.

[100] "Again the Big Stick" (edit.), *The Nation*, May 29, 1954, p. 453. "The Administration has blown it up [the *Alfhem* episode] into an international incident of impressive magnitude, and by doing so has crudely revealed the town-bully attitude it tried so hard to hide at Caracas under a camouflage of pan-American 'unity.' But what kind of attitude is this? How does it differ from the attitude of Russia toward one of its lesser satellites? The State Department is angry at Guatemala for pursuing a left-wing policy. . . . It is also annoyed by Guatemala's stubborn, tough dealings with big American companies operating there. And so, obsessed with its role as boss-defender of the hemisphere, it [the State Department] refuses to sell arms to Guatemala, refuses to allow Guatemala to buy arms from friendly nations, and then denounces Guatemala as a threat to security when it gets arms where it can."

[101] Smathers (D-Fla), May 20, 1954, *CR*-Senate, p. 6916.

[102] McCormack (D-Mass), May 25, 1954, *CR*-House, p. 7092; Lantaff (D-Fla), May 24, 1954, ibid., p. 7016; Sikes (D-Fla), May 25, 1954, ibid., pp. 7091–92.

mission [in Guatemala]." What consistency is there, he asked, in "having a mission and at the same time being concerned about the shipment of arms for the army there?"[103]

Dulles sprang into action. First he phoned his brother. Allen was not in his office, and so by 11:42 a.m. he was on the phone with Allen's deputy, Wisner:

> The Secretary mentioned that he had talked with AWD re keeping the missions in Guatemala, and now thinks new thought could be given to it. AWD has thought up to now it is desirable to keep it there. . . . The Sec. referred to Knowland's call. . . . The Sec. said maybe we should pull them right out. W. said one of the Pentagon's thoughts and theirs is that the strongest single bulwark against the Communist-controlled government is the army, and this could be used for discussion with the Congressman. . . . The Sec. said he has to let his friends on the Hill know what to say. W. said they can say we don't know if the arms are for the army. The effect of this might be good as it might make the army mad. Confidentially the Sec. can say that the mission, like others we have behind the Iron Curtain, is used as eyes and ears for us.[104]

Dulles immediately reported the conversation to Knowland.[105] In the afternoon, Allen returned his brother's call. "AWD said he is opposed to taking the fellows [the military missions] out of Guatemala. He will be glad to help on the Hill—talk to Knowland, etc. . . . The only hope [for PBSUCCESS] is defection there [among the Guatemalan officers]."[106] The CIA prevailed: the military missions were not mentioned in Congress.

The furor provoked by the *Alfhem* in the United States was heightened by the fact that a strike had broken out in early May among the forty thousand workers of United Fruit and Standard Fruit in Honduras, the two American giants that monopolized banana production there. By the time the *Alfhem* reached Guatemala, the entire northern region, the heart of Honduras's economy, was paralyzed. It was without precedent. Honduras, noted *Business Week*, had been "an employers' paradise": there were no unions for rural workers "and little labor legislation beyond some paper government machinery for settling labor disputes."[107]

From Tegucigalpa, Ambassador Willauer had cabled on May 9 that "while the Honduran Government was likely to maintain control, he had important reservations." That day, the State Department had "declined to predict de-

[103] TelConv (Knowland, JFD), May 18, 1954, 11:38 a.m., DP:TCS, Box 2, EL.

[104] TelConv (JFD, Wisner), May 18, 1954, 11:42 a.m., ibid.

[105] TelConv (JFD, Knowland), May 18, 1954, 11:46 a.m., ibid.

[106] TelConv (JFD, AWD), May 18, 1954, 5:10 p.m., ibid.

[107] "Banana Battle," *Business Week*, May 22, 1954, p. 166. The best studies of the strike are Posas, *Luchas*, pp. 95–185, and Meza, *Historia*, pp. 67–98. See also La-Barge, "A Study of United Fruit," pp. 294–304.

velopments.''[108] On May 13, the Dulles brothers commented, "We may want to send forces [into Honduras] . . . but this is not yet necessary." They both hoped that the strike would be broken.[109] Instead, it spread to Tegucigalpa and other towns. On May 23, a panicky President Gálvez asked that two U.S. warships be stationed off the north coast, ready to land marines should the need arise.[110] The State Department agreed. The Pentagon had already drawn up plans.[111]

From the outset, the Hondurans had claimed that international communism lay behind the strike, and they had singled out Guatemala for blame. There was no proof, but none was needed: every major labor conflict was, by definition, communist inspired. The Hondurans also knew that the most effective way to discredit the strikers, and to elicit the support of the United States, was to brandish the Red threat and, in particular, the "Guatemalan Connection."

In fact, neither the Guatemalan government nor the PGT had fomented the strike. Their association with it was insignificant: *Diario de Centro América* expressed support for the strikers, and the CGTG collected a few hundred dollars for them and served as a conduit for a similar amount sent from Mexico by the *Confederación de Trabajadores de América Latina*.[112]

To the Americans—journalists, congressmen, officials—the strike was too

[108] Memorandum for the Chairman, Joint Chiefs of Staff, May 13, 1954, DDI-12-54, quoted p. 1.

[109] TelConv (JFD, AWD), May 13, 1954, 9:46 a.m., DP, JFD:CS, Box 7, EL.

[110] Secretaría de Relaciones Exteriores de la República de Honduras, Memorandum Confidencial, May 23, 1954, enclosed in AmEm Tegucigalpa, Coerr to DOS, no. 495, May 28, 1954, NA 714.001. See also Willauer to Holland, May 24, 1954, 1 a.m.

[111] JFD to President, "Unsettled Labor and Political Conditions in Honduras," May 11, 1954, WF, Dulles/Herter Series, Box 2, EL. There is a wealth of documentary material on this matter. See, for instance, Hall, "Assistant Secretary Henry Holland's Remarks on Latin America in the Planning Board Meeting on Monday, May 24, 1954," White House Office, Special Assistant for National Security Affairs: Records, 1952–61, NSC Series, Administrative SubSeries, Box 4, EL; Op-30 to Op-03, May 28, 1954, Op-303E/csv Ser. 000510P; Chief of Naval Operations to Joint Chiefs of Staff, May 29, 1954, Op-383/aas Ser. 0005-81; CINCLANTFLT no. 516, June 8, 1954. For relevant NSC documents, see: NSC 5419, May 24, 1954, *FRUS*, 1952–1954, 4:1129–31; "Memorandum of Discussion at the 199th Meeting of the National Security Council, May 27, 1954," ibid., pp. 1131–35; NSC 5419/1, May 28, 1954, ibid., pp. 1135–36.

[112] See, for instance, *DCA*: "En huelga contra la United Fruit trabajadores de la costa norte de Honduras," May 5, 1954, p. 8; "Más mensajes de apoyo," May 17, 1954, p. 1; "Jóvenes con trabajadores de Honduras" and "Primeros aportes para los huelguistas de Honduras," May 18, 1954, p. 1. See also Lombardo Toledano to Gutiérrez, June 4, 1954, *GT*, Box 24, and Gutiérrez to Lombardo Toledano, June 10, 1954, ibid. Boxes 25 and 44 of the *GT* include two folders dealing with the efforts of the CGTG and the CNCG to assist the Honduran strikers.

sudden, too well organized, too widespread not to reek of international communism. "This strike," proclaimed Senator Mike Mansfield on May 28, "has been conducted in the Communist manner, with workers thoroughly organized, disciplined and carrying out precise orders completely uncharacteristic of the natives of Honduras and Guatemala." And it would not stop there: "Reports now reach Washington," revealed Representative Hale Boggs, "that Guatemalan agents are now attempting to foment strikes in Panama. The canal itself may be threatened."[113]

Two incidents that had attracted little attention when they were first announced were reinterpreted in the light of the *Alfhem*. In the words of Representative Clark Fisher, "The Communist hand was shown last April . . . in the attempt to assassinate the vehement anti-Communist President Anastasio Somoza of Nicaragua. . . . About the same time Nicaraguan agents discovered Soviet marked guns, believed to have been smuggled in by submarines."[114] Even the *New York Times*, albeit more tentatively than Fisher, could not resist the temptation to see a grand Guatemalan conspiracy linking the *Alfhem*, the Honduran strike, the plot against Somoza, and the Nicaraguan arms cache.[115]

Many Congressmen and journalists were tired of the passivity of the Eisenhower administration. "With its head-in-the-sand attitude . . . [the State Department] has chosen to ignore the dangers of the situation," charged Representative Lantaff. "We might well do away with diplomatic niceties right away," urged Senator Margaret Chase Smith. The gentlewoman was bitter. The previous February she had introduced a resolution "toward placing a ban against importing Guatemalan coffee. . . . What happened? The State Department, playing the game of timidity and fear of offending someone—and a game dangerously close to appeasement of the Reds—expressed its opposition to my anti-Communist legislation against the Guatemalan Reds. By such op-

---

[113] Mansfield (D-Mont), May 28, 1954, *CR*-Senate, p. 7337; Boggs (D-La), May 25, 1954, *CR*-House, p. 7092. The first official U.S. statement implicating Guatemala in the Honduran strike was made by Secretary Dulles at his May 11 news conference. (See *The Department of State Bulletin*, May 24, 1954, p. 801.)

[114] Fisher (D-Texas), June 14, 1954, *CR*-House, p. 8193. But perhaps none said it as well as an article in *Harper's* one year later: "Evidence has been found that a razzle-dazzle triple play was planned for April and May 1954. In Nicaragua, Somoza was to be assassinated. The underground Communist organization would rise, and one-third of the *Alfhem* arms would give it a good chance of crushing all opposition. In Honduras, a general strike was starting, led by expert agitators from abroad. It was to be turned into a revolution by arming the strikers. . . . If Nicaragua, Honduras, and Guatemala were quickly welded together into a new Red dominion, then the United States would face the hard choice of fighting another Korean War close to home or letting Central America go the way of Indochina." (Monroe, "Guatemala: What the Reds Left Behind," p. 63.)

[115] "Arming of Guatemala Alarms Its Neighbors," *NYT*, May 23, 1954, D9.

position the State Department stymied action by the Senate Foreign Relations Committee."[116]

Representative Sikes sought guidance in America's past: "In other days, America has acted promptly and vigorously to protect her interests and her friends. The incident of the Barbary pirates, the campaign of Andrew Jackson, the courage of Teddy Roosevelt are all part of our glorious heritage. In those days we did not hesitate to act, we did not allow ourselves to become entangled in diplomatic red tape, we got results."[117]

Behind the scenes, the Eisenhower administration sought to restrain overzealous congressmen from pushing through measures that would openly violate the principle of nonintervention, while hinting to key congressmen that more discreet activities to eliminate the Guatemalan threat were underway. The administration did not discourage, however, the uproar in the Congress and the press. The tumult added to the psychological warfare of PBSUCCESS. For, as the *Christian Science Monitor* concluded, it sent a clear message: "The United States is determined that the pro-Communist government in Guatemala must go."[118] The morale of the Guatemalans could not fail to be shaken, particularly the morale of the institution on whom PBSUCCESS depended: the armed forces.

"Guatemala Has Not Bought Weapons From the Soviet Union or Poland," the Arbenz administration announced on May 21, after days of silence[119]—a moot point, since the arms had been bought in Czechoslovakia. While refusing to identify the source of the shipment, Foreign Minister Toriello and other officials stressed their government's right to acquire weapons wherever it wished, particularly in light of the American embargo.[120] "Guatemala is not a colony of the United States," stated *Diario de Centro América*.[121]

[116] Lantaff, May 24, 1954, *CR*-House, p. 7016; Smith, "It is Time to Stifle Guatemala's Reds," *Star Ledger* (Newark, N.J.), May 24, 1954, p. 10.

[117] Sikes, May 25, 1954, *CR*-House, p. 7092. See also Mansfield, May 20, 1954, *CR*-Senate, pp. 6915-18; Boggs, May 25, 1954, *CR*-House, p. 7092; McCormack, May 25, 1954, ibid.; Henry Reams (Ind.-Ohio), June 2, 1954, ibid., p. 7534; Patrick Hillings (R-Calif), June 10, 1954, *CR*-Senate, pp. 8018–19; Fisher, June 14, 1954, *CR*-House, pp. 8192–94; Bourke Hickenlooper (R-Iowa), June 17, 1954, *CR*-Senate, pp. 8442–44; Senate Minority Leader Lyndon Johnson (D-Texas), quoted in "Problem Is Communism," *Time*, June 7, 1954, p. 41.

[118] Hallett, "U.S. Views on Guatemala Find Latin America Wary," *CSM*, May 25, 1954, p. 1.

[119] For the text of the communiqué, see *DCA*, May 21, 1954, p. 8.

[120] See "Declaraciones de la cancillería," *DCA*, May 21, 1954, p. 1; "Guatemala Says U.S. Tried to Make Her Defenseless," *NYT*, May 22, 1954, p. 1; "Guatemala Hints U.N. Case on Arms," *NYT*, May 23, 1954, p. 1.

[121] "Guatemala no es una colonia norteamericana" (edit.), *DCA*, May 22, 1954, p. 3.

The brave words and half-truths could not change reality: the gamble had backfired. Not only had Arbenz and the PGT handed Washington an excuse to escalate its aggression, but their hope of secreting arms for workers' militias was dashed. Senior Guatemalan military officers who had been informed of the shipment by the United States appeared at the pier to take charge of the cargo. Arbenz had to approve. The weapons, he explained, were for the armed forces; their communist origins were due only to the American embargo.[122]

Under normal circumstances, the officers would not have objected to the fact that the shipment came from Czechoslovakia or even to the secrecy surrounding its arrival because they had wanted arms for so long. But the circumstances were not normal, and the price—the wrath of the United States—was staggering. Publicly, the military proclaimed its gratitude to Arbenz: the acquisition of weapons had been an "urgent necessity."[123] Privately, the officers were increasingly distressed by the president who was leading them to a head-on collision with Washington.

The loyalty of the officer corps had been faltering since the arrival of Peurifoy. On November 23, 1953, Bill Krieg, the DCM of the embassy, had written: "The officers may not yet be said to have abandoned their often-reported loyalty to Arbenz, but at the moment they are wondering and speculating more than hitherto about his actions."[124] In late December, Colonel Anselmo Getellá repeatedly conveyed his fears to sources close to the U.S. embassy: "If he [Arbenz] keeps on, he will bring us to ruin with him." Getellá, noted another report, "is frustrated, discontented and apparently has no faith that the country can go on much longer under the present circumstances." His malaise was particularly significant, Peurifoy remarked, because he was considered deeply loyal to Arbenz.[125] "Getellá will tell me the truth," Arbenz used to say.[126] (But if Getellá did not lie, he could also be silent. It was not until June 25, a week after the invasion had begun, that he expressed his fears to Arbenz. By then, it was too late.)

Getellá's complaints were quietly echoed by many of his colleagues. "A

[122] Interviews with Fortuny, María de Arbenz, and two senior Guatemalan officers who asked not to be identified.

[123] "Estamos prontos a sacrificar nuestras vidas, si fuera necesario, en defensa de los caros intereses de la patria," statement read over the radio by Army Chief of Staff Parinello, *DCA*, May 27, 1954, p. 1 (quoted from p. 12); see also "Voto de gratitud del Consejo de la Defensa al Presidente," *El I*, June 2, 1954, p. 1.

[124] Krieg to DOS, no. 443, Nov. 23, 1953, p. 3, NA 714.00.

[125] Quotations from Plihal and Herrera, "Report," Dec. 31, 1953, p. 2, and Plihal, "Report," Dec. 26, 1953, p. 2, both enclosed in Peurifoy to Leddy, Jan. 5, 1954, NA 714.00.

[126] Interviews with María de Arbenz and Fortuny. Getellá was a *Centenario* of Arbenz and was one of the very few officers who addressed him with the familiar "vos" form.

great number of officers are extremely unhappy about the Communists in the government and the poor U.S.-Guatemalan relations,'' reported the assistant air attaché at the U.S. embassy in mid-February; yet, he added, ''none dares to speak out for fear of jeopardizing his personal security.''[127] Two weeks later, as the Caracas conference opened, a CIA report pointed out the ambivalence of many officers, torn between their growing fear of the United States and their reluctance to plot against Arbenz: ''The loyalty of certain key officers . . . to President Arbenz apparently is wavering. . . . There is no conclusive evidence that the officers are yet prepared to oust Arbenz.''[128] Following the Caracas conference, reported Krieg, the officers were ''in a highly nervous state, anticipating U.S. action against Guatemala.''[129]

Guatemalan officers confirm these reports. Even before the conference opened, the psychological pressure was brutal. Caracas only heightened their fears: ''The army was in profound disarray''; it was ''a minefield.''[130] To the threats that rained from Washington were added threats from U.S. officials in Guatemala. ''Many officers,'' recalls Colonel Rubén González Siguí, ''were approached by the U.S. embassy and by the U.S. military mission.''[131] The message, be it explicit or implicit, was always the same: the United States could no longer tolerate Arbenz; should the Guatemalan army fail to act, Washington would resort to extreme measures. ''We were,'' laments Colonel Ernesto Paiz Novales, ''under enormous pressure. The U.S. military mission even hinted that the United States would invade.''[132] Bill Krieg concurs: the possibility of a direct military intervention was ''only hinted—but I'm sure that the Guatemalan officers got the point, and they inferred from it even more than was implied: they exaggerated everything we told them.''[133]

Fear spread among the Guatemalan officers and their families. Fear and confusion. Amid the growing demoralization, no one knew who could be trusted, who would betray. Many, indeed, no longer knew where they themselves stood. Arbenz's defense minister, Colonel José Angel Sánchez, was no

[127] Lt. Col. McAdam to Peurifoy, enclosed in Krieg to DOS, no. 722, Feb. 19, 1954, NA 714.00. See also Col. McCormick to Ambassador et al., Feb. 15, 1954, RG84 G&C, Box 3, NA-S.

[128] CIA report (title and number deleted), Mar. 5, 1954.

[129] Krieg to Peurifoy, Mar. 29, 1954.

[130] Quotations from interviews with Col. Parinello and Maj. Paz Tejada.

[131] Interview with Col. González Siguí, who claims that he refused to join in a plot against Arbenz—a statement that many officers dispute. In early June 1954, Arbenz dismissed González Siguí from the army. For González Siguí's account, see ''Battle of the Backyard,'' *Time*, June 28, 1954, pp. 43–44.

[132] Interview with Paiz Novales (who claims that he withstood the pressure). Also useful were interviews with the following officers: Parinello, Montenegro, Cruz Salazar, Paz Tejada, Mendoza.

[133] Interview with Krieg.

exception. An embassy official told Peurifoy of a conversation between the minister, his brother (Colonel Rodolfo Sánchez) and his cousin (Srta. Barrilla):

> Srta. Barrilla, who has much influence on the Minister, asked him if he did not realize what the situation was here and what would happen to the whole family in the event that Arbenz was overthrown. Colonel Rodolfo Sánchez asked if there was nothing the Minister could do to bring about a change in the situation here. Colonel José Angel Sánchez replied that there was nothing he could do. . . . [He] himself no longer had any idea of how the Army would react in the event of a move against the government. He imagined that some officers would stand by the government and others would be disposed to oppose it, but at present it was impossible to know which ones were which. It was, therefore, useless to try to do anything. Besides, he added, President Arbenz had told him that he would not leave the National Palace unless he were shot out of it.[134]

The men behind PBSUCCESS knew that fear was spreading through the Guatemalan officers, yet they were unable to assess its impact. They had drummed up only a few collaborators from the officer corps—none of whom held a key position—and they were not sure how the Guatemalan army would respond to Castillo Armas's invasion. Even three days after the invasion had begun, the CIA noted: "The controlling factor in the situation is . . . the position of the Guatemalan armed forces, and thus far this group has not given any clear indication of whether it will move, and if so, in which way."[135]

U.S. reports in the months preceding the invasion stressed that the Guatemalan officers were afraid of Arbenz. This was true. They feared dismissal; they feared disgrace. But there was more than fear. There was also, for many, a sense of nationalism and respect for Arbenz; several also felt gratitude for personal favors they had received. This respect, this gratitude, this warmth, were still evident thirty years later as Colonel González Siguí spoke of Arbenz. Arbenz, he remembered, was a magnificent officer, a charismatic military leader, a man of deep intelligence, a fervent nationalist who dared stand up to the Yankees and to Peurifoy, "the arrogant and abusive ambassador." The same respect for Arbenz was expressed by other officers who, like González Siguí, ultimately betrayed him.[136]

Until late May, Guatemalan officers had refrained from expressing their growing reservations to Arbenz. In the words of González Siguí, "No one said anything to Arbenz, but we all knew that things were going badly." Now,

[134] Hill to Peurifoy et al., Feb. 26, 1954.

[135] DCI to President, "The Situation in Guatemala as of 20 June," *FRUS*, 1952–1954, 4:1174–75. See also below, pp. 334–38.

[136] Particularly instructive were interviews with Cols. González Siguí (quoted), Mendoza, Parinello, and with Lt. Col. Paiz Novales.

under the avalanche of threats from the United States that followed the arrival of the *Alfhem*, fear of Washington overwhelmed them. ''We could smell the invasion, and we knew that Castillo Armas was Washington's man.''[137]

On the first of June, Arbenz called an officers' meeting, one of the very few he held during his presidency. He wanted to strengthen their morale. During the meeting, no one challenged Arbenz, but even he, who had lost touch with the officer corps, realized that his audience was uneasy, restless, unconvinced. Aware that he was not at his best addressing large groups, Arbenz thought that he would be able to reassure the officers through the power of the written word. He invited them to give him a list of questions expressing all their concerns; he would respond promptly.[138]

On June 5, the list, prepared by Army Chief of Staff Parinello and other senior officers, was presented to Arbenz.[139] It was a peculiar document. Cast in a very respectful tone, it began by stressing the army's loyalty to ''Señor Presidente.'' The officers would obey him ''absolutely and without reservation''; the questions were formulated only ''to comply with the wishes of Señor Presidente.'' There followed twenty questions. They addressed one issue only: communism. Did the president not think that communist influence in Guatemala was excessive? Did the president agree that the communists, ''who defame and insult foreign governments,'' were a threat to the country's well-being? ''Might not Señor Presidente rely only and exclusively on his army— which is unconditionally loyal''—and eliminate the communists from the positions of influence they occupied? How did the president interpret article 32 of the constitution, which forbade organizations of an international character? Wouldn't the country's domestic and foreign policies be better served if the Communist party were marginalized?

Arbenz and the Secretariat of the PGT still failed to grasp the depth of the officers' dissatisfaction.[140] They believed that the officers were merely voicing doubts, doubts they could allay. Arbenz outlined the responses, and Fortuny fleshed them out. They reiterated what Arbenz had so often stated in public: ''I am not now, nor will I be, a communist, but . . . neither am I, nor will I be, an anticommunist.'' Communist influence in the bureaucracy was extremely limited. ''There are communists in the agrarian reform department,'' he conceded, ''but they are the best workers and the most honest.'' Beyond

[137] Interview with González Siguí.

[138] Interviews with Parinello, González Siguí, and (for Arbenz's reactions) María de Arbenz and Fortuny. See also ''El ocho de junio comenzó revolución interna,'' *La Hora*, July 26, 1954, p. 1.

[139] ''Pliego de consultas de la oficialidad del Estado Mayor del Ejército, preparado por sugestión del señor Presidente de la República,'' June 5, 1954, *GT*, Box 11. Also useful were interviews with Col. Parinello, Lt. Col. Cruz Salazar, and Lt. Peralta Méndez.

[140] Interviews with María de Arbenz, Fortuny, Guerra Borges, Alejandro, Charnaud.

this refrain, Arbenz struck one theme: there would be no change in his policies. He considered the army's support decisive, but to rule "only and exclusively" with the army, as the officers had suggested, "is what is done by dictators like Pérez Jiménez and Somoza."[141]

There was no open break between the president and the officers; there was no further exchange of views. Arbenz and the Secretariat of the PGT thought they had reassured the officers. But only a pledge from Arbenz that he would immediately expel the PGT from the government could have satisfied the officers who cowered in the shadow of Washington's big stick. As it was, Arbenz's responses heightened the officers' exasperation with him and their fear of the United States.

While the army's morale was faltering, and while American journalists and congressmen demanded that Eisenhower halt Red aggression, only the blind and the gullible could have failed to notice that an armed attack on Guatemala was imminent. On May 19, Nicaragua had broken diplomatic relations with Guatemala. "This break," explained the *Washington Post*, "had been building up for some time because of the Guatemalan plotting against the Nicaraguan regime."[142] Encouraged by Washington, Somoza called for a meeting of OAS foreign ministers to discuss Guatemala's threat to the peace and security of the region. He was joined by Figueres; the foes united.[143] Meanwhile, Haiti declared the two ranking officials at the Guatemalan embassy in Port-au-Prince *persona non grata*, and in Havana, Batista ordered army, navy, police, and intelligence chiefs to be particularly alert to communist subversion emanating from Guatemala.[144] Given that Arbenz had made a special effort to cultivate good relations with Haiti and to maintain correct relations with the unsavory Batista, these diplomatic snubs were ominous.[145] Adding "to the

---

[141] A copy of Arbenz's written answers is in *GT*, Box 11. The document is undated, but it was delivered by June 10 at the latest. (Interviews with Fortuny and Parinello.)

Rumors about the officers' meeting with Arbenz spread, but the United States had no clear idea of what went on. See, for instance, TelConv (JFD, AWD), June 15, 1954, 10:17 a.m., DP, JFD:CS, Box 8, EL.

[142] "Communist Beachhead" (edit.), *WP*, May 21, 1954, p. 22.

[143] See MemoConv (Holland, Sevilla Sacasa), May 21, 1954, NA 714.00; "Gobiernos del Istmo consultan," *El I*, May 20, 1954, p. 1; "Consultas en el Caribe," *El I*, May 21, 1954, p. 1; "El embajador Sevilla Sacasa habla de consultas a la OEA," *La Hora*, May 21, 1954, p. 1; "Guatemala Hints U.N. Case on Arms," *NYT*, May 23, 1954, p. 1; "U.S. Detains Ship for Arms Search," *NYT*, May 27, 1954, p. 6; Herron and Wieland to Holland, Memo no. 208, June 9, 1954.

[144] See "Cuba Tightens Security," *NYT*, May 25, 1954, p. 12, and "Non grato encargado de negocios A.I. en Haiti," *El I*, May 25, 1954, p. 1.

[145] For Guatemala's overtures toward Haiti, see "Saludo y homenaje a Haiti," *DCA*, May 18, 1953, p. 4; "Pueblo haitiano concede a Arbenz la más alta prueba de amis-

impression that Guatemala was rapidly becoming isolated internationally," Panama and Costa Rica recalled their ambassadors for consultations.[146]

On May 25 the Honduran ambassador to Guatemala left abruptly, "on the urgent instructions of his government." Guatemalan officials explained that the hasty departure did not presage a break in diplomatic relations, but the opposition *El Imparcial* was keen to dispel false illusions. "Well-informed sources," it pointed out, "note that Ambassador Duran will not return. . . . The Ambassador has left with everything, even his reserves of wine and alcohol. His baggage included five cases of champagne, four of whiskey, and five of French table wine."[147] As the ambassador crated his wine, the press in the other Central American republics was sounding the tocsin: Guatemalan troops were massing at the Honduran border; equipped with the *Alfhem* weapons, Guatemala stood poised to attack peaceful, defenseless Honduras.[148]

In Guatemala, everyone knew that this was nonsense. Such an attack would have been suicidal, for it would have triggered the American response. What, then, lay behind these rumors? Pieced together "with other reports that the United States was flying arms into Honduras and Nicaragua," there was, for the Guatemalans, only one possible explanation: Honduras was about to attack, this attack would be presented as Guatemalan aggression against Honduras, and U.S. military intervention would thereby be justified.[149]

On May 26, an unmarked C-47 flew over Guatemala City dropping leaflets that informed the Guatemalans that their liberation was at hand. "If they had been napalm bombs and not leaflets, we wouldn't be here to talk about it," *El Imparcial* wrote for the benefit of the dim-witted.[150] On the succeeding days,

---

tad," *DCA*, Dec. 28, 1953, p. 8; "Haiti condecora a Arbenz," *Tribuna Popular*, Dec. 30, 1953, p. 1; "Buena impresión dejó en Haiti nuestra delegación especial," *DCA*, Feb. 1, 1954, p. 8.

[146] *JW* 21, May 28, 1954, p. 2.

[147] "Embajador hondureño sale subito," *El I*, May 25, 1954, pp. 1, 5.

[148] For relevant articles, see "Fuerzas militares a frontera con Honduras," *La Prensa*, Managua, May 23, 1954, p. 8; "Inminente la guerra entre Honduras y Guatemala," *Diario de Costa Rica*, San José, May 25, 1954, p. 1; "La guerra entre Honduras y Guatemala es inminente," *La Nación*, San José, May 25, 1954, p. 1. For a lucid critique of this war scare, see Alberto Quinteros, "Serenidad y espíritu fraternal en estos momentos difíciles para Centro América," *El Diario de Hoy*, San Salvador, June 2, 1954, p. 6. ("Many Central American newspapers . . . have exacerbated the climate of fear by announcing the movement of Guatemalan troops to the Honduran border, by discussing the possibility of an attack on the Panama Canal from bases in Guatemala and by printing other alarming stories.")

[149] Quoted from *JW* 21, May 28, 1954, p. 2. Meanwhile in Washington, "It was agreed that there would be wide publicity in connection with the visit to the U.S. by the Honduran military man, Velasquez, in order to create further nervousness in Guatemala." (DOS, Meeting of Guatemalan Group, June 2, 1954, p. 2.)

[150] "Avión desconocido voló dejando caer propaganda contra el comunismo," *El I*,

other "mystery planes" appeared over the capital in what seemed to be an "obvious rehearsal for the dropping of bombs."[151]

One of the commando groups trained by the CIA in Nicaragua had already sprung into action. On May 20, a train carrying the *Alfhem* weapons from Puerto Barrios to the capital "was almost blown up" (the explosion produced very little damage; unexploded sticks of dynamite were later found); there was a shootout; one soldier was killed, three were wounded; one of the saboteurs was also killed, and the others escaped. The attack was praised by the U.S.-controlled *Voz de la Liberación*. There were further attempts to sabotage trains linking Puerto Barrios with the capital on May 21 and May 25.[152] Both attempts failed, but another, less violent form of warfare was waged in the capital in the last week of May. At night, "leaflets were pushed under the doors . . . telling people to prepare lists of communists and known communist-sympathizers. Immediately after the government was overthrown, the leaflets said, the people were to take the lists to the new authorities, who would deal out 'justice.' "[153]

While journalists in the United States and Central America described Honduras as the innocent victim, it was an open secret that Castillo Armas was preparing to attack Guatemala from Honduras. By late May "his soldiers in uniform swaggered around the streets of Tegucigalpa," *U.S. News and World Report* later wrote. "Correspondents visited his headquarters and filed dispatches saying that the revolution was going to start."[154] And when Rodolfo Mendoza, formerly chief of the Guatemalan air force, fled Guatemala on June 4 aboard a private aircraft, everyone assumed that he had defected to join Castillo Armas. More ominously still, with him was an American citizen, Major (ret.) Ferdinand Schupp, who had been the deputy chief of the U.S. Air

May 27, 1954, p. 1, quoted from p. 5. For a less enthusiastic account, see "Avión extranjero provoca al gobierno de la revolución," *DCA*, May 27, 1954, p. 1.

[151] William Krehm, "A Victory for the West in Guatemala?" *International Journal*, Autumn 1954, p. 300.

[152] "Tren estuvo a punto de ser dinamitado," *El I*, May 21, 1954, p. 1 (quoted); "Ferrocarrileros indignados por el atentado dinamitero," *DCA*, May 21, 1954, p. 1; "Terrorismo dinamitero: Pieza de un engranaje," *DCA*, May 22, 1954, p. 1; "Investigase atentado dinamitero," ibid.; "Atentado a convoy con armamento," *El I*, May 22, 1954, p. 1; "Guatemala Says U.S. Tried to Make Her Defenseless," *NYT*, May 22, 1954, p. 1; "Radio clandestina felicitó a los terroristas el sabado," *DCA*, May 24, 1954, p. 1; "Nuevo acto de sabotaje a tren de Barrios," *El I*, May 26, 1954, p. 1. On the role of the CIA, see Schlesinger and Kinzer, *Bitter Fruit*, p. 151.

[153] Gruson, "Guatemala Grim as Tension Rises," *NYT*, May 30, 1954, p. 16.

[154] "A Revolt U.S. Couldn't Win," *U.S. News and World Report*, July 2, 1954, pp. 22, 24. For an admiring interview with Castillo Armas in Tegucigalpa by a prestigious Central American newspaper, see "Por la patria y por nuestra religión," *La Nación*, San José, June 9, 1954, p. 19.

Force Mission in Guatemala until 1952.[155] Mendoza was not just a retired colonel. He had been "the most experienced and capable pilot in the Guatemalan Air Force."[156] Nor was Schupp just a U.S. citizen. Because of his previous position, many Guatemalans saw him as an agent of the U.S. government. Mendoza and Schupp would be back in a few days, flying over the capital as part of Castillo Armas's air force.

Perhaps the dramatic departure of Mendoza and Schupp had been timed by the CIA to reap maximum psychological advantage; perhaps the timing was due to fear that their participation in PBSUCCESS had been discovered. In any case, they left when tension was at a peak. The mood in Guatemala City that week was captured by Sidney Gruson:

> The climax of the crisis in the immediate future is widely expected. There is talk of a possibility of an economic boycott or of an armed invasion by Guatemalan exiles, or even the possibility of a landing of United States troops to sweep the Communists from political power. . . . The nervousness is not confined to the ordinary people here. The government's concern is apparent. . . . Even more apparent are the jitters spreading among leaders of the non-Communist revolutionary parties. As a result of the crisis, the leaders, for the first time, are talking guardedly of the dangers . . . [of] having allowed the Communists to gain wide powers.[157]

In vain did the Arbenz administration seek to quell the storm. On May 27, Foreign Minister Toriello sent a cable to his Honduran counterpart urging the immediate conclusion of a pact of friendship and nonaggression. The cable had been sent, the *New York Times* pointed out, at 3:30 a.m., "about nine hours after an unidentified C-47 plane had showered the City of Guatemala with anti-government leaflets."[158]

Toriello's offer was spurned. In Tegucigalpa, officials explained to sympathetic journalists that "Guatemala was using an old communist trick: it was just trying to put the Honduran people off guard so that it would be easier to

[155] "Rodolfo Mendoza huyó por aire," *El I*, June 5, 1954, p. 1; "Coronel Mendoza desaparece en una avioneta particular," *DCA*, June 5, 1954, p. 1; "Rodolfo Mendoza obtuvo el asilo político en la república salvadoreña," *El I*, June 7, 1954, p. 1; "Quien es el incógnito personaje que voló con el coronel Mendoza," *La Hora*, June 7, 1954, p. 1; "Top Flyer Escapes," *NYT*, June 7, 1954, p. 6; "U.S. Ex-Officer Joins Guatemalan in Flight," *NYT*, June 8, 1954, p. 1; Peurifoy to SecState, no. 910, June 7, 1954, NA 714.00; *JW* 23, June 11, 1954, p. 4.

[156] HQs Panama Canal Department, "Weekly Intelligence Summary" no. 274, Oct. 2, 1947, p.8, RG319 ID 0402769, NA-S.

[157] "Guatemala Grim as Tension Rises," *NYT*, May 30, 1954, p. 16.

[158] "Guatemala Proposes Pact with Honduras," *NYT*, May 28, 1954, p. 1 (quoted); "Pacto de amistad y no agresión con Honduras propone el gobierno de Guatemala," *DCA*, May 27, 1954, p. 1; "Amistad y no agresión" (edit.), *DCA*, May 28, 1954, p. 1.

attack them later.'' In the U.S. Congress, Representative Ray Madden damned the offer as further proof of the true intentions of ''the Communist conspirators in Guatemala.'' The Guatemalan proposal, he revealed, followed ''exactly the same blueprint used to place Lithuania, Latvia, and Estonia, and other captive nations under Kremlin slavery.''[159]

Guatemala called for talks with the United States to reduce tensions. Toriello declared his ''well-founded hope'' that the problems between the two countries would be settled ''in the most amicable fashion'' and even claimed that Peurifoy ''has always behaved like a gentleman.'' Peurifoy's rejoinder was ''No comment,'' while from Washington flowed further indications that the decision was irrevocable: Arbenz must go.[160]

''U.S. Detains Ship for Arms Search,'' announced the *New York Times* on May 27, as the State Department disclosed that a French merchant vessel was being searched by U.S. customs officials in the Canal Zone ''with the knowledge and the approval of the French Government and the French line.''[161] The Eisenhower administration had imposed a naval quarantine. No weapons and no ammunition would be allowed to reach Guatemala. ''If it is necessary as a last resort to damage them [the suspect ships] to cause them to stop . . . that will be done,'' read the instructions to the task force that had been patrolling the Gulf of Honduras since May 24. Operation Hardrock had begun.[162]

[159] ''La proposición de Guatemala a nuestro gobierno suscita conjeturas en Panama,'' *El Día*, Tegucigalpa, June 3, 1954, p. 1; Madden (D-Ind), June 8, 1954, *CR-House*, p. 7881.

[160] Quotations from ''Embajador de EE.UU: Sostuvo conferencia con Toriello,'' *El I*, May 24, 1954, pp. 1, 2. See also ''Guatemala Eases Stand toward U.S.,'' *NYT*, May 25, 1954, p. 12; ''Guatemalans Fail to Grasp Concern of U.S. over Reds,'' *NYT*, May 26, 1954, p. 13; ''Guatemala for Talks,'' *NYT*, May 29, 1954, p. 5; ''Reunión personal con Eisenhower podría aliviar situación de C.A.,'' *DCA*, May 31, 1954, p. 1; ''Guatemala Aide Meets U.S. Envoy,'' *NYT*, June 2, 1954, p. 10; *JW* 21, May 28, 1954, pp. 2–3; *JW* 22, June 4, 1954, pp. 1–3; Peurifoy to SecState, no. 860, June 1, 1954, NA 714.00; Peurifoy to SecState, June 2, 1954, *FRUS*, 1952–1954, 4:1155–56.

Guatemala did not intend to make concessions on the communist issue. Furthermore, while Toriello expressed willingness to hold talks with United Fruit officials, he also stated ''that his government would put . . . one limitation on negotiations with the company. The agrarian reform law . . . 'is not a subject for negotiation or discussion.' '' (''Guatemala for Talks,'' *NYT*, May 29, 1954, p. 5.)

[161] ''U.S. Detains Ship for Arms Search,'' *NYT*, May 27, 1954, p. 1. (The article includes the text of the State Department's communiqué.)

[162] U.S. Atlantic Fleet, Cdr. Honduras Patrol, no. 003-54, June 28, 1954, p. A4. On Operation Hardrock, see esp. DOD, Annual Report of the Cdr.-in-Chief U.S. Atlantic Fleet (Supplementary), Part 4; U.S. Atlantic Fleet, Cdr. Honduras Patrol, no. 001-54, May 24, 1954, report of Cdr. USS Fessenden, ''Operation Hardrock Baker,'' June 1, 1954; U.S. Atlantic Fleet, Cdr. Honduras Patrol, no. 001-54, June 1, 1954; report of Cdr. Escort Squadron 10, ''Operations of the Honduras Patrol Group,'' June 8, 1954; U.S. Atlantic Fleet, Cdr. Honduras Patrol, no. 002-54, June 12, 1954.

In London, the quarantine was considered particularly insulting. Accustomed to ruling the waves, and jealous of their "special relationship" with the United States, the British sought assurances that they would not be treated like mere Frenchmen—that British ships would not be boarded. Foster Dulles was unmoved. He could offer no promises, he told the British ambassador. The Foreign Office began to prepare a paper on the legality of the blockade, only to be told by Prime Minister Churchill, who did not consider the issue worth jeopardizing American goodwill, to forget it. Britain would comply.[163]

Secretary Dulles and his brother Allen, the prime movers behind the measure, knew that they were violating international law. The legal adviser of the State Department had said as much, and not one of the officials consulted had claimed otherwise.[164] None, however, had opposed the measure except Robert Murphy, deputy assistant secretary of state, who had not been consulted, but had learned of the decision "by a casual reference" at lunch. In a memo to Secretary Dulles, Murphy did not mince words. "Now that the President and you have decided on this action it must, of course, be seen through," he wrote, "but I would like you to know that I believe the philosophy back of the action is wrong and that it may be very expensive over the longer term. My instinct, and perhaps my ignorance of Guatemalan problems, tells me that to resort to this action confesses the bankruptcy of our political policy vis-à-vis that country. Instead of political action inside Guatemala, we are obliged to resort to heavy-handed military action on the periphery of the cause of trouble."[165]

During the quarantine, which ended only with the fall of Arbenz, U.S. warships found no weapons or ammunition destined for Guatemala. Yet Operation Hardrock was not mere bravado; it packed a psychological punch. To anxious Guatemalans, the spectacle of U.S. warships patrolling the Gulf of Honduras and openly flouting international law stirred disturbing memories of the marines landing on the shores of Central America.

More recent memories—those of Caracas—were rekindled by rumors that the United States was seeking a special OAS conference to vote sanctions against Guatemala. On June 1, the Guatemalan chargé d'affaires in Washing-

---

On the decision to establish the quarantine, see TelConv (JFD, AWD), May 18, 1954, 9:05 a.m., DP:TCS, Box 2, EL; TelConv (JFD, AWD), May 19, 1954, 8:56 a.m., DP, JFD:CS, Box 7, EL; MemoConv, May 22, 1954, *FRUS*, 1952–1954, 4:1122–23; "Memorandum of Discussion at the 199th Meeting of the National Security Council, May 27," ibid., pp. 1131–35.

[163] Meers, "Pebble on the Beach," pp. 44–49; Young, "Great Britain's Latin American Dilemma," pp. 577–79.

[164] See TelConv (JFD, Anderson), May 19, 1954, 9:00 a.m., DP, JFD:CS, Box 7, EL; TelConv (JFD, Holland), May 19, 1954, 9:05 a.m., ibid.; English to Holland, May 20, 1954, NA 714.00; Holland to Donnelly and Pawley, May 27, 1954, NA 714.00.

[165] Murphy to SecState, May 25, 1954, NA 611.14.

ton informed Toriello that the preparatory work "had progressed very far."[166] The conference, the *New York Times* stated a few days later, would be held at Montevideo on July 1. U.S. officials, it added, seemed "confident of support by a majority of other Latin American Republics."[167]

The *Times'* information was accurate. When the article appeared, on June 10, Washington could count on the required two-thirds majority to pass two types of sanctions: the prohibition of travel by agents of international communism to and from Guatemala and the prohibition of the importation of military equipment into Guatemala. A special task force within the State Department, the Guatemalan Group, had been at work since early May (that is, before the arrival of the *Alfhem*) coaxing and pressuring the Latin American republics to support these sanctions.[168]

Guatemala alone of the OAS members had been excluded from the prelim-

[166] Peurifoy to SecState, no. 870, June 2, 1954, NA 714.00, quoting Toriello.

[167] "Panama Favoring Guatemala Talks," *NYT*, June 10, 1954, p. 12.

[168] For the creation of the Task Force, see "OAS Action against Communism in Guatemala," May 10, 1954, *FRUS*, 1952–1954, 4:1102–5. For the draft resolution, see "The Secretary of State to Diplomatic Offices in the American Republics," June 5, 1954, ibid., pp. 1157–60.

Rabe writes, "In a straw vote, the State Department found it could count on only eleven Latin American votes." (*Eisenhower and Latin America*, p. 53.) This was two votes short of the required two-thirds majority. Other votes were, however, in the pipeline: on June 19, Panama pledged its vote. (MemoConv [Heurtematte, Holland], June 19, 1954, NA 714.00.) And, of course, there was Brazil: as Foster Dulles noted, Brazil had enthusiastically supported the U.S. position against Guatemala at Caracas (U.S. Congress, *HCFA*, p. 502), and had warmly endorsed the draft resolution against Guatemala prepared by the United States for the Montevideo conference. (MemoConv [Dulles, Muñiz, Holland] May 11, 1954; MemoConv [Dulles, Muñiz, Holland] May 24, 1954; MemoConv [Dulles, Muñiz, Holland] May 27, 1954; MemoConv [Muñiz, Holland] May 28, 1954. All NA 714.00.) That Brazil had not yet officially joined the co-sponsors of the draft resolution was not due to sudden scruples about the principle of nonintervention. It was because the foreign minister was "very irritated" with the State Department; he had asked that Brazil be granted the honor "to take the lead in approaching Uruguay, Paraguay, Bolivia and Chile" on behalf of the draft resolution, but the emissary he had appointed for the purpose had been delayed by illness, and the State Department proceeded without him. (Quotations from MemoConv [Muñiz, Holland] June 10, 1954, p. 1, and DOS, "OAS Action against Communism in Guatemala," May 29, 1954, p. 1. Both NA 714.00.) After he had vented his frustration, the foreign minister softened: if the State Department would accept two changes in the draft resolution, Brazil would not only endorse it, but also "try to get others" to support it. "These [two amendments] are acceptable to the U.S. . . . Brazil's joinder should bring in several waverers and give us more than the required fourteen votes." (Quotations from: TelConv [JFD, Holland] June 16, 1954, 11:29 a.m., DP, JFD:CS, Box 8, and from Holland to Undersecretary, June 16, 1954, NA Lot 58D18 & 58D78, Box 2.)

inaries. No Latin American government had informed the Arbenz administration of the nature of the sanctions under discussion. "It was a miracle," marveled Assistant Secretary Holland on June 10, "that the secrecy of the resolution had been preserved."[169] To the Guatemalans, Holland's miracle was a nightmare: they could only speculate about the gravity of the sanctions that were being hammered out even before the conference began, and they imagined the worst.[170] On June 9, Minor Keilhauer, an upper-class friend of Arbenz, appeared in desperation at the U.S. embassy. He and other prominent supporters of the administration, among them Foreign Minister Toriello, "were greatly disturbed over the possibility of sanctions. All of them," Peurifoy reported,

> realize that the government could not operate if sanctions were applied. He [Keilhauer] stated that many of Arbenz's friends had been working on him to change the

---

These fourteen countries had accepted the draft resolution in its entirety *in advance of* the conference and it is very unlikely that all the other countries would have voted against the resolution. On June 17, an OIR report concluded, "There is no doubt that the substance of the anti-Guatemala resolution proposed for Montevideo will be approved by more than two-thirds of the OAS nations." (Intelligence Report, June 17, 1954, p. 1, NA 714.00.)

[169] MemoConv (Holland, Jara, Suarez, Barrell), June 10, 1954, p. 1, NA 714.00. Interviews with María de Arbenz, Fortuny, and Toriello confirm that the government did not know what sanctions were being planned.

Even democratic Uruguay, considered an ardent supporter of the principle of nonintervention, expressly excluded Guatemala—and included the United States—in its deliberations about the conference. Ambassador José Mora told Holland that his government would send a special ambassador to Guatemala before the conference "to investigate on the ground." This envoy, Holland noted, "would get in touch with our ambassador there, but would not report to the local government." Uruguay had earlier informed the State Department "that it would support the calling of the conference" and agreed to have it in Montevideo. (Quotations from MemoConv [Mora, Holland] June 10, 1954, and MemoConv [Mora, Holland] June 7, 1954. Both NA 714.00.) It was only after Castillo Armas's invasion had begun that Uruguay expressed "strong opposition to going ahead with the plans" for the conference and warned that it might "revoke permission to use Montevideo as a site." (CIA, *Current Intelligence Digest*, June 25, 1954, p. 16.)

[170] Confirmed by all the Guatemalans interviewed on this point. See also *JW* 21, May 28, 1954, p. 1. "Action by the [OAS] Foreign Ministers might include an agreement to stop all trade with Guatemala," opined *Newsweek*. ("U.S. Showdown on Guatemala?" June 14, 1954, p. 54.) While *DCA* barely mentioned the forthcoming conference, the opposition press speculated about it recklessly. See, for instance, *El I*: "Hacia consulta interamericana," May 27, 1954, p. 1; "El Salvador no admite el envio," May 28, 1954, p. 1; "Senador Johnson predijo planteamiento de las sanciones contra Guatemala," May 29, 1954, p. 1; "Canciller colombiano declara que debe convocarse junta de América," June 2, 1954, p. 1; "La ilusión de la solidaridad," June 3, 1954, p. 1; "Montevideo posible sede," June 8, 1954, p. 1.

government's attitude and actions. Keilhauer asked me if I would see the President [Arbenz] and attempt to bring about a change in the situation. . . . He said . . . time was running short in view of the proposed meeting of the OAS. He and his conferees knew this conference would vote economic sanctions against Guatemala, and that the government would not survive.[171]

Peurifoy, however, had neither the time nor the inclination to chat with Arbenz. He was too busy trying to convince Washington to do more to destabilize the government before Castillo Armas's invasion began.[172]

Three decades later, in a Georgetown sitting room, a man who had been a senior member of the Guatemalan Group looked back at the curious timing of the Montevideo conference. "I am beginning to think that the preparations for Montevideo were part of a cover-up and that there was never any intention of holding the conference," Deputy Assistant Secretary Woodward mused.[173] The conference was planned for early July, that is, after the date set for the invasion of Guatemala. If the invasion succeeded, it would have been unnecessary to have held the conference; if the invasion failed, it would have been foolhardy. Arbenz would have become a hero in Latin America, Dulles himself noted, and it would have been difficult to have held the Latin American governments in line.[174] Those State Department officials who, like Woodward, were not privy to PBSUCCESS and who, like Woodward, labored hard for a conference that would never take place, were unwitting pawns of PBSUCCESS.

In theory, the United States could have held the Montevideo conference before the invasion, used the sanctions to further weaken the Guatemalans' morale and then launched Castillo Armas's band. But there is no indication that this was considered.[175] Perhaps they reasoned that preparing for a paper conference would strengthen the figleaf: the United States was acting responsibly within the framework of the Organization of American States; it was not indulging in covert operations. Perhaps they reasoned that the threat of unspecified sanctions was, for the Guatemalans, more frightening than the imposition of the specific sanctions that were planned.

And the Guatemalans were indeed frightened. Tension and anguish escalated among the *Arbencistas*, and finally "something like hysteria took

[171] Peurifoy to SecState, no. 945, June 10, 1954, NA 714.00.

[172] See Peurifoy to SecState, June 2, 1954, *FRUS*, 1952–1954, 4:1155–56 and Peurifoy to SecState, no. 956, June 11, 1954, NA 714.00.

[173] Interview with Woodward.

[174] "The Secretary believed that on the assumption that [Castillo] Armas failed, Arbenz and Toriello would become heroes and we may not succeed in obtaining our resolution. Such a diplomatic defeat would be a great blow to the US prestige." (DOS, Meeting of Guatemalan Group, June 25, 1954, p. 1.)

[175] Interviews with Bissell and Kirkpatrick.

over."[176] In despair and self-defense, the regime began to lash out at the only foe that it could reach—the internal opposition—in an attempt to destroy the fifth column before the invasion began. On June 8, constitutional guarantees were suspended.[177] Censorship was imposed, and the opposition media ceased their furious attacks on the regime. "They had reported sensationally the developing political crisis in Guatemala" until the day the decree was announced, reported the U.S. embassy.[178]

A wave of arrests had begun in the last days of May.[179] In the final four weeks of the regime several hundred suspects were detained. Among them were many plotters, but also many who were not involved in any conspiracy. "Prisoners were tortured. At least seventy-five were killed and hastily buried in mass graves."[180]

In the United States, the repression provoked an uproar. Congressmen and journalists inveighed against a "tyrannical Communist minority" that was trying "to maintain itself against the will of the people."[181] Secretary Dulles "spoke out bluntly" against the "reign of terror," and President Eisenhower "added the weight of his disapproval and deep regret."[182]

The depth of the indignation that seized so many in the United States who

[176] Krehm (see n. 151 above), p. 300. This is an excellent article by a first-rate journalist.

[177] "Restringidas las garantías," *DCA*, June 8, 1954, p. 1; "Garantías restrictas un mes," *El I*, June 8, 1954, p. 1; "Guatemala Calls Emergency and Suspends Civil Liberty," *NYT*, June 8, 1954, p. 1.

[178] *JW* 23, June 11, 1954, p. 3.

[179] See "Tras cateos, cinco asilados," *El I*, May 31, 1954, p. 1; "Capturas por complot siguen," *El I*, June 1, 1954, p. 1; "Dos capturas más," *El I*, June 2, 1954, p. 1; "Inseguridad de las personas" (edit.), ibid.; "Descubierto el más grande complot," *DCA*, June 3, 1954, p. 1; "El aventurismo golpista" (edit.), ibid., p. 3; "No tardaré en el destierro, dijo Goicolea Villacorta," *El I*, June 4, 1954, p. 1; "Nuevas capturas quedan en misterio," *El I*, June 5, 1954, p. 1; "Salvoconductos a dos exilados más," *El I*, June 7, 1954, p. 1; Peurifoy to SecState, no. 873, June 2, 1954, NA 714.00; Peurifoy to SecState, no. 903, June 5, 1954, NA 714.00; "Plot in Guatemala Charged as 5 Flee to Embassy Haven," *NYT*, June 1, 1954, p. 1; "Plot Still Fought by Guatemalans," *NYT*, June 3, 1954, p. 1. For a letter that vividly conveys the tension of the time, see Charnaud to Toriello, June 15, 1954, CO:G, June 1954, pp. 408–10, AGCA.

[180] Krehm (see n. 151 above), p. 300. This is the most accurate estimate. After Arbenz's fall, the bodies of many "communists" executed by the *Liberacionistas* were displayed to foreign journalists as the victims of the defeated regime. See below, pp. 333–34.

[181] Hickenlooper, June 17, 1954, *CR*-Senate, p. 8843.

[182] Quotations from "Dulles Pictures Guatemalan Fear," *NYT*, June 16, 1954, p. 8, and "Guatemala, Battle in the Backyard," *Time*, June 28, 1954, p. 43. For the transcript of Eisenhower's press conference see *NYT*, June 17, 1954, p. 14.

were usually philosophical about violence in Latin America is somewhat surprising. Arbenz, however, was the enemy. For too long, his government had posed a disquieting paradox for the Americans: riddled with communists, it had nevertheless upheld political democracy and civil liberties to a degree that was highly unusual in Latin America.

In the words of Senators Wiley and Hickenlooper, the "Communist wolves" had finally shed their "sheep's clothing." Now, at last, the communists were moving "to crush the free spirit of the Guatemalan people." Representative Javits expressed the views of many when he proclaimed, "The suspension of constitutional guarantees by the Government of Guatemala is a final confirmation of the grave threat to the peace and security of the Americas due to the Communist-infiltrated government of that unhappy country."[183]

Many rushed to condemn the Arbenz administration to eternal opprobrium. If this required that history be rewritten, so be it. By claiming that the crimes perpetrated in the last weeks of the regime were unusually atrocious ("treatment I have never heard of before, nor imagined"), by claiming that these were "unLatin" acts,[184] they sought to convey the unprecedented nature of the threat: "For a suitable analogy [to these crimes] one must look behind the Iron Curtain."[185] Like the weapons on the *Alfhem*, they were stamped with a hammer and sickle.

[183] Wiley, June 16, 1954, *CR*-Senate, p. A4443; Hickenlooper, June 17, 1954, ibid, p. 8443; Javits, June 7, 1954, *CR*-House, p. 8107.

[184] Quotations from Monroe, "Guatemala: What the Reds Left Behind," p. 60, and Martz, *Communist Infiltration*, p. 101.

[185] James, *Red Design*, p. 263.

CHAPTER 14

The Fall of Arbenz

ON JUNE 18, 1954, the Tegucigalpa daily *El Cronista* published a statement issued by Eduardo Valenzuela, the foreign minister of Honduras. He had informed Lt. Colonel Castillo Armas that if he violated the neutrality of Honduras he would be expelled. "The Honduran public can be confident," Valenzuela pledged, "that the government is firm and will be firm in maintaining and honoring its neutrality."[1]

The *New York Times* told a different story. In a "virtual wide-open movement," it reported, Guatemalan exiles were being flown in Honduran planes to the Guatemalan border.[2] The story was out of date before it appeared; on June 17, the invasion of Guatemala had begun.[3]

For the next ten days the international press bandied about contradictory reports of the war, the Guatemalan army released confident communiqués, and Castillo Armas's American patrons began to fear the worst. On the twenty-sixth, an army bulletin announced that the rebels were on the run, and *Diario de Centro América* blared: "Government Triumphs!"[4]

On June 27, Arbenz resigned. A game of musical chairs began in Guatemala City. At each pause, Castillo Armas was closer to the throne. Meanwhile, hundreds of *Arbencistas*, and Arbenz himself, sought refuge in foreign embassies, and repression swept the country. "The years of spring in the land of eternal tyranny" had abruptly concluded.

Throughout his exile, Arbenz would be subjected to the reproaches of former supporters and to the thinly disguised contempt of a new generation of Latin American leftists who grew in the shadow of Fidel Castro. During his presidency, these critics argued, Jacobo Arbenz had proudly challenged the

[1] "Castillo Armas recibió la prevención en el despacho de nuestra cancillería," *El Cronista*, Tegucigalpa, June 18, 1954, p. 1. For a vehement apology of the official position of the Honduran government, see Moya Posas, *La jornada épica*.

[2] "Anti-Arbenz Men Move in Honduras," *NYT*, June 18, 1954, p. 7.

[3] American authors, following the *NYT*, regularly cite June 18 as the beginning of the invasion; Guatemalan authors, the Guatemalan press and Guatemalan participants assert that Castillo Armas's men crossed the border in the early hours of June 17 and occupied El Florido, Jocotán, and other hamlets along the road to Chiquimula later in the day.

[4] Quotations from "Persecución de los agresores ha continuado sin cuartel," *El I*, June 26, 1954, p. 1, and "Fuerzas de la revolución triunfantes," *DCA*, June 26, 1954, p. 1.

American colossus—only to surrender as if he were the abject president of a banana republic. For months on end, they asserted, that stubborn, enigmatic man had imposed a steady course on those who had wavered, but at the moment of crisis he had sought refuge in a foreign embassy. The marines had not been necessary; economic sanctions had not been necessary; a handful of exiles had sufficed. No major battles had been fought and on the two occasions when the rebels had met resistance, they had been defeated. Arbenz, the indictment ran, gave up without even going to the front, without even attempting to arm the people. He was a petty bourgeois, not a revolutionary, concluded those who sought wisdom in simplistic class analysis.[5] And yet Arbenz was not a coward: "Military attachés, diplomats and journalists who have met the Guatemalan President," *Time* reported on June 28, 1954, "are in striking agreement that the mainspring of his character is dogged, stubborn, self-willed courage."[6]

THE INVASION

Arbenz's initial response to the invasion was based on his belief that Castillo Armas posed no military threat. His informers in Honduras had assured him that there were only a few hundred rebels.[7] To defeat them would not be difficult.[8]

His assessment of the rebels' strength was correct. Castillo Armas's "rather ramshackle army" of *Liberacionistas* consisted of about 250 men: approximately 150 rebels crossed the border on June 17 and headed in the direction of Zacapa; the others attacked Puerto Barrios, to the north, a few days later.[9]

[5] See, for example, Cardoza y Aragón, *La Revolución Gualtemalteca*; Cardoza, "A treinta años," p. 92; and Góngora, *Introducción*, pp. 92–93.

[6] "Guatemala: Battle in the Backyard," *Time*, June 28, 1954, p. 38.

[7] See the numerous reports by Chargé d'Affaires Paredes Moreira, Military Attaché Col. Morales, and Amb. Chinchilla Orellana in *GT*, Boxes 7 and 72. These reports cover Oct. 1953 to June 1954.

[8] Interviews with María de Arbenz, Fortuny, Guerra Borges, Alejandro, Toriello, Charnaud, and Cols. Parinello and Guillén.

[9] Quoted from Allen W. Dulles, "My Answer to the Bay of Pigs," p. 16, AWD Papers, Box 138, ML. The figure usually given—150 to 200—does not include the hundred rebels who attacked Puerto Barrios. On the main force, see Putzeys Rojas, *Así se hizo la Liberación*; L.A.H.A., *Así se gestó la Liberación*; Santa Cruz Morales, "El Ejército de Liberación."

Liberacionista accounts of the invasion are rare, florid and fantastic. The most useful are Putzeys Rojas, *Así se hizo la Liberación* and L.A.H.A., *Así se gestó la Liberación*. See also Flores Avendaño, *Memorias*, 2:401–45; Guatemala, *Efemérides*; López Villatoro, *Por qué fué derrotado el comunismo en Guatemala?* pp. 47–53. Works that do not deal with the invasion but perpetuate the *Liberacionista* myth include López Vil-

Not only were the rebels a mere handful, but their weapons were of the same quality as those of the Guatemalan army, that is, World War II vintage—a nod to the figleaf that still rankles many who had expected to be given sophisticated arms.[10] Only in communications equipment and in aircraft did the rebels enjoy a marked advantage.

Arbenz's realistic assessment of the military insignificance of the rebel challenge had a perverse effect on his overall assessment of the invasion. Throughout the previous months, he had believed that the army would remain loyal if faced with an exile attack in which the United States did not directly participate. The military weakness of the invasion reinforced his illusions. Arbenz, his wife recalls, "believed that the army would defend the motherland. Our army would refuse to submit to Castillo Armas, a traitor who had been defeated in 1950 and who was leading a motley band of outlaws—not even soldiers. The army would not dishonor itself. The officers would not capitulate to a traitor."[11]

Thus, Arbenz concluded that an attempt to arm the population would be unnecessary and dangerous, unnecessary because the army would defeat Castillo Armas and dangerous because the officers might refuse to distribute the weapons. The very weakness of the rebel force aggravated this danger. Lacking any military justification, an order to arm the civilians would strike the officers as a blatant insult, or betrayal—that is, proof that Arbenz intended to establish workers' militias.[12]

On June 18, and again two or three days later, Armed Forces Chief Díaz told Arbenz and leading politicians that a decision to arm the civilians "would deeply disturb the army. It is their job to defeat Castillo Armas, and they can do it alone. Be confident," he urged. "The army will do its duty."[13] Díaz was sincere. But he failed to mention what everyone feared: if ordered to arm the population, the officers might rise in revolt—a boon to Castillo Armas.

Arbenz decided not to arm the civilians. The PGT and the other administration forces concurred. Until June 25, when the army's betrayal was flagrant, no political party or labor confederation asked for weapons. Consistently expressing their confidence in the army, they voiced their eagerness to assist in any way the military might deem useful. The workers were ready to act "under the direction of the army," declared Gutiérrez for the CGTG; "all the

latoro, *Por los fueros de la verdad histórica*; Comisión permanente, *El libro negro*; Nájera Farfán, *Cuando el árbol cae*; de la Guarda, *Castillo Armas*.

[10] Interview with Taracena.

[11] Interviews with María de Arbenz (quoted), Fortuny, Guerra Borges, Alejandro, Charnaud, Toriello, and Cols. Parinello and Guillén.

[12] Interviews with María de Arbenz, Fortuny, Guerra Borges, Alejandro, Charnaud, Toriello, and Col. Parinello.

[13] Interviews with Fortuny (quoting Díaz) and Charnaud, both of whom were at the meetings.

peasants are eager to be led by the army,'' Castillo Flores pledged on behalf of the CNCG.[14]

To all but a select few, Arbenz expressed only confidence that Castillo Armas would be defeated. To his wife and Fortuny, he confided his anguish. The thought that had haunted him since Caracas tormented him now. What would the United States do after the defeat of Castillo Armas? Would Eisenhower send in the marines? Or would Honduras attack on Washington's behalf, only to be followed by U.S. troops sent to punish the ''aggressor''? Or would the United States turn to economic strangulation? Eisenhower, Arbenz told Fortuny, ''could cut off our oil supplies.'' What would happen then? Guatemala imported all its oil. Mexico was not even self-sufficient in oil; would it dare defy the Americans? Oil-rich Venezuela was ruled by Pérez Jiménez.[15] On June 3, Arbenz had invited Roberto Saravia, the manager of Esso in Guatemala, to the presidential palace. Arbenz ''asked about stocks on hand, rate of consumption and expected deliveries . . . [and] whether it would be possible for the Guatemalan Government to purchase one million gallons of gasoline in barrels.'' Saravia told the president that it would not be possible and hastened to report the conversation to the U.S. embassy.[16] How long could Guatemala survive without oil? ''The economy could not withstand it, nor would the army,'' Arbenz told Fortuny.[17]

Fortuny and Doña María shared Arbenz's fears. Like him, they had no answers, only tenuous hopes: perhaps the United Nations would help; perhaps international pressure would restrain Eisenhower. Latin American public opinion was already responding with fury to an invasion that reeked of Washington. ''We had heard,'' recalls Toriello, ''about protest marches across the continent, rallies of 100,000 people in Mexico, huge demonstrations in Chile.''[18] These reports heartened Arbenz. The dispatch of U.S. troops to Guatemala, he believed, would do untold damage to Eisenhower's carefully cultivated international image: ''the hero of the Second World War pummeling

[14] Quoted from ''Inconmovible alianza de los obreros y campesinos,'' *Nuestro Diario*, June 22, 1954, p. 5. Communiqués by political parties echoed the same line; see, for instance, the PAR's statements in *Nuestro Diario*, June 23, 1954, p. 4 (''Unidos defenderemos Guatemala''), and June 25, 1954, p. 10 (''Comunicado del PAR a las bases del país''). See also the speech by Edelberto Torres Rivas, secretary general of the PGT's youth, ''Cuatrocientos jóvenes juraron fidelidad a la causa del pueblo,'' *Nuestro Diario*, June 26, 1954, p. 5.

[15] Interviews with Fortuny (quoted) and María de Arbenz.

[16] Wardlaw to Ambassador and Krieg, ''President Arbenz' Concern About Gasoline Supplies,'' June 4, 1954, pp. 1–2 (quoted), and Wardlaw to Ambassador and Krieg, ''Conversation with Roberto Saravia,'' June 9, 1954. Both RG84 G&C, Box 3, NAS.

[17] Interview with Fortuny.

[18] Interview with Toriello.

a small and defenseless nation!'' Economic sanctions would provoke a wave of hatred throughout Latin America, shattering the myth of the Good Neighbor Policy and forcing even timid governments to adopt a firmer stance against the aggressor. Even Western Europe would not find it easy to remain aloof. Therefore, might not Eisenhower conclude after Castillo Armas's defeat that it was prudent to leave Guatemala alone?[19] Arbenz himself has recalled that he had hoped that ''the formidable mobilization of the peoples of Latin America and the outcry of the whole world would stop the United States from intervening in an even more flagrant manner.''[20]

As hope and despair spun in a debilitating vortex, Arbenz dismissed Castillo Armas's attack as a sideshow. The battlefront was the capital: it was from Guatemala City that the international effort to restrain Eisenhower would be launched. Why, then, should he leave to lead his troops against Castillo Armas's puny band? No one suggested that he do so: not Fortuny and his PGT friends, who were convinced that the army would crush the rebels; not the leaders of the revolutionary parties, who feared not Castillo Armas, but U.S. retribution after his defeat. Nor did Arbenz's senior military aides ever suggest that he go to the front—not Colonel Díaz, not Defense Minister Sánchez, and not Army Chief of Staff Parinello.[21]

Arbenz remained in the capital and asked Díaz to select the men who would lead the troops against the rebels. He approved Díaz's choices, for they seemed eminently reasonable. Díaz had selected three close friends. He placed in overall command Colonel Víctor M. León, the inspector general of the army, who was thought to be a loyal *Arbencista*. Colonels Pablo Díaz and José Barzanallana completed the trio. Pablo Díaz, who had held only desk jobs prior to his appointment as head of the Base Militar, was reputed to be a man of personal integrity. Barzanallana, the commander of the Guardia de Honor, had been in command of the Base Militar in 1950 when Castillo Armas had attacked it. He had routed the rebels and earned their hatred; Barzanallana, Castillo Armas had written, was a murderer who ''had forsaken his honor as a soldier, and as a man.'' Self-preservation, Arbenz and Díaz believed, dictated that Barzanallana would be eager to defeat Castillo Armas again.[22]

On the night of June 19, most of the troops from the Guardia de Honor and the Base Militar left for Zacapa, a town thirty miles west of the Honduran border. Small army detachments from the departments of Quetzaltenango, Es-

[19] Interviews with María de Arbenz (quoted) and Fortuny.

[20] Arbenz, ''Jacobo Arbenz relata detalles,'' p. 9.

[21] Interviews with María de Arbenz, Fortuny, Guerra Borges, Alejandro, Charnaud, Toriello, and Cols. Parinello and Guillén.

[22] Quoted from L.A.H.A., *Así se gestó la Liberación*, p. 53. Interviews with Parinello, Paz Tejada, and Peralta Méndez. The PGT had no say in these appointments, nor did it offer any suggestions ''because we knew very little about the army.'' (Interview with Fortuny.)

cuintla, and Cobán followed suit. Zacapa, Arbenz had decided, would be the headquarters of the troops sent against Castillo Armas; from there, León and his colleagues would launch the counteroffensive against the rebels. But first they had to let Castillo Armas penetrate several miles deep into Guatemala: "This invasion is a farce," Arbenz told Fortuny. "We can shoo them away with our hats. What I'm afraid of—and this is why I ordered Díaz to let the mercenaries advance into our territory—what I'm afraid of is that if we defeat them right on the border, the Honduran government will manufacture a border incident, declare war on us, and the United States will invade."[23]

The countryside was rife with rumors that the fifth column was preparing to strike. Local peasant unions were flooding the national offices of the CGTG and the CNCG with requests for weapons. "We beg you to send guns for the defence of the government," pleaded the union of Santa Teresa; "Comrade, convince them to send us arms; we want to fight beside the army," urged the union from Catarina. All received the same reply: there was no need to arm the population; the "army is successfully defending our country"; the peasants should remain vigilant "day and night" against possible acts of sabotage and provide whatever assistance the army might require.[24]

The peasants did what they could. In late May and early June, saboteurs trained by the CIA had infiltrated into Guatemala; they would join hands with the "internal front" and weaken the regime's grip at home. But throughout the invasion, as the U.S. embassy pointed out, the fifth column failed to materialize and the only acts of sabotage were occasional disruptions of the telegraph lines between Zacapa and the capital.[25] Even before the invasion had begun, the peasants had started manning roadblocks. They were "polite but firm."[26] They searched for weapons that rebel planes had been dropping since June 14, and they dutifully handed them over to the local army and police

[23] Interviews with Fortuny (quoted), María de Arbenz, Col. Parinello, and Lt. Col. Mendizabal were particularly useful for this paragraph. See also Toriello, *La batalla de Guatemala*, p. 121. For the troops' departure from the capital, see Peurifoy to SecState, no. 1054, June 20, 1954, NA 714.00, and CIA, *Current Intelligence Digest*, June 24, 1954, p. 14.

[24] Quotations from: Moises Hernández to CGTG, Santa Teresa, June 20, 1954, *GT*, Box 5; Edrulfo Morales Arreaga to Castillo Flores, Catarina, June 20, 1954, *GT*, Box 11; Castillo Flores to Morales Arreaga, June 20, 1954, ibid.; Castillo Flores to the Secretaries General of the Federaciones Campesinas de la República, June 19, 1954, *GT*, Box 5. The *GT*, esp. Boxes 5, 11, and 71, include a wealth of documents that illuminate the response of local peasant unions to the invasion.

[25] *JW* 25, June 25, 1954, p. 3.

[26] Peurifoy to SecState, no. 1012, June 16, 1954, NA 714.00. See also Wardlaw to Ambassador et al., "Conditions in Pacific Coast Area," June 17, 1954, RG84 G&C, Box 3, NA-S; "Anti-Arbenz Men Move in Honduras," *NYT*, June 18, 1954, p. 7; *JW* 25, June 25, 1954, p. 3.

Guatemala Hotspots: A Map of the Invasion. (From the United States Information Service files in the National Archives, June 23, 1954.)

authorities.[27] "Travelers from the provinces," stated the *New York Times* on June 22, "reported that labor syndicate officials and agricultural committees were exercising control in the villages."[28] This remained true until Arbenz fell.

Eager to show its support for the army, the CGTG urged the population to donate blood for "our soldiers wounded in the line of duty," and to give cigarettes to the troops "as a gesture of gratitude to the Army of the Revolution."[29] Meanwhile rebel planes strafed the capital for a few minutes every day and occasionally dropped a bomb, causing little damage but unnerving the populace. "The last seven days," wrote a *New York Times* correspondent from Guatemala City on June 24, "have been filled with anxiety and confusion." Yet, he added, "the effect on normal living has been slight. A gasoline shortage was indicated last week, but this appears to have ended. Food prices have risen slightly, but the Government acted early to institute price controls."[30] The city was quiet but tense. The government radio and the *Voz de la Liberación* were broadcasting contradictory reports and rumors were rampant: had Castillo Armas been routed or were the rebels several thousand strong, advancing relentlessly?

In fact, very little was happening at the front. Between June 17 and June 19 the rebels advanced unopposed along a strip of territory five to fifteen miles deep and twenty to thirty miles wide in the general direction of Zacapa.[31] Then at Gualán, on June 20, they fought their first battle. Gualán, a small town fifteen miles west of the Honduran border, was defended by Lieutenant César Augusto Silva Girón and thirty soldiers. Receiving neither instructions nor assistance from Zacapa, the stubborn lieutenant fought for thirty-six hours— until the rebels withdrew in defeat.[32] The victory of an isolated and outnum-

[27] See *GT*, esp. Boxes 5, 11, and 71; see also CIA, "Current Unrest in Guatemala," CS-40-75, June 21, 1954, p. 1, and *JW* 24, June 18, 1954, pp. 3–4.

[28] "Battle for Port," *NYT*, June 22, 1954, p. 3.

[29] Quoted from CGTG, Circular, June 23, 1954, *GT*, Box 19. See also José Alberto Cardoza, no. 187, June 23, 1954, *GT*, Box 61; Cardoza to Estado Mayor del Ejército Nacional, June 25, 1954, *GT*, Box 71; Col. Víctor Quilo to Cardoza, June 26, 1954, ibid.

[30] "Capital near Normal," *NYT*, June 25, 1954, p. 3.

[31] See DOS, Circular 499, June 22, 1954, NA 714.00. *Liberacionista* accounts do not claim otherwise.

[32] Silva Girón provides a turgid but accurate account in his *La batalla de Gualán*. Understandably, *Liberacionista* sources are far more discreet. They either summarily explain the defeat by claiming that Silva Girón had "ten times more men" than they did (L.A.H.A., *Así se gestó la Liberación*, pp. 184 and 188 [quoted]), or they don't mention Gualán. Silva Girón's version was confirmed in interviews with Guatemalan officers of differing political sympathies, including González Siguí, Parinello, Mendizabal, and Paiz Novales.

bered outpost strengthened Arbenz in his belief that the army would trounce this band of traitors, just as it had defeated those who had attacked Salamá the year before.

On June 21, approximately one hundred rebels launched a surprise attack on Puerto Barrios. One third had come by sea on a Honduran vessel; the others had infiltrated from Honduras. Within a few hours the rebels were on the run, leaving behind twenty prisoners (including eleven Hondurans and one Salvadoran), several dead, their ship, and their weapons. They had been defeated by the police of Puerto Barrios and by hastily armed civilians, mainly labor union members.[33]

By the time the rebels had fled from Gualán and Puerto Barrios, over two thousand soldiers entrusted to Colonel León had assembled at Zacapa. Arbenz expected that they would now rout what was left of the rebel force, but León reported that his offensive would be delayed; a rebel plane had attacked a train bringing additional supplies and equipment to Zacapa. (The attack had indeed occurred, but the damage had been slight.) There was no reason to worry, he stressed. He would attack very soon; morale was good; Castillo Armas was doomed. In the capital, Colonel Carlos Enrique Díaz, who was in charge of communication with Zacapa, relayed these assurances to Arbenz. Díaz was confident: Víctor M. León, Pablo Díaz, and José Barzanallana were his friends.[34]

Arbenz, the PGT, and most government leaders believed these promises.[35] Others knew better—and said nothing. Army Chief of Staff Parinello was sent by Díaz to inspect the front on the twenty-third. He stayed only a few hours ("it was a whirlwind tour") and returned convinced that the army would not fight.[36] He did not, however, tell this to Arbenz or Díaz. It was not that he was

[33] For the names and nationalities of the prisoners, as well as a summary of their depositions and other useful information, see Jaime Rosenberg to Arbenz, June 23, 1954, *GT*, Box 1. See also Francisco Vásquez to Arbenz, *GT*, Box 71; T. Alvarado N., memo 564, ibid.; Cornelio Lone Mejía, memo 565, *GT*, Box 4. All June 21, 1954. For the size of the force that attacked Puerto Barrios, see also L.A.H.A., *Así se gestó la Liberación*, p. 188.

[34] Interviews with Cols. Parinello and Guillén, and with Fortuny, María de Arbenz, and Charnaud. For the attack on the train, see also Peurifoy to SecState, nos. 1060 and 1068, both June 21, 1954, NA 714.00.

[35] There were, of course, exceptions. On June 22, Marcos Antonio Franco Chacón, a PAR leader and the president of the Guatemalan Congress, told Major Paz Tejeda "that he was very worried and did not believe Díaz's optimistic reports." (Interview with Paz Tejada.) But this was a minority viewpoint. (Interviews with María de Arbenz, Fortuny, Guerra Borges, Alejandro, Toriello, Charnaud, and Parinello; see also CIA, *Current Intelligence Digest*, June 28, 1954, p. 15.)

[36] Interview with Parinello. Parinello's trip to the front was recorded in the *Boletín* no. 6 of the *Alto Mando Militar*. (See *El I*, June 24, 1954, p. 1.)

afraid of Castillo Armas; he was afraid of the United States. Eisenhower, he believed, had decided that Arbenz had to go, and the Americans "would most likely send in the marines if Castillo Armas failed."[37] Parinello was not ready to join in any plot—not yet, at least—but neither was he willing to take any risks. He epitomized the "loyal" officer.

While professions of loyalty and promises of victory continued to flow from Zacapa, Arbenz focused on the diplomatic battle—Guatemala's only hope, he believed, against the United States.

The Guatemalan government asked El Salvador to lend its good offices with Honduras, but the Salvadoran ambassador merely leaked the request to Peurifoy, spicing it with spiteful comments about the Arbenz regime.[38] Guatemala's emissaries were dispatched to Mexico to seek its diplomatic support, but Mexico remained aloof.[39] Arbenz and Toriello placed their hopes, above

[37] Interview with Parinello, who related an episode that sheds light on his own attitude. In the spring of 1954, he was approached by a Guatemalan officer who told him: "Colonel, there are some people from the U.S. Secret Service who want to overthrow Arbenz. They want to meet you in Antigua for a very confidential lunch. Arbenz is going to fall." Parinello refused to go—but he did not denounce the officer. (Interview with Parinello.)

[38] See Peurifoy to SecState, no. 1102, June 24, 1954, 7 p.m., NA 714.00. The evidence suggests that President Osorio, while clearly wanting Arbenz overthrown, preferred to watch the spectacle from the sidelines and spare his country Honduras's demeaning role. (See AmEm San José, MemoConv [Canessa, Cohen], Feb. 4, 1953, enclosed in Fleming to DOS, no. 743, Feb. 5, 1953, NA 713.00; AmEm San Salvador, McDermott to Cabot, Oct. 2, 1953, NA Lot 58D18 & 58D78, Box 1; DOS, "Briefing on El Salvador," Apr. 23, 1954, NA 716.00. Also helpful was interview with Sol.)

[39] Interviews with Toriello, Fortuny, Guerra Borges, and Cardoza y Aragón (who had close contacts with high Mexican officials). Since its glorious revolution, Mexico's support for the principle of nonintervention has been exemplary; this, at least, is what Mexican officials assert. Their country, they note, provided a haven for Sandino. Their country was the only member of the OAS to refuse to impose sanctions against Castro's Cuba. And their country said no to Foster Dulles at Caracas in defense of Guatemala's sovereignty.

In fact, Mexico's support for the principle of nonintervention has been undermined by its fear of Washington and by the conservatism of its leaders. Mexico was a treacherous friend to Sandino, it colluded with the CIA against Cuba, and it turned against Arbenz's Guatemala. (On Mexico and Sandino, see Macaulay, *Sandino Affair*, pp. 146–50, 156–60. On Mexico and Cuba in the 1960s, see Pellicer de Brody, *México y la Revolución Cubana*.)

Mexico did abstain at Caracas and this abstention did contrast favorably with the spinelessness of the other Latin American countries, but in the weeks that followed, the Mexican authorities responded complacently to the State Department's preparations for another OAS conference to vote sanctions against Guatemala. On June 11, the

all, in the United Nations. Guatemala's case was so solid and the evidence of Honduras's and Nicaragua's complicity was so glaring that the United Nations would have to intervene.[40] On June 18, Toriello asked the UN Security Council "to take the measures necessary . . . to put a stop to the aggression," which he blamed on Nicaragua, Honduras, and "certain foreign monopolies whose interests have been affected by the progressive policy of my government."[41]

It seemed for a moment that the august body would consider Guatemala's plight. On June 20, the Security Council approved a French motion calling for "the immediate termination of any action likely to cause bloodshed" and requesting "all Members of the United Nations to abstain . . . from rendering assistance to any such action."[42] Publicly, the United States supported the motion, but Secretary Dulles was furious. The behavior of the French was

---

Mexican government announced that it would attend the Montevideo conference. "Mexico," U.S. Ambassador White was told, "had decided that it . . . would cooperate with the United States there, but that it would not commit itself in advance to any actions." Significantly, the Mexican authorities did not inform Guatemala of the contents of the draft resolution. (See MemoTel [White, Holland], June 1, 1954; MemoConv [Tello, Holland], June 7, 1954; MemoConv [White, Holland], June 7, 1954; MemoConv [White, Holland], June 9, 1954; MemoConv [White, Holland], June 10, 1954, quoted; MemoConv [Tello, Nieto, Holland], June 19, 1954; all NA 714.00. See also AmEm Mexico City, White to Holland, May 14, 1954, NA Lot 57D295, Box 4; AmEm Mexico City, White to Holland, May 26, 1954, NA 714.001; AmEm Mexico City, White to Holland, June 1, 1954, NA Lot 57D295, Box 4.)

When Washington's verbal assault on Guatemala reached unprecedented levels, the Mexican government was silent, and it maintained its "cautious reserve" after the invasion had begun. The government-controlled organizations and media were equally discreet—all the while loudly proclaiming their country's anticommunism. The press castigated former President Lázaro Cárdenas for voicing his solidarity "with the people and the government of Guatemala," and the First Congress against Soviet Intervention in Latin America heaped abuse on Arbenz. The congress, which opened in Mexico City in late May, was organized by the CIA with the financial assistance of the Mexican government. (Pellicer de Brody and Mancilla, *Historia de la Revolución Mexicana*, pp. 102–10, quoted from pp. 109, 104. This book provides the only scholarly discussion of Mexico's attitude toward Guatemala in the last months of the Arbenz administration. See also AmEm Mexico City, White to SecState, no. 1345, May 16, 1954; AmEm Mexico City, White to SecState, no. 1348, May 17, 1954; AmEm Mexico City, White to SecState, no. 1362, May 19, 1954; Hughes to Holland, "Monthly Summary—Mexico," June 29, 1954, NA 712.00; "Guatemala Issue Disturbs Mexico," *NYT*, June 14, 1954, p. 7; "Officials' Kin in Mexico," *NYT*, June 17, 1954, p. 8.)

[40] Interviews with María de Arbenz, Toriello, and Fortuny.

[41] "Guatemala's Note and U.N. Charter Articles Cited," *NYT*, June 20, 1954, p. 2.

[42] United Nations, Security Council Official Records, June 20, 1954, p. 38. For the debate, see pp. 1–41.

330 · Chapter 14

"shabby," he told Henry Cabot Lodge, the U.S. ambassador to the United Nations. "We have . . . held up putting Indochina in the UN in deference to their request. And then without prior understandings etc., they jump right in when another international body should have been used."[43] Dulles's position was that only the Organization of American States was competent to address the Guatemalan complaint. The United Nations must not interfere in the affairs of the Western Hemisphere. His stance was immediately endorsed by Honduras and Nicaragua. Indignantly, they asked that the Inter-American Peace Committee of the OAS investigate Guatemala's slanderous charges.[44] They knew, of course, that no OAS body would conduct any investigation against the will of the United States.

On June 21, Toriello turned again to the Security Council, asking it to take "whatever steps are necessary" to stave the flow of foreign assistance to the rebels.[45] Four days of frantic activity followed, as Dulles lined up the votes and instructed Lodge, the Council's president, to delay a meeting.[46] "Lodge Holds Off on Guatemala Bid," blared the *New York Times* on June 24.[47] "I will have to have a meeting, probably tomorrow," Lodge told Dulles at 9:55 a.m. that same morning.[48] Eisenhower was ready "to use the veto if necessary," Dulles informed the ambassador a few hours later. It would be the first U.S. veto in the history of the United Nations, and, as such, a severe propaganda defeat: "If they vote against us, that will raise 'hell,' " Dulles fumed.[49]

Dulles was referring to France and England. They wanted the Security Council to consider the Guatemalan matter and to dispatch UN observers to the area.[50] Both were concerned with the legal ramifications of the case, not

[43] TelConv (JFD, Lodge), June 22, 1954, 4:30 p.m., DP:TCS, Box 2, EL.

[44] "Inter-American Commission Defers Action on Guatemala," *NYT*, June 22, 1954, p. 1.

[45] "Guatemala Asks U.N. to Carry Out Cease-Fire Order," *NYT*, June 23, 1954, p. 1. For the text of the Guatemalan note, see p. 2.

[46] TelConv (Lodge, JFD), June 24, 1954, 9:11 a.m., DP:TCS, Box 2, EL; see also Lodge to SecState, no. 870, June 24, 1954, 11 a.m., NA 714.00.

[47] "Lodge Holds Off on Guatemala Bid," *NYT*, June 24, 1954, p. 1.

[48] MemoTel (Dulles, Lodge), 9:55 a.m., *FRUS*, 1952–1954, 4:1185.

[49] Quotations from TelConv (JFD, Lodge), June 24, 1954, 4:01 p.m., DP, JFD:CS, Box 8, EL, and TelConv (Hagerty, JFD), June 25, 1954, 10 a.m., DP:TCS, Box 10, EL. See also: MemoConv (Dulles, Bonnet, de Juniac, Key), June 24, 1954, NA Lot 58D18 & 58D78, Box 3; Minutes of Cabinet Meetings, July 9, 1954, WF, Cabinet Series, Box 3, EL; Hagerty Diary, June 24, 1954, EL.

[50] "Lodge informed Holland that the British and French representatives to the Security Council are prepared to go along with a Soviet proposal that the Council send peace observers to Central America." ("Notes of a Meeting of the Guatemalan Group," June 23, 1954, *FRUS*, 1952–1954, 4:1178.) See also Lodge to SecState, no. 870, June 24, 1954, 11 a.m., NA 714.00, and Lodge to SecState, June 24, 1954, 6 p.m., *FRUS*, 1952–1954, 4:1185.

with the fate of Arbenz. At issue was the jurisdiction of the United Nations. Their concern was shared by many other UN delegations and by the UN secretary general, Dag Hammarskjöld, who bitterly opposed the U.S. position and was subjected in turn to harsh and relentless pressure from Lodge to remain silent.[51]

"The president," Dulles told Lodge, "said he thinks you should let the British and French know that if they take [an] independent line backing [the] Guatemalan move in this matter . . . we would feel entirely free without regard to their position in relation to any such matters as any of their colonial problems in Egypt, Cyprus, etc."[52] The same threats were delivered by the American ambassadors in France and England, and by Dulles himself to Foreign Secretary Anthony Eden, who arrived in Washington with Churchill on June 25 for an untimely visit. In the limousine from the airport, Dulles upbraided the cornered Eden. "He said that if the first thing that happens after they [Eden and Churchill] arrive is that we split on this, they better pack up and go home."[53]

On the evening of June 25, after five hours of debate, the Security Council refused to consider the Guatemalan matter. Four countries—the Soviet Union, Denmark, Lebanon, and New Zealand—voted in favor. Among the five who voted against were the council's two Latin American members, Colombia and Brazil. England and France abstained.[54] The American position, Hammarskjöld later told the British delegate, "was the most serious blow so far aimed at the Organization."[55]

[51] "U.N. Bars Debate over Guatemala Pending Inquiry," NYT, June 26, 1954, p. 1. For Hammarskjöld's clash with Lodge, see Urquhart, Hammarskjöld, pp. 88–94.

[52] MemoTel (Dulles, Lodge), 9:55 a.m., June 24, 1954, FRUS, 1952–1954, 4:1184.

[53] TelConv (JFD, Lodge), June 25, 1954, 9:56 a.m., DP, JFD:CS, Box 8, EL. See also TelConv (Lodge, JFD), June 25, 1954, 9:11 a.m., ibid.; TelConv (JFD, Lodge), June 25, 1954, 11:22 a.m., ibid.; Lodge to SecState, no. 880, June 25, 1954, 7 p.m., NA 714.00; Shanley Diaries, Box 2, July 9, 1954, p. 1599, EL; Handwritten Minutes of Cabinet Meetings, July 9, 1954, p. 3, White House Office, Staff Secretary: Records, 1952–61, Cabinet Series, Box 2, EL; Hagerty Diaries, June 25–26, 1954, EL. For a sanitized version, see Eden, Full Circle, pp. 133–38.

For an excellent account of Anglo-American tensions focusing on the role of the Security Council in the resolution of the Guatemalan crisis, see Meers, "Pebble on the Beach," pp. 55–67. See also Young, "Great Britain's Latin America Dilemma," pp. 581–86.

[54] For the debate see United Nations, Security Council Official Records, June 25, 1954, pp. 1–34. See also "U.N. Bars Debate over Guatemala Pending Inquiry," NYT, June 26, 1954, p. 1; Munro, "Oral History Interview," pp. 5–7; Connell-Smith, Inter-American System, pp. 231–37.

[55] Quoted by Urquhart, Hammarskjöld, p. 92. Hammarskjöld considered lodging a formal complaint about the behavior of the United States but was dissuaded by the British delegate. (Meers, "Pebble on the Beach," pp. 71–72.)

For Arbenz, the council's decision was shattering. And yet how could a vote in New York have affected the fast-moving events in Guatemala? On June 25, as the Security Council was rejecting the Guatemalan case, other news reached Arbenz: the army at Zacapa had rebelled.

After the battles of Puerto Barrios and Gualán, the front had been quiet, except for occasional attacks by rebel planes. On June 23, Castillo Armas established a provisional government at Esquipulas, six miles from the Honduran border. León continued to send reassuring messages from Zacapa: he would move soon against Castillo Armas. Carlos Enrique Díaz remained confident. But as the promised offensive failed to materialize, Arbenz grew uneasy. León seemed overly cautious. Arbenz did not, however, suspect betrayal. His attention was elsewhere. During the first week of the invasion, "Jacobo was constantly on the phone with New York, wanting news about the Security Council: 'What's happening? How's it going? When are they going to meet?' We were grasping at straws," remarks his wife. "But what else could we do? How else could we hope to stop the United States?"[56]

It was the PGT that broke the spell. Many party leaders, like Guerra Borges, were wrapped "in irresponsible optimism." Others, though confident that the army would crush the rebels, wanted more information. On the evening of June 23, without consulting either Arbenz or the Secretariat, Acting Secretary General Alvarado Monzón sent Octavio Reyes, a member of the PGT's Central Committee, to Zacapa. Early on the twenty-fifth Reyes was back in Guatemala City, exhausted physically and emotionally. The officers at Zacapa, he reported, were demoralized, afraid, unwilling to fight; when he had chastised them, he had barely escaped arrest.[57]

Fortuny took Reyes to Arbenz. After listening to Reyes, the president turned to his friend: "Do you trust him?" he asked. "Absolutely," responded Fortuny.[58]

Stunned but not persuaded—Reyes was, after all, unfamiliar with military matters—Arbenz summoned Colonel Getellá, a trusted officer. He must leave for Zacapa at once and return with a detailed report.

Getellá left immediately, and he was back late that same night. He confirmed Reyes's account, and he brought a message from the officers at Zacapa: "*Centenario*, the high command asked me to tell you that you must resign. The situation is hopeless. The officers don't want to fight. They think that the Americans are threatening Guatemala just because of you and your communist

---

[56] Interviews with María de Arbenz (quoted), Fortuny, Parinello, Toriello, and Charnaud.

[57] Interviews with Guerra Borges (quoted), Pellecer, Alejandro, and Fortuny. See also Fortuny, "Observaciones," p. 68.

[58] Interview with Fortuny. See also Arbenz, "Jacobo Arbenz relata detalles," p. 9.

friends. If you don't resign, the army will march on the capital to depose you. They have already begun to arrest peasants."[59]

Getellá had not sought to reason with the mutinous officers. "He was known to be a brave man," recollects an eyewitness, "but in Zacapa I saw him shaking."[60] Getellá himself says: "I returned [to the capital] depressed and scared. Defeat was inevitable. There was no way to stop the gringos."[61]

Getellá did not actively betray Arbenz, but neither did he stay to support him. As he left the presidential palace, he had one piece of advice for Arbenz: "You must decide quickly. Otherwise the army will make a deal with Castillo Armas and move against the capital."[62] That same day, in grim confirmation of his words, came the news that Chiquimula had fallen to Castillo Armas on the twenty-fourth. Chiquimula, the first important town between the Honduran border and Zacapa, had been defended by several hundred well-armed soldiers led by Lt. Colonel Jorge Hernández, a loyal officer—or so Arbenz had believed.

Searching for tales of glory in a barren campaign, the *Liberacionistas* present the battle of Chiquimula—the only encounter they won—as a noble victory: "seven hours of fighting against forces ten times larger than ours."[63] For his part, Lt. Colonel Hernández, grasping for excuses if not for glory, claims that at Chiquimula he fought a hard battle, resisting for long hours against "five hundred or more" rebels, while Zacapa spurned his pleas for assistance. The morale of his soldiers, he says, was good, and "our weapons were satisfactory."[64]

In truth, what happened at Chiquimula could hardly be called a battle. Hernández, who had only 150 men and received no assistance from Zacapa, was

[59] Interview with Fortuny. My major sources on the Getellá mission are interviews with: Getellá; Lt. Col. Mendizabal and another senior officer (who asked not to be identified), both of whom were at Zacapa; Fortuny, Charnaud, Guerra Borges, and María de Arbenz, all of whom related what they learned from Arbenz; Cols. Parinello, Mendoza, and Lorenzana, all of whom related what they learned from other officers. In 1955, Arbenz noted: "On Friday, June 25, the troops led by officers in whom I had complete trust sent me an ultimatum: either I resign, or they would side with Castillo Armas." (Arbenz, "Jacobo Arbenz relata detalles," p. 9.) Getellá's mission has gone virtually unnoticed in the literature; for two exceptions, see the cursory reference in Sierra Roldán, *Diálogos*, p. 109, and Torres Rivas, "Crisis," p. 65, n. 15.

[60] Interviews with Lt. Col. Mendizabal (quoted) and with the aforementioned senior officer from Zacapa.

[61] Interview with Getellá.

[62] Interview with Fortuny.

[63] Flores Avendaño, *Memorias*, 2:439. See also L.A.H.A., *Así se gestó la Liberación*, pp. 231–35, and the fanciful account in Putzeys Rojas, *Así se hizo la Liberación*, pp. 211–51.

[64] Interview with Hernández.

eager to surrender. Those who resisted—"doggedly," recalls a *Liberacionista*—were a few dozen poorly armed peasants. "They fought with old hunting rifles. They were the ones who killed our people. When we captured them, we shot them. Hernández didn't arm the peasants. If he had, then the capture of Chiquimula would have been much more difficult." After Castillo Armas's victory, Hernández was allowed to remain in the army; the dead peasants were eulogized as innocent victims of communist terror.[65]

Treason at Zacapa

It is difficult to reconstruct the details of the events at Zacapa in the days that preceded Getellá's visit and the surrender of Chiquimula. Two of the three commanding colonels are dead. The third, Pablo Díaz, prefers "not to talk about these things";[66] he has maintained an exemplary discretion—as did, as long as they lived, León and Barzanallana. CIA reports reveal only how little the agency knew. Nevertheless, the story can be reconstructed, even though many details will be forever hazy.

When the invasion began, observes Eduardo Taracena, a senior *Liberacionista*, "a group of officers was on our side." They were, however, "very few," and they occupied posts of secondary importance. Their leaders were Enrique Closse de León, a lieutenant colonel who had a desk job, and Antonio Montenegro, a young lieutenant.[67] Other officers, such as Colonels Cruz Salazar, Elfego Monzón, and Mauricio Dubois, "were sapping the spirit of the army, but for their own ends, not to help Castillo Armas," remembers Taracena. Cruz Salazar concurs: "My friends and I were on bad terms with Castillo Armas due to personal differences."[68]

Although Castillo Armas garnered more respect among the officers than did his rivals in the exile movement, the dominant attitude toward him was hostility. Officers like Monzón and Cruz Salazar, who hoped that someday, somehow, they would replace Arbenz, saw Castillo Armas as a rival. But the hostility had other roots as well: many still liked or respected Jacobo Arbenz; others, though unsympathetic to the regime, resented the exiles' strident as-

[65] Particularly useful were interviews with Taracena (quoted)—a *Liberacionista* who fought at Chiquimula—and with Col. Parinello and Lt. Silva Girón. In his memoirs, Col. Monzón mentions "the defection of the officer in command at Chiquimula." (Sierra Roldán, *Diálogos*, p. 107; see also pp. 109, 116.)

[66] Telephone conversation with Col. Pablo Díaz.

[67] Interviews with Taracena (quoted) and Montenegro. The only difference between them is that Montenegro claimed that he had not been plotting with Castillo Armas—a denial that greatly amused former *Liberacionistas* and army officers when they were told of it. Bissell noted that very few Guatemalan officers were involved in the plot. (Interview with Bissell.)

[68] Quotations from interviews with Taracena and Cruz Salazar.

sertions that the army was serving a communist government; the exiles' blatant courtship of Trujillo and Somoza offended many Guatemalan officers who were proud that their country was no longer Ubico's tropical dictatorship. Moreover, by seeking to overthrow the Arbenz regime, Castillo Armas and his fellow exiles threatened the well-being of the officer corps.

Those officers who disliked Arbenz even more than they resented Castillo Armas were but a small minority. Had they felt free to choose, most Guatemalan officers would have rallied to Arbenz in June 1954 and crushed the rebels. But fear gnawed at them—fear of the United States.

When the invasion began, the planners of PBSUCCESS knew that they had shaken the morale of the Guatemalan army, but they could not assess to what degree. In addition to the handful of active plotters, "various officers" had promised that they would "take action against the regime given just a little more time or just a little more justification," the CIA reported with some exasperation.[69] Washington did not know when these officers would act—or if they would ever act. Hence they had to be prodded, cattlelike, with the spark of Castillo Armas's invasion.

It is striking, in retrospect, how unsure U.S. Intelligence was of how the army would respond to the rebel attack. A CIA official who participated in the operation has stated that he had thought the chances of success to be about even.[70] A June 17 analysis, cast in a slightly more optimistic mold, reveals the tentativeness of Washington's predictions:

> The political scene [in Guatemala] is dominated by President Arbenz, his Communist advisors, and his sizable but relatively passive popular following. . . . In a position to decide the political issue is the 6,000-man Guatemalan Army. This is a newly professionalized Army, proud of its military efficiency developed during the past ten years. Its officers and men enjoy numerous privileges granted by the Arbenz government. The officer corps has personal ties to Arbenz who emerged from it into political life. . . .
>
> So far as the Army is concerned, its preferred choice unquestionably would be to keep Arbenz and dispose of his Communist Advisors. If the leaders of the officer corps could not persuade Arbenz to go along, they might carry off a coup and set up an Army regime as at least a stop-gap. Or, if they came to believe that opposition political groups could command some popular support and also could be counted on to protect the Army's position and perquisites, then the officers might install a new civilian government manned by members of the present opposition.
>
> The probability is that the Army will take one of these three courses. Its officers will calculate, as will Latin Americans generally, that the US could not embark on

[69] DCI to President, "The Situation in Guatemala as of 20 June," *FRUS*, 1952–1954, 4:1175.

[70] Bissell, "Oral History Interview," p. 13.

the project of ridding Guatemala of Communist domination without intending to carry through any action necessary. This being the case, the Guatemalan Army can be expected . . . to exert its dominant power to the end of preventing a showdown with the US.[71]

That very day, the *Liberacionistas* entered Guatemala. They advanced a few miles, unopposed, were defeated at Gualán and Puerto Barrios, and settled down on their puny strip of "liberated" territory. Meanwhile, the fifth column failed to materialize, and the country remained under government control. The cautious optimism of Castillo Armas's American patrons gave way to uneasiness. A CIA memorandum to Eisenhower warned:

> As of 20 June the outcome of the efforts to overthrow . . . Arbenz . . . remains very much in doubt. The controlling factor in the situation is still considered to be the position of the Guatemalan armed forces, and thus far this group has not given any clear indication of whether it will move, and if so, in which way. . . . If it remains loyal . . . Castillo Armas . . . will be defeated. . . .
>
> The position of the top-ranking military officers is constantly shifting. . . . It is probable that the rising pressure of events will compel this group to declare its position, one way or the other, at any time from now on—although the possible result could be a split in the ranks. . . . The action of Colonel Castillo Armas is not in any sense a conventional military operation. . . . The entire effort is thus more dependent upon psychological impact rather than actual military strength, although it is upon the ability of the Castillo Armas effort to create and maintain for a short time the *impression* of very substantial military strength that the success of this particular effort primarily depends. . . . If the effort does not succeed in arousing the other latent forces of resistance within the next period of approximately twenty-four hours, it will probably begin to lose strength.[72]

From his command post in the U.S. embassy, Peurifoy "was like a ship running through a dense fog."[73] His dispatches show that he attempted, with some success, to intimidate Guatemalan officials—not a new game for him.[74] But Peurifoy's dispatches also betray his frustration. On June 20, he cabled Washington: "Embassy is able to report accurately only on events in Guatemala City and even here it is difficult to verify enormous numbers of rumors mostly false which are circulating. . . . No reliable information is available

[71] OIR, Intelligence Report, June 17, 1954, pp. 2–3, NA 714.00.

[72] "The Situation in Guatemala as of 20 June" (see n. 69 above), quoted from pp. 1174–75, 1176 (italics in the original).

[73] Interview with Krieg.

[74] See, for instance, Peurifoy to SecState, no. 1053, June 20, 1954, NA 714.00; Peurifoy to SecState, June 23, 1954, *FRUS*, 1952–1954, 4:1180–82; Peurifoy to SecState, no. 1120, June 26, 1954, NA 714.00. Throughout the invasion, no U.S. official spoke with Arbenz. (Interviews with María de Arbenz, Fortuny, and Krieg.)

about progress of rebels but they are not known to hold any important town."[75] The capital was but a secondary front. Those army officers who had remained in the city were unwilling to act on their own, and while they waited for news of Zacapa, their sullen passivity and nervousness were little comfort to an ambassador who craved action.[76] Meanwhile, Castillo Armas's supporters in Guatemala City were beginning to fear that the invasion might collapse. Among them was the proud Rossell y Arellano, archbishop of Guatemala, who on June 21 appealed to Peurifoy "for direct U.S. intervention."[77] Until the twenty-fifth, the mood in the embassy was one of pessimism: "It looked as if Arbenz had won. . . . We were all very discouraged."[78]

In Washington, too, the mood was somber. On the twenty-second, Assistant Secretary Holland stated that Castillo Armas had "counted on the defection of the Guatemalan Army, [and] that since this defection did not occur he would probably lose."[79] CIA headquarters was equally grim: "The feeling was that things were going very badly."[80] Addressing the situation up to and including the twenty-fourth, the CIA observed that Castillo Armas had occupied "only limited and relatively unimportant territory," and that "local recruiting" by his forces appeared to be "slow." Little was known of developments at Zacapa, but "there appear to have been no wholesale desertions from the Guatemalan army and key commanders apparently remain loyal."[81] And yet, it was on the twenty-fourth that Chiquimula fell!

Only on the twenty-fifth did the CIA discern some grounds for optimism: "Guatemalan army officers are reported . . . to be 'slowly realizing' the extreme gravity of the situation and are becoming convinced that getting rid of President Arbenz and the Communists would be 'an easy way out.' " However, there was still "no evidence of defections from the Guatemalan army."[82] And yet, it was on the twenty-fifth that Getellá delivered the army's ultimatum to Arbenz!

[75] Peurifoy to SecState, no. 1052, June 20, 1954, NA 714.00.

[76] On the mood of the officers in the capital, interviews with the following officers, all of whom were in the capital, were helpful: Parinello, Cruz Salazar, Paiz Novales, González Siguí, Getellá, Montenegro, and Peralta Méndez. Parinello adds an interesting story that illustrates the demoralization of the officers. A few days after the beginning of the invasion, "the G-2 of the army, Colonel Víctor Manuel Gordillo, told me: 'Colonel, things are very bad. It's very hard to make ends meet. Why don't you ask the President to give us two months' salary in advance?' In other words," Parinello explains, "he knew that the government would not last long."

[77] Peurifoy to SecState, no. 1063, June 21, 1954, NA 714.00.

[78] Interview with Krieg.

[79] DOS, Meeting of Guatemalan Group, June 22, 1954, p. 1.

[80] Interviews with Amory (quoted) and Bissell.

[81] CIA, *Current Intelligence Digest*, June 25, 1954, p. 16.

[82] CIA, *Current Intelligence Digest*, June 28, 1954, p. 15.

Thus, throughout the first week of the invasion, the CIA underestimated the confusion and demoralization that gripped Zacapa. All the available evidence indicates that when the senior officers left the capital for Zacapa, on June 19, they had not yet decided to turn against Arbenz. They were, however, angry: why had they been chosen? "I can't understand Carlos Enrique [Díaz]. Why is he sending his friends to fight against Castillo Armas?" Colonel Pablo Díaz complained before leaving the capital. "Why can't he send someone else?"[83]

At Zacapa the colonels neither surrendered nor fought. "They were paralyzed." They kept Arbenz at bay with reassuring telegrams, and they avoided any move—such as crushing the rebels—that might further provoke the Americans. "The High Command was made of jelly."[84] A few junior officers complained about their superiors, but only among themselves.[85] And so, the troops remained at Zacapa, many kilometers from the "front." This was not due to any secret deal with the CIA. The reason for the army's behavior is more prosaic: "Fear defeated them," a Guatemalan officer explains. "They were terrorized by the idea that the United States was looming behind Castillo Armas." The U.S. army attaché concurs: "The Guatemalan officers were definitely afraid of the possibility of U.S. intervention against Arbenz and with good reason. That fear was the stabilizing influence that kept them from coming to Arbenz's support when the chips were down."[86] This is why the only battle the army fought was at Gualán, where a young lieutenant had acted on his own initiative.[87]

The situation was indeed untenable. The army at Zacapa was lying to Arbenz, and these lies could not long remain hidden. Every day, every hour increased the gravity of this disobedience and led, inexorably, to betrayal.

[83] Interview with Lt. Col. Cruz Salazar, to whom Díaz was speaking. In addition, my most important sources for this paragraph are interviews with: Cols. Mendoza, Parinello, González Siguí, Lorenzana, and Getellá; Lt. Cols. Paiz Novales and Hernández; Maj. Paz Tejada; Lt. Montenegro; and Taracena.

[84] Quotations from interviews with Lt. Col. Mendizabal and Lt. Silva Girón.

[85] Of these officers, those most often mentioned are Lt. Juan García and Captain Prudencio López.

[86] Quotations from interviews with Lt. Col. Mendizabal and Col. McCormick.

[87] After the army at Zacapa had surrendered to Castillo Armas, Silva Girón was assisted by Lt. Col. Mendizabal to return to the capital disguised as a nurse. Later, he was arrested and jailed for a year without trial and then sent into exile. He returned in 1957 after Castillo Armas's death and was eventually reinstated into the army. But while several officers, including some of Arbenz's foes, respected him for his resistance at Gualán, his military career was in fact over. He retired in 1972. He had finally made it to colonel, but had never again been given command over troops. "They made me into a desk officer." (Quoted from interview with Silva Girón. Interviews with Col. González Siguí, and Lt. Cols. Mendizabal and Paiz Novales were particularly useful. See also Silva Girón, *Cuando gobiernan las armas*, esp. pp. 79–115.)

Then Castillo Armas attacked Chiquimula. Hernández surrendered and Zacapa remained aloof. The surrender of the one and the passivity of the other were treason. Getellá arrived at Zacapa: Arbenz was demanding an account. The charade could be sustained no longer. Zacapa told Arbenz to step down.

Only against this backdrop of officers who were demoralized before they reached the front, officers who feared the consequences of victory more than defeat, can the significance of the rebels' air force and superior communication equipment be appreciated.

If Castillo Armas's air force was puny, that of the government was practically nonexistent. Guatemala's planes were as antiquated and unsuited for battle as their pilots were unreliable. With the exception of Lieutenant Juan Adolfo Castillo, who died on June 18 when his AT-6 crashed, the pilots had no desire to fight. One defected with his aircraft to Castillo Armas, several sought asylum in foreign embassies, and the remaining few were grounded to prevent more desertions.[88]

The rebel air force inflicted only minimal damage. In the capital, a P-47 knocked out a radio station, but the station belonged to an American evangelist.[89] The intended target, the nearby government radio transmitter, emerged from the war unscathed. Rebel aircraft also damaged a few bridges and railroad tracks between the capital and Zacapa, but none too seriously. Little harm was done at the front—at Zacapa, Gualán, Puerto Barrios, and Chiquimula. The American pilots were apparently reluctant to risk their lives; the Guatemalans had more ardor, but less skill; the planes were old, and on occasion they met "very heavy anti-aircraft fire."[90]

By June 22 the rebels had lost two planes. One had been brought down by hostile fire, and the other had run out of gas. On that day Eisenhower met with the Dulles brothers and Assistant Secretary Holland to decide whether the planes should be replaced. Nearly a decade later, in an account of the meeting, Eisenhower acknowledged that the United States had provided material assistance to Castillo Armas: "I considered the matter carefully," he wrote. "It seemed to me that to refuse to cooperate in providing indirect support to a strictly anti-Communist faction in this struggle would be contrary to the letter

[88] "The Situation in Guatemala as of 20 June" (see n. 69 above), p. 1175; Peurifoy to SecState, no. 1045, June 19, 1954, NA 714.00; AmEm San Salvador to SecState, no. 192350Z, June, NA 714.00; AmEm San Salvador, McDermott to SecState, no. 160, June 22, 1954, NA 714.00; "Advance 9 Miles," NYT, June 20, 1954, p. 1.

[89] "Estragos por avión pirata en la radio La Voz Evangelica," El I, June 22, 1954, p. 1; "Wrong Radio Bombed," NYT, June 25, 1954, p. 3.

[90] "The Situation in Guatemala as of 20 June" (see n. 69 above), p. 1175. My main sources for this paragraph are (1) interviews with protagonists; (2) reports of the U.S. embassy; (3) press reports (the New York Times had a reporter, Paul Kennedy, in Guatemala City during the invasion, as did other major newspapers).

and spirit of the Caracas resolution. I had faith in the strength of the inter-American resolve therein set forth. . . . our proper course of action—indeed my duty—was clear to me. We would replace the airplanes." The original planes, Eisenhower averred disingenuously, had been provided to Castillo Armas by another (unnamed) country.[91]

In material terms, the major achievement of the rebel air force was the sinking of a British freighter on June 27. "Someone gave us the information that there was an unidentified ship in San José [Guatemala]," recalls Phil Roettinger, a CIA agent who was involved in the incident. "Robertson [another CIA agent], who was a wild man, said: 'They must be unloading weapons. Let's sink it.' So we got Schupp, and he did it."[92] In fact, there were no weapons on board, only bales of cotton and bags of coffee. It was this incident that the general counsel of the CIA first remembered when asked about PBSUCCESS. "Dealing with it was my office's main task associated with PBSUCCESS. I remember the captain of the ship well. He was a nice man."[93] This "sub-incident," as Bissell called it, "mercifully turned out to be of little significance and to do no political, and minor financial damage to [the] United States."[94] The British government was eager not to antagonize Washington, U.S. responsibility was not publicly discussed, and the claim was eventually settled *sub rosa* for $1 million.[95]

Another bombing error did no financial damage to the United States and was, in fact, a political boon. On June 22, a P-47 dropped a couple of bombs on the Honduran town of San Pedro de Copán, eight miles from the Guatemalan border. Secretary Dulles, who knew better, transformed this mistake of a rebel pilot into a Guatemalan attack on its peace-loving neighbor. The Honduran government enthusiastically denounced this Guatemalan "aggression" and threatened retaliation.[96]

[91] Eisenhower, *Mandate*, pp. 425–26. For the loss of the two planes, see "Guatemala Links U.S. Fliers to Raid," *NYT*, June 21, p. 2; "Capturada en Puerto Barrios goleta enemiga," *DCA*, June 21, p. 1; Peurifoy to SecState, no. 1067, June 21, NA 714.00; "Aviador americano se estrelló," *La Prensa*, Managua, June 22, p. 3; AmEm Tegucigalpa, ALUSNA to SecState, DTG 030230Z, July 3, NA 714.00. All 1954.

[92] Interview with Roettinger.

[93] Interview with Houston.

[94] Bissell, quoted in "The Science of Spying," May 4, 1965, p. 9, AWD Papers, Box 141, ML.

[95] For the incident, see: Tiburcio Avila, Alcalde Municipal San José, to Charnaud, June 27, 1954, CO:G, June 1954, p. 640, AGCA; TelConv (JFD, AWD), June 28, 1954, 9:39 a.m., DP, JFD:CS, Box 8, EL; Peurifoy to SecState, no. 1127, June 28, 1954, NA 714.00; "British Ship Sunk Off Guatemala," *NYT*, June 28, 1954, p. 1; "Pérdida completa del barco Springfjord," *El I*, June 29, 1954, p. 1; AmEmG to DOS, "Economic Summary—June 1954," no. 10, July 9, 1954, p. 2, NA 814.00; Meers, "Pebble on the Beach," pp. 81–82.

[96] TelConv (Holland, JFD), June 22, 1954, 5:12 p.m., DP:TCS, Box 2, EL; Tel-

The rebels' planes and broadcasts have often been presented as the decisive psychological weapons that brought Arbenz and his army to their knees. This is hardly plausible. Arbenz, the PGT, and the other leaders of the government coalition remained confident of Castillo Armas's defeat until the betrayal of the army had become plain, rebel planes and radio broadcasts notwithstanding. Nor did the planes and broadcasts disrupt military operations. They were of no value against those who were willing to fight: Lieutenant Silva Girón with his handful of soldiers at Gualán, the police and the armed civilians at Puerto Barrios, and the peasants at Chiquimula. (Indeed, in his colorful account of the battle, Lt. Colonel Hernández did not even mention the planes.)[97] "Chiquimula stands in its entirety," wrote Marroquín Rojas. "Not one house, not one building, not one shack was destroyed. The capital, as we all know, suffered not at all, except for the bomb that fell on the old Fort Matamoros and the strafing of some gasoline storage tanks. All the rest, except for the sinking of the ship in San José harbor, is pure fantasy."[98] If León failed to attack, this was not because he believed that Castillo Armas had thousands of men, as the *Voz de la Liberación* claimed, or because rebel planes were sowing panic and death among his troops. The Guatemalan officers knew "very well" that the rebel force was paltry, and, at Zacapa, Castillo Armas's aircraft provoked neither desertions nor panic among the rank and file. On the contrary, the soldiers patiently awaited their officers' orders.[99]

The planes and radio broadcasts have been useful, however, to a Guatemalan officer corps that has sought to justify its surrender to Castillo Armas. In conversation after conversation with Guatemalan officers, the rebel air force and radio broadcasts were initially cited as the critical causes of defeat, but they receded as the conversations proceeded, and the true explanation emerged: "The officers were aware," Colonel Paiz Novales admitted with marked understatement, "that it might be better if Arbenz stepped down. . . . The propaganda of the U.S. was devastating. . . . This is why Zacapa did not fight."[100] The broadcasts and the planes were a sideshow. Washington pro-

---

Conv (JFD, Holland), June 23, 1954, 6:24 p.m., DP, JFD:CS, Box 8, EL; "Tres bombas dejó caer el avión en San Pedro de Copán," *El Día*, Tegucigalpa, June 23, 1954, p. 1; "Honduras Reports Bombing," *NYT*, June 23, 1954, p. 1; "Honduran Regime Protests to U.N. on Town Bombing," *NYT*, June 24, 1954, p. 1; "Guatemala rechazó la protesta de Honduras," *El I*, June 24, 1954, p. 1; "Honduran Ouster of Envoy Hinted," *NYT*, June 25, 1954, p. 3; AmEm Tegucigalpa, ALUSNA to SecState, DTG 030230Z, July 3, 1954, NA 714.00.

[97] Interview with Hernández.

[98] Marroquín Rojas, *La derrota*, p. 129.

[99] Interviews with Krieg (quoted), Montenegro, Mendizabal, González Siguí, Parinello, Silva Girón, Hernández.

[100] Interview with Paiz Novales. In a three-hour conversation, Col. González Siguí also began by stressing the impact of the rebels' planes and radio broadcasts. Then, after noting that "actually it was not an impressive invasion," he went on to explain

vided Castillo Armas with a far more powerful weapon: the Guatemalan officers' conviction that the defeat of the motley rebel band would lead to prompt and cruel revenge.

THE RESIGNATION OF ARBENZ

On the night of June 25, Jacobo Arbenz summoned the leaders of the government parties and the labor confederations to the presidential palace; also present was Colonel Carlos Enrique Díaz. The army at Zacapa had deserted, Arbenz explained; the population must be armed; the political parties and the trade unions must gather their supporters at dawn to receive weapons and training. Díaz raised no objections. He asked only that the distribution of weapons be orderly. The party leaders pledged four to five thousand volunteers; the CGTG at least as many.[101]

Of the thousands of volunteers anticipated by the party leaders and the CGTG, no more than two hundred materialized. At the Campo de Marte, where the CGTG had called its troops, only two hundred showed up. There they waited for weapons that never came. All that appeared "was a decrepit colonel who began to lead them in exercises"—and so they passed the day, doing push-ups.[102] A similar scene took place at the Maya Club, where the revolutionary parties had summoned their members. Those few who arrived waited in vain for weapons. They were spared, however, the calisthenics; the few officers who were present "kept them anxious and huddled together doing nothing—yet these were people who could have been organized."[103]

An equally depressing scene occurred at the Hipódromo del Norte, where the teachers of the STEG (one of the country's most combative unions) had been called by their secretary general, Rafael Tischler, a member of the PGT's Central Committee. Many teachers arrived, but when Tischler told them that the army at Zacapa had rebelled and asked for volunteers, only three or four came forward. The others explained that they had families and that it was hopeless anyway. For Arbenz and the PGT, it was "another disheartening blow."[104]

On two earlier occasions—on October 20, 1944 and July 18, 1949—the population of the capital had been summoned to fight, and it had done so

---

that it was fear of the United States that brought about the surrender of the Guatemalan officers.

[101] Interviews with Fortuny and Charnaud, who were present, and with María de Arbenz, who related what Arbenz told her. See also Fortuny, "Observaciones," p. 66.

[102] Interviews with Fortuny (quoted) and Pellecer. Pellecer, who was also at the Campo de Marte, asserts that "no more than one hundred volunteers came."

[103] Interviews with Maj. Rosenberg (quoted) and Paz Tejada.

[104] Interview with Fortuny (quoted), and Cardoza, "A treinta años," p. 92.

eagerly. On this twenty-sixth of June, 1954, however, the response was apathetic.

On those two previous occasions, troops had fought alongside civilians; they had passed out the weapons, and officers had led the volunteers. This time, the military had no intention of fighting, and it opposed arming the people. Moreover, the government's sudden appeal for volunteers—when communiqué after communiqué had spoken of victory—gave credence to the rebel radio's claims that Castillo Armas was advancing with thousands of well armed men. Above all, in October 1944 and July 1949, Guatemalans had been fighting Guatemalans. Now, they faced a formidable foe. Rumors were rife: the Marines had landed on the Caribbean coast and would march on the capital to eliminate Arbenz; "at the front it was raining U.S. paratroopers."[105] Why else, it was asked, would Arbenz call so abruptly for volunteers?

Some have argued that had Arbenz addressed the people on that twenty-sixth of June, had he convoked a mass demonstration, thousands of civilians would have marched on the military barracks in the capital to seize the weapons. But this is highly unlikely. A week of mounting rumors, of growing tensions, had sapped the will of a population bruised by months of psychological warfare. Guatemala City was no Madrid. There were no International Brigades, and the fledgling labor unions had not been hardened in a daily, bloody struggle like their Spanish counterparts eighteen years earlier. Nor was the capital the bastion of the young revolution. It was to the countryside, rather than the cities, that Arbenz had brought the greatest benefits. Thousands of peasants might have fought on that twenty-sixth of June. For them, Arbenz meant freedom and land. But they had no weapons. Unaware that their government was collapsing, they continued to man roadblocks, to search for weapons dropped by rebel planes, and to flood the capital with telegrams pledging their loyalty.[106]

Jacobo Arbenz was exhausted. He remained closeted in his office on the twenty-sixth of June, listening to hourly reports that were increasingly disheartening: the population was immobilized, and the officers in the capital were becoming mutinous. Perhaps, he began to think, he should step down. Perhaps, then, the army would rout Castillo Armas. Perhaps, if he accepted Zacapa's ultimatum, some part of the revolution could be saved. In the late afternoon, Arbenz told Fortuny that he was considering resigning. That evening, the Secretariat of the PGT met in his office. "Several of us spoke. We told Arbenz that resistance was still possible, that we could still win—if we

---

[105] Lt. Eugenio Dedette of the Presidential Guard quoted by Paz Tejada. (Interview with Paz Tejada.) On the role of the U.S. embassy in this disinformation campaign, see Schlesinger and Kinzer, *Bitter Fruit*, pp. 192–93.

[106] See *GT*, esp. Boxes 5, 11, and 71.

armed the people.'' As if he were shaking off a trance, Arbenz said, ''You've convinced me. Now help me. We have to start at once.''[107]

It was 11 p.m. when the leaders of the PGT left the presidential palace. They had talked with Arbenz about organizing a group of about a hundred PGT members who would be armed with machine guns, but they had no suggestions as to how to seize the weapons from the army and transform untrained civilians into an effective fighting force. They were ready to die for their beliefs, and many have died since, under torture.[108] They had no idea, however, how to organize the defense of the capital. In the words of Guerra Borges, ''The situation was so grave and so complex that the party could no longer deal with it. We were overtaken by events.''[109]

Fortuny stayed with Arbenz. They talked for two or three hours, ''discussing the telegrams and messages of support that had arrived from abroad. We talked about how we should handle the U.N. and the diplomatic offensive. We talked about how we could make the military arm the people.'' But Arbenz took no action during those hours he spent with Fortuny, ''other than talking.''[110]

Nearly thirty years later, Fortuny comments: ''We were escaping from reality. Arbenz was exhausted; he didn't even try to implement the plans he had discussed with the leaders of the PGT.'' The same was true of Fortuny, who failed (as he acknowledges) to point out to Arbenz that they had to do more than talk.[111] After months of terrible tension, two brave men were unwilling to concede defeat and were paralyzed by despair.

It was to be Arbenz's last night in the presidential palace. While he daydreamed with Fortuny, others in the capital prepared to act—all with one objective, to remove the president and appease the United States. On the morning of Sunday the twenty-seventh, Foreign Minister Toriello, on his own initiative and without informing Arbenz, sought out Peurifoy. He asked whether the United States would be satisfied if Arbenz were replaced by a military *junta*, but not by Castillo Armas. He too would resign, if Washington so desired, although, he hastened to add, ''he personally . . . had always been very anti-Communist and . . . as far as he was concerned the Junta could take all the Communists in Guatemala and send them to Moscow.''[112]

As Toriello pleaded with Peurifoy, several unconnected plots were brewing

---

[107] Interviews with Fortuny (quoted) and Guerra Borges, who were both present, and with María de Arbenz, who relates what Arbenz told her. See also Fortuny, ''Observaciones,'' pp. 67–68. The major discrepancy is that in Fortuny's account, Gutiérrez and one or two other members of the PGT's Political Commission were also present.

[108] See below, p. 388.

[109] Interview with Guerra Borges.

[110] Interview with Fortuny.

[111] Interview with Fortuny.

[112] Peurifoy to SecState, June 27, 1954, 2 p.m., *FRUS*, 1952–1954, 4:1188–89.

among the officer corps in the capital. There was the handful of supporters of
Castillo Armas, biding time and busily spreading rumors. There were also
those perennial plotters who were hostile to both Arbenz and Castillo Armas—
senior officers like Cruz Salazar, Monzón, and Dubois, who were ambitious
yet had lacked the courage to act. And there were those senior officers who
were considered particularly loyal to Arbenz and who had never plotted
against him—men like Armed Forces Chief Díaz, Defense Minister Sánchez,
Army Chief of Staff Parinello, Air Force Chief Luis Girón, and the president
of the Consejo Superior de la Defensa, Carlos Sarti. These five colonels met
on the morning of the twenty-seventh at Díaz's house, and their conclusion
was swift and unanimous: Jacobo must go.[113] Thereupon Díaz phoned Peurifoy, who had just finished listening to Toriello's entreaties. "Situation appears
breaking rapidly," commented the ambassador, after listening to Díaz's plea
that they meet "at earliest possible moment." It was 2 p.m., June 27, 1954.[114]

Accompanied by Colonels Martin and McCormick, and by DCM Krieg,
Peurifoy went to Díaz's house. There he met Díaz and his four confederates.
Díaz said that he and his colleagues were ready to force Arbenz to resign; he
would become president and would immediately outlaw the PGT and exile its
leaders. In return, the United States must no longer champion Castillo Armas.
In ringing tones (rather hollow under the circumstances), Díaz, "strongly sec-
onded by others, [stated] that direct negotiations with Castillo [Armas] were
out of question; they would rather die than talk with him." Washington would
no longer need Castillo Armas, they pledged: their Guatemala would be stable, anticommunist and pro-American.[115]

The first order of business was the removal of Arbenz, Peurifoy pointed
out. The rest could be settled later. Nor did his interlocutors think to insist on
a guarantee as to the future role of Castillo Armas. Finding solace in Peurifoy's promise that as soon as Arbenz had been deposed he would arrange a
truce with the rebels, "Díaz said that they had decided to act at once." There
was, however, one last problem, Díaz added, "the tough problem. Who is
going to bell the cat? Who will talk to Jacobo?" Peurifoy's report continues:

> With but moment's hesitation he [Díaz] made decision: "Col. Sánchez will visit all
> garrisons and announce I have assumed presidency. Colonel Girón will inform air
> force. I will go to Palace with Parinello and Sarti and we will tell Jacobo." After
> some other talk, Díaz said, "Arbenz may answer two ways. He will either say 'Yes,'

[113] Interview with Parinello.

[114] Peurifoy to SecState, June 27, 1954, 2 p.m., *FRUS*, 1952–1954, 4:1188–89.

[115] Peurifoy to SecState, June 27, 1954, 11 p.m., ibid., pp. 1189–91, quoted from
p. 1190. "At one point Díaz asked whether any members of present Cabinet were
unacceptable to US. I said I could not attempt to dictate his Cabinet and that if he
appointed reasonable men I was sure all our secondary problems could be worked out,
such as difficulties of American Companies." (Ibid., p. 1191.)

or he will say, 'This is insubordination,' and call the guard. In latter case we will not emerge from Palace. If we are not out in reasonable period, Sánchez will bring up artillery.''[116]

Díaz and his friends departed, with Peurifoy insisting on the "necessity of acting quickly to round up leading Communists.''[117]

Peurifoy's account is confirmed by two of the U.S. officials who were present and by Colonel Parinello.[118] Once the meeting had ended, Parinello went with Díaz and Girón to the presidential palace: "I was trembling, Arbenz could have had us shot.''[119] (The possibility was remote: the small Presidential Guard, the only military force within the presidential palace, was commanded by Lt. Colonel Dubois, who was himself busily plotting against Arbenz.)

In the palace, they found the president virtually alone. While Parinello and Girón waited, Díaz went into Arbenz's office and emerged half an hour later. "It's settled. He will resign today." Leaving the palace, they rushed to tell the good news to Peurifoy: Arbenz had agreed to step down in favor of Díaz and would announce his resignation at 9 p.m. It was approximately 5 p.m.[120]

Fortuny, who had arrived at the palace while Arbenz was with Díaz, saw his friend as soon as the colonels had left. This time, Arbenz refused to reconsider his decision. Instead, he asked Fortuny to write his resignation speech. At first Fortuny refused, but Arbenz insisted: "Please, do this last favor for me, the last favor I will ask you in my life." Fortuny relented, and together they outlined the speech.[121]

Shortly thereafter, in the late afternoon, Arbenz met with the cabinet. At least two ministers were absent. Aldana Sandoval had already sought asylum in the Salvadoran embassy,[122] and Defense Minister Sánchez was busy drumming up support for his friend Carlos Enrique Díaz in the barracks of the capital.

Throughout the Arbenz presidency, the cabinet had been an institution of only modest importance. It had not met since the beginning of the invasion.

[116] Ibid., pp. 1190–91.

[117] Ibid., p. 1191.

[118] McCormick to SecState, no. C-14, 280145Z, NA 714.00; interviews with Krieg, Parinello, and McCormick.

[119] Interview with Parinello, who says that Girón, not Sarti, went with them to the palace.

[120] Interview with Parinello. See also Peurifoy to SecState, no. 1123, June 27, 1954, 7 p.m.; McCormick to SecState, no. C-14, 280145Z. Both NA 714.00.

[121] Interviews with Fortuny (quoted) and María de Arbenz.

[122] Krieg to DOS, no. 41, July 21, 1954, p. 3, NA 714.00; "Expresidente Arbenz ya se encuentra en México," *Tribuna Libre*, San Salvador, Sept. 11, 1954, p. 5. On Aldana Sandoval's demoralization and his fears, see also Peurifoy to SecState, no. 1107, June 25, 1954, NA 714.00, and CIA, *Current Intelligence Digest*, June 28, 1954, p. 15.

As the ministers convened, at Arbenz's request, not one knew he intended to resign. Interior Minister Charnaud, perhaps the most influential cabinet member, had not seen Arbenz since the twenty-fifth; others had not seen him since June 17. Now they were informed of his decision. Arbenz did not ask for their advice, nor did they offer it.[123] The session was short, which suited many of the ministers who were in a hurry to leave—to seek asylum in foreign embassies.

Arbenz also left, but for his personal residence, Casa Pomona. It was 8 p.m., June 27, 1954. He had already taped the short speech that Fortuny had prepared. It was broadcast at 9 p.m. Speaking "with a voice full of emotion,"[124] President Arbenz bade farewell to the Guatemalan people: "I say goodbye to you, my friends, with bitterness and pain, but firm in my convictions." He was resigning to eliminate "the pretext for the invasion of our country." He had reached his decision with his "eyes on the welfare of the people" and he would hand over power to his friend Carlos Enrique Díaz "with the hope of saving the democratic gains of the October revolution. . . . A government that, although different from mine, is still inspired by our October revolution is preferable to twenty years of bloody tyranny under the men whom Castillo Armas has brought into the country."[125]

Arbenz's words, words of immense sadness and dignity, were as enigmatic as the man himself. He did not explain his decision, he remained silent about developments at the front, and he made no reference to any ultimatum from his officers. Indeed his speech included no attack on the army that had betrayed him. His criticism, and it was scathing, was reserved for Castillo Armas and the United States.

Many have branded Arbenz's resignation as the surrender of a frightened man. These critics include Guatemalans and foreigners, people of the right and of the left. They have passed judgment but have seldom sought to understand what hopes and what fears might have led him to this desperate step. Even Peurifoy's dispatches show greater insight into Arbenz's motivations.

[123] Interviews with Charnaud and Toriello, who were at the meeting. Their account is confirmed by Monzón, who was also present (see Sierra Roldán, *Diálogos*, pp. 89, 99), and by interviews with Fortuny and María de Arbenz (providing Arbenz's version of the session). Also at the meeting were a number of party leaders and trade union officials, one of whom has left a self-serving account of it. (See Díaz Rozzotto, *El carácter de la Revolución Guatemalteca*, pp. 291–92.)

[124] "Sucesivos cambios en el Ejecutivo," *El I*, June 29, 1954, p. 1.

[125] The Guatemalan press printed only short excerpts of the speech. The full text, from the original tape, was later published in Putzeys Rojas, *Así se hizo la Liberación*, pp. 297–300. Arbenz's previous broadcast, on June 19, had been full of confidence. ("Tenemos confianza en la unidad del pueblo, en el ejército, en la victoria," *DCA*, June 21, 1954, p. 5.)

As Peurifoy reported, Díaz and his four cohorts had offered to get rid of Arbenz but had insisted that the United States abandon Castillo Armas. Peurifoy had "avoided any comment."[126] The five colonels transformed this ambiguity into a promise.[127]

Díaz went to the presidential palace. He told Arbenz that the army units in the capital would attack the palace by 5 p.m. unless he resigned. Whether out of fear or shame, Díaz stressed that he was merely "the messenger"[128] and that he remained loyal to his friend and president: "This was decided without me, Jacobo, and I was merely asked to inform you; I will not participate in this coup."[129]

Beyond these lies, Díaz told Arbenz the truth, or rather, his version of the truth: Peurifoy had promised, he asserted, that the United States would accept him as Guatemala's next president if Arbenz resigned and the PGT was banned.

Díaz said that he had been sent by the officers in the capital; in fact, he represented no one but himself and his four colonel cronies.[130] Earlier he had told the same tale to Peurifoy. ("Solution desired by all army officers was that he should assume presidency," the ambassador had cabled, quoting Díaz.)[131] Vain and unintelligent, Díaz overestimated his influence in the army. Mistaking superficial camaraderie for loyalty and respect, he believed that the army would rally behind him; his four confederates shared his illusions. ("We, too, believed that Díaz could hold onto power," recalls Parinello.)[132] Díaz was not consciously lying. He was stating what he thought would occur, and his confidence was reinforced by what he believed to be Peurifoy's blessing. He would prove wrong, on both counts.

Arbenz knew even less about the true feelings of the officers than did Díaz. He believed that Díaz was his friend, and he believed that he was telling him the truth. Díaz was the most senior officer in the armed forces and was, Arbenz thought, well regarded by his fellow officers. Had he not been selected as the new president? Furthermore, according to Getellá, the officers at Zacapa were rebelling against Arbenz because they refused to be dragged into "his" war

[126] Interview with Krieg.

[127] Interview with Parinello.

[128] Interview with María de Arbenz.

[129] Interview with Fortuny, confirmed by interviews with María de Arbenz and Charnaud (all giving Arbenz's account) and interview with Parinello (giving Díaz's account); see also Arbenz, "Jacobo Arbenz relata detalles." Several months later, Arbenz still believed Díaz's tale and praised his "exemplary conduct." (Arbenz, "Tiene la palabra Jacobo Arbenz," p. 50.)

[130] Confirmed by interview with Parinello.

[131] Peurifoy to SecState, June 27, 1954, 11 p.m., *FRUS*, 1952–1954, 4:1190 (quoted); McCormick to SecState, no. C-14, 280145Z, NA 714.00 ("Díaz claimed entire support army"); interviews with Krieg and Parinello.

[132] Interview with Parinello.

against the United States. They had not attacked Díaz; indeed León and his two colleagues were Díaz's friends. Therefore, Arbenz concluded, if the United States was willing to accept Díaz, Zacapa would follow suit, and the ascent of Castillo Armas would be blocked.[133]

Díaz had told Arbenz that as president he would have to ban the PGT, exile its leaders, and halt the agrarian reform; but he had stressed that he would retain as many of the benefits of the revolution as he could—including leaving the land that had been distributed under Decree 900 in the peasants' hands. Arbenz saw himself confronted with a cruel choice. A Díaz presidency would spell the end of the revolution, and it would abort his attempt to transform Guatemala into an independent nation. The alternative, however, was worse. A victory of Castillo Armas meant the surrender of all national dignity, the obliteration of all the reforms undertaken since 1944, the return to power of the landed elite, and an orgy of repression. Reports were already coming in that the *Liberacionistas* were killing "subversives." Arbenz could no longer protect the Guatemalan peasants. He had lost, and they with him. His timely resignation could lighten the burden of their defeat.[134]

And so Arbenz was lulled by Díaz's promises. Later, he said: "I agreed to withdraw in favor of a loyal officer, Colonel Díaz, under two conditions: that there were no deals with Castillo Armas and that the achievements of the October revolution were preserved."[135] Corroboration is afforded by the embassy of the United States. After listening to Díaz's account of his conversation with Arbenz, Colonel McCormick cabled that "Arbenz had accepted Díaz ultimatum provided Díaz promise not [to] negotiate with Castillo Armas. Díaz agreed." In the same vein, Peurifoy reported: "As condition for peaceful turnover Arbenz demanded and Díaz gave his word of honor that he would not enter into negotiations with Castillo Armas."[136]

[133] Interviews with María de Arbenz, Fortuny, and Charnaud were particularly helpful for this paragraph.

[134] For Arbenz's perceptions, interviews with María de Arbenz, Fortuny, Guerra Borges, and Charnaud were particularly useful. (Charnaud was not close to Arbenz at the time, but they became close in the 1960s.) See also PGT, *La intervención*, p. 20. The reports of peasant executions were confirmed in interviews with officers who were in the Zacapa area, such as Hernández, Silva Girón, and Mendizabal; see also Peurifoy to SecState, no. 1157, June 30, 1954, NA 814.062, and Santa Cruz Morales, "La invasión a Guatemala." Putzeys Rojas blandly refers to "those peasants who fled in fear to the mountains." (*Así se hizo la Liberación*, p. 265.) The fate of the peasants, the main beneficiaries of his government, weighed particularly heavily on Arbenz in those dark hours. "Arbenz was afraid that if he resisted the army's ultimatum there would be a bloodbath in the countryside, and he knew that the peasants had no way to defend themselves." (Interview with Charnaud.)

[135] Arbenz, "Tiene la palabra Jacobo Arbenz," p. 50; see also Arbenz, "Jacobo Arbenz relata detalles."

[136] Quoted from McCormick to SecState, no. C-14, 280145Z, and Peurifoy to

This explains why, in his resignation speech, Arbenz did not condemn the officers who had betrayed him. "It is as if Jacobo had said to the army, 'I am resigning, but please continue to fight against this traitor [Castillo Armas]. Do not surrender to these bandits.' Clinging to his last hope, he was appealing to the army's sense of honor."[137]

What alternative was open to Jacobo Arbenz at that late hour? Should he, as some have claimed, have left the capital and become a guerrilla leader? His failure to do so "was a crude error of grave historical consequences," stated Luis Cardoza y Aragón, a Guatemalan writer who lived in Mexico.[138]

But even if Arbenz had been able to leave the capital for the countryside (not a foregone conclusion, since the army could have tried to prevent his departure, and the Presidential Guard was commanded by the disloyal Dubois), how could he have built his guerrilla force? True, many peasants would have joined him, but they had neither weapons nor training. The adventure would have ranked among the most senseless of the many guerrilla efforts attempted in the hemisphere in the twentieth century. Arbenz would have led a host of peasants to their slaughter in the name of what? Revolutionary glory? Personal heroism?

Is the argument that Arbenz should have ennobled the collapse of the revolution through his own death? If such were the aim, rather than staining his own martyrdom with the blood of defenseless peasants, he should have met his fate by attempting to hold out in the presidential palace. As with Salvador Allende, death in the palace would have glorified his memory. And death might have been preferable, for Arbenz, to the seventeen years that awaited him.

But Arbenz's decision must be seen in the light of the alternatives as they appeared to him on that fateful twenty-seventh of June: he believed that his timely resignation would lead to the presidency of Carlos Enrique Díaz and thwart the triumph of Castillo Armas. His resignation was not an act of cowardice, but the desperate attempt to save what might still be saved. "Perhaps many people will think that I am making a mistake," he conceded in his farewell speech. "From the bottom of my heart I do not believe this. Only history will decide."[139]

As his words were broadcast on the evening of the twenty-seventh, Arbenz was at his home, Casa Pomona, where he spent the night—he had no need to seek refuge, he reasoned, since Díaz was in command.[140]

SecState, no. 1123, June 27, 1954, 7 p.m. Both NA 714.00. See also Burrows to Woodward, June 28, 1954, NA 714.00 and CIA, *Current Intelligence Digest*, June 28, 1954, p. 16.

[137] Interview with María de Arbenz.

[138] *La Revolución Guatemalteca*, p. 187.

[139] Putzeys Rojas, *Así se hizo la Liberación*, p. 300.

[140] Interviews with María de Arbenz, Fortuny, and Lilly Zachrisson (who was living

Before leaving the presidential palace, he had urged the revolutionary politicians present to assist the new president. Some did not dally; they fled to foreign embassies. Others stayed, among them Charnaud and Castillo Flores, who remained "calm"—confident that Díaz would remain in control.[141]

"The peasant organizations," Castillo Flores proclaimed, "must cooperate fully with Colonel Díaz, since he has promised to uphold the laws of the October Revolution."[142] In a speech that was broadcast immediately after that of Arbenz, Díaz had indeed pledged that he would honor the social reforms enacted since 1944, and he had also promised that he would continue to fight against Castillo Armas "until he is defeated."[143]

FROM DÍAZ TO CASTILLO ARMAS

Díaz was an opportunist, but he was not utterly disloyal to the men with whom he had hobnobbed when he had been Arbenz's protegé. On the evening of the twenty-seventh, he freed Gutiérrez, who had been arrested a few hours earlier. "You, Pellecer and Gutiérrez should seek asylum tonight," he warned Fortuny, who was still lingering in the presidential palace. "Your lives are in danger, and there are things I cannot control." Díaz, concludes Fortuny, "was not prepared to kill communists."[144]

Díaz was doomed. The United States had not launched Castillo Armas's invasion in order to hand the presidency to a friend of Arbenz. Washington intended to impose its own man, a man with unblemished anticommunist credentials, a man who would not urge communist leaders to seek asylum, but who would destroy them.

A game of musical chairs began. By the time the music stopped, on July 7, Castillo Armas was in control.

To accomplish this feat, the United States, in Secretary Dulles's apt words, had to "crack some heads together,"[145] a task for which Peurifoy was partic-

---

at Casa Pomona). Their version is confirmed by a fiery supporter of Castillo Armas: "Arbenz went to 'Pomona.' " (Del Valle Matheu, *La verdad*, p. 30.) Arbenz sought asylum in the Mexican embassy the following day, once it had become obvious that Díaz was unable to maintain control. He did so under strong pressure from his wife, who urged him: "Don't let them kill you for no reason. Don't make a vain sacrifice. You're still young; you can fight again for Guatemala." (Interview with María de Arbenz.) The fact that Arbenz sought asylum only on the twenty-eighth is also confirmed by the testimony of a Mexican official who was at the embassy: see Guillén, *Guatemala*, p. 77.

[141] Interviews with Fortuny (quoted), who was still at the palace, and with Charnaud.

[142] Castillo Flores to Sec. Gen. de la Unión Campesina "La Brigada," June 28, 1954, *GT*, Box 5.

[143] "Exito en la gestión del nuevo gobierno," *DCA*, June 28, 1954, p. 1.

[144] Interview with Fortuny.

[145] Peurifoy, "Memorandum of Negotiations Leading to Signing of Pact of San Salvador, July 2, 1954," July 7, 1954, *FRUS*, 1952–1954, 4:1202.

ularly well suited. It was not an exacting undertaking. Arbenz and his communist friends had been removed from the stage, and a crowd of officers had rushed into their places. Deeply demoralized, fragmented, aware that their conduct appeared ignominious—but too worried about their own survival to behave with dignity—the Guatemalan officers were easy prey.

In the eleven days following Arbenz's resignation, five provisional governments (staffed entirely by officers) succeeded one another, each more amenable to Castillo Armas than its predecessor. Some officers served in more than one *junta*. (Colonel Monzón set the record by serving in four.) In this squalid minuet, the dancers jostled one another, each with his hopes and delusions, moving to a foreign beat. Some, damned by their *Arbencista* past, were quickly shoved off the floor by an impatient Peurifoy. Others met with his approval: the fervent anticommunists who had disliked Arbenz and had served him only out of opportunism. But theirs was only a supporting role: to pave the way for Castillo Armas. Those who performed gracefully were later rewarded. None proved more supple than Lt. Colonel Cruz Salazar (two *juntas*). When the invasion began, he was hostile to Castillo Armas; two weeks later he was working on his behalf. According to Cruz Salazar, he was "under unbelievable psychological pressure": John Doherty, the CIA station chief, "would appear at any hour, day and night; he didn't let me sleep."[146] But the Americans were reasonable men. Doherty's threats were accompanied by promises, and the promises would be kept. Cruz Salazar became Castillo Armas's first ambassador to the United States and received a generous "bonus"—the beginning of an enriching career.[147]

Colonel Monzón was not as astute as Cruz Salazar. Peurifoy and other U.S. officials had praise for him: he was a fervent anticommunist and a hard worker. Had Monzón understood his role, he too could have savored the sweet blessings of obedience. But he persisted in believing that he could deal with Castillo Armas as an equal. He was soon brought to heel, of course, and his importunities cost him dearly. On September 1, 1954, he was forced out of the *junta*; a few months later he was eased out of the country. When he tried to return, in August 1955, he was informed "that his papers were not in order, and that he regretfully could not be permitted to enter the country."[148] He even

---

[146] Interview with Cruz Salazar.

[147] "Most reports place the figure at $100,000." (Cehelsky, "Guatemala's Frustrated Revolution," p. 63.) "The new Ambassador has expended his efforts in directions which appear to offer little general benefit to Guatemala," a U.S. official reported. (Leddy to Mann, Nov. 12, 1954, p. 1, NA 611.14.)

[148] Cehelsky, "Guatemala's Frustrated Revolution," p. 107. See also Sierra Roldán, *Diálogos*, p. 125. For U.S. impressions of Monzón, see Peurifoy to SecState, no. 1142, June 29, 1954, NA 714.00; CIA, *Current Intelligence Digest*, June 30, 1954, p. 7; Dulles to AmEm Paris, June 30, 1954, NA 714.00/6-2354; Bowdler to Pearson,

suffered the indignity—for a man of his stamp—of being refused a U.S. visa.[149] Monzón's memoirs, *Diálogos con el coronel Monzón*, are the bitter lamentations of a failed opportunist.

The dance that brought Castillo Armas from Chiquimula to the presidency can be quickly described; it is a sordid footnote to Arbenz's resignation. On the night of June 27, Colonel Díaz was awakened by two CIA agents who ordered him to resign at once. Stunned—hadn't Peurifoy given him his word?—Díaz asked to see the ambassador. But when he was brought to Peurifoy, it was only to hear the same sentence again: he must resign. "They were quite rough with Díaz that night," recalls DCM Krieg.[150] Peurifoy upbraided the hapless colonel for having allowed Arbenz to denounce the United States in his resignation speech and told him to step aside in favor of Monzón, who was "well-known for his anti-Communist feelings."[151] In his illusion that Peurifoy would accept him as president of Guatemala, Díaz had chased the mirage of a promise. The tone of Arbenz's farewell speech only abbreviated the span of a presidency that would, in any case, have been ephemeral.

Chastened, Díaz withdrew. He dared not disobey Peurifoy, but neither was he ready to jettison his ambitions. He reappeared before the ambassador a few hours later, flanked by his friend, Colonel Sánchez, and by Monzón. Hoping to placate Peurifoy, Díaz had traded the presidential mantle for that of the head of a three-man *junta* composed of himself, Sánchez and Monzón. Stressing that Monzón would be completely in charge of security matters—that is, of "carrying out vigorous program [to] clean out Communists"—Díaz and Sánchez "promised [to] take no action without his approval."[152]

The *junta* lasted less than twenty-four hours. Peurifoy continued to insist that Díaz resign. His threats were delicately summed up by Monzón in his memoirs: "There will be no peace in Guatemala until the men in power can guarantee the eradication of communism." This was why, Monzón argued,

"ARA Monthly Report for July," Aug. 4, 1954, NA 714.00; Memo for Record ("Situation in Guatemala"), Aug. 24, 1954, NA 714.00.

[149] See Sierra Roldán, *Diálogos*, p. 130. Monzón was allowed to return to Guatemala in 1957, after Castillo Armas's death.

[150] Interview with Krieg.

[151] Peurifoy to SecState, June 28, 1954, noon, *FRUS*, 1952–1954, 4:1192.

[152] Quotations from Peurifoy to SecState, June 28, 1954, 5 p.m., ibid., p. 1193. Peurifoy's view of the Díaz *junta* was shared by the CIA: "It would appear that the Guatemalan government is attempting by the maneuver of ousting Arbenz and outlawing the Workers' Party [PGT] to remove the stigma of Communism from the government and thereby take from Castillo Armas the reason for his campaign. Most of those calling for support of the new government have long pro-Communist records." (*Current Intelligence Digest*, June 29, 1954, p. 15.)

"I suggested to Carlos Enrique Díaz that he resign in my favor."[153] Díaz hesitated, and was overtaken by events. On the night of the twenty-eighth, a group of officers arrived unbidden at the house of his ally, Army Chief of Staff Parinello. Unceremoniously, they woke him up: "You are dismissed. Give us the keys to your office."[154] Parinello docilely handed over the keys, thereby exiting from center stage. Meanwhile, another group of officers rose against Díaz and Sánchez. At 4:45 a.m. a new *junta* was proclaimed, composed of Monzón (as president), Cruz Salazar, and Dubois. Not one drop of blood had been shed and no resistance had been offered. Díaz and Sánchez meekly hastened off the stage. Their departure was described by the indefatigable Peurifoy: "Returning to Díaz's office at 4 a.m., I found Monzón had not yet appeared. Just as I was about to leave, Díaz received telephone call from Palace and he and Sánchez left to confer with several officers. . . . Shortly thereafter Díaz returned and wearily informed me that things had changed: he and Sánchez had decided resign from Junta."[155]

This was, applauded Peurifoy, a healthy change, which guaranteed that there would no longer be any wavering in the persecution of communists.[156] Castillo Armas, however, was still at Chiquimula and still waiting for his turn.

When Monzón installed himself in the presidential palace, Castillo Armas controlled only a speck of Guatemalan territory. His was the parody of an invasion, but he faced the parody of an army. In any case, his strength was elsewhere: he was the candidate of the United States in a country that was rapidly regressing to a banana republic. Negotiations had opened on June 27 between Castillo Armas and the colonels at Zacapa. They ended, three days later, with the *Pacto de las Tunas*, whereby the troops at Zacapa placed themselves under Castillo Armas, receiving in exchange "full guarantees . . . of life and property" and the assurance that "they would suffer no discrimination . . . in their military careers." The pact asserted that "the honor and the dignity of the army were untarnished"[157]—a fantasy that convinced no one, and

[153] Sierra Roldán, *Diálogos*, p. 101; see also Peurifoy to SecState, June 28, 1954, 8 p.m., *FRUS*, 1952–1954, 4:1194–95, and Peurifoy to SecState, no. 1138, June 28, 1954, 9 p.m., NA 714.00.

[154] Interview with Parinello.

[155] Quoted from Peurifoy to SecState, June 29, 1954, 7 p.m., *FRUS*, 1952–1954, 4:1197; see also Peurifoy to SecState, no. 1139, June 29, 1954, NA 714.00, and Urist, "Monday Night Meeting," June 29, 1954, RG84 G&C, Box 3, NA-S. For Monzón's account, see Sierra Roldán, *Diálogos*, pp. 105–6. Interview with Cruz Salazar was useful.

[156] MemoTel (Peurifoy, Leddy), June 30, 1954, NA 714.00; Peurifoy to SecState, no. 1153, June 30, 1954, NA 714.00.

[157] The full text of the pact is published in Putzeys Rojas, *Así se hizo la Liberación*, pp. 309–11; for the negotiations, see pp. 98, 100, 118, 293–96, and 300. See also Sierra Roldán, *Diálogos*, p. 117, and Flores Avendaño, *Memorias*, 2:441–45.

certainly not the officers at Zacapa. Within a few days, they returned to their barracks "despondent, with a terrible sense of defeat."[158]

Though eager to crush communists and relentless in his professions of loyalty to the United States, Monzón was reluctant to hand power to Castillo Armas. He enjoyed the timid support of a great many officers who felt that they would be better protected by a *junta* of fellow colonels than by their erstwhile foes; none, however, was willing to challenge the United States. Meanwhile other officers, including *junta* members Dubois and Cruz Salazar, were discreetly working for the triumph of Castillo Armas.

The United States opened the next act. The State Department asked President Osorio to invite Monzón and Castillo Armas to talks in San Salvador. Osorio complied, and the two rivals arrived on June 30 aboard U.S. planes; both were disgruntled, wary, and anxious.[159] Two days of quarrels ensued. Then, at 4:45 a.m. on July 2, Monzón and Castillo Armas embraced, to the edification of a crowd of photographers, and signed the *Pacto de San Salvador*; they had, wrote the *New York Times*, "tears in their eyes."[160] The pact established a new *junta*, which included Monzón, Dubois, and Cruz Salazar, as well as Castillo Armas and another *Liberacionista*, Major Enrique Trinidad Oliva. For the moment, Monzón would continue as president, "but the *junta* would select a new president in not more than two weeks."[161] In Washington, Holland concluded, "Since Cruz [Salazar] and Oliva are Castillo men, Castillo has control."[162]

The most colorful character at San Salvador was Peurifoy, who arrived in the early afternoon of July first, with a planeload of journalists. Acting like a stern father, he brought the recalcitrant pair to a swift agreement. He first received Castillo Armas, whom he had never met. Setting diplomatic niceties aside, he scolded the Guatemalan for his intransigence. Peurifoy explained:

[158] Interview with Col. Mendoza, who was appointed army chief of staff in early July. "Therefore," as he said, "I saw all this very closely."

[159] AmEm San Salvador, McDermott to DOS, "Negotiation in San Salvador of Guatemalan Peace Pact," July 5, 1954, NA 714.00. See also: MemoTel (McDermott, Holland), June 29, 1954, NA 714.00; MemoTel (Willauer, Holland), June 29, 1954, NA 714.00; MemoTel (Peurifoy, Holland), June 29, 1954, *FRUS*, 1952–1954, 4:1195; MemoTel (Peurifoy, Holland, Whelan, McDermott, Castro), June 29, 1954, NA 714.00; Peurifoy to SecState, no. 1148, June 29, 1954, NA 714.00.

[160] "Guatemala Chiefs Vow to Fight Reds," *NYT*, July 3, 1954, p. 1.

[161] Point 6 of the *Pacto de San Salvador*. The best sources on the negotiations are McDermott, "Negotiation" (see n. 159 above), and Peurifoy, "Memorandum of Negotiations" (see n. 145 above), pp. 1202–8. For Monzón's account see Sierra Roldán, *Diálogos*, pp. 114–23, 132–34; for the Salvadoran government's account see El Salvador, *De la neutralidad vigilante a la mediación con Guatemala*.

[162] DOS, "Meeting of Guatemalan Group," July 2, 1954, p. 1.

I then told him I was going to speak with absolute frankness. "You know, and I know," I told him, "how the American people feel about you. Many American people think you should be the president of Guatemala, and . . . I personally will do all in my power to help you. For the present, I think you should be taken into the Junta. And, confidentially, I'll tell you something else. Col. Cruz Salazar . . . told me that he was on your side, so you should have no problem at all." He seemed to be pleased and reassured by these last statements.[163]

Next it was Monzón's turn to be lectured by the ambassador. "In all due modesty," Peurifoy later boasted to Holland, "within an hour—after talking for about 30 minutes with each man . . . [I] had a basic agreement. The rest of the time—all night long—they were fighting over details."[164]

While Peurifoy held center stage, Somoza bombarded the State Department with suggestions and complaints, claiming that Castillo Armas was being placed "at a disadvantage" in the negotiations with Monzón.[165] Ambassador Whelan cabled that Somoza was "hurt and angry" because Castillo Armas had been told upon landing in Managua while enroute to San Salvador "that he was under orders see no one but me. . . . I told President [Somoza] I knew of no such order and thought it misunderstanding. I then phoned airport and learned such order had been received from somewhere. . . . I told airport disregard their orders."[166]

In San Salvador Peurifoy was interrupted in his peacemaking by the untimely visit of the Nicaraguan ambassador, Carlos Duque, who carried an urgent message from his master. Peurifoy reported:

President Somoza wished to advise me that in view of the "breakdown" in negotiations between Castillo Armas and Monzón, he urged the entire negotiating party to come to Managua as his guests to continue their discussions there. If this were not feasible, he said, then he strongly advised that Col. Castillo Armas be made president of Guatemala, and that Col. Monzón be made Minister of Defense. He mentioned several other Cabinet appointments, which I do not recall. I thanked Ambassador Duque. . . . I told him, however . . . that I did not believe it would be necessary to trouble President Somoza with any of the negotiations.[167]

Eager to mask its interference, the State Department downplayed its role at San Salvador. Thus, it was initially thought that Peurifoy should not attend the meeting, much to his disappointment; but the stubbornness of Castillo Armas

---

[163] Peurifoy, "Memorandum of Negotiations" (see n. 145 above), pp. 1203–4.

[164] MemoTel (Peurifoy, Holland), July 2, 1954, 10:50 a.m., p. 2, NA 714.00.

[165] AmEm Managua, Whelan to SecState, no. 237, June 29, 1954, 9 p.m., NA 714.00.

[166] AmEm Managua, Whelan to SecState, no. 240, June 30, 1954, 4 p.m., NA 714.00.

[167] Peurifoy, "Memorandum of Negotiations" (see n. 145 above), p. 1206.

and Monzón forced Washington to reconsider.[168] Once Peurifoy had done the job, U.S. officials informed Osorio, who had merely housed and fed the guests, that the credit for the agreement was all his. Commendable modesty also led the United States to abstain from signing the pact, "thus giving the Salvadoran government recognition as the principal mediator." The agreement was signed by only Castillo Armas, Monzón, and El Salvador's acting foreign minister. (The foreign minister was " 'indisposed' because of alcoholic excesses.")[169]

On July 3, a triumphant Peurifoy brought Monzón and Castillo Armas—with a crowd of boisterous journalists—back to Guatemala City in the embassy plane. If Castillo Armas still doubted that he had won, his misgivings were soon dispelled. On July 7, in accordance with their secret pledges, Cruz Salazar and Dubois resigned from the *junta*. To Monzón, it came as a surprise; to Peurifoy, as a foreordained conclusion. Left with Castillo Armas and Oliva, the hapless Monzón dutifully added his vote, a few hours later, to theirs, making Castillo Armas's election as *junta* president unanimous. "Things are going to work out beautifully," a confident Peurifoy told Holland the following day.[170] And so they did. On September 1, again by unanimous vote, the *junta* dissolved itself, and Castillo Armas became president of Guatemala.

Only one incident disturbed the careful choreography that brought Castillo Armas from Chiquimula to Guatemala City. At dawn, on August 2, "a vigorous exchange of gunfire awoke those who lived in the southeastern sector of the capital." About a hundred of the 136 cadets of the Escuela Politécnica were attacking the Roosevelt Hospital, which housed seven hundred armed *Liberacionistas* who had come from Zacapa and Chiquimula to participate in a victory parade.[171]

[168] See McDermott, "Negotiation" (see n. 159 above), p. 4; Dulles to Peurifoy, no. 259, June 29, 1954, 8:07 p.m.; MemoTel (Peurifoy, Holland), June 30, 1954, 10 a.m.; MemoTel (Holland, McDermott), June 30, 1954, 9 p.m.; Holland to Wisner, no. 371, June 30, 1954, 9:25 p.m. All NA 714.00.

[169] Quoted from Peurifoy, "Memorandum of Negotiations Leading to Signing of Pact of San Salvador, July 2, 1954," July 7, 1954, p. 4, NA 714.00. The parenthetical sentence has been deleted in *FRUS* 1952–1954 (see 4:1206); see also MemoTel (Peurifoy, Holland), July 2, 1954, 10:50 a.m., NA 714.00.

[170] MemoTel (Peurifoy, Holland), July 8, 1954, NA 714.00; see also Peurifoy to SecState, no. 32, July 6, 1954, NA 714.00. Apparently Dubois received the same financial reward as Cruz Salazar. (See Cehelsky, "Guatemala's Frustrated Revolution," p. 63.)

[171] "Información sobre los sucesos habidos hoy temprano en el sur de la ciudad," *La Hora*, Aug. 2, 1954, p. 1 (quoted). Castillo Armas's troops swelled "with imaginary combatants" after his victory. "These new recruits, many of them children of the upper class, had never fired a shot because they had never been near the fighting." (Col. Pinto Recinos, "Sublevación," July 23, 1988, p. 3.)

Peurifoy, Castillo Armas, and the officers in the city were caught by surprise. Also surprised were the cadets' officers, who did not join their charges in the attack on the hospital.[172]

Taking off from the nearby military airport, Castillo Armas's planes strafed the cadets, who had been reinforced by about two hundred soldiers sent by the Base Militar. But the cadets and soldiers held their ground, demonstrating once again that the rebel air force was of little use against troops willing to fight.

The *Liberacionistas* were isolated. No army unit came to their assistance. On the contrary, the Base Militar sent a detail to occupy the military airport later in the morning, thus grounding Castillo Armas's planes. The Base Militar, however, "never openly raised the banner of insurrection against Castillo Armas." During the day, the army units in the capital broadcast both proclamations of loyalty to the ruling *junta* and words of praise for "the glorious efforts of the cadets to vindicate the honor of the army."[173]

It was Peurifoy who dominated the scene in Guatemala City. He held court, appropriately enough, in the presidential palace. He threatened, cajoled, admonished. He told the officers who came to pledge their loyalty that the United States was irrevocably behind Castillo Armas.[174] He was not unduly excited by the rebellion. It had no leftist tinges, he told Holland, and "there were no signs of Communist activity"; rather, he stressed, "anti-Communists were fighting anti-Communists"[175]—and Guatemala's anticommunists had a comforting tendency to obey U.S. orders.

The immediate cause of the revolt, Peurifoy cabled, was a tawdry incident that had occurred on the night of August 1: "Liberation elements forced two cadets into local bawdy house, made them strip and attempted perpetuate gross indignities on their persons and reportedly killing one of them in ensuing brawl."[176] His information was accurate except for a few details. The unlucky cadets—who were four or five rather than two—had gone to the brothel on

[172] The best sources on the revolt are (1) Peurifoy's cables to DOS and memos of telephone conversations between him and Holland, Aug. 2–4, 1954, in NA 714.00; *JW* 32, Aug. 6, 1954; (2) *El I* and *La Hora* (despite a pronounced bias in favor of Castillo Armas); (3) Second Lt. Girón, "La rebelión de los cadetes"; Santa Cruz Morales, "Secuela"; Pinto Recinos, "Sublevación." Also useful are Monzón's account in Sierra Roldán, *Diálogos*, pp. 140–44, and Samayoa Coronado, *La Escuela Politécnica*, 2:243–49. Interviews with Lorenzana, Mendizabal, Peralta Méndez, and Krieg were particularly valuable.

[173] Quotations from *JW* 32, Aug. 6, 1954, p. 3, and Santa Cruz Morales, "Secuela," p. 9.

[174] Interview with Krieg, who acted as Peurifoy's interpreter.

[175] Quotations from: MemoTel (Peurifoy, Holland), Aug. 2, 1954, 11:05 p.m.; Peurifoy to SecState, no. 146, Aug. 2, 1954, 11 p.m. Both NA 714.00.

[176] Peurifoy to SecState, no. 142, Aug. 2, 1954, 6 p.m., NA 714.00.

their own initiative, and, although they were forced to dance naked in front of the prostitutes and other clients, none had been killed.[177]

This was merely one in a series of humiliations. Castillo Armas's supporters had found it difficult to hide their contempt for an army that had surrendered without fighting. On August 6, the U.S. embassy pointed out that behind the cadets' uprising

> was dissatisfaction in the Army resulting from the rankling sense of humiliation of the Officer's Corps, . . . the uneasiness which naturally extended through the armed forces as officers wondered what their fate would be in the shake-up expected from the new government, . . . and the jeers to which uniformed Army personnel are reported to have been subjected by the populace, and especially by the swaggering youngsters carrying the brassard of the "Liberation Army."[178]

The rebellious cadets were not challenging the United States. Even as they besieged the Roosevelt Hospital, they informed Peurifoy of their loyalty to the *junta*—they wanted only an "end to insults" from the *Liberacionistas*.[179]

At 5:30 p.m. on August 2, while his men still held out at the Roosevelt Hospital against a smaller force,[180] Castillo Armas informed Peurifoy that he intended to go to Zacapa where he had another five hundred men under arms, but Peurifoy told him to stay in the capital.[181]

One hour later, the besieged *Liberacionistas* surrendered. They were disarmed and forced "to rip off their military badges . . . and throw them on the floor."[182] Then they were "marched as prisoners of war through the city, and loaded into trains."[183] After spending the night in the wagons, the defeated rabble departed for Zacapa, from whence it had come as conquerors a few days earlier.

At dusk, on August 3, the confidence of the ambassador was vindicated. The commander of the Base Militar and his deputy went meekly to the presidential palace to give themselves up while the other army units in the capital declared that they were ready to attack the cadets. Obligingly, the cadets sur-

---

[177] See esp. Santa Cruz Morales, "Secuela," p. 10. Among the dancers was Benedicto Lucas, a future general and chief of staff (1980–1982) of the Guatemalan army. (Villagrán Kramer, "Los pactos," July 19, 1987, pp. 18–19.)

[178] *JW* 32, Aug. 6, 1954, p. 2.

[179] Peurifoy to SecState, no. 138, Aug. 2, 1954, 1 p.m., NA 714.00.

[180] With the passing of the years, the attackers have multiplied in the *Liberacionista* lore; by 1986, they had grown from some three hundred to 1,800 ("2 de agosto: versión del MLN," *La Hora*).

[181] Peurifoy to SecState, no. 145, Aug. 2, 1954, 9 p.m., NA 714.00; see also Peurifoy to SecState, no. 146, Aug. 2, 1954, 11 p.m., NA 714.00.

[182] Santa Cruz Morales, "Secuela," p. 9.

[183] *JW* 32, Aug. 6, 1954, p. 2.

rendered forthwith in exchange for a guarantee that they would not be punished.

The Guatemalan press, which was no longer free, celebrated the end of the revolt as another glorious *Liberacionista* victory: "Second Battle against Communism Won," crowed *El Imparcial*.[184] The U.S. embassy was more sober: the events had demonstrated "that there was very little active support for Castillo Armas in the Armed Forces"; Castillo Armas himself had shown "little imagination or resolution," and the "civilian anti-Communist and 'Liberation' organizations [had] lost all semblance of discipline [during the crisis]."[185]

The cadets had attempted the impossible. They had tried to recover the dignity of the army without standing up to the United States. As in June, opportunism proved stronger than honor; fear of Washington more powerful than national pride. One hundred Guatemalans, including many innocent bystanders, were killed or wounded on August 2 and 3 as the cadets indulged in their senseless pursuit of the lost dignity of the Guatemalan army. Castillo Armas's retribution followed. In violation of the terms of surrender, the Escuela Politécnica was closed, and the rebellious cadets and several officers were cashiered or jailed. The Pax Americana was reestablished.

[184] "Segunda batalla contra el comunismo ganada," *El I*, Aug. 5, 1954, p. 1.
[185] *JW* 32, Aug. 6, 1954, pp. 4, 1.

CHAPTER 15

Conclusion

EVER SINCE Jefferson cast his gaze toward Cuba, three forces have shaped U.S. policy toward the Caribbean: the search for economic gain, the search for security, and imperial hubris. These were the forces that shaped the American response to the Guatemalan revolution. Consider the stage: there is Jack Peurifoy, that "abusive, arrogant ambassador,"[1] there is the Red Jacobo, and there are the bananas.

Behind the bananas looms the United Fruit Company, with its platoon of "influential lobbyists and talented publicists."[2] In Washington, a Republican president heads a probusiness administration whose upper echelon is studded with friends of United Fruit. Foster Dulles had been a senior partner in the law firm that had represented UFCO. His deputy, Walter Bedell Smith, was toying with the idea of taking a job with UFCO (which he indeed did when he retired in 1955). The assistant secretary for Latin America was a Cabot, as was the ambassador to the United Nations—and the Cabots were major UFCO stockholders. Eisenhower's personal secretary, Ann Whitman, was the wife of UFCO's director of public relations.

From Washington's perspective, Arbenz perpetrated outrages against UFCO. If one recalls the fury of the Truman administration when Arévalo sought to enforce the labor code, one can appreciate the gravity of Arbenz's crime when he seized UFCO's lands. It is not surprising, then, that some critics have seen in the decision to overthrow Arbenz the heavy hand of UFCO. "Without United Fruit's troubles," write the authors of *Bitter Fruit*, "it seems probable that the Dulles brothers might not have paid such intense attention to the few Communists in Guatemala, since larger numbers had taken part in political activity on a greater scale during the postwar years in Brazil, Chile and Costa Rica without causing excessive concern in the U.S. government."[3]

---

[1] Quoted from interview with Col. González Siguí.

[2] Schlesinger and Kinzer, *Bitter Fruit*, p. 77.

[3] Ibid., p. 106. The view that United Fruit was instrumental in the U.S. decision to overthrow Arbenz has its legion of ardent adherents—from Schlesinger and Kinzer, who provide its most compelling presentation, to lovers of the sensational, such as Rodman, "Operation Diablo," who scarcely bothers to cover his lies. Some portray a U.S. government that is putty in the hands of the company, conveniently overlooking evidence that might temper or complicate their thesis, including the fact that the government initiated an antitrust suit against UFCO shortly after the fall of Arbenz. On this, see Miller to Attorney General, Dec. 4, 1951, NA 814.062; Redmond to Miller,

UFCO had a motive, and it had the contacts. It is tempting to survey the scene of the crime, find this smoking gun, and arrest the fruit company. There is, however, more evidence. After studying the Guatemalan primary sources and juxtaposing them with U.S. reports, it becomes clearer and clearer that while the U.S. embassy's concern with communism under Arévalo owed much to UFCO's smoke and mirrors, its concern with communism under Arbenz owed little to the company.

Arbenz's sympathy for the communist cause was obvious, as was the growth in strength and prestige of the Community party. It is true, as *Bitter Fruit* points out, that the communist parties of Brazil, Chile, and Costa Rica had acquired significant influence in their respective countries. The Communist Party of Chile had ministers in the cabinet, that of Costa Rica was an important part of the government coalition, and that of Brazil won 10 percent of the vote in the December 1945 presidential elections. By 1948, however, all three parties had been banned. The PGT, by contrast, gained influence in the early 1950s, when in the United States, McCarthyism was at a peak and when, in Latin America, all other communist parties were waning. Not in Brazil or in Chile or in Costa Rica had the communists ever been the president's intimates; never had they been part of his inner circle, privy to his most closely guarded secrets.[4] In no country of Latin America had the communists ever been as influential as they were in Guatemala. And no president had ever been as close to the communists as was Arbenz. It required no manipulations by UFCO minions for U.S. officials to appreciate these truths. As Ambassador Schoenfeld noted, "One had only to read the articles carried by the official *Diario de Centro America*."[5]

Just as scholars frequently fail to see the depth of the change from Arévalo to Arbenz, so they have failed to see the change in the U.S. government's reporting on Guatemala from the late forties to the early fifties. The reports of the late forties reveal, beyond their arrogance and ethnocentrism, immense ignorance. Many are simply bizarre, particularly those discussing the communist issue—those convoluted papers, for example, on whether Arévalo was

---

Dec. 4, 1951, NA 814.062; MemoConv (Barnes, Phleger, Metzger), May 22, 1953, NA Lot 58D18 & 58D78; TelConv (JFD, Brownell), June 30, 1954, DP, JFD:CS, Box 8, EL; "United Fruit Sued," *NYT*, July 3, 1954, p.1; "Oil on the Fire," *Business Week*, July 10, 1954, p. 128. See also Leddy to Holland, Oct. 12, 1954; Barnes to Baggett, Nov. 9, 1954; Sparks to Murphy, Nov. 18, 1954; Sparks to JFD, Dec. 3, 1954; Sherwood to Radius and Pearson, Dec. 6, 1954, and enclosed memo by Cutler. All NA Lot 58D18 & 58D78.

[4] See Alexander, *Communism*, and Goldenberg, *Kommunismus*. See also Halperin, *Nationalism and Communism in Chile*, pp. 52–59; Skidmore, *Politics in Brazil*, pp. 60–67; Aguilar Bulgarelli, *Costa Rica*.

[5] MemoConv (Schoenfeld, Toriello), Feb. 5, 1953, p. 2, RG84 G&C, Box 8, NA-S.

a communist. These reports bear no relationship to the reality of Guatemala; they inhabit a deranged world of nightmares. In the fifties, the embassy dispatches, despite their inaccuracies and ethnocentrism, reveal a grasp of the country and of the situation. A core of Guatemala hands had emerged in the Office of Intelligence and Research of the State Department, in the Directorate of Intelligence of the CIA, and in the embassy in Guatemala. Very often, when these people pointed to cases of communist influence, they were right. This shift from an embassy that knew nothing to an embassy that was reasonably well informed reduced UFCO's power to influence the picture of Guatemala. In the forties, UFCO was, to a great extent, the interpreter of matters Guatemalan. In the fifties, its role had become marginal.

The figure of the loud and arrogant Jack Peurifoy distorts a temperate assessment of U.S. reporting on Guatemala in the months before the overthrow of Arbenz. It is difficult not to be overwhelmed by this embodiment of imperial hubris, particularly when he is contrasted with his poised and urbane predecessor, Rudolph Schoenfeld. Schoenfeld is remembered to this day as a gentleman;[6] the contrast with Peurifoy could not be more stark. There was no contrast, however, between Schoenfeld's and Peurifoy's assessment of Guatemalan politics. Schoenfeld had hardened his stance on the Arbenz administration with each passing year, and his reports to the Department were increasingly hard-hitting. "During the first year of its application the Agrarian Reform caused a perceptible alteration in the political balance in Guatemala," Schoenfeld reported in 1953. "In its simplest terms, this change was the progressive atrophy of the opposition and a further growth and consolidation of Communist influence. This was the natural result of the Communists' position in the Agrarian Reform, of President Arbenz' attitude and of the continued unawareness and indifference of the Guatemalan Army to the currents of the time."[7] Temperamentally, Schoenfeld was not the man to oversee the bullying warfare of PBSUCCESS, but his analysis of what was happening in Guatemala helped to provide the operation's impetus.

Peurifoy was well cast for his role. His bad manners shine through his own report of the conversation he had with Arbenz when the two officials and their wives dined together on December 16, 1953. This oft-cited report has clinched the man's reputation, and indeed, it is difficult not to feel sympathy for Arbenz and respect for his quiet dignity as he faced the American's cross-examination.

[6] Interview with María de Arbenz. Schoenfeld's reports of his conversations with Arbenz reveal two men who were able to converse politely but were utterly unable to converse meaningfully. Arbenz would express his interest in technical assistance programs; Schoenfeld would respond with comments about communism. They were two ships in the night. (See: MemoConv [Arbenz, Schoenfeld], May 7, 1952, RG84 CF, Box 15; MemoConv [Arbenz, Schoenfeld], Sept. 25, 1952, ibid.; MemoConv [Arbenz, Schoenfeld], Mar. 4, 1953, RG84 G&C, Box 2. All NA-S.)

[7] Schoenfeld to DOS, no. 31, July 31, 1953, p. 11, NA 814.20.

This is not, however, the only conclusion to be derived from the report. It is also undeniable that the ambassador had been well briefed.

"Our talks lasted approximately six hours," wrote Peurifoy, six hours during which the focus of his interest was communist influence in Guatemala—not UFCO's plight. Indeed, when Arbenz sought to raise the subject of UFCO, Peurifoy retorted that "we should consider first things first."[8]

First things first. As Peurifoy pressed Arbenz with precise questions about communists in the administration, the pro-Soviet slant of the government media, the PGT's influence in the agrarian reform, Arbenz's answers were lame, unconvincing. Nor was he helped by his wife who acted as interpreter and volunteered answers that were manifestly untrue. This was the case when María stated, in response to Peurifoy's questioning, that neither the deputy director of the agrarian reform department nor the director general of radio broadcasting was a communist—only to be quickly corrected by Arbenz. (It was public knowledge that both officials belonged to the PGT.) Further, when Peurifoy asked why the Guatemalan Congress had held memorial services for Stalin, "Mrs. Arbenz interjected to state that the reason for this was that the people of Guatemala had regarded Roosevelt, Churchill and Stalin as saviors of the world and that perhaps when Mr. Churchill passes on, Congress will hold memorial services for him"[9]—a singularly ecumenical position.

Twenty-eight years later, after reading Peurifoy's report, María de Arbenz commented ruefully that on that most unpleasant evening she and her husband had not been persuasive. "The truth," she explained, "is that we were in a very difficult situation because Peurifoy's information was essentially correct."[10]

Survey the scene again. There is UFCO, boasting from the sidelines; there is Peurifoy loudly, rudely, reporting home. These two cloud the crux of the is-

[8] MemoConv (Pres. Arbenz, Mrs. Arbenz, Amb. Peurifoy, Mrs. Peurifoy), Dec. 17, 1953, p. 1, enclosed in Peurifoy to DOS, no. 522, Dec. 18, 1953, NA 611.14.

[9] Ibid., p.4.

[10] Interview with María de Arbenz. In Washington, as ambassador, the able Willy Toriello had been in a somewhat similar predicament. Relentlessly questioned by State Department officials about communist influence in Guatemala, he tried to placate them with a patently incredible message: "Arbenz's policy was directed toward allowing the Communists to discredit themselves," he told Acheson in December 1952; "the Guatemalan government was following a policy of discrediting the Communists and thereby containing their influence," he told State Department officials the following January, and again and again until his departure from Washington. (Quotations from Schoenfeld to Clark, Dec. 19, 1952, p. 1, NA 611.14, and from MemoConv [Toriello, Clark, Leddy], Jan. 27, 1953, p. 1, NA 714.001. See also MemoConv [Toriello, Schoenfeld], Feb. 5, 1953, RG84 G&C, Box 8, NA-S; MemoConv [Toriello, Rubottom, Leddy, Fisher], Mar. 11, 1953, NA 714.001; MemoConv [Toriello, Mann, Fisher], June 26, 1953, NA 611.14.)

sue: U.S. officials were alarmed by the rising influence of communism in Guatemala. And yet they knew that the communists were not in control of Guatemala. Neither the CIA nor embassy officials nor the military attachés ever claimed that the Guatemalan army was infiltrated by communists—and the army, they noted, was Guatemala's key institution.

But they were worried about the future. "The Communists," the CIA had warned as early as 1952, "will attempt to subvert or neutralize the Army."[11] The agency also feared that, under pressure from Arbenz and the PGT, the army "might eventually be unable to retain the monopoly of weapons, and, although very reluctantly, agree to release weapons to a people's militia."[12]

More immediately, Arbenz's Guatemala threatened the stability of the region. It was the only country in the hemisphere that offered a friendly abode to persecuted communists, and it was actively engaged, U.S. officials believed, in subverting its neighbors. On this point, Washington was wrong. Unlike Arévalo, Arbenz did not meddle in the internal affairs of other countries.[13] But his agrarian reform was far more dangerous than Arévalo's Caribbean Legion had ever been: "Guatemala has become an increasing threat to the stability of Honduras and El Salvador. Its agrarian reform is a powerful propaganda weapon; its broad social program of aiding the workers and peasants in a victorious struggle against the upper classes and large foreign enterprises has a strong appeal to the populations of Central American neighbors where similar conditions prevail." Central America was small, the borders were porous, news traveled fast. "It was impossible to escape the contagion," asserted Marroquín Rojas, as the May 1954 strike paralyzed the north coast of Honduras, while from El Salvador, Osorio sent a message of fear. His country, he warned, "would be next on the list."[14]

Even without the hazy prospect of a communist takeover of Guatemala—and the more real threat to Guatemala's neighbors—Arbenz posed an intolerable challenge. In the heart of the American sphere of influence, in an upstart

[11] CIA, "Present Political Situation in Guatemala and Possible Developments during 1952," NIE-62, March 11, 1952, p. 5, Truman Papers, President's Secretary's File, Intelligence File, Box 254, TL.

[12] Interview with Bissell.

[13] Not surprisingly, neither U.S. officials nor Guatemala's neighbors were able to garner any proof of Guatemala's subversive efforts. The following is representative: "Despite repeated efforts on our part in Washington and San Salvador, the Salvadoran Government has not produced any . . . concrete evidence of Guatemalan aggression." (Leddy to Cabot, "Salvadoran Evidence of Guatemalan Aggression," July 31, 1953, p. 1, NA 714.00. See also AmEm San Salvador, McDermott to Cabot, Oct. 2, 1953, NA Lot 58D18 & 58D78, Box 1.)

[14] Quotations from: Burrows to Cabot, Dec. 23, 1953, NA Lot 57D95, Box 5; Clemente Marroquín Rojas, "Tal como lo dijimos está sucediendo," La Hora, May 17, 1954, p. 4; MemoConv (Krieg, Trigueros), May 13, 1954, RG84 G&C, Box 6, NA-S.

banana republic, there stood—proud, defiant—a president whose procom-munist sympathies were obvious, a president whose closest collaborators were communists. Worse, this president and his communist friends were success-ful. The agrarian reform was proceeding well, the PGT was gaining popular support, and basic freedoms were being upheld. It was an intolerable chal-lenge to America's sense of self-respect. Fortuny was right when he said, "They would have overthrown us even if we had grown no bananas."[15]

Eisenhower's Guatemala policy was no aberration; it was derailed neither by UFCO nor by Peurifoy nor by Senator Joseph McCarthy. It fit within a deeply held tradition, shared by Democrats and Republicans alike and centered on the intransigent assertion of U.S. hegemony over Central America and the Ca-ribbean. This intransigence, which climaxed in the series of military interven-tions linking the presidencies of Theodore Roosevelt, William Taft, and Woodrow Wilson, seemed tempered in the 1930s by the Good Neighbor Pol-icy of Franklin D. Roosevelt. But FDR's neighborliness was tested only once, for the dictators who infested the area during his presidency never questioned Washington's hegemony. The exception was Cuba, where in late 1933 the United States worked for the downfall of a young nationalist government, helping to usher in the long era of Batista's tyranny.[16]

Would Truman, had he remained in the White House for another term, have tried to overthrow Arbenz? In this realm of speculation, there are several guideposts. His administration became fiercely hostile to Arévalo, yet Aréva-lo's sins were trifling compared to those of Arbenz. Truman did approve a plan to unseat Arbenz, OPERATION FORTUNE, that was canceled only at Ache-son's urging. Would he have reactivated it as the agrarian reform unfolded? Would he have held back, as communist influence in Guatemala grew?[17]

---

[15] Interview with Fortuny. Many have explained the difference in attitude of the Eisenhower administration vis-à-vis the Guatemalan and the Bolivian revolutions by pointing out that there were no U.S. economic interests affected in Bolivia—a proof *a contrario*, therefore, of the economic motivation behind the U.S. intervention in Gua-temala. In fact, as the U.S. government correctly understood, the administration of Paz Estenssoro was not procommunist. It is also interesting, in this context, to note that Bolivia voted "correctly" at Caracas, that Bolivia agreed to cosponsor the Montevideo resolution and that it pledged its vote in advance to the United States.

[16] See Aguilar, *Cuba 1933*, pp. 152–229; Thomas, *Cuba*, pp. 634–88; Pérez, *Cuba*, pp. 266–75.

[17] The contrast between Truman's and Eisenhower's use of covert operations should not be drawn too starkly. While the heyday of covert operations was during the Eisen-hower administration, under Truman the agency launched a number of covert opera-tions in the Soviet Bloc, including the attempt to overthrow the government of Albania. Helms's comment is apt: "Truman okayed a good many decisions for covert operations

What is certain is that Truman never considered a *modus vivendi* with Guatemala except on his own terms: an end to the "persecution" of American companies and a comprehensive purge of those whom Washington deemed communists. This is what he had demanded of Arévalo, and this is what he demanded of Arbenz. Truman and Eisenhower, Democrats and Republicans were unable to think of Guatemala in terms other than the relationship between metropole and banana republic. America's imperial hubris was no aberration. It preceded Truman and continues well beyond Eisenhower.

As the Eisenhower administration's broadsides against Guatemala reached their crescendo, Republicans and Democrats sang the appropriate chorus in impressive bipartisan harmony. On June 22, as the invasion was underway, the minority leader, Lyndon Johnson, addressed the Senate. The Soviet Union had supported Guatemala's demand that the United Nations, rather than the OAS, handle the crisis. This, he declared, "was open, flagrant notice that the Communists are reserving the power to penetrate the Western Hemisphere by every means—espionage, sabotage, subversion, and ultimately open aggression." Johnson introduced Senate Concurrent Resolution 91, which reaffirmed that the United States must "prevent interference in Western Hemisphere affairs by the Soviet Communists."[18] The resolution was approved with a lone negative vote, that of William Langer, the maverick senator from North Dakota. "The Senate," Langer warned, "does not know all the facts."[19] This was the one expression of humility and the one call for restraint in U.S. policy toward Guatemala heard in the U.S. Congress between 1949— when the attacks on Arévalo began—and 1954. (In the House, Johnson's resolution was lauded as the expression of "the true courage and resolve which is embedded so strongly in the hearts of our countrymen." It passed without dissent.)[20]

If the Congress of the United States mistook the aggressor for the victim, so too did the American press. It had paid very little attention to the country in the Arévalo years. As a result, it had been easy prey for the helpful UFCO representatives. Then came Arbenz. As the "Red Jacobo" became notorious in the United States, journalists began to visit Guatemala more frequently. Many remained ignorant, ethnocentric, and shrouded in Cold War paranoia. Others relied less on obliging sources and gained a better understanding of the

---

that in later years he said he knew nothing about. It's all presidential deniability." (Interview with Helms.)

[18] June 22, 1954, *CR*-Senate, p. 8564. In its final form, the words "Soviet Communists" were replaced by "International Communist movement." (See ibid., June 25, 1954, pp. 8921–27.)

[19] Langer (R-N.Dak.), June 28, 1954, ibid., p. 9066.

[20] Jackson, June 29, 1954, *CR*-House, p. 9177; for the vote see p. 9179.

country.[21] But even they remained convinced that, whatever the peccadillos of a receding past, U.S. respect for the principle of nonintervention had been exemplary since Franklin Delano Roosevelt.

This self-righteousness became all the more shrill as PBSUCCESS gathered momentum: brutal Guatemala was bullying the long-suffering United States. When, in January 1954, the Arbenz government provided proof that the United States was plotting against it, the American press leaped into collective self-delusion and ardently embraced the lies of the State Department. While the Latin Americans stood transfixed in the weeks that followed Caracas, American journalists scoffed at their fears.

Given this attitude, the CIA did not have to do much to mask the involvement of the United States. "The figleaf was very transparent, threadbare," in the words of a CIA official.[22] During the invasion of Guatemala and after Arbenz's overthrow, a magic curtain was drawn around the United States. "There is no evidence that the United States provided material aid or guidance," Milton Bracker assured his readers. Castillo Armas, the *New York Times* explained, had enjoyed merely "the moral support of the United States," just as Arbenz had "the moral support of the Soviet Union."[23] The *New Republic*'s comment was equally penetrating: "It was just our luck that Castillo Armas did come by some second-hand lethal weapons from Heaven knows where."[24]

Even those journalists who hinted that they were not so gullible heeded what John Kennedy later called "the duty of self-restraint."[25] *Newsweek*'s remark

---

[21] Among these journalists was Sydney Gruson, of the *New York Times*. Gruson was intellectually honest, and by 1952 he knew Guatemala well. His articles "infuriated" Peurifoy, for they told of the popularity of the Arbenz regime, the success of the agrarian reform, the dedication of the Guatemalan communists, and the sterility of the opposition; in a May 1954 NSC meeting, Secretary Dulles "expressed very great concern about the Communist line" of Gruson's articles. Clearly, Gruson was not a mouthpiece of United Fruit, yet he himself had announced, in a November 1953 article, that Arbenz had become "a prisoner of the embrace he so long ago gave the Communists"— the kiss of death in the America of the 1950s. (Quotations from: Salisbury, *Without Fear*, p. 479; "Memorandum of Discussion at the 199th Meeting of the National Security Council," May 27, 1954, *FRUS*, 1952–1954, 4:1132; "Guatemala Reds Increase Powers," *NYT*, Nov. 6, 1953, p. 3.) In early June, the Dulles brothers successfully asked the *Times* to remove Gruson from the Guatemalan story. (See Salisbury, *Without Fear*, pp. 478–83.)

[22] Interview with Kirkpatrick.

[23] Bracker, "The Lessons of the Guatemalan Struggle," *New York Times Magazine*, July 11, 1954, p. 39; "Guatemala: Out Leftists" (edit.), *NYT*, July 4, 1954, D2.

[24] "We Won't Turn the Clock Back—Maybe," *New Republic*, July 19, 1954, p. 10.

[25] Kennedy to newspaper publishers, Apr. 27, 1961, quoted by Houghton, "The Cuban Invasion," p. 426. "The press," Richard Bissell observed dryly, "had not yet gotten into the habit of blaming everything on the CIA." (Interview with Bissell.)

is typical of this style of the fleeting and unprobed innuendo: "The United States, aside from whatever gumshoe work the Central Intelligence Agency may or may not have been busy with, had kept hands strictly off." Washington could have cleaned up the situation "overnight if necessary: by halting coffee purchases, shutting off oil and gasoline from Guatemala, or as a last resort, by promoting a border incident and sending Marines to help the Hondurans. Instead it followed the letter of the law." Arbenz had been overthrown "in the best possible way: by the Guatemalans."[26] James Reston adopted a similar, cryptic style: "If somebody wants to start a revolution against the Communists in, say, Guatemala, it is no good talking to Foster Dulles. But Allen Dulles, head of the Central Intelligence Agency, is a more active man. He has been watching the Guatemalan situation for a long time."[27] Reston quickly moved onto other, less contentious subjects. The discreet works of the CIA were of no concern to patriotic journalists.[28]

The credulity and the complicity of the American press allowed the Eisenhower administration to broadcast the big lie, to present the fall of Arbenz "as dramatic evidence that the idea of freedom was one for which men were willing to fight and die."[29] For Eisenhower, notes one of his closest aides, "it was very important not only to achieve the objective, but how it would be achieved."[30] It was important, that is, for Eisenhower to be able to boast: "The people of Guatemala in a magnificent effort have liberated themselves from the shackles of international communist direction and reclaimed their right of self-determination."[31] The press took up his cry, joining in the celebration of what the *New York Times* called "the first successful anti-Communist revolt since the last war."[32] It was a time for rejoicing, not for questioning. What Oswald Garrison Villard wrote in 1918 about the American press's handling of the U.S. occupations of Haiti and the Dominican Republic, held true thirty-six years later:

[26] "Guatemala: The Price of Prestige," *Newsweek*, July 26, 1954, p. 40. For articles in a comparable vein, see "A Place where Reds Didn't Win," *U.S. News and World Report*, July 30, 1954, pp. 44–45 and "Guatemala," *Time*, July 12, 1954, pp. 38–39. Even *The Nation*, which had been critical of U.S. policy in Guatemala, drew back at the moment of intervention with the lame, "but now we simply do not know the facts." ("Guatemala Guinea Pig," edit., July 10, 1954, pp. 21–23, quote p. 22.)

[27] "With the Dulles Brothers in Darkest Guatemala," *NYT*, June 20, 1954, D8.

[28] There is no study of the failure of the American press to investigate beneath the figleaf of PBSUCCESS, but there are several studies of its similar blindness during the months that preceded the Bay of Pigs. See Bernstein and Gordon, "Press"; Aronson, *Press*, pp. 153–69; Salisbury, *Without Fear*, pp. 137–64.

[29] Vice President Nixon quoted in "Nixon Leads Fiesta on Party Centenary," *NYT*, July 7, 1954, p. 1, quoted from p. 16.

[30] Interview with Goodpaster.

[31] "Transcript of Eisenhower Press Conference," *NYT*, July 1, 1954, p. 10.

[32] "Red Defeat in Guatemala" (edit.), *NYT*, July 1, 1954, p. 24.

There were not more than five journals in this country which took the trouble to examine into the facts, or the reasons for the Government's action, or that sought for independent knowledge as to what led up to this development. There was the usual chorus of absolute approval. America could do no wrong; why inquire? If the desideratum is a watchful, well-informed, intelligent, and independent press, bent upon preserving the liberties of ourselves and our neighbors, then truly are our newspapers sorely lacking.[33]

The press in Western Europe and Latin America was not so flaccid. The figleaf allowed those who did not want to see the truth to avert their eyes, but the others—the majority—were not so coy. "At a time when diplomatic successes are rare in the United States," remarked *Le Monde* on July 2,

> it was predictable that the Secretary of State would not forego the opportunity to celebrate the victory of Good versus Evil in Guatemala. This he did in last night's televised speech. . . . The speech will not endure as a masterpiece of eloquence. But it will endure as evidence of the Americans' "clean conscience," of the hypocrisy with which some Americans condemn the colonialism and the subversive plots of others, but never reflect on the modern forms of economic colonialism or on the methods they themselves use to get rid of governments that they do not like.[34]

Few in Western Europe believed that Guatemala had been on the verge of becoming a communist bastion. Many thought that Eisenhower had brought down Arbenz on behalf of United Fruit; others thought his behavior that of the lord of the manor using "a cannon . . . to render a poacher harmless."[35] It is not surprising, then, that Assistant Secretary Holland complained of "the bad European press."[36]

But the irritation of the Europeans was tempered by fatalism: the Caribbean was the Americans' backyard. The Europeans might wish that the United States behaved in a more mature, more generous manner in the region, but in the final analysis, it was Washington's affair. Europe was a distant bystander, and no direct European interests were at stake. "Criticism of and doubts about U.S. policy" are widespread, reported the Foreign Broadcast Information Ser-

[33] "The Press and the International Situation," *The Nation*, Mar. 21, 1918, p. 315. Nancy Mitchell, currently working on a book on Wilson's Caribbean policy, kindly called this article to my attention.

[34] "M. Foster Dulles célèbre le succès de la vertu," *Le Monde*, Paris, July 2, 1954, p. 4. For the text of Dulles' speech, see the *NYT*, July 1, 1954, p. 2.

[35] *Nieuwe Rotterdammer* (edit.), quoted in Foreign Broadcast Information Service (FBIS), "World Comment on the Guatemalan Revolution," June 25, 1954, p. 8.

[36] TelConv (Holland, JFD), June 28, 1954, 5:45 p.m., DP, JFD:CS, Box 8, EL. Franco's Spain, Salazar's Portugal and autocratic Greece were significant exceptions. (FBIS [see n. 35 above], p. 8.)

vice, but the criticism "is neither heated nor large in volume."[37] A U.S. official predicted calmly, "It will die within the next few days."[38] And so it did.

The one European country in which the Guatemala story left more than a fleeting impression was England. For the British, who prided themselves on their "special relationship" with the United States, the crisis had been doubly humiliating. The quarantine had been a slap to England's maritime pride and American browbeating for their Security Council vote had added to the insult. For several weeks, the opposition kept the issue alive, but by late summer it had faded from the British press and from the minds of the British people.[39]

The Latin Americans were less philosophical. "Washington was shocked by the wave of pro-Guatemalan and anti-U.S. demonstrations that swept over Latin America," noted *Newsweek*.[40] Only those countries where the dictator's rule was absolute, like Trujillo's Dominican Republic and Somoza's Nicaragua,[41] remained quiet. "Our people . . . are frightened by reactions all over," Foster Dulles told his brother,[42] while the *New York Times* reported from Brazil that it was "difficult" to find anyone who did not believe that the United States was involved in the fall of Arbenz.[43] PBSUCCESS, most analysts now agree, left a lasting legacy of anti-Americanism in the region.

This conclusion must be tempered. Those who spat on Vice President Nixon in Lima in May 1958 and those who threw stones at him a few days later in Caracas did surely reflect Latin America's deep anger at the Eisenhower administration and, more generally, at the United States. But grievances beyond

[37] FBIS (see n. 35 above), p. 6.

[38] McBride to Merchant and Tyler, "French Reactions to Guatemalan Affair," June 29, 1954, NA Lot 58D18 & 58D78, Box 3.

[39] See the excellent account in Meers, "Pebble on the Beach," pp. 68–82.

[40] "Guatemala: The Strange Revolt," *Newsweek*, July 5, 1954, p. 46.

[41] Even the independent Nicaraguan daily *La Prensa* espoused the U.S. position with enthusiasm worthy of Somoza. During the Caracas conference, it lambasted Toriello, accusing him of "being Moscow's plaything, disrupting inter-American solidarity, and hurling ridiculous charges against the United States." ("Ha sido un fracaso diplomático el del canciller Toriello," Mar. 13, 1954, p. 2.) According to *La Prensa*, no one could accuse the United States of one single violation of the principle of nonintervention. Since the days of FDR, Washington had, if anything, "erred on the side of caution, scared of awakening even the slightest suspicion of interventionism." ("El tabú de la no intervención," Mar. 16, 1954, p. 2.) Not once did *La Prensa* consider the possibility that the United States might be behind the Guatemalan rebels. It praised the overthrow of Arbenz as "the liquidation of the Red threat." ("Guatemala: índice y termometro," July 6, 1954, p. 2.)

[42] TelConv (JFD, AWD), June 24, 1954, 2:01 p.m., DP:TCS, Box 2, EL. See also "Unofficial Reactions in Latin America to the Guatemalan Situation, June 18–22," enclosed in Burgin to Raine, June 23, 1954, NA 714.00 and CIA, *Current Intelligence Review*, SC no. 13342, July 8, 1954, pp. 8–9.

[43] "U.S. Prestige Ebbs in Latin America," *NYT*, June 27, 1954, p. 10.

PBSUCCESS had stoked this fury: the embrace of Latin America's dictators, the support for any and all American companies, the denial of economic aid. Had Eisenhower refrained from PBSUCCESS and maintained the rest of his hemispheric policy, it is doubtful that the reception of Nixon in Lima and Caracas would have been less angry. Furthermore, given his hemispheric policy, had Eisenhower refrained from ousting Arbenz, his restraint would have been seen by many as weakness.

No doubt, geography and history made Guatemala's plight more poignant in Havana than, say, in Buenos Aires. The Guatemalan drama contributed to the radicalization of Che Guevara—who was in Guatemala when Arbenz fell. And it embittered Cuban nationalists like Fidel Castro. The fall of Arbenz, we are told, taught the Cubans and Che Guevara a precious lesson: "We cannot guarantee the Revolution before cleansing the armed forces," Che told Castro.[44]

The Cubans' quarrel with the United States, however, had deep roots. What would have been different had PBSUCCESS not occurred? Not the bitterness over the past—the Platt amendment, the overthrow of Grau, the coddling of Batista. Not the shame of seeing Havana a brothel for American tourists and vast sectors of the country's economy in U.S. hands. The nationalism of Fidel Castro and those who surrounded him had no need of Arbenz's drama. Nor did Castro need to learn from Arbenz's experience that he should not trust Batista's army.

PBSUCCESS had, however, a more real cost for the United States. It inflated the self-confidence of the CIA. ("It induced euphoria: we can do anything if we want to!")[45] Coming in the wake of the overthrow of Mossadegh, it strengthened confidence in the agency's abilities and so contributed to the disaster of the Bay of Pigs, the Cuban nemesis of Washington's victory in Guatemala.

"I don't think that when we were planning the Bay of Pigs we had a clear understanding of why Arbenz had resigned," Richard Bissell muses. "All too seldom," he adds, "did the CIA conduct postmortems of successful covert operations. I never saw a postmortem of AJAX and, to the best of my knowledge, there was no postmortem of PBSUCCESS."[46] His point is enlarged by Lyman Kirkpatrick, the inspector general of the CIA, whose office was expressly excluded from PBSUCCESS. "After I got wind of the operation," he recalls, "I wrote a memo to Allen Dulles: I wanted him to let two men from my office observe PBSUCCESS. That memo got the fastest turnaround I've ever seen. Within an hour the thing was back on my desk: 'Permission refused,'

---

[44] Schlesinger and Kinzer, *Bitter Fruit*, p. 184 (quoted); Immerman, *CIA in Guatemala*, pp. 187–88.

[45] Interview with Kirkpatrick.

[46] Interviews with Bissell (quoted), Helms, and Kirkpatrick.

signed AWD.''[47] After Arbenz fell, the CIA made no effort to probe the Guatemalan officers and other protagonists to find out what really had happened in Guatemala, what really had brought down Arbenz. Even in the absence of this, notes Bissell, a careful internal study would have been very useful. It was not done.[48]

Flushed with victory, the CIA transformed PBSUCCESS into an impressive exploit. Relief swept away any consideration of the flaws of the operation—the failure to penetrate the military, the failure of the fifth column,[49] the failure to plan beyond the first stage of the invasion. Only seven years later was there a postmortem of sorts of the Guatemalan operation. In his review of the Bay of Pigs, Inspector General Kirkpatrick looked back at PBSUCCESS. ''I can still remember Allen Dulles' face after I had gone over everything and told him: 'The Agency did a miserable job.' ''[50]

Boastful operatives have spun the image of an omnipresent CIA that had penetrated every nook and cranny of Guatemala—the army, in particular. We are told, for example, ''a CIA staff officer, documented and disguised as a European businessman, entered Guatemala and achieved the defection of a senior officer on Arbenz's staff. Through him we were able to gain up-to-the-minute situation intelligence concerning Arbenz's intentions and the disposition of his troops.'' Elsewhere we read that during the invasion ''the CIA had authorized its paramilitary teams at the front lines to promise cash payments to any officer thinking of defecting, and one army commander reportedly accepted $60,000 to surrender his troops.''[51]

The truth is more banal. Throughout PBSUCCESS, the CIA was poorly informed about developments in the Guatemalan army; once the invasion began, it was unsure how the officers would respond. As for the authorization to the CIA ''paramilitary teams on the front lines,'' notes Bissell, ''we couldn't have done it, because we didn't have anyone on the government side at the front.''[52] Nor, for that matter, did the CIA have anyone on the rebel side at the front.

[47] Interview with Kirkpatrick.

[48] Interview with Bissell.

[49] ''From the beginning, I thought that those who were counting on a fifth column were a bit unrealistic,'' comments Bissell. The arrests of January, May, and June 1954 destroyed whatever shaky infrastructure the CIA had managed to build in Guatemala. Yet the hope remained that Arbenz's foes would be galvanized into action by the invasion, by the radio propaganda, and by the saboteurs who had infiltrated the country. ''I don't know how much the CIA appreciated that it could not succeed,'' DCM Krieg remarked later. (Interviews with Bissell and Krieg.)

[50] Interview with Kirkpatrick. On Kirkpatrick's postmortem of the Bay of Pigs, see Ranelagh, *Agency*, pp. 380–81 and Kirkpatrick, ''Paramilitary Case Study.''

[51] Quotations from Hunt, *Undercover*, pp. 99–100, and Schlesinger and Kinzer, *Bitter Fruit*, p. 189.

[52] Interview with Bissell.

"We weren't allowed to go with them," recalls a CIA agent who had trained the rebels in Honduras. "We weren't supposed to have anything to do with them. It would have been a disaster if one of us had been captured."[53]

But this nod to the figleaf was not what caused the agency to remain ignorant, over the next week, of what went on in Zacapa and even in the capital. Very few officers had joined PBSUCCESS, and not one of them occupied a sensitive position. This failure is illuminated by Richard Bissell. In the Directorate of Plans, he explains, there was

> a lack of expertise about Central America. I would be surprised if there was anyone at Opa Locka—or at the CIA Washington headquarters of PBSUCCESS—who had a thoughtful understanding of what was going on in Guatemala. Once PBSUCCESS started rolling, the CIA sent more agents to Guatemala. But they were new to the country, so they weren't the best men to penetrate the armed forces. This is a slow, professional job that requires a lot of time; all our concentration was on things that could bring quick results. The CIA gained very few officers for PBSUCCESS. In fact, to the very limited extent that the U.S. was able to penetrate the Guatemalan armed forces, this was mainly through the military attachés and the military missions, rather than through the CIA.[54]

But the military attachés, too, had their problems. Like the embassy and the State Department, they understood the obvious: the Guatemalan army was not communist; it was opportunistic, nationalistic (especially the younger officers), and loyal to Arbenz despite its uneasiness about his ties to the communists. PBSUCCESS demanded that the military attachés scare the Guatemalan officers, and they were the right men for the job—brash and burly.[55] Subtlety was not their strong card. They succeeded in scaring, but not in understanding. "Socially, we knew the Guatemalan officers very well," the army attaché remembers. "They were very gracious, easy to talk to, but when you tried to pin them down, it was very difficult." DCM Krieg concurs, "For decades, the fear of speaking against the government had been instilled in the officer corps. It was extremely difficult to break down their exterior friendliness. They didn't mind coming to your house, having a drink—but when it came to important questions, they hid behind a wall of clichés and generalities."[56] This broad failure to penetrate the Guatemalan armed forces and to grasp the extent of their demoralization led the CIA to underestimate the chances of success before Castillo Armas crossed the border and to grow increasingly despondent during the first week of the invasion. It explains why Eisenhower's decision

---

[53] Interview with Roettinger.

[54] Interview with Bissell. Confirmed by interview with Kirkpatrick.

[55] Based on the reports of the military attachés, on Col. Hanford's "Communist Beachhead," and interviews with Col. McCormick and Maj. Chavez.

[56] Quotations from interviews with Col. McCormick and Krieg.

on June 22 to replace the two planes lost by the rebels has been presented as an historic moment when the fate of the operation hung in the balance.[57] This notion that, as Kirkpatrick himself has written, the Guatemalan operation "only succeeded by the narrowest of margins," remains the established truth.[58] In fact, Castillo Armas had won before he crossed the border. He had won because the Guatemalan army was convinced that his defeat would trigger a U.S. intervention.

Taking into account how insecure the CIA had been about the operation, it is striking how little contingency planning had been done. To some degree this was inevitable: "In a covert operation," argues Bissell, "one can plan the first phases, but not what happens next." In PBSUCCESS, the detailed planning of the CIA had extended only until the moment Castillo Armas's force crossed into Guatemala. And after that? "Very little." Through the first week of the invasion, "as the fog of war was pretty dense," and Castillo Armas floundered, the CIA waited passively and with growing pessimism. Finally, as the second week began, Allen Dulles and Wisner spun into action. In a meeting in Allen Dulles' office, they decided "to take all Castillo Armas' troops, to withdraw them from Guatemala, and to shift the attack around into a seaborne operation against Puerto Barrios." This was a plan born of despair. "We thought Armas was going to lose," comments Bissell, who was at the meeting and was told "to go to New York to commission a ship." The operation, he recalls, was called off "when we learned that Arbenz was resigning."[59] Whatever it might say about the CIA's lack of foresight, it is eloquent testimony to the agency's ignorance of developments at the front.

Likewise, Bissell remarks, "No thought had been given to what to do should Castillo Armas fail."[60] Given the U.S. assessment of the threat posed by the Arbenz government, the humiliation that Castillo Armas's defeat would have represented, and the fact that it would have strengthened Arbenz, it is hard to imagine that Eisenhower would have accepted failure. Passivity would have been humiliating abroad. The Guatemalan military and the Latin American governments, who knew that Castillo Armas was Washington's man, would have seen it as weakness, not wisdom. And passivity would have been humiliating at home, where Republicans and Democrats would have railed against the administration that had come to power promising to roll back communism.

[57] Eisenhower, *Mandate*, pp. 425–26. See also Schlesinger and Kinzer, *Bitter Fruit*, pp. 177–78; Ambrose and Immerman, *Ike's Spies*, pp. 232–33; Ranelagh, *Agency*, pp. 266–67; Higgins, *Perfect Failure*, p. 32.

[58] Kirkpatrick, "Paramilitary Case Study," p. 37.

[59] Quoted from interview with Bissell. An operation against Puerto Barrios had been attempted, with disastrous results, on June 21 (see above, p. 327).

[60] Interview with Bissell.

Domestic pressure and the immense imbalance between the two countries would have sparked Eisenhower's imagination. Perhaps he would have imposed unilateral sanctions. Guatemala was totally dependent on imported oil, shipped in by three American companies and Shell. As the general counsel of the CIA remarked, "The oil companies were very cooperative at that time. Very cooperative." On June 16, 1954, Allen Dulles met with representatives of one of the four to discuss "the small country down south."[61] Was this a harbinger, should Castillo Armas fail? Or perhaps a direct military intervention would have been justified by inventing, first, a border incident between Honduras and Guatemala. Eisenhower "firmly believed that the presence of a communist-controlled regime in our backyard was unacceptable," a close aide recalls. "He had a great inventory of principles in order, some would say, to rationalize whatever he wanted to do."[62]

Eisenhower faced no awkward decision. Arbenz fell. The ease with which his regime collapsed helped pave the way for the Bay of Pigs. Overconfidence, lack of reflection on the lessons of PBSUCCESS, and what Kirkpatrick has called the "amateurishness" of the young agency[63] caused the CIA to launch the Cuban operation as if it were a grand sequel to the Guatemalan one. This, despite the fact that the two situations were fundamentally different: Castro had his own army; Arbenz did not. Therefore, PBSUCCESS was a psychological operation that needed only a minimum paramilitary component—the "spark"; the Bay of Pigs was, or should have been, a military operation. If the CIA had paused to reflect on the former, they would have recoiled from the latter. Instead, the agency wallowed in euphoria.

The ease with which Arbenz collapsed held another cost for U.S. policymakers. As Eisenhower's assistant secretary of state for Latin America said, it "tended to blind a little bit the eyes of all us."[64] It reinforced Washington's complacency: no radical challenge would succeed in the American Mediterranean; no changes were necessary in U.S. policy toward the region. It is conceivable that, had Eisenhower refrained from PBSUCCESS, the United States might have learned that an unsympathetic regime need not represent a threat to its security, that coexistence was possible. It might further be argued that,

[61] Quotations from interview with Houston and from TelConv (JFD, AWD), June 16, 1954, 11:20 a.m., DP:TCS, Box 2, EL. Commenting on this document, Bissell stressed that to the best of his knowledge, the oil weapon had never been considered as part of PBSUCCESS. (Interview with Bissell.) As already noted, the United States wanted to appear to be refraining from unilateral sanctions and to be scrupulously respecting the OAS charter.

The three American companies were California Standard, Esso, and Texaco. (Peurifoy, Jan. 26, 1954, U.S. Congress, HCFA, pp. 466, 476.)

[62] Interview with Goodpaster.

[63] Interview with Kirkpatrick.

[64] Rubottom, "Oral History Interview," p. 48.

had Arbenz been allowed to end his term, the example of Guatemala's successful agrarian reform would have forced the neighboring regimes—in El Salvador, above all—to introduce reforms. One might retort, however, that without PBSUCCESS, Washington would have remained just as intransigent and narrow-minded, and that the Hondurans and the Salvadorans would have responded to the Guatemalan contagion with repression, not reform. Beyond these speculations, one conclusion remains: the cost of victory was, for the United States, very low. Those who paid were the Guatemalans.

In 1944, the fall of the dictators had opened the possibility of hope in the country of eternal tyranny. To the eloquent and charismatic Juan José Arévalo fell the task of defining the meaning of the revolution. Arévalo was honest, eager, and confident. His immense ego shines through his countless speeches, his flowery statements about Spiritual Socialism, and the adulatory biographies that rolled off the government presses during his presidency. Yet he failed to address the problem of American control of vital sectors of the country's infrastructure; he failed to address the problem of the country's retrogressive tax structure; and he failed to address the problem of land distribution. He benefited from a period of high coffee prices, and he enacted some worthwhile economic measures, but he lacked a coherent economic program. As the World Bank noted in 1950, "The developmental efforts are so haphazard that resources are dissipated in a number of inadequate and uncoordinated projects."[65]

There could have been no Arbenz, however, without first an Arévalo who introduced political freedoms and social reforms. The men who would form Arbenz's kitchen cabinet—and Arbenz himself—awoke politically in the Arévalo years. Yet there is a clear break between the two presidencies. "Arevalismo and Arbencismo were two very different things—two very different ways of governing," Arévalo himself has stated. "Arbencismo warped the revolution . . . and welcomed the communist leaders into the president's office."[66]

Arbenz did more than welcome the communist leaders into his office. With their help, he brought agrarian reform to the Guatemalan countryside. This is the crucial difference between the two leaders. As the Office of Intelligence and Research had concluded, "no positive action" had been taken by the Arévalo administration to correct the extremely skewed land tenure system that rotted the Guatemalan countryside, home to 80 percent of the country's population.[67] The "revision of the Labor Code was virtually the only incursion which the revolution made in the countryside under Arévalo."[68]

[65] MemoConv (Britnell, Miller, Siracusa), Aug. 28, 1950, p. 1, NA 714.00.
[66] Arévalo, *Carta Política*, pp. 2–3.
[67] OIR, "Agrarian Reform in Guatemala," no. 6001, Mar. 5, 1953, p. 1, NA.
[68] Alexander, "Guatemalan Revolution," pp. 5–6.

True, it would have been very difficult for Arévalo to implement a comprehensive agrarian reform program, at least until the death of Arana, since he did not control the army. The impression that emerges from the written evidence, however, and from Arévalo's own statements on the land tenure problem in Guatemala, and from interviews with men who were close to Arévalo is that it was neither the army nor the upper class that restrained him. He was a middle class Ladino; his family owned land. The world of the Indian was distant and fearsome. Agrarian reform was not in his plans—whether on privately owned lands or on the Fincas Nacionales. This should provoke neither surprise nor indignation; it was typical of his class.

Less typical was Arbenz's behavior. Like Arévalo before him, he wanted Guatemala to be a nation, not a banana republic. But unlike Arévalo, Arbenz—this white son of a Swiss-German father, this military officer—loosened the knots that stifled his country. As he prepared Decree 900, he was moved by his own beliefs, not by external pressure. The revolutionary parties had no desire for such a step, and the rural masses were too weak to demand it. When Arbenz sought to justify the agrarian reform to his officers by saying, "If we don't do it ourselves, the peasants will do it themselves—with machetes,"[69] they rightly understood that he was dissembling: the peasants, so long oppressed, were not demanding what they so desperately needed. Indeed, many peasants were initially deeply wary of Decree 900. The impetus came from Arbenz.

Arbenz's partner was the PGT. No other partner was possible, for no political party shared Arbenz's commitment to social reform and his willingness to put the interests of the nation before his own. The dedication, honesty, and selflessness of the leaders of the PGT were noted even by the U.S. embassy.

A hybrid regime evolved that was unprecedented in the region. A small group of idealists—Arbenz and the leaders of the Communist party—promoted a revolution from above, but not a doctrinaire program that would have been disastrous for their country. The communists spearheaded the agrarian reform, but they did not seek collectivization.

Some American intellectuals who were sympathetic to the reforms complained at the time that the PGT was perverting the revolution. How nice it would have been to have the revolution without the communists![70] This is

[69] Interview with Col. Guillén, quoting Arbenz.

[70] Alexander, for example, wrote, "The Communists . . . were able to divert the Guatemalan Revolution from its course and convert it into one more weapon of Soviet foreign policy." (*Communism*, p. 362.) Alexander, then a young professor at Rutgers University, had been one of the most sensitive U.S. observers of the Guatemalan revolution, clearly sympathetic to social reform and critical of United Fruit and the State Department's support of it. His several excellent articles include: "Revolution in Guatemala," "The Guatemalan Revolution and Communism," "Communists Gain Strength in Guatemala," and "The Guatemalan Communists."

unrealistic. The PGT's role—as advisers and as implementors—was essential. As Arbenz's widow observed, "Alone, he could not have done it."[71]

Granted, Arbenz could have had communists as allies and not been one of them. The evidence, however, indicates that the communists were his closest personal and political friends and that, at least by 1952, he felt like one of them, even though he did not join the party until 1957.

Nearly forty years after his overthrow, Jacobo Arbenz remains an elusive, enigmatic figure. He left no books and no articles presenting his views, arguing his case—only a few reticent interviews. His photographs as an officer, as president, show a teutonic man—good looking but with a distant expression. A different Arbenz emerges in conversations with his few close friends and in yellowed letters that his wife may read aloud but will not lend—personal passages that provide a glimpse of the man who had a soft smile and who had wanted to be a reformer without knowing exactly what it meant, a man who did not become a cold ideologue, but who dreamed a passionate dream. Introverted and brilliant, as the CIA noted.[72] And shy, and modest. "Jacobo never talked of Arbencismo," his wife has written. "Very rarely, in fact almost never, did he give interviews to the television, press or radio. He abhorred personality cults."[73] During his presidency, the government presses printed no book extolling his merits. Here, too, he was unlike Arévalo.

Jacobo Arbenz is not one of history's giants. He made serious mistakes; he was naive. Irrespective of his political beliefs, he should have kept a tight rein on the administration media. The tone of *DCA*, other government publications, and the radio was needlessly provocative, as were actions such as the minute of silence for Stalin. He underestimated the threat from the United States until late 1953 when the documents provided by Delgado made it irrefutable that the United States was plotting against him.

Arbenz, who had renounced Arévalo's activist foreign policy, failed to grasp how completely the Inter-American system was dominated by the United States, how completely Bolívar had been replaced by Monroe. He believed—tenaciously, naively—that other Latin American governments would stand up to Foster Dulles at Caracas. Later, he turned his hopes to the United Nations, blind to the fact that international law was as impotent to help him as it would be for the Hungarians in 1956, the Dominicans in 1965, or the Czechs in 1968.

The complexities of Arbenz's personality and of his position are distilled in his relationship with the army, a relationship that embodied the strain, the distance he had traveled in his own life. He was a respected officer, and, in-

[71] Interview with María de Arbenz.

[72] CIA, "Guatemala," SR-46, July 27, 1950, p. 39, Truman Papers, President's Secretary's File, Intelligence File, Box 261, TL.

[73] María de Arbenz, letter to the author, Jan. 27, 1988, p. 19.

creasingly, he was a communist. These two worlds—the communist and the military—were bridged by Arbenz alone. He alone was the fulcrum. His handling of the officers was deft. By doling out perks, by maintaining the army's monopoly of weapons, by not spreading communist propaganda in the ranks, and by wielding his prestige and power, he established an effective *modus vivendi* with them. This was the best that could have been expected: there was no way he could have subverted the army, that is, indoctrinated the officers. Nevertheless, the officers—conservative, contemptuous of the Indians, anticommunist—accepted Decree 900.

Arbenz's behavior was also naive and contradictory, traits that are crystallized in the story of the *Alfhem*. His decision to break the army's monopoly of the weapons reveals his doubts and fears that the army, under the strain of growing U.S. pressure, would betray him; at the same time, however, he had earmarked some of the weapons to strengthen the very army he was beginning to distrust. Furthermore, he continued to overestimate the loyalty and the nationalism of his officers. He failed to grasp the meaning of their list of demands of June 5, 1954, and persisted in his belief that the army would fight an exile invasion as long as there was no direct U.S. participation.

If Arbenz underestimated the U.S. threat and overestimated the loyalty of the military, so too did the PGT. If Arbenz believed that the Organization of American States and the United Nations could give pause to the American aggressor, so too did the PGT. "If we had been more mature, we would have faced the threat of intervention squarely, and we would have gotten organized to work underground. That would have been the true mark of maturity: to have prepared for winter."[74]

And so we return to the words of Alfredo Guerra Borges with which this book began: "It wasn't a great conspiracy, and it wasn't a child's game. We were just a group of young men searching for our destiny."[75] It was a revolution from above; it was the feat of a small group of men. They proceeded alone, in an international environment that became increasingly inhospitable. "We were a little skiff in a raging tempest," recalls María de Arbenz. "We were pitted against enormous waves."[76] These waves, this tempest were not of Guatemalan origin. For one fact is clear, and makes the Guatemalan tragedy all the more poignant, just as it made intervention seem all the more necessary to the United States: the civilian opposition had no chance of overthrowing the government, and there was no hope that the military would move against Arbenz. The plotters within the army were weak and ineffectual. The officers' betrayal had one cause only: fear of U.S. intervention.

Jacobo Arbenz provided Guatemala with the best government it has ever

---

[74] Interview with Fortuny.
[75] Interview with Guerra Borges.
[76] Interview with María de Arbenz.

had. He embarked on the first comprehensive development plan in the history of Guatemala whereas his predecessor had not even outlined such a plan, and he presided over the most successful agrarian reform in the history of Central America. Within eighteen months, "the agrarian reform had reached its half-way mark":[77] five hundred thousand peasants had received land without disrupting the country's economy. Decree 900 brought more than land to the poor: it broadened political freedom in the countryside. Serfs were becoming citizens.

By the end of Arbenz's term, hundreds of thousands of peasants would have been solidly established on land granted them by Decree 900. In a fundamental sense, Arbenz's successor would have inherited a Guatemala far different from that Arévalo had bequeathed to him in 1951. But the Pax Americana prevailed. Nowhere in Central America or the Caribbean has U.S. intervention been so decisive and so baneful in shaping the future of a country.

By the time Castillo Armas died, in July 1957, he had accomplished, in the words of a close aide, a "herculean feat": all but two hundred of the "squatters"—the beneficiaries of Decree 900—had been chased off the land they had received under Arbenz.[78]

In the early summer of 1954, several American newspapers had demanded that Arbenz not be replaced by a regime of the far right. The *New York Times* had intoned, "We have a right to expect . . . that revolts against the tyranny of the Left shall not bring in a tyranny of the Right."[79] Many U.S. officials had also expressed the hope that the new regime would not be embarrassingly reactionary. Castillo Armas, cabled Peurifoy, should proceed at once to "some land distribution" and a "prompt reorganization of non-Communist labor movement should be genuinely and intelligently encouraged to prevent workers from looking back on Communist unions as only protectors of their rights."[80]

There was no way, however, that the United States could have replaced Arbenz with a centrist, moderate government—even if it had truly wanted to—for the center and the moderates had supported Arbenz. The only Guatemalans who had been eager to overthrow him, and the only Guatemalans who were not tainted by collaboration with his regime, were those who bitterly opposed all social reform. To oust Arbenz was to return them to power.

Neither the press nor U.S. officials faced this unpleasant fact. Waving the

[77] Krieg to DOS, no. 818, Mar. 29, 1954, p. 1, NA 814.20.

[78] Montenegro, "El capitán Montenegro defiende." The figure is approximate; see also Handy, "Reform," esp. pp. 11–12. On the Castillo Armas government see Handy, *Gift*, pp. 149–52; Bishop, "Guatemalan Labor," pp. 162–99; McClintock, *American Connection*, 2:28–45; Toriello, *A dónde va Guatemala?*

[79] "As Guatemala Settles Down" (edit.), *NYT*, July 6, 1954, p. 22.

[80] Peurifoy to SecState, no. 157, Aug. 4, 1954, p. 2, NA 714.00.

wand of rhetoric, American journalists eagerly transformed Castillo Armas into a progressive leader—or one who was, at least, not altogether unsavory. Castillo Armas, pronounced the *New York Times* in a September 1954 editorial, "has made a number of sound decisions and is following progressive policies."[81]

The U.S. embassy was, initially, more honest. In the summer of 1954, it noted "the mass arrests of small agrarian leaders," the flouting of the labor laws and "panic, bitterness and disillusionment" among urban and rural workers. After Castillo Armas enacted "a statute reversing the Agrarian Reform Law," DCM Krieg commented, "there is no blinking at the fact that the new Statute is a long step backwards from the agrarian policies of the previous regime."[82] Some embassy officials were not surprised. In a 1952 memo calling for the overthrow of Arbenz, Second Secretary Hill had concluded, "the Department must . . . face up to the probability that an 'undemocratic' regime is the only one which in the near future could hope to succeed the present one. There will be no immediate 'salvaging of the original aims of the revolution.' "[83]

What mattered, however, was that Castillo Armas be fervently anticommunist and pro-American. As U.S. officials decided that there was no longer any immediate communist threat in Guatemala, their lingering hesitations about Castillo Armas's social policies were papered over with complacency. Within a year, they had convinced themselves that their man was a moderate.[84]

[81] "Guatemala without Arbenz" (edit.), *NYT*, Sept. 11, 1954, p. 16. *The Nation* and *Christian Century* stated that Arbenz had been replaced by a tyranny of the right, but they were the exceptions. (See "The Right of Asylum," *The Nation*, July 17, 1954, pp. 41–42; "Guatemala Bulletin," *The Nation*, July 24, 1954, pp. 63–64; "Guatemala Takes Land From Peasants," *Christian Century*, Sept. 8, 1954, p. 1060; "Second Thoughts on Guatemala," *Christian Century*, Dec. 8, 1954, p. 1490.)

[82] Quotations from: Hill to SecState, no. 231, Sept. 1, 1954, p. 1, NA 714.00/9-2154; *JW* 33, Aug. 20, 1954, p. 5; Krieg to DOS, no. 73, July 29, 1954, p. 2, NA 814.20. See also Peurifoy to SecState, no. 160, Aug. 4, 1954; Krieg to SecState, no. 181, Aug. 11, 1954; Peurifoy to SecState, no. 194, Aug. 17, 1954; Peurifoy to SecState, no. 238, Sept. 2, 1954 (all NA 814.062); MemoConv (Hill, Celli), Dec. 29, 1954, RG84 G&C, Box 3, NA-S. Cursory references to peasant protests against the regime appear in the press in the first month after the fall of Arbenz: "Grupos rojos hacen masacres," *La Prensa*, Managua, July 2, 1954, p. 1; "Los campesinos levantan a los propietarios en contra del ejército," ibid., p. 3; "Troops Ordered Out," *NYT*, July 5, 1954, p. 3; "Castillo trasladará por aire a sus tropas," *La Prensa*, Managua, July 6, 1954, p. 3; "Nuevo zafarrancho comunista en Covadonga, Chiquimulilla," *La Hora*, July 26, 1954, p. 1.

[83] Hill to Ambassador, Oct. 2, 1952, p. 3, RG84 CF, Box 15, NA-S.

[84] One of the few exceptions was a June 19, 1956, CIA memo that bluntly noted that Castillo Armas "removed the Communists . . . but he has failed thus far to offer peasants and workers a constructive alternative." (*FRUS*, 1955–1957, 7:120–21.) A sense

In October 1954, Castillo Armas had himself enthroned as president for a six-year term after a plebiscite in which he received 99.99 percent of the vote.[85] He ruled with the support of the upper class, a purged army, and the Eisenhower administration[86] until his death in a murder that has never been solved. By then, the peace and social harmony that Arbenz had disturbed had returned to Guatemala, and the country had long ceased to be in the news in the United States. It was again the joy of American tourists with its pro-American elite, its Mayan ruins and its smiling, humble Indians who lived their quaint traditional life.

This comforting image masks the reality of Guatemala since the "liberation." Guatemala is a foreboding world of repression and violence; it holds the macabre record for human rights violations in Latin America.

Torture and death have been the final arbiters of Guatemalan society, the gods that determine behavior. Fear torments the oppressed and the oppressor. Fear gnaws even at the upper class: fear of the communists and fear of the Indians, fear of the military and fear of the future. Guatemala is ruled by the culture of fear.

It is the keynote that cuts through the cacophony of the many Guatemalan cultures—the Indian and the Ladino, the elite few and the miserable many, the town dweller and the peasant, the civilian and the military. It hails from the long night that began with the Spanish conquest, a conquest that is, for the Indians, a trauma from which they have not yet recovered.[87]

The Guatemalan revolution—Arbenz, above all, with his communist friends—challenged the culture of fear. In eighteen months, five hundred thousand people were given land. The culture of fear was loosening its grip over the great masses of the Guatemalan people. In a not distant future, it might have faded away, a distant nightmare.

---

of urgency returned to State Department dispatches only in the wake of Castillo Armas's death, as the acting president allowed a number of exiles, such as Guillermo Toriello, to return to Guatemala: "You should seek audience immediately with President Flores and emphasize to him my own concern over communist threat and potential which return of these undesirable elements presents for Guatemala," Foster Dulles ordered the American ambassador. "There is no room for complacency." (Dulles to AmEmG, Nov. 8, Dec. 6 [quoted] and Dec. 12, 1957, ibid., pp. 147–48, 150–52.)

[85] Conceding that the election had not been free, the *New York Times* advised its readers: "It is doubtless unfair to expect anything else so soon after a revolution against a Communist-dominated regime." ("Voting in Guatemala" [edit.], Oct. 12, 1954, p. 26.)

[86] The Eisenhower administration gave the Castillo Armas government close to $100 million in direct aid. "This was during a period when total U.S. aid to all of Latin America was under $60 million annually." (Handy, *Gift*, p. 189.)

[87] On the culture of fear, see Gleijeses, *Politics and Culture*.

The Guatemalan upper class responded with cries of pain and anger and fear, and the United States intervened. Arbenz was overthrown, the communists were persecuted, the army was purged, the peasants were thrown off the land they had received. As the culture of fear descended again over the great many, the elite few strengthened their resolve. Never had they felt as threatened as they had under Arbenz; never before had they lost land to the Indians; never would it happen again. For them, the 1944–1954 interlude had confirmed that democracy was dangerous, that reformers were communists, that concession was surrender. To this belief they have held, with fierce resolve, to this day.

And so Guatemala has grown—like a deformed body, wracked with pain and fear—with a land tenure system that is the most skewed in Latin America, a fiscal system that is among the most regressive in the hemisphere, a labor force that suffers from illiteracy, malnutrition, and ill health. Meanwhile, barbarians press at the gates, threatening the enchanted world of the Guatemalan upper class: guerrillas, seeking to destroy the system; middle-class politicians, seeking to reform it; priests, who no longer seek charity from the rich, but justice for the poor.[88]

Under such conditions, violence alone could maintain the status quo. Journalists, professors, priests, men and women of the political center lost their lives to feed the culture of fear. They died alongside members of rural cooperatives, grassroots organizers, labor leaders, left-wing students and armed guerrillas. "Tortures and murders are part of a deliberate and long-standing program of the Guatemalan Government," Amnesty International stated in 1981.[89] Periods of selective violence have alternated with waves of greater violence. The particular characteristics of the man who sat in the presidential palace have not been decisive. The intensity of the repression has depended on the intensity of the fear felt by the upper class and the military.[90]

[88] On the post-1954 period, see Handy, *Gift*, pp. 149–281; Aguilera Peralta, *Dialéctica del terror*; Brintnall, *Revolt of the Dead*; Falla, *Quiché rebelde*; Gleijeses, *Politics and Culture*; Hough, *Land and Labor*; Lovell, "Surviving Conquest"; McClintock, *American Connection*, vol. 2; Jonas, *Battle for Guatemala*.

[89] Amnesty International, *Guatemala . . . Political Murder*, p. 3.

[90] Thus, as a presidential candidate, Julio César Méndez Montenegro was a well-respected moderate of the centrist *Partido Revolucionario* (PR). But upon winning the election, Méndez Montenegro was allowed to assume the presidency only after signing a written guarantee that the armed forces—not he—would in fact rule the country. For four long years (1966–1970), he provided a veneer of legitimacy while the social reforms promised by the PR never materialized and the armed forces massacred thousands of peasants in order to eliminate a handful of guerrillas. (The text of the secret pact was eventually published in *La Hora* of Nov. 26 and 27, 1973, by Clemente Marroquín Rojas, who, as Méndez Montenegro's vice president, had been a signatory to it.)

I remember an evening in September 1982 in the house of Ricardo Barrios Peña, Arana's upper-class friend and adviser. "Look how beautiful all this is," he said as he took me to a window that overlooked his luxuriant garden. "I know that it won't last forever, but I will fight as long as I can to preserve it for myself and for my children." Barrios Peña spoke calmly, with no sense of guilt—just as he had when telling me of his plotting with Arana in 1949.[91]

As he spoke, a whirlwind of death was swirling through the Indian highlands of Guatemala. Left-wing guerrillas had mounted an unprecedented challenge and "the repression was pitiless." The mountains and the valleys were littered with corpses of men, women, infants. Rape was a banal event; charred villages a fact of life.[92]

Terror proved effective, but victory carried a price: the drama of the Guatemalan upper class is that, alone, it cannot safeguard its world. The privileged have sought a series of protectors: dictators to control the masses; the United States to topple Arbenz; and now, the army to defeat the guerrillas. They would like the army to be humble, subordinate—as it was to Ubico. But the mercenaries have grabbed power for themselves; they have encroached upon the political and economic preserves of the upper class.

In June 1954, the Guatemalan officers had returned from the "front" after their surrender to Castillo Armas "despondent, and with a terrible sense of defeat."[93] They, who had sympathized with the nationalism of the revolutionary years, had capitulated like officers of a banana republic. They were subjected to the contempt of those whom they had betrayed and of those who had benefited from their betrayal. On August 1, in a military parade, the army was jeered by the masses and by the upper class, by the defeated and by the victors alike, traitors to the former and cowards to the latter. It was a moment that the Guatemalan officers neither forgot nor forgave. Henceforth, they vowed, they might be cursed, but never again would they be jeered.[94]

It was the far left, the guerrillas, that helped them to recover their pride. As

[91] Interview with Barrios Peña. For Barrios Peña and Arana, see above pp. 62–63.

[92] Interview with the Guatemalan Bishop Juan Gerardi, Guatemala City, Jan. 5, 1985. On the slaughter of the early 1980s, see the reports of Americas Watch and Amnesty International listed in the bibliography; Carmack, *Harvest of Violence*; Davis and Hodson, *Witnesses*; Gleijeses, *Guatemala: The Struggle for Democracy*; Montejo, *Testimony*; Capt. Ruiz Morales, "Por qué solos?" According to the Guatemalan government, "the violence left no fewer than forty thousand widows and two hundred thousand orphans in its wake." ("40 mil viudas y 200 mil huérfanos," *La Hora*, Sept. 24, 1988, p. 3.) Since married men were not the only victims, an estimate of fifty thousand dead is conservative.

[93] Interview with Col. Mendoza.

[94] This paragraph is based on interviews with the following officers: González Siguí, Mendoza, Paiz Novales, Peralta Méndez, Silva Girón, Getellá, Lorenzana.

their pride swelled, so did their power. Until 1944, they had been the instrument of the dictators; after 1954, they were the bride of the upper class. As the army battled successfully against the guerrillas, the marriage underwent a subtle transformation: "the army gradually grew whiskers and developed strong muscles."[95] By the late 1970s, the army controlled both the country and the national budget. It had become the country's strongest "political party," ruled by a Central Committee of a few senior officers. It even instituted its own agrarian reform: the State gave land to generals and colonels.

The army is still the *macho* in Guatemalan society. It wields awesome power, and it exudes an institutional pride and a mystique that set it sharply apart from its counterparts in Honduras and El Salvador. The Guatemalan officers are proud of their impunity; they are not prosecuted for crimes against civilians. They are proud of the fear they inspire. "The army is untouchable. They are mightier than God. They are everywhere, they see everything, they know everything."[96] And yet, the army cannot escape the culture of fear. Too much blood has been shed in Guatemala for its officers to sleep peacefully; too many enemies lurk.

In 1985, the army organized elections to lend an aura of legitimacy to a regime in which it would retain power but be relieved of the burden of coping with the economic morass into which it had sunk the country. A "democratic" Guatemala, moreover, would be better able to obtain foreign economic assistance. And so, in January 1986, a civilian president was inaugurated. He boasts about Guatemala's new human rights legislation and its new institutions to protect human rights. But the laws are not enforced and the institutions are spineless. Torture and murder are still the alternative to social reform in Guatemala, and the human sacrifice continues. Hence the cry of pain of the chief justice of Guatemala: "In this country we are drowning in demagoguery and in laws that will never be enforced. I say this in full knowledge of the situation, and it pains me to say it. . . . As a judge, I am filled with shame."[97]

Perhaps someday the process that the United States crushed in 1954 will resume.[98] Perhaps someday the social reforms that the upper class and the

[95] Interview with a Guatemalan intellectual, who prefers to remain anonymous. Guatemala City, Jan. 15, 1985.

[96] Interview with a Guatemalan priest, who prefers to remain anonymous. Guatemala City, Jan. 2, 1985.

[97] Chief Justice Edmundo Vásquez Martínez, quoted in " 'Pena y vergüenza . . .' en Presidente del Poder Judicial," *La Hora*, Nov. 15, 1988, p. 6. See also, Americas Watch, *Closing the Space*; Americas Watch, *Persecuting*; OAS, *Informe anual*; Castellanos Cambranes, *Democratización*; Gleijeses, "Guatemala."

[98] In the 1960s, the Johnson and Nixon administrations provided the Guatemalan army with military assistance against the guerrillas and winked at its crimes, but U.S. assistance was in no way decisive. Unlike Carter, Reagan sought to assist the Guate-

military now oppose will become possible, and the culture of fear will, again, loosen its grip over the land of Guatemala. At present, there is the reality, a reality that was expressed in the 1988 Pastoral of the Guatemalan bishops: ''The cry for land is, without any doubt, the loudest, the most dramatic and the most desperate sound in Guatemala. . . . The hunger for land is the root of the injustice of our society.'' The bishops paid homage to the man their predecessors had reviled: Arbenz's agrarian reform program, they asserted, was ''the only serious attempt to reform this situation of profound injustice.''[99] Since 1954, at least one hundred thousand Guatemalans have been killed, and over forty thousand have disappeared to preserve the fruits of Castillo Armas's victory.

---

malan army against the guerrillas, but could not overcome congressional resistance and was obliged to cheer from the sidelines.

[99] Penados del Barrio, *El clamor por la tierra*, p. 1.

The Fate of the Defeated

THROUGH the summer and the autumn of 1954, while Castillo Armas arrested thousands in the name of anticommunism, the U.S. embassy bitterly complained that five of the eleven members of the PGT's Political Commission were still at large.[1]

Of these eleven men, three are alive today. Not one of the others died a natural death; all were murdered by their government in cold blood. Víctor Manuel Gutiérrez, the "Franciscan," was seized by the police on March 5, 1966. He was tortured and killed. His corpse and those of several other prisoners were "sewn into burlap sacks and dropped into the ocean from an army transport plane."[2]

Bernardo Alvarado Monzón, Mario Silva Jonama, and other PGT leaders "disappeared" in September 1972. Six weeks later, *Le Monde* told their story:

> Eight leaders of the PGT . . . disappeared on September 26 from the capital of Guatemala. Since then, no one . . . has been able to say where they are or even whether they are still alive. . . . Except for the feeble protests, quickly hushed, of family members and a few friends, silence has reigned. . . . Yet there were witnesses to the "disappearance" of September 26. The eight PGT leaders were attending a secret meeting . . . when the police came to abduct them. Witnesses wrote down the license plate numbers of the police cars. . . . Nevertheless, Colonel Alvarado Robles, chief of police, has denied that the eight were arrested, and officials claim that the allegations are a "plot" to discredit the government. "Many people," they explain, "disappear because they have left illegally for the United States in search of work; others have accidents in inaccessible places; others die in shoot-outs with the forces of law and order and must be buried at once because they don't have identity papers." . . .
>
> The "disappeared of September," are they still alive? Or, as the U.S. Embassy suggests, have they been tortured, killed, hacked in pieces and tossed from a plane into the grey waters of the Pacific ocean—the discreet and welcoming grave of so many "disappeared" more anonymous than these men of the PGT?[3]

[1] See *JW* 33, Aug. 13, 1954, p. 4; *JW* 35, Sept. 3, 1954, p. 3; *JW* 38, Sept. 4, 1954, p. 3; *JW* 43, Oct. 29, 1954, p. 6; *JW* 47, Nov. 26, 1954, p. 3.

[2] "28 in Guatemala Reported Slain by Police in Peralta's Regime," *NYT*, July 18, 1966, p. 12.

[3] "Peut-être en prison, peut-être dans le Pacifique," *Le Monde*, Paris, Dec. 13, 1972, p. 2. See also Cáceres, *Aproximación*, pp. 184–90.

While his former friends were tortured, killed, and hacked in pieces, Carlos Manuel Pellecer lived well. In the Arbenz years, he had been an influential member of the PGT's Political Commission, but he broke with the party in 1962.[4] Not only did he turn into a rabid anticommunist, he soon began to sing the praises of those who ruled Guatemala and to applaud the liberation of 1954. He was appointed ambassador to Israel, consul general in Houston, and chargé d'affaires in Paraguay.[5]

Alfredo Guerra Borges, too, broke with the party in the mid-1960s.[6] But he never recanted, and he never praised the liberators. Although he was allowed to live in Guatemala, he lived in fear, and he subjected himself to rigorous self-censorship. In 1981 he left his country, as the repression rose to a new frenzy, threatening even a man who had long ago renounced all political activity, but who had refused to surrender his dignity.

Unlike Pellecer, Fortuny never betrayed his beliefs; unlike Guerra Borges, he never ceased fighting for them. He has remained pugnacious, stubborn, cantankerous—a poor diplomat and a warm human being. He demonstrated his political courage in Cuba in the 1960s. As the PGT's representative, he clashed repeatedly and doggedly with his hosts on behalf of his party's independence. And he demonstrated his physical courage during four years of clandestine life in Guatemala (1971–1974), where capture meant death.

Fortuny now lives in Mexico—modestly, as he always has. He earns his living as a journalist and freelance editor. In mediocre health, but always active politically, far more attracted by the evolution of the Italian Communist Party than by the dogmatism of the Cubans, Fortuny looks with pride at his forty years of political struggle—from the heady days of the Guatemalan revolution to the long exile that began as he left his country with the defeated Jacobo Arbenz.

ARBENZ

Guatemala City, September 11, 1954, 10 p.m.: several cars speed from the Mexican embassy. Jacobo Arbenz and his wife are driven to the plane that will

---

[4] See "Carlos M. Pellecer rompe con el comunismo," *El I*, Nov. 27, 1962, p. 1, and Pellecer, "Repudio al comunismo."

[5] I draw this portrait reluctantly, as Pellecer received me graciously and is a witty and intelligent conversationalist. Contrary to what many have asserted, there is no indication that he worked for the CIA in the Arbenz years. At least until the fall of Arbenz, the CIA was unable to infiltrate the hierarchy of the PGT. After his "conversion," Pellecer published several turgid diatribes, including: *Renuncia al comunismo*; . . . *camino equivocado, Che!* and *Caballeros sin esperanza*. For a revealing interview of Pellecer, see "Utiles después de muertos."

[6] The portraits of Guerra Borges and Fortuny are based on interviews with them and with a broad spectrum of individuals who have seen them at various times in their years of exile. This spectrum spans Guatemalans and non-Guatemalans, friends and enemies.

take them to Mexico; after a delay of more than two months, Castillo Armas has granted them safe-conduct. At the airport, Arbenz is searched. The defeated president "had to take off all his clothes and hand them to the Immigration officials." As he undressed, journalists and photographers pressed around him, "the former taking notes; the latter, photos of every step of the proceedings: the surrender of the overcoat, the surrender of the jacket, the surrender of the pants, etc." Throughout the ordeal, Arbenz remained composed, and when he spoke, briefly responding to the questions of the immigration officials, he did so "in a sober and serene manner."[7] He left his country with dignity.

In Mexico, "the welcome was cold." The Mexican authorities were sensitive to pressure from Washington, and they had, in any case, little sympathy for the Red Jacobo. They told him that he could remain in the country only if he abstained from all political activity. They wanted to be rid of Arbenz, but without the opprobrium of deporting him. Thus, when he told them in December 1954 that he wanted to go to Europe for a few weeks, they promised that he would be allowed back, but when he tried to return, the Mexican embassy in Paris refused to give him a visa. "The time is not right," they told him. He must wait.[8]

And wait he did: a year in Prague, a few months in Moscow and Paris. At last, in 1957, he and his wife were able to return to the Western Hemisphere. They settled in Uruguay, the only Latin American country willing to receive them. It was there that Arbenz formally joined the PGT.[9]

Those were painful years. Arbenz had to endure more than the hatred and the scorn of those whom Washington had enthroned in Guatemala. When he had been president, Guatemala's revolutionary politicians had been respectful. Now they vented their anger and their frustration: had Arbenz been like Arévalo, had he not unleashed the agrarian reform and befriended the communists, he would still be in power, and they with him. "You are to blame for the defeat of the revolution," a former friend told him in early 1955; "Jacobo was deeply hurt," his wife remembers.[10] And, in a widely read book, the prominent Gua-

---

[7] Quoted from "Expresidente Arbenz ya se encuentra en México," *Tribuna Libre*, San Salvador, Sept. 11, 1954, pp. 1, 4. See also Arbenz's terse account in "Arbenz revela su secreto a 'Siempre!' "

[8] Quotations from interview with María de Arbenz. For Arbenz's reception in Mexico, see "Guatemalan Ex-President in Exile," *NYT*, Sept. 11, 1954, p. 1; "México acogió ayer al desterrado ex presidente J. Arbenz," *Excelsior*, Mexico City, Sept. 11, 1954, p. 1; "Salió a descansar el ex presidente Jacobo Arbenz," *Excelsior*, Mexico City, Sept. 12, 1954, p. 1.

[9] See above, p. 147.

[10] Quoted from interview with María de Arbenz. Interviews with Fortuny, Capuano, and Paz Tejada were also helpful.

temalan writer Cardoza y Aragón—a self-proclaimed revolutionary who sat out the revolution—pronounced Arbenz a coward and a petty bourgeois.[11]

In 1960, Jacobo and María moved to Havana. Cuba offered Arbenz a place to live, the fleeting hope that he could be useful, and enduring humiliations. For the triumphant Castroites, he was the symbol of failure. In their exuberant arrogance, they overlooked that Arbenz, unlike Castro, had come to power without his own army and had received no support from the Soviet Union. They paid him brief homage for his efforts as president of Guatemala and then stressed how they would avoid his mistakes. "The Cubans were very condescending," recalls María. "It was humiliating for Jacobo." He asked them "to give him something constructive to do, even if it wasn't related to politics—he offered to teach math in a school." But the Cubans demurred. "They made him feel useless. All they did was to call on him every once in a while to give interviews or to deliver speeches."[12]

While Arbenz was in Cuba, young guerrilla leaders raised the flag of revolt in Guatemala. They had been children in 1954; they grew to manhood as Castro triumphed. To them, Fidel was the present and the future; Arbenz, the past. Arbenz respected their courage but was critical of the *foco* theory they had borrowed from the Cubans. His relations with them were friendly but distant; his offer to join them was accepted in principle but postponed to a future that never arrived.[13]

Personal tragedy struck. Arabella, the eldest of Arbenz's three children, shot herself in October 1965, at age twenty-seven. She was, like her mother, beautiful and very intelligent, and she was renowned for her high-strung spirits. In Mexico, at the funeral, friends who had not seen Arbenz in ten years remarked how he had aged. "He was very thin and smoking like a chimney." He looked haggard and sick, "like a tired old man."[14]

[11] Cardoza y Aragón, *La Revolución Guatemalteca*. Cardoza y Aragón had missed the boat from the beginning: he had crossed the border into Guatemala, "ready for anything," on October 22, 1944. (Cardoza y Aragón, *Guatemala*, p. 7.) As Marroquín Rojas has pointed out in a sardonic essay, Cardoza y Aragón's bravery was unnecessary. The struggle against the dictators was over; Ponce had been overthrown on October 20. (*En el mundo de la polémica*, pp. 129-36.)

[12] Interviews with María de Arbenz (quoted) and Fortuny, who was also in Cuba. Che Guevara, who had been in Guatemala as a "revolutionary tourist" in the last months of the Arbenz regime and had witnessed Arbenz's fall from the sidelines, shared this condescending attitude: "We must thank Arbenz and the democracy that perished for the valuable lessons we have learned from our correct analysis of all the weaknesses that that government was unable to overcome." ("Al Primer Congreso Latino Americano de Juventudes," Aug. 1960, in Guevara, *Che*, p. 309.) For embellished accounts of Guevara's stay in Guatemala, see Gadea, *Ernesto*, pp. 1–72, and Mencía, "El Che Guevara en Guatemala."

[13] Interviews with María de Arbenz, Fortuny, and a Guatemalan guerrilla leader.

[14] Quotations from interviews with Paz Tejada and Guillén. See also "Fue sepultada

A few months later, Arbenz left Cuba for Paris and then Lausanne. He was still a member of the PGT, but his health was declining, and he was increasingly lost in his own thoughts, tormented by a sense of failure—and by the ghost of Arabella. At last, in 1970, he was allowed back into Mexico, but on a visa that had to be renewed abroad every six months. ''My longing is to live the last moments of my life near Guatemala,'' he told a journalist in October.[15]

He died on January 27, 1971, in Mexico, a lonely man. He was alone the night he died, for his wife had gone to El Salvador on family business.[16] His last known conversation had been with Fortuny, his loyal friend in success and in defeat.[17]

ARÉVALO

Soon after his inauguration, Arbenz appointed Arévalo roving ambassador— a pleasant sinecure. For the next three years, the ex-president passed his time in Europe and Latin America at his government's expense. He was neither consulted about policy in Guatemala nor did he influence developments there.[18]

Arévalo was in Chile when Arbenz fell. He remained there, later moving to Uruguay and, in 1959, to Venezuela. He resumed his academic career and wrote three books that constituted a passionate—if clumsy—indictment of U.S. policy in the hemisphere.[19] By 1961, however, his criticism of Eisenhower and Foster Dulles was accompanied by attacks on Castro and praise for Kennedy.[20]

In 1963, Arévalo joined in a bizarre tango with his old foe, General Ydígoras, who had been president of Guatemala since 1958. The stench of corruption and incompetence permeated his administration. As the end of his term

---

ayer la actriz Arabella Arbenz,'' *Excelsior*, Mexico City, Oct. 12, 1965, p. 24. Arbenz received an eight-day visa to attend the funeral for his daughter. (Interviews with María de Arbenz and Ernesto Capuano, a Guatemalan lawyer who had become a Mexican citizen and was instrumental in obtaining the visa for Arbenz.)

[15] ''Murió el ex Presidente Arbenz, de Guatemala,'' *Excelsior*, Mexico City, Jan. 28, 1971, p. 1. On Arbenz's visa, interviews with María de Arbenz and Capuano were helpful.

[16] María's share of the family estate had been their sole source of income since 1954.

[17] Interviews with Fortuny and María de Arbenz.

[18] Interviews with Arévalo, Osegueda, Galich, Charnaud, Toriello, Fortuny, Guerra Borges, and María de Arbenz. See also Arévalo, *Escritos complementarios*, pp. 9–33. These memoirs cover 1951 to 1963. They provide useful, if not always accurate information, and are eloquent testimony to the resilience of Arévalo's ego.

[19] *Guatemala: La democracia y el imperio*; *Fábula del tiburón y las sardinas*; *Antikomunismo en América Latina*.

[20] See Arévalo, *Escritos complementarios*, pp. 71–73, 76–77, 100–101.

grew close, Ydígoras groomed his successor, Roberto Alejos, who was unpopular in his own right and further burdened by his champion's disrepute. The upper class opposed Alejos and splintered its support among half a dozen other hopefuls. Elections were scheduled for November 1963. Ydígoras intimated that he would allow Arévalo to run and announced that the elections would be free.

From Mexico, where he had lived since early 1962, Arévalo was campaigning. Seeking to assuage the fears of the upper class and the military, he stressed that he was—and had always been—an anticommunist. For good measure, he indulged in personal attacks on Arbenz. He also swore that he, Arévalo, had had nothing to do with the death of his good friend, Arana. "Everybody in Guatemala knows who killed Arana, why he was killed and who benefited from it."[21] Arévalo made no apology for his past criticism of the United States, but he explained that it was different now: "There has been a changing of the guard. The dinosaurs have been defeated, and the Great Republic is ruled by new men—men who studied at Harvard."[22]

In Guatemala, tensions rose. If Arévalo were to run in unfettered elections, he would win, reported the U.S. embassy, for he would receive the votes of all those who were critical of the liberation of 1954. Yet neither the upper class nor the army would countenance a second presidency of Juan José Arévalo, the man who had delivered them to the Red Jacobo.[23]

On March 30, 1963, the country awoke to the news that Arévalo had returned. He had come to lead his supporters, he announced, and he would remain in Guatemala "even if it cost him his skin."[24] Two days later, however, Arévalo was back in Mexico. On March 31, the army had ousted Ydígoras and installed a military *junta*. The elections were canceled.

Poor Ydígoras. Free elections had never been in his thoughts. He had merely hoped to blackmail the upper class and the military: "He raised the specter of Arévalo in order to frighten us into accepting his candidate," observes an upper-class Guatemalan. "But his little ploy backfired."[25]

[21] Arévalo, *Carta política*, p. 4. This is Arévalo's most detailed campaign statement. For an interesting diatribe in response by a prominent conservative, see Marroquín Rojas, *La "Carta política."*

[22] Arévalo, *Carta política*, p. 10.

[23] See McNeil to SecState, A-283, Nov. 10, 1962; Bell to SecState, no. 521, Feb. 28, 1963; *JW* 9, Mar. 2, 1963; Corrigan to SecState, no. 551, Mar. 12, 1963; *JW* 11, Mar. 16, 1963; *JW* 14, Apr. 5, 1963. See also the press of the first four months of 1963, and Marroquín Rojas, *La "Carta política."*

[24] "Arévalo en Guatemala," *Prensa Libre*, Mar. 30, 1963, p. 2. On the evening of the twenty-ninth, Arévalo had given a press conference to selected journalists in the house of a "crony" of Ydígoras. (*JW* 14, Apr. 5, 1963, p. 2.)

[25] Interview with Barrios Peña, another presidential candidate.

The coup neither surprised nor displeased Washington.[26] More than a decade had passed since Truman's days, and much had changed in the world. But Central America was still at the heart of the American empire, and imperial reflexes die hard. For Guatemala, the "dinosaurs" were still in power in Washington, Harvard educated or not.[27] "The Department considers Arévalo's return to power adverse to U.S. interests," Undersecretary George Ball wrote on January 5, 1963. As president, Arévalo "had allowed the infiltration of Communists," Secretary Dean Rusk noted, while from Guatemala the U.S. ambassador joined the chorus: "Arévalo is totally bad from U.S. standpoint."[28]

Arévalo may have been deprived of the presidency, but he had no intention of enduring the lonely fate of Jacobo Arbenz. Lesser honors were available to him, if he was willing to pay the price.

He was willing. In 1969, Guatemala's president offered Arévalo the ambassadorship to Chile. Arévalo accepted the kind offer, turning a blind eye to the fact that the army had just slaughtered thousands of unarmed civilians.[29] Through the next decade, he served under military governments that were notorious for their brutality, their venality, and their illegitimacy.[30] Juan José Arévalo, the honored elder statesman, lives today in Guatemala; he has adjusted well to fear, repression, and forgetting.

[26] Many plotters had visited the U.S. embassy in the preceding weeks. They had been received by very discreet officials who had expressed no disapproval of their schemes. See MemoConv (Dreyfuss, Maldonado), Nov. 25, 1962; Corrigan to SecState, no. 551, Mar. 12, 1963; *JW* 11, Mar. 16, 1963; Bell to SecState, no. 605, Mar. 30, 1963.

[27] In 1963, the Kennedy administration condemned Juan Bosch, the moderate president of the Dominican Republic, as soft on communism in terms strikingly similar to those Truman had earlier used against Arévalo. See Gleijeses, *Dominican Crisis*, pp. 86–99, and Martin, *Overtaken by Events*, pp. 282–614.

[28] Quotations from: Ball, "Telegram to all American Diplomatic Posts in Central America, Caracas, Mexico, Panama and Santo Domingo," Jan. 5, 1963, p. 1; Rusk to All ARA Diplomatic Posts, Jan. 24, 1963, NA 714.00; Bell to SecState, no. 511, Feb. 22, 1963.

[29] See "Doctor Juan J. Arévalo por ser designado embajador en Chile," *El I*, Jan. 13, 1969, p. 1, and "Guatemala Names Arévalo, Long Exiled, Envoy to Chile," *NYT*, Jan. 16, 1969, p. 4.

[30] In the 1970s, Arévalo served as ambassador to Chile, Venezuela, and Israel. He retired in 1978 due to poor health.

Bibliography

THE AIM of this bibliography is to provide the reader with a readily accessible list of the sources I have used and to give the full citation of sources which, for simplicity's sake, have been cited in abbreviated form in the footnotes.

Every book cited in the footnotes, including those that are incidental, is listed in the bibliography. When the author is the same as the publisher, I list only the place and date of publication.

Given the quantity of newspaper and magazine articles cited in the notes, it seemed sensible to follow a different procedure: no article that appeared between January 1, 1930, and January 1, 1955, is listed unless it is of particular historical importance; articles that appeared after January 1, 1955, are included only when they would be of use to a scholar of the revolution.

Articles that appeared in scholarly journals between January 1, 1930, and January 1, 1955, are listed in the bibliography.

UNPUBLISHED PAPERS AND DOCUMENTS

I have used six major depositories of documents.

The *Eisenhower Library* in Abilene, Kansas, is a researcher's dream. Superbly organized, with a staff of highest quality, its only drawback is that it deprives the researcher of the pleasure of the search. Upon arrival, I was handed a list of the files that would be relevant to my study—and whenever I ventured beyond these files, I came up empty-handed. Thus, I had been warned that the library's massive Walter Bedell Smith collection would be of no use to me. I tried anyway, acquired an intimate knowledge of the general's love of fishing—but not a whisper about Guatemala.

In the *Truman Library*, Independence, Missouri, the researcher will have to show some spirit of initiative and search for files on his own, but this, too, is a well-organized, professionally run library.

In the *National Archives* in Washington, the researcher should go systematically through all the decimal files relating, even peripherally, to Guatemala. Particularly valuable is the generally overlooked *Joint Weeka*, especially for the 1952–1954 period, when it not only sheds light on U.S. perceptions, but also presents a reasonably accurate picture of Guatemala. Whenever appropriate, I have also looked at the decimal files of the other Central American countries and the general file for Central America. The researcher should also look beyond the decimal files to the usually neglected lot files.

If the Eisenhower Library is the Concorde, the *National Archives at Suitland, Maryland*, are an Edsel. The confusion of the staff is surpassed only by that of their files. It is, however, worth the considerable pain. Suitland houses the reports of the military attachés, internal embassy memos, and reports that were never sent to Washington, as well as other material that by some mysterious plan of Providence has found its way there.

The Guatemalan Transcripts are located in the Manuscript Division, *Library of Congress*, Washington D.C. They consist of ninety-four boxes of documents (sixty-three reels of microfilm) captured by the CIA in Guatemala after the fall of Arbenz. A mishmash, they include some truly trivial detritus and a mass of important documents. They are indispensable to the study of Guatemala in 1944–1954.

The *Archivo General de Centro América* in Guatemala City houses documents that help to convey the flavor of the time, but the researcher will have to weed through unorganized files to find them.

In addition to these six major depositories, I acquired documents through the Freedom of Information Act and benefited from the generosity of Steven Schlesinger and Blanche Wiesen Cook, who shared their FOIA documents with me. I have also had access to the private papers of some individuals—such as several letters by Jacobo Arbenz and his wife, and the personal papers of other Guatemalans.

Eisenhower Library

John Foster Dulles Papers.
Eisenhower: Papers as President, 1953–1961 (Ann Whitman File).
Eisenhower: Records as President, 1953–1961 (White House Central Files).
Milton Eisenhower Papers.
James Hagerty Papers.
C. D. Jackson Papers.
Bernard Shanley Diary.
White House Office, Office of the Special Assistant for National Security Records.

Truman Library

Nathaniel P. Davis Papers.
Edward G. Miller, Jr. Papers.
Richard Patterson Papers.
Harry S. Truman Papers: Official File.
Harry S. Truman Papers: President's Secretary's Files, Intelligence File.

National Archives

RG59 Decimal Files
RG59 Lot Files
RG59 Research and Analysis Files

National Archives at Suitland (Washington National Record Center)

RG84 Foreign Service Posts: Guatemala, Confidential File. (The box for 1949–1952 is labeled "Classified, General Records," but it is clearly part of the Confidential File.)
RG84 Foreign Service Posts: Guatemala, General and Classified Records.
RG84 Foreign Service Posts: Guatemala, General Records.
RG165 Military Intelligence Division, Regional Files 1922–1944: Guatemala.
RG319 Army Intelligence, Project Decimal File: Guatemala.
RG319 Records of the Army Staff, Intelligence Document Files.

Library of Congress
Guatemalan Transcripts

Archivo General de Centro América
Correspondencia del Presidente de la República (through 1947)
Departamento Administrativo del Trabajo:
  Contratos de Trabajo
  Correspondencia Sindical Campesina
Gobernación:
  Copiador de Oficios
  Correspondencia Dirigida al Señor Ministro (through 1947)
  Informes Mensuales de Jefes Políticos (through Oct. 1947)
  Ministerio Público (through 1946)
Inspección General de Trabajo
Jefaturas Políticas (through 1947)
Organismo Judicial de la República

Other Depositories

Archives of the Nicaraguan Embassy, Washington, D.C.: following the overthrow of
  Somoza, I was given access to the documents stored in the embassy. They were of
  modest use.
Archivo Histórico Arquidiocesano "Francisco de Paula García Pelaez," Guatemala
  City: some useful documents are buried among the baptismal records in the Corre-
  spondencia file.
Adolf Berle Papers, Franklin D. Roosevelt Library, Hyde Park, New York.
Allen W. Dulles Papers, Seeley G. Mudd Library, Princeton University.
Edwin J. Kyle Papers, Cornell University: unilluminating memorabilia.
Bernardo Vega File: documents from the Private Archive of Rafael Trujillo (Archivo
  Particular del Generalisimo), National Palace, Santo Domingo. These documents
  were culled by the Dominican historian, Bernardo Vega, who, with characteristic
  generosity, shared them with me.
Whiting Willauer Papers, Seeley G. Mudd Library, Princeton University.

THE PRESS

The Guatemalan press has never been freer than in the 1944–1954 decade—particularly
the Arbenz years, when all shades of opinion were expressed openly. The contrast with
the Guatemalan press of the 1980s—officially uncensored, but crippled by self-censorship—is striking.

The essential newspapers are the official *Diario de Centro América*, the leading
opposition daily *El Imparcial*, the opposition *La Hora* (especially the editorials of its
owner, Clemente Marroquín Rojas), the communist weekly *Octubre*, and the communist daily *Tribuna Popular*. I have read these Guatemalan newspapers systematically.
I have also consulted about twenty others; they are cited in the footnotes.

I have consulted several newspapers from elsewhere in Central America—both for
incidents that involved their countries, and for their slant on Guatemalan developments. Again, they are cited in the footnotes.

I have used South American and European newspapers only very occasionally. Mexican coverage of Guatemala was disappointingly shallow.

The U.S. press covered Guatemala very poorly during most of the revolutionary period. Over time, however, some newspapers improved, particularly the *New York Times* and the *Christian Science Monitor*. But the U.S. press is not the place to learn about the Guatemalan revolution. Nor is it even the place to learn about U.S. policy toward Guatemala. Its usefulness lies in its reflection of American perceptions of matters Guatemalan. This applies equally to American magazines—with the exception of a handful of articles that soar above the rest and are cited in the bibliography.

INTERVIEWS

Unless otherwise noted, the position given for each person interviewed is that held on June 1, 1954. Individuals interviewed about post-1954 Guatemala are not listed.

Alejandro [pseud. of Severo Aguirre Cristo]: Member of the Central Committee of the Cuban Communist Party. Adviser to the Secretariat of the Guatemalan Communist Party, 1951–1954. Havana, Feb. 24, 1982; Mar. 20, 1986.

Aldana Sandoval, Carlos: Colonel (ret.), Guatemalan army. A leader of the 1944 revolution. Chief of Staff of the Guatemalan army (1945–1948). Minister of Public Works (1948–1951; 1952–1954). Ambassador to Washington (1951–1952). Guatemala City, Aug. 22, 1990.

Amory, Robert: CIA, Deputy Director for Intelligence. Washington, D.C., Oct. 17, 1983.

Arévalo Bermejo, Juan José: President of Guatemala, 1945–1951. Guatemala City, Aug. 25, 1979.

Arriola Ligorría, Jorge Luis: Colleague of Jacobo Arbenz when a professor at the Escuela Politécnica under Ubico. Minister of Education in the Revolutionary *Junta*. Minister of Health (1951–1953). Guatemala City, Oct. 13, 1988.

Arvelo Delgado, Tulio: Dominican exile involved in the Caribbean Legion in the late 1940s. Santo Domingo, Dominican Republic, May 24, 1971.

Barrios Peña, Ricardo: Adviser to Col. Francisco Arana in the late 1940s. A leader of the *Liberacionistas*. Guatemala City, Sept. 8, 1982.

Bauer Paiz, Alfonso: President of the National Agrarian Bank. Senior administration politician. Managua, Nov. 26, 1982.

Bendaña Perdomo, Ricardo: A Jesuit priest who is an authority on the Church in the revolutionary period. Guatemala City, Aug. 21 and 22, 1978.

Bissell, Richard: CIA, assistant to Allen Dulles. Participated in PBSUCCESS. Farmington, Conn., Nov. 10, 1983; May 24, 1989.

Capuano del Vecchio, Ernesto: Senior administration politician. Senior official of the National Agrarian Bank. Mexico City, Aug. 11, 16, 20, 1981; Aug. 7, 13, 18, 1982.

Cardoza y Aragón, Luis: Leading Guatemalan intellectual. Mexico City, Aug. 15, 1982.

Castañeda de Guerra Borges, Elsa: Mid-level official of the Guatemalan Communist Party. Mexico City, Aug. 10, 1982.

Charnaud MacDonald, Augusto: Minister of the Interior. One of the most powerful administration politicians. Mexico City, Aug. 12, 15, 18, 23, 1982.

Chavez, Manuel: Major, assistant U.S. Air Force Attaché, 1950–1953. Telephone interview, June 2, 1989.

Coerr, Wimberley: Deputy Chief of Mission, U.S. embassy in Honduras. Telephone interview, May 23, 1985.

Cruz Salazar, José Luis: Lt. Colonel, Guatemalan army. Guatemala City, Aug. 20, 1978; Sept. 6, 1982.

Dillon, Dorothy: CIA analyst. Washington, D.C., Sept. 15, 1984.

Figueres Ferrer, José: President of Costa Rica. San José, Costa Rica, June 6, 1982.

Fortuny Arana, José Manuel: Secretary General of the Guatemalan Communist Party. Mexico City, frequently in Aug. 1980, in Aug. 1981, Aug. 1982; July 16, 1984; Jan. 17–19, 1985; Jan. 19–20, 1987; Apr. 21–23, 1988.

Galich López, Manuel: Senior administration politician in the Arévalo years. Foreign Minister of Guatemala, 1951–1952. Havana, Aug. 25, 1980; Jan. 11, 1981.

García Zepeda, Amadeo: Lieutenant, Guatemalan army and aide to Arbenz, 1945–1950. Guatemala City, Aug. 8, 10, 13, 18, 24, 1978; Aug. 24, 1979; Aug. 21, 22, 1990.

Getellá Amezquita, Anselmo: Colonel, Guatemalan army. Guatemala City, Sept. 4, 1982.

González Orellana, Carlos: Senior official of the Guatemalan Foreign Ministry. Member of the Guatemalan delegation to Caracas. San José, Costa Rica, May 20, 1986.

González Siguí, Rubén: Colonel, Guatemalan army. Guatemala City, Sept. 11, 1982.

Goodpaster, Andrew: General, Staff Secretary to President Eisenhower (Oct. 1954–Jan. 1961). Washington, D.C., Sept. 24, 1983.

Guerra Borges, Alfredo: Member of the Secretariat of the Guatemalan Communist Party. Guatemala City, Jan. 9–13, 1973; Aug. 22, 1979. Mexico City, Aug. 10, 14, 19, 22, 28, 30, 1982.

Guillén Corletto, Terencio: Colonel, Guatemalan army. Governor of Escuintla. Mexico City, Aug. 11, 13, 16, 1981; Aug. 13, 1982.

Helms, Richard: CIA, Chief of Operations, Directorate of Plans. Washington, D.C., Sept. 7, 1989.

Hernández Méndes, Jorge: Lt. Colonel, Guatemalan army. Guatemala City, Sept. 5, 1982.

Houston, Lawrence: CIA, General Counsel. Washington, D.C., Sept. 14, 1989.

Hyman, Elizabeth: State Department, Office of Intelligence and Research. Alexandria, Va., Oct. 25, 1984.

Jamison, Edward: State Department, Deputy Director of the Office of Regional Latin American Affairs. Washington, D.C., Oct. 6, 1983.

Kirkpatrick, Lyman: CIA, Inspector General. Middleburg, Va., June 2, 1989.

Krieg, William: Deputy Chief of Mission, U.S. embassy in Guatemala. Washington, D.C., June 18, 20, 23, 1983; Sept. 22, 26, 29, 1983.

Lorenzana Salazar, Roberto: Colonel, Guatemalan army. Antigua, Guatemala: Aug. 20, 23, 1978.

McCormick, Aloysius: Colonel, U.S. Army Attaché. Telephone interview, June 12, 1989.

Martínez Bonilla, José Rolando: a Dominican exile involved in the Caribbean Legion in the late 1940s. Santo Domingo, Dominican Republic, Jan. 3, 1975.

Mendizabal Pérez, Antonio: Lt. Colonel, Guatemalan army. Mexico City, Aug. 28, 1982.

Mendoza Azurdia, Oscar: Colonel, Guatemalan army. Guatemala City, Sept. 6, 1982.

Monteforte Toledo, Mario: Senior administration politician in the Arévalo years. President of the Congress, 1948–1950. Guatemala City, Oct. 13, 1988.

Montenegro Morales, Manuel Antonio: Lieutenant, Guatemalan army. A leader of the *Liberacionistas*. Guatemala City, Sept. 7, 1982.

Morgan García, Héctor: Senior administration politician. Guatemala City, Aug. 21, 1990.

Noriega Morales, Guillermo: Senior official of the National Agrarian Bank. Member of the Guatemalan delegation to Caracas. Guatemala City, Sept. 6, 1982.

Osegueda Palala, Raúl: Foreign Minister of Guatemala (Nov. 1952–Jan. 1954). Guatemala City, Sept. 3, 5, 1982.

Paiz Novales, Ernesto: Lt. Colonel, Guatemalan army. Guatemala City, Sept. 8, 1982.

Parinello de León, Enrique: Colonel, Chief of Staff of the Guatemalan army. Guatemala City, Sept. 9, 1982.

Paz Tejada, Carlos: Major (ret.), Guatemalan army. Chief of the Armed Forces, 1949–1951. Mexico City, frequently in Aug. 1980, Aug. 1981, Aug. 1982; July 17, 1984; Jan. 17–19, 1985; Jan. 19, 1987; Apr. 22–24, 1988.

Pellecer Durán, Carlos Manuel: Member of the Political Commission of the Guatemalan Communist Party. Antígua, Guatemala, Aug. 15, 19, 1990.

Peralta Méndez, Ricardo: Lieutenant, Guatemalan army. Washington, D.C., Mar. 4, 1986.

Phillips, David: CIA official who participated in PBSUCCESS. Washington, D.C., Nov. 14, 1984.

Ramírez Alcantara, Miguel Angel: a Dominican exile involved in the Caribbean Legion in the late 1940s. Santo Domingo, Dominican Republic, May 16, 1971.

Roettinger, Phillip: CIA agent who participated in PBSUCCESS. Washington, D.C., March 21, 22, 1990.

Rolz Bennett, Federico: A civilian leader of the 1944 revolution and a childhood friend of Arbenz. Guatemala City, Aug. 17, 1990.

Rosenberg Rivera, Jaime: Deputy Chief of the Guatemalan police. Mexico City, Aug. 20, 1980.

Silva Girón, César Augusto: Lieutenant, Guatemalan army. Guatemala City, Sept. 9, 1982.

Sol Castellanos, Jorge: Finance Minister of El Salvador, 1951–1953. Washington, D.C., Nov. 7, 1983.

Steins, Kenedon: Political officer, U.S. embassy in Guatemala, 1947–1951. Washington, D.C., Oct. 15, 1983.

Taracena de la Cerda, Eduardo: a leader of the *Liberacionistas*. Guatemala City, Aug. 15, 18, 23, 1978; Sept. 4, 10, 1982; Aug. 17, 1990.

Toriello Garrido, Guillermo: Guatemalan Ambassador to Washington (Sept. 1952–Jan. 1954). Foreign Minister of Guatemala. Cuernavaca, Mexico, Aug. 21, 1982.

Torres Espinoza, Edelberto: Nicaraguan exile involved in the Caribbean Legion in the late 1940s. San José, Costa Rica, Mar. 4, 1982; Nov. 28, 1982.

Vásquez, Miguel Angel: A leader of Guatemala's first Communist party, 1923–1932. Mexico City, Aug. 24, 1982.

Vilanova de Arbenz, María: Wife of President Arbenz. San José, Costa Rica, March 1–9, 1982; June 1–13, 1982; June 6–15, 1984; May 18–21, 1985; May 14–17, 1986; Aug. 12–13, 1989.

Wardlaw, Andrew: First Secretary, U.S. embassy in Guatemala. Telephone interview, May 29, 1989.

Woodward, Robert: Deputy Chief of Mission, U.S. embassy in Guatemala, 1944–1946; Deputy Assistant Secretary of State for inter-American affairs. Washington, D.C., Oct. 6, 10, 13, 18, 1983; Dec. 12, 1988.

Wright, Lydia: Cultural Attaché, U.S. embassy in Guatemala. Washington, D.C., July 31, 1984.

Ydígoras Fuentes, Miguel: Guatemalan exile leader. Major rival of Castillo Armas. Guatemala City, Aug. 15, 1978.

Zachrisson de Vilanova, Lilly: Sister-in-law of President Arbenz. San José, Costa Rica, Feb. 28, 1982; Mar. 4, 1982.

WORKS CITED

Acuña, Miguel. *El 48*. San José, C.R.: Lehmann, 1974.

Adams, Richard [Stokes Newbold, pseud.]. "Receptivity to Communist Fomented Agitation in Rural Guatemala." *Economic Development and Cultural Change* 5, no. 4 (July 1957): 338–61.

Adams, Richard. *Crucifixion by Power: Essays on Guatemalan National Social Structure, 1944–1966*. Austin: University of Texas Press, 1970.

Adler, John, Eugene Schlesinger, and Ernest Olson. *Public Finance and Economic Development in Guatemala*. Stanford, Calif.: Stanford University Press, 1952.

Aguilar, Luis. *Cuba 1933: Prologue to Revolution*. Ithaca, N.Y.: Cornell University Press, 1972.

Aguilar Bulgarelli, Oscar. *Costa Rica y sus hechos políticos de 1948*. San José: Editorial Costa Rica, 1978.

Aguilar P., J. Humberto. *Vida y muerte de una dictadura*. Mexico City: Linotipografía Nieto, 1944.

Aguilera Peralta, Gabriel, Jorge Romero Imery, et al. *Dialéctica del terror en Guatemala*. San José, C.R.: EDUCA, 1981.

Alexander, Robert. *Communism in Latin America*. New Brunswick, N.J.: Rutgers University Press, 1957.

———. "Communists Gain Strength in Guatemala." *New Leader*, May 24, 1954.

———. "The Guatemalan Communists." *Canadian Forum*, Toronto, July 1954, pp. 81–83.

———. "The Guatemalan Revolution and Communism." *Foreign Policy Bulletin* 33 (Apr. 1954): 5–7.

———. "Revolution in Guatemala." *New Leader*, Jan. 5, 1953, pp. 6–8.

Alonso, Isidoro, and Gines Garrido. *La Iglesia en América Central y el Caribe*. Madrid: Centro de Información y Sociología de la Obra de Cooperación Sacerdotal Hispanoamericana, 1962.

Altolaguirre Ubico, Arturo. "Entrevistamos al coronel Altolaguirre." *La Hora*, Oct. 3, 1962, p. 4.

Alvarado Arellano, Huberto. *Apuntes para la historia del Partido Guatemalteco del Trabajo*. Guatemala City: Ediciones del PGT, 1975.

———. *Esbozo histórico del PGT*. Guatemala City: n.p., 1971.

Alvarado Rubio, Mario. *El asesinato del coronel Arana*. Guatemala City: n.p., 1983.

Alvarez Elizondo, Pedro. *El Presidente Arévalo y el retorno a Bolívar*. Mexico City: Ediciones Rex, 1947.

Ambrose, Stephen. *Eisenhower*. Vol. 1: *Soldier, General of the Army, President-Elect, 1890–1952*. Vol. 2: *The President*. New York: Simon and Schuster, 1983, 1984.

Ambrose, Stephen, and Richard Immerman. *Ike's Spies: Eisenhower and the Espionage Establishment*. Garden City, N.Y.: Doubleday, 1981.

Americas Watch. *Closing the Space: Human Rights in Guatemala, May 1987–October 1988*. New York, 1988.

———. *Creating a Desolation and Calling It Peace*. New York, 1983.

———. *Guatemala: A Nation of Prisoners*. New York, 1984.

———. *Human Rights In Guatemala: No Neutrals Allowed*. New York, 1982.

———. *Persecuting Human Rights Monitors*. New York, 1989.

Ameringer, Charles. *The Democratic Left in Exile*. Coral Gables, Fla.: University of Miami Press, 1974.

———. *Don Pepe: A Political Biography of José Figueres of Costa Rica*. Albuquerque: University of New Mexico Press, 1978.

Amnesty International. *Guatemala: A Government Program of Political Murder*. London, 1981.

———. *Guatemala: Massive Extrajudicial Executions in Rural Areas under the Government of General Efraín Ríos Montt*. London, 1982.

Anderson, Thomas. *Matanza: El Salvador's Communist Revolt of 1932*. Lincoln: University of Nebraska Press, 1971.

Arbenz, Jacobo. "Arbenz revela su secreto a 'Siempre!' " *Siempre!* Mexico City, Oct. 27, 1954, pp. 8–11.

———. *Exposición del Presidente de la República, ciudadano Jacobo Arbenz, ante la opinión pública nacional y el Consejo Nacional de Economía sobre su programa de gobierno*. Guatemala City: Secretaría de Publicidad de la Presidencia de la República, 1951.

———. "Habla Arbenz." *Alero* 8 (Sept./Oct. 1974): 116–24. (Interview by Marta Cehelsky.)

———. *Informe del ciudadano Presidente de la República coronel Jacobo Arbenz Guzmán*. Guatemala City: Secretaría de Propaganda y Divulgación de la Presidencia, 1954.

———. *Informe del ciudadano Presidente de la República, coronel Jacobo Arbenz Guzmán, al Congreso Nacional en su primer periodo de sesiones ordinarias del año de 1953*. Guatemala City: Tipografía Nacional, 1953.

———. "Jacobo Arbenz relata detalles de la causa de su caída del gobierno de Guatemala." *La Prensa Libre*, San José, C.R., Oct. 25, 1955, pp. 9, 14. (Interview by Ronaldo Ramírez.)

————. "Tiene la palabra Jacobo Arbenz." *Bohemia*, Havana, Nov. 14, 1954, pp. 48–50. (Interview by Raúl Roa.)

Ardón, Enrique. *El señor general Ubico*. Guatemala City: n.p., 1968.

Arévalo, Juan José. *Antikomunismo en América Latina*. Buenos Aires: Editorial Palestra, 1959.

————. *La Argentina que yo viví (1927–1944)*. Mexico City: Costa-Amic, 1974.

————. *El candidato blanco y el huracán. 1944–1945*. Guatemala City: EDITA, 1984.

————. *Carta política al pueblo de Guatemala*. Guatemala City: El Imparcial, 1963.

————. *Discursos del doctor Juan José Arévalo y del teniente coronel Jacobo Arbenz Guzmán en el acto de transmisión de la Presidencia de la República, 15 de marzo de 1951*. Guatemala City: Tipografía Nacional, 1951.

————. *Discursos en la presidencia (1945–1948)*. Guatemala City: Tipografía Nacional, 1948.

————. *Escritos complementarios*. Guatemala City: José de Pineda Ibarra, 1988.

————. *Escritos pedagógicos y filosóficos*. Guatemala City: Tipografía Nacional, 1945.

————. *Escritos políticos*. Guatemala City: Tipografía Nacional, 1945.

————. *Fábula del tiburón y las sardinas*. Santiago de Chile: Ediciones América Nueva, 1956.

————. *Guatemala: la democracia y el imperio*. Rev. ed., Buenos Aires: Editorial Renacimiento, 1955.

————. *La inquietud normalista*. San Salvador: Editorial Universitaria de El Salvador, 1970.

————. "De Juan José Arévalo a Carlos Manuel Pellecer." *El Imparcial*, Sept. 9, 1982, p. 2.

————. *Memorias de aldea*. Mexico City: Editorial Orión, 1963.

————. "La revolución le enseñó al pueblo que se puede luchar." *7 Días*, Oct. 22, 1988, p. 9.

————. "No sé si la ayuda que dimos a Figueres en 1948 fué para bien." *Diario de Costa Rica*, San José, Jan. 31, 1972, p. 16.

Arévalo Martínez, Rafael. *Ecce Pericles!* 1945. 2 vols. San José, C.R.: EDUCA, 1971.

————. *Ubico*. Guatemala City: Tipografía Nacional, 1984.

Argüello, Rosendo hijo. *Quiénes y cómo nos traicionaron*. N.p., n.d.

Arias Gómez, Jorge. *Farabundo Martí*. San José, C.R.: EDUCA, 1972.

Aronson, James. *The Press and the Cold War*. New York: Bobbs-Merrill, 1970.

Arvelo, Tulio. *Cayo Confite y Luperón: Memorias de un expedicionario*. Santo Domingo, D.R.: Universidad Autónoma de Santo Domingo, 1981.

Asociación General de Agricultores. *Proyecto de ley agraria de la Asociación General de Agricultores*. Guatemala City: Sánchez & de Guise, 1952.

Avila Ayala, Manuel María. "La muerte del coronel Arana." *La Hora*, 14 articles, July 27–Aug. 13, 1954.

Aybar de Soto, José. *Dependency and Intervention: The Case of Guatemala in 1954*. Boulder, Colo.: Westview, 1978.

Baker, George. "The Woodrow Wilson Administration and Guatemalan Relations." *The Historian* 27, no. 2 (Feb. 1965): 155–69.

Barrios Archila, Jaime. *Biografía mínima del doctor Juan José Arévalo Bermejo*. Guatemala City: Ministerio de Educación, 1985.

Bauer Paiz, Alfonso. *Como opera el capital yanqui en Centroamérica: El caso de Guatemala*. Mexico City: Ed. Ibero Mexicana, 1956.

———. "La Electric Bond and Share Company." *Alero* 2.2 (Nov. 1970): 20–34.

———. *La Frutera y la discriminación*. Guatemala City: Ministerio de Economía y Trabajo, 1949.

Bayo, Alberto. *Tempestad en el Caribe*. Mexico City: n.p., 1950.

Bell, John Patrick. *Crisis in Costa Rica: The 1948 Revolution*. Austin: University of Texas Press, 1971.

Bemis, Samuel. *The Latin American Policy of the United States*. 1940. New York: Norton, 1967.

Bendaña Perdomo, Ricardo. "Historia general de la Iglesia de América Latina: Parte correspondiente a Guatemala, 1821–1976." Unpublished ms. in author's files.

Benites, Tulio. *Meditaciones de un católico ante la reforma agraria*. Guatemala City: Ministerio de Educación Pública, 1952.

Berle, Beatrice Bishop, and Travis Beal Jacobs, eds. *Navigating the Rapids, 1918–1971*. New York: Harcourt, Brace, Jovanovich, 1973.

Bernays, Edward. *Biography of an Idea: Memoirs of a Public Relations Counsel*. New York: Simon and Schuster, 1965.

Bernstein, Barton. "Election of 1952," in Arthur Schlesinger Jr., ed., *History of American Presidential Elections, 1789–1968*. New York: Chelsea House, 1971, 4:3215–66.

Bernstein, Victor, and Jesse Gordon. "The Press and the Bay of Pigs." *Columbia University Forum* 10, no. 3 (Fall 1967): 5–13.

Betancourt, Rómulo. "La opinión continental frente a la X Conferencia Interamericana." *Cuadernos Americanos*, Mexico City, vol. 71 (Sept.–Oct. 1953): 7–37.

Biechler, Michael. "The Coffee Industry of Guatemala: A Geographic Analysis." Ph.D. diss., Michigan State University, 1970.

Birkett, Blair. "Confidence in Guatemala Restored by Settlement of Labor Dispute." *Foreign Trade*, Ottawa, no. 124 (May 14, 1949): 1008–11.

Bishop, Edwin. "The Guatemalan Labor Movement, 1944–1959." Ph.D. diss., University of Wisconsin, 1959.

Bishop, Jefferson Mack. "Arévalo and Central American Unification." Ph.D. diss., Louisiana State University and Agricultural and Mechanical College, 1971.

Bissell, Richard. "Oral History Interview." Columbia University, 1973.

Blanco, Ramón. *25 galeras*. Guatemala City: Unión Tipográfica, 1954.

Blasier, Cole. *The Hovering Giant: U.S. Responses to Revolutionary Change in Latin America*. Pittsburgh: University of Pittsburgh Press, 1976.

Bosch, Juan. "Errores de la política norteamericana en el Caribe." *Bohemia*, Havana, Oct. 16, 1949, pp. 57, 62.

Bosch, Juan, et al. "Cayo Confites y la lucha contra Trujillo." *Política: teoría y acción*, Santo Domingo, D.R., 44 (Nov. 1983): 1–28.

Brands, H. W. *Cold Warriors: Eisenhower's Generation and American Foreign Policy*. New York: Columbia University Press, 1988.

Brintnall, Douglas. *Revolt of the Dead: The Modernization of a Mayan Community in the Highlands of Guatemala*. New York: Gordon and Breach, 1979.

Bulmer-Thomas, Victor. *The Political Economy of Central America since 1920*. Cambridge: Cambridge University Press, 1987.

Bush, Archer. "Organized Labor in Guatemala, 1944–1949." M.A. thesis, Colgate University, 1950.

Cabot, John Moors. *First Line of Defense: Forty Years' Experiences of a Career Diplomat*. Washington D.C.: School of Foreign Service, Georgetown University, [1979].

———. *Toward Our Common American Destiny*. Boston: Fletcher School of Law and Diplomacy, [1955].

Cáceres, Carlos. *Aproximación a Guatemala*. Culiacán, Mexico: Universidad Autónoma de Sinaloa, 1980.

Calder, Bruce. *Crecimiento y cambio de la Iglesia Católica Guatemalteca, 1944–1966*. Guatemala City: José de Pineda Ibarra, 1970.

Cardona, Rokael. "Cooperativismo y modernización agrícola en Guatemala (1945–1975)." Thesis, University of Costa Rica, 1977.

Cardoza, José Alberto. "A treinta años de la Revolución de Octubre de 1944." *Alero* 8 (Sept./Oct. 1974): 89–93.

Cardoza y Aragón, Luis. *Guatemala, las líneas de su mano*. Mexico City: Fondo de Cultura Económica, 1955.

———. *Retorno al futuro*. Mexico City: Letras de México, 1948.

———. *La Revolución Guatemalteca*. Mexico City: Cuadernos Americanos, 1955.

Carmack, Robert. *Historia social de los Quichés*. Guatemala City: Seminario de Integración Social Guatemalteca, 1979.

Carmack, Robert, ed. *Harvest of Violence: The Maya Indians and the Guatemalan Crisis*. Norman: University of Oklahoma Press, 1988.

Carpio, Cayetano. *Secuestro y capucha*. San José, C.R.: EDUCA, 1979.

Carrillo Ramírez, Alfredo. *Evolución histórica de la educación secundaria en Guatemala*. 2 vols. Guatemala City: José de Pineda Ibarra, 1971, 1972.

Casey, Dennis. "Indigenismo: The Guatemalan Experience." Ph.D. diss., University of Kansas, 1979.

Castellanos Cambranes, Julio. *Café y campesinos en Guatemala, 1853–1897*. Guatemala City: Editorial Universitaria, 1985.

———. *Democratización y movimientos campesinos pro-tierra en Guatemala*. Madrid: Centro de Estudios Rurales Centroamericanos, 1988.

———. *Desarrollo económico y social de Guatemala: 1868–85*. Guatemala City: IIES, Universidad de San Carlos, 1975.

———. "Los empresarios agrarios modernos y el Estado en Guatemala." *Mesoamérica* 10 (Dec. 1985): 243–91.

———. *El imperialismo alemán en Guatemala*. Guatemala City: IIES, Universidad de San Carlos, 1977.

Castillo Armas, Carlos. "Organización del ataque a la Base Militar." *El Espectador*, July 3, 1955, p. 3.

Catalán M., Juan Carlos. "Huelga universitaria contra Ubico." *La calle donde tú vives*, Sept. 16, 1977, pp. 10–15.

Cehelsky, Marta. "Guatemala's Frustrated Revolution: The 'Liberation' of 1954." M.A. thesis, Columbia University, [1967].

Childs, Marquis. *Eisenhower, Captive Hero: A Critical Study of the General and the President*. New York: Harcourt, Brace, Jovanovich, 1958.

Cline, Ray. *Secrets, Spies and Scholars: Blueprint of the Essential CIA*. Washington, D.C.: Acropolis Books, 1976.

Clissold, Stephen, ed. *Soviet Relations with Latin America 1918–1960: A Documentary Record*. New York: Oxford University Press, 1970.

Colby, Benjamin, and Pierre van den Berghe. *Ixil Country: A Plural Society in Highland Guatemala*. Berkeley: University of California Press, 1969.

Comisión permanente del primer congreso contra la intervención soviética en América Latina. *El libro negro del comunismo en Guatemala*. Mexico City, 1954.

Comité Interamericano de Desarrollo Agrícola. *Tenencia de la tierra y desarrollo socio-económico del sector agrícola*. Washington, D.C.: Unión Panamericana, 1965.

Connell-Smith, Gordon. *The Inter-American System*. London: Oxford University Press, 1966.

Cook, Blanche Wiesen. *The Declassified Eisenhower: A Divided Legacy*. Garden City, N.Y.: Doubleday, 1981.

Corado, Carlos Daniel. "Yo no firmé la rendición el 20 de octubre." *La Tarde*, Oct. 17, 1970, p. 9.

Corominas, Enrique. *In the Caribbean Political Areas*. New York: University Press of Cambridge, 1954.

Couloumbis, Theodore. *Greek Political Reaction to American and NATO Influences*. New Haven: Yale University Press, 1966.

Crassweller, Robert. *Trujillo: The Life and Times of a Caribbean Dictator*. New York: Macmillan, 1966.

Cruz Salazar, José Luis. "El ejército como una fuerza política." *Estudios Sociales* 6 (Apr. 1972): 74–98.

Dalton, Roque. *Miguel Mármol*. San José, C.R.: EDUCA, 1982.

Davis, Shelton, and Julie Hodson. *Witnesses to Political Violence in Guatemala: The Suppression of a Rural Development Movement*. Boston: Oxfam America, 1982.

Dawson, Frank Griffith. "Labor Legislation and Social Integration in Guatemala: 1871–1944." *American Journal of Comparative Law* 14 (1965–1966): 124–42.

De la Guarda, Manuel César. *Castillo Armas, libertador y mártir*. Lima: Editorial Indoamérica, 1957.

De León Aragón, Oscar. *Los contratos de la United Fruit Company y las compañías muelleras en Guatemala*. Guatemala City: Ministerio de Educación Pública, 1950.

Delli Sante-Arrocha, Angela. *Juan José Arévalo: Pensador contemporáneo*. Mexico City: Costa-Amic, 1962.

De los Rios, Efraín. *Ombres contra hombres*. 2 vols. Guatemala City: Tipografía Nacional, 1969.

Del Valle Matheu, Jorge. *La verdad sobre el "caso de Guatemala."* Guatemala City: n.p., 1956.

De Santis, Vincent. "Eisenhower Revisionism." *Review of Politics* 38 (Apr. 1976): 190–207.

De Wiche, Josefina. "El comunismo en Guatemala." *Estudios sobre el comunismo*. Santiago de Chile, vol. 1, no. 1 (July/Sept. 1953): 92–96.

De Zirión, Grace H. *Datos biográficos del general e ingeniero Miguel Ydígoras Fuentes*. Guatemala City: José de Pineda Ibarra, 1961.

Díaz Rozzotto, Jaime. *El carácter de la Revolución Guatemalteca*. Mexico City: Ediciones Revista "Horizonte," 1958.

Dinerstein, Herbert. *The Making of a Missile Crisis: October 1962*. Baltimore: Johns Hopkins University Press, 1976.

Dinwoodie, David. "Expedient Diplomacy: The United States and Guatemala, 1898–1920." Ph.D. diss., University of Colorado, 1966.

Dion, Marie Berthe. *Las ideas sociales y políticas de Arévalo*. Mexico City: Editorial América Nueva, 1958.

Divine, Robert. *Eisenhower and the Cold War*. New York: Oxford University Press, 1981.

———. *Foreign Policy and U.S. Presidential Elections, 1952–1960*. New York: New Viewpoints, 1974.

Dominican Republic, Ministry for Home Affairs. *White Book of Communism in Dominican Republic*. Madrid: Gráficas Rey, n.d.

Donaldson, Robert. *Soviet Policy toward India*. Cambridge: Harvard University Press, 1974.

Dosal, Paul. "The Political Economy of Guatemalan Industrialization, 1871–1948: The Career of Carlos F. Novella." *Hispanic American Historical Review* 68, no. 2 (May 1988): 321–58.

Early, John. *The Demographic Structure and Evolution of a Peasant System: The Guatemalan Population*. Boca Raton: University Presses of Florida, 1982.

Ebaugh, Cameron. *Education in Guatemala*. Washington, D.C.: GPO, 1947.

Eden, Anthony. *Full Circle*. London: Cassell, 1960.

Eisenhower, Dwight. *Mandate for Change, 1953–1956*. Garden City, N.Y.: Doubleday, 1963.

El Espectador. July 3, 1955. (Special issue on Castillo Armas.)

El Salvador, Secretaría de Información de la Presidencia. *De la neutralidad vigilante a la mediación con Guatemala*. Rev. ed. San Salvador, 1955.

Escuela Politécnica. *Centenario de la Escuela Politécnica, 1873–1973*. Guatemala City, 1973.

———. *La Escuela Politécnica, 1 de Septiembre 1873–1 de Septiembre 1941*. Guatemala City, 1941.

Estrada Monroy, Agustín. *Datos para la historia de la Iglesia en Guatemala*. 3 vols. Guatemala City: Sociedad de Geografía e Historia de Guatemala, 1973, 1978, 1979.

Fabela, Isidro. "La conferencia de Caracas y la actitud anticomunista de México." *Cuadernos Americanos*, Mexico City, vol. 75, no. 3 (May–June 1954): 7–44.

Falla, Ricardo. *Quiché rebelde*. Guatemala City: Editorial Universitaria, 1978.

Ferrell, Robert, ed. *The Diary of James C. Hagerty*. Bloomington: Indiana University Press, 1983.

———, ed. *The Eisenhower Diaries*. New York: Norton, 1981.

Figueres, José. *El espiritu del 48*. San José, C.R.: Editorial Costa Rica, 1987.

———. "Oral History Interview." Truman Library, 1970.

Figueroa Ibarra, Carlos. "Contenido de clase y participación obrera en el movimiento antidictatorial de 1920." *Política y Sociedad* 4 (July–Dec. 1977): 5–51.

———. "La insurrección armada de 1920 en Guatemala." *Política y Sociedad* 8 (July–Dec. 1979): 91–146.

Flores Avendaño, Guillermo. *Memorias (1900–1970)*. 2 vols. Guatemala City: Editorial del Ejército, 1974.

Fortuny, José Manuel. "Autocrítica." Mexico City, Feb. 15, 1955, unpublished ms. in author's files.

———. *Informe sobre la actividad del Comité Central del Partido Comunista de Guatemala, 11 de diciembre de 1952*. Guatemala City: Ediciones del Partido Guatemalteco del Trabajo, 1953.

———. "Observaciones al trabajo de Edelberto Torres Rivas." *Historia y Sociedad*, Mexico City, 15 (1977): 55–69.

———. *Por un frente único de masas: Informe al Pleno Ampliado del Comité Central del Partido Guatemalteco del Trabajo: 16 de octubre de 1953*. Guatemala City: n.p., 1953.

Frankel, Anita. "Political Development in Guatemala, 1944–1954: The Impact of Foreign, Military and Religious Elites." Ph.D. diss., University of Connecticut, 1969.

Fuentes Mohr, Alberto. "Land Settlement and Agrarian Reform in Guatemala." *International Journal of Agrarian Affairs*, London, vol. 2, no. 1 (Jan. 1955): 24–32.

Gadea, Hilda. *Ernesto: A Memoir of Che Guevara*. Garden City, N.Y.: Doubleday, 1972.

Gaitán, Héctor. "Los mártires del sindicalismo." *La calle donde tú vives*, Apr. 28, 1978, pp. 2–9.

Galich, Manuel. *Del pánico al ataque*. 1949. Guatemala City: Editorial Universitaria, 1977.

———. *Por qué lucha Guatemala?* Buenos Aires: Elmer, 1958.

García, Graciela. *Las luchas revolucionarias de la nueva Guatemala*. Mexico City: n.p., 1952.

———. *Páginas de lucha revolucionaria en Centroamérica*. Mexico City: Ediciones Linterna, 1971.

García Añoveros, Jesús. "El 'caso Guatemala' (junio de 1954): La Universidad y el campesinado," *Alero* 28 (Jan./Feb. 1978): 133–234.

———. *Jacobo Arbenz*. Madrid: Historia 16 Quorum, 1987.

———. *La reforma agraria de Arbenz en Guatemala*. Madrid: Ediciones Cultura Hispánica, 1987.

García Granados, Jorge. *Evolución sociológica de Guatemala*. Guatemala: Sánchez & de Guise, 1927.

Geiger, Theodore. *Communism versus Progress in Guatemala*. Washington, D.C.: National Planning Association, 1953.

Gillin, John, and K. H. Silvert. "Ambiguities in Guatemala." *Foreign Affairs* 34 (Apr. 1956): 469–82.

Girón, José Ernesto. "La rebelión de los cadetes." *La Hora Dominical*, July 27, 1975, pp. 19–22.

Gleijeses, Piero. *The Dominican Crisis*. Baltimore: Johns Hopkins University Press, 1978.

―――. "Guatemala." In James Malloy and Eduardo Gamarra, eds., *Latin America and Caribbean Contemporary Record*. Vol. 7. New York: Holmes & Meier, 1990, pp. B259–74.

―――. *Guatemala: The Struggle for Democracy*. Cork, Ireland: University College, 1986.

―――. *Politics and Culture in Guatemala*. Ann Arbor: Center for Political Studies, University of Michigan, 1988.

Goldenberg, Boris. *Kommunismus in Lateinamerika*. Stuttgart: Kohlhammer, 1971.

Góngora, Mayra. *Introducción a la sociedad guatemalteca contemporánea*. Havana: Centro de Estudios sobre América, 1982.

González, Mario Aníbal. "Recuerdos de la dictadura del general Jorge Ubico." *La Hora*, Feb. 15, 1986, pp. 3, 11.

González Campo, José. "La caída del presidente Jorge Ubico." *Estudios Centroamericanos*, San Salvador, vol. 19, no. 192 (Apr. 1964): 84–98.

―――. "El general Jorge Ubico, un dictador progresista." *Estudios Centroamericanos*, San Salvador, vol. 18, no. 187 (Nov. 1963): 345–55.

González Orellana, Carlos. *Historia de la educación en Guatemala*. Guatemala City: José de Pineda Ibarra, 1970.

Greenstein, Fred. *The Hidden-Hand Presidency: Eisenhower as Leader*. New York: Basic Books, 1982.

Grieb, Kenneth. "American Involvement in the Rise of Jorge Ubico," *Caribbean Studies* 10, no. 1 (Apr. 1970): 5–21.

―――. *Guatemalan Caudillo: The Regime of Jorge Ubico*. Athens: Ohio University Press, 1979.

Griffith, William. "A Recent Attempt at Educational Cooperation between the United States and Guatemala." *Middle American Research Records* 1, no. 12 (May 15, 1949): 171–92.

―――. "Santo Tomás, anhelado emporio del comercio en el Atlántico." *Anales de la Sociedad de Geografía e Historia*, Jan./Dec. 1958, pp. 40–61.

Guatemala, Congress of. "Actas del Congreso," 1952–1953.

―――. *Diario de las Sesiones del Congreso de la República de Guatemala*. 1953–1954.

Guatemala, Government of. *Censo agropecuario 1950*. Guatemala City: Dirección General de Estadística, 1954.

―――. *Crítica al proyecto de ley agraria de la Asociación General de Agricultores*. Guatemala City: Secretaría de Propaganda y Divulgación de la Presidencia de la República, May 1952.

―――. *La democracia amenazada. El caso de Guatemala*. Guatemala City: Tipografía Nacional, Secretaría de Propaganda y Divulgación de la Presidencia de la República, 1954.

―――. *Efemerides del Movimiento de Liberación Nacional: junio y julio de 1954*. Guatemala City: Secretaría de Divulgación, Cultura y Turismo, 1955.

―――. *Primera colonia agrícola de Poptún*. Guatemala City: Departamento de Publicidad de la Presidencia de la República, 1950.

Guatemala, Government of. *El triángulo de Escuintla*. Guatemala City: Tipografía Nacional, 1946.

Guerra Borges, Alfredo. "Apuntes para una interpretación de la Revolución Guatemalteca y de su derrota en 1954." *Anuario de Estudios Centroamericanos*, San José, C.R., vol. 14, no. 1–2 (1988): 109–20.

――――. *Pensamiento económico social de la Revolución de Octubre*. Guatemala City: Universidad de San Carlos, 1977.

Guevara, Ernesto. *Che: Obra revolucionaria*. Mexico City: ERA, 1967.

Guillén, Fedro. *Guatemala: prólogo y epílogo de una revolución*. Mexico City: Cuadernos Americanos, 1964.

Gunther, John. *Inside Latin America*. New York: Harper & Brothers, 1941.

Gutiérrez, Víctor Manuel. *Apuntes para la historia del Partido Comunista de Guatemala*. Guatemala City: n.p., 1965.

――――. *Breve historia del movimiento sindical de Guatemala*. Mexico City: n.p., 1964.

Halperin, Ernst. *Nationalism and Communism in Chile*. Cambridge: MIT Press, 1965.

Handy, Jim. *Class and Community in Rural Guatemala: Village Reaction to the Agrarian Reform Law, 1952–1954*. Occasional Papers Series, no. 59. Miami: Latin American and Caribbean Center, Florida International University, 1985.

――――. *Gift of the Devil: A History of Guatemala*. Boston: South End Press, 1984.

――――. "The Guatemalan Revolution and Civil Rights." *Canadian Journal of Latin American and Caribbean Studies*, Toronto, vol. 10, no. 19 (1985): 3–21.

――――. " 'The Most Precious Fruit of the Revolution': The Guatemalan Agrarian Reform, 1952–54." *Hispanic American Historical Review* 68, no. 4 (Nov. 1988): 675–705.

――――. "Reform and Counter-Reform: Agrarian Policy in Guatemala, 1952–1957." Presented at Latin American Studies Association, 15th Congress, Miami, Dec. 1989.

Hanford, Thomas. "The Communist Beachhead in the Western Hemisphere." Presented at Army War College, Carlisle Barracks, Pa., Mar. 15, 1955.

Hendon, Robert. "Some Recent Economic Reforms in Guatemala." M.A thesis, Colgate University, 1949.

Hennessey, John. "National Economy of Guatemala." *Commercial Pan America* 16, no. 2 (Feb. 1947): 43–96.

Henríquez Vásquez, Alberto. "Cayo Confites (ahora más completo y menos dulce)." *Ultima Hora*, Santo Domingo, D.R., 26 articles, Jan. 2–Apr. 13, 1984.

Hernández de León, Federico. *Viajes presidenciales*. 2 vols. Guatemala City: Publicaciones del Partido Liberal Progresista, 1940, 1943.

Hernández Sifontes, Julio. *Realidad jurídica del indígena guatemalteco*. Guatemala City: José de Pineda Ibarra, 1965.

Higbee, Edward. "The Agricultural Regions of Guatemala." *Geographic Review* 38 (Apr. 1947): 177–201.

――――. "Guatemala's Agrarian Problem." Ph.D. diss., Johns Hopkins University, 1949.

Higgins, Trumbull. *The Perfect Failure: Kennedy, Eisenhower, and the CIA at the Bay of Pigs*. New York: Norton, 1987.

Hill, Robert. "Oral History Interview." Princeton University, 1964.

――――. "Oral History Interview." Columbia University, 1973.

"History: Damn Good and Sure." *Newsweek*, Mar. 4, 1963, p. 17.

Holleran, Mary. *Church and State in Guatemala*. New York: Columbia University Press, 1949.

Hough, Jerry. *The Struggle for the Third World: Soviet Debates and American Options*. Washington, D.C.: Brookings, 1986.

Hough, Richard, et al. *Land and Labor in Guatemala: An Assesssment*. Guatemala City: United States Agency for International Development and Development Associates, 1982.

Houghton, Neal. "The Cuban Invasion of 1961 and the U.S. Press, in Retrospect." *Journalism Quarterly* 42 (Summer 1965): 422–32.

Hughes, John Emmet. *The Ordeal of Power: A Political Memoir of the Eisenhower Years*. New York: Atheneum, 1963.

Hunt, Howard. *Undercover: Memoirs of an American Secret Agent*. New York: Putnam, 1974.

Hurtado Aguilar, Luis Alberto. *Así se gestó la Liberación*. Guatemala City: Secretaría de Divulgación, Cultura y Turismo de la Presidencia de la República, 1956.

Immerman, Richard. *The CIA in Guatemala: The Foreign Policy of Intervention*. Austin: University of Texas Press, 1982.

———. "Eisenhower and Dulles: Who Made the Decisions?" *Political Psychology* 1 (Autumn 1979): 21–38.

Inman, Samuel Guy. *Inter-American Conferences, 1826–1954: History and Problems*. Washington, D.C.: University Press of Washington D.C. and the Community College Press, 1965.

———. *A New Day in Guatemala*. Wilton, Conn.: Worldover Press, 1951.

International Bank for Reconstruction and Development (World Bank). *The Economic Development of Guatemala*. Washington, D.C., 1951.

James, Daniel. *Red Design for the Americas: Guatemalan Prelude*. New York: John Day, 1954.

Jimenez, Ernesto. *La educación rural en Guatemala*. Guatemala City: José de Pineda Ibarra, 1967.

Joes, Anthony James. "Eisenhower Revisionism: The Tide Comes In." *Presidential Studies Quarterly* 15 (Summer 1985): 561–71.

Jonas, Susanne. *Battle for Guatemala*. Boulder, Colo.: Westview, 1991.

———. "Guatemala: Land of Eternal Struggle." In Ronald Chilcote and Joel Edelstein, eds. *Latin America: The Struggle with Dependency and Beyond*. New York: John Wiley, 1974, pp. 89–219.

Jonas, Susanne, and David Tobis, eds. *Guatemala*. New York: North American Congress on Latin America, 1974.

Jones, Chester Lloyd. *Guatemala: Past and Present*. Minneapolis: University of Minnesota Press, 1940.

Kanet, Roger, ed. *The Soviet Union and the Developing World*. Baltimore: Johns Hopkins University Press, 1974.

Kaufman, Burton. *Trade and Aid: Eisenhower's Foreign Economic Policy, 1953–1961*. Baltimore: Johns Hopkins University Press, 1982.

Kepner, Charles. *Social Aspects of the Banana Industry*. New York: Columbia University Press, 1936.

Kepner, Charles, and Jay Soothill. *The Banana Empire: A Case Study of Economic Imperialism.* New York: Vanguard Press, 1935.

Kirkpatrick, Lyman. "Paramilitary Case Study: The Bay of Pigs," *Naval War College Review*, Nov.–Dec. 1972, pp. 32–42.

———. *The Real CIA.* London: Macmillan, 1968.

Kolb, Glen. *Democracy and Dictatorship in Venezuela, 1945–1958.* Hamden, Conn.: Archon Books, 1974.

Krehm, William. *Democracies and Tyrannies of the Caribbean.* Westport, Conn.: Lawrence Hill, 1984.

LaBarge, Richard. "Impact of the United Fruit Company on the Economic Development of Guatemala, 1946–1954." In LaBarge, et al., *Studies in Middle American Economics.* New Orleans: Middle American Research Institute, Tulane University, 1968, pp. 1–72.

———. "A Study of United Fruit Company Operations in Isthmian America, 1946–1956." Ph.D. diss., Duke University, 1959.

LaCharite, Norman, et al. *Case Study in Insurgency and Revolutionary Warfare: Guatemala, 1944–1954.* Washington D.C.: American University, 1964.

L.A.H.A.: See Hurtado Aguilar.

Larsen, Douglas. " 'Sulfato': Nemesis of the Guatemalan Reds." *Flying*, July 1957, pp. 50–51, 86–88.

Leary, William. *Perilous Missions: Civil Air Transport and CIA Covert Operations in Asia.* University: University of Alabama Press, 1984.

LeBaron, Alan. "Impaired Democracy in Guatemala, 1944–1951." Ph.D. diss., University of Florida, 1988.

López Larrave, Mario. *Breve historia del movimiento sindical guatemalteco.* Guatemala City: Editorial Universitaria, 1976.

López Villatoro, Mario. *Por los fueros de la verdad histórica, una voz de la patria escarnecida.* Guatemala City: n.p., 1956.

———. *Por qué fué derrotado el comunismo en Guatemala?* Guatemala City: n.p., 1957.

Lovell, George. "Surviving Conquest: The Maya of Guatemala in Historical Perspective." *Latin American Research Review* 23, no. 2 (1988): 25–57.

McAuliffe, Mary. "Eisenhower, The President." *Journal of American History* 68 (1981): 625–32.

McCann, Thomas. *An American Company: The Tragedy of United Fruit.* New York: Crown Publishers, 1976.

McClintock, Michael. *The American Connection.* Vol. 1: *State Terror and Popular Resistance in El Salvador.* Vol. 2: *State Terror and Popular Resistance in Guatemala.* London: Zed Books, 1985.

McCreery, David. "Debt Servitude in Rural Guatemala, 1876–1936." *Hispanic American Historical Review* 63, no. 4 (1983): 735–59.

———. *Development and the State in Reforma Guatemala 1871–1885.* Athens: Ohio University Center for International Studies, 1983.

———. "An 'Odious Feudalism': *Mandamiento* Labor and Commercial Agriculture in Guatemala, 1858–1920." *Latin American Perspectives* 13, no. 1 (Winter 1986): 99–117.

McLellan, David, and David Acheson, eds. *Among Friends: Personal Letters of Dean Acheson*. New York: Dodd, Mead, 1980.

McMahon, Robert. "Eisenhower and Third World Nationalism: A Critique of the Revisionists." *Political Science Quarterly* 101, no. 3 (1986): 453–73.

Macaulay, Neill. *The Sandino Affair*. New York: Quadrangle Books, 1967.

Marroquín Rojas, Clemente [Canuto Ocaña, pseud.]. *La "Carta política" del ciudadano Juan José Arévalo*. Guatemala City: Editorial San Antonio, 1965.

Marroquín Rojas, Clemente. *Crónicas de la Constituyente del 45*. 1945. Guatemala City: Tipografía Nacional, 1970.

———. *La derrota de una batalla*. Guatemala City: n.p., n.d.

———. *En el mundo de la polémica*. Guatemala City: n.p., 1971.

Martin, John Bartlow. *Overtaken by Events: The Dominican Crisis from the Fall of Trujillo to the Civil War*. Garden City, N.Y.: Doubleday, 1966.

Martínez Estévez, Alfonso. "En México se pelea duro el arevalismo y Martínez Estévez," *La Hora*, Mar. 4, 1963, pp. 4, 7.

Martz, John. *Central America: The Crisis and the Challenge*. Chapel Hill: University of North Carolina Press, 1959.

———. *Communist Infiltration in Guatemala*. New York: Vantage Press, 1956.

Matthews, Herbert. *A World in Revolution*. New York: Scribner's, 1971.

May, Stacy, and Galo Plaza. *The United Fruit Company in Latin America*. Washington, D.C.: National Planning Association, 1958.

Meers, Sharon. "A Pebble on the Beach: Guatemala, British Decline and the Fall of Jacobo Arbenz." B.A. thesis, Harvard University, 1988.

Mejía, Medardo. *Juan José Arévalo o el humanismo en la presidencia*. Guatemala City: Tipografía Nacional, 1951.

———. *El movimiento obrero en la Revolución de Octubre*. Guatemala City: Tipografía Nacional, 1949.

Melville, Thomas, and Marjorie Melville. *Guatemala—Another Vietnam?* Harmondsworth: Penguin Books, 1971.

———. *Guatemala: The Politics of Land Ownership*. New York: Free Press, 1971.

Mencía, Mario. "El Che Guevara en Guatemala." *Alero* 27 (Nov.–Dec. 1977): 99–111.

Méndez Montenegro, Julio César. *444 años de legislación agraria, 1513–1957*. Guatemala City: Imprenta Universitaria, 1960.

Meza, Víctor. *Historia del movimiento obrero hondureño*. Tegucigalpa: Editorial Guaymuras, 1980.

Miller, Hubert. "Catholic Leaders and Spiritual Socialism during the Arévalo Administration in Guatemala, 1945–1951." In Ralph Lee Woodward, Jr., ed., *Central America: Historical Perspectives on the Contemporary Crises*. New York: Greenwood Press, 1988, pp. 85–105.

Monroe, Keith. "Guatemala: What the Reds Left Behind." *Harper's*, July 1955, pp. 60–65.

Monteforte Toledo, Mario. *Una democracia a prueba de fuego*. Guatemala City: Tipografía Nacional, 1949.

———. *Guatemala: Monografía sociológica*. Mexico City: Universidad Nacional Autónoma de México, 1959.

Montejo, Victor. *Testimony: Death of a Guatemalan Village.* Willimantic, Conn.: Curbstone Press, 1987.

Montenegro, Arturo. "El capitán Montenegro defiende la obra del ex-Presidente Castillo Armas." *La Hora,* Apr. 1, 1958, p. 4.

Morales, Baltasar. *Derrocamiento de una tiranía.* Guatemala City: Tipografía Nacional, 1958.

Morán, Francisco. *Las jornadas cívicas de abril y mayo de 1944.* San Salvador: Editorial Universitaria, 1979.

Morazán, Francisco. "Apuntes de Francisco Morazán." Unpublished ms. in author's files.

———. "Los siete primeros y el hombre de la CIA." 2 vols. Unpublished ms. in author's files.

Mosley, Leonard. *Dulles: A Biography of Eleanor, Allen, and John Foster Dulles and Their Family Network.* New York: Dial Press, 1978.

Moya Posas, Emma. *La jornada épica de Castillo Armas vista desde Honduras.* Tegucigalpa: Imprenta La República, 1955.

Muñoz Meany, Enrique. *El hombre y la encrucijada.* Guatemala City: Tipografía Nacional, 1950.

Munro, Dana. *Intervention and Dollar Diplomacy in the Caribbean, 1900–1921.* Princeton: Princeton University Press, 1964.

Munro, Leslie Knox. "Oral History Interview." Princeton University, 1964.

Nájera Farfán, Mario Efraín. *Cuando el árbol cae . . . (un presidente que murió para vivir).* Guatemala City: n.p., 1958.

———. *Los estafadores de la democracia: Hombres y hechos en Guatemala.* Buenos Aires: Editorial Glem, 1956.

Náñez Falcón, Guillermo. "Erwin Paul Dieseldorff, German Entrepreneur in the Alta Verapaz of Guatemala, 1889–1937." Ph.D. diss., Tulane University, 1970.

Noval, Joaquín. *Tres problemas de la educación rural en Guatemala.* Guatemala City: José de Pineda Ibarra, 1959.

Obando Sánchez, Antonio. *Memorias.* Rev. ed. Guatemala City: Editorial Universitaria, 1978.

Oquelí, Ramón. "Un señor Juan Pablo Wainwright." *Revista Ariel,* Tegucigalpa, May–June 1974, pp. 11–13.

Ordóñez Argüello, Alberto, ed. *Arévalo visto por América.* Guatemala City: Ministerio de Educación Pública, 1951.

Organization of American States. *Annals of the Organization of American States.* Vol. 5. Washington D.C., 1953.

———. *Informe anual de la Comisión Interamericana de Derechos Humanos 1987–1988.* Washington, D.C., 1988.

———. *Tenth Inter-American Conference, Caracas, Venezuela, 1954. Chronological Collection of Documents.* Washington, D.C., 1954.

Ornes, Horacio. *Desembarco en Luperón.* Mexico City: Ediciones Humanismo, 1956.

Osegueda, Raúl. *Operación Guatemala $$ OK $$.* Mexico City: Editorial América Nueva, 1955.

Ovalle, N. K. *Industrial Report on the Republic of Guatemala.* Washington, D.C.: Inter-American Development Commission, 1946.

Palacios, José Antonio. "Formas de redistribución del ingreso en Guatemala." *Trimestre Económico*, Mexico City, vol. 19 (July–Sept. 1952): 422–51.

Paredes Moreira, José Luis. "Aspectos y resultados económicos de la reforma agraria en Guatemala." *Economía* 12 (Dec. 1966): 26–61.

———. *Aplicación del Decreto 900*. Guatemala City: IIES, Universidad de San Carlos, 1964.

———. *Reforma agraria: Una experiencia en Guatemala*. Guatemala City: Imprenta Universitaria, 1963.

Parkman, Patricia. *Nonviolent Insurrection in El Salvador: The Fall of Maximiliano Hernández Martínez*. Tucson: University of Arizona Press, 1988.

Parmet, Herbert. *Eisenhower and the American Crusade*. New York: Macmillan, 1972.

Partido Guatemalteco del Trabajo. *Estatutos del Partido Guatemalteco del Trabajo*. Guatemala City, 1952.

Partido Guatemalteco del Trabajo, Comisión Política del Comité Central. *La intervención norteamericana en Guatemala y el derrocamiento del régimen democrático*. Guatemala City, 1955.

Pearson, Neale. "The *Confederación Nacional Campesina de Guatemala* (CNCG) and Peasant Unionism in Guatemala, 1944–1954." M.A. thesis, Georgetown University, 1964.

———. "Guatemala: The Peasant Union Movement, 1944–1954." In Henry Landsberger ed., *Latin American Peasant Movements*. Ithaca, N.Y.: Cornell University Press, 1969, pp. 323–73.

Pellecer, Carlos Manuel. *Caballeros sin esperanza*. Guatemala City: Editorial del Ejército, 1973.

———. *. . . . camino equivocado, Che!* Guatemala City: Editorial del Ejército, 1971.

———. "Crónica de mi lucha por la tierra." Unpublished ms. in author's files.

———. "Dos yanquis más contra Guatemala." *El Imparcial*, 10 articles, Aug. 27–Sept. 7, 1982.

———. *Memoria en dos geografías*. Mexico City: Costa-Amic, 1964.

———. *Renuncia al comunismo*. Mexico City: Costa-Amic, 1963.

———. "Repudio al comunismo." *El Imparcial*, 8 articles, Nov. 28–Dec. 6, 1962.

———. "Utiles después de muertos." *La Hora*, Feb. 20, 1986, p.3.

Pellicer de Brody, Olga. *México y la Revolución Cubana*. Mexico City: El Colegio de México, 1972.

Pellicer de Brody, Olga, and Esteban Mancilla. *Historia de la Revolución Mexicana, 1952–1960*. Mexico City: El Colegio de México, 1978.

Penados del Barrio et al. *El clamor por la tierra*. (Pastoral Letter of the Guatemalan Bishops.) Guatemala: n.p., 1988.

Pérez, Luis. *Cuba: Between Reform and Revolution*. New York: Oxford University Press, 1988.

Pérez, Silverio. "Los oscuros acontecimientos de hace 37 años." *La Hora*, July 21, 1986, pp. 4, 11.

Phillips, David A. *The Night Watch: 25 Years of Peculiar Service*. New York: Atheneum, 1977.

Piedra-Santa, Rafael. "La construcción de ferrocarriles en Guatemala y los problemas financieros de la IRCA." *Economía* 15 (Jan.–Mar. 1968): 5–48.

Pike, Frederick. "The Catholic Church in Central America." *Review of Politics* 21 (Jan. 1959): 83–113.

Pinto Recinos, Ricardo Alberto. "Lo que yo sé del '20 de Octubre de 1944.' " *La Hora*, Oct. 25, 1984, pp. 2, 11.

———. "Sublevación de los caballeros cadetes." *La Hora*, 14 articles, July 22–Aug. 8, 1988.

———. "La rebelión de la Guardia de Honor, el 18 de Julio de 1949." *La Hora*, 15 articles, June 18–July 4, 1985.

Pitti, Joseph. "Jorge Ubico and Guatemalan Politics in the 1920's." Ph.D. diss., University of New Mexico, 1975.

Pollan, A. A. *The United Fruit Company and Middle America*. New York: New School for Social Research, 1944.

Posas, Mario. *Luchas del movimiento obrero hondureño*. San José, C.R.: EDUCA, 1981.

Powers, Thomas. *The Man Who Kept the Secrets*. New York: Pocket Books, 1981.

"Proyecciones de la Revolución del 44." *El Gráfico*, May 20, 1982, p. 5.

Pruessen, Ronald. *John Foster Dulles: The Road to Power*. New York: The Free Press, 1982.

Putzeys Rojas, Guillermo. *Así se hizo la Liberación*. Guatemala City: Tipografía Nacional, 1976.

Quan Rossell, Stella de la Luz. *Guatemala: una cultura de la ignominía*. 2 vols. Mexico City: Escuela Nacional de Antropología e Historia, 1972.

"Que pasó el 20 de Octubre?" *El Gráfico*, Oct. 20, 1973, p. 7.

Quintana, Epaminondas. *La generación de 1920*. Guatemala City: Tipografía Nacional, 1971.

Rabe, Stephen. *Eisenhower and Latin America: The Foreign Policy of Anticommunism*. Chapel Hill: University of North Carolina Press, 1988.

———. "The Elusive Conference: United States Economic Relations with Latin America, 1945–1952." *Diplomatic History* 2 (Summer 1978): 279–94.

Ramos Guzmán de Schmoock, María Eugenia. "El movimiento sindical en el decenio revolucionario (1944–1954)." Thesis, Universidad de San Carlos (Guatemala City), Escuela de Historia, 1978.

Ranelagh, John. *The Agency: The Rise and Decline of the CIA*. Rev. ed. New York: Touchstone, 1987.

Reichard, Gary. "Eisenhower as President: The Changing View." *South Atlantic Quarterly* 77 (Summer 1978): 265–81.

Reina, Ruben. "Chinautla, A Guatemalan Indian Community." In Richard Adams, ed., *Community Culture and National Change*. New Orleans: Middle American Research Institute, Tulane University, 1972, pp. 55–110.

"Resumen seleccionado del 'Estudio económico-contable sobre los Ferrocarriles Internacionales de Centro América, correspondiente a los años 1954 a 1957.' " *Economía* 16 (Apr.–June 1968): 30–55.

Richard, Pablo, and Guillermo Meléndez, eds. *La Iglesia de los Pobres en América Central*. San José, C.R.: Departamento Ecuménico de Investigaciones, 1982.

Rivas, Ernesto. "Versión inédita sobre la renuncia del general Ubico." *La Tarde*, Oct. 16, 1970, p. 9.

Rodman, Robert. "Operation Diablo." *Soldier of Fortune*, Summer 1976, pp. 16–19, 28, 58, 60, 77–78.

Rodríguez Loeche, Enrique. "Por qué fracasó la expedición a Santo Domingo." *Bohemia*, Havana, Aug. 21, 1949, pp. 58–59, 80–81, 89–90.

Roosevelt, Kermit. *Countercoup: The Struggle for the Control of Iran*. New York: McGraw-Hill, 1979.

Rosenthal, Mario. *Guatemala*. New York: Twayne Publishers, 1962.

Rostow, W. W. *Eisenhower, Kennedy, and Foreign Aid*. Austin: University of Texas Press, 1985.

Roy, M. N. *M. N. Roy's Memoirs*. Bombay: Allied Publishers, 1964.

Rubio Sánchez, Manuel. "Breve historia del desarrollo del cultivo del café en Guatemala." *Anales de la Sociedad de Geografía e Historia* 27 (Mar. 1953–Dec. 1954): 169–238.

Rubottom, Richard. "Oral History Interview." Princeton University, 1966.

Ruiz Franco, Arcadio. *Hambre y miseria*. Guatemala City: Tipografía Nacional, 1950.

Ruiz Morales, César Augusto. "Por qué solos?" *Revista Militar* 4 (1981): 89–93.

Saker-Ti. *Enrique Muñoz Meany*. Guatemala City, 1952.

Salazar, Carlos. *Memoria de los servicios prestados a la nación por el licenciado Carlos Salazar*. Guatemala City: Tipografía Sánchez & de Guise, 1945.

Salisbury, Harrison. *Without Fear or Favor: An Uncompromising Look at the New York Times*. New York: Ballantine Books, 1980.

Samayoa Chinchilla, Carlos. *El dictador y yo*. Guatemala City: Imprenta Iberia, 1950.

———. *El Quetzal no es rojo*. Guatemala City: n.p., 1956.

Samayoa Coronado, Francisco. *La Escuela Politécnica a través de su historia*. 2 vols. Guatemala City: Tipografía Nacional, 1964.

Sandoval Vásquez, Carlos Alberto. *Leifugados*. Mexico City: Impresora Periodística y Comercial, 1946.

Santa Cruz Morales, Raúl. "El Ejército de Liberación." *La Hora Dominical*, Aug. 20, 1978, pp. 5–16.

———. "Hace 42 años: Levantamiento indígena en Patzicía." *La Hora*, Oct. 31, 1986, pp. 7, 26.

———. "La invasión a Guatemala." *La Hora*, June 21, 1986, pp. 4, 11.

———. "Secuela del 2 de agosto." *La Hora Dominical*, Aug. 6, 1978, pp. 7–14.

Schifter, Jacobo. *Las alianzas conflictivas: Las relaciones de Costa Rica y Estados Unidos de la segunda guerra mundial a los inicios de la guerra civil*. San José, C.R.: Libro Libre, 1986.

Schlesinger, Arthur, Jr. "The Ike Age Revisited." *Reviews in American History* 9 (Mar. 1983): 1–11.

Schlesinger, Jorge. *Revolución comunista*. Guatemala City: Unión Tipográfica Castañeda, Avila y Cia, 1946.

Schlesinger, Stephen, and Stephen Kinzer. *Bitter Fruit: The Untold Story of the American Coup in Guatemala*. Garden City, N.Y.: Doubleday, 1982.

Schneider, Ronald. *Communism in Guatemala: 1944–1954*. New York: Praeger, 1959.

Selser, Gregorio. *El guatemalazo: La primera guerra sucia.* Buenos Aires: Iguazú, 1961.

Shoup, Laurence, and William Minter. *Imperial Brain Trust: The Council on Foreign Relations and United States Foreign Policy.* New York: Monthly Review Press, 1977.

Sierra Roldán, Tomás. *Diálogos con el coronel Monzón.* Guatemala City: Editorial San Antonio, 1958.

Silfa, Nicolás. *Guerra, traición y exilio.* 3 vols. Barcelona: n.p., 1980–1981.

Silva Girón, César Augusto. *La batalla de Gualán.* Guatemala City: n.p., 1977.

———. *Cuando gobiernan las armas.* Guatemala City: Oscar de León Palacios, 1987.

———. *12 horas de combate.* Guatemala City: Oscar de León Palacios, 1981.

Silva Jonama, Mario. Unpublished diary in author's files.

Silvert, Kalman. *A Study in Government: Guatemala.* New Orleans: Middle American Research Institute, Tulane University, 1954.

Skidmore, Thomas. *Politics in Brazil, 1930–1964.* New York: Oxford University Press, 1967.

Skinner-Klée, Jorge. *Legislación indigenista de Guatemala.* Mexico City: Instituto Indigenista Interamericano, 1954.

Slater, Jerome. *The OAS and United States Foreign Policy.* Columbus: Ohio State University Press, 1967.

Smith, Robert F. *The United States and Cuba.* New Haven, Conn.: College and University Press, 1960.

Solis, César. *Los ferrocarriles en Guatemala.* Guatemala City: Tipografía Nacional, 1952.

Stewart, Watt. *Keith and Costa Rica.* Albuquerque: University of New Mexico Press, 1964.

"Los sucesos de 1932." *Abra*, San Salvador, no. 13 (June 1976): 1–48.

Suslow, Leo. "Aspects of Social Reforms in Guatemala, 1944–1949." M.A. thesis, Colgate University, 1949.

———. "Social Security in Guatemala." Ph.D. diss., University of Connecticut, 1954.

Szulc, Tad. *Compulsive Spy: The Strange Career of E. Howard Hunt.* New York: The Viking Press, 1974.

Taracena Arriola, Arturo. "Les Origines du Mouvement Ouvrier au Guatemala, 1878–1932." Ph.D. diss., Ecole des Hautes Etudes en Sciences Sociales (Paris), 1982.

———. "El primer Partido Comunista de Guatemala (1922–1932)." *Araucaria de Chile*, Madrid, no. 27 (1984): 71–91.

Tax, Sol. *Penny Capitalism: A Guatemalan Indian Economy.* Chicago: University of Chicago Press, 1963.

Thomas, Hugh. *Cuba: The Pursuit of Freedom.* New York: Harper & Row, 1971.

Toriello, Guillermo. *La batalla de Guatemala.* Santiago de Chile: Editorial Universitaria, 1955.

———. *A dónde va Guatemala?* Mexico City: Editorial América Nueva, 1956.

Toriello, Jorge. "Revelaciones de Jorge Toriello." *La Semana*, Oct. 9, 1970, pp. 15–21.

Torres Moss, Clodoveo. "La justicia salomónica del general Jorge Ubico." *La Hora* (Suplemento cultural), Feb. 8, 15, 22, and Mar. 1, 1986.

Torres Rivas, Edelberto. "Crisis y coyuntura crítica: La caída de Arbenz y los contra-tiempos de la revolución burguesa." *Política y Sociedad* 4 (July–Dec. 1977): 53–83.

Travis, Helen Simon, and A. B. Magil. *The Truth about Guatemala*. New York: New Century Publishers, 1954.

Treverton, Gregory. *Covert Action: The Limits of Intervention in the Postwar World*. New York: Basic Books, 1987.

Tully, Andrew. *CIA: The Inside Story*. New York: William Morrow, 1962.

Turner, Frederick. *Catholicism and Political Development in Latin America*. Chapel Hill: University of North Carolina Press, 1971.

"2 de agosto: Versión del MLN." *La Hora*, Aug. 9, 1986, p. 4.

Unión Panamericana, Departamento de Estudios Jurídicos. *Tratado Interamericano de Asistencia Recíproca*. Vol. 1. Washington, D.C., 1973.

Unión Patriótica Guatemalteca. *Guatemala contra el imperialismo*. Havana, 1964.

United Nations. *El transporte en el istmo centroamericano*. Mexico City, 1953.

United Nations, Economic Commission for Latin America. *Economic Development of Guatemala*. Mexico City, 1951.

———. *La política tributaria y el desarrollo económico en Centroamérica*. Mexico City, 1956.

United Nations, Food and Agriculture Organization. *The World Coffee Economy*. Rome, 1961.

United Nations, Security Council. *Official Records*.

United States Congress. *Congressional Record*.

United States Congress, House Committee on Foreign Affairs. *Selected Executive Session Hearings of the Committee, 1951–1956*. Vol. 16: *Middle East, Africa, and Inter-American Affairs*. Washington, D.C.: GPO, 1980.

United States Congress, House Select Committee on Communist Aggression. *Communist Aggression in Latin America*. Hearings before the Subcommittee on Latin America, 83rd Congress, 2d session, Washington, D.C.: GPO, 1954.

United States Congress, Senate Committee of the Judiciary. *Communist Threat to the United States Through the Caribbean*. Hearings before the Subcommittee to Investigate the Administration of the Internal Security Act and Other Internal Security Laws, 87th Congress, 1st session, Washington, D.C.: GPO, 1961.

United States Congress, Senate Committee on Foreign Relations. *Executive Sessions of the Senate Foreign Relations Committee (Historical Series), 1951–1954*. Washington, D.C.: GPO, 1976–1977.

United States, Department of State. *Department of State Bulletin*. Washington, D.C.: GPO.

———. *Foreign Relations of the United States*. Washington, D.C.: GPO.

———. *Intervention of International Communism in Guatemala*. Washington, D.C.: GPO, 1954.

———. *Penetration of the Political Institutions of Guatemala by the International Communist Movement*. Washington, D.C.: GPO, 1954.

———. *Tenth Inter-American Conference*. Washington, D.C.: GPO, 1955.

United States Tariff Commission. *Economic Controls and Commercial Policy in Guatemala*. Washington, D.C.: GPO, 1947.

———. *Mining and Manufacturing Industries in Guatemala*. Washington, D.C.: GPO, 1949.

United States Treasury Department. *Census of American-Owned Assets in Foreign Countries*. Washington, D.C.: GPO, 1947.

Urquhart, Brian. *Hammarskjöld*. New York: Knopf, 1973.

Valdes López, Julia. "Aspectos socioculturales de la educación en Guatemala." Thesis, Universidad de San Carlos (Guatemala City), Facultad de Humanidades, 1976.

Vega, Bernardo, ed. *Los Estados Unidos y Trujillo–1947*. 2 vols. Santo Domingo: Fundación Cultural Dominicana, 1984.

Vilanova de Arbenz, María. "Aclaración." *La Prensa Libre*, San José, C.R., July 26, 1984, p. 3.

Villagrán Kramer, Francisco. "Los pactos políticos en la historia contemporánea." *Prensa Libre Domingo*, July 12, 19, and 26, 1987.

Villegas Rodas, Miguel. "Como se produjo la renuncia del general Jorge Ubico." *El Imparcial*, July 26, 1961, pp. 3, 11.

Wagner, Regina. "Actividades empresariales de los alemanes en Guatemala, 1850–1920." *Mesoamérica* 13 (June 1987): 87–123.

Wangüemert y Máiquez, J. L. "El diario de Cayo Confites." *Carteles*, Havana, Oct. 12, 19, 26, and Nov. 2, 1947.

Wasserstrom, Robert. "Revolution in Guatemala: Peasants and Politics under the Arbenz Government." *Comparative Studies in Society and History* 17 (Oct. 1975): 443–78.

Whetten, Nathan. *Guatemala: The Land and the People*. New Haven: Yale University Press, 1961.

———. "Land Reform in a Modern World." *Rural Sociology* 19 (1954): 329–36.

Williams, John. "The Rise of the Banana Industry and Its Influence on Caribbean Countries." M.A. thesis, Clark University, 1925.

Wise, David, and Thomas Ross. *The Invisible Government*. New York: Bantam, 1965.

Wood, Bryce. *The Dismantling of the Good Neighbor Policy*. Austin: University of Texas Press, 1985.

———. "Self-Plagiarism and Foreign Policy." *Latin American Research Review* 3, no. 3 (1968): 184–91.

Ydígoras Fuentes, Miguel. *My War with Communism*. Englewood Cliffs, N.J.: Prentice-Hall, 1963.

Young, John. "Great Britain's Latin American Dilemma: The Foreign Office and the Overthrow of 'Communist' Guatemala, June 1954." *International History Review* 8, no. 4 (Nov. 1986): 573-92.

Zamora Alvarez, José. *Las memorias de Andrés*. Guatemala City: Editorial del Ejército, 1975.

Zamora Castellanos, Pedro. *Nuestros cuarteles*. Guatemala City: n.p., 1972.

Zea Carrascosa, Manuel Octavio. *Semblanzas: Ministros de la guerra y de la defensa nacional de Guatemala*. Guatemala City: Ministerio de la Defensa Nacional, 1971.

Zea González, Emilio. *El espejismo de la democracia en Guatemala*. Guatemala City: n.p., 1989.

Zorrilla, Luis. *Relaciones de México con la República de CentroAmérica y con Guatemala*. Mexico City: Editorial Porrúa, 1984.

Zoumaras, Thomas. "Eisenhower's Foreign Economic Policy: The Case of Latin America." In Richard Melanson and David Mayers, eds., *Reevaluating Eisenhower*. Urbana: University of Illinois Press, 1987, pp. 155–91.

Index

Acheson, Dean, 115, 128, 226, 229–31, 236, 237, 366
Aguirre, Severo [pseud. Alejandro], 3, 6, 185, 189, 283, 285
Aldana Sandoval, Carlos, 28, 50, 51n, 69, 140, 198, 203, 346
Alejandro. *See* Aguirre, Severo
Alejos, Roberto, 393
Alemán, Miguel, 148
Alexander, Robert, 378n
Alfhem, 295–97, 299, 300, 302
Alianza Femenina Guatemalteca, 193, 197
Allende, Salvador, 350
Altolaguirre Ubico, Arturo, 62, 69
Alvarado Fuentes, Roberto, 174
Alvarado Jérez, Carlos, 180, 182
Alvarado Monzón, Bernardo, 76, 80, 141, 194, 283, 285, 332, 388
American Federation of Labor (AFL), 259–60
Amory, Robert, 244
Anzueto, Roderico, 26
Arana, Francisco, 4, 109, 137; death of, 64–71; and 1944 revolution, 28, 30, 50–51; presidential ambitions of, 51–64; and U.S., 123–24
Arbenz, Jacobo, 3, 4, 108, 180, 184, 186, 224–25, 266, 308, 365–66, 368, 383; agrarian reform program of, 143–46, 149–64, 210; and *Alfhem*, 279, 281–83; and army, 198–206, 221, 279, 287, 303, 304, 305n, 306–8, 379–80; assessment of, 377–81; background of, 134–39; and Caracas conference, 258, 273, 277–78, 286–87; and Church, 212–13; and death of Arana, 64–71; as Defense Minister, 53, 58–59, 60–63; economic program of, 149–50, 167–70, 209; in exile, 389–92; and invasion of Guatemala, 319–24, 327–29, 332–35, 338–39, 341; and labor unions, 189–90; and 1944 revolution, 28, 30, 50–53, 139–40; and Peurifoy, 255, 363–64; and PGT, 182–83, 191, 203, 286, 362, 378–79; political evolution of, 140–48; as presidential candidate, 73–75, 80–81, 83–84; public works program of, 165–66; resignation of, 342–51;

and revolutionary parties, 172, 174–76. *See also* Truman, Harry S
Arbenz, María. *See* Vilanova de Arbenz, María
Arbenz Vilanova, Arabella, 139n, 391
Arenas, José Luis, 251
Arévalo, Juan José, 3, 4, 28, 100n, 186n, 221n, 365; and Arana, 51, 52–57, 59, 62–65, 68–71; and Arbenz, 51, 74–75; assessment of, 377–78; background of, 32–33; and Caribbean Legion, 64, 107–16; and communists, 78, 81, 102, 119–20; after 1951, 392–94; as president, 38–48, 50, 161, 163; as presidential candidate, 34–36. *See also* Truman, Harry S; United Fruit Company
Argentina, 32–35, 108, 271, 274, 275, 277
army, Guatemalan: under Arbenz, 196–207, 221, 279, 303–8, 365, 378; under Arévalo, 50, 67–69, 72–73, 201; and invasion of Guatemala, 319, 321, 323–28, 332–42, 345–47, 352–55, 374–75; and 1944 revolution, 25–29, 31–32; after 1954, 385–88; and revolt of cadets, 357–60; under Ubico, 14–17, 137, 198. *See also* Arana, Francisco; Base Militar; Guardia de Honor; PBSUCCESS; Zacapa
Arriola, Jorge Luis, 139n
Asociación General de Agricultores (AGA), 145–46, 151, 209, 216
Asociación General de Industriales de Guatemala (AGIG), 209
Atlantic Highway, 166

Ball, George, 394
Banco Nacional Agrario (BNA), 156–58, 176
Bannell, Marshall, 260–63
Barahona Streber, Oscar, 97
Barrios Klée, Waldemar, 182, 194n
Barrios Peña, Ricardo, 55n, 56, 60, 63, 385, 393n
Barrios Peña, Roberto, 16n, 222, 248
Barzanallana, José, 323, 327, 334
Base Militar, 60, 68, 82–83, 322, 358–59
Batista, Fulgencio, 22, 185, 223, 274, 308
Bauer Paiz, Alfonso, 157, 176

Cognitive Task Analysis

Cognitive Task Analysis

Edited by

Jan Maarten Schraagen
TNO Human Factors

Susan F. Chipman
Office of Naval Research

Valerie L. Shalin
Wright State University

LAWRENCE ERLBAUM ASSOCIATES, PUBLISHERS
2000   Mahwah, New Jersey   London

Lawrence Erlbaum Associates, Inc., Publishers
10 Industrial Avenue
Mahwah, NJ 07430

Cover design by Kathryn Houghtaling Lacey

Library of Congress Cataloging-in-Publication Data

Cognitive task analysis / edited by Jan Maarten Schraagen,
Susan Chipman, Valerie Shalin.
    p. cm.
Includes bibliographical references and index.
  ISBN 0-8058-3383-8 (alk. paper)
  1. Cognition. 2. Task Analysis. I. Schraagen, Jan Maarten.
II. Chipman, Susan F. III. Shalin, Valerie L.
  BF311 .C55345 1999
  153.4—dc21   99-042583
                                       CIP

Printed in the United States of America
10 9 8 7 6 5 4 3 2 1

CONTENTS

CONTRIBUTORS

John Annett
University of Warwick

David P. Baker
American Institutes for Research

Sandrine Balbo
Commonwealth Scientific and Industrial Research Organisation

Philip J. Barnard
MRC Cognition and Brain Sciences Unit

Elizabeth Blickensderfer
Naval Air Warfare Center Training Systems Division

Guy A. Boy
European Institute of Cognitive Sciences and Engineering

Janis A. Cannon-Bowers
Naval Air Warfare Center Training Systems Division

Susan F. Chipman
Office of Naval Research

David Cunningham
Centre for Human Sciences, Defence Evaluation and Research Agency

Henk van Doorne
TNO Human Factors

David DuBois
Psychological Systems and Research, Inc.

Alan Lesgold
University of Pittsburgh

Jon May
University of Sheffield

David E. Meyer
University of Michigan

Mark A. Neerincx
TNO Human Factors

Thomas C. Ormerod
Lancaster University

Nadine Ozkan
Commonwealth Scientific and Industrial Research Organisation

Cecile Paris
Commonwealth Scientific and Industrial Research Organisation

Wilfried M. Post
TNO Human Factors

Scott S. Potter
MindSim, Inc.

Peter C. Rasker
TNO Human Factors

Richard E. Redding
University of Virginia

William C. Elm
MindSim, Inc.

Ludger van Elst
University of Heidelberg

Peter J.M.D. Essens
TNO Human Factors

John M. Flach
Wright State University

Wayne D. Gray
George Mason University

Fraser Hamilton
University of Brighton

W. Ian Hamilton
Human Engineering Limited

James H. Hicinbothom
CHI Systems, Inc.

Earl Hunt
University of Washington

Hilary Johnson
University of Bath

Peter Johnson
University of Bath

Susan Joslyn
University of Washington

George L. Kaempf
Sun Microsystems

Emilie M. Roth
Roth Cognitive Engineering

Mark Ruijsendaal
TNO Human Factors

Joan M. Ryder
CHI Systems, Inc.

Eduardo Salas
The University of Central Florida

Alma Schaafstal
TNO Human Factors

Franz Schmalhofer
University of Heidelberg

Jan Maarten Schraagen
TNO Human Factors

Thomas L. Seamster
Cognitive & Human Factors

Valerie L. Shalin
Wright State University

Valerie J. Shute
Air Force Research Laboratory

Lisa A. Torreano
National Research Council Fellow at AFRL

Kim J. Vicente
University of Toronto

Kent E. Williams
The University of Central Florida

David E. Kieras
University of Michigan

Susan S. Kirschenbaum
*Naval Undersea Warfare Center Division
Newport*

Gary Klein
Klein Associates, Inc

Ross E. Willis
Galaxy Scientific, Corp.

David D. Woods
The Ohio State University

Wayne W. Zachary
CHI Systems, Inc.

FOREWORD

This volume represents the state of the art in cognitive task analysis (CTA). Therefore, the chapters are about expertise and proficiency from a methodological perspective. Various methods of CTA are described in chapters that report research in diverse domains, and a number of important methodological issues are discussed along the way: What types of CTA methods are being used? What types of domains are being studied? What are the differences in the emphases and goals of the various schools of thought? What makes for a good CTA method? Exactly how does one conduct CTA? How does one pick a CTA method to use in a particular project?

In the United States, from the mid-1970s to the early 1980s, educational, cognitive, and human factors psychology researchers recognized a need to place the adjective "cognitive" before the phrase "task analysis." It seemed a natural thing to do. To some, the phrase "task analysis" might harken back to behaviorism and the so-called "knobs-and-dials era" of human factors psychology in the years following World War II. However, task analysis, which dates back to the late 1800s, was never purely behavioral, and applied psychology was never void of cognition. Indeed, the very concept of the human–machine system dates back to British industrial psychology of the 1920s. The foundations of applied psychology were set by the first generation of European PhD experimental psychologists in domains such as psychometrics, aviation, and industrial psychology. Despite interruptions to and changes in applied psychology brought on by the World Wars, the traditions, or one might say "styles" of European applied psychology, continued on course and led to current schools of thought—the Dutch tradition of ergonomics, the French tradition of work analysis, the British tradition of functional task analysis, and so on.

Whatever tapestry we may weave to place history in relief, today the foreground is information technology. The goal is human-centered computing, user-friendly interfaces, graphics displays that support direct perception and understanding, systems that support situation awareness, and intelligent decision aids and expert systems. As technology becomes more complex, the goals of human-centered computing become more salient and important.

It is perhaps ironic that much of the modern work that claims to rely on CTA is aimed toward design of machines and tools. The first generation of applied psychologists did not spend all of their time developing psychometric tests; they spent it designing machines—from the shape of screwdriver handles, to the construction of simulators to test candidate railroad conductors, to redesign of controls for lathes and other machine tools (see Barnes, 1937; von Drunen, 1997). In redesigning even simple tools such as shovels, industrial psychologists such as Frederick W. Taylor began by studying the performance of experts (see Taylor, 1911). An expert laborer or machinist was often brought in, their behavior studied, their knowledge elicited, and their goals and tasks specified. The next step would be to redesign the tool (and often even an entire workspace).

Modern information technology has changed the nature of the research and development enterprise. Whereas performance at the level of action (i.e., the keyboard) remains important, cognition is ever more critical. A primary goal of research is to build machines and design jobs and training methods that make people smarter (see Norman, 1993), or that turn ordinary folks into domain experts. Broadly construed, CTA can embrace the efforts at "knowledge elicitation," conducted by applied psychologists who are involved in the construction of expert systems or the preservation of corporate knowledge. CTA embraces the use of "software-assisted knowledge acquisition" tools that conduct knowledge elicitation and go on to generate implementable representations of knowledge. CTA embraces the methods used to develop training programs that are based on a gold standard—knowledge and skill elicited from domain experts. CTA embraces the efforts of cognitive psychologists who build millisecond-by-millisecond models of how particular mental operations chain together in the conduct of complex tasks. It embraces the methods of think aloud problem solving used in cognitive research on expert–novice differences. It embraces the different interviewing techniques anthropologists and sociologists use in studies ranging from the activities of design teams to the knowledge of tribal healers.

The focus of this volume is on *method* and *methodology* in the analysis of cognition within the context of applied work that, in one way or another involves real-world domains where proficiency and expertise are critical. Therefore, the volume serves as an invitation to cognitive psychologists who may be interested in getting into this avenue of research. This volume is a useful source for courses on cognitive psychology and applied cognitive psychology. It will also serve as an impetus to reinforce and build on the palette of methods that are used to study experts.

—Robert R. Hoffman

REFERENCES

Barnes, R. M. (1949). *Motion and time study* (3rd ed., 1st ed., 1937). New York: Wiley.

Norman, D. A. (1993). *Things that make us smart: Defending human attributes in the age of the machine.* Reading, MA: Perseus.

Taylor, F. W. (1911). *Principles of scientific management.* New York: Harper & Row.

von Drunen, P. (1997). *Psychotechnics.* In W. G. Bringmann, H. E. Lock, R. Miller & C. E. Early (Eds.), *A pictorial history of psychology* (pp. 480–484). Chicago: Quintessence.

PREFACE

For almost a century, psychologists have been interested in matching tasks with human capabilities. The ultimate goal of this endeavor was, and still is, to make work safe, productive, and healthy. Matching tasks with human capabilities requires a deep understanding both of the task domain and the human practitioner. Over the past 100 years, various techniques have been at the psychologist's disposal, depending on the nature of the work. Before World War II, psychologists mainly analyzed manual work with the aim of improving the efficiency of every step in the work process. This changed in the 1950s when the number of white-collar workers started to exceed the number of blue collar workers. New techniques were refined for analyzing mental rather than manual work. Cognitive Task Analysis (CTA) is a broad area consisting of tools and techniques for describing the knowledge and strategies required for task performance. CTA has implications for the development of expert systems, training and instructional design, expert decision-making, and policy-making. It has been applied in a wide range of settings, with different purposes, for instance: specifying user requirements in system design or specifying training requirements in training needs analysis.

Although CTA has emerged as a new branch of applied psychology, there is as yet no single book describing the various perspectives that exist in the field, nor is there a book that can be used for graduate courses or for practitioners. Our goal in this book is to present in a single source a comprehensive, in-depth introduction to the field of CTA. We have attempted to include as many examples as possible in the book, making it highly suitable for those wishing to undertake a CTA themselves. The book also contains a historical introduction to the field and an annotated bibliography, making it an excellent guide to additional resources. The book is therefore suitable for graduate students taking courses in CTA and instructors teaching such courses. It is also of interest to practitioners in industry looking for techniques and tools that can be applied in the course of specifying user requirements for system or interface design. Those interested in training and instructional design should also benefit from reading this book. Finally, the book will be of interest to those working in the areas of job analysis and job design.

Most of the chapters in the volume have evolved from talks originally presented at the NATO-ONR Workshop on Cognitive Task Analysis held between October 30–November 1, 1997, in Washington, D.C. The chapters have benefitted from a subsequent extensive review process, and most were actually completed in late 1998, early 1999. The workshop itself was one of the activities of a NATO research Study Group on Cognitive Task Analysis[1], initiated by TNO Human Factors research Institute and chaired by Jan Maarten Schraagen of that institute. The Study Group started in 1996 by reviewing the state-of-the-art of the field of CTA. It turned out that the field was quite fragmented, and that not much guidance could be provided to analysts wanting to carry out a cognitive task analysis. CTA was more of an art than a science. Because the review was heavily focused on the early

Study Group wanted to get a better appreciation of more recent developments, and therefore decided to organize a workshop with experts in the field. The workshop was by invitation only; although most contributors were directly invited to submit an abstract, there also was an open invitation on a bulletin board to solicit a wider response. Of the 50 abstracts received, 23 were finally selected for a presentation. As reflected by the chapters in this book, a wide range of nationalities was involved, primarily from the United States and Great Britain, but there were contributions from The Netherlands, France, Germany, Canada, and Australia. More importantly, contributors who would normally not speak to each other because of their widely differing viewpoints, now started to listen to each other. The presentations were longer than the regular 20-minute conference presentation, and more time was available for discussion. Moreover, there were no parallel sessions, so everyone could participate in the discussions. The Workshop was held in the stately Hay-Adams Hotel, opposite the White House, and this choice of venue (by Valerie Shalin) undoubtedly added to the success of the Workshop.

ACKNOWLEDGMENTS

I thank NATO/RTO for their support of the Research Study Group on Cognitive Task Analysis. I would like to thank Susan Chipman of the Office of Naval Research for financing the Workshop, reviewing the chapters, and being such a loyal and well-informed member of the NATO Research Study Group. Without her, this book would simply not exist. I also would like to thank Valerie Shalin of Wright State University for organizing the Workshop and for spending a great deal of effort in reviewing all chapters. My thanks also go to the members of the NATO Research Study Group who have contributed in one way or another to the genesis of this book: John Annett, Colin Sheppard, Bob Taylor, Susan Chipman, Mike Strube, Valerie Shute, Jean-Yves Ruisseau, Nicolas Graff, and Gert Dörfel. Robert Hoffman did his best to persuade us to "do the book you want to do." Last, but not least, my sincere thanks to Erica van Kooij for her tremendous efforts in producing the camera ready copy of this volume, and to Willeke Roodenburg and Loes Meijer for substituting for Erica when she "was working on the book."

—*Jan Maarten Schraagen*

---

[1] Research Study Group 27 was part of the Human Factors and Medicine Panel of the NATO Research and Technology Organization. RSG 27 was active from 1996 until 1998.

INTRODUCTION AND HISTORY

1

INTRODUCTION TO COGNITIVE TASK ANALYSIS

Susan F. Chipman
Office of Naval Research

Jan Maarten Schraagen
TNO Human Factors

Valerie L. Shalin
Wright State University

Modern work, with its increasing reliance on automation to support human action, is focusing attention on the cognitive aspects of work that are not accessible to direct observation. For example, it is obvious that the physical acts of button pushing that occur in the command center of a modern ship are of less intrinsic importance than the mental decision processes executed via those actions. The mental processes organize and give meaning to the observable physical actions. Attempts to analyze a task like air traffic control with traditional behavioral task analysis techniques made the shortcomings of those techniques strikingly clear (Means, 1993). Starting in the 1960s, the cognitive revolution in academic psychology has both increased our awareness of the extensive cognitive activity underlying even apparently simple tasks and provided research techniques and theories for characterizing covert cognition. Hence, the term *cognitive task analysis* is coming into use to describe a new branch of applied psychology. The relative newness of this enterprise is evidenced by the fact that, as of this writing, a search of the entire Psyc INFO database with the term yielded only 28 items, some irrelevant, and a search in the Science Citation Index yielded 30 items. The high current interest in cognitive task analysis is evidenced by recent literature review efforts undertaken by a British aerospace company (confidential) and by the French military (Doireau, Grau, & Poisson, 1996) as well as the NATO Study Group effort reported here.

Cognitive task analysis is the extension of traditional task analysis techniques to yield information about the knowledge, thought processes, and goal structures that underlie observable task performance. Some would confine the term exclusively to the methods that focus on the cognitive aspects of tasks, but this seems counterproductive. Overt observable behavior and the covert cognitive functions behind it form an integrated whole. Artificially separating and focusing on the cognitive alone is likely to produce information that is not very useful in understanding, aiding, or training job performance. The tension between traditional behavioral task analysis techniques and newer cognitive task analysis is largely a U.S. phenomenon. Elsewhere, behaviorism never took hold as it did in the U.S., where military regulations governing training development have forbidden talk of processes that go on inside the head almost until the present day. Annett, Duncan, Stammers, and Gray's (1971) hierarchical task analyses, for example, often segued smoothly from the domain of observable behavior to the internal world of perception and cognition (see also Duncan, 1974). The changing nature of work, however, is universal throughout the developed world. Even those who did not eschew analysis of the cognitive aspects of work now need more powerful tools and techniques to address the large role of cognition in modern work. Chapter 2 (this volume) reviews the history of task analysis more fully.

Analyses of jobs and their component tasks may be undertaken for a wide variety of purposes, including the design of computer systems to support human work, the development of training, or the development of tests to certify job competence. An emerging frontier of modern task analysis is the analysis of entire working teams' activities. This is done for purposes such as the allocation of responsibilities to individual humans and cooperating computer systems, often with the goal of reducing the number of humans who must be employed to accomplish the team function. Given the purposes and constraints of particular projects, several (cognitive) task analysis approaches merit consideration. Savvy customers and practitioners of cognitive task analysis must know that one approach will not fit all circumstances. On the other hand, a thorough-going cognitive task analysis may repay the substantial investment required by proving applicable to purposes beyond the original intent. For example, Zachary, Ryder, and Hicinbothom (Chap. 22, this volume) analyzed the tasks of the AEGIS antiair warfare team in order to build an artificially intelligent training system, but these same analyses are being used to guide the design of advanced work stations and new teams with fewer members.

This book is the ultimate product of a NATO study group aiming to capture the state of the art of cognitive task analysis. The intent is to advance it toward a more routine engineering discipline—one that could be applied reliably by practitioners not necessarily educated at the doctoral level in cognitive psychology or cognitive science. To that end, two major activities were undertaken. One was a review of the state of the art of cognitive task analysis, focusing on recent articles and chapters claiming to review cognitive task analysis techniques. This effort produced a bibliographic resource appearing as chapter 28 in this book. We hope that this chapter gives sufficient information to help students and other readers decide which of these earlier contributions to the field they should read for their particular purposes. The second major activity of the NATO study group was an international workshop intended to provide an up-to-date snapshot of cognitive task analyses, emphasizing new developments. Invitations were extended to known important contributors to the field. The opportunity to participate was also advertised widely through electronic mailing lists to capture new developments and ongoing projects that might not be known to the study group members organizing the workshop. This book is largely the product of that workshop, sharing its insights into the state of the art of this new field. This introduction provides an overview of these two activities. First, we sketch a prototypic cognitive task analysis, based on results from the NATO study group. Next, we describe the organization of the chapters in this book that resulted from the international workshop.

THE PROTOTYPIC COGNITIVE TASK ANALYSIS PROCESS AS SEEN IN PRIOR LITERATURE

Ironically, the cognitive analysis of tasks is itself a field of expertise like those it attempts to describe. Reviewing recent discussions of cognitive task analysis reveals that the explicitly stated state of the art is lacking specification of just those kinds of knowledge most characteristic of expertise. A large number of particular, limited methods are described repeatedly. However, little is said about how these can be effectively orchestrated into an approach that will yield a complete analysis of a task or job. Little is said about the conditions under which an approach or method is appropriate. Clearly, the relevant conditions that need to be considered include at least the type of task being analyzed, the purpose for which the analysis is being done (human-computer interaction design, training, testing, expert system development), and the resources available for the analysis, particularly the type of personnel available to do the analysis (cognitive scientists, cognitive psychologists, educational specialists, subject-matter experts). The literature is also weak in specifying the way in which the products of task analysis should be used in designing either training or systems with which humans will interact. The prior literature on cognitive task analysis is also limited by a focus on the tasks of individuals, almost exclusively existing tasks for which there are existing task experts.

Nevertheless, the literature review effort did, within these limits, provide the image of a prototypic ideal case of the cognitive task analysis process, as it might be when unhampered by resource limitations. What emerges as the ideal case, assuming that resource limitations are not a problem? Although the answer to this question may vary somewhat, depending on the purpose for which the analysis is being done, we set aside that consideration for a while or assume that the purpose is training and associated proficiency measurement. Several of the articles we reviewed are strong in their presentation of an inclusive recommended approach to cognitive task analysis (e.g., Hall, Gott, & Pokorny, 1995; Hoffman, Shadbolt, Burton, & Klein, 1995; Means, 1993; DuBois & Shalin, 1995). In the present volume, the following chapters also present reasonably inclusive descriptions of the process: chapter 3 by DuBois and Shalin, chapter 6 by Flach, and chapter 9 by Seamster, Redding, and Kaempf.

Preliminary Phase

One should begin a cognitive task analysis with a study of the job or jobs involved to determine what tasks merit the detailed attention of a cognitive task analysis. Standard approaches from personnel psychology are appropriate for this phase of the effort, using unstructured interviews and/or questionnaires to determine the importance, typicality, and frequency of tasks within job performance. Hall et al. (1995) discussed this preliminary phase, as did DuBois and Shalin (1995) with somewhat more methodological detail. DuBois and Shalin also pointed out the importance of focusing on the tasks or problems within general tasks that discriminate more expert performance from routine performance, even though these may not be high-frequency events. Klein Associates' approach seems to embody the same view, with an emphasis on gathering data about past *critical incidents* in experts' experience.

Depending on the availability of written materials about the job or task, such as existing training materials, the first step for those responsible for the analysis probably should be to read those materials to gain a general familiarity with the job or task and a knowledge of the specialized vocabulary (this is referred to as *bootstrapping* by Hoffman et al. [1995], and *table-top analysis* by Flach [chap. 6, this volume]). The major alternative is to begin with informal, unstructured interviews with persons who have been identified as experts. In the ideal case, the task analysis becomes a team effort among one or more experts in cognitive task analysis and several subject-matter experts. Of course, it is important to obtain the time, effort, and cooperation of experts who are in fact expert. Hall et al. (1995) discussed the issue of the scarcity of true experts and the selection of appropriate experts in moderate detail. Hoffman et al. (1995) were also concerned with the gradations of expertise. Articulate experts with recent experience in both performing and teaching the skill are particularly useful. For example, the MYCIN (Buchanan & Shortliffe, 1984) expert was reknowned for his ability to teach medical diagnosis.

It is also true that not just anyone is suitable for acting as a cognitive task analyst—not even just anyone who is educated in cognitive psychology and cognitive science. Analysts must have the social skills to establish rapport with the subject-matter experts (SMEs), sometimes across the barriers of different social, cultural and economic backgrounds. If doing unstructured or even structured interviews, they must be verbally adept to adapt to the changing circumstances of the interview. They must be intelligent, quick learners because they have to learn a great deal about the task to analyze it effectively. Hoffman et al. (1995) and Crandall, Klein, Militello, and Wolf (1994) discussed some of these issues about the requirements for cognitive task analysts. Forsythe and Buchanan (1993) also appears to be a reference of interest on these points. There is also a good deal of literature from the expert systems community dealing with the practicalities of interviewing and with requirements that both the knowledge engineer and the expert must meet (e.g., Firlej & Hellens, 1991; McGraw & Harbison-Briggs, 1989; Meyer & Booker, 1991; Waterman, 1986).

Identifying Knowledge Representations

A major goal for the initial unstructured interviews with the SMEs should be to identify the abstract nature of the knowledge involved in the task, that is, the type of knowledge representations that need to be used. This can order the rest of the task analytic effort. This point is not explicit in the literature, but the more impressive, convincing approaches are organized around a knowledge representation or set of knowledge representations appropriate for the job or task. For example, DuBois and Shalin (1995, chap. 3, this volume) use a goal/method graph annotated with additional information about the basis for method selection and the explanation of the rationale or principles behind the method. Less explicitly, the PARI method (Hall et al., 1995) gathers essentially the same information supplemented by information about the experts' mental organization of device structure and function. Crandall et al. (1994) advocated collecting mental models of the task and of the team context of work, as well as of the equipment. For eliciting knowledge about how a device or system works, Williams and Kotnur (1993) described Miyake's (1986) *constructive interaction*. Benysh, Koubek, and Calvez (1993) proposed a knowledge representation that combines procedural information with conceptual information. Similarly, in ongoing work, Williams, Hultman, and Graesser (1998) have collaborated on ways to combine the representations of declarative and procedural knowledge.

Semantic networks are probably overrepresented in reviews of knowledge acquisition methods relative to their actual utility. Although measures of conceptual relatedness or organization are sensitive to growth in expertise, they may actually be derived from more complex knowledge organizations in the experts' minds, such as those mentioned earlier that integrate procedural and declarative knowledge. For example, it might be a mistake to attempt to directly train the conceptual organizations one deduces from studies of experts. However, semantic networking or clustering techniques have been successfully used to structure more effective computer interfaces (Patel, Drury, & Shalin, 1998; Roske-Hofstrand & Paap, 1986; Vora, Helander, & Shalin, 1994). As we gain experience with cognitive task analysis, it may become possible to define a taxonomy of tasks that, in effect, would classify tasks into types for which the same abstract knowledge representations and the same associated knowledge-elicitation methods are appropriate. However, we should always keep in mind the possibility that the particular task of concern may involve some type of knowledge not in the stereotype for its assigned position in the classification scheme.

Knowledge-Elicitation Techniques

Having identified the general framework for the knowledge that has to be obtained, the analysts can then proceed to employ the knowledge-elicitation techniques or methods discussed in the articles reviewed. Structured interviews can be used to obtain information—an approach that is well discussed in Hoffman et al. (1995), Randel, Pugh, and Reed (1996), and Crandall et al. (1994). The extreme of the structured interview is the computer-aided knowledge-elicitation approach, discussed in reviews by Williams and Kotnour (1993) and Cooke (1994) and exemplified by Shute's (chap. 5, this volume) DNA cognitive task analysis software and Williams' (chap. 11, this volume) CAT and CAT-HCI tools. The latter structure and support a generalized version of a GOMS-style analysis, generating much the same sort of goal/method representation recommended by DuBois and Shalin. Of course these interviews and other methods must be focused on an appropriate representative set of problems or cases previously identified, as alluded to earlier. The PARI method (Hall et al., 1995) features the participation of SMEs to develop appropriate problems. The importance of an appropriate sample of problems or tasks is perhaps most obvious for the simple case of the use of GOMS analysis to evaluate alternative keyboard/display designs. The basis for evaluation would be differences in the predicted execution times—for a representative sample of tasks. In training development, the issue is providing adequate coverage of essential knowledge and skills.

Structured interviews and their extensions into computer-aided methods used by SMEs assume that the experts have direct conscious access to their relevant knowledge and skill. However, research on expertise has shown that this cannot be assumed. Much goes on below the level of conscious awareness, especially in skills that are exercised under time pressure or have significant perceptual and/or motor aspects. (For this reason, although the true ideal case might seem to be having the cognitive analyst and SME combined in one person, as has been true for many of the successful intelligent tutoring projects, it is never safe to assume that experts can directly explicate task knowledge.) Often one may simply extract the expert's naive psychological theory of how the task is performed—a theory that will not stand up to empirical investigation. (Obviously even expert cognitive psychologists often propose theories of task performance that do not stand up to empirical investigation.) For this reason, the use of process-tracing methods (cf. Cooke, 1994) is recommended.

Observation of expert performance, which may be videorecorded and carefully and elaborately coded, belongs in this category. Observation tends to contribute primarily to an analysis of the overt, observable aspects of the task. However, if the task involves communication among team members, cognitive aspects of the task may be revealed. Observation of apprenticeship training is likely to reveal such information, and there is a variation of this in which the expert is asked to coach an analyst in task performance. Most conspicuous among the cognitive process tracing methods is the collection of verbal think aloud protocols while the SMEs perform a representative set of task problems. (The PARI method involves the use of SMEs to simulate problems—fault effects, test results etc.—for other experts attempting unfamiliar problems.) To increase the information yield for practical applications, protocols may be supplemented with probe questions or retrospective review of videotapes with probe questions (cf. Dubois & Shalin, chap. 3; Zachary, Ryder, & Hicinbothom, chap.22, this volume). There is also a variant approach called *interruption analysis* that several reviews mention. The goal of these methods is to bring out relevant knowledge in the context of use. Of course, verbal protocol methods and other verbal methods are relatively ineffective in getting at nonverbal types of knowledge, although one may discover that a surprising amount of specialized perceptual vocabulary has been developed for purposes of training and teamwork. Experimental psychology has provided other process tracing methods, such as the collection of eye fixations, that may prove useful in getting at aspects of task performance not represented verbally.

If a semantic network of concepts seems to be an appropriate part of the representation of task knowledge, a large number of knowledge-elicitation techniques are available for this purpose. Olson and Biolsi (1991) provide the best discussion of these—the associated data analysis methods, and the relations among them—along with a useful diagram of those relationships. These methods generally can be used with only a small set of concepts, a serious limitation given the large number of concepts actually involved in any area of expertise. Cooke (1994) and Benysh, Koubek, and Calvez (1993) are the only authors who give much attention to the problem of selecting the set of concepts to be used with these methods.

Choosing target knowledge representations provides guidance to the overall cognitive task analysis effort. A wide variety of techniques from experimental psychology, including novel ones invented for the purpose, might be used to fill in the information needed in one's chosen knowledge representations. Hoffman et al. (1995) referred to this deliberate modification of the familiar task as the use of *contrived techniques*. Although contrived techniques can make the expert feel uncomfortable and may sometimes give misleading results, Hoffman et al. noted that they can be informative and tend to be more efficient in yielding information. Once they have been developed, it is usual to present the knowledge representations to the SMEs to review for reasonableness and to gather other comments. Of course if the analysis becomes the basis of an expert system or expert cognitive model, one may also be able to evaluate its performance for its resemblance to the performance of human experts.

Using CTA Products

Once you have done a cognitive task analysis, how do you make use of the products in your application? This is a definite weak point in the literature. Using the output of PARI analyses to develop training systems has proved problematic for the U.S.

Air Force. If one has a detailed goal/method analysis down to the production system level, an analysis of the type that Williams' CAT tool is designed to support, this can probably be converted into a running computational model that can function as the student model of an intelligent tutoring system. John R. Anderson (personal communication, 29 August, 1995) has claimed that, once such a cognitive model has been developed, the actual development of a tutoring system is quite trivial, given the tools available in his lab. Of course the process described here would also have yielded a set of problems that could be used in the tutoring system. DuBois, Shalin, and their associates have developed a method for using task analysis results to generate test items. An elaboration of the same method applies to the identification of information requirements for interface design (Shalin & Geddes, 1994, 1998; Shalin, Geddes, Mikesell, & Ramamurthy, 1993). The ACTA cd-rom (1997) developed by Klein Associates for training cognitive task analysis methods contains useful suggestions for the ways in which the information developed can be used to improve training (Militello & Hutton, 1998; Militello et al., 1997). From the work of Schvaneveldt (1990) and his associates, it appears that any of the techniques for analyzing concept organization can be readily used to provide crude assessments of the development of expertise by measuring the resemblance of learners' conceptual organization to that of experts.

In the present volume, the chapters by Boy (chap. 18); Johnson, Johnson, and Hamilton (chap. 13); Neerincx, van Doorne, and Ruijsendaal (chap. 21); Ormerod (chap. 12); Paris, Balbo, and Ozkan (chap. 16); and Potter, Roth, Woods, and Elm (chap. 20) attempt to bridge the gap between cognitive task analysis and system design using task models. Task models are formal ways of describing standard task elements. They serve to structure knowledge acquisition and bridge the gap between cognitive task analysts and software engineers.

As in the case of training, applications of cognitive task analysis to human–system interaction began by analyzing the interactions of experienced users with existing systems, often to identify problematic features of existing interfaces. These methods could be extended rather readily to evaluate detailed designs for new interfaces or to compare multiple designs for a future interface, as was done with the GOMS engineering model approach developed by Card, Moran, and Newell (1983). The GOMS approach (analysis into Goals, Operators, Methods, and Selection criteria for methods) (John and Kieras, 1994) is conceptually similar to the tradition of hierarchical task analysis dominant in the United Kingdom.

UPDATING THE STATE OF THE ART
THE ORGANIZATION OF THIS BOOK

After a chapter by Annett (chap. 2) that deals with the history of task analysis methods, this book is organized into three primary sections. The first deals with applications of task analysis to training of individuals, including related applications to testing. The second section deals with applications to the design of human–system interaction, primarily considering the case of individual operators. These chapters display significant advances in cognitive task analysis for the design of truly new systems, rather than mere modifications of existing systems. Training and systems design applications, of course, interact in interesting ways. Design inadequacies can generate major training problems, and minimizing training requirements is an important criterion for system design. The third section cuts across these major application areas, focusing on task analysis methods for situations involving work teams rather than individuals. This is now a major frontier for new developments in cognitive task analysis methods. Although cognitive psychology, which provides the basic scientific foundations for cognitive task analysis, has focused on the individual learner, thinker, and performer, actual work typically involves interacting teams of at least a few and often many individuals. Finally, the book closes with a discussion by Lesgold. As mentioned earlier, the resources provided by the book's own chapters are supplemented by a chapter reviewing prior contributions to the field. We hope that this will be useful in selecting additional readings for courses or self-study.

Cognitive Task Analysis for Individual Training, Performance Assessment, and Selection

Most often when the purpose of task analysis is for training or test development, there are existing task experts whose knowledge and performance potentially can be analyzed to provide guidance in developing training or testing products. The prototypic task analysis process outlined earlier is most clearly applicable here.

The first chapter in Section II (chap. 3, by DuBois and Shalin), provides an introduction to the use of such methods. It is organized and oriented by a general theoretical framework provided by the cognitive science characterization of human problem solving. This theoretical framework almost provides a set of blanks for the analyst to fill in, suggesting a way in which cognitive task analysis might become a more routinized form of engineering. The original purpose of their approach when it was developed was to enable the development of new tests that better predict job performance by assessing the cognitive aspects of job skills. The analytic approach has now been supplemented by software to aid test authors in developing test items based on the analyses. The analytic approach would be equally applicable to applications in training development. However, as presented, it does not go on to the level of detail needed for developing fine-grained running computational models of cognitive skill, such as those underlying the artificially intelligent tutors developed by Anderson and his associates at Carnegie-Mellon University. It is theoretically consistent with such applications and could undoubtedly be extended to support them.

Chapter 4 by Schaafstal and Schraagen provides less detail about the cognitive task analysis processes used, but their work is in the same general theoretical framework. It presents an inspirational case in which cognitive task analysis was dramatically successful in improving training efficiency, leading to large-scale applications of the methods in reforming additional training courses. It is an example that others would hope to emulate. Furthermore, it is an example that can be used to allay the concerns of those who fear that doing a cognitive task analysis will result in longer training.

Shute et al. (chap. 5) describe an early effort to provide computer support to an SME in analyzing a skill, in an attempt to decrease the personnel resources required to conduct a task analysis. The computer support is quite similar to the software described by Williams in the next section on human–system interaction. In a flexible sense, both are providing blanks for the analyst to fill, resulting in a record of the analytic product. Both bear strong resemblances to Annett's earlier hierarchical task analysis method. Both tend to be limited by the tacit assumption that the expert has conscious insight into the basis of his or her own expertise, but they could also be used as tools by a cognitive task analysis expert using a variety of methods to get around those limitations.

Chapter 6 by Flach provides an ecological perspective on cognitive task analysis. Accordingly, the goal of the analysis is to uncover the significant patterns within a particular domain, which experts discover after years of practice. By focusing on domains with a heavy perceptual-motor component, Flach addresses the perceptual aspects of expertise that are most vulnerable to the limitations of task analysis methods inspired by information-processing views of cognition. His task analysis methods reflect concern for obtaining a comprehensive view of the work situation by sampling multiple experts. Flach suggests using a variety of techniques for discovering the significant patterns, including a recommendation that analysts attempt to perform the task in question to experience first hand the constraints that may be difficult for the expert to describe.

Chapter 7 by Vicente also challenges the theoretical predispositions that motivate many of the methods described in this book. Like Flach, Vicente suggests that the demands of the task domain should be the focus of analysis. By focusing on domain constraints and goals that shape task activities, Vicente promotes task descriptions that allow specific details and individual strategies to influence observed behavior. By equating expertise with an understanding of domain constraints and goals, Vicente also provides another entry in a long-standing debate concerning the optimal nature of training—whether it should focus on developing understanding of the task domain or train specific procedures. Such understanding holds the promise of flexible response to novel situations, but there is always the question whether the trainees will be able to generate actions from that understanding—or to generate them fast enough to be useful.

Finally, chapter 8 by Hunt and Joslyn describes a different form of task analysis that produces not a detailed description of task performance but a description at the level of general information-processing abilities or capacities. This form of description is useful in developing less knowledge-intensive tasks that can serve as selection tests to predict which candidates will be successful in learning and performing the target tasks. We find counterparts to this alternate perspective in applications to the design of human–system interaction as well.

Cognitive Task Analysis for Applications to the Design of Human–System Interaction

In section III, Seamster, Redding, and Kaempf (chap. 9) provide a framework for cognitive skills and associate these with appropriate cognitive task analysis methods. They strive for a practical approach to cognitive task analysis that is accessible to a domain expert lacking academic training in cognitive task analysis. Their approach avoids extensive analysis of knowledge apart from the context of skill performance—analysis that could prove wasted effort. The chapter concludes by describing a cognitive task analysis conducted to assist in the redesign of a menu for a speech-based information system.

Chapter 10 by Barnard and May seems to exemplify an alternative perspective in the context of applications to human–system interaction. That is, their emphasis is on determining whether the information-processing requirements imposed on the human operator by the design of the system are going to stress or exceed the human's capacities. Barnard and May present a comprehensive theory of human cognitive architecture, which is rather different in character from the American theories of cognitive architecture underlying many of the other chapters in the book.

Chapter 11 by Williams, which describes a computer tool—CAT-HCI— that supports GOMS-style analyses, reflects the relatively mature state of this approach. This tool incorporates data from the research literature that enable detailed predictions of the time required to execute practiced actions with a real or designed interface. The same analyses can also be used to support the development of production system models of skill for an intelligent tutor and to predict the amount of training time that will be required. Detailed analyses and predictions of execution time are, of course, tied to the particulars of an interface design. However, they can be important and worthwhile when a workstation operation will be repeated many times by many users so that even fractions of a second can translate into millions of dollars of costs. They can also be important in time-critical military applications. For example, a predictive GOMS analysis was done on a new design for a U.S. missile launch system. It predicted that the new system would be too slow; the analysis was rejected and locked away. Some years later, the system failed an acceptance test because it was too slow, as predicted.

Ormerod (chap. 12) describes a rather similar approach; it is also accompanied by supporting computer tools, but emphasizes the need to avoid analyses that are excessively tied to the particulars of an existing system. If one is seeking guidance in the design of a new system, he points out, it is important to halt the task analysis at a higher level of description open to alternative specific implementations. This chapter also presents some interesting case examples.

Chapter 13 by Johnson, Johnson, and Hamilton describes another line of development—from hierarchical task analysis to tools supporting the design of new systems and interfaces. They developed the theoretical notion of *task knowledge structures* to model conceptual, declarative, and procedural knowledge in terms of the roles, goals, objects, and actions concerned in executing work tasks. Their emphasis on task knowledge is consistent with DuBois and Shalin, but contrasts with Barnard's emphasis on archictecture. Johnson et al. also developed a related software tool—ADEPT—that shows how these models can be used to guide the design of prototype interfaces.

Chapter 14 by Hamilton draws on the history of hierarchical task analysis, the theory of task knowledge structures, and the GOMS tradition in developing a computer tool, ATLAS, to support cognitive task analyses and maintain results. Hamilton emphasizes the possibility that one may want to look at a cognitive task analysis from multiple perspectives—training as well as system design— and also emphasizes the importance of maintaining consistency of the analysis across different applications. ATLAS begins the goal description process well above what would ordinarily be considered a task, with levels called *mission, phase,* and *function. Task* appears below *function* and is elaborated with three classes of attributes: behavioral requirements, training-related issues such as criticality and knowledge required, and associated hazards. Other tools such as CAT-HCI seem to support more detailed decomposition of tasks, but do not provide for specification of some of these other attributes.

Chapter 15 by Kieras and Meyer attempts to build a bridge between the human factors tradition of task analysis and the relatively recent development of computational models of human cognitive architecture in basic cognitive psychology. They present their cognitive architecture, EPIC, which incorporates models of some aspects of perception and motor activity, making it particularly useful for modeling human–computer interaction. To date, this system has mainly been used to model human performance in simple experimental tasks, primarily accounting for phenomena in what is known as the *dual-task* literature. Even in these simple tasks, however, Kieras and Meyer encountered the complexity that emerges because of the maneuvering room that the human operator has between the constraints inherent to the task situation and the constraints imposed by the limitations of human information processing: Typically, multiple strategies are possible for accomplishing the task requirements. It is difficult to predict which strategy will emerge and what actual task performance, such as execution times, will look like. To address this problem, Kieras and Meyer propose a bracketing approach for predictive evaluations of alternative interface designs, developing an estimate of the range of likely task execution times.

Chapter 16 by Paris, Balbo, and Ozkan takes a further step toward incorporating task analysis methods into the software development process. The authors provide examples of two case studies using different task formalisms to bridge task analysis and software development. One of these cases has an interesting reflexive character because it involves developing a computer aid for writers of technical documentation for software systems. Thus, a representation of software systems and their functionality is an intrinsic part of the technical writers' task. Both cases suggest that task models have a promising role not only as tools for interface design, but as communication tools to support interaction among HCI specialists, system designers, and end users—consistent with Boy's chapter.

Chapter 17 by Gray and Kirschenbaum provides a cautionary tale about what may happen when one attempts to develop a detailed computational model of a much more complex military task. Despite their tribulations, the work has provided insights into the design of a future console for the submarine approach officer, whose work has not previously been supported by displays. In addition, it has provided a quantitative illustration of complaints about the amount of effort involved in manipulating information systems as compared with effort truly devoted to task performance.

Boy (chap. 18) is particularly concerned with representing the rationale for a system design, including design constraints associated with the intended human user. Boy proposes active design documents as a form of computer-based representation that captures such constraints. Active documents allow users and developers to interact with and comment on simulations of proposed designs, thereby facilitating participatory design and modification. The interactive capabilities of active design documents also encourage a view of task representations and the computers on which they are hosted as collaborators in the design process.

Schmalhofer and van Elst (chap. 19) provide a perspective on cognitive task analysis driven by concern for the open-ended problem of knowledge management. They first consider the suitability of current CTA methods, including several presented in this volume, for designing future information systems. The authors then combine research from artificial intelligence with a multilevel analysis of anticipated work practices to develop the Oligo-Agent system that assists users in document comprehension and knowledge distribution.

Chapter 20 by Potter, Roth, Woods, and Elm exemplifies the cognitive systems engineering approach to task analysis. Like Boy and Paris, Potter et al. emphasize the integration of cognitive task analysis into the software and system development process. They are particularly concerned with understanding the way people operate in their world and in identifying opportunities for more effective support. In the typical application areas they address, the domain is always too complex and too rich to be described by one single technique or approach. Consequently, the heuristic choice of eclectic techniques serves to deepen the understanding of the domain and the practitioner, leading to successive cycles of prototyping and empirical testing.

Neerincx, van Doorne, and Ruijsendaal (chap. 21), are interested in predicting workload in a future Ship Control Center on the basis of current task performance. This raises the interesting issue whether cognitive task analysis can contribute to the design of novel systems, if it is necessarily based on an analysis of experts carrying out tasks with current systems. Their solution is to present scenarios to a simulated Ship Control Center team and have naval experts predict the actions taken by the team. These actions are then assessed against a simplified model of human cognition to determine workload. The next step would be to assess whether the future systems alleviate workload.

Cognitive Task Analysis for Teamwork Situations

Many of the cognitive task analyses directed at individuals and their jobs or tasks actually involve individuals working as participants in teams. Today, attempts to extend cognitive task analysis to deal with working teams are clearly one of the most active areas of new development. Many of these efforts focus on military command teams with the goals of improving performance, often while simultaneously reducing the required person power through better allocation of task responsibilities among humans and between humans and automated support systems.

In Section IV, Zachary, Ryder, and Hicinbothom (chap. 22) discuss cognitive task analyses of the antiair warfare team of an AEGIS ship. The original goal of these analyses was to produce running computational models of each of the team members, including their participation in teamwork activity, in order to provide the expert component of an artificially intelligent tutoring system for the entire team. That training system, known as the Advanced Embedded Training System, was planned to assess teamwork through such means as a speech recognition and understanding system that would determine whether the right information was being asked for and communicated at the right time. Another challenge in modeling team performance is that some task components, such as investigating and classifying radar tracks, might be accomplished acceptably by any one of several individuals. Indeed, appropriate shifting of such task components to share workload is one aspect of effective teamwork. As of this writing, this effort was not quite complete and it was not yet clear how successful the modeling of team aspects would be. At the same time, these models were already being applied for other purposes, such as the design of an advanced work station and task reallocation to a command team of smaller size, exemplifying Hamilton's point about the multiple potential uses of a single cognitive task analysis.

Two additional chapters also address the analysis of command teams: chapter 23 by Essens, Post, and Rasker, and chapter 24 by Annett and Cunningham. The modeling being done by Essens et al. does not involve the level of detail required by the running computational models of the Advanced Embedded Training System, but the analysis addresses the tasks of the entire ship command team of 15 individuals. Essens et al. argue that the Combat Information Center may be viewed as a cognitive system because the information that is received undergoes various transformations before it results in a decision. Numerous agents contribute to the processing of information, and the authors stress the necessity of taking multiple perspectives on this system.

Annett and Cunningham conducted a hierarchical task analysis of a command team to identify objective performance criteria with which to assess the team. The goal of their study was to improve the quality of the team training. Although the authors obtained some insight in determinants of successful team performance, they admit that their use of self-report questionnaires was less than successful.

Zachary et. al. focused on first modeling individuals and then added teamwork features. In contrast, Klein (chap. 25) focuses on analyzing team aspects almost to the exclusion of individual cognitive task analyses. Perhaps this is because the area of greatest challenge is currently there. A strong theoretical framework specifying what one should be looking for is yet to be developed. There is not yet the degree of consensus represented by, for example, the cognitive science account of problem solving. The work of the U.S. Navy lab in Orlando, NAWCTSD, described in chapter 26 by Blickensderfer, Cannon-Bowers, Salas, and Baker—the knowledge elements critical for successful team performance—may represent the beginnings of such a conceptual framework.

FUTURE DIRECTIONS FOR COGNITIVE TASK ANALYSIS RESEARCH AND DEVELOPMENT

The enterprise of cognitive task analysis exists in a region of tension between the basic research in psychology and cognitive science that provides its theoretical foundations and many of its methods, and the applied purposes and needs that drive it. From a basic research perspective, researchers are concerned about the difficulty of being certain about what really goes on in the internal cognition of trainees or system operators. Often the evidence seems indeterminate with respect to several possible internal mechanisms. Basic researchers are aware of cases in the history of cognitive research such as the decades-long debate over the interpretation of performance on Piaget's relatively simple cognitive tasks. Certainly there are also examples much closer to the enterprise that could give pause. For example, Anderson built an intelligent tutor of geometry-proof skills (Anderson, Boyle, & Yost, 1985), the expert module of which was based on a considerable background of research into geometry proof skills that he and Greeno had done. Yet, only a few years later, Koedinger (Koedinger & Anderson, 1990a, 1990b), one of Anderson's students, built a new tutor incorporating a significantly different model of expertise. Perhaps the act of building the computational model for the first tutor highlighted the significance of some aspects of expertise—spatial thinking with diagrams—that had been neglected. Rouse and Morris (1986) expressed some of these doubts in a review of research on mental models.

Sometimes it can be difficult to draw the distinction between a basic research investigation and a cognitive task analysis. If nothing like it has been done before, a cognitive task analysis may become, de facto, a basic research investigation. However, some areas have been heavily investigated in cognitive psychology and cognitive science so that a general consensus on the nature of knowledge or skill in those areas is well developed. The cognitive science theory about the nature of human problem solving drawn on in the chapter by DuBois and Shalin is the prime example of this. In such a case, the theory almost provides a set of blanks to be filled in: At least one knows what sort of knowledge one is looking for. Conceptual networks and associated methods for getting at knowledge in this form are another well-developed area of cognitive research (Olson & Biolsi, 1991). However, for that very reason, they may have been over-represented in attempts at cognitive task analysis. It is less than clear how conceptual networks actually function in complex task performance. They may be a distorted and incomplete view of the knowledge actually supporting performance. This issue is worthy of investigation.

Knowledge Representations for Spatial and Perceptual Thinking

Some aspects of cognition have not been so well investigated by the basic research community. Here there is a need for basic research investigations to bring our understanding of appropriate knowledge representations to the same level as the generic view of problem-solving knowledge. A prime example of this is the cognitive representation of space and associated spatial reasoning processes. These are not well understood. We do know that objective Euclidean space is not a good representation of psychological space, however. Spatial representations and spatial thinking play an important role in many significant jobs, such as air traffic control, the submarine approach officer task addressed by Gray and Kirschenbaum, and architectural design. Yet the cognitive modeling system, Anderson's ACT-R (Anderson, 1993; Anderson & Lebière, 1998), which Gray and Kirschenbaum are using, has no provision now for representing the demanding three-dimensional spatial aspects of the approach officer's problem-solving task. This should be considered a high-priority area for research.

Similarly, there may be room for more development in the representation of other perceptual aspects of knowledge. Researchers such as Flach (chap. 6, this volume), and Klein and Hoffman (Klein & Hoffman, 1992) have attended to perceptual knowledge, but more formal theoretical development is needed. In basic cognitive research, there has been a great deal of activity in neural network approaches to perceptual recognition and classification. This approach has not yet found its way into cognitive task analysis. However, Marshall pioneered the use of neural net recognition modules in more complex hybrid models of both math word problem solving (Marshall, 1995) and tactical decision making (Marshall, Christensen, & McAllister, 1996; Marshall, Wilson, & Page, 1998). No doubt this approach will become more prominent in cognitive task analyses of the future. In such neural net models of recognition, *features* are unanalyzed input to the net. It may be that further work is also needed on what kind of thing a perceptual feature can be, linking models of cognitive processing to computational theories of perception that have undergone substantial development in recent years.

Better Approaches to Cognitive Task Analysis for Working Teams

Moving up the descriptive hierarchy, it is already evident that cognitive task analysis as applied to entire working teams is a major area for new developments. Here, too, the basic research foundations are largely lacking. Cognitive psychology and cognitive science have primarily examined the interior workings of individual human beings. The study of teams and organizations belongs to entirely different and largely unconnected fields of psychology, social psychology, and organizational psychology. For the most part, these fields have not attended to the cognitive aspects of human behavior, although the rise of cognitive psychology as a major force within psychology generally has begun to change that. To support team cognitive task analyses, there is a need to develop generic theoretical frameworks for the knowledge and skill specifically involved in teamwork so that analysts in this area will have rather well-defined blanks to fill in. A major challenge is to integrate the individual and team-oriented perspectives on task analysis.

Novel Jobs and Systems: A Major Challenge for Cognitive Task Analysis

For the most part, the existing practice of cognitive task analysis is based on the premise that one has existing jobs with experts and existing systems with experienced users to be analyzed. One can then use the results of the analysis to help design training for those jobs or to tweak existing systems in improved directions. However, especially in military applications, new systems for which there are no experts frequently occur. It is highly desirable to develop the capability for designing radically new systems that will prove well adapted to human use. In the case of training, one can now imagine addressing the problem of training for a new system by writing a cognitive model for performance of the tasks in a strong theoretical framework like ACT-R. This would provide assurance that the task actually can be performed by a learner. In fact, development of an artificially intelligent training system on this foundation is relatively straightforward. Considering this case can even provide some reassurance about the problem of indeterminacy that was raised earlier. Although one's cognitive task analysis may not yield the one right answer about how the task is done by current experts or will be done by experts who will emerge in the future, for training purposes, it is probably sufficient to define *a* way to do the task that humans are capable of learning. Strong cognitive theories will enable us to do that.

In some respects, cognitive task analysis for the design of new systems seems to be further progressed because it is possible to view the cognitive task analysis as much the same thing as the software design process. Theoretical constructs such as *task knowledge structures* have been developed. An interesting question is how these relate to theories of human cognitive architecture emerging in basic cognitive science. Perhaps an important direction for future development is the integration of these two approaches so that the analytic or design tools are constrained to assign doable and readily learnable functions to humans. As yet, it seems unclear how useful these design tools actually are.

Making the Products of Cognitive Task Analysis More Usable

The usability of the products of cognitive task analysis is another major issue for the future. Perhaps the output of the analysis can be a software design; several of our chapter authors are making progress in that direction. For training, cognitive task analysis presumably provides cognitive objectives for instruction, but it is not always clear how we should train toward those objectives or how we should test their attainment. For example, the use of Bayesian inference networks to assess mastery of a fine-grained production rule within a cognitive model of skill—as is common in modern intelligent tutoring systems—is a very different type of assessment from conventional test items. Probably the question of how to train to cognitive objectives should be declared beyond the scope of the cognitive task analysis problem, but should be used instead to set a major agenda for instructional research.

It is obviously important that we develop more explicit understanding of the way in which cognitive task analysis products can and should be used in our target applications. Not only do we need to realize our purposes, the vastness of expert knowledge—commented on by several authors—further increases the importance of solving this problem. One could spend a great deal of time/effort/money extracting and analyzing knowledge that will never be used. On the other hand, no matter how large the effort, it is likely that only a fraction of expert knowledge will ever be explicated. It is important to become efficient at extracting the knowledge actually needed for our purposes. Currently, too little is being said about the use of cognitive task analysis products in discussions of cognitive task analysis. Future reports of cognitive task analyses should be certain to cover this topic.

Some of the original ambitions of the NATO study group on cognitive task analysis proved overambitious. Attempting to define a taxonomy of tasks that points to appropriate task analysis methods to use for each type is clearly premature. Today, cognitive task analysis seems to be a domain in which case-based reasoning is the most appropriate tactic for the would-be practitioner. Somewhat similar cases of apparently successful and useful cognitive task analyses can be studied for what they suggest toward an approach for one's new task analysis problem. We hope that this book is a useful resource for that purpose. We expect that the future will bring digital library case resources to further facilitate analysts' work, as our readers add their contributions to the expanding field of cognitive task analysis.

REFERENCES

Anderson, J.R. (1993). *Rules of the mind*. Hillsdale, NJ: Lawrence Erlbaum Associates.

Anderson, J.R. (Personal communication, 29 August, 1995). Proposal to ONR entitled, "A tutor development kit based on the ACT-R cognitive simulation"

Anderson, J.R., Boyle, C.F., & Yost, G. (1985). The geometry tutor. *Proceedings of the IJCAI*, 1–7.

Anderson, J.R., & Lebière, C. (1998). *The atomic components of thought*. Mahwah, NJ: Lawrence Erlbaum Associates.

Annett, J., Duncan, K.D., Stammers, R.B., & Gray, M. J. (1971). *Task analysis*. London: Her Majesty's Stationary Office.

Benysh, D.V., Koubek, R.J., & Calvez, V. (1993). A comparative review of knowledge structure measurement techniques for interface design. *International Journal of Human-Computer Interaction, 5(3)*, 211–237.

Buchanan, B.G., & Shortliffe, E.H. (Eds.). (1984). *Rule-based expert systems: The MYCIN experiments of the Stanford Heuristic Programming Project*. Reading, MA: Addison-Wesley.

Card, S., Moran, T. P., & Newell, A. (1983*). The psychology of human-computer interaction*. Hillsdale, NJ: Lawrence Erlbaum Associates.

Cooke, N.J. (1994). Varieties of knowledge elicitation techniques. *International Journal of Human-Computer Studies, 41*, 801–849.

Crandall, B., Klein, G., Militello, L. G., & Wolf, S. P. (1994). *Tools for applied cognitive task analysis* (Contract Summary report on N66001-94-C-7008). Fairborn, OH: Klein Associates.

Doireau, P., Grau, J.Y., & Poisson, R. (1996*). Cognitive task analysis: A literature review*. Rapport de Recherche No. 96-03, January. Centre D'Etudes et de Recherches de Medecine Aerospatiale, Service de Santé des Armées. IMASSA/CERMA, Bretigny-sur-Orge Cedex.

DuBois, D., & Shalin, V.L. (1995). Adapting cognitive methods to real-world objectives: An application to job knowledge testing. In P. D. Nichols, S. F. Chipman, & R. L. Brennan (Eds.), *Cognitively diagnostic assessment* (pp. 189–220). Hillsdale, NJ: Lawrence Erlbaum Associates.

Duncan, K.D. (1974). Analytical techniques in training design. In E. Edwards & F.P. Lees (Eds.*), The human operator in process control* (pp. 283–320). London: Taylor & Francis.

Firlej, M., & Hellens, D. (1991). *Knowledge elicitation: A practical handbook*. Hemel, Hempstead: Prentice-Hall.

Forsythe, D.E., & Buchanan, B.G. (1989). Knowledge acquisition for expert systems: Some pitfalls and suggestions. *IEEE Systems, Man and Cybernetics, 19(3)*, 435–442.

Hall, E.P., Gott, S.P., & Pokorny, R.A. (1995). *A procedural guide to cognitive task analysis: The PARI methodology* (Technical Report AL/HR-TR-1995-0108). Brooks Air Force Base, TX: AFMC.

Hoffman, R.R., Shadbolt, N.R., Burton, A.M., & Klein, G. (1995). Eliciting knowledge from experts: A methodological analysis. *Organizational Behavior and Human Decision Processes, 62(2)*, 129–158.

John, B.E., & Kieras, D.E. (1994). *The GOMS family of analysis techniques: Tools for design and evaluation* (Report CMU-CS-94-181). Pittsburgh, PA: Carnegie-Mellon University, School of Computer Science.

Klein, G.A., & Hoffman, R.R. 1992. Seeing the invisible: Perceptual-cognitive aspects of expertise. In M. Rabinowitz (Ed.), *Cognitive science foundations of instruction* (pp. 203–226). Mahwah, NJ: Lawrence Erlbaum Associates.

Koedinger, K.R., & Anderson, J.R. (1990a). Abstract planning and perceptual chunks: Elements of expertise in geometry. *Cognitive Science, 14,* 511–550.

Koedinger, K.R., & Anderson, J.R. (1990b, March 27–29). *Theoretical and empirical motivations for the design of ANGLE: A New Geometry Learning Environment.* Working notes of the 1990 AAAI Spring Symposia on Knowledge-Based Environments for Learning and Teaching, Stanford, CA .

Marshall, S.P. (1995). *Schemas in problem solving.* New York: Cambridge University Press.

Marshall, S.P., Christensen, S.E., & McAllister, J.A. (1996, June). Cognitive differences in tactical decision making. In *Proceedings of the 1996 Command and Control Research and Technology Symposium* (pp. 122–132). Monterey, CA: Naval Post-graduate School.

Marshall, S.P., Wilson, D.M., & Page, K.V. (1998*). Sharing decision-making knowledge in tactical situations: Extended analyses* (Technical Report CERF No. 98-02). Cognitive Ergonomics Research Facility, San Diego State University, San Diego, CA.

McGraw, K.L., & Harbison-Briggs, K. (1989*). Knowledge acquisition: Principles and guidelines.* Englewood Cliffs, NJ: Prentice-Hall.

Means, B. (1993). Cognitive task analysis as a basis for instructional design. In M. Rabinowitz (Ed.), *Cognitive science foundations of instruction* (pp. 97–118). Hillsdale, NJ: Lawrence Erlbaum Associates.

Meyer, M.A., & Booker, J.M. (1991). *Eliciting and analyzing expert judgement: A practical guide.* London: Academic Press.

Militello, L.G., & Hutton, R.J.B. (1998). Applied cognitive task analysis (ACTA): A practitioner's toolkit for understanding cognitive task demands. *Ergonomics, 41(11),* 1618–1641.

Militello, L.G., Hutton, R.J.B., Pliske, R.M., Knight, B.J., Klein, G., & Randel, J. (1997). *Applied Cognitive Task Analysis (ACTA) methodology* (Tech. Report NPRDC-TN-98-4). Navy Personnel Research and Development Center, San Diego CA.

Miyake, N. (1986). Constructive interaction and the iterative process of understanding. *Cognitive Science, 10(2),* 151–177.

Olson, J. R., & Biolsi, K. J. (1991). Techniques for representing expert knowledge. In K.A. Ericsson & J. Smith (Eds*.), Toward a general theory of expertise* (pp. 240–285). Cambridge, England: Cambridge University Press.

Patel, S., Drury, C.G., & Shalin, V.L. (1998). Effectiveness of expert semantic knowledge as a navigational aid within hypertext. *Behavior and Information Technology, 17,* 313–324.

Randel, J.M., Pugh, H.L., & Reed, S.K. (1996). Differences in expert and novice situation awareness in naturalistic decision making. *International Journal of Human-Computer Studies, 45,* 579–597.

Roske-Hofstrand, R.J., & Paap, K.R. (1986). Cognitive networks as a guide to menu organization: An application in the automated cockpit. *Ergonomics, 29(11),* 1301–1311.

Rouse, W.B., & Morris, N.M. (1986). On looking into the blackbox: Prospects and limits in the search for mental models. *Psychological Bulletin, 100,* 349–363.

Schvaneveldt, R.W. (1990). *Pathfinder associative networks: Studies in knowledge organization.* Norwood, NJ: Ablex.

Shalin, V.L., & Geddes, N.D. (1994, October). *Task dependent information management in a dynamic environment: Concept and measurement issues.* Proceedings of the 1994 IEEE International Conference on Systems, Man and Cybernetics, San Antonio, TX.

Shalin, V.L., & Geddes, N.D. (1998, March). *Pilot performance with mid-flight plan-based display changes.* Proceedings of HICS '98: 4th annual symposium on human interaction with complex systems, Dayton, OH.

Shalin, V.L., Geddes, N.D., Mikesell, B.G., & Ramamurthy, M. (1993, April). *Performance effects of plan-based information displays in commercial aviation.* Proceedings of the 7th International Symposium on Aviation Psychology, Columbus, OH.

Vora, P.R., Helander, M.G., & Shalin, V.L. (1994, April). *Evaluating the influence of interface styles and multiple access paths in hypertext.* Proceedings of CHI '94, ACM/ SIGCHI, Boston, MA.

Waterman, D.A. (1986*). A guide to expert systems.* Reading: Addison-Wesley.

Williams, K. E. (1998, May). *The transfer of complex knowledge: A cognitive task analysis approach.* In Proceedings of the 34th International Applied Military Psychology Symposium, Paris, France.

Williams, K.E., Hultman, E., & Graesser, A.C. (1998). CAT: A tool for eliciting knowledge on how to perform procedures. *Behavior Research Methods, Instruments, & Computers, 30,* 565–572.

Williams, K. E., & Kotnur, T. G. (1993). *Knowledge acquisition: A review of manual, machine-aided and machine-learning methods* (Technical report on Office of Naval Research contract N00014-91-J- 5-1500). Blacksburg, VA: Virginia Polytechnic Institute and State University, Management Systems Laboratories.

2

THEORETICAL AND PRAGMATIC INFLUENCES ON TASK ANALYSIS METHODS

John Annett
Warwick University, United Kingdom

The term *task analysis* and variants such as *hierarchical task analysis* and *cognitive task analysis* represent a wide range of approaches and methods that reflect both current theories of human performance and the practical demands made on the analyst by the sociotechnical context. The aim of this short introduction is to explore the origins of the ideas that have inspired some of the more popular methods; this is done to gain a perspective on current practice and future possibilities. The historical origins of modern analytical methods are outlined and related to some of the broad theoretical positions that have inspired practice.

CLASSICAL METHODS

Early attempts at a scientific analysis of work by F.W. Taylor (Taylor, 1911) and John and Lilian Gilbreth (Gilbreth, 1911) were directed toward optimizing the use of labor primarily in terms of time and effort. The industrial world was emerging from an indefinitely long period in which skill was a characteristic of the individual worker or craftsman—into a new world in which the firm or the company owned not only the means of production, the materials, and tools but also the methods by which goods were to be produced. Wealth comprises not just the possession of resources but the means of adding value by efficiently turning resources into merchantable products. In short, Taylor and others realized that the human contribution to the means of production was an important source of wealth, and so it became necessary to describe and codify human performance in a scientific manner. Taylor investigated work by experimentally comparing different work methods—discovering empirically, for example, an optimal use of human labor (carefully costed) to move pig iron.

The Gilbreths, a builder and a psychologist with engineering training, saw the need for a system of behavioral units for describing all work. The Therbligs (Gilbreth spelled backwards) were a set of universal elements that could be used to describe a wide range of semiskilled or routine activities, such as bricklaying and laundering, in a way that made it possible to reduce the number of movements required to achieve a given result. Most of the therbligs referred to physical movements such as grasp, transport loaded, and assemble but the list of approximately 18 basic elements (the number varied over the years) included some mental or cognitive elements such as search, select and find. Lilian Gilbreth as a psychologist may well have been influenced by the experimental psychology newly arrived from Germany,[1] which made it possible to measure choice or decision time, and by the discovery that this was a major component in response time—a finding that was to assume even greater theoretical significance 50 years later. Time and motion study continued for over half a century as a methodology for determining optimal work layout and soon became used in production engineering and job evaluation and as a tool for determining the likely labor cost of a new product.

PSYCHOLOGY AND HUMAN FACTORS

Initially the input of psychology to the analysis of human tasks was secondary to the requirements of production engineering. During and after World War I, studies of the effects of fatigue, working conditions, and the environment became popular.[2] By the 1940s, and especially in the context of aviation with an emphasis on instrument flying, sensory psychology and the classical psychophysical methods had a major impact on the emerging field of Human Factors. The methods described in Chapanis's (1959) classic text extended the units of analysis beyond the traditional therbligs to encompass any recognizable activity that might be of interest. At the same time, the conception of analyzable work had extended well beyond routine manufacturing tasks to encompass the monitoring, control, and fault finding on increasingly complex equipment.

For example, the tasks of an air navigator are not entirely routine. However by using activity sampling (Christiansen, 1949), the analyst—being free to select any activity such as taking instrument readings and making calculations, which made sense in the given context—was able to determine how the individual typically spent his time. These data could be used to draw conclusions about which tasks might be off-loaded to another individual or piece of equipment because task allocation between crew members and between human operators and machines was beginning to be a major question in system design.

---

[1] Hugo Munsterberg, who some regard as the founder of applied psychology, spent the years 1892-1895 at Harvard at the invitation of William James. His *Psychology and Industrial Eficiency* was published in 1913,

[2] In the United Kingdom, an Industrial Fatigue Research Board (later the Industrial Health Research Board) was set up in 1916.

A similar freedom in the choice of a unit of analysis was offered by Critical Incident Technique (CIT), which was developed in the context of military aviation tasks by Fitts and Jones (1947) and Flanagan (1954). The method identifies those incidents such as accidents and near accidents; which are are meaningful in a given context and requires participants to provide plain language accounts of events leading up to the incident. Given appropriate data, CIT led to conclusions such as the need to modify or redesign multirevolution altimeters and artificial horizons or relocate important controls.

Link analysis, another observational technique described by Chapanis (1959), likewise required only a commonsense unit of analysis—namely, any act involving the passing of materials or information between different people or locations. Like other methods developed by experimental social psychologists in the tradition of Bales (1950), link analysis provides counts of various types or categories of interaction between people or between people and objects. These counts could then be used to shorten and in other ways improve lines of communication (e.g., by redesigning the work-space layout). Other graphical representations such as process charts, signal flow graphs, and Petri-nets can all provide useful insights in complex tasks characterized by the flow of materials or information, and the data they provide may be used as the basis for simulations used in design and evaluation of complex systems (Kirwan & Ainsworth, 1992).

INFORMATION THEORY & MENTAL WORKLOAD

A significant development in the 1950s, which laid one of the important foundations of what we now know as cognitive psychology, was the demonstration that the human operator could be described as a transmitter of information with a measurably fixed maximum rate or channel capacity of 10 to15 bits per second. The work of W.E. Hick in the United Kingdom (Hick, 1952) and Paul Fitts in the United States (Fitts, 1954; Fitts & Posner, 1967) soon made it clear that it was often information processing rather than physical effort that determined the time taken to complete a task. Indeed, it was the perceptual therbligs that limited the rate at which even simple manual tasks could be performed (Annett, Golby, & Kay 1958). In Birmingham, United Kingdom, Crossman (1956) and Seymour (1954) adapted the classical process chart to include not only the physical actions of the right and left hands but also the use of sensory information and decision making. The concept of limited channel capacity, with respect to both sensory information processing and decision making, had a profound influence on theories of attention (Broadbent, 1958). This led to the concept of *mental workload*. The assessment of mental workload remains a central consideration in the analysis of tasks. Yet, despite extensive research effort over many years, there is no agreed single metric of mental work. Practical analysts typically rely on either subjective estimates of mental effort or measures of performance decrement on a simultaneous secondary task (Pew, 1978).

SYSTEMS THEORY, PROCESS CONTROL
AND HUMAN ERROR

The late 1940s and early 1950s saw the adoption by engineering psychologists of systems concepts especially in relation to the design of military systems and process control engineering. From the engineering viewpoint, the human operator became an element whose properties need to be known in order to build a viable system in which the operator played a key role. R.B. Miller's (1953, 1962) Method for Man–Machine Task Analysis was seminal in applying systems thinking to the analysis of human tasks. Miller adopted a cybernetic or information-processing model with an emphasis on the operator's task in data processing. The human operator was shown to be best adapted to act as a simple amplifier in a control loop, but was often required to act, in analogue computing terms, as an integrator or differentiator to take account of both stored and currently available information and to generate responses that met future as well as current demands (see Morgan, Cook, Chapanis, & Lund, 1963). A key question was this: Which functions should be allocated to the human and which to the machine? Hence, the important aim of task analysis was to identify operator functions within the system context to assist the optimal allocation of functions between human operators and machines.

The manual control problems in tasks such as flying high-performance aircraft are complemented by those of controlling large-scale chemical and other industrial processes—notably, nuclear power production. It became increasingly apparent during the 1960s that the skills of the process control operator required a new approach. Physical actions were often limited to the manipulation of switches, but knowledge of the system to be controlled—including its internal dynamics and physical layout—were essential to the early identification of problems which, if left unattended, could have disastrous consequences. Indeed, a number of well-publicized disasters involving chemical and nuclear plant during the 1970s focused attention on the need to understand the problem-solving strategies and specialized knowledge bases of process controllers (Rasmussen & Rouse, 1981; Reason, 1990; Sheridan & Hennessy, 1984). These problems provided an impetus to develop new methods of task analysis that could lead to a better understanding of the important cognitive skills underlying both success and failure in controlling complex plant (Bainbridge, 1978; Duncan, 1972).

HIERARCHICAL DECOMPOSITION

The dominant behaviorist psychology gave no credence to mentalistic concepts. However, psychologists such as Broadbent (1958) at Cambridge, United Kingdom, and Fitts (1951) at Ohio State, who worked in an engineering context, were concerned with the problem of describing the cognitive components of work. The concepts of systems engineering, and functional analysis were highly consistent with the emerging cybernetic view of human performance (Miller, Galanter, & Pribram, 1960). A group at Hull (United Kingdom) (Annett & Duncan, 1967; Annett, Duncan, Stammers, & Gray, 1971) developed an approach, now known as Hierarchical Task Analysis (HTA), in the context of process control tasks—notably, in the petrochemical and power-generation industries. The emphasis in HTA was not so much the recording of overt behavior *per se* but the systematic decomposition of goals. Its purpose was to identify potential failures of goal attainment in complex tasks due to problems connected with either physical actions or the information-processing and knowledge requirements of operators and to remedy these either by training or redesigning the system.

HTA was premised on the view proposed by Miller, Galanter, & Pribram (1960) that behavior is fundamentally goal directed and can be understood in terms of a hierarchical goal structure in which the attainment of primary goals is served by the attainment of sub-goals, which may in turn be decomposed into ever more detailed or specific sub-sub-goals.

In HTA, the unit of analysis is an operation—conceptually the same as Miller et al.'s Test-Operate-Test-Exit unit. The operation, like the T-O-T-E, is a feedback loop. However, operations are not primitives in the sense that they are not further analyzable, for they can be decomposed into sub-operations, each of which has the same T-O-T-E structure. The extent of decomposition is determined by a pragmatic stop rule (see Annett et al., 1971) that ensures that the effort of analysis is devoted principally to aspects of the task that are most likely to require remedial attention if the system goals are to be reliably met.

EDUCATIONAL TECHNOLOGY, ARTIFICIAL INTELLIGENCE AND KNOWLEDGE ENGINEERING

The late 1950s saw the introduction of *teaching machines* and the concept of *educational technology*, in which computers would play an important role in education and training. The term was coined by B.F. Skinner (1954) and the technology initially relied on his version of behaviorist learning theory. Any subject matter to be taught was seen from the behaviorist viewpoint as a string of elementary stimulus-response connections, each of which had to be individually reinforced by the provision of a symbolic reward. This required the programmer to analyze the most complex subject matter into very small steps to be presented in a way that would result in a high probability of eliciting a correct response and consequent reward. However, it soon became apparent that a more cognitive theory was required to identify the key skills and knowledge to be taught and to structure the material embodied in automatic teaching devices.

These issues were addressed by educators such as R.M. Gagné at Princeton (Gagné, 1962, 1965) and R. Glaser at the Learning Research and Development Center, Pittsburgh (Glaser, 1976). The term cognitive task analysis came into general use among the educational technology community by the early

1970s. It refers to a variety of techniques for analyzing and structuring the content of course materials. Some of these techniques resembled the way in which a computer programmer might create problem-solving algorithms.

Among the important developments in cognitive psychology in that period was the theory of problem solving by Newell and Simon (1972). The theory was based on the identification of elementary information-processing mechanisms called *production systems* and ways of describing how these were brought into play in solving problems. The production system concept is quite explicitly based on T-O-T-E unit (Miller et al. 1960). When expressed as a set of condition—action statements it is comparable to the *operation* of Annett et al. (1971). Newell and Simon used these concepts to describe paths through a problem space taken by novice and expert problem solvers. These reveal the strategies and heuristics used, and the resulting problem behavior graphs resemble the diagrammatic representations of HTA analyses of process control operators tasks (Duncan, 1972; Shepherd, 1985).

In the 1970s and certainly by the early 1980s, cognitive psychology became more prominent, even dominant, in academic psychology under influences from linguistics and artificial intelligence (AI) and especially knowledge-based systems. A major insight of the AI community was that machines (i.e., computers) were only likely to perform tasks requiring intelligence if, instead of following inflexible programs or algorithms, they could make use of stored knowledge of the world in which they were required to operate (Winograd, 1972). Intelligent knowledge-based teaching systems such as SOPHIE (Brown, Burton & Bell, 1975) were able not only to detect errors but to explain to students why their answers were incorrect on the basis of stored knowledge of the domain.

Expert systems, such as DENDRAL (Lindsay, Buchanan, Feigenbaum, & Lederberg, 1980) are programs that could encapsulate the knowledge of an expert in such a way as to be usable by novices to guide them through complex decision-making tasks. An expert system needs to incorporate the knowledge and strategies of the expert. This development in computer science led to a more general interest in ways of capturing human expertise. For the most part, the classical time-and-motion study analyst could simply observe and record expert behavior with clipboard and stopwatch, but the behavior of skilled problem solvers typically reveals little of the underlying mental processes. Problem solving is often opaque to the external observer, and frequently the expert finds it difficult to articulate the processes by which a solution is attained. This drew attention to the distinction between declarative and procedural knowledge. The former comprises facts, rules and principles that are known and can be expressed in response to a verbal inquiry, whereas the latter is primarily exhibited in successful performance; it often requires careful self-examination or even a controlled experiment to bring to light the principles or processes underlying performance. Thus, knowledge-elicitation techniques such as observation, coupled with probe questions and the systematic (experimental) control of cues, now play an essential role in the analysis of complex cognitively loaded tasks.

HUMAN—COMPUTER INTERACTION AND TASK ANALYSIS

During the 1970s, the increasing complexity of computer programs and the concern for their integrity led to the development of systematic methods of specifying and measuring the tasks that computers do. *Software engineering*, as it came to be known, developed notations that permitted formal checks to be made on the logical consistency, integrity, and efficiency of software, and some of these ideas have counterparts in the specification of tasks in which humans interact with computers. An early and notable example was Goals, Operators, Methods, and Selection rules (GOMS), (Card, Moran, and Newell, 1983; see also Kieras, 1991). GOMS, although developed independently from Newell and Simon's theory of problem solving, shares many of the principles of HTA. For example, in GOMS, a goal has much the same meaning as in HTA—namely, a statement of some state of affairs that is to be attained. In HTA, the term *operation* refers to the unit of behavior comprising a goal and the conditions under which the goal is activated (or the input), the action by which the goal is achieved, and feedback, (i.e., the conditions indicating successful goal attainment). Operators in GOMS are equivalent to the actions (physical or mental) required to achieve the goal; the starting conditions (if—then) are normally specified, but the feedback term, explicit in HTA, usually remains implicit. In GOMS, the control structure that produces purposive behavior is described by methods and selection rules, the former being groups of elementary operators and the latter rules specifying the conditions under which operators are brought into play. In HTA, the role of methods and selection rules is taken by the concept of a *plan*, which shows how a superordinate operation is decomposed into subordinate operations or tasks.

Productions, which form the core element of GOMS, are essentially items of compiled or procedural knowledge conceived of as if—then statements, (i.e., a production specifies what action should occur under specified conditions, much as a computer program will execute a primitive operation according to the state of a memory register). Although the production systems approach is not formally presented as a task analysis method, it is nonetheless seen as a way to model cognitive tasks. In a sense, this is what all task analysis methods try to do. Neither GOMS nor production systems pay much attention to the requirement to specify feedback explicit in HTA, and it is arguable whether the hierarchical decomposition principle is exploited such as to reveal significant higher level cognitive structures. These differences aside, the three approaches have much in common and ought, in most cases, lead to similar results.

COGNITIVE TASK ANALYSIS

The term Cognitive Task Analysis (CTA) began to emerge in reports in the late 1970s (Gallagher, 1979; Scandura, 1982; Rothkopf, 1986). It encapsulates attempts to apply current concepts in cognitive psychology to the analysis of complex tasks. In the 1950s and 1960s, the major emphasis was on control tasks (flying, steering, managing chemical plant), whereas CTA is primarily concerned with decision-making tasks such as air traffic control and military command and control (C2). The basis of CTA in cognitive theory is not necessarily fixed because models of cognition are still somewhat fluid. However, recent implementations have been strongly influenced by writers such as Anderson (1985) on learning and Johnson-Laird (1983) on mental models, with one group strongly identified with Newell's (1990) SOAR as both a unified theory of cognition and a method. Recent authors (e.g., Seamster, Redding & Kaempf, 1997) sometimes treat CTA as if it involved entirely new concepts compared with an outdated 'behavioral' task analysis. Such a contrast would be an oversimplification of the intellectual history of task analysis principles and methods as outlined in this chapter. However, CTA does make explicit the cognitive involvement that was implicit in the formulations of Miller (1962) and Annett et al. (1971). Shepherd (1998) argued that cognition and action are so intimately related that a specialist form of cognitive task analysis is not necessary if a conventional HTA were correctly carried out.

Simply observing overt behavior can sometimes give only a superficial understanding of what an operator is doing and why. Furthermore, even questioning the expert does not always reveal the underlying cognitive structure, which, if known, would be a better predictor of performance in as yet unobserved situations, such as a novel emergency. Only a detailed, correct cognitive model that specifies the necessary procedural *and* declarative knowledge will do if we are to predict potential failures and formulate effective training procedures. It has long been recognized that, although experts can sometimes verbally formulate the rules and facts underlying their performance, this is not always the case. The skill or procedural knowledge underlying performance may have to be teased out by more subtle means. On occasion, the present writer has resorted to setting up miniature experiments to test the hypothesis that the expert is in fact making use of a particular rule or getting information from a particular cue even though unable to express this as declarative knowledge. Kieras and Meyer (1998) discussed the relevance of HTA and CTA to cognitive modeling express the view that a demonstration is needed that one can start with an HTA or GOMS analysis and then proceed systematically to a usefully accurate computational cognitive model.

DESCRIPTION VERSUS ANALYSIS

Although cognitive psychology and computer science have strongly influenced the development of modern task analysis methods, there are other factors that affect the approach taken. These have to do with the way in which the socio-technical system is organized. A variety of specialists from engineers and designers to instructors and human resource managers have an interest in task analysis. However, each individual or sub-group has limited responsibility—some for selection, others for training, others for equipment design, others for health and safety. The methods they use reflect the different types of question they are required to answer. A consequence of this division of labor is that each specialist is required to contribute to a common database that may be referred to by an individual or small team responsible for the development of the whole project. This risks spending effort on unnecessary detail or failing to collect important information

The proceduralization of task analysis using computer programs of tools such as ACTA (Militello & Hutton, 1998), ATLAS (Hamilton, chap. 14, this volume), CAT (Williams, chap. 11, this volume), Micro-SAINT (Laughery, 1984), PARI (Hall, Gott, & Pokorny, 1995), and many others is in part a response to this diversity of uses and users. However, it does have a downside—namely, that it becomes easy to lose sight of the essential problem-solving nature of the task analysis process. The seldom made distinction between description and analysis is crucial. When a number of different practitioners are expected to feed information into a common database, they are almost bound to use a common agreed language in which to describe their findings, whether these be empirical descriptions of how people actually perform the tasks in question or how they might ideally be performed. They are also obliged to be thorough and include in the description anything that might conceivably be of interest to other users of the database. Task analysis is in this case, simply the collection of data, subsequently to be used by someone else for purposes which are not always clear to those collecting the data. By contrast, true analysis should be viewed as a problem-solving process in which the questions asked and the data collected are all aimed at providing answers to the questions posed. Task analysis, as opposed to task description, should be a way of producing answers to questions (i.e., identifying potential performance failures or training needs and indicating how these problems might be solved). The methods used should be adapted to the questions asked.

Essens, Fallesen, McCann, Cannon-Bowers, and Dorfel (1994) produced a valuable framework for cognitive analysis, design, and evaluation (COADE). It includes both description and analysis. COADE identifies task analysis with a behavioral model, in the sense of list of duties or activities, and cognitive task analysis with a further stage in which underlying cognitive processes are considered. The COADE process is iterative and thus accepts the role of analysis rather than simple description.

In a comprehensive practical guide to cognitive task analysis methods in aviation, Seamster, Redding, and Kaempf (1997) made it clear that the analysis should be undertaken with some purpose in mind and were at pains to point out where particular techniques are likely to be of value. Nevertheless, practical administrative procedures tend to dictate that, where processes are seen as separate, they can be carried out by different individuals or groups, and this could defeat the primary object of analysis as feeding into possible solutions to identified human factor problems.

THE ANALYSIS OF INDIVIDUAL AND TEAM TASKS

Much of the task analysis literature focuses on the tasks of individuals. Increasingly, however, work is carried out by teams, (i.e., a groups of individuals who, while often having different roles and performing different activities, have a shared overall goal). Viewed from the perspective of the hierarchical decomposition of goals, higher level goals are typically achieved through teamwork and lower level goals through individual work. For example, in Command and Control (C2) tasks, individuals collect and classify information using their individual skills and expertise but communicate with other team members to coordinate responses appropriate to the overall team goals. The distinction between individual and team tasks is, in practice, somewhat fuzzy, and the question arises as to whether different principles and techniques should be applied. Hierarchical methods seem appropriate and methods of collecting and describing interactions are already available. However, concepts such as coordination, communication, and collaboration appear to require a consistent taxonomy if they are to be useful as descriptors of team tasks (Guzzo & Salas, 1995). These in turn may require the development of a theory of team performance (Brannick, Salas, & Prince, 1997). This is currently an active research area driven by some pressing practical needs to define, analyze, and measure collective performance.

ACKNOWLEDGMENTS

The author wishes to thank Robert Hoffman, Peter Essens, Alan Lesgold, and the editors for their valuable comments and suggestions.

REFERENCES

Anderson, J. R. (1985). *Cognitive psychology and its implications*. New York: W.H. Freeman.

Annett, J., & Duncan, K.D (1967). Task analysis and training design. *Occupational Psychology, 41*, 211–221

Annett, J., Duncan, K.D., Stammers, R.B., & Gray, M.J. (1971). *Task analysis*. London:

HMSO.

Annett, J., Golby, C.W., & Kay, H. (1958). The measurement of elements in an assembly task: The information output of the human motor system. *Quarterly Journal of Experimental Psychology, 20,* 1–11.

Bainbridge, L. (1978). The process controller. In W.T. Singleton (Ed.) *The analysis of practical skills* (pp. 236–263). Lancaster: MTP Press.

Bales, R.F. (1950). *Interaction process analysis: A method for the study of small groups.* Cambridge, MA: Addison-Wesley.

Brannick, M.T., Salas, E., & Prince, C. (Eds.) (1997). *Team performance, assessment and measurement: Theory, methods, and applications.* Mahwah, NJ: Lawrence Erlbaum Associates.

Broadbent, D. (1958). *Perception and communication.* London: Pergamon Press.

Brown, J.S., Burton, R.R., & Bell, A.G. (1975). SOPHIE A step towards a reactive learning environment. International Journal Man-Machine Studies, 7, 675–696.

Card, S., Moran, T.P., & Newell, A. (1983). *The psychology of human-computer interaction.* Hillsdale, NJ: Lawrence Erlbaum Associates.

Chapanis, A. (1959). *Research techniques in human engineering.* Baltimore: Johns Hopkins Press.

Christiansen, J.M. (1949). Arctic aerial navigation: A method for the analysis of complex activities and its application to the job of the arctic aerial navigator. *Mechanical Engineering, 71,* 11–16, 22.

Crossman, E.R.F.W. (1956, February). Perception study: A complement to Motion Study. *The Manager,* (pp. 141–145).

Duncan, K.D. (1972). Strategies for the analysis of the task. In J. Hartley (Ed.), *Strategies for programmed instruction* (pp. 19–81). London: Butterworths.

Essens, P.J.M.D. Fallesen, J.J. McCann, C.A. Cannon-Bowers, J., & Dörfel, G. (1994). *COADE: A framework for cognitive analysis, design and evaluation.* Final report of Panel 8 on the Defence Applications of Human and Bio-Medical Sciences/RSG.19 on Decision Aids in Command and Control. Soesterberg NL: TNO Human Factors Research Institute.

Fitts, P.M. (1951). Engineering psychology and equipment design. In S.S. Stevens (Ed.), *Handbook of experimental psychology* (pp. 1287–1340). New York: Wiley.

Fitts, P.M. (1954). The information capacity of the human motor system in controlling the amplitude of movement. *Journal of Experimental Psychology, 47,* 381–391.

Fitts, P.M., & Jones, R.H. (1947). Analysis of factors contributing to 460 "pilot error" experiences in operating aircraft controls. Report TSEAA-694-12, AML, Wright-Patterson Air Force Base, Dayton Ohio (Reprinted in W.H. Sinaiko [1961]. *Selected papers on human factors in the design and use of control systems.* New York: Dover Books.)

Fitts, P.M., & Posner, M.I. (1967). *Human performance.* Belmont CA: Brooks/Cole.

Flanagan, J.C. (1954). The critical incident technique. *Psychological Bulletin, 51,* 327–358.

Gagné, R.M. (1962). The acquisition of knowledge. *Psychological Review, 69,* 355–365.

Gallagher, J.P. (1979). Cognitive/information processing psychology and instruction: Reviewing recent theory and practice. *Instructional Science, 8,* 393–414.

Gilbreth, F.B. (1911). *Motion study.* Princeton, NJ: Van Nostrand.

Glaser, R. (1976). Cognitive psychology and instructional design. In D. Klahr (Ed.), *Cognition and instruction* (pp. 303–315). Hillsdale, NJ: Lawrence Erlbaum Associates.

Guzzo, R.A., & Salas, E. (1995). *Team effectiveness and decision making in organisations.* San Francisco, CA: Jossey-Bass.

Hall, E.M., Gott, S.P., & Pokorny, R.A. (1995). *A procedural guide to cognitive task analysis: The PARI methodology* (Report No. AL/HR-TR-1995-0108). Brooks Air Force Base, TX: US Air Force Materiel Command.

Hick, W.E. (1952). On the rate of gain of information. *Quarterly Journal of Experimental Psychology, 4,* 11–26.

Johnson-Laird, P. (1983). *Mental models.* Cambridge, England: Cambridge University Press.

Kieras, D. (1991). Towards a practical GOMS model methodology for user interface design. In M. Helander (Ed.), *Handbook of human-computer interaction (2nd. ed., pp. 135–137).* Amsterdam: Elsevier Science Publishers.

Kieras, D.E., & Meyer, D.E. (1998). The role of cognitive task analysis in the application of predictive models of human performance (University of Michigan EPIC Report No. 11. TR-98-ONR-EPIC-11).

Kirwan, B., & Ainsworth, L.K (1992). *A guide to task analysis.* London: Taylor & Francis.

Laughery, K.R. (1984). Computer modeling of human performance on microcomputers. *Proceedings of the Annual Meeting of the Human Factors Society, 884–888.*

Militello, L.G., & Hutton, R.J.B. (1998). Applied cognitive task analysis (ACTA): A practitioners toolkit for understanding task demands. *Ergonomics, 41,* 164–168.

Miller, G.A, Galanter, E., & Pribram, K. (1960). *Plans and the structure of behavior.* New York: Holt.

Miller, R.B. (1953). *A Method for Man-Machine Task Analysis* Dayton, OH: Wright Air Development Center. (Technical Report 53–137).

Miller, R.B. (1962). Task description and analysis. In R.M. Gagné (Ed.), *Psychological principles of system development* (pp. 187–228). New York: Holt.

Morgan, C.T., Cook, J.S., Chapanis, A., & Lund, M.W. (1963). *Human engineering guide to equipment design.* New York: McGraw-Hill.

Newell, A. (1990). *Unified theories of cognition.* Cambridge, MA: Harvard University Press.

Pew, R.W. (1978). Secondary tasks and workload measurement. In N. Moray (Ed.), *Mental workload: Its theory and measurement* (pp. 23–28). New York: Plenum.

Rasmussen J., & Rouse, W. (1981). *Human detection and diagnosis of system failures.* New York: Plenum.

Reason, J. (1990). *Human error.* Cambridge, England: Cambridge University Press

Rothkopf, E.Z. (1986). Cognitive science applications to human resource problems. *Advances in Reading/Language Research, 4,* 283–289.

Scandura, J.M. (1982). Structural (cognitive task) analysis: A method for analyzing content: I. Background and empirical research. *Journal of Structural Learning, 7,* 101–114.

Seamster, T.L., Redding, R.E., & Kaempf, G.L. (1997). *Applied cognitive task analysis in aviation.* Aldershot: Ashgate Publishing.

Seymour, W.D. (1954). *Industrial training for manual operations*. London: Pitman.

Shepherd, A. (1998). HTA as a framework for task analysis. *Ergonomics, 41*, 1537–1552.

Sheridan, T.B., & Hennessy, R.T. (Eds.) (1984). *Research and modeling of supervisory control behavior*. Washington, DC: National Academy Press.

Skinner, B.F. (1954). The science of learning and the art of teaching. *Harvard Educational Review, 24*, 86–97.

Taylor, F.W. (1911). *Principles of scientific management*. New York: Harper & Row.

Winograd, T. (1972). Understanding natural language. *Cognitive Psychology, 3*, 1–191.

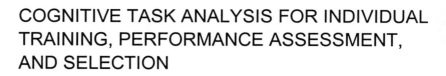

COGNITIVE TASK ANALYSIS FOR INDIVIDUAL TRAINING, PERFORMANCE ASSESSMENT, AND SELECTION

3

DESCRIBING JOB EXPERTISE USING COGNITIVELY ORIENTED TASK ANALYSES (COTA)

David DuBois
Psychological Systems & Research, Inc.

Valerie L. Shalin
Wright State University

Years of experience are typically required to achieve high levels of performance for most jobs, even when extensive job knowledge is acquired from formal education and training. Considerable time must be spent adapting learned principles and methods to new or more complex situations arising from the changing requirements of the job. This even appears true for jobs such as ditch digging, which generally do not involve substantial cognitive demands. From job experience, skilled ditch diggers develop effective strategies for identifying and managing risky situations, for making work efficient, and so forth (Shalin & Verdile, 1998). Jobs that involve dynamic work conditions and multiple team participants require additional knowledge to accommodate changing work conditions and constraints and to manage interactions between multiple tasks and task contexts. These additional knowledge requirements, beyond those defined by traditional education and training curricula, are essential to effective job performance and comprise most of what is meant by the term *job expertise.*

For example, consider the following episode taken from our work with navy computer technicians. While observing a technician aboard a ship at sea, his routine work of loading new tapes onto the computers was interrupted by a computer fault. Because these computers were involved in recording the data for an eminent missile launch, several of the ship's officers quickly entered the computer room to monitor and discuss the problem. The technician responded to direct queries and suggestions from the officers while intermittently switching between completing the tape-loading task and beginning the troubleshooting process. He appeared hesitant and unsure of how to proceed.

A subsequent debrief of the computer technician revealed an impasse concerning how to deal with the officers. He did not know an effective way to request that they refrain from interfering with the troubleshooting process.

Their insistence on discussing areas outside their expertise was impeding progress. Further, the computer technician was uncertain of the relative priorities for the multiple tasks facing him, given the change in circumstances (i.e., a system fault that could delay or end the entire missile launch). The knowledge requirements imposed by this situation involved communicating effectively with officers and decision making about the relative task priorities in novel contexts. More experienced technicians' described the solutions they had generated from similar work experiences, such as assigning one team member to brief the officers while keeping them from interfering with troubleshooting.

This episode illustrates our view of job expertise by demonstrating the unique knowledge requirements that emerge in real-world contexts (i.e., interactions between tasks, and between tasks and the context); it also emphasizes the importance of this knowledge for effective job performance. Consistent with research in personnel psychology (e.g., Campbell, McCloy, Oppler, & Sager, 1993; Peterson, Mumford, Borman, Jeanneret, & Fleishman, 1995), this focus on job performance in context reveals that job performance and job expertise are multidimensional in nature. Cognitive task analysis elaborates this claim by making explicit the implicit knowledge and cognitive-processing requirements of jobs.

The choice of methods for cognitive task analysis are primarily influenced by two considerations: (a) the assumptions made about the nature of job expertise and human cognition, and (b) the adaptations and constraints imposed by the application goal (e.g., personnel testing, training, software design). Our approach to cognitive task analysis (CTA) assumes that the multidimensional expertise acquired from job experience involves interactions between the technical core tasks (i.e., loading new tapes onto computers to record data, monitoring computer performance, and, when required, diagnosing and repairing computer faults) and: (a) other major work tasks (e.g., teamwork, communications) or (b) changes in the work context (e.g., changes in missions, environments, equipment). Our approach to CTA emerged from an application goal to improve assessments of job expertise and performance (e.g., DuBois & Shalin, 1995; DuBois, Shalin, Levi, & Borman, 1997). We outline below the basic knowledge-elicitation and representation procedures of this approach. We then illustrate how the CTA results are utilized in the design and development of tests of job knowledge, expertise, and performance. We conclude by discussing the impact of CTA results on application design principles and the impact of application goals on CTA methods.

AN OVERVIEW OF COGNITIVELY ORIENTED TASK ANALYSIS (COTA)

COTA is a collection of procedures flexibly applied to describing the expertise that supports overall job performance. It may be distinguished from other approaches to CTA in terms of four characteristics. First, the emphasis of COTA methods is on describing the contents of knowledge, rather than the processes of cognition. This reflects both the testing application for which it was originally developed and a recognition of the importance of knowledge in guiding effective work performance (e.g., Hunter & Hunter, 1984). Knowledge content consistently has been a major determinant of performance effectiveness (Campbell, 1971; Campbell et al., 1993). Consequently, COTA uses verbal evidence to identify (a) the standard methods used for accomplishing tasks; (b) how these methods are selected, initiated, and completed; and (c) how these methods are adapted to novel situations.

A second distinguishing feature of COTA is its focus on whole jobs rather than isolated technical tasks. This preference is based on the assumption that much of what comprises job expertise consists of learning how to manage multiple tasks and goals. Although instruction frequently addresses individual tasks, much additional expertise must be acquired to perform successfully in a complex, dynamic setting. Knowing the relative priority of tasks, options for satisficing some tasks, relative timelines for completion of intermediate steps, and so forth are but a few examples of the knowledge that comprises job expertise and that typically are acquired from job experience.

Based on this same assumption about the nature of job expertise, a third distinguishing characteristic of COTA is its emphasis on observing competent job performance in its natural setting. The rationale for these preferences is the importance of understanding expertise in adapting instructed methods to the physical, social, and psychological environments of the workplace. Hence, COTA examines performance in the job setting to elicit implicit aspects of job expertise that arise from the constraints imposed on tasks by the context of missions, environments, resources, and so forth.

Fourth, sampling is used to ensure that CTA results fairly, completely, and accurately represent the target domain. Reliance on theory and preliminary task analysis interviews ensures that subsequent data gathering samples the relevant persons, tasks, and contexts. For example, we have identified substantive differences in persons' expertise due to both contextual factors (e.g., environments or missions) and experience (experts vs. decayed experts, whose knowledge and skills have faded due to lack of recent practice). Further, the data-collection plan for the job analysis incorporates procedures to ensure that all major tasks (including teamwork, administration, communications, etc.) are sampled as well as major contextual factors represented by changes in missions, environments, and resources. Additionally, the task analysis interviews are used to identify important task characteristics that affect knowledge requirements. These include the amount, relative influence, and stability of time and outcome pressures, as well as task consistency and complexity.

In our choice of protocol analysis and in its implementation, COTA is reasonably representative of mainstream cognitive science methods. The COTA process can be summarized in three phases of task analysis activities—planning, describing job expertise, and developing COTA products.

PLANNING

The planning phase is directed toward achieving three interrelated goals. The first goal is to define the project goals, resources, and constraints. The second goal is to develop a preliminary description of the work context and tasks performed for the job. The third goal is to specify a sampling plan for conducting knowledge-elicitation activities. The primary method for achieving these goals is to conduct interviews with management and with subject matter experts (SMEs).

The first step involves developing a comprehensive description of the work context and job duties and tasks. In initial interviews and meetings with clients, we inquire about the range of missions, projects, environments, and other contextual characteristics of the job. This information guides a representative sampling of people, contexts, and tasks for the task analysis. We then conduct a series of 1-hour, one-on-one interviews with SMEs selected to represent the range of salient contexts and varieties of expertise comprised in the job. Interviews with three to five job experts typically result in a converging set of job duties and task characteristics.

After providing an introduction to the project and obtaining background information about the SME, we conduct the interview using a series of open-ended questions and follow-up probes about duties, tasks, and work contexts. Open-ended questions allow SMEs to provide their own conception and terminology about their work. The questions are general at first, such as "What are your primary job duties?" or "What do you do on a typical day?" After clarifying the interviewee's responses, follow-up probes are used to expand and articulate the description. To ensure a comprehensive description of the job, we use follow-up questions to probe about the performance of other tasks, such as oral and written communications, teamwork, guiding or leading others, initiative, and skill development. Additional questions concern the effects of task and contextual characteristics. For example, we ask about which tasks have time and outcome pressures associated with them, which tasks are the most difficult, and which ones may be performed in routine fashion.

This information is consolidated into a representation of job expertise. This usually takes two forms: one a task list, and the other a graphic display of the hierarchical structure of goals and methods. We refer to this figural representation as a plan–goal graph, which is described in the next section. We use the list format to develop a sampling plan of tasks and contexts for the knowledge-elicitation phase. This is accomplished by obtaining ratings from a group of SMEs on the relative importance and performance variability of each task and in each context. The information from these two ratings is combined and used to prioritize and sample tasks for more detailed study. These ratings are also used in the test development process as described in a later section.

DESCRIBING JOB EXPERTISE

We utilize videotaped protocol analysis (adapted from Ericsson & Simon, 1993) of job performance in the natural work environment to identify and describe the knowledge that supports effective performance. Videotaping captures important features of the work context such as the work and physical environments, physical movements, and facial expressions. This visual documentation provides a rich source of information about how work gets initiated (e.g., from recognition of patterns of cues), structured, and constrained. Whenever possible, we capture these protocols in the actual work environment. This focus allows us to identify those characteristics of the work context that contribute to the knowledge requirements of the job. Often the effects of these features are pervasive, yet subtle enough that they are not recalled by SMEs when they provide descriptions and explanations to others away from the job context. These contextual characteristics include the physical organization of the work space, time and outcome pressures on performance, the effects of managing and performing multiple tasks, and adaptation to changes in mission or environment. These contextual characteristics can impose substantial demands on knowledge requirements.

Knowledge Elicitation

Table 3.1 illustrates how we conduct knowledge elicitation. The table provides an excerpt from our knowledge-elicitation activities for an electronics repair task of a navy computer technician. The session from which this illustration was drawn included two observers and two instructors (a navy chief and a civilian instructor). The session occurred in a land-based laboratory used for instructional purposes. The equipment in this laboratory closely resembled the computer room of ships, but also included capabilities for inserting simulated faults. The civilian's role in the session was to select and program faults into the equipment and to discuss alternative faults with the observers. As a SME, the chief's role was to conduct his ordinary diagnostic activities while thinking aloud.

We chose this excerpt because it provides a suitable foundation for the application development (a job knowledge test in this example) by capturing content essential to job expertise. For example, in several cases, the SME criticizes and overrides the technical documentation, providing one set of instances of how job expertise can differ from descriptions of knowledge contained in formal job documentation. Because the SME worked on a problem that was not immediately obvious to him, he utilized both fault isolation flowcharts and timing diagrams.

The table indicates the speakers in the leftmost column, which includes numbers for later reference. The transcription of their verbalizations is also provided in this column. The right column contains our interpretations of the speaker's verbalizations. The excerpt begins in the middle of the chief's attempt to localize a fault. He is just completing a test with the voltmeter with some assistance from the civilian instructor. Following the protocol excerpt, we discuss our interpretation of these data and then show how we organize these protocols into a formal representation of job expertise.

TABLE 3.1
A Protocol Excerpt From Computer Technician Repair Task

Dialogue	*Discussion*
(1) Chief: I'm gonna say it stops soon after being picked up. Replace auto-thread module A-9.	The SME uses a fault-isolation flowchart as a method for identifying the cause of a fault. The chief assigns an interpretation to his observations, indicating the challenge of interpreting observations using domain terminology.
(2) Civilian: Do you wanna replace it?	
(3) Chief: Hold on, I don't want to replace anything yet. Ok. Problem still exists. There's something you can check! Let's go in and look at that. It comes down here and tells you to replace the A-9 module. And then it comes down here and tells you more places to go. To me, it would make more sense to go down here. It's silly.	This comment reveals a preference for gathering more information by conducting more observations before swapping faulty parts, despite the instructions in the flowchart. The chief refers to the documentation as silly, perhaps suggesting a concern for efficiency.
(4) Chief: Looking for the THS light. The red one right here. Now me, I don't think it is gonna light.	The informant states the purpose of his action, points out the object of interest, and states his expectations.

(continued)

(5) Obsvr: You don't think this is the problem?	The observer is not quite sure what the chief means, but echoes a response to indicate her attention.
(6) Chief: It didn't light. No. Replace the tape threaded sensor. Now that would be. That doesn't make sense though. Tape threaded sensor. Why would that cause that problem. Why would that cause that problem. I've got to think about this.	The chief provides a response to the observer's prompt. The informant reveals a preference for reasoning before doing. He also warns the experimenter that he does not have a ready explanation and that this will take some time.
(7) Obsvr: You don't see how it could cause that problem?	The observer acknowledges his difficulty but won't let the SME remain silent while he solves the problem.
(8) Chief: No.	The chief treats the prompt as a question that could be satisfied with a short, nonsubstantive answer.
(9) Obsvr: What does the threaded tape sensor do?	The observer tries a more substantive prompt that cannot be satisfied with a one-word reply.
(10) Chief: It's saying that the tape is. I'm trying to think of when that tape threaded sensor light comes on. I don't know when it comes on. Where's our little time chart? I'm trying to think when it comes on.	The SME complies with the obligation to reply and fortunately begins to verbalize on his own again. The absence of verbalization in the past few turns leaves us with the idea that the chief is pondering a difficult problem. We have no idea of his reasoning during the silence.
(11) Chief: Turn on, vacuumed sensed.	The SME begins to read the timing chart.

As long as the SME is fairly verbal, the observer indicates her engagement with *uh-huh*. The observer's comments largely indicate her continued attention generally by paraphrasing or responding to the SME's most recent comment (5). The observer becomes intrusive when the periods of silence increase (7, 9). The silence is associated with complex reasoning, which is exactly the place we would like to get the most verbalization. In all of these cases, the questions and comments are not intended to elicit specific information, but rather to indicate sufficient engagement to require continued verbalization from the SME.

Knowledge Representation

Our approach to analyzing the protocol data involves interpreting each segment and encoding it as a method or a goal in a representation of knowledge. We also elaborate the goals and methods with other knowledge, such as decisions (e.g., choosing which goal to pursue next or which method to use), cues or conditions that initiate the use of a method, or criteria that indicate that a goal has been completed.

At this stage of cognitive task analysis, we use a plan–goal graph for organizing the knowledge-elicitation results. Plan–goal graphs are graphical depictions of task structure (Rouse, Geddes, & Hammer, 1993; Sewell & Geddes, 1990). The overall purpose of a work activity is decomposed into sub-goals and methods (i.e., plans) for accomplishing the goals. The decomposition can be continued to any desired level of detail as may be required by the application. Goals are represented by ovals and methods are shown as boxes. Methods specify alternative procedures for accomplishing a goal; only one method is needed to satisfy a goal. Goals are conjunctive; each one must be completed to satisfy the higher level parent goal. This approach to representing job expertise is shown in Fig. 3.1 using information from the protocol excerpted in the previous section. To illustrate how we approach analyzing protocols, we continue the computer technician example by interpreting the protocol and translate this interpretation into the plan–goal graph representation in Fig. 3.1.

We infer that the goal of the SME's activity is to find the cause of an observed failure. The support for this inference comes from statements like (4), in which the SME suggests that he has not yet found the problem. Note that the goal here is not simply a state of the world, but a state of the SME's mind. If he believed he had found the failure, we would not expect any further diagnostic activities. The full protocol illustrates four methods for finding this failure, defined by four different representations (see four methods under Goal A in the plan–goal graph). One method is to follow the instructions in a fault-isolation flow chart (1). A second method is to examine a timing diagram to determine the sequence and duration of events that should occur (10). A third method involves a functional block diagram. A fourth method involves a schematic diagram.

Each of the methods identified can be further decomposed. The full protocol provides information to help us decompose using Flowchart B in the plan–goal graph, which is much more complicated than we expected. Although not illustrated in the excerpt, one subgoal for using these flowcharts is simply to locate the correct flowchart (C in the plan–goal graph). This is often established by using an index that maps descriptions of problems onto flowchart numbers (D).

We became aware of this subgoal for two reasons. First, we have observed trainees who have difficulty using the index for locating the correct flowchart.

Second, the session from which the excerpt was drawn includes an episode in which the chief notices after some time that he is using the wrong flowchart. In both cases, the failure to achieve the goal of having the correct figure halts any progress on using the flowcharts. We infer that this step must be present to use the flowcharts properly.

We name goals choosing words that convey states of the world rather than procedures for achieving these states. For these reasons, we avoid goal names that use present tense verbs suggesting action. For example, we named the sub-goal *flowchart applied* to avoid the procedural connotation of the name *apply flowchart*. This convention helps maintain the distinction between goals and plans.

The observed difficulties in locating the correct flowchart illustrate how mistakes inform the task analysis by indicating knowledge requirements that may not be obvious when performance is perfect. In addition, the chief's episode suggests the presence of knowledge for confirming that the appropriate flow-chart is in use. Without such knowledge, the chief could not have identified and corrected his error.

Representing this knowledge in a plan–goal graph suits the intermediate level of analyses appropriate to the development of a job knowledge test. By encoding knowledge into the structure of a plan–goal graph, we confirm that each knowledge element is relevant to a goal of task performance. Thus, we did not formally analyze the protocol data, nor did we implement a computational cognitive model. Rather, we developed an initial plan–goal graph model and refined it through several protocol-gathering sessions. This approach substantially reduces the time, personnel, and other costs that occur with more formal data analytic methods.

DEVELOPING CTA PRODUCTS

The final stage of the COTA process involves transforming the knowledge representation into appropriate inputs for the intended application. For written knowledge tests, the cognitive task analysis results provide two major outcomes: the content for tests of knowledge and a useful set of design principles for test development. Both outcomes require additional steps to transform COTA results into the appropriate products.

Developing Test Content

In the section on planning, we discussed the use of expert ratings as inputs to the sampling plan for knowledge elicitation. Expert ratings across a matrix of tasks and knowledge provide a blueprint for test development. For this use, the per-

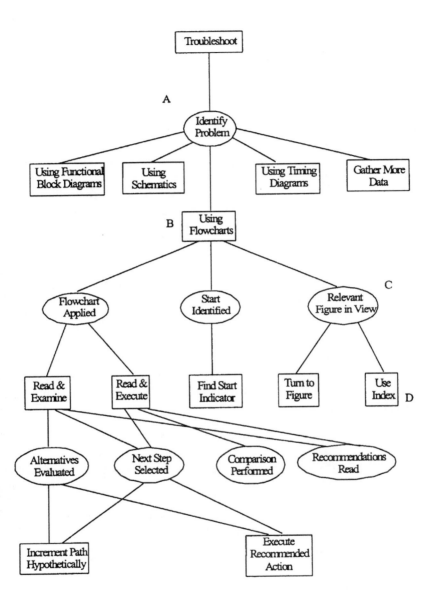

FIG. 3.1   Portions of a plan–goal graph for computer technicians (from DuBois, Shalin, Levi, & Borman, 1997). Reprinted by permission.

centages in the body of the matrix specify the proportion of the test that should be devoted to each knowledge facet for each task.

Before use as a set of test specifications, two additional steps are needed. First, the task analysts should review these preliminary ratings based on the results of the cognitive task analysis. In addition to providing a detailed elaboration of job expertise, the cognitive task analysis may also have revealed aspects of expertise that are not reflected in the experts' ratings. This can occur because of discrepancies between experts' implicit theories of job expertise and the knowledge they actually use on the job. If such a discrepancy seems apparent, another iteration of the ratings can be useful. For this rating exercise, the raters should be provided with a summary of the task analysis results with any discrepant or anomalous results described. The ratings should then again be combined into a revised matrix.

In the next step, the task by knowledge matrix is elaborated into more detailed descriptions of expertise. To provide additional specificity to the test writer, test specifications should also be provided at the method level of analysis. For example, as shown in the plan–goal graph in Fig. 3.1, the troubleshooting task was decomposed into five methods. Using the plan–goal graph representation, a list of methods should be developed for all tasks. Detailed test specifications can then be developed for methods by obtaining additional ratings from job experts.

At a third and finest level of detail, the plan–goal graph information is converted into a list of the steps required for performing each method, the initiating conditions, constraints, choice of method, and completion criteria. Additionally, the type and frequency of errors for performing each method are gathered and presented with this list of knowledge elements.

Together, these three levels of detail for test specifications provide specific guidance for which test questions to construct, what the content of the question should entail, and which response options should be written (i.e., for multiple-choice tests). It should be noted that, although all of the knowledge content was identified in the knowledge-elicitation stage, some additional processing of this information was required to provide the appropriate inputs to the test development application. Specifically, the information contained in the plan–goal graph was converted into lists at three levels of analysis; ratings were then obtained and processed for the items in each list. The contribution of cognitive task analysis to this process is to specify in detail which aspects of knowledge should be assessed by each test question. In knowledge tests that we have developed, this approach led to a shift in test content from questions assessing facts and procedures to a much stronger emphasis on decisionmaking, problem-solving, and pattern recognition. This systematic approach to cognitive test design has been organized into a set of software tools to aid test developers

(DuBois, Levi, & Shalin, 1997).

Adapting Test Design Principles

In addition to providing the content for test questions, another useful contribution of cognitive task analysis is its refinement of test design principles. Test development normally proceeds according to a plan that specifies the number of test questions for each category of content and/or instructional objective. These plans are often defined by topics in educational settings and by tasks in training settings. More elaborated methods have also been proposed where distinctions have been made about content within tasks and topics (Millman & Greene, 1989). For example, Ellis and Wulfeck (1982) proposed that instructional objectives and test questions should identify whether recall or recognition was required to achieve the desired level of understanding or performance. This approach results in a test specification matrix, where the number of test questions is defined by a set of content categories within the task or topic categories.

We adapted this matrix approach by using distinctions about the content of knowledge instead of the processes of retrieval of information from memory. We elaborated the traditional distinction between declarative (facts, concepts) and procedural (how to perform a task) knowledge to incorporate two additional distinctions about knowledge content: generative (knowledge supporting transfer and problem solving in new contexts) and team/self knowledge (knowledge about the capabilities, strategies, and preferences of individuals). Additionally, we made numerous additional distinctions within each of these major distinctions. For example, we elaborated procedural knowledge as comprising the following subcategories of knowledge: goal choice, conditions/constraints, method choice, method execution, goal standards, and pattern recognition. Cognitive task analyses of job performance in several domains indicated that these substantive distinctions about knowledge content were more relevant than distinctions about cognitive processes or test methods (i.e., multiple choice, open response, true–false) for specifying test content. This strategy has been shown to significantly improve the predictive validity of job knowledge tests (DuBois & Shalin, 1995). Thus, in addition to supplying the content for test development, cognitive task analysis results were used to refine and constrain the principles of test design. By specifying precisely which aspects of knowledge should be tested, test writing becomes more efficient, systematic, and valid.

DISCUSSION

The COTA approach evolved from work to develop a principled approach to the development of measures of performance. The work to date suggests that it is effective for this purpose (DuBois & Shalin, 1995). Additional research is needed to determine the boundary conditions for the usefulness of this and other strategies of cognitive task analysis across a range of applications, jobs, and features of job expertise and human cognition. Given the practical relevance of further understanding of which CTA methods are suitable for particular situations, we conclude by commenting on the interrelationships between COTA methods and the application for which they were developed.

Impact of the Application on COTA

In addition to our theoretical predispositions concerning the nature of job expertise, the application of developing written performance measures had substantial effects on our selection of task analysis methods. The emphasis on representative sampling has a long history in test design for both psychometric and legal reasons. For this application, it was natural to extend this notion to sampling test questions across knowledge requirements in addition to sampling across essential job duties. We also employed representative sampling in selecting people, tasks, and contexts to examine during the knowledge- elicitation stage of the task analysis.

Our focus on knowledge content also reflects the application of test development. Test results are used to diagnose, assess, and prescribe instruction. Consequently, content is especially relevant for this application. Coupled with our theoretical position on the importance of the work context, the choice of protocol analysis for identifying the contents of expertise reflects the application purpose.

Impact of COTA on Application Design Principles

Although psychometrics has provided sophisticated statistical techniques for evaluating properties of test questions, guidance for the conception and writing of test questions consists of a loose collection of rules of thumb (Sechrest, Kihlstrom, & Bootzin, 1993). The implementation of cognitive task analysis defined a set of distinctions about job expertise content that constrain the test design process. In translating the task analysis results into appropriate inputs for test design, the resulting test specifications provided useful, specific constraints on the content of question stems, response options, scenarios, and accompanying graphics.

This situation of highly principled methods for analysis and evaluation, coupled with somewhat informal approaches to design, appear to characterize other design domains such as software design, systems engineering, architecture, and so forth. Using the adaptations we made to the test design process as an analogy, it may be possible that similar improvements in the design process can be achieved for other design disciplines. Although the application domains are different, the essential feature of the design problem is the same—how to usefully describe the user. That is, our experience in test design suggests that a more principled, efficient, and effective design process can result from formally incorporating essential aspects of cognition into the design process. The use of cognitive task analysis to address issues in design principles may represent an important contribution of these methodologies for describing expertise.

REFERENCES

Campbell, J. P. (1971). Personnel training and development. *Annual Review of Psychology, 22*, 565–602.

Campbell, J. P., McCloy, R. M., Oppler, S. H., & Sager, C. E. (1993). A theory of performance. In N. Schmitt & W. C. Borman (Eds.), *Personnel selection in organizations* (pp. 35–70). San Francisco, CA: Jossey-Bass.

DuBois, D., & Shalin, V. L. (1995). Adapting cognitive methods to real world objectives: An application to job knowledge testing. In P. Nichols, S. Chipman, & R. Brennan (Eds.), *Cognitively diagnostic assessment* (pp. 189–220). Hillsdale, NJ: Lawrence Erlbaum Associates.

DuBois, D., Levi, K., & Shalin, V. L. (1997). *Aid for designing evaluations of performance and training (ADEPT).* Kent, OH: Psychological Systems and Research, Inc.

DuBois, D. A., Shalin, V. L., Levi, K., & Borman, W. C. (1997). A cognitively oriented approach to task analysis. *Training Research Journal, 3*, 103–142.

Ellis, J. A., & Wulfeck, W. H. (1982). *Handbook for testing in Navy schools* (NPRDC SR 83-2). San Diego, CA: Navy Personnel Research and Development Center.

Ericcson, K. A., & Simon, H. A. (1993). *Protocol analysis: Verbal reports as data* (rev. ed.). Cambridge, MA: MIT Press.

Hunter, J. E., & Hunter, R. F. (1984). Validity and utility of alternative predictors of job performance. *Psychological Bulletin, 96(1)*, 72–98.

Millman, J., & Greene, J. (1989). The specification and development of tests of achievement and ability. In R. L. Linn (Ed.), *Educational measurement* (3rd ed.), (pp. 335–366). New York: Macmillan.

Peterson, N. G., Mumford, M. D., Borman, W. C., Jeanneret, P. R., & Fleishman, E.A. (1995, September). *Development of prototype occupational information network (O*Net) content model: Volume I* (Report, Contract #94-542). Utah Department of Employment Security.

Rouse, W. B., Geddes, N., & Hammer, J. M. (1993, March). Computer aided fighter pilots. *IEEE Spectrum*, pp. 38–41.

Sechrest, L., Kihlstrom, J. F., & Bootzin, R. R. (1993). How to develop multiple-choice tests. *APS Observer*, pp. 10ff.

Sewell, D. R., & Geddes, N. (1990). A plan and goal based method for computer-human system design. In *Human Computer Interaction, INTERACT 90* (pp. 283–288). New York: North-Holland.

Shalin, V. L., & Verdile, C. L. (1998, April). *Knowledge content and function in manual labor.* Presented at the Symposium for Industrial and Organizational Psychology (SIOP), Dallas, TX.

4

TRAINING OF TROUBLESHOOTING: A STRUCTURED, TASK ANALYTICAL APPROACH

Alma Schaafstal and Jan Maarten Schraagen
TNO Human Factors

Naval ships are equipped with a large number of systems with a combat function, varying from sensor systems (radar, sonar) to weapon systems (guns, missile launchers) and communication systems (computers). To maintain optimal combat readiness, it is essential that the integrity of these systems be maintained at all times. The Weapon Engineering Service is responsible for this task. The weapon engineers on board carry out periodic preventive maintenance, much like car mechanics do when you bring your car to a garage at certain intervals. They also do corrective maintenance, i.e., troubleshooting in case a malfunction occurs. The corrective maintenance task is carried out under high time pressure, particularly under operational conditions. Often, the command team is waiting anxiously for the weapon engineers to find the fault and bring the defective system back to operational status. Therefore, it is essential that the weapon engineers are well trained and able to troubleshoot effectively and efficiently.

In the 1990s, complaints started to emerge from the operational Dutch fleet concerning the speed and accuracy of the weapon engineers. At a macrolevel, a number of reasons could be given for the apparent suboptimal performance of the engineers. First, expert troubleshooters are in high demand in the civilian world, and a sizable number leave the navy each year. Second, fewer candidates for the weapon engineering branch are entering the Weapon Engineering School. Whatever the precise reasons, in 1990 the Royal Netherlands Navy asked TNO Human Factors Research to look at these complaints and come up with possible solutions to the problems.

OBSERVATIONAL STUDIES

We carried out a number of observational studies on actual troubleshooting. It has always been our aim to stay as closely as possible to the tasks that technicians actually carry out, to get at their actual reasoning strategies. We investigated how well technicians were able to solve malfunctions they were confronted with. These malfunctions were deliberately introduced into the actual systems the school has available for training purposes. Two systems were studied: radar and computer.

Radar Study

For the radar system, technicians with various levels of expertise were asked to solve four different problems they had not encountered. We included a theory instructor, practice instructor, trainee who just finished the course, technician with a lot of practical experience in this particular radar system, and technician with a lot of practical experience in a different radar system. The latter person was included to observe and understand functional thinking about systems, because all radar systems function similarly down to a certain level of abstraction. The technicians were asked to think aloud while troubleshooting. Details they could not easily find in the documentation were provided to them by the radar expert present.

The study showed some remarkable results. First, it turned out that the theory instructor was not a good troubleshooter. This turned our attention to a gap in the method used for course design between theoretical instruction and bringing theory into practice. Second, there was not as much functional thinking as we had expected and virtually no transfer of knowledge from one radar system to the other. This turned our attention to the contents of the training courses, which were component-oriented instead of functionally oriented. Third, the trainee knew all sorts of details about the system, but was unsystematic in his approach to troubleshooting. Again, this confirms the point made about the contents of the training courses, but also indicates a lack of practice in actual troubleshooting. Theoretically, it was interesting to distinguish between system knowledge and a general troubleshooting strategy. Some experts apparently exhibited the latter in the absence of the former. Fourth, problems were mainly solved, if at all, by recognition of a similarity to a previous problem. Although efficient, this approach should not be the basis of one's training philosophy, because problems are too numerous to train on. A more principled and systematic approach to troubleshooting should be taught during the training courses. At this stage in our project, however, we were still unable to implement this philosophy in actual training courses.

Computer Study

The second preliminary study was carried out on a computer system. We wanted to replicate the results obtained in the radar study under more controlled conditions. Among other things, this meant a larger sample of subjects. This necessitated a switch from the radar system to a system that larger numbers of trainees are trained to maintain. The SMRμ is a computer system that forms the basis for a large number of other systems and so most weapon engineers have to take the course on this system. Twelve students—without practical experience on board, who had just finished their course on this system—were asked to solve four representative problems of intermediate difficulty selected by the school. Before they started troubleshooting, the students were also asked to fill in a knowledge test containing 20 open questions on various aspects of the system. Two independent observers rated the number of problems solved correctly.

The results of the computer study showed that, on average, only 40% of the problems were solved accurately. Second, only a small correlation was found between the knowledge test and fault-finding performance (Pearson $r = .27$). This confirms the results of the radar study, showing a gap between theory and practice.

COGNITIVE TASK ANALYSIS

To understand and appreciate in a theoretical framework the difficulties the students have, a cognitive task analysis was carried out. A basic assumption in this analysis is that troubleshooting is first and foremost a cognitive task. It requires a lot of knowledge about the system the engineer is supposed to maintain and a lot of skill in taking measurements and carrying out repairs. Systems mostly look deceptively simple from the outside, but most carry an impressive amount of electrical and electronic circuitry inside. Troubleshooting is a search for a likely cause through an enormous problem space of possible causes. To be able to search selectively, it is essential that the representation of the system is highly structured. One likely candidate for such a structuring is a functional, hierarchical representation. Although this has been known for a long time in the literature on expertnovice differences in general, and even in the domain of troubleshooting, it turned out to be surprisingly difficult to find the correct functional representation for the systems we were working on. We return to the techniques we used later. First, a second element in our approach to cognitive task analysis should be mentioned; a control strategy that governs the troubleshooting process.

Research by Schaafstal in the domain of paper making has shown that expert troubleshooters use a structured approach to troubleshooting consisting of a number of steps they take in a particular order (Schaafstal, 1991). This structured approach is discussed later in more detail. For now, suffice it to say that its function is primarily memory management. Particularly with novel faults not previously encountered, the control strategy is essential for preventing working memory overload. Novice troubleshooters, who lack such a strategy, do not see the forest for the trees, although their lack of a functional representation of the system may also contribute to their problems.

At TNO Human Factors Research Institute, a theoretical framework for cognitive task analysis has been developed (Merkelbach & Schraagen, 1994; Schaafstal & Schraagen, 1992). A cognitive task analysis is an analysis of the knowledge and skills required for a proper performance of a particular task. The framework consists of three elements: (a) an analysis of the tasks that have to be carried out to accomplish particular goals (the goal of troubleshooting can be described as bringing the system back to its normal state), (b) an analysis of the knowledge and skills required to accomplish these tasks (e.g., system knowledge and measurement skills), and (c) an analysis of the cognitive (thought) processes of experienced and less experienced technicians.

Research has been carried out on the third element—technicians' thought processes (see Schaafstal, 1993; Schraagen & Schaafstal, 1991). For instance, it has been found that experienced technicians have a more systematic approach to troubleshooting than less experienced technicians (Schaafstal, 1991), that experienced technicians mentally represent a system at multiple levels of abstraction (Frederiksen & White, 1993), and that experienced technicians use more efficient strategies than less experienced technicians (Reed & Johnson, 1993). The following paragraphs discuss the first two elements in more detail.

At a global level, troubleshooting can be subdivided in the following four subtasks: (a) formulate problem description, (b) generate causes, (c) test, and (d) evaluate

Formulate Problem Description

The process of troubleshooting is started when the technician observes abnormal system behavior or receives a notification of abnormal system behavior. Besides recognizing abnormal behavior, the technician also needs to identify correct behavior. This is an important task because determining correct aspects of system behavior can limit the number of possible causes. By determining what aspects of system behavior are still normal, the technician eliminates certain parts that do not need to be investigated further.

Generate Causes

When generating causes, it is important to keep the search for a possible cause within bounds. At the lowest level, thousands of pins, transistors, and relays could be the possible cause. It is clear that not all components have the same chance of causing the malfunction. To constrain this process of searching for possible causes, a technician needs to be able to look at the system at several levels of abstraction. The higher levels are often called the *functional levels* because at those levels blocks are distinguished that fulfill a particular function. At the lowest levels, functions are realized in a particular structure (hardware).

For the course on the SMRμ computer, we have distinguished four levels of abstraction. At the highest level, Level 1, the SMRμ consists of four blocks: power supply, central processor, memory, and peripheral equipment. Level 1 was developed for educational purposes only: The student needs to learn that troubleshooting can take place at different levels of detail and that with particular faults complete functional blocks can be eliminated at Level 1. At the level immediately below, Level 2, the block 'power supply' is subdivided into four blocks and the blocks 'central processor', 'memory', and 'peripheral equipment' are also further subdivided. When signals need to be measured during the testing phase, Level 2 is insufficient. That is why Level 2 extra was developed. At Level 2 extra, no new functional blocks are distinguished. Level 2 extra adds the signals that run among the different blocks distinguished at Level 2. If one needs to know how the signals are generated within the blocks, one needs to fall back on the so-called electrical principle (EP) schemata. These EP schemata can be considered as Level 3. The knowledge that is required for generating possible causes is mainly knowledge of Levels 1 and 2.

Test

When possible causes have been generated, they need to be tested. The technician needs to choose the right testing method and testing means. By testing means we mean all tools and equipment that can provide clarity to a technician concerning the status of the system. The next task is performing the test. This amounts to the correct setting up and operating of testing means and the correct reading of the test's outcome. After this, the outcome of the test needs to be interpreted. This implies that the technician needs to formulate an expectation before performing the test and subsequently relates the outcome of the test to this expectation. If a technician expects, on the basis of the proper functioning of the system, a low level (0V) and he measures and observes a high level (5V), the cause that was tested needs to be accepted provided all boundary conditions for the proper execution of the test have been fulfilled. However, if on the basis of the outcome of a test a possible cause is rejected, the next possible cause needs to be tested. When all possible causes have been rejected, the technician needs to back up to the task of generating causes, brcause he has probably overlooked something. When the correct cause has been identified, it needs to be evaluated.

The technician needs to possess the following skills: executing several tests, creating preconditions to be able to measure (for instance, safety measures), and handling measurement tools. These measurement skills are of great importance because our research has shown that corporals who have just finished the function course do not yet possess all of these skills (Schaafstal & Schraagen, 1993; Schraagen & Schaafstal, 1996).

Evaluate

If a technician thinks he has identified the correct cause, this cause needs to be eliminated. The goal of troubleshooting is to return the system to its normal state of working. The necessity to eliminate the cause means that the cause needs to be brought back to line replaceable unit (LRU) level. Faultfinding at a lower level (mostly until a component on a circuit board has been identified) can only serve as a justification for replacing a particular circuit board. When a technician is certain that a particular circuit board is faulty (has identified the cause), it is senseless to further localize the cause on the circuit board (with the exception of particular operational circumstances). Instead, the technician needs to change the circuit board with an intact circuit board and subsequently test whether the abnormal behavior still occurs. If the abnormal behavior does not occur anymore, the fault has been found. If the abnormal behavior still occurs, either the circuit board was not faulty after all or the problem consists of several causes that mask each other. In that case, the technician needs to test and evaluate the remaining causes. When evaluating a particular cause, one needs to possess the skills of localizing the faulty circuit board and replacing and possibly tuning a new component.

Recommendations for the Training of Troubleshooting

If the results of the two preliminary studies are combined with the results of the cognitive task analysis, two conclusions can be drawn about the troubleshooting performance of beginning technicians: (a) Beginning technicians lack a systematic approach in troubleshooting, resulting in a lack of goal-directed problem solving; and (b) they lack a functional understanding of the equipment they have to maintain. As a result, several recommendations for the training of troubleshooters have been put forward:

1.   The training of a systematic approach to troubleshooting should be embedded in regular training courses; this systematic approach then becomes second nature for technicians. This is a different approach to the training of troubleshooting than taken by, for example, Kepner and Tregoe (1966). These authors claim it is possible to train a systematic approach to troubleshooting independent from any specific knowledge of equipment. However, recent research in

cognitive psychology has shown that general strategies are ineffective when trained in isolation, i.e., separated from domain-specific knowledge (Singley & Anderson, 1989). We have demonstrated the same in the domain of troubleshooting (Schraagen & Schaafstal, 1996).

2. The theory incorporated in training courses, and the relation between theory and practice, should be geared toward the job and should be fine tuned to the task that technicians have to fullfill in their daily routine. The training should be geared toward the acquisition of troubleshooting skill and the necessary knowledge of the equipment should be related to the acquisition of this troubleshooting skill and should not be isolated.

3. The knowledge of equipment should be taught at a functional level, not at a component level.

Innovation of the Course on the SMRμ Computer

We tried to implement the recommendations stated earlier into a pilot training, in which an extra week of training was added to an existing course. A systematic evaluation of this innovation took place after a group of rather inexperienced corporals had taken the course. The course chosen for the innovation is the course that results in the qualification *technician SMRμ*. The SMRμ is a computer that is installed on board certain types of frigates. As far as troubleshooting is concerned, the system can be described as an electronic system. In a normal situation, the parts to be replaced (so-called line replaceable units [LRUs]) are mostly circuit boards. This course was chosen because it is one most frequently taken at the Naval Weapon Engineering School. The advantage of this choice is that a potentially positive educational innovation has a lot of impact. Besides there is a substantial number of students whose performance can be evaluated. The existing function course lasts for 6 weeks. It consists of theoretical and practical parts, given by different instructors. For the practical part, practice equipment is available.

On the basis of the aforementioned task analysis and the knowledge and skills required, training goals have been formulated. These training goals explicitly mention the ability to troubleshoot. The training goals have been implemented in a 1-week training course that is characterized by a systematic approach to troubleshooting and a lot of practice in structured troubleshooting. The 1-week training course was added onto the existing function course as a first step. If this proved successful, the existing course would be modified completely according to our principles and the modified course would also be evaluated empirically.

EVALUATION OF THE COURSE ON THE SMRµ COMPUTER

To obtain an objective impression of the effect of this training innovation compared with the old situation, an experimental evaluation of the new course took place.

Method

Twenty-one participants (corporals) took part in the experiment. Ten of these participants had passed the regular function course SMRµ at the Naval Weapon Engineering School (control group). The remaining 11 participants took a 1-week course specifically aimed at training structured troubleshooting in addition to the regular function course (Structured Troubleshooting [ST] group). Participants had no practical experience on board ships in their current function as corporal. Four unfamiliar problems were used to measure the participants' troubleshooting performance. According to instructors, the problems were of a reasonable degree of difficulty and were representative of the types of problems that may occur in this piece of equipment. Participants were asked to think aloud while troubleshooting. Their verbalizations were recorded with a cassette recorder. The maximum time allotted to solve each problem was 1 hour. Before troubleshooting on these four problems, participants were asked to take a knowledge test to measure their theoretical knowledge. This test consisted of open-ended questions to minimize the amount of guessing. The most important variables measured include:

The score on the knowledge test. The knowledge tests were rated by the practice instructor. This rating was blind with respect to the name of the participant to ensure as much objectivity in rating as possible.

Verbal protocols. The verbal protocols were typed literally without further elaboration. The protocols were rated blindly: the two raters (expert troubleshooters) did not know whose protocols they were rating and the condition in which the subjects participated. The Spearman rank order correlation coefficient between the two raters was .72, which is sufficiently high to be satisfying. Each rater was asked to rate each protocol on three aspects:

1. The quality of the *solution* (on a scale from 0 to 1): Has the right LRU been localized? As a measure for having solved a particular problem, a measure for quality of solution of .75 or higher was taken.

2. The quality of *reasoning* (on a scale from 1 to 5): Has the reasoning process been systematic?

3. The quality of *system knowledge* (on a scale from 1 to 5): How do the subjects reason about the system?

TABLE 4.1

Performance of the Control Group and the Structured Troubleshooting (ST) Group, Averaged Over Four Malfunctions

Aspects	Control Group	ST-Group
Quality of solution (0-1)	0.39	0.86
Percentage problems solved (%)	40	86
Quality of reasoning (1-5)	2.60	4.64
Quality of system knowledge (1-5)	2.87	4.59

Judgment of trainees about the extra 1-week course. The subjects in the ST condition were asked, after having finished the extra week but before the actual experiment started, to fill out anonymously an evaluation form about their experience with the extra week of training.

Results

Score on Knowledge Test. The control group scored on average 55% correct on the knowledge test and the ST group 63%. This is not a statistically reliable difference ($F(1,10)=2.36$, $p=.14$). Thus, the ST group did not score significantly higher on the knowledge test than the subjects who had taken the regular course.

Rating of Verbal Protocols. The ratings of the verbal protocols are shown in Table 4.1.

The results show a clear difference on all aspects between the control group and the ST group. Statistical analyses confirmed there was a significant effect on all rated aspects: All *p*-values exceeded .01-level [the $F(1,19)$ values being 31.72 for quality of solution, 26.07 for percentage problems solved, 77.57 for quality of reasoning, and 43.00 for quality of system knowledge]. There was no significant interaction on any of the dependent variables between group and type of problem: The ST group performed equally better than the control group on all problems.

Evaluation Form. All 11 trainees of the ST group entirely agreed with this statement: The content of this course is a useful addendum to the knowledge I already possessed. The most frequently mentioned points of which one felt the course was a useful addendum were: *more practice oriented* (nine times) and *better troubleshooting method* (four times). The most frequently used terms to describe the course as a whole were: *it trains you to troubleshoot faster due to the systematic approach, the training is geared towards practice,* and *a useful addendum to the regular course.* The course was judged to be *useful* and *very good.*

Modified Course. On the basis of the results reported previously one could still argue that the significant improvements obtained were due to the fact that students in the ST condition received 1 week more education than the regular students. Therefore, our results might not be attributed to the contents of the education but rather to the duration. To counter this criticism, we have completely modified the existing function course SMRµ according to our principles of ST. This has resulted in a course with a duration of 4 weeks instead of 6 weeks—a 33% reduction in duration. Several groups of corporals have taken this modified course, and we have evaluated this course along the same lines as reported earlier (i.e., the same four malfunctions were given and the same measurements were taken with 11 corporals).

The results (see table 4.2) show that the percentage of malfunctions correctly identified was 95, the quality of reasoning was 4.84, and the quality of system knowledge was 4.77. Statistical analyses confirmed that these numbers were significantly higher compared with those obtained with the control group that received the old 6-week course. In fact, the corporals who received the modified and shortened course did not perform worse than the corporals who took the 7-week course, which contained the 1 additional week. At some measures, they even performed better than the corporals who took the 7-week course. This means that, although the course length is reduced from 7 to 4 weeks, troubleshooting performance remains at high levels. Therefore, we conclude that our initial results obtained with the 1-week extra course were not due to the fact that students received more education, but rather to the contents of the education. In particular, designing the course according to principles of ST is the critical factor behind the great improvement in troubleshooting performance.

DISCUSSION

After an extra week of training designed according to the principles of ST corporals solved twice as many problems compared with corporals who did not

TABLE 4.2
Performance of the Control Group, Structured Troubleshooting (ST) Group, and the Structured Troubleshooting Group After Shortening of the Course, Averaged Over Four Malfunctions

Aspects	Control Group	ST-Group	Shortened
Percentage problems solved (%)	40	86	95
Quality of reasoning (1-5)	2.60	4.64	4.84
Quality of system knowledge (1-5)	2.87	4.59	4.77

take this extra week. This supports the idea that ST is a general plan applicable across problems. The quality of reasoning improves with 78% and the quality of system knowledge with 60%. These results are based on a thorough analysis of verbal protocols of corporals during troubleshooting. The effects are all of a large size and are all statistically significant at the .01 level. The analysis of verbal protocols is reliable because a second rater arrives at similar results independent of the first rater.

The trainees who took the extra 1-week course were all pleased with the contents of the training. Remarkably, trainees expected that the ST method would lead to faster troubleshooting. Although this hypothesis has not been tested formally in this experiment, we have the strong impression that this in fact is true. The reason for not incorporating time to solution as a dependent variable in the analysis is that there was a time limit of 1 hour and many corporals in the control condition had not finished their troubleshooting within this hour. A pure estimate of time to solution is therefore impossible. However, it is clear that corporals in the ST group often solved at least the first three problems within a half hour and sometimes even within 5 to 10 minutes. Thus, there is at least a reduction of 50% in time to solution when someone has been trained according to ST principles. From an operational viewpoint, this is an important result.

One of the limitations of the present study is the emphasis on only one type of equipment—a computer system digital and electronic in nature. Hence, the question to be asked is whether the method equally applies to other types of systems (e.g., those more mechanical in nature). A recent project—in which a course is redesigned for maintenance training of the Oto Melara, the big gun on some of the frigates, a system with much more mechanical aspects—shows that the method equally applies to this system and is therefore not dependent for its results on electronical systems.

The possible criticism that the positive results are due to the lengthening of the course has been countered by redesigning the course—and in this way shortening the course from 7 to 4 weeks. An experimental evaluation of this shortened course results in at least as high a troubleshooting performance as the 7-week course, as shown in Table 4.2.

The practical implications of the present results for training of troubleshooting in technical systems include the following. Training designed and given according to the principles of ST results in an enormous performance improvement. On the basis of this, the Naval Weapon Engineering School uses this method for the design of all their courses, resulting in a more practice and job-oriented training. This includes less emphasis on the detailed functioning of equipment and its components, but more emphasis on the actual skill of troubleshooting. Now that a large number of training courses on a variety of systems have been redesigned according to this method, we have even more convincing results about the validity of the method. Almost all courses that have been redesigned have resulted in good troubleshooting performance and substantial reductions of training time (i.e., 30% on average, with reductions sometimes up to 60%). During this process of redesign, we acted as consultants and took the experiences we obtained with us for the design of guidelines with respect to the implementation of ST. Certain parts of the method are easier to grasp for training designers than others. In general, it takes them time to design functional schemata for systems. This is understandable, because it requires self-elicitation of knowledge. Second, they are so used to training design on the basis of available documentation, that learning to think in terms of task analyses is difficult. Finally, there are all sorts of (administrative) procedures that should be adapted to fit the new scheme of training design. However, after they have gone through the process of redesign, instructors feel that their students are better trained for the job situation and have better skills.

Structured Troubleshooting is also useful in civilian industry. First of all, ST makes the process of troubleshooting explicit. Hence, companies can show their clients how their technicians troubleshoot. Second, technicians can more easily communicate with and learn from each other when they record their troubleshooting on the fault-isolation form that was developed as part of ST. Finally, ST leads to faster and better performance. Ultimately, this saves a lot of money.

REFLECTION ON COGNITIVE TASK ANALYSIS METHODS USED

Looking back on this project, it became clear to us that we oscillated between understanding the domain and understanding the practitioner. In this process, we have used multiple techniques. In understanding the domain, we have, of course, resorted to documentation analysis and interviews. We firmly believe, however, that what has made this project convincing and successful has been our collection of empirical data. The following techniques were used for behavioral observation:

1. Obervational studies of real-life tasks. As a starting point, it is often very useful to observe experts perform the task they are familiar with. However, added value is provided by introducing a quasi-experimental manipulation. (e.g., by using experts with different perspectives, backgrounds, or areas of expertise, and by contrasting expert with novice performance). In our radar observation study, for instance, we observed both theory and practice instructors, and experts with varying familiarity with a particular radar system. This study yielded important insights: Possessing theoretical knowledge was not sufficient for good troubleshooting, and, presumably due to

training practices, there was no such thing as general radar knowledge.

2. Use of verbal protocols. We made extensive use of verbal protocols in our observation studies. Analysis of the verbal protocols was greatly facilitated by our generic model for troubleshooting, decomposing the task into the subtasks: formulate problem description, generate causes, test, and evaluate. We also used the verbal protocols to assess troubleshooting performance by experts

3. Controlled experiments. To assess whether our proposed training innovation actually had the intended effect, we conducted a number of controlled experiments. These were not laboratory experiments with artificial tasks. Rather, they were experiments under naturalistic conditions with the stimuli (faults) under control. This allowed us to obtain quantitative data on the effectiveness of the different courses we compared. For practical purposes, these data have served us well in convincing others of our approach to innovating training courses.

Interestingly, the most challenging and still ongoing task has been the domain modeling. Troubleshooting as a behavioral activity is more or less the same regardless of the particular equipment. However, our approach places a lot of emphasis on modeling the equipment at a functional level. This part has also been difficult to convey to the technicians, who tend to confuse functions and design. After applying the functional decomposition technique to various systems, we discovered that there is not one model that fits all. Rather, there are at least causal models and component models. Moreover, the electronic and mechanical parts of a system each require a different approach to modeling. In summary, our experience reflects Simon's (1981) parable of the ant: The apparent complexity of behavior is a reflection of the complexity of the environment, not of the human.

REFERENCES

Frederiksen, J. R., & White, B. Y. (1993, August). The avionics job-family tutor: An approach to developing generic cognitive skills within a job-situated context. In P. Brna, S. Ohlsson, & H. Pain (Eds.), *Proceedings of the World Conference on Artificial Intelligence in Education* (pp. 513–520). Edinburgh, Scotland.

Kepner, C. H., & Tregoe, B.B. (1966). *Analytic trouble shooting (ATS)*. Princeton: NJ, Princeton Research Press,

Merkelbach, E. J. H. M., & Schraagen, J.M.C. (1994). *A framework for the analysis of cognitive tasks* (Technical Report TNO-TM 1994 B-13). Soesterberg, The Netherlands: TNO Human Factors Research Institute.

Reed, N. E., & Johnson, P. E. (1993). Analysis of expert reasoning in hardware diagnosis. *International Journal of Man-Machine Studies, 38*, 251–280.

Schaafstal, A .M. (1991). *Diagnostic skill in process operation: A comparison between experts and novices*. Unpublished Doctoral Dissertation, University of Groningen, The Netherlands.

Schaafstal, A. M. (1993). Knowledge and strategies in diagnostic skill. *Ergonomics, 36*, 1305–1316.

Schaafstal, A. M. & Schraagen, J. M. C. (1992). *A method for cognitive task analysis* (Technical Report IZF 1992 B-5). Soesterberg, The Netherlands: TNO Human Factors Research Institute.

Schaafstal, A. M., & Schraagen, J. M. C. (1993). *Knowledge-based support for the training of troubleshooting in a Sensor, Weapon, and Command subsystem: the SMR_μ* (Technical Report IZF 1993 A-49). Soesterberg, The Netherlands: TNO Institute for Perception (in dutch).

Schraagen, J. M. C. & Schaafstal, A. M. (1991). *Fault diagnosis in a Sensor, Weapon and Command subsystem: the LW08 radar*. (Technical Report IZF 1991 A-36). Soesterberg, The Netherlands: TNO Institute for Perception (in dutch).

Schraagen, J. M. C. & Schaafstal, A. M. (1996). Training of systematic diagnosis: A case study in electronics troubleshooting. *Le Travail Humain, 59*(1), 5–21.

Simon, H. A. (1981). *The sciences of the artificial* (2nd ed.). Cambridge, MA: The MIT Press.

Singley, M.K. & Anderson, J.R. (1989). *The transfer of cognitive skill*. Cambridge, MA: Harvard University Press.

5

DNA: PROVIDING THE BLUEPRINT FOR INSTRUCTION

Valerie J. Shute
Air Force Research Laboratory (AFRL)

Lisa A. Torreano
National Research Council Fellow at AFRL

Ross E. Willis
Galaxy Scientific, Corp.

Cognitive task analysis (CTA) refers to a diverse collection of methods for obtaining information from expert sources. The techniques are united by the common goal of representing the underlying knowledge, skills, and goal structures of a particular domain or task performance (e.g., Dehoney, 1995; Gordon & Gill, 1992; Hall, Gott, & Pokorny, 1995; Schraagen et al., 1997). Recently, conventional CTA methods have come under attack for a variety of reasons. Most notably, the great expense (in time, personnel, and money) associated with conducting a CTA is often cited as a major obstacle to employing them more widely. That is, a typical CTA process involves the support of many individuals, such as instructional designers, cognitive psychologists, knowledge engineers, and subject-matter experts (SMEs), across long periods of time (e.g., Durkin, 1994; Gordon, Schmierer, & Gill, 1993; Hayes-Roth, Waterman, & Lenat, 1983). A more subtle, but important criticism of CTA has to do with a general sense of vagueness and imprecision. For example, in their recent review of the field, Schraagen et al. (1997) concluded, "that little attention is being paid to the conditions under which methods are appropriate, and that often it is unclear how products of cognitive task analysis should be used" (p. 5).

This chapter describes our response to these issues. Specifically, can we automate any part of this process without sacrificing accuracy and do so in a principled manner? Other researchers have tackled this issue of automating knowledge acquisition and representation (for excellent reviews of such tools, see Lethbridge, 1994; Williams & Kotnur, 1993). Generally, these knowledge-elicitation tools have not made it into the mainstream for various reasons–most notably due to limitations in the breadth of data that may be captured (e.g., only conceptual knowledge by Lethbridge's CODE4 program) and being difficult to be used by persons other than programmers. We describe a computer-based cognitive tool that has been designed to aid in knowledge elicitation and organization for instruction and training purposes, capturing a range of data in a user-friendly manner. Our tool is called DNA, which stands for decompose a domain into its constituent elements, network the elements into an inheritance hierarchy, and assess the ensuing knowledge structure for validity and reliability (for a detailed description of the program, see Shute, Torreano, & Willis, in press-a).

DNA's particular target application, in relation to CTA, is to obtain curriculum elements to be used within instructional systems—specifically, intelligent tutoring systems (ITSs) that generally contain three distinct core components: expert model, student model, and instructor model. The expert model contains a curriculum map consisting of expert knowledge and skills. The student model monitors a learner's prior and emergent knowledge and skills and gauges whether he or she has demonstrated mastery of the elements included in the expert model. Basically, the student model is an online report card that indicates whether a student has mastered the curriculum elements contained in the expert model. Finally, the instructor model determines a student's path through the instructional content based on discrepancies between the expert model and the student model. These three components interact to individualize instruction based on a learner's needs. DNA's job, then, is to facilitate expert model development.

The organization of our chapter is as follows. First, we briefly discuss the two previously cited CTA-related issues in relation to DNA design features. We continue with a description of DNA's structure and components, followed by an illustration of how the program works in the context of dealing with a real-world situation (i.e., obtaining elements for a specific curriculum). We conclude with a summary of the general CTA-related issues and our program's fit in the realm of CTA.

CTA ISSUES

As mentioned, the design of DNA was motivated, in part, as a response to some of the problems cited earlier. The following paragraphs discuss DNA in relation to these CTA-related issues.

Maximizing Cost–Benefit Ratio

The first issue influencing DNA's design concerns improving the cost–benefit ratio of analyzing a domain. That is, typical CTA methods involve numerous steps and personnel. First, the instructional designer employs a trained cognitive task analyst. The analyst prepares for upcoming interviews with experts by becoming familiar with the target domain (e.g., via document analysis).

Subsequently, the analyst conducts extensive interviews with one or more experts in the field. Following the interviews, the analyst transcribes the protocols and translates and organizes the knowledge and skill elements into individual curriculum elements (CEs). Finally, the instructional designer needs to transform individual CEs into a coherent curriculum. This process typically requires several months and many person hours to achieve (e.g., Gordon, Babbitt, Sorensen, Bell, & Crane, 1993). Thus, the cost–benefit ratio has room for improvement.

DNA attempts to automate the bulk of the interview process, thus improving efficiency by decreasing the personnel resources required to conduct the analysis. Additional time is saved because lengthy transcription sessions are eliminated. That is, DNA immediately stores all SME input in a database of CE records. In addition, the two common phases of CTA–elicitation and organization of knowledge–have been collapsed into a symbiotic process to decrease the time required for the SME. The SME, working with the DNA program, not only identifies various CEs, but also arrays them into a hierarchical structure.

Specifying Purpose, Domain, and Representation

To avoid the vagueness issue cited previously, throughout the design process, we have been careful to explicate DNA's purpose, including suitable domains and desired representation. DNA's primary purpose is to obtain curriculum for use in intelligent instructional software. It was not designed to be an all-purpose tool. Within instruction, there are some domains for which it is appropriate and others for which it is not. The most fitting domains or tasks are those containing structured, explicit knowledge and skills. There are many domains that fall into this category in academic, military, and industrial settings. Domains or tasks where DNA is less suitable include those that place a large emphasis on psychomotor skill and those that contain a lot of implicit knowledge. In the former case, observational techniques such as videotaping on-the-job perfor-mance may be appropriate to capture relevant psychomotor data. In the latter case, acquiring implicit knowledge may be achieved via card sorting and other multidimensional scaling techniques or think-aloud protocols. Finally, we have considered the needed representation given the domains to be analyzed for our purposes of instruction. As is described in greater detail in the next section, because DNA is intended to help build instruction across a variety of topics, it was designed to capture a range of knowledge and skill types. Consequently, DNA represents information in a hybrid structure—combining aspects of production systems (i.e., if–then rules related to procedural knowledge and skills; see Anderson, 1993) as well as conceptual graphs (e.g., semantic nets of concepts and their relationships; see Gordon et al., 1993).

DNA COMPONENTS AND STRUCTURE

DNA is a software program designed to streamline development of ITSs by automating part of the process of constructing the expert model or curriculum map. Although DNA can theoretically provide the foundation for any curriculum, computer administered or not, it was specifically designed to interface with a student-modeling paradigm called *SMART* (Student Modeling Approach to Responsive Tutoring; Shute, 1995).

DNA and SMART are intended to work together. DNA provides the blueprint for instruction by obtaining curriculum elements directly from the responses and actions of SMEs who answer structured queries posed by the computer. That is, it supplies the instructional system with an expert model by eliciting and organizing knowledge and skills from human experts. SMART uses the resulting blueprint (knowledge structure) as the basis for assessment, cognitive diagnosis, and instruction, managing the learning environment based on the discrepancies between the expert and student models. To optimally manage such divergences, SMART requires the identification of individual units of instruction (i.e., the curricular elements) as well as their relationships (hierarchical dependencies). Hierarchical dependencies indicate prerequisite knowledge and skills that are used when developing the instructional path through the curriculum. Given these requirements, the goals for DNA's output are to identify CEs and their relationships (Shute et al., in press-a).

Because they are meant to work collaboratively, SMART influenced key DNA design decisions affecting the intended nature of the tool's knowledge representation or output. In particular, SMART is intended to be useful across a large array of instructional content. Consequently, it recognizes and monitors a variety of knowledge types (symbolic, procedural, and conceptual). In addition, SMART is intended to manage instruction in a principled manner based on dependency relations among knowledge elements. Thus, it uses information from hierarchical knowledge structures to select curriculum units for instruction.

As a result, DNA was designed to capture a range of knowledge types as well as their hierarchical structure. Specifically, DNA operates via a series of interactive modules for decomposing, networking, and assessing experts' knowledge structures in relation to a topic. The Decompose module acquires and classifies experts' knowledge into the knowledge types that are recognized and monitored by SMART. Its focus is to analyze the domain, breaking its knowledge down into constituent elements. The Network module, an organizational tool, allows experts to connect their extracted knowledge components into an integrated hierarchical structure of CEs. Its focus is the synthesis of the knowledge units. Finally, the Assess module (when implemented) will allow the instructional designer to ascertain the validity and reliability of the extracted knowledge structures obtained from SMEs–an important aspect of any CTA approach. Collectively, the DNA-elicited elements and hierarchical structure provide guidance to SMART in terms of how to structure, track, and modify the ensuing curriculum.

We now present more detail on the particular knowledge types and structures that both SMART and DNA distinguish. The purpose is to extend the range of applicability across domains, as well as provide a coherent basis on which to make principled decisions regarding instruction.

Knowledge Types

SMART and DNA recognize three knowledge types: symbolic, procedural, and conceptual (also known as what, how, and why knowledge, respectively). Symbolic knowledge refers to fundamental information including definitions, symbols, formulas, and other basic depictions. Procedural knowledge relates to specific steps and conditionals underlying a particular procedure or way to accomplish a goal. Conceptual knowledge provides the rationale or "big picture" relating lower level elements together into a system or whole (e.g., Kyllonen & Shute, 1989; Shute, 1994). The reason DNA makes these knowledge-type distinctions is because of its interface with SMART, which provides differential instruction and assessment based on the categorization. To illustrate the differential instruction, consider one piece of knowledge—the statistical mean. Symbolic knowledge elements, such as the formula for the mean (e.g., $\Sigma X/N$), are introduced in a straightforward, didactic manner and assessed by requiring the recognition and/or generation of an answer. Instruction and assessment of procedural elements, however, can focus either on the knowledge of the rules of a procedure (procedural knowledge) or the competency with which the procedure is executed (procedural skill). For example, procedural knowledge may require the generation of the procedure's relevant steps (e.g., add all numbers in a distribution of data, then divide by the total sample size). In contrast, procedural skill might be instructed in the context of an interactive, problem-solving environment and assessed via the application of some rule or procedure (e.g., calculate the mean of a given data set). Finally, instruction of conceptual knowledge may use analogies or the explicit presentation of the big picture, whereas assessment requires extrapolation, induction, deduction, and transfer to novel areas. For example, conceptual knowledge of the mean involves understanding and articulating its relationship to other measures of central tendency within various distributions.

As we have shown, the knowledge-type distinction is important to SMART in that it allows for more customized instructional and assessment techniques to be employed. Consequently, DNA is responsible for acquiring and categorizing data in accord with these three knowledge types. This is accomplished via queries embedded within the program that are specifically crafted to focus on eliciting what, how, and why knowledge. We now turn our attention to the importance of knowledge structures.

Knowledge Structures

Although the Decompose module of DNA is intended to elicit and embellish a variety of curriculum elements, the Network module is designed to capture the structure of the experts' knowledge (Chi, Glaser, & Rees 1982; Dochy, 1992; Jonassen, Beissner, & Yacci, 1993). These structures contain inheritance relationships among CEs that can provide the basis for assessment (i.e., What is the current status of a particular CE?), cognitive diagnosis (i.e., What is the source of the problem, if any?), and instruction (i.e., What needs to be taught now?). To enable the structuring of the range of CE types captured during the decomposition, the Network module includes provisions for approximating both a production system framework to represent procedural elements and a conceptual graph structure to reflect conceptual elements, as well as the relationship between the two.

Ultimately, it is structured knowledge that provides the curriculum that we, as educators, research scientists, and/or designers of intelligent instructional software, wish to impart to learners (Jonassen, Beissner, & Yacci, 1993; Reigeluth, 1983). The reason for doing so is straightforward: "Structured knowledge enables inference capabilities, assists in the elaboration of new information, and enhances retrieval. It provides potential links between stored knowledge and incoming information, which facilitates learning and problem solving" (Glaser & Bassok, 1989, p. 26).

Sound CTA approaches consider the nature of the knowledge of the domain being analyzed and use an appropriate representation to reflect it. Given that DNA is designed for developing curriculum for a range of topics, both conceptual and procedural in nature, it is important that this tool be able to accommodate a range of knowledge types. Having been designed to accommodate the knowledge classification used by SMART, and by providing an organizational aid to support structuring of procedural and conceptual knowledge domains, our CTA tool should be readied to accomplish this goal.

DNA: How Does it Work?

The Situation. Two of the authors were posed with the task to develop a 2-hour training program for medical personnel on how to use the Internet to access pertinent data. To develop the curriculum, we used the Decompose module of DNA to collect relevant elements and procedures on this topic. We present our actual interactions with the system to illustrate how DNA operates to obtain relevant symbolic, procedural, and conceptual knowledge for the domain "getting data from the Internet." This illustration should provide a general sense of how the program works. For more details on design and functionality, see Shute, et al. (in press-a).

Interaction Among DNA Program Components

As mentioned, DNA consists of several modules that interact with one another. The instructional designer (ID) begins with the Customize module and answers a fairly short series of questions. During the process, he or she specifies the domain of interest, delineates the learning goals for the course, identifies the incoming knowledge and skills of the learner population (targeted to receive the course), and indicates the desired flavor of instruction (e.g., teaching the curriculum from a predominately procedural perspective). After the ID completes the Customize module, the program automatically generates a customized form letter that is sent to prospective SMEs, in conjunction with the DNA program, initialized to reflect the input by the ID. Table 5.1 shows the actual letter produced by the customize module, which is generated to reflect the requirements of this Internet curriculum.

TABLE 5.1
Edited Output From Customize Module Detailing the Curriculum for the Expert

Dear [Expert's Name],

We're writing today to get your help in designing a course on getting data from the Internet. Before you begin working with the enclosed program, please sit down and think about the critical things that make you good at getting data from the Internet.

As you go through the enclosed program and respond to our questions, try to respond in terms of how you currently perform the job or think about the particular task. Please don't respond with how you originally learned to get data from the Internet; you have probably developed much better ways of performing this task since then.

The ultimate goals of the course are for our trainees to:

(1) Identify the components used to access the WWW
(2) Identify the syntax and semantics of a URL
(3) Identify various search engines
(4) Know how to connect to the Internet
(5) Know how to bring up various search engines

(continued)

(6) Know how to input keywords for efficient searching (strategies & tricks)
(7) Know how to navigate to a web site from a hot link
(8) Know how to navigate to a web site given any URL
(9) Know how to get information from the WWW in your hands or into your PC
(10) Know how to download files from a web page
(11) Know how to bookmark page(s) for later viewing
(12) Understand the relationship among elements that allow you to view a page on the WWW
(13) Understand how search engines retrieve relevant data

How specific should you get? You can presume that our trainees will have the following knowledge and skills: (1) familiarity with Windows 95/98 environment, (2) basic knowledge of the Internet, and (3) basic typing skills. Therefore, you will not need to define knowledge or skills at a detailed level in relation to these elements.

When answering questions during the program, please make your responses consistent with the following distribution: What: 34%; How: 54%; Why: 12%. As you can see, the curriculum is intended to emphasize procedural knowledge, but also includes "what" and a bit of the "why" knowledge.

Thanks very much for your time.

Sincerely,

[Signature]

The SME receives the letter and begins the program. DNA starts with a 5- to 10-minute orientation that provides a general overview of the program and includes a description of the different knowledge types (introduced as what, how, and why kinds of knowledge). There is also a summary of how the program operates. After the brief orientation, the expert begins the Decompose module.

Decompose Module

The Decompose module asks what, how, and why questions via a semi-structured, interactive dialogue with the expert. A different set of questions is posed to the expert depending on whether symbolic, procedural, or conceptual knowledge is currently being decomposed. That is, to differentiate the knowledge comprising a domain, different paths of interrogation have been designed to capture information relevant to each particular knowledge type. Each path (i.e., What—Symbolic knowledge, How—Procedural knowledge, and Why—Conceptual knowledge) has its own interface to accomplish that goal. For example, to elicit symbolic knowledge, DNA probes for definitions, examples, and supplemental multimedia links. To elicit procedural knowledge, DNA probes for detailed, step-by-step information, logical and temporal relations among steps, and subprocedures. For obtaining conceptual knowledge, DNA focuses on obtaining relational information among concepts. Responses in all paths are made via selecting items from list boxes and typing directly into text boxes.

One of the three inquiry paths is launched when the SME selects a question listed in the Main Question Queue–the first screen of the Decompose module. To initialize the list of questions, the program restates the ID-provided learning goals in question formats consistent with the three knowledge types. For example, the fourth goal (see Table 5.1) for the topic "getting data from the Internet" was for students to "know how to connect to the Internet"–a procedural knowledge goal. The restated question listed in the Main Question Queue, which would launch the How path, became: "What are the steps that you go through when you connect to the Internet?"

The following paragraphs illustrate portions of each path in action when surfing the Internet was being decomposed. We start with the How path because the dominant flavor of the curriculum to be achieved is procedural (i.e., 8/13 of the listed learning goals are procedural knowledge).

How Path. The How path is used to elicit procedural knowledge. The primary interface is the Step Editor (see Fig. 5.1), which the expert uses to build procedures using options to list steps, establish conditional statements (i.e., If/Then), and include necessary connectors (i.e., and–or). Fig. 5.1 presents the steps for finding information on the Internet corresponding to Goal 6 in table 5.1.

Notice that If/Then items are automatically grouped and function as a single unit of information. The numbers (i.e., 1, 2, 3) in the Grouping column indicate that elements sharing identical numbers belong to the same group. For example, the user cannot separate an If statement from its associated Then statement. Other features include tagging steps with additional information, such as whether a step is optional or required.

A series of follow-up questions will be implemented in the next version of the Decompose module. They are intended to clarify procedures that may be ambiguous. For example, if an expert outlined the procedure: DO A AND B OR C (without adequate grouping), the program would ask if the procedure was: {DO (A AND B) OR C} or {DO A AND (B OR C)}. Follow-up questions also require the expert to consider *alternative* conditions and consequences. For instance, suppose the expert created the conditional: IF X, THEN Y. The program would ask if

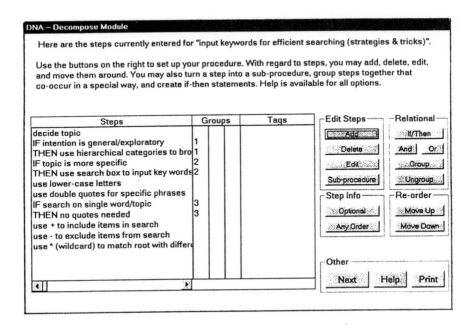

FIG. 5.1. The Step Editor interface from DNA's How path illustrating a
procedure.

there are other conditions, besides X, that could invoke Y, and whether there are
actions, other than Y, that may ensue from X.

With these follow-up questions, in conjunction with the user-friendly interface, we anticipate that even individuals who are naive to control structure (or
logic) will be able to provide descriptions that will enable context-dependent
reasoning. This is important because it is conceptual knowledge (i.e., the underlying *why* and *how* a step is important toward reaching the goal state) that constrains a procedure. Therefore, having a conceptual understanding of a procedure
enables one to make inferences during task performance and thus respond appropriately when faced with novel circumstances.

What Path. The What path is a series of screens used to elicit symbolic
knowledge. Fig. 5.2 depicts the interface after the expert has entered some relevant terms and definitions related to the topic being decomposed. For instance, in
Fig. 5.2, the expert defined the term "client" and attached a graphics file to this
definition (i.e., an image of a personal computer). This associated picture attachment is denoted by the Mona Lisa icon located below the definition. Experts

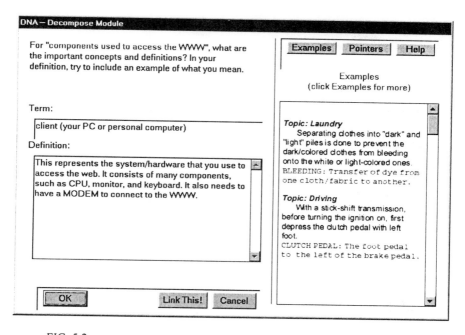

FIG. 5.2.   Interface from DNA's What path defining an Internet-related term.

are free to attach sound files, videos, and other multimedia embellishments in computer or hard-copy format.

Additional features in the What path, shown on the right-hand side of Fig. 5.2, include examples to help guide the expert when composing definitions. Additionally, the expert can view answering pointers that explain how to best phrase responses so the wording in future questions posed by DNA will flow smoothly. Similar support is available throughout each path of inquiry.

Why Path.   The Why path is used to elicit conceptual knowledge. The interface consists of a series of questions that asks for information that enables the expert to successively build up the concept currently in focus. The first question asks the expert to list the main components underlying the current concept or topic being decomposed (e.g., architecture of the internet). The expert identified several components that comprise the Internet, such as: PC (personal computer, or client), phone lines (copper, fiber optic), server's modem, PC's modem (internal, external), and so on. Fig. 5.3 shows the second screen of the Why path. The list of components entered on the first screen are presented and the

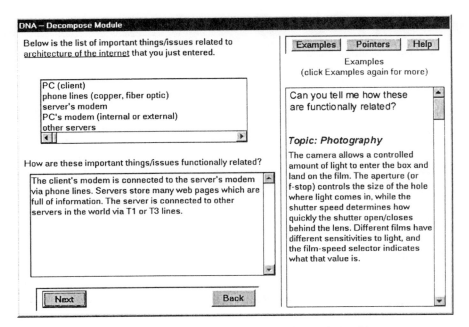

FIG. 5.3.   Interface from DNA's Why path describing relationships among components.

expert is asked to describe how these components are functionally related to one another. The experts accomplish this via input to the text box that can hold up to 16,000 characters.

The third question/screen asks, "Why is having a functional understanding of Internet architecture (i.e., the current topic of query) important in relation to getting data from the Internet" (i.e., the overall domain being decomposed)? One expert response was, "The Internet is comprised of millions of individual web pages, each connected to its own server, and each server is connected to all other servers. This provides a framework for understanding the notion of 'the Internet' and thus how a search engine can travel to so many sites in response to a database inquiry."

All CE-related information is stored in a Microsoft Access 7.0 database containing multifarious fields such as the CE's description, unique number, knowledge type, higher order relations, and so on. When the expert has answered the initial queries from the main question queue, as well as those generated from the various paths, he or she may begin the network module.

Network Module

The Network module represents CEs from the Decompose module as graphical nodes and lets the expert arrange and link them, thereby resulting in a CE hierarchy. New CE nodes can be added, deleted, and edited, and the changes are communicated to the Decompose module via a shared database. Alternatively, if the expert wants to return to the Decompose module to make CE-related changes, that is also possible.

Nodes differ by knowledge type. That is, symbolic knowledge elements are represented as squares, procedural elements by circles, and conceptual ones as rounded rectangles. Links between nodes differ by type of association (e.g., is a, part of, parent of), strength of association (weak, moderate, and strong), and directionality (uni, bi, or none), which is shown by labels, thickness of line, and arrowheads, respectively. Finally, nesting can occur where one can zoom in or out from a particular node to see more or less detail. Rightclicking successively expands nodes that have other nodes (i.e., CEs) subsumed within.

We view one of the primary functions of the network representation as an organizational aid—to both IDs and SMEs. In general, we expect that this graphical array will make errors salient to an expert viewing the array. Problem areas may then be repaired either in the Network or Decompose module. The other main function of the graph is in terms of providing an indication of knowledge structure–whether it resembles a production system or conceptual graph dependent on the underlying content. The dependency relationships, as embodied in the hierarchical structure, should provide the basis for subsequent instructional decisions.

Assess Module

This last module of DNA, once implemented, is intended to validate conceptual graphs in terms of content, relationships, and associated material generated by different experts on the same topic. This module can be implemented in a number of ways, each offering different strengths and weaknesses. To illustrate, after the initial expert (SME-1) has created a database of elements and associated network, he or she sends the output (database and graphical array) back to the ID who sends that out to the subsequent expert (SME-2). SME-2 uses SME-1's data as the point of departure to modify, clarify, and validate the externalized knowledge structure. Alternatively, the program can be sent to multiple experts in parallel, who complete the Decompose and Network modules independently and return the knowledge structures to the ID. The former option could potentially result in an anchoring bias to the initial expert's output. Although the latter option avoids this potential anchoring problem, it offers other difficulties in the synthesis of multiple knowledge structures. Indeed, a combination of methods may prove to be the best option; multiple experts independently use the tool to represent their knowledge, followed by a series of reviews of each output by other experts for checks on consistency and validity. In short, the assessment module will allow experts to review and edit the database listing of curricular elements and graphs of other experts.

Although we have outlined assessment criterion based on consensus, we believe that additional checks of the output should also be conducted where appropriate. For example, procedural knowledge, after having been validated by a panel of experts, can be further assessed by executing the procedures outlined and determining whether, in fact, the actions produce the desired effect or accomplish the intended goal. Successful real-world implementation of outlined procedures offers independent, empirical validation of the knowledge structure.

We have attempted to provide a cursory depiction of DNA's functionality in the context of developing a real-world curriculum. Although acquisition and organization of knowledge elements constitute just a part of the overall development of the expert model, they are substantially important. Furthermore, we believe they are good candidates to be rendered more efficient. Thus we continue our attempts to automate these processes.

CONCLUSION

In conclusion, we have discussed issues that have motivated DNA's design. Specifically, our goal is to increase efficiency in the acquisition and organization of knowledge and to do so in a principled way. Our approach has been to create a new cognitive tool that automates the bulk of the interview, transcription, and organization processes, thus enhancing efficiency.

We have also responded to the criticisms of vagueness and imprecision within the CTA field by specifying the conditions under which DNA is appropriate and how its products should be used. Specifically, DNA was designed to fill a particular niche in the realm of CTA—that of providing the knowledge structure (or domain expertise) for ITSs. In contrast to the typical CTA focus on expert performance in relation to some task, DNA's purpose is to develop curriculum for a broad range of topics, procedural or conceptual in nature. The consideration of DNA's purpose and intended topics of analysis led to the implementation of principled design features (e.g., capturing a variety of knowledge types and structuring them in a hybrid representation). This infrastructure, in addition to being principled, contributes to efficiency as it was designed to fit with an existing student modeling paradigm that should streamline ITS development.

The Decompose module has now been used to elicit data from experts across various domains, including using the email software program Microsoft Exchange, descriptive statistics, and surfing the Internet. We have completed one formative evaluation of the Decompose module (see Shute, Torreano, & Willis, in press-b) and the results are quite encouraging. However, we are aware, with each new research study and subsequent version of the program, that the road to automating these processes is not on the map.

REFERENCES

Anderson, J. R. (1993). *Rules of the mind*. Hillsdale, NJ: Lawrence Erlbaum Associates.

Chi, M. T. H., Glaser R., & Rees, E. (1982). Expertise in problem solving. In R. Sternberg (Ed.), *Advances in the psychology of human intelligence* (Vol. 1, pp. 7–75). Hillsdale, NJ: Lawrence Erlbaum Associates.

Dehoney, J. (1995). *Cognitive task analysis: Implications for the theory and practice of instructional design*. Proceedings of the 1995 annual national convention of the Association for Educational Communications and Technology (AECT), Anaheim, CA.

Dochy, F. J. R. C. (1992*). Assessment of prior knowledge as a determinant of future learning*. Utrecht, The Netherlands: Lemma.

Durkin, J. (1994). Knowledge acquisition. In J. Durkin (Ed.), *Expert systems: Design and development* (pp. 518–599). New York: Macmillan.

Glaser, R., & Bassok, M. (1989). *Learning theory and the study of instruction* (Technical Report No. 11). Pittsburgh, PA: University of Pittsburgh Press.

Gordon, S.E., Babbitt, B.A., Sorensen, H.B., Bell, H. H., & Crane, P. M. (1993, November–December). *Cognitive task analysis for development of an intelligent tutoring system*. Proceedings of the 15th Interservice/Industry Training Systems and Education Conference, Orlando, FL.

Gordon, S. E., & Gill, R. T. (1992). Knowledge acquisition with question probes and conceptual graph structures. In T. Lauer, E. Peacock, & A. Graesser (Eds.), *Questions and information systems* (pp. 29–46). Hillsdale, NJ: Lawrence Erlbaum Associates.

Gordon, S. E., Schmierer, K. A., & Gill, R. T. (1993). Conceptual graph analysis: Knowledge acquisition for instructional systems design. *Human Factors, 35,* 459–481.

Hall, E. P., Gott, S. P., & Pokorny, R. A. (1995). *A procedural guide to cognitive task analysis: The PARI methodology* (Report No. AL/HR-TR-1995-0108). Air Force Materiel Command, Brooks Air Force Base, TX.

Hayes-Roth, F., Waterman, D. A., & Lenat, D. B. (1983*). Building expert systems*. Reading, MA: Addison Wesley.

Jonassen, D. H., Beissner, K., & Yacci, M. A (1993). *Structural knowledge: Techniques for representing, conveying, and acquiring structural knowledge*. Hillsdale, NJ: Lawrence Erlbaum Associates.

Kyllonen, P. C., & Shute, V. J. (1989). A taxonomy of learning skills. In P. L. Ackerman, R. J. Sternberg, & R. Glaser (Eds.*), Learning and individual differences* (pp. 117–163). New York: Freeman.

Lethbridge, T. C. (1994). *Practical techniques for organizing and measuring knowledge*. Unpublished doctoral dissertation, Computer Science Department, University of Ottawa, Ontario, Canada.

Reigeluth, C. M. (1983). Meaningfulness and instruction: Relating what is being learned to what a student knows. *Instructional Science, 12,* 197–218.

Schraagen, J. M. C., Chipman, S. E., Shute, V. J., Annett, J., Strub, M., Sheppard, C., Ruisseau, J. Y., & Graff, N. (1997). *State-of-the-art review of cognitive task analysis techniques.* Deliverable Report of NATO Defense Research Study Group 27 on Cognitive Task Analysis. Soesterberg, The Netherlands: TNO Human Factors Research Institute (Report TM-97-B012).

Shute, V. J. (1994). Learning processes and learning outcomes. In T. Husen & T. N. Postlethwaite (Eds.), *International encyclopedia of education* (2nd ed., pp. 3315–3325). New York: Pergamon.

Shute, V. J. (1995). SMART: Student modeling approach for responsive tutoring. *User Modeling and User-Adapted Interaction, 5*, 1–44.

Shute, V. J., Torreano, L. A., & Willis, R. E. (in press-a). DNA: Towards an automated knowledge elicitation and organization tool. In S. P. Lajoie (Ed.), *Computers as cognitive tools* (Vol. 2). Hillsdale, NJ: Lawrence Erlbaum Associates.

Shute, V. J., Torreano, L. A., & Willis, R. E. (in press-b). Preliminary evaluation of an automated knowledge elicitation and organization tool. *International Journal of AI and Education.*

Williams, K. E., & Kotnur, T. G. (1993). *Knowledge acquisition: A review of manual, machine-aided and machine-learning methods.* Technical report of Office of Naval Research. Blacksburg, VA: Virginia Polytechnic Institute and State University (Interim Technical Report N00014-91-J-5-1500).

6

DISCOVERING SITUATED MEANING: AN ECOLOGICAL APPROACH TO TASK ANALYSIS

John M. Flach
Wright State University

"Experts perceive large meaningful patterns in their domain."
—Cooke, (1992, p. 33).

What does it mean for a pattern to be "meaningful"? It is surprising to me that the issue of meaning is often overlooked in studies of cognition and expertise. For example, *meaning* is not included as an index item in Hoffman's (1992) edited volume on the psychology of expertise. Further, it is not included in the indexes of other cognitive texts (Anderson, 1995; Gardner, 1985; Mayer, 1992). Halpern (1996) has two references to meaning. In one citation, Halpern claimed, in a discussion of memory, that "we can add meaning to information by elaborating on it" (p. 47). The other reference included the claim that "meaningful information is more easily remembered than nonmeaningful information" (p. 80). Solso (1995) has two index entries to meaning. Both entries refer to the interpretation or meaning of words.

It seems that, in cognitive psychology, the term *meaning* is synonymous with interpretation. The meaning of something is the interpretation of a particular agent. In this context, it makes sense to talk about *adding meaning* by the act of interpretation. Meaning comes into being when an observer relates one observation to previous experiences. This use of meaning probably has its roots in the linguistic and verbal learning traditions of cognitive psychology, where the stimuli were often words. In this context, the statement at the beginning of this section might suggest that the *meaningful patterns* exist in the mind of the expert. In other words, meaning is added to the pattern as a result of the expert's knowledge—meaning is the product of information processing.

An alternative perspective would be to define *meaning* as synonymous with *significance*. Meaningfulness might be defined independent of any particular observer or interpretation. For example, the pattern may be significant because of its implications for some function. The pattern might signify some threat or opportunity relative to the functional goals within a work domain. In this sense, the pattern would be meaningful regardless of whether that meaning was appreciated by any particular observer. One would expect that patterns that were significant with respect to domain functions would also be perceived as significant by experts. However, the fact that the pattern was not perceived as significant by a particular observer would not diminish its meaningfulness with respect to domain functions. From this perspective, meaning is the raw material available to be picked up by an information-processing system.

An ecological approach to cognition adopts the significance perspective to meaning. Thus, meaning has a basis in the situation. Objects, events, or situations are meaningful (significant) relative to the functional goals of a work domain. In this sense, meaning exists regardless of whether it is perceived or appreciated by a particular observer. One might characterize meaning as *normative*, in that it represents authoritative standards that characterize a work domain. It is still possible to talk about significance with respect to a particular observer (i.e., awareness). However, it would not be consistent to talk about adding or creating meaning through interpretation or processing. Rather, the focus is on discovery of the significance with respect to the functional goals of the work domain. Experts are people who have discovered the meaningful relations within a work domain.

For classical approaches, information is processed and meaning is added as a result of the processing. Meaning is a product; it is constructed. For an ecological approach, meaning is the raw material; it exists independent of any processing. It is available to be discovered and acted on by an agent. Thus, agents are viewed as meaning-processing systems as opposed to the classical notion of an information processing system (Flach, 1995, 1998; Flach, in press; Flach & Rasmussen, in press).

EXPERTISE

"It would be hard to overemphasize the importance for perceptual learning of the discovery of invariant properties which are in correspondence with physical variables. The term *extraction* will be applied to this process, for the property may be buried, as it were, in a welter of impinging stimulation."

—E. Gibson, (1969, p. 81; italics added)

For an ecological approach to expertise, the keywords in the prior statement are *correspondence* and *discovery*. An expert is someone whose awareness is in correspondence with the situation. In other words, patterns that are, in fact, significant with regard to functional goals of the domain correspond to what the expert sees, recognizes, or thinks are significant. The expert is one who has discovered many of the meaningful patterns within a particular domain.

The terms *correspondence* and *discovery* fit nicely within a dynamic systems perspective for characterizing expertise. Discovery characterizes a dynamic interaction between an agent and environment. Correspondence characterizes a state of that process. High correspondence results in a well-balanced process or a tight coordination between agent and environment. Low correspondence results

in an unbalanced process or discoordination between agent and environment. With time, the discovery process typically progresses
from low correspondence, where the agent may depend on behavior patterns developed in other contexts (assimilation), to increasing correspondence (accommodation).

Fig. 6.1 is a qualitative representation of the dynamics of exploration. Note that the classical order—perception then action—is reversed in this diagram. For the discovery diagram, action is given precedence over perception. In fact, there is no fixed precedence because action and perception are coupled in a circular feedback loop. However, giving precedence to action can have radical effects on how the cognitive system is perceived. It turns the problem of cognition inside–out, such that the ecology (i.e., environment/situation) becomes the heart of the problem. Action is coupled with perception—not through the brain, but through the environment. Meaning arises within the ecology and reflects the constraints on action in that ecology. The ecology at the heart of Fig. 6.1 represents the environment—but not in terms of extrinsic physical dimensions, but rather in relation to action. It is this relation that gives rise to meaning. As J. Gibson (1979) noted: "The world of physical reality does not consist of meaningful things. The world of ecological reality, as I have been trying to describe it, does. If what we perceive were the entities of physics and mathematics, meaning would have to be imposed on them. But if what we perceive are the entities of environmental science, their meanings can be discovered". (p. 33)

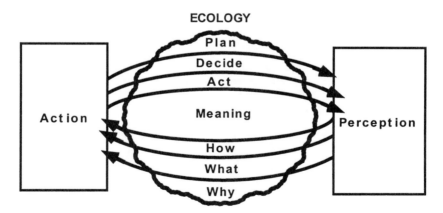

Fig. 6.1   Cognition is illustrated as an active process in which action and perception are coupled, through the ecology, by a set of nested control loops. Meaning resides within the ecology at the heart of the cognitive process.

Another important feature of Fig. 6.1 is the nested set of loops that couple action and perception. This reflects different levels of action. The act loop represents motor responses. The decide and plan loop are also considered actions in a general sense. Classically, the relations—particularly between deciding and acting—have been represented as sequential, independent stages in an information-processing system. However, Fig. 6.1 represents planning, deciding, and acting as nested control loops. This suggests a dynamic that is different from classical information processing. In this representation, planning, deciding, and acting are operating simultaneously (as opposed to sequentially). The order of the nesting represents different time constants (i.e., the lag between an action and the feedback relative to that action). The outermost loop has the longest time constant. The inner loop has the smallest time constant.

At this point, it would be premature to make any claims about the actual number of loops. The important point is that the dynamic of exploration and discovery is a nested control process. There is a loose coupling between these nested control loops. One type of interaction is that outer loops might set the reference or equilibrium point for inner loops (e.g., Powers, 1973). However, this is not the only type of coupling. Outer loops might also influence parameters of the transfer function of inner loops (e.g., locking out degrees of freedom to simplify the control problem at lower levels; e.g., Fowler & Turvey, 1978). Also, the coupling occurs in both directions. Adjustments in the dynamics of inner loops (e.g., Runeson's [1977] smart mechanisms or Shiffrin & Schneider's [1977] automatic processing) can change the nature of outer loop control.

Another important implication of the nested action loops is that there are multiple levels of meaning. What is significant depends in part on the nature of the control process. Things that are significant for the act loop may or may not be significant in terms of the planning loop. For example, two routes to the airport may be indistinguishable with respect to the planning loop (e.g., they both take about the same time). However, they may be distinct with respect to the act loop (e.g., one route is highway and the other is over surface streets with many traffic lights). This reflects Rasmussen's (1986) insight (Rasmussen, Pejtersen, & Goodstein, 1994) that meaning within work ecologies must be described at multiple levels of abstraction.

The evolution of skill reflects the plasticity of the loose coupling across the nested control loops and the ability of humans to adapt the mode of control to the specific demands of a particular work domain (e.g., Kugler & Turvey's [1987] notion of softly assembled constraints; see also Flach, 1990). In general, for novices, the inner loops are not attuned to the meanings within the novel domain. Therefore, they depend heavily on knowledge-based generalizations. In other words, they utilize general problem-solving skills that have been developed across many different domains of experience. For example, their processing might reflect what Piaget called *assimilation*—an American dad might utilize the schema that he developed playing basketball when he tries to coach his kids in soccer. With experience, the inner loops become better attuned to the specific meanings in the now familiar domain (Piaget's *accommodation*). For example, the American dad begins learning the rules of soccer and becomes better attuned to the meaningful patterns specific to soccer and thus relies less on analogies to other sports.

In summary, the phenomenon of cognition is an active, nested control process where the coupling between action and perception and across control loops happens in the ecology (as opposed to in the head). Expertise reflects discovery of significant constraints within the ecology (work domain or situation) and attunement of the control loops to that meaning. This turns the classical problem of cognition inside–out. In the classical view, perception is linked to action by a brain. The problem for cognitive science has classically been to discover the structural links (either in terms of neural mechanisms or knowledge/schema) that connect perception and action. However, in an ecological approach, action is linked to perception through the situation. From this perspective, it is natural to search for the structural links that support expertise in the situation. The next section considers the implications of this inside–out perspective on cognitive task analysis.

ANALYSIS

Cognitive task analyses that have been motivated by classical theories of cognition have typically been associated with knowledge elicitation or knowledge engineering. The goal has been to tap into the knowledge (schema, mental models, representations, strategies) that differentiates experts from novices. From this perspective, the focus has been on awareness. The goal is to discover the cues that experts use to interpret a situation. This makes sense if meaning is treated as if it were synonymous with interpretation and if the coupling between perception and action happens in the head. However, if one takes an ecological orientation to the problem, where meaning is synonymous with significance and where action and perception are coupled through the ecology, the focus shifts to the situation. The goal is to discover the constraints on action, the consequences of actions, and the information that specifies the constraints and consequences.

Cognitive task analysis has typically been directed at discovering and describing how the expert's interpretation (awareness) is different from a novice's interpretation. In this section, the question is framed differently. The point of the analysis is to discover what patterns in the work domain (situation) are significant (meaningful). The product of this analysis is not a description about how a particular expert thinks and acts, but rather a normative model that describes the ecological basis for skilled control. This ecological basis for control has three dimensions:

1. What are the constraints on action? What can be done?
2. What are the consequences of action? What are the functional

constraints, or costs and benefits, associated with actions?

3.   What are the constraints on feedback (information)? How are the constraints on and consequences of actions specified in the perceptual array?

The key word in the previous list is *constraint*. Constraints within the ecology are what makes skill possible. Constraint (consistency or invariance) is essential to skilled control. An expert utilizes the constraints within a work domain to simplify the control problem. An ecological task analysis is directed at uncovering the constraints within a problem domain. Rasmussen's (1986; Rasmussen, Pejtersen, & Goodstein, 1994) abstraction hierarchy is one formalism for identifying different classes of constraints.

The remainder of this chapter looks at some of the activities involved in an ecological task analysis. On the surface, these activities are similar to traditional approaches. However, the focus is on the situation rather than awareness.

TABLE-TOP ANALYSIS

It is important to do your homework at the start of a cognitive task analysis. Most work domains have a published literature that describes the nature of the work. For example, in aviation, this literature might include texts on aerodynamics, general training manuals, and procedural manuals for specific aircraft or specific applications/missions. The kinds of information that might be found include: (a) constraints on action like the dynamics of stalls or the optimal approach angle for landing a particular aircraft; (b) functional constraints like the costs of fuel, the costs of time, or passenger comfort; and (c) constraints on information like the h-angle associated with the optimal glide-slope (Flach & Warren, 1995) or the types of displays available to the pilot (Hutchins, 1995). For surgery, this literature might include texts on general anatomy and physiology and/or on specific surgical procedures. Here useful information would include: (a) constraints on action like the reach and functionality of surgical instruments like an endo-grasper or the relative position of ducts to be cut (e.g., the cystic duct) and ducts that must not be cut (e.g., the common bile duct); (b) functional constraints like the consequences of tissue damage relative to the consequences of prolonged exposure to anesthesia; and (c) information constraints like the field of view of an endoscope or the location, shape, and color of a particular organ (e.g., the gall bladder or the cystic duct). These sources of conventional wisdom help identify well-established constraints within the work domains. They also help guide and ground observations in naturalistic settings. They also facilitate communication with experts by helping the analyst become familiar with the jargon of a domain.

The analyst should not completely trust conventional wisdom; there are many examples where conventional wisdom does not generalize to specific contexts. For example, Crandall and Calderwood (1989) discovered that some of the clinical symptoms for identifying sepsis (infection) in neonates (premature infants) were different than the symptoms listed in medical texts. The text identified irritability as a symptom, whereas the experiences of clinical nurses suggested just the opposite. Low affect and unresponsiveness were repeatedly identified as early signs of a problem. Uncovering the limitations of conventional wisdom has been one of the motivating reasons for cognitive task analysis. Nevertheless, the published literature is a valuable source of information that should not be ignored. It provides a baseline of standards of practice and well-understood constraints that can be a valuable foundation for further analyses.

KNOWLEDGE ELICITATION

Often the world of textbooks is only abstractly related to the world of practice. There are many reasons for this. One is that many aspects of practice may be highly dependent on context, thus it is difficult to abstract a general principle of the sort that can easily be communicated in a textbook. Further the context assumed by the text may have changed due to advances in technology, social climate, or other factors. For example, the decision to convert from a laparoscopic procedure (minimally invasive, small incisions) to an open procedure (large incisions) during a cholecystectomy (gall bladder removal) is a prototypical case (Dominguez, 1997; Dominguez, Flach, Lake, McKellar, & Dunn, in press). In the case of this conversion decision, the absence of discussion in textbooks reflects both the recent evolution of laparoscopic (minimally invasive) procedures as well as the highly contextual and controversial nature of the decision.

We found that expert surgeons expressed diverse opinions about the significance of various dimensions for the conversion decision. In one case of an aged patient, one expert argued that doing the surgery laproscopically was essential to prevent extensive tissue damage and avoid an extended hospital stay with the possibility of pneumonia and other complications. Another expert argued that, due to the patient's age, it was essential to do an open procedure because a laparoscopic procedure would mean longer time under anesthetic and this might lead to complications in an older patient. Thus, there is no consensus or conventional wisdom with respect to how the consequences of laparoscopic surgery change as a function of age. With more experience with laparoscopic procedures, consensus about the implications of age may emerge and age may interact with a host of other factors (e.g., the skill level of the particular surgeon, the skill of the anesthesiologist, the skill of the nursing staff at a particular hospital, as well as the mobility and living situation of a particular patient). Further, it may be impossible to articulate a simple principle of the sort that can be communicated in a text.

The issues of age and the risks and benefits of a laparoscopic procedure for cholecystectomy raise another important issue: Who is the expert? Who is the authority with respect to the amount of anesthesia an older patient might tolerate—the surgeon or anesthesiologist? Who is in a better position to predict the consequences of an extended hospital stay—the surgeon, nurse, or general practitioner? In aviation, who has a better knowledge of the performance envelop of a particular aircraft—the pilot or aeronautical engineer? Most complex domains involve multiple experts each with different perspectives on the domain. Who should be the target for the knowledge elicitation?

Classically, because the goal of task analysis would be to understand how expert surgeons interpret situations, it would be natural to interview surgeons exclusively. However, because the goal of ecological task analysis is to understand meaning within the domain, not in any particular head, the input from many different perspectives is essential. Talking to multiple experts helps differentiate those aspects that are significant with respect to the work domain from those aspects that are significant to a particular perspective or level of awareness. The goal of an ecological task analysis is to discover the invariance with respect to the work domain. Consensus across multiple experts, with multiple perspectives on the problem, indicates that an issue is significant with respect to the domain. Disagreements across different perspectives on a problem might provide cues for contextual factors or information factors that interact to determine the significance of a particular issue within the domain.

A similar logic applies to the methods for knowledge elicitation. Over the past few years, a number of methods for knowledge elicitation have been developed (e.g., concept maps, plan–goal graphs, knowledge audits, critical incident reports, etc.). Each method might provide a different perspective on a work domain. From an ecological point of view, no single perspective is privileged. Different methods might tap into different levels of meaning within the situation. Further, the consistencies and differences across the perspectives can provide insights not available from any single perspective.

In summary, the goal is to get a comprehensive, authoritative, and/or normative view of the situation. We are not interested in the particulars of anyone's awareness. Rather, we are looking for invariants associated with the work space. The goal is to generalize about the situation. What is meaningful with respect to the situation? The analysis is more representative of the actual situation if we sample multiple experts using a variety of interviewing tools.

NATURALISTIC OBSERVATION

Although published reports and expert accounts provide important windows on a work domain, they typically will not provide a comprehensive view; in some cases, they actually may provide misleading information about the domain. There are many reasons for this. For example, highly practiced perceptual motor skills, such as those involved in flying or surgery, tend to become automated so they happen independent of any conscious awareness. Thus, it is difficult for many pilots to explain how they know when they are on the right glideslope or how they know when to flare to achieve a soft touchdown (for an exception, see Langeweische's [1944] rich account of the approach to landing).

Because of limitations of experts' awareness and possible misconceptions about their own behavior, it is essential to observe in the actual work context. Again, the goal is to understand the situation. Thus, observing situated performance is essential. In our work on surgery, we spent many hours observing actual surgeries. A heated exchange between surgeon and resident holding the laparoscope ("Goddamit, keep the horizon steady!") helped us appreciate the importance of a consistent orientation of the laparoscope. Being present when a monitor failed and the functionally blind surgeon had to hold perfectly still while a new monitor was located and hooked up to the scope helped us appreciate the brittleness of the technology. Seeing the variations in anatomy helped us appreciate the difficulty of the discriminations that have to be made to identify critical structures (e.g., the cystic duct and common bile duct). These are aspects of the domain that are difficult to appreciate from reading texts and talking with surgeons.

It is also important to realize that many constraints within a work domain are difficult to appreciate from passive observations. Often to get a full appreciation, it is important for the analyst to be a participant observer. Early in my career, I was involved in a project to evaluate the appropriate orientation for an electronic map for low-level navigation in helicopters. Our research group was split based on our experiences driving cars—on whether we thought track-up or north-up was the best solution. During the project, we got an opportunity to fly a low-level mission in a helicopter, and one of our team members took the map and functioned as navigator. Immediately we saw clearly that a track-up orientation was preferable for this application. What we discovered in practice was the correspondence problem. When driving cars, the correspondence between landmarks in the world (e.g., the exit from the highway) and landmarks on the map can be resolved spatially or using numerical or verbal labels that are on both the highway and the map. However, when flying in natural terrain using a topographic map, the correspondence problem must be solved spatially. The spatial problem is significantly easier if the map orientation is aligned with the view of the landscape. Thus, a track-up orientation was clearly better. Later I got the opportunity to take my sons orienteering—again, we quickly learned, in practice, the value of orienting the map track-up.

We also had an opportunity in our surgery work to perform a laparoscopic cholecystectomy (on a pig). This was incredibly valuable in helping us appreciate the difficulties of orienting to the displaced view created by the laparoscope. When separating the gall bladder from the liver bed, surgeons had mentioned the importance of tension points. I did not appreciate the significance of this until I was doing the cutting myself. There is a tangle of tissue connecting the gall bladder to the liver bed that has to be dissected to remove the gall bladder. When the assistant pulls the gall bladder away from the liver, it creates points of ten-

sion in this tissue. If you gently touch the tension points with the tip of an endoscopic cautery tool, they separate easily. However, if you try to separate the tissue at nontension points (which I naively did), the tissue gives but does not separate. The danger is that you push through the tissue and hit the liver (which I
did). The liver is highly vascular and prone to bleeding (which it did). This can
create a serious complication for laparoscopic surgery. Fortunately, in this case,
the bleeding was minor and we were able to complete the surgery successfully
(to the great surprise of the surgeons who were instructing us). The point of these
examples is that some constraints that are difficult to appreciate based on abstract, logical analysis of passive observations become clearly evident to an active observer.

LABORATORY EXPERIMENTS

Natural work domains tend to be complex. Also, some events that might be important to a complete understanding of the domain (e.g., equipment failures)
might occur only rarely. Thus, there can be advantages to more controlled observations where the phenomenon can be parsed into more manageable chunks or
where the same event can be observed repeatedly. For ecological task analysis,
the critical concern is to parse the work domain into chunks that preserve meaningful aspects of the situation. Again, the goal is to understand the situation.
Classical cognitive psychology has designed experiments based on a parsing of
awareness. The meaning associated with particular situations was considered a
confound. As a result, these experiments end up being literally nonsense tasks
with respect to the goals of ecological task analysis. They may provide important
insights about the structure of cognitive mechanisms, but they provide little useful information about the meaning of situations.

The key to experimentation from an ecological perspective is to design the
experimental tasks to capture meaningful chunks of the situation. Thus, in our
experiments on flight control, we examine control problems associated with
flight (e.g., speed, altitude, control of collisions). We analyze the situation to
identify potential sources of information for closing the loop on these control
problems. Then we systematically manipulate control constraints (e.g., flight
dynamics) and sources of information (e.g., global optical flow, splay angle, etc.)
to determine the significance of the action and information constraints for performance. The laboratory tasks are greatly simplified relative to the actual domain. They target narrow, but potentially significant, features of the work domain (e.g., Flach, Hagen, & Larish, 1992; Flach, Warren, Garness, Kelly, &
Stanard, 1997; Larish & Flach, 1990; Stanard, 1998; Stanard, Flach, Smith, &
Warren, 1996).

The laboratory context also allows tinkering with an expert's task so that
transfer paradigms can be used to make inferences about an aspect of expertise
that may not be observable or open to verbal report (Hoffman, 1992). We have

utilized this to understand how surgeons orient to the displaced vision associated with laparoscopic surgery. Holden, Flach, and Donchin (1999) used a simple simulation and transfer paradigm to explore the relation between motor (position of the surgeon) and visual (position of the laparoscopic camera) orientations to the workspace. The results show neither motor orientation nor visual orientation alone were critical to the spatial orientation. Rather, it was a consistent relation between motor and visual constraints that was critical.

Thus, reductionistic experiments can lead to important insights about meaning within a work domain. The key is to parse the phenomenon so that significant constraints with respect to the work domain are preserved. The goal is not to understand interpretation processes, but to understand how the constraints within a situation shape performance.

SYNTHETIC TASK ENVIRONMENTS

The availability of high-fidelity simulations and virtual reality systems creates a great opportunity for an ecological approach to cognitive task analysis. These synthetic environments allow the semantics of complex environments to be brought into the laboratory (e.g., Dalrymple & Schiflett, 1996). These simulations allow constraints at various levels of abstraction to be controlled and manipulated in attempts to identify performance invariants. For example, goals, displays, context, resources, or plant dynamics can be manipulated independently or in combination. Finally, they allow simultaneous measurement at multiple levels that reflect the multiple levels of meaning in a situation. Thus, performance can be scored in terms of overall success (e.g., did the patient survive?), normative expectations (were standard procedures followed?), and by more general performance indexes (how long did the procedure take?).

The simultaneous measurement of the microstructure of behavior (e.g., eye and hand movements) and performance with regard to macroscopic functional goals (e.g., safe landing, successful operation) is critical from a dynamic systems perspective. Examining the patterns in time across these multiple levels may be the key to understanding the coupling across the different nested control loops that is critical to the adaptation and evolution of skill (e.g., see Kelso, 1995; Kugler & Turvey, 1987; Thelen & Smith, 1994). This multilevel measurement is an opportunity to empirically link the microstructure of behavior (e.g., a msec delay in activating a control) to functional consequences in a domain (e.g, probability of a crash).

The synthetic task environment also offers a safe place for the analyst to experience the domain constraints without endangering patients or passengers. Again, these kind of experiences may be critical for gaining a full appreciation of the situation. However, there is a chicken–egg problem associated with synthetic task environments. What constitutes a high-fidelity simulation? The whole point of ecological cognitive task analysis is to discover the meaningful aspects of a domain. Unless you fully understand the domain constraints, you do not know what *high fidelity* means. Thus, synthetic task environments must be part of an iterative analysis process that includes table-top analyses, knowledge elicitation, field observations, and lab experiments. These analyses help define *high fidelity* for a particular domain. The synthetic task environment can then be used to test hypotheses about what *high fidelity* means. Transfer experiments between real and synthetic tasks can help test the fidelity of the simulation.

SUMMARY

A skilled cognitive agent uses information to guide action and uses action to create information. Because perception and action are linked in a circular feedback system, there is no natural precedence relation between action and perception. Traditionally, precedence has been given to perception. Perception is considered to inform action. An ecological approach gives precedence to action. Cognition is modeled as an active process of exploration and discovery. Neither perspective is true or complete. They are different perspectives on the phenomenon of cognition and both perspectives contribute unique insights.

This chapter outlined the implications of an ecological perspective to cognitive task analysis. The goal of that analysis is to uncover the meaning within situations. That is, to discover the significant constraints in a particular domain with regard to the nested control problem. To identify these constraints it is necessary to integrate across multiple perspectives. These perspectives include published accounts of standard practices, the opinions of various experts, field observations within the particular domain, lab experiments, and experiments within synthetic task environments. Nome of these views is privileged. At the end of the day, the product of the cognitive task analysis should be an understanding of what is meaningful or significant in terms of the situation or workspace. The hope is that an understanding of situations, might be a foundation for eventually framing sensible (as opposed to nonsense syllable) questions about awareness. Thus, although there is no natural precedence between situations and awareness, there may be an advantage to beginning an assault on expertise from the perspective of situations.

ACKNOWLEDGMENTS

Ecological task analysis is a monumental task that typically requires a team of researchers. Many students and colleagues have contributed to the difficult work of exploring the aviation and surgical domains. In particular, I would like to acknowledge Cindy Dominguez, who dragged me into surgery and is responsible for most of what I know about surgery. Also, Chris Wickens did the navigating on our helicopter flight. Chris was principal investigator for that project. Also, a sincere thanks to Valerie Shalin, Susan Chipman, and Jan Maarten Schraagen for organizing the CTA symposium and managing the production of this book. It was generous of them to provide a forum for this crazy ecological perspective.

REFERENCES

Anderson, J.R. (1995). *Cognitive psychology and its implications* (4th ed.). New York: Freeman.

Crandall, B., & Calderwood, R. (1989). *Clinical assessment skills of experienced neonatal intensive care nurses.* Yellow Springs, OH: Klein Associates. (Final Report prepared for the National Center for Nursing, NIH under contract No. 1 R43 NR01911 01.)

Cooke, N.J. (1992). Modeling human expertise in expert systems. In R.R. Hoffman (Ed.), *The psychology of expertise* (pp. 29–60). New York: Springer-Verlag.

Dalrymple, M., & Schiflett, S. (1996, June*). Measuring situational awareness of AWACS weapons directors.* Paper presented at the International Symposium on Situational Awareness in the Tactical Air Environment, Patuxent River, MD.

Dominguez, C.O. (1997). *First, do no harm: Expertise and metacognition in laparoscopic surgery.* Unpublished doctoral dissertation, Wright State University, Dayton, OH.

Dominguez, C.O., Flach, J.M., Lake, P., McKellar, D., & Dunn, M. (in press). The conversion decision: Knowing your limits and limiting your risks. In K. Smith, J. Shanteau, & P. Johnson (Eds.), *Psychological explorations of competent decision making.* Cambridge, England: Cambridge University Press.

Flach, J.M. (1999). Ready, fire, aim: Toward a theory of meaning processing systems. In D. Gopher & A. Koriat (Eds.), *Attention & performance XVII* (pp. 187–221). Cambridge, MA: MIT Press.

Flach, J.M. (1998). Cognitive systems engineering: Putting things in context. *Ergonomics, 41*(2), 163–167.

Flach, J.M. (1995). Situation awareness: Proceed with caution. *Human Factors, 37,* 149–157.

Flach, J.M. (1990). Control with an eye for perception: Precursors to an active psychophysics. *Ecological Psychology, 2*(2*),* 83–111.

Flach, J.M., & Rasmussen, J. (in press). Cognitive engineering: Designing for situation awareness. In N. Sarter & R. Amalberti (Eds.), *Cognitive engineering in the aviation domain.* Mahwah, NJ: Lawrence Erlbaum Associates.

Flach, J.M., & Warren, R. (1995). Low altitude flight. In P.A. Hancock, J.M. Flach, J. Caird, & K. Vicente (Eds), *Local applications of the ecological approach to human–machine systems* (pp. 65–103). Hillsdale, NJ: Lawrence Erlbaum Associates.

Flach, J.M., Warren, R., Garness, S.A., Kelly, L., & Stanard, T. (1997). Perception and control of altitude: Splay & depression angles. *Journal of Experimental Psychology: Human Perception and Performance, 23,* 1764–1782.

Flach, J.M., Hagen, B.A., & Larish, J.F. (1992). Sources of information in optic flow for the regulation of altitude. *Perception & Psychophysics, 51*(6), 557–568.

Fowler, C.A., & Turvey, M.T. (1978). Skill acquisition: An event approach with special reference to searching for the optimum of a function of several variables. In G.E. Stelmach (Ed.), *Information processing in motor control and learning* (pp. 1–54). New York: Academic Press.

Gardner, H. (1985). *The mind's new science.* New York: Basic Books.

Gibson, E.J. (1969). *Perceptual learning and development.* New York: Appleton-Century-Crofts.

Gibson, J.J. (1979). *The ecological approach to visual perception.* Boston: Houghton Mifflin.

Halpern, D.F. (1996). *Thought & knowledge* (3rd ed.). Mahwah, NJ: Lawrence Erlbaum Associates.

Hoffman, R.R. (Ed.). (1992). *The psychology of expertise.* New York: Springer-Verlag.

Holden, J.G., Flach, J.M., & Donchin, Y. (1999). Perceptual-motor coordination in an endoscopic surgery simulation. *Surgical Endoscopy, 13,* 127–132.

Hutchins, E. (1995). How a cockpit remembers its speeds. *Cognitive Science, 19,* 265–288.

Kelso, J.A.S. (1995). *Dynamic patterns: The self-organization of brain and behavior.* Cambridge, MA: MIT Press.

Kugler, P.N., & Turvey, M.T. (1987). *Information, natural law, and the self-assembly of rhythmic movement.* Mahwah, NJ: Lawrence Erlbaum Associates.

Langeweische, W. (1944). *Stick and rudder.* New York: McGraw-Hill.

Larish, J., & Flach, J.M. (1990). Sources of optical information useful for perception of speed of rectilinear self-motion. *Journal of Experimental Psychology: Human Perception and Performance, 16,* 295–302.

Mayer, R.E. (1992). *Thinking, problem solving, cognition* (2nd ed.). New York: Freeman.

Powers, W.T. (1973). *Behavior: The control of perception.* Chicago: Aldine.

Rasmussen, J. (1986). *Information processing and human-machine interaction: An approach to cognitive engineering.* New York: North Holland.

Rasmussen, J., Pejtersen, A.M., & Goodstein, L.P. (1994). *Cognitive systems engineering.* New York: Wiley.

Runeson, S. (1977). On the possibility of smart perceptual mechanisms. *Scandinavian Journal of Psychology, 18,* 172–179.

Shiffrin, R.M., & Schneider, W. (1977). Controlled and automatic information processing: II. Perceptual learning, automatic attending, and a general theory. *Psychological Review, 84,* 127–190.

Solso, R. L. (1995). *Cognitive psychology* (4th ed.). Boston: Allyn & Bacon.

Stanard, T.W. (1998). *The visual information used in collision avoidance.* Unpublished doctoral dissertation, Wright State University, Dayton, OH.

Stanard, T.W., Flach, J.M., Smith, M., & Warren, R. (1996). Visual information use in collision avoidance tasks: The importance of understanding the dynamics of action. In *Third Annual Symposium on Human Interaction with Complex Systems* (pp. 62–67). Los Alamitos, CA: IEEE Computer Society Press.

Thelen, E., & Smith, L.B. (1994). *A dynamic systems approach to the development of cognition and action.* Cambridge, MA: MIT Press.

7

WORK DOMAIN ANALYSIS AND TASK ANALYSIS: A DIFFERENCE THAT MATTERS

Kim J. Vicente
University of Toronto

Work analysis methods have been around for many decades (e.g., Taylor, 1911), and many different types of techniques have been developed. Therefore, it should not be surprising that different types of methods are appropriate for different types of work situations (Rasmussen, 1988). Accordingly, we should focus our attention on understanding which techniques are most suitable for particular classes of problems.

This chapter is concerned with the relatively unique challenges imposed by complex, sociotechnical systems (e.g., nuclear power plants, intensive care units, financial markets). These work environments are placing an increasing premium on worker adaptation to novelty (Rasmussen, Pejtersen, & Goodstein, 1994). More and more, workers are being required to play the role of adaptive problem solvers whose ingenuity is required to deal with situations that were not anticipated by system designers. How can we design systems that explicitly help workers play this challenging, but vital, role?

Rasmussen and colleagues (Rasmussen, 1986; Rasmussen et al., 1994) have developed a framework for cognitive work analysis (CWA) that is intended to address this problem. CWA represents a grand vision for how to analyze human work so as to derive implications for designing computer-based systems that explicitly support adaptation to novelty (Vicente, 1999). Unfortunately, grand visions make for incomprehensible book chapters. Thus, this chapter focuses on a much more modest goal.

Specifically, my aim is to explain the distinction between two different classes of work analysis methods: work domain analysis and task analysis. This distinction is an important one, having implications for designing information systems that support adaptation to novelty. Most work analysis approaches that have been developed to date are variants of task analysis. Although task analysis has a significant role in supporting adaptation, the role of work domain analysis is at least as important, if not more. Because the complementary advantages of work domain analysis are relatively unappreciated, it is important to bring them to the fore.

TASK ANALYSIS

What Is Task Analysis?

Task analysis actually represents a diverse set of methods. These methods can be used to identify and examine "the tasks that *must* be performed by users when they interact with systems" (Kirwan & Ainsworth, 1992, p. vii; italics added). Despite their many differences, task analysis techniques generally share this rational quest for identifying the ideal way(s) in which the job should be performed.

To be sure, the precision with which this objective is sought differs considerably among task analysis techniques. Three different levels can be identified.

1.   *Input/Output Constraints.* This first level identifies the inputs that are required to perform the task, the outputs that are achieved after it is completed, and the constraints that must be taken into account in selecting the actions that are required to achieve the task. An example is illustrated in Fig. 7.1 for the task of determining the rate of gasoline consumption in km/l for an automobile. The two inputs and the single output for the task are shown, but the steps that are used to achieve the task are not specified. The inputs are specified in miles and gallons so a conversion process is required to perform the task correctly. Thus, certain constraints must be obeyed to reach the goal state. For the example in Fig. 7.1, two relevant constraints are the number of kilometers in a mile and the number of liters in a gallon. Even for such a simple task, there are several different sets of actions that one could adopt to perform the same task. For example, we could use a calculator, in which case the main steps are reading off numbers from the odometer and the gas pump and then typing those numbers into the calculator. Alternatively, we could use mental arithmetic, in which case some cognitive steps are also required to arrive at the correct answer. The input–output analysis deliberately ignores these process details. It only provides a high-level product description of the task.

There are several points worth noting. First, the constraints on action can be of different types. In the example presented in Fig. 7.1, the constraints were relationships among variables. However, they could also be sequential in nature (e.g., there must be water in the kettle before you turn on the stove). Second, it is not possible to perform the task correctly without factoring in these constraints.

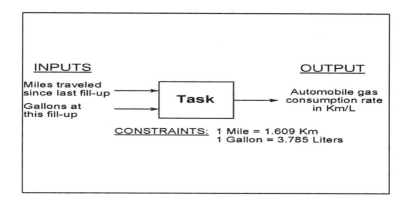

FIG. 7.1   Example of input–output constraints task analysis for determining the rate of gasoline consumption in an automobile.

They must be taken into account independent of how the task is actually performed. Third, the constraints frequently do not specify a unique action flow sequence. They merely limit the options (degrees of freedom) on viable action sequences (i.e., allsequences that do not factor in the correct conversion factors are ruled out). In the words of Kugler, Kelso, and Turvey (1980), "it is not that actions are caused by constraints, it is rather that some actions are excluded by them" (p. 9).

2.   *Sequential Flow.* This level identifies a temporally ordered sequence of actions that is required to complete the task. Such a description is equivalent to a flowchart of the process that workers should follow to perform the task, much like the specification of a computer algorithm. Such analyses are usually based on a behavior taxonomy such as the classic Berliner taxonomy (Meister, 1985). These taxonomies provide a periodic table of elemental action verbs that can be used to compose a flow sequence for a particular task. For example, one specific sequence of behaviors for performing part of the task in Fig. 7.1 could be:

> *Read* current odometer value,
>
> *Read* odometer value at last fill-up, and
>
> *Calculate* the difference to obtain miles traveled since last fill-up.

The result would be an algorithm for performing the task in a particular way. Note that, because it is more detailed, this level of task analysis is usually dependent on the device workers currently have available to do the task. For example, if we had a trip odometer in our car, the action sequence specified earlier would be unnecessary as long as we reset the odometer the last time we filled our tank. Instead of calculating the miles traveled since the last fill-up, we could simply read off this value from the trip odometer.

3.   *Timeline*. This final level identifies a temporally ordered sequence of actions that is required to achieve the task, with duration estimates for each action. This is the most detailed level of all. Sticking with the example used previously, we might obtain the following task description (the time estimates are purely hypothetical):

> 0 – 1s: *Read* current odometer value
>
> 1 – 2s: *Read* odometer value at last fill-up, and
>
> 2 – 3s: *Calculate* the difference to obtain miles traveled since last fill-up.

Not only is the sequence of actions that should be performed specified, but so is the duration of each of those actions. If we are to believe this analysis, there is only one right way to perform this task, because all of the discretion has essentially been eliminated, leaving only a single, well defined procedure for workers to follow.

Constraints Versus Instructions

These three levels of task analysis, represented graphically in Fig. 7.2, differ in their specificity. If we adopt a multidimensional state space as a frame of reference, the first level of task analysis (input–output) shown in Fig. 7.2a merely identifies a point in the space (i.e., the goal state), the inputs that are required to get to that point (not shown in the figure), and the constraints that must be respected (i.e., the areas that must be avoided) if workers are to get to the goal state. The second level of task analysis (flow sequence), shown in Fig. 7.2b, represents a marked increase in specificity. Not only is the goal state identified, but so is a sequence of actions for getting to the goal state. However, there is still some leeway, because the timing of the actions is not specified. Therefore, in terms of a state-space representation, this level of task analysis corresponds to a path that must be followed (see Fig. 7.2b). Finally, the third level of task analysis (timeline) is the most specific of all. It prescribes a sequence of actions, each with a particular duration. This level of analysis can be represented as a unique trajectory in the state space for reaching the goal (see Fig. 7.2c).[1]

The graphical comparison in Fig. 7.2 clearly reveals an otherwise subtle qualitative distinction among the three levels of task analysis. The first level, based on constraints, specifies what should not be done, whereas the other two

a) Level 1 - Input/Output:

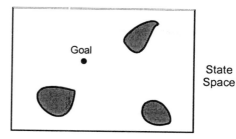

State
Space

b) Level 2 - Flow Sequence:

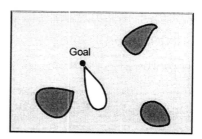

State
Space

c) Level 3 - Timeline:

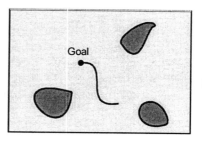

State
Space

FIG. 7.2   Three types of task analysis. See text for description.

levels, based on instructions, specify what should be done (cf. Kugler et al., 1980). This qualitative difference, although perhaps unfamiliar, is of fundamental importance.

---

[1]Note that the distinction between a path and trajectory is a relative one. For example, if we adopt a more fine-grained level of analysis (i.e., if we zoom in), what looked like a trajectory becomes a path. Conversely, if we adopt a more coarse level of analysis (i.e., if we zoom out), what looked like a path can look like a trajectory.

Implications

Different forms of work analysis make different assumptions about the nature of work. Hence, they lead to different designs, which, in turn, lead to different types of guidance for workers. For example, constraint- and instruction-based approaches to task analysis have different implications for workers.[2] First, instruction-based approaches are more detailed so they leave less discretion to workers (cf. Leplat, 1989). At the lowest level (timeline; see Fig. 7.2c), the analyst must make decisions about what actions should be performed to accomplish the task, how they should be sequenced together, and how long each will take. There is little left for the worker to do except follow the resulting procedure or work flow reliably and consistently (Reed, 1996). In contrast, with constraint-based approaches, none of these decisions are made up front by the analyst. Only guidance about the goal state and the constraints on action are provided, not about how the task should be accomplished (Fig. 7.2a). Consequently, workers are given the discretion to make decisions online about how to perform the task. This contrast shows that constraint-based approaches to task analysis provide more worker discretion than instruction-based approaches.

Of course, we could just as easily turn these observations around by examining not the discretion, but the guidance offered to workers by the two types of task analysis. We could argue that instruction-based approaches provide more detailed guidance and thus are less likely to lead to human error. In contrast, constraint-based approaches offer minimal guidance and thus are more likely to lead to human error. Thus, if we view people in a positive light, we may want to adopt the constraint-based approach: Provide a computer system with information about the goal to be achieved, the current state of affairs, and the constraints to be obeyed, and then let workers decide how to achieve the goal. If we view people in a negative light, we may want to adopt the instruction-based approach: Identify up front the "correct" way to perform the task and then build the results of that analysis into a computer-based workflow that leads workers along and enforces that "proper" way of doing the job (e.g., Marsden, 1996).

Second, this difference between levels of analysis can also be viewed from the perspective of accommodating performance variability. As shown in Fig. 7.2, constraint-based analyses accommodate a great deal of variability in worker

---

[2]The instruction-based approaches to task analysis described in this chapter are from the human factors literature, whereas the instruction-based approaches to cognitive task analysis described in several other chapters in this book are from the cognitive science literature. Additional research would have to be conducted to determine to what extent the limitations of the former extend to the latter.

behavior (i.e., many ways of doing the task), whereas instruction-based analyses accommodate little variability in worker behavior (i.e., in the extreme, only one way of doing the task). This observation has implications for two important factors. By accommodating variability, we provide workers with opportunities that foster learning (e.g., Bernstein, 1996; Gibson, 1991; Norros, 1996). Also, by accommodating variability, we provide workers with the flexibility required to deal with novel circumstances. After all, if the conditions under which a task is to be performed vary from one situation to the next (e.g., starting to the right of the goal in Fig. 7.2 rather than to the left), the actions that are required to get to the goal must differ for the two cases (cf. Bernstein, 1996). This relationship is explored in detail in the next section.

Third, because they are more detailed, instruction-based analyses must be based on assumptions about the device that workers have available to perform the task. We saw this in the simple case of figuring out the gas consumption for an automobile. Therefore, instruction-based analyses are more device-dependent (Benyon, 1992) because their content and form change as a function of the tools people have available to perform the task.

In contrast, because constraint-based analyses merely provide an envelope on task achievement, they are more device-independent. For example, the requirements shown in Fig. 7.1 must be taken into account if the task is to be accomplished correctly and consistently. If the fact that there are 3.785 liters in a gallon is not taken into account somehow, whether it be by the worker or the device (e.g., a calculator), the correct answer cannot possibly be consistently obtained. It is worthwhile emphasizing that this statement is true even if the actor performing the task is not a person. In general terms, some relationships are properties of a task and quite independent of any particular device (Diaper & Addison, 1992). By constraining rather than instructing workers, constraint-based analyses describe properties of the task, rather than properties of how to do the task with a particular device. Therefore, constraint-based analyses are generally less device dependent than instruction-based analyses.

Consequently, instruction-based analyses are plagued by a fundamental logical problem that Potter et al. (chap. 20, this volume) refer to as the *envisioned world problem*. If an instruction-based task analysis is going to be performed, then assumptions about the design of the device (e.g., computer interface and automation) available to workers must be made. The reason for this is that the particulars of the timeline or flow sequence will change as a function of the device that is available. However, the reason we want to do a task analysis in the first place is to figure out how the device should be designed. Thus, we are faced with an infinite regress that is apparent, albeit implicit, in the practical guide to task analysis by Kirwan and Ainsworth (1992):

- task analysis defines what a worker is required to do (p. 1)
- task analysis can be used by designers at an early stage of design to decide how to allocate functions between workers and machines (p. 2)
- some tasks are better performed by workers, whereas other tasks are better performed by machines (p. 17)

What is left implicit is that different function-allocation policies lead to different worker responsibilities. For instance, if a task is completely automated, there may be no worker activities at all for that task. The same logic applies to interface design. Returning to the trip odometer example, with one interface, a worker may have to perform one action (calculate the difference between current and previous km), whereas with a different interface, a worker may have to perform a different action (read the trip odometer) to perform the same task. Hence we are left with a conundrum where what the worker is required to do is both an input to and an output of the design process. Note that it is not possible to escape this dilemma completely by iteration because any design decision can result in a change in worker activities or responsibilities (Carroll, Kelogg, & Rosson, 1991).

Conclusions

The primary advantage of the instruction-based approach seems to be that more guidance is provided. By following the steps laid out in a flow sequence or time-line, workers may be less likely to forget a step, perform the wrong step, or perform the right steps in the wrong order. In short, by providing workers with a precompiled solution to task demands, there may be less chance of human errors arising from human information-processing limitations.

The constraint-based approach has several advantages. First, more discretion is given to workers to decide exactly how the task should be performed. There is substantial evidence to suggest that this enhanced discretion leads to better worker health (Karasek & Theorell, 1990). Second, constraint-based approaches also accommodate greater variability in behavior. As a result, workers have more opportunities to learn and better chances of coping with unusual or changing circumstances. Thus, constraint-based approaches foster learning and support greater flexibility. Third, constraint-based approaches make fewer assumptions about the properties of the device (i.e., the computer information system) available to workers. Consequently, it is more likely that the new design will result in new functional possibilities, rather than being constrained by designers' current assumptions about functionality. There is evidence to suggest that new functionality is a prerequisite for substantial improvements in productivity (Landauer, 1995).

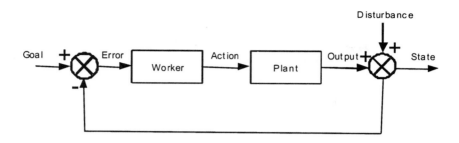

FIG. 7.3   A simple model of goal-directed behavior.

CONSTRAINTS OR INSTRUCTIONS? THE VIEW FROM CONTROL THEORY

Control theory provides a generic language for understanding behavior. Hence, it is used here to resolve the apparent conflict between constraint- and instruction-based approaches to task analysis. Although control theorists have developed sophisticated mathematical formalisms for analyzing systems, I only use qualitative concepts from control theory in an informal way. In this subsection (based on the work of Powers, 1973), I present a simple model of goal-oriented behavior. Although it is not a realistic representation of human behavior in complex systems, the model can nevertheless be used to uncover a number of useful insights.

Negative Feedback Loop With a Disturbance

Fig. 7.3 shows a negative feedback loop with a disturbance. The variables in the loop are:

Goal (g) - the desired state to be achieved and maintained
Output (o) - the output from the plant
Disturbance (d)–unpredictable disturbances that affect the state of the system
State (s) – the current state of the world
Error (e) - the difference between the desired state and the current state
Action (a) - the behavior of the worker

Although the notation does not make this explicit, each of these variables is dynamic. In addition to these four variables, the negative feedback loop is also characterized by two parameters:

W - the control strategy used by the worker
P - the dynamics of the plant (the control-theoretic term for the system being controlled)

It is important to discuss the relevance of disturbances because they play such an important role. A simple example of a disturbance is the wind that can push our car when we are driving. The wind gusts (d) are added to the output (o) of our car and thereby cause a different state of the world (s) (i.e., the car is in a different position than it would have been in without the wind). Many kinds of disturbances can be found in complex sociotechnical systems: an unanticipated change in the economy in the financial industry, a rush order in the manufacturing industry, and an unexpected allergic reaction of a patient to an antibiotic in the medical domain (cf. Norros, 1996). The severity of these examples should make it clear that it is important to understand the implications of disturbances for the control of complex sociotechnical systems.

A number of deductions can be made from this simple model. The actions are a function of the error signal and strategy used by the worker:

$$a = W\,e \quad (1)$$

The error signal is the difference between the goal state and the state of the world:

$$e = g - s \quad (2)$$

The output of the plant is determined by the actions performed by the worker and the dynamics of the plant:

$$o = P\,a \quad (3)$$

Also, the state of the world is a simple function of two variables—the disturbance and the output from the plant:

$$s = o + d \quad (4)$$

Substituting Equation (4) into Equation (2) leads to the following:

$$e = g - (o + d) \quad (5)$$

If we substitute Equation (3) into Equation (5), we get:

$$e = g - (P\,a + d) \quad (6)$$

For the goal to be satisfied, the error signal must go to zero. If we let $e = 0$ in Equation (6), we can see what relationship must be true for the goal to be achieved:

$$g = a\,P + d \quad (7)$$

Solving for the actions that the worker must perform, we get:

$$a = (g - d)\,/\,P \quad (8)$$

Equation (8) has a straightforward, yet important, qualitative interpretation. The actions that workers must perform (a) to achieve the goal are a function of the goal (g), the dynamics of the plant (P), and the disturbance acting on the system (d). As mentioned before, the disturbance—by definition—cannot be predicted. It follows that the actions workers need to take to satisfy the goal also cannot be predicted.

The example mentioned earlier of driving a car under windy conditions gives an intuitive appreciation for this fact. If the goal (g) is to be satisfied (e.g., stay in your lane), the actions (*a*) performed by the driver must oppose the disturbances (*d*) caused by the wind. However, because nobody (including the driver) can predict what the pattern of disturbances will be, the precise actions that the driver must take, as well as their timing, cannot be planned up front. Instead, they must be generated online, in real time, as the wind acts on the car.

There are several points that follow from this observation. First, the same set of actions have different effects at different times because the pattern of disturbances is rarely repeated (cf. Bernstein, 1996). Each situation is a unique context characterized by a different set of contingencies (cf. Suchman, 1987). Second, as a result of this situated context, if the same goal is to be achieved on different occasions, a different set of actions is required to perform the same task. Thus, the actions have to vary if the outcome is to remain the same. This phenomenon has been referred to as *context-conditioned variability* (Turvey, Shaw, & Mace, 1978).

Critical Analysis

We are now in a position to resolve the conflict between constraint- and instruction-based approaches to task analysis described earlier. The feasibility of the two types of analysis can be understood by distinguishing between closed and open systems. *Closed systems* are completely isolated from their environment. From the viewpoint of the analyst, the behavior of the system can be well understood by examining influences that are internal to the system. Conversely, *open systems* are subject to influences (i.e., unpredictable disturbances) that are external to the system.[3]

With this distinction in hand, the conflict between conducting an instruction-based analysis to reduce human error and a constraint-based analysis to support safety, flexibility, and health may be resolved in a systematic way.

---

[3] The system is defined by the analyst (i.e., it is an epistemological entity, not an ontological entity). As a result, if the model adopted by the analyst has gross deficiencies, the system is open because it is being affected by factors that are not accounted for in the analyst's model. Therefore, at any one point in time, it is generally not possible to distinguish between the following two situations: (a) external factors are affecting the behavior of the system, and (b) internal factors not accounted for by the analyst's model are governing the behavior of the system. Only when better models are developed can it be established that a situation that looked like Case (a) actually turned out to be Case (b). For our purposes, it is sufficient to include both cases under the definition of *open system* because each presents the analyst with sources of disturbance that, by definition, cannot be anticipated.

The more closed a system is, the more amenable it is to instruction-based forms of task analysis. More concretely, in cases where the analyst can anticipate the conditions under which the work is done, a flow sequence or timeline may be specified. Conversely, the more open a system is, the less amenable it is to an instruction-based form of task analysis. Because there are unpredictable external disturbances acting on the system, it is not possible to accurately pre-identify the different flow sequences or timelines that lead to the satisfaction of the goal. Open systems give rise to context-conditioned variability. Workers must adapt online in real time to disturbances that cannot possibly be foreseen by analysts (Hirschhorn, 1984).

Given this insight, we can understand why instruction-based task analysis has been used effectively by system designers for many years and why it is much more prevalent than constraint-based approaches. In the past, the demands on workers have been comparatively procedural in nature. Consequently, analysts could treat such systems as being essentially closed for practical purposes. In these cases, instruction-based analyses were feasible and captured task demands in a way that was sufficiently accurate to derive useful design implications. More recently, as the demands on workers have become more cognitive and social in nature, systems are becoming more and more open. Specifically, complex sociotechnical systems are subject to external disturbances (e.g., faults, changes in demands) that must be compensated for; they are subject to various forms of uncertainty that must be accommodated; their demands are primarily cognitive and social in nature, so there is no one right way of getting the job done; their behavior is dynamic, requiring workers to adapt to moment-by-moment changes in context. Collectively, these factors create a need for context-conditioned variability that is substantial enough in magnitude that it cannot be meaningfully ignored (cf. Norros, 1996). In complex sociotechnical systems, then, it becomes essentially impossible to conduct an instruction-based task analysis that does justice to the richness of the set of behaviors that are required to cope with the entire set of job demands. The flow sequence and timing of the actions that satisfy the goals are not fixed, are too numerous to enumerate, and are subject to factors that cannot be identified a priori.

Constraint-Based Approaches: A Partial Savior

Fortunately, constraint-based approaches to task analysis can accommodate some of the context-conditioned variability required to achieve goals in open systems. As discussed earlier, that is one of the primary advantages of constraint-based analyses—they are flexible enough to accommodate variability in worker behavior. Because they only specify the goal to be achieved and the constraints on achieving that goal, such analyses are indifferent to variations in precisely how the goal is to be achieved. In fact, the negative feedback model discussed earlier (see Fig. 7.3) is a constraint-based structure, not instruction-based. There is no preplanned set of actions built into the control loop. Instead, the actions that are required to achieve the goal emerge on the spot in realtime as a function of the initial conditions and disturbances of the moment. In other words, the negative feedback loop is capable of an elementary form of context-conditioned variability (or situated action; Suchman, 1987).

The only factors that remain constant in the control loop are the goal to be achieved and the constraints on goal achievement. Although this vagueness can be considered by some to be a disadvantage (see the earlier discussion on the relationship between the level of detail of guidance and the likelihood of human error), the preceding analysis shows that this vagueness is actually an advantage for open systems. The only way to adapt to disturbances is to leave decisions about how the task should be performed to the worker, rather than specify such details up front based on idealized (and unrealistic) assumptions about what should be done.

It is extremely important to note, however, that discretion is not the same as complete freedom. I am not advocating that workers be allowed to do whatever they want. This would be irresponsible because it would include unintentional errors, not to mention deliberate acts of sabotage. The discretion and flexibility I am advocating is bounded by constraints. Errors and acts of sabotage fall into the areas of the state space that workers are required to avoid. Thus, the position I am advocating is to give workers discretion within the boundaries of safe and effective operation.

An Unresolved Problem

Constraint-based forms of task analysis can be meaningfully conducted for complex sociotechnical systems and go part way toward addressing the challenges imposed by such systems. However, they are not capable of meeting all of those challenges. This important qualification can be recognized if we uncover an implicit assumption that is buried in the control-theoretic model presented earlier. The model assumes that the goal to be achieved is well defined and can be established ahead of time, although the sequence and timing of actions that are required to achieve the goal cannot be predicted. There are some situations in complex sociotechnical systems where even the particular goal to be achieved may not be identifiable beforehand. The prototypical example is an unanticipated emergency in a nuclear power plant. If the event that triggers the emergency cannot be known beforehand, how can we know what the goal should be? Although it is not widely recognized, this problem can exist in many comparatively more mundane situations. A good example is provided by Shepherd

(1992) in an application of task analysis to maintenance training for mechanical fitters in a chemical company: "A major problem that had to be dealt with at the outset was that fitters, like most craftsmen, are supposed to do anything they are called upon to do: there is apparently no one task to analyze" (p. 328).

One way to deal with this dilemma is to specify the task goal at a high (i.e., vague) level. For example, Shepherd (1992) identified one task goal as requiring workers to "Note any problems" (p. 335). This tactic tries to overcome ignorance about the precise goal to be pursued by specifying a broad goal that subsumes all of the more specific goals that might be associated with unanticipated events. The problem with this approach is that it merely provides a placeholder for what workers are supposed to do. It does little to identify the information or knowledge that workers require to cope with the novelty imposed by unanticipated events.

The crux of the problem seems to be that all task analysis methods are event-dependent (Vicente & Tanabe, 1993). They require a specification (or assumption) of at least a class of initiating events before the analysis can even get off the ground. Otherwise, the precise goal to be pursued cannot be identified. Therefore, even constraint-based forms of task analysis do not provide a satisfactory basis for dealing with unanticipated events.

This is an unacceptable situation for complex sociotechnical systems because unanticipated events pose the greatest risk to safety in such systems (Vicente, 1999). We need some other form of work analysis if we are to support workers in these challenging situations. More specifically, we need event-independent work analysis techniques (Vicente & Tanabe, 1993) whose relevance and utility are not tied to a specific, finite class of anticipated events.

DEALING WITH UNANTICIPATED EVENTS

This section derives insights about how to conduct an event-independent work analysis by drawing on an activity with which everyone is familiar—namely, spatial navigation.

Directions Versus Maps

In finding our way in our everyday environments (e.g., while walking or driving in a city), we are all familiar with relying on two kinds of support: directions and maps. Directions represent the sequence of actions that people are required to take to follow a particular route. Maps represent the spatial relationships between locations and routes in an environment.

TABLE 7.1

Relative Advantages and Disadvantages of Task Analysis and Work Domain Analysis

Criterion	Task	Work Domain
Mental economy	Efficient	Effortful
Ability to adapt to unforeseen contingencies	Brittle	Flexible
Scope of applicability	Narrow	Broad

The distinction between these two forms of navigational aids has an analogue in two forms of work analysis. Like directions, task analyses tell workers what goals they should be trying to achieve or how they should be achieving them. Like maps, work domain analyses merely describe the structure of the controlled system. More intuitively, a task is what workers are trying to achieve and actions are how they achieve it, whereas a work domain is what workers act on (i.e., the object of action).

As shown in Table 7.1, task and work domain analysis have complementary advantages and disadvantages. Just as directions are more efficient than maps because the former tell you what to do, so task analysis representations are more efficient than work domain representations because the former provide workers with a set of actions to get from a particular starting point to a particular goal state. Because an analyst has already done most of the thinking for us, all we have to do is follow the actions in the task representation. In contrast, a work domain representation is like a map because we have to do the thinking ourselves to derive a particular set of actions (like a route) from where we are to where we want to be.

However, this decrease in efficiency is compensated for by an increase in both flexibility and generality. Like maps, work domain representations are more flexible because they provide workers with the information they need to generate an appropriate response online in real time to events that have not been anticipated by designers. This is particularly useful when an unforeseen event occurs because task representations, by definition, cannot cope with the unanticipated.

Work domain representations also have another related advantage— namely, their generality. Just as maps are independent of any particular route, work domain representations are independent of any particular event. They merely show what the system is capable of doing. Thus, they provide workers with the discretion to meet the demands of the job in a variety of ways that suit their preferences or the particular needs of the moment. This is an obvious advantage, especially if we frequently have to deal with novelty and change, as workers in complex sociotechnical systems need to do. This provides a stark contrast to the limited possibilities made available by task representations.

CONCLUSIONS

The concern in this chapter has been to discuss a viable technique for work analysis in complex sociotechnical systems. The arguments that have been presented indicate that work domain analyses are absolutely essential. They provide a way to support worker adaptation to novelty, thereby addressing the criterion of safety. They also provide discretion—not complete freedom—to workers, thereby addressing the criterion of health. The chapter has also shown that task and work domain analysis have complementary strengths and weaknesses. Thus, it would be useful to include both in a single, integrated framework for work analysis. In this way, work analysis can provide the breadth and generality to cope with unanticipated events.

The Rasmussen et al. (1994) framework for CWA achieves this goal by including a work domain analysis phase and a constraint-based task analysis phase in one integrated, overarching framework (Vicente, 1999). Also included are analyses of the strategies that can be used to perform each task, the competencies that workers require, and the form and content of the organizational structure of work. Therefore, CWA provides a framework that is explicitly suited to the demands of complex sociotechnical systems, endeavoring to support the ever-increasing need for worker adaptation to the unanticipated.

ACKNOWLEDGMENTS

This chapter is a revised and condensed version of chapter 3 of Vicente (1999). The writing of this chapter was sponsored by research and equipment grants from the Natural Sciences and Engineering Research Council of Canada. I would like to thank John Hajdukiewicz for creating the figures and Jan Maarten Schraagen for inviting me to participate in the workshop.

REFERENCES

Benyon, D. (1992). The role of task analysis in systems design. *Interacting With Computers, 4*, 102–123.

Bernstein, N. A. (1996). On dexterity and its development. In M. L. Latash & M. T. Turvey (Eds.), *Dexterity and its development* (pp. 1–244). Mahwah, NJ: Lawrence Erlbaum Associates.

Carroll, J. M., Kellogg, W. A., & Rosson, M. B. (1991). The task-artifact cycle. In J. M. Carroll (Ed.), *Designing interaction: Psychology at the human-computer interface* (pp. 74–102). Cambridge, England: Cambridge University Press.

Diaper, D., & Addison, M. (1992). Task analysis and systems analysis for software development. *Interacting With Computers, 4*, 124–139.

Gibson, E. J. (1991). *An odyssey in learning and perception.* Cambridge, MA: MIT Press.

Hirschhorn, L. (1984). *Beyond mechanization: Work and technology in a postindustrial age.* Cambridge, MA: MIT Press.

Karasek, R., & Theorell, T. (1990). *Healthy work: Stress, productivity, and the reconstruction of working life.* New York: Basic Books.

Kirwan, B., & Ainsworth, L. K. (1992). *A guide to task analysis.* London: Taylor & Francis.

Kugler, P. N., Kelso, J. A. S., & Turvey, M. T. (1980). On the concept of coordinative structures as dissipative structures: 1. Theoretical lines of convergence. In G. E. Stelmach & J. Requin (Eds.), *Tutorials in motor behavior* (pp. 3–47). Amsterdam: North Holland.

Landauer, T. K. (1995). *The trouble with computers: Usefulness, usability, and productivity.* Cambridge, MA: MIT Press.

Leplat, J. (1989). Error analysis, instrument and object for task analysis. *Ergonomics, 32,* 813–822.

Marsden, P. (1996). Procedures in the nuclear industry. In N. Stanton (Ed.), *Human factors in nuclear safety* (pp. 99–116). London: Taylor & Francis.

Meister, D. (1985). *Behavioral analysis and measurement methods.* New York: Wiley.

Norros, L. (1996). System disturbances as springboard for development of operators' expertise. In Y. Engeström & D. Middleton (Eds.), *Cognition and communication at work* (pp. 159–176). Cambridge, England: Cambridge University Press.

Powers, W. T. (1973). *Behavior: The control of perception.* Chicago: Aldine.

Rasmussen, J. (1986). *Information processing and human-machine interaction: An approach to cognitive engineering.* New York: North-Holland.

Rasmussen, J. (1988). Information technology: A challenge to the Human Factors Society? *Human Factors Society Bulletin, 31*(7), 1–3.

Rasmussen, J., Pejtersen, A. M., & Goodstein, L. P. (1994). *Cognitive systems engineering.* New York: Wiley.

Reed, E. S. (1996). *The necessity of experience.* New Haven, CT: Yale University Press.

Shepherd, A. (1992). Maintenance training. In B. Kirwan & L. K. Ainsworth (Eds.), *A guide to task analysis* (pp. 327–339). London: Taylor & Francis.

Suchman, L. A. (1987). *Plans and situated actions: The problem of human-machine communication.* Cambridge, England: Cambridge University Press.

Taylor, F. W. (1911). *The principles of scientific management.* New York: Harper & Row.

Turvey, M. T., Shaw, R. E., & Mace, W. (1978). Issues in the theory of action: Degrees of freedom, coordinative structures and coalitions. In J. Requin (Ed.), *Attention and performance VII* (pp. 557–595). Hillsdale, NJ: Lawrence Erlbaum Associates.

Vicente, K. J. (1999). *Cognitive work analysis: Toward safe, productive, and healthy computer-based work.* Mahwah, NJ: Lawrence Erlbaum Associates.

Vicente, K. J., & Tanabe, F. (1993). Event-independent assessment of operator information requirements: Providing support for unanticipated events. In *Proceedings of the American Nuclear Society Topical Meeting on Nuclear Plant Instrumentation, Control and Man-Machine Interface Technologies* (pp. 389–393). LaGrange Park, IL: ANS.

COGNITIVE TASK ANALYSIS FOR APPLICATIONS TO THE DESIGN OF HUMAN-SYSTEM INTERACTION

8

A FUNCTIONAL TASK ANALYSIS OF TIME-PRESSURED DECISION MAKING

Earl Hunt and Susan Joslyn
University of Washington

Two key issues appear and reappear in industrial and applied cognitive psychology. Psychologists are asked to find out what people are doing when they are assigned to a particular workstation and how personnel officers can find people who have the skills needed to accept these assignments. The first question provides the motivation for cognitive task analysis. The second question motivates the development of personnel screening measures. Logically, the second question presumes that the test developer knows the answer to the first. How can a psychologist design a test to identify people who would be good at a job unless the psychologist knows what skills the job demands? In practice, many personnel testing programs avoid the task analysis phase by relying on measures of general cognitive competence. This is especially likely when task-specific measures, such as work samples, are not feasible. This situation arises when applicants do not have sufficient training to perform in appropriate test situations. In addition, developing work samples or similar tests for every job in the workplace obviously would not be economically feasible. Therefore, there is a role for the development of job-related tests that apply to a class of workplace situations and that can be administered to applicants without extensive training. To develop such tests, it is necessary to conduct a cognitive task analysis to begin test design and then match the results of that analysis to the test development effort.

We describe here the development of one such test; it is intended to identify people who do well in situations characterized by multitasking and decision making under considerable time pressure. We began with an analysis of the skills being used in one such situation. We then developed measures that appeared to capture these skills. The measures were tested by determining whether they predicted performance in simulations of the original task and two other, somewhat dissimilar tasks that also required time-pressured decision making. We have reported the details of our empirical work elsewhere (Joslyn & Hunt, 1998). This chapter concentrates on the task analysis involved and the methods used to validate our efforts.

THE TASK ANALYZED: PUBLIC SAFETY DISPATCHING

We needed a context in which to study time-pressured decision making. Initially, two industrial tasks were suggested: air traffic control (ATC) and public safety (911) dispatching. After a brief investigation, in which we visited ATC centers and the Federal Aviation Administration (FAA) research office at Oklahoma City, we concluded that it would be difficult for us to do very much work in ATC. The difficulties were largely administrative, not the least being that so many psychologists wished to study ATC that the FAA was faced with something of a psychologist traffic control. In addition, there were some problems with studying the task. Therefore, although we did make some use of ATC simulations as test vehicles, we decided to focus on public safety (911) dispatching.

Most of our work was done with a communication center in a mixed residential–industrial area in the Seattle metropolitan area, but outside the city of Seattle. We refer to it as *Valley Comm*. Valley Comm handles communications for several contiguous incorporated areas. We also visited another center similar to Valley Comm and did some work with a smaller center that served a large, sparsely populated county in a mountainous region in southern Washington State. Our remarks are based on our observations of Valley Comm unless otherwise noted.

Valley Comm is responsible for dispatch of police, fire, and medical units throughout its jurisdiction. The center operates 24 hours a day, in three 8-hour shifts. Shift assignments are rotated over a month. Shifts are staffed by two to three call receivers, two or three police dispatchers, a fire-medical dispatcher, and a shift supervisor. There is also a center supervisor who visits the operations room frequently, but on an irregular schedule.

When a 911 call is received from a reporting party (RP), the call receiver ascertains the details of the incident and types a description of it into a networked computer. The description includes relevant details and a classification in legal and administrative terms (e.g., DomV = domestic dispute, verbal). The description is then forwarded to a dispatcher. The priority of the incident is reflected in the code assigned to it. The call receiver has a sophisticated call-waiting system, which tells the receiver how many unanswered calls are in the queue. This information is relevant when the receiver is dealing with a minor or administrative call. In addition, the call receiver has a call-identifier display that shows both the calling number and the street address listed for that number.

The dispatcher's computer display is considerably more complicated than the call receiver's. It includes the call receiver's description of the current incident, a list of available and assigned police units, and a record of all incidents that have been assigned or are waiting handling. Incidents are listed by number and code type. Priorities are indicated by the code and a color showing the priority level. If the dispatcher decides to change the call receiver's classification of an incident (which does happen from time to time), the incident takes the priority of the new classification. In addition, the dispatcher can interrogate a public safety database for information about people or vehicles. The dispatcher can also request the display of descriptions of previously handled incidents.

Dispatchers use radio to receive reports of incidents encountered by an officer in the field. In this case, the officer is the RP, but talks directly to the dispatcher. Most of these incidents are traffic stops, but other events are common. In addition, the radio is used to transmit information about the handling of an active incident (e.g., acknowledgment of assignment, report of arrival on scene, request for information or backup). The dispatcher logs this information into the computer as it is received. Dispatchers are also responsible for checking periodically after an officer has been assigned to an incident. The frequency of the check depends on the type of assignment. For instance, dispatchers request information if they do not hear from an officer within 5 minutes after a traffic stop. The radio is also used for a good deal of administrative traffic and casual conversation.

Dispatchers have a telephone they use if they wish to speak with the RP. This is usually done in complicated cases, especially when the RP is involved in the incident. Although most of this communication is prosaic, it can be dramatic. We witnessed one case in which a dispatcher spent more than 15 minutes talking to an armed woman who was threatening suicide. Eventually the dispatcher persuaded her to put down the weapon, unlock her door, and allow the police outside to take her to a hospital. In our opinion, the RP could not have received better service had she called a professional psychotherapist.

The dispatchers are men or women from 25 to 40 years old who have some postsecondary education, but who are usually not college graduates. A few are police or firefighters who have had to retire from the active force usually because of a physical disability. They go through a 6-week training course and receive periodic evaluations. One of us (EH) attended a managerial review that centered on dispatchers reliability and problem-solving skills. There is about a 25% attrition rate in training. The dispatchers we worked with had from 2 to 5 years of experience.

THE COGNITIVE TASK ANALYSIS

Four observers (the two authors of this article, an industrial-organizational psychologist, and a graduate student who had had considerable experience in industry) visited the dispatch centers for several hours at a time. Although most visits were by a single observer, at times we intentionally went in pairs so that we could compare notes afterward. We met regularly during this period, to formulate a picture of what we thought was happening. We concluded that the basic tasks in dispatching are classifying and assigning resources. This much could be determined by reading the job description. Underlying the classification and assignment tasks, however, are two other processes.

The first is gathering information so that a classification can be made. We saw this as a major distinction between dispatching and ATC. In ATC, the analogue of an RP is a pilot who is almost always a reliable provider of required information. This is definitely not true of RPs. We witnessed one case in which a RP vehemently maintained that all that was needed was a medical response in a situation where shots had been fired. This example is obviously extreme. Most calls are more prosaic. However, call receivers and dispatchers routinely have to ask for some of the information that they need before a call can be handled.

The most common call is a traffic stop reported directly to the dispatcher by an officer on patrol. Traffic stops initiate two important dispatcher actions. The dispatcher searches the vehicle identification database to determine if the car being stopped is wanted for any reason. This is usually done before the officer approaches the vehicle. When the officer calls in identifications of the driver or any other person in the vehicle, the dispatcher searches the person database for a similar reason.

Dispatchers typically deal with several active incidents at a time, each of which can generate multiple messages. The urgency and complexity of the response can vary greatly. Therefore, it is essential that the dispatcher be able to prioritize his or her actions. Incidents constituting a threat to human life are given higher priority than those threatening property. Active incidents, such as a report of a burglar on the premises, are given higher priority than investigation of past incidents, such as a report of a burglarized home. All else being equal, the nearest appropriate and available unit(s) is assigned to an incident. In fact, the computer program recommends a unit based on these principles. The recommendation is usually accepted, but it is not at all unusual for the dispatcher to override it. New incidences may be reported at any time. Active incidents may change their priority as they develop. For instance, a routine traffic stop will go to a higher priority and may generate a call for backup if a weapon is reported in the car. As this example suggests, dispatchers must be aware of developing events even to the point of intentionally not assigning an available unit to a low-priority incident if the dispatcher anticipates a call for backup. Sometimes the dispatcher must break off dealing with one incident to deal with another and then return to the first incident.

We now return to our psychological question. We were interested in complex decision making in general and not dispatching in particular. Individual differences in such an ability are suggested by the attrition in ATC and 911 training programs in which such decision making is required.[1] However, we do not know whether this reflects the lack of a general ability for time-pressured decision making or an inability to master other specialized demands of the jobs. To answer this question, we turned to the experimental laboratory.

ABSTRACT DECISION-MAKING (ADM) TEST

We constructed a stripped-down task that had the elements of rapid decision making in a multiple task environment but without the specifics of any one environment. The reason for avoiding environment specificity was to predict performance in a variety of time-pressured decision-making situations, not just dispatching. As a result of our task analysis, we concluded that the test situation should require allocation of resources based on classification of incidents. The attributes used to make the classification should be hidden, in the sense that the decision maker would receive a partial description of a situation, and then decide what further information was needed to classify it. The task should demand multitasking, in the sense that several classification problems should be presented simultaneously. The Abstract Decision-Making (ADM) task was designed with to meet these goals.

ADM is a computer game in which participants earn points by sorting objects into bins as rapidly as possible. The sorting is done based on object attributes (size, shape, and color). However, the objects are not shown. First the participant is shown a list of the characteristics of objects allowed in each of the bins. Then, when an objects presence is announced, the participant asks questions about object attributes until enough information is accumulated to determine the proper bin. The score reflects the difficulty of the classification and the time it took the participant to make it. As described, this sounds like an exceptionally easy task. What makes the task difficult is the speed with which objects arrive, the brevity of message displays (30 seconds), and the need to ask questions efficiently.

At the end of a sequence of classifications, participants are shown two measures of their performance—the average time it took them to assign an object to the appropriate bin and their point score—totaled over successful assignments. Feedback was provided to enhance motivation and aid in correcting and improving performance (Wickens, 1993). More points were awarded for matches that required knowing more features. Points were deducted for errone-

---

[1] There is a reported 29% attrition rate in ATC training (Sells, Dailey, & Pickrel, 1984) that is comparable to that estimated in public safety dispatch training (25%).

ous assignments commensurate with the number of features that did not match (e.g., a large yellow triangle wedged into a small yellow triangle bin resulted in a point deduction for the size error but not for the two other features). It was possible to earn a negative final score for an ultimately successful match by preceding the correct answer with wrong assignments. The more quickly the participant worked, the more objects were sorted into bins and the higher the final score (for more details, see Joslyn & Hunt, 1998).

LABORATORY STUDIES

To evaluate ADM, we conducted a series of experiments in which we compared the performance of participants (in some cases college students and in others professional dispatchers) on ADM and simulations of jobs thought to require the same abilities (e.g., 911 and ATC). Public safety dispatching was simulated using the DISPATCHER program described next. TRACON[2] (Terminal radar approach control), a commercially available computer game was used to simulate ATC performance. The hypothesis was that if ADM captured the decision-making ability in which we were interested, performance on ADM and the job simulations would be positively correlated.

DISPATCHER Simulation

The DISPATCHER simulation is a C++ computer program designed to simulate the task of a Valley Comm dispatcher. The program was designed for Macintosh computers using the System 7 operating system (Franklin & Hunt, 1993). The display screen for DISPATCHER, which corresponds closely to that used in the dispatch center on which it was modeled, is shown in Fig. 8.1a.

DISPATCHER presents participants with a sequence of emergency incidents and scores their ability to handle them. Each incident appears on the display screen as if it had been transmitted by the call receiver. Participants handle a maximum of 20 incidents over a 15-minute period, at which point the simulation ends and the participant is told his or her score. The score is based largely on the time required to resolve incidents, weighted by priority. The scoring algorithm was based on information provided by public safety supervisors regarding optimal dispatching performance and the severity of various errors. Additional details are available in Joslyn and Hunt (1998).

---

[2]TRACON is licensed software by Robert B. Wesson, Wesson International, Austin Texas.

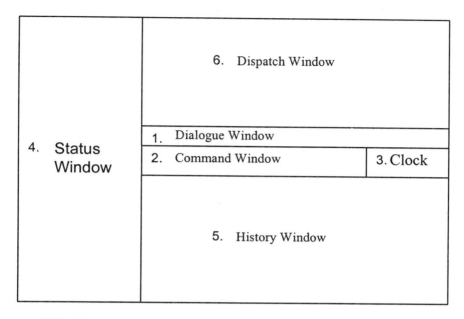

FIG. 8.1a DISPATCHER screen. A complete description of the incident at the top of the waiting list was displayed in the Dispatch Window. Additional information such as the history of incidents or units, license plate information, and criminal records was found in a third section.

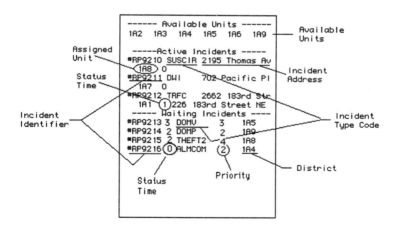

FIG. 8.1b Enlargement of status window of DISPATCHER screen. Incidents on the waiting list were ordered according to when they were reported. This list also indicated priority, location, and the number of minutes incidents had been on the waiting list.

At the beginning of the game, 10 police units are available for dispatching. Incident reports then begin to appear on the screen. The participant's goal is to evaluate the available information, decide which emergency incident to deal with next, and which unit to dispatch. Participants are instructed to attend to high-priority incidents first. When several units are available, the best dispatching strategy was to send the unit closest to the incident. In the more difficult scenarios, the participant will run out of units while still having a sizable list of pending incidents. At this stage, the best strategy is to simply dispatch units to high-priority incidents as soon as a unit is available with less regard for unit location.

The DISPATCHER display screen closely resembles the screen used by Valley Comm dispatchers. Incidents and police units are listed on the display using alphanumeric codes indicating their classification and status. Incidents on the waiting list are ordered according to when they were reported. This list also indicates priority, location, and the number of minutes incidents have been on the waiting list. A more complete description of the incident at the top of the waiting list is displayed in another portion of the screen. Additional information, including incident and unit history, license plate information, and criminal records, was found in a third section (see Fig. 8.1a, History and Dispatch Windows).

Participants received a preliminary training session in which they worked through practice scenarios. Lists of procedures and commands were posted on the wall above the workstation during both training and testing sessions. Because looking up commands took time, it was to participants advantage to remember as many of these as possible.

In addition to dispatching, participants were responsible for maintaining a log of operations and monitoring all dispatched police units. The status of a dispatched officer was to be checked at least once every 5 minutes. Participants also provided information to officers in the field about criminal records and license plate numbers. Real dispatchers receive incoming requests from police units, such as these, over a radio head set. In the simulation, messages from police units appeared in the dialogue window at the center of the screen (Fig. 8.1a, Dialogue Window). The substitution of visual input for radio messages represents the biggest difference between a DISPATCHER simulation screen and the screen of an actual dispatcher. The Dialogue Window was designed to model auditory information input as closely as possible. Each new message was announced by a beep and then appeared at the bottom of the Dialogue Window. Because the window could hold only three messages, an incoming message could write over an old one. Because messages from the field can be important, participants had to monitor this screen carefully. Overwritten messages could be retrieved in a process analogous to asking an officer to repeat a radio transmission, but the procedure was time-consuming and therefore costly.

Emergency Incidents

More than 230 codes are used in dispatching. To save on training time, only 15 were used in DISPATCHER. These codes reflected the incidents most frequently encountered in an analysis of Valley Comms log. Incidents were combined into sequences that were presented over the 15-minute period. Participants trained on relatively simple sequences and were tested on more complex ones. All participants were presented the same order of sequences.

SUMMARY OF RESULTS WITH ADM, DISPATCHER, AND TRACON

The ADM task had reliable and substantial correlations with performance in both job simulations. Table 8.1 shows the results of two experiments involving college students trained on the mini-dispatching task. The statistic shown is the raw correlation without any correction for (or assumption about) such unobservables as restricted variance or unreliability of measures. As can be seen, the correlations vary from .50 to .70 and are reliable in both studies. In other words, the ADM scores reliably predicted both the dispatching and ATC job simulation performance.

We also conducted a study in which professional dispatchers performed on both ADM and the dispatching simulation task. This allowed us to validate the job simulation as well as test the ADM–dispatcher relationship in a different population. The professional dispatchers, without preliminary training, performed the simulation task at a level comparable to that of trained student subjects. In addition, the professional dispatchers commented on the realism of the task. Nevertheless, dispatchers do vary in their performance. This variation was predicted by their ADM scores (r = .61, preliminary test; .49, final test). This result increases the confidence with which we generalize the results based on studies with college students.

DISPATCHER, TRACON, and ADM, are computer games. One could argue that we merely demonstrated that some people are good at playing computer games regardless of the interface involved. Could we predict performance in a situation where the decision making and prioritization take place in the context of person-to-person interaction rather than person-to-compu-ter interaction? To answer this question, we developed a simulation of the call-receiver task that depended on person-to-person, rather than person-to-computer, interaction.

CALL-RECEIVER SIMULATION

In the call-receiver simulation, participants fielded calls from live actors playing scripted roles of RPs. Participants gathered information from the RPs, which

TABLE 8.1
Correlations Between ADM and Job Simulation tasks

VARIABELE	DISPATCHER (Experiment 1)	DISPATCHER (Experiment 2)	ATC
ADM	.70	.68	.50
DISPATCHER (Experiment 1)			.67
DISPATCHER (Experiment 2)			

they entered on a computer screen (Fig. 8.2). The screen closely resembled the screen used by actual call receivers. It is essentially a form that a call receiver filled out while talking to an RP. Once sufficient information was entered, it was forwarded to a dispatcher. There was no actual dispatcher in this simulation.

A HYPERCARD 2.0 (@) program for Macintosh generated the screen and collected information about the participants' performance. The program, which was much simpler than either DISPATCHER or TRACON, kept track of the

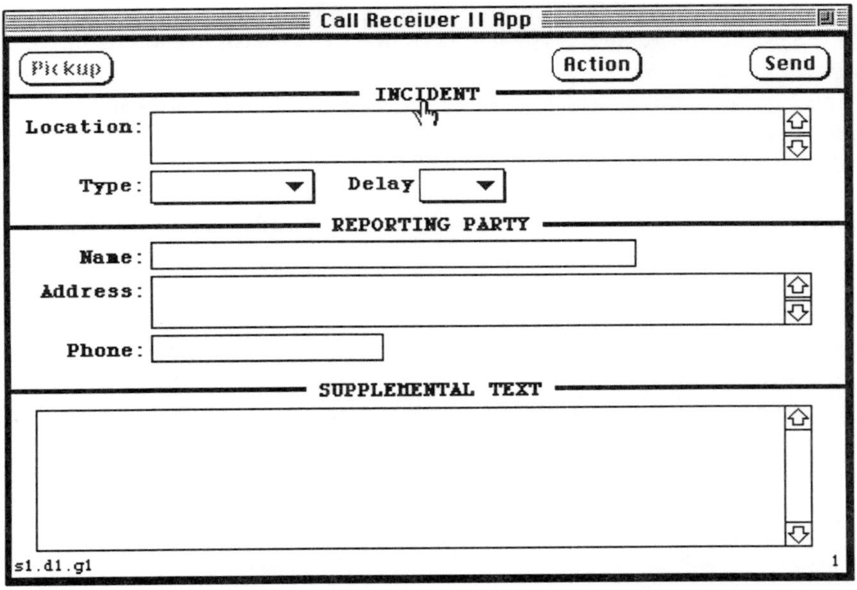

FIG. 8.2   Call receiver screen.

length of time it took each participant to handle an incident. When a call was received, participants clicked a pick-up button on the computer screen and the time was recorded. (As a check, the RP [an actor], at the experimenter's direction, also recorded the time of the call.) When participants wished to transmit a completed description to the dispatcher, they clicked a send button on the screen, again recording the time. The program also recorded the incident code selected by the participant from a pull-down menu. The rest of the information was entered using the Supplemental Text Window.

The major task of the call receiver is to determine what code to assign the incident. As with the prior dispatcher simulation, our training dealt with only a 15 of the 230 possible incident types. However, we took care to retain some codes that were similar to one another because a common mistake made by call receivers is to confuse related codes.

Participants asked the RP a series of questions in an effort to ascertain the proper code for the incident. They were told to work as rapidly as possible, asking for key information in a specified order. The first thing the participant asked the RP was the address of the incident so that, if contact with the RP was lost, the dispatcher could still take action. (To appreciate the need for this outside of the laboratory, recall that the RP may be the target of an assault.) The participant then asked a series of questions to determine the priority of the call and finally questions about other details, such as descriptions of persons or vehicles. These were to be asked in a prescribed order, as they are in actual call receiving.

Generation of Calls From RPs

Three professional actors, two men and a woman, played the role of RPs. Each actor played three different roles, reporting three different emergency incidents. Accordingly, each participant played call receiver for nine different incidents. Actors varied accents, voices, and personalities across incidents. During debriefing, participants said they were unaware that they had heard the same actor more than once.

The incident scenarios were based on actual incidents. Of course, names and locations were changed. The actors initial description of a given incident was always the same. Their subsequent responses were determined in part by what questions the participant asked. However, considerable effort was made to keep these responses uniform across participants. Responses to basic questions were scripted. This ensured that all participants received the same information with regard to the aspects of the event that determined the code: time delay, addresses, names, as well as suspect, weapon, and vehicle descriptions. Actors gave answers to these questions only when queried specifically. Otherwise they gave a vague response or expressed their failure to understand the question.

Because we could not be certain that participants would ask only the appropriate questions, the actors were prepared to make ad lib responses. Before the experiment began, the actors created a coherent background for each character so they could answer any unanticipated questions based on these facts. They made an effort to keep responses to such questions as consistent as possible for each role across participants.

People reporting emergencies are often upset and confused. Moreover, the RPs idea of what information is relevant to the call receiver is not always accurate. The actors emulated such characteristics in their roles. Some characters were extremely excited, gave a lot of irrelevant information, and were difficult for participants to question. Others were confused and slow to respond. These aspects of the role were also held constant across participants. As a result, the actors gave exceptionally realistic performances. In fact, they were so realistic that after pretesting we had to revise our consent form to acknowledge that the task could be emotionally stressful.

Job Score

Two measures of call-receiving performance were taken. *Time* was the total time taken from the point at which the pick-up call button was pressed until the send button was pressed. *Score* was a point system in which participants were given points for the information collected and transmitted.. The score obtained by each participant was then divided by the overall time required to resolve the incident. This constituted a measure of information gathered per unit time. This measure was weighted by the priority of the incident, emphasizing high-priority incidents. As such, this measure reflected the key features of call receiving, accuracy of information, and efficient use of time especially on high-priority incidents (which was stressed to the participants). This incident score was averaged across incidents to assign an overall job score.

Results

The correlation between performance in the call receiver and ADM tasks was .52, $p < .05$. This generalized our studies to prediction of performance in a task that is qualitatively different from the computer-oriented interactions typical of the other two analogue tasks.

GENERAL CONCLUSIONS

Our conclusions can be considered under two rather separate headings: what we learned about the psychology of time-pressured decision making and what we learned about the interplay between cognitive task analyses and laboratory studies.

Conclusions Concerning Psychological Variables

We are confident that there does exist a reliable trait for making decisions under seconds-to-minutes time pressure. Further research is required to relate this trait to other abilities, such as general intelligence, the ability to make decisions without time pressure, or the ability to make rapid perceptual decisions.

Conclusions Concerning the Interplay Between Laboratory and Field Studies

We also believe that our studies represent a useful addition to the current spate of studies on naturalistic cognition. To us, understanding public safety communications was a means of advancing toward a scientific goal, not a goal in itself. (We were, of course, aware of the applied value of our research.) Therefore, we were able to ignore a number of important aspects of the task, which, although important in understanding public safety, were not central to our own goal. For instance, call receivers and dispatchers keep aware of each others activities. One reason for doing this is that two apparently unrelated calls received at about the same time and from roughly the same place may represent the same incident seen from different viewpoints. We witnessed one particularly dramatic incident, in which a dispatcher realized that a minor disturbance call and a medical aid call, taken together, indicated that a serious assault might have taken place. The officer who had responded to the disturbance was instructed to return to the scene and told that he had "probable cause to believe that a crime had been committed," thus allowing him to enter a premise without a warrant. Tragically, on entering, the officer discovered that a child had been killed. We made no attempt to deal with this sort of impromptu communication and reasoning. Similarly, we did not attempt to model any of the social interactions among dispatchers, public safety officers, and management. These are clearly an important part of the job, broadly defined, but they do not directly impact on the narrower aspects of technical performance. These limitations are not limitations on our restricted psychological conclusions. They would have been serious limitations if our intent had been to understand dispatching for its own sake.

Our work has combined features of field studies and laboratory experimentation. We attempted to investigate a complex, ecologically valid decision-making environment and maintain a level of experimental control that would allow us to test a specific hypothesis. Although from the perspective of ecological validity it would have been ideal to use professional dispatchers and actual job performance, such performance would have been far too complex to measure accurately. In addition, it would have been impossible to ensure that each participant was tested in a situation of comparable difficulty. Instead, we used professional dispatchers performance on a realistic simulation task to verify the results of nonprofessional subjects on the same simulation. We do not apologize for these compromises. They permitted us to check our analyses far more rigorously than would otherwise have been possible.

Finally, we are pleased that some of the material that we developed for our experimental work could be and, in some cases, has been used by our participating organizations. Both DISPATCHER and, quite serendipitously, the training materials we used to teach call receivers how to interrogate RPs proved of some interest to communication centers as practical training devices. Of course, we have provided these materials although we do not monitor their use. We believe, quite without proof, that one of the reasons that we received the cooperation that we did was that we were perceived as trying to help the organizations we worked with, not just to study them.

ACKNOWLEDGMENTS

The research reported here was supported by the Office of Naval Research (ONR) under a contract to the University of Washington; Earl Hunt, Principal Investigator. The views expressed here are those of the authors and not of the ONR. We thank Thomas Sanquist (Batelle Corporation), A. Lynn Franklin, and David Smith for their assistance. We also express our particular thanks to the personnel of Valley Comm for their cooperation and suggestions throughout our studies.

REFERENCES

Franklin, A. L., & Hunt, E. (1993). An emergency situation simulator for examining time-pressured decision making. *Behavior Research Methods, Instruments & Computers, 25*(2), 143–147.

Joslyn, S. L., & Hunt, E. (1998). Evaluating individual differences in response to emergency situations. *Journal of Experimental Psychology: Applied, 4*(1), 16–43.

Wickens, C. D. (1993). *Engineering psychology and human performance* (2nd ed.). Columbus, OH: Charles Merrill.

9

A SKILL-BASED COGNITIVE TASK ANALYSIS FRAMEWORK

Thomas L. Seamster
Cognitive & Human Factors

Richard E. Redding
University of Virginia

George L. Kaempf
Sun Microsystems

Jobs are placing greater cognitive demands on workers. In job environments such as aviation, operating rooms, and command and control centers, especially where time-constrained decisions are critical to overall performance, there is a growing demand for cognitive task analysis (CTA) to support the design of job aids and training systems. Within these operational environments, CTA is evolving from research and development projects to applied cognitive analyses integrated with traditional methods such as the Instructional Systems Development (ISD) process (Redding & Seamster, 1994).

Although CTAs have been used in a range of job environments, the number of CTAs is still relatively small when compared with the number of task analyses performed throughout industry. Most CTAs have been designed and conducted by researchers with substantial experience in cognitive science. The limited number of qualified researchers and the high cost of these CTAs have constrained the number of cognitive analyses performed to date. Most analysts experienced with the ISD process would be unable to perform a full CTA. However, given a set of explicit steps, they could conduct a cognitive analysis on a narrow, well-defined problem area.

CTA could be used in operational settings if there were a simplified approach to identifying key job elements that could then be analyzed by a small set of methods. One approach has been proposed by Seamster, Redding, and Kaempf (1997), guided by a skill-based CTA framework, for analyzing the cognitive aspects of performance. The main contribution of this skill-based framework is that it proposes a simplified hierarchy of cognitive skill types linking each type to several established CTA methods. The framework is most useful in well-defined task areas where routine as well as nonnormal tasks have been specified through a job analysis or the ISD process. Recognizing the wide range of cognitive analysis methods, this framework avoids the controversial methods, concentrating on relatively established methods most suited to the efficient analysis of certain cognitive skill types.

SKILL-BASED CTA FRAMEWORK

The skill-based CTA framework is intended to facilitate the evolution of CTA from its current research orientation to a specified set of methods that can be applied by personnel in operational settings. This framework is guided by an operational definition of skill grounded in Ericsson and Lehmann's (1996) concept of expert performance and modified by Proctor and Dutta's (1995) review of skill research. A cognitive skill includes the content, organization, and mental manipulation essential for good or superior performance. A cognitive skill is acquired through task or job practice and therefore can be trained. This framework bypasses the research communities' controversy over what is knowledge and what is skill by concentrating on elements essential to good or superior performance. Although theoretically complex, operationally, the knowledge—skill distinction can and should be simplified. If the task element is more efficiently trained in the context of complete or part-task performance, it is skill. If the element is more efficiently trained as a concept, it is knowledge.

The skill-based CTA framework has three features that help transition cognitive task analysis from the research lab to operational environments. First, its emphasis on skill types helps limit the scope of the CTA and makes the results operationally relevant. This is done by linking each skill type to specific analysis techniques that then link to specific training and assessment techniques (see Seamster, Redding, & Kaempf, 1997). A CTA organized around a hierarchy of skills, supports job aid design and training that is structured and sequenced along a continuum of skill complexity (see Gagné, Briggs, & Wager, 1992).

Second, this framework facilitates CTA analysis within the context of an existing task analysis or task listing. The traditional task analysis based on the ISD process can provide a broad task listing with gaps especially in the cognitive areas. Analysts can use the existing listing as a starting point to locate the tasks, subtasks, or skills that require further analysis. This skill-based framework allows the analyst to probe specific cognitive skills in more depth than can be done using traditional task analysis methods, while maintaining a point of reference to other job tasks, especially those that may require the same or similar skills.

Third, the skill-based framework uses methods that are most practical in operational settings, where time is limited and analysts may have little training in statistics, research methods, or cognitive science. The data collection and analysis methods used in this framework have been selected and modified so they can be readily used in operational environments. By focusing the effort on one or more specific cognitive skills, the skill-based CTA framework can significantly reduce the time required to perform a cognitive analysis. However, the framework does encourage the use of multiple methods to validate results.

The use of two different methods permits a systematic comparison without substantially increasing the cost of the overall CTA.

Skill Types in Cognitive Performance

The skills framework begins with the identification of five skill types covering a substantial range of expert performance, and proposes a small set of efficient methods that can be used to analyze the different skill types. Cognitive performance usually includes some aspects of automaticity, procedural skills, representational skills, decision making, and strategies. Each of these skill types requires different analysis methods, different training approaches, and different assessment methods, as well as different considerations when designing job aids or computerized support systems. For instance, the instructional techniques for training automaticity, with its requirement for a large number of exposures to consistent stimuli, are different from those to train strategies or metacognitive skills.

The skill-based CTA framework assumes that simpler cognitive skills form the basis of more advanced skills. A hierarchy of skill complexity is important to system design and training because complex skills require that sets of simpler skills be established before the more complex skills can be efficiently trained. Motivated by Gagné, Briggs, and Wager's (1992) intellectual skills framework, Seamster, Redding, and Kaempf (1997) identify five cognitive skill types forming a hierarchy list starting with the most complex skill type:

- Strategies
- Decision-Making Skills
- Representational Skills
- Procedural Skills
- Automated Skills

Automated skills, a basic cognitive skill type, produce rapid job performance with a minimum of cognitive processing, thus providing the foundation of skilled performance by contributing to the efficient execution of multiple tasks. Automated skills exhibit rapid and effortless performance, are based on a consistent relationship between the condition and the response, and require substantial practice to train. Automated skills must be trained so that the conditions that activate the skill are recognized and then practiced over a substantial number of trials on consistent components (Myers & Fisk, 1987), with the stimuli mapped to a specific context or response and presented so that consistency is evident.

Procedural skills are the building blocks of skilled performance. They produce constrained sequences of physical and cognitive activities performed in predictable situations, but without requiring a close mapping between the condition and response. Procedural skills are performed rapidly, but do not facilitate the execution of simultaneous tasks because they require some controlled processing and thus are not automated. Procedural skills can only be acquired by doing (Anderson, 1983). This begins with some form of declarative knowledge that is gradually compiled into a preliminary form of the skill and then strengthened for increased speed and performance improvement.

Representational skills are an element of mental models that improve performance by providing an efficient simulation of a key aspect of a system or process. It is hypothesized, based on Newell's (1990) articulation of model representations, that representational skills contribute to superior performance because they are "limited in scope" and relatively "easy to process." These representations reduce the complexity of a system in the context of specific tasks by substituting a complete representation for one that is accurate and simplified to meet the needs of the task or tasks.

Decision-making skills facilitate choosing among alternatives and are learned through experience. As decision makers experience an increasing number of situations, they learn which patterns in the environment provide relevant cues, and they obtain feedback about what does and does not work in each situation. By providing simple steps or rules of thumb that can be used in repeatable contexts, tactics help decision makers decompose and better understand complex environments. Klein and his colleagues describe a model of these recognitional decisions that characterize proficient performance in naturalistic settings (see Kaempf, Klein, Thordsen, & Wolf, 1996).

Strategies or metacognitive skills enhance performance by providing the self-monitoring and integration of other skills. Strategies are the most complex and generally the last skill type to be fully developed in the skill hierarchy. With automated skills as the foundation, and procedural skills as the building blocks of skilled performance, strategies can be thought of as the coordination or management of other skill types. Because of the key role that strategies play in proficient performance, their analysis is essential for identifying critical requirements for training and systems design.

CTA Methods by Skill Types

Each of the cognitive skill types has unique analysis requirements and methods (see Seamster, Redding, & Kaempf, 1997, for a detailed description). The following briefly describes methods for efficiently analyzing the components of each cognitive skill type.

Automated Skills. The analysis of automated skills involves a comparison between expert and novice performance because this skill type is often difficult to detect when observing only expert performance. Because automated skills are rapid and require minimal or no conscious attention, they are difficult to detect in observing expert performance alone and are difficult for experts to verbalize and explain. Automated skills are often easier to detect by their absence in novice performance, where actions are slower and more effortful, as compared with expert performance. Automated skills can be analyzed by the Consistent Component and Verbal Report Methods.

The Consistent Component Method identifies the consistent task elements that allow for the training of automated skills. Although originally presented as a set of guidelines (see Fisk & Eggemeier, 1988), consistent component analysis has been refined into a CTA methodology with steps that have been developed and tested on aviation jobs (see Seamster, Redding, & Kaempf, 1997). This CTA method, generally used as an intermediate or final form of analysis in the identification of automated skill components, includes six steps. Steps 1 and 2 decompose tasks or subtasks into their main elements and identify the high-level skills for each element. In Steps 3 and 4, analysts work with novices and experts to identify decision points for each element. An analysis of the differences in their decision points can identify possible automated skills. If novices make a decision at a given point and experts do not, it can indicate that the experts have automated that component. Finally, Steps 5 and 6 examine task components where novices have difficulty under higher workload and identify the consistent information or context for each automated skill.

The Verbal Report Method is based on the collection of a running commentary of the subject-matter expert's (SME's) task performance, which is recorded for later analysis. Verbal reports can either be concurrent or retrospective (collected shortly after the task has been performed). Although concurrent verbal reports provide more accurate data from working memory, they are not appropriate for tasks that have substantial communication, working memory, or auditory requirements. In such cases, retrospective verbal reports may be collected after task performance using a replay of the performance to stimulate memory. When verbal reports are used to identify consistent decision components, only elements relating to the decision must be simulated. The verbal report method is used to probe for key decisions relating to particular subtasks. Data collection requires planning the task simulation and developing the probes that elicit the verbal reports. The verbal report method is also recommended when the consistent component analysis has identified a number of novice decision points, but has failed to identify the content of those decisions.

Procedural Skills. Procedural skills can be analyzed by the Simplified PARI Method in addition to the Verbal Report Method. The PARI (Precursor, Action, Result, Interpretation) Method is based on a structured interview process designed to elicit a finer level of skill detail than afforded by traditional task analysis. The full PARI methodology includes nine stages (Hall, Gott, & Pokorny, 1995). The Simplified PARI Method, tailored to operational environments (see Seamster, Redding, & Kaempf, 1997), includes only three steps. At least one SME should be identified as the problem designer and presenter, and a second SME should be the problem solver. The problem designer participates in all three steps of the method, whereas the problem solver only participates in the third step. In the first step, the problem designer provides a complete problem or scenario description to include the subtasks, a problem statement that describes all the initial conditions, and all required problem—solution working aids such as documentation. In the second step, the PARI interview is conducted by the analyst, with the problem designer SME solving the problem. In the final step, the PARI interview is conducted by having the problem designer working with the problem solver. The analysis decomposes the data into actions that provide the elements in the procedure, along with the precursor and interpretation data, which provide the cognitive context.

Representational Skills. Representational skills are elements of mental models used to predict or anticipate required actions, and can be analyzed using the Diagramming and Rating/Sorting Methods. The Diagramming Method has an SME diagram a particular visual/dynamic representation associated with the context of the task. For example, Lesgold, Rubinson, Feltovich, Glaser, Klopfer, and Wang (1988) asked expert radiologists to diagram on X-ray film all the structures they could see in the diagnostically significant area. First, the SME is given a set of instructions and a diagramming form to help structure the resulting diagram. Second, the SME is given some practice and feedback in problem solving and diagramming. Third, the SME is presented with a short written problem statement describing the general conditions and actual symptoms of the problem. Fourth, the SME is asked to solve the problem while thinking aloud and then to write numbers on the form, indicating the position of the elements and the order in which they were attended. Finally, the SME labels each of the numbers with a name for the element, drawing an arrow from one element to the next to verify both their identity and order of the elements.

The Rating/Sorting Method can be used to determine the mental relationship between items in a system, the organization of specific functions, or the grouping of steps in a process. It is based on an SME's estimate of the degree of relatedness between two concepts or other job-related elements. Primary considerations are the specification of how the SMEs are to simulate task performance and the development of instructions on how to conduct the ratings. The three steps in data collection start with the SME simulating or performing the task related to the items being rated. Then the SME is instructed on the rating procedure and is given some practice sessions. Finally, the SME is asked to rate all, or just the key pairs of items. The ratings are then placed in proximity matrixes that can be analyzed by different scaling methods.

Decision-Making Skills. Decision-making skills can be analyzed through the Critical Decision, Error Analysis, and Verbal Report Methods. The Critical Decision Method (CDM) is a semistructured interview technique (Klein, Calderwood, & MacGregor, 1989) developed to elicit information about decisions made by experts in dynamic field settings. Focused probes help experts describe aspects of their task performance normally only tacitly understood. The CDM concentrates on critical incidents experienced by domain experts, applying a set of probes to elicit the expert's perceptual discriminations, pattern recognition, expectancies, and cues. In a way, the CDM interview is a storytelling technique guided by the interviewer. The interviewer uses the incident as a framework to probe decisions, judgments, and problem solving and may need to ask numerous questions to extract information sufficient to define all the cues used to make a decision.

The Error Analysis Method is the systematic analysis of operational or performance error data, as collected through observation, accident records, self-report, or simulator performance measures. Although error analysis has been used for years in traditional task analysis, a CTA-based error analysis focuses on the underlying cognitive processes linked to particular error types. This method provides data about decision making, particularly in critical situations, that would not be gained through the study of routine performance. Error analysis is particularly useful for developing judgment or critical incident decision-making training (see Redding, 1992) and identifying trouble spots in human–machine interfaces (Norman, 1984). For example, Redding (1992) conducted a content analysis on the incident reports made by air traffic controllers and classified each report according to the underlying cognitive operation contributing to the incident.

Strategies. A strategy may be thought of as a plan that directs complex job performance (Gott, 1990), including the regulatory or self-monitoring aspects often critical in complex, time-constrained environments. Strategies can be analyzed through the Team Communication, Structured Interview, Verbal Report, and Error Analysis Methods.

The Team Communication Method involves the analysis of communication among team members during their performance on a real or simulation scenario. The analyst must identify the measures of team processes and outcomes that are captured during the analysis. The stream of communication is decomposed into discrete, meaningful units based on a predetermined coding scheme depending on the goals of the analysis (see Seamster, Cannon, Pierce, & Redding, 1992). Inferences can be made about performance strategies based on frequencies and patterns that correlate with team performance. For example, Seamster, Cannon, Pierce, and Redding (1992) recorded the performance of air traffic controller teams working different types of simulator scenarios and transcribed their communications from each session. These transcripts were decomposed into their relevant speech turns, with each speech turn coded into 1 of 15 categories. Frequencies for each speech turn were computed and analyzed by comparing differences among team member positions, type of problem, and level of performance.

The Structured Interview Method elicits information about high-level strategies. Structured interviews (see Kirwan & Ainsworth, 1992) can be used to analyze declarative knowledge, procedural skills, or strategies. In this framework, the structured interview method is used primarily to analyze advanced strategies—the metacognitive skills that direct expert performance. Interviews must be carefully planned and designed to obtain useful data that go beyond what is already known about the lower level skills (such as procedural skills) from the front-end analysis of job manuals and documents, and it is useful to interview a variety of SMEs. A series of questions are designed to elicit increasingly specific information about specific job tasks or problem situations. In many cases, SMEs read case vignettes or recall past performance and then answer questions designed to elicit information about their strategies. The questions selected are often based on a particular cognitive theory of expertise or are designed to provide answers suitable for the format selected for representing the results.

APPLICATION OF THE FRAMEWORK

This section illustrates how simple CTA methods can be applied to have sometimes dramatic impacts on systems design in high-technology domains. The Rating Method was used to define users' skilled representations of their work environment. This produced a significant impact on the design of a commonly used software tool—an interactive voice response (IVR) system used by the human resources department of a large company.

Problem. How people conceptually organize their work is an important component of interface design. For an IVR system to work effectively, it must categorize the information and options in a way meaningful to callers. Information is most readily accessed when grouped into meaningful categories, thus designers must develop a structure that reflects users' cognitive organization of the domain. This is where the company's IVR system failed. Soon after implementing the system, the company received a large number of complaints about problems experienced by employees using the IVR system. Of the complaints received, 47% indicated that the employee had entered the system with a well-specified objective but had not been able to discover the means to act on that objective. Another 28% of the complaints indicated that the employee found the desired segment of the IVR system but was unable to achieve the desired result. How did smart designers create such a problem? The designers focused on what the human resource department wanted to accomplish with this system rather than on how the average employee would use the system.

This study took the first step toward identifying specific representational skills of a variety of company employees. The objective was to describe how employees represented the quality and strength of relationships among the various options in the IVR system. System designers could then develop menu structures and navigational paths through the IVR system that were more consistent with how the system's users represent their human resource needs.

Data Collection. The Sorting Method was used to identify employees' representations of the human resources information contained in the IVR system. Two hundred and twenty-six items were extracted from the IVR scripts (e.g., "For education and training press two"). Each term was printed on an index card and presented to 20 company employees, who were instructed to "sort the cards into groups of terms that you believe belong together." When finished, the employees labeled each stack with a term that they believed best described the category. The card sort took an average of 20 minutes for each employee. Analysts scored the sort, demanding an 80% agreement level between employees, before concluding that two terms were associated with one another.

Results. The original IVR system provided access to all of the system's information through five major categories :
- Time management
- Benefits
- Enterprise self-service
- Absence management
- More options

The card sort scoring identified a hierarchical structuring of related terms. Although the entire structure is beyond the scope of this chapter, the sort identified 10 key categories having at least six associated terms, accounting for 144 of the terms presented in the sort:
- Time management
- Benefits
- Group Life Insurance
- Employee and Health Assistance Programs
- Employee Stock Ownership Plan
- Savings
- Wage Garnishments and IRS termsHealth promotion
- Fitworks
- Lifeworks

Furthermore, the sort recognized multilevel dependencies among groups. For example, Group Life Insurance and Employee and Health Assistance Programs were associated with Benefits. These findings were consistent with the organization of the existing IVR, but the consistencies ended there. A number of terms linked together in the card sort crossed categories in the previous IVR hierarchy. There were 82 terms in the card sort that showed no strong association with the 10 categories or with each other. Curiously, these included two major categories in the original IVR structure: Enterprise Self-Service and Absence Management. Employees clearly had little concept of what types of information might be accessed through these major categories.

The findings resulted in several recommendations. The first was to revise the terms used in the IVR structure so they were more meaningful to the average employee. The second recommendation was to conduct a second card sort using the revised terms and with a broader representation of employees. The third recommendation was to revise the IVR structure to reflect the hierarchy generated by the card sort. The final recommendation was to conduct iterative user testing of the structure and its implementation. These recommendations led to a second version of the IVR system that was much easier to use, resulting in far fewer complaints and enhanced user success. This example demonstrates the ease with which CTA methods can be applied in a work setting to identify representational skills: how employees structure their work and work environment. This relatively simple effort, conducted in a matter of several weeks, had a dramatic impact on the effectiveness of a costly and important piece of software.

DISCUSSION

CTA helps understand and better prepare for the changing nature of work resulting from system automation and the increasingly cognitive nature of many job tasks. Like other approaches to CTA, the skill-based framework can be used to support training design, systems design, and human resource management. The skill-based framework provides a more efficient and focused approach to encourage cognitive analyses in operational settings.

CTA evolved into a powerful methodology providing detailed understanding of complex and critical elements of human performance. However, until recently, the practice of CTA has been limited to the research community. CTA has been too expensive, difficult, and time-consuming to be used by those in operational environments—exactly the people who require efficient ways to analyze targeted areas of cognitive performance.

The skill-based framework summarized here distills a set of efficient CTA methods that can be readily applied in operational settings. These methods meet several criteria. First, they provide an effective means to address specific skill types. Second, they can be implemented within the time constraints of operational environments. Most operations do not have the time to perform a complete, extended CTA. Finally, these skill-based methods are relatively simple to perform. Most industrial staffs, whether for training or software development, do not have the experience required to perform the full range of CTA methods used by researchers. Yet cognitive skills are a critical component of success in the workplace and must be analyzed by training developers and system designers without extensive experience in cognitive science.

The success of this skill-based CTA framework depends on additional efforts from the research community. Further development of valid tests for assessing cognitive skills is needed, such as cognitive diagnostic tests that authentically capture cognitive performance skills (see Nichols, Chipman, & Brennan, 1995). The skill-based framework can both benefit from, and contribute to, the development of authentic cognitive assessment because of its emphasis on the performance of particular job tasks and skills. For example, Seamster, Redding, and Broach (1996) used the Structured Interview and Verbal Report Methods to identify the four key procedural and automated skills characteristic of good performers on an air traffic control selection test. The skills approach links performance data to specific cognitive skills so that problems in particular performance areas indicate a direct link to specific skills requiring additional or modified training.

The skill-based framework described in this chapter provides a useful guide for industrial analysts along with a set of relatively simple methods that can be used to improve product design and training systems. Furthermore, this framework organizes cognitive skills in a way that is consistent with more traditional methods that address motor and perceptual skills. This ensures that the results from a skill-based CTA can be more easily integrated into operational design and development efforts.

REFERENCES

Anderson, J. R. (1983). *The architecture of cognition.* Cambridge, MA: Harvard University Press.

Ericsson, K. A., & Lehmann, A. C. (1996). Expert and exceptional performance: Evidence of maximal adaptation to task constraints. *Annual Review of Psychology, 47,* 273–305.

Fisk, A. D., & Eggemeier, F. T. (1988). Application of automatic/-controlled processing theory to training tactical command and control skills: 1. Background and task analytic methodology. In *Proceedings of the Human Factors Society 32nd annual meeting* (pp. 1227–1231). Santa Monica, CA: Human Factors Society.

Gagné, R. M., Briggs, L. J., & Wager, W. W. (1992). *Principles of instructional design* (4th ed.). New York: Harcourt Brace Jovanovich.

Gott, S. P. (1990). The assisted learning of strategic skills. In N. Frederiksen, R. Glaser, A. Lesgold, & M. G. Shafto (Eds.), *Diagnostic monitoring of skill and knowledge acquisition* (pp. 173–189). Hillsdale, NJ: Lawrence Erlbaum Associates.

Hall, E. M., Gott, S. P., & Pokorny, R. A. (1995). *A procedural guide to cognitive task analysis: The PARI methodology* (AL/HR-TR-1995-0108). Brooks Air Force Base, TX: Air Force Materiel Command.

Kaempf, G., Klein, G., Thordsen, M., & Wolf, S. (1996). Decision making in complex naval command and control environments. *Human Factors, 38,* 220–231.

Kirwan, B., & Ainsworth, L. K. (Eds.). (1992). *A guide to task analysis.* London: Taylor & Francis.

Klein, G. A., Calderwood, R., & MacGregor, D. (1989). Critical decision method for eliciting knowledge. Special issue: Perspectives in knowledge engineering. *IEEE Transactions on Systems, Man, and Cybernetics, 19*, 462–472.

Lesgold, A., Rubinson, H., Feltovich, P., Glaser, R., Klopfer, D., & Wang, Y. (1988). Expertise in a complex skill: Diagnosing X-ray pictures. In M. T. H. Chi, R. Glaser, & M. J. Farr (Eds.), *The nature of expertise* (pp. 311–342). Hillsdale, NJ: Lawrence Erlbaum Associates.

Myers, G. L., & Fisk, A. D. (1987). Application of automatic and controlled processing theory to industrial training: The value of consistent component training. *Human Factors, 29*, 255–268.

Newell, A. (1990). *Unified theories of cognition.* Cambridge, MA: Harvard University Press.

Nichols, P. D., Chipman, S. F., & Brennan, R. L. (Eds.). (1995). *Cognitively diagnostic assessment.* Hillsdale, NJ: Lawrence Erlbaum Associates.

Norman, D. A. (1984). Stages and levels in human-machine interaction. *International Journal of Man-Machine Studies, 21*, 365–370.

Proctor, R. W., & Dutta, A. (1995). *Skill acquisition and human performance.* Thousand Oaks, CA: Sage.

Redding, R. E. (1992). Analysis of operational errors and workload in air traffic control. *Proceedings of the Human Factors Society 36th annual meeting* (pp. 1265–1269). Santa Monica, CA: Human Factors Society.

Redding, R. E., & Seamster, T. L. (1994). Cognitive task analysis in air traffic control and aviation crew training. In N. Johnston, N. McDonald, & R. Fuller (Eds.), *Aviation psychology in practice* (pp. 190–222). London: Ashgate.

Seamster, T.L., Cannon, J.R., Pierce, R.M., & Redding, R.E. (1992). The analysis of en route air traffic controller team communication and controller resource management (CRM). *Proceedings of the Human Factors Society 36th annual meeting* (pp. 66–70). Santa Monica, CA: Human Factors Society.

Seamster, T. L., Redding, R. E., & Broach, D. L. (1996). Effects of performance strategies on the air traffic control simulation test. *Proceedings of the Human Factors and Ergonomics Society 40th annual meeting* (pp. 1092–1096). Santa Monica, CA: Human Factors and Ergonomics Society.

Seamster, T. L., Redding, R. E., & Kaempf, G. L. (1997). *Applied cognitive task analysis in aviation.* London: Ashgate.

10

TOWARD A THEORY-BASED FORM OF COGNITIVE TASK ANALYSIS OF BROAD SCOPE AND APPLICABILITY

Philip J. Barnard
MRC Cognition and Brain Sciences Unit, Cambridge

Jon May
University of Sheffield

All forms of task analysis rely on the idea that human action can be decomposed and that the decomposition can be used to reason about what people should do and know to complete a task. With simple technologies, the process of developing an analytic focus was readily tractable. The allocation of function among people in a team and between people and technology was straightforward. Tasks were thought of as primarily involving vigilance, perceptual-motor skill, memory, decision making, communications, or some simple combination of these capabilities. Today, the situation is less straightforward. As tasks have become more intricate, knowledge-intensive, and subject to increasingly integrated forms of technological support, traditional forms of task decomposition appear to have an overly restricted scope.

It is unlikely that there will be a universally applicable form of cognitive task analysis (CTA). Indeed, in this volume, the diversity of approaches to the definition of CTA and its conduct at individual and team levels well illustrates the extent of the wider problem. Methods or models developed to deal with specific situations are of undeniable value in that they are used to generate predictions about performance times, human error, or to support other forms of reasoning about how tasks are best carried out by a team in a setting. However, any method is likely to remain of limited utility if its use is restricted to a specific type of task, application domain, or technology. Ideally, the methods and models we develop should generalize from one task context to another and from one generation of technology to the next. They should also be able to address, at least to some level of approximation, the complete web of relationships that bind together the perceptual, motor, cognitive, and emotional facets of human performance. The requirement of being able to generalize implies a role for theoretical principles. The requirement of being able to address all facets of mental life implies a role for an integrated, macrotheory of our mental architecture rather than relying on a collection of microtheories. We follow Newell's (1990) vision that more unified forms of cognitive theory are not only desirable but a tractable research problem. As with the EPIC mental architecture (Kieras et al., chap. 5, this volume), we also assume that practical forms of CTA with enhanced scope can be approached from the standpoint of theoretical constraints on human mental representation and information processing.

THE UNDERLYING COGNITIVE THEORY

Our approach is thus cast within an applied science framework. Evidence from behavior in laboratory and real-world tasks has been used to derive and validate aspects of a body of macrotheory (interacting cognitive subsystems (ICS); see Barnard, 1985, 1999; Barnard & May, 1995; Teasdale & Barnard, 1993). ICS is a multiprocessor architecture with nine subsystems encompassing sensory, central, and effector processing activity (Fig. 10.1). Each subsystem contains processes that transform information from one type of mental representation to another and incorporates a local memory (image record), which represents past inputs. The theory makes three substantive contributions, the details of which are beyond the scope of this chapter. First, it defines how information flows between the subsystems. Second, it defines the form and content of the different types of mental representation handled by each subsystem (Table 10.1). Third, it specifies principles governing: (a) the transformation of inputs to a given subsystem into a form that can be used by another subsystem, (b) the storage of information in memory and its re-use, (c) the hierarchical and temporal structure of mental representations, and (d) the acquisition of new knowledge and processing potential.

Fig. 10.2 illustrates the extensive range of mental processing activity that occurs when people engage in conversation. In the visual subsystem, they see the other people while attending to one face at the level of Object representation. Simultaneously, speech is processed through various levels of interpretation. The black flow in Fig. 10.2 highlights the relevant configuration of activity. Successive transformations of information go from Acoustic (speech sounds), through Morphonolexical (words and syntax) and Propositional (meaning) representations, until an overall, abstract schematic model of discourse content and setting is constructed at the level of Implicational representation. Whereas Propositional representation is purely cognitive and cold, Implicational representation is cognitive affective (see Table 10.1) and is the level at which an emotion would be experienced, such as an apprehensive reaction to what had been said (Teasdale & Barnard, 1993).

Processes within the architecture operate concurrently. Information concerning facial expression and tone of voice maps directly from the sensory subsystems to the Implicational subsystem from where it can influence the propositional meaning of the words actually heard. Similarly, bodily sensations such as

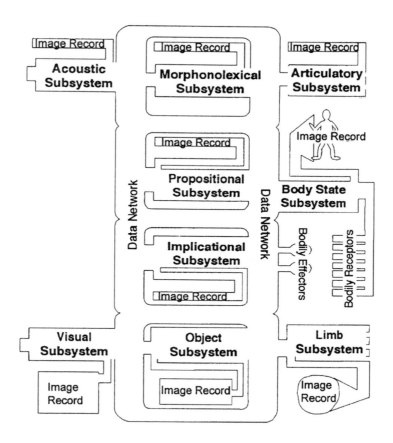

FIG. 10.1   The interacting cognitive subsystems architecture in outline.
Copyright, 1999, reprinted by permission of Cambridge University Press,
Cambridge, UK.

alertness, exhaustion, or hunger can be fed into the implicational synthesis via
feedback from the Body State subsystem. When required to alter posture or control the production of overt speech, flows to the Articulatory and Limb subsystems can be initiated from the central subsystems.

The flows shown in Fig.10.2 are not restricted to verbal exchanges. The
same configurations are applied when modeling use of multimodal computer
interfaces. Multimodal effects occur when information from different sources
arrive at the same subsystem and undergo integration. In the conversation example, information derived from speech content was integrated, at an Implicational

TABLE 10.1
Types of Information Handled by Each Subsystem Within The Architecture

Subsystem Description

Peripheral
Sensory
    Acoustic (AC): Sound frequency (pitch), timber, intensity etc.
Subjectively, what we hear in the world.
    Visual (VIS): Light wavelength (hue), brightness over visual space, etc.
Subjectively, what we see in the world as patterns of shapes and colors.
    Body State (BS): Type of stimulation (e.g., cutaneous pressure, temperature, olfactory, muscle tension), its location, intensity, etc.
Subjectively, bodily sensations of pressure, pain, positions of parts of the body, as well as tastes and smells, etc.
Effector
    Articulatory (ART): Force, target positions, and timing of articulatory musculatures (e.g., place of articulation).
Subjectively, our experience of subvocal speech output.
    Limb (LIM): Force, target positions, and timing of skeletal musculatures.
Subjectively, mental physical movement.
 	
Central
Structural
    Morphonolexical (MPL): An abstract structural description of entities and relationships in sound space. Dominated by speech forms, where it conveys a surface structure description of the identity of words, their status, order, and the form of boundaries between them.
Subjectively, what we hear in the head, our mental voice.
    Object (OBJ): An abstract structural description of entities and relationships in visual space, conveying the attributes and identity of structurally integrated vidual objects, their relative positions, and dynamic characteristics.
Subjectively, our visual imagery.
Meaning
    Propositional (PROP): A description of entities and relationships in semantic space conveying the attributes and identities of underlying referents and the nature of relationships among them.
Subjectively, specific semantic relationships (knowing that).
    Implicational (IMPLIC): An abstract description of human existential space, abstracted over both sensory and propositional input, and conveying ideational and affective content: schematic models of experience.
Subjectively, senses of knowing (e.g., familiarity or causal relatedness of ideas), or of affect (e.g., apprehension, desire).

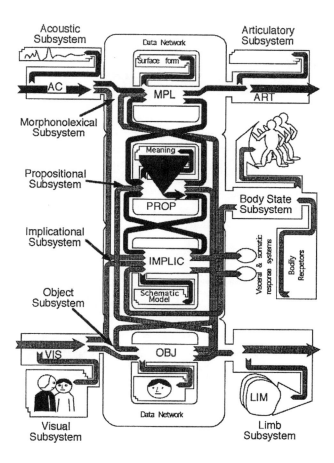

FIG. 10.2 The interacting Cognitive subsystems architecture illustrating data flow interactions.

level of understanding, with information derived from facial expression, tone of voice, and bodily feelings. A generic sense of presence in virtual reality systems would be synthesized and experienced at this same Implicational level as a result of exactly the same flow patterns. In contrast, speech level integration occurs at the Morphonolexical subsystem. When the soundtrack of a film goes out of synchrony, we effectively hear one data stream and see another because data flows arriving at the Morphonolexical subsystem from acoustic sources are not appropriately timed for integration with visually derived information about the associated lip movements. A theoretical treatment of all levels of perceptual and conceptual integration within ICS is provided elsewhere (Barnard & May, 1995).

A key simplifying assumption is that all subsystems share a common internal structure and processing principles; representations introduced in Table 10.1 can all be analyzed using common principles. All representations are assigned a three-level characterization organized around their basic units. The basic units are formed out of constituent elements and are organized into a superordinate structure that captures the interrelationships among them. For example, a sentence is made up of basic units in the form of word parts. These can be decomposed into their phonological constituents. The basic units are also part of the phrases and clauses that make up the superordinate structure of the complete utterance. Similarly, visual objects or sounds can both be decomposed into their constituent parts and have structural relationships to other basic units within a wider visual or auditory scene.

The flow of information among subsystems is connected to the way in which representations are formed at each level. When auditory speech sounds are transformed into Morphonolexical code, detailed information in the speech signal is discarded and a new, more abstract structure is created (Fig. 10.3). The

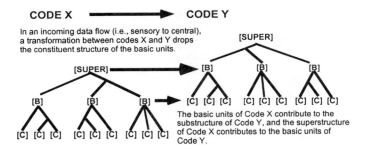

FIG. 10.3   The representational shift accomplished in input transformations.

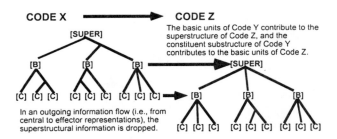

FIG. 10.4   The representational shift accomplished in output transformations.

constituent elements of the source information are discarded, and the basic units created within that code become constituent elements of the output representation. The added value of the transformation is the new superordinate structure that is created to capture interdependencies among these new units.

The opposite applies in transformations that generate representations for output (Fig. 10 4). The superordinate structure of the source representation is discarded and its basic units provide the superordinate structuring for the next level of representation. The added value of the transformation is to provide the new constituents of the next type of representation in the sequence. In language production, the Articulatory subsystem transforms its input to elaborate the specification of motor commands for the speech musculature.

Although easiest to understand for sensory and effector representations, the same principles hold for exchanges among the four central subsystems. An output from one subsystem contributes to the representation of information being constructed in another. Information received during early learning acts to constrain the coding space developed at the receiving subsystem. Propositional coding is determined by three inputs. From the products of Morphonolexical processing, it is constrained by relationships expressed in language; from the products of Object processing, it is constrained by visuospatial relationships; and from the Implicational subsystem, it is constrained by influences on interpretation embodied in abstract schematic models. The information we are capable of encoding at the various levels is partly determined by genetic endowment, as with the capability of our sensory receptors, and partly by our experience, as with the acquisition of the phonology of a particular language.

The organization of information into basic units, their constituent elements, and their superordinate structuring captures the form and content of mental representations. However, representations of this type do not suddenly appear as complete entities—they are constructed over time. When telling a story, we may introduce a topic and say something more detailed about it, then focus on one of the details and say a little more about that. Similarly, when scanning a visual scene, we may look for one object within a scene, zoom in, pay attention to its detail, and then move on to something else in the scene. These thematic transitions are also captured within the framework.

The left-hand diagram in Fig. 10.5 depicts an office. This scene can be decomposed hierarchically into the walls, ceiling and floor components, and so on. The right-hand diagram shows the decomposition of the desktop area. In real time, our visual attention can be directed around this scene. In scanning the desktop, an observer might look at the central pad, then the stack of paper to its left, and then look at one of the books to its right.

By generalizing from systemic grammar (Halliday, 1970), all mental representations within ICS are regarded as having a psychological subject and predicate. The subject of a representation is what the representation is about, whereas the predicate specifies the relationships of other basic units either to the sub-

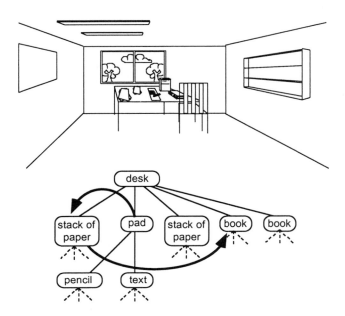

FIG. 10.5   Illustrative thematic transitions for mentally moving the focus of attention within a scene.

ject itself or among entities within the predicate. If we are looking at a specific object in a visual scene, that will typically be the current psychological subject of processing activity within the Object subsystem. Other objects mentally represented within the scene are represented in the relevant predicate, as will the spatial relationships they bear to the subject. As attention moves around the scene, these relationship dynamically reconfigure. Fig. 10.6 notates a series of thematic transitions as attention moves around the office scene. The basic unit equated with the current psychological subject is shown surrounded by the bold black border—the pad. The predicate incorporates those basic units surrounding it on the desk top—the stack of papers and books. The component shown on the leftmost end of the row represents the entity within the hierarchy that is superordinate to the current psychological subject, whereas the components in the rightmost box represent those items in the hierarchy that are constituents of the current psychological subject.

Successive rows in Fig. 10.6 capture processing over time in Transition Path Diagrams (TPDs). In the first transition, attention moves up a level from the pad to its superordinate (desk); attention then shifts to the window, a transition at an equivalent level in the hierarchy; then to a constituent of the window segment (tree). Within each row, the representation of the current subject—predicate spe-

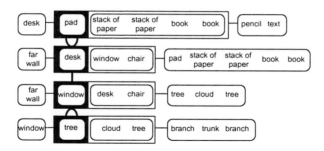

FIG. 10.6   Successive transitions in the focus (psychological subject) of visual attention within a scene.

cification adjusts to capture the current state of the various interrelationships. The successive rows capture a history of processing at the Object level and also the immediate potential for deriving and constructing Propositional meaning from the scene at each stage (e.g., the semantic relationship "the desk is under the window").

The theory of information flow is thus coupled directly to the hierarchical structure of mental representations and their thematic processing over time. Many of the principles are generic and can be applied to any level of mental representation. What differs is how the principles are bound to the properties of different mental codes. Because the analysis is based on the general properties of mental activity, it can be applied across tasks, domains of knowledge, and technologies.

The theory-based analyses of information flow,—of hierarchical decomposition of mental representations and their thematic processing over time,— provide the essential foundation and several explicit methods for supporting CTA and cognitive engineering. Two of these methods have considerable technical detail. In one, the principles of flow and representation are encapsulated in a AI production system. This production system generates cognitive task models that describe the properties of mental activity that might occur during goal formation, action specification, and action execution; it then uses these models to generate behavioral predictions or design advice (Barnard & May, 1999). In a second methodology, called syndetic[1] modeling the operation of the ICS architecture is represented axiomatically in formal logic. The operation of some technological artifact is also represented axiomatically. A third set of syndetic axioms represents the theory of their interaction. This

---

[1]This comes from the Greek term syndesis, meaning to combine

method allows a software designer or task analyst to represent their assumptions about users, systems, and their interaction in abstract terms, but with sufficient precision to support a mathematical proof that the behavior of the envisaged combination of users and technologies should exhibit desirable (or undesirable) properties (Duke, Barnard, Duce, & May, 1998). In the remainder of this chapter, we illustrate a third, more informal method for CTA based on ICS. This involves a tutorial package to guide the use of hierarchical and thematic notations for analyzing how mental activity across subsystems constrains human performance.

THREE ILLUSTRATIONS OF ICS-BASED COGNITIVE TASK ANALYSES

The tutorial package includes a set of software animations. These illustrate the dynamic functioning of the ICS architecture, introduce the principles of flow and mental representation, and exemplify them across a range of task contexts (AnimICS v7.2). An accompanying manual describes how to construct structure diagrams and TPDs for different types of mental representation and how to reason theoretically about tasks and technology design (May, Scott, & Barnard, 1995). By constructing TPDs for different levels of mental representation, the methodology can identify attributes of task-relevant representations or patterns of information integration that may either facilitate or inhibit effective performance of that task. With a basic understanding of the theory, such analyses can support design decision making and provide substantive pointers about how to improve task performance (May & Barnard, 1995).

Our first illustration is derived from an experiment on the learning of an e-mail system (Barnard, MacLean, & Hammond, 1984). Users were asked to learn two sequences of eight commands, one each for incoming mail and outgoing mail, but the conceptual structures of the sequences were manipulated. In one structure, subjects were required to establish four parameters such as addresses, times, and cost and then perform four specific actions that required these parameters. In the alternative structure, the sequence was organized into four pairs of operations, within each of which users established a parameter, like an address, and then used it immediately to carry out an action, such as dispatch. The data show that users took less time and were less likely to access the help system with the four pairs of operations than with the two groups of four operations. Somewhat paradoxically, users were more likely to confuse semantically related commands like display and show when using the paired structure that otherwise produced more effective performance.

It is assumed that this type of task is typically represented at the Propositional level. Hierarchical descriptions are shown in Fig. 10.7 for the two versions of the task. For the paired structure (lower diagram), the parameter must be established immediately before an action can be performed. Given this constraint,

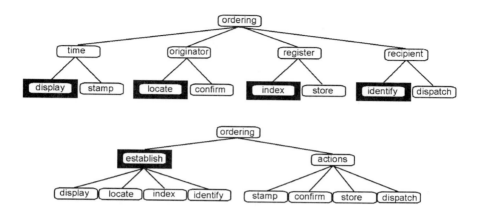

FIG. 10.7   Structure diagrams for two interfaces with identical task steps but different structures. Reprinted from Barnard & May, 1999.

users are unlikely to get the order of operations within a pair wrong. Given primacy and recency effects, they are also likely to remember the first pair and the last pair. Therefore, the potential ambiguity of ordering the basic units is low—they might perhaps transpose the two central pairs. The superordinate conceptual structure relates domain-specific concepts like time and recipient to the basic units. Thus, there is a strong semantic relationship between the superordinate nodes and the basic units. The situation is different with the grouped structure (upper diagram). Here there are no pragmatic constraints on the order in which parameters should be obtained nor the order in which actions should be carried out. There is thus a higher ambiguity of ordering with the grouped structure. The superordinate nodes within this hierarchy also bear a more abstract semantic relationship to the basic units than those within the paired structure because they merely specify establishing parameters or carrying out actions.

In task performance, the mental mechanism has to transform the propositional level of task representation into a structure of lexical commands in a particular order. With the paired structure, the cognitive task model would incorporate attributes characterizing the task as having a low level of order ambiguity and a helpful superordinate description for accessing the referential identity of the basic command operations. In contrast, the grouped structure has high-order ambiguity and poor superordinate nodes for accessing the referential identities of the individual operations. The resolution of order and item uncertainty requires more processing transactions among subsystems, increasing complexity in the dynamic control of cognitive activity. When attributes associated with uncertainty are high, as with the grouped structure, it implies that the propositional representation of the task is problematic and people may access other

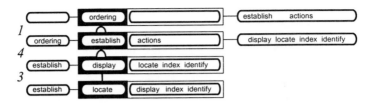

FIG. 10.8   A transition path diagram for the two sets of four structure, showing the temporal sequence of the focus of processing for the first two operations. Reprinted from Barnard & May, 1999.

representations, like the surface form of the command words preserved within the image record of the Morphonolexical subsystem. This accounts for the higher incidence of semantic confusion errors with the paired structure. Items that are otherwise semantically confusable can be distinguished on the basis of their phonological identities.

The TPD shows how the detailed argument can be developed (Fig. 10.8). It shows the transitions as a user correctly carries out the start of the two groups of four task structure. The psychological subject is in the highlighted box, and the predicate units are shown immediately to its right. To its left is the superordinate that the subject and predicate belong to, and to the far right is the constituent decomposition of the subject component. Each row of the TPD details all of the elements that could potentially become the subject on the next row. The user starts with the overall ordering task as the psychological subject of mental processing and then proceeds down into its constituent structure.

Because the establish element is a pragmatic subject, it becomes the new focus of processing directly. This is reflected by the ambiguity value of 1 for the transition, shown at the left of the figure. The next change is a move into the constituent structure of the establish group to focus on the four individual task steps. At this point, the designer constructing the TPD can note that there is no pragmatic subject, and so there is ambiguity about the transition. Because there are four constituent elements, all equally likely to be chosen, the ambiguity value of this transition is 4. Once this element has been dealt with, there are still three predicate elements to choose among for the next task step, and so the ambiguity of that next step is 3. The complete diagram would continue with each of the four establish actions being represented as the subject of a row, followed by a transition up the structure to their parent element and a transition across to the action element. The four action operations would then have to be processed in the same way as the establish actions, with corresponding ambiguity values.

In Fig. 10.9, the initial section of the TPD for the four pairs option is shown. The first subject is again the ordering task, but its constituent elements are now the four pairs instead of the two groups. The first transition is to one of these; because they have no pragmatic subject, this has an ambiguity value of 4.

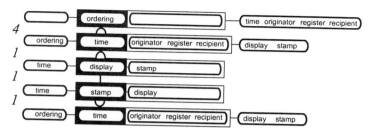

FIG. 10.9   A transition path diagram for the 'four pairs' structure, showing the temporal sequence of the focus of processing for the first two operations. Reprinted from Barnard & May, 1999.

The next step into its constituent structure does have a pragmatic subject because one of its elements is an establish action, whereas the other is the related action operation. Both of these transitions are unambiguous and have the value of 1, as does the fifth transition back up to the pairing element. The next transition to another pair of operations would have a value of 3 and so on.

The overall order uncertainty attribute of these alternative structures is obtained by multiplying the ambiguity values. This delivers a metric of the likelihood that someone would carry out operations in the correct sequence if they had no prior experience of the command sequence and were guided entirely by their pragmatic knowledge. The full TPD for the two groups of four option has

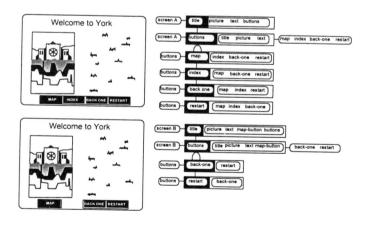

FIG. 10.10   Two versions of a hypertext with different navigation buttons (after Hammond & Allinson, 1988), and the respective TPDs for the selection of the back one button. Reprinted from Barnard & May, 1999.

the values of 4 x 3 x 2 x 4 x 3 x 2 = 576, and four pairs option results in 4 x 3 x 2 = 24. For accurate prediction of learning, these initial estimates need downward correction for primacy and recency effects in memory. In the present context, our point is simply to show how the notation can be used to assist reasoning about cognitive activity and its relationship to human performance.

Many techniques for analyzing the conceptual structure of tasks could perhaps achieve the same outcome, whereas few would generalize directly to a consideration of other aspects of human mentation. Because they are based on a theory of mental representation, the structure diagrams and TPDs can, in principle, be generalized to support CTA of visual, auditory, or multimodal constraints on task performance. However, our two remaining examples are restricted to the analysis of properties of complex visual displays and the role of TPDs topicalized on Object representations.

Fig. 10.10 shows two versions of a hypertext guide to the city of York (Hammond & Allinson, 1988). These versions differ only in the structural decomposition of the menu of navigation options at the base of the display. The uppermost variant includes an option to access an alphabetical Index that is absent in the other design. The respective TPDs suggest that the one of the more frequent operations carried out in hypertext environments, returning to the previous screen (using the back one option in this system), is accomplished differently in the two variants. By including the index button as the second element of a line of options, users are likely to locate the back one button by scanning across the linear menu from left to right. The third line of the uppermost TPD represents the start of scanning pattern, with the Map button as the psychological subject linked to a three component predicate. As the lower TPD shows, without the index option, the back one option can be located more directly as the psychological subject of smaller structure, including the restart option as its only predicate component. The Map button gave access to a graphical overview of the Hypertext, and the designers found that removing the index button had the side effect of reducing people's use of, and knowledge about, the availability of the Map. The TPD for the indexless version suggests why this may have happened: Users are unlikely to attend to this button in their primary navigation tasks of going back one and going home. Therefore, they fail to experience the Map button in the context of navigation. It also suggests how this particular problem may be remedied—by bringing the Map, back one, and restart options into an integrated linear menu.

Our final example of a dynamic screen change is shown in Fig. 10.11. When a user clicks on Baden-Baden in a small-scale map of this region of Germany, the screen changes to show a more detailed, larger scale map of the area. The change in the user's Object representation in this case has been caused externally, by a change in the interface, rather than internally, by a change in their propositional task representation. Therefore, it is essential that the new Object

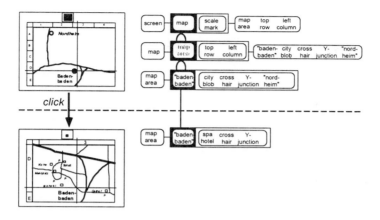

FIG. 10.11   Dynamic changes in an interface result in externally driven changes in an object representation, as shown in the TPD. Reprinted from Barnard & May, 1999.

representation is thematically coherent with the existing propositional task structure. Without such coherence, additional mental activity is required to enable the user to establish how new structures are related to the prior ones. The TPD in Fig. 10.12 shows that the designers have indeed incorporated thematically coherent components. The psychological subject prior to the transition (Baden-Baden) has its constituents elaborated after that transition. Coherence is further supported by the presence of common components in the predicate (cross hairs and the y-junction road lay out).

CONCLUSION

The introductory section of this chapter briefly outlined the case for seeking to develop theory-based CTA of broad scope and applicability. The central sections sought to illustrate how the Interacting Cognitive Subsystems model has been used to work toward this objective by outlining the most informal of three methodologies currently under development. Given the ambitious nature of this project, readers are referred to longer articles on each method for greater justification and detail. Although we have explored the applicability and breadth of the theoretical principles using a significant range of examples, much further work needs to be done to validate and extend the principles and refine the relationships they bear to specific real-world task domains. In the best traditions of human factors, we have also sought to consider our own target users, by conducting empirical studies of the usability of the AI production system model and students learning the techniques from tutorial instruction (e.g., Jørgensen & May, 1997).

To date, the theory and its associated methodologies have only been applied in an academic context. They have not been used independently in commercial settings, although they have contributed to design exercises on a significant scale (e.g., see Bellotti et al, 1996).

We cannot claim that we are soon to attain our objective of having fully validated principles and methods of broad scope and applicability. We do believe that we have demonstrated that the development of a body of macrotheory to support practical forms of CTA is a perfectly tractable and realizable proposition. We believe that practical methods can benefit from the substance of underlying information-processing theory without necessarily requiring intricate specifications of task knowledge (e.g., Johnson & Johnson, 1991). Representations of the abstract properties of that knowledge and the consequences for human information processing can support useful reasoning about practical issues. To that extent, we believe further developments along these lines could well compare favorably, on the one hand, with generic, nontheory-based techniques for task decompositions and, on the other hand, with more traditional forms of cognitive modeling of narrower scope and more substantial requirements for implementation (e.g., Kieras & Polson, 1985; Kieras et al., chapter 15, this volume; Young et al., 1989).

REFERENCES

Barnard, P. J. (1985). Interacting cognitive subsystems: A psycholinguistic approach to short term memory. In A. Ellis (Ed.), *Progress in the psychology of language* (Vol. 2, pp. 197–258) London: Lawrence Erlbaum Associates.

Barnard, P. J. (1999). Interacting cognitive subsystems: Modelling working memory phenomena within a multi-processor architecture. In A. Miyake, & P. Shah (Eds.), *Models of working memory*. (pp. 298–339). Cambridge: Cambridge University Press.

Barnard, P., & May, J. (1995). Interactions with advanced graphical interfaces and the deployment of latent human knowledge. In F. Paterno (Ed.), *The design specification and verification of interactive systems* (pp. 15–49). Berlin: Springer Verlag.

Barnard, P., & May, J. (1999). Representing cognitive activity in complex tasks. *Human-Computer Interaction, 14*, 93–158.

Barnard, P. J., MacLean, A., & Hammond, N. V. (1984). User representations of ordered sequences of command operations. In B. Shackel (Ed.), *Proceedings of Interact '84: First IFIP Conference on Human-Computer Interaction* (Vol. 1, pp. 434–438). London: IEE.

Bellotti, V., Blandford, A., Duke, D., MacLean, A., May, J., & Nigay, L. (1996). Controlling accessibility in computer mediated communications: A systematic analysis of the design space. *Human Computer Interaction, 11*, 357–432.

Duke, D. J., Barnard, P. J., Duce, D. A., & May, J. (1999). Syndetic modelling. *Human Computer Interaction, 13*, 337–393.

Halliday, M. A. K. (1970). Language structure and language function. In J. Lyons (Ed.), *New horizons in linguistics*. (pp. 140–165). Middlesex, England: Penguin.

Hammond, N., & Allinson, L. (1988). Travels around a learning support environment. In E. Soloway, D. Frye & S. B. Sheppard (Eds.), *Proceedings of CHI '88* (pp. 269–273). New York: ACM.

Johnson, P., & Johnson H. (1991). Knowledge analysis of tasks: Task analysis and specification for human-computer systems. In A. Downton (Ed.), *Engineering the human-computer interface* (pp. 119–144). London: McGraw Hill.

Jørgensen, A. H., & May, J. (1997) Evaluation of a theory-based display guide. Proc. HCI'97: San Francisco, Aug. 24-29, 1997. In: Smith, M. J., Salvendy, G., & Koubek, R.J. (Eds.). *Advances in human factors/ergonomics: Vol. 21B. Design of computing systems: Social and ergonomic considerations*. Amsterdam: Elsevier.

Kieras, D. E., & Polson, P. G. (1985). An approach to formal analysis of user complexity. *International Journal of Man-Machine Studies, 22,* 365–394.

May, J., & Barnard, P. (1995). The case for supportive evaluation during design. *Interacting with Computers, 7,* 115–143.

May, J., Scott, S., & Barnard, P. (1995). Structuring displays: A psychological guide. (Eurographics Tutorial Notes Series). Geneva: EACG.

Newell, A. (1990) *Unified theories of cognition*. Cambridge, MA: Harvard University Press.

Teasdale, J. & Barnard, P. J. (1993). *Affect, cogntion and change*. Hove: Lawrence Erlbaum Associates.

Young, R. M., Green, T. R. G., & Simon, T. (1989). Programmable user models for predictive evaluation of interface designs. In *Proceedings of CHI'89, Human Factors in Computing Systems* (pp. 15–19). New York: ACM.

11

AN AUTOMATED AID FOR MODELING HUMAN–COMPUTER INTERACTION

Kent E. Williams
The University of Central Florida

Typically the representation of knowledge units making up cognitive task models takes two forms: declarative knowledge units and procedural knowledge units (Anderson, 1993). These are associated with two types of memory: declarative and procedural. Declarative units represent facts about a domain or relations between objects, such as "Washington was the first president of the United States". The units of declarative knowledge, which organize objects such as Washington and the United States by way of the relation "president of", are sometimes referred to as *propositions* or *chunks*. Procedural knowledge units, consist of associations of these facts or chunks in specific patterns, which are bound to specific actions. The actions may be overt behavioral actions or covert mental actions, such as retrieving something from memory, deciding between alternatives, setting up a motor response for execution, deleting information from working memory, adding information to working memory, or setting a new goal. These procedural units are referred to as *production units* or *production rules* and are characterized by their automaticity. That is, production units are not interpreted but are fired off automatically in sequences, which produce skilled performance. They are automatic to the extent that experts at a specific skill may not be able to recall why they perform the skill as they do. They have lost their ability to interpret their behavior. Theoretically, these different units of knowledge can represent knowledge about any type of task.

COGNITIVE MODELS AS PRODUCTION SYSTEMS

The technology of modeling cognitive tasks has developed over the past 30 years in various research settings. A predominant architecture for the instantiation of these cognitive models is the production system. A production system employs production rules to realize how a cognitive skill is represented and executed as knowledge in human memory. The production rule consists of a set of conditions, which are initially represented as chunks of declarative knowledge in long-term declarative memory. One of these conditions is always a goal because it is assumed that all behavior is purposeful. These conditions become associated with each other to form a pattern of information elements, which in turn are associated with some action. As repeated exposure to these conditions and their associated action is experienced, the condition—action pattern becomes strengthened as a memory unit in and of itself. Each of these production rules then takes the form of: IF < Goal and Conditions> THEN < some Action>. As a skill is learned, many of these condition—action patterns become strengthened and referred to as *production rules* or *production units*. The whole set of units making up a skill is then referred to as a *production system*.

When a skill is executed, information comes into working memory. The information in working memory then gets matched to the conditions of production rules in procedural memory where these production rules reside. More than one rule may have its conditions matched. As a result of resolving the conflict of which production unit to select, a single rule is chosen and the action associated with that rule is deposited into working memory for execution. Again, the action may be setting a new goal, placing an instruction to execute a motor response in working memory, deleting some information from working memory, instructing to attend to something, retrieving something from long-term declarative memory, and so on. The action is executed and the contents of working memory change. From this change in working memory, a new set of information elements or chunks is now present in working memory and a new production unit may then be matched and fired dependent the pattern of chunks in working memory. The result of this chain reaction is the execution of the skill.

To date there have been many different applications of this general production system architecture to model a variety of human cognitive skills. Research employing the production system as a model for simulating human cognitive skill has included such areas as human problem solving (Newell & Simon, 1972; Simon, 1978; Langley, Simon, Bradshaw, & Zytkow, 1987; VanLehn, Jones, & Chi, 1991; Newell, 1991, Anderson, 1993), intelligent tutoring systems (Anderson, Conrad, & Corbett, 1989; Corbett, & Anderson, 1989), structuring curriculum (Williams, & Reynolds, 1991; Williams, Reynolds, Carolan, Anglin, & Shrestha, 1990), and modeling human–computer interaction performance (Bovair, Kieras, & Polson, 1990; Kieras, & Meyer, 1994; Kieras and Polson, 1985; Meyer & Kieras, 1994).

Developing Cognitive Models From a Cognitive Task Analysis

To develop these cognitive models, a detailed cognitive task analysis must be conducted to identify and structure information in the production rule form required to simulate the domain task of concern. Prior research by Williams (1993a) involved a review of cognitive task analysis techniques. This review and analysis was conducted to determine whether techniques for the conduct of a cognitive task analysis had been systematized and formalized as a structured interview process, such that the processes could be implemented in computer software as an authoring aid for the generation of cognitive task models. As a result of this review and analysis, a practical cognitive task analysis technique developed by Kieras (1988, 1991) was identified for implementation in computer software.

The Cognitive Analysis Tool

The system developed (Williams, Hultman, & Graesser, in press) is referred to as the cognitive analysis tool (CAT). The CAT can elicit from users their descriptions of how they would perform a specific task independent of the task domain; it can also structure those descriptions as isomorphes of production rules. However, the level of detail of task descriptions is left to the judgment of the user. To create highly detailed cognitive task models for predicting human performance in terms of the time to execute a task, as is the case when assessing the cognitive complexity of a human–computer interaction, a lower level of analysis is required. For CAT to evolve into a general-purpose tool for conducting cognitive task analyses for any type of cognitive task, it must be capable of capturing knowledge units associated with this microlevel of detail. This microlevel of detail consists of primitive cognitive, perceptual, and motor operations that are triggered by production units and whose execution times are of millisecond duration.

An evaluation of CAT (Williams, 1993b) with secretaries expert in a word processing task demonstrated that users could accurately and consistently describe overt behavioral operations consistent with the GOMS analysis process. However, these users were unable to describe the more primitive cognitive and perceptual operations required to develop detailed cognitive models of their interactions with a word processing application. Getting at the right level of detail would then require that CAT be imbued with specific knowledge regarding the primitive operations that could apply in modeling such a task. Of course, this requires that CAT have some knowledge about the task domain, such that it can elicit specific information from the user and make inferences regarding underlying perceptual and cognitive operations. This low-level grain of analysis incorporating perceptual and cognitive operations is required to make predictions regarding the complexity of a human–computer interaction. From such detailed models, accurate estimates of the time to execute a task and the time to learn a task employing a specific human–computer application can be made.

The Benefits of Cognitive Models for HCI Design and Evaluation

The result of predictions of time to execute specific tasks has been shown to have a significant impact the cost of operations employing a specific human–

computer interface design. As several empirical studies have demonstrated, using a GOMS cognitive analysis technique can result in considerable savings and improved efficiency in human performance by assessing the complexity between candidate interface designs. The IRS used this technique to assess the differences in terms of complexity between competing work station designs for the processing of returns (B. John, personal communication, September 12, 1998). They awarded the contract for the work station to the highest bidder. This was protested by the other candidates. The analysis of the complexity of competing work station designs demonstrated that, although the highest bidder was awarded the contract, their work station design would save the government over $ 30 million per year in greater efficiency with which returns could be processed. This savings more than compensated for the higher initial cost of the system as compared with that of the competitors.

NYNEX was considering a new operator call-handling work station. They compared the old and new designs and found that the old design would result in a cost savings of $ 2.5 million a year compared with the new work station under consideration. Needless to say, they opted not to purchase the work station under consideration (Gray, John, & Atwood, 1992). As another example, the Austrian Surveying and Mapping Agency used this technique to develop a change in the interface of a manual map-digitizing system. The single change resulted in a projected cost savings for the mapping project of $ 730,000 dollars in terms of increased productivity (Haunold, & Kuhn, 1994). Beard, Smith, and Denelsbeck (1996) also employed a simplification of GOMS in the design of the interface for a computed tomography medical imaging system—*cat scan*. The result of using their analysis significantly improved the productivity of this multimillion dollar equipment. John and Kieras (1994) summarized other examples of the application of GOMS models to the design and development of computing system interfaces.

GOMS ANALYSIS PROCESS

The GOMS methodology for creating psychological models of human–computer interaction was first defined in Card, Moran, and Newell (1983). Card et al. proposed that, by using this methodology to define how tasks were organized by an expert user, detailed task models of human–computer interaction could be generated, such that predictions of human task performance could be made. GOMS is an acronym for goals, operators, methods, and selection rules. Goals are an end state, that must be achieved to accomplish a task. On the way to goal attainment, there may be many subgoals that must be achieved, with each subgoal bringing one closer to the accomplishment of the task. Operators are the task actions, that one must perform to attain a goal or subgoal. Methods are a sequence of these operators used to accomplish a specific goal or subgoal. Selection rules are sets of discriminating conditions or decision rules that are used to determine which specific method should apply to accomplish a goal if more than one method is available to accomplish that goal. All human–computer interaction can be defined as some organization of these goals, operators, methods, and selection rules. Card et al. also proposed that there was a finite set of primitive operators that could define any human–computer interaction task. Consequently, one could analyze the interactions using this GOMS methodology and these primitive level operators and predict time to execute a task without having to collect execution time. The interactions could be simulated using these GOMS models without the need to gather data for each conceivable type of interaction a human could perform with a computer interface.

GOMS and the Model Human Processor

This small set of primitive operators were classified under three subsystems that made up what Card et al. (1983) referred to as the model human processor (MHP). The three subsystems consisted of the motor subsystem, the perceptual subsystem, and the cognitive subsystem. All interactions with a computer required the execution of these primitive operations associated with these subsystems. Moreover, because empirical evidence was available regarding the time it takes the human information-processing system to execute this small set of subsystem operators, the time it takes to execute any human–computer interaction could be predicted once the sequence of primitive operators for that interaction were defined. Theoretically, this approach can apply universally to all of human performance if the task can be defined in terms of these primitive operators.

Card et al. (1983) demonstrated that this GOMS analysis technique could predict human performance in terms of time to execute a task on a wide variety of human–computer interactions. In general, these predictions were within 80% of observed behavior on those tasks investigated. There have been numerous investigations of the application of this method to the prediction of human–computer interaction performance (John, & Kieras, 1994; Olson, & Olson, 1990). Some of the more recent research conducted by Meyer and Kieras (1994) has extended this technology to the prediction of multiple-task performance.

CAT-HCI DESIGN METHODOLOGY

As was apparent from the evaluation of CAT (Williams, 1993b), users of CAT could accurately and consistently describe their interactions with an application in terms of the overt behavioral operations. The more implicit perceptual and cognitive operations were not readily elicited from these lay subjects selected for the evaluation. The challenge was to develop and extend the interface of CAT, such that inferences regarding these primitive perceptual and cognitive operations could be made from the descriptions readily elicited by CAT.

To proceed, it was necessary to design a set of menus and their associated items, which describe specific classes of operations descriptive of interactions with a human–computer interface. These classes of operations were associated with a set of questions when a selection is made from the list. The questions must be designed such that answers to the questions satisfy specific conditions, which in turn would be associated with specific inferences regarding the absence or presence of primitive level motor, perceptual, and cognitive operations. To define such a set of menus and questions, a set of constraints that delimit the domain of human–computer interaction description was identified. This identification of constraints was the first step in arriving at a set of menus and questions, which could be integrated into CAT to make the appropriate inferences regarding the insertion of primitive cognitive and perceptual operations. Fortunately, there are natural classes of events in the domain of human–computer interaction that allow specific inferences to be made by inheritance given knowledge of those classes of activities and device interaction technologies.

The first set of constraints identified were those, that the user of CAT imposes the process of eliciting cognitive task models of human–computer interaction. These constraints constitute what we can expect on the part of the user in terms of the kinds of inputs the user can provide to the system and the kinds of questions we can reasonably expect the user to respond to accurately. As our previous evaluation of CAT indicated, we can expect accurate descriptions of the more overt behavioral and perceptual operations to be described as a worst case. This is what the system must start with as input to the process of making deeper, more detailed inferences regarding primitive perceptual and cognitive operations. Consequently, the system would have to infer from user descriptions of overt behaviors exactly what these primitive level perceptual and cognitive operations are.

We could also expect that the user can identify classes of activities that can be accomplished while interacting with a computer (e.g., typing, drawing, keying in numbers, speaking, listening, reading, etc.). Additionally, we expected that users could identify sources of information and category types within each of the sources. For example, a source of information may be perceptual and would include visual and auditory types of information.

The next set of constraints identified were inherent in the MHP architecture with its three subsystems: motor, perceptual, and cognitive (Card et al., 1983). That is, step descriptions must fall within one of these subsystems, albeit we anticipated that the majority of descriptions would be motor. Additional constraints can be imposed within each of these subsystems because there are different classes of activity, that can be identified within each subsystem. For example, the perceptual subsystem can consist of the auditory, visual, or tactile processes. The motor subsystem can consist of the eye-head subsystem, the finger-hand-arm subsystem, and the motor speech subsystem. The cognitive subsystem can consist of retrieval operations, retention activities, decision activities, and so on. Each one of these subsystems has its own set of constraints in terms of how much information can be processed within a given period of time (e.g., in the case of working memory, there are limits to how much information can be heeded at any given period of time).

The last set of constraints included what was known about the execution time of specific human–computer interaction activities, which were dependent on the different types of physical interface devices. The cognitive task modeling performance prediction capability is strongly dependent on past research, which has determined the execution time of specific interactions with a computer. Additionally, researchers have defined specific heuristics about the absence or presence of specific primitive, perceptual, motor, and cognitive operations dependent on the type of activity being described and the interface technology, which determines the activity. All of these constraints had to be considered in the development of the menus and questions to be presented to the user of CAT. From these constraints, however, specific inferences can be made to generate models from which relatively accurate predictions regarding human performance could be computed.

As a result of these constraints and the classes of activity for which execution times could be identified, once a class of activity is known and the source of the information for that activity is indicated, the space of possible operators is drastically reduced. Other more specific questions can then be asked; these converge on the type(s) of primitive operations, that must be involved, along with their execution times. The classification process allows the system to make specific inferences by inheritance, which in turn provides the opportunity for other questions to be presented and answered. The logical flow of the questions and answers converges on the appropriate inference regarding the primitive operator or sequence of operators required to adequately model the activity in a fashion, which is transparent to the user.

Classification of Subsystem Operations and Empirical Execution Time Data

The activity of generating cognitive task models from which predictions of human–computer interaction performance can be made is heavily dependent on: (a) the data available regarding the execution time of specific primitive operators, and (b) the heuristics that have been developed concerning sequences of primitive operators involved in specific interactions with computer applications.

Consequently, a review of the available literature addressing primitive operator execution times and heuristics was conducted. The data were classified with respect to the various subsystems of the MHP and human–computer interaction task activities to which the data were associated. The primary sources of information for this task were: Card et al. (1983), John (1988, 1990), John and Newell (1989), John and Gray (1992), Kieras (1988), Kieras and Bovair (1986), Kieras and Elkerton (1991), Meyer and Kieras (1994), Anderson (1993), and Olson and Olson (1990). The research reported by Olson and Olson (1990) is an analysis of the various efforts of researchers who have experimentally derived execution time data on various primitive operations consistent with the MHP. The data were reviewed and median values of the execution time parameters were calculated to give a best approximation wherever there was variation in the data reported. A complete listing of the research for these classes of operations, along with their execution times, is presented in Williams (1998).

Inferring Primitive Operators and Heuristics for Sequences of Operations

Given the classification of execution times for primitive operators and interaction activities as they are associated with the specific subsystems and sub-subsystems of the MHP, the majority of human–computer interaction tasks can be modeled such that predictions of the time to perform such tasks can be made. These predictions are restricted to interactions employing the kinds of interface devices for which execution time data are available or from which generalizations of these execution times can be made. This extends the kinds of interactions, which were modeled by Card et al. (1983), because other researchers have provided additional data after that time.

With the set of execution times and the classification of activities related to human–computer interactions, an interface dialogue was designed to infer primitive perceptual and cognitive operations. The result of this classification scheme and interface dialogue allows users to generate a detailed cognitive task model, which can predict human performance as the time to execute a modeled task.

Example Dialogue

The interaction dialogue of the system designed progressively constrains the space of primitive operators, which may potentially underlie the execution of a step as described by a user expert in the use of the application being modeled. This is accomplished by (a) identifying the subsystem of the MHP under which the step of a method would be classified, and (b) selecting the appropriate menu representing that subsystem. If the user omits the specification of perceptual and cognitive operations from his or her descriptions, the dialogue eventually infers them as a result of querying the user about the more overt motor operations, which they can more readily describe.

The subsystems are arm-hand-finger operations, visual operations, auditory operations, cognitive operations, or motor speech operations. Additionally, there is a class of operations, that refer to system execution time, which is labeled as *waiting for system response*. Having selected the appropriate menu, a step description is selected from the menu for potential insertion in the method being described. Following this, the primitive operator or sequence of operators that are responsible for executing the step are defined by a variety of queries and heuristics. The execution times generated are inserted into the method description (Fig. 11.1). Last, the source of the information, which triggered that step selection, is determined (Fig. 11.2). The following presents some examples of this process. A detailed report presenting the heuristics for the entire system, as well as the dialogue presented to the user to make inferences regarding any human–computer interaction task, appears in Williams (1998) as an ONR technical report.

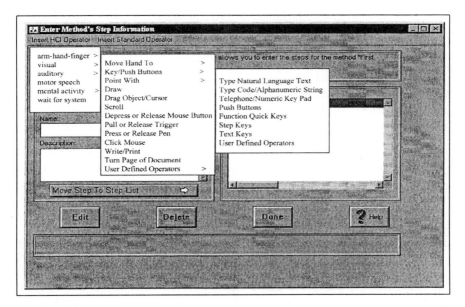

FIG. 11.1 Specific activities which can be performed given the selection of Key/Push Buttons from the class of high level activities with Arm-Hand-Finger operations.

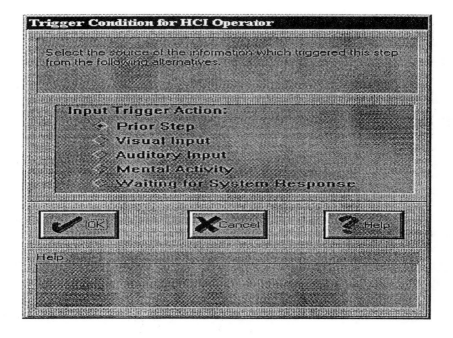

FIG. 11.2   Dialogue box for eliciting the source of the information which triggered the current step being described by the user.

An Example of CAT-HCI Heuristics for Inferring Primitive Operators and Execution Times.

The examples presented in the following describe the inferences, that would automatically be made regarding the presence of primitive operations as the user describes the low-level steps of a method. The symbol ">" in the material presented indicates a nested menu.

The first step of a method being described must have been preceded by a cognitive operation, which pushes a subgoal on the goal stack of the cognitive architecture. This operator is automatically inferred and inserted as the first operation of a method as a result of research conducted by Anderson, Kushmerick, and Lebière (1993). Anderson et al. reported the results of a study designed to empirically establish the existence of goal structures and, in particular, a goal stack in the control of behavior. These investigators found ample evidence for the existence of goal structures in explaining the data recorded from test subjects involved in performing the Tower of Hanoi task. Their data indicate a strong relationship between the number of subgoals set and the time taken to make a move. The time taken to make a move in the solution to the task appeared to be invariant across many versions of the task and showed little learning across repeated trials. However, wherever it could be inferred that a subgoal was directing the behavior of the subjects, an additional 2 seconds was added to the time to make the move. As more subgoals could be inferred to have been placed on the stack to make the move, the time to make the move was incremented by 2 seconds per subgoal inferred. Anderson et al. (1993) cited others such as Ruiz (1987) and Egan and Greeno (1974), who have similarly reported data that indicate this relationship between the number of subgaol firings and the time to make a move. Consequently, it shall be inferred that, in the execution of a given method for accomplishing a task, a 2-second cognitive operator is charged prior to the execution of the first step of the method to account for the time to push the subgoal on the goal stack of the architecture. This 2-second period of time to push the goal on the stack may be what underlies the Card et al. (1983) estimate of preparation to execute a method, which was proposed to be 1.35 seconds.

Therefore, the heuristic for inferring a cognitive operator for the first step of a method is: If first step of a method, then insert a 2-second cognitive operator to push the goal on the stack (Anderson, Kushmerick, & Lebière, 1993; Egan & Greeno, 1974; Ruiz, 1987).

If a specific method is selected from a set of alternative methods, the system employs Kieras's (1991) technique of assigning 100 msec to each statement in the selection rule set. Each statement requires one cycle of the cognitive processor, which equates to 100 msec per cycle. Counting selection rule statements is in accordance with the following convention (Kieras, 1991):

- 1 cycle for the Selection Rule Set statement
- 1 cycle for each If-Then statement in the set
- 1 cycle for the terminating statement of the Selection Rule "Return With Specific Selection Rule Satisfied"

The following is a description of the nested menu for the "Move Hand To" operation:

- Mouse
- Lightpen/gun
- Pen/pencil
- Joystick
- Trackball
- Keyboard
- Numeric keypad
- Telephone keypad
- Push button array
- Other to be defined

Dependent on the user's selection, the following operator execution times are inserted:

- For Mouse, Lightpen/gun, Pen/pencil, a 50 msec cognitive operator is charged to initiate the motor response and a 360 msec motor
- operator to move the hand to the device (Card et al., 1983).
- For Joystick and Trackball charge, a 50 msec cognitive operator to initiate the motor response and a 260 msec to move the hand to the device (Card et al., 1983).
- For Keyboard, Numeric keypad, Telephone keypad, and Push buttons, a 50 msec cognitive operator charge is inserted to initiate the motor response and a 270 msec motor operator charge to move the hand (Card et al. 1983). Here the midpoint between text keys and step keys from page 237 of Card et al. (1983) is used for the execution time and generalized to push buttons as on a tactical console.
- If the user selects "Other to be defined" the system presents the dialogue box of Fig. 11.3, which elicits information relative to computing execution time to Move The Hand employing Fitt's Law.

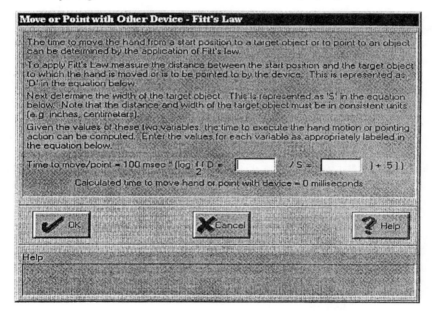

FIG. 11.3 Dialogue box for eliciting parameters to compute the execution time for moving the hand to an object using Fitt's law.

SUMMARY

As demonstrated by the examples given herein, CAT-HCI incorporates considerable knowledge regarding the architecture of cognition and how that architecture can be applied to modeling human–computer interactions. Furthermore, the design of the system has implemented assumptions about a typical user and anticipated that a typical user would not be knowledgeable regarding the nuances of cognitive modeling at this level of analysis. As a result, considerable thought and effort went into designing a dialogue with queries, which could readily be responded to by users such that the appropriate inferences could be made regarding underlying primitive operators. The ease with which such complex models can be generated by individuals not skilled in the underlying analysis technique and the consistency of models generated by different individuals for the same complex task must be subjected to an empirical evaluation.

As shown by Williams et al. (in press), naïve users of the first phase of CAT system development consistently generated simple cognitive models of word processing tasks using the structured interview process of GOMS. However, these users failed to describe even high-level perceptual and cognitive activities. The extensions to CAT as embodied in CAT-HCI were designed specifically to make inferences regarding such high- and low-level primitive operations and can only improve on the accuracy with which complex detailed models can be generated.

Additional work has focused on further development of an interface for cognitive task modeling; it would allow virtually any step to be conditionalized, such that attention can shift from that step/subgoal to another step/subgoal. This allows for the modeling of highly dynamic tasks, such as in tactical decision making, where attention can shift between subgoals dependent on the actions of an opponent. This capability allows one to model tasks that would be consistent with the COGNET architecture of Zachary, Ryder, and Le Mentec (1995), which has been applied to a number of highly dynamic tactical tasks. Within this framework, theoretically any task step can be interrupted and a new subgoal can be set dependent on conditions in the environment.

This newer version of CAT focuses on modeling declarative knowledge. It takes each rule generated and breaks up the condition—action patterns into a list of declarative chunks. Each chunk represents a node. Each node can be assigned to one of five different classes of node: style, goal, state, event and concept (Graesser, Gordon, & Brainard, 1992). Once the user classifies each node, the user may define which nodes are related by drawing an arch between any two nodes. Given the two related nodes and their class types, the kinds of relations that can hold between the nodes is constrained. The space of relations is then presented to the user as a list from which the appropriate relation can be selected. Directionality of the relation can be specified as well as the strength of the relation. The result is a semantic network of declarative chunks from which the production rules evolved. These extensions to the system need to be debugged, as well as subjected to an evaluation as to the facility with which users can conduct such a complex analysis.

REFERENCES

Anderson, J. R. (1993). *Rules of the mind*. Hillsdale, NJ: Lawrence Erlbaum Associates.

Anderson, J. R., Conrad, F. G., & Corbett, A. T. (1989). Skill acquisition and the LISP tutor. *Cognitive Science, 13,* 467—506.

Anderson, J. R., Kushmerick, N., & Lebière, C. (1993). The Tower of Hanoi and goal structures. In J. R. Anderson (Ed.), *Rules of the mind*. Hillsdale, NJ: Lawrence Erlbaum Associates.

Beard, D. V., Smith, D. K., & Denelsbeck, K. M. (1996). Quick and dirty GOMS: A case study of computed tomography interpretation. *Human Computer Interaction, 11,* 157–180.

Bovair, S., Kieras, D. E., & Polson, P. G. (1990). The acquisition and performance of text-editing skill: A cognitive complexity analysis. *Human Computer Interaction, 5,* 1–48.

Card, S.T., Moran, T. P., & Newell, A. (1983). *The psychology of human-computer interaction*. Hillsdale, NJ: Lawrence Erlbaum Associates.

Corbett, A. T., & Anderson, J. R. (1989). Feedback timing and student control in the LISP Intelligent Tutoring System. *Proceedings of the Fourth International Conference on AI and Education,* 64–72.

Egan, D. E., & Greeno, J. (1974). Theory of rule induction: Knowledge acquired in concept learning , serial pattern learning and problem solving. In L. W. Gregg (Ed.), *Knowledge and cognition* (pp. 43–104). Hillsdale, NJ: Lawrence Erlbaum Associates.

Graesser, A. C., Gordon, S., & Brainard, L. E. (1992). QUEST: A model of question answering. *Computers & Mathematics With Applications, 23,* 733–992.

Gray, W. D., John, B. E., & Atwood, M. E. (1992). The precise of project Ernestine or an overview of a validation of GOMS. In *Proceedings of ACM CHI'92 Conference on Human Factors in Computing Systems* (pp. 307–312).

Haunold, P., & Kuhn, W. (1994). A keystroke level analysis of a graphics application: Manual map digitizing. In *Proceedings of ACM CHI'94 Conference on Human Factors in Computing Systems* (pp. 337–343).

John, B. E. (1988). *Contributions to engineering models of human-computer interaction*. Unpublished doctoral dissertation, Carnegie Mellon University.

John, B. E. (1990). Extensions of GOMS analyses to expert performance requiring perception of dynamic visual and auditory information. *In Proceedings of CHI 1990* (pp. 107–115). New York: Association of Computing Machinery.

John, B. E., & Gray, W. D. (1992). *GOMS analyses for parallel activities*. CHI 1992 Tutorial.

John, B. E., & Kieras, D. E. (1994). The GOMS family of analysis techniques: Tools for design and evaluation (Technical Report # CMU-HCI-94-106). School of Computer Science, Carnegie Mellon University, Pittsburgh PA.

John, B. E., & Newell, A. (1989). Cumulating the science of HCI: From S-R compatibility to transcription typing. In *Proceedings of CHI 1989* (pp. 109–114). New York: Association of Computing Machinery.

Kieras, D. E. (1988). Toward a practical GOMS model methodology user interface design. In M. Helander (Ed.), *Handbook of human-computer interaction* (pp. 135–158). Amsterdam: North Holland Elsevier.

Kieras, D. E. (1991). *A guide to GOMS task analysis*. CHI '91 Tutorial.

Kieras, D. E., & Bovair, S. (1986). The acquisition of procedures from text: A production-system analysis of transfer of training. *Journal of Memory and Language, 25*, 507–524.

Kieras, D. E., & Elkerton, J. (1991*). How to do a GOMS analysis for interface and documentation design*. CHI'91 Tutorial Notes.

Kieras, D. E. & Meyer, D. E. (1994). *The EPIC architecture for modeling human information-processing and performance: A brief introduction* (Office of Naval Research Technical Report Contract Number N00014-92-J-1173).

Kieras, D. E., & Polson, P. G. (1985). An approach to the formal analysis of user complexity. *International Journal of Man-Machine Studies, 22*, 365–394.

Langley, P. H., Simon, H. A., Bradshaw, G. L., & Zytkow, J. M. (1987). *Scientific discovery: Computational explorations of the creative process*. Cambridge, MA: MIT Press.

Meyer, D. E., & Kieras, D. E. (1994). *EPIC computational models of psychological refractory-period effects in human multiple-task performance* (Office of Naval Research Technical Report Contract Number N00014-92-J-1173).

Newell, A. (1991). *Unified theories of cognition*. Cambridge, MA: Harvard University Press.

Newell, A., & Simon, H. A. (1972). *Human problem solving*. Englewood Cliffs, NJ: Prentice-Hall.

Olson, J. R., & Olson, G. M.(1990). The growth of cognitive modeling in human-computer interaction since GOMS. *Human Computer Interaction, 5*, 221–265.

Ruiz, D. (1987). Learning and problem solving: What is learned while solving the Tower of Hanoi? (Doctoral dissertation, Stanford University, 1986). *Dissertation Abstracts International, 42*, 3438B.

Simon, H. (1978). An information processing theory of human problem solving. In W. K. Estes (Ed.), *Handbook of learning and cognitive processes: Human information processing* (Vol. 5). Hillsdale, NJ: Lawrence Erlbaum Associates.

VanLehn, K., Jones, R. M., & Chi, M. T. H. (1991). Modeling self-explanation effect with Cascade 3. In K. Hammond & D. Gentner (Eds.), *Proceedings of the 13th annual conference of the cognitive science society*. Hillsdale, NJ: Lawrence Erlbaum Associates.

Williams, K. E. (1993a). Knowledge acquisition: A review of manual, machine aided and machine learning methodologies (Office of Naval Research Technical Report Contract N00014-91-J-5-1500).

Williams, K. E. (1993b). The development of an automated cognitive task analysis and modeling process for intelligent tutoring system development (Technical Report: Contract No. N00014-91-J-5-1500). Office of Naval Research, Cognitive Sciences Program, Arlington, VA.

Williams, K.E. (1998). An automated aid for the conduct of a detailed cognitive task analysis for modeling human computer interaction performance. The Office of Naval Research, cognitive sciences program technical report. Contract # N00014-95-C-0112.

Williams, K. E., Hultman, E. G., & Graesser, A. C. (in press). CAT: A tool for eliciting knowledge on how to perform procedures: Behavior research methods, instrumentation, and computers.

Williams, K. E., & Reynolds, R. E. (1991). The acquisition of cognitive simulation models: A knowledge-based training approach. In Fishwick & Modjeski (Eds.), *Knowledge-based simulation: Methodology and application*. New York: Springer-Verlag.

Williams, K. E., Reynolds, R. E., Carolan, T. F., Anglin, P. D., & Shrestha, L. B (1990). An evaluation of a methodology for cognitively structuring and adaptively sequencing exercise content for embedded training (TR 89-035). Cognitive Science Program, Office of Naval Research, Arlington, VA.

Zachary, W., Ryder, J., & Le Mentec, J.-C. (1995). A cognitive architecture, description language and execution engine for modeling real-time multi-tasking human computer interaction. Unpublished manuscript, CHI Systems Inc.

12

USING TASK ANALYSIS AS A PRIMARY DESIGN METHOD: THE SGT APPROACH

Thomas C. Ormerod
Lancaster University

The development of technological systems typically proceeds through a series of stages—from conception through requirements specification, conceptual design, detailed design, and implementation to testing, documentation, marketing, and maintenance. The success of all of these stages is perhaps most strongly determined by the quality of the requirements specification. This should detail all that the new system is expected to do, and it should include "analysis of customer needs, as well as specification of both the functional behaviour of the proposed system and the non-functional requirements that must be met" (Borgida, Greenspan, & Mylopoulos, 1985, p.82). The requirements specification is often the basis for a contract between the client and the designers: The designers use it to guide their design and the client uses it to ensure that the final design meets their needs.

Until relatively recently, technological systems were typically targeted at specialist user groups and Hence the focus was placed on the specification of functional requirements,—on the assumption that the costs associated with operating and learning to use complex devices were relatively low compared with the advantages of extensive system functionality. Whether this assumption was ever justifiable is questionable, but it is certainly unjustifiable given the mass availability of technological systems to nonspecialist user populations. The shift from specialist to nonspecialist user populations creates a need to consider the information requirements that arise in the use of systems. Information requirements comprise the types of display objects, signals, indicators, and feedback that are required for successful use of an interface in pursuit of its functional values.

Many methods support only the specification of functional requirements (Harker, Olphert, & Eason, 1990). Indeed, the design of the interface between user and system often ends up as an afterthought in the design process, occurring well after the rest of the system has been designed. In some cases, the specification of information requirements is ignored or at best implicit. For example, a specification for a process plant that we examined (Shepherd & Ormerod, 1992) offered this as a full statement of interface requirements: "The new system will present the operator with the plant parameters and variables and enable him to make any adjustment as necessary to control the plant." This neither informs the designer nor allows the client to assess the final system rigorously. Poor information requirement specifications result in users confronting systems that are difficult to operate and that may not fully meet their needs.

Frequently, the specification of information requirements is included in a specification simply as a corollary of the functional requirements. For example, for every component in a process plant, there should exist a valve, alarm and dial. For every function that a word processor offers, there should be a command, menu item, or keystroke shortcut. However, to associate interface design with hardware components is a recipe for disaster. For example, Lansdale Ormerod (1994) described the problems associated with replacing older pneumatically linked panel displays with VDU displays in operations rooms. An obvious approach is to replicate the old display (e.g., using an electronic rather than pneumatically controlled floating indicator to show the level in a tank). However, the amount of information that can be viewed at any one time is highly restricted by the size of the VDU screen. We know of at least one case in a waste reprocessing plant, where the old panel displays had to be reinstalled because operators were unable to carry out plant monitoring tasks using the new VDU displays. In another case, the panel display was re-created by having banks of VDU screens stacked on top of each other.

It is in the specification of information requirements that task analysis should gain prominence as a design method. Almost by definition, it is necessary to specify the tasks that a user must undertake before it is possible to specify the information that users need for these tasks. However, the design community has been slow to take up task analysis. Consequently, it has often failed to recognize the importance of specifying information requirements. This chapter begins by examining three potential problems in using task analysis for design: (a) the possibility that task analysis might inhibit innovative design, (b) the difficulty of situating relatively informal methods in the design process, and (c) the usability of task analysis methods in nonspecialist hands. A new approach to task analysis, the Sub-Goal Template (SGT) method, is then presented, which, we argue, addresses the problems of integrating task analysis into the design process.

DEVICE INDEPENDENCE

By definition, design is the development of new artefacts under constraints. Constraints range from obvious ones such as required functionality, cost, and safety to more subtle ones such as originality and (conversely) compatibility with existing practices. However, in developing innovative interfaces, it is critical that designers are not unnecessarily constrained by adherence to existing and potentially outmoded or inefficient existing artefacts.

One of the main criticisms that has been leveled at the use of task analysis in interface design is that, because it implies the analysis of tasks carried out on existing artefacts, it is impossible for future designs to break out from current design constraints. Benyon (1992) argued that task analysis should only play a limited role in the design process. He argued for the use of systems analysis methods such as SSADM, which provides logical specification of the system structures needed to deliver the required functionality independent of data flow. He suggested that task analysis is not device-independent because it incorporates details on the order of tasks and the control of data flow. He believed that these details embody facets of the current system and therefore restrict the originality of the new design.

Benyon's arguments have not gone unchallenged (e.g., Diaper & Addison, 1992; Lansdale & Ormerod, 1994). Recently, we argued (Richardson, Ormerod, & Shepherd, 1998) that a data centered approach can be achieved by both systems analysis and task analysis methods, and that systems analysis methods on their own cannot provide a sufficient data specification for interface design. There is an asymmetry between the data required by the system and the data required by the user: The data that the system deals with do not necessarily entail all of the information required by the user to operate that system.

CLARITY OF PROCEDURES AND APPROPRIATE STOPPING RULES

One reason for the absence of widespread use of task analysis in design is that it requires expertise that is not necessarily available in engineering, computing, or production-oriented design teams. Many task analysis methods do little to alleviate this problem: They are craft skills that require experience and practice, as well as conceptual knowledge and skill in using methods and notations. A number of methods have been developed for specifying user requirements (e.g., Card, Moran, & Newell, 1983; Lim & Long, 1994; Payne & Green, 1986). Almost all user-oriented interface design methods embody some aspect of task analysis, whether explicitly or implicitly, and some provide notations for describing the products of task analysis. Yet few, if any, of these methods provide a notation that is developed to support the process of task analysis. For example, the task-action grammar (TAG) method of Payne & Green (1986) provides a notation for assessing the consistency of alternative interface designs, yet there is no guidance as to how TAG might be used in an ongoing design process. Like many other task analytic methods, it is a research tool that has not had a major impact outside the laboratory.

The process of specifying information requirements requires some degree of guidance and formalism. This can be gained through adherence to formal or semiformal design methods. Design methods provide a structure within which the design process can occur, which ensures completeness and breaks the task of design down into manageable units. Furthermore, some methods incorporate human factors techniques into the design process from the outset and thus make explicit the importance of early interface design (e.g., Walsh, Lim, & Long, 1989). However, the extent to which one can produce a rigidly formal task analytic method is questionable. Lansdale and Ormerod (1994) argued that task analysis should be seen as an ongoing process in which the resulting specification is a product of negotiation and reanalysis. There is no such thing as a unique correct task analysis for any design project, only a number of alternatives that have varying strengths. Thus, in common with other methods such as SSADM, alternative outcomes should not only be expected but should be actively sought as a way of pursuing optimal requirements specifications.

A key problem that faces task analysts is knowing the correct stopping point: Too little detail, and the designer does not receive a full specification of requirements; too much, and the designer's options are overly constrained. Typically, task analysts have adopted some form of cost–benefit decision as the criterion for deciding when to proceed or discontinue analysis, such as the P x C rule (probability of inefficiency x cost of inefficiency) of Annett and Duncan (1967). However, this kind of stopping rule is inherently subjective. It is also vulnerable to criticism of Benyon (1992), who stated that task analysis can become device-dependent if based on an evaluation of existing artefacts, as the P x C rule must surely be (although to be fair, in the context of training design in which the P x C rule was devised, problems of subjectivity and device-dependence are either lessened or irrelevant).

USABILITY OF METHODS

Although methods aimed at the design of usable interfaces have a worthy aim, they are often curiously insensitive to the usability issues they generate. For example, Benyon (1992) claimed that the diagrammatic output produced by systems analysis methods such as SSADM is simple for designers to understand and can be easily used as input to later stages of design. However, Diaper and Addison (1992) argued that diagrams, such as those produced by data flow or systems analyses, can be misleading; if users are unfamiliar with the conventions used in their construction, they can be misinterpreted. Usability problems also affect task analysis methods. Notations that are intended to enhance the specification of requirements are often developed without regard to their own usability (see Richardson, 1996, for examples where methods would have benefited from more careful notational design). Research has shown the potential value of evaluating notations, such as the evaluation by Greene, Devlin, Cannata, and Gomez (1990) of alternative notations for the database query language SQL. Similar importance should be attached to the ergonomic design of notations and tools for task analysis if it is to become more widespread as a design method, especially for nonspecialist users.

THE SGT APPROACH TO INFORMATION REQUIREMENTS SPECIFICATION

The Sub-Goal Template (SGT) scheme was developed by Shepherd and Ormerod (1992; Shepherd, 1993) to allow a hierarchical task analysis (HTA) to form the basis for an information requirements specification. Our concern has been to produce a task analysis method that addresses the issues of device-independence, clarity of procedures, and usability in an integrated approach to specifying interfaces. There are six elements to our approach, which are discussed in turn: (a) adoption of HTA, (b) SGT task elements, (c) the SGT sequencing elements, (d) provision of information requirements, (e) core design cycle, and (f) situating the SGT method within a computer-based tool.

Hierarchical Task Analysis

Task analysis is used to analyze system function in terms of the user's goals and subgoals inherent in performing the task. It provides a simple method for allowing constituent tasks and their order to be discovered. The main distinction between systems analysis and task analysis methods is that the former focus on specifying the logical structure of the system to be built, whereas the latter focus on the structure of the tasks to be performed by users. Task analysis can be used for interface design, training, job design, ensuring safety, and assessing cost-effectiveness. A wide range of techniques exist for task analysis (see Kirwan & Ainsworth, 1992, for a review). Hierarchical task analysis (HTA), developed by Annett, Duncan, Stammers, and Gray (1971), is one technique that is well established. We have chosen HTA as the basis for our work for two reasons. First, it is one of the most simple approaches, having relatively few notational formalisms and conceptual structures. Second, HTA makes no assumptions about the knowledge structures of users, unlike many cognitive task analysis methods, which are explicitly designed to model user knowledge.

HTA involves taking a task and identifying its subgoals. For example, the task of operating a process plant might have the immediate subgoals "Clean out plant," "Start up plant," "Monitor and maintain parameters," and "Carry out shutdown." Each of these subgoals has associated tasks that can be further redescribed in the same manner, until a level of analysis is reached that is appropriate for the design of the system to begin (although, as argued earlier, the decision as to what constitutes an appropriate level for designers is problematic in existing formulations of HTA and other task analytic methods). Plans are used to describe the relationships between the tasks and constraints on them. Thereby capturing sequence information. Sequence information can then be used to assess the feasibility of tasks and determine contiguous information requirements. There are two key aspects to HTA: information gathering, which emphasizes the process of HTA, and task representation, which emphasizes the products of the HTA process. For details on these aspects, see reviews by Shepherd (1985), Diaper (1989), and Kirwan and Ainsworth (1992).

SUB-GOAL TEMPLATES (SGTs)

To derive an information requirements specification from an HTA, a method is needed that provides three things. First, the information needs associated with each task must be detailed. Second, standardized rather than idiosyncratic descriptions are required for the tasks emerging from HTAs. Third, a degree of rigor must be introduced into the process of producing an HTA to ensure that the analysis ceases at a level of description that can usefully contribute to design. Subgoal templates (SGTs) are a set of standard task elements that capture the tasks that users (e.g., control operators) encounter at any interface and that provide such a method. The scheme provides a vocabulary for redescribing the outcomes of task analysis, facilitating the process of task identification and introducing a degree of systematicity and rigor into task labeling and organization. Under the SGT scheme, each of the lowest level tasks in the HTA is described by an SGT task element. The SGT task elements fall into four classes, as illustrated in Table 12.1 (although extensions to the scheme are discussed later). These correspond to stereotypical operational tasks. Each of the lowest level subgoals in an HTA corresponds to a single operational task and can therefore be redescribed using an SGT task element. For example, the subgoal "Close valve 1" can be described using the SGT element "A1: Prepare equipment." Thus, the SGT task elements allow for a standardized HTA to be produced.

A key aspect of the SGT task elements is that they specify the stopping point for the analysis at the level where tasks are technology-independent single goals. For example, the subgoal "Close valve 1" could be redescribed in terms of the individual actions carried out to close the valve. However, these actions would be dependent on the existing technology. Thus, by prescribing a stopping point, the SGT scheme prevents the analysis from becoming a description of the existing implementation. This is illustrated in Fig. 12.1, in which part of an HTA of a telephone customer service task by Shepherd (1995) is redescribed in terms

TABLE 12.1
SGT Task Elements (after Richardson, Ormerod & Shepherd, 1998,
© Taylor & Francis Ltd).

Action elements		
Code	*Label*	*Information Requirements*
A1	prepare equipment	• Indication of alternative operating states, feedback that equipment is set to required state
A2	activate	• Feedback that the action has been effective
A3	adjust	• Possible operational states, feedback confirming actual state
A4	de-activate	• Feedback that the action has been effective
Communication Elements		
C1	read	• Indication of item
C2	write	• Location of record for storage and retrieval
C3	wait for instruction	• Projected wait time, contact point
C4	receive instruction	• Channel for confirmation
C5	instruct or give data	• Feedback of receipt
C6	remember	• Prompt for operator-supplied value
C7	retrieve	• Location of information for retrieval
Monitoring Elements		
M1	monitor to detect deviance	• Listing of relevant items to monitor, normal parameters for comparison
M2	monitor to anticipate change	• Listing of relevant items to monitor, anticipated level
M3	monitor rate of change	• Listing of relevant items to monitor, template against which to compare observed parameters
M4	inspect plant and equipment	• Access to symptoms, templates for comparison with acceptable tolerances if necessary
Decision Making Elements		
D1	diagnose problems	• Information to support trained strategy
D2	plan adjustments	• Planning information from typical scenarios
D3	locate contaminant	• Sample points enabling problem bracketing between a clean input and a contaminated output
D4	judge adjustment	• Target indicator, adjustment values

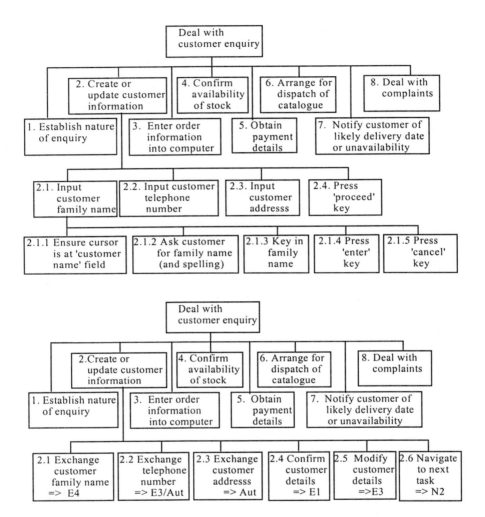

FIG. 12.1 An HTA for the task "Deal with customer enquiry." The upper hierarchy is from Shepherd (1995) and the lower hierarchy shows a revised SGT analysis. Note that the codes on the lowest level of the SGT analysis correspond with SGT task elements as described in Table 12.3. The code "Aut" refers to a job-allocation decision to automate that task.

of SGT task elements. The key point of the redescription is that it stops at a level above that given by Shepherd, because his analysis included implementation-specific actions. For example, there are other ways to gain a register of the in-

TABLE 12.2
The SGT Sequencing Elements (from Ormerod, Richardson & Shepherd, 1998,
©Taylor & Francis Ltd)

Code	Label	Syntax
S1	Fixed	*S1 Then X*
S2	Choice/contingent	*S2 if Z Then X if not Z Then Y*
S3	Parallel	*S3 Then do together X and Y*
S4	Free	*S4 In any order X and Y*

formation entailed in the task "Exchange customer address" apart from inputting it by keyboard. It may be (indeed, it is commonly the case) that completion of the task "Exchange customer family name" enables the automated access of the address from computer-based records.

Sequencing Elements

The possible orders in which the operational tasks can be carried out are specified by translating the information contained within the HTA plans using sequencing elements (shown in Table 12.2). The SGT sequencing elements provide a notation for describing task plans in terms of four different relationships between tasks: fixed, contingent, parallel, and free sequences. The function of these elements is to specify the way in which information should be arranged for presentation to the user. For example, if two operations are carried out in parallel, the information needs of both must be displayed together. The importance of capturing the orders, dependencies, and contingencies that exist in user tasks

Informal plan description	SGT re-description
Shut off the input to the mixer tank and switch the output to the storage tank. Monitor the level of liquid in the mixer tank, when it falls to zero then switch off the output.	S3 In any order A4 Shut off input and A3 Switch output S3 Then do together M2 monitor level and S2 If zero then A4 switch off If not zero then C3 wait for instruction.

FIG.12.2 A re-description of an informal plan in the SGT notation.

was highlighted by Shepherd (1986) in his use of plans for HTA. Plans describe the logical order in which the subtasks that constitute a task must be undertaken depending on the conditions of task performance. Fig. 12.2 shows a redescription in the SGT scheme of an embedded task sequence. An interesting aspect of combining task elements with sequence elements is that tasks that are implicit in informal plan descriptions are made explicit in the redescription (e.g., the task C3—of waiting for an appropriate instruction where an appropriate tank level is not reached).

The inclusion of sequence information goes strictly against the edicts of many systems design methods, which maintain the strict separation of data and control flow found in structured programming approaches (e.g., Jackson, 1980; Wirth, 1971). Indeed, it is one of the criticisms of task analysis offered by Benyon (1992). We believe that sequence information cannot be divorced from task descriptions in an information requirements specification, because constraints on the order in which users carry out tasks are an essential component of the information that users must have for successful task completion. Shepherd (1993) illustrated this with respect to two problems that occur when sequence information is ignored in interface design: "breaking the loop," when control information is separated from the point at which control actions must be executed, and "information fragmentation," when information must be drawn from several sources (e.g., different plant components) in performance of a single task. These problems are commonly seen in the situation described previously, where traditional panel displays are replaced by VDU technology. The need for sequencing elements in the scheme arises because of the asymmetry between system data specification and user specification. In essence, constraints on task order are part of the data that users need to perform tasks with an interface.

Stereotypical Information Requirements

The SGT elements have associated information requirements in the form of templates that must be filled in. For example, in the template for the SGT element, "A1: Prepare equipment," the user must specify the nature of the information that will indicate the alternative operating states and provide feedback indicating whether the equipment is set to the required state. In the case of the task "Close valve 1," the alternative operating states are open and closed; feedback would be required to show whether the valve was in fact open or closed. Therefore, these templates capture the information requirements associated with each task. Labeling tasks with SGT elements entails the automatic specification of information requirements for successful task completion without constraining the design options that deliver the task's information needs. In this way, the SGT scheme provides a full requirements specification for the interface designer as an automatic outcome of HTA.

A key point of the SGT scheme is that each task element should have a unique set of information needs (for examples, see Lansdale & Ormerod, 1994). Indeed, the determination of distinct SGT task elements is operationalized by this requirement. There are no information requirements associated with sequencing elements. Instead, their function is to specify the way in which information should be arranged contiguously for presentation to the user.

The Core Design Cycle

The SGT scheme was originally conceived as a notation for redescribing a completed HTA so that information requirements for all tasks could be collated (Shepherd & Ormerod, 1992). Thus, the original method of applying the scheme was to translate task plans from completed HTAs into the SGT notation. However, there are a number of advantages to making the application of SGTs an integral part of HTA. For example, it makes requirements specification a single- rather than a two-stage process; it also provides a structure around which the

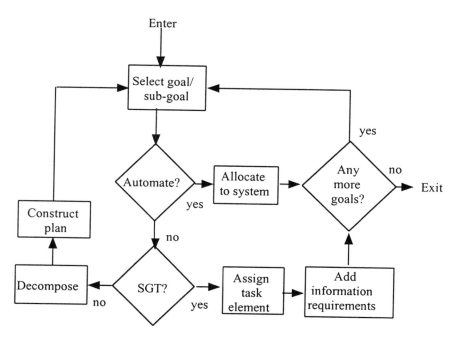

FIG. 12.3   The core design cycle underlying the SGT method (from Ormerod, Richardson, & Shepherd, 1998, © Taylor & Francis Ltd)

process of HTA can be carried out in a rigorous fashion. Hence, the SGT scheme, which describes the notation, was extended by Ormerod et al. (1998) to give the SGT method, which outlines the application of the scheme during an ongoing design process. Fig. 12.3 shows the design cycle that forms the basis of the SGT method. The cycle operates as follows: The analyst searches for the highest level task to emerge from interviews with designers and operators during an initial information-gathering phase. An attempt is then made to assign one of the SGT task elements to it. If this fails, the task must be decomposed into sub-tasks (again based on data gathering and rational decomposition of complex tasks). At this stage, a plan must be constructed using the SGT sequencing elements that shows how subtasks are ordered for successful task completion in each possible contingency. The process then cycles, with an attempt to assign an SGT to each subtask or further decomposition and data collection where necessary. When an SGT is assigned successfully to a task, decomposition ceases at this level and a set of stereotypical information requirements is assigned to the task.

EXTENDING THE SCHEME

The SGT method was originally developed for the specification of process control interfaces (see Shepherd, 1993, for examples). However, there is no reason in principle why the scheme cannot be extended to any interface design task in any domain. A key issue in extending the method to other domains is one of emphasis. In process control, the task type of monitoring is perhaps one of the domain's defining features. In other domains, such as using office information systems, one also encounters monitoring, action, communication, and decision-

Level			Field system main menu		
1	Customer records	Office records	Engineer job sheet	Comms.	Stock catalogue
2	Contact details	Maps	Today list	Call H.O	Parts cat.
	Service record	Service sheets	Week list	Call depot	Equipment cat.
	Client account	Client records	Priority list	Call Reg. HQ	Servicing cat.
	Job request	Staffing	Outstanding	Contact F.E.	Place order
	Client history	Accounts	Bonus sheet		Check avail.
	Promotions?		Employee data		Search

FIG. 12.4   Client's proposed menu hierarchy for a portable computer system for field engineers. Only the first two levels of the hierarchy are shown. Each menu item at the lowest level has between one and three levels of command menus beneath it before the required data/function is accessed.

TABLE 12.3

Extending the SGT Task Elements for Navigation and Information Exchange

Exchange elements

Code	Label	Syntax
E1	Enter from discrete range •	Item position & delineation, advance descriptors, choice recovery
E2	Enter from continuous range •	Choice indicator, range/category delineation, advance descriptors, end of range, range recovery
E3	Extract from discrete range •	Information structure (e.g. criticality, weight, frequency structuring), feedback on current choice
E4	Extract from continuous range •	Available range; information structure (e.g., criticality, weight, frequency structuring), feedback on current choices

Navigation elements

Code	Label	Syntax
N1	Locate a given information set •	Organization structure cues (e.g., screen set/menu hierarchy, catalogue, etc.), choice descriptor conventions, current location, location relative to start, selection indicator
N2	Move to a given location •	Layout structure cues (e.g., screen position/menu selection, icon, etc.), current position, position relative to information coordinates, movement indicator
N3	Browse an information set •	Information (e.g., screen/menu hierarchy, catalogue, etc.) organization cues, information scope, choice points, current location, location relative to start, selection indicator

making tasks. The emphasis, however, is typically rather different. For example, in exploring the Internet, two key aspects of task performance are the need to navigate and exchange data. In principle, navigation and data exchange can be subsumed within the SGT task elements by redescribing them as a combination of actions, communication, and monitoring tasks. However, in practice, it is appropriate to isolate these task types as separate SGTs so that designers are given specific information requirements to support them.

Table 12.3 describes the extension of the SGT scheme to include navigation and exchange elements. For information exchange, there are two orthogonal dimensions on which tasks vary: Users may be extracting or imparting data, and data may be discrete or continuous. For navigation, there are two dimensions—data and location—but they are not orthogonal. Essentially, users can navigate to find predetermined data in an unknown location, they can navigate to a predetermined location to find unknown data, or they can browse (when neither data nor location are predetermined). This gives a set of seven additional SGT task elements. Each of these has unique (although overlapping) information requirements, although these are different from those of the original task element set in that they dictate the organization of information rather than the nature of the information.

The extended SGT scheme was recently applied in a project run by a major energy supply company, for whom we acted as consultants, to design the interface for a portable computer for field engineers. As is fairly typical in such projects, we were called in at a late stage—when the hardware platform had already been purchased and decisions about the main interface features had already been taken and fixed. The clients had already designed an interface consisting of a text menu hierarchy of commands (part illustrated in Fig. 12.4) grouped according to an informal analysis carried out by the clients of commonalities among system functions and user tasks. Thus, our principal task, from our client's perspective at any rate, was to evaluate the menu hierarchy and suggest regrouping tasks according to an HTA.

In turned out that our analysis revealed problems inherent in the menu hierarchy that went beyond the mere reorganization of menu items across levels. The complete menu hierarchy had over 500 entries organized across five levels (and this was just the first module of a 9-module project). The grouping of items was logical in the sense that all commands concerning communications with head office were together, all customer record commands were together, and so on. However, in terms of the goals of the interface users (the field engineers), the commands necessary to execute everyday tasks were fragmented across the hierarchy. One task involved checking with head office about rescheduling a field engineer's job schedule in response to a customer request during an on-site visit. We estimated that this would entail over 60 individual menu selections, with

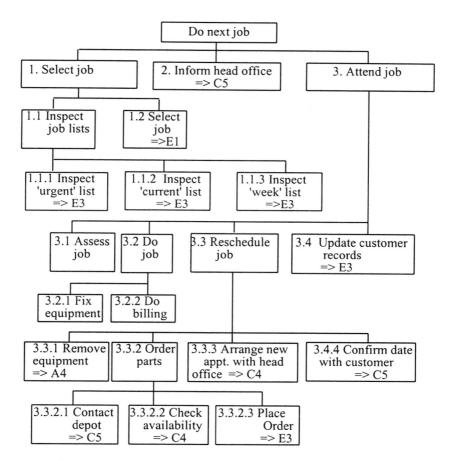

FIG. 12.5   Hierarchy from an SGT analysis of the field engineer task "Undertake next job" (plans are omitted for brevity).

unspecified but presumably lengthy delays between each as a result of the need for telephonic communications for some commands.

Fig. 12.5 shows an SGT analysis of one task to be undertaken by field engineers using the system, illustrating how tasks are built up from elements scattered across the original menu hierarchy. On the basis of our analysis and the resulting information requirements, it was clear that the original hierarchy would be extremely unwieldy and the design solution chosen by the clients was impracticable. Significantly, the client's representation of the tasks faced by the field engineers did not include any notion navigating around the system and did not distinguish among different forms of navigation. We proposed a revised design in which certain tasks, such as communication with head office, were separated from the main menu hierarchy in the form of fast paths (e.g., using function keys), because these formed repeated and common units within the field engineers' task repertoire. Typically, the repeated tasks were to do with information exchange. We also proposed a variable menu hierarchy to reflect the presence of different types of navigation, in which options that supported browsing were given qualitatively different displays and selection modes from options that necessitated search and movement. It would be nice to say that the interface was subsequently changed according to our suggestions and was shown to be successful. However, by the time we were contracted, most of the software had already been written and was dependent on the interface imposed by the original menu hierarchy.

As well as demonstrating the important role played by navigation and exchange in information system interfaces, this example also illustrates two pitfalls that task analysis can help overcome in the design of interfaces. First, grouping system functions and commands according to surface commonalities can be problematic: They must be grouped according to their pattern of use in tasks, and this can only be revealed by task analysis. Second, our clients had read around issues of usability in the literature and had fixated on the importance of consistency in interface design. What could be more consistent than a single mode of command selection (viz. navigation and command selection) by making discrete choices from a series of on-screen menus that were identical in all but command names? The problem is that, although the system learning overheads might seem low, the lack of task-oriented organization of the interface meant that the system was extremely cumbersome.

USABILITY PROBLEMS AND THE NEED FOR AN SGT TOOL

The SGT method provides a relatively simple way to carry out task analysis to the point where information requirements are provided directly to the interface designer. However, as a paper-based scheme, it has its limitations. These made us aware of the vital importance of making the method usable if it were to contribute successfully to the design of other usable systems (Ormerod, Richardson, & Shepherd, 1998).

There are several reasons that a computer-based tool may make the SGT method easier to execute. First, Green (1989) argued that the environment in which a design method is used should provide the necessary features to support the use of its notations. Second, a computer-based tool provides a formalism for applying the SGT scheme. The designer can be guided through complex tasks to ensure accuracy and completeness, progress can easily be measured, and design projects are managed more efficiently (Parnas & Clements, 1986). Third, tools can be used to trap errors or check the completeness of the finished specification (Tse & Pong, 1991)

The SGT tool adopts the core design cycle as its underlying process model. The tool has two main components: a goal information window, which controls the design cycle underlying the SGT method, and a plan construction window, in which a plan can be drawn up using the sequencing elements. The plan construction window is illustrated in Fig. 12.6. The window contains a field in which the plan is written, a menu of sequencing elements, a field displaying information about the currently selected sequencing element, and a menu of

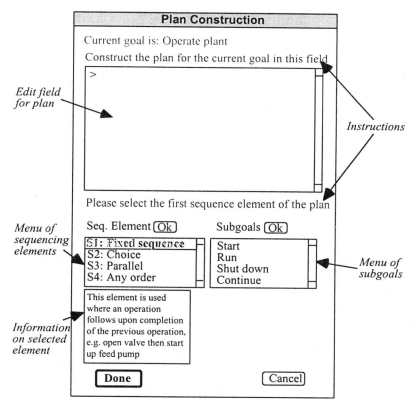

FIG. 12.6   Plan construction window in the SGT tool (from Ormerod, Richardson, & Shepherd, 1998).

subgoals. The user constructs the plan by selecting a point in the construction field, selecting an element or subgoal from one of the menus, and clicking the "OK" button next to the menu. The SGT tool was designed to reduce errors in two ways: first, the templates prevent users from missing out parts of the elements or adding unnecessary items. Second, the tool automatically checks the validity of the insertion point when a new item is added to the plan.

The tool was evaluated against a paper-based environment for using the SGT scheme using the redescription problems from the earlier notation evaluation. Subjects using the computer environment solved more problems correctly on the first attempt than subjects using the paper environment. Perhaps more important, subjects using the computer environment made significantly fewer syntactic errors (Ormerod, Richardson, & Shepherd, 1998). Richardson (1996) also reported a case study of an experienced designer of process control displays using the SGT tool successfully to produce an information requirements specification for a control display.

The redesign of the SGT notation and the development of the SGT tool demonstrates the importance of addressing usability issues in the design of task analysis tools. An apparently minor change in syntax to a form that was more in keeping with the regular use of linguistic choice structures made a large difference in the usability of the SGT method; its embodiment within a supportive environment greatly enhanced the usability of the method.

CONCLUSIONS

The SGT method has been developed for the specification of information requirements to address the problems using task analysis as a design method. Device-independence is maintained by the use of SGT task elements that provide explicit stopping points for task decomposition to prevent the analysis from becoming implementation-dependent. The need for clear and integrated design procedures is dealt with by having a core design cycle, from which an information requirements specification is an end product. Usability has been addressed by the careful and systematic evaluation of the notation and tool that support the SGT method. Much remains to be done before we can be confident of its use by a wider community. For example, the information requirements demand further validation. We have been deliberately cautious in releasing the SGT method and tool for commercial use until we are confident that we have established the viability of the notation and core design cycle. The next step is for the tool and SGT method to be evaluated through a longitudinal study on a commercial design project.

REFERENCES

Annett, J., & Duncan, K. D. (1967). Task analysis and training design. *Occupational Psychology*, *41*, 211–221.

Annett, J., Duncan, K. D., Stammers, R., & Gray, M. J. (1971). *Task analysis*. London: HMSO.

Benyon, D. (1992). The role of task analysis in systems design. *Interacting With Computers*, *4*, 102–139.

Borgida, A., Greenspan, S., & Mylopoulos, J. (1985). Knowledge representation as the basis for requirement specifications. *IEEE Computer*, 82–90.

Card, S. K., Moran, J. P., & Newell, A. (1983). *The psychology of human computer interaction*. Hillsdale, NJ: Lawrence Erlbaum Associates.

Diaper, D. (Ed.). (1989). *Task analysis for human-computer interaction*. Chichester: Ellis Horwood.

Diaper, D., & Addison, M. (1992). Task analysis and systems analysis for software development. *Interacting with Computers*, *4*, 124–139.

Green, T. R. G. (1989). Cognitive dimensions of notations. In A. Sutcliffe & L.Macaulay (Eds.), *People and Computers V* (pp. 443–459). Cambridge: Cambridge University Press.

Greene, S. L., Devlin, S. J., Cannata, P. E., & Gomez, L. M. (1990). No IFs, ANDS, or ORs: A study of database querying. *International Journal of Man-Machine Studies*, *32*, 303–326.

Harker, S. D. P., Olphert, C. W., & Eason, K. D. (1990). The development of tools to assist in organizational requirements definition for information technology systems. In D. Diaper (Ed.), *Human-computer interaction—INTERACT '90* (pp. 295–300). New York: Elsevier.

Jackson, M. (1980). The design and use of conventional programming languages. In H.T. Smith & T.R.G. Green (Eds.), *Human interaction with computers* (pp. 321–347). London: Academic Press.

Kirwan, B., & Ainsworth, L. K. (1992). *The task analysis guide*. London: Taylor & Francis.

Lansdale, M. W., & Ormerod, T. C. (1994). *Understanding interfaces: A handbook of human-computer interaction*. London: Academic Press.

Lim, K. Y., & Long, J. (1994). *The MUSE method for usability engineering*. Cambridge: Cambridge University Press.

Ormerod, T. C., Richardson, J., & Shepherd, A. (1998). Enhancing the usability of a task analysis method: A notation and environment for requirements specification. *Ergonomics*, *41*, 1642–1663.

Parnas, D. L., & Clements, P. C. (1986). A rational design process; how and why to fake it. *IEEE Transactions on Software Engineering*, *SE-12* N.2.

Payne, S. J., & Green, T. R. G. (1986). Task-action grammars: A model of the mental representation of task languages. *Human-Computer Interaction*, *2*, 93–133.

Richardson, J., Ormerod, T. C., & Shepherd, A. (1998). The role of task analysis in capturing requirements for interface design. *Interacting with Computers*, *9*, 367–384.

Shepherd, A. (1986). Hierarchical task analysis and training decisions. *Programmed Learning and Educational Technology*, *22*, 162–176.

Shepherd, A. (1993). An approach to information requirements specification for process control tasks. *Ergonomics*, *36*, 805–817.

Shepherd, A. (1995). Task analysis in HCI. In A. F. Monk & N. Gilbert (Eds.), *Perspectives on HCI: Diverse approaches*. London: Academic Press.

Shepherd, A., & Ormerod, T. C. (1992). *Development of a formal method of user requirements specification for process plant displays*. Final report for British Gas plc.

Tse, T. H., & Pong, L. (1991). An examination of requirements specification languages. *The Computer Journal*, *34*, 143–152.

Walsh, P., Lim, K. Y., & Long, J. B. (1989). JSD and the design of user interface software. *Ergonomics*, *32*, 1483–1498.

Wirth, N. (1971). Program development by stepwise refinement. *Communications of the ACM*, *14*, 221–226.

13

GETTING THE KNOWLEDGE INTO HCI: THEORETICAL AND PRACTICAL ASPECTS OF TASK KNOWLEDGE STRUCTURES

Peter Johnson and Hilary Johnson
University of Bath

Fraser Hamilton
University of Brighton

A significant focus of cognitive task analysis (CTA) has been toward, its application in HCI. In general the HCI community, has been striving for a theoretical base and the ability to contribute to design theory and practice, such that better-designed, more usable systems result. From a theoretical perspective, we developed Task Knowledge Structures (TKS; Johnson, 1992; Johnson and Johnson, 1991a; Johnson et al., 1988) to model conceptual, declarative, and procedural knowledge in terms of the roles, goals, objects, and actions concerned in executing work tasks. To contribute to design practice, we have developed methods that could be applied by designers in collecting and analyzing data and constructing TKS models. As a result of the development of TKS, a task-based approach to user interface design (ADEPT; Johnson, Johnson, & Wilson, 1995) was conceived to enable the transition between task modeling and designing interactive systems to support work tasks.

HCI is an applied discipline, bringing together science and engineering with craft knowledge and skills. Solutions to HCI problems need to be based on sound science and engineering and applicable by practitioners of HCI. A central concern for CTA in HCI is the role it can play in the generation of design solutions and the evaluation of interactive computer systems. Therefore, methods, techniques, and tools need to be developed to support the practitioner in using CTA in design and evaluation.

A core concern for HCI design has been the recognition that interactive systems are useless if they do not support users in performing their work tasks. To this end, the representation and modeling of users' work-task knowledge is a major concern. Modeling users' task knowledge enables designers not only to make informed design decisions, but also to predict the effects of those decisions upon users. This has led to an interest in the design process and how to approach design from a user-work-centered perspective. Moreover, it causes us to movefrom a descriptive and analytical input to design to a more prescriptive and predictive form of HCI design.

In later sections of this chapter, we demonstrate briefly, using our past research on TKS, our descriptive, analytical, and prescriptive contributions to HCI design theory and practice. An extract from an example TKS is used to drive the empirical research on predictive principles for user interface design. Our current research on the further development of TKS is also outlined to show our contribution to more predictive forms of HCI design. A number of predictive principles are described and validated empirically within this chapter. The empirical study briefly outlined demonstrates usability benefits in applying the predictive principles. For the sake of generality, validity, and greater understanding, a further example from a well-known application is provided. This second example is used to show that a formal modeling approach to HCI can be employed in conjunction with a TKS model—to formally specify, compare, and evaluate existing user interface designs in terms of given usability principles.

TASK KNOWLEDGE STRUCTURES (TKS)

The TKS approach to analyzing users' work tasks was developed to provide input to design generation by identifying and modeling users' task knowledge. The overriding aim was to develop an approach with a theoretical base (see Johnson & Johnson, 1991a), but with an associated method that could be used early in a design process by designers and developers of interactive systems.

The various approaches to task analysis (TA) that have been developed in HCI (e.g., Card, Moran, & Newell, 1983) were primarily designed to play an evaluative role and have less to contribute to design generation. These approaches assume that decisions about what tasks the system should support have been made elsewhere and also that design solutions have already been proposed. There are three important distinctions between other TA approaches in HCI and TKS. First, many TA approaches tend to focus on the evaluation and prediction of user performance and do not detail any particular method of task analysis. In contrast, TKS provides a method for identifying, analyzing, and modeling task knowledge that can be usefully applied to the generation of design solutions. Second, the range and complexity of tasks with which we are concerned is creative work tasks in complex domains well beyond the level of simple tasks. Finally, TKS models actual user performance; it is a performance rather than a competence model.

A basic tenet of the TKS approach is that task knowledge structures are functionally equivalent to the knowledge structures that people possess and use when performing a task (Johnson et al., 1988). Task knowledge is represented in conceptual or general knowledge structures in long-term memory and processed in working memory. The TKS approach assumes that human activity associated with tasks is non-random and follows a structured pattern determined by the context, domain, organization, task, and person's experience. We also assume that people develop task knowledge from these structured patterns of activity. With increasing experience, people impose fine-tuned organizing structures on tasks. Some behaviors are carried out together, precede or follow other behaviors, and, in some cases, prime or are primed by other behaviors. Violating the organizing structure that people impose on task activity is one cause of usability problems. The TKS approach also includes knowledge about objects and their associated actions, which differ in how representative they are of the TKS of which they are a part. Furthermore, it is important to identify knowledge about objects and actions and how central they are to the task because not supporting these object/action pairings can also lead to usability detriments.

A TKS is a summary representation of the different types of knowledge that are recruited and used in task behavior. A TKS is related to other TKSs by a number of possible relations. One form of relation between TKSs is in terms of their association within a given role. A person may take on a number of roles and there are tasks associated with each of these roles. For each task that a role may be required to perform, there is a TKS. A second form of relation between TKSs is in terms of the similarity between tasks across roles (between role relations). This occurs when a person is performing a similar task under different roles.

Within each TKS, there are other knowledge representations. The goal structure represents the goals and subgoals identified within the TKS. The goal structure also includes the enabling and conditional states that must prevail if a goal or subgoal is to be achieved. Because there may be alternative sets of procedures for achieving a particular subgoal, there are also conditional and contextual groupings of procedures. The action and object knowledge is represented in a taxonomic structure. Within the taxonomic structure, information about the properties of the actions and objects are represented. This includes the representativeness of the object or action, the class or categorical membership and other characteristics such as the procedures in which it is commonly used, its relation to other objects and actions, and its attributes.

The theory of TKS requires information gathering about the following knowledge components for a given task: roles, plans, goals, subgoals, procedures, actions and objects, and their representativeness. (For definitions of the various TKS components, see Johnson et al., 1988; for their use in scenario-based design, see Johnson et al., 1995). TKS at this level provides a descriptive and analytical approach to CTA: It describes, analyzes, and subsequently models users' task knowledge. In addition to the theoretical basis of TKS research, a supporting method has been developed to help designers carry out TKS analyses. This supporting TKS method provides a more prescriptive approach to CTA. It indicates how the specific knowledge modeled can and should be used in design. An extract from an example TKS for the task of ordering a book from a bookshop is given in Fig. 13.1.

The output from a TKS analysis is a series of representations at different levels of abstraction. At the object level, the taxonomic structure identifies representative objects within the domain and the features of those objects. This information can be used prescriptively by designers in making decisions about how to provide a visible representation of the task.

At the next level of representation, the TKS model identifies the knowledge a person has about how to achieve their subgoals and plans they construct for achieving the identified goal of the task. The procedures represented at this level of the TKS provide a description of the rules or pattern of behaviors that people performing the task would normally attempt to execute and the alternative procedures they would execute under particular conditions. This information can be used prescriptively by the system designer to decide how the user will expect to use the objects and actions (functions) in the application. The TKS also identifies what is the most frequent or preferred procedure for achieving a subgoal. This information can be used to set up default modes of operation in the system design.

The next level of the TKS represents an overall summary of the plan, procedures, and objects and actions people associate with a particular task. This information may be of interest to the designer because it provides an overview of particular contexts in which specific procedures of activity might occur. It could also be used to provide the user with a summary representation of how the designer assumes or expects a user task to be performed. At the highest level, the TKS shows the relations between tasks and roles. This information provides the designer with a view as to how different roles or jobs might expect to have access to the same task functions and to those task functions that are specific to particular roles. This task/role information is also of use to designers who may be concerned with configuring a system to suit the needs of a particular organization, since it shows the task/role match of the organization.

For designers and developers of interactive systems to be able to make use of the TKS approach, it is necessary to consider how the prescriptive nature of TKS might be supported within a design process and to provide tools to aid in this activity.

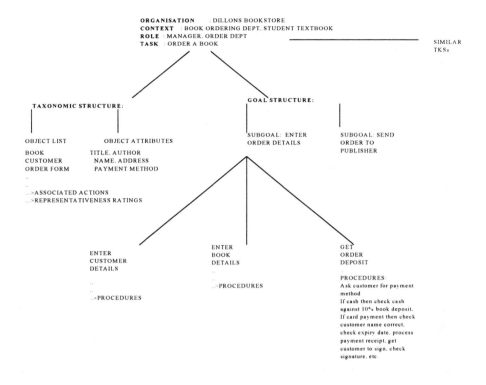

FIG. 13.1   An example extract from a TKS for ordering a book.

SUPPORTING THE USE OF TASK KNOWLEDGE STRUCTURES

From our earlier work (Johnson & Johnson, 1991a, 1991b), it is clear that if designers are to be expected to prescriptively apply task analysis, they need more than just the detail of the TKS theory and a method for carrying out task analyses. Moreover, the aim for TKS is that it should be applied to the creation and development of user interface designs. It is our belief that task-based approaches to user interface design are important and help progress usability engineering in design. From this position, it follows that the analysis and modeling aspects of TKS should form part of an integrated approach to user interface design. This has resulted in the development of an Advanced Environment for Prototyping with Task Models (ADEPT; see Johnson et al., 1995). A primary goal of this research was to investigate how descriptions of users' tasks should further prescribe the design of systems to support those tasks and to show how tool support might assist the designer in following such an approach. A main purpose of producing the task models is to add to the designers' understanding of the task domain.

Task-based design emphasizes the importance of designers developing an understanding of users' existing work tasks, the requirements for changing those tasks, and the consequences for users' work tasks that are brought about by new designs. Fig. 13.2 summarizes a minimal task-based design process.

The approach starts from an analysis of the existing user tasks and continues with the development of a description of the envisioned tasks as an early design activity. The envisioned task model is a description of how work goals could be achieved if a system were to be designed to support it. It is a specification of the tasks that users could perform with a new system. From this, the process continues with the development of an 'abstract interface model'. This is a high-level description of an interface to support those tasks, expressed in terms of abstract interaction objects, groupings of these objects, and dialogue information. Further design decisions at the level of the abstract interface model may have consequences for the envisioned tasks. The final stage in the process is the progression from abstract interface model to prototype interface, or low-level, executable form of the proposed design. Prototype design tools have been provided in ADEPT to support all stages of the design process, but only this final step is automated under the influence of a set of modifiable design guidelines. The designer may then choose to modify the generated interface using an interface builder tool.

The research conducted on TKS (described herein) has shown that we are able to contribute to design generation. The contribution is descriptive, analyti-

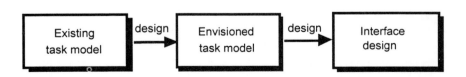

FIG. 13.2   Overview of task-based design.

cal, prescriptive, and constructive. We further believe that TKS can be used to make predictions about usability. To this end, we have developed some basic principles for task-based design that arise from TKS. In addition, we have investigated the use of formal methods in conjunction with TKS to provide a stronger formal engineering background to task-based design.

PRINCIPLES AND FORMAL METHODS

Principles for Supporting Users' Tasks

We have identified four basic principles that provide a predictive approach to task-based user interface design. The first and second principles arise from Hamilton, Johnson, & Johnson (1998); the third and fourth principle arise from the work of Markopoulos, Johnson, & Rowson (1997). The four basic principles are:

- Categorical structuring: Objects that are the same or similar are conceptually grouped together and actions on the same or similar objects are carried out together.
- Procedural dependency: Actions that are causally related to each other through a task goal structure are conceptually grouped together.
- Conformance: User interfaces that conform to the users' conceptual grouping are easier to use.
- Transformation: Transforming a conceptual grouping to accommodate changes in the level or structure of concepts is cognitively expensive.

In a series of experiments, Hamilton et al., (1998) investigated the validity of the first two of these principles. It is not our intention in this chapter to provide detailed descriptions of these experimental tests. Interested readers are referred to Hamilton et al., (1998). Rather, we aim here to show that the "Order a book" TKS was able to identify relevant dimensions of the users' task knowledge; this knowledge, applied in conjunction with the predictive TKS principles of categorical structuring and procedural dependency, resulted in directly predicted and observed usability benefits and costs.

Further research into the use of formal methods in HCI (Markopoulos, 1995; Markopoulos et al., 1997) has shown that formal languages can be used to assess whether user interfaces meet the third and fourth principles.

1. Principle 1–Categorical structuring: In essence, this principle states that the grouping of similar objects results in a subsequent grouping of actions on those objects. It further assumes that users create higher level knowledge constructs of the object group structure (declarative knowledge) and this influences their task-action sequenc-

ing.

This grouping of knowledge facilitates better recall because people retrieve the group as a composite whole. This leads to quicker task-completion times when the user interface reflects this organizing structure.

2. Principle 2–Procedural dependency: In carrying out actions, people form associations among those actions that contribute to a given procedural and goal state. Thus, the sequencing relations of actions are developed, learned, and structured via the goal structure. When this is directly supported by the interface, it facilitates improved recall and results in quicker, more accurate task-completion times.
Hamilton et al., (1998) used these two principles in conjunction with the "Order a book" TKS to generate hypotheses with both qualitative and quantitative predictions of task performance. Four different user interfaces were designed; three governed by the predictive TKS principles using the spatial and temporal groupings
of the display to reflect those principles and a fourth control condition.

In the control condition, spatial grouping followed an alphabetical ordering of left to right, top to bottom. In the categorical structuring condition, the display grouped actions to the same object (e.g., book, customer, etc.). In the procedural condition, actions that were connected within a goal (or subgoal) were grouped together. Finally, in a combined categorical structuring and procedural dependency principles condition, the actions were grouped around objects and, within that grouping, were located around the same goal or subgoal.

Four groups of subjects (one group per condition) with 12 subjects per group carried out a series of trials on the system. Their performance was measured across each trial collecting data in the form of times, sequences, intervals, and errors. In addition, further tests of recall and grouping were carried out in pre- and post-tests using card sorting and forced choice questions.

The results show that, although the control group of subjects had the greatest number of errors to start with, these errors gradually decreased over the trials and the task times gradually improved. The subjects initially followed the sequenced order of actions as they were presented in the display (i.e., alphabetical left to right, top to bottom). However, over the trials, different groupings of action sequences began to appear in the subjects' task behaviors (i.e., they ceased following the display structure). Interestingly, the control subjects began to impose a task structure of their own. Moreover, there was a common task structure imposed across the subjects in this group and the structure imposed was as predicted and supported by the predictive principles.

Subjects in the categorical structuring group made a number of sequence errors and these did not improve. However, their task-completion times did gradually improve and these were much faster than the control group. Of particular interest is that the subjects in this condition continued to follow the structure of the display and did not attempt to impose any other task structure upon it. It appears that subjects recognized that the task and display structure were compatible and so their task behavior followed the one provided by the display.

The procedural dependency principled group of subjects had very few sequencing errors throughout; their task times also gradually improved and were much faster than those of the control group. Again, subjects continued to follow the structure of the display and did not attempt to impose an alternative task structure onto it. The final condition, supporting both categorical structuring and procedural dependency principles, produced similar results.

It appears that the control (unprincipled) design required users to impose their own task structure, whereas the principled conditions allowed the users to follow the task structure that was already supported by the display. There were direct usability consequences of not supporting the predictive principles. Some implications of these findings for user interface design are that the designer should categorize objects and actions based on object similarity and reflect this category structure in the user interface through perceptual properties of the display (such as the spatial grouping of objects in the display). Actions should be categorized according to their goal-related, sequential, and causal relations and this should be reflected in the user interface display through the temporal and perceptual properties of the user interface design. Users can and do follow the user interface structure to build their own task knowledge structures provided that the user interface does support a task structure. Where the user interface does not support a task structure, the user will impose their own task structure but this will take longer to achieve and their performance with the user interface will be less efficient (i.e., slower and with more errors) than if the interface reflected a conceptually meaningful task structure.

The third and fourth principles—namely, conformance and transformation—have been investigated in conjunction with the use of formal methods in HCI. The intention of using formal methods in HCI is to provide rigorous and systematic ways of reasoning about properties of concern. In the following section, we apply formal methods to the principles of conformance and transformation. A new domain has been used to demonstrate the general applicability of the principles and provide greater understanding from employing an example in an application domain with which many readers are likely to be familiar.

APPLYING PREDICTIVE PRINCIPLES TO FORMAL MODELS
OF TASKS AND INTERFACES

Markopoulos et al., (1997) developed a formal modeling approach for human–computer interface software and demonstrated how this can be used in conjunction with a TKS model to formally specify and evaluate user interface design in terms of given usability principles. These formal models are known as *interactor models*. Interactor models can be used analytically for modeling properties of interactive systems, but also as building blocks in the specification of interface software. The ADC interactor model (Markopoulos, 1995) is named after its main components: the Abstraction, the Display, and the Controller. ADC is characterized by the specification in distinct modules of the data operations and the temporal ordering of the behavior of the interactor. The ADC approach provides a framework that defines the scope of the dialogue representation. Furthermore, it facilitates the verification of dialogue properties in a modular fashion.

Interactors are seen as basic communication entities that cooperate with each other to manage the dialogue between a user and an application. Interactors are modeled as LOTOS (a formal language of temporal operators) processes that can communicate with each other and possibly with the user or application. Interactions take place over the gates of the process; they have no duration, but may have a structure that models the transfer of data into or out of the interactor. The interface can be modeled as a graph whose nodes are the interactors and whose edges correspond to connections between them over a pair of gates. Interactors may also be connected to agents representing the application and user.

Using the ADC model in conjunction with TKS, we have been able to test the degree to which any interface conforms to a given task model and the degree to which a given user interface will correspond to the conceptual level equivalence of the task model (i.e., the less conceptual equivalence there is, the greater the transformation required by the user). We have specified the user's task and interface in a common formalism (LOTOS; Markopolous, Rowson, & Johnson, 1997). The interface is defined in terms of an ADC model. The interactive behavior of an ADC is then defined by a series of interactors between the components of an ADC and other ADC. The interactive behavior is then specified using LOTOS process algebra. Temporal behavioral aspects of task models can also be specified using the same process algebra. Comparisons between interfaces and tasks can then be made by applying the predictive principles of conformance and transformation and testing the interfaces in the following manner:

Conformance testing—Does the interface behavior allow the task to be performed?

Transformation (or conceptual equivalence) testing—Is the conceptual level of the user–interface equivalent to the conceptual level of the users' tasks?

To demonstrate this, Markopoulos et al. (1997) took two versions of a commonly found word processing application, Microsoft Word versions 5.1 and 6.0, and a frequently undertaken task in word processing—that of altering the margins and orientation of a document and viewing the results to see whether the document has the desired layout. An idealized TKS model of an optimum way to perform this task was produced by asking five experienced document authors how they currently perform the task and how they would like to perform it. We then developed ADC models for each of the versions of Word 5.1 and 6.0 and wrote LOTOS process algebras for the idealized task models and each of the two versions of the application. This gave us six LOTOS algebras: two for the idealized versions of the two tasks and two for each of the Word 5.1 and Word 6.0 versions of the two tasks. This allowed us to compare properties of each of the designs and each of the tasks, to see whether either of these corresponded to the idealized task models in terms of the level of objects, actions, and proce-dures that were required.

Both versions of the word processor allow you to alter margins, view the results, change the orientation, and then view the results. However, Word 5.1 requires a lower level knowledge of how to manipulate alternative modes of the word processor. The ADC model and LOTOS algebra of Word 5.1 showed that there are two modes of use: normal view and print preview. The user can alter orientation and margins in normal view but cannot see the effects of those changes. In preview, the user can see all the changes but can only alter the mar-gins. Consequently, the user has to switch repeatedly between normal view and preview to carry out the alterations to the orientation. In contrast, the ADC model and LOTOS algebra of Word 6.0 showed that both orientation and mar-gins can be viewed and altered in preview mode, and both can be altered but not viewed in normal mode. Consequently, the user does not need to know about the distinction between orientations and margins relative to the different modes. Furthermore, the user does not have to repeatedly switch between the two modes.

The two idealized activities of altering margins and altering the orienta-tion were specified as two LOTOS processes. These are shown next in a simpli-fied version of LOTOS:

Process 1. [preview,observe,margins,satisfied,close,success]:exit:=
        preview; observe; margins; observe; satisfied; close;
        success;exit end proc.

This translates as enter preview mode, observe the state of the document, change the margins, observe the new state of the document, decide if satisfied with new state, close preview mode, document margins successfully changed, and exit from word processor.

> Process 2. [preview,observe,orientation,satisfied,close,success]:exit:=
>   preview; observe; orientation; observe; satisfied; close; success;
>   exit end proc.

This translates as enter preview mode, observe state of document, change the orientation of the document, observe the new state of the document, decide if satisfied, close preview mode, document orientation successfully changed, and exit from word processor.

When the two word processor ADC model specifications, for the activities of altering orientation and margins were tested for their conformance to the idealized task processes shown earlier, the following results were produced: Word 5.1 succeeds on Process 1 but fails on Process 2, and Word 6.0 succeeds on Process 1 and succeeds on Process 2. Thus, although both word processors allowed the tasks to be performed, they are not equal in the degree to which they support the tasks. Word 5.1 was not equivalent to the users' level of conceptualizing the task and therefore failed the transformation principle. Furthermore, Word 5.1 also failed the conformance principle because it did not conform to the structure of the idealized task model for the orientation task activity because it did not allow the user to alter orientation while viewing the effects of the alterations on the document. Consequently, Word 5.1 would be harder to use for this task than Version 6.0. This demonstrates that formal methods—TKS models and TKS derived usability principles—can support both comparative and isolated testing of user interface designs for their ability to support efficient task performance.

In summary, the development of principles for user interface design changes the ability of task analysis from being descriptive and prescriptive, to being able to predict the usability consequences of designs in terms of their adherence to TKS principles.

CONCLUSION

This chapter began by outlining a number of concerns and issues related to the employment of CTA in HCI. The TKS approach was developed to model conceptual, declarative, and procedural knowledge concerned in executing work tasks. In addition, we developed methods for collecting data and constructing TKS models and a basis for using TKS models in user interface design. This provided a descriptive and prescriptive approach to the use of CTA in HCI.

However, a more predictive approach was needed; consequently, task-related design principles have been developed. These principles relate to both conceptual and sequential structures of task knowledge (Hamilton et al., 1998) and have implications for display and interactive design.

The principles provide a theoretical basis for making predictions about the learning and use of interface designs intended to support users' tasks. The research on task principles and predictive evaluation is further developed in our use of formal methods to enable us to specify user tasks and user interface designs using a formal notation (LOTOS) and by applying the TKS principles to assess the user interface design. Together these principles and formal methods provide theoretical and practical advancement in task-based design.

TKS was initially developed to provide a theoretical and practical input to HCI. This motivation also underpins our current research activity into complex and creative collaborative tasks. One such activity involves the analysis and modeling of tasks in collaborative work systems over multimedia, distributed networks to support improved health care for diabetes patients. In this research, we are applying our past research and current extensions to TKS to address considerations such as how the use of media and group working can be analyzed and modeled to further support user interface design.

ACKNOWLEDGMENTS

We are grateful to EPSRC for currently funding the following research projects contributing to TKS: RESCUED grant no. GR/K79154, ARAMIS grant no. GR/K7976, and PRIDE grant no. GR/L93874.

REFERENCES

Card, S.K., Moran, T.P., & Newell, A. (1983). *The psychology of human-computer interaction*. Hillsdale, NJ: Lawrence Erlbaum Associates.

Hamilton, F., Johnson, P., & Johnson, H. (1998, June). *Task-related principles for user interface design*. Proceedings of the Schaerding Workshop on Task Analysis.

Johnson, P. (1992). *Human computer interaction: Psychology, task analysis and software engineering*. New York: McGraw-Hill.

Johnson, H., & Johnson, P. (1991a). Task knowledge structures: Psychological basis and integration into system design. *Acta Psychologica, 78*, 3–26.

Johnson, P., & Johnson H. (1991b). Knowledge analysis of tasks: Task analysis and specification for human-computer systems. In A. Downton (Ed.), *Engineering the human-computer interface* (pp. 119–144). London: McGraw-Hill.

Johnson, P., Johnson H., Waddington, R., & Shouls, A. (1988). Task related knowledge structures: Analysis, modeling and application. In D.M. Jones & R.Winder (Eds.), *People and computers: From research to implementation* (pp. 35–62). Cambridge: Cambridge University Press.

Johnson, P., Johnson, H., & Wilson, S. (1995). Rapid prototyping of user interfaces driven by task models. In J. Carroll (Ed.), *Scenario-based design* (pp. 209–246). New York: J. Wiley.

Markopoulos P. (1995). On the expression of interaction properties within an interactor model. In P. Palanque & R. Bastide (Eds.), *Design, specification, and verification of interactive systems '95* (pp. 294–311). New York: Springer.

Markopoulos, P., Johnson, P. Rowson, J. 1997. Formal aspects of task based design. In M.D. Harrison & J.C. Torres (Eds.), *Design, specification and verification of interactive systems '97* (pp. 209–224). New York: Springer.

Markopoulos, P. Rowson, J., & Johnson, P. (1997). On the composition of interactor specifications. In C. Roast & J. Siddiqi (Eds.), *Formal aspects of the human computer interface* (pp. 132–161). New York: Springer.

14

COGNITIVE TASK ANALYSIS USING ATLAS

W. Ian Hamilton
Human Engineering Limited

THE GOAL OF HUMAN FACTORS INTEGRATION

The early and effective integration of human factors requirements into systems engineering has been a primary goal among human factors practitioners for decades. Fundamental to achieving this objective is the development of techniques that are capable of (a) supporting the management of large quantities of task analysis data, and (b) exploiting these data to deliver rational and objective outputs that are capable of supporting decision making in design.

The task analysis methods are well documented in a book by Kirwan and Ainsworth (1992). This work covers both observational techniques and representational methods, some of which are merely descriptive (such as hierarchical task analysis [HTA]; Annett, Duncan, Stammers, & Gray, 1971; link analysis; Chapanis, 1959). Others have attempted to be predictive (e.g., GOMS; Card, Moran, & Newell, 1983; cognitive complexity theory; Kieras & Polson, 1986).

Whatever the analyst's goals, he will be faced with the problem of managing the large quantity of task analysis data that inevitably emerges. The response to this problem has been the emergence of a plethora of computer tools that address one or other of these needs (e.g., HOS V, Micro Saint, and Wincrew, all of which are available through Micro Analysis & Design Inc.; MIDAS; Corker & Smith, 1997; IPME, which is a UK MOD research development; IPME, 1997).

THE NEED FOR AN INTEGRATED APPROACH

Such computer database techniques have begun to allow the human engineer to manage and utilize task data more efficiently. At the same time, however, the range of inputs demanded for human factors integration has expanded. Human factors practitioners are typically asked to contribute to systems development in a range of ways including: requirements capture, crew complement specification,

215

allocation of functions and job design, training needs analysis (TNA), information requirements specifications, optimization of command and control systems, analysis of HCI complexity, operator performance modeling, workload prediction, and human reliability assessment.

Historically, to meet these various demands, the analyst would need to develop several representations of the description of the task content. This is likely to be extremely labor intensive and almost certainly prohibitively expensive. Even where the analysis has been done at the outset of a project, it has been the author's experience that the data are not maintained as the design develops and so they quickly lose relevance and value.

There is also the added difficulty that, with several representations of task data, there is a risk of inconsistencies emerging. This makes it difficult to track design decision making with any degree of precision. Consequently, there is likely to be a poor audit trail of the human factors contribution. At best, this means that the value added by the human factors practitioners may not be recognized. At worst, it could mean that the human factors contribution is overlooked, resulting in a poorly optimized design.

The required solution to these problems is to create a task data management tool that will allow task analysis data to be developed efficiently, easy to maintain, and capable of delivering the widest possible range of outputs for systems specification and design.

ATLAS

This chapter deals with the ongoing development of the ATLAS tool set which was an attempt to create just such an integrated platform to guide the application of human factors to systems design (Human Engineering Limited, 1996). From the outset, ATLAS was developed with the objective of maximizing the value that can be extracted from task analysis data.

In what follows, a brief description of ATLAS is provided to illustrate its structure and the philosophy adopted in its development. Following this, a more detailed account of the development of a cognitive task analysis capability for the tool is described. This account includes a description of some of the early attempts to integrate cognitive task analysis into ATLAS and their failure. It then goes on to relate how a practical solution was finally created, based on task knowledge structures theory (Johnson, 1992). By adding a transaction analysis rule, it illustrates what has been accomplished with this solution by reference to recent work.

THE STRUCTURE OF ATLAS

Interface

The ATLAS tool set emphasizes the use of convenient graphical interaction techniques for the input and representation of the task data (see Fig. 14.1). The analysis data structure was based on the GOMS theory (Card et al., 1983). GOMS was chosen for its consistency with cognitive theory and because it allows the analysis of the structure and organization of task goals while supporting the prediction of skilled behavior. This offered the best prospect for the creation of a broad-based taxonomy of task data.

The ATLAS task data are held centrally as a database but can be viewed in three main ways: as a hierarchical diagram of task goals, as a time line model, and as tabular data. There are also a variety of data entry options, including the ability to manipulate task data through interaction with the images of the workstation objects and operators that are displayed in the workstation graphic window. The data can also be exported in a variety of ways, including some predefined formats that are specifically tailored to the needs of system evaluation and specification.

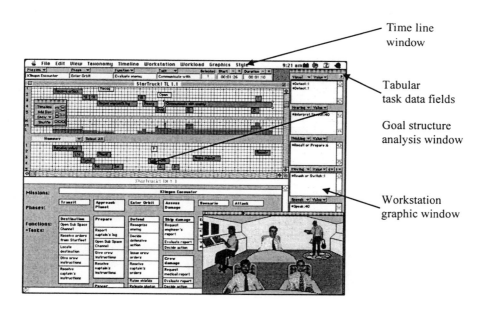

FIG. 14.1   The ATLAS interface, showing Star Truck data.

Using Atlas

The analyst can begin with whichever data format is most appropriate. However, the typical sequence of application for system development is described in the following sections. The analyst creates a goal structure of the mission or job role of interest (Fig. 14.2). The goal structure is fixed at five levels of decomposition, which has proved to be sufficient for all applications so far. These levels are arbitrarily labeled: Mission, Phase, Function, Task, and Attribute. There is no limitation to the breadth of analysis at any of these levels. The analyst works in a graphical editor that utilizes a *post-it note* metaphor.

Mission or Job Role

The Mission level of description can also be labeled the *Job Role*. This is the highest level of description and is used to represent the primary goals of the activity. The following examples of Mission and Job Role items are taken from a range of applications: Missions—Operate Boiler Plant, Operate Incinerator Plant, Ground Attack, Advance to Contact, and Klingon Encounter (see Fig. 14.2), and Job Roles—Mission Planner, Pilot, Navigator, Train Driver, and Tank Commander.

ATLAS implies no properties by the labels *Mission* or *Job Role* other than that this is the top level of the goal structure. The analyst can attach a comment

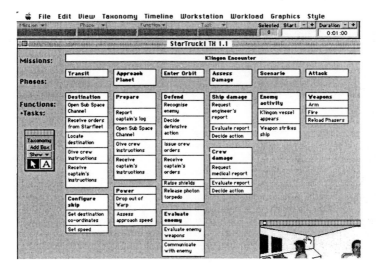

FIG. 14.2   The goal structure analysis window in ATLAS.

to this level of data, and typically this is used to identify certain parameters that have been assumed for the mission or job analysis scenario.

Phase or Responsibility

The Phase level of description can also be labeled *Responsibility*. This is the first level of task subgoals and typically relates to the major sequential elements of the Mission or the primary areas of Job Role responsibility. Phases can be serial or overlapping as required, and the analyst enters (selection) rules to define when a phase or responsibility is invoked. Examples include (from various applications): Shift Hand-over, Maintenance Activities, Prepare for Action, Fault Repairs, and Attack. The analyst has the option to assign the Phases to any operator (within a mission) or move Responsibilities between Job Roles. The order of Phases in the goal structure window is unimportant (because sequence information is defined in the time line window).

Function

Phases or Responsibilities are made up of a number of Functions. Functions are the second level of task subgoals. All relevant Function goals must be accomplished to complete a Phase or Responsibility. Typically these might be (examples drawn from various applications): Accept coordination of aircraft into sector, Agree to changes to traffic management plan, Replenish supplies, Move vehicle, and Observation. Here, too, the analyst can allocate Functions to any operator or even to the system. In other words, the goal structure is largely independent of any specific system design concept or team structure. Consequently, it can be used to explore options for these. Again there are selection rules to define when a Function is performed.

Task

Tasks are effectively behavioral methods for the accomplishment of Functions. Typically there are between 2 and 10 Tasks per Function, although there is, of course, no limit to this number. Selection rules determine when each Task applies. Examples of Tasks are (from a range of applications): Review documentation, Discuss system hand-over, Assess vertical separation, Establish RT contact, Monitor radar screen, and Open file.

Attributes

Tasks are elaborated using Attributes. Attributes are the lowest level of description in ATLAS and refer to the features or properties of tasks. Attributes is a more general classification than the GOMS keystroke level Operators, although the ATLAS Attributes do include behaviors. The full list of Attributes that can be assigned to a Task is extensive; it is organized into three main categories as shown in Table 14.1.

TABLE 14.1
The Attribute Categories in ATLAS

Behavioral	Training	Hazards
Operator (any number as defined in the workstation or timeline)	Criticality (3-point scale)	Hazard type (2 options)
Demand level (typically a 5-point scale)	Frequency (30 options)	Description (text)
Speed setting (also duration calculated)	Difficulty (4 options)	Probability rating (5 options)
Visual behaviors (7 options)	Knowledge required (text)	Consequence rating (8 options)
Hearing behaviors (7 options)	Skills (24 options)	Nature of hazard (11 options)
Thinking behaviors (7 options)	Performance standards (text)	Risk (calculated)
Move behaviors (10 options)	Trade/experience level (text)	Impact rating (user definable)
Speech (specify word number or text)	Training solution questions (user definable, any number allowed)	MAE Impact (user definable)
Leader tasks (5 relationship types)	Training solution recommendation (calculated)	Control measures (text)
Follower tasks (5 relationship types)	Comment (text)	Effectiveness (text)
Comment (text)		Mitigation measures (text) Comment (text)

As indicated in parentheses in Table 14.1, many of the Attributes have predefined value lists. For example, cognitive task analysis was supported in this version of ATLAS by the provision of a list of cognitive behavioral attributes as follows:

- Recall/Prepare
- Simple RT
- Recognition
- Choice RT
- Mental calculation

- Decision (up to five variables)
- Judgment (multiple variables)

The training analysis attributes also support the identification of task knowledge and training goals, albeit in a relatively unstructured format.

Outputs

The behavioral attributes are based on a version of a Visual, Auditory, Cognitive, & Psychomotor (VACP)[1] classification created by Margaret Shuck (1988). Every behavioral attribute is associated with a performance algorithm that is capable of returning a triangular distribution (i.e., fast, medium, and slow) of performance times. In all, there are 32 performance algorithms. These are mostly based on the GOMS human information-processing model (Card et al., 1983) plus other models that are reported in the general literature. Skill development is also acknowledged by virtue of the fact that, for slow times, all behaviors are performed in series. However, for medium and fast times, those behaviors that do not compete for cognitive resources are carried out in parallel. These algorithms can be used to automatically generate timelines for task performance (see Fig 14.3).

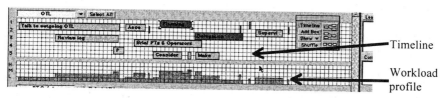

Timeline

Workload profile

FIG. 14.3   A task timeline showing a workload (demand) profile.

The demand attribute is also used for workload assessment (see Fig. 14.3), although there are three other workload calculation techniques that make use of look-up tables or rule-based computational methods. These techniques range from a simple T model (Parks & Boucek, 1988) to demand and conflict models

---

[1]This is a variation on the Visual, Auditory, Cognitive, & Psychomotor behavioral classification system developed by McCracken and Aldrich (1984).

(Aldrich, Szabo, & Bierbaum, 1988; McCracken & Aldrich, 1984); a custom technique combines working memory and divided attention limitations by application of a rule base to the task data. This technique was developed specifically for application to air traffic management tasks (Hamilton, White, & Gosling, 1995). Similarly, many of the risk and training Attributes are supported by lookups, rule bases, and calculation algorithms to deliver objective data on human reliability and basic training solution recommendations.

The tool set has been applied successfully to domains as diverse as process control, air traffic management, military fast jet operations, armored vehicle combat, civil flight deck tasks, train driving, and analysis of hazardous work activities. ATLAS has a demonstrated utility for the investigation of allocation of functions solutions and for the delivery of operator performance modeling, workload analyses, and error assessment data.

THE NEED FOR CTA

The original cognitive task analysis (CTA) component of ATLAS was simplistic. Mental tasks were represented using a simple taxonomy of behaviors. The advantage of this approach was that it allowed the use of performance modeling and workload algorithms. However, it did not capture task knowledge in a formal way. Therefore, ATLAS could not be used effectively to deliver learning objectives for TNA (training needs analysis—a formal approach to the specification of training goals and methods for a new system) or for examining information needs, interaction complexity, and communication issues.

As a first attempt to address this weakness, we added a method for matching training solutions to tasks using a network model of training solution selection criteria. The network method was based on Annett's TEAS[2] algorithm, and the rule base could be edited to emphasize the particular training priorities and constraints of a given project. The full details of this work were reported by Annett and Hamilton (1996).

However, this approach was by no means a comprehensive solution to training needs analysis, and it did not even begin to address the other requirements for CTA (i.e., the specification of communication and information needs

---

[2]TEAS (Training Equipment Advisory System) is a computer-administered checklist that interrogates the equipment design team on various characteristics of the proposed equipment and tasks; on the basis of the answers given, it issues an advisory report on the types of training equipment that may be needed.

and the evaluation of interaction complexity). Also, the training needs specifica-tions were fuzzy and simplistic. This was primarily because the knowledge and skill attributes were recorded simply as text descriptions. Consequently, they were not amenable to any form of objective treatment and the knowledge de-scriptions in particular were not usable in defining learning objectives.

Goals for CTA

It is worth clarifying the goals for a CTA method. They were to: (a) be able to capture and deliver a formal training needs specification, (b) identify informa-tion flow and communications dependencies, and (c) deliver a measure of the complexity of the system interaction for use in assessing design alternatives. Fundamentally, it is necessary to capture the way in which knowledge is used in task performance. Therefore, the first step was to improve the formality of the tool's knowledge representation. More important, however, the knowledge data had to be captured in a way that was consistent with the rest of the ATLAS data structure. The value of a CTA capability would be eroded if it came at the cost of sacrificing the simplicity and transparency of the tool.

HOW TO REPRESENT KNOWLEDGE

Cognitive Theory

According to cognitive theory (Anderson & Bower, 1973), *knowledge* may be defined in terms of units called *propositions*. This is simply the smallest unit of knowledge that can stand as a separate assertion (Anderson, 1980). Typically propositions are made up of objects, agents, properties, and relations. These components represent the concrete objects and operations that make up the world. Therefore, any proposition arranges instances of these components into statements that describe our perception of the objects and events around us.

This notion has attracted a great deal of attention in the context of repre-senting the user's model of complex systems, especially for the analysis of hu-man computer interaction. In the early 1980s, there were numerous attempts to produce formal grammars; these borrowed from the ideas of propositional repre-sentation to create formal measures of the complexity of a computer interface (e.g., Task Action Language; Reisner, 1981) or precisely specify the interaction language that a user has to learn to operate computer software (e.g., Command Language Grammar; Moran, 1981). These grammars were therefore an obvious starting point in the search for a more practical form of CTA.

In addition, knowledge concerned with skilled behavior is represented in the form of rules or production systems (Newell & Simon, 1972). The application of this knowledge in problem solving is goal directed; that is entirely compatible with GOMS, which already uses selection rules for strategy options. Consequently, it would also be necessary for our solution to be capable of capturing and representing procedural task knowledge in a rule-based form.

Practical CTA Using Task Knowledge Structures

We first looked at Task Analysis for Knowledge Descriptions (TAKD; Diaper & Johnson, 1989). This method of task analysis was originally developed in the early 1980s as a way to specify syllabus content. It was later developed into a format for use in the analysis of human–computer interaction. This line of research led to the Task Knowledge Structures (TKS) theory, which was posited by Johnson, Johnson, Waddington, & Shouls (1988).

TKS theory describes task knowledge as being made up of three components: (a) goal structure, (b) procedural structure, and (c) taxonomic substructure. The theory also suggests appropriate forms of representation for each of these components. When examined, these appeared to offer a highly practical approach to knowledge analysis that was also a good fit to the existing ATLAS data structure.

The goal structure can be represented as a hierarchical structure of goals and subgoals that can be shown diagramatically. This is clearly compatible with the task goal structure in ATLAS. The procedural component can be represented as a set of production rules that describe the procedural knowledge and conditions for task execution. There is an obvious parallel with GOMS here, and the rules can be used to describe both the selection of plans and the procedures. This is compatible with the way in which the rules are nested within the ATLAS goal hierarchy. ATLAS places the information about goal/task selection rules into the Phase, Function, and Task levels of data as appropriate.

The final component is the taxonomic substructure. This is where the knowledge about the objects in the task world and their features is represented. This is also referred to as *declarative* or *propositional knowledge*. This representation is accomplished using a formal grammar. Johnson (1992) suggested that any appropriate propositional type grammar can be applied depending on the analyst's objectives. It was necessary to extend ATLAS to incorporate this type of representation, therefore a range of candidate grammars were examined: Task Action Grammar (Payne & Green, 1986), TAKD (Diaper & Johnson, 1989), and Knowledge Analysis of Tasks (Johnson & Johnson, 1991). None of these met the requirements for a flexible and practical method of knowledge analysis. Either their precise syntax for application was inadequately defined to be usable or they were simply too complicated and unwieldy. In the end, it was decided that we should use a tailor-made grammar that has the essential features required for the taxonomic representation but that also allows a certain amount of user adaptation.

The majority of ATLAS applications involve the following elements:

- Agents (or operators who perform the work);
- Objects (or items of hardware, software, and information used in the interaction);
- Relationships (or operations performed on Objects by Agents—e.g., open, close, select, etc.); and
- Properties (and states or features of both Agents and Objects—e.g., ISA, HASA, ON, OFF, etc.).

Therefore, it was decided that these categories of knowledge elements would constitute a fixed portion of the ATLAS system for propositional knowledge representation.

At a lower level, however, the specific instances of each of these categories is likely to vary from one application domain to another. For example, the objects and operations performed on them in a process control room are quite unlike those in an armored fighting vehicle. Consequently, it was decided that this level should be user definable. In fact, the ATLAS user already enters information about operators, objects, and their properties in the workstation window, and this is made available in pop-up menus elsewhere in the program. This functionality simply had to be extended to the propositional analysis window (once one was added).

The next issue was how to incorporate this facility. It seemed clear that the propositional data should be orthogonal to the goal and procedural data (because knowledge about objects would apply across tasks), thus it was not obvious how to embody it within the existing data structure. The solution was to create a new propositional analysis window that would be used to enter the knowledge data into a related data file. To be consistent with the graphical interface philosophy of the program, this was created in a drawing tool format that could be used to edit a propositional network diagram (see Fig. 14.4).

On entering the network editor, the user can select a category using the tools shown in Fig. 14.4 on the left of the windows. Circles are Agents, squares are Objects, the house shape represents Properties, and the line is a Relationship. A menu appears and the analyst can select from the existing list of options in each case or, alternatively, select Edit to define a new instance. Once this selection is made, clicking anywhere inside the drawing area drops the selected item, which is labeled appropriately. To enter a relationship, the analyst selects a relationship type and then the cursor is simply dragged between an Agent and Object. The analyst then repeats these actions to represent the domain knowledge as

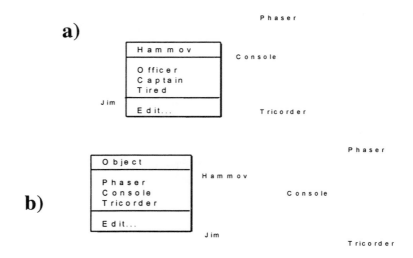

FIG. 14.4 The ATLAS propositional network editor: (a) editing the properties of a defined object, and (b) selecting the type of object to be added.

Agent	Relation	Object	Property
Panel Operator	Select	Turbine No. 2	Start
Panel Operator	Inspect/Check	Annunciator panel	ISA(display)
Panel Operator	Select	Alarm Signal	OFF
...			

FIG. 14.5 An extract from propositional network data.

necessary. At any time, the entire propositional network can be printed or, alternatively, the data that it represents can be printed out in the format shown in Fig. 14.5.

APPLICATIONS

Three case studies illustrate what has been accomplished with this integration of CTA into the ATLAS data structure. Unfortunately, it was not entirely successful. The first case illustrates the failure of the orthogonal structure of the taxonomic representation. The second and third applications illustrate how this problem was ultimately solved by making the taxonomic data a task attribute and by introducing a transactional analysis rule. The limitations of the final solution are then discussed along with the conclusions.

Case Study 1: The Failure of Orthogonal Knowledge Structures

As mentioned previously, the ATLAS tutorial makes use of a make-believe star ship development project known as *Star Truck* (see Fig. 14.1). These data were used to test the utility of the CTA facility. When the ATLAS CTA method is applied to the analysis of the tasks to be performed by the Star Truck crew, however, a major weakness is revealed. It is impossible to map the data from the propositional network to the performance sequence for tasks. Consequently, the data cannot be used for the purposes of a training needs specification.

This problem is caused by the fact that the propositional knowledge data are separated from the goal and procedural knowledge data. Although the analyst can obtain an output of the propositional knowledge, this cannot be used to create effective training specifications because it is not easily related to task goals. The approach successfully captures the relevant task knowledge. However, by divorcing it from the goals and procedures, this cannot be translated into a plan of learning objectives that would form the basis for a syllabus specification.

This weakness would also limit the usefulness of the tool for information requirements analysis. Divorcing the description of the manipulation of information from the goals and procedures description omits vital information on the timing of information transactions. Therefore, it was clear that the taxonomic component could not be arranged orthogonally to the goal structure. Consequently, we had to find a way to integrate the two.

A further problem was the boundary for the analysis of knowledge. The analyst was left to consider all possible interactions between agents and objects and the resulting changes in state, without any guiding principle or end rule. This would be especially difficult for the synthesis of task data for a new application. The analyst would be forced to consider the validity of all possible knowledge relationships. This would result in a large and unwieldy body of analysis data, which would further exacerbate the problems of deriving useful outputs.

An Integration of Task Knowledge Structures

The task taxonomic knowledge had to be captured along with the goal and procedural knowledge. Procedural knowledge was already captured in the task goal structure, therefore the declarative knowledge was added to this by creating a new task attribute field. The analyst creates the goal structure as normal; adds the procedural knowledge at the Phase, Function, and Task levels as required;

and then adds the propositional knowledge data to the Tasks.

This approach certainly solved the problem of relating the propositional data to the goal and procedural data because it was now all part of a single hierarchical data set. However, a further problem was created by virtue of the fact that there was now an enormous amount of redundancy within the propositional data. Consider, for example, frequency with which a common piece of equipment is used in an activity (e.g., a mouse in a word processing task). This approach would require the analyst to describe all the relationships involving the mouse on every occasion.

Of course it is not necessary to describe all the relations and properties of the agents and objects on every occasion, but the problem is then how to keep track of what has been described already and what must still be added. It was necessary to control the level of redundancy without losing anything in completeness. This creates a data management problem that is merely a distraction from the real job of task analysis. What was needed was some form of guiding principle that would help determine the scope of what to include and exclude at each step.

This principle was found in the notion of transactional analysis. This is a simple rule that says it is only necessary to analyze those aspects of knowledge that are directly relevant to the accomplishment of the specific goals for the Task. This rule specifies the scope of the analysis required, ensures essential data are included, and controls redundancy. Determining the knowledge capture requirement from the specific low-level goals of the task appeared to be a parsimonious solution to both the knowledge data integration and end rule problems.

The Transaction Analysis Method

The purpose of the transaction analysis approach was to capture the process that occurs within a task and the knowledge relevant to this. This requires that the task goals are made explicit, that the starting state is specified, that the mental operations and knowledge involved in creating the change to be effected are defined, and that the end states and their consequences for action are recorded. To achieve this, the analysis was supported by a tabular database with the fields defined in Table 14.2.

The format of the data recorded in each field is shown in Table 14.3. This is Task level data. The rules concerning which task is relevant in particular circumstances are stored at the Function level. In the case shown, the task would have been selected as a result of the alarm conditions. For example, the rule involved in this case is:

"IF < Auditory alert: ON: Tone (Continuous, high pitch) AND Annunciator board: Alarms lit> THEN < Task: Invesigate new alarms>"

TABLE 14.2
The Data Fields for Transaction Analysis of Tasks

Data Field	Description
Goal	The primary objectives to be accomplished by the task, described in a Task Goal: *\<goal\>* format
Initiation	The external and internal events that initiate the task (which can be *Outcomes* from preceding tasks), described using the Agent-Relation-Object-Property grammar
Input	The system or event state at the start of the task, described using the Agent-Relation-Object-Property grammar
Knowledge elements	Stored knowledge related to the task goal, described using the Agent-Relation-Object-Property grammar, but also including procedural rules if required
Transactions	The physical and mental processes that alter the state of the information and the specific knowledge variables involved, described using the ATLAS behavioral taxonomy and incorporating the Agent-Relation-Object-Property grammar
Translation	The change to the *Input* data that arises from the *Transactions*; this includes the goals for the selection of an action plan, described using the Agent-Relation-Object-Property grammar, plus the task goal format
Outcomes	Points to the required actions arising directly from the *Translation*, usually in the form Go To: *\<function name\>*

In the example shown in Table 14.3, an operator is responding to an alarm. He must first acknowledge the alarm, determine its cause, and choose an appropriate action to correct the problem. The task begins with the onset of an auditory alarm tone that is accompanied by an indicator light on an annunciator board. The tone, location, and color of the signals all convey information about the nature of the problem, that the operator can check against knowledge elements. He also knows certain condition–action rules that he can apply to the situation. The task ends with the alarms having been silenced and turned–off and the operator having arrived at a hypothesis about the cause and required action.

In Table 14.3, the dashes indicate that parts of the Agent-Relation-Object-Property statements are absent; usually because they are not needed. The statements enclosed in brackets are the property variables. Sometimes there can be more than one property, as in the following case, where both Tone and Meaning are properties of the Object Auditory alert:

TABLE 14.3
The Data Formats and Examples Used for Transaction Analysis of Tasks

Field	Data Format Examples
Goal	Task: Investigate new alarms Task goal: Acknowledge alarm Task goal: Determine alarm cause Task goal: Choose action required
Initiation	- - Auditory alert: ON: Tone (Continuous, high pitch) - - Annunciator board: Alarms lit Operator: Detect: Auditory alert - Operator: Detect: Annunciator board lights -
Input	- - Auditory alert: ON: Tone (Continuous, high pitch) - - Annunciators: ON - - Alarm state cause: *unknown*
Knowledge elements	- - Auditory alert: Tone (Continuous, high pitch): Meaning (New alarm) - - Auditory alert: Cancel button: Location (Annunciator key pad) - - Auditory alert: Cancel button: Color (Red) - - Annunciator board: Location (Top panel) - - Annunciators: Signal (Indicate alarm when lit) - - Annunciators: Codes: Meaning() - - Action options - - - - Alarm condition() - - - Remedy() - - Boiler steam levels: Output pressure () IF <Steam generation: Normal> THEN <Raise steam line pressure> IF <Steam generation: Not normal> THEN <Reduce plant steam demand>
Transactions	Operator: Recognition: Auditory alert: Tone (Continuous, high pitch): Meaning (New alarm) Operator: Recall: Auditory alert cancel: Location (Annunciator key pad) : Color (Red) Operator: Search (display): Auditory alert cancel: Location (Annunciator key pad): Color (Red) Operator: Reach/Switch: Auditory alert cancel: OFF Operator: Recall: Annunciator board: Location (Top panel) Operator: Inspect/Check: Annunciators: Signal (Indicate alarm when lit)

(continued)

	Operator: Text symbology: Annunciators: Codes: Meaning(Low low pressure 125 steam line)
	Operator: Recognition: Annunciators: Codes: Meaning(Low low pressure 125 steam line)
	Operator: Recall: Action options: Alarm condition (Low low pressure 125 steam line)
	Operator: Decide: Action options: Remedy (Raise steam line pressure, Reduce steam demand)
	Operator: Inspect/Check: Boiler steam levels: Output pressure ()
	Operator: Text symbology: Boiler steam levels: Output pressure (Normal)
	Operator: Recall: Action options: Remedy (Raise steam line pressure)
Translation	- - Auditory alarm: OFF
	- - Annunciators: OFF
	- - Alarm state cause: Low low pressure 125 steam line
	Task goal: Raise steam line pressure
Outcomes	Go to Function: Steam control

Operator: Recognition: Auditory alert: Tone (Continuous, high pitch): Meaning (New alarm).

There is no limit to the number of properties that can be associated with an Object or Agent. The following two case studies illustrate the success that has been achieved with this solution.

Case Study 2: An Offshore Heavy Lift Operation

ATLAS was applied to the analysis of the command and control requirements for an offshore heavy lift operation (Hamilton & Charles, 1998). The lift involved using an oil platform's drilling draw works to hoist two modules, totaling 220 tons in weight, from a supply vessel onto the platform deck. There were 19 people involved in this operation; they located on the platform, supply vessel, and standby (rescue) vessel. Although in engineering terms the operation was quite straightforward, it had been recognized that the coordination of the lift team would be crucial to safety.

A full analysis of the operation was performed using ATLAS. A timeline was constructed and the CTA was particularly helpful in elaborating the command and decision-making process for the coordination of all 19 participants. The analysis revealed the information flow and timing of communications between operators.

The cognitive task data proved to be extremely valuable. Not only were the data used for a human reliability study and a communications analysis, but they were also used to design and deliver a set of training packs, each of which focused on a specific role within the lift team. The training packs each included a timeline of actions and a set of checklists and key facts to support their execution. This was a direct output from the transaction analysis. The transaction analysis data were also used to (a) specify a complete communications protocol for the lift operation, and (b) identify the requirements for a comprehensive system of backups and fail safes.

The transaction rule facilitated the analysis to be performed quickly and efficiently. Each task within the coordination process was analyzed from its goals and initiation to its outcomes and relationship to the next task. This process also proved to be transparent enough for the data format to be disseminated throughout the project team for comment. None of the other team members were human factors practitioners, yet they found the data to be meaningful and unambiguous. On the successful completion of the lift, the project manager referred to the human factors analysis as having made a significant and professional contribution to the lift planning.

Case Study 3: ATM Performance Prediction

Recently, the ATLAS CTA capability has been validated for use in predicting air traffic management (ATM) activities. A cognitive task model was constructed for a Tactical Controller in an advanced ATM simulation. This model was then used to predict controller behavior and performance for a new traffic management scenario.

The purpose of this work was to demonstrate that the CTA could be used to derive a prediction of the strategy that the controller would follow. The study was also intended to demonstrate the validity of the ATLAS performance modeling algorithms and workload calculations for this application. The work was conducted on behalf of the Eurocontrol agency in Paris; it is reported in full in Cullen (1999).

For the purposes of this chapter the finding of interest is the accuracy of the strategy prediction. The sequence of actions that were predicted for the test scenario were compared against those observed to occur when a controller was presented with the traffic scenario in a simulation exercise. Although not perfect, the results show that the model accurately predicted the number and timing of RT tasks, monitoring tasks, and conflict-resolution tasks.

The task model failed to predict all instances of dealing with outgoing aircraft, overestimated the number of occasions when the controller was expected to consult his colleague, and underestimated the number of routing instructions issued and housekeeping tasks performed. However, all of these errors were attributable to limitations in the scenario data supplied and to a few omissions from the CTA. If these were corrected, the errors in prediction would not recur. Nothing in the results indicates that the method was fundamentally invalid, and the work is currently proceeding to a second phase of study.

CONCLUSIONS

Usability of the TKS-Based Method

The aim of the work reported here was to create a practical CTA method that would deliver objective human factors integration outputs and to integrate this within an existing GOMS-like task analysis data structure. The solution that was adopted was to utilize the TKS theory, which is highly compatible with GOMS combined with a transactional analysis rule.

This approach offers two key advantages: (a) the knowledge data are tied to the task goal structure, and (b) the transaction rule guides the analyst to identify and describe those knowledge elements involved in the accomplishment of the task. The CTA knowledge representation appears to have worked successfully. Because the knowledge data are closely associated with the task goal structure, more effective training needs analyses can be produced by virtue of the fact that the data are already organized into a Goal-Method-Knowledge structure, which is easy to translate into learning objectives. In addition, the CTA data have shown that they can be used to support task and performance prediction for even complex tasks such as ATM.

The Wider Aim for Human Factors Integration

With regard to the wider goal of creating an integrated data analysis tool to support the full range of human factors integration work, the results so far suggest that ATLAS represents a promising start. Recent applications have demonstrated that the integrated data structure is capable of delivering the following human factors integration outputs:

- Job role definitions,
- Training needs analyses,
- Communications analyses, and
- Task strategy prediction.

This is accomplished without compromising other outputs such as performance modeling data, workload analyses, and human reliability analyses. The graphical interface has also proved to be both efficient to work with and highly intuitive.

The primary advantage that these qualities bestow is that it is possible to develop even large sets of task data for complex team-based activities quickly and reliably. The point and click data entry means that the analyst has to do the minimum amount of typing, and the extensive use of pop-up menus for data entry further improves data consistency.

The graphical presentation also allows several analysts to share the work because each is building on the highly transparent result of earlier work. As well as encouraging consistency by virtue of a common and visible task model, this also has advantages for continuity because not all of the task analysis expertise is invested in one or two individuals. The clear presentation also assists with data verification.

The efficiency of the approach also means that task data development need not be simply an up-front activity, but can be ongoing throughout the design process. Consequently, the task data can be used to lead design decision making through the use of the tool's specification and evaluation outputs. Also, because a wide range of rational and objective outputs can be obtained conveniently from a common set of task data, a comprehensive audit trail of human factors integration decisions can be developed easily.

Limitations of These Results

Unfortunately, there has not yet been an opportunity to test the full range of outputs that the ATLAS CTA method can provide. Consequently, there is still further work to be done to demonstrate that the method has value for the specification of information requirements, especially in the context of military command and control systems, and to establish the feasibility of obtaining outputs that can be used in the assessment of human--computer interaction complexity.

More fundamentally, however, there remains one further overriding obstacle. In the area of knowledge analysis for training needs specification, the data interpretation process is still heavily reliant on the skill and expertise of the analyst. The tool contains algorithms for performance modeling, workload analysis, and reliability analysis, but none for translating knowledge data into training needs specifications. Instead, the analyst relies on skilled judgment and the structure of the data to suggest recommendations. Further work is required to improve the objectivity of this area of output through the use of theoretically based tools to generate training prescriptions.

Availability of the ATLAS Software

The ATLAS software was originally written for the Apple Macintosh. It is currently being rewritten for Windows. A Windows version of the functionality described here should be available in late 1999. It is not intended that this will be a retail product, but that the tool should continue to be used in support of the human factors integration work being conducted by the author and his colleagues.

REFERENCES

Aldrich, T., Szabo, S., & Bierbaum, G. R. (1989). The development and application of models to predict operator workload during system design. In G. R. McMillan, D. Beevis, E. Sallas, M. H. Strub, R. Sutton, & L. van Breda (Eds.), *Applications of Human Performance Models to System Design* (pp. 65–80). New York: Plenum Press.

Anderson, J. R. (1980). *Cognitive psychology and its implications.* San Francisco: W. H. Freeman & Company.

Anderson, J. R., & Bower, G. H. (1973). *Human associative memory.* Washington, DC: V. H. Winston & Sons Inc.

Annett, J., Duncan, K. D., Stammers, R. B., & Gray, M. J. (1971). *Task analysis.* Training Information Paper No. 6, London, HMSO.

Annett, J., & Hamilton, W. I. (1996). *Using ATLAS for training needs analysis.* NATO Panel 8 Defence Applications of Human & Biomedical Sciences AC 243, Workshop: Task Analysis & Training Systems Design, Soesterberg.

Card, S. K., Moran, T. P., & Newell, A. (1983). *The psychology of human–computer interaction.* Hillsdale, NJ: Lawrence Erlbaum Associates.

Chapanis, A. (1959). *Research techniques in human engineering.* Baltimore: Johns Hopkins University Press.

Corker, K. M., & Smith, B. R. (1997). *An architecture and model for cognitive engineering simulation.* Paper published on the WWW. http://ccf.arc.nasa.gov.

Cullen, E. (1999). *Validation of a methodology for predicting performance & workload.* Human Engineering Limited, HEL/EC/97152/RT3, Issue 01, January 1999.

Diaper, D., & Johnson, P. (1989). Task analysis for knowledge descriptions: Theory and application in training. In J. Long & A. Whitefield (Eds.), *Cognitive ergonomics and human computer interaction.* Cambridge, England: Cambridge University Press.

Edmonds, J. C. (1997). PUMA Modelling of ASTRATS Conflict. TOSCA II WP 8.1, TOSCA/NAT/WPR/08.1, Air Traffic Management Development Unit.

Hamilton, W. I., & Charles, P. (1998). Case study: A human factors safety assessment of a heavy lift operation. In M. Hanson (Ed.), *Contemporary ergonomics 1998: Proceedings of the Ergonomics Society Annual Conference.* London: Taylor & Francis.

Hamilton, W. I., White, J., & Gosling, P. (1995). *Final report & validation of workload algorithms and inputs to PUMA WAT.* EPP/HF/CAA/9448a-e, Engineering Production Planning Limited.

Human Engineering Limited. (1996). *ATLAS user guide.* HEL/ATLAS/UG01, Human Engineering Limited.

IPME. (1997). *Integrated performance modelling environment.* http://www.ipme@-maad.com.

Johnson, P. (1992). *Human computer interaction: Psychology, task analysis and software engineering.* New York: McGraw-Hill.

Johnson, P., & Johnson, H. (1991). Knowledge analysis of tasks: Task analysis and specification for human-computer systems. In A. Downton (Ed.), *Engineering the human-computer interface* (pp. 119–144). London: McGraw-Hill.

Johnson, P., Johnson, H., Waddington, R., & Shouls, A. (1988). Task related knowledge structures: Analysis, modelling and application. In D. M. Jones, & R. Winder (Eds.), *People & computers IV: From research to implementation* (pp. 35–62). Cambridge: Cambridge University Press.

Kieras, D., & Polson, P. G. (1986). An approach to the formal analysis of user complexity. *International Journal of Man-Machine Studies, 22,* 365–394.

Kirwan, B., & Ainsworth, L. K. (1992). *A guide to task analysis.* London: Taylor & Francis.

McCracken, J., & Aldrich, T. B. (1984). *Analysis of Selected LHX mission functions.* Technical Note ASI 479-024-84(b) Anacapa Sciences.

Moran, T. P. (1981). The command language grammar: A representation for the user interface of interactive computer systems. *International Journal of Man-Machine Studies, 15,* 3–50.

Newell, A., & Simon, H. (1972). *Human problem solving.* Englewood Cliffs, NJ: Prentice-Hall.

Parks, D. L., & Boucek, G. P. (1989). Workload prediction, diagnosis, and continuing challenges. In G. R. McMillan, D. Beevis, E. Sallas, M. H. Strub, R. Sutton, & L. van Breda (Eds.), *Applications of Human Performance Models to System Design* (pp. 47–63). New York: Plenum Press.

Payne, S. J., & Green, T. R. G. (1986). Task action grammars. *Human-Computer Interaction, 2,* 93–133.

Reisner, P. (1981). Formal grammars & human factors design of an interactive graphics system. *IEEE Transactions on Software Engineering, 5,* 229–240.

Schuck, M. M. (1988). *A new method for the development of task conflict matrices.* Unpublished manuscript.

15

THE ROLE OF COGNITIVE TASK ANALYSIS IN THE APPLICATION OF PREDICTIVE MODELS OF HUMAN PERFORMANCE

David E. Kieras and David E. Meyer
University of Michigan

TWO TRADITIONS IN HUMAN PERFORMANCE MODELING

Two communities have been interested in modeling and predicting human performance. The *Human Factors Engineering* community has long applied methods for predicting human performance for the purpose of arriving at better designs of systems. For example, past applications have been based on methods and modeling tools such as SAINT and HOS (Elkind, Card, Hochberg, & Huey, 1989; McMillan, Beevis, Salas, Strub, Sutton, & Van Breda, 1989). These approaches are based on analyzing the task that the system operator performs, using systematic task analysis methods that have developed over many years of practical experience in system analysis and design (Beevis et al., 1992; Kirwan & Ainsworth, 1992). In addition, modeling tools use well-established theoretical concepts from human information processing to generate performance predictions. Overall, this approach has been successful enough that considerable effort has been expended to implement computer-based tools for constructing and using models of human performance in system design.

Concomitantly, the *Cognitive Psychology Research* community has developed a new generation of concepts for modeling human cognition and performance. These promise considerably more detail and precision and provide a more theoretically unified and coherent framework than traditional human information-processing theory. These advanced approaches are based on computational modeling packages that implement an overall structure for human cognition, a *cognitive architecture*, which is analogous to the hardware architecture of a computer. Within such a framework, models for a specific task or type of task can be implemented. Because the focus has been on developing the scientific basis of the architectures, rather than practical application, the tasks chosen for study have not typically involved actual systems, and systematic methods of task analysis have not been applied.

PRACTICAL VALUE OF PREDICTIVE MODELING

The further development of predictive modeling methodology in human factors work should have a strong impact on system design because it will enable the design of systems that will perform well with considerably less cost and greater success than the current standard methodology, which centers on empirical user testing. User testing is necessarily slow and expensive and, to be most accurate, requires a fairly complete prototype or mockup of the system under design. In contrast, predictive models can produce results on human performance while a future system is still in the earliest design phase, as when SAINT-family models are applied during functional analysis and function allocation. To use the models at their greatest level of precision requires only a detailed design specification. No mockups, prototypes, or human testing are necessary to evaluate a design early enough to get the system design in the right ballpark before the necessary and costly next steps of actual user testing. Current experience with newer approaches to performance modeling, such as MIDAS (Hoecker, Roth, Corker, Lipner, & Bunzo, 1994; Smith & Tyler, 1997) and GOMS (John & Kieras, 1996a, 1996b), is especially encouraging. It would seem that applying the new cognitive architectures from the Cognitive Psychology Research community to the work of Human Factors Engineering would be an obvious and direct step. However, the two communities have been severely compartmentalized. Despite the shared interest in human performance modeling, there is a huge gap in both theory and practice between the researchers building sophisticated cognitive models and the human factors designers of large-scale systems.

PURPOSE OF THIS CHAPTER

This chapter is an effort to begin bridging the gap. We focus on certain problems that arise in applying a modern cognitive modeling approach to predicting performance in somewhat complicated tasks. Our cognitive modeling work has revealed a deficiency in both task analysis methodology and cognitive modeling methodology. We propose an initial solution to the problem and point to how the more general issues could be addressed.

The remainder of this chapter first describes the general approach for using cognitive architecture in system design, including what is required to apply a cognitive architecture to predict human performance in a system design setting. The chapter then presents the critical problem of identifying the task strategy to be used in the model, which is complicated by the presence of optional aspects of how the task is performed. We present a solution to the problem of strategy options, the *bracketing heuristic*, and a test of its application. We conclude with remarks about how the bracketing heuristic can be applied, the requirements it places on task analysis, and the relation of cognitive modeling and task analysis in general.

USING COGNITIVE ARCHITECTURES IN SYSTEM DESIGN

Task-Independent Architecture and Task-Specific Procedures

Currently, the three most important cognitive architectures relevant to this chapter are ACT-R (Anderson, 1993), Soar (Laird, Newell, & Rosenbloom, 1987), and EPIC (Kieras & Meyer, 1997; Kieras, Wood, & Meyer, 1997; Meyer & Kieras, 1997a, 1997b, 1999). All of these involve representing the *"how to do it"* knowledge (procedural knowledge) for a task with a set of production rules, —a simple and elegant formalism. A production rule representation is a set of if–then rules that the architecture mechanisms run to perform the task. Thus, the structures and mechanisms postulated in the architecture represent the fixed or constant mechanisms of human cognition and performance, whereas the production rules represent the task-specific programming, which is analogous to the distinction between computer hardware and software. These architectures make a clear distinction between the fixed versus the task-specific aspects of behavior, and so provide a software reuse capability in constructing models of human performance. If the architecture is accurate, then only the new task-specific components need to be specified to generate performance predictions for a new design problem.

In this chapter, the term *task instance* is used to refer to an exact specific task situation or a specific scenario, whereas a *task* is a *type* or *class* of task situations. Cognitive models are normally programmed to execute a task, not a specific task instance. That is, a typical cognitive psychology experiment involves a general task of responding in a specified way to a variety of different stimuli that arrive in a variety of different contexts. Each such individual stimulus-context situation defines a task instance. A cognitive model is programmed so that it responds properly to all possible task instances. Thus, it is a model for the whole task, not for a specific stimulus-in-context situation. Such models can be termed *generative* after the usage in linguistics: The model contains a set of rules that generate behavior in all possible task instances subsumed by the model. The generative use of cognitive models is central to their value as scientific theories, but it also contrasts sharply to common task analysis practice that tends to focus on a few individual scenarios, which are basically task instances. The important practical implications are discussed later in this chapter.

Current proposed cognitive architectures differ in their detailed assumptions about the components of human cognition and performance. However, these differences are not relevant for the purposes of this chapter, which therefore uses only the EPIC architecture. Nevertheless, the main points herein apply equally to models constructed with any other architecture whose goal is modeling human performance in detail and predictively.

Requirements for Architecture-Based Predictive Modeling

To construct and apply an architectural model of human performance, three elements are necessary:

- *A specified architecture.* There must be a specified architecture that represents the fixed, constant, human abilities that generalize across tasks. The architecture can be extremely simple, as in those underlying GOMS methodology (see John & Kieras, 1996b), or very complex, as in ACT-R (Anderson, 1993) or Soar (Laird, Newell, & Rosenbloom, 1987). In addition, the architecture must include some way to represent task-specific parameters of architectural components in addition to task-specific procedural knowledge. For example, a specific task might involve specialized symbols on a display that will take some amount of time to recognize. These recognition times need to be represented in the architecture by numerical values of parameters chosen for the task domain, even if the recognition is assumed to be handled by standard components of the architecture.

- *A representation of task strategy.* There must be some representational scheme, such as production rules, through which the assumed procedural knowledge for performing a task—here called a *task strategy*—can be stated and used along with the architecture to generate predictions about task activities and performance. This representation is essentially the "programming language" for the architecture; it is the major mechanism that adapts the fixed architecture to deal with tasks and the variety of task instances.

- *A strategy-identification methodology.* Third, there must be a methodology for identifying what strategy is be used to perform the task. This strategy can then be expressed in the representational scheme. The strategy-identification methodology, and the problems in developing it, are one major focus of this chapter.

If all three of these elements can be developed and fielded appropriately, cognitive architecture models could be used routinely in system design to predict human performance for a particular system design. The steps in this routine application would be: (a) determine and represent the task-specific processes and their parameters, (b) identify a strategy for performing the task and then program the architecture to follow the task strategy, (c) run the resulting model through a selected set of representative task instances to obtain predicted human performance, (d) evaluate a proposed system design by comparing the predicted performance against either performance requirements or the performance predicted for alternative system designs, and (e) if necessary, revise the system design and repeat the assessment.

THE STRATEGY-IDENTIFICATION PROBLEM

This proposed process for routine application of cognitive modeling sounds straightforward and simply echoes conventional wisdom in the application of simpler models (e.g., Card, Moran, & Newell, 1983; Elkind, et al., 1989; John & Kieras, 1996a; McMillan et al., 1989). However, identifying the task strategy is the stumbling block. Even in putatively simple laboratory tasks, the task strategy can be very non-obvious, and the difficulties of understanding expert performance in the real world are legion. The extreme detail and precision of modern cognitive architectures exacerbates the problem because it is even harder to identify a detailed strategy than a coarse-grained one. Finally, we know from certain long-standing formal results in computation theory that veridical identification of a task strategy is in principle impossible (e.g., Moore, 1956), so strategy identification is at best only a heuristic process. What heuristic knowledge can be brought to bear on strategy identification from cognitive modeling and human factors?

Cognitive Modeling Practice

In most academic cognitive modeling research, the method for identifying the task strategy is intuitive, informal, and normally unstated. Typically, the researcher makes an intuitive guess about what the task strategy is and then sees whether the predictions generated from the assumed strategy and architecture fit the data. If not, the researcher modifies the strategy or architecture and repeats until a good fit is obtained between the data and predictions.

Thus, the researcher tinkers with a model until its predictions fit the data. The model predicts only in the statistical sense of the term—conceptually, the process is fundamentally post hoc. The scientific lessons learned from this heuristic exercise are based on the vicissitudes experienced in achieving the fit. For example, if the model can be made to fit only with implausible assumptions, the plausibility of the proposed architecture is seriously weakened. If modifications to the architecture are required for a good fit, the question becomes whether these changes are general and lead to a more accurate architecture or whether they are purely ad hoc. However, if applying the architecture to a variety of task domains reveals recurring patterns of strategies, important lessons have been learned about the "software" of human performance as well as the "hardware" (see Meyer & Kieras, 1999). Ultimately, the research endeavor is deemed successful if the lessons learned from the data-fitting exercise are generalizable and useful.

Application Requires True Prediction

However, in trying to predict performance of a human–machine system during system design, the truth is unknown. There are no data to be fit because the system has not yet been constructed. The modeler must construct a model that truly predicts the human–machine performance of a system that does not exist—real prediction is required, not a statistical account of existing data. Granted, some basic parameters may require empirical measurement, such as how long it takes to interpret system-specific symbols on a display screen. Nonetheless, the predictive model must produce results similar to what full-scale measurement of an actual system would yield, but using a simulated system and simulated users. Consequently, the task strategy cannot be determined simply by post hoc data-fitting tinkering. Rather, the analyst must try to guess the task strategy in advance by considering the user interface of the proposed system and the overall task requirements that the user is trying to meet.

This need for a priori determination of the task strategy poses great problems. Practical system design involves tasks of high complexity, and the strength of cognitive modeling supposedly stems from its ability to deal with complex tasks. Yet cognitive modelers cannot perform seat-of-the-pants task analysis fast enough, accurately enough, or reliably enough to yield a practically useful model in a usefully short time. Thus, a crucial future objective for both the scientific and practical application of a cognitive architecture is to develop a priori strategy-identification methods that are powerful, accurate, and reliable enough for practical application.

Will Task Analysis Methodology Help?

Given that task analysis in human factors practice has a long and successful history (Beevis et al., 1992; Kirwan & Ainsworth, 1992), conventional task analysis methods should be applicable to identifying task strategies for use in cognitive models. For example, task flow models like SAINT can be applied directly to a fairly high-level and undetailed task analysis (Laughery, 1989). More detailed models like HOS (Harris, Iavecchia, & Dick, 1989) can be routinely applied when the exact sequence of user actions or user procedures is specified in selected situations or scenarios. Many of the techniques in sources like Kirwan and Ainsworth (1992) and Beevis et al. (1992) supply methods and notation for identifying and recording task procedures and other aspects of the task situation.

However, there is a historical gulf between cognitive modeling and human factors methodology. The considerable experience in practical task analysis has yet to be applied in a systematic fashion to the construction of computational cognitive models. Conversely, the modern approach to computational cognitive architecture modeling is not at all in the mainstream of human factors practice. In short, human factors task analysis experts do not build architected cognitive models, and cognitive modelers do not apply the established and principled methods of task analysis.

The Problem of Optional Aspects of Task Strategy

The thesis of this chapter is that fully exploiting modern cognitive architectural modeling requires some innovation in how we do both task analysis and modeling. The reason is that human task strategies can be more difficult to identify than our previous experience with simple architectures and straightforward tasks would lead us to believe. More specifically, in our own work (Meyer & Kieras, 1997a, 1997b), we have seen that task performance is very heavily influenced by optional aspects of task strategy. These are aspects of how the task is performed that are at the discretion of the human operator, being constrained neither by the task requirements nor the cognitive architecture. These optional aspects of task strategy can occur and cause powerful effects even in very elementary tasks, which have traditionally been assumed to depend solely on the architectural structure of the human information-processing system (see Meyer & Kieras, 1999). Moreover, humans can be remarkably subtle, creative, and even confused in exactly how they choose to do a task. These considerations pose the human factors analyst with a fundamental question: How can performance be predicted when the analyst is forced to guess about how clever or confused the future users of a system will be?

The remainder of the chapter helps answer this question. Here we present an example of an interesting task in which strategy options are involved when modeled with the EPIC architecture. Our work shows how performance can be predicted by bracketing the range of performance produced through the different strategy options. However, first a brief introduction to the EPIC architecture and its representation of task strategies is necessary.

THE BRACKETING HEURISTIC FOR PERFORMANCE PREDICTION

The EPIC Architecture

Fig. 15.1 presents the overall structure of the EPIC architecture. The philosophy and many details of EPIC are irrelevant to this chapter and so are not presented here. The reader is referred to Kieras, Wood, and Meyer (1997); and Kieras and Meyer (1997) for detailed descriptions of the architecture; more complete information is also available from the authors. For present purposes, it suffices to say that EPIC postulates separate processors for perceptual, cognitive, and motor systems, which operate in parallel with each other and interact to produce simulated human performance. Task strategies are represented as sets of production rules executed by the cognitive processor. The perceptual processors rely on pa-

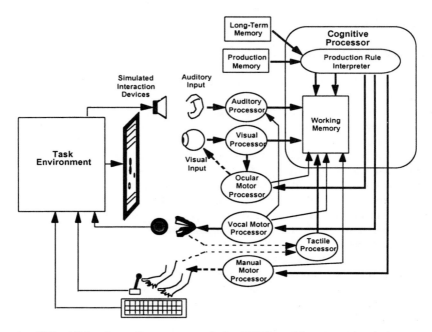

FIG. 15.1 Overall structure of the EPIC architecture simulation system. Task performance is simulated by having the EPIC model for a simulated human (on the right) interact with a simulated task environment (on the left) via a simulated interface between sensory and motor organs and interaction devices. Information flow paths are shown as solid lines and mechanical control or connections as dashed lines. The processors run independently and in parallel with both each other and the Task Environment module.

rameter estimates for task-specific encodings, such as the time required to recognize display symbols.

EPIC's cognitive processor allows fully parallel processing, and the perceptual and motor mechanisms permit a larger set of parallel activities than most architectures have previously entertained. For example, recognition of a visual stimulus object can occur while the eye is being moved to the next object. The physical execution of a movement can be overlapped with the motor programming for the next movement. The hand might be prepared for a movement well in advance of when the movement is fully specified or executed. Our work has repeatedly revealed how such extreme parallelism is required to fit task data (Meyer & Kieras, 1999). If full advantage of this parallelism is taken and task activities are overlapped as much as possible, performance is much faster than if more conservative strategies are followed.

Identification of Task Strategies in EPIC Modeling

In Kieras, Wood, and Meyer (1997), we applied EPIC to model telephone operator task times. We found that not only did we have to identify the required task procedures and implement them as task strategies, but we also had to devise a set of *modeling policies* that specified optional strategy features, such as which processes the task strategy would overlap. Because we could not choose a single policy based on either the task analysis or the EPIC architecture, we explored several of the large number of possibilities by constructing strategies according to selected combinations of modeling policies and then comparing the model predictions to observed task performance. We discovered that all of the EPIC models using these strategies were usefully accurate in predicting the data. However, we also observed that some policies resulted in models that overpredicted the task times, whereas others underpredicted. We were encouraged: Predictions based on the different modeling policies had fallen both above and below the target data, but were also fairly close to them. In what follows, we describe an extension of this approach using a much more strategically complex task as an example.

The Ballas Task and Results

Now that the basics of the EPIC architecture have been presented, we present an example of how optional aspects of task strategy appear in our EPIC model for a complex task. Here we have applied EPIC to predicting performance using data collected by James Ballas and his collaborators at the Naval Research Laboratory (Ballas, Heitmeyer, & Perez, 1992a, 1992b). The experimental task was a dual-task paradigm in which subjects had to track a target with a joystick and concurrently classify other targets presented on a radarlike display.

Fig. 15.2. shows a sketch of the dual-task display; the tracking task is performed in the right-hand window and the tactical classification task (termed the *tactical task* hereafter) in the left-hand window. During these tasks, "blips" would appear on the tactical display, then change color, whereupon the subject had to classify the blips as being hostile or neutral as fast as possible according to a set of prespecified decision rules. Each response to a blip consisted of two keystrokes—one to identify the blip by its "track number" and the second to designate whether it was hostile or neutral. Periodically, an onboard computer would take over the tactical task and classify the blips automatically, leaving the subject free to perform the tracking task by itself. After a time, the computer signaled the subject to resume the tactical task and classify the blips manually.

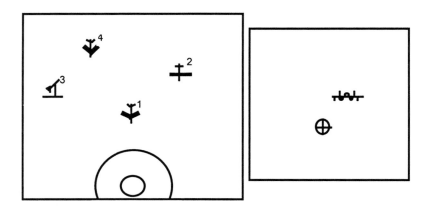

FIG. 15.2 Sketch of the display for the graphical keypad interface
in the Ballas et al. task. The tracking task is performed in the window on the right. Here the aircraft icon moves around and the joystick is used to try to keep the cross-hairs on it. The tactical classification task is performed in the window on the left. Here the center
of the small circle at the bottom of the display represents the "ownship" point; the "blips" appear in the display and generally move
toward the bottom. Initially they are black, but then they change
color and must be responded to, with red meaning confirm as hostile, blue meaning confirm as neutral, and amber meaning classify
based on the speed and direction of the blip. Each blip is identified
by a "track" number. Two keystrokes are made on the keypad—one
for the hostile/neural designation and the other for the track number.

The basic effect observed by Ballas et al. (1992a, 1992b) appears in Fig.
15.3, which shows the observed reaction times of the first and second keystroke
responses for each blip color-change event following the resumption of the manual tactical task. Responses to the blips were slower for a period of time after
task resumption, compared to a matched set of blips events during later steady-
state performance. Thus, there was an interesting automation deficit associated
with getting back into the tactical task when the subject had to resume performing it manually.

Required and Optional Aspects of the Task

The details of our work on modeling the Ballas task are presented elsewhere. For
present purposes, the main point is that getting a close fit to the empirical data
from the model requires assuming that the subject follows a subtle and complex
strategy that is modulated in real time depending on the task workload

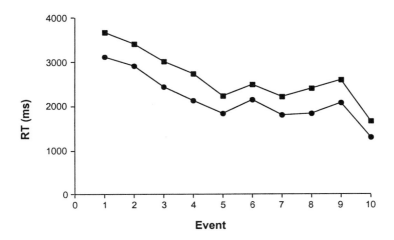

FIG. 15.3 Observed reaction times in the Ballas task for each event after tactical task resumption. The lower curve, plotted with circles, are the times for the first keystroke; the higher curve, plotted with squares, are for the second keystroke. The automation deficit effect appears as longer times for the first few color-change events after the task is resumed (Events 1–3) compared with a matched set of events during steady-state task performance (Events 7–9) .

Fig. 15.4 shows the Ballas task strategy as a hierarchy of tasks and subtasks that we formulated intuitively by the usual cut-and-try approach practiced in most cognitive modeling. Logically, the Ballas task requires alternating between the tracking task and the tactical task according to some task-switching rule, and the tactical task requires choosing a blip and making the appropriate responses to it. However, the specific task-switching criterion, the structural relationships of the task processes, and the extent to which they can be overlapped are constrained by neither the logical requirements of the task nor the EPIC architecture. There are a variety of options that could be chosen by the subjects. We arrived at a specific combination of these options that seems empirically and theoretically plausible by iteratively proposing strategies and comparing their performance to observed data. Of course, there is no guarantee that our final inferred strategy is the actual strategy followed by the subjects. However, because of how difficult it was to fit the data quantitatively, we doubt that there are many other possibilities within the EPIC architecture.

Task Strategy Organization. The strategy shown in Fig. 15.4 can be described in more detail. The dual-task executive supervises the two main subtasks. As well as a third auxiliary task that can monitor events on the tactical

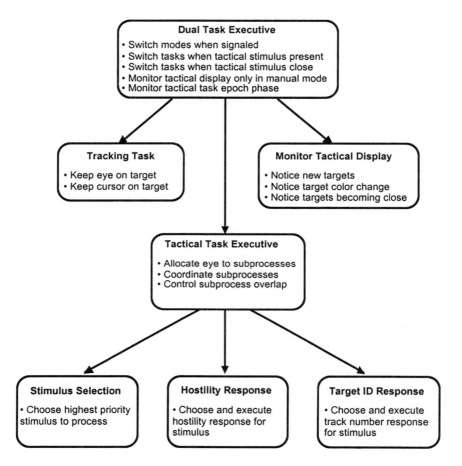

FIG. 15.4 Hierarchical structure of the task strategy used in the models for the Ballas task. Each box represents a task process that performs the functions listed in the box. The executive processes control the task processes below them.

executive can apply a variety of rules for when to switch tasks depending on ancillary contextual details. Under a conservative rule, the dual-task executive waits until some tactical-task blip changes color before suspending tracking and starting the tactical task. Alternatively, an enterprising rule is to anticipate the color-change events by switching to the tactical task when a threatening blip gets close to the "ownship" circle, and thus is likely to change color soon. The eye is placed on the threatening blip, so the response to its color change can be made more quickly.

Performing the tactical task involves an executive process that coordinates three subtasks; one to select a blip for processing, a second to select and produce the hostility designation response for the selected blip, and a third to select and produce the target ID (track number) response for the selected blip. Under EPIC, these three subtasks could run simultaneously depending on the overlapping policy implemented in the task strategy. If the task strategy overlaps the processing heavily, performance is very fast. If not, performance is substantially slower. Generally speaking, once basic perceptual and motor delays have had their effect, the performance speed depends primarily on the extent to which the task processes are overlapped by the task strategy.

Dynamic Modulation of Optional Aspects. To fit the observed task data, we had to postulate that subjects followed the task strategy shown in Fig. 15.4, but dynamically modulated the dual-task executive's task-switch rule and the degree of tactical-task process overlap as a function of current workload. During high load periods, such as those for Events 1–3 and 7–9 in Fig. 15.3, the task strategy is more aggressive with overlapping and anticipation, whereas during lower load periods, less overlapping and anticipation is used.

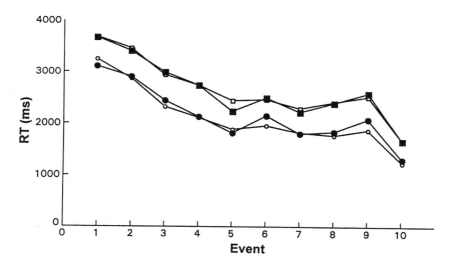

FIG. 15.5 Observed and predicted reaction times in the Ballas task based on the fitted model for each event after tactical task resumption. Observed times are shown as solid points, predicted times as open points. The lower curves (circles) are the times for the first keystroke, the higher curves (squares) for the second. The close fit was obtained as a result of the task strategy dynamically modulating the overlapping and anticipation options as a function of workload.

The resulting model using the dynamically modulated task strategy fits the data very well, as shown in Fig. 15.5. This model is termed the *fitted model* in the rest of this chapter. For present purposes, the fitted model serves to show that EPIC is a reasonably successful architecture under the usual scientific criteria that allow the task strategy to be iteratively modified to fit the data.

Strategy Options Complicate Prediction. Despite the apparent success of this modeling with EPIC, there is a serious limitation with such work. The fact that one can program models using a cognitive architecture to fit data accurately does not mean that models built with the architecture are useful in system design. There are many technical obstacles to making model-based predictions in a practical context, but the chief problem of concern in this chapter is dealing with the optional aspects of the task strategy. These must be resolved before practical model-based predictions are possible. For example, the modulation decisions in the fitted model are not dictated by either the task requirements or the architecture constraints, but rather depend on how the subjects chose to do the task strategically, and this was determined with post hoc data-fitting iterations. The problem for practical prediction is to determine in advance how enterprising the system operator will be: Will operators use a task strategy that aggressively optimizes performance speed, or will they take a more leisurely approach? In combat, it would be reasonable for operators to try to work rapidly, but what if they have to function for hours at a time? Wouldn't they slow down to a sustainable level of effort? These questions are much more difficult to deal with than the typical task analysis because their answers cannot be derived in any obvious a priori way from the task requirements, system design, or cognitive architecture. Rather, such strategy issues involve as yet unknown aspects of human metacognition.

THE BRACKETING HEURISTIC

Given these considerations, this chapter presents a basic new insight: Rather than try to guess the actual task strategy, it is easier and more reliable to characterize the extremes of the possible task strategies using the following *bracketing heuristic*. First, identify a *base strategy* for performing the task. This should be dictated by the logical requirements of the task and a systematic approach to representing the strategy in a well-organized and structured form, and which incorporates plausible estimates for important task-specific parameters. Second, define a *slowest reasonable* version of the base strategy; this strategy consists of nominal adherence to the task requirements, but without use of enterprising strategy options. Such a task strategy is neither haphazard nor lazy. Rather, it is deliberate and unhurried. Third, define a *fastest possible* version of the base strategy, which, given the limits represented by the cognitive architecture, exploits that architecture to its fullest to produce the fastest performance. According to the bracketing heuristic, actual human performance on the fielded system should lie somewhere between the extremes of the fastest possible and slowest reasonable strategy. Exactly where actual performance lies will depend on the level of training, stress, motivation, and fatigue, as well as the extent to which the operators are clever, enterprising, or simply lucky in their choice of strategy. Thus, instead of trying to guess what specific optional strategy the operators will devise, we can simply bracket their performance.

A TEST OF THE BRACKETING HEURISTIC

To test the viability of the bracketing heuristic, we first applied it to the same data set that we used originally to formulate the fitted model. Next we applied it to a new set of data collected for a similar version of the task. In each case, we used the fitted model as the base strategy, and from it created fastest possible and slowest reasonable versions that worked for both cases. In the first case, we were bracketing data that we already had examined extensively; in the second case, we did not even examine the data until the bracketing predictions had been obtained. Thus, we were able to approximate the situation of using a cognitive model predictively.

The Bracketing Strategies

Of course, the bracketing heuristic has to be elaborated in the context of a multi-task situation like the Ballas et al. (1992a, 1992b) task—what is the meaning of "slowest reasonable" and "fastest possible" when there are two tasks that must compete for processing resources? We resolved this in terms of the relative priorities of the two tasks. The tactical task was designated as the highest priority. Thus, fastest possible means that the tactical task is executed as fast as possible regardless of the effect on the lower priority tracking task. Slowest reasonable means that the higher priority of the tactical task should be honored, but no more so than the overall task instructions explicitly require.

More specifically, the slowest reasonable task strategy implements a nominal adherence to the task instructions. The instructions imply that the tracking task should be performed until a blip changes color in the tactical task. Hence, under the slowest reasonable strategy, there is no attempt to anticipate when the tactical task needs attention. Likewise, the instructions imply that when the tactical task is automated, there is no need to monitor the tactical display. Therefore, the slowest reasonable strategy lacks the optional enterprising features we have often had to include in our fitted models (Meyer & Kieras, 1999). Hence, it omits movement prepositioning, advance preparation, and overlapping for the three subprocesses of the tactical task—each response movement must be complete before the next step in processing for the tactical task began.

In contrast, the fastest possible task strategy corresponds to the most extreme interpretation of the task instructions. Because the tactical task supposedly has higher priority than the tracking task, this strategy ignores the tracking task if there is anything useful to be done on the tactical task. For example, if there is even a single blip on the tactical display, the eye is kept on it until it changes color, resulting in faster responding than if the eye had been moved back to the tracking task display. In addition, the tactical display is monitored at all times, even while the tactical task is automated and tracking being performed, because this speeds up identifying relevant blips when the tactical task is resumed. Furthermore, the fastest possible strategy overlaps the three tactical task subprocesses as much as possible, maximizing advance movement prepositioning, preparation, and overlapped movement execution.

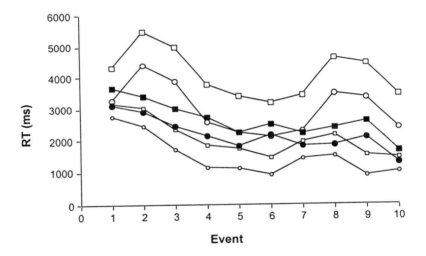

FIG. 15.6 Observed and predicted reaction times in the Ballas task obtained from the bracketing models for each event after tactical task resumption. Observed times are the same data as shown in Fig. 15.3 and are shown as solid points; predicted times are shown as open points. The curves plotted with circles are the times for the first keystroke; the curves plotted with squares are for the second. The slowest reasonable model is plotted with large open points, the fastest possible with small open points. Note how the observed times for each keystroke across events are bracketed between the slowest reasonable and fastest possible predicted times.

Bracketing Results

We derived predictions from the two models that implemented the fastest possible and slowest reasonable strategies using the same perceptual parameter estimates as in the fitted model. The corresponding predicted and observed times are shown in Fig. 15.6. The observed times are the same as those shown in Fig. 15.3. The predictions based on the fastest possible and slowest reasonable strategies do a good job of bracketing the observed times—both in absolute magnitude and sequential trends across events. We obtained similarly good bracketing results for another version of the Ballas task that involved a touch-screen interface.

After this initial success, we next attempted to bracket a new set of data collected by Ballas and his current coworkers for a task that had the same structure and requirements as the previously modeled one, but that involved different event scenarios and different properties of the targets to be classified.

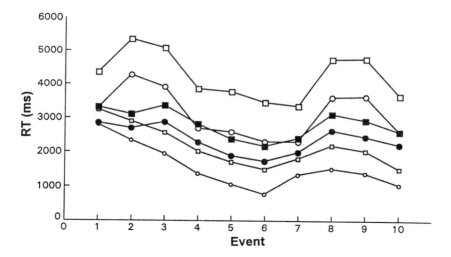

FIG. 15.7 Observed and predicted reaction times in the Ballas task obtained from the bracketing models for each event after tactical task resumption. Observed times are the new data described in the text and are shown as solid points; predicted times are shown as open points. The curves plotted with circles are the times for the first keystroke, the curves plotted with squares are for the second. The slowest reasonable model is plotted with large open points, the fastest possible with small open points. Note how the observed times for each keystroke across events are bracketed between the slowest reasonable and fastest possible predicted times.

For this purpose, Ballas also collected single-task, single-target classification reaction times, in which a single blip was presented and subjects had to classify it as hostile or neutral by pressing a single key. We used these supplementary data to obtain new estimates of the perceptual processing parameters for the new target properties. This was done with a simple model for doing just this tiny task, and the perceptual processing parameters were adjusted to match the differences in the time to classify the single targets.

Then we generated bracketing predictions from the same fastest possible and slowest reasonable models with these perceptual parameters for the new experimental scenarios. Finally, we got the actual data from Ballas's laboratory, and compared the predicted with the observed times. The predicted and observed reaction times from this a priori bracketing are shown in Fig. 15.7. Again, the fastest possible and slowest reasonable predictions do a good job of bracketing the observed performance—both in absolute magnitude and sequential trends across events. We also obtained similarly good bracketing results for a second scenario in the same experiment. Because we had not previously modeled these data, we are highly encouraged about the value of the bracketing heuristic. We hope to conduct more ambitious applications of it in the future.

CONCLUSIONS

Conclusions About the Bracketing Heuristic

Bracketing as a Scientific Tactic. These results suggest a tactic for future scientific work in the post hoc model-fitting mode, in which the goal is to arrive at a well-fitting model by iterative testing. The bracketing predictions could help arrive at a well-fitting task strategy more rapidly. For example, as previously described, our fitted model strategy in the Ballas task adjusted the overlapping dynamically as a function of workload. We arrived at this strategy by tediously iterating through a large number of models and finally achieving the insight that an apt strategy had to perform at nearly top speed during high workload and much more leisurely during low workload.

However, we might have achieved this insight much sooner if we had obtained the bracketing predictions first. For example, in Fig. 15.6, during the high-workload portions of the scenario (Events 1–3 and 7–9), performance is close to the predictions from fastest possible strategy; during the low-workload times, performance is closer to predictions from the slowest reasonable strategy. These results support our final conclusion about dynamic overlapping adjustment, but they also would have made the need for dynamic adjustment rather obvious at the outset. Future work with EPIC will allow us to test this a priori constrained approach further.

The Bracketing Heuristic in System Design. The bracketing heuristic could be used during system design as a way to obtain performance predictions for a proposed system despite the indeterminacy about what final strategies the human operators will learn and apply. The fastest possible and slowest reasonable strategies correspond to the range of variation that could be attributed to differences in levels of training, experience, or motivation on the part of the ultimate operators of the system.

For two system designs being compared to see which produces the best performance, if they are consistently ordered in terms of the fastest and slowest task strategies, the best design can be chosen despite the unknown future effects of operator strategy. There is a more interesting case of predicting system performance, in which there are absolute requirements for the overall speed of performance of the human–machine system. If the bracketing predictions both fall inside the acceptable range of performance, the design is acceptable. However, if the fastest possible performance is too slow, the system design is seriously flawed—no human operator will be able to do the task fast enough. In this situation, the analyst can examine the model and its activity to identify the obstacles to faster performance and then consider alternative system designs to relieve the problem, such as additional automation or a different user interface design.

However, if the fastest possible performance is adequate, but the slowest reasonable is not, then the system design is marginal—its success will depend on whether the human operators are able or willing to perform according to a more efficient task strategy. This problematic situation could be addressed by considering the demands of the faster strategies and assessing whether they could be easily and consistently trained and then reliably executed under actual field conditions. Of course, the safest and most robust approach would be to change the system design so that even the slowest reasonable strategy produces acceptable performance.

Required Task Analysis for Bracketing Prediction

Mandatory Versus Optional Requirements of the Task. The bracketing heuristic is a way to obtain performance predictions in spite of variations in human task strategies. However, to devise the bracketing strategies, we need to know the mandatory and optional task demands so that the bounds on the possible ways of doing the task can be defined. This requirement is not normally an objective of task analysis—we are not asking "how is the task done?", but rather "what absolutely must be done in the task?" Providing an answer to the latter question requires a much more thoughtful analysis than simply observing and recording how users operate an existing system or working through a few specific scenarios of how a system might be operated in the future.

Why Don't Operators Work as Fast as Possible? For the bracketing heuristic to be most useful, we also need a greater understanding of when people will try to achieve the fastest possible performance and when not. Our models of telephone operator performance strongly suggested that some operators optimized their performance with respect to energetic, "ergonomic", or fatigue-based criteria in their task strategy, rather than maximizing their performance speed. How can we tell when and in what ways to take account of such considerations when predicting performance?

Relation of Task Analysis to Cognitive Modeling

Using Computational Models to Express a Task Analysis. Many commonly used task analysis notations are difficult to check for accuracy and completeness due to their informality and reliance on interpretation by the human analyst. In contrast, expressing the result of a task analysis as a computational model would go far toward making task analysis more accurate and complete. By attempting to construct the model, the analyst gains more insight into what the task requirements actually are. By attempting to run the model, the analyst is able to check whether the analysis accurately captures a correct understanding of the task. In short, a computational model is an excellent target for task analysis methods. If the task analysis is complete and accurate enough to specify a running computational model of performance, the essential features of the task have almost certainly been captured. Furthermore, with appropriate tools, a model-based task analysis approach can integrate task analysis, system design, performance evaluation, and system implementation. Both the task analysis and the system design are represented in the computational model, which can both predict performance and potentially help generate the actual user interface implementation (see Byrne, Wood, Sukaviriya, Foley, & Kieras, 1994).

What Is a "Formal" Task Analysis? Traditional task analysis can be fairly informal because the knowledge and intuition of the audience can make up for vagueness and incompleteness in the analysis. However, computational modeling requires a very formal representation of a task and so suggests a distinction between what is and is not formalizable in a task analysis. That is, understanding a user's task is inherently an informal, intuitive process in which the task analyst attempts to arrive at an understanding of the user's task and situation. Once this understanding has been achieved, it must be recorded and communicated in some notational scheme that should be at least formal enough to be standardized and documented. Thus, the task analysis methods developed in the Human Factors community consist essentially of suggestions about what to observe, measure, or record about the user's activities and useful human-readable notations for recording the information so collected. The methods are nothing more, nor less, than guides to make the analysis process more systematic, dependable, and communicable, but the analyst's intuition and expertise is still the actual source of the understanding of the user's task. Thus, having a computational cognitive model to express the results of the task analysis would extend the value and test-ability of this intuitively derived information by representing it in a more rigor-ous and executable form.

How Reliable is Task Analysis? Conventional applications of task analy-sis make only limited claims to rigor and objectivity; it suffices that the analysis helps to develop a good system design. However, if task analysis is to be coupled with computational predictive models for rigorous engineering in system design, it is important to know how much the results of task analysis depend on the idio-syncrasies of the analyst and the vagaries of the analysis process. Unfortunately, there has been little work on assessing the reliability of standard task analysis methods. Clearly, a computational model can be no more reliable than the task analysis used to construct it, and the power of a computational model can be es-pecially dangerous if the reliability of the task analysis from which it came is suspect. This concern has led some researchers to question the value of modeling approaches such as GOMS, but their concern is misplaced—the basic reliability problem lies with the task analysis, not with the modeling approach. High prior-ity should be given to studying the reproducibility and reliability of task analysis methods.

Generative Models are Essential. A major contribution of computa-tional cognitive modeling approaches is its potential for overcoming a serious practical limitation in most task analysis approaches. Typical current task analysis practice is either gross-level analysis or severely limited detailed analysis. That is, the analyst considers only a small number of task instances or scenarios and either records at a detailed level how users operate an existing system or forecasts at a gross level how a future system might be operated.

However, fundamental human performance abilities and limitations can only be addressed at the detailed level of analysis, and for a valid assessment of system performance, a large variety of task instances must be analyzed. How-ever, a typical detailed task analysis method requires enumerating, by hand, every operator action in every specific task instance for every system design un-der consideration. The time and labor requirements are simply prohibitive.

However, as discussed earlier in this chapter, computational cognitive models are generative. Once programmed with a general strategy, a computa-tional model can be run to automatically generate predicted operator behavior and performance for any number of representative situations. Modifications to the system design typically require only small modifications to the model, and the same task instances can then be rerun to quickly obtain a new set of predic-tions. In addition, the explicit representation of the procedural knowledge in a general form allows the proposed system design to be studied and analyzed in considerable depth, such as assessing interface consistency and the potential for transfer of training. The advantages of generative models are presented in more detail in Kieras, Wood, and Meyer (1997) and John and Kieras (1996b).

Can Task Analysis Support Modeling Directly? Clearly, the effort to apply predictive human performance modeling to system design requires more theoretical and practical work on computational cognitive architectures and overcoming the technical difficulties in programming models using these architectures. However, the real bottleneck is in the task analysis process. It would seem that traditional cognitive task analysis at least focused on the proper subject matter and so it should dovetail nicely with the needs of model building. For example, *Hierarchical Task Analysis* (HTA; Annett, Duncan, Stammers, & Gray, 1971; see Kirwan & Ainsworth, 1992), the single most popular task analysis method, represents task procedures in ways similar to GOMS models, which it predates by many years and vastly surpasses in amount of practical application and guidance available to the analyst. However, we do not really know whether methods such as HTA will work in support of model building because, in fact, there is little past experience. What is missing, and badly needed, is a demonstration that one can start with a conventional task analysis such as HTA and then proceed systematically to a usefully accurate computational cognitive model, with no "hand-waving" in between. If so, prospects are good that task analysis methods and computational models can be combined to increase the range and power of the tools available to help design more effective systems.

ACKNOWLEDGMENT

This work was supported by grants to the authors from the Office of Naval Research, Grant No. N00014-92-J-1173, and Grant No. N00014-96-1-0467 in collaboration with James Ballas, Naval Research Laboratory.

REFERENCES

Anderson, J. R. (1993). *Rules of the mind.* Hillsdale, NJ: Lawrence Erlbaum Associates.
Annett, J., Duncan, K. D., Stammers, R. B., & Gray, M. J. (1971). *Task analysis.* London: Her Majesty's Stationery Office.
Ballas, J. A., Heitmeyer, C. L., & Perez, M. A. (1992a). *Direct manipulation and intermittent automation in advanced cockpits* (Techn. Rep. NRL/FR/5534--92-9375). Washington, DC: Naval Research Laboratory.
Ballas, J. A., Heitmeyer, C. L., & Perez, M. A. (1992b). Evaluating two aspects of direct manipulation in advanced cockpits. In *Proceedings of the CHI'92 Conference on Human Factors in Computing Systems* (pp. 127–134). New York: ACM.
Beevis, D., Bost, R., Doering, B., Nordo, E., Oberman, F., Papin, J. P., Schuffel, H., & Streets, D. (1992). *Analysis techniques for man-machine system design* (Report AC/243(P8)TR/7). Brussels, Belgium: Defense Research Group, NATO HQ.
Byrne, M. D., Wood, S. D., Sukaviriya, P., Foley, J. D., & Kieras, D. E. (1994). Automating interface evaluation. In *Proceedings of CHI '94,* Conference on Human Factors in Computing Systems (pp. 232–237). New York: ACM.

Card, S.K., Moran, T.P., & Newell, A. (1983). *The psychology of human-computer interaction,* NJ: Lawrence Erlbaum Associates.

Elkind, J. I., Card, S. K., Hochberg, J., & Huey, B. M. (Eds.). (1989). *Human performance models for computer-aided engineering.* Committee on Human Factors, National Research Council. Washington, DC: National Academy Press.

Harris, R., Iavecchia, H. P., & Dick, A. O. (1989). The Human Operator Simulator (HOS-IV). In G. R. McMillan, D., Beevis, E., Salas, M. H., Strub, R., Sutton, & L., Van Breda (Eds.), *Applications of human performance models to system design* (pp. 275–280). New York: Plenum Press.

Hoecker, D. G., Roth, E. M., Corker, K. M., Lipner, M. H., & Bunzo, M. S. (1994, October). Man–machine design and analysis system (MIDAS) applied to a computer-based procedure-aiding system. In *Proceedings of the 38th annual meeting of the Human Factors and Ergonomics Society.* Memphis, TN.

John, B. E., & Kieras, D. E. (1996a). Using GOMS for user interface design and evaluation: Which technique? *ACM Transactions on Computer-Human Interaction, 3,* 287–319.

John, B. E., & Kieras, D. E. (1996b). The GOMS family of user interface analysis techniques: Comparison and contrast. *ACM Transactions on Computer-Human Interaction, 3,* 320–351.

Kieras, D. E., & Meyer, D. E. (1997). An overview of the EPIC architecture for cognition and performance with application to human-computer interaction. *Human-Computer Interaction, 12,* 391–438.

Kieras, D. E., Wood, S. D., & Meyer, D. E. (1997). Predictive engineering models based on the EPIC architecture for a multimodal high-performance human-computer interaction task. *ACM Transactions on Computer-Human Interaction, 4,* 230–275.

Kirwan, B., & Ainsworth, L. K. (1992). *A guide to task analysis.* London: Taylor & Francis.

Laird, J. E., Newell, A., & Rosenbloom, P. S. (1987). Soar: An architecture for general intelligence. *Artificial Intelligence, 33,* 1–64.

Laughery, K. R. (1989). Micro SAINT—A tool for modeling human performance in systems. In G. R. McMillan, D., Beevis, E., Salas, M. H., Strub, R., Sutton, & L., Van Breda (Eds.), *Applications of human performance models to system design* (pp. 219–230). New York: Plenum Press.

McMillan, G. R., Beevis, D., Salas, E., Strub, M. H., Sutton, R., & Van Breda, L. (1989). *Applications of human performance models to system design.* New York: Plenum Press.

Meyer, D. E., & Kieras, D. E. (1997a). A computational theory of executive cognitive processes and multiple-task performance: Part 1. Basic mechanisms. *Psychological Review, 104,* 3–65.

Meyer, D. E., & Kieras, D. E. (1997b). A computational theory of executive control processes and human multiple-task performance: Part 2. Accounts of psychological refractory-period phenomena. *Psychological Review, 104,* 749–791.

Meyer, D. E., & Kieras, D. E. (1999). Precis to a practical unified theory of cognition and action: Some lessons from computational modeling of human multiple-task performance. In D. Gopher & A. Koriat (Eds.), *Attention and performance XVII* (pp. 15–88), Cambridge, MA: MIT Press.

Moore, E. F. (1956). Gedanken experiments on sequential machines. In C. E. Shannon & J. McCarthy (Eds.), *Automata studies* (pp. 129–153). Princeton, NJ: Princeton University Press.

Smith, B. R., & Tyler, S. W. (1997, March). *The design and application of MIDAS: A constructive simulation for human-system analysis.* Paper presented at the second Simulation Technology and Training Conference, Canberra, Australia.

16

NOVEL USES OF TASK MODELS: TWO CASE STUDIES

Cécile Paris, Sandrine Balbo, and Nadine Ozkan

Commonwealth Scientific and
Industrial Research Organisation

Our work is concerned with the use, adaptation, and refinement of task analysis methodologies for a variety of different situations, believing that so far their exploitation has been needlessly limited. Our emphasis is on novel uses of task models, their introduction into industrial contexts, and their integration into the software design process.

Software engineering (SE) and human factors disciplines find their common ground in the design of user interfaces (UI). Unfortunately, the results of academic research have tended to be too complex or too specific to be seen as useful in industry. Thus, the gap between academia and industry remains large, and industry is not yet fully aware of the benefits of human–computer interaction (HCI) techniques and principles. Similarly, in practice, user requirements analysis and UI design are neither fully nor formally integrated within SE development; hence, there is still a gap between SE and HCI.

We are concerned with bridging these gaps. We feel that task models can bridge SE and UI design, because they are sufficiently formal to support specifications for SE. We also believe they can be used to introduce HCI techniques in industrial contexts. We try to determine the different and innovative uses to which task models can be applied within the software design process and other contexts. We also try to introduce HCI techniques and task models in industrial contexts whenever possible.

In this chapter, we describe two projects in which we are making extensive uses of task models, including in situations where they had not been exploited before. One of the projects also involves the successful introduction of a task analysis in an industrial context.

CASE STUDY: APLCRATES

Our first case study involves the introduction of task analysis and task modeling in a real-world setting; it demonstrates their acceptance by both industrial end users and software engineers. The aim of the APLCRATES[1] project was to design a decision support system for spare parts assessment for the Royal Australian Navy (RAN). In this project, our team was working in collaboration with software engineers and technical writers from IBM Global Services Australia. Our specific responsibilities were knowledge acquisition, design and development of the system, and design of its graphical user interface (GUI).

We do not describe in detail the specifics of the project, its constraints, problems, or the resulting system[2]. Instead we focus on our use of a task model in this industrial context and on the lessons learned from the experience. The decision support system to be developed was to replace an existing system that had a number of limitations and a poor UI. In addition to addressing the limitations and replacing the UI, the objectives for the new system were to significantly reduce training time and encourage higher quality and more standardized performances. These new functional requirements resulted in the following user requirements: (a) automate decisions and provide support for obtaining information from existing external databases, (b) provide a context-sensitive help facility, and (c) provide guidance in the decision-making process by asking questions rather than directing choices.

These requirements meant that it was necessary for the development team to have a good understanding of the tasks to be performed and of the requirements pertaining to those tasks. The group of target end users was not homogeneous. We realized early on that there was a considerable lack of consistency in the end users' understanding of the tasks. A major aspect of the analysis phase became the development of a common and agreed model of assessment expertise among all the end users and the whole software development team.

Originally, the knowledge engineers decided to employ flowcharts for knowledge acquisition and representation. The fact that they could only represent strict sequential activities was found to be too restrictive for this application. Therefore, we turned to an explicit task formalism, with the objective that the task model would contribute significantly to user requirements analysis. We thought that a task model would be a good communication tool among all parties involved (end users, software engineers, knowledge engineers, UI designers, and technical writers), and that an iterative task modeling process would ensure that everyone agreed with and understood the final model. We felt that it would also provide a systematic foundation for subsequent system design and implementation, including detailed knowledge engineering activities.

---

[1] Assembly Part List Creation Reassessment and Tracking Expert System.
[2] See Balbo & Lindley (1997) for partial descriptions.

The APLCRATES project schedule allowed 2 months to complete the user requirements and develop the first prototype. Given the short time available and the size of our task, we chose MAD[3] (Scapin & Pierret-Golbreich, 1990) as the task formalism with the following criteria in mind:

- It had to be appropriate for user requirement analysis and user interface design;
- It had to be task-oriented, because we wanted to model the users' tasks;
- It had to be readable because we hoped to use it to communicate with users; and
- It had to represent a variety of temporal relations among subtasks and actions.

These criteria are issued from a taxonomy developed by Balbo et al. (1998).

There are a number of task models that fit these requirements, such as UAN (User Action Notation; Hix & Hartson 1993), MAD, and DIANE+ (Tarby & Barthet, 1996). Our choice was finalized with two other (more informal) requirements:

- *Simplicity:* We were going to use this formalism in a real-world context with real users and had little time for training users in the use and comprehension of the formalism. Although there have been claims of readability for the various models, to our knowledge, there had not yet been, any experiments performed to validate these claims. Given the time pressures we were facing, we could not test the hypothesis of readability, nor could we risk delays due to miscommunication. Thus, we opted for the formalism that seemed the simplest;
- Our own experience level with the formalism: This is clearly a subjective criterion. However, given the tight schedule, good expertise with one formalism was a clear advantage. Although we were familiar with many of the formalisms proposed in the HCI literature, we had extensive hands-on experience with only a few.

Literature on MAD has described using this method in the early stage of the software UI interface design. However, like several other task analysis methods developed in HCI, previously MAD had been used only in research environments. Thus, this project was going to serve as a validation of these claims.

---

[3]MAD is a French acronym for Analytical Description Method.

Our Uses of MAD in APLCRATES

The use of MAD turned out to be a key feature of the project (Balbo & Lindley 1997). The task model was exploited in a variety of ways, including some unexpected ones. More specifically, we used MAD to:

- Organize our understanding of the spare assessment task in a reliable way, given an explicit and formal representation of the task.
- Perform knowledge acquisition. This resulted in a specific UI interface for the system to provide specific decision support for subtasks. Important, MAD allowed us to structure the knowledge-acquisition task by providing a high level of modularization of the task knowledge. This modularization formed a framework within which detailed knowledge acquisition could occur.
- Communicate with all the parties involved. While performing the first rounds of interviews, we employed MAD as a tool for presenting the results of the analysis to the RAN managers and staff (our users and stakeholders) to demonstrate that we understood their tasks. It turns out that everyone converged to the MAD formalism to communicate their current understanding of the task and knowledge (including the software engineers).
- Help us agree on a common vocabulary to be employed subsequently within the APLCRATES project.
- Perform a complete task analysis. This resulted in the definition of the UI design and structure. More specifically, the task models provided the basis for screen design, with specification of detailed functions associated with each screen. From these specifications, the UI was developed rapidly.
- Help the technical writers design the help system and tutorial. They exploited the task hierarchy to structure the documentation and define help topics.

Thus, MAD was exploited in situations for which it was not originally intended. In fact, this application in general represented a novel domain of application for MAD.

The APLCRATES system is now in use. From some initial feedback, its users show a high level of satisfaction and have in fact nominated it for an industry award. It reduces training time from 6 months to just a couple of weeks, cuts supervisory time by 75%, and may save tens of millions of dollars in excess inventory.

In conclusion, the system that was developed answers the users' needs and shows that the development team had a good understanding of the task. This successful understanding critically relied on a strong collaboration with the end users and an explicit means of representing this understanding. We believe this experience shows that task models can be used to bridge the gap both between SE and HCI and between research and industry.

Second Case Study: The Isolde Authoring Tool

We are currently using task modeling in the Isolde[4] project, whose aim is to design and develop an authoring tool for online help (Paris et al., 1998). The increased needs for online help in software systems and the short time span in which it usually has to be produced are two factors that motivate the development of tools to support technical writers in this task–beyond simple text processing tools. In Isolde, we are developing an interactive, online help drafting tool to be integrated into both the technical writers' working environment and the software design process. The tool is intended to be used by technical writers to help them produce online documentation. Besides the issues of generating hypertext-based online help automatically, we are also addressing the issue of the integration of documentation production into the software design process.

Online help and documentation typically refers to end users' tasks—that is how they can achieve their goals with the system. Given an explicit representation of the system's functionality in terms of these end users' tasks, Isolde produces a draft of the online help for the tasks. Using a system like Isolde, a technical writer needs to manipulate the representation of the task to be documented instead of constructing text. Thus, the nature of the technical writer's work would change (Paris et al., 1998). Isolde's interface to the technical author in Isolde must provide support for this new documentation task. Because constructing these task models from scratch is likely to be a long process, we are also investigating how partial models can be obtained automatically from the underlying software specifications, thus linking documentation production into the software design process (Lu et al., 1999).

The Isolde scenario is as follows. Starting from the specifications of a software application as embodied in a CASE[5] tool, Isolde derives a draft task model for the application. Because the automatically derived model is typically not sufficient to obtain a full task model, a technical writer subsequently augments the model. Hypertext-based online help is then generated. The draft produced is presented to the technical writer for corrections or approval.

---

[4]Isolde is an Integrated Software Online Documentation Environment. Isolde is partially funded by ONR under Grant N0001496-1-0465.
[5]Computer Aided Software Engineering.

In contrast with the ALPCRATES project, Isolde was not done at the instigation of users seeking a solution to a problem: It is a research project whose outcome is a proof-of-concept prototype. Nevertheless, we feel that, given the nature of the work, it was crucial to involve the Isolde's target user population (i.e., technical writers) to guide its design and establish its interaction principles. We worked with two groups of technical writers: experienced indus-trial technical writers from IBM Global Services Australia and under-graduate students of technical writing from University of Western Sydney. In the context of Isolde, our work on task models addresses a number of issues:

- Can task analysis be used to shape our understanding of the process of writing online help as it is carried out in an industrial setting, and can a task model represent that process?
- Can task models describing the functionality of a software system be exploited to generate online help automatically?
- Can such task models be obtained automatically from formal software specifications, such as those embedded in a CASE tool?
- Can end users such as technical writers create and manipulate such task models, and how?

We do not discuss all these issues here. Instead, we focus on the analysis and modeling of the cognitive task of technical writing after motivating our choice of a specific task model to address all these issues.

Choosing a Task Model in Isolde

Our first concern was to choose a task model to be used within Isolde as a representation of a software system's functionality in terms of the end users' tasks. We wished to have a model with high representational power. Instead of using an AI-type representation (as in Paris & Vander Linden 1996), we turned toward the task models developed in the HCI community because we felt that:

- These models would be more appropriate to represent end user tasks (as opposed to an AI system's problem-solving activities) because they had been developed with the end users in mind.
- A number of task models with high representational power already existed, and there was no need for us to define a new one.
- Some of the task models developed in HCI make the claim of readability and usability. Because the users of Isolde would be required to create and manipulate the task models, readability and usability were important.

Our specific criteria to choose a task model among those put forth in the HCI community were the following:

- A formalism suited for user requirement specifications and system design.

- A task representation that would require minimal training on the part of technical writers.
- A powerful representation with specific task attributes represented formally and explicitly.

Based on these desiderata, we chose the DIANE+ formalism (Tarby & Barthet 1996). In addition to fitting our criteria, DIANE+ has two other characteristics that make it desirable for our purposes:

- DIANE+ is intended to be sufficiently formal to be exploited in an automatic way for dialogue monitoring. Thus, DIANE+ attempts to bridge the gap between SE (code generation) and human factors (task perspective on systems). This is particularly well aligned with our goal for Isolde's integration into the software design process.
- DIANE+ is currently being used to generate some simple features of contextual help (Tarby 1994). Again, this is well aligned with our work of generating the documentation automatically from the task model.

To assess the readability and usability of DIANE+ and inform the design of Isolde's UI, we studied the understanding of DIANE+ models by technical writers and their strategies for creating these models (Ozkan et al., 1998). The results of this study show that: (a) the technical writers understood the concepts expressed in task models (task decomposition, task sequencing, task parallelism, etc.), (b) task models are readable by technical writers, and (c) the usability of task models was more problematic (i.e., for the creation of task models, DIANE+ induces a confusion between two types of links between tasks–sequencing links, which express the sequencing of tasks in time, and decomposition links, which expand a task into its subtasks). The results of the study validate that DIANE+ is appropriate for our purposes even if the results about the usability of DIANE+ are somewhat mitigated. The study has also guided us in the design of Isolde's UI.

Studying the Task of Technical Writing

Still with the objective of gaining guidance in the design of Isolde's UI, we used task analysis to shape our understanding of the process of writing online help as it is carried out in an industrial setting. Task modeling was used to capture this understanding and to communicate and validate it with technical writers.

In APLCRATES, the system was designed to support the users' current work practices. Therefore, task analysis was used to reflect user task description. This is not the case with Isolde. In fact, the use of Isolde by technical writers would require a substantial change in their current work practices, as mentioned previously, because they would manipulate task models instead of text. Task analysis was therefore used in Isolde in a prospective way. First, Isolde's UI cannot be designed to closely match an existing task description. Second, the analysis of the technical writing activity was used to yield an understanding of current work practices to better anticipate the changes that will be brought about by Isolde. Abundant literature exists on technical writing, which describes how documentation and, more specifically, online help should be written (e.g., Horton, 1994). Although these manuals are quite specific in characterizing good documentation, they are quite vague as to the process of technical writing. Our aim was to be more specific than what the manuals provide. In addition, based on previous studies of the writing process (e.g., Pemberton et al., 1996), we suspected that real-world industrial constraints shape the actual practice of technical writing in a way that is different from the idealized practice described in the literature. This is why we undertook some task analysis.

Our Process for Task Elicitation. We conducted three 90-minute individual task-elicitation sessions with three expert technical writers (each with more than 10 years of experience). These sessions included both semistructured interviews and observations of simulations of the task on writing online help. The results are captured in three DIANE+ models, each representing the activity of writing online help for one technical writer. We then analyzed the individual models against each other to produce a generalized model. This generalized model was presented to the three initial technical writers and to three others in a general round-table discussion. This lead to further revision and refinement.

It quickly became apparent that we had to focus our analysis in two ways:

1. We decided to restrain our analysis of the task of writing online help to its cognitive, individual (as opposed to collective) aspect. In fact, writing online help also includes collaborative work between technical writers, end users, and the SE team. All these participants may contribute in some way to the specifications of the system at hand or to the revision of its functionalities in the course of the development process. The nature and degree of this collaborative aspect vary from project to project. Isolde's objectives as they currently stand (namely, a single-user authoring tool) motivated us to exclude the aspect of collaborative work from our analysis.

2. The task of writing online help requires two major activities (or subtasks): building a mental model of the software to be documented and producing the text. However, because of the time constraints faced by industrial technical writers, mental model construction and writing are actually done concurrently (i.e., in a manner that is so intertwined that technical writers do not consider them as two separate processes). To further our understanding of the task, however, we had to conceptually distinguish these two. Thus, most interviews were conducted around two themes: mental modeling

and writing. Making this distinction was part of our own learning process of the task of writing online help. In the end, our comprehension of this task collated together these two activities (in accordance with the technical writers' views), and the final version of our model reflects this reconciliation.

The Resulting Task Model of Technical Writing and Reactions From the Technical Writers

According to our model, technical writing consists of one sequence of tasks intertwined with four other tasks that can occur at any time, as shown in Fig. 16.1.

The sequence consists of the following phases:
- A preparation phase, where the technical writers find background information about the system to be documented and start designing the help: its structure and a standard wording. At this point, technical writers may inquire about the general context of the application and start documenting that. This is a necessary step in the production of online help, but it may occur at this early stage or later;

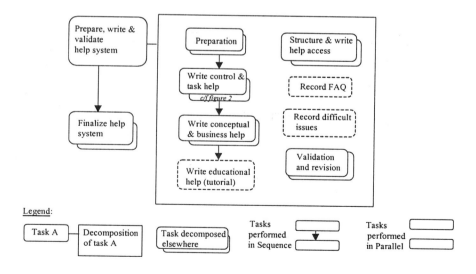

Fig. 16.1   Task model for the task of writing online help.

- A phase where the help on system functionalities is produced, namely (in the terminology used by technical writers): (a) control help, which pertains to buttons, menus, fields, and so on; (b) window help, which pertains to windows; and (c) task help, which pertains to the steps involved in performing a task.

Out of the three technical writers, two undertook this phase in similar ways: the third used quite a different approach, as reflected in the decomposition shown in Fig. 16.2. We decided to make this difference in strategies explicit in our generalized model: The trade-off was between having a generic but fairly bland model and having a model that was not completely generalized but retained all the interesting information. We opted for the second option.

The two strategies that are used to undertake this phase can be qualified as task-driven and features-driven. The task-driven strategy consists of writing control, window, and task help for each task in turn, with no particular order between them. The features-driven strategy consists of writing the control help for the whole application, then the window help, and finally the task help.

It is important to note that, depending on the project, system functional specifications are not always available, finalized, or even accurate when the documentation is undertaken. However, a prototype is frequently available. In

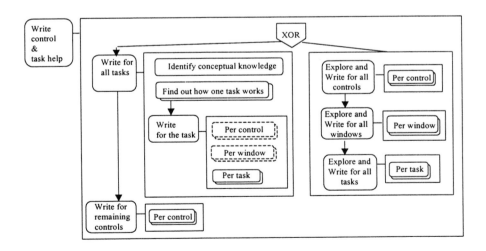

Fig. 16.2   Decomposition of the task "Write control & task help."

the absence of useful written material, this phase of documenting system func-tionalities is often done through active exploration of a prototype, rather than by consulting system specifications.

- The third phase involves writing help or completing the help on what the technical writers call the conceptual and business issues, which includes the purpose of the system, its place in the work context, the concepts that are used, and so on. This help is not di-rectly related to functionality, but relates to global system use.
- The fourth phase involves writing tutorials and educational type of help. This type of help is not required in most applications.

In parallel with this sequence of phases, three other activities take place:

- Writing access to the help: table of contents and the index. This is done throughout the process and is finalized at the end.
- Accumulating system issues that can later be documented as fre-quently asked questions (FAQ).
- Accumulating problematic aspects of the system to address them specifically in the help on system functionalities.

All these phases are iterative, and their output is subject to validation and revi-sion.

The technical writers were both interested and intrigued by the resulting model. To see an explicit and structured representation of their work process seems to have been a shock to them, at least at first.

Discussion

Our analysis shows that, as suspected, the practice of technical writing does not conform to the ideal methods prescribed in textbooks. It is customary to say that a good global comprehension of the system to be documented should be attained before the writing actually begins. This is not the case in industrial environ-ments, given time pressures. For example, the ideal technical writing practice stipulates that the documentation table of contents should be written first, whereas it is left to the end of the actual technical writing process, as is any text pertaining to the global objectives of the system. Similarly, another example of the discrepancy between the ideal practice and the actual practice is that writing is distinct from revision, although we observed that they are completely inter-twined.

We found that the process of building a mental model of the system to be documented is fed and structured by the writing process. For example, the same exploration strategies are used both to discover system functionalities and con-currently write the task-oriented help. Similarly, field help is generated as the technical writer tries various input data types in the system.

We observed two distinct strategies for writing the core online help: features-driven and task-driven writing. This difference cannot be attributed to varying degrees of experience from the technical writers, nor to varying types of projects, SE process, or technologies. At this point, we can only conjecture that this difference is related to different cognitive styles. We hypothesize that the two strategies correspond to two distinct mental model-building strategies. The features-driven strategy is an aggregation strategy, where small, easily manageable units are compounded into larger units, which are themselves compounded. The task-driven strategy is centered on a core concept, the task, to which the various characteristics and attributes are gradually linked.

In conclusion, we have stretched the range of application of task models on another account. Traditional task models à la DIANE+ are intended to closely guide system design based on existing work practices for well-determined tasks, as in APLCRATES. In Isolde, we used DIANE+ in the design of a system that would require substantial changes in current work practices. The use of task models to analyze the technical writing activity in Isolde has expanded the traditional applications of these models in two directions: First, task modeling was applied to an open-ended task and, second, it was used in a prospective way.

CONCLUSIONS

This chapter described various innovative uses of task models:

- As a communication tool between software engineers and HCI specialists.

  This communicational function of task models contributes, albeit in an informal way (e.g., if compared with code generation), to bridging the gap between the disciplines of SE and HCI. Furthermore, it indicates that the integration of task analysis in industrial SE practices is a realistic and beneficial goal to pursue, and thus paves the way to a formalization of this communicational function of task models in the setting of software development. For example, a research direction to be explored from here is the analysis of the ways in which task models can act as a repository of common team understanding and support collaborative system design.

- As a communication tool with end users in an industrial context.

  We have seen the successful introduction of task models in an industrial context with the APLCRATES system. The successful integration of APLCRATES in its target organizational setting can be attributed, in good part, to the development team's comprehension of work organization using the MAD description.

- To help in the design of online help. This was done manually in the APLCRATES project: The structure of the help closely reflected the structure of the task. In Isolde, we investigate the automatic exploitation of task models for the generation of online help.

- To help in system design for both functionalities and user interface. We saw, with the APLCRATES experience, that system design based on task models coming from the HCI community, and therefore intended to guide UI design, can be quite successful even in the case of nontraditional systems such as decision support systems. The decisive factor for success does not seem to be the type of system involved, but rather the close alignment of the system's objectives with current work practices described in the task model. This is in line with current criticism of task models on the ground that they are, by nature, of limited value for the design of innovative systems whose introduction results in changing work practices. However, our position is not so extreme. We have seen with the Isolde project that task modeling can yield useful—and even critical—insight into current work practices. The design of systems that introduce new work practices can then proceed from this basis in an informed way.

- To model open-ended cognitive processes. Task formalisms are normally employed to model systematic, well-structured tasks. In stretching their application to an open-ended task, we have encountered difficulties of representation and some incomprehension on the part of the people who perform this task. This may indicate that the family of task models that we have examined is not fully appropriate to this type of task.

ACKNOWLEDGMENTS

We thank the team of technical writers from IBM Global Services Australia for their enthusiastic participation in our experiments, and Marsha Durham and Necola Hoare from University of Western Sydney, Nepean, for their useful insights. We are grateful to the other members of the Isolde team: Shijian Lu and Keith Vander Linden. Finally, we are thankful to Jean Claude Tarby for his involvement in our discussions about the DIANE+ formalism.

REFERENCES

Balbo, S., & Lindley, C. (1997, July). Adaptation of a task analysis methodology to the design of a decision support system. In Proceedings of Interact'97 (pp. 355–361).

Balbo, S., Paris, C., & Ozkan, N. (1998). Characterising task formalisms: Towards a taxonomy (Tech. Rep. CMIS 98/221). Sydney: CSIRO-MIS.

Hix, D., & Hartson, R. (1993). *Developing user interfaces, ensuring usability through product & process*. New York: Wiley.

Horton, W. (1994). *Designing and writing online documentation*. New York: Wiley.

Lu, S., Paris, C., & Vander Linden, K. (1999, September). Towards the automatic generation of task models from object oriented diagrams. In P. Dewan & S. Shatty (Eds.). Proceedings of the IFIP Working conference on Engineering for Human-Computer Interaction, Crete, Greece (pp. 169–190).

Ozkan, N., Balbo, S., & Paris, C. (1998, September). Can users understand task models? An experiment. In People and Computer XIII—Proceedings of HCI'98 (pp. 123–137). Sheffield, England: Springer-Verlag.

Paris, C., & Vander Linden, K. (1996, July). An interactive support tool for writing multilingual manuals. *IEEE Computer*, 29(7), 49–56.

Paris, C., Vander Linden, K., & Lu, S., (1998, August). Automatic documentation creation from software specifications. In Proceedings of the Third Australian Document Computing Symposium. University of Sydney, Technical Report 518. Sydney, Australia.

Pemberton, L., Gorman, L., Hartley, T., & Power, R., (1996). Computer support for producing software documentation: Some possible futures. In T. Geest and M. Sharples (Eds), *The new writing environment: Writers at work in a world of technology*. (pp. 59–72). Berlin: Springer-Verlag.

Scapin, D., & Pierret-Golbreich, C. (1990). Toward a method for task description: MAD. In L. Berlingvet & D. Berthellete (Eds.), *Proceedings of Work with Display Units 89* (pp. 371–380). New York: Elsevier Science Publishers.

Tarby, J.-C. (1994, August). The automatic management of human-computer dialogue and contextual help. In Proceedings of the 1994 East-West International Conference on Human-Computer Interaction (pp. I-233–I-243). St. Petersburg, Russia.

Tarby, J.-C., & Barthet, M.-F. (1996, June). The DIANE+ method. In J. Van der Donckt (Eds.). Proceedings of the Second International Workshop on Computer-Aided Design of User Interfaces (pp. 95 –119). Namur, Belgium: Presses Universitaires de Namur.

17

ANALYZING A NOVEL EXPERTISE: AN UNMARKED ROAD

Wayne D. Gray
George Mason University

Susan S. Kirschenbaum
Naval Undersea Warfare Center Division Newport

There are many varieties of task analysis—each with its advantages and disadvantages, each with its adherents and detractors (e.g., see the recent collections published by Annett & Stanton, 1998; Kirwan & Ainsworth, 1992). Most published descriptions focus on how to apply the technique or why it is a good technique to apply. Few accounts written by advocates of a technique are specifically directed at problems and pitfalls in applying the technique. This account is different. Although we are unabashedly enthusiastic advocates of the theory-driven combination of task analysis and protocol analysis that we employ, we hope that by identifying problems and obstacles that we encountered that more people will be better prepared and, therefore, more successful at applying these techniques.

Beware—knowing that the road is narrow, winding, and unmarked does not make the trip easy. It might, however, discourage someone from setting out in the family sedan. For those who are better equipped, knowledge of the hazards ahead may help them avoid blindly plunging forward into a known problem. It is in this spirit that we write this chapter.

The following section provides a brief overview of the techniques we employ. Our introduction concludes with a discussion of the known obstacles to these techniques. The main part of the chapter discusses these obstacles in the context of a specific project—Project Nemo.

Theory-Driven Task Analysis and Protocol Analysis

Theory-driven task analysis decomposes the procedural and declarative knowledge required to perform a task into components supported by the theory. With some additional work on the part of the analyst, the control structure provided by the theory can use the elements of the analysis to form a model of how a user performs the task. Theories with weak or rigid control structures, such as key-stroke-level GOMS or CPM-GOMS (for an overview, see John & Kieras, 1996a, 1996b), may produce models that are only capable of performing the exact task that was analyzed. Theories with more powerful control structures, such as NGOMSL, ACT-R, Soar, or EPIC (see Gray, Young, & Kirschenbaum, 1997), may respond adaptively to perform variations of the analyzed task.

Cognitive theories provide constraints to the final form of the analysis—that is, for how the components must fit together. However, the components per se vary widely, and the analysis of expertise into such components is an underconstrained problem. For example, the expertise exhibited by a chess master in plotting his next move is different from that shown by a medical expert diagnosing a rare disease (VanLehn, 1989). Once the components (i.e., the knowledge structures and strategies) of expertise have been delineated, they can be cast into the mechanisms of a cognitive theory. However, existing cognitive theory provides few a priori constraints for deriving the components of a hitherto unstudied expertise.

Given a rare form of expertise, one that has been subject to few published reports (Kirschenbaum, 1990, 1992, 1994), how does the analyst proceed? The method adopted here is a form of bootstrapping. As shown in Fig. 17.1, an initial task analysis[1] guides a protocol analysis. The task analysis is revised and used as the basis of the next round of protocol analysis. When the analyst deems that the results of the analysis are as good as the existing data permit, the analyst moves to the next phase of the effort.

The story told in this chapter is the story of an iterative loop around the stages shown in Fig. 17.1. The project has now moved to the next phase. Its story is given Ehret, Gray, and Kirschenbaum (in press).

Dead Ends and Wrong Turns

Studying an expertise that has not been extensively analyzed is like traveling on an unmarked road—one with many intersections and forks. What aspects of the expertise are important for the goals of the analysis? Can knowledge of the components of other expertise guide and inform the current analysis or does this knowledge serve to lead us astray? If the expertise is a dynamic expertise—problem solving that takes place over a period of time and that is responsive to

---

[1]The initial task analysis can be as informal as it has to be, but should be as formal as possible. For Project Nemo, the initial task analysis was based on the published literature (Kirschenbaum, 1990, 1992, 1994).

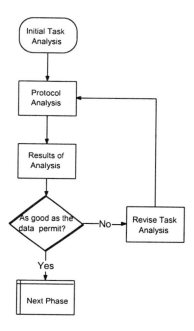

FIG. 17.1 Bootstrapping.

events in the environment—what is the best way to capture key aspects of the expertise without distorting it due to artifacts of data collection?

These problems are common in analyzing expertise. Indeed, others have warned that an almost inevitable danger of doing the first, deep-level cognitive analysis of a hitherto unstudied expertise is that "the final interpretation of the data and its matching against the theory [i.e., task analysis] may appear to reflect mainly hindsight – pulling out of the data the hypotheses that have been implic-itly hidden in it by the data interpretation process" (Ericsson & Simon, 1993, p. 286).

Although we have read (and heeded) the warnings, what we have not read is a detailed discussion by analysts of their encounters with problems that threaten the validity of their conclusions. This chapter fills that void. In it, we provide an autobiographic description of the problems encountered in our analy-ses for Project Nemo. We feel no shame at admitting to having problems. In-deed, when the road is rocky and unmarked, problems must be expected. The shame lies not in having problems, but in not recognizing problems. The shame falls to the analyst who mistakes a dead end for the end of the trip or a wrong turn for the right path.

THE TASK AND OUR GOALS IN ANALYZING IT

Different cognitive task analyses may have different goals. The goal of Project Nemo was to analyze the knowledge and cognitive processes used by submarine approach officers (AOs) as they tried to localize an enemy submarine hiding in deep waters. The project is a collaboration between a navy and a university researcher. An important role played by the navy researcher was to feed the results of the project, as they came in, to those parts of the submarine research community that could make the most use of them. From the beginning of the project, the most interested parties have been the designers of the command workstation for the next-generation submarine.

Knowing that the results of the analysis would be used for interface design provided an important constraint on the knowledge and cognitive processes that Project Nemo analyzed. The AO possesses specialized knowledge that is acquired over a 20-year period. Rather than focus on the acquisition, depth, and breadth of this knowledge, we focused on how it is used as the AO makes progress in his goal of localizing the enemy submarine. Our effort focused on the knowledge, structures, and strategies unique to the dynamic problem-solving process of localizing an enemy submarine hiding in deep water.[2]

Any given task takes place in the context of the artifacts and organization used to perform the task. The goal of many task analyses, including most GOMS analyses, is to analyze task interactions at this *activity level*. Such analyses can either assess the problems with the current way of performing the task or provide specifications for a new system. The goal of the current analysis is different. We are neither involved in critiquing the current system nor directly involved in designing the new system. Rather, our intent is to provide the designers of the new system with a detailed description of the information processing performed by the AO as he localizes an enemy submarine. Hence, in our analysis, we seek to abstract from the activity level to the *functional level* (Gray, John, & Atwood, 1993, pp. 244-257).

---

[2]After a target is detected, it must be localized. Detection tells the AO that a target is out there. Localizing tells him where it is in terms of bearing from own ship, range, course, and speed. Due, in part, to the physics of sound transmission underwater and the need to remain covert, localizing a target is a mathematically underconstrained problem. Passive sonar is the only tool available to the AO. From passive sonar, the AO can directly compute the bearing of the target. Computing the target's range, course, and speed is a difficult process.

ISSUES

We had two sets of problems in understanding AO expertise. The first set included issues in understanding the control structure of the cognitive processes used by the AO to perform the localizing task. The second set entailed understanding the nature and limits to the data we had collected.

The Control Structure of AO Expertise

A common metaphor is to conceptualize problem solving as a search in a problem space (Newell & Simon, 1972). Tasks involving expertise are often thought of as being both wide and deep. At each step in the problem space, there are many alternative next steps (width). Solving a problem involves solving many subproblems, and each subproblem can be decomposed into another subproblem that needs to be solved (depth). In contrast to expertise, the accepted wisdom is that, for everyday tasks, the search space is limited. The problem spaces for everyday tasks are either shallow and wide (like choosing a flavor from the menu in an ice cream store) or narrow and deep (like following a recipe from a cookbook; Norman, 1989).

Clearly, localizing targets hiding in deep water is not an everyday activity. Therefore, we reasoned, that rather than being shallow and wide or narrow and deep that the AOs' expertise must be both wide and deep. This bias led us to make our first and most fundamental mistake regarding the control structure of the AOs' cognitive processes for this task.

Matrix? Subgoals? One of the most basic control structures used in cognitive task analysis is hierarchical, or goal—subgoal, decomposition. From discussions with experts, however, it was clear that AOs kept track of many different pieces of several different tasks. Hence, a classic, hierarchical control structure did not seem accurate.

Our alternative was a matrix goal structure. Although we abandoned the matrix notion before working out the details, its basic elements were as follows. Imagine a cube with AO goals along the x axis, information elements about the target, own ship, and ocean conditions along the y axis, and rules that capture the AOs' procedural knowledge along the z axis. A given rule would yield information regarding one or more information element. In turn, a given information element would be applicable to one or more AO goals. In such a system, one could imagine that the rules that fired (i.e., the actions that the AOs take) would be those rules that yielded the greatest amount of new information for the greatest number of AO goals.

Unfortunately, for our preconceptions, we found little in our data that would support a matrix organization. We gradually abandoned this idea and, for a while, ignored the larger control structure issue to concentrate on how and why one rule rather than another is selected. Our explorations of rule selection led us, albeit a bit unwillingly, to the realization that most AO actions could be characterized as small steps in a shallow goal hierarchy. However, unlike the everyday task of choosing one flavor from a wide but shallow ice cream store menu, AOs′ make many successive choices. It is the nature of these successive choices that characterize the AOs′ procedural expertise.

Our current theory of how AOs solve the localizing problem can be summarized by the rather awkward phrase "schema-directed problem solving with shallow and adaptive subgoaling" (SDPSSAS). The schema is the task-relevant knowledge accumulated over 20 years of experience as a submariner (half of it at sea). It is a knowledge structure[3] that contains both declarative and procedural knowledge. An implication of shallow subgoaling is that the knowledge available to AOs is so rich that the steps required to supplement this knowledge can be fairly shallow.

The second implication is that the problem the AO is constantly solving is "what is the state of the world – *NOW*" (where NOW is somewhere on the order of 30 to 300 s). The AO is trying to find a quiet target hiding in a noisy environment while remaining covert and undetected himself. What we see him doing is taking short steps that either (a) assess the noise from the environment or signal from the target—NOW, or (b) attempt to reduce the noise or increase the signal from the target by maneuvering own ship. As shown in Fig. 17.2, these short steps result in shallow subgoaling. When a subgoal pops, the schema is reassessed. The result of this reassessment directs the next step (i.e., selects the next subgoal). This step is accomplished, it returns information to the schema, the schema is reassessed, and so on.

The process of subgoaling is adaptive in two senses. First, the subgoal that is chosen next reflects the current reassessment of the schema. Second, this choice is sensitive to both the long-term importance of the subgoal as well as its recent history of success or failure. Regardless of a goal's long-term importance,

---

[3]As we think of the schema in terms of ACT-R mechanisms, the schema would be a body of task-specific, declarative memory elements and productions. Any given declarative memory element is relatively small and limited. However, the set of task-relevant, declarative memory elements have high interitem association values (see Anderson & Lebière, 1998).

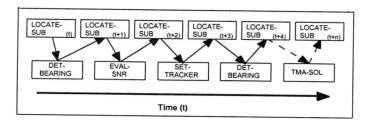

FIG. 17.2   Schema-directed problem solving with shallow and
adaptive subgoaling (SDPSSAS).

AOs will not continue to attempt a goal if successive tries fail. Instead, they will,
choose another goal and return to the more important goal later.[4] The dynamic
aspect of the AO's task plays an important role in this view of schema-directed
problem-solving with shallow and adaptive subgoaling. First, the state of the
AO's world is continually changing—both own ship and target are moving at a
given depth, direction, and speed. For own ship, the value of these attributes can
be changed, but neither own ship nor the target can be stopped. Consequently,
time is an important part of the picture. Second, subgoals are not accomplished
once and then discarded. In the AO's world, subgoals bring in certain types of
information or accomplish certain changes to own ship. As the world changes,
any given subgoal may be revisited (e.g., DET-BEARING in Fig. 17.2).

Choosing What to Do Next: Goal-Driven? Event-Driven?   When we put
aside the issue of the larger organization of the AO's actions—subgoal or matrix
(at this point, we had not hit on SDPSSAS)—we focused on the more local issue
of how or why an individual rule was chosen. For problems such as arithmetic,
physics problems, and Tower of Hanoi, the pacing of the solution is entirely under the control of the person solving the problem. The problem can be decomposed into a deep and increasingly wide series of goals and subgoals. At any
given place in this goal—subgoal hierarchy, the action chosen next completely
depends the plans and knowledge of the problem solver. Such tasks are said to
be *goal-driven.*

---

[4]As described by Lovett (1998), this adaptive subgoaling can be modeled in ACT-R 4.0
as the temporary depression and recovery of the expected value of a goal.

We recognized from the beginning that the AO's problem is not simply goal-driven in that the problem state changes without the intervention of the person. Some part of what the AO does is clearly an event-driven process. The issue is not event-driven versus goal-driven, but what combination of the two controls the AO's problem-solving behavior and how this combination can be represented in a cognitively plausible manner.

As we were struggling with the goal-driven versus event-driven interpretations, we were having problems supporting another early idea—localizing a target as a diagnostic process. The literature suggests that an important first stage in solving many tasks is diagnosing the problem. This stage ends when the correct schema is selected (VanLehn, 1989).

We fully expected that the first stage of localizing the target would entail diagnosing the situation to determine the correct target-finding schema. Indeed, for about the first 18 months, our encodings had a goal called IDENTIFY-POSSIBLE-INITIAL-SCHEMA. Believing that the "absence of evidence is not evidence of absence," we struggled mightily to find support for a diagnostic process. However, we could not find evidence in our protocols or elsewhere (e.g., from any of the other AOs and experts whom we consulted) that we could interpret as evidence that schema selection required extended deliberation. Our tenacity in clinging to the notion of schema selection is, in part, attributable to evidence that suggested that AOs used different schemas when the target was a submarine than when the target was a merchant. Unfortunately, this evidence turned out to be bogus.

In brief, our analyses indicate that when LOCATE-MERCHANT was the goal, fewer subgoals were pushed and popped than when LOCATE-SUBMARINE was the goal (see the left side of Fig. 17.3). More important, most of the subgoals for LOCATE-MERCHANT were similar to, but qualitatively different from, those for LOCATE-SUBMARINE. As discussed later, what turned out to be bogus was the apparent qualitative difference between similar subgoals for different goals. Once this spurious qualitative difference was eliminated, we concluded that the same LOCALIZE-THE-TARGET schema guided the processing of localizing either a hostile submarine or a friendly merchant. This conclusion converged with our failure to find any evidence of schema selection. We currently believe that schema selection is not a problem. Whether the goal is LOCATE-SUBMARINE or LOCATE-MERCHANT, our expert AOs have one schema, LOCALIZE-THE-TARGET, that is automatically chosen.

Schema-Directed Problem Solving. Conceptualizing the AOs' task as schema instantiation, not selection, was the key to a parsimonious account of the general structure of the AOs' cognitive processes. Localizing the target was not

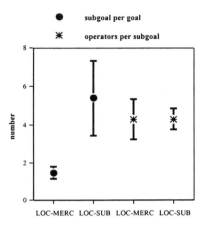

FIG. 17.3   Mean number of subgoals per goal (left two) and mean number of operators per subgoal (right two) for LOCALIZE-MERC and LOCALIZE-SUB. Also shown are the 95% confidence intervals for the standard error of the mean.

driven by goals or events, but was directed by a schema. The data gathered were used to instantiate attributes of this schema. On each cycle of problem solving, the schema was reevaluated, the currently most critical attribute–value pair was identified, and instantiating this pair became the current subgoal. New events were incorporated into the schema and affect problem solving only to the extent that they affect the identification of the currently most critical attribute–value pair.

   This view of schema instantiation as schema-directed problem solving fits in nicely with our emerging awareness of shallow subgoaling. Each time the AO returned to the top-level goal (LOCATE-SUBMARINE in Fig. 17.2), the schema was reevaluated. The subgoal chosen was one that would return information regarding one attribute–value pair. Hence, localizing a target is a wide and shallow task. The width is represented by a well-learned schema. The shallowness is represented by shallow subgoaling. Localizing the target involves dozens of iterations of schema evaluation and shallow subgoaling. These iterations continue until the AO has confidence that the schema as currently instantiated provides accurate information regarding the target's location.

Data Analysis: Levels of Analysis and Limits to the Data

Changes in our taxonomy of goals, subgoals, and operators were driven by three sources: our changing understanding of the general structure of AO cognition (discussed earlier), our failure to understand the limits to our data (discussed next), and our tendency to embed specifics of interacting with the simulation in our analysis of the task—that is, a failure to distinguish between task and artifact (discussed later).

Distinctions Not Supported. Our final encodings resulted in nine categories of operators (Gray, Kirschenbaum, & Ehret, 1997; Kirschenbaum, Gray, & Ehret, 1997). Each of these categories can be considered as representing many subcategories. For example, at one time, we tried to distinguish subcategories of things that could be queried and sources from which information could be received. An AO could query a display, the own ship operator,5 his own memory, an instrument reading, and so on. Likewise, information could be received from long-term memory, from short-term memory, from reading a table, from viewing a graphic, from inferring a relationship among other information, from the own ship operator, and so on. At one time or another, each of the above subcategories was considered—if only briefly—as a candidate for inclusion in the analysis.

In deriving our encoding categories, we focused on two transcripts—one from each of two AOs. New encoding categories could be proposed by any of our three encoders. Typically, the encoder would present a rationale for why the subcategory was needed, along with a particular instance from the transcript that the encoder felt represented that subcategory. If the other two encoders were convinced by the instance, much discussion would be spent defining criteria by which other instances could be identified. Two or three of the encoders would together go through one of the two sample transcripts. New instances of the encoding category would be identified and debated until consensus was achieved. After this, two or three of the encoders would independently go through the other sample transcript in an attempt to identify instances of the new category.

More often than not, each independent encoding would yield a handful of instances (out of about 300 encoded operators) that could be considered members of the new category. However, there would be little or no agreement about which encodings were exemplars of the new category and which were not. At this point, the candidate would be abandoned. We considered it a plausible distinction, but a distinction for which the data were at too coarse of a level to support.

Problem Solving the Tool as Opposed to Problem Solving the Task. We collected data from AOs who localized targets presented on a dynamic simulation of the ocean environment—CSEAL (for more information, see Gray, Kirschenbaum, & Ehret, 1997; Kirschenbaum et al., 1997). However, our task was not to describe how AOs used the simulation (the artifact or tool) to localize the target (the task), but to separate the specifics of the simulation from the more general aspects of their problem-solving process (i.e., a functional level of analysis). Time and again, we found ourselves encoding specifics of using the simulator to localize targets rather than simply localizing targets.

We attempted to encode every segment of the transcript, but realized early on, that a significant number of segments simply had nothing to do with the problem. The fact that many of the segments in a verbal protocol have nothing to do with the problem being solved is not news and, indeed, we expected this. These NAs (not applicable) were easy to identify because they represented comments about the desirability of eating lunch soon, the drive to the base, the weather, the room in which the simulation was run, and so on. Of the 2,882 segments encoded, 946 were in this NA category.

More difficult to distinguish were the segments that did not refer to solving the problem but to some aspect of the simulation. An analogy to this is talking to a co-author about how to format a table in Microsoft Word™ as opposed to discussing the data that would go into the table. A simple example is represented by the following query from the AO to the own ship operator asking about the units (relative or true) in which a particular display represented the data

Protocol:	"and so this (display) is relative or true? (AO points to TB16 block)?"

At some point, we realized that what we were seeing was a ubiquitous phenomenon that was not limited to our paradigm but that represented a type of usability issue. We saw this as problem solving in the tool space, as opposed to the task space, and proposed the tool:task ratio as a usability metric (Kirschenbaum, Gray, Ehret, & Miller, 1996). Following this insight, our transcripts were recoded with a new operator— instrumentation. Most instrumentation operators were found in groups of one to three amid a series of task operators. These small groups of instrumentation operators are essentially asides that are embedded among operators concerned with a particular task goal. Occasionally, both the AO and the own ship operator abandoned the task of localizing the target and became engaged in an episode of collaborative problem solving— attempting to figure out how to get the simulation to take a particular input or to

display a particular type of data. Such episodes were recoded as a new goal—
that of supervising the use of the tool (supervisory).

Over our entire set of encoded data, 421 goals and 2,882 operators were
required to encode the nine scenarios from our six AOs (for more details, see
Gray, Kirschenbaum, & Ehret, 1997; Kirschenbaum et al., 1997). After removing all supervisory goals, their operators, all instrumentation operators, and all
NA operators, we were left with 397 goals and 1,269 operators. We refer to this
remainder as our *clean set*. The clean set of encodings was used in all subsequent
analyses.

The significance of this reduction cannot be overstated; over half of our
encoded utterances had nothing to do with localizing per se. Having these in the
analyses confounded our efforts to make sense of the data. Once these were removed, regularities that had been obscured became apparent. For example, the
scenarios we studied involved two targets: a hostile submarine and a friendly
merchant. Given the shallow subgoaling we were beginning to believe in, it
made sense to us that there would be more subgoals involved in localizing the
quiet submarine than in localizing the noisy merchant. Indeed, this is what our
encodings suggested (see the left two data points in Fig. 17.3). However, the
same subgoal seemed to involve many more steps if its supergoal was LOCATE-
SUBMARINE rather than LOCATE-MERCHANT.

Initially, it did not seem unreasonable that more steps were needed for a
subgoal such as determine the signal-to-noise ratio (determine-SNR) when it was
a subgoal of LOCATE-SUBMARINE than when it was a subgoal of LOCATE-
MERCHANT. Indeed, as discussed earlier, such differences supported our belief
that different schemas were used for different targets. By inference, this finding
supported the belief that schema selection was an important component of the
AO's problem-solving process.

However, once the instrumentation operators and supervisory goals were
removed, regularities appeared. As shown in the right two data points of Fig.
17.3 the subgoals used in LOCATE-MERCHANT required the same number of
operators as the subgoal of LOCATE-SUBMARINE. (An extended discussion of
this point is provided in both Gray, Kirschenbaum et al., 1997, and Kirschenbaum et al., 1997.)

Completed versus Successful Goals. Another part of our struggle to define
the number of levels and depth of the goal stack resulted from an implicit assumption that a completed goal was synonymous with a successful goal. In our
initial attempts to shoehorn reality, we viewed a completed goal as one that returned the information queried. For example, if the AO queried the bearing rate
on a particular target, this goal would not be completed until the target's bearing
rate was determined. Attempting to trace the path from initial query to comple-

tion led us to postulate a tangled web of semi-infinite subgoaling. Stepping back and listening to the data led to a different conclusion. We discovered that, for the AO, knowing that, at a given point in time under current conditions, the bearing rate (or course, speed, etc.) cannot be determined is an important and complete piece of information.

The insight that a goal can be considered *completed* without being considered *successful* supports the shallow subgoaling component of schema-directed problem solving. The AO launches a continuing stream of short queries. Each query returns some information. In the early stages of localizing (immediately after the target has been detected), the information typically is something such as the data are too noisy to answer that question (the SNR is literally too low). This leads the AO to take actions to increase the SNR.

Summary of Issues

Understanding the control structure of the AOs' cognition, together with understanding the nature and limits of the data, were major obstacles in our attempts to do a cognitive analysis of the AOs' task. Before beginning this project, we knew that understanding the control structure of cognition would be the key to the cognitive task analysis (this concern was reflected in the original proposal to ONR).

At each iteration around the loop (see Fig. 17.1), each component of our analysis seemed plausible. What troubled us were our efforts to fit the parts together into a coherent whole. Although, during this period we were not building ACT-R models, we were constantly asking ourselves how the disparate parts could fit into an ACT-R model. It was the failure to answer this question positively that kept driving us around the loop and deeper into the data.

At this point, we have exited the loop (Fig. 17.1) and moved onto the next phase of the project. Although the current hypothesis—schema-directed problem solving with shallow and adaptive subgoaling—is coherent, we are collecting additional data in the hopes of capturing finer grained data on key aspects of AO problem solving in a dynamic environment.

CONCLUSIONS

The current chapter has concentrated on the difficulties of doing a deep-level cognitive task analysis of a novel expertise. The difficulties are all the more notable in that our team of researchers brought to the study considerable expertise in cognitive theory and in applying cognitive theory to real-world tasks. Prior to working on Project Nemo, the authors of this chapter had conducted research on

COBOL programmers, HAWK Air Defense maintenance workers, small-unit tactical team training, phone company operators, as well as more traditional decision-making studies of submariners and school children.

Although the road was difficult and unmarked, we have arrived at our destination. Our current characterization of the AOs' expertise—schema-directed problem solving with shallow and adaptive subgoaling—is both simpler and more profound than what we had envisioned when we began our journey. As far as we can tell, this characterization is unlike any that appears in the literature on expert performance. As such, it is important that those who are designing the command workstation understand this characterization of the AOs' expertise rather than designing an interface that will support the consideration of multiple hypotheses (as in medical diagnoses) or the in-depth exploration of several alternative courses of action (as in chess playing).

Instead of telling stories about how difficult our trip was, we would rather give the reader a sure-fire guide to plotting a safe path to any destination, on any road, marked or unmarked. We do not know if such a guide can be written. However, we are sure that we cannot write one. Unfortunately, the truth remains that, whatever may be done differently, the task of understanding a hitherto unstudied expertise will never be quick or easy. The problems discussed in this chapter can be anticipated but not avoided.

ACKNOWLEDGMENT

More than usual, we thank our agency sponsors and our scientific officer for understanding that if we knew what we were doing, it would not be called research. We believe that the emerging results justify their long-term support of this effort. However, we also understand that there were times when they might have thought that a successful outcome was unlikely. We thank Brian D. Ehret who joined our project about two thirds of the way through the events recounted here. Brian was the third encoder on each of the final encodings of the transcripts. His diagnoses have guided the current phase of data collection. The work on this project at George Mason University was supported by a grant from the Office of Naval Research (#N00014-95-1-0175) to Wayne D. Gray. Susan S. Kirschenbaum's work has been jointly sponsored by Office of Naval Research (ONR) (Program element 61153N) and by Naval Undersea Warfare Center's Independent Research Program as Project A10328.

REFERENCES

Anderson, J. R., & Lebière, C. (Eds.). (1998). *Atomic components of thought.* Hillsdale, NJ: Lawrence Erlbaum Associates.

Annett, J., & Stanton, N. (1998). Introduction to this special issue on task analysis. *Ergonomics, 41*(11), 1529–1536.

Ehret, B. D., Gray, W. D., & Kirschenbaum, S. S. (in press). Contending with complexity: Developing and using a scaled world in applied cognitive research. *Human Factors.*

Gray, W. D., John, B. E., & Atwood, M. E. (1993). Project Ernestine: Validating a GOMS analysis for predicting and explaining real-world performance. *Human-Computer Interaction, 8*(3), 237–309.

Gray, W. D., Kirschenbaum, S. S., & Ehret, B. D. (1997). The précis of Project Nemo, phase 1: Subgoaling and subschemas for submariners. *In Nineteenth Annual Conference of the Cognitive Science Society* (pp. 283–288). Hillsdale, NJ: Lawrence Erlbaum Associates.

Gray, W. D., Young, R. M., & Kirschenbaum, S. S. (1997). Introduction to this special issue on cognitive architectures and human-computer interaction. *Human-Computer Interaction, 12*(4), 301–309.

John, B. E., & Kieras, D. E. (1996a). The GOMS family of user interface analysis techniques: Comparison and contrast. *ACM Transactions on Computer-Human Interaction, 3*(4), 320–351.

John, B. E., & Kieras, D. E. (1996b). Using GOMS for user interface design and evaluation: Which technique? *ACM Transactions on Computer-Human Interaction, 3*(4), 287–319.

Kirschenbaum, S. S. (1990). Command decision making: *Lessons learned* (NUSC TM No. 902149). Naval Underwater Systems Center.

Kirschenbaum, S. S. (1992). The effect of level of experience on information gathering strategies. *Journal of Applied Psychology, 77,* 343–352.

Kirschenbaum, S. S. (1994). *Command decision-making: A simulation study* (Tech. Rep. 10,350). Naval Undersea Warfare Center Division Newport.

Kirschenbaum, S. S., Gray, W. D., & Ehret, B. D. (1997). *Subgoaling and subschemas for submariners: Cognitive models of situation assessment* (Tech. Rep. 10,764-1). Newport, RI: NUWC-NPT.

Kirschenbaum, S. S., Gray, W. D., Ehret, B. D., & Miller, S. L. (1996). When using the tool interferes with doing the task. In M. J. Tauber (Ed.), *Conference companion of the ACM CHI'96 Conference Human Factors in Computing Systems* (pp. 203–204). New York: ACM Press.

Kirwan, B., & Ainsworth, L. K. (Eds.). (1992). *A guide to task analysis.* Washington, DC: Taylor & Francis.

Lovett, M. (1998). Choice. In J. R. Anderson & C. Lebière (Eds.), *Atomic components of thought* (pp. 255–296). Hillsdale, NJ: Lawrence Erlbaum Associates.

Newell, A., & Simon, H. A. (1972). *Human problem solving.* Englewood Cliffs, NJ: Prentice-Hall.

Norman, D. A. (1989). *The design of everyday things*. New York: Doubleday.

VanLehn, K. (1989). Problem solving and cognitive skill acquisition. In M. I. Posner (Ed.), *Foundations of cognitive science* (pp. 527–579). Cambridge, MA: MIT Press.

18

ACTIVE DESIGN DOCUMENTS AS SOFTWARE AGENTS THAT MEDIATE PARTICIPATORY DESIGN AND TRACEABILITY

Guy A. Boy
European Institute of Cognitive Sciences and Engineering

CONSEQUENCES OF THE COMPUTERIZATION OF WORK

The computerization of work and living interferes with evolved human capabilities for interacting with a physical environment. Humans evolved to change their locations, change their environment, accomplish their own goals, and execute tasks by relying on feedback from their natural sensory motor capabilities. Increasingly, natural human capability is artificially amplified. Natural capability for action is amplified through tools such as hammers or pointing devices. Natural capability for attributing meaning to input is amplified through interpretive processes that mediate between the physical environment and a human recipient. In the ideal case, the interpretive process provides outputs that make contact with the recipient's knowledge and skills. In this sense, human–human and human–machine interactions in work and everyday life have evolved from physical, energy-based interactions to abstract, information-based interactions, and they are often stripped of the multimodal richness that promotes a coherent understanding.

Moreover, the artificial amplifications need not follow real-world requirements and constraints. For example, a flight simulator may permit travel through the center of the earth and a new attempt at landing. This is not possible in the real world. Human learning in simulated safety-critical scenarios might benefit from abstract information-based feedback regarding real-world constraints. However, such feedback requires knowledge-based intepretation and transformation. An alternative approach is to provide feedback through artifacts that re-create more primitive energy-based feedback, making more direct contact with the human sensorimotor system.

THE NEED FOR MULTIAGENT MODELS IN THE
ALLOCATION OF COGNITIVE FUNCTION

Artificial intelligence and cognitive engineering of the early 1980s led to over-simplified and closedworld applications. The disappointing results may be attributed to an intentional attempt to generalize contextual detail. The alternative notion of a machine agent, and more specifically a software agent, arises from developments in automation. A machine agent executes tasks for other agents, usually human, according to the intentions of its design team. A machine agent is composed of an appearance and internal mechanism. A design team defines three attributes of an agent: (a) functions transferred to the agent; (b) the contexts in which the agent is valid, and (c) resources necessary for using the agent.

A realistic context around a machine agent includes other agents, including at least one human agent if not groups of other machine agents. Together human and machine agents accomplish a set of functions coordinated through explicit interactions. Thus, multiagent models are required to enable the analysis, design, and evaluation of cognitive function allocation in human–machine systems.

This chapter presents an approach to the allocation of cognitive functions to agents based on concpets of delegation, cooperation, and coordination. An extension of the Computer Integrated Documentation (CID) project (Boy, 1991) originating at NASA provides an example of a role for software agents in documenting the lifecycle and evolution of an artifact. First, this chapter describes the notion of an active document as background for the notion of an active design document. A subsequent section on active design documents identifies their defining aspects. The largest portion of the chapter is devoted to the consideration of active design documents in use.

ACTIVE DOCUMENTS

Documents provide a framework for the exchange of information between people. The category of *document*, such as a meeting report or technical note, allows a recipient to anticipate content and suggests interpretive strategies. The category of *document* also generates an attitude in the recipient (i.e., a mental state that anticipates a class of actions in response to certain inputs from the document). An active document has a dynamic function. An active document can include software agents that assist user comprehension. For instance, a lab exercise concerning electrical circuits might contain a diagram with missing parts that the students must add to complete a consistent electrical circuit. A paper version of the diagram might contain a text explanation of instructions. When hosted on a computer, the same diagram can be active so that clicking on parts activates

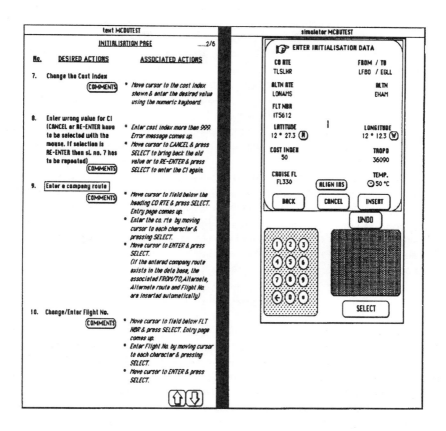

FIG.18.1   An active design document.

hypertext instructions.

ACTIVE DESIGN DOCUMENTS

An active design document is a hypermedia application used by a community. An active design document describes the various attributes of an artifact whose design is either defined or in progress. An active design document is defined by three aspects and exemplified by the textual description of operational procedures in Fig. 18.1:

- *Interaction descriptions* represent the symbolic aspect, which conveys ideas and information such as the description of a procedure in the left part of Fig. 18.1. This aspect of an active design document is related to the task involved in the use of the artifact. The interaction description defines the task space.
- *Interface objects* connected to interaction descriptions support an emotive aspect, which expresses, evokes, and excites feelings and attitudes (e.g., a software prototype of a flight management system [FMS] interface in the right part of Fig. 18.1). This aspect is related to the interface of the artifact that provides interactive capabilities. The interface objects define the activity space.
- *Contextual links* between the interaction descriptions and the interface objects (e.g., annotations or comments contextually generated during tests). This aspect is related to the user and environment in which the artifact is used. Contextual links define the cognitive function space.

Although interaction descriptions and interface objects can be superimposed, in this chapter they are separate entities available in two different windows. These three aspects are discussed further herein.

INTERACTION DESCRIPTIONS

The interaction descriptions of an active design document define the user–artifact dialogue. These descriptions express content (semantics) as well as use (pragmatics). The simplest form of interaction descriptions included in a document is a list of concepts. When they are related to each other, concepts constitute a semantic network called a *thesaurus*. The thesauras guides search into documentation. Content may be expressed using natural language or a domain-specific technical language. The latter can range from simplified English to a knowledge representation, such as an interaction block (Boy, 1998). In practice, interaction descriptions can be strings or multimedia entitities. They may be used as triggering conditions to activate other parts of an active design document.

Fig. 18.2 illustrates the active design document for a prototype interface for a flight management system of a commercial aircraft. Interface objects provide an active design document with an appropriate, useful, and natural illusion that assists the user in understanding the document and artifact in question. In particular, users must determine the functionality of the artifact subject to documentation. This requirement suggests the need for an appropriate level of detail from the user's perspective. One form of interface object that is particularly compatible with dynamic artifacts is simulation, which allows document users to engage in the manipulation of artifacts in question. Manipulation allows users to

INTERFACE OBJECTS

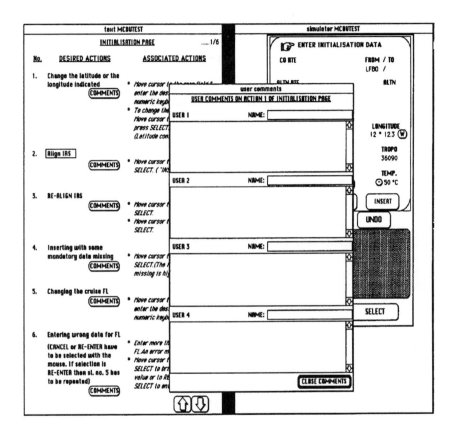

FIG. 18. 2   An example of comments as contextual links.

experience the possibilities that an artifact provides; in so doing, it makes contact with the user's sensorimotor capabilities. The hope is that the enhanced interaction that active documents provide relative to static documents reduces the possibility for unmet expectations that result in cognitive dissonance (Festinger, 1957).

Two types of simulation are possible. Shallow-global simulations provide a global view of the artifact being designed. They do not have full, deep functionality. However, they retain multiple possibilities in the realization of the artifact, such as options for cognitive functions involving supervisory control, management, and coordination. Deep-local simulations provide a local, active view of the proposed artifact and retain somewhat restricted options for cognitive functions, such as control and monitoring. This multilevel view of simulation acknowledges the need to reverse a standard design practice in which narrow experiments drive design modification. Instead, a global perspective at the initial stages of design, considering the functionality of the artifact in its broad environment, can suggest difficult problems that require more detailed local analysis and experimentation.

CONTEXTUAL LINKS

Contextual links provide active design documents with mechanisms for indexing, annotating, and browsing to interrelate interface objects to interaction descriptions. In the CID system, a document becomes active when its descriptors are activated via connections to other documents. In CID, a contextualized thesaurus is incrementally generated through interpreting and annotating the documentation. An interpretation usually leads to an annotation that contextualizes a document and organizes its reading. When necessary, integrated methods such as the Group Elicitation Method (GEM) may prompt the generation of comments from a design team (Boy, 1997). A version of GEM for active design documents specifically enable argumentative annotations (Boy, 1998). Annotations are incrementally generated by users and automatically processed by a machine-learning mechanism. For example, interaction descriptions of an author-designer and a reader-user are often not the same even when the same person performs both functions. As illustrated in the figure, an analysis of cognitive function extends an approach to contextualization that originated in the CID project.

Users select descriptors on the active design document. For example, a descriptor interface object can be an instrument or a part of an instrument such as a speed bug in the cockpit. This part–whole distinction illustrates that the selection of strings or drawings is ambiguous. To reduce this ambiguity, when users select a descriptor, they obtain a list of possible referents. Contextual links can be used to determine the best candidate referent. Contextual links also provide access to the design rationale of a descriptor. A design rationale for the speed indicators might indicate its purpose and ground its analogue design in ergonomic principles.

Incrementally generated contextual links specify requirements, comments, and perceived design flaws in a proposed artifact. The context of use may include the user profile, the design rationale of an interface object, the situation in which the active design document is being used, and user intention. Contextual links can be evaluated according to their success at identifying appropriate interface objects for a given interaction. Users may provide such evaluations directly or, given a context-matching model, a machine can provide evaluations automatically.

ACTIVE DESIGN DOCUMENTS IN USE

Advantages of Active Design Documents

Sketches on the corner of a bistro table can be used to explain ideas to others. In an academic setting, a blackboard provides the same functionality as the table. Both are cheap and easy ways to promote discussion and formalize ideas, but may fail to make contact with sensorimotor pathways involved in interactions with a physical environment. Simulations also promote discussion particularly regarding the usability of an artifact, but simulations are expensive. Active design documents provide a compromise between these two extremes. Appropriate prototyping tools facilitate the generation of active design documents, which can capture artifact behavior at multiple levels of abstraction.

The Role of Active Design Documents

The purpose of a design document is to predict the usability of the artifact. The predictive capability hinges on the level and nature of detail. Several dimensions require testing, such as learnability, retention power, efficiency, the number of errors and recovery possibilities, and user subjective satisfaction (Nielsen, 1993). Of course, the level of detail impacts the level of development effort. Predictive capability also hinges on the number of individuals evaluating the proposed design.

Assessment of Active Design Documents

Because active design documents are software entitites, their evaluation might logically lead to the verification and validation of software requirements and design specifications (Boehm, 1984). The approach advocated here bases evaluation on users' attitudes, suggested by interface objects and interaction descriptions. Target users can assess the affordances of a proposed design by examining the usability of corresponding active design documents with resepect to criteria for safety, robustness, user-friendliness, efficiency, and retention.

The primary challenge in assessment is attributing complaints to either a flawed simulation or a flawed design. The former case may yield to explanation, but reinforces the need for users to understand the nature of prototyping and the inherent limitations in a prototype. The latter case may require a reconsideration of the design.

Active Design Documents in Top–Down and Bottom–Up Design

Design may be approached top–down or bottom–up. A top–down approach leads to a structured development process. This common engineering approach limits the involvement of users, who may be dissatisfied with the results. In the KADS approach to knowledge acquisition for the design of knowledge-based systems (Wielinga, Schreiber, & Breuker, 1992), expertise is analyzed at the knowledge level independently from the implementation details. It is formalized at the symbolic level and results in a model. Test results of the operational knowledge base are accessible only after the implementation of the model (Linster, 1992). Thus, the time between model design and implementation is too long to enable appropriate usability testing.

A bottom–up approach involves rapid prototyping and enables end users' participation during the earliest stages of the design process. Evaluation is incremental. However, the rationale for the resulting artifact may be confusing and difficult to maintain. Domains that lack a priori expertise necessitate a bottom–up approach, whereas the expertise is incrementally developed. The SAOTS project for the design of an intelligent assistant system for the European space robotic arm exemplifies bottom–up design (Mathé, 1990). The development process encourages the articulation of operational procedures. For example, the design of the interface determines how the user will interact with the artifact.

Fensel et al. (1991) tried to combine the two design approaches to optimize the advantages and disadvantages trade-off. Active design documents provide an alternative approach to combining top–down and bottom–up approaches to design. Design remains top–down, because successive active design documents represent the traditional chronological steps of an artifact lifecycle. Yet design retains the advantages of a bottom–up process because each active design document version can be evaluated, documented, and revised by a wide range of actors.

Participatory Design

Design often focuses on the technology rather than how it will be used. Design engineers are generally not trained in human factors. Nevertheless, design teams have involved human factors consultants, but generally late in the design cycle. The incorporation of human factors earlier in the design cycle requires a capability in combining diverse sources of expertise, a formal ownership, and commitment by all participants in design or use of the artifact and participation of all affected parties in the decision-making process (Muller, 1991). Active Design Document Generation and Maintenance (ADDGM) facilitates the involvement of the individuals that compose an organization. ADDGM is intended to replace the simple notion of an information system that fails to acknowledge users. Active design doucments result in a prototype that is easily shared among users and keeps the design team focused on a common vision. Active design documents also enable the design team to share concepts represented as multimedia objects that undergo modification to harmonize the mutual understanding of the design team members. A basic difference between classical human-factors-oriented design and participatory design hinges on the source of insight. Classical human factors design revolves around observing and analyzing an existing user organization and application area. Participatory design revolves around interaction with design team members.

Active Design Document Evolution and Traceability

Active design documents are incrementally modified according to possible design options, human factors criteria, and organizational requirements. Traceability is the process that retains design decisions, including the alternatives and rationale for their dismissal (Carroll et al., 1994).

Fig. 18.3 provides an illustration of traceability. In the beginning of the design process, active design documents have design-centered interaction descriptions that document a preliminary task analysis, roughly sketched interface objects, and contextual links associated with the design rationale. Interaction with interface objects benefits from short, crisp interaction descriptions. Later in the lifecycle of the artifact, interface objects become more sophisticated and user-friendly, interaction descriptions become minimal, and contextual links are enriched by comments and test results. However, the growth in contextual links challenges traceability and requires a scheme for classification, generalization, and eventual simplification. A promising approach to this challenge is to group contextual links by viewpoint. CID provides a descriptor browser that enbales the user to navigate in a documentation system and see the documents from different viewpoints. The use of CID demonstrates the improvement of traceability due to contextual information retrieval.

Users retrieve active design documents to retrieve information, create new documents, modify existing documents, and organize sets of documents. Users are expected to identify relevant documents through a process of analogical reasoning that relates a current problem to previous experience. The relevance of a

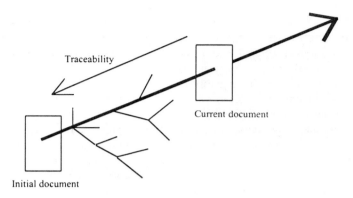

FIG. 18.3   Evolution of a document.

retrieved document to a current problem can help users refine their retrieval strategies. At the same time, indexing is crucial for retrieving appropriate documents. The list of candidate descriptors should address content, (i.e., by extracting words from the text or by eliciting descriptors that are not formally included in the text, or graphics for that matter, but summarize the document). Finally, each descriptor should represent reinforcement according to its observed relevance to the goals motivating retrieval.

Hypermedia as a Programming Tool

Hypermedia technology plays two roles in the development of an active design document. First, hypermedia technology provides multiple windows for the three components of an active design document.

Figure 18.4 presents an example of an active design document for the Level Change procedure of a new-generation commercial aircraft. This example was developed with Hypercard software and its scripting language, Hypertalk. The figure includes an interaction description window (right side of the Hypercard stack) and an interace objects window (left side of the Hypercard stack). The user has already selected and executed seven items of those procedures indicated by highlighting. Each time a procedure item (i.e., an interaction description) is selected, a contextual link automatically sends a message to the corresponding interface objects window that displays the hypertext systems, such as Hypercard. These are often excellent implementation tools for sketching a useful cognitive simulation.

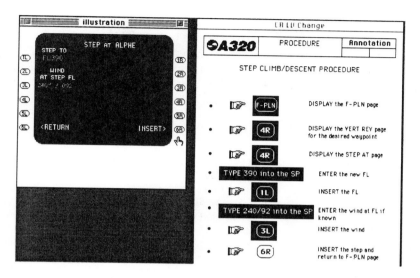

FIG. 18.4   Example of an active design document that includes an aircraft procedure (interaction descriptions) and the illustration of the corresponding information display in the cockpit (interface objects).

Conclusion

Technical documentation is evolving from an output of the design process to guide for the design process. An active design document provides interaction descriptions, interface objects, and contextual links. Active design documents are designed and refined from the beginning to the end of the lifecycle of an artifact. Active design documents are used to elict descriptions of the interaction with the artifact being designed (i.e., active design document interface objects). Active design documents enable design teams to run cognitive simulations to take into account human factors during design. Generation and use of active design documents enable the elicitation of interaction descriptions and the design of interface objects. Contextual links enable people to trace the origins of design rationale and support participatory design. Relative to other approaches such as DODE (Fischer et al., 1995), the current approach integrates human factors evaluations in the incremental definition of design rationale. Active design documents benefit from hypermedia technology. This approach is currently used in three applied research projects in the aeronautics domain. In these projects, designers, trainers, pilots, and human factors specialists cooperate to design new cockpits using active design documents.

ACKNOWLEDGMENTS

Many people contributed to the current state of EURISCO user-centered design using active documents project. Among them, I owe thanks to Hubert L'Ebraly, Thierry Broignez, and Krishnakumar, who greatly contributed to the development of the first versions of active design documents. Valerie Shalin provided astute advice toward improving the quality of this chapter.

REFERENCES

Boehm, B. W. (1984). Verifying and validating software requirements and design specifications. *IEEE Software, 1* (1), 75–89.

Boy, G.A. (1991, December). *Indexing hypertext documents in context.* Proceedings of the Hypertext'91 Conference, San Antonio, TX.

Boy, G.A. (1997, March). The group elicitation method for participatory design and usability testing. *Interactions Magazine.*

Boy, G.A. (1998). *Cognitive function analysis.* Stamford, NJ: Ablex.

Carroll, J.M., Alpert, S.R., Karat, J., Van Deusen, M.S., & Rosson, M.B. (1994, April). Raison d'Etre: Capturing design history and rationale in multimedia narratives. In *Proceedings of the ACM CHI'94 Conference* (pp. 192–197). New York: ACM Press.

Fensel, D., Angele, J., & Landes, D. (1991). KARL: A knowledge acquisition and representation language. *Proceedings Expert Systems and their Applications, 11th International Workshop, Conference "Tools, Techniques and Methods",* Avignon.

Festinger, L. (1957). *A theory of cognitive dissonance.* Evanston, IL: Row, Peterson.

Fischer, G., Nakakoji, K., & Ostwald, J. (1995). *Supporting the evolution of design artifacts with representations of context and intent. Proceedings of ACM DIS'95,* Ann Arbor, MI.

Linster, M. (1992). L'ingénierie de la connaissance: Une symbiose de deux perspectives sur le développement des modèles. *Actes des 3èmes Journées d'Acquisition de Connaissances du PRC-IA,* Dourdan, 14-16 April.

Mathé, N. (1990). *Assistance Intelligente au Controle de Processus: Application a la Telemanipulation Spatiale.* Unpublished doctoral dissertation, Toulouse, France.

Muller, M. (1991). Participatory design in Britain and North America: Responding to the "Scandinavian Challenge." In S.P. Robertson, G.M. Olson, & J.S. Olson (Eds), *Reading through technology, CHI'91 Conference Proceedings* (pp. 389–392).

Nielsen, J. (1993). *Usability engineering.* London: Academic Press.

Wielinga, B. J., Schreiber, A. Th.., & Breuker, J. A. (1992). KADS: A modeling approach to knowledge engineering. *Knowledge Acquisition, 4,* 5–53.

19

COGNITIVE ANALYSES WITHIN INCREASINGLY LARGER ORGANIZATIONAL CONTEXTS

Franz Schmalhofer and Ludger van Elst
University of Heidelberg

In the currently emerging knowledge society, knowledge is seen as the most important success factor for industrial enterprises. Just as manufacturing technologies are extremely important during the industrial age, knowledge creation, knowledge management, and organizational innovations play the pivotal role in future businesses (Drucker, 1993). Therefore, the construction of novel knowledge as well as its efficient utilization and distribution is the most decisive factors for maintaining or achieving the leading edge in successful markets. Under these circumstances, it makes perfect sense to talk about successful products as being the coordinated and reified knowledge of some business enterprise. In an environment where markets are shifting, technology proliferating, competitiors multiplying, and products becoming obsolete overnight (cf. Nonaka & Takeuchi, 1995), we certainly also have a worry—whether the various techniques for cognitive task analyses that have been developed and successfully applied over the last 20 years will, by themselves, be sufficient for mastering the demands of the emerging knowledge society or whether additional progress is indeed required.

Many prominent cognitive task analyses as well as cognitive modeling research have been performed for clearly circumscribed task environments such as editing a manuscipt with a word processing system (Card, Moran, & Newell, 1983). For these comparably small task domains, it thereby became possible to predict the learnability and usability of various word processors by the application of a cognitive theory. For example, the cognitive complexity theory (Kieras & Polson, 1985) predicted the learnability of a word processor by the number of cognitive production rules that, according to the theory, the user had to learn. The ease of use of a system was similarly predicted by the number of mental production rules that, according to the theory, needed to be executed for completing a specific task.

The research of the last 15 years has matured this approach into more complex cognitive task analyses, more complete cognitive architectures (Anderson & Lebière, 1998), and into respective cognitive guidelines for system design

(Lewis et al., 1990). Thus, the research in cognitive psychology and artificial intelligence (AI), progressed along parallel paths, often without taking much notice from one another. Both areas developed generic task models for somewhat different purposes. In AI, there are now elaborate libraries of generic task structures and corresponding processing architectures for expert systems (Breuker & Van de Velde, 1994). Similarly, cognitive psychology research has produced several architectures for describing human cognition: e.g. SOAR (Laird, Newell, & Rosenbloom, 1987), ACT-R (Anderson & Lebière, 1998), EPIC (Meyer & Kieras, 1997), and C-I (Kintsch, 1998) architectures. These capture the most significant cognitive constraints that shape human task performances under various circumstances.

   With computational models like EPIC, new user-friendly information systems can indeed be developed with considerable less cost than by performing direct empirical tests. An additional advantage of applying computational models lies in the fact that they can be employed before or while a new information system is being developed. In contrast, direct empirical tests require that the information system already be in use (cf. Roberts & Moran, 1983; Schmalhofer, 1987). Due to the rapid technological developments, the particular system that is being investigated may soon be outdated. Of course, this raises the important questions of whether and how the respective empirical findings can be transferred to the information systems currently in use. For achieving a broad scope of applicability of psychological results, Barnard and May (chap. 10, this volume) used the behavioral evidence obtained from various laboratory and real-world tasks to specify the interacting cognitive subsystems that are most important for cognitive task analyses.

   As Vicente (chap. 7, this volume) pointed out, such task analyses are quite useful when the goal to be achieved by some worker is clearly specified and the worker is basically operating within a closed task environment so that a fixed set of operations will accomplish the given goal. On other occasions, however, one needs to accommodate variability within repeated executions of similar tasks and thereby provide workers with opportunities that foster learning. This is especially true in the emerging knowledge society. Knowledge workers need to have the flexibility to deal with novel circumstances as well as to develop novel goals. Vicente's proposed work domain analysis is therefore an adequate first step toward preparing for change and the need for organizational learning in the emerging knowledge society.

   The new kind of task analysis that is proposed in this chapter is strongly rooted in the research on cognitive architectures and models as briefly summarized. More important, it is geared toward the requirements of the knowledge society. James Watt's invention of the steam engine in 1769 led to the Industrial Revolution—dramatic reorganizations of work resulting in the well-known division of (industrial) labor (Taylor, 1911). Likewise, the advent of the computer in the first half of the century, with its subsequent developments of inter- and intranets, has fostered information and knowledge processing, which are leading to the globalization of (knowledge) work.

To accommodate this development, we propose that cognitive models should not only be used to automate human performance (Schmalhofer & Thoben, 1992) and human learning processes (Reinartz & Schmalhofer, 1994), but also to use such cognitive models for developing more global visions for the open-ended and therefore ill-defined task environment of knowledge workers. We first describe how model-based visions can be developed for the tasks of information comprehension and knowledge distribution. Thereafter we present how a general comprehension-based model of knowledge acquisition was utilized for developing a specific oligo-agent system for knowledge classification and knowledge distribution on the basis of intranet technologies. An oligo-agent system is a computer environment with a relatively small number of different types of intelligent computer agents that behave in accordance to some assigned individual and social responsibilities. Finally, we discuss this work in relation to other research and system developments.

COGNITIVE TASK ANALYSES FOR THE KNOWLEDGE SOCIETY

The knowledge society is driven by the vision that knowledge, and not so much techniques for manufacturing material goods, will yield the capital income and economic growth of the future. The creation of novel knowledge as well as the effective and efficient distribution of the already available knowledge within an organization are therefore the pivotal tasks in the knowledge society that will drive the innovation and rapid changes of the future. Thus, an important vision for the knowledge society is efficient and effective knowledge management in intra- and internets. With intra- and internets, geographically dispersed individuals or groups of people all have access to the documents and information that are electronically stored in some kind of corporate, organizational, group, or universal memory (in the case of the World Wide Web). The access to information is therefore almost instantaneous and only limited by the assigned privileges that a given user possesses. Therefore, knowledge distribution and document comprehension will become central functionalities within any modern intranet, and cognitive task analyses will again play a significant role for developing these functionalities.

When we performed a cognitive task analysis for the knowledge management problem of getting the right documents to the right people at the right time, we applied the cognitive architectures and cognitive models in quite a different manner than what had been done before. Instead of deriving precise performance predictions for some closed-task environment, we needed to develop a vision and system architecture for future knowledge work. The openness and unpredictability of the rampering knowledge society requires different levels of abstraction to be introduced. The more abstract levels are used to establish some permanence. They do not become obsolete as quickly as the more concrete levels do. Therefore, it is of particular importance to establish a vision at the most abstract level possible. Such a cognitive task analysis was performed by four steps—namely, identifying a feasible AI vision, performing a levels analysis of task performances, analyzing the current work practices, and selecting a cognitive model of the core tasks to guide the system development. We now describe these four basic steps that we have performed for developing the oligo-agent system, which assists a community of practice with document comprehension and knowledge distribution.

The Two Visions of Artificial Intelligence

Research in AI (cf. Charniak & McDermott, 1985) has been driven by the vision that human information processes, such as thinking, language comprehension, and learning, can also be performed by computers and that human knowledge can similarly be represented and maintained in a computer system. With respect to human work, there are basically two different suggestions for the application of AI techniques. Stated in a provocative manner, these two suggestions are to replace people by machines in the workplace or keep the people in charge and empower them with supporting computer tools. The first suggestion is driven by the ideal of complete and correct systems as we know them from mathematics. The second suggestion has more of a biological flavor. Here systems may change in quite unpredictable ways through their interaction with some environment.

According to the first suggestion, one may represent the knowledge of human experts in computer systems and subsequently automate the human information processes that are needed to perform knowledge work. Difficult tasks can thus be automatically performed by computer systems, and humans are alleviated from performing mental work—similar to the alleviation from physical work, which occurred as a consequence of the Industrial Revolution. According to the second suggestion, human workers are supported by intelligent computer assistants that are particularly designed for the human needs. Thus, the human workers definitely remain in charge of the tasks to be performed. This second vision is the one we used for performing our task analyses.

Levels Analyses of Knowledge Tasks

Following the general suggestions and various demonstrations by Newell (1982), Anderson (1990), Schmalhofer (1998), Vicente (chap. 7, this volume) and others, a levels analysis was performed for the knowledge management problems. At the most abstract level, we thereby distinguished among the document providers, document distributors, document librarians, and information consumers with their specific interests, goals, and duties who live and continuously shape some information landscape that is built on top of the intra- or internet. Most important, this information landscape with its agents forms a multiagent world with preestablished and/or emerging cooperations and competitions. The distinction between individual and social objectives is therefore of equal importance as the (explicit or implicit) representation of existing entitlements, permissions, and obligations for the various individuals and groups.

Currently Available Knowledge Management Techniques

News readers, alias lists for e-mail distribution and search engines, are already widely available and can indeed be used for performing information-distribution tasks more effectively than what had been previously available. Therefore, we analyzed the strengths and weaknesses of these techniques. We determined that news reader systems usually have some sort of representation of the stored documents (i.e., the news groups), but no user profile of their potential readers. However, alias lists also (at least implicitly) represent the people who have similar functions or interest by assigning them to a particular group alias. Nevertheless, they do not maintain any representation of the information that has been or is to be distributed. Finally, search engines have an incomplete and relatively surface-oriented representation of the documents in an information web.

By combining the presented AI vision with the described levels analyses of tasks and the conceptualizations of the currently available tools (news readers, e-mail aliases, inter- and intranets with search engines), the idea of an innovative knowledge-management system emerged. More specifically, it is suggested to employ a cognitive model of document comprehension for developing the core components of personal and social assistants for document comprehension and document distribution in an intranet. We now describe the specific cognitive model selected and then present the resulting oligo-agent system for knowledge management.

A Cognitive Model of Document Comprehension

The KIWi model (see Schmalhofer, 1998), which is a unified model for the comprehension of knowledge from different types of information materials, was selected as the candidate system for developing the comprehension assistant. Such information materials may be texts or cases, (e.g., a table that occurs within a given document). The KIWi model consists of a number of implemented simulation modules from which empirical predictions can be obtained. The empirical validity of the model has been confirmed by several experiments, in which subjects had to learn a new programming language and their knowledge was subsequently tested by different types of tasks. Figure 19.1 presents an overview of the representation and processing assumptions of the KIWi model. It shows the particular information processes and the resulting symbol structures that are formed and utilized in different tasks. In learning from text, a textbase is formed en route to the construction of a situation model. A textbase is a coherent structure of propositions that represents the meaning of a text. Propositions are cognitive units that represent the meaning of elementary sentences. A situation model represents the state of affairs that is described by the text. A situation model consists of situation units and their interconnections. For the construction of a situation model, related domain knowledge as well as commonsense knowledge are utilized. In learning from cases, a template base is formed en route to the construction of a situation model, whereas related domain knowledge and commonsense knowledge are similarly employed. A template base consists of templates that are generalizations of real or possible examples. The templates represent the structure of these examples.

In learning from text, the following information processes may thus be distinguished: (a) parsing of a text and the textbase formation, (b) selection of prior knowledge (domain or commonsense knowledge), (c) situation-oriented instantiation of prior knowledge, and (d) operationalization of abstract situation knowledge for some specific purpose. In learning from cases, we distinguish the following processes: (a) generalization of cases and formation of templates, (b) selection of prior knowledge (domain or commonsense knowledge), and (c) formation of abstractions that are then stored as part of the situation model.

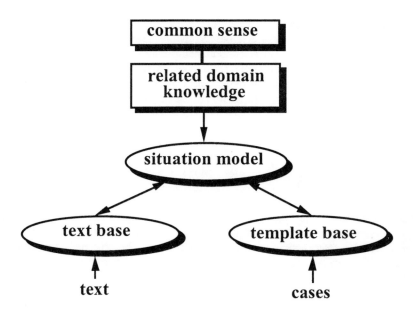

FIG. 19.1 Overview of the representational assumptions of the KIWi model (Schmalhofer, 1998).

One of the most central learning components of the KIWi model has been termed *explanation-based abstraction* (EBA). It has been successfully applied in the PABS system for building abstractions in various application domains (cf. Bergmann & Wilke, 1995; Schmalhofer, Bergmann, Boschert, & Thoben, 1993; Schmalhofer, Reinartz, & Tschaitschian, 1995). Unlike the generalization of examples (e.g., replacing constants by variables) that are stored as part of the template base, EBA constructs true abstractions (i.e., descriptions in a more abstract representation language) that are then stored as part of the situation model. Thus, we follow the distinction that was pointed out by Michalski and Kodratoff (1990). Whereas generalizations transform a description along a set–superset dimension, abstractions change a description's level of detail. Therefore, abstraction involves the change from a detailed representation space (e.g., the example and template representation space) to a more coarse-grained representation space (e.g., the representation of situation models). Because the application of EBA requires prior domain knowledge, it is predicted that novices would not be able to perform such knowledge-construction processes. Thus, the KIWi-model clearly predicts that prior domain knowledge is necessary for constructing a situation model. Without such prior knowledge, only material-related representations may be formed.

The knowledge-utilization processes that occur in performing some given task are similar to the respective knowledge-acquisition processes. The major difference concerns the last processing component. In knowledge acquisition, a memory storage is performed as the last processing component, whereas a decision or performance component is executed in the knowledge-utilization tasks. The different simulation components can be performed in any meaningful order. Thus, one can simulate any arbitrary sequence of learning from text, learning from examples, or learning by exploration. Also, each learning component can be applied to learning materials of any length. Thus, the simulation program provides a high degree of flexibility for modeling human learning.

An Oligo-Agent System for Knowledge Management With Intranet Technologies

The KIWi model was thus used for core components of the oligo-agent system for knowledge management. Figure 19.2 shows the task structure of the information assistance that must be supplied by the oligo-agent system. There are various documents that can be described by its contents as well as by a metalevel description (e.g., is location within an intranet or the type of document). The different employees or users of the intranet are similarly characterized by user profiles and user stereotypes. From these document and user descriptions, the relevance or interestingness of some given information for a given person may then be assessed by a binary relation (i.e., relevance). Based on feedback from the users, document and user representations may be updated by various ma-

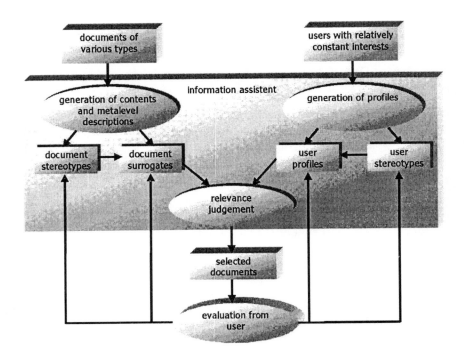

FIG. 19.2   Task structure of the information assistance.

chine-learning procedures (Schmalhofer & Aitken, 1995).

When an intranet is used as an organizational memory, one usually distinguishes among the authors (or information providers) who supply the various documents, the *administrators* who maintain the news or memory system (i.e., they serve the function of librarians), and the users (or information *consumers*) who read some of the stored documents. Because the *distribution* of documents is a separate task in its own right, it requires responsible action. This role is taken by a so-called distributor (of information) who is equipped with the required privileges.

The core task of the integrated distribution and comprehension assistant involves assigning groups of information consumers to groups of documents. These functions are implemented by the oligo-agent system with two types of agents—namely, the primary manager (PriMa) and individual agents (PersonA, PersonB, etc.) for each user or information consumer. These agents live in a three-tier client–server architecture. PriMa is located at an application server and has access to the central information database (e.g., organizational memory). The

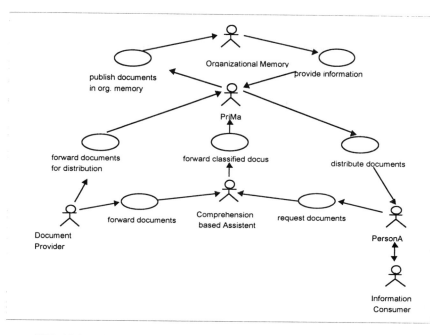

FIG. 19.3   Distribution and comprehension assistance within the organizational memory.

individual agents (PersonA, PersonB, etc.) are located at the clients and communicate with the central information database via PriMa by using the standard intranet protocols.

Figure 19.3 presents an overview of the distribution and comprehension assistance within the organizational memory. The proposed solution for knowledge dissemination in an organization (i.e., the right documents to the right people at the right time) can be characterized by the following description:

1.   The Coordination of individual and global concerns occurs in an oligo-agent's system that is embedded in an organizational memory (based on intranet technologies). Although the individual agents (PersonA, PersonB, etc.) are clientbased, the global agent lives at an application server.

2.   The agent PriMa uses a relational database system to keep and maintain repositories that are used for the definition of user profiles (information consumers), document groups, and distribution (interests lists). Thus, it is possible to use the available information, consisting of document attributes, document contents, and organizational structures as a whole. Concerning the distribution and interest

identification tasks, PriMa maintains a continually updated representation of the organizational memory at the relevant level of abstraction.

3.   Based on the described cognitive model of human comprehension processes (i.e., the KIWi model), a fully automated comprehension assistant with three levels of representations is used to achieve mutually shared representations between the oligo-agent system and their different users. With more people applying the oligo-agent system, the mutual understanding may be shared among increasingly more people and more documents. A detailed description of the comprehension assistant, and especially of its three levels of representation, is described by van Elst (1998).

4.   The decoupling of definition time, information-identification time, and presentation time allows distribution to be determined either by the individual or as a common responsibility of the administrator, author, distributors, and information consumers. These responsibilities may concern one-shot distributions as well as periodical repetitions of some general distribution specification.

From an application point of view, the functions provided by the distribution and comprehension assistant can be compared to the Fishwrap system (cf. Chesnais et al., 1997). The information consumer gets a personalized view of the organizational memory. This view consists of individual aspects that are based on a semantic document analysis as well as on organizational aspects (distribution lists), in which a distributor determines the portion of information that is delivered to the consumer. However, unlike an individualized newspaper, the proposed oligo-agent system has a sophisticated representation about the ripeness and expiration time for relevant information. The combination of these elements leads to a flexible tool for handling different aspects of information distribution and information gathering—two of the core problems of knowledge management. In short, the proposed oligo-agent system knows about the right time when information should be presented.

We now explain how the different components interact for the distribution- and comprehensionbased tasks of the proposed assistant. Based on these repositories, specific distribution and interests lists are constructed (or chosen) and refined. These tasks also specify information as to when the information should be delivered. A demon acts on this information. Whenever a specific distribution or interests list reaches its distribution time, this demon computes the delivery information, which basically consists of a table of (user, document info) pairs. This table is processed by standard e-mail, sending the document notifications to the user's inbox. The delivered information is filtered by the consumer agent (PersonA) and thus categorized individually. Each category has presentation time information, which is used by a PersonA-demon to initiate presentation via a special user interface. This allows for individualized ranking and selection of documents.

How the document providers and information consumers of the organizational memory can employ the distribution and comprehension assistant to improve their consensual understanding of documents in the organizational memory can be seen in Figure 19.3. Document providers (who may either be authors or distributors) can publish a document in the organizational memory in one of two ways. They may have their own suggestions as to where in the organizational memory (i.e., the virtual library) the document should be stored and to whom it should be distributed. In this case they would directly forward the documents and/or distribution list to PriMa. Alternatively, they can call on the comprehension assistant, which will then make suggestions as to where the document is to be stored and who should be informed about its publication. In either case, PriMa will eventually store the newly published information in the organizational memory and distribute the information via the personal agents (PersonA) to the potential information consumers.

In addition to this push-oriented approach to knowledge management, the integrated assistant also provides a sophisticated information pull solution that is based on content and metacontent descriptions of the documents as well as user interests. With the personal agent (PersonA) and a dynamic queries interface (cf. Williamson & Shneiderman, 1992), the users can specify their interests to the comprehension assistant, which will in turn communicate to PriMa and then provide the specific documents.

Discussion

Lesgold (chap. 27, this volume) convincingly argues that cognitive tasks that are well understood and formally described become candidates for automation by AI techniques. As an example, the editing of a manuscript that has been investigated by cognitive research has been partially automated by the spelling-correction programs now available in most word processing systems. With such computer automations, a new cogntive task analysis should also determine a new and better balance between the newly automated cognitive function and the other functions that remain allocated to humans, but that will change as a consequence thereof. Boy's (chap. 18, this volume) cognitive function analysis provides a method for such agent-based cognitive engineering within larger contexts. Understanding the principles that underly the behavior of multiple entities in the world (i.e., agents) and their interactions with one another is also one of the new and central issues in AI (Sycara, 1998). Work domain analyses (Vicente, chap. 7, this volume) similarly investigate the behavior-shaping constraints in complex, multiagent environments, where changes occur over time and produce unpredictable demands (Clancey, 1997).

When we viewed the results from psychological experiments (Gertzen & Schmalhofer, 1987; Schmalhofer, 1987) and a model like KIWi in the larger context of knowledge management with intranet technologies, we were confronted with new demands that could not be predicited from the previous cognitive research. Due to the demand of scaling up to large sets of documents, we had to derive a somewhat different comprehension assistant. This assistant is embedded in an oligo-agent system and an organizational memory for knowledge management. Although a given cognitive model may be succesfully applied for predictive modeling in the context that was anticipated at the design time of the cognitive model, the significantly larger frame of reference of knowledge management required the behavior description of the system (Schmalhofer, Aitken, & Bourne, 1994) to be reworked according to the new demands. Despite the significant changes, this redescription of behavior nevertheless provided numerous re-use possibilities of the earlier model at least at the conceptual level. Therefore, cognitive models and architectures are not only useful for making precise predictions within a fixed frame of reference, but they can also lead the way to an increasingly larger and quite open-ended context—as the presented research has shown.

ACKNOWLEDGMENTS

We would like to thank Jan Maarten Schraagen, Susan Chipman, and Valerie Shalin for their valuable suggestions for revising this chapter as well as their invitation to participate in the workshop.

REFERENCES

Anderson, J. R. (1990). *The adaptive character of thought.* Hillsdale, NJ: Lawrence Erlbaum Associates.

Anderson, J. R., & Lebière, C. (1998). *The atomic components of thought.* Mahwah, NJ: Lawrence Erlbaum Associates.

Bergmann, R., & Wilke, W. (1995). Learning abstract planning cases. In N. Lavrac & S. Wrobel (Eds.), *Machine learning: ECML-95* (pp. 55–76). Berlin: Springer-Verlag.

Breuker, J. A., & Van de Velde, W. (Eds.). (1994). *The Common-KADS library for expertise modelling.* Amsterdam, Netherlands: IOS Press.

Card, S. K., Moran, T. P., & Newell, A. (1983). *The psychology of human-computer interaction.* Hillsdale, NJ: Lawrence Erlbaum Associates.

Charniak, E., & McDermott, D. (1985). *Introduction to artificial intelligence.* Reading, MA: Addison-Wesley.

Chesnais, P. R., Mucklo, M. J., & Sheena, J. A. (1997). *The Fishwrap Personalized News System.* http://fishwrap-docs.www.media.mit.edu/docs/dev/CNGlue/cnglue.html.

Clancey, W. J. (1997). *Situated cognition: On human knowledge and computer representations.* New York: Cambridge University Press.

Drucker, P. F. (1993). *Post-capitalist society.* Oxford: Butterworth-Heinemann.

van Elst, L. (1998). *Ein kooperativer Informationsassistent zum gemeinsamen Verstehen von Textdokumenten (An information assistant for the cooperative comprehension of text documents).* Unpublished master's thesis, Department of Computer Science, University of Kaiserslautern.

Gertzen, H., & Schmalhofer, F. (1987). Auswirkungen von gleichzeitiger oder sequentieller Darbietung am Bildschirm auf Entscheidungen (Effects of parallel or sequential screen presentation on decisions). In W. Schönpflug & M. Wittstock (Eds.), Software-Ergonomie '87 (pp. 187–196). Stuttgart: B. G. Teubner.

Kieras, D. E., & Polson, P. (1985). An approach to the formal analysis of user complexity. *International Journal of Man-Machine Studies, 22,* 365–394.

Kintsch, W. (1998). *Comprehension: A paradigm for cognition.* Cambridge, MA: Cambridge University Press.

Laird, J. E., Newell, A., & Rosenbloom, P. S. (1987). Soar: An architecture for general intelligence. *Artificial Intelligence, 24,* 169–203.

Lewis, C., Polson, P. G., Wharton, C., & Rieman, J. (1990). Testing a walkthrough methodology for theory-based design of walk-up-and-use interfaces. *Human Factors in Computing Systems, Special Issue of the SICHI Bulletin,* pp. 235–242.

Meyer, D. E., & Kieras, D. E. (1997). A computational theory of executive cognitive processes and multiple-task performance: Part 1. Basic mechanisms. *Psychological Review, 104,* 3–65.

Michalski, R. S., & Kodratoff, Y. (1990). Research in machine learning: Recent progress, classification of methods, and future directions. In Y. Kodratoff & R. S. Michalski (Eds.), *Machine learning: An artificial intelligence approach* (Vol. 3, pp. 3–30). San Mateo, CA: Morgan Kaufmann.

Newell, A. (1982). The knowledge level. *Artificial Intelligence, 18,* 87–127.

Nonaka, I., & Takeuchi, H. (1995). *The knowledge-creating company.* Oxford: Oxford University Press.

Reinartz, T., & Schmalhofer, F. (1994). An integration of knowledge acquisition techniques and EBL for real-world production planning. *Knowledge Acquisition Journal, 6,* 115–136.

Roberts, T. L., & Moran, T. P. (1983). The evaluation of computer text editors: Methodology and empirical results. *Communications of the ACM, 26* (4), 265–283.

Schmalhofer, F. (1987). Mental model and procedural elements approaches as guidelines for designing word processing instructions. In H.-J. Bullinger & B. Shakel (Eds.), *Human-Computer Interaction INTERACT '87* (pp. 269–274). Amsterdam: North-Holland.

Schmalhofer, F. (1998). *Constructive knowledge acquisition: A computational model and experimental evaluation.* Mahwah, NJ: Lawrence Erlbaum Associates.

Schmalhofer, F., & Aitken, S. (1995). Beyond the knowledge level: Behavior descriptions of machine learning systems. In D. Fensel (Eds.), *Knowledge level modelling and machine learning: Proceedings of the MLnet Sponsered Familiarization Workshop,* Crete, Greece: Heraklion (III.1.1–III.1.15).

Schmalhofer, F., Aitken, St., & Bourne, L. E. (1994). Beyond the knowledge level: Descriptions of rational behavior for sharing and reuse. In L. Steels, G. Schreiber & W. Van de Velde (Eds.), *A future for knowledge acquisition* (pp. 83–103). Berlin: Springer-Verlag.

Schmalhofer, F., Bergmann, R., Boschert, S., & Thoben, J. (1993). Learning program abstractions: Formal model and empirical validation. In G. Strube & K. F. Wender (Eds.), *The cognitive psychology of knowledge* (pp. 203–232). Amsterdam, Elsevier.

Schmalhofer, F., Reinartz, T., & Tschaitschian, B. (1995). A unified approach to learning in complex real world domains. *Applied Artificial Intelligence, An International Journal, 9* (2), 127–156.

Schmalhofer, F., & Thoben, J. (1992). The model-based construction of a case-oriented expert system. *AI Communications, 5,* 3–18.

Sycara, K. P. (1998). The many faces of agents. *AI Magazine, 19* (2), 11–12.

Taylor, F. W. (1911). *The principles of scientific management.* New York: Harper & Row.

Williamson, C., & Shneiderman, B. (1992, June). *The dynamic homefinder: Evaluation of dynamic queries in a real-estate information exploration system.* Proceedings of the ACM SIGIR'92 Conference, Copenhagen, Denmark.

20

BOOTSTRAPPING MULTIPLE CONVERGING COGNITIVE TASK ANALYSIS TECHNIQUES FOR SYSTEM DESIGN

Scott S. Potter
MindSim, Inc.

Emilie M. Roth
Roth Cognitive Engineering

David D. Woods
The Ohio State University

William C. Elm
MindSim, Inc.

The goal of cognitive task analysis (CTA) is to uncover the cognitive activities that are required for task performance in a domain to identify opportunities to improve performance through better support of these cognitive activities. Since at least the early 1980s, the desire to enhance human performance in cognitive work has led researchers to develop techniques for CTA either as the basis for intelligent tutoring systems (e.g., Lesgold et al., 1985) or online computer-based support systems (Hollnagel & Woods, 1983; Roth & Woods, 1988; Woods & Hollnagel, 1987).

A variety of specific techniques drawing from basic principles and methods of cognitive psychology have been developed. These include structured interview techniques, critical incident analysis methods, field study methodologies, and methods based on observation of performance in high-fidelity simulators. Comprehensive reviews of CTA methods can be found in Cooke (1994), Hoffman (1987), Potter, Roth, Woods, and & Elm (1998), and Roth and Woods (1989).

To support development of computer-based tools intended to aid cognition and collaboration, we and others have found that CTA is more than the application of any single CTA technique. Instead, developing a meaningful understanding of a field of practice relies on multiple converging techniques. We have used this approach to model cognition and collaboration, as well as to develop new online support systems in time-pressured tasks such as situation assessment, anomaly response, supervisory control, and dynamic replanning across domains such as military intelligence analysis (Potter, McKee, & Elm, 1997), military aeromedical evacuation planning (Cook, Woods, Walters, & Christoffersen, 1996; Potter, Ball, & Elm, 1996), military command and control (Shattuck & Woods, 1997), commercial aviation (Sarter & Woods, in press), operating rooms (Cook & Woods, 1996; Sowb, Loeb, & Roth, 1998), space shuttle mission control (Patterson, Watts-Perotti, & Woods, in press), railroad dispatching (Roth, Malsch, Multer, Coplen, & Katz-Rhoads, 1998), and nuclear power plant emergencies (Roth, Lin, Thomas, Kerch, Kenney, & Sugibayachi, 1998).

This chapter presents a CTA framework that orchestrates different types of specific CTA techniques to provide design-relevant CTA results. It integrates the results into the software development process. We illustrate the approach with a specific case study pointing to requirements for software tools that support the CTA process and facilitate seamless integration of CTA results into the decision support system software development process.

CURRENT STATE OF PRACTICE

We recently reviewed the state of the practice of CTA in terms of the approaches and methodologies currently in use (Potter, Roth, Woods, & Elm, 1998). The review revealed wide diversity in the techniques that are employed, the conditions under which domain knowledge is obtained, the type of information generated, and the manner in which the information is represented. Some of the techniques, such as the PARI method, focus primarily on eliciting knowledge from domain practitioners (Hall, Gott, & Pokorny, 1995). Other techniques, such as function-based task analyses and cognitive work analyses methods, focus more on understanding the inherent demands of the domain (e.g., Rasmussen, 1986; Rasmussen, Pejtersen, & Goodstein, 1994; Roth & Mumaw, 1995; Vicente, 1998; Vicente & Rasmussen, 1992). Some of the techniques, such as the critical decision method, are empirical, involving observations or interviews of domain experts (Klein, Calderwood, & MacGregor, 1989). Others (e.g., the table-top analysis method described by Flach, chap. 6, this volume) are more analytic, involving reviews of existing documents (training manuals, procedures, system drawings). Some techniques, such as the concept mapping method, involve structured interviews outside the context of practice, such as in a conference room (e.g., McNeese, Zaff, Citera, Brown, & Whitaker, 1995). Others entail observations in realistic work contexts (e.g., Di Bello, 1997; Jordan & Henderson, 1995; Roth, 1997; Roth, Mumaw, Vicente, & Burns, 1997). Some techniques focus primarily on the knowledge-elicitation aspect of CTA (e.g., the critical decision method), whereas other methods such as conceptual graph analysis (Goron, Schmierer, & Gill, 1993), influence diagrams (Bostrom, Fischhoff, & Morgan, 1992), and COGNET (Zachary, Ryder, Ross, & Weiland, 1992) focus on a representation formalism for capturing and communicating the results of the analysis. Further, most methods include elements of all these approaches.

The potential effect of this diversity in approaches is confusion as to what the term *CTA* refers to, what type of results are expected to be produced from a CTA effort, and how these results will impact system development or evaluation efforts. Further, the approaches to CTA are typically labor intensive, paper-based, and only weakly coupled to the design and development of advanced decision support systems. Often the CTA generates a large amount of data (e.g., audio and video data that must be transcribed) that are time-consuming to analyze, and it produces outputs that are not easily integrated into the software development process.

CTA as a Modeling Process

The review of CTA methods might leave the impression that CTA encompasses a collection of diverse approaches with little connection or cohesiveness. However, at a deeper level, all approaches to CTA share a common goal——to uncover the cognitive activities that underlie task performance in a domain to specify ways to improve individual and team performance (be it through new forms of training, user interfaces, or decision aids). The diversity in techniques used for knowledge acquisition may be thought of as responses to different pragmatic constraints and system goals.

We contend that CTA is inherently a discovery and modeling activity. The focus is on building a model that captures the analysts evolving understanding of the demands of the domain, the knowledge and strategies of domain practitioners, and how existing artifacts influence performance. Specific CTA techniques are employed in the service of this goal and vary in accordance with the particular pragmatic constraints confronted.

Our approach to CTA is depicted in Fig. 20.1. The left side of this figure is intended to convey how CTA is an iterative, bootstrapping process focused on understanding both the domain (mapping the cognitive demands of the fields of practice) and practitioners (modeling expertise and cognitive strategies) through a series of complementary (empirical and analytical) techniques. As indicated by the right side of Fig. 20.1, the CTA process continues into the design/prototype development process. The CTA model (the output of the left side) becomes the initial hypothesis for artifacts embodied in the design prototypes, which in turn are used to discover additional requirements for useful support (Woods, in press). Phases within the CTA process are represented by the two columns, and the domain world/practitioner distinction (within the field of practice) is represented by the two rows. Time is on the abscissa and growth of understanding is on the ordinate. CTA products/artifacts are represented by the nodes along the activity trajectory.

- Critical issues addressed by this framework include the need for: multiple, coordinated approaches to CTA. No one approach can capture the richness required for a comprehensive, insightful CTA.
- However, in an iterative manner, a set of approaches can succes-

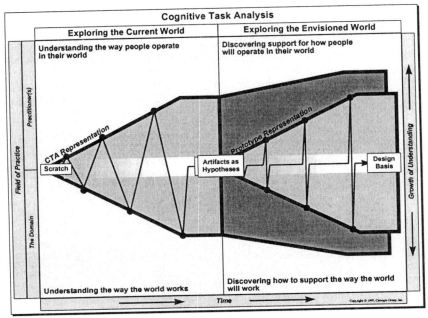

FIG. 20.1 Overview of an integrated approach to CTA within a system de-
velop-ment process. CTA is an interactive process focused on understanding both the cognitive demands of the domain and the knowledge and cognitive strategies of domain practitioners. The left side of the figure depicts
CTA activities intended to understand how domain practitioners operate in
the current work environment. Results of CTA activities are represented by
the nodes along the activity trajectory. The right side of the figure emphasizes that the analysis process continues into the design/prototype development phase. The results of the analysis of the curent work environment (the
output of the left side) generate hypotheses for ways to improve performance (the envisioned world). The hypotheses are embodied in design prototypes, which are in turn used to discover additional requirements for useful support.

sively (and successfully) build the required understanding.

- *analytical and empirical evidence to support the CTA.* Analytical
  models need to be refined and verified through complementary empirical investigations.
- *tangible products from CTA that clearly map onto artifacts used by
  system designers.* CTA must work within a system development
  process and support critical system design issues.
- *prototypes as tools to discover additional CTA issues.* CTA cannot
  be viewed as a stand-alone analysis. It needs to be an iterative process that learns from subsequent design activities.

In performing a CTA, two mutually reinforcing perspectives need to be considered (as depicted by the two dimensions on the ordinate axis in Fig.20.1). One perspective focuses on the fundamental characteristics of the domain and the cognitive demands they impose. The focus is on understanding the way the world works today and what factors contribute to making practitioner performance challenging. Understanding domain characteristics is important because it provides a framework for interpreting practitioner performance (Why do experts utilize the strategies they do? What complexities in the domain are they responding to? Why do less experienced practitioners perform less well? What constraints in the domain are they less sensitive to?). It also helps define the requirements for effective support (What aspects of performance could use support? What are the hard cases where support could really be useful?). It also clarifies the bounds of feasible support (What technologies can be brought tot bear to deal with the complexities inherent in the domain? Which aspects of the domain tasks are amenable to support? Which are beyond the capabilities of current technologies?).

The second perspective focuses on how todays practitioners respond to the demands of the domain. Understanding the knowledge and strategies that expert practitioners have developed in response to domain demands provides a second window for uncovering what makes todays world hard and what are effective strategies for dealing with domain demands. These strategies can be captured and transmitted directly to less experienced practitioners (e.g., through training systems) or they can provide ideas for more effective support systems that would eliminate the need for these compensating strategies. Examining the performance of average and less experienced practitioners is important because it can reveal where the needs for support are.

In selecting and applying CTA techniques, the focus needs to be on the products to be generated from the techniques rather than on the details of the method. Some CTA methods focus on uncovering specific domain expertise, whereas other methods focus more on analyzing the demands of the domain. In performing a CTA, it is important to utilize a balanced suite of methods that enable both the demands of the domain and the knowledge and strategies of domain experts to be captured in a way that enables clear identification of opportunities for improved support.

CTA AS A BOOTSTRAP PROCESS

We contend that CTA is fundamentally an opportunistic bootstrap process. The selection and timing of particular techniques to be deployed depend on the detailed constraints and pragmatics of the particular domain being addressed. Figure 20.1 provided an overview of this process, whereas Fig.20.2 illustrates additional details of this idea. One starts from an initial base of knowledge regarding the domain and how practitioners function within it (often very limited). One then uses a number of CTA techniques to expand on and enrich the base under

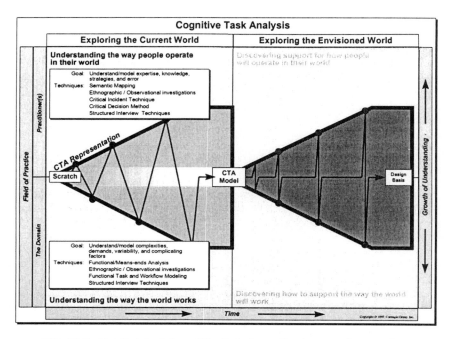

FIG. 20.2   Detailed depiction of the first phase of an integrated approach to
CTA within an iterative system development process. A critical element is
the use of mutually reinforcing analyses that work toward an understanding
of the practitioner(s) and the domain. The goal is to develop a model that
captures the analyst's evolving understanding of the demands of the domain,
the knowledge and strategies of domain practitioners, and how artifacts influence perfor-mance—with the ultimate goal of deriving requirements for
improved performance.

standing and evolve a CTA model from which ideas for improved support can be
generated. The process is highly opportunistic. Which techniques are selected—
whether one starts by focusing on understanding the domain or by focusing on
the knowledge and skills of domain practitioners—depends on the specific local
pragmatics. The key is to focus on evolving and enriching the model as you go to
ultimately cover an understanding of both the characteristics of the domain and
an understanding of the way practitioners operate in the domain. This means that
techniques that explore both aspects will most likely need to be sampled. However where one starts and the path one takes through the space depend on what is
likely to be most informative and meet the local constraints at a particular point
in time.

    The phrase *bootstrapping process* is used to emphasize that the process
builds on itself. Each step taken expands the knowledge, base providing opportunity to take the next step. Making progress on one line of inquiry (understand-

ing one aspect of the field of practice) creates the room to make progress on another. For example, one might start by reading available documents that provide background on the field of practice (e.g., training manuals, procedures). The knowledge gained will raise new questions or hypotheses to pursue; these can then be addressed in interviews with domain experts. It will also provide the background for interpreting what the experts say. In turn, the results of interviews may point to complicating factors in the domain that place heavy cognitive demands and opportunities for error. This information may provide the necessary background to create scenarios to be used to observe practitioner performance under simulated conditions. It can also guide search for confirming example cases and support interpretation of observations in naturalistic field studies.

The selection of which technique(s) to use and how many techniques to employ should be motivated by the need to produce a model of the field of practice and how domain practitioners operate in that field. In practice, the modeling process generally requires the use of multiple converging techniques, including those that focus on understanding the domain demands as well as those that focus on understanding the knowledge and strategies of domain practitioners. The particular set of techniques selected are strongly determined by the pragmatics of the specific local conditions. For example, access to domain practitioners is often limited. In that case, other sources of domain knowledge (e.g., written documents) should be maximally exploited before turning to domain experts. In some cases, observing domain experts in actual work practice (e.g., using ethnographic methods or simulator studies) may be impractical, in those cases using structured interview techniques (such as concept mapping), and critical incident analysis may be the most practical methods available. Still in other cases, domain experts may not be accessible at all (e.g., in highly classified government applications); in those cases, it may be necessary to look for surrogate experts (e.g., individuals who have performed the task in the past) or analogous domains to examine.

It should be stressed that the practitioner and domain are merely different access points that provide complementary perspectives. We present them here as distinct to stress the importance of considering both perspectives, but in practice the lines are not so clearly drawn. It is possible to uncover characteristics of the domain through interviews with domain practitioners or field observations. It is also possible to gain perspective on expert strategies by understanding the affordances provided by structural characteristics of the domain. If resources are limited, it is more effective to utilize several techniques that sample from both portions of the space (analysis of the domain and analysis of practitioner), even if done cursorily, than to expend all resources utilizing one technique. Unexpected complexities and surprises are more likely to be uncovered when multiple techniques are employed than when the focus is on only one technique. When the results using several techniques reinforce each other and converge, it increases confidence in the adequacy of understanding. If differences are found, it signals the need for a deeper analysis.

A second point to emphasize is that the goal of the CTA is to develop a productive model that points to contributors to performance difficulty, opportunities for improved performance, and concepts for aiding. The focus of the CTA throughout the process must be on developing concepts related to the goal of the project/system. If the issue is training, then a valid focus is on understanding differences between the knowledge of experts and novices that allow experts to handle cases that novices cannot and developing training concepts for how to transition novices to eventually perform at a more expert level. If the goal is to develop support systems, the focus needs to be on disentangling inherent complexities in the domain that the system needs to deal with—from more superficial aspects that result from characteristics/limitations of existing artifacts. It also requires differentiating features of an existing environment and artifacts that practitioners rely on and need to be preserved even as new technologies are introduced—from noncritical features that can be changed or eliminated.

GETTING STARTED: THE ROLE OF INITIAL CONCEPTS AND RESEARCH BASE

Fortunately for an experienced researcher conducting a CTA, one rarely has to start from scratch for each analysis. Lessons learned from previous research inform the CTA process and provide an interpretive background for understanding the specific findings of the CTA. Guiding insights can come from research on similar worlds, research using similar methods, as well as basic research on human cognition, biases, and errors. For example, previous research on nuclear power process control environments can provide considerable insights on issues in multiagent (person and machine) decision making in dynamic, high-risk worlds that can guide analysis and interpretation of analogous worlds, such as space shuttle mission control, medical emergency crisis management, or train dispatch center operations.

The research base can support the CTA effort in a variety of ways, including guiding:

- *What approach(es) to use*—Similarities between the target and previous worlds can provide insights into what CTA method(s) may be most appropriate.
- *Where to focus attention*—Issues that arise in related worlds can point to potential points of complexity or vulnerability. For example, the research base documenting problems with automation in aviation (e.g., Sarter & Woods, in press) suggests the importance of focusing attention on humanautomation coordination issues in domains where a high degree of automation exists (or is contemplated).
- *What types of scenarios to build*—Experience with analogous domains can suggest characteristics to incorporate in scenarios to reveal the knowledge and strategies that domain practitioners have

developed to cope with domain demands. For example, in some domains, the tempo of the world or the cascade of disturbances may be important attributes to capture in a scenario. In other domains, information uncertainty may be a critical issue that needs to be addressed.

- One of the first steps in the CTA process should be an assessment of the target domain in terms of relationships to analogous worlds and relevant research bases that can inform the CTA. For example, in the case study presented next, it was recognized that the work on making automation activity visible (Ranson & Woods, 1996; Woods, Elm, & Easter, 1986) and the work on decomposing complex systems into multiple levels of abstraction (Rasmussen, 1986; Vicente & Rasmussen, 1992; Woods & Hollnagel, 1987) would provide useful starting points.

USING PROTOTYPES AS TOOLS FOR DISCOVERY

The introduction of new technology necessarily transforms the nature of practice. New technology introduces new error forms, new representations change the cognitive activities needed to accomplish tasks and enable the development of new strategies, and new technology creates new tasks and roles for people at different levels of a system. Changing systems change what it means for someone to be an expert and the kinds of errors that will occur.

Because the introduction of new technology transforms the nature of practice, developers face the envisioned world problem (Woods, in press):

- How do the results of CTA that characterize cognitive and cooperative activities in the current field of practice inform or apply to design activities that will produce a world different from the one studied?

- How does one envision or predict the relation of technology, cognition, and collaboration in a domain that does not yet exist or is in a process of becoming?

- How can we predict the changing nature of expertise and new forms of failure as the workplace changes?

The envisioned world problem means that effective CTA must face a challenge of prediction: How will the envisioned technological change shape cognition and collaboration? How will practitioners adapt artifacts to meet their own goal given mismatches to the actual demands and pressures they experience? The goal of such predictions is to influence the development process so that new tools are useful, support practitioners, and are robust.

One approach to dealing with the envisioned world problem is to extend the CTA process into the design/prototype development phase. This is illustrated in Fig. 20.3. The CTA model (output of the first phase of the CTA effort) becomes the initial hypothesis for aiding concepts. These concepts are embodied in

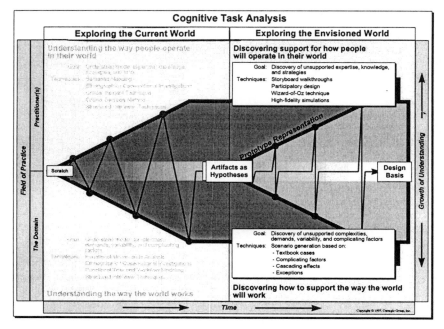

FIG. 20.3   The transition to the second phase of CTA. One of the critical distinctions between the two phases of the CTA is the shift from exploring the current world to exploring the envisioned world. In the second phase, prototypes that embody hypotheses that are derived from the first phase regarding what will be useful support are used as tools for further discovery of the requirements for effective support.

the design prototypes, which in turn are used to discover additional requirements for useful support (Woods, in press).

As indicated by the figure, each opportunity to assess the utility of the design artifacts provides additional understanding of requirements for effective support. It also serves to enrich and refine the initial CTA model. CTA techniques appropriate for this phase of the analysis include storyboard walkthroughs, participatory design, wizard-of-oz techniques, rapid prototype evaluations, and observation of performance using simulations of various degrees of fidelity.

A key element in the success of the envisioned world phase of the analysis is the design of scenarios to be used in exploring the impact of the proposed design artifacts on practitioner performance. To effectively evaluate the degree of support provided by the new technology, it is important to create scenarios that reflect the range of complexity and cognitive and collaborative demands resident in the domain. In addition to scenarios that embody routine situations, it is important to sample scenarios that reflect the range of complicating factors, cascading effects, and exceptions that can arise in the domain.

Note that extending the CTA to encompass exploration of the envisioned world contrasts with the narrow view of CTA as an initial, self-contained technique whose product is handed off to system designers. A second, related point is that it is only when we are able to design appropriate support that we truly understand the way a world works and the way that people will operate in that world. This is the flip side of the claim by Winograd (1987)—that designing things that make us smart depends on "developing a theoretical base for creating meaningful artifacts and for understanding their use and effects" (p. 10).

CASE STUDY: DECISION - CENTERED VISUALIZATION FOR THE NATIONAL GROUND INTELLIGENCE CENTER'S (NGIC) MILITARY CAPABILITIES SPECTRUM MODEL (MCSM)

This section walks through a case study in which we conducted a CTA to provide design concepts for a next generation decision support system (DSS). The application was to design a graphic user interface for the National Ground Intelligence Centers (NGIC) Military Capabilities Spectrum Model (MCSM). The MCSM is a mathematical model being developed to assess patterns of military capability potential worldwide. MCSM enables decision makers and commanders to assess military strengths and weaknesses of other countries and compare potential military capabilities.

The case study is intended to illustrate the use of multiple converging methods in conducting a CTA, and the link between CTA results and design concepts. The focus of the CTA activities was on discovering support requirements—what would be useful to enhance decision making in this domain and reduce the paths to ineffective decisions. Although considerable detail and scope has been omitted, it is hoped that the case study illustrates the steps involved in performing a CTA and the link between CTA activities and design.

The case study traces a CTA process that is now performed largely manually—with minimal computational support. One of the objectives of the case study is to bring to bold relief the requirements for tool support for the CTA process so as to make the transition from CTA insights to design requirements and DSS software development more seamless.

Cognitive Task Analysis

The MCSM employs the tenets of complexity theory and nonlinear dynamics to model military capability potential as a function of 14 critical factors in a countrys military posture. The goal of this mathematical modeling is to provide a common yardstick for assessing the impact of change in any of these factors on that countrys military capability potential, especially with reference to shifts in the balance of power. The CTA effort was a small-scale project that was focused on establishing initial, innovative concepts that illustrated decision-centered visualizations of the target domain. The objective was to create visualizations to support rapid assessment of global military capability.

A decision-centered CTA of the military intelligence domain addressed by the MCSM was conducted. The analysis consisted of: (a) constructing a functional goal-means representation of the domain; (b) identifying decision requirements and the resulting information requirements; (c) defining the relationships between information requirements and user interface design concepts; (d) explo-ring techniques to implement these design concepts into powerful, flexible visualizations of domain semantics.

A functional goal-means representation provided the core framework for identifying the decision and information requirements (Rasmussen, 1986; Roth & Mumaw, 1995; Vicente, 1998). This representation structures the domain in terms of the goals to be accomplished, the relationships between goals, and the means to achieve these goals. This approach consists of an analysis of system objectives that determine higher order functional properties that need to be conveyed to the human operator. The result is a functional decomposition of system behavior, a description of decision requirements to achieve these system goals, and information requirements for assessing goal state and determining courses of action. As detailed next, the steps taken to build the goal-means representation involved both analytic activities and structured interviews of domain practitioners.

Visualization Design

We then created a set of display designs that translated the CTA results into support concepts. The product of this effort was a storyboard consisting of screen mock-ups and supporting design rationale.

A critical element of this task was to establish a mapping that communicated information on the state and behavior of the domain (i.e., critical decision and information requirements uncovered in the first phase of the CTA) through the syntax and dynamics of the support system visualizations (i.e., the form and behavior of the graphical user interface). The objective was to develop breakthrough concepts to move to decision-centered visualizations.

Display task descriptions provided an intermediate step between the CTA results and graphic visualizations. Intermediate design process artifacts included:

- Display task descriptions—a specification of the ideal information needed to fulfill the decision requirement(s) and an explicit description of the goal(s) of a particular display to meet these requirements.
- Graphical depictions—display concepts that translate the display task descriptions into graphic visualizations.

Scenario Development

As a parallel effort, we developed a realistic, operational scenario to provide a basis for design decisions. This operational scenario contains hypothetical input data, potential starting points into the MCSM DSS, and strategies and paths through the information and data space as well as through the control structure of the user interface. Scenarios are used not only to provide data for future prototype development, but also to create incidents to address the predefined cognitive demands of the domain (identified in the CTA) and identify potential modifications to the user interface mechanisms that are used to interact with the domain. The following describes the process that was used to move from CTA results to graphic visualizations step by step. Fig. 20.4 provides a graphic depiction of the process.

Step 1—Initial Functional Description

The first step of the CTA was to build an initial functional goal-means representation of the domain (Rasmussen, 1986; Vicente, 1998). The functional representation specifies the underlying, unchanging system functions and relationships that form the basis for system complexity and goal achievement. This domain model is critical for understanding the context (in terms of goals to be achieved, strategies for achieving these goals, etc.) in which practitioner(s) must perform.

The functional representation is intended to provide a robust model of a complex environment independent of specific events, tasks, and strategies. One of the strengths of this modeling approach is that it enables identification of person–machine and interperson information requirements to support operator decision making and problem solving in unanticipated situations that systemdesigners have not explicitly foreseen and addressed (as opposed to approaches based on predefined task sequences or incidents).

Figure 20.5 presents the initial functional description developed after an interview with domain experts and model developers. This provided a starting point in understanding fundamental relationships, scope of the application, and system objectives. Even this austere representation conveys the structure of physical entities (specific military components) contributing to generalized capability, which collectively comprise each of the terms of reference (TORs). These TOR ratings determine entropy and complexity, which in turn determine military capability potential. At the functional purpose level is the abstract concept of stability monitoring.

One of the interesting points raised by this example is the concept of *entropy*. In this application, entropy is used in a manner consistent with the origins of the concept——as a measure of the degree of disorder within the system. Specifically in this example, entropy is an indication of the variability of the ratings (for a given country) on the different factors or terms of reference. As is evident

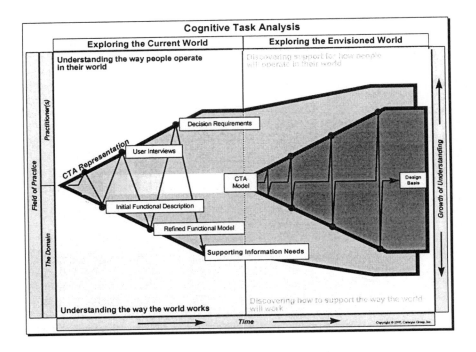

FIG. 20.4   A tracing of the steps that were conducted as part of the CTA for the MCSM decision support system development project. The process began with an initial functional description of the domain. User interviews were then used to refine and enrich the functional description. The result provides the basis for specifying decision requirements and in turn supporting information needs.

from Fig. 20.5, entropy was not initially seen as a contributor to any higher order functions. This provided a cue for the need for additional investigation into the role of this concept within the system functioning.

Step 2—User Interviews

Subsequent to the initial functional description, interviews with potential users were conducted to understand their information needs, knowledge, and strategies. The MCSM model was a unique and novel approach to providing support that was not familiar to the target user population. As a result, user interviews focused on the decision requirements and information needs of the users and the potential for this new tool to support these needs. A wide range of domain experts and potential users were included in this step.

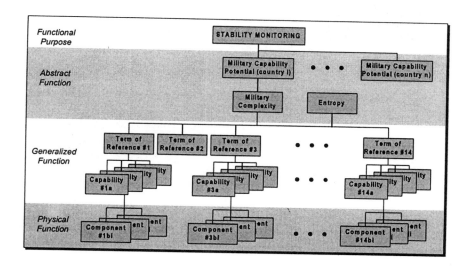

FIG. 20.5   Initial version of a functional goal-means abstraction hierarchy model of the military capability potential domain. In accord with the work of Rasmussen (1986) and Vicente (1998), four levels of abstraction were used to model the work domain.

Figure 20.6 presents a small sample of user comments that were provided in response to probes about specific aspects of the system under development. The functional model provided a framework for identifying information to collect based on areas of uncertainty and/or ambiguity in the initial model and inconsistencies in the model (e.g., no higher order goal making use of entropy). The insights from these interviews were then used to refine and expand the model.

One of the primary uses of the initial model in this stage of the CTA was as a mechanism for resolving discrepancies among different interviews. In some cases, this resulted from inaccuracies as to the designed functionality of the system. In other cases, it was due to an immature functional representation that did not reflect some of the subtle issues within the domain. In the case of entropy, the user interviews provided insights into needed visualizations. Users did not understand the concept of entropy, and therefore if it was to be helpful to them it needed to be explained through the user interface. This led to concepts for graphically depicting the underlying mathematics for users to be able to interpret the results of the calculations.

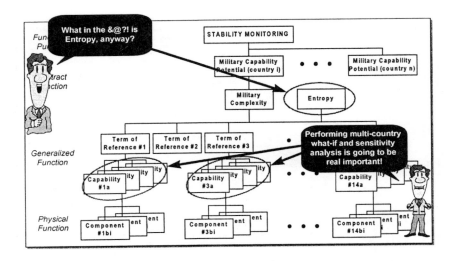

FIG. 20.6   Use of the initial functional model as a guide for interviews with potential users.

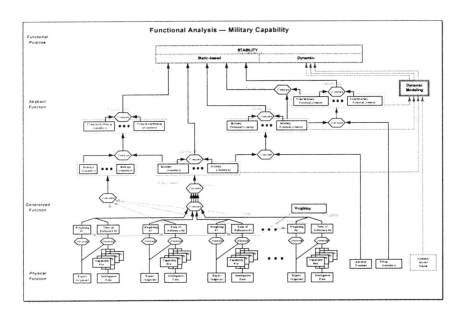

FIG. 20.7   Enhanced version of the functional model for this military capability potential environment.

Measurement of Entropy — Display Task Description

- **User(s) —** Intelligence analysts responsible for:
  - Assessing the impact of events in terms of military complexity.
  - Monitoring global military complexity for critical differences.

- **Context —** Entropy, as a variability metric for the TOR ratings, provides a measure of disorder within the ratings. The impact of what-if changes in TORs can be assessed in the context of changes in entropy. The goal of this display is to provide a framework for comparisons of an individual country in terms of entropy.

- **Cognitive Tasks / Critical Decisions —**
  - D1 - Assess degree of disorder for a given country and given time interval.
  - D2 - Understand the underlying math behind Entropy in order to predict effect of potential changes.
  - D3 - Determine the most influential TORs from an "Entropy calculation" perspective.
  - D4 - Determine impact of what-if changes on complexity/entropy for a given country and time interval.

- **Supporting Information Needs —**
  - Graphical depiction/explanation of Entropy calculation with TOR ratings as input and entropy value as output. (D2, D3)
  - Past, current, and projected TOR and entropy values for the countries of interest. (D1; D2)
  - Validated and what-if TOR and entropy values for the countries of interest. (D2; D4)

FIG. 20.8 An example of a display task description. This display task description specifies the critical decisions and supporting information needs related to the calculate entropy node of the abstraction hierarchy functional model.

Step 3—Refined Functional Model

The next step in the CTA modeling process was to refine the initial functional model of the domain based on information obtained from the user interviews. As such, the functional model begins to capture some of the practitioner side of the world (the upper part of Fig. 20.4) in terms of expertise, knowledge, and strategies. This also begins to identify decision and information requirements. Figure 20.7 presents the revised functional model developed after interviews with potential users and domain experts. As is apparent from this figure, considerable content and detail were added relative to the initial model. For a specific example—entropy—one can now see that it is the joint relationship between entropy and complexity that is compared across the different countries to provide an indication of military stability. In addition, the calculation of entropy was defined as its own node, separating the comparison of entropy and complexity from the underlying calculation of the abstract concept.

Step 4—Decision Requirements

Just as the insights gained from user interviews provided input for refining the functional model, they also helped identify critical decisions within the work domain. These decisions must then be supported by the resulting system design. In this step, the critical decisions for each active node in the functional model (e.g., generate, calculate, compare) were defined and attached to that particular region of the model. Figure 20.8 presents the first part of a display task description, which describes, for a given node within the functional model, the associated decisions to be supported and the information requirements for these decisions. The display task description is for the entropy calculation node. As can be seen within this example, one of the decisions (D2) addresses the need to understand the calculation of entropy to predict the impact of changes. This is designed to address the lack of knowledge on the part of users as to what information this metric was conveying.

Step 5—Supporting Information Needs

Information needs for the identified critical decisions can then be defined to provide the basis for any resulting representation designed to support these decisions. In some cases, information needs may be defined that do not exist in the current system (e.g., lack of sensors, uncomputed metric, etc.). Figure 20.8 presents the supporting information needs for each of the critical decisions identified in the previous step. This defines the information that needs to be contained within the support system and provides the link to the decisions being supported. In this case, one of the critical pieces of information was a graphical depiction of the entropy calculation in terms of input and output relationships (as well as any intermediate calculations).

Step 6—Visualization Design

Figure 20.9 presents the visualization design to support the information needs for each of the critical decisions identified in the previous step. As previously mentioned, one of the critical pieces of information was a graphical depiction of entropy calculation in terms of input and output relationships (as well as any intermediate calculations). The critical part of the entropy calculation is the distribution of the ratings on the different terms of reference. This is explicitly represented in the middle of the bottom portion of the display. Modifications to the ratings (what-if analyses) are represented throughout the transformation from rating to distribution to probability to entropy.

INTEGRATING CTA INTO THE SYSTEM DEVELOPMENT PROCESS

The case study provided earlier illustrated the CTA process and the link between insights gained from the CTA and the resulting support system concepts. The case study illustrated the use of multiple converging CTA methods that included both analytical and empirical approaches to mapping the demands of the domain and extracting the requirements for expert practitioner performance. The case study made salient the use of display task descriptions as a mechanism to transition the insights gained from the CTA into display design requirements that could inform the DSS development process.

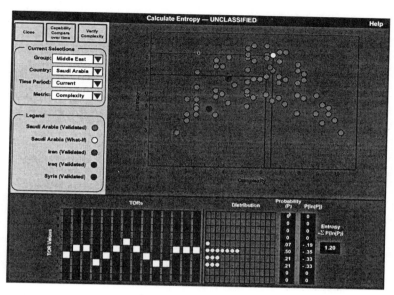

FIG. 20.9   Resulting visualization design for the calculate entropy node within the functional model.

Although the case study illustrated how the results of a CTA could be linked to the DSS development process, the CTA to software transition is currently far from seamless. A critical bottleneck occurs at the transition from CTA analysis to system design, where insights gained from the CTA effort must be crystallized into design requirements and specifications to impact the characteristics of the resulting system. In the best of current practice, system developers typically read through volumes of descriptions of behavior-centered insights and must translate these into software methodology compliant formats. In the case study presented earlier this hurdle was finessed because the individual who created the graphic visualizations was the same person who performed the CTA and generated the display task descriptions.

To more efficiently transition to the design/development phase, the CTA must define the information requirements and system support needed to more effectively accomplish mission objectives. This means that CTA efforts must be focused on efficiently integrating into software development artifacts and go beyond descriptions of cognitively difficult situations. Among the primary conclusions from our analysis of the current state of CTA practice, and our experience in conducting CTAs within a software development environment, are the need for:

- CTA to go well beyond an initial CTA model. A CTA needs to provide concrete, decision-centered design concepts (e.g., information requirements, proof-of-concept storyboards) to provide sufficient support for system design. Initial CTA artifacts such as semantic maps, functional models, and decision requirements are inadequate for software developers.

- an understanding of the artifacts used by software engineers (e.g., system requirements, object model) and how results from a CTA can be integrated into these artifacts (and effectively support system design activity). Given these artifacts form the underlying specification for system development, they are the critical targets if CTA is to effectively impact design.

- a mechanism for capturing design rationale to provide underlying basis for design concepts resulting from CTA effort (to separate the design concept from the instantiation). This is important from several dimensions; first, to separate the information from the presentation (to isolate the source of the problem in an ineffective design); and second, given the inevitable trade-offs within implementation, to identify the critical aspects of the design concepts.

- scenario development to be a central part of CTA. Scenarios become a critical part of system development (e.g., concept of operations documents, event trace diagrams, test case generation) and need to be

- designed around complexities, variability, and complicating factors of the domain.

In developing and evaluating a CTA process, the focus should be on the products to be derived from the CTA. The question one should ask is, Are the demands of the domain and how domain practitioners are responding to those demands being captured in a way that enables concepts for improved support to be generated? Criteria to consider in developing and evaluating a CTA process should include:

1. *efficiency* of the CTA in itself (Are the resources being invested in the CTA activities commensurate with the value of the results being obtained?)

2. *validity* of CTA (Does it capture what it is like to function in the field of practice?)

3. *effectiveness* of CTA in design (Does the CTA point to what is likely to be useful support? Does it help generate new aiding concepts and innovations? Does the CTA help identify the bounds of aiding? Does it help avoid typical design errors? Does it generate ideas that can be readily converted to system requirements to guide system design and testing?)

4. *tractability* of CTA results in design (Are the products of the CTA documented in a way that can be meaningfully reviewed, tracked, and updated not only throughout the CTA phase but also throughout the entire system design lifecycle? Does it support distributed communication and coordination of design team members within and

across organizational boundaries? Do the products of the CTA make contact with artifacts utilized in the software design process, and can the results of the CTA be integrated into the software and product development process?)

5. *predictive power* of CTA (Does it help anticipate the impact of the introduction of new technologies and aiding concepts on practitioner performance? Does it predict how new technological power can change roles, expertise, and error? Does it help address the envisioned world problem?)

These criteria help elucidate the requirements for software tools to support the CTA process. The major benefits of applying software technology to the CTA process will not come from improving the efficiency of use of any given CTA technique. The real value of applying software technology comes from providing tools to support the modeling and documentation activities that are the products of the CTA that feed into the system development process.

Our vision is to develop software tools that aid the CTA analysts in the modeling and documentation aspects of the CTA process. This should yield a more useful product that makes direct contact with the software development process and supports communication and coordination of CTA results among design team members distributed within and across development organizations.

We envision a tool that:

- streamlines the production of software engineering artifacts (i.e., provides support for directly contributing a CTA perspective into established software engineering artifacts);
- makes these software engineering artifacts more focused on defining requirements for building effective, practice-centered decision support (i.e., system requirements that defines solutions to the cognitive demands imposed on the user by the complexities of the domain); and
- provides a mechanism for updating and maintaining related downstream design stages (e.g., a change in the underlying CTA structure triggers a change in the information requirements and thus a change in the resulting display and vice versa).

In this way, it would support cognitive task analysts in capturing and maintaining the essential cognitive issues and relationships developed through a CTA. Yet it will also be a tool for software developers to maintain awareness of the design basis underlying the resulting system requirements and specifications by forming a maintainable, traceable component of the functional design. The primary benefit of an integrated, tool-supported process is the radical advance in the impact of CTA results on the resulting decision support system design.

ACKNOWLEDGMENT

This work was performed under USAF Armstrong Laboratory contract #F41624-97-C-6013. We gratefully acknowledge insights from Michael McNeese (Technical Monitor) and Robert Eggleston from AFRL/HECI.

REFERENCES

Bostrom, A., Fischhoff, B., & Morgan, G. (1992). Characterizing mental models of hazardous processes: A methodology and an application to Radon. *Journal of Social Issues, 48(4)*, 85–100.

Cooke, N. J. (1994). Varieties of knowledge elicitation techniques. *International Journal of Human-Computer Studies, 41*, 801–849.

Cook, R. I., & Woods, D. D. (1996). Adapting to new technology in the operating room. *Human Factors, 384*, 593–613.

Cook, R. I., Woods, D. D., Walters, M., & Christoffersen, K. (1996, August). Coping with the complexity of aeromedical evacuation planning: Implications for the development of decision support systems. In *Proceedings of the 3rd Annual Symposium on Human Interaction with Complex Systems*. Dayton, OH: IEEE.

Di Bello, L. (1997). Exploring the relationship between activity and expertise: Paradigm shifts and decision defaults among workers learning material requirements planning. In C. Zsambok, & G. Klein (Eds.), *Naturalistic decision making* (pp. 121–130). Mahwah, New Jersey: Lawrence Erlbaum Associates.

Gordon, S. E., Schmierer, K. A., & Gill, R. T. (1993). Conceptual graph analysis: Knowledge acquisition for instructional system design. *Human Factors, 35(3)*, 459–481.

Hall, E. M., Gott, S. P., & Pokorny, R. A. (1995). A procedural guide to cognitive task analysis: The PARI method (Tech. Rep.-AL/HR-TR-2095-0108). Brooks AFB, TX: USAF Armstrong Laboratory.

Hoffman, R. R. (1987, Summer). The problem of extracting the knowledge of experts from the perspective of experimental psychology. *The AI Magazine, 8*, 53–67.

Hollnagel, E., & Woods, D. D. (1983). Cognitive systems engineering: New wine in new bottles. *International Journal of Man-Machine Studies, 18*, 583–600.

Jordan, B., & Henderson, A. (1995) Interaction analysis: Foundations and practice. *The Journal of the Learning Sciences, 4*, 39–103.

Klein, G. A., Calderwood, R., & MacGregor, D. (1989). Critical decision method for eliciting knowledge. *IEEE Transactions on Systems, Man, and Cybernetics, 19(3)*, 462–472.

Lesgold, A. M., Glaser, R., Lajoie, S, Eastman, R., Eggan, G., Greenberg, L., Logan, D., Magone, M., Weiner, A., Wolf, R., and Yengo, L. (1985). *Guide to cognitive task analysis*. Pittsburgh, P.A: University of Pittsburgh, LRDC.

McNeese, M. D., Zaff, B. S., Citera, M., Brown, C. E., & Whitaker, R. D. (1995). AKADAM: Eliciting user knowledge to support participatory ergonomics. *International Journal of Industrial Ergonomics, 15(5)*, 345–364.

Patterson, E. S., Watts-Perotti, J., & Woods, D. D. (in press). Voice loops as coordination aids in space shuttle mission control. *Computer Supported Cooperative Work.*

Potter, S. S., Ball, R. W., Jr., & Elm, W. C. (1996, August). Supporting aeromedical evacuation planning through information visualization. In *Proceedings of the 3rd Annual Symposium on Human Interaction with Complex Systems* (pp. 198-215). Dayton, OH: IEEE.

Potter, S. S., McKee, J. E., & Elm, W. C. (1997). *Decision centered visualization for the military capability spectrum project.* Unpublished technical report. Pittsburgh, PA: Carnegie Group, Inc.

Potter, S. S., Roth, E. M., Woods, D. D., & Elm, W. C. (1998). *Toward the development of a computer-aided cognitive engineering tool to facilitate the development of advanced decision support systems for information warfare domains.* (Tech. Rep. # AFRL-HE-WP-TR-1998-0004). Wright-Patterson AFB, OH: Human Effectiveness Directorate Crew System Interface Division, USAF Armstrong Laboratory.

Ranson, D. S., & Woods, D. D. (1996). Animating computer agents. In *Proceedings of the 3rd Annual Symposium on Human Interaction with Complex Systems* (pp. 268-275). Dayton, OH: IEEE.

Rasmussen, J. (1986). *Information processing and human-machine interaction: An approach to cognitive engineering.* New York: North Holland.

Rasmussen, J., Pejtersen, A. M., & Goodstein, L. P. (1994). *Cognitive systems engineering.* New York: Wiley.

Roth, E. M. (1997). Analysis of decision-making in nuclear power plant emergencies: A naturalistic decision making approach. In C. Zsambok & G. Klein (Eds.), *Naturalistic decision making,* Mahwah, NJ: Lawrence Erlbaum Associates.

Roth, E. M., Lin, L., Thomas, V. M., Kerch, S., Kenney, S. J., & Sugibayashi, N. (1998). Supporting situation awareness of individuals and teams using group view displays. In *Proceedings of the Human Factors and Ergonomics Society 42nd Annual Meeting* (pp. 244–248). Santa Monica, CA: HFES.

Roth, E. M., Malsch, N., Multer, J., Coplen, M., & Katz-Rhoads, N. (1998). Analyzing railroad dispatchers' strategies: A cognitive task analysis of a distributed team planning task. In *Proceedings of the 1998 IEEE International Conference on Systems, Man, and Cybernetics* (pp. 2539–2544). San Diego, CA: IEEE.

Roth, E. M., & Mumaw, R. J. (1995, October). Using cognitive task analysis to define human interface requirements for first-of-a-kind systems. In *Proceedings of the Human Factors and Ergonomics Society 39th Annual Meeting* (pp. 519–524). San Diego, CA: HFES.

Roth, E. M., Mumaw, R.J., Vicente, K. J., & Burns, C. M. (1997, September). Operator monitoring during normal operations: Vigilance or problem-solving? In *Proceedings of the Human Factors and Ergonomics Society 41st Annual Meeting.* Albuquerque, NM: HFES.

Roth, E. M., & Woods, D. D. (1988). Aiding human performance: I. Cognitive analysis. *Le Travail Humain, 51(1),* 39–64.

Roth, E. M., & Woods, D. D. (1989). Cognitive task analysis: An approach to knowledge acquisition for intelligent system design. In G. Guida & C. Tasso (Eds.), *Topics in expert systems design* (pp. 233–264). New York: Elsevier.

Sarter, N., & Woods, D. D. (1997). Teamplay with a powerful and independent agent: A corpus of operational experiences and automation surprises on the Airbus A-320. *Human Factors, 39,* 553–569.

Shattuck, L., & Woods, D. D. (1997, September). Communication of intent in distributed supervisory control systems. In *Proceedings of the 41st Annual Meeting of the Human Factors and Ergonomics Society,* Albuquerque, NM: HFES.

Sowb, Y. A., Loeb, R. G., & Roth, E. M. (1998). Cognitive modeling of intraoperative critical events. In *Proceedings of the 1998 IEEE International Conference on Systems, Man, and Cybernetics* (pp. 2533–2538). San Diego, CA: IEEE.

Vicente, K. (1998). *Cognitive work analysis: Towards safe, productive, and healthy computer based work.* Mahwah, NJ: Lawrence Erlbaum Associates.

Vicente, K. J., & Rasmussen, J. (1992). Ecological interface design: Theoretical foundations. *IEEE Transactions on Systems, Man, and Cybernetics, 22,* 589–606.

Walters, M., Woods, D. D., & Christoffersen, K. (1996, August). Reactive replanning in aeromedical evacuation: A case study. In *Proceedings of the 3rd Annual Symposium on Human Interaction with Complex Systems,* Dayton, OH: IEEE.

Winograd, T. (1987). *Three responses to situation theory* (Techn. Rep. CSLI-87-106). Stanford CA: Center for the Study of Language and Information, Stanford University.

Woods, D. D. (1998). Designs are hypotheses about how artifacts shape cognition and collaboration. *Ergonomics, 41,* 168–173.

Woods, D. D., Elm, W. C., & Easter, J. R. (1986). The disturbance board concept for intelligent support of fault management tasks. In *Proceedings of the International Topical Meeting on Advances in Human Factors in Nuclear Power.* American Nuclear Society/European Nuclear Society.

Woods, D. D., & Hollnagel, E. (1987). Mapping cognitive demands in complex problem-solving worlds. *International Journal of Man-Machine Studies, 26,* 257–275.

Zachary, W., Ryder, J., Ross, L., & Weiland, M. Z. (1992). Intelligent computer-human interaction in real-time, multi-tasking process control and monitoring systems. In M. Helander & M. Nagamachi (Eds.), *Human factors in design for manufacturability* (pp. 377–401). New York: Taylor & Francis.

21

ATTUNING COMPUTER-SUPPORTED WORK TO HUMAN KNOWLEDGE AND PROCESSING CAPACITIES IN SHIP CONTROL CENTERS

Mark A. Neerincx, Henk van Doorne, and Mark Ruijsendaal

TNO Human Factors

In process control, operator workload is an important performance determinant. The operator's task is process paced, and changes in the process can accumulate so that the operator has to carry out a lot of complex actions in a short time. New developments in information technology bring about new possibilities to provide users with information and task support in such situations. However, due to the introduction of this technology, task demands change and new bottlenecks appear. Automation is changing operator tasks substantially, from real time in the loop control to supervision and (re)planning of complex processes. For example, this planning can involve a high mental load in nonroutine situations such as fault diagnosis during operation.

The working conditions of platform control in naval ships provide a good example of such changes in task load and computer utilization. Separate platform systems, such as the systems for energy supply, propulsion and fire handling, are more and more supervised from one control room, the Ship Control Center (SCC), using an integrated software system. The user interface and its support functions can have a major impact on the task load. The overall effect of support interfaces is determined by loading and off loading factors. For example, the support facility of the interface can guide, complement, or take over operator actions involving a load decrease, whereas the extra interaction with the interface required for consulting the support facility can cause a load increase. Human factors expertise and techniques are required to attune the platform automation to the SCC personnel so that personnel's knowledge and processing capacities are well employed and the overall human machine performance meets the operational requirements. However, a comprehensive and empirically validated method that applies current knowledge of cognitive psychology to the analysis of complex computer-supported tasks has not (yet) been developed (Schraagen et al., 1997).

In the domain of railway traffic control, recent research aimed at such a method (i.e., a cognitive task analysis [CTA]). First, Neerincx & Griffioen (1996) developed and applied a method for task (re)allocation for traffic controllers of the Netherlands Railways. Subsequently, this method was combined with a design method for user interfaces providing cognitive support in high-task load situations (Neerincx, 1997; Neerincx & de Greef, 1998). This method is further developed to be used for optimizing task load, user interfaces, and cognitive support in future SCCs of the Royal Netherlands Navy (RNN). The RNN is maintaining and developing various classes of frigates, starting with the standard frigate, succeeded by the multipurpose frigate, to the future Air Defense and Command (ADC) frigate. For this last frigate, an Integrated Monitoring and Control System (IMCS) is being developed to establish a reliable and safe operation, control, and monitoring of the platform systems with the related and available crew size, under all specified operational and wartime conditions, and missions (Otto et al., 1997). This chapter provides the general framework of the CTA method, comprising human factors principles and techniques for the specification and assessment of cognitive task demands, and presents the first application to the early phase of the IMCS development. It then describes the cognitive engineering approach to software development in which cognitive task load and support are analyzed in successive development stages. Next it discusses the techniques for the specification and assessment of cognitive task demands exemplified with the analysis for the future ADC frigate. Finally, it provides the conclusions and indicates the state of the art of the method for the CTA that we used.

COGNITIVE ENGINEERING

Cognitive engineering aims at optimal human perception, information processing, decision making, and control in the overall human machine system performance (cf. Norman, 1986; Rasmussen, 1986). To realize such an optimal human task involvement, human factors aspects are addressed in all stages of software development. Software development is an iterative process in which the artifact is specified in more and more detail and specifications are assessed more or less regularly to refine the specification, test it, and adjust or extend it. For the assessment, analytical tests are used in early phases and empirical tests in later phases. Figure 21.1 presents one iteration cycle that can take place at all stages in software development.

The human factors involvement in this process consists of providing relevant expertise (human factors principles and guidelines) and techniques for specification, and assessment. In the specification these principles and guidelines must be ad-

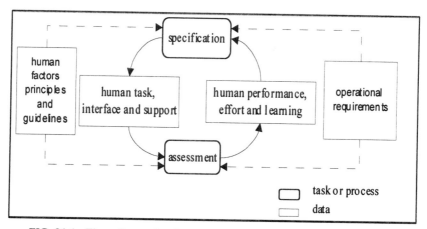

FIG. 21.1 The software development guided by human factors principles and guidelines on the one hand and operational requirements on the other hand (Neerincx & van Doorne, 1997).

addressed as well as the specific operational requirements for the human task performance. The assessment checks whether specifications agree with these principles, guidelines, and requirements. An assessment provides qualitative or quantitative results in terms of human performance, mental effort, and learning. These results are used to refine, adjust, or extend the specification. Eventually, the process of iterations stops when the specification proves to be attuned to the knowledge and processing capacities of the human task performers (e.g., as assessed with a prototype) so that performance, mental effort, and learning are satisfactory.

Cognitive Task Load

Cognitive task load is defined by the cognitive requirements of the tasks allocated to the human operators. The cognitive load of tasks is determined by comparing the required human information processing (i.e., the task demands) with the processing capacities that are available at that moment. Three situations can occur: (a) the required processes exceed the available capacities (i.e., task load is too high), (b) the required cognitive processes agree with the capacities (i.e., task load is fine), or (c) the capacities are not or hardly required (i.e., task load is too low). Task demands can be defined in terms of various variables, such as time, information processing resources, and attention (shifts).

Time. The simplest approaches calculate workload in terms of time on the basis of:

"Workload (%) = (time required for tasks / time available for tasks) x 100"

for sequences of tasks lasting several seconds. Typically, this approach for timeline analysis incorporates capacity limits (i.e., overload) of 70% to 80% time occupied (Beevis, 1992). However, the technique does not deal adequately with tasks that have to be performed continuously (e.g., monitoring), nor with cognitive tasks, although these two task aspects are becoming more and more important in process control (such as railway traffic control and platform control). In process control, due to automation, *mental* workload has increased because fewer people are required to control and supervise multiple, complex systems and processes simultaneously. To address this task demand, Neerincx & Griffioen (1996) extended the timeline approach with the SRK framework.

The SRK framework. The SRK framework of Rasmussen (1986) and Reason (1990) is used to specify human information processing by distinguishing skill-, rule-, and knowledge-based actions. Figure 21.2 shows a simplified overview of this framework that is used for the analysis of complex mental actions in terms of the human goals, knowledge, and the situation, distinghuising three load levels.

1. At the *skill-based level*, information (signals) is processed automatically, resulting in actions that are hardly cognitively demanding (sensor motor shortcut). After a statement of intention, these actions take place as smooth and highly integrated patterns of behavior. Monitoring is an example of skill-based behavior that can be interrupted by attention attracting events (e.g., an alarm).

    Working memory, with its limited capacity, is involved in the rule- and knowledge-based actions that are guided by the user's attention. In addition to the situation, these actions are directed largely by the user's goals and knowledge.

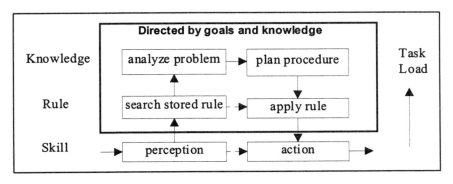

FIG. 21.2 The three levels of information processing and task load.

2. At the rule-based level, input information (signs) triggers routine solutions (i.e., procedures) resulting into rather efficient problem solving in terms of required cognitive capacities (rule short-cut). For these problem-solving actions, the solutions are governed by stored rules of the type *if* <event/state> *then* <actions>, e.g., *if* fire is confirmed *then* set crash stop ventilation in a ship.

3. At the *knowledge-based level*, based on input information (symbols), the problem is analyzed and solution(s) are planned, in particular to deal with new situations. This type of information processing can involve a heavy load on the limited capacity of working memory. Based on a mental model, the person sets local goals, initiates actions to achieve them, observes the extent to which the actions are successful, and, if needed, poses new subgoals to minimize the discrepancy between the present and the desired state. An example is planning a route for approaching a fire.

In addition to the task characteristics, the training and experience of the task performers determine the level of information processing. For example, an operator who has never dealt with a fire will have to use his or her knowledge about fire to infer the correct action (i.e., the ventilation will fan the fire and, consequently, has to be stopped via the previously-mentioned crash stop ventilation). Such a new action takes place at the knowledge-based level. Neerincx & Griffioen (1996) provided a detailed example of an SRK analysis for an existing railway traffic control system and established a load standard.

Task-Set Switching. In complex task situations, several goals have to be accomplished that require adjustments in human behavior (task strategy); this appeals to different sources of human knowledge and capacities and refers to different objects in the environment. Shifts in attention to other goals, memory structures, and environmental objects increase the task load (Gaillard, 1996). It should be noted that our study centers around complex, real-world tasks, compared with the research on simple, laboratory tasks in experimental psychology (e.g., Rogers & Monsell, 1995). Figure 21.3 shows the model for multiple task performance that we use to specify the goal-directed and situation-driven elements of computer-supported human behavior. Three abstraction levels of human behaviour are distinguished:

- An activity is the combination of tasks and actions that are performed to accomplish a general goal in a definite period and for a specific scenario (e.g., damage control on a ship in stormy weather during thenight). A scenario consists of an initial state of the ship and environment and a sequence of events that trigger tasks.

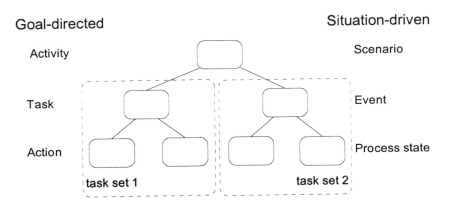

FIG. 21.3 The model of multiple task performance by one operator.

- Tasks are performed to accomplish a subgoal. The term *task set* is used to denote the composite of goal, knowledge, and processing resources of the operator and the corresponding objects in the environment. A task is activated by an event and/or a predefined goal of the task executor.
- Actions are the elements of observable behavior that affect the state of a specific object in the environment. They are a kind of elementary units and, for establishing the corresponding subgoal, the action has to be performed, in one run, from start to finish (cf. unit task in GOMS; Card et al., 1983). The process state determines which action is active or should be activated.

Task Load Analysis. The combination of the three measures (i.e., time, level of information processing, and task-set switches) determines the cognitive task load: the higher the time occupied, the higher the processing level, the more switches, the higher the load will be, and vice versa. In the cognitive task load analysis, two types of time scales are used. First, a general indication of task demands is surveyed (i.e., the general load of a scenario for each person involved). Second, the process of task execution is surveyed to detect bottlenecks for specific moments in the scenario (i.e., continuous monotonous work and high momentary task load).

Because classic workload quantification does not apply to cognitive task load as defined earlier and well-founded measures are still lacking, establishing the exact criteria for cognitive load is part of the method. Table 21.1 presents the general objectives of a cognitive task load analysis for which the standard should be estab-

TABLE 21.1
Objectives of Cognitive Task Load Analysis.

1	There should be sufficient time to carry out the actions, and the time should be sufficiently filled up.
2	The task must call for several levels of information processing. Skill-based actions are barely cognitively demanding; the percentage of knowledge-based actions should be optimized.
3	The number of task-set switches should not impose so heavy a load that the performance on these task sets deteriorates.
4	There should be no long-term period in which only one sort of skill-based action is performed continuously (e.g., performance may decrease after 10 minutes of continuous vigilance).
5	Momentary overloading due to continuous knowledge-based action execution and many task-set switches should be avoided.

lished and, subsequently, met. For each job, the standard is determined empirically in terms of time, processing level, and task-set switches with scenario-based assessments. In system development, the specification should comprise these load parameters so that it can be tuned to the standard.

Cognitive Support

So far, cognitive load has been described in terms of the task and the operator. However, when human tasks are performed with a computer, the user interface— possibly consisting of support functions—determines task load too. There is a trade-off between the costs and benefits of support facilities: The costs can even outweigh the benefits (Kirlik, 1993; Adelman et al., 1993; Neerincx & de Greef, 1993). An optimal benefit can be established when the support function is directed at major determinants and bottlenecks of human task performance, and when it is consistent with the training. The costs, consisting of the overhead of utilizing it, can be minimized, first, by integrating support into human task performance. Using support should not be a separate activity, apart from normal work, and getting support should require minimal investment. Second, the support should be well integrated into the user interface so that the support interface is easy to learn and easy-to-use. Based on these two general requirements, principles have been established for the four cognitive support functions that can be distinguished within the SRK framework: rule provision, information handling, problem exploration, and rule checking (see Figure 21.4). These principles provide the data of the left box in Figure 21.1 so that the user interface and cognitive support can be analyzed in terms of cognitive task load and the corresponding human factors objectives in Table

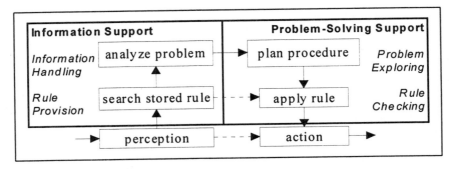

FIG. 21.4   Four cognitive support functions that complement human resources.

21.1.

Rule Provision. Due to training and experience, people develop and retain
procedures for efficient task performance. Performance deficiencies may arise when
the task is performed rarely so that procedures are not learned or are forgotten, or
when the information does not trigger the corresponding procedure in human
memory. For these situations, rule provision aims to supplement human procedural
knowledge (i.e., providing the shortcut on rule-based level, see Figure 21.2; De
Greef & Neerincx, 1995). Neerincx & de Greef (1998)) showed that rule provision
can improve human performance especially when task load is high.

Information Handling. When procedural knowledge is lacking, the problem
and solution must be analyzed. Based on information about the environment (state,
process) and information from memory, a procedure must be planned for solving
the problem. Due to the increasing quantity of available information, situation
assessment and awareness can deteriorate without support. Information support
comprises functions for retaining and/or providing knowledge, data filtering, data
transformations, or data arranging, such as integrated information presentation. For
example, it can help to display the object structure with dependencies and functions,
provide a mnemonic device, and present context specific information about the
relations between symptoms and causes (Rasmussen, 1986; Raaijmakers & Verduyn, 1996; Kerstholt & Passenier, 1997).

Problem Exploration. For novel situations, when complete procedures are
not available, actions have to be planned. Based on a mental model, the person sets
local goals, initiates actions to achieve them, observes the extent to which the
actions are successful, and, if needed, poses new subgoals to minimize the discrep-

ancy between the present and desired states. A problem-exploration function consists of a knowledge-based component that can execute some problem-solving activities such as the generation of questions in a diagnosis process. One possibility is hypotheses generation and the selection of an urgent and most promising one. Another possibility is to provide predictions of future states based on the current user actions. In process control, system components can respond slowly and sometimes, initially, in a backward direction so that current action must be based on future states. Given the high mental load of anticipating future states and keeping track of current actions for which the consequences are not yet displayed, the use of predictive displays can be of considerable value (Wickens, 1992). In addition to real-time support, prediction functions can help plan actions, such as travel time predictions for ship voyage planning or estimates of the closest point of approach. Taken together, the benefits of providing predictions of future states can be large for a number of tasks if the predicted path is explicitly presented and well integrated into the overall presentation of state information.

Rule Checking. Rule checkers or critics.

> "use knowledge bases of heuristics to affect the judgment and performance of users doing a task they are capable of recognizing when their human collaborator has strayed from the normative problem-solving path. In such a case, the critics are triggered, and they help influence, de-bias, and otherwise affect the human's biased judgment to reach a more correct task outcome. (Silverman, p. 170, 1992)"

However, as task difficulty increases, a point is crossed at which subject-matter experts can no longer be assisted by critiquing alone. Thus, under conditions of high task load critiquing is not the best type of support. A further restriction is that the users must have some knowledge to start their task execution. If they do not know which goals to perform, they cannot be critiqued.

SPECIFICATION OF COGNITIVE TASK DEMANDS

Corresponding to the iterative software engineering methods, the CTA method starts with abstract specifications that are assessed and refined in the development process until the task demands are established in detail (i.e., quantified). Neerincx et al. (1998) described the first phase of this process for the specification of human–computer task performance in which the specification of general, hierarchical-ordered task sets is combined with the specification of combinations of task-set instances (i.e., activities). Figure 21.5 shows the specification process of the goal- and situation-driven task elements with their mutual relations:

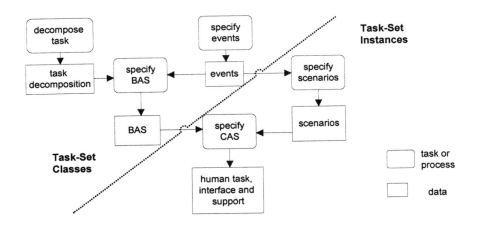

FIG. 21.5 Processes and data flows for the specification of task demands in the analysis stage of user interface development.

- A task decomposition describes the task classes and provides an overview of the goal-directed elements.
- An (hierarchically ordered) event list describes the event classes that trigger task classes and provides an overview of the situation-driven elements.
- A set of Basic Action Sequences (BAS) describes the general relationships between event classes and task classes as general procedures.
- A set of Compound Action Sequences (CAS) describes the relationships between event instances and task instances for specific situations as activities with the corresponding interface support.

Task-Set Classes

The *task decomposition* defines the breakdown structure of tasks and provides an overview of the general task objectives assigned to persons and related to detailed descriptions of human actions with the corresponding information needs. The task decomposition can be enriched with data flow diagrams that show the information that has to be communicated between the tasks. The data flows between human tasks and machine tasks provide a high-level specification of the user interface. For the ADC-frigate, three platform functions are distinguished: provide survivability; provide mobility; and support hotel functions, weapons, and sensors (Otto et al., 1997). In the first instance, the task breakdown stops when all task allocations to the SCC-crew can be designated within it (see Figure 21.6). In correspondance with operation rooms, three types of SCC-activities can be distinguished: planning, monitoring and execution (Passenier & van Delft, 1997). In the present situation, the planning and part of the monitoring functions are allocated to the managers, whereas the monitoring functions and the functions at the execution level are performed by the operators (and a personnel coordinator). The tasks to perform depend on the actual state of the ship (e.g., in harbor or transit) and the environment (e.g., narrow water or ocean). If more tasks have to be done, more persons are present in the SCC. The Royal Netherlands Navy distinguishes 7 Readiness States (RS) for SCCs. The task allocation in Figure 21.6 shows the occupation in RS1 the crew is complete and prepared to perform all tasks. For lower RSs and/or if critical events do not occur, fewer tasks have to be performed by less persons; these task allocations can also be designated within Figure 21.6.

After establishing the jobs as a set of tasks that have to be performed by one person, decomposition continues until the subtask can be mapped on to a specific IMCS function of the ADC-frigate so that either the human computer interaction or an observable human action is specified. In this model, the corresponding information flows have to be established, that is, the information that the human task performers need for their task performance (e.g., with data flow diagrams).

Classes of *events* are specified that trigger the actions of the task breakdown. The event refers to a change in an object that can take place in specific situations and has specific consequences. The events are placed in a hierarchical tree to acquire an overview of the environmental conditions that affect task performance.

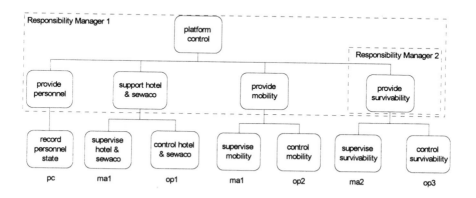

FIG. 21.6 The first task breakdown of platform control with tasks allocated to two managers (ma1 and ma2), three operators (op1, op2, and op3), and one personnel coordinator (pc) in Readiness State 1 (sewacosensor, weapon, and communication).

Events that occur in specific situations determine the SCC work and the corresponding cognitive demands. A distinction can be made between internal events (i.e., events that arise in the ship such as a malfunction in the electricity supply) and external events (i.e., events that arise in the ship's environment such as the appearance of another ship). These classes can be subdivided further with increasing level of detail. Table 21.2 shows some brief examples.

The general procedures for dealing with the events are specified without situation specifics (i.e., in terms of event classes) in so-called *Basic Action Sequences* (BAS). Action sequence diagrams define the dynamic or control aspects of task performance (i.e., the events and conditions that trigger task execution sequences). These diagrams are a combination of specifications for timelines (e.g., Kirwan & Ainsworth, 1992), operational sequences (e.g. Kirwan & Ainsworth, 1992), and cooperation processes (e.g., de Greef & Neerincx, 1995). The task procedures are mainly provided by the applications. Further sections show an example action sequence, with two simple procedures for fire control and dealing with an engine shutdown.

TABLE 21.2
Examples of Events and Consequences for five event Types.

Event Types	Example Event	Example Consequence
System malfunction • Sensor/weapon /communication	E-supply cable broken in harbor	Black-out E-power
• mobility	Leakage propulsion pipe	Oil pressure low
• survivability	Valves defect for smoke boundary	Smoke diffuses in ship
• hotel	Lightning defect	Bad sight
Calamity • fire (ignition)	Large fire in engine room	Damage to engine room
• structural damage	Structural damage by missile hit	Leakage, flooding
Casualty	Call casualties in engine room	Cannot close room's door
Personnel missing	Call cannot find fire fighter x	Fire out of control
Change readiness state	Harbor to transit	More persons in SCC

Task-Set Instances

Events are selected, instantiated, and combined for future working environments into envisioned *scenarios* to determine possible critical event compositions. Scenarios show a particular combination of events and conditions that cause one line of user actions. Scenarios can be a valuable tool to envision computer-supported work and estimate the costs and benefits of the support for the human task performance (Carroll, 1995). In particular, scenarios can provide a bridge between the software engineering focus on software's functionality and human factors focus on users' goals and information needs (cf. use cases in object-oriented software engineering; Jacobson, 1995). In the cognitive engineering method, the term *scenario* is used for a mission type of description (i.e., scenarios consist of a sequence of events that occur in a specific state). However, the purpose of this description is not restricted to the general mission of an abstract function, such as damage control. Scenarios are formulated for a large set of action triggering events, and therefore they can be rather specific.

For the specific purpose of the first analysis for the IMCS development, two scenarios were selected and specified. The initial state of these scenarios differs completely. The first consists of an unexpected calamity with extra complications occurring in a quiet situation. The second consists of severe damage in wartime, comprising a hectic situation that the SCC crew, completely occupatied, must be able to deal with. Table 21.3 presents a brief example of one scenario, called Fire in the galley in harbor, for Readiness State (RS) 5 (foreign harbor).

Per scenario, the Basic Action Sequences (BAS) of the events are instantiated and integrated into a Compound Action Sequence (CAS). The same BAS appears more than once in a scenario when the scenario consists of similar events. Compound Action Sequences do not contain feedback loops and selection mechanisms (such as if x then y), so that the timeline and corresponding task load can be established per chart. Scenario's 1 and 2 are transformed CAS for handling the events of this scenario. The CAS provides an overview of actions and processes performed during the scenario. For each action, the execution time is estimated for *fast* and *slow* performances (i.e., for each scenario, a fast action sequence and a slow action sequence is specified). The duration of action times varies between 5 seconds and 10 minutes. Figure 21.7 presents a part of SAC for Scenario 1. The following components can be distinguished:

- *Actors.* In the SCC, there are three operators (op1 to op3), two managers (ma1 and ma2), the personnel coordinator (pc), the IMCS, and other.
- *Timeline.* The vertical axis shows the timeline. It should be noted that the timeline is not linear (a block sometimes represents 6 minutes,

TABLE 21.3
Example of a Scenario: Fire in the Galley in Harbor.

Scenario: Fire in the Galley in Harbor					
Initial situation:					
1.　　Readiness State: 5 (foreign harbor)					
2.　　Platform configuration					
- Energy generation: one diesel generator running in Front Engine Room; others standby (manual)					
- Survivability: Riser fire main system in Zone 4 defect and fixed fire fighting system in gallery defect					
- Door between kitchen and cafeteria open					
Time	*Event*	*Location*	*Details*	*Consequences*	*Info Source*
0.0	Calamity: ignition	Galley (H-deck, zone 4) + cafeteria (H-deck, zone 5)	Cause: frying fat overheat	Fire Kitchen door not reachable	IMCS + human human
1.5	Malfunction boundary control	Ventilation room 4 (E-deck, zone 5)	Fire causes ventilation room 4 not reachable	Smoke disperses	Human
2.0	Casualty: report	Location of fire	Six casualties—2 in fire-fighting party	Fire-fighting party incomplete	Human
3.0	Malfunctionsensor/ weapon	Load center 2 (E-deck, zone 3)	Failure of transformer unit	Lighting off	IMCS

whereas at another place it represents ½ minute), so the diagram can provide a finer grained view when more actions are performed.

- *Events.* Events occur at a specific moment and directly or indirectly trigger actions.
- *Actions.* At a certain moment, the operator performs rule- or knowledge-based actions.
- *Processes.* The IMCS supports the users with their task performance by rule provision, information handling, problem exploring, or rule checking.

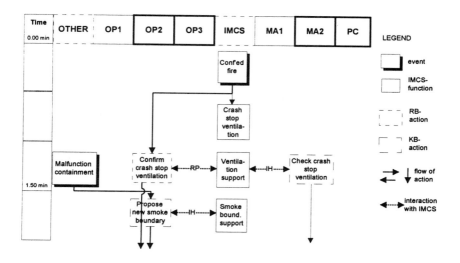

FIG. 21.7 Example CAS for scenario fire in the galley in harbor (op operator, ma manager, pc personnel coordinator, RB rule-based, KB knowledge-based, IH information handling, RP rule provision).

The CAS of Figure 21.7 is a simple example for illustration purposes. The actual action sequences consisted of more actors, the action times were presented in them, and the individual BAS's were coded separately to get an overview of the number of switches between task sets in an activity. Four CAS's were specified. For Scenario 1, the fast version had a duration of 1,090 seconds (more than 18 minutes) and the slow version a duration of 3,380 seconds (more than 56 minutes). For Scenario 2, the fast version had a duration of 1,475 seconds (less than 25 minutes) and the slow version a duration of 4,340 seconds (more than 72 minutes).

ASSESSMENT OF COGNITIVE TASK DEMANDS

In the analysis stage, the technique of scenario-based assessments is used to establish the task demands and detect possible situations of low or high task load. Based on this analytical assessment, the system specification can be adjusted and/or an empirical test can be conducted to zoom into the bottlenecks and detect the exact user behavior consequences. For the first assessment, in addition to the specification of task demands and the human factors principles of the previous section, information was used from a first IMCS System Specification and a set of operational requirements provided by the RNN. The assessment procedure consists of identifying high task load and surveying the human computer interaction. Neerincx et al. (1998) provided the results. The following gives a brief overview.

Identification of High Task Load

In the first step of the assessment, general patterns and extremes of task load are identified. Load is defined by the composite of three parameters: percentage time occupied, percentage KB actions, and number of task-set switches. Differences in the *time* a person is occupied appear mainly between scenarios. There is a large variance: between 8% and 71% occupied. Time occupied does not appear to be a cause of overload on its own, although one operator is at the time load criterion of 70%. Overall, the tasks of managers and operators have a large *knowledge-based* component for which system and process knowledge is required. The work is complex and cognitively demanding for the complete SCC crew. Managers' tasks comprise planning, supervision, priority determination, and coordination, whereas operators have to assess, diagnose, and solve specific technical problems. The current situation requires that the operators have knowledge of the specific part of the platform control system and tasks in which they are involved. The percentage of KB actions differs between the two types of scenarios, in particular for Operator 3: Scenarios 1 and 2 involve 100% and 42% of KB actions respectively. In the CTA method, a *task set* is defined as BAS for a specific event. For example, when the same BAS's appear more than once in a CAS, they are viewed as different task sets because they apply to different events (i.e,. different objects in the environment). Task-set switching often appear's, varying for the two scenarios and among the persons. In particular, for Manager 1, task-set switching can be a problem in the fast Scenario 2: 54 switches in an hour (i.e., a switch every 67 seconds). The number of switches increases in Scenario 2, when action times are longer, because the operational requirements are more difficult to satisfy in this condition. In general, it is the composite of time occupied, percentage of KB actions, and the number of task-set switches that determines the task load. With respect to the general load, two conclusions can be draw. First, the load of the personnel coordinator is relatively high: He performs only KB actions and also has a relatively high score on the other two measures. Second, Manager 1 has a high load in Scenario 2 due to many KB actions with many task-set switches.

The CAS's show the action times of each person and the interrelationships between the actions: the critical path. Often more than one person is on the critical path so that worse performance of one person at a specific moment will often have a major effect on the overall SSC crew performance. Therefore, it is of utmost importance to detect possible peak loads for all persons. Compared with the general load, for momentary peak loads, the time scale of occurrences of almost continuous

KB actions with a lot of switches is much shorter (between 5 and 15 minutes) and the load limit is higher. Table 21.4 presents the detection of some peak loads in particular, the momentary load of Operator 2 in the fast condition of Scenario 2 is high. In a period of 5 minutes, he has to switch every 20 seconds to a new taskset that almost always comprises a KB action. It can be expected that he will not be able to fulfill these task demands; because he is on the critical path, this will have an impact on the overall SCC crew performance. Further, in this period, the operator performs 19 interactions with the IMCS. For this specific action sequence of Operator 2, it is important that the dialogue with the IMCS be as efficient as possible (i.e., the user interface structure should map very well on this sequence).

Survey of Human-Computer Interaction

First, the allocation of actions to the actors is checked. Based on the analysis of action sequences, some task allocations were modified (i.e., this analysis provided an update of the first task allocation).

Second, the map of the users, tasks on the system functions is assessed (see the earlier human factors principles. This mapping of the users, task specification on the IMCS specification was not always direct: Sometimes user requirements did not appear in the IMCS specifications and vice versa. In general, the human computer interaction specification was rather meager so that the general interface structure was not explicitly evident. Third, the cognitive support is identified according to the SRK framework, and it is checked if the corresponding human factors principles are addressed. For each interaction, the support type was established in terms of rule provision, information handling, problem exploring, and rule checking. Some rule provision (mainly consisting of checklists providing the procedure steps to follow) and a lot of information handling was present. For most functions, the corresponding human factors principles were insufficiently addressed: The specification should

TABLE 21.4
High Momentary Load in the Two Scenarios for Fast and Slow
Action Times in Seconds (s).

Scenario	Person	Start	Duration	KB (%)	Task Sets	Switches
6 fast	Operator 2	360s	570s	100	2	4
6 slow	Manager 2	80s	390s	51	4	4
30 fast	Operator 2	30s	300s	93	5	15
30 slow	Operator 2	30s	455s	87	4	8
	pers. coord.	760s	635s	100	5	6

be extended with these principles. For example, one must specify whether the human or computer has the initiative for the data transfer in the human computer interaction.

CONCLUSIONS AND RECOMMENDATIONS

This chapter provides the first result of the development of a CTA method for the analysis of cognitive task load and cognitive support in SCC's. Table 21.5 summarizes the result (i.e., the general framework consisting of the human factors principles and specification techniques and assessment techniques for each software development stage discussed above).

At the analysis stage, the focus is on attuning the user interface at the task level to users' goals and corresponding information needs to their knowledge and processing capacities (i.e., extra support needs), and to the context in which the task is performed. The cognitive requirements are specified with a task breakdown, task allocation, data flows, scenarios, and the corresponding action sequences in terms of the SRK framework. This specification is based on information acquired with interviews, questionnaires, task observations, documents consultations, and critical incident analysis. Based on the action sequences, situations of high task load are identified and the human computer interaction is surveyed. At the design stage, the focus is on attuning the user interface at the communication level to current principles and guidelines with respect to compatibility, consistency, memory, structure, feedback, interaction load, and individualization. To establish a user interface design, the goals, information needs, and support needs are mapped on a specific interaction style. For the assessment, this specification can be prototyped into a mock-up, and the result can be tested analytically with a structured walkthrough and empirically with questionnaires or user interaction evaluations. At the implementation level, the human factors and operational requirements have to be realized by an adequate software application code (i.e., the implementation specification). Then a complete empirical evaluation can be applied with questionnaires or user interaction evaluations.

Many ingredients of Table 21.5 have been used in prior Human System Integration (HSI) approaches (Beevis & Essens, 1997). The new aspects are the focus on a coherent analysis of cognitive task load and cognitive support, and the combination of techniques to make an efficient method for the design of tasks and user interfaces. The CTA method that was developed and applied for the railway traffic control task was the starting point of this research. The basic approach and the cognitive foundations prove to apply to the domain of SCC's. However, the CTA version that was applied to railway traffic control centered mainly around assessing task load for the actual situation and generating recommendations for task re-allocation and procedural support (i.e., rule provision). To affect early software

TABLE 21.5

The Method for Cognitive Task Analysis Consisting of Human Factors Principles, Specification Techniques, and Assessment Techniques for Each System Development Stage.

Development Stage	Human Factors Principles	Specification Techniques	Assessment Techniques
Analysis	Attune user interface at the task level to: • user's goals • information needs • support needs • context	Submodeling: • task decomposition • task allocation • data flows • scenarios • SRK actions Information elicitation • interview • questionnaire • observation • document consultation • critical incidents	Analytical: • identify high load • check human computer co-operation
Design	Attune user interface at the communication level to principles and corresponding guidelines: • compatibility • consistency • memory • structure • feedback • interaction load • individualization	Refine and map analysis specification on specific interaction style (e.g., WIMP)	Analytical: • walk-through Empirical: • question naires • user interaction with mock-up
Implementation	Realize human factors and operational requirements	Software application code	Empirical • questionnaires • user interaction with-interface

specifications and encompass all SCC crew actions, the CTA method had to be extended and detailed substantially. The model of mental load was improved by including task-set switches, human factors principles for the design of cognitive support were added, techniques for the specification of task demands were refined, and an analytical assessment technique was added. It should be noted that the current results apply to the first stage of the IMCS-development for the ADC frigate. In subsequent stages, these results (such as action sequences with time estimations) will be validated and the load standard will be quantified (i.e., the percentage time, the percentage KB actions, and the number of taskset switches for a scenario and short time periods).

Based on the results of the CTA, the specification of the Integrated Monitoring and Control System for the ADC frigate should be improved by describing a general coherent user interface structure and establishing the dialogue principles for its components. In particular, the interface should enable efficient task switching and may even provide support to keep track of task sets that run in the background and return to these task sets. The CTA encompasses an enormous amount of domain expertise. The specification is divided into a coherent set of submodels to keep it manageable. However, the submodels should not be standing completely on their own. Software tools are required for constructing, maintaining and updating these submodels to keep the acquired task knowledge alive and coherent. Furthermore, tools are needed to utilize the information that is present in the specification of CAS's as much and as possible. The specification should be moldable to assess alternative solutions (e.g., by comparing the general and momentary load for each alternative).

ACKNOWLEDGEMENTS

Research is teamwork. We are very grateful to the Royal Netherlands Navy for their contribution to the cognitive task analysis. In particular, we would like to thank ir. K. Visser, ir. E. Otto, ir. H. Sebel, ir. W. Helleman, and ing. T. Bolland for their provision of domain knowledge and their comments on previous parts of the method.

REFERENCES

Adelman, L., Cohen, M.S., Bresnick, T.A., Chinnis, J.O., & Laskey, K.B. (1993). Real-time expert system interfaces, cognitive processes, and task performance: An empirical assessment. *Human Factors, 35,* 243 261.

Beevis, D. (Ed.). (1992). *Analysis techniques for man-machine systems design, Vol 1 & 2* (NATO/Panel 8-RSG.14, Tech. Rep. AC/243 Panel 8 TR/7). Brussels: NATO.

Beevis, D., & Essens, P. (1997, October*). The NATO defense research group workshop on function allocation.* Proceedings of the Int. Conf. on Revisiting the Allocation of functions, Issue: New Perspectives, Galway, Ireland.

Card, S., Moran, T., & Newell, A. (1983). *The psychology of human-computer interaction.* Hillsdale, NJ: Lawrence Erlbaum Associates.

Carroll, J.M. (Ed.). (1995). *Scenario-based design: Envisioning work and technology in system development.* New York: Wiley.

De Greef, H.P., & Neerincx, M.A. (1995). Cognitive support: Designing aiding to supplement human knowledge. *Int. J.of Human-Computer Studies, 42,* 531–571.

Gaillard, A.W.K. (1996). *Stress, produktiviteit en gezondheid* [Stress, productivity and health]. Amsterdam: Uitgeverij Nieuwezijds.

Jacobson, I. (1995). The use-case construct in object-oriented software engineering. In J.M. Carroll (Ed.), *Scenario-based design: Envisioning work and technology in system development* (pp. 309-336). New York: Wiley.

Kerstholt, J., & Passenier, P. (1997). Design and evaluation of decision support for integrated ship operation. In P.A. Wilson (Ed.), *Proceedings of the Eleventh Ship Control Systems Symposium: Vol II* (pp. 39–51). Boston: Computational Mechanics Publications.

Kirlik, A. (1993). Modeling strategic behavior in human-automation interaction: Why an aid can (and should) go unused. *Human Factors, 35,* 221–242.

Kirwan, B., & Ainsworth, L.K. (Eds.). (1992). *A guide to task analysis.* London: Taylor & Francis.

Neerincx, M.A. (1997). Employing and extending human knowledge and processing capacities. In D. Harris (Ed.), *Engineering psychology and cognitive ergonomics: Volume I Transportation systems* (pp. 413–419). Aldershot: Ashgate.

Neerincx, M.A., & de Greef, H.P. (1993). How to aid non-experts. In S. Ashlund, K. Mullet, A. Henderson, E. Hollnagel, & T. White (Eds.), *Proceedings of INTERCHI 93* (pp. 165–171). New York: ACM.

Neerincx, M.A., & de Greef, H.P. (1998). Cognitive support: Extending human knowledge and processing capacities. *Human-Computer Interaction, 13,* 73–106.

Neerincx, M.A., & Griffioen, E. (1996). Cognitive task analysis: Harmonizing tasks to human capacities. *Ergonomics, 39*(4), 543–561.

Neerincx, M.A., & van Doorne, H. (1997). *Cognitive task analysis for user interface development in naval ship control centers* (Report TM-97-A079). Soesterberg, The Netherlands: TNO Human Factors Research Institute.

Neerincx, M.A., van Doorne, H., & Ruijsendaal, M. (1998). *Scenario-based analysis of the platform control task demands in the future Air Defense and Command frigate* (Memo TNO-HFRI 1998-M01). Soesterberg, The Netherlands: TNO Human Factors Research Institute.

Norman, D.A. (1986). Cognitive engineering. In D.A. Norman & S.W. Draper (Eds.), *User-centered system design: New perspectives on human-computer interaction* (pp. 31-65). Hillsdale, NJ: Lawrence Erlbaum Associates.

Otto, E., Visser, K., & Wolff, Ph.A. (1997). Application of functional analysis in naval platform automation specification. In P.A. Wilson (Ed.), *Proceedings of the Eleventh Ship Control Systems Symposium: Vol. 1* (pp. 353–364). Boston: Computational Mechanics Publications.

Raaijmakers, J.G.W., & Verduyn, W.W. (1996). Individual differences and the effects of an information aid in performance of a fault diagnosis task. *Ergonomics*, *39*(7), 966–979.

Rasmussen, J. (1986). *Information processing and human-machine interaction: An approach to cognitive engineering*. Amsterdam: Elsevier.

Reason, J. (1990). *Human error*. Cambridge: Cambridge University Press.

Rogers, R.D., & Monsell, S. (1995). Costs of a predictable switch between simple cognitive tasks. *Journal of Experimental Psychology: General*, *124*, 207–231.

Schraagen, J.M.C., Chipman, S.E., Shute, V., Annett, J., Strub, M., Sheppard, C., Ruisseau, J.-Y., & Graf, N. (1997). *State-of-the-art review of cognitive task analysis techniques* (Report TM-97-B012, TNO-HFRI). Soesterberg, The Netherlands: TNO Human Factors Research Institute.

Silverman, B.G. (1992). Human-computer collaboration. *Human-Computer Interaction*, *7*, 165–196.

Wickens, C.D. (1992). *Engineering psychology and human performance (2nd ed.)*. New York: HarperCollins.

IV COGNITIVE TASK ANALYSIS FOR TEAMWORK SITUATIONS

22

BUILDING COGNITIVE TASK ANALYSES AND MODELS OF A DECISION-MAKING TEAM IN A COMPLEX REAL-TIME ENVIRONMENT

Wayne W. Zachary, Joan M. Ryder,
and James H. Hicinbothom
CHI Systems, Inc.

The Advanced Embedded Training System (AETS) is an intelligent tutoring system that required a large-scale application of cognitive task analysis (CTA) to produce executable cognitive models of a team of human decision makers in a ship-based combat information center (see Zachary, Cannon-Bowers, Burns, Bilazarian, & Krecker, 1998). The team is responsible for maintaining and coordinating ship self-defense/air-defense warfare—an extremely fast-paced, information-rich task domain. The scope of the AETS application required that the CTA and resultant executable cognitive models deal with the full range of individual human activity in the combat information center—from high-level strategy to situation awareness to low-level keystroke sequences and eye movements, as well as the interactions among team members in collaboratively creating and maintaining an air-defense solution. The real-time nature of the work environment and the need to produce detailed executable cognitive models placed strong requirements and constraints on the CTA process for AETS. The need to analyze and model not a single individual but a whole team added further complexity. This chapter describes the methods by which these challenges were met in the AETS research. The general problem of performing CTA leading to executable cognitive models is discussed first, after which a general method for conducting team-level CTA in real-time environments is presented. The application of this general method to the development of AETS is then presented in a case study format and is followed by some concluding thoughts.

General Approach to CTA in Real-Time Environments

Building executable cognitive models in a complex real-time domain requires a CTA method that captures the range of knowledge, procedures, and strategies that reliably characterize adaptive expertise in that domain. The specificity required for building computational models is much greater than that needed for other representation formats (e.g., concept maps, decision tables). This requires more effort for knowledge acquisition and model development, but yields a computable representation that can be used as an embedded model in a tutoring system or as an embedded intelligent agent in an operational system. The resultant model must be accurate and complete enough to reliably predict expert behavior given an unfolding problem situation. Furthermore, it must be robust enough to handle situations other than the scenarios used in knowledge elicitation. To support embedded training and cognitive diagnosis, the cognitive model must also relate decision-maker actions to decision-maker cognitive processes and cognitive states. Thus, the CTA must decompose and describe not just cognitive processes, but also the way in which those cognitive processes are linked to observable behavior.

Traditional task analysis, concerned as it is with description of behavior, can rely on direct observation of actions taken in given situations to gather the data needed for analysis. Cognitive task analysis, however, seeks to relate the behavioral concerns of traditional task analysis with the internal knowledge concerns of cognitive science. Consequently, it must incorporate some method for eliciting the internal information used by a person in a specific task context. Two approaches are commonly used for this purpose, both based on verbal introspection. The retrospective approach, championed by Klein (Klein, Calderwood, & MacGregor, 1989), anchors the subject on specific behavioral instances in the past (often long in the past) and guides the subjects through a verbal introspection process. The thinking-aloud approach, which began with the early cognitive science research of Newell and Simon (1972) and later became a distinct methodology (Ericsson & Simon, 1984), has the subjects solve a representative problem in a realistic setting and verbally introspect while solving the problem. Each of these approaches raises problems for real-time environments where attention demands are high and the task performance requires multi-tasking.

However, the thinking-aloud approach is simply too intrusive. Either the subject is unable to provide the verbal protocol because of high task work load or the verbal protocol task intrudes into the performance of the underlying task and changes the performance and strategy to the point where the resulting data are problematic. These concerns are especially true in highly verbal, event-driven task domains such as ship self-defense/air-defense warfare. Klein's retrospective approach was developed in the context of real-time problems (e.g., fire fighting) and avoids the intrusion problem by relying on retrospection. However, the collection of retrospective protocols well after the fact (often months or years) brings into question the reliability of the subject's recall. The reliability of memories of events long after the fact have consistently been challenged in laboratory and empirical studies (see, e.g., overviews by Bernard, Killworth, Kronenfeld, & Sailer, 1984; Loftus, 1991). Given these data, the ability of subjects to reliably recall the details of cognitive processes and the use of individual knowledge elements long after the fact seems dubious.

The research team at CHI Systems began to develop a solution to this problem nearly 10 years ago (see Zachary, Ryder, & Zubritzky, 1989), in which the two approaches were essentially combined. In essence, this approach presented next has subjects solve real or realistic problems in a naturalistic problem-solving environment in an uninterrupted manner. During this process, all actions (of the subject and in the relevant environment) are recorded so that the problem-solving instance can be replayed. Then, immediately after the problem session is complete, the subjects review their own problem-solving behavior and are guided through a variant of a think-aloud protocol called a question—answering protocol (Graesser & Murray, 1990).[1] In those cases where access to the subjects who did the work is restricted, this approach can be augmented through replay of this recorded session to other more available subject matter experts. In training settings like AETS, having the instructors who participated in the recorded training sessions act as subjects reviewing the performance using the question—answering protocol has shown significant additional benefits in both ease of knowledge elicitation and quality of expertise captured. This approach has been refined and applied to a number of major cognitive task analyses since its inception,[2] including the case study discussed in detail next.

Even within this framework, it is important to recognize that conduct of a CTA to build an executable cognitive model is essentially an iterative process of refinement, in which each iteration provides greater detail, corrections of model components based on incomplete understanding, and refinement for consistency and conformity among parts and links between parts. Although it is difficult to describe this process as a sequence of steps that can be followed in a procedural fashion (because model development is itself a cognitive task), the following paragraphs describe the general method and issues guiding the operationalization

---

[1]Discussions in Hoffman (1987) on unstructured and structured interviews and in Diaper (1989) on posttask walkthroughs describe related methods.

[2]Some of these analyses include antisubmarine warfare (Zachary, Ryder, Ross, & Weiland, 1992), en-route air traffic control (Seamster, Redding, Cannon-Bowers, Ryder, & Purcell, 1993), telephone operator services (Ryder, Weiland, Szczepkowski, & Zachary, 1998), and helicopter pilot-vehicle interaction (Hicinbothom et al., 1995).

of the hybrid approach discussed earlier. The overall method currently involves six broad steps:

1. Performing an a priori domain analysis.
2. Defining subjects, settings, and example problems/scenarios.
3. Recording subject performance in real or simulated problem solving, followed as quickly as possible by verbal question—answering protocol using problem replay.
4. Analyzing and representing the data, repeating Step 3 as necessary.
5. Developing the executable cognitive model, repeating Steps 3 and 4 as necessary to achieve the level of detail and quality of elicited expertise required.
6. Validating the CTA result.

A more detailed discussion of this method is given next, followed by a detailed case study showing how this method was used and customized to produce the executable models of a team of experts needed by the AETS application.

1. *Performing an a priori domain analysis.* In complex real-world environments, it is difficult to gain access to domain experts from whom task analysis data can be collected. When the constraint is added that the access must be in a real or realistically simulated, problem-solving environment, the difficulty is often increased. Therefore, it is critical for the analyst to become thoroughly familiar with the essential principles, terminology, and processes of the domain. This material can usually be obtained from training materials, elementary texts, web sites, or other similar materials and guided, when possible, by an interested party familiar with the domain. The goal is not to attempt to become an expert, but rather to become a reasonable novice. This step is key for two reasons. The first reason is pragmatic—it saves precious time. Without this a priori learning, the limited time with the subjects (during the verbal protocols) will be occupied with elementary information exchanges rather than issues of deeper expertise. The second reason is more qualitative. It is essential that the analyst establish a productive rapport with the CTA subject. Taking the time to learn the essentials of the domain often helps establish this rapport, and just as often failing to do so destroys it. Subjects who are busy experts taking time from other activities quickly tire of elementary questions about basic terms and definitions; they become less cooperative or even terminate the process as a waste of their time.

2. *Defining subjects, settings, and example problems/scenarios.* Before collecting data, care must be taken to define the setting and problems for which data will be collected and the subjects who will be used in this process. Subjects should be selected to represent the same level of expertise. The authors have argued elsewhere (Zachary & Ryder, 1997) that experts,

novices, and intermediate-level individuals vary not (just) in the amount of knowledge but in the organization and representation of that knowledge. For experts, there is typically a high degree of commonality imposed by the domain and by sociology of knowledge in the operational community (novices and intermediate-level individuals have less coherent knowledge structures and exhibit more variability in knowledge content and strategies). For the following discussion, it is assumed that experts are the focus.[3] This method has empirically been found to work well with a sample of 5 to 10 individuals (more are usually required at nonexpert levels because the lower the level of expertise, the greater the variability in knowledge organization and content).[4] In Step 3, the subjects are asked to solve representative problems in their domain of expertise in the setting in which these problems are naturally encountered. Although this can be accomplished in either the actual environment or a simulated equivalent, a simulated equivalent is usually chosen because it affords more experimental control and more accessible data recording. The selection of both the scenarios and the operational personnel must reflect the range of problem-solving challenges and the strategies to meet those challenges posed by the actual environment. This scope ensures that the diversity and complexity of the environment are captured by the analysis.

3.   *Recording subject performance and using verbal question—answering protocol.* During each real or simulated scenario, the activities of each subject are observed and recorded for subsequent analysis in such a way that the problem-solving session can be played back. Ideally, the real environment or simulator can provide this data-capture and replay capability. When this is not the case, synchronized audio/video recordings

---

[3]It is difficult to define *expertise* in absolute or quantitative terms. The authors' criteria include amount of experience in the job (roughly top quarter) and citation by others in the field as most respected. Within the military, trainers often meet these criteria.

[4]The estimate of 5 to 10 is only empirical and represents the point where the authors have found that new knowledge seems to cease coming into the analysis.

have been successfully used (see Ryder et al., 1998).[5] Pragmatically, the ability to capture and replay the data may be a determinant in the choice (in Step 2) between a real or simulated environment. The verbal data, in the form of thinking-aloud protocols and question—answering protocols, are taken immediately after the problem or simulation has been completed. The authors' experience has shown that high-quality protocols can be obtained in response to recordings of actual behavior, particularly when taken immediately afterward while the problem is still fresh in the subject's mind. When immediate replay is not possible, useful protocols can still be obtained up to several weeks later with rapidly diminishing quality. In these verbal protocols, subjects are asked to introspect and recount their internal decision processes used to solve the problem. Specific verbal probes are often made to clarify these accounts (at which time the replay of the problem is paused). For example, probes are inserted when the subject: (a) uses an unfamiliar term or concept, (b) appears to take an action different than a past situation that appeared to be the same (or vice versa), and (c) seems to be switching from one task to another. These verbal probes are key to exploring certain parts of the knowledge space in depth. These primary verbal data can be supported by unstructured debriefs by participants, as well as interviews and critiques by subject matter experts (SMEs) from the domain, particularly during the data analysis process.

4.   *Analyzing and representing the data.* Once the problem-solving and verbal data have been collected, the analysis of the data proceeds. This step is the bridge between the knowledge-acquisition portion of the CTA and the representation of that knowledge in a summary form, converging the differing views among subjects and the differing strategies across problems. Particularly when the goal of the CTA is construction of an executable model, this step necessarily involves transforming the verbal and performance data into a formal representation language. This method was developed in conjunction with a specific representation language called COGNET (Zachary, Ryder, Ross, & Weiland, 1992), which was specifically developed to capture cognitive processes in real-time, multiple-task-

---

[5]When recording equipment cannot be used, an analysis can be conducted with a series of static snapshots or other representations of the problem-solving process at frequent intervals. This was used in an analysis of air traffic control (Seamster et al., 1993), in which the contents of the main radar display was printed at 60-second intervals as a record of the problem-solving activity. This is clearly a less desirable case, however.

demand environments. However, the authors believe that the method described here can be applied with other representational formalisms as well. The analysis of the raw verbal and performance data is an iterative process in which major model components are initially defined, then further detail is added, sometimes necessitating revision of the major components. The initial stage of the analysis using COGNET notation decomposes the decision processes in the problem domain into a set of cognitive tasks and high-level goals that organize the decision maker's procedural knowledge and a set of categories/entities that encompass the decision maker's declarative knowledge. This is done by reviewing the sequences of problem-solving behavior (either through video/audio recordings or use of computer-generated problem replays) in conjunction with verbal protocols from the subject experts. Following the general principles of exploratory sequential data analysis (see Sanderson & Fisher, 1997), a time-based record of each session is created, decomposed, and annotated to identify basic declarative, procedural, perceptual, and motor knowledge components. The initial pass at task/goal definition involves identifying recurring sets of activities from each subject expert. Similarly, the initial declarative knowledge definition is based on representing the elements of the problem domain that are used in the problem-solving process. In addition, an initial pass is made at defining perceptual processes (i.e., identifying information in the environment that the expert responds to in performing the tasks) and motor processes (i.e., the actions the expert takes on the external world).

Unlike artificial intelligence knowledge engineering, which often focused on capturing the knowledge of a single expert, a cognitive task analysis should seek to capture shared understanding across individuals at a common level of expertise. In reality, this requires identifying the differences as well as the commonalities among the subjects. Differences among experts should be noted during the analysis of the raw data and resolved with follow-up discussions among the subject experts. This is where it is important to have multiple sources of expertise, not just one. Differences in strategy, procedures, and problem representation that are uncovered in the initial analyses must be presented to multiple experts to determine if they represent:

- competing approaches within the community of experts (with no agreed-on preferred approach)
- idiosyncratic methods of a single individual (which may be accepted by the broader group of experts or not), or
- different instances of a more abstract, common underlying approach.

Ultimately, the problem comes down to one of either:
- accepting one variation over the others,
- allowing multiple variations, or
- revising the analysis to a higher level of abstraction that incorporates what appeared to be variants into a single model.

5.   *Developing the executable cognitive model.* Each model component undergoes progressive refinement and elaboration until it is completely defined in the relevant representation language (COGNET or some other). Each component must be specified with the precision and formality needed for an executable model. That entails, for example, specifying all relevant attributes of each domain object, as well as conceptual relationships among domain objects. In addition, the refinement process includes ensuring consistency across model components. For example, all cognitive operations manipulate the information stored in the declarative problem representation. Thus, the cognitive operations have to be consistent across model components. At this stage, the model must be executed under different conditions and tested, to ensure that its behavior is appropriate and timely, under different problem conditions. This blends into the next step.

6.   *Validating the model.* Validating the model is actually a process that occurs throughout the time the model is being developed; however, a more formal validation process is usually undertaken when the model has been completed. There are two primary foci for validation. First, it is necessary to ensure that tasks are activated in the appropriate conditions (and not in inappropriate ones). Second, it is necessary to ensure that the complete expertise model generates valid and reasonable behavior. Methods for model validation include walkthroughs with domain experts or running the models and comparing the results with human expert performance. For a formal model validation, the models are run using new domain problems (rather than ones that were used in the data collection process) to determine the generality of the model's behavior for a wider variety of situations.

Team Issues in Real-Time CTA

Few individuals actually perform their work in true isolation, especially in high-risk, real-time, multitasking (RTMT) domains. Whenever multiple individuals must work together as a team, effort must be invested in creating and maintaining a shared team conceptual model (e.g., who does what under which set of circumstances, prearranged plans requiring synchronized sequences or simultaneous actions by multiple team members, etc.). Thus, the CTA of issues like communication, coordination, competition, and cooperation plays an important part in such domains.

Identifying and characterizing all of the means of communication among coworkers is often not as simple as it might at first seem. All communications need not be direct nor need they occur in real-time—even in RTMT domains. Some communications may be carried out via posting important information in the work environment as notes, general announcements, or other nonreal-time means of communication. Other communications may be indirect, such as computer-mediated communication among team members. Whenever and however communications occur, they are essential to enabling any team of individuals to perform as one while still retaining the abilities of all of the individuals.

Teams of workers often coordinate their individual actions to achieve team objectives through a combination of prior arrangements (e.g., prebriefings and team meetings), on-the-fly cueing of situations covered by prearranged plans, and on-the-fly coordination in unanticipated situations. Competition for shared resources is also a fact of most teamwork, requiring shared understanding of the: (a) relative priorities of each competing task, and (b) implications and effects of each team member's actions on other team members and the ability of the team as a whole to achieve its objectives. Cooperation among team members further clouds the CTA by causing individuals to perform actions not normally thought of as part of their job, as they step in to aid or correct a teammate (e.g., compensatory behaviors).

Asking open-ended probing questions about communication, coordination, competition, and cooperation during performance of a given task is one way to deal with these team issues. Unfortunately, some experts limit their answers to textbook descriptions of how they think the job should be performed, completely overlooking the true complexity involved in how they actually perform the job. Going beyond these self-imposed limits is often difficult. The general approach described earlier—of combining recorded performance with verbal protocol data—can often help overcome these limits, as can pointed investigation of the source of each piece of information or data used during observed performance of the job (e.g., an information environment audit). The most reliable method of identifying and characterizing all of these team issues is, in our experience, to augment the aforementioned approaches with an extensive informant-guided physical audit of the information environment. Such an audit includes inspection of all common areas, documents, filing cabinets, bulletin boards, telecommunications equipment, meeting or briefing rooms, and other shared resources used by any of the team members. Videotaping actual work performance (as well as any briefings or meetings) is useful in supporting this integrated approach, especially when all team members are not co-located in the same workplace. Audiotaping verbal communications is also useful for analyzing the explicit communication patterns and how they relate to accomplishment of team goals. The use of these data is discussed in more detail in the following AETS case study.

Case Study: Advanced Embedded Training System (AETS)

The AETS project[6] was undertaken to demonstrate the ability to turn an existing embedded team-training simulator,[7] specifically that provided by the AEGIS control system on (some) navy ships, into an intelligent training system by adding automated instructional technology. This automated instructional technology was dependent on a capability to monitor and diagnose the behavior of human watchstanders in an AEGIS-equipped ship's Combat Information Center (CIC) during training exercises. This was done using embedded executable cognitive models of the watchstander roles as the standard against which trainee performance would be compared (see Zachary et al., 1998, for an overview of the AETS architecture). These embedded cognitive models were developed from a detailed CTA of human watchstander teams.

AETS was designed to provide both individual- and team-level training (i.e., training on how the various individuals should work together as a team to accomplish the complex air defense function). Thus, the models (and the underlying CTA) had to include the knowledge used to generate both the work functions of the individual watchstander role and the collaborative knowledge on how to interact and cooperate with the other team members.

The primary focus of AETS was on one of several teams working within the (25+ persons) CIC, specifically on the core of the Air Defense Warfare

---

[6]AETS was funded by the Office of Naval Research and the Naval Air Warfare Center Training Systems Division, under contracts N61339-97C-405 and N61339-96-C0055. The early portions of the cognitive task analysis were supported by the Naval Air Warfare Center Training Systems Division, under subcontract to Micro Analysis and Design, Inc.

[7]That is, a simulator that is embedded within a software/hardware system used by a team of people, and allows the system to be exercised in simulation mode for training purposes. Typically, such embedded training simulators provide no training function other than problem simulation and practice—diagnosis, feedback, and remediation, if any, are provided by human instructors.

(ADW) team, which is responsible for protecting their own ship and others from airborne attacks from aircraft and missiles. The CTA of the ADW team was undertaken using the general method described earlier and produced detailed, executable cognitive models of the ADW team. These models are discussed in Zachary et al. (1998) and Zachary, Ryder, Hicinbothom, and Bracken (1997). The AETS team CTA was a complex undertaking, having to be conducted in field (rather than laboratory) settings and requiring many pragmatic adjustments and extensions of the general framework. These are summarized next using the same six-step organization as presented previously.

Domain Analysis

The AETS CTA had access to a large volume of past analyses of the ADW domain. In particular, a multiyear study of the domain that had been done in the early 1990s (see Cannon-Bowers & Salas, 1998) provided a great deal of material on the AEGIS-based ADW from a decision-making, training, and human–computer-interaction basis. However, this proved a mixed blessing. ADW proved to be a rapidly changing domain, and by the late 1990s, the strategies, equipment, and tasks of ADW watchstanders were found to have evolved substantially from what had been studied even 3 to 5 years earlier. As a result, the CTA team sought out documentation of systems and tactics that were current at the time of the AETS analysis. In addition, the CTA team interviewed various SMEs, including writers of the then-current documentation, to further round out the needed a priori background in the problem domain.

Defining Subjects, Settings, and Example Problems/Scenarios

The AETS CTA was by definition a team CTA. This meant that the unit for which performance data had to be collected and recorded was the team, not just the individual watchstander. This imposed substantial logistical problems. Gaining access to individual human domain experts for CTA is generally difficult, and gaining access to whole ADW teams simultaneously was a daunting prospect. It was soon realized that the only way in which whole teams could be observed and recorded performing ADW tasks was in the context in which these activities naturally occurred—on board ships and at periodic onshore team training. Various factors precluded the former—the cramped space on board ship, the difficulty in using recording equipment there, and the tremendous demands on crew members' time while at sea. The shore-based training setting presented a much more attractive data-collection setting (although also adding some other challenges, as discussed in the next section).

Shore-based training took place in a facility that used the same equipment as on board ship, but in a less cramped setting.[8] Moreover, to support the human trainers, the training setting had existing facilities to capture the primary display contents of the various watchstanders on videotape and add audiotracks from the various (closed-circuit radio) communication networks with which team members communicated. These screen and audio recordings were supplemented by a second camera placed over the shoulder of each watchstander in the ADW team. This camera captured the actions of the watchstanders' hands and showed head movements between and among the various display units, particularly those not able to be captured by the existing data-logging facility.[9]

The use of the training facility as a performance-capture setting largely removed the problem of selecting the problems to be presented to the subject teams. The problems worked by the teams were those that were provided as part of their regular training exercises. However, over the 2 weeks of intensive training that each team received, there were many different problem scenarios that were simulated, and the CTA team had the opportunity to record the ones it deemed most useful for the analysis (including all of them).

Collecting Performance and Verbal Protocol Data

The nature of work in the navy is that individual sailors are placed into crews for a period of time at sea (called a *deployment*) and then potentially reassigned between deployments as new ships are commissioned or to replace crew members whose obligation has expired and who leave the service. Thus, team membership is dynamic, and a new crew (i.e., for a new ship) is typically formed from a mix of experienced and inexperienced members. This new crew is put through 2-week team training prior to commissioning of the new ship. It is this precommission training that was observed and captured for the AETS CTA. Over a 12-month period, seven such crews were studied; between two and five problem sessions were recorded for each of these crews. Thus, for any crew running a specific problem simulation, the performance-collection process yielded a series of videotapes, two per watchstander, showing (on the first) the main dis-

---

[8]Full-fidelity was important in the CTA because the models that resulted from it ultimately had to be embedded into, and therefore to fully reflect the constraints, strategies, and interactions needed to carry out ADW in the full AEGIS environment. The need for full fidelity led the team to discount any use of existing low-fidelity simulation environments for the CTA performance-data capture.

[9]For some crews, the use of this over-the-shoulder camera was not permitted.

play and main auxiliary display contents and (on the second) the hand and head movements, as seen by someone looking over the shoulder of that watchstander (as an instructor would). The audio tracks on these tapes captured the radio and speech communications within the team and among the larger CIC staff.

This approach to performance data collection raised some serious issues for the verbal protocol portion of the analysis. Clearly, although some individuals in each crew might be expert at their individual role, these were not expert teams. They were still learning how to interact and work as a team.[10]
Taking verbal protocols from them would not yield the expert-level insights that were sought. In fact, the recorded performance was rarely expert level at least for team behaviors. On reflection, it was realized that the purpose of the cognitive models in AETS was not to actually automate the watchstander roles, but to automate the observation, assessment, and diagnosis process now performed by human instructors who stand over the shoulder of human trainees. This helped frame the goals of the verbal protocol portion of the analysis.

If the AETS-embedded cognitive models needed to observe and diagnose the actions of watchstander trainees, the kind of knowledge that needed to be elicited via the verbal protocol was that which human instructors observing actual trainees would evaluate, (i.e., high-level actions). Thus, it was decided to modify the verbal protocol task from one of thinking aloud about your own performance to one of asking a human instructor to think aloud about the (recorded) performance of this trainee. With this revised definition, various experienced instructors were used as subjects in the verbal protocol task, where they provided data on what they thought the trainee was and should be doing. The verbal data covered both the trainee's specific watchstander responsibilities (i.e., the task work) and interactions with other team members (i.e., the team work).

Analysis and Representation of Data

The data were first analyzed by session—that is, the combined verbal protocol and recorded performance data for a single member of a single team working a single simulated problem. Each session was analyzed to identify the following elements:

- use of core concepts involved in domain reasoning,
- identification of and pursuit of intermediate and final goals to be achieved in each aspect of the job,

---

[10]To help compensate for this, the main recordings of performance were taken near the end of the 2-week intensive training, when the crews were at their best level of performance both as individuals and as a team.

- procedures or sequences of related actions in service of a goal,
- use of specific elements of the displays and/or specific communications in domain-reasoning procedures,
- performance of specific actions (both manual actions to invoke system functions and verbal communicative actions to share information or make requests with other team members),
- application of prearranged procedures and actions to be coordinated with other team members,
- initiation and completion of compensatory behaviors intended to aid or correct a teammate,
- formation of expectations about future events and initiation of action based on achievement or failure of such expectations to materialize,
- reference to or reasoning about underlying (system or environmental) processes that had to be understood to predict implications of actions for self and teammates, and
- resources shared with others or otherwise affected by others' actions.

From the session decompositions, a number of parallel and interrelated analyses were undertaken, the goal of which was to formalize the information in the COGNET representation language. In general, these analyses involved combining specific types of information in the annotations across multiple session records.

Using outlining tools, the core concepts were organized into a hierarchical structure of information categories and concepts, and the goals were organized into a hierarchical task/goal/subgoal structure. Both of these processes could be considered top–down analyses informed by the a priori domain analysis of the ADW domain and team-training objectives. A parallel bottom–up analysis was undertaken using the set of possible actions to determine what decisions had to be made to select those actions and what data had to be available to make those decisions, building up to link them with low-level, intermediate-level, and ultimately top-level goals. Similarly, the elements in the information environment were analyzed to determine which specific items in the environment were being internalized and used either to trigger or complete the reasoning/action procedures, as well as how they were being used. These analyses led to the initial characterization of declarative, procedural, and perceptual knowledge as represented in the COGNET notation (see Zachary et al., 1992; Zachary, Ryder, & Hicinbothom, 1998, for notational details).

Each watchstander's declarative, procedural, and perceptual knowledge incorporated elements that contributed to teamwork behaviors. These included knowledge of prearranged procedures and coordinated actions, of how and when to undertake compensatory behaviors, of underlying processes and their implications for other task-work responsibilities, and of resources subject to competition among the team members and of how to account for that competition in task work. This phase of analysis was highly iterative and often required additional interviews with SMEs to clarify concepts or resolve issues in the analysis, especially teamwork issues as each individual watchstander's job became more clear.

For AETS, it was necessary to converge on a single representation of expert strategy and knowledge organization for each watchstander role. When the prior analysis process yielded alternative solutions, two final authority subject experts were consulted and asked to review the alternative analyses. If they agreed on one as superior over the other, that preferred solution was accepted. When they disagreed, they were questioned again to determine whether they were responding to different characteristics of the situation, which would lead to a differentiation of strategies based on more specific situational nuances. When this failed to achieve consensus, the strategy that was preferred by a majority of the instructors who provided the verbal protocols was used.

Developing Executable Models

The AETS CTA results were translated into executable cognitive models using the COGNET notation (Zachary et al., 1992), as discussed earlier, as supported by the iGEN[TM] software system. The iGEN[TM] software allowed graphical authoring, editing, and inspection of the models. It also supported their interaction with the AEGIS work station emulators. This permitted any model (or all of them) to act as a watchstander and solve a simulated ADW problem through the actual AEGIS work station emulator, thus supporting incremental testing and debugging. During the AETS CTA, the processes of data analysis, formalization, and executable model development were undertaken simultaneously.

To support the model development process, various strategies were employed to divide the analysis/modeling effort. For some ADW watchstanders, the analysis and modeling were divided between two individuals, each focusing on a different level of knowledge. One focused on task-level knowledge and skills, whereas the other focused on tool-level (i.e., HCI) knowledge and skills. For other ADW watchstanders, the analysis and modeling were done by one individual, but with access to the models created for the other ADW watchstanders. This allowed the effective reuse of model components such as general domain knowledge. In general, both strategies seemed effective, but further research is needed to compare these and other strategies and relate them to characteristics of the role and task being modeled.

Validation

The cognitive models that were created through the AETS CTA were complex, particularly in their ability to engage in team behaviors as well as individual problem solving. Validation of these models was an ongoing part of the development process and was done using SMEs (typically ADW instructors and team trainers). Validation consisted of two types of activities:

- *Model execution inspections*—as noted earlier, the iGEN™ software permitted any model to assume the watch for a particular role during a problem simulation. The iGEN™ software also permitted the internal processing and knowledge states of the model to be examined while it was executing and allowed the execution to be paused at any time for more detailed internal inspection. Subject matter experts observed the execution of the model and examined its internal basis for taking specific actions, decisions, and so on to determine if the model were acting as a reasonable expert watchstander would. This amounted to a modified Turing test form of assessment and was the primary means of validation.
- *CTA/model walkthroughs*—the graphical nature of the model representation in iGEN™ permitted SMEs to walk through the model's knowledge (declarative, procedural, and perceptual) and comment on it. In many cases, this process identified problems that might only occur under occasional or rare conditions (i.e., those not observed during the execution inspections).

In both the inspections and walkthroughs, the validation focused on both individual and team behaviors. For the latter, a major concern was the ability of the model to generate appropriate communications with the remainder of the team, to respond to other team members' communications (which were made accessible to the model through a speech-recognition system), and to take compensatory actions when some other team member made an error of omission or commission.

CONCLUSION

AETS represented an ambitious effort to apply CTA and cognitive modeling approaches to a team of individuals in a complex task domain. Among the many things learned in the process, the following four are of the most general relevance:

1. *CTA is the vehicle not the driver*—in AETS it was essential to focus on why the CTA was being done to produce a useful analysis. This is, in the authors' experience, typically the case. Each CTA must be

tailored to fit the purpose for which it was undertaken. However, a thorough CTA may prove to be useful for additional purposes—either as it stands or as the starting point for further analysis.

2. *Knowledge is dynamic*—over a 5-year, and even a 1-year, period, substantial evolutions were found in the way front-line human teams perform the ADW task. This has serious implications for CTA—specifically, that it must be considered as a function of a point in time, as well as a specific system, domain, and so on. When the CTA is embodied in a system, interface, or agent, the knowledge must be maintained and updated or it may quickly become stale and outdated. Although the overall characteristics and work goals of the domain are stable, weapons, sensors, or platforms may be upgraded or replaced and tactics change over time.

3. *The level of abstraction is not under your control*—in AETS, the concern was not with low-level HCI knowledge, but rather with high-level domain knowledge and teamwork issues. Unfortunately, it was impossible to avoid the low-level HCI knowledge in the CTA. Thus, the AEGIS system did not permit a clean separation of tool knowledge and task knowledge for its human operators, thus many aspects of strategy were inextricably interwoven with arcane HCI details and functionality. Unfortunately, this is often true, leading to cases where the analysis and model have to incorporate details that were not originally felt necessary.

4. *Individual versus team CTA is a continuum, not a dichotomy*—in AETS, the CTA process began with an individual-oriented approach and was extended to capture features of team-level behaviors (e.g., communication, compensatory actions, proactive guidance, and information sharing). In doing so, the underlying CTA framework grew from one that considered only individual task performance to one that incrementally included knowledge of team roles, meta-cognitive processes, and organizational cognitive processes. These represent incremental steps on a continuum that may have, at opposite ends, pure individual task performance (e.g., isolated HCI) and pure team processes (e.g., organizational dynamics). However, it may well prove that most needs for team CTA will fall, as did AETS, somewhere in the middle of this continuum, rather than at either end.

REFERENCES

Bernard, H. R., Killworth, P., Kronenfeld, D., & Sailer, L. (1984). The problem of informant accuracy: The validity of retrospective data. *Annual Review of Anthropology, 13*, 495–517.

Cannon-Bowers, J., & Salas, E. (Eds.). (1998). *Decision making under stress: Implications for training and simulation.* Washington, DC: American Psychological Association.

Diaper, D. (1989). Task observation for human-computer interaction. In D. Diaper (Ed.), *Task analysis for human-computer interaction* (pp. 210–237). Chichester, England: Ellis Horwood.

Ericsson, K.A., & Simon, H.A. (1984). *Protocol analysis: Verbal reports as data.* Cambridge, MA: Bradford Books/MIT Press.

Graesser, A., & Murray, K. (1990). A question-answering methodology for exploring a user's acquisition and knowledge of a computer environment. In S. Robertson, W. Zachary, & J. Black (Eds.), *Cognition, computing and cooperation* (pp. 237–267). Norwood: Ablex.

Hicinbothom, J. H., Weiland, W., Santarelli, T., Fry, C. A., Voorhees, J. W., & Zaklad, A. L. (1995, May). *AMMI: Intelligent support for alarm systems in advanced rotorcraft.* Paper presented at the American Helicopter Society 51st Annual Forum, Fort Worth, TX.

Hoffman, R. R. (1987, Summer). The problem of extracting the knowledge of experts from the perspective of experimental psychology. *The AI Magazine, 8,* 53–64.

Klein, G., Calderwood, R., & MacGregor, D. (1989). Critical decision method for eliciting knowledge. *IEEE Transactions on Systems, Man, and Cybernetics, 19* (1), 462–472.

Loftus, E. (Ed.). (1991). Science watch. *American Psychologist, 46,* 16–48.

Newell, A., & Simon, H. (1972). *Human problem solving.* Englewood Cliffs, NJ: Prentice-Hall.

Ryder, J.M., Weiland, M.Z., Szczepkowski, M.A., & Zachary, W.W. (1998). Cognitive engineering of a new telephone operator workstation using COGNET. *International Journal of Industrial Ergonomics, 22,* 417–429.

Sanderson, P. M., & Fisher, C. (1997). Exploratory sequential data analysis: Qualitative and quantitative handling of continuous observational data. In G. Salvendy (Ed.), *Handbook of human factors and ergonomics* (2nd ed., pp. 1471–1513). New York: Wiley.

Seamster, T.L., Redding, R. E., Cannon, J.R., Ryder, J.M., & Purcell, J.A. (1993). Cognitive task analysis of expertise in air traffic control. *International Journal of Aviation Psychology, 3* (4), 257–283.

Zachary, W., Cannon-Bowers, J., Burns, J., Bilazarian, P., & Krecker, D. (1998). An intelligent embedded tutoring system for tactical team training: The advanced embedded training system (AETS). In B. Goettl & H. Halff (Eds.), *Intelligent tutoring systems* (pp. 544–553). Berlin: Springer-Verlag.

Zachary, W.W., & Ryder, J.M. (1997). Decision support systems: Integrating decision aiding and decision training. In M.G. Helander, T.K. Landauer, & P. Prabhu (Eds.), *Handbook of Human–computer interaction* (2nd ed., pp. 1235–1258). Amsterdam: Elsevier.

Zachary, W.W., and Ryder, J.M., & Hicinbothom, J.H. (1998). Cognitive task analysis and modeling of decision making in complex environments. In J. Cannon-Bowers & E. Salas (Eds.), *Decision making under stress: Implications for training and simulation* (pp. 315–344). Washington, DC: American Psychological Association.

Zachary, W., Ryder, J., Hicinbothom, J., & Bracken, K. (1997). The use of executable cognitive models in simulation-based intelligent embedded training. In *Proceedings of Human Factors Society 41st Annual Meeting* (pp. 1118–1122). Santa Monica, CA: Human Factors Society.

Zachary, W., Ryder, J., Hicinbothom, J., Santarelli, T., Scolaro, J., Szczepkowski, M., & Cannon-Bowers, J. (1998). Simulating behavior of tactical operators and teams using COGNET/GINA. In *Proceedings of the 7th Symposium on Computer-Generated Forces and Behavioral Representation* (pp. 365–376). Orlando, FL: Institute for Simulation and Training.

Zachary, W.W., Ryder, J.M., Ross, L., & Weiland, M.Z. (1992). Intelligent computer-human interaction in real-time multi-tasking process control and monitoring systems. In M. Helander & M. Nagamachi (Eds.), *Design for manufacturability* (pp. 377–401). New York: Taylor & Francis.

Zachary, W., Ryder, J., & Zubritzky, M. (1989). *A cognitive model of human-computer interaction in Naval Air ASW Mission Management* (Tech. Rep. 891215.8704). Spring House, PA: CHI Systems Inc.

23

MODELING A COMMAND CENTER

Peter J.M.D. Essens, Wilfried M. Post,
and Peter C. Rasker

TNO Human Factors

The role of human factors in the design of complex systems has grown from a focus on local physical ergonomic issues and individual human–machine interaction to an approach where organizational, technological, and human factors are being integrated into the system. This can be seen in the approach to design of ships by the Royal Netherlands Navy (RNLN) over the last 15 years. The layouts of ship bridges, operations rooms, and command centers are now being based on design concepts driven by task organization and team factors (Post & Punte, 1997). For operator interface design, a similar development can be described. In addition to using human vision characteristics as a basis for information display requirements, cognitive requirements derived from tasks, responsibilities, and operational conditions are now driving the specification of which information should be displayed and in what format (Essens et al., 1994; Neerincx, 1995; Passenier & van Delft, 1996). A third development concerns the design approach. The RNLN wants to take account of human characteristics at an early stage in the design process (Huisman, 1995; Otto, Visser, & Wolff, 1997). A major motivation for this is the requirement to reduce manning levels. The goal is to base early design decisions on the most influential operational and human performance constraints and opportunities. With a more formalized approach, one can better control the complex design process and its outcome.

The human engineering approach advocated by the NATO Study Group RSG.14 (Beevis et al., 1992) was adopted as a framework for including human factors into design decisions. This approach builds on a functional design methodology, which starts its analysis with a specification of the functions the system should perform to achieve its mission. The functions represent the whole system on an abstract level. The human factors input in the early design phases shows itself in particular in the allocation of functions process. Function allocation is the design activity that specifies what roles humans and technology have in the realization of the functions. Criteria for function allocation are traditionally focused on the information-processing capabilities of humans and machines (Fitts, 1951; Essens, Martens, & Helsdingen, 1997). These are still applied in current practice, but considerations are being broadened to human–human allocations including teamwork, rank structures, job design criteria, user well-being, and, even broader, to sociotechnical and organizational criteria and system efficiency and cost-effectiveness issues (Beevis, Essens, & Schuffel, 1996; Beevis & Essens, 1997; Fallon et al., 1997).

Traditional human factors evaluation of complex prototype or operational systems usually focuses on operator performance instead of system performance (Meister, 1998) or limits evaluation to a subsystem, such as the human–computer interface, or a single criterion, such as work load. Outcome measure approaches take the result of the total system; however, by treating the system as black box, it fails to provide an understanding of the factors leading to that outcome. Command and control effectiveness methods—such as the Headquarters Effectiveness Assessment Tool and Army Command and Control Performance Measurement—take the systems' underlying functions and apply diagnostic measures to them (HEAT and ACCES; e.g., Castro et al., 1991; both cited in Engel & Townsend, 1991). Sample underlying functions are monitor and plan alternatives; sample diagnostic measures are percentage of out-dated unit locations and number of changes in plans. Despite the problem linking these measures directly to battle outcome, the research did provide significant insights into factors of command group performance (Engel & Townsend, 1991).

Although performance-oriented evaluation is understandably the primary perspective in judging the effectiveness to systems' functioning, especially for military systems, other perspectives such as user well-being, satisfaction, and control are receiving increasing attention in the evaluation of complex systems. These changes can be characterized as a shift toward an integrated systems perspective. The systems approach is conceptually not so new (see Checkland, 1993; Meister, 1991). What is new is this: the high-level support for human factors as an integral part of design, test, and evaluation (such as the US DOD Human Systems Integration directives 5000 series and the UK MOD Human Factors Integration Program); the sponsors' attention to cognitive analysis as a basis for design decisions (Essens et al., 1994); the attention for the team as a system element (HFES, 1998); the broad effort to integrate people, technology, and organizational factors into the evaluation of existing systems and analysis and design of future systems reflected in recent conferences (see Fallon et al., 1997; Vink, Koningsveld, & Dhondt, 1998), and new journals (such as *Cognition, Technology & Work*).

A typical example of a complex system is the command center (operations room or combat information center) of a frigate, where information from the air, surface, and subsurface worlds is gathered, analyzed, and acted on. The system is built to respond to a wide variety of situations and signals from external *worlds*. The worlds that the command center monitors and tries to control are dynamic and change with varying time horizons. The system is complex because it is comprised of multiple people and multiple technologies organized in several subsystems that have to tune their processes and combine and collate the information produced to achieve the ship's mission. A command center can be characterized as a *human activity system* (Checkland, 1993) designed for human information processing, decision making, and execution; it is supported by technologies such as interfaces to sensor and weapon systems and the combat information system. More specifically, the command center can be seen as a complex *cognitive* system: It takes situation-specific information, knowledge from training and experience, mental constructs (hypotheses and assumptions), and norms and values and then combines those into new information entities. These have abstract labels such as *intention, situation description*, and *threat*, which are complex elements of a shared mental model.

A complex system is not just a collection of individuals and technology. Adding up the products of each subsystem would undervalue the integrative contribution of the system as a whole. Analysis of individual command center operators focuses on what goals they have in performing their tasks, what information is used, what mental transformations are applied, and the resulting output. The same questions are asked when analyzing a system as a whole, with a unit of analysis that may cover more than one individual or subsystem. Analysis of a human activity system requires the identification of entities that comprise the task-related structure of the system on the one hand and performance indicators on the other hand.

Recently, the RNLN launched several studies for the analysis and design of command centers: One is an assessment of the *current* command of the M-frigate class, whereas the other is a *future command* study aimed at reduced manning concepts for command centers of future frigates. The aim of the assessment of the current command center was to measure work load and quality of information processing, system handling, communications, and team performance. The study should provide insight into what determines command team performance as it is currently configured. The assessment does not address the strategic or tactical qualities of the systems' outcome nor the performance of the technology systems. Rather it focuses on the processes, on how well the cognitive system responds to changes in the worlds, how well information is handled and communicated, how well decisions are implemented, and how well these processes are managed and controlled. The *current command* study had two parts—a descriptive modeling part and a performance assessment part. (The performance assessment part looked directly into the work load and quality of performance of several operational command teams from RNLN M-frigates, who performed three realistic warfare scenarios under controlled conditions. Measures were taken and scored directly during the process and linked to video registrations.)

The modeling was primarily intended to establish a common framework of concepts for the assessment team (naval experts and researchers). In particular, we focused on the specification of the entities that comprise the task-related structure of the system and captured those in descriptive models.

MODELING THE RNLN COMMAND CENTER

Modeling serves several purposes in system analysis. For one, modeling is analysis in the sense that it breaks up a whole into its essential elements. In this way, modeling reduces complexity of analysis. Modeling a system is complex because the essential elements and their relationships are not readily given and have to be abstracted from the many details of the system. Modeling is a good way to learn to understand a system. A model provides a visualization of the system, which can facilitate communication about the system, and functions as a vehicle for verifying the correctness of understanding.

The most important requirement of the command center modeling is that it should identify the information entities and the functions that generate or transform them. A function may be associated with what one person does, but it may also cover the activities of a team either in interaction with technical systems or not. Other requirements are that the model should be communicable with domain experts and that it provides a common terminology (in a glossary or data dictionary) for proper communication. The model should be correct in the sense of being agreed on by a representative group of domain experts. The modeling process should be manageable and, in this particular study, it should be completed within months and with limited resources. To manage the process, the modeling process should progress in iterations—top–down and breadth-first—so that at each iteration the complete picture is available. The description of the resulting models and the experiences from developing and validating them form the core of the rest of this chapter.

MODELING APPROACH

Modeling is no sinecure of a system where more than 20 persons are interacting with each other and with technical systems, in an adaptive organization, using communications lines often in parallel, reacting and pro-acting to the dynamically changing worlds. The sheer complexity of a command center makes performance-oriented task network modeling a precarious affair. The benefit of combining understanding the system and measuring its performance in simulations in unlimited parameter variations is offset by the risk of getting stuck into detail and the problems of validating the predictions. Moreover, the indispensable adaptive and compensatory capabilities of the humans are a challenge for simulating system performance. Information on the quality of performance in the study was covered by controlled observations. The role of the modeling effort was to compile an easily accessible map of the task-related structure of the command center: the functions, tasks, dependencies between functions, distribution of tasks over operators, and information used and generated in the tasks—all linked to each other. This map should provide insight in the structure and global processes before the performance assessment effort. Additionally, after the assessment, with acquired knowledge about hotspots in the performance, the model(s) should allow us to point at the structural elements and process steps that require more detailed analysis.

Beevis et al. (1992) listed a number of analysis techniques and qualified a subset as highly applicable for analysis of complex man–machine systems. The techniques stress the sequential relationships of functions (function flow diagrams; sequence, and timing diagrams); the input, control, and resource requirements of the functions (structured analysis and design technique); or the processes and decisions involved in information flow (behavior graphs, operational sequence diagrams). Other analysis approaches focus on the goal structure that drives the behavior of the system (e.g., GOMS, HTA; Kirwan & Ainsworth, 1992). The hierarchical task analysis (HTA) method represents the system activities in terms of goal hierarchies and in what order subgoals are realized. The method has been applied in several studies (Kirwan & Ainsworth, 1992), including the analysis of naval command teams (Annett & Cunningham, this volume). Goals are in fact compatible with functions in a human activity system; in that sense, a functional decomposition represents a goal hierarchy. However, one perspective, that is not modeled explicitly in an HTA is the information. Information is the core product of a command center's internal process. Knowing what information units are flowing through the system and what processes act on them is crucial for understanding the functioning of the system.

In our approach, we designed a suite of models that provides different perspectives of the system: function model, information model, organization model, technical means model, human agent model, knowledge model, function-information model, task model, and event handling model (Fig. 23.1). The first six models are hierarchically organized. The function-information model shows the information dependencies of the functions on the different hierarchical levels. The event handling model shows the response to a tactical event in a temporal sequence of functions that are distributed over agents. The task model takes the end nodes of the functional hierarchy and couples these with the end nodes of the information hierarchy (as input and output), the technical means and agents as resources, and the knowledge entities as controls. The next section covers a more detailed description of the models.

The Suite of Descriptive Models

The representation language and graphics used in the models consist of a restricted set of descriptors with a consistent form (syntax) and a consistent meaning (semantics). The objects described are shared by the models, and by the modelers, through a terminology base (a glossary). The graphical representation of the descriptors was partially derived from the work of Rumbaugh et al. (1991) and Yourdon (1989): An arrow means data dependency, small circle with line means part-of relationship, rounded box represents a function, square shaded box represents an information entity and circle represents a mechanism. Right-shadowed boxes have a hierarchically lower layer (see Fig. 23.2).

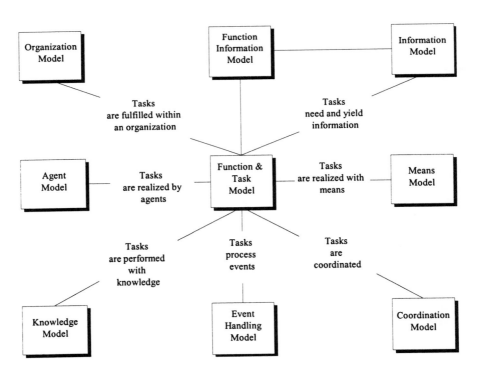

FIG. 23.1 Suite of models for the description of a complex system.

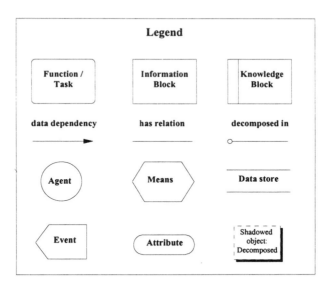

FIG. 23.2 Symbols used in the modeling.

Function Model.   The top-fighting function of the ship is distributed over
three warfare functions: Anti-air (AAW), Anti-submarine (ASW), and Anti-
Surface warfare (ASuW). Each such function has a subset of functions that can
be clustered in a similar way. Similarities in parallel branches reduce the complexity of the representation. The subsets of functions can be organized using a
model developed for command and control. Models of command systems use a
set of basic functions for decomposing the process into chunks of related activities. The OODA loop uses terms like observation, orientation, decision, and action. The SHOR model stands for stimulus, hypothesis, option, response (Wohl,
1981). Some models use more detailed terminology (Engel & Townsend, 1991).
The terminology we used is situation awareness, threat assessment, decision
making, and direction and control (Van Delft & Schuffel, 1995; Passenier & van
Delft, 1996). The processes they focus on are (a) knowing what is going on by a
permanent process of compilation, monitoring, and maintenance of the actual
situation often with fusion of additional information sources; (b) knowing what it
means for the mission by appraisal and interpretation of the current situation
from a tactical perspective; (c) knowing what to do by selecting an option and
planning (counter)measures; and (d) knowing how to do it and making it work
by giving directives and allocating resources. The four functions from the C2
model were used as primary functions in the modeling of the M- frigate command center. The secondary functions are those needed to achieve the goals formulated in the primary function. Fig. 23.3 (top) shows the functions in a hierarchical representation.

Task Model. Functions were decomposed until they could be assigned to a human agent or a technical means. This level is called the *task level* because of the coupling with human agents. Tasks in the task model realize the functions from the function model. A representational form of the basic SADT diagram (structural analysis and design technique) was used (described in Beevis et al., 1992). This diagram represents a function/task in terms of inputs, outputs, controls (knowledge), and mechanisms to realize the function (technical systems and human agents). Input and output are information entities. Mechanisms are crews, persons, or technical systems that transform the input information into output information. This transformation is directed and controlled by knowledge of mission goals, tactics, and orders (Fig. 23.3 bottom). The figure shows a task model of AAW subfunctions using a particular class of sensors. Information inputs are (in this example) radar signals and sensor and communications settings. Control comes from knowledge about the air picture. Several operators and technical systems are involved in the task. The output is an established air contact (in particular, a radar air contact).

The sample shows a subset of the decomposition. In the task model, the lowest level of the function decomposition is combined with details from the other models: the information input and output, the resources (i.e., means and human agents), and the knowledge used. Decomposition was stopped at the task level. Further decomposition would get us into individual cognitive and sensory–motor tasks, which was not the general intention of the current decomposition. Further decomposition is only conducted for the tasks identified as critical in the performance assessment.

Function-Information Integration Model. We have argued that information is the core product of the command center. In interviews with domain experts, abstract information concepts were used to indicate general information concepts that are important in the command center processes, and detailed concepts were used for task descriptions. This suggested a representation of the functions combined with these abstract concepts. In Fig. 23.4, an integration of the two hierarchies is presented. The AAW function is shown with the basic command and control concepts (rounded boxes) together, with the information concepts as input and output of these functions. Some information comes from outside the AAW function (e.g., intelligence, staffwork), whereas some is generated internally (e.g., situation description). The arrows indicate data dependencies, not a flow that starts at some point and ends at another. This means that decision making needs information concerning the threat. This is not to say that threat is not known to the other functions, but the other functions do not depend on it for their operation. It can be seen that situation description is a central concept in this function, which is fed by the four command and control functions.

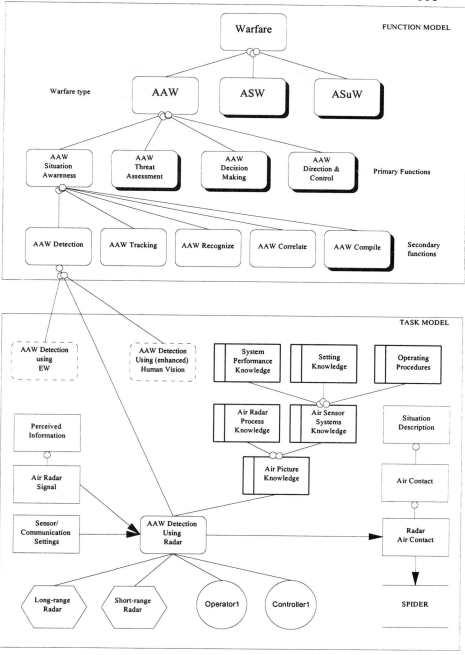

FIG. 23.3 Function model and task model

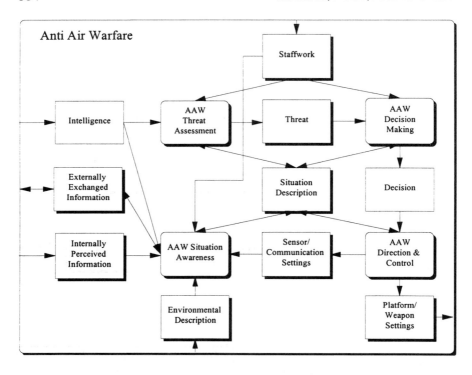

FIG. 23.4 Sample of one level of the Function-Information integration model.

Functions are linked with their information input and output entities. The diagram shows the data dependencies among the functions.

Event-Handling Model. The event-handling model provides a generic representation of the flow of tasks (the lowest function level) performed successively and in parallel by the human agents as a response to an external event, such as a contact or a threat. No particular time unit is defined; only the order is conveyed. For the three warfare functions, a set of critical event diagrams were developed. The representational format is similar to the sequence and timing (SAT) diagrams (described in Beevis et al, 1992). The arrows represent information flow. Information can also come from or go to external agents (Fig. 23.5).

The Other Models. The organization model describes how the M-frigate as an organizational unit relates to the task group and other organizational units. The agent model represents the human actors in the organization. The means model represents the set of technological systems and tools to support the agents to carry out their work. The knowledge model represents what the agents need to know to carry out their tasks. This could be called *school knowledge*. The diagram shows the flow of functions of the command center and its distribution over human agents as a response to a critical event.

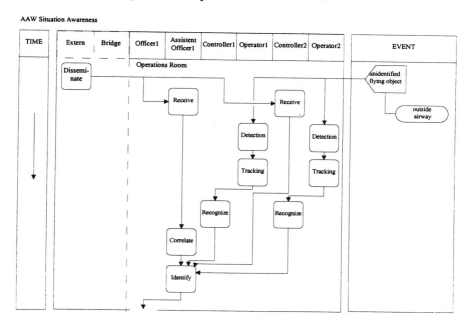

FIG. 23.5 Sample of an event-handling model.

The Modeling Process

Development of the models was expected to be iterative. Modeling started with the basic command and control functions: situation awareness, threat assessment, decision making, and direction and control. On the basis of available documents, such as NATO protocols and training material, own domain knowledge, and formative interviews with two domain experts, a first arrangement of concepts was made. In 4 half-day sessions with two pairs of other domain experts, this was extended into a first *strawman*. One pair dealt with AAW and the other pair with ASW and ASuW. The split along warfares proved to be necessary because specialization and expertise of the experts in a particular warfare resulted in different concepts of the other warfare. An intentional restriction was made for situational-bound tactical knowledge, which was outside the focus of our modeling effort. The order of development was, roughly, first the function and the function-information model for the three war fares, subsequently the task model, and, in parallel, the knowledge model and other models. Finally, the flow of functions over personnel was described for a number of basic events from each warfare. Between the sessions, corrections were worked into the models, consistency checking between the models was done, and models were updated.

It was also anticipated that the officers' perspective would be substantially different from the controllers' and operators' perspectives. To cover all perspectives without getting into the *as many experts as many opinions* consensus problem, a norm group of six naval experts was formed: It consisted of trainers, evaluators, operational experts, officers, and noncommissioned officers. This group's task was to check and correct the content of the finalized models and to sanction it. This was done in two group sessions. Because of the size of the model set, a number of full-day sessions were needed.

Tools

A relatively simple flowchart tool with a chart layer function and active navigation buttons (ABC flowcharter) was used to draw the models. This gave us a quick start and freedom of representation compared with more complex modeling tools, but required gradually substantial bookkeeping, version management, consistency checking, and glossary maintenance. We used special hardware (interactive large screen displays) to speed up development, adjustment, and verification of the (intermediate) models during elicitation group sessions with domain experts.

SUMMARY AND CONCLUSIONS

The modeling effort demonstrated its value in eliciting task-related structural knowledge from the domain experts, which had not been specified previously in a formal way for this class ship. The modeling forced the researchers to specify precisely what their understanding was of the system. The domain experts differed in the mental models they used, which made it necessary to establish a norm group of experienced naval experts to come to a consensus. The need of a norm group was not anticipated in advance, but proved to be essential for establishing an authoritative representation. Additionally, the discussion on what the norm is helped tune the ideas of the norm group experts, which was beneficial for the performance assessment in which they also participated. As a side effect, the value of the norm group was that the models were more widely recognized and are now being applied in other applications too (e.g., for information system design and for training specification).

The domain experts needed some time to get acquainted to the syntax used. In particular, the data dependency diagrams (function-information model) were initially read as process flowcharts. Most discussion, however, went into the concepts used and their precise meaning. The use of interactive large-screen displays, together with the graphical modeling language, became well accepted within the expert teams and proved to be an effective way to gather information and build the models. Although the domain experts noted that the models had become complex at first sight, they recognized that this was inevitable because the model suite represents a complex system.

The large quantity of information (changes, annotations, new branches) elicited in the group sessions was difficult to process afterward. Because the models are strongly interrelated, adapting them became a major enterprise. Further technical support to the process should be helpful for consistency checking, glossary update, version management, and for having navigational overview within and between the models.

One of the concerns at the start of the study was the way details explode when modeled. This was controlled by the top–down, breadth-first approach, which kept us on track and prevented pet branches from being developed first. On the negative side, the detail covered to date is not sufficient for a simulation or deduction of potential bottlenecks in the information flow. For example, if several arrows join at a function, this does not imply that there is a bottleneck. However, if, from observations and measurement of critical incidents, it is concluded that there is a problem at a particular function, the model provides insight into what information is involved, where information is coming from, and from whom the context is readily available. Overall, the modeling effort required input from some 12 domain experts (about one week each) and occupied five human factors researchers (one person year); it resulted in more than 400 interrelated graphical representations (implemented with a browser on a CD-ROM).

The suite of models was developed with the purpose of understanding the complex system and its essential elements. The information-transformation functions and their information products are seen as essential cognitive elements of a command center. The modeling effort has been successful in three ways. First, it provided a common and consistent picture of the task-related structure of the command center. The focus on functions and their information input and output was crucial in understanding the functioning structure of the command center. Second, it yielded a common vocabulary among researchers and domain experts (the role of the norm group has been essential in this). Third, the use of different models provided a comprehensive but manageable view on the task structure. In particular, the combination of different perspectives, such as in the function information and the task model, provided insight into the information processing of the command center. As a spin-off, the suite of models is currently being used in the definition of training requirements, as educational material, and for the design of future command centers.

ACKNOWLEDGMENT

The authors wish to thank Mr. David Beevis from the Canadian Defence and Civil Institute for Environmental Medicine for helpful comments on this chapter.

REFERENCES

Beevis, D., & Essens, P. (1997). The NATO Defense Research Group Workshop on function allocation. In E.F. Fallon, L. Bannon, & J. McCarthy (Eds.), ALLFN'97: *Revisiting the allocation functions issue — New perspectives. Proceedings of the first international conference on allocation of functions* (Vol. I, pp. 1–15). Louisville: IEA Press.

Beevis, D., Essens, P., & Schuffel, H. (Eds.). (1996). *State-of-the-art report: Improving function allocation for integrated systems design.* Wright-Patterson Air Force Base, OH: Crew Systems Ergonomics Information Analysis Center.

Beevis, D., Bost, R., Döring, B., Nordø, E., Oberman, F., Papin, J.-P., Schuffel, H., & Streets, D. (1992). *Analysis techniques for man-machine system design* (AC/243[Panel-8]TR/7). Brussels: NATO Defense Research Group.

Checkland, P. (1993). *Systems thinking, systems practice.* Chichester: Wiley.

Engel, R., & Townsend, M. (1991). *Division command and control performance measurement* (DCIEM report). North York, CA: Defence and Civil Institute of Environmental Medicine.

Essens, P.J.M.D., Fallesen, J.J., McCann, C.A., Cannon-Bowers, J., & Dörfel, G. (1994). *COADE — A framework for cognitive analysis, design and evaluation* (AC/243[Panel-8] TR/17). Brussels: NATO Defense Research Group.

Essens, P.J.M.D., Martens, M.H., & Helsdingen, A.S. (1997). *The application of function allocation in the analysis of platform functions of the F124/F100 Air Defense Command Frigate* (TNO-report TM-97-A091). Soesterberg, The Netherlands: TNO Human Factors Research Institute.

Fallon, E.F., Bannon, L., & McCarthy, J. (Eds). (1997). *ALLFN'97: Revisiting the allocation functions issue — New perspectives. Proceedings of the first international conference on allocation of functions* (Vol. I & II). Louisville: IEA Press.

Fitts, P.M. (1951). Some basic questions in designing an air navigation and traffic control system. In D. Beevis, P. Essens, & H. Schuffel (Eds.), *State-of-the-art report: Improving function allocation for integrated systems design* (pp. 295–311). Wright-Patterson Air Force Base, OH: Crew Systems Ergonomics Information Analysis Center.

HFES. (1998). Proceedings of the Human Factors and Ergonomics Society, 42nd Annual meeting. Santa Monica, (CA): The Human Factors and Ergonomics Society.

Huisman, J. (1995). Ship design process for the Royal Dutch Navy. Schip & Werf de Zee, July/Aug, 1995.

Kirwan, B., & Ainsworth, L.K. (1992). *A guide to task analysis.* London: Taylor & Francis.

Meister, D. (1991). *Psychology of system design*. Amsterdam: Elsevier.

Meister, D. (1998). Basic principles of behavioral test and evaluation. *In Technical proceedings of the NATO RSG.24 Workshop on emerging technologies in human engineering testing and evaluation* (NATO R&T document AC/243 [Panel 8] TP/17). Brussels: Defense Research Group.

Neerincx, M.A. (1995). Harmonizing tasks to human knowledge and capacities. Dissertation University of Groningen. The Netherlands.

Otto, E., Visser, K., & Wolff, Ph.A. (1997). Application of function analysis in naval platform automation specification. In P.A. Wilson (Ed.), *Eleventh Ship Control Systems Symposium*, (Vol. 1, pp. 353–364). Southampton: Computational Mechanics Publications.

Passenier, P.O., & van Delft, J.H. (1996, April). *The combat information centre. The interface between warfare officers and sensor and weapon systems*. Proceedings INEC 96, Third International Naval Engineering Conference and Exhibition, Part II Poster Session Paper, Den Helder, The Netherlands.

Post, W.M., & Punte, P.A. (1997). *Conceptual layout of the operations room of the Air Defense and Command Frigate* (TNO-report TNO-TM-97-A015). Soesterberg, The Netherlands: TNO Human Factors Research Institute.

Rumbaugh, J., Blaha, M., Premerlani, W., Eddy, F., & Lorensen, W. (1991). *Object oriented modeling and design*. Amsterdam: North-Holland.

Van Delft, J.H., & Schuffel, H. (Eds.). (1995). Human factors research for future RNLN operations rooms. (TNO-report TNO-TM 1995 A-19). Soesterberg, The Netherlands: TNO Human Factors Research Institute.

Vink, P., Koningsveld, E.A.P., & Dhondt, S. (Eds.). (1998). Proceedings of the 6th International Symposium on Human Factors in Organizational Design and Management, The Hague, The Netherlands, 19-22 August 1998. Amsterdam: Elsevier Science.

Wohl, J.G., (1981). Force management decision requirements for Air Force tactical command and control. *IEEE Transactions on Systems, Man, and Cybernetics, 11 (9)*, 618–639.

Yourdan, E. (1989). *Modern structured analysis*. Prentice Hall, Englewood Cliffs: New Jersey.

24

ANALYZING COMMAND TEAM SKILLS

John Annett
Warwick University

David Cunningham
Centre for Human Sciences
Defence Evaluation and Research Agency, Portsdown

A naval command team comprises a group of 20 or more individuals who man the ship's action information (AI) system, compiling a picture of the underwater, surface, and air environments from data derived from the ship's sensors and by data link from other ships and aircraft. The command (i.e., the captain, advised by the warfare officers who analyze and interpret the picture), uses this information to direct defensive and offensive actions typically in collaboration with other friendly ships and aircraft. During the course of an action, the team deals with hundreds of verbal messages and items of electronic information. Although there are standard operating procedures to deal with most contingencies, no two actions are alike, and complex decisions have to be made, often under time stress. In short, the command team is a highly complex entity, and the description and analysis of the work of the command team is itself a challenging task.

It is obviously of great value to any commander to know how well his team is performing and, where necessary, to improve performance by appropriate and cost-effective training. Team assessment is carried out on a regular basis using shore-based simulation facilities and during sea-going exercises. Assessment depends on the judgment of experienced observers and is admittedly subjective. However, both the evaluation of training procedures and a better understanding of the factors that affect team performance depend on the development of scientifically based objective measurement of team performance. This chapter describes some recent work in the United Kingdom on analyzing and measuring command team skills, which complements the considerable research effort on teamwork currently in progress in the United States. It is based on a particular approach to task analysis and a tentative theoretical model of team performance.

HIERARCHICAL TASK ANALYSIS

Hierarchical Task Analysis (HTA) was developed during the late 1960s at the University of Hull, United Kingdom. (Annett & Duncan, 1967; Annett, Duncan, Stammers, & Gray, 1971; Cunningham & Duncan, 1967). Prompted by the need to describe complex nonrepetitive tasks in the petrochemical industry, it owed much to the systems approach to the study of human factors problems promoted by pioneers of engineering psychology such as Chapanis (1949) and Fitts (1951). HTA is not so much a procedure as a philosophy that can incorporate a number of techniques. However, its defining feature is that it is based on the decomposition of the system goals into subgoals. Failure to attain or maintain system goals is regarded as system error, but sources of error are often distributed unevenly throughout the system. As Chapanis (1949) pointed out, total variation (error) in system performance is the sum of the variation contributed individually by uncorrelated system components as shown in the equation.

$$\sigma^2_T = \sigma^2_a + \sigma^2_b + \sigma^2_c$$

This means that the error contributed by any component increases quadratically with its size relative to other components. Therefore, the aim of analysis must be to identify system goals and measures which represent variation in goal attainment. The decomposition process is intended to reveal a nested hierarchy of system goals such that any higher order goal can be redescribed in terms of a number of subgoals. This is a practical strategy because any complex system is likely to comprise some elements which are robust and others which are vulnerable to error. In a complex system the devil is often in the detail and analysis by hierarchical decomposition is the shortest and most reliable route to the devil, or devils, which threaten system performance.

Systems, and hence system goals, can be decomposed in a variety of ways. For example, Fitts (1951) was concerned with distinguishing the human and machine components and their relative contribution to system error, but in task analysis we are usually interested in identifying error due to human interventions—in short, the goals humans attain with ease and those they find difficult. However, the reliability of human performance in different tasks must also be considered in relation to the effect that human error has on the system as a whole. In some instances the results of human intervention on system performance are trivial, whereas in others it is critical. This is the rationale for determining the level of goal decomposition—referred to as the *p x c* rule, that is the product of the *p*robability (or in some cases, the magnitude) of error and the *c*ost

until the source of error is identified and a solution proposed.

The second defining feature of HTA concerns the unit of analysis—that is, what components of performance we are to identify. The classical approach was to develop a taxonomy of task elements (e.g., the *therbligs* of time and motion study). The new approach adopted in HTA is based on the premise that all human interventions in complex systems are acts of control—that is to say the fundamental human operator function is that of controller or servo. Any servomechanism requires three elements: a goal or set point, a power source that varies output, and a feedback loop providing data on output error to the power source. In psychological terms, the three elements translate to the task goal, the processes required to attain the goal and an indication of error or attainment. In practice, the operator's task may be described in terms of (a) the stimulus or input conditions, which, in the case of any control action being required, is a representation of the current goal discrepancy: (b) the control action required to correct the goal discrepancy and (c) the feedback indicating the goal discrepancy has been eliminated. This unit of analysis is referred to as an *operation*. Not only does it avoid the problems inherent in task taxonomies, but it directly relates to the notion of system error and hence to the underlying logic of hierarchical decomposition. The reader will note similarities with GOMS and productions, which it predated by more than a decade, and with the TOTE unit of Miller, Galanter, and Pribram (1960).

The basic *input-action-feedback* (I-A-F) structure of operations is capable of being interpreted at different levels of system function—from individual psychomotor and cognitive abilities to social or team interactions. At the psychomotor level, a typical input might be a simple warning signal, the required action turning a switch and the feedback the removal of the warning signal. At the cognitive level, the input may be a pattern of symptoms, the action a series of investigative or remedial actions, and the feedback a change in the symptom pattern that indicates the problem has been diagnosed and remedied. At the social level, the input comprises the problem faced by the group or team, and the action comprises the way the team must act together to solve the problem (e.g., by sharing information and coordinating individual actions). Different levels of analysis are appropriate to different problems. In tasks that appear to be of a primarily perceptual-motor character, detailed analysis of stimuli and responses would be the main focus. In tasks that are cognitively more complex, sources of human error are likely to be found in the interpretation of complex stimulus arrays or the organization of action based on rules, strategies, and knowledge. In team tasks where it is suspected that problems may lie not so much in individual skills and knowledge as in the ability of team members to communicate with each other and coordinate their actions, the analysis will focus on those goals and subgoals that are crucially dependent on team communication and coordination. HTA has been used extensively in the analysis of both perceptual-motor and cognitive tasks (Ainsworth & Marshall, 1998; Drury, Paramore, Van Cott, Grey, & Corlett. 1987; Kirwan & Ainsworth, 1992; Shepherd, 1998). This chapter describes some preliminary work on the application of HTA to team tasks.

HTA APPLIED TO TEAMWORK

A team has been defined as "a distinguishable set of two or more people who interact, dynamically, interdependently and adaptively toward a common and valued goal/objective/mission" (Salas et. al., 1992, pa.4). Because HTA begins with the decomposition of goals, we can just as easily ask, What is the goal sought by this set of people? We previously asked, What is the goal sought by this individual?

Teams come in many different forms; one way to characterize them is in terms of the roles individual team members have in achieving team goals (cf. Steiner, 1972). In some teams, roles are flexible and may depend on the specific task or problem presented. In navy teams, individuals generally have closely specified roles. However, in varying degrees, they also carry some responsibility for team functioning by monitoring each other's behavior and helping to prevent misunderstandings and errors. In general, the quality and extent to which the individual communicates and collaborates with fellow team members is thought to be both additional to the exercise of individual skills and relevant to the effective functioning of the team as a whole (Cannon-Bowers, Tannenbaum, Salas, & Volpe, 1995). When we identify a problem in individual performance, we begin by asking questions such as, Is the operator aware of signals indicating a goal discrepancy requiring action? or Does the operator know what action is most suited to reducing the goal discrepancy and, if so, is he or she capable of performing it? When we are satisfied that individual team members appear to be capable of performing their designated tasks, but still the team is not functioning well, we may begin to ask questions about team processes—such as whether team members communicate well and if they collaborate with each other, these features of teamwork may become the focus of the analysis.

A MODEL OF TEAMWORK

Just as the control theory model of input, action and feedback was applied to the attainment of individual goals, so we need a model of team performance to apply to the attainment of team goals. The model of teamwork proposed by Annett (1996) meets this requirement, but it is a generic model in the sense that it may apply to any sort of team carrying out any sort of task. The main function of the model is to qualitatively represent the kinds of behavioral, cognitive, and affective processes believed to operate in teams, (i.e., working groups that have a common goal).

The model distinguishes between team product—the goal or goals the team members are aiming at—and process—the behavioral, cognitive, and affective factors that contribute, along with task-specific activities (or taskwork), to the attainment of the specified goal(s). A task analysis can provide not only details of the specific or individual tasks, but also identifies the specific team goals or product variables and the specific team processes required to attain those goals. The behavioral processes are overt and observable and especially in-

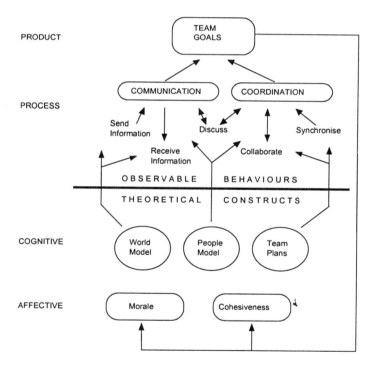

FIG. 24.1 The teamwork model distinguishes product from process; within processes, it distinguishes between observed and inferred constructs, which may be either cognitive or affective. The arrows indicate the presumed directions of influence.

clude acts of communication, both formal and informal. Further, a case can be made for identifying coordination behavior as actions which are related in some systematic way to actions of other team members. Fig. 24.1 indicates a number of ways in which these behaviors may be manifest, including various ways in which communication may play a role in teamwork and ways in which individual behavior may be coordinated with that of other team members, depending on the team objective.

Underlying these observables are some important constructs suggested by current theories of team behavior. The cognitive constructs, generally referred to as *mental models* represent the knowledge held by individuals that appears to be relevant to team performance. The *world model* is the individual's understanding of the environment or problem space in which the team finds itself. For example, individual team members may or may not be aware of the location of the ship and other friendly and hostile units. Depending on the tasks required of the individual, this knowledge may be relevant to the significance of received and transmitted information. The *people model* represents the individual's understanding of colleagues, what they do, what they know, what state they are in, and whether their support can be relied on. The *team plan* represents the individual's knowledge of team goals and strategies to attain those goals. This, like the other two types of mental models, may be used by the individual to determine an appropriate course of action under circumstances in which decisions are subject to ambiguity.

In a sense, the model is incomplete until we include information about the task, Hence, an important step is to show how specific task information is incorporated into the general model. Only when this is done is it possible to generate specific predictions about factors contributing significantly to team performance. Steiner (1972) pointed out that the relationship between team process and team product can only be understood in the context of the specific team task and team structure and the roles of individual members. Naval command teams are highly structured and individuals have specific roles. However, the structure does allow, and in certain circumstances even encourages, some role flexibility to the extent that team members are expected to help each other. Some members have a supervisory role, which permits them to support or even take over the role of another team member—in a sense, to add their skill to that of the individual. We may also classify teams in other relevant ways, such as whether the team is of uniform or mixed ability, is long established or newly formed, is highly cohesive, or is subject to internal disruptive stresses. These features can also affect the ways in which individuals behave within their given role, and therefore they are variables of interest to the analysis of team performance. In summary, the basic model is generic. To generate predictions about the performance of teams of a specific composition performing specific tasks, information is needed from a task analysis that indicates which team processes are critical to the team product.

An Example

The basic aim in conducting the analysis outlined next is to develop a set of objective measures to assess command teams and evaluate alternative training procedures. The current method of assessing teams involves expert assessors—normally instructors—observing the teamwork during an exercise that may take place either in a shore-based simulator or at sea. Assessment usually takes the form of written comments on a number of performance dimensions related to the different warfare disciplines or subteams, such as anti-submarine, anti-surface, anti-air and electronic warfare, along with assessments of briefing and preparation, communication, and general organization, which apply to the whole team. Written assessments are supplemented by ratings on a 5-point scale (1 = *unsatisfactory*, 3 = *satisfactory,* and 5 = *very good*). Although the system is well understood by its users, it has certain shortcomings as a measuring instrument which limits its use as a basis for evaluating the responses of teams to different training regimes. First, there is a tendency to use only the middle numerical categories (3 and 4), but, more important, there is no reliability check. Whereas validity is guaranteed by the professional standing of those making the assessments, the relative importance of these dimensions to overall system performance is unknown. Task analysis can deal with both these problems by establishing the criterion behaviors and clearly specifying agreed measurement dimensions, thus moving from the realm of subjective impression toward objective measurement.

If we begin by asking what are the goals of naval command teams, there is a ready answer—that is, to float, move, and fight. The goal of fighting might be decomposed into gathering information, using it to assess the threat and respond appropriately to it, and disseminating it to others who might need it. Figure 24.2 shows, in a simplified form, the initial decomposition of command team goals during a typical exercise. The analysis is carried down to three or four levels and could be continued into much greater detail. Although some of the boxes in Fig. 24.2 describe the goals of specific disciplines or subteams, many more are goals that can only be achieved by interaction between different subteams and individuals.

At this stage of the analysis, we ask who is involved in attempts to attain the team goal—that is, the *de facto* team for that goal—and what is the nature of

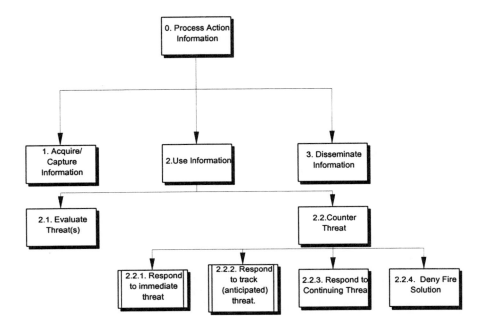

FIG. 24.2   Partial goal hierarchy for the command team task. The diagram
locates Operation 2.2.4. to deny the hostile contact a fire control solution
within the overall goal hierarchy.

the interaction that has to occur for the team goal to be attained. Table 24.1 gives
an example of the notes that describe Operation 2.2.4. In this instance, the goal is
to deny the enemy a fire solution. This is a critical goal because, if the team gets
it wrong, they are liable to be sunk. It is possible to compute from speeds, dis-
tances, and angles precisely whether the maneuver ordered by the command
team will achieve that objective; in this case, recording of success or failure is
unequivocal.

We also note which team members are principally involved in deciding on, planning and ordering the maneuver and in what ways teamwork is
manifested. In this case, reports of critical incidents collected from experienced
warfare officers during the initial stages of the analysis suggest that, in executing
this task, there can be a conflict of interest between the various disciplines. In
addition, there can be conflicts of interest between the control room and the
bridge, where the Officer of the Watch (OOW) is responsible for navigation

TABLE 24.1
Summary of Operation 2.2.4

Variable	Description
Deny fire solution	Action (other than preparing to launch offensive or defensive weapons) may be taken to deny the enemy a fire control solution to protect the ship or a high-value unit. The appropriate action will depend on the judgment of the command team (PWO/captain or force commander) in the light of information provided from various sources. Once a decision has been made, directions are conveyed to OOW and/or captain/PWO of other units to effect the plan.
Goal	To deny the enemy a valid fire control solution as determined by relative location, course, and speed.
Team members	Principal Warfare Officer (PWO), Anti-Air Warfare Officer (AAWO) with the Officer of the Watch (OOW), the Action Picture Supervisor (APS), and Missile Gun Directors (MGDs).
Teamwork	Reconciling any conflict of interest as between air, surface, and subsurface teams, and the weapons directors (MGDs) and communication with OOW.
Performance measures	Ship deployed to best advantage with respect to fire control solutions.

subject to the overriding authority of the Principal Warfare Officer (PWO) under certain conditions. Both need to be in communication with the Action Picture Supervisor (APS), who is in the control room not on the bridge. The situation illustrates several features of the model. Clearly, communication has to occur; this may be complicated by discussion in the event that there is any conflict of interest between those who have responsibility for other warfare disciplines such as air defense or between the bridge and the operations room. The activities of those team members who are responsible for executing the response must be coordinated, but, perhaps most important, all those involved in the decision and response must share compatible world models, people models, and understanding of the team plan.

Measurement Problems

The analysis enables us to establish two kinds objective measures of command team performance. First, the high-level goals as determined by the analysis provide criteria for team success. In terms of our model, these are the product variables. Second, because we are interested in the contribution of teamwork skills to team product, the analysis can show, in as much detail as necessary, exactly how team members need to interact for team goals to be achieved, Thus, we have a source for the measurement of the behavioral team process variables. Both types of measure, however, present problems.

In a world ideally designed for the experimentalist who needs an unambiguous dependent variable against which to test alternative treatments, there would be one overarching product variable determined by the top goal in the hierarchy, which would stand for the level of team performance. In this ideal world, we would have a means of ordering teams along some dimension that represents their productivity or general excellence. In reality, there are a number of different product variables, any one of which could be critical to survival in warfare depending on the opponent and circumstances. HTA is, in part, a matter of eliciting from recognized experts a general consensus about the goals of the system and the relative values of different goals in the hierarchy. It is probably not possible to achieve total agreement, but at least the process of analysis brings the issues into focus and enables the researcher to say to the sponsor, "if these are the values you want to optimize I can now design trials which will permit you to distinguish between options, such as different training regimes." This may seem a less than ideal conclusion, but classical experimental design is not the only approach. As is seen, a different approach based on multivariate analysis may prove a more comfortable match to the problem.

As noted earlier, the currently used methods of assessing command teams employ a mixture of product and process variables—that is, measures of what the team achieves and how it sets about it. The most commonly recognized process variable in this context is communication. Experts refer to the smooth flow of information between members of the team as being especially indicative of a good team. Clearly, if this were the case, a measure of communication would be a useful indicator of team performance, or at least of how the team was progressing under training, but the question is how to devise a suitable objective measure. During the course of an exercise, many messages of varying significance are passed between members of the operations room team and between them and the outside world. Not all communication is useful and to the point, but HTA enables the analyst to identify specific instances like that shown in Fig.

24.2 and Table 24.1, where communication is crucial to team success. HTA also indicates what information is or should be passing between certain individuals, thus providing a specific set of data points to use in a subsequent assessment of team performance or indeed a statistical analysis. As with the product variables, no single measures are likely to be adequate for either assessment or evaluation purposes, but at least HTA provides a selection of instances of process behaviours that have been shown to be relevant to one or more product variables.

The sheer complexity of team activities during even a routine practice exercise creates serious problems for performance measurement, and thus for any kind of research aimed at evaluating operational or training systems. Shore-based simulators typically provide electronic recording, such that an exercise can be replayed during debriefing. The typical record shows how ships and aircraft maneuvered on a general operations plot (GOP). Although this shows the outcome of the command team decisions, it may not reveal how these decisions were reached. For training purposes, more detail is required. At another extreme, some simulators provide for a recording of all operator keypresses. Because a dozen operators may each key in hundreds of items of information during the course of an exercise, these data are often left unused on file simply because there is not enough time to carry out an analysis between the end of one exercise and the beginning of the next. Voice recordings of communication circuits are sometimes made, but a great deal of informal interaction by voice and gesture goes unrecorded and unanalyzed for much the same reasons. Clearly, there is a need for some kind of strategy for recording those classes of events that illuminate those aspects of team performance that, according to the theoretical model in Fig. 24.1, are believed to have a significant effect on team success.

STATISTICAL MODELING OF TEAM PERFORMANCE

In a preliminary study of 16 naval command teams under training, Annett, Cunningham, and Dowsett (1997) examined a number of possibilities for recording data. The standard performance ratings on eight dimensions were provided by instructors who also agreed to record the times at which certain critical events occurred. These events were selected on the basis of an HTA as being critical to the attainment of key team goals of reporting, classifying, and making a response to a radar contact. Instructors recorded the times at which teams responded to contacts presented to the ship's sensors (one submarine and one air attack), time to report these contacts, to make a classification and assessment and to initiate an appropriate response. These were taken to be representative of the product variables referred to in the theoretical model.

For the reasons given earlier, recording of team behaviour was much more difficult. Hence, as a first approximation to measuring process variables, a questionnaire method was used at de-briefing. All team members were asked questions such as whether they had received all the information they needed from colleagues (communication), whether they felt confident in knowing what was going on (situation awareness), and whether they were able to get the help and advice they needed (mutual support and collaboration) during the course of the exercise.

Each team member was also asked to provide information on his or her own level of experience with the equipment and procedures being used in the exercise and duration of team membership and attitudes toward the rest of the team (morale and team cohesiveness). In all some 270 naval personnel at all levels—from captain to junior operator—responded to some 30 questions relating to their experiences during a 2-hour training exercise.

The overall aim of the study was to see if either of the two product measures—the objective time scores derived from the HTA or the subjective assessments of the instructors—could be predicted from the process measures derived from the questionnaire responses. As a preliminary data-reduction procedure, the instructor ratings and questionnaire results were subjected to factor analysis. Although the instructors provided ratings on eight dimensions, the factor analysis showed that only two dimensions accounted for 69% of the total variance. The first factor (55% of variance) was most heavily loaded on collaboration and quality of supervision, and the second factor (14% of total variance) was connected with equipment handling and communication. However these two dimensions were found to be predictive of actual response times in one aspect of the exercise, dealing with an air attack (AAW), but not in the other, dealing with a submarine threat (ASW). Interestingly, these two aspects of the exercise involve different procedures and therefore may tap rather different qualities of team performance.

The questionnaire measures of team process were reduced by factor analysis to eight factors. These accounted for 66% of the total variance (see Table 24.2), some of which distinguished significantly between teams which had been in existence for some time and others which had been assembled on an *ad hoc* basis for the purpose of the exercise. We found virtually no significant relationships between these process variables and overall team performance as measured objectively by key event times. Thus, although some teams showed high levels of knowledge of, and liking for, each other and of better situational awareness when compared with other teams, it was only the breadth of their technical experience that was predictive of performance in the AAW scenario.

TABLE 24.2
Factors Measured by Team Process Questionnaire

#	Factor Name	Variance %	Factor Description
1	Team familiarity	18.6	Knowledge of and liking for other team members, especially ratings, self-assessed ability to work with the team and duration of team membership
2	Technical familiarity	12.4	Familiarity with the AI system and equipment and experience with other systems and fits
3	Communication	10.1	Self-assessed situational awareness; getting information and advice from other team members
4	Technical breadth	6.2	Experience with other AI systems and equipment
5	Team regard	5.5	Team spirit and cohesion and perceived team competence
6	Management regard	5.1	Liking to work with this set of officers and senior rates
7	Self-confidence	4.3	Confidence in self and team
8	Compliance	3.8	Perceived willingness of other team members to accept advice and familiarity with officers

These results are modestly disappointing in relation to the claims made for some theories of team performance, but they do indicate a possible way forward by combining the results of task analysis with statistical modeling techniques. In this example, HTA was used to identify objective performance criteria. In HTA terms, these are high-level system goals or, in terms of the model, team product variables. However, the questionnaire method of establishing process variables appears relatively coarse-grained. In the next phase of this research, we hope to use the detailed results of HTA to identify those team process measures (e.g., actual acts of communication, etc.), that can be more directly related to team product or outcome measures. It is probable that different team tasks depend on different team processes. For example, the difference we found between the AAW and ASW exercises could well reflect the different procedures involved and hence test different aspects of team communication and coordination skills.

Finally, neither team product nor the processes that underlie them can be reasonably represented by simple numerical indices. Just as the teamwork model indicates a number of different process variables, so also team product is not unidimensional except in simple tasks in which the team is pursuing a unique and easily defined goal state. Team product is a concept more like health or intelligence than, say, height or weight. In the next phase of this work, we hope to explore the potential of structural equation models in shedding further light on the complex relations between how teams behave, what they know and believe, and what they achieve.

REFERENCES

Ainsworth, L., & Marshall, E. (1998). Issues of quality and practicability in task analysis: Preliminary results from two surveys. *Ergonomics, 41,* 1607–1617.

Annett, J. (1996). Recent developments in hierarchical task analysis. In S.A. Robertson (Ed.), *Contemporary ergonomics* (pp. 262–268). London: Taylor & Francis.

Annett, J., Cunningham, D.J., & Dowsett, D. (1997). Team skill development at HMS Dryad. PLSD/CHS/HS3/CR97047/1.0 (U.K. Restricted)

Annett, J., & Duncan, K.D. (1967). Task analysis and training design. *Occupational Psychology, 41,* 211–221.

Annett, J., Duncan, K.D., Stammers, R.B., & Gray, M.J. (1971). *Task analysis.* London: Her Majesty's Stationery Office.

Cannon-Bowers, J. A., Tannenbaum, S.I., Salas, E., & Volpe, C.E. (1995). Defining competencies and establishing team training requirements. In R.A. Guzzo, E. Salas et al. (Eds.), *Team effectiveness and decision making in organizations* (pp. 333–380). San Francisco: Jossey-Bass.

Chapanis, A. (1949). Theory and methods for analysing errors in man-machine systems. *Annals of the New York Academy of Sciences, 51,* (6).

Cunningham, D.J., & Duncan, K.D. (1967). Describing non-repetitive tasks for training purposes. *Occupational Psychology, 41,* 203–210.

Drury, C.G., Paramore, B., Van Cott, H.P., Grey, S.M., & Corlett, N. (1987). Task analysis. In G. Salvendy (Ed.), *Handbook of human factors (*pp. 370–401). New York: Wiley.

Fitts, P.M. (1951). Engineering psychology & equipment design. In S.S. Stevens (Ed.), *Handbook of experimental psychology* (pp. 1287–1340). New York: Wiley.

Kirwan, B., & Ainsworth, L.K. (Eds.). (1992). *A guide to task analysis.* London: Taylor & Francis.

Miller, G.A., Galanter, E., & Pribram, K. (1960). *Plans and the structure of behavior.* New York: Henry Holt.

Miller, R.B. (1962). Task description and analysis. In R.M. Gagné (Ed.), *Psychological principles of system development* (pp. 187–228). New York: Holt.

Salas, E., Dickinson, T.L., Converse, S.A., & Tannenbaum, S.I. (1992). Toward an understanding of team performance and training. In R.W. Swezey & E.Salas (Eds.), *Teams: Their training and performance* (pp. 3-29). Norwood, NJ: Ablex.

Shepherd, A. (1998). HTA as a framework for task analysis. *Ergonomics, 41,* 1537–1552.

Steiner, I.D. (1972). *Group processes & productivity.* New York: Academic Press.

25

COGNITIVE TASK ANALYSIS OF TEAMS

Gary Klein
Klein Associates Inc.

A team Cognitive Task Analysis (CTA) is a description of the cognitive skills needed to perform a task proficiently. A behavioral account of a team's performance would tell us which team member is responsible for which subtasks. A behavioral account would show how the responsibility for a subtask shifts throughout the performance cycle. A behavioral account would help us observe the team and see if it was following the procedures. However, a behavioral account would not help us understand how the team was interpreting the situation, how the team was making decisions, how the team was confused about roles and functions of different members, or how the team was monitoring itself so that it could adapt or improvise when necessary. That is why a team CTA can be helpful— it can describe the way the team is thinking as opposed to the steps it is following.

Researchers have been performing versions of a team CTA for many years. One of the early examples was performed by Pew, Miller, and Feehrer (1982) in their study of nuclear power plant operations. This chapter presents a theoretical framework for a team CTA, linking it to CTAs of individuals. The chapter also suggests some methods for conducting a team CTA.

This chapter is concerned with situations where tasks are decomposed and assigned to different team members, to be performed in parallel and overlapping fashion, often by personnel who are not in direct contact with each other. Thordsen and Klein (1989) suggested that we can consider a team as an intelligent entity. Teams process information, make decisions, solve problems, and make plans. If we treat teams as intelligent entities, we can try to identify the key cognitive processes required by tasks that depend on teamwork. Based on a number of research projects, we have identified a small set of cognitive processes for teams:

- control of attention
- shared situation awareness
- shared mental models
- application of strategies and heuristics to make decisions, solve problems, and plan
- metacognition

Before discussing these five cognitive processes, it may be helpful to consider a distinction between two types of teams: planning teams and action teams.

Klein, Zsambok, and Thordsen (1993) presented a model of team decision making for planning teams (also see Klein & Miller, 1999), and Thordsen, McCloskey, Heaton, and Serfaty (1996) adapted this model to describe action teams. The job of a planning team is to produce a plan. In the military, we find planning teams that generate air tasking orders and other types of products that are distributed for implementation. The job of an action team is to accomplish a task. An action team may carry out a plan (as in a regiment that carries out the plan created by the higher echelons) or perform a task (as in a team of air traffic controllers moving airplanes across the country). Many teams have both functions. An airplane crew develops a flight plan, carries it out, and is prepared to react to unplanned emergencies. The reason for making this distinction is that the cognitive processes discussed herein are often performed differently by planning teams and action teams.

The control of attention for a team refers to the way it engages in information management including information seeking. Some teams are ineffective at information management, and may fail to distribute important messages, filter irrelevant messages, properly distribute messages, allocate attention to important functions, or seek missing information. In contrast, skilled teams have learned how to carry out these activities. Management of information would include the team's working memory—the way it uses limited resources for processing simultaneous messages.

Information management is important for a group that is co-located and working on the same task at the same time. It is even more important for a team whose members are dispersed. It is important for planning teams if the situation they face is dynamic and complex so that different team members are learning about new developments and are having to debate which messages to distribute. Information management is critical for action teams in all of the settings we have encountered.

The shared situation awareness of a team refers to the degree to which the members have the same interpretation of ongoing events (Cannon-Bowers, Salas, & Converse, 1992). In static environments, this may not be particularly critical. However, in dynamic environments, it is easy for the different team members to form divergent impressions without realizing it and for discrepant assumptions to create difficulties. In dynamic situations, shared situation awareness is important both for planning and for action teams.

On the surface, it would seem that the remedy for discrepant situation awareness is to ensure that each team member is given all the data. However, this just creates data overload. Teams can also benefit from having different members hold different interpretations of the situation, in cases where the uncertainty is high. Individuals have a tendency to preserve a preferred interpretation by explaining away inconsistent data (De Keyser & Woods, 1993). If the team members have a diversity of interpretations, then, even if the leader is mistaken, the team has a greater chance that someone will see what is going on. Somehow the team has to be able to efficiently update its members on critical events without overloading them and provide the dominant interpretation without eliminating alternative explanations for the events.

A team has shared mental models to the extent that the members have the same understanding for the dynamics of key processes. These processes can include the roles and functions of each team member in accomplishing the task, the nature of the task, the use of equipment, and so forth. In most settings, a critical factor is the degree to which the team members have a shared mental model of their own roles and functions.[1] One common source of difficulty for teams is when the members are confused about who is supposed to do what. Confusion about roles and functions leads to wasted effort or a failure to carry out essential subtasks. Effective teams understand the functions, including the common routines, much as a professional football team knows the plays in the game plan. The difference between shared situation awareness and shared mental models is that the former refers to the current and projected situation, whereas the latter refers to the configuration of the team and the way it is supposed to perform routines.

In our observations, planning teams often struggle with the shared mental models, but action teams do not. Planning teams typically are experimenting with new procedures and approaches and often are introducing inexperienced staff members into the mix. The planning teams we have observed, such as upper echelon military teams and nuclear power plant emergency response teams, appeared to struggle greatly with confusion over roles and functions and the inadequate mental models of how the planning process was supposed to work. For the military settings, part of the difficulty was due to high rates of turnover and new procedures being incorporated. For the nuclear power plants, the problem stemmed primarily from the limited opportunities to practice for emergencies, as well as changes in procedures.

In contrast, the action teams we observed did appear to have shared mental models of the roles and functions and the way the task is to be performed. Perhaps this is because of their high level of expertise (e.g., aircrews, air traffic controllers, U.S. Navy landing signal officers). Perhaps it is because of the nature of their work. They are not disrupted by turnover the way the planning teams are. In fact, aircrews are prepared to work together despite continual turn

---

[1]The concept of mental models (e.g., Gentner & Stevens, 1983; Rouse & Morris, 1986) is not particularly clear at the level of individual cognition; when applied to teams (e.g., Cannon-Bowers, Salas, & Converse, 1992), it does not gain in clarity. Nevertheless, there may be face validity to the assertion that team members may be more or less congruent in their understanding of phenomena such as their roles and responsibilities, the operation of equipment, and so forth.

over. Because of the difficulties of scheduling, a flight crew typically works together for only a few days. Landing signal officers also work in teams that have
regular turnover. In response, these action teams make sure that the roles and
functions are well understood by all.

A team learns strategies and routines as it gains experience. Even if the
team has prepared a list of steps and procedures, in most complex cases these
procedures are inadequate. A skillful team typically has learned the work-
arounds—the shortcuts—that are not codified in procedures. A skillful team has
learned who the key decision makers are (who need to be supported) and who
the key sources of expertise are (who need to be consulted). If a team CTA is
intended to show us how a team thinks, the strategies it has developed for moving ideas and information around (information management) and the strategies it
has developed for drawing inferences from different data sources help us get
inside the teams mind.

The processes of decision making, problem solving, and planning obviously apply for planning teams. They also are relevant for action teams, which
need to make rapid decisions, to generate new courses of action if the standard
ones do not work, and sometimes plan even if the time horizon is only a few
minutes long. A fireground commander arriving at a large incident will need to
formulate a plan in just a few minutes or less.

A team needs to monitor itself and determine when it is running into difficulty, how the difficulty is linked to its vulnerabilities and limitations, and where
it needs to shift its strategies. We can refer to this as metacognition. Effective
teams can both self-monitor and make the changes. Ineffective teams typically
are unaware of why they are getting in their own way. If a team does not even
realize where its inefficiencies are, it will be unable to adapt itself to improve.

The process of metacognition seems more important for planning teams
than action teams. This may be because the action teams we have observed are
more skilled and have a clearer sense of roles and functions. In contrast, the
planning teams are usually still working out their routines and so have a greater
need to scrutinize themselves.

A team CTA is a method to capture these five processes. In addition, a
team CTA needs to represent the findings to others. This is another difficult requirement. Behavioral analyses are sometimes performed to capture all of the
elements of information flow among all of the nodes in the team network and
represent these in painful detail. The results are typically not useful. These types
of representations are referred to as spaghetti diagrams. The people who develop
these spaghetti diagrams may argue that everything is captured in them, but their
complexity makes it hard to use them.

Therefore, a team CTA needs to elicit findings about the way the team
performs the five processes described earlier, and to represent these findings so
they can be put into action. One way to represent the findings of a team CTA is
to present the overall decision requirements for a team. These are the critical and

difficult decisions, why they are difficult (the barriers to effective decision making), and the skills of good teams (perhaps contrasting skilled and ineffective teams).

A team CTA is a reflection and representation of the team mind. It is an elaboration of the team decision requirements. It is a determination of the types of expertise found in effective teams. Given that a team CTA provides these types of insights, the next question is what impact can a team CTA have.

WHY WOULD WE NEED TO PERFORM A TEAM CTA?

The primary reason to conduct a CTA on a team is to improve its performance. A basic achievement is to be able to assess a team's performance and gauge its strengths and weaknesses. The type of performance that is best addressed by a team CTA is, obviously, cognitive performance—the way the team makes decisions, makes judgments, solves problems, formulates plans, and develops situation awareness. The team CTA would have less value in improving more behavioral or procedural aspects of performance, such as making routines more automatic or addressing motivational and emotional issues (e.g., strengthening morale, reducing absenteeism, etc.). A team CTA would have more value for designing a command post for managing emergencies.

There are several standard strategies for converting the results of a team CTA into performance gains. The functions of a team CTA include finding ways to improve performance by:

- Restructuring the team
- Changing the size of the team
- Designing better:
  information technology
  information management strategies
  human-computer interfaces
  decision support systems
  communications
- Developing methods for team training

One common mistake is to specify these strategies in advance because the preferred strategy may not be known until after the team CTA is performed. It is important to specify the desired outcome in advance, such as reducing errors, cutting costs, speeding up reaction time, or increasing readiness. These are important types of goals and are worth striving for by conducting a team CTA. Research projects appropriately specify one type of strategy, such as exploring ways to accomplish a team task with fewer personnel. This type of work can lead researchers to develop a wider range of tools. However, in an operational setting, the strategies should be determined by the dynamics of the team task. The functions of a team CTA are to recommend the strategies to be used in trying to reach a goal (e.g., more careful selection, reduced team size, or better information management procedures), as well as guiding the way those strategies would be carried out.

EXAMPLES OF TEAM CTA STUDIES

This chapter has covered what a team CTA is and why it would be carried out. This section briefly describes two recent team CTA efforts that were conducted. The efforts recounted in this section are a study of U.S. Marine Corps (USMC) regimental command posts and the emergency response organization of a nuclear power plant. The intent is to illustrate different team CTA strategies. The following section discusses the components of a team CTA.

USMC Command Posts

Klein, Schmitt, McCloskey, Heaton, Klinger, and Wolf (1996) performed a study of Marine Corps command posts at the regimental level. This effort was funded by the Marine Corps with the goal of improving the decision-making process in command posts.[2]

The study of USMC regimental command posts was primarily observational. We observed four regimental exercises. The data-collection strategy was to collect specific incidents that appeared to be relevant to decision making. The observers collected more than 200 critical decision-making incidents from the key players in the command posts. We identified the key decision requirements, treating the command post as an organizational entity (along the lines of a team mind).

In addition to observations, we conducted more than 70 interviews with command post personnel. Many of these interviews were follow-ups to the incidents we observed to obtain more details and clarify the events. Another data-collection strategy was a simulated regimental event that required decision making. A tactical decision game was developed and presented to the key decision makers in three separate regiments. We obtained the responses of the primary operations officers in all cases, along with the responses of the commanding officers for each of the regiments. The experienced senior officers (colonels and lieutenant colonels) needed only 5 to 10 minutes to study a situation and grasp its dynamics. The majors took 45 minutes and longer and still had not perceived the dynamics very well. In the rapid pace of battle, the requirement to rapidly size up a situation is critical.

The findings were reported in several ways. First, we prepared a set of 40 decision requirements detailing the critical decisions, reasons for the difficulty,

---

[2]Contract USC P.O. 681584 for the Naval Command, Control and Ocean Surveillance Center.

types of common errors, and cues and strategies used for effective decision making. We found that the top-level decision requirements were fairly generic. It was only by describing the reasons for difficulty and the barriers that the marines could see where to improve operations. Second, we compiled a list of approximately 30 primary barriers to effective decision making. The decision requirements clustered into the following categories: (a) building and maintaining situational awareness, (b) managing information, and (c) deciding on a plan.

Building and Maintaining Situational Awareness. It was striking to see how many barriers the current command posts placed in the way of forming a big picture. The essence of seeing the big picture is to track the interconnections between friendly and enemy units, between air and artillery, and so forth. Yet each of these was presented on a separate mapboard, and these mapboards were sometimes placed in different parts of the command post, separated by furniture and personnel. The system of overlays was archaic and cumbersome. In a setting rife with interruptions, the command post staff members trying to integrate a big picture had to rely on memory as they shifted from one display to another.

Situational awareness is dynamic and maintained through a succession of messages and communications. Yet these messages were often transmitted through extremely inexperienced marines, who were prone to making errors, missing nuances, and failing to gain clarifications where needed. The command post forced a series of handoffs for messages; each handoff increased the chance for error or interruption.

Managing Information. Information becomes obsolete with the passage of time. Therefore, a source of inefficiency is sending messages that are no longer relevant, which ties up the communication lines and reduces alertness to new messages. Another source of inefficiency is passing along data reports that have not been checked for validity, thereby adding noise and confusion to the system. Thus, the information management function also requires filtering. However, if the filtering takes too long, the data become obsolete.

The information routing function was often performed by relatively inexperienced personnel who did not understand the roles and functions of the decision makers, and this may have contributed to the proliferation of messages. In turn, the blizzard of messages required more staff members to monitor the communications, and these were usually inexperienced personnel, which compounded the problem.

Some of the information explosion may have stemmed from the demand features of this setting because marines can be blamed for failing to send important messages, but they are rarely blamed for sending irrelevant information. Therefore, the safest strategy is: When in doubt, send it out. The command post staff tried to manage the message traffic by defining and searching for high-value data and information. They identified Commanders Critical Information Requirements (CCIRs), which were intended to prioritize the information-seeking and disseminating tasks. Because of our interest in information-management strategies, we examined the way these CCIRs were used. We found that they were not having much impact. We found that the staff members were misapplying the concept of CCIRs. In one setting, we counted more than 80 CCIRs, which raises the question of what critical means. How was a list of 80 CCIRs going to prioritize information-management activities? We observed that the CCIRs were rarely updated once the simulated battle began. As a result, the CCIRs quickly became obsolete and were ignored.

Deciding on a plan. The command post staff ran into difficulty making modifications as the plan was put into action. The USMC communications systems we observed in the field were so unreliable that it was too risky to begin an adaptation when there was a chance that not everyone could be informed in time. A related difficulty was that there were usually a great many people to coordinate with, further complicating the process. In several incidents, the commander realized that the plan needed to be changed, but decided to stay with the existing plan because he could not reliably communicate and coordinate the changes in time.

This project was a front-end analysis of the command post decision making, and the findings were being used in several different ways. One application was a recommendation about reengineering the command post. We concluded that there were too many marines in the command post, and this made it harder to get the job done. Therefore, we recommended a reduced staffing. Not only would this save on manpower and the size of the command post, but we believed it would actually improve the speed and quality of the decisions. Many of these suggestions were tested at different USMC locations, and some have been adopted by individual units. For example, one regiment reduced the size of its forward command post from 34 to 24 and found that performance was improved.

Emergency Response Organization of a Nuclear Power Plant

Klinger and Klein (in press) described a project to improve the performance of an emergency response organization. The customer for this effort was Duke Power Company—a highly respected organization that was having unexpected difficulty at one of its nuclear power plants. The Nuclear Regulatory Commission (NRC) has mandated that each nuclear power plant set up an Emergency Response Organization (ERO), and the NRC conducts periodic evaluations of these. At this plant, although routine operations were highly satisfactory, the ERO was running into difficulties during the NRC drills. Consequently, the NRC was threatening to increase the number of drills and exercises each year, which would have been expensive for the plant.

The plant managers were aware of the high workload in the ERO. They wanted to increase the number of staff members, but the room was physically not large enough to accommodate additional staff. That was why they commissioned a team CTA study. The goals identified by the plant managers were twofold: for the emergency coordinator, who was the head of the ERO, to make quicker and better decisions; and to find ways for the rest of the team to better support the emergency coordinator. The plant managers did not believe that anything was broken. They were just looking to tweak the system, not to get a complete overhaul.

We used a model of effective team decision making (Klein, Zsambok, & Thordsen, 1993) to understand the key functions that were causing most of the problems. The primary methodology consisted of observations of emergency exercises and interviews with the personnel in the ERO. During a simulated emergency, the observers traced the number of steps it took to accomplish specific actions and the value added to each interaction along the chain. The observations also attempted to trace the decision makers and clarify the roles and functions of the team members. For example, if team members needed to go to several different people to find out a critical fact, that might indicate that the roles and functions were not sufficiently clear. Similarly, if messages were sent out to a wide audience indiscriminately, rather than to the few people who needed the information, that might also indicate a lack of understanding of the roles and functions of different players. Finally, the observations attempted to identify key incidents or stories that could be used to illustrate effective as well as questionable practices that could be discussed later during interviews.

The observers attempted to write down major events (e.g., the possible starting point of an incident) and time tag these. The observers did not know which of these starting points would be useful later. Most were not relevant, but some turned into incidents. The starting points for these incidents were events that could impact others. If an operations manager said "the fire is out," that was worth tagging to see how long it would take for others to get the message. Another criterion for a starting point of an incident was that if someone made a decision that would affect someone else, it could be worth studying how long it took for the implications to be worked out.

After the drill was completed, the personnel performing the team CTA conducted interviews. They began their interviews with the five team members who had been defined as the key decision makers. The goal of these interviews was to further clarify the decision-making flow in the ERO. The interviewers discovered that only one of the five was actually making decisions. One was so marginal that he was eventually moved out of the ERO.

The form of the interview was a simple presentation of incidents, along with questions about why these happened. In trying to answer these questions, the emergency coordinator realized how many inefficient and irrelevant procedures had accumulated over the years. A subsequent observation trip validated many of the initial hypotheses about who was making decisions and who was not. The observers identified unnecessary lags in the system that showed ineffective information management. Also, simple operations were requiring too many handoffs.

With this base of observations and interviews, the personnel performing the team CTA identified several primary difficulties. One was that there were too many people in the ERO. During the next months, successive tryouts showed that the number of staff members could be reduced from more than 80 down to fewer than 35. The impact was an improvement in performance and a reduction in noise and workload. The people with expertise were able to work more effectively.

Another problem was a lack of shared situation awareness. For example, many people would stare at the status board and explain away what they saw (e.g., "Oh, that guy just wrote it wrong"). Thus, there was not a good shared situation awareness even when they started with the same data. Everyone was generating his or her own stories and not conveying or checking these stories. There was real confusion, with many different interpretations. No one knew the goals and priorities in the ERO. People closer to the emergency coordinator knew the goals better, but they did not know why those goals had been selected. The recommended solution here was a magnetic board— to let the team shift priorities and allow everyone to see these revisions. Previously, the status board had been ignored. After making this change, the ERO found that the status board was used. People discussed it: "If that's now our priority, what should we be doing?" They caught implications down the road: "You also need to check that pump while you're out there." They became proactive.

Another primary difficulty was that the crews were not clear about their roles and functions. The personnel performing the team CTA worked with the crews to redefine the roles and functions and to redesign the workspace layout in the ERO to help people coordinate better. In all, more than 50 recommendations were put into place during the 10-month period of this project.

The outcome was highly favorable. After watching the team in action during the next exercise, the NRC reduced the number of required drills at the plant down to one every 2 years. The NRC also wiped the slate free from the previous deficiencies and designated the plant as a model of ERO performance.

HOW CAN WE DO A CTA OF TEAMS?

There are several ways to examine the cognitive processes of teams: through the use of guided observation, through simulations, and through interviews. In many settings, we have been able to conduct observations. The work with nuclear power plants, described earlier was based on guided observations. We have found that the most useful strategy is to collect critical incidents. This process was used in both of the projects described in the previous section, the work with marines, and the work with nuclear power plants. With experience, observers learn to identify the starting point for incidents that have to do with the five processes of interest. The observers record the events within the incident, including the times when each event occurs and the personnel involved at each stage. This account can be deepened through subsequent interviews. The output of this type of observation is a set of critical incidents that illustrate strengths and weaknesses in accomplishing the five primary factors of interest. Hutchins (1995) described the use of observations to gain insight into cognition, attentional control, and memory by examining task settings that distribute these functions across team members.

In some settings, we have been able to conduct or participate in simulations. In the work with the marines, we developed a regimental tactical decision game and presented it to three different regiments to find commonalities. In other projects (e.g., Miller & Lim, 1993), we used simulations to study information management in teams that consisted of F-117 pilots, intelligence analysts, and structural engineers.

For most of our projects, we have used interviews. We usually conduct interviews in conjunction with the observations and simulations, but in some settings we are restricted to interviews. Here, we might ask the interviewee to describe critical incidents that relate to the five key processes; we would probe the team's decision making along the lines of a critical decision interview with an individual (Hoffman, Crandall, & Shadbolt, 1998). We have learned that it is not effective to ask a team, "Do you have good shared situation awareness?" This is a hard thing to gauge. It is easier to work from specific events (e.g., "Write down how many people were injured during this simulated accident"). Then the team members can see for themselves if they have a common understanding. If not, they are usually motivated to try to figure out why they arrived at different answers and what needed to be done differently.

Regardless of how the data are collected, the team CTA is an attempt to gather information about the way the team makes decisions and the way it manages itself. The critical incidents are data points and vehicles for communicating the findings. We can put the results into the form of decision requirements tables, presenting the key decision requirements, the reasons the team has difficulty with them, and the strategies developed by skillful teams. We can break out the barriers from these, if the list of barriers is useful.

The output of the team CTA—whether in the form of decision requirements, barriers, or just a collection of incidents—needs to describe the five key processes. First, it needs to describe how the team manages information. If there are inefficiencies here, they need to be explained. If the team has to depart from procedures, this can be important. If the team has learned some clever strategies, these have to be described. Second, the output needs to describe how the team tries to maintain shared situation awareness. If important team members are left out of the loop, that has to be explained. If the procedures for sharing situation awareness are excessive and cumbersome, that is an important finding. If the team has learned to make good use of status boards or other artifacts, that is worth mentioning. Third, the output needs to describe the degree to which mental models are shared. We have found that the most common problem here is a lack of understanding about the roles and functions of the team members. These inconsistencies can be detected through the observations (people do not know who to ask for information or who to pass information to), but they can also be discovered during simulations and interviews. Fourth, the output should document the strengths of the team, the expertise it has developed, and the strategies it has learned. These may already be covered in the way the team manages information and maintains shared situation awareness, but other types of strategies can emerge such as the way domain experts are used. Fifth, the output can appraise the degree of metacognition. Often teams have no mechanism for observing themselves; as a result, they are unable to spot problems and make adaptations. The level of metacognition can be gauged by observing when a team runs into a problem—to see who notices the problem and how it is labeled. Often the impact of the problem is seen, but the team does not make any attempt to diagnose the problem.

This chapter suggested that many teams are decision-making entities. A team CTA can probe the way the team makes decisions and can make visible the workings of the team mind. The analysis needs to be sufficiently comprehensive so as to provide an accurate account. However, the analysis should not be so exhaustive that it obscures the main findings. For this reason, only a small set of cognitive processes have been identified as worth studying. The output of a team CTA should be a compelling, storylike account of how a team carries out the critical cognitive processes and where the team struggles the most. By being selective and focused, a team CTA would make it easier to determine what types of remediation, if any, are appropriate, and the team CTA would guide the way in which the remediation is carried out.

REFERENCES

Cannon-Bowers, J. A., Salas, E., & Converse, S. (1992). Shared mental models in expert team decision making. In N. J. Castellan, Jr. (Ed.), *Current issues in individual and group decision making.* (pp. 221–246). Hillsdale, NJ: Lawrence Erlbaum Associates.

De Keyser, V., & Woods, D. D. (1993). Fixation errors: Failures to revise situation assessment in dynamic and risky systems. In A. G. Colombo & A. Saiz de Bustamente (Eds.), *Advanced systems in reliability modeling.* Norwell, MA: Kluwer Academic.

Gentner, D., & Stevens, A. L. (Eds.). (1983). *Mental models.* Mahwah, NJ: Lawrence Erlbaum Associates.

Hoffman, R. R., Crandall, B. W., & Shadbolt, N. R. (1998, June). Use of the critical decision method to elicit expert knowledge: A case study in cognitive task analysis methodology. *Journal of Human Factors and Ergonomics Society, 40*(2), 254–276.

Hutchins, E. (1995). *Cognition in the wild*. Cambridge, MA: MIT Press.

Klein, G., & Miller, T. E. (1999). Distributed planning teams. *International Journal of Cognitive Ergonomics, 3*(3), 203–222.

Klein, G., Schmitt, J., McCloskey, M., Heaton, J., Klinger, D., & Wolf, S. (1996). *A decision-centered study of the regimental command post*. Fairborn, OH: Klein Associates.

Klein, G. A., Zsambok, C. E., & Thordsen, M. L. (1993, April). Team decision training: Five myths and a model. *Military Review*, pp. 36–42.

Klinger, D. W., & Klein, G. (in press). Emergency Response Organizations: An accident waiting to happen. *Ergonomics in Design*. Santa Monica, CA: HFES.

Miller, T. E., & Lim, L. S. (1993). *Using knowledge engineering in the development of an expert system to assist targeteers in assessing battle damage and making weapons decisions for hardened-structure targets*. Fairborn, OH: Klein Associates.

Pew, R. W., Miller, D. C., & Feehrer, C. E. (1982). *Evaluation of proposed control room improvements through analysis of critical operator decisions*. Palo Alto, CA: Electric Power Research Institute.

Rouse, W. B., & Morris, N. M. (1986). On looking into the black box: Prospects and limits on the search for mental models. *Psychological Bulletin, 100*(3), 349–363.

Thordsen, M. L., & Klein, G. A. (1989, November). Cognitive processes of the team mind. In *Proceedings of IEEE International Conference on Systems, Man, and Cybernetics* (pp 46–49). New York, NY: IEEE.

Thordsen, M. L., McCloskey, M. J., Heaton, J. K., & Serfaty, D. (1996). *Decision-centered development of a mission rehearsal system* (Contract N61339-95-C-0101 for Naval Air Warfare Center Training Systems Division, Orlando, FL). Fairborn, OH: Klein Associates.

26

ANALYZING KNOWLEDGE REQUIREMENTS IN TEAM TASKS

Elizabeth Blickensderfer and Janis A. Cannon-Bowers
Naval Air Warfare Center Training Systems Division

Eduardo Salas
The University of Central Florida

David P. Baker
American Institutes for Research

Teams and their associated cognitive requirements have received an increasing amount of attention over the last 10 years (e.g., Cannon-Bowers, Salas, & Converse, 1993; Orasanu, 1990). Numerous articles and books address critical issues related to team decision making (Guzzo & Salas, 1995), team training (Swezey & Salas, 1992), and team performance measurement (Brannick, Prince, & Salas, 1997). However, it is only recently that researchers have begun to analyze teamwork in terms of its component tasks and associated knowledge, skill, and attitude requirements (e.g., Baker, Salas, & Cannon-Bowers, 1998; Bowers, Baker, & Salas, 1994; Campion, Medsker, & Higgs, 1993; Stevens & Campion, 1994). In particular, a thorough analysis of the cognitive components that underlie effective team performance is lacking. Such an analysis—cognitive task analysis for teams—would be useful for decisions regarding team selection, design, and training and would also be useful for building more complete and accurate models of team performance (Salas, Dickinson, Converse, & Tannenbaum, 1992).

Cognitive task analysis (CTA) for teams differs from that of individuals in two major areas. First, this analysis must identify, define, and describe the cognitive processes and knowledge associated with teamwork processes (e.g., communication, coordination, adaptability). Second, it must be capable of addressing the issue of team knowledge. The purpose of the present chapter is to assess and describe CTA methods to capture team knowledge. To accomplish this, we begin with a theoretical overview of team knowledge. We next review knowledge-elicitation methods that have been used previously to tap team knowledge. Finally, we suggest alternative methods to enhance team CTA.

What Is Team Knowledge?

A major requirement of team CTA is to identify, define, and describe team knowledge. Team knowledge (referred to as *shared mental models* by Cannon-Bowers and her colleagues) is thought to relate directly to team performance (Cannon-Bowers et al., 1993; Orasanu, 1990). Team knowledge is knowledge that is shared across members of the team. Cannon-Bowers and her colleagues suggested that this knowledge has the potential to affect teamwork at two levels. First, when communication channels are limited, team knowledge enables team members to anticipate other team members' behavioral and informational requirements. Second, team knowledge of the team task enables team members to perform these tasks from a common frame of reference (see Cannon-Bowers et al., 1993, for a detailed discussion). Other authors refer to team knowledge as schema similarity (Rentsch & Hall, 1994), shared cognitive schema (Moussavi & Evans, 1993), and shared cognitive maps (Langfield-Smith, 1992). Despite terminology differences, researchers tend to agree that team knowledge of this sort seems to help teams coordinate smoothly and effectively (Rouse, Cannon-Bowers, & Salas, 1992; Cannon-Bowers et al., 1993; Hinsz, 1995; Kraiger & Wenzel, 1997; Rentsch & Hall, 1994). In fact, several researchers have attempted to assess the degree of sharedness in knowledge and have found evidence that suggests a positive relationship between the degree of team knowledge and team performance (Blickensderfer, Cannon-Bowers, & Salas, 1997; Mathieu, Heffner, Goodwin, Salas, & Cannon-Bowers, in press; Minionis, Zaccaro, & Perez, 1995).

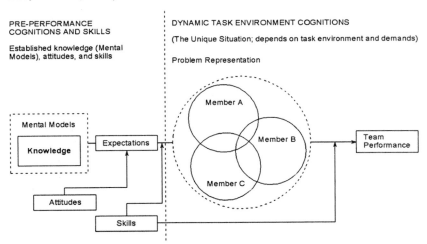

FIG. 26.1   Model of shared cognition.

Although the prior description gives an overview of team knowledge, we next provide specific definitions. Consider the conceptual model in Fig. 26.1. Based on Stout, Cannon-Bowers, and Salas (1996), this model depicts team knowledge as composed of two major elements: knowledge existing prior to task activities (pretask team knowledge) and knowledge and understanding that develops dynamically during performance. Researchers believe that both types of knowledge have implications for team performance (Cannon-Bowers et al., 1993; Klimoski & Mohammed, 1994; Rentsch & Hall, 1994). The fundamental argument behind sharing each type of knowledge is that this knowledge enables teammates to attend to, interpret, communicate about, and respond to the world more similarly than individuals with discrepant or incomplete knowledge (Rentsch & Hall, 1994).

Pretask Team Knowledge

Pretask knowledge is knowledge that resides in long-term memory. Team members carry it with them into task performance. The extent to which team members come to the task with compatible knowledge and mental models we consider their level of pretask team knowledge. Many researchers have postulated about the specific content of pretask shared knowledge that is most beneficial. First, teammates who possess compatible knowledge of the overall mission objectives (Cannon-Bowers, Tannenbaum, Salas, & Volpe, 1995) and team goals (Kraiger & Wenzel, 1997) may help team performance. The basic premise for this is straightforward: Team members need to understand the team's objectives to ensure everyone is working toward the same goal. For example, consider a basketball team. In a particular game, if the overall objective is showing off particular players for recruitment scouts, the focus of the plays could be different from those used to win the game. If the players involved do not focus on the same overall objectives, they may have different expectations concerning plays. Conflicting expectations could cause them to misinterpret plays and play against each other rather than performing as a team.

In addition, team knowledge of teammates' roles and responsibilities may also be vital for effective team performance (e.g., Cannon-Bowers et al., 1993, 1995; Orasanu, 1990; Rentsch & Hall, 1994; Stout et al., 1996/1997; Volpe, Cannon-Bowers, Salas, & Spector, 1996). Pretask knowledge of roles and responsibilities should help ensure that each team member understands the interdependencies inherent to the team, and that teammates understand how to help each other and, in turn, to help the team (Cannon-Bowers et al., 1993). Furthermore, teammates who understand each other's duties will be able to predict the team's behavior in frequently encountered situations (Rentsch & Hall, 1994). For example, Orasanu (1990) examined two-member pilot crew aircraft flights.

She observed that effective teams talked in detail during preflight plans about possible situations the crew may encounter and what the team should do if those situations occur. Orasanu (1990) argued that this planning includes building an understanding of roles and responsibilities.

Teammates may also need to be familiar with teammate characteristics (e.g., the knowledge, skills, attitudes [KSAs], preferences and other task-relevant attributes of their teammates; Cannon-Bowers et al., 1993). Teammates' expectations of behaviors vary as a function of the individuals who compose the team. A basic example would be performance speed: Some individuals will perform the task slightly slower or faster than other individuals. This may require their teammates to adjust their expectations of when certain events will happen. The specific characteristics teammates should be aware of vary with the task.

Other preperformance knowledge important for team members to share may be knowledge of the equipment, relationships among equipment, and task operations (Orasanu, 1990; Rouse et al., 1992). This includes declarative knowledge about the task such as typical situations and decision criteria. However, Rouse et al. (1992) argued that this knowledge is important only as much as it helps individuals form expectations about the task, equipment, and team, and that those expectations enable individuals to perform more effectively. Knowledge of acceptable team behaviors also may be useful for effective team performance (Jenkins & Rentsch, 1995; Rentsch & Hall, 1994; Smith-Jentsch, Zeisig, Acton, & McPherson, 1998). Rentsch and colleagues argued that teams develop schemas (or scripts) that enable them to perform effectively. One type of schema of particular interest to these researchers has been schemas describing acceptable team behavior and teamwork processes (e.g., asking for help, leader behavior, team goal setting). Rentsch and Hall (1994) contended that a similar understanding of these behaviors among teammates will enhance team processes by improving communication among team members. They predict that team members will be better able to anticipate information that other team members will need and give it to them in the most useful form. In a related vein, Smith-Jentsch et al. (1998) advocated that team members must understand the definition of effective teamwork. They argued that teammates will not be able to communicate effectively, for example, if they do not have a clear mental model of effective communication.

Cannon-Bowers and colleagues (Cannon-Bowers et al., 1995; Rouse et al., 1992; Stout et al., 1996) posited that shared knowledge of sequences and timing related to task actions and behaviors are both useful for teams to possess. Rentsch and Hall (1994) agreed that the sequence or temporal ordering of team behaviors is key. Klimoski and Mohammed (1994) postulated that learned response patterns may be part of a team mental model. Duncan et al. (1996) considered knowledge of how teammates perform their respective duties and knowledge of how teammates perform together important for team performance. Finally, Kraiger and Wenzel (1997) argued that shared procedural knowledge is useful in team tasks with high interdependencies, but may not be as important for tasks with fewer interdependencies. The bottom line is that knowledge of task procedures, sequences, and timing enables the team to expect or predict what will happen next and thus what should be their next action.

Although not focusing on procedures per se, Hinsz (1995) argued that we need to focus on the exact view the individual has of the implications of his or her interactions for the system. If an individual does not have accurate expectations, it is likely that he or she will interact ineffectively with the system. Consider an individual with an unclear cause-and-effect model of using a calculator. That individual may hit the clear key repeatedly even although once is enough. Similarly, in a team task, an individual may have incorrect beliefs about the outcomes of various behavior patterns. Believing that certain behaviors yield desired results, this person may act in a manner that actually adds nothing or even hinders the team. To avoid this problem, researchers argue that it is critical to assess each individual's understanding of outcomes that result from behavior patterns (Cannon-Bowers et al., 1993; Hinsz, 1995). In other words, we need to examine what the individual expects to happen as a consequence of his or her actions.

In general, a knowledge of procedures and patterns of team interactions and functions drives procedural expectations. For example, if team members understand the normal procedures, they can predict when teammates will need information passed to them, when a teammate may need help, and when something is wrong. If teammates can make these predictions, they reduce their need for overt communication (Kleinman & Serfaty, 1989). In addition to building expectations, understanding procedures enables individuals to explain why certain events are occurring. For example, consider a team member who understands why an event occurred when it did. The team member knows that Event A caused Event B. The next time a particular event occurs (Event A), the team member will predict or expect what will happen down the road (Event B). Although not all expectations and explanations are products of procedural knowledge, procedural knowledge does seem to foster many expectations and explanations.

Dynamic Team Knowledge

In addition to preperformance knowledge, another element of team knowledge develops when the team is actually performing the task (Orasanu, 1990; i.e., the right side of Fig. 26.1). As previously noted, we refer to this as *dynamic task understanding*—it occurs dynamically during the performance episode. Dynamic understanding is the degree to which teammates develop compatible assessments of cues and patterns in the situation, the implications of these for the team and task, how the team is proceeding, and particular actions that certain team members need to take. We consider this dynamic understanding qualitatively different from, but related to, the sharedness or compatibility of the preexisting knowledge discussed previously. Dynamic understanding combines preperformance knowledge with cognizance of the specific characteristics of the current situation. During performance, team members interpret cues and patterns in a situation (Stout, Cannon-Bowers, & Salas, in press). These interpretations are influenced by preexisting knowledge and by the execution of appropriate team processes (e.g., clear team communications; Stout et al., 1996). The degree to which teammates develop compatible interpretations on the fly is crucial. For example, although an aviation crew may have a high degree of knowledge going into a flight, the situation may change suddenly from an average flight to an unusual situation that requires changes in team strategy. Similarly, an organization project team may have a high degree of shared knowledge going into a new task; however, once the task has begun, it may not match their expectations. Unexpected problems may occur, changes in procedures may be needed, the team may lose a member and gain a new member, and so on. Teams that are able to develop a shared understanding of these issues (and act accordingly) are likely to perform better than those that do not (Orasanu, 1990).

In summary, team knowledge may provide the foundation for certain team skills. Teammates with team knowledge know what to do when, know when and how to compensate for their teammates, know which materials and information to provide to their teammates, and can fulfill responsibilities and manage their resources without prompting by other members. When the task demands it, teammates with team knowledge can work together effectively with a limited amount of overt communications (Kleinman & Serfaty, 1989). Therefore, it is crucial for a cognitive team task analysis to identify team knowledge requirements for a team task. This includes identifying both the essential pretask knowledge in addition to the much more elusive dynamic performance understanding.

Analyzing Team Knowledge

To date, there has been little or no research on which specific cognitive task analysis methods are useful for eliciting team members' knowledge about their team and its task. Most approaches to analyzing cognitive task requirements have focused on individuals as opposed to teams. Indeed, research is needed to determine methods that best identify the knowledge needed by team members, including a determination of how much of this knowledge must be shared by team members to maximize task performance. It may be that some knowledge needs to be shared, whereas other knowledge simply needs to be compatible. Further effort is needed to sort out this important issue and develop methods to assess the sharedness or overlap required in the knowledge of various team members.

Another issue that must be addressed is the manner in which the elicited information is represented. As is the case with CTA data at the individual level, there are several representational formats that might be useful as a means to describe knowledge elicited from a team CTA. For example, task-action hierarchies, concept maps, semantic nets, concept graphs, task network models, or simple lists or tables could be useful as means to represent team CTA data. At the team level, it might also be useful to employ communication or link analyses to describe the flow of information among team members, models of shared knowledge, or analyses of knowledge overlap among team members. These latter techniques have not received much attention in the literature, but are crucial if a true picture of team-level cognitive concepts is desired. In fact, the issue of how to cast individual- and team-level knowledge stemming from a team CTA is a central question that must be addressed if team-level CTAs are to be useful. This includes an understanding of what each team member needs to know to function effectively, as well as an understanding of what information must be dynamically shared among members. Research aimed at addressing this issue is clearly needed.

Despite the gaps in research, a number of knowledge-elicitation methods available from research on individual CTA seem adaptable to a team environment. Some of these have been used in the team performance arena, whereas others have not. This section suggests potential methods for the different types of team knowledge described in the previous section: methods for eliciting pretask team knowledge and dynamic team knowledge. We list the type of team knowledge and discuss previous attempts (if any) to elicit this knowledge. We also suggest other methods that have potential to tap this knowledge. Although a detailed description of all potential methods is beyond the scope of this chapter, we have attempted to include a brief description of a variety methods. This information is summarized in Table 26.1.

Task Objectives and Goals

Although it has not been tested in team research, we suggest separate interviews of all team members, observations of the team performing the task, and examination of documents regarding the team task to gather this information. To represent this knowledge, we suggest using a variation of taskaction mapping (e.g., Coury, Motte, & Seiford, 1992) or goal-directed analysis (Woods & Hollnagel,

TABLE 26.1
Potential Methods to Elicit Team Knowledge

Pre-Task Team Knowledge Element	Possible Elicitation	Possible Representation	Possible Agreement Comparison
Knowledge of task objectives and goals	• Document analysis • Observation • Separate interviews • Group interviews	• Adaptation of task-action mapping (e.g., Coury et al., 1992) • Adaptation of goal-directed analysis (e.g., Woods & Hollnagel, 1987)	• Agreement metric (e.g., Minionis et al., 1995)
Knowledge of task procedures, sequences, and timing	• Document analysis • Observation • Separate interviews • Group interviews • Concept rating tasks (Stout et al., in press)	• Adaptation of task-action mapping (e.g., Coury et al., 1992) • Adaptation of goal-directed analysis (e.g., Woods & Hollnagel, 1987) • Knowledge structures (e.g., Cooke et al., 1996; Stout et al., in press)	• Agreement metric (e.g., Minionis et al., 1995) • Pathfinder agreement metric (Schvaneveldt et al., 1987)
Knowledge of roles and responsibilities	• Document analysis • Observation • Separate interviews • Group interviews	• Basic tables, lists • Adaptation of task-action mapping (e.g., Coury et al., 1992) • Adaptation of goal-directed analysis (e.g., Woods & Hollnagel, 1987)	• Interrater agreement metrics applied to responses to specific scenarios developed by knowledge engineer or teammates (e.g., Blickensderfer et al., 1997) • Agreement metric (e.g., Minionis et al., 1995)

Pre-Task Team Knowledge Element	Possible Elicitation	Possible Representation	Possible Agreement Comparison
Knowledge of roles and responsibilities	• Questionnaires (Smith-Jentsch et al., 1998) • Adapted critical incident (Flanagan, 1954) or critical decision method (Klein et al. 1989)	• Lists of characteristics	• Interrater agreement metrics applied to responses on questionnaires (Smith-Jentsch et al., 1998) • Comparisons of characteristics lists
Knowledge of teamwork	• Numeric similarity ratings of teamwork concepts (Mathieu et al., 1998) • Sorting teamwork concepts (Smith-Jentsch et al., 1998) • Questionnaires	• Knowledge structures (Mathieu et al., 1998; Smith-Jentsch et al., 1998) • Lists, tables	• Knowledge structure agreement metrics • Concept grouping agreement metric (Smith-Jentsch et al., 1998) • Interrater agreement metrics applied to questionnaire responses (Jenkins & Rentsch, 1995)
Dynamic Performance Understanding: During actual task performance: compatible assessments of cues and patterns in the environment, the implications of those for the team and task, how the team is proceeding, and particular actions that certain team members need to take.	• Adaptation of SAGAT (Endsley, 1995) • SALIENT (Muniz et al., 1998) • Retrospective protocol analysis of videotape performance (Means, 1993) • Structured interview during videotape-simulated mission (Fowlkes et al., in press)	• Tables, charts, and lists (e.g., Baker et al., under review; Muniz et al., 1998)	• Basic comparisons of cues and information elicted

1987), where team members identify the task goals, subgoals, and actions needed for the team to complete each task element. This should include the team goals, the goals and actions of each team member, and how the individual actions enable the team to accomplish the task. This decomposition of goals in terms of action sequences provides the level of detail necessary to specify the interactions that must occur among the team members and between the team members and the system. Once a basic task structure (in terms of goals, relationships among the goals, and means to achieve the goals) is achieved, we suggest a follow-up group interview of the team to ensure the structure is accurate and to fill in any gaps that may be present. The emphasis of the group interview should be to obtain different team members' perspectives on what should happen during those crucial moments where teammates must coordinate and/or communicate with each other.

Knowledge of Task Procedures, Sequences, and Timing

Similar to the overall task objectives and goals, we suggest interviews with information represented in a variation of task-action mapping (Coury et al., 1991) or goal-directed analysis (Woods & Hollnagel, 1987) for knowledge of task procedures, sequences, and timing.

Once knowledge of task procedures was obtained, Minionis et al. (1995) used a simplified variation of the concept mapping approach to assess agreement among team members regarding the domain elements and relationships among those domain elements. They asked team members to complete basic concept maps of the team procedure and then computed agreement among team members. Agreement on team procedures was related to aspects of team performance that required heavy interdependence.

Other researchers have used knowledge structure assessment to elicit sequential understanding. Although not focusing on teams, Cooke, Neville, and Rowe (1996) used Pathfinder (Schvaneveldt, Durso, & Dearholt, 1987) to analyze sequential data. In the team performance arena, Stout, Cannon-Bowers, Salas, and Milanovich (1999) had some success using Pathfinder assessments of knowledge structures of team communication sequences. Their results indicate that teams with effective preperformance planning had higher degrees of agreement in terms of knowledge structures of team sequences.

Team Member Roles and Responsibilities

To elicit the roles and responsibilities of the various team members, we suggest first bootstrapping (Hoffman, Shadbolt, Burton, & Klein, 1995) to gain basic task knowledge via analysis of documentation and job observation. We then reccommend conducting individual interviews of the team members and, finally, a group interview. The individual interviews should be used to elicit individual position processes and knowledge—information that team members who had never performed that exact position would not necessarily know. Again, the group interview should focus on moments of inter-dependence revealed in the initial interviews and obtain different team members' perspectives on what should happen during those crucial moments where teammates must coordinate and/or communicate with each other.

If basic task knowledge of roles and responsibilities of team members is available, the knowledge engineer could also create a probing test or questionnaire to assess degree of knowledge overlap. For example, Blickensderfer et al. (1997) used a questionnaire to assess team members' degree of agreement on expectations concerning aspects of the teammate roles, responsibilities, and communications with respect to a variety of task situations. The questionnaire described scenarios that might occur during task performance. Participants were asked to give estimates regarding the likelihood of various team member actions and communications. Degree of agreement was related to team processes and overall team task performance.

Teammate Characteristics

To elicit knowledge of teammate characteristics, Smith-Jentsch, Kraiger, and Cannon-Bowers (1998) used a questionnaire approach. Each team member answered items with respect to his or herself and every other team member. The questions focused on task-related preferences and abilities, responses to stress, knowledge of the tasks, and personal characteristics such as flexibility, competitiveness, and willingness to accept feedback. Overall ratings of these characteristics may then be obtained by combining the teammates' ratings (e.g., Alice's and Tom's ratings of Susan's characteristics).

For a more detailed assessment of teammate characteristics, we suggest using probed recall of past events, situations, or salient cases. This is a variation of Flanagan's (1954) critical incident and Klein, Calderwood, and MacGregor's (1989) critical decision method. Instead of recalling a decision that was made or cue that occurred, team members would be asked to describe how their teammates responded in terms of task-related knowledge and/or personal characteristics. For example, when considering how a teammate responds to stress, the other teammates could think of stressful incidents that occurred in the past and recall how the particular teammate responded to that situation. Alternatively, a fictional scenario could be presented to a team member and that team member asked to predict how a teammate would respond.

Teamwork Behaviors

One method to elicit knowledge of teamwork behaviors has been structural analyses (Mathieu et al. in press; Smith-Jentsch et al., 1998). Two studies were found that used teamwork-related concepts extracted from previous taxonomies of team skills. To elicit knowledge organization of the teamwork related-terms, Mathieu et al. (in press) asked team members to rate a number of teamwork concepts in relation to other teamwork concepts (e.g., coordination of action, liking, team spirit, cooperation, roles). This was followed by a network analysis of the data, which included obtaining agreement metrics among teammates. Smith-Jentsch et al. (1998) required team members to sort the teamwork-related concepts into relatedness groups (via card sorting). The groups were then compared to an expert model and level of agreement with the expert model computed. The Mathieu et al. (in press) results indicate a positive relationship between team agreement and team performance. Although performance data were not available, the Smith-Jentsch et al. (1998) results indicate that team members' understanding of teamwork did change as a result of a team training program.

Dynamic Performance Understanding

A second issue in team CTA is how to assess dynamic shared understanding. The ideal measure would be one that allows dynamic assessment of shared understanding during task performance. Even with current human performance modeling technology, however, this is not yet possible. Until dynamic assessment is possible, two basic approaches come to mind. First, the researcher could stop the task at a particular point and assess shared understanding at that point. A variety of knowledge-elicitation methods might be used during task performance intermissions. For example, although not assessing overlap among teammates, Endsley's (1995) Situation Awareness Global Assessment Technique (SAGAT) method to assess situation awareness is an example of this type of task-interruption approach. In SAGAT, the knowledge engineer freezes a simulated mission after various intervals of time and asks the operator to recall certain pieces of information pertaining to the mission. Although used previously for individuals, this technique could be expanded to a team setting by asking all team members the questions individually and then comparing where the members agree and disagree. Further work along these lines is required, along with methods that involve multiple team members in the elicitation process.

The other basic approach is to avoid performance interruptions. For example, Muniz, Stout, Bowers, and Salas (1998) used an observation and inference approach. Muniz et al. examined team behaviors in key task situations and, based on the behaviors observed, inferred the degree of knowledge of the team situation (i.e., situation awareness) that was present. In another approach, Fowlkes, Baker, Salas, Cannon-Bowers, and Stout (in press) avoided task performance interruption by eliminating actual task performance altogether. In this study, pilots observed a videotaped mission and answered questions as if they were actually performing the mission. First, each pilot was given a description of the planned flight and the weather conditions of the route, in addition to approach plates, charts, a pocket checklist, and a cockpit diagram. The pilots then watched a videotape of a helicopter flight (from the initial briefing through the flight). The tape was stopped at specific times and the participants responded verbally to questions. The probing questions elicited task, team, and environmental cues that appeared during the mission and information regarding which knowledge was important to be shared among teammates during the mission.

In addition, a variation of a retrospective protocol methodology may also be useful. For example, a researcher could videotape a team task performance and later replay the performance for that particular team while stopping it periodically to ask questions (e.g., Means, 1993). Consider a training run in a flight simulator that is later replayed for the crew to review the run. At certain points during the replay, the researcher could use any of the shared knowledge assessment methods to assess team members' understanding of the situation and then calculate the degree of agreement among the teammates. This type of replay approach seems particularly useful for tasks performed under severe time pressure—a characteristic of many team tasks. Although not examining agreement between team members, Means (1993) used this method as a form of CTA for air traffic control. Means noted that air traffic controllers make hundreds of individual decisions in an hour, and that they do this often with little conscious awareness of the many criteria they are combining to arrive at a solution. Wanting to elicit controller understanding of these situations, yet realizing that task interruptive forms of CTA would not be possible, Means used the strategy of videotaping experts performing realistic air traffic control scenarios on full-scale simulators and later eliciting commentary on the situation from other expert controllers. Using some assessment of agreement, this same strategy seems a strong candidate to assess shared dynamic performance understanding in a team task.

SUMMARY

Clearly, the challenge of optimizing team performance is a formidable one. At the team level, a rich understanding of the cognitive demands of a task requires that information at both the individual and team levels must be elicited. Moreover, evidence suggests that, to understand fully the nature of team functioning, it is crucial to delineate those knowledge elements that must be common among team members as a precursor to performance as well as the team's ability to construct a shared picture of the task during the performance episode. In this chapter, we attempted to specify the nature of these types of knowledge and provided recommendations regarding promising team CTA methods to capture and represent such knowledge. The benefits of developing techniques that provide valid, useable team CTA data are many. In fact, such data are required so that team selection, training, task design, and management systems can be optimized. Our hope is that work in this crucial area will continue.

ACKNOWLEDGMENTS

The view expressed herein are those of the authors and do not necessarily represent the official positions of the agencies with which they are affiliated.

REFERENCES

Baker, D. P., Salas, E., & Cannon-Bowers, J. A. (1998). Team task analysis: Lost but hopefully not forgotten. *The Industrial - Organizational Psychologist, 35,* 79–83.

Blickensderfer, E. L., Cannon-Bowers, J. A., & Salas, E. (1997, April). *Training teams to self-correct: An empirical investigation.* Paper presented at the 12th annual conference of the Society for Industrial and Organizational Psychology, St. Louis, MO.

Bowers, C. A., Baker, D. P., & Salas, E. (1994). The importance of teamwork in the cockpit: The utility of job/task analysis indices for training design. *Military Psychology, 4,* 205–214.

Brannick, M. T., Prince, C., & Salas, E. (1997). *Team performance assessment and measurement.* Mahwah, NJ: Lawrence Erlbaum Associates.

Campion, M. A., Medsker, G. J., & Higgs, A. C. (1993). Relations between work group characteristics and effectiveness: Implications for designing effective work groups. *Personnel Psychology, 46,* 823–850.

Cannon-Bowers, J. A., Salas, E., & Converse, S. A. (1993). Shared mental models in expert team decision making. In N. J. Castellan, Jr. (Ed.), *Current issues in individual and group decision making* (pp. 221–246). Hillsdale, NJ: Lawrence Erlbaum Associates.

Cannon-Bowers, J. A., Tannenbaum, S. I., Salas, E., & Volpe, C. E. (1995). Defining competencies and establishing team training requirements. In R. Guzzo & E. Salas (Eds.), *Team effectiveness and decision making in organizations* (pp. 333–380). San Francisco, CA: Jossey-Bass.

Cooke, N. J., Neville, K. J., & Rowe, A. L. (1996). Procedural network representations of sequential data. *Human-Computer Interaction, 11,* 29–68.

Coury, B. G., Motte, S., & Seiford, L. M. (1991). Capturing and representing decision processes in the design of an information system. *Proceedings of the Human Factors Society 35th annual meeting* (1223–1227). Santa Monica, CA: Human Factors Society.

Duncan, P. C., Rouse, W. B., Johnston, J. H., Cannon-Bowers, J. A., Salas, E., & Burns, J. J. (1996). Training teams working in complex systems: A mental model-based approach. In W. B. Rouse (Ed.), *Human/technology interaction in complex systems* (Vol. 8, pp. 173–231). Greenwich, CT: JAI Press.

Endsley, M. R. (1995). Measurement of situation awareness in dynamic systems. *Human Factors, 37,* 65–84.

Flanagan, J. C. (1954). The critical incident technique. *Psychological Bulletin, 51,* 327–358.

Fowlkes, J. E., Baker, D. P., Salas, E., Cannon-Bowers, J. A., & Stout, R. J. (in press). The utility of interviews and guided verbal reports for knowledge elicitation. *Human Factors.*

Guzzo, R., & Salas E. (1995). *Team effectiveness and decision making in organizations.* San Francisco, CA: Jossey-Bass.

Hinsz, V. B. (1995). Mental models of groups as social systems: Considerations of specification and assessment. *Small Group Research, 26,* 200–233.

Hoffman, R. R., Shadbolt, N. R., Burton, A. M., & Klein, G. (1995). Eliciting knowledge from experts: A methodological analysis. *Organizational Behavior and Human Decision Making, 62*(2), 129–158.

Jenkins, N. M., & Rentsch, J. R. (1995, May). The effects of teamwork schema similarity on team effectiveness and fairness perceptions. In J. Mathieu (Chair), *Mental models and team effectiveness: Three empirical tests.* Symposium presented at the 10th annual conference of the Society for Industrial and Organizational Psychology, Orlando, FL.

Klein, G. A., Calderwood, R., & MacGregor, D. (1989). Critical decision method for eliciting knowledge. *IEEE Transactions on Systems, Man, and Cybernetics, 19,* 462–472.

Kleinman, D. L. & Serfaty, D. (1989). Team performance assessment in distributed decision making. In R. Gilson, J. P. Kincaid, & B. Goldiez (Eds.), *Proceedings of the Symposium on Interactive Networked Simulation for Training* (pp. 22–27). Orlando, FL: The Institute for Simulation and Training/University of Central Florida.

Klimoski, R., & Mohammed, S. (1994). Team mental model: Construct or metaphor? *Journal of Management, 20,* 403–437.

Kraiger, K., & Wenzel, L. H. (1997). Conceptual development and empirical evaluation of measures of shared mental models as indicators of team effectiveness. In M. T. Brannick, E. Salas, & C. Prince (Eds.), *Team performance assessment and measurement: Theory, methods, and applications* (pp. 63–84). Hillsdale, NJ: Lawrence Erlbaum Associates.

Langfield-Smith, K. (1992). Exploring the need for a shared cognitive map. *Journal of Management Studies, 29(3),* 349–367.

Mathieu, J. E., Heffner, T. S., Goodwin, G. F., Salas, E., & Cannon-Bowers, J. A. (in press). The influence of shared mental models on team process and performance. *Journal of Applied Psychology.*

Means, B. (1993). Cognitive task analysis as a basis for instructional design. In M. Rabinowitz (Ed.), *Cognitive science foundations of instruction* (pp. 97–118). Hillsdale, NJ: Lawrence Erlbaum Associates.

Minionis, D. P., Zaccaro, S. J., & Perez, R. (1995, May). Shared mental models, team coordination, and team performance. In J. Mathieu (Chair), *Mental models and team effectiveness: Three empirical tests*. Symposium presented at the 10th annual conference of the Society for Industrial and Organizational Psychology, Orlando, FL.

Moussavi, F., & Evans, D.A. (1993). Emergence of organizational attributions: The role of a shared cognitive schema. *Journal of Management, 19(1),* 79–95.

Muñiz, E. J., Stout, R. J., Bowers, C. A., & Salas, E. (1998). A methodology for measuring team situation awareness: Situation awareness linked indicators adapted to novel tasks (SALIANT*). Proceedings of the RTO Meeting: Collaborative Crew Performance in Complex Operational Systems* (pp. 11-1–11-8). Quebec, Canada: Canada Communication Group.

Orasanu, J. (1990, October). *Shared mental models and crew performance*. Paper presented at the 34th annual meeting of the Human Factors Society, Orlando, FL.

Rentsch, J. R., & Hall, R. J. (1994). Members of great teams think alike: A model of team effectiveness and schema similarity among team members. In M. M. Beyerlein & D. A. Johnson (Eds.), *Advances in interdisciplinary studies of work teams: Theories of self-managing work teams* (Vol. 1, pp. 223–262). Greenwich, CT: JAI Press.

Rouse, W. B., Cannon-Bowers, J. A., & Salas, E. (1992). The role of mental models in team performance in complex systems. *IEEE Transactions on Systems, Man, and Cybernetics, 22,* 1296–1308.

Salas, E., Dickinson, T. L., Converse, S., & Tannenbaum, S. I. (1992). Toward an understanding of team performance and training. In R. W. Swezey, & E. Salas (Eds.), *Teams: Their training and performance* (pp. 3–29). Norwood, NJ: Ablex.

Schvaneveldt, R. W., Durso, F. T., & Dearholt, D. W. (1987). *Pathfinder: Networks from proximity data*. Memorandum in Computer and Cognitive Science, MCCS-87-9, Computing Research Laboratory, New Mexico State University.

Smith-Jentsch, K. A., Kraiger, K., & Cannon-Bowers, J. A. (1998, April). A data driven model of precursors to teamwork. In K. Kraiger (Chair*), Team effectiveness as a product of individual, team, and situational factors*. Symposium presented at the 13th annual conference of the Society of Industrial and Organizational Psychology, Dallas, TX.

Smith-Jentsch, K. A., Zeisig, R. L., Acton, B., & McPherson, J. A. (1998). Team dimensional training: A strategy for guided team self-correction. In J. A. Cannon-Bowers, & E. Salas (Eds*.), Making decisions under stress: Implications for individual and team training* (pp. 271–297). Washington, DC: American Psychological Association.

Stevens, M. J., & Campion, M. A. (1994). The knowledge, skill, and ability requirements for teamwork: Implications for human resource management. *Journal of Management, 20,* 503–530.

Stout, R. J., Cannon-Bowers, J. A., & Salas, E. (1996). The role of shared mental models in developing team situational awareness: Implications for training. *Training Research Journal, 2,* 85–116.

Stout, R. J., Cannon-Bowers, J. A., & Salas, E. (in press). Team situational awareness (SA): Cue recognition training. To appear in M. McNeese, E. Salas, & M. Endsley (Eds.), *New trends in collaborative activities.* Santa Monica, CA: Human Factors and Ergonomics Society.

Stout, R. J., Cannon-Bowers, J. A., Salas, E., & Milanovich, D. M. (1999). Planning, shared mental models, and coordinated performance: An empirical link is established. *Human Factors, 41,* 61–71.

Swezey, R. W., & Salas, E. (1992). *Teams: Their training and performance.* Norwood, NJ: Ablex.

Volpe, C. E., Cannon-Bowers, J. A., Salas, E., & Spector, P. (1996). The impact of cross-training on team functioning. *Human Factors, 38,* 87–100.

Woods, D. D., & Hollnagel, E. (1987). Mapping cognitive demands in complex problem-solving worlds. *International Journal of Man-Machine Studies, 26,* 257–275.

V DISCUSSION

27

ON THE FUTURE OF COGNITIVE
TASK ANALYSIS

Alan Lesgold
University of Pittsburgh

Specifying the specific actions required to do a job has been with us since the dawn of history. For example, the Bible contains specific instructions for certain activities, such as the offering of sacrifices in the Temple. However, as work has evolved, the requirements for job analyses and the forms in which job content are expressed have changed considerably. Today's jobs often require complex thinking and the solution of problems that cannot be stated explicitly in advance. They often involve groups of people with different knowledge and skills working together to solve problems. They sometimes involve the use of intelligent systems, either as part of work teams or for training team members. Those systems require a much more formal and structured specification of the knowledge that is needed to be a coach or member of a work team. To some extent, the underlying assumptions embedded in the culture of cognitive task analysts are being challenged today. For example, task analyses are generally done in part by interviewing current job experts. This used to work very well. Today, however, training is often being built for tasks no one has ever done before. Hence, there may be no subject-matter expert (SME) to interview. We know that the engineers who design tools and work processes are not universally good at telling us what the work is about. That is why we went to interviewing job incumbents in the first place.

Further, we know that some work teams experience considerable turnover. For example, in a one-year project we did jointly with a large high-technology company, we had three turnovers in a four-person programming team. Clearly part of the group work process that would need to be analyzed in a cognitive task analysis (CTA) of that team's work is the training activity embedded in daily work. That is, part of being a team member is knowing how to improve the relevant knowledge of other team members on a continuing basis. No account of the team's work goals will reveal this training requirement, yet it is essential to the team's success in getting work done.

The work reported herein is some of the best done on CTA; it has taken us a long way from the behavioral schemes that existed before cognitive psychology addressed the task analysis problem. Researchers like Annett laid a strong foundation for the field, and the newer approaches discussed in this book have made CTA an important aspect of modern job and system design. However, I think we need even more to address the hard parts of the CTA problem, including:

- The processes whereby team activity is maintained in the face of turnover and language barriers among workers with different knowledge and expertise,
- The processes whereby transferable knowledge is acquired that can be used to deal with novel problems that keep arising in complex enterprises, and
- The processes that support the individual and organizational learning that seems to be necessary in the modern work world.

In addition, we need to attend to a paradox produced by the emergence of machine intelligence. To the extent that we succeed in analyzing a work process into a set of formally specifiable rules, we may have rendered the job obsolete. The reason for that is that, once you really understand a task and really understand what it takes to do it, it is a good candidate for automation. The only reason that it might not be automated is if the supply and price of labor is such that you are better off having humans do it than having machines do it.

That being the case, we need to find ways to analyze the unanalyzable. We need to pay more attention to the way in which people mediate between systems of knowledge that do not fit together very well—the key role for people that machines seldom can fill. The telephone operator is a sensible challenge for the CTA world. The telephone operator may mediate between the system of thought of a person who calls up on the telephone to order 16 Elvis recordings and some system of production, distribution, and banking that allows a transaction to take place. The person who answers the telephone for a medical insurer may mediate among the insurance system, the medical system, and the models of both that consumers tend to have. Similarly, diagnosis of system failures is a human role because failed systems, like Dostoevsky's failed marriages[1], tend to be unique and not fully describable in advance of the failure. Such are the uniquely human roles in the future. Consequently, paying more attention to how different system of knowledges are interconnected and interrelated may become a more important part of any CTA.

Cognitive task analysis is also needed to support just-in-time learning. I visited a plant in Helsinki that made motor drives. Every motor drive that comes down the line is different from the previous one. Somebody had the clever idea

---

[1] See the first sentence of *Anna Karenina*

that if you could figure out what adaptive knowledge a person would need to build a motor drive different from the ones he had built before, you could provide the needed information on the same screen that displays the parts list. When a piece of motor drive arrives at a work station, the worker flashes a bar code reader at the tag on that piece. This prompts the computer system to tell him what parts to install on that drive chassis. If he is not sure how to do this, he scans another bar code in front of him and the needed advice appears on his screen. Such is the nature of modern work—mostly it is doing a task you have never done before that bears some family resemblance to tasks you have done. Understanding and supporting this adaptability has to be part of the CTA world in the future.

One approach that has been mentioned two or three times in the course of this conference is the work of Jens Rasmussen (Rasmussen et al., 1994), who proposed a hierarchy of skills, rules, and knowledge. Rasmussen's hierarchy raises the question of how skills, rules, and conceptual knowledge get interconnected. How is it that someone confronting a novel situation can pop up to the knowledge level, cobble together a plan from existing rules and skills, and then execute it? In medical education, future physicians have to learn to bounce around among rule-based medical knowledge about finding out what is wrong with somebody, an array of cost–benefit issues, and a physiological understanding of medicine. How do they learn this, and what does that imply for task analysis?

Boshuizen and Van de Wiel (1999) proposed that cases are the experiences that allow us to make connections among knowledge at the different levels. If that proposal continues to be supported by data, it may suggest that, for complex domains, a complete CTA will include not only a decomposition of the skills, rules, and conceptual knowledge the domain requires, but also a specification of the kinds of case experiences that can integrate these bodies of knowledge. Perhaps this would help contain the difficulty observed in midlevel medical fellows, who sometimes did worse on a case in midcareer than on the same case earlier in their training. In midcareer, they were confronting the knowledge-integration problem, where earlier they had minimal knowledge to integrate but could often guess correctly on a case by using rules that almost fit (Lesgold, 1984).

In that same spirit, I again return to Barnard's chapter (chap. 10) and the notion that part of a task analysis is a collection of models of different levels of knowledge and performance capabilities., In some of his figures, Barnard had little cards, one in front of the other, with different levels of instantiated cognitive theory attached to them, such as theories of novice and expert performance. That prompted me to think about another training problem for which I think CTAs are important: Understanding the pattern of experiences that can facilitate achieving high levels of understanding and skill. We have a strong sense that concrete or situated knowledge is easy to acquire. Further, concrete knowledge often provides a base that supports acquisition of more abstract knowledge. Perhaps we should be paying some attention to the collections of novice competencies that provide a potential pathway to expertise.

Similarly, in our analyses, I think we are going to keep facing some new puzzles. Lévi-Strauss (1966) made a distinction between engineering and bricolage. Bricolage performance is tightly bound to the artifacts of a task. The bricoleur can make something happen when the physical entities of a domain are in his hands. However, according to Lévi-Strauss, he often cannot solve the same problem when the relevant physical artifacts are not in front of him. He contrasted that with the notion of engineering, which he saw as a much more principled activity where people planned out what they were going to do and dealt in abstractions. The striking thing about the information age is that it becomes more difficult to understand the difference between these two types of performances.

Increasingly we see things that look concrete but are responded to abstractly. The biggest puzzle is the other direction. We see people finding ways to engage in bricolage with abstractions. The hacker that you do not want working on your software engages in bricolage of abstracted artifacts—programs. This suggests that all three of Rasmussen's levels are inherently cognitive and not behavioral, both in terms of the underlying knowledge and the mental actions that can be taken. Cognitive task analysis partly takes this into account, but we do not consider whether the experts we choose as SMEs are engineers or bricoleurs. Some very useful people have acquired most of their knowledge at the skill level. Tapping their expertise will not reveal conceptual knowledge that could support transfer to new but related work. Other experts deal purely in abstractions, and basing an analysis only on their input may result in omission of skills that make real work a lot easier.

DIFFERENT REQUIREMENTS FOR DIFFERENT CTA PURPOSES

Although researchers such as Gary Klein (chap. 25, this volume) have made important steps in this direction, there remains work to be done defining the task analytic approaches suitable for different purposes. For example, many task analyses are performed to support the development of interfaces to computer and other systems. Others are performed as a starting point in developing an improved work procedure in a business. Many others are performed as part of the design of new training systems or materials. Different purposes require somewhat different procedures. Indeed, whole areas of CTA develop and are meant to serve a particular purpose, with other purposes not necessarily being considered.

Three of the most common foci for CTA today are the design of interfaces to equipment and software, design of work procedures for individual workers in a businesses, and design of business processes that involve multiple, collaborating actors.

DESIGN OF INTERFACES

When task analyses are performed to support interface development, the primary concerns are efficiency and transparency of the interface. Usage is modeled so that inefficient actions can be simplified through better locations of interface components. Also, observational studies may be developed to identify circumstances in which the user apparently does not know how to find or use a particular interface component. At a deeper level, it is possible to perform task analyses with the purpose of examining the match between the layout of an interface and the mental models held by the user.

Often modeling related to interface development can benefit from CTAs that produce runnable user models. Such modeling affords an opportunity for estimating the amount of time that using various alternative interface forms will take for a given activity. Although it can be time-consuming to develop models for each of several alternative interfaces, once they are developed, it is likely that design principles will emerge that can shape future interface enhancements. My general sense is that CTA for interface development is well developed—it is the most complete expression of cognitive science applied to task analysis that we have.

This particular application is also the closest point of connection between the technologies of CTA and those of software engineering. One more recent step in the evolution of CTA is the realization that object-oriented design approaches in software engineering bear a strong resemblance to some of the emerging schemes for analyzing the procedures of thought as well as the ways in which experts represent the environments within which they work (cf. Richards & Menzies, 1997). Consider a bank teller and an automated teller machine. To train bank tellers, instructional designers might do a CTA of the expertise of existing tellers. To develop the software for an automated teller machine, an analyst might do an object-oriented analysis based on a preliminary requirements analysis or list of the constraints and functionality desired in the ATM machine.

In fact, the two tasks—cognitive analysis of the human performer and object-oriented analysis of the work requirements for the machine—overlap substantially; thus it makes sense for analysts in one field to look at the work of those in the other. The emerging vocabulary of task analysis includes rules, objects or concepts, and system specifications that indicate the relationships among objects in a work environment (see, e.g., Shadbolt, 1992; Shadbolt, O'Hara, &

Schreiber, 1996). The main differences between the two analysis forms are in the criteria for a successful system representation. Object-oriented analysis is followed by design activity focused on controlling the computational demands of the program being designed. In contrast, CTA focuses on building an intelligent system description in which the needed computation and representation must fit with the known limitations of human cognitive capability and human learning mechanisms. Because cognitive knowledge must be learned and is not simply loaded into a person, it must be designed to be learnable. Still, cognitive analysts on the psychology side may have ignored the merits of object-based formalisms at least as often as analysts on the software engineering side have ignored human learning and performance constraints.

A number of other representational forms have been used in task analysis, but the object-oriented approaches seem to be the most powerful at the moment, at least when knowledge of a system is a major part of an expert's domain knowledge. Certain special concerns in task analysis have provoked the use of other computer science formalisms as well, such as Petri Nets (Palanque et al., 1993; Van Biljon, 1988). The need to reify a process or an interaction is quite general, so we can count on a number of analytic processes being developed for that purpose. The emerging field of business process engineering is also now driving further connections between CTA and basic software systems engineering.

DESIGN OF GROUP WORK PROCEDURES

There are some areas of task analysis that need, and seem to be receiving, considerable additional work. Specifically, I refer to the analysis of tasks to be performed by groups. Rasmussen et al. (1994) suggested two different viewpoints on group work: the work components viewpoint and the social organization viewpoint. In any organization, the official command structure and socially perceived organization of job structure often deviates considerably from the actual pattern of knowledge and performance that is observed when the group's performance is analyzed. Rasmussen et al. pointed out that often the same cognitive activity can be seen at three different levels, corresponding to rationale (why), goal structure (what), and (possibly cognitive) actions (who). For example, in analyzing a group activity, we can ask who works on the rationale (why), who works on the goal structure and basic plan (what), and who carries out the activity (how).

Consider the example of flying a plane. The basic procedures for many piloting activities are mandated in various governmental (e.g., the Federal Aviation Administration [FAA] in the United States) and company policies. So, the what layer is pretty clear. The why layer often requires work, and it is important to the extent that carrying out the FAA and company mandates is sometimes not possible or dangerous. The how layer is important to the extent that a pilot or some other party may not be sufficiently familiar with a particular aircraft or airport and how procedures are carried out in certain situations.

This all becomes a social or group task analysis issue when we take account of the fact that multiple parties are involved in flying a plane. The air traffic controllers issue orders, the pilot has to act, and additional orders and advisory information come from the company flight operations center. To analyze a particular procedure, it is necessary to look not only at the three levels of the work, but also at how the work is divided. There are several issues that arise only when work is split among multiple actors.

Different actors may have different mental models of what is going on, and those models need to be coordinated to some extent. The air traffic controller has a model of the air space in which the priority actions are those needed to keep planes separated and keep the take-off and landing processes running smoothly and efficiently. The pilot, in turn, has a model of his own aircraft, the space immediately surrounding it, and the schedule he is supposed to keep. The company flight operations center sees each airplane as a line—a particular aircraft that has to carry out a sequence of flights over the course of the day. To the controller, a delay in a particular landing might allow a more efficient overall pattern. To flight operations, it might mean that a later flight in another city that uses the same aircraft will now be delayed. Part of a CTA for group activity then is to understand the individual jobs and their interactions, as well as the ways in which the overall mental models of individual actors influence both their immediate performances and the level to which their individual performances coordinate to produce an overall effective team performance. This, in turn, is complicated because there are often gaps between the organization of work roles as a set of social conventions or doctrine and the actual interactions that occur during group work.

Rasmussen et al. (1994) addressed this distinction between the functional model of team effort and the social model. An example may help clarify this. Consider a naval battle group, which might have a carrier, several frigates, and some escort destroyers. An admiral might sit on the carrier. Each ship has a captain. There is a deep hierarchy of rank aboard each ship and throughout the group. The admiral provides an overall strategy and issues specific guidance to his officers. Those officers, in turn, issue orders to the enlisted men under them. The enlisted men carry out those orders. This, at least, is how the social order is defined. Actual military plan development—the orchestration of group activity in military contexts—proceeds through alternating cycles of top-level planning and lower level review of plans for their executability. When this works well, a lower level officer receives a what instruction combined with some why information; his job is to determine the how, test to see that the personnel he commands accomplish the what in a manner consistent with the why, and possibly to recursively send requests for further vetting of this type to subordinates.

That is how it is supposed to happen. However, consider what happens when, as the fleet is steaming along in the middle of the night, a low-ranking seaman looking at an Aegis screen notices a possible intruder. For all practical purposes, that seaman controls what the fleet will do, at least until the commanders get a clear sense of what is happening. The model of a group task from the standpoint of functions does not necessarily match the model of the task in terms of social order and structure. That is, the low-level person who is supposed to just execute the how part of a job suddenly needs the guidance of some why information (e.g., should he wake the captain?). The standard answer to this apparent dilemma is that it is the commander's job to train his crew in an established doctrine—a preplanned agreement about how everyone will act in the course of any potential situation that might arise. From this point of view, the command hierarchy asserts control by training everyone to follow a specific set of rules when a situation arises. At the top levels of command, the training passed down might be broad guidance about objectives and general strategy. At lower levels of command, procedures are a lot more specific. At the bottom levels, in traditional doctrines, the orders are extremely directive.

Same Task, Different Responsibilities or Viewpoints

In reality, however, groups that have more shallow command structures increasingly encounter novel situations. For example, we train Seals and Rangers to work on their own to achieve broad goals. Those people may do the same actions as a private in an infantry company in some situations. Hence, at one level, one could claim that a single task analysis would characterize both the private's and the Ranger's performance in that situation. However, the two differ in the mental models behind their actions, in the level of processing at which the actions are potentiated/triggered, and in the kinds of responsibility and social relationships they have with superiors. A central part of effective CTA is to capture these differences along with the basic performances.

We need to develop more powerful tools for dealing with these situations in which multiple mental models must be flexibly used by a single individual as part of a team effort. One source of possible new approaches is the work being done in computer science on multiple agents who must work together to solve complex problems. These agents, each seeing different information, must somehow merge that information into a shared model that can be the basis for negotiation of temporary roles for each of them. Projects are now underway to design agents that maintain local situation models, negotiate shared models, and broker or matchmake the sharing of tasks that arise as situations change (cf. Sykara et al., 1996, for an example of this approach).

Multiple, Independent Agency

The design approach taken in such software design projects also may be a good source for us to get ideas about how to model the skills of model updating, knowledge negotiation, and task brokering that are a central part of modern work. This is partly because computer software designs have long been a good source of ideas for cognitive modeling and task analysis. More important, the intelligent agent research world is addressing virtually the same problems that I believe are faced in building a richer methodology for analysis of human work activity. In both cases, the fundamental issue is the manner in which somewhat independent sources of expertise, within or between machine or human actors, are coordinated.

One general trend as management structures flatten is to compress the why—what—how sequence from three layers of hierarchy into one or two. For this to happen, the why level, in terms of knowledge-based processing, must be incorporated into the CTA of worker responsibilities. In addition, techniques for testing whether the why is being satisfied as the what is carried out are also required. In the multiple agent world, it is also a common finding that more representation of deeper levels of knowledge and purpose is required to support any sort of sharing of responsibilities. It is not that multiple agent systems cannot evolve in ways that demand little representation of the why of activity. Bees have evolved this way, as have swarms of minimal robots. Rather, it is that modern applications seldom permit the luxury of evolving coordination of actors rather than designing systems of work to be coordinated through some mixture of process design and individual worker knowledge.

FURTHER THOUGHTS ON MODELING THE SOCIAL
ASPECTS OF WORK

- A somewhat different metaphor helped me consider the problem of teamwork from yet another angle. Consider a football team's playbook[2]. In a sense, this is a CTA as well as a strategic plan. It has some interesting properties:
- On each play, the responsibility patterns are different,
- The play will only work if each player gets the signal (i.e., recognizes the special situation to which the play applies), and
- Even within the play, there are differential expectations about opportunistic behavior for each player.

The ball carrier can choose to do something different if a hole opens up[3]. The ends (i.e., players on the outside of the formation who run ahead to catch the football if it is passed) can choose to follow a slightly different path, but they have to be sure the passer knows where they are. A defensive player can only switch roles if he is absolutely confident that no one is counting on him to be in his assigned place.

Overall, then, we can speak of commitments that roles imply, terms under which commitments can be broken, situations that trigger one pattern or another of commitment, and differential conventions regarding the range of deviation that a given actor has in a given circumstance.

Commitments

Commitments go a step beyond the message passing of object-oriented design, because, in principle, they are constraints expected to apply independent of whether the actor counting on a commitment actually sends a message to the person the actor is counting on. It seems to me that commitments are important to identify in a CTA of a group task. That is, one should be probing not only for all of the goal structure for the group task and the roles played by different actors, but also for the commitments that are implicit or explicit in the various goal-seeking actions that different actors take. For each commitment, it is important to know:

- Who is making it;
- Who the commitment is to;
- What signals the commitment;
- What exactly is being committed to—a specific action, an assured outcome, or a range of acceptable actions; and

---

[2]U.S. football consists of a sequence of relatively short periods of activity, called *plays*. Major football teams do extensive planning of the patterns of activity that will occur on a given play. A notation system is used to describe these patterns, and the complete set of patterns that a team plans to use is bound into a volume called a *playbook*. Players study these playbooks and memorize the play patterns so that the quarterback can *call* for a given pattern by number just before a given play begins.

[3]The team with the ball is trying to move it forward while the other team is trying to block this movement. Sometimes the player carrying the ball will see a hole in the line of defenders trying to stop him.

- What are the circumstances under which the commitment can be abrogated, and what is the protocol for abrogation.

In principle, if the overall CTA results in a runnable model, it should be possible to verify the extent to which commitments are necessary for goal attainment. When a group task contains commitments that turn out not to be necessary, this is useful to know about. It is often worth probing at some length to be sure that there is no current reason for the commitment to be preserved.

This can be complex because some commitments relate to background tasks that are not the direct object of a particular task analysis. For example, suppose I am the captain of a ship. I might expect people under me to report certain kinds of situations to me although they are not relevant to the task at hand. For example, my maintenance responsibilities might make it essential that all observed equipment problems be reported to me even if they are noticed at a time when the equipment is not currently needed. Similarly, I might expect those under me to respond to all information requests even if the current situation makes the information irrelevant. Identification of commitments that relate to background concerns is often important in developing overall understanding of organizational successes and failures.

Resource Pools

A somewhat different kind of situation arises when a team is large enough that not all of its members need be assigned to each task that comes along. In such cases, it is easy to overlook aspects of the situation that might relate to who the right people to handle it might be. Also, it can be important to know how resources are allocated from a resource pool. Who decides? Do actors volunteer? Is there a rotation scheme? Is a manager supposed to make the allocation?

All of us have had the experience of being in a restaurant where resource allocation has broken down. In such a situation, one server might be running way behind, but the others will not assist because they are not supposed to take orders outside their assigned tables. Notice that a CTA in such a situation would need to capture the assignment process as well as the relevant background information concerning how tips are handled (i.e., the incentive structure for helping other workers). This specific problem might be addressed, for example, by changing the rules for tip handling to a scheme that encourages generally happy customers (e.g., sharing of tips by all workers on the dining room floor).

Notice then that commitments are a lot like goals, in the sense that they have purposes (why) and are discharged by executing (how) a plan (what) of some form. The difference is that a commitment supports the mental models under which the actors to whom the commitment is made are operating. Violating a commitment means that some other actor is going to be working with a mental model that is flawed.

Commitment Triggers

Finally, state or situation modeling can often be useful as a means of identifying the circumstances under which commitments come into being and the circumstances under which they can disappear. It can also be useful to determine how a commitment is remembered by an organization. Sometimes commitments are remembered only in individual actors' minds, but other times artifacts capture some or all of the commitments (e.g., in a shared project Gantt chart that displays the deadline for each subgoal of a project and, often, who is responsible for assuring that the subgoal is met).

DRIVING FORCES

Information Ubiquity

To reflect on where CTA work should next proceed, I found it useful to think a bit about the changing nature of the environments in which we work and live. Clearly, the single biggest change in those environments is the ubiquity of information and the explosion of bandwidth for conveying information from one place to another. The change is so dramatic that it makes sense to speak of the velocity of both information and money (which exists mostly as data these days). Those velocities are increasing. As a result, processes that were not time bound before the computer age suddenly become time bound. When the same activity that once took place on a relatively long time scale suddenly needs to happen more quickly, the organization of work changes dramatically, and new requirements for task analyses to support work design and worker training become necessary.

Tasks can sometimes be done faster by having more people do more pieces of the task in parallel. In addition, as more information is potentially available, the processes of work change. In particular, some tasks are split among multiple people and done more in parallel than before. This, in turn, changes the nature of work, making it more social in character. Compared with 20 or 30 years ago, an adequate CTA today is likely to require analyses of the interactions among people as they share work, the management of large amounts of information, and the speed at which various mental processes unfold. More generally, the complexity of work becomes a bigger task analysis issue than it was in the past.

Task Complexity

Because improved communications enable more complex social structuring of work, circumstances more commonly arise in which we are able to see, post hoc, how a combination of numerous actions, each of which was reasonably safe, led to a catastrophe (see Dörner, 1996; Reason, 1995). Complexity then is both a scale problem for CTA and a specific aspect of the environment within which tasks are carried out. I see three important issues that must be considered here.

Information moves much more quickly than ever before. Hence, situations change more quickly because situations are constrained by available information. A simple case is buying shares of stock. There may have been a time when an investor who noticed a particular company had considerable time in which to decide on whether to invest in that company. Larger companies' shares were sold on an exchange, but even that exchange was part of a relatively slow information environment. Today, on finding out something important about a company, an investor must consider not only the reliability of the information but also how quickly other investors will find out the same thing and whether, at a given moment, the price of shares already reflects the new information.

This example also illustrates a special aspect of the velocity of information, which is the velocity of money. Because money is really only information about who owns what, the faster information can move, the faster money can move. Today, the same funds can be involved in many transactions per day in certain sectors, such as currency arbitrage. This means that the situation being faced as well as the value of various outcomes changes continually. Therefore, part of being competent to perform certain tasks is having means for continually building and reflecting on mental models of unfolding situations while deciding on actions to take.

Of course, the information age also allows us to automate processes—to replace people with computers—whenever we have fully understood a particular competence. This leads to an important conclusion—one that may seem to contradict what I have just said. Anything fully analyzed is a candidate for automation, so the human systems task is to handle the incompletely analyzable. One reaction to this is to decide not to worry about all the concerns I have raised because they do not apply to the jobs remaining for humans to do. A more productive conclusion, however, might be to decide that a special area of focus in task analysis must be understanding the means humans use to fill their special role in the information age of mediating among systems that are each understood but that do not neatly interconnect.

Sometimes this mediation can be seen clearly in even the most mundane jobs. For example, a person handling complaints for a health care provider is often in the position of trying to mediate between a patient's understanding and goal structures and the requirements of a medical insurance system, which are partly grounded in issues not immediately relevant to the patient's goals. This role is often assigned to people with minimal training, although companies are coming to realize that explicit understanding of the role's complexity is important to performing successfully.

A general conclusion driven by this discussion is that metacognitive skill, the ability to monitor one's performance and even one's modeling of work situations, is a central part of the competence needed for many kinds of work. Consequently, CTA must take account of such skills and explicitly capture capabilities that arise when work breaks out of routine. After all, the special role for humans in the information age is to handle the nonroutine. Unless our analytic tools rise to this new challenge, we end up with technologies for designing robots but not adequate technologies for teaching human workers or for building effective and efficient systems for human work in this age of complexity and information velocity and ubiquity.

REFERENCES

Boshuizen, H.P.A., & Van de Wiel, M.W.J. (1999). Using multiple representations in medicine: How students struggle with it. In M.W. van Someren, H.P.A. Boshuizen, T. de Jong, & P. Reimann (Eds.), *Learning with multiple representations* (pp. 237–262). Amsterdam: Elsevier.

Dörner, D. (1996). *The logic of failure: Why things go wrong and what we can do to make them right.* New York: Metropolitan Books (Henry Holt).

Lesgold, A.M. (1984). Acquiring expertise. In J.R. Anderson & S.M. Kosslyn (Eds.), *Tutorials in learning and memory: Essays in honor of Gordon Bower* (pp. 31–60). San Francisco, W. H. Freeman.

Lévi-Strauss, C. (1966). The *savage mind*. Chicago: University of Chicago Press.

Palanque, P., Bastide, R., Dourte, L., & Sibertin-Blanc, C. (1993). Design of user-driven interfaces using petri nets and objects. In *Proceedings of Advanced Information Systems Engineering: 5th International Conference, CAiSE 93* (pp. 569–585). New York: Springer-Verlag.

Rasmussen, J., Pejtersen, A.M., & Goodstein, L.P. (1994). *Cognitive systems engineering.* New York: Wiley.

Reason, J. (1995). A systems approach to organizational error. *Ergonomics, 38(8),* 1708–1721.

Richards, D. & Menzies, T. (1997). Extending knowledge engineering to requirements engineering from multiple perspectives. Perth: Third Australian Knowledge Acquisition Workshop. [available from http://www.cse.unsw.edu.au/~timm/pub/-docs/97akawre.ps.gz]

Shadbolt, N. (1992). Facts, fantasies and frameworks: The design of a knowledge acquisition workbench. In F. Schmalhofer, G. Strube, & T. Wetter (Eds.), *Contemporary knowledge engineering and cognition.* Heidelberg: SpringerVerlag.

Shadbolt, N.R., O'Hara, K., & Schreiber, G. (1996). *Advances in knowledge acquisition.* New York: Springer-Verlag.

Sycara, K., Decker, K., Pannu, A., Williamson, M., & Zeng, D. (1996). Distributed intelligent agents. *IEEE Expert, 11,* 36–46.

Van Biljon, W.R. (1988). Extending petri nets for specifying man-machine dialogues. *International Journal Man-Machine Studies, 28,* 437–455.

28

STATE-OF-THE-ART REVIEW OF COGNITIVE TASK ANALYSIS TECHNIQUES

Jan Maarten Schraagen
TNO Human Factors

Susan F. Chipman
Office of Naval Research

Valerie J. Shute
Wright State University

As part of its Programme of Work, RSG.27 on Cognitive Task Analysis undertook the task of reviewing existing cognitive task analysis techniques and computer tools. RSG.27 restricted itself to a "review of reviews", in order to keep the work manageable. Therefore, descriptions of individual methods and techniques were explicitly excluded from the review. A literature search was conducted, starting with references from 1990 onwards. Twenty reviews were deemed useful for further reading. This chapter contains a brief description of the contents of each review, listed by year of appearance. A more elaborate description may be found in Schraagen, Chipman, Shute, Annett, Strub, Sheppard, Ruisseau, and Graff (1997).

Grant, S., & Mayes, T. (1991). Cognitive task analysis? In G.R.S. Weir & J.L. Alty (Eds.), *Human-computer interaction and complex systems* (pp. 147–167). London: Academic Press.

The focus in this chapter is on cognitive task analysis (CTA) for human–computer interaction in complex systems. The authors argue that because humans will continue to play a key role in controlling or supervising complex systems, these systems need to be designed taking into account the human's information needs. "A CTA will properly involve an analysis of the information flow and the required knowledge states throughout the entire system" (p. 149). The authors distinguish three approaches to CTA:

1. An analysis of a task in terms that relate to human cognition (decomposition formalisms),
2. Theories and models of human cognition that specify the terms in which the task has to be analyzed, and
3. Observations on salient features of human cognition in complex processes.

Examples of the first approach that are discussed are: GOMS, Cognitive Complexity Theory, Command Language Grammar, and Task-Action Grammars. The main shortcoming of these formalisms, according to the authors, is that they have been restricted to simpler systems and highly proceduralized behavior. The authors are also skeptical about representing knowledge in terms of an unrestricted production system precisely because multiple solutions are equally possible. Therefore, it is unclear whether any particular production system bears any resemblance to actual cognitive behavior.

The models of cognition that are discussed as examples of the second approach are: The Model Human Processor, Programmable User Models, ACT*, and Interacting Cognitive Subsystems. Again, these models are more suitable for analyzing short-term simple tasks than longer term subtler cognitive abilities involving problem solving or decision making. Models such as ACT* (and SOAR) need a way of finding those production rules that best represent a particular human approach to a particular task. These models do not help focus an approach to analysis, but rather leave this aspect of the analysis open (in general, it is possible to analyze a task in terms of production rules in many widely differing ways). The authors are clearly in favor of Interacting Cognitive Subsystems.

Among the important features of cognition in complex systems mentioned are Rasmussen's Skills, Rules, and Knowledge framework; Roth and Woods' Mapping Cognitive Demands framework, and Moray's Quasi-independent subsystems. Although the authors find the Rasmussen framework useful, it does not amount to a complete CTA technique. Roth and Woods' attempt to map cognitive demands independently of representation and cognitive agent is difficult given the possibility of individual differences and uncertainty about how the domain problem is to be described in the first place. The problem with Moray's analysis is that he offers no evidence about the extent to which actual models of operators match up with the methodical analyses.

The authors conclude from their review that none of the approaches discussed is fully adequate for a CTA in the context of complex systems: They either lack sufficient input from cognitive psychology or they lack sufficient relevance to the realities of complex tasks, or both. The aim of CTA must be to integrate an investigation of tasks independently of human cognition and an investigation of cognitive processes involved in complex control tasks.

Overall, this is more a philosophical than a practical chapter, and it is also somewhat outdated. The only practical advice offered is to "investigate the information requirements of specific operators in specific situations" (pp. 165–166). The good point is that the authors are concerned with actual cognitive behavior as displayed by human operators. They offer some critical comments about cognitive modeling enterprises that seemingly ignore actual cognitive behavior. In a current version of their chapter, the authors would need to include EPIC (Meyer & Kieras) and ACT-R (Anderson), although many of their comments would remain the same.

Olson, J.R., & Biolsi, K.J. (1991). Techniques for representing expert knowledge. In K. Anders Ericsson & J. Smith (Eds.), *Toward a general theory of expertise* (pp. 240–285). Cambridge, England: Cambridge University Press.

This chapter cites a great deal of methodological work that extends quite far back; it seems to provide coverage up to about 1989. It reviews quite a number of knowledge-elicitation techniques, along with their associated analysis methods and resulting output representations of knowledge. The techniques are divided into direct (interview, think-aloud, observation, interruption analysis, commentary, drawing of groupings in a spatial array, card sorting) and indirect methods (direct judgments of similarity or relatedness, confusion probabilities, cooccurrence probabilities, repertory grid and recall orders). Useful diagrams bring out the relationships among the members of these two families of methods. The direct methods are not treated in any detail: They are described as a way to discover the vocabulary and concepts in an area of expertise and as the only way to uncover problem-solving strategies. For example, there is no discussion of ways to design or structure interviews. Some comments are made about the domains in which think-aloud methods are suitable (those naturally involving verbal concepts) and not suitable (perceptual, motor, highly automatized). In contrast, the indirect methods are discussed in considerable detail both with respect to procedures and assumptions about the underlying knowledge representations and assumptions about the way in which subjects may be generating the data collected by the method from the underlying representation. A table summarizing experience with these methods (p. 274) reveals that most are suited when it is reasonable to assume a hierarchical representation of concepts. The text also comments that multidimensional scaling has proved more suitable to the analysis of perceptual similarities, whereas the other methods seem more appropriate for semantic concepts. Some concern is expressed about the psychological reality of the representations emerging from these methods and about the desirability of obtaining convergent evidence from multiple methods. A useful general comment is made about the importance of paying attention to the extent to which the data-collection task appears to be easy and natural for the subjects. There are also a few useful comments about the orchestration of these different approaches into a total approach—the use of interviews to identify important concepts, the use of indirect methods to explore relations among these concepts, and the possible integration of think-aloud or similar methods into indirect data-collection techniques to ease interpretation of the results. However, some points that are rather obvious from the discussion are not brought out strongly and explicitly. Although the chapter begins by pointing out the richness of true expert knowledge, the implications of this are not brought out. In particular, the problem of the small number of concepts that can typically be studied with the indirect techniques is not discussed. Also, despite the emphasis on the importance of the nature of the representations and the assumptions on this point, nothing is said about a direct focus on this issue.

Wilson, B. & Cole, P. (1991). A review of cognitive teaching models. *Educational Technology, Research and Development, 39*(4), 47–64.

This article reviews (from primarily an instructional design perspective) nine teaching programs developed by cognitive psychologists over the last dozen years or so. Among these models, Collins' cognitive apprenticeship model has the most explicit prescriptions for instructional design. This cognitive apprenticeship model is analyzed, and then components of the model are used as an organizing framework for understanding the remaining models. Differences in approach are noted between traditional ID prescriptions and the cognitive teaching models. Surprisingly, no design strategies were found to be common to all the model programs. Key differences among programs included: (a) problem solving versus skill orientations, (b) detailed versus broad cognitive task analysis (CTA), (c) learner versus system control, and (d) error-restricted versus error-driven instruction. The article concludes with an argument for the utility of continuing dialogue between cognitive psychologists and instructional designers.

Alm, I. (1992). *Cognitive tasks: A meta-analysis of methods* (FOA report C 50098.5.5). Sundbyberg, Sweden: National Defense Research Establishment, Department of Human Studies.

This report does not fully deliver what it promises—namely, a meta-analysis of methods for cognitive task analysis (CTA). Only two methods are discussed in some detail: the generic-error modeling system (GEMS) and hierarchical task analysis (HTA). The major claim is that these and other methods for CTA generally ignore the context in which cognitive behavior takes place. This is similar to Simon's claim that the task environment to a large extent determines the representations used by problem solvers. For instance, according to Alm, "it is not the same thing to drive alone on a road on a sunny day and drive a car during a rush hour on a rainy day" (p. 11). The task, driving a car, is the same on both occasions, but the change in context leads to quite different demands on the driver and consequently to quite different driving behavior.

The report distinguishes between two types of contexts: physical and social structures. In the first, a cognitive system interacts with a noncognitive system; in the second, two or more cognitive systems interact. Furthermore, two different types of tasks are distinguished: iterative or repetitive tasks and open-ended or dynamic tasks. Iterative tasks in either a physical or social structure require a different approach when being analyzed than open-ended tasks. Iterative tasks require that the analyst find out what instruction is valid for task performance, what the performer's mental representation of the task and/or the instruction is, and what biases cause the two to differ. Open-ended tasks performed in a physical or social structure require the observer to find out the system's function, the organization of the task, and the system's relation to the environment. Next, a context for a particular task performance is selected and studied during some period of time (space-time structure). This analysis should be checked with the performers. Finally, the mental representations of the task and the space-time structure should be examined.

The major conclusion of the report is that there does not exist any universal method that can analyze, describe, and explain all cognitive tasks performed in different contexts. Therefore, prior to analyzing a particular task's demands on the cognitive system, it is extremely important to differentiate among various kinds of purposes, situations, tasks, structures, and organizations.

Kirwan, B., & Ainsworth, L.K. (Eds.). (1992). *A guide to task analysis*. London: Taylor & Francis.

Although it is sometimes claimed (e.g., by Gordon & Gill, 1997) that this book solely contains traditional behavioral task analysis methods, this is certainly not the case. Various methods that are usually claimed to be cognitive in nature, are discussed (e.g., critical incident technique, GOMS, hierarchical task analysis, structured interviews, verbal protocols, walk-through/talk-through analyses, withheld information). Admittedly, the authors briefly list a technique that they describe as *cognitive task analysis* on page 392 only (this is the TAKD technique). Because the only reference to cognitive task analysis (CTA) in the book is to this short paragraph, the authors must view the other methods listed earlier as noncognitive. This is strange because, without a doubt, both GOMS and verbal protocols are purely cognitive in nature. The guide is stronger, then, on the behavioral techniques, although the description of verbal protocols, for instance, is useful and balanced.

The guide contains descriptions of 25 techniques and illustrates the practical use of these techniques in 10 case studies. The case studies clearly show lessons learned and are very powerful illustrations of what task analysis techniques can provide for an organization.

Redding, R.E. (1992). *A standard procedure for conducting cognitive task analysis.* McLean, VA: Human Technology, Inc. (ERIC Document Reproduction Service No. ED 340 847).

The Instructional Systems Development (ISD) model has been widely used and found effective for analysis and training of psychomotor skills. It includes five phases: (task) analyze, design, develop, implement, and control. However, the ISD model has not been effective for jobs requiring complex cognitive skills (e.g., decision making, problem solving, attention switching, and/or the effective organization and retrieval of large amounts of knowledge). As Redding points out, cognitive methods need to be incorporated into ISD task analysis, and this book provides a standard procedure for conducting such an analysis.

The guidelines given in this document provide a method for accomplishing a CTA and preparing the deliverables (i.e., research proposal, optional interim report, and final report). Redding outlines critical actions that are described next. Additionally, he includes some sections regarding what should be reported in documentation (e.g., proposals and reports), data-collection methods used for CTA (i.e., protocol analysis, psychological scaling, performance modeling, and observation of job performance and interviewing), controlled experimental design, measures and experimental treatments, data analysis methods, and validation of results. The five critical actions are the following: (a) Identify key job tasks and training issues. This includes determining the goals and foci of the task analysis, specific training problems, justifications for job task selections (e.g., tasks where frequent errors are made, high-performance skills, tasks requiring large amounts of knowledge), what is already known about the nature of expertise in the job task (e.g., through manuals, operating procedures, expert interviews), and describing the population to be used in the analysis (i.e., defining *expert* on the task, determining sample size, determining the range of ability or experience levels in sample). (b) Develop visual representations of knowledge structures. One should present the organization of experts' (and/or less experienced persons') knowledge structures about the task in a visual model using a network of linked concepts, a tree diagram, or a schema depicting interrelationships between knowledge. (c) Describe cognitive processes underlying performance. This includes the skills, conceptual and procedural knowledge, and learning and performance strategies that result in effective task performance (e.g., effective mental models for the task, types of skills required for competent performance, effective cognitive-optimizing strategies, visual representations, conceptual and procedural knowledge needed for the task as a whole and as they interrelate, important task components or subgoals, and strategies, heuristics, algorithms, or aids used for learning or during job performance—that is, production rules, If—Then rules, GOMS, decision trees). (d) Identify differences between experts and novices. This includes differences in knowledge structures (optional), skills, conceptual and procedural knowledge, and learning and performance strategies. This also aids in determining effective job performance skills, knowledge, and knowledge structures. (e) Determine implications of results for design phase. The results of a CTA (i.e., curricular guts) should allow one to recommend a training structure (e.g., improve understanding of interrelationships, improve organization to support problem solving, diagnose and remedy novice errors), a training sequence (i.e., according to skill, knowledge, and knowledge structure progressions), and the instructional setting, media, and strategies that will facilitate learning.

Benysh, D.V., Koubek, R.J., & Calvez, V. (1993). A comparative review of knowledge structure measurement techniques for interface design. *International Journal of Human-Computer Interaction, 5*(3), 211–237.

The authors state that the purpose of their article is to provide researchers in human–computer interaction with a comparative review of available techniques and to summarize their potential application for aiding designers at various stages of interface design. They classify techniques into three classes: verbal reports, clustering techniques, and scaling methods. (In fact, the latter two classes are not that cleanly separated in the actual review.) For each class, they discuss the manner of data gathering and concept elicitation, the method used to derive the knowledge structure, and the analysis procedures used. The category of verbal reports includes interviewing, questionnaires, interruption analysis, and protocol analysis. These are discussed briefly, but the authors do make an important point about the significant role of the analyst in determining how the knowledge structures are represented. They point out that cognitive modeling schemes such as GOMS, Task-Action Grammar, or production rules are sometimes used in the representation. In discussing clustering methods, the authors give much more attention to the problem of developing the list of concepts to be studied than do most reviewers, and they review several methods for this purpose. The methods of cluster elicitation discussed are card sorting, ordered recall, closed-curve analysis (drawing curves around things that go together), and spatial reconstruction. They point out that closed-curve analysis has revealed overlapping clusters, whereas most methods of analysis assume discrete or hierarchical clusters. Scaling methods involve the same problem of creating concept lists. The methods of obtaining concept similarity that are discussed are similarity ratings, repertory grid, co-occurrence analysis (e.g., in card sorting), and proximity in recall. Methods of analysis for these data include conversion to general weighted networks (e.g., by Pathfinder), multidimensional scaling, and hierarchical clustering. They briefly discuss the problem of comparing the resulting representations across individuals. Throughout the article, a few brief remarks are made about how this information could be useful in interface design (e.g., in grouping menu items). They comment that, with the exception of the verbal report methods, these methods primarily get at declarative knowledge.

Means, B. (1993). Cognitive task analysis as a basis for instructional design. In M. Rabinowitz (Ed.), *Cognitive science foundations of instruction* (pp. 97–118). Hillsdale, NJ: Lawrence Erlbaum Associates.

This chapter effectively makes the case for the need to focus on cognitive aspects of many tasks to supplement the information provided by more traditional behavioral task analyses, using the example of air traffic control. It also points out the problems often posed by experts' lack of explicit conscious access to much of their task knowledge. It advocates a team approach to CTA in which the instructional and/or cognitive experts work with collaborating SMEs who both design example tasks or scenarios to bring out necessary expertise and serve as subjects in solving problems, providing protocols, and so on. Two case examples are described—one involving avionics troubleshooting and the other air traffic control. These differ greatly in task pacing and thus in the techniques that are feasible for studying task performance. The air traffic control case also provides interesting examples of the role of metacognitive knowledge or skills. The analytic approach draws heavily on the tradition of expert/novice studies in cognitive science, both as a theoretical foundation and as a source of experimental (or knowledge-elicitation) techniques. Quite a number of such techniques were used in the cases described, but they are not explicitly called out or separately described.

Williams, K.E., & Kotnur, T.G. (1993*). Knowledge acquisition: A review of manual, machine-aided and machine-learning methods* (Tech. Rep. on Office of Naval Research contract N00014-91-J-5-1500). Blacksburg, VA: Virginia Polytechnic Institute and State University, Management Systems Laboratories.

"This review and classification of knowledge-acquisition methods was conducted as part of a design process in the development of an automated aid for creating detailed cognitive models of procedural tasks consistent with a production system architecture of cognition. The target application for the automated aid was the authoring of ideal student models for intelligent tutoring systems. The review was conducted to identify the various kinds of methods that have been developed for knowledge-acquisition because ideal student model generation is a knowledge-acquisition process. As a result of this review, approximately 40 different methods were identified and classified. The methods are classified along a continuum of the degree to which automation is employed in implementing the knowledge-acquisition process. Three classes of methods were defined: manual methods, machine-aided methods, and machine-learning methods. (portion of authors' abstract)"

A useful graph showing the classifications and subclassifications of the methods reviewed, as well as naming those specific methods, appears on page 6 of the report. The review is more comprehensive than most because of its inclusion of machine-aided and machine-learning methods, but it does not claim to be exhaustive. In particular, the review tends to present one example of a machine-aided version of a method rather than discuss all versions that may be available. Some effort is made to provide worked out examples of the various fundamentally different methods for instructional purposes. More detail is provided for the machine-aided methods. In the description of methods for getting at conceptual organization, the report relies heavily on Olson and Reuter (1987). It credits Carbonell (1990) and, to a lesser extent, Michalski (1991) for the taxonomy of machine learning methods. Among the CTA methods, it includes Miyake's (1986) *constructive interaction* method for getting information about how a device or system works, which does not seem to be mentioned in most reviews. The report ends with a conclusion and discussion focused on the system design purpose for which the review was done. However, this section also contains a number of remarks about which methods are suited to obtaining various kinds of information.

Cooke, N.J. (1994). Varieties of knowledge elicitation techniques. *International Journal of Human-Computer Studies, 41,* 801–849.

This article provides an extensive review of some 70 knowledge-elicitation techniques. The list of references contains 231 books and articles on the subject. Relatively brief reference is made to CTA approaches or methodologies (organized sets of methods or techniques). This notwithstanding, many of the techniques discussed in this article appear in the CTA methods proposed in the literature. Moreover, quite a few of the techniques discussed are useful for practitioners conducting CTAs.

The author views knowledge acquisition as a modeling, not a mining, activity. The major problem in this activity involves the abstracting of adequate models of expert knowledge from the data gathered during elicitation. The validity of the data gathered is limited because much knowledge is tacit and not subject to conscious introspection and subsequent verbalization. Therefore, the validity of verbal reports has been subject to controversy. Other problems in knowledge acquisition concern the unavailability of experts and the communication blocks that arise when experts try to convey their knowledge to nonexperts (in an attempt to satisfy the elicitor, the expert communicates whatever knowledge is accessible).

The article organizes knowledge-elicitation techniques according to the process of elicitation, rather than to elicitation stage or type of knowledge elicited. Three families of techniques are distinguished: (a) observations and interviews, (b) process tracing, and (c) conceptual techniques.

(a)   *Observations and interviews.* The first family involves rather direct methods of watching experts and talking with them. These methods seem well suited to the initial phases of knowledge elicitation, although the results are often unwieldy and difficult to interpret.

(b)   *Process tracing.* The second family involves techniques that are generally performed concurrently with expert task performance. The data that are recorded are of a prespecified type (verbal reports, eye movements) and are used to make inferences about the cognitive processes or knowledge underlying task performance. The validity of the data is highly dependent on a number of factors that should be carefully considered before using the techniques (e.g., whether the task involves verbal communication or has high cognitive demands). The selection of cases presented to the expert to solve is highly critical: The cases should be neither too routine (because the expert uses mainly tacit, unverbalizable knowledge) nor too unfamiliar (because the expert cannot use his or her knowledge and the result will not be representative). Process-tracing techniques result in large and often unmanageable data sets that are often difficult to interpret. On the positive side, the techniques are generally carried out easily.

(c)   *Conceptual techniques.* The third family involves indirect techniques that produce representations of domain concepts and their structure or interrelations. These techniques are limited in the types of knowledge they yield; the focus is on concepts and their relations rather than on heuristics, rules, and strategies. For this reason, a combination with process-tracing techniques is recommended. In addition, the analyst requires some background knowledge to employ these techniques. Experts may often regard these techniques with suspicion due to their artificiality. On the positive side, these techniques rely less on verbal reports; they are more suitable for dealing with data from multiple experts and they center on data reduction.

The article concludes that more empirical comparisons among techniques are required. In the meantime, it advises to employ multiple techniques (with the caution that sequencing of techniques may influence the outcome of techniques) or use iterative prototyping and evaluation for the purpose of refining the knowledge base.

Essens, P.J.M.D., Fallesen, J.J., McCann, C.A., Cannon-Bowers, J., & Dorfel, G. (1994*). COADE: A framework for cognitive analysis, design and evaluation.* Final Report of RSG-19 (Decision Aids in Command and Control), Panel 8 (Defense Applications of Human and Bio-Medical Sciences), NATO Defense Research Group.

This report is concerned with the broader topics of system design and evaluation within the application area of decision support for military command and control. Only a portion of the report is devoted to a review of CTA techniques. Cognitive task analysis is covered in Sections 5.1.3 (pp. 43–45) and 6.3 (pp. 113–129). The report assumes that CTA will be done in the context of prior, more traditional behavioral task analyses. Relatively brief reference is made to CTA approaches or methodologies (organized sets of methods and techniques) that have been proposed by other workers. More attention is given to reviewing a large number (about 35) of specific knowledge-elicitation techniques that are grouped according to whether they yield information about declarative knowledge (e.g., semantic nets), procedural knowledge, or strategic knowledge (defined as knowing when and how to apply the other kinds of knowledge, as well as metacognitive or monitoring capabilities). Useful concise tables briefly describe these techniques, the type of knowledge representation they assume, their strength and weaknesses, whether they are direct, explicit approaches or indirect approaches to knowledge extraction, and references to publications discussing the techniques.

John, B.E., & Kieras, D.E. (1994). *The GOMS family of analysis techniques: Tools for design and evaluation* (Report CMU-CS-94-181). Pittsburgh, PA: Carnegie-Mellon University, School of Computer Science.

This report synthesizes the previous work on GOMS to provide an integrated view of GOMS models and how they can be used in design. The major variants of GOMS that have matured sufficiently to be used in real-world design and evaluation situations are described and related to the original GOMS proposal and to each other. A single example (text editing) is used to illustrate all of the techniques. Guidance is provided to practitioners who wish to use GOMS for their design and evaluation problems, and examples of actual applications of GOMS techniques are presented.

Insofar as this report constitutes a review, it is a review solely of GOMS models. However, because the GOMS family is one of the most influential types of CTAs in the HCI field, it is worthwhile to review this report here. GOMS models are best viewed as engineering models of human–computer interaction, in contrast with research-oriented cognitive models. First, these models must be able to make predictions early in the design process when actual data cannot yet be obtained from users. Second, the models need to be used by computer system designers not trained in psychology or human factors (the authors claim that most GOMS techniques can be taught in single-class sessions up to a full-day tutorial). This brings with it the need for explicit procedures for use and canned psychological knowledge in the form of tables of parameter values. Third, engineering models must address a useful range of design issues. GOMS models cover the procedural aspects of a user interface well, together with lower level, perceptual-motor issues. Fourth, engineering models for HCI must be approximate in nature: With 20% of the effort, 80% accuracy should be obtained. This is what GOMS models do.

The authors provide useful background information on the concepts used by GOMS (e.g., the difference between goals and operators) and the conceptual framework underlying GOMS (being representative of stage models of human information processing). It is made clear that GOMS is a form of task analysis that describes the procedural, how-to-do-it knowledge involved in a task. GOMS does not deal with declarative knowledge (e.g., device knowledge) or analogical reasoning. GOMS is a form of task analysis that only deals with routine operating procedures, not with problem solving and exploration. However, because most tasks have some elements of routine cognitive skill, GOMS techniques may be used widely. An important aspect of using GOMS, which sets it apart from other task analysis techniques, is that the analyst must start with a list of top-level tasks or user goals. GOMS does not provide this list; other task analysis techniques (interviews, observations, intuition) should provide it (the authors do not consider the opinion that a list with top-level tasks is more important and more difficult to get than carrying out a GOMS analysis once you have defined the goals).

The report attempts to classify the various GOMS techniques in terms of task type (user control versus system control, sequential vs. parallel) and the type of design information required (e.g., does the system provide a method for every user goal; are the same methods used throughout for the same goals; what sequence of overt physical operators will a user perform; what will be the learning time and execution time). Using this classification scheme, analysts can choose a particular GOMS technique.

Merkelbach, E.J.H.M., & Schraagen, J.M.C. (1994). *A framework for the analysis of cognitive tasks* (Report TNO-TM 1994 B-13). Soesterberg, The Netherlands: TNO Human Factors Research Institute.

The report is based on a literature search that yielded 20 usable techniques or methodologies for CTA. Based on the literature search, a framework is presented that integrates three views on CTA: Task modeling, knowledge modeling, and cognitive modeling. The task modeling view concentrates on the decomposition of tasks into goals and subgoals. Hierarchical task analysis is discussed in some detail as an example of this view. The knowledge modeling view concentrates on the knowledge and strategies that are required to accomplish the task's goals. The KADS methodology for knowledge-based system development is discussed as an example of this view. The cognitive modeling view concentrates on the knowledge and strategies actually used to accomplish the task's goals. The GOMS method is discussed as an example of this view.

Whitefield, A., & Hill, B. (1994). Comparative analysis of task analysis products. *Interacting with Computers, 6*(3), 289–309.

By *products* this article means the outcome product of task analysis processes. Four task analysis processes are reviewed from the perspective of applications to human–computer interaction (HCI): hierarchical task analysis, task knowledge structures, GOMS, and cognitive task analysis/interacting cognitive subsystems.

The authors seem to be primarily concerned with tasks of low cognitive complexity, such as word processing or other document manipulation tasks. To be more precise, they are concerned with interactive work systems (IWS) for such tasks. They have developed a schema for use in discussing task analysis products that they use to characterize the prior processes, asserting that a task analysis product should contain descriptions of the following components: IWS behaviors, IWS behavior sequences, task goals, a decomposition, work domain objects (e.g., documents) and their attributes, abstract IWS structures, physical IWS structures, performance, and cross-references among these components. The authors seem to be somewhat dissatisfied with all of the task analysis processes they review because all are focused on the human user and do not provide independent descriptions of the work objects or the physical characteristics of the IWS. They comment that this can make it difficult to ascertain whether alternative work station designs could perform the same work. They believe that the GOMS approach can handle only serial operations—a view that is not up to date with current versions of the GOMS approach. They characterize Barnard's approach as being totally concerned with specifying internal cognitive processes of the user, as having aspirations to psychological reality in those descriptions, and as giving a description only at that base level, without retaining any hierarchical description. This approach and GOMS are characterized as tending to a fixed vocabulary of low-level operations, whereas the other approaches are more free-form and therefore perhaps more dependent on the specialized expertise of the analyst.

Dehoney, J. (1995). *Cognitive task analysis: Implications for the theory and practice of instructional design.* Proceedings of the annual national convention of the Association for Educational Communications and Technology (AECT), Anaheim, CA. (ERIC Document Reproduction Service No. ED 383 294).

Dehoney's CTA review is broken up into three sections: (a) summary of the underlying theory of CTA, with a focus on problem solving and expertise, (b) review of

CTA models and techniques (including weaknesses), and (c) description of the implications of CTA techniques for instructional design. The state of current instructional design (ID) task analysis results in a linear description or hierarchical ordering of skills required to achieve the task, which are fine for top–down or bottom–up analyses. Cognitive psychologists have extended such analyses into methods for describing how people solve difficult problems, with the most important skills being "metacognitive strategies for selecting relevant information, prioritizing and revising goals, and working between multiple versions of the problem representation". The underlying theory of CTA in terms of problem solving involves the problem representation of experts (or novice–expert comparisons). Learners internally represent objects, actions of objects, strategies to use with those objects, and any constraints of those objects, actions, and strategies. In experts, these representations are linked to the specific domain knowledge. The process of solving a problem is working through the problem space from the initial state (i.e., givens of the problem) to the goal state (i.e., problem solution). Performance by experts has been characterized with several consistent features (e.g., broader and better organized domain knowledge, better able to recognize patterns, focus on underlying principles instead of surface features), and it is the goal of CTA to extricate their representations and strategies. Several researchers describe various procedures for CTA focusing on different aspects of experts' problem solving (e.g., deriving an implicit rule base for problem solution; Ohlsson, 1990) or determining expert organization of domain knowledge into schemata, semantic webs, or mental representations (Lesgold, Lajoie, Logan, & Eggan, 1990; Means, 1993; Nelson, 1990). However, Gardner (1985) and Roth and Woods (1989) proposed formal CTA models. Gardner (1985) stated that the purpose of CTA is to identify performance components, knowledge structures, and metacognitive knowledge underlying a task. Roth and Woods (1989) defined CTA as a two-part process. The first part is to create a competence model (i.e., define competent performance on the task or create a model of the problem-solving environment), which enables the analyst to identify problem areas. The second part is to derive a performance model of how the task is actually achieved in practice, whereby domain-specific knowledge is elicited through interviewing and other observational techniques. Dehoney describes these two models as compatible, with Gardner's viewed as part of a performance model for CTA and Roth and Woods' as a broad competency model. Dehoney grouped CTA strategies for conducting CTA into three general categories: (a) methods for using domain knowledge to structure the analysis (i.e., review existing materials on the task, interview practitioners, hold discussions with panels of experts), (b) development of focus problems (i.e., to gain an understanding of cognitive skills required for task, study/create/discuss representative or critical scenario problem solving in the domain by experts), and (c) knowledge elicitation (i.e., at the performance level: observing and acquiring information about the task;

at the knowledge structure level: interviews, discussions, protocol analysis, simulations; at the metacognitive skills level: protocol analysis, reconstruction, developing mental models). Results from these methods are then organized in a manner that is useful for task performance (e.g., tables with each knowledge type and examples listed). Although there are similarities in the ID and CTA procedures (e.g., hierarchical task descriptions), differences in terminology and emphasis make it difficult (but not insurmountable) for the instructional designer. Although cognitive psychologists may not find any benefit from ID literature (e.g., the literature already shows some CTA-designed instruction that successfully remediates declarative and procedural knowledge: Sherlock), instructional designers would benefit from current CTA methods (e.g., by addressing metacognitive skills required in the task, and providing more specific dimensions to the current task analysis methods). Cognitive psychologists continue to identify, research, and instructionally manipulate complex mental models, and thus will continue to discover worthwhile instructional techniques for complex problem-solving domains. Instructional designers also need to capitalize on this contribution of cognitive research.

DuBois, D., & Shalin, V.L. (1995). Adapting cognitive methods to real-world objectives: An application to job knowledge testing. In P.D. Nichols, S.F. Chipman, & R.L. Brennan (Eds.), *Cognitively diagnostic assessment* (pp. 189–220). Hillsdale, NJ: Lawrence Erlbaum Associates.

This chapter is not really a review of CTA methods, but the presentation of an approach to CTA with the purpose of improving the quality of job knowledge tests by including questions that probe types of knowledge revealed by CTA. It also presents a case example involving Marines' land navigation skill. The approach begins with a larger perspective than is usual, employing relatively standard personnel psychology methods for the analysis of jobs to identify the tasks that are worthy of detailed analysis. Current test development methods, they say, conceptualize knowledge as an accumulation of facts, concepts, and skills and provide little information about how knowledge is organized and used in job performance. Existing test development methods are based on ratings of job importance, saliency, or frequency of use and do not serve well to differentiate novices from expert performers. In fact, they generate approximately the same results whether experts or novices are used as informants. The methods of knowledge elicitation discussed and used included protocol analysis, coaching of a collaborator by the expert, and analysis of naturally occurring team communication, as well as supplementary use of retrospective probe questioning and critical incident methods.

This chapter gives much more attention to the resulting knowledge representation than most: The knowledge representation organizes most of the task analysis and test development activity. The chapter reviews the characteristics of knowledge that have been shown to differentiate expert and novice knowledge: ontology (cf. Chi, Feltovich & Glaser, 1981: differences in objects, relations, and attributes), explanatory knowledge (understanding why procedures are constructed the way they are and what principles must be respected in modifying them), tacit knowledge (relevant conditions for task goals, knowing how to integrate bits of knowledge and information into performance), and recognition of goal attainment (which involves identifying both final states and—sometimes—whether proper process was used in getting there). It is noted that representing novice knowledge may require the addition of buggy knowledge or misconceptions. The knowledge representation used was a plan (or method)/goal graph similar to a GOMS analysis. The nodes of this graph were annotated with additional information: (a) concepts and principles explaining why the method works, (b) procedure-selection knowledge, (c) pattern-recognition knowledge of contexts required to select or execute task procedures, (d) procedure-execution knowledge such as steps or subgoals, and (f) goal attainment knowledge, including priority, sequencing, and standards. The nodes were also annotated with candidate test questions and descriptions of typical mistakes.

In conducting the task analysis of land navigation skill, several different experts of varying skill were used, along with two novices and two decayed experts who had not actually practiced the skill recently. Videotaped think-aloud protocols were supplemented with retrospective questioning (How did you know? Why did you select?) to fill in missing information. Analysis of team communication revealed the existence of vocabulary for many perceptual aspects of the task. The study was done in two different terrains, and retrospective interviews were used to explore the effects of different terrains and conditions. The critical incident technique was used primarily to identify errors and buggy knowledge.

The authors comment that they were aiming for a practical, cost-effective method so that there were some methodological trade-offs: Relatively few protocols were collected in relation to the procedures involved (65 identified), the analysis was not taken to the level of detail required for computational modeling, and no experimental analyses of expertise were done. (In other words, they did not use most of the techniques for knowledge acquisition described in most reviews.) For the purposes of test development, the method/goal graph information was converted to a matrix with domain-specific methods as rows and the types of annotated knowledge described earlier (e.g., procedure selection) as columns. This matrix specified the types of test questions to be developed. In addition, expert ratings of diagnosticity, rather than importance or frequency of use, were used in selecting which questions to use. The authors also note that the method/goal graph representation is useful for practical purposes in demonstrating that one is testing job-relevant knowledge.

Hall, E.P., Gott, S.P., & Pokorny, R.A. (1995). A procedural guide
to cognitive task analysis: The PARI methodology (Tech. Rep. No.
1995-0108). AFMC. Brooks Air Force Base, Texas USA.

Developing effective instruction for complex problems-solving tasks requires
analysis of the cognitive processes and structures that contribute to task performance. This report describes in great detail the exhaustive data-collection procedures
associated with a CTA technique known as the PARI methodology (for: precursor,
action, result, and interpretation). The method was developed at Brooks AF Base
(Basic Job Skills program, originally headed by Sherrie Gott). The PARI method
represents one component of an integrated technology for developing and delivering training of cognitively complex tasks. The specific data collection procedures
they discuss in this report can be considered an extension of existing task analysis
techniques and are based on studies of over 200 AF technicians in aircraft maintenance specialties whose primary task is troubleshooting. The procedures derived
from these studies impose a structure on the knowledge-acquisition task that
captures the cognitive as well as the behavioral components of troubleshooting skill.
The structured interview approach yields data that allow qualitative comparisons
of problem-solving performances within and across technical skill levels (novices,
experts, shades of gray in between). Such analyses have informed instruction
developed under the program by revealing the developmental course of skill
acquisition and the components of expertise, which are the training targets. That is
a definite plus. More recent analyses have identified skill and knowledge overlaps
across maintenance specialties and are informing training designed to facilitate
knowledge transfer. A future goal of the program is to examine the generality of the
PARI methodology and the extent to which it can be applied to problem-solving
tasks in nonmaintenance domains. The claim of the authors is that this PARI
method represents a general purpose tool, but it is currently quite bound to eliciting
and structuring troubleshooting knowledge and skills.

Hoffman, R.R., Shadbolt, N.R., Burton, A.M., & Klein, G. (1995).
Eliciting knowledge from experts: A methodological analysis. *Organizational Behavior and Human Decision Processes, 62*(2), 129–
158.

This article is a generalized review of approaches for capturing expert knowledge
for purposes ranging from reduction of performance error to conventional training
to the creation of artificial expert systems. The methods considered range from the
use of texts, reports, and courses (which they call *indirect*) to the analysis of experts
performing naturalistic tasks, various types of interviews, and various types of
contrived techniques. It is relatively stronger on the less formal methods, such as

interviews, than on the contrived techniques, which are mostly experimental methods from cognitive psychology.

It discusses degrees and kinds of expertise and, briefly, ways of identifying experts to use in knowledge elicitation, as well as several different approaches for finding case examples to be used in studying experts' problem-solving behavior. The value of structured (vs. totally unstructured) interviews is discussed and references on this subject are given, along with a detailed example of generic probe questions. The contrived techniques discussed include some unusual ones like decision analysis and the use of group decision-making situations, as well as the more usual rating and sorting tasks, repertory grid, and explicit construction of conceptual graphs. The use of experimentally constrained problem-solving conditions, in which time or information is abnormally constrained, is also mentioned. There is little detail on these techniques, although there is some mention of and references to computerized knowledge-acquisition tools that implement such techniques. The latter portion of the article discusses experience with knowledge-elicitation approaches and some comparative evidence. It is admitted that contrived tasks seem to be more efficient providers of information than interviews. Some possible problems are discussed: Inaccessible expert knowledge, interactions between the method of elicitation and the knowledge or strategies that are evoked in the expert, and biases that are introduced by the structure of the interview or contrived task. Toward the end of the article, there is a suggestion of an overall approach: study of documentary sources or courses to familiarize the analyst with the concepts and vocabulary of the domain, followed by unstructured interviews, expert review of the resulting first-pass knowledge base, followed by structured interviews, think-aloud problem solving, and contrived tasks for refinement. Throughout, some useful comments on the social niceties of working with experts are made. At the end, the possibility of a taxonomy of tasks that could be associated with recommended knowledge-elicitation techniques is raised.

Crandall, B., Klein, G., Militello, L.G., & Wolf, S.P., (1997). *Tools for applied cognitive task analysis* (Contract Summary report on N66001-94-C- 7008). Fairborn, OH: Klein Associates.

This is a summary report on a Phase I Small Business Initiative Research (SBIR) contract intended to draw on the experience of Klein Associates in conducting CTA to produce CTA methods that could be used by training developers as well as other researchers. The work of the project included a review of the CTA literature as well as a compilation of Klein Associates' inhouse experience in conducting CTAs. Other professionals in the area were also interviewed. (The report contains an annotated bibliography of summaries similar to this, as well as an appendix of reports of the interviews of other CTA experts.) On this basis, a generic applied cognitive task analysis (ACTA) was developed. The methods reviewed included: unstructured interviews, functional analysis system technique (FAST), concept maps, conceptual graphs, cognitive interviews, critical decision method, constructed scenarios, repertory grid, modeling methods, and experimental methods. The authors report that concept maps are quite easy to do but can become excessively complex. Klein Associates uses concept maps in initial interviews, developing one for the task, one for the equipment, and one for the teamwork. They report that more formalized conceptual graph analysis requires more time and specialized training to conduct. Although Klein Associates favors the use of the critical decision method, they find that conducting the necessary interviews requires at least a 6-month apprenticeship and that some experts also have difficulty participating in this method. They view cognitive modeling methods such as COGNET and GOMS as being extremely time-consuming and mostly applicable to tasks that involve interacting with a keyboard. They view the use of experimental psychology tasks (like scaling of similarity) as tedious and inappropriate for applied projects. Of the possible ways to represent extracted knowledge, the authors prefer the *decision requirements table* and the *critical cue inventory* that they developed. They have not found concept map representations or other methods that focus on extracting declarative knowledge to be useful. Instead, the cognitive literature on the nature of expertise has proved more useful. Within the critical decision method, they seek this information: (a) expert–novice differences in dealing with a situation, as seen by the expert; (b) decision points; (c) goals versus nongoals; (d) critical cues, patterns, and relationships; (e) response to hypotheticals, including Marvin Cohen's crystal ball method; and (f) triggers. With respect to goals, they look at how goals get defined, adopted, modified, or not adopted as an important part of the process. *Critical cues* refer to the perceptual aspects of tasks. *Triggers* refer to violations of expectations of either type. The report discusses the difficulties that some people have had in developing the necessary interview skills for the methods that Klein Associates and others typically use.

In this project, they aimed to develop simplified methods that educational specialists can use to interview, observe, and help SMEs articulate the basis of their skills. They wanted to develop a method that would get at aspects of expertise, mental models, judgment, and decision making. For this purpose, they developed corresponding knowledge-elicitation methods: knowledge audit interviews, schematics of equipment, tasks and team/organization, and scenarios that probe key decisions and associated cues. They also developed corresponding knowledge analysis and representation methods: (a) inventory of expertise and compilation of specific examples, (b) aggregate schematics and task function, clusters, and (c) the decision requirements table. They estimate that interviewing and analyzing four to five SMEs would require about a week's work by educational specialists, and they assert that some have reacted to this approach as potentially reducing the work typically involved in a course development effort. The knowledge audit, for example, is a structured interview with suggested probe questions tied to aspects of expertise and is to include the collection of examples and incidents—*sea stories*. These are later used for instructional materials. The schematics are intended to be relatively simple. For example, the team schematic involves identifying the significant team members that the SME interacts with, the type of information exchanged with them, and the criticality of that information. These schematics are potentially useful as advance organizers for sections of instruction. To look at judgment and decision making, SMEs are presented with challenging scenarios and asked about the embedded judgments and decision points. This is an easy method to learn, and scenarios are frequently already available in military training contexts. For analysis, the decisions involved in the task are identified. SMEs are probed about the information, cues, and other factors important in making the decision. They are asked which decisions are most difficult. This information can help set training objectives, and the information about what experts do can serve as models for trainees.

Gordon, S.E., & Gill, R.T. (1997). Cognitive task analysis. In C.E. Zsambok & G. Klein (Eds.), *Naturalistic decision making* (pp. 131–140). Mahwah, NJ: Lawrence Erlbaum Associates.

This short chapter's origins lie in a panel discussion that was held in 1994 during the second Naturalistic Decision Making Conference held in Dayton, Ohio. Unfortunately, the panel members are not mentioned in the chapter. They were Hoffman, Kaempf, Gott, Gordon, Ryder, and McNeese.

The chapter contrasts CTA with traditional behavioral task analysis methods. Because many jobs are beginning to involve complex cognitive processing, CTA methods are better suited to modern-day jobs than behavioral task analysis methods. Tasks that are cognitively complex are well suited for CTA (Gordon claims to have developed a software tool that helps an analyst estimate the cognitive complexity of a task). In practice, many tasks contain both cognitively complex and more behavioral subtasks at the same time, such that a variety of task analysis methods is most useful. It is also recommended to use a variety of CTA methods because each method may get at different types of knowledge or is biased in different ways.

The chapter discusses five CTA methods in some detail: concept mapping and expert design storyboarding, COGNET, conceptual graph analysis, PARI, critical incidents, tough cases, and constrained/contrived cases. Overall approaches are not discussed. The discussion of these methods is fairly shallow and nonevaluative. The authors note that these methods differ along a number of dimensions, such as how and by whom scenarios or test cases are generated, the type of cases analyzed, and the types of representational formalisms used.

The chapter concludes with issues for the future. One is the issue of when to use what method. The authors propose that system designers evaluate the type of information required for a particular project first and then select a CTA method that yields that type of information (the authors do not specify what they mean by *type of information*, so this advice is not really helpful). A second issue concerns the validity and reliability of various CTA methods. Validity concerns the question of whether the domain expertise is adequately captured. Because the authors view CTA as a modeling enterprise, the model of expert performance can be used to generate predictions, and these can be tested empirically. A second way to validate the model is to look at the success of the artifact it has supported (e.g., the training program designed with the aid of the model). Unfortunately, the artifact may be a confounding factor (e.g., the training program could have led to improved results without the CTA being conducted in advance). Reliability of CTA methods concerns the issue of whether different analysts using the same method end up with the same results. The authors note that there is a scarcity of publications, seminars, and courses on how to conduct a CTA. This may lead to low reliability of methods. Relatively simple methods that can be taught to training and system analysts should be identified. Finally, an issue for the future is the translation of CTA results into a final system, training program, or interface. There is still a gap here that may have more ramifications than the choice of any particular CTA method.

REFERENCES

Schraagen, J.M.C., Chipman, S.E., Shute, V., Annet, J., Strub, M., Sheppard, C., Ruisseau, J.-Y., & Graff, N. (1997). State-of-the-art review of Cognitive Task Analysis Techniques: Deliverable of RSG.27 on Cognitive Task Analysis (Tech. Rep. TM-97-B012). Soesterberg, The Netherlands: TNO Human Factors Research Institute.

AUTHOR INDEX

Locators annotated with *f* indicate figures.
Locators annotated with *n* indicate notes.
Locators annotated with *t* indicate tables.

SUBJECT INDEX

Locators annotated with *f* indicate figures.
Locators annotated with *n* indicate notes.
Locators annotated with *t* indicate tables.

A

Abstract decision-making (ADM), as
    time-pressured test
    laboratory studies on, 124-127, 125*f*
    principles of, 123-124
    summary of, 127
Abstract interface model, task-based,
    155-156, 206, 206*f*
Abstraction
    decomposition of, 60, 155, 305-306, 325
    in knowledge management, 204, 206,
        305-306, 309
    in problem-solving, 60-62, 454
    in software designing, 155-156, 204,
        206, 297
Abstraction hierarchy
    of constraints, 92, 96
    of functional goal-means, 329-330,
        331*f*-333*f*
ACCES (Army Command and Control
    Performance Measurement), 386
Accommodation, expertise relationship to,
    91, 106-107
Acoustic representations, cognitive, 148,
    149*f*, 150*t*
ACT–R model, of cognitive task perfor-
    mance, 18-19, 239
    with novel expertise, 276, 280*n*-281*n*,
        287
ACTA, *see* Applied cognitive task analysis
Action
    cognitive models of, 155, 157, 157*f*,
        165-166
    computer amplification of, 291
    constraint interpretations on, 91-92,
        102-104
    expertise relationship to, 89-91, 89*f*
    PARI method and, 7, 9, 33, 139-140,
        483, 486

in task knowledge structures, 203-204, 205*t*
    in transaction analysis, 228-231,
        229*t*-231*t*
Action teams
    Cognitive processes of, 417-421
    Marine Corps example, 422-424
Active Design Document Generation and
    Maintenance (ADDGM), 299
Active design documents
    advantages of, 297
    artifacts in, 291, 294-298
    assessment of, 297-298
    bottom-up design of, 298
    contextual links component, 294, 295*f*,
        296-297
    definition of, 293-294
    description of, 292-293, 293*f*
    evolution of, 299-300, 300*f*
    interaction descriptions component,
        294, 295*f*, 301*f*
    interface objects component, 294-296
    job simulations and, 291-292, 294-295,
        301
    participatory design of, 298-299
    programming tool for, 300, 301*f*
    purpose of, 297, 301
    top-down design of, 298
    traceability of, 299-300
Activity classification
    in group work designs, 451, 456-459
    for human–computer interactions,
        169-172, 255-256
Activity sampling, in task analysis, 26, 387
Adaptation
    by subgoaling, in problem solving,
        280-283, 281*f*, 283*f*, 286-288
    of workers
        in modern work, 452-453
        promotion of, 101, 107-108,
            113-114, 116